Panic Disorder with Agoraphobia

Agoraphobia Without History of Panic Disorder

Specific Phobia

Social Phobia

Obsessive-Compulsive Disorder

Posttraumatic Stress Disorder

Acute Stress Disorder

Generalized Anxiety Disorder

SOMATOFORM DISORDERS

Somatization Disorder

Undifferentiated Somatoform Disorder

Conversion Disorder

Pain Disorder

Hypochondriasis

Body Dysmorphic Disorder

FACTITIOUS DISORDERS

DISSOCIATIVE DISORDERS

Dissociative Amnesia

Dissociative Fugue

Dissociative Identity Disorder

Depersonalization Disorder

SEXUAL AND GENDER IDENTITY DISORDERS

Sexual Dysfunctions

Sexual Desire Disorders

Hypoactive Sexual Desire Disorder

Sexual Aversion Disorder

Sexual Arousal Disorders

Female Sexual Arousal Disorder

Male Erectile Disorder

Orgasmic Disorders

Female Orgasmic Disorder

Male Orgasmic Disorder

Premature Ejaculation

Sexual Pain Disorders

Dyspareunia (Not Due to a General Medical Condition)

Vaginismus (Not Due to a General Medical Condition)

Paraphilias

Exhibitionism

Fetishism

Frotteurism

Pedophilia

Sexual Masochism

Sexual Sadism

Transvestic Fetishism

Voyeurism

Gender Identity Disorders

Gender Identity Disorder in Children

Gender Identity Disorder in Adolescents or Adults

EATING DISORDERS

Anorexia Nervosa

Bulimia Nervosa

SLEEP DISORDERS

Primary Sleep Disorders: Dyssomnias

Primary Insomnia

Primary Hypersomnia

Narcolepsy

Breathing-Related Sleep Disorder

Circadian Rhythm Sleep Disorder

Primary Sleep Disorders: Parasomnias

Nightmare Disorder

Sleep Terror Disorder

Sleepwalking Disorder

IMPULSE-CONTROL DISORDERS NOT ELSEWHERE CLASSIFIED

Intermittent Explosive Disorder

Kleptomania

Pyromania

Pathological Gambling

Trichotillomania

ADJUSTMENT DISORDERS

Adjustment Disorder

With Depressed Mood

With Anxiety

With Mixed Anxiety and Depressed Mood

With Disturbance of Conduct

With Mixed Disturbance of Emotions and Conduct Unspecified

PERSONALITY DISORDERS

Note: These are coded on Axis II.

Paranoid Personality Disorder

Schizoid Personality Disorder

Schizotypal Personality Disorder

Antisocial Personality Disorder

Borderline Personality Disorder

Histrionic Personality Disorder

Narcissistic Personality Disorder

Avoidant Personality Disorder

Dependent Personality Disorder

Obsessive-Compulsive Personality Disorder

MULTIAXIAL SYSTEM

Axis 1

Clinical Disorders

Other Conditions That May Be a Focus of Clinical Attention

Axis II

Personality Disorders

Mental Retardation

Axis III

General Medical Condition

Axis IV

Psychosocial and Environmental Problems

Axis V

Global Assessment of Functioning

UNDERSTANDING ABNORMAL BEHAVIOR

UNDERSTANDING ABNORMAL BEHAVIOR

FIFTH EDITION

DAVID SUE

Western Washington University

DERALD SUE

California School of Professional Psychology, Alameda
California State University, Hayward

STANLEY SUE

University of California, Los Angeles

HOUGHTON MIFFLIN COMPANY   **Boston**   **New York**

To our parents, Tom and Lucy Sue, who never suspected they would produce three psychologists, and to our wives and families, who provided the emotional support that enabled us to complete this edition.

Sponsoring Editor: David C. Lee
Senior Associate Editor: Jane Knetzger
Senior Project Editor: Carol Newman
Senior Production/Design Coordinator: Sarah Ambrose
Senior Manufacturing Coordinator: Priscilla Bailey
Marketing Manager: David Lenehan

Cover design by Harold Burch, Harold Burch Design, NYC

Cover image by Georges-Pierre Seurat, *Seated Boy with a Straw Hat,* Yale University Art Gallery, Everett V. Meeks, B. A. 1901, Fund.

Credits
Chapter opening photos: Ch. 1, p. 2 Weinberg/Clark/The Image Bank; *Ch. 2, p. 32* Todd Davidson/The Image Bank; *Ch. 3, p. 70* Ian Miles/The Image Bank; *Ch. 4, p. 98* Tate Gallery/Art Resource; *Ch. 5, p. 122* Giraudon/Art resource, NY; *Ch. 6, p. 158* VAGA; *Ch. 7, p. 188* Roy Wiemann/The Image Bank; *Ch. 8, p. 218* Giraudon/Art Resource; *Ch. 9, p. 250* Weinber/Clark/The Image Bank; *Ch. 10, p. 284* Scala/Art Resource; *Ch. 11, p. 324,* Scala/Art Resource; *Ch. 12, p. 358* Howard Berman/The Image Bank; *Ch. 13, p. 388* Scala/Art Resource; *Ch. 14, p. 408* 1996 Marisol Escobar/VAGA; *Ch. 15, p. 438* Elle Schuster/The Image Bank; *Ch. 16, p. 466* National Museum of American Art, Washington DC/Art Resource, New York; *Ch. 17, p. 506* G and V Chapman/The Image Bank; *Ch. 18, p. 542* Gary Gay/The Image Bank.

All other credits appear in the Credits section at the end of the text.

Printed in the U.S.A.

Library of Congress Catalog Card Number: 96–76574

ISBN: 0-395-78826-9

2 3 4 5 6 7 8 9–VH–00 99 98 97

Brief Contents

Contents

FEATURES

PREFACE

This is an exciting time to be learning about abnormal behavior, its causes, and its treatment. Researchers have made major advances in understanding genetic and other biological influences on mental disorders. At the same time, psychological models of psychopathology have become increasingly sophisticated and much research has been conducted on effective forms of psychotherapy. In our society, health-care reform is altering the provision of mental health services, and new ethical issues concerning the delivery of mental health interventions have been raised. Looking beyond our society, we are becoming more familiar with other cultures and peoples, and more aware of variability in the way emotional distress is expressed and in the way problems are treated. This dynamic environment is the context in which we study abnormal behavior.

In writing and revising this book we have sought to engage students in the exciting process of understanding abnormal behavior and the ways that mental health professionals study and attempt to treat it. In pursuing this goal, we have been guided by three major objectives:

- To provide students with scholarship of the highest quality.

- To offer an evenhanded treatment of abnormal psychology as both a scientific and a clinical endeavor, giving students the opportunity to explore topics thoroughly and responsibly.

- To make our book inviting and stimulating to a wide range of students.

In each edition we have strived to achieve these objectives, working with comments from many students and instructors and our own work in teaching, research, and therapy. The Fifth Edition, we believe, builds on the achievements of previous editions and surpasses them.

OUR APPROACH

We take an eclectic, multicultural approach to the field, drawing on important contributions from various disciplines and theoretical stances. The text covers the major categories of disorders listed in the *Diagnostic and Statistical Manual of Mental Disorders IV* (DSM-IV), but is not a reiteration of DSM. We believe that different combinations of life experiences and constitutional factors influence behavioral disorders, and we project this view throughout the text.

One vital aspect of life experience comprises cultural norms, values, and expectations. Because we are convinced that cross-cultural comparisons of abnormal behavior and treatment methods can greatly enhance our understanding of disorders, we pay special attention to cultural phenomena. Indeed, *Understanding Abnormal Behavior* was the first textbook on abnormal psychology to integrate and emphasize the role of multicultural factors, and although many texts have since followed our lead, the Fifth Edition continues to provide the most extensive coverage and integration of multicultural models, explanations, and concepts available. Not only do we discuss how changing demographics have increased the importance of multicultural psychology, but we introduce multicultural models of psychopathology in the opening chapters. As with other models of psychopathology (e.g., psychoanalytic, cognitive, behavioral, biological), we address multicultural issues throughout the text whenever research findings and theoretical formulations allow. For example, cultural factors as they affect assessment, classification, phobias, stress disorders, suicide, sexual disorders, schizophrenia, and so forth are provided to students. Such an approach adds richness to our understanding of mental disorders.

As psychologists (and professors) we know that learning is enhanced whenever material is presented in a lively and engaging manner. We achieve these qualities in part by providing case vignettes and clients' descriptions of their experiences to complement and illustrate research-based explanations. In addition, we highlight and explore controversial topics in depth. Among these are:

- Do women have higher rates of anxiety and depressive disorders? (Chapters 5 and 11)

- What are the causes of sexual aggression in society? (Chapter 10)

- Is psychotherapy effective and useful? (Chapter 17)

- Should we assist in suicide and allow the "right to die"? (Chapter 18)

■ Should therapists maintain confidentiality with AIDS clients? (Chapter 18)

We have also strived to present complex material with clarifying examples. Two instances include our discussion of the phenomenon of recovered memories, which includes case descriptions and research findings, and our careful examination of the various factors that affect clients with mood disorders. We try to encourage students to think critically about the knowledge they acquire in the hope that they will develop an appreciation of the study of abnormal behavior rather than merely assimilate a collection of facts and theories.

SPECIAL FEATURES

Contributing to the strength of the Fifth Edition are a number of features popularized in earlier editions.

■ *Disorder charts* illustrate the relationships among categories of disorder, based on DSM-IV criteria. Students find the charts extremely useful in organizing disorders and in gaining a graphic overview of the chapters where they are discussed.

■ *Focus On boxes* examine in depth various high-interest issues, research findings, or clinical implications, providing stimulating and informative reading for students.

■ *Critical Thinking boxes* provide factual evidence and thought-provoking questions that raise key issues in research, examine widely held assumptions about abnormal behavior, or challenge the student's own understanding of the text material. This feature prompts students to think about issues as a psychologist would, weighing the evidence and applying theoretical perspectives and personal experiences to arrive at an evaluation. The feature can spark lively class discussion and debate.

■ *First Person essays* written mainly by therapists or researchers give first-hand accounts of experiences in the mental health field that personalize research and therapy issues and portray the wide range of careers in psychopathology.

■ *A chapter outline* on the first page of every chapter gives students an overview of the topics that will be discussed.

■ *Chapter summaries* provide students with a concise overview of the chapter's most important concepts and ideas.

■ *Key terms* are highlighted in the text, and definitions appear at the end of each chapter and in the glossary at the back of the book.

NEW TO THE FIFTH EDITION

Our foremost objective in preparing this edition was to update thoroughly and present the latest trends in research and clinical thinking. This has led throughout the text to expanded coverage of dozens of topics, including:

■ The growing ethnic and cultural diversity in the United States and the implications for mental health research, theory, and practice.

■ Research strategies to study the influence of heredity and the latest research findings on genetic factors in mental disorders.

■ New developments concerning the implications of managed health care on mental health services and the use of empirically validated treatments.

■ Research findings concerning the rates of each mental disorder and the prevalence of disorders according to gender, ethnicity, and age.

■ Identification of psychotherapies and treatments that are likely to increase or decrease in use in the future.

■ Developmental and clinically significant decline in memory associated with aging.

■ Ethical and legal issues raised by recent cases involving insanity pleas, courtroom testimony by psychologists, and assisted suicide.

The format and design of the book have been enhanced as well. The Fifth Edition contains many more tables, illustrations, figures, and photographs than previous editions. They graphically show research data, illustrate comparisons and contrasts, or enhance the understanding of concepts or controversies in the field.

New Focus On boxes include:

■ Should we challenge delusions and hallucinations? (Chapter 13)

■ Some types of therapy groups (Chapter 17)

■ Was Ellie Nesler insane when she shot Daniel Driver to death? (Chapter 18)

New Critical Thinking topics include:

■ Can we accurately assess the status of members of different cultural groups? (Chapter 3)

■ Can memories be recovered during hypnosis? (Chapter 4)

■ Illness: Are psychological or physical factors more important? (Chapter 7)

- Should electroconvulsive shock therapy for depression be banned? (Chapter 11)

- "Am I Losing It as I Get Older?" (Chapter 15)

- "What Kind of Therapist Do You Want?" (Chapter 17)

Two new First Person narratives have been added:

- Elizabeth Loftus, a researcher well-known for her work on repressed memory questions the validity of this phenomenon. (Chapter 6)

- Psychologist Lenore Walker describes her forensic work on battered women. (Chapter 18)

In addition to updating the book's coverage, its look, and its special features, we have considerably streamlined the organization of the book, as described below.

ORGANIZATION OF THE TEXT

To make covering the book's contents over the course of a quarter or semester more manageable, the text has been streamlined from twenty chapters to eighteen chapters, in keeping with feedback from users of the book. Whereas previously two chapters were devoted to models of abnormal behavior, they are now featured only in Chapter 2. Moreover, the chapter on community psychology has been eliminated. Some of the topics in that chapter (prevention and managed health care, for example) now appear in Chapter 17 (Individual and Group Therapy). We found that it was possible to condense materials and to exclude topics that were not central to the field of abnormal psychology without sacrificing our major objectives for writing the textbook.

Chapters 1 through 4 provide a context for viewing abnormal behavior and treatment by introducing students to definitions of abnormal behavior and historical perspectives (Chapter 1), the key theoretical perspectives used to explain deviant behavior (Chapter 2), methods of assessment and classification (Chapter 3), and the research process involved in the study of abnormal behavior (Chapter 4).

The bulk of the text, Chapters 5 through 16, presents the major disorders covered in DSM-IV. In each chapter, symptoms are presented first, followed by diagnosis, theoretical perspectives, etiology, and treatment. Highlights of the coverage in this part of the book include an entire chapter devoted to suicide (Chapter 12) and two chapters covering schizophrenia (Chapters 13 and 14). The chapter on suicide was conceived in light of current issues involving the right to die, assisted suicide, and our aging population. It presents information on not only the reasons for suicide but also the moral, legal, and ethical implications. The first chapter on schizophrenia describes the interesting array of symptoms and the attempts to assess and categorize this complex and debilitating disorder. The subsequent chapter is devoted to etiological factors and treatment considerations. Because schizophrenia is one of the most well-researched mental disorders, the two-chapter treatment seems wise.

Chapters 17 and 18 conclude the book with a look at therapy and the legal and ethical issues in psychopathology. Discussions of treatment approaches are included in each of the chapters on disorders, allowing students some closure in covering particular disorders. Chapter 17 then looks at treatment more broadly. Chapter 18 covers the issues and controversies surrounding topics such as the insanity defense, patients' rights, confidentiality, and mental health practices in general.

ANCILLARIES

We once again thank Richard L. Leavy of Ohio Wesleyan University for continuing his outstanding work revising the *Instructor's Resource Manual, Study Guide,* and *Test Bank.* All three of these supplements continue to be unified not only by Professor Leavy's authorship but also by a single set of learning objectives.

For each chapter of the text, the *Instructor's Resource Manual* includes an extended chapter outline, learning objectives, discussion topics, classroom exercises, handouts, and a list of supplementary readings and multimedia resources. For instructors switching from the Fourth to the Fifth Edition, a transition guide highlights changes within every chapter. In addition, the examination of the case of Steven V., formerly a part of several chapters in the book, now appears in the *Instructor's Resource Manual.*

The *Test Bank* features one hundred multiple-choice questions per chapter, of which half are new. In items repeated from the previous edition, answer choices have been scrambled. For each question, the corresponding learning objective, text page number, question type (fact/concept or application), and page number are provided. At least half of the questions in every chapter ask students to apply their knowledge. New to every chapter are three essay questions with sample answers.

The *Study Guide* provides a complete review of each chapter in the text through the use of chapter outlines, learning objectives, a fill-in-the-blank review of key terms, and practice multiple-choice questions.

Answers to the test questions include an explanation of each incorrect answer as well as the right answer, which has proved to be a particularly helpful feature for students.

A *Computerized Test Bank* available in both IBM and Macintosh formats allows instructors to create their own exams from the test bank questions and integrate their own questions with those on disk.

Houghton Mifflin's *Internet Guide for Psychology,* by David Mahony of St. John's University, is available at no cost to students who purchase *Understanding Abnormal Behavior.* This handy manual introduces students to electronic mail, discussion groups, on-line journals, Usenet newsgroups, the World Wide Web, APA Reference Style for the Internet, and more, and it provides students with step-by-step exercises and a wealth of addresses and sites relevant to psychology.

A set of full-color transparencies, including images from outside the text, is available to all adopters.

Finally, a selection of videos on topics in abnormal psychology is available to qualified instructors. Your Houghton Mifflin sales representative can provide the details.

ACKNOWLEDGMENTS

We continue to appreciate the feedback by reviewers and colleagues. The following individuals helped us prepare the Fifth Edition by sharing valuable insights, opinions, and recommendations with us:

Dorothy M. Bianco, *Rhode Island College*

Winfield Brown, *Florence-Darlington Technical College*

Lorry J. Cology, *Owens Community College*

Robert E. Francis, *North Shore Community College*

Louis E. Gardner, *Creighton University*

Cheryl Golden, *LeMoyne-Owen College*

Ricki Kantrowitz, *Westfield State College*

Phil Lau, *DeAnza College*

William E. Roweton, *Chadron State College*

Nancy Simpson, *Trident Technical College*

R. Bruce Tallon, *Niagara College*

Josh Weinstein, *Humboldt State University*

We would also like to acknowledge the continuing support and high quality of work by Houghton Mifflin personnel; in particular, Senior Associate Editor Jane Knetzger for her vision regarding our book; Sponsoring Editor David Lee, Gwen Fairweather, Sheralee Connors, and Nancy Fleming for their helpful comments and suggestions; and Senior Project Editor Carol Newman for her dedication and attentive supervision of the production process.

D. S.

D. S.

S. S.

About the Authors

David Sue is Professor of Psychology at Western Washington University, where he is an associate of the Center for Cross-Cultural Research and chairperson of the Mental Health Counseling Program. He received his Ph.D. in Clinical Psychology from Washington State University. His research interests revolve around issues in cross-cultural counseling. He, his wife, and their three children enjoy tennis, hiking and snowshoeing.

Derald Wing Sue is Professor of Psychology at the California School of Professional Psychology and at California State University, Hayward. He has written extensively in the field of counseling psychology and multicultural counseling/therapy and is author of a best-selling book, *Counseling the Culturally Different: Theory and Practice*. He received his Ph.D. from the University of Oregon. Dr. Sue is married and the father of two children. Friends describe him as addicted to exercise and the Internet.

Stanley Sue is Professor of Psychology at the University of California, Los Angeles and Director of the National Research Center on Asian American Mental Health, an NIMH-funded research center. He received his Ph.D. from UCLA and served for ten years on the psychology faculty at the University of Washington. At UCLA, he was also Associate Dean of the Graduate Division. His research interests lie in the areas of clinical-community psychology and ethnicity and mental health, and his hobbies include working on computers, which has also fostered an addiction to the Internet, and jogging with his wife.

UNDERSTANDING ABNORMAL BEHAVIOR

ABNORMAL BEHAVIOR

The study of abnormal psychology is a journey into known and unknown territories of the mind and body. To help you understand the scope and dynamics of this field, we would like to introduce you to an incident one of the authors encountered early in his career.

My first introduction to working with severely disturbed patients began in the psychiatric ward at the University of Oregon Medical School. I had just finished all doctoral coursework and was beginning my internship at the medical school. Along with a group of other trainees, I was being given a tour of the ward facilities by the supervising psychologist. To our left was a nurse's station from which medication was dispensed, and near it was a group of small rooms separated by a glass partition. Later that day I was to discover that these rooms were used primarily for electroconvulsive shock therapy (ECT). Sitting to my immediate right in a semicircle was a group of about twenty patients, a licensed psychiatric nurse, and the head psychiatrist, who was conducting a ward meeting.

I recall making eye contact with one particular patient: Chung, a Chinese male, of short stocky build. His eyes followed me throughout the orientation session, making me feel quite self-conscious. I assumed Chung was interested in me because I was probably one of the few Asian American mental health professionals he had ever seen. With considerable effort, I tried to turn my attention away from him and to concentrate on what our guide was saying.

As we approached the nurse's station, I heard a low gutteral growl and caught a quick movement of a fast-approaching figure on my right. Chung had launched himself toward me, striking me with his left shoulder and driving me against the glass partition. I collapsed on the floor, completely stunned as he stood over me, appearing equally surprised at what he had done. We stared at each other for what felt like hours before the attending psychiatrist and nurses gently but firmly pulled Chung away.

While I was in no way injured (except for a few bruises on my forearm and a deflated ego), I was baffled by what had happened. No amount of reading and coursework could have prepared me for such an experience. My head filled with questions:

1. What was wrong with Chung? His behavior certainly seemed unexplainable and quite bizarre.

2. What role did my culture and race—and his—play in the manifestation of his problems? I was later to discover that my Chinese ancestry did play a part in his reaction to me.

3. What disorder did he suffer from? I learned shortly thereafter that Chung had once been diagnosed with manic depression but it was changed to paranoid schizophrenia when admitted.

4. Why did he attack me? After all, I had never seen him before and had been on the ward for less than an hour.

5. Was he dangerous? My professors had always reassured us that fears of violence and injury from mentally disturbed individuals were unfounded.

6. What type of therapy was he receiving? Apparently, Chung was not only being treated with a combination of medication and individual therapy but was scheduled for another series of electroconvulsive shock treatment.

In a sense, the purpose of this book, *Understanding Abnormal Behavior,* is to help you answer such questions. To do so, however, requires us first to examine some basic aspects of the study of abnormal behavior, including some of its history and emerging changes in the field. Periodically, we will return to the case of Chung, for it illustrates many complex issues in the field.

THE CONCERNS OF ABNORMAL PSYCHOLOGY

Abnormal psychology is the scientific study whose objectives are to describe, explain, predict, and control behaviors that are considered strange or unusual. Its subject matter ranges from the bizarre and spectacular to the more commonplace—from the violent homicides and "perverted" sexual acts that are widely reported by the news media to such unsensational (but more prevalent) behaviors as stuttering, depression, ulcers, and anxiety about examinations.

Describing Abnormal Behavior

The description of a particular case of abnormal behavior must be based on systematic observations by an attentive professional. These observations, usually paired with the results of psychological tests and with the person's psychological history, become the raw material for a **psychodiagnosis,** an attempt to describe, assess, and systematically draw inferences about an individual's psychological disorder. For example, Chung had a long psychiatric history and had, at various times, been diagnosed as suffering from paranoid schizophrenia, manic depression, and other mental disorders.

Diagnosis is obviously an important early step in the treatment process. But a diagnosis that is not developed with great care can end up as nothing more than a label that tends to hinder rather than aid treatment. Such labels present two major problems. First, like the term *manic-depressive* (a term once used to refer to a particular mood disorder) applied to Chung, labels can cover a wide range of behaviors and can mean different things to different psychologists. A label may therefore be too general—it may describe something other than a client's specific behaviors. Second, a label describes only a current condition rather than a past or changing circumstance. A person's psychological problems (especially those of a young person) are likely to change over time. A previous diagnosis can quickly become obsolete, a label that no longer describes that person. To guard against these problems, sensitive therapists ensure that labels, either old or new, are not substitutes for careful investigation of a client's condition.

Explaining Abnormal Behavior

To explain abnormal behavior, the psychologist must identify its causes and determine how they led to the described behavior. This information, in turn, bears heavily on how a program of treatment is chosen.

As you will see in later chapters, explanations of abnormal behavior do vary, depending on the psychologist's theoretical orientation. For example, Chung's therapist might stress his client's *intrapsychic conflicts* and the need to resolve and control extreme feelings of rage and hostility, due primarily to early childhood experiences of abandonment. (Chung's mother had sent him to the United States to live with his uncle.) Other psychologists might concentrate on his *social* and *cultural isolation* (stemming from his recent immigration to the United States from Taiwan), his culture conflicts, and his experiences of discrimination, leading to suspiciousness and paranoia. Explanations offered by still other psychologists might be more *biological* in nature, emphasizing genetics or a biochemical imbalance. And still others might see and treat Chung's behavior as resulting from *a combination* of these causes.

Predicting Abnormal Behavior

If a therapist can correctly identify the source of a client's difficulty, he or she should be able to predict the kinds of problems the client will face during therapy and the symptoms the client will display. But therapists have difficulty predicting the future course of many disorders. Even an experienced professional

During a therapy session, the therapist not only hears about the client's problems, but also carefully observes the client's behavior and emotional reactions. These observations can help to form the basis of a psychodiagnosis and a method of intervention. This photo depicts a group therapy session.

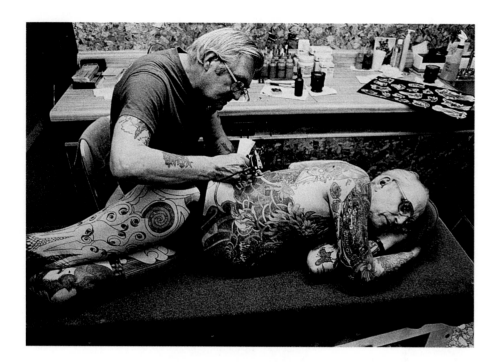

By most people's standards, the full-body tatoo of this man would probably be considered unusual at best and bizarre at worst. Yet, despite the way his body appears, this person may be very functional in his work and personal life. This leads to an important question: What constitutes abnormal behavior and how do we recognize it?

finds it hard to foretell how a particular client will behave.

For example, consider Chung's behavior. Was he a danger to people? His physical attack on one of the authors might certainly indicate an affirmative response. Yet, although Chung had a history of suicidal attempts, he had never directly assaulted or even made verbal or physical threats to others before that incident. Research shows that mental health professionals do a poor job of predicting dangerousness; they tend to greatly overpredict violence.

Controlling Abnormal Behavior

Abnormal behavior may be controlled through **therapy,** which is a program of systematic intervention whose purpose is to modify a client's behavioral, affective (emotional), and/or cognitive state. For example, many therapists believe that allowing Chung an opportunity to get in touch with and to vent his anger would reduce his chances of doing harm to others. Some mental health professionals might also recommend family therapy, culture-specific therapy, social skills training, or medication. Those who see schizophrenia as caused by a chemical imbalance might rely on a primarily biological means of intervention and prescribe antipsychotic drugs. As we shall shortly see, the treatment for abnormal behavior generally follows from its explanation. Just as there are many ways to explain abnormal behaviors, there are many proposed ways of controlling or ameliorating them.

DEFINING ABNORMAL BEHAVIOR

Implicit in our discussion so far is the one overriding concern of abnormal psychology: abnormal behavior itself. But what exactly is abnormal behavior, and how do psychologists recognize it? To answer this question, we will examine four types of definitions of abnormal behavior: conceptual, practical, integrated, and DSM-IV. Figure 1.1 summarizes the criteria for each of these definitions.

Conceptual Definitions

Conceptual definitions define abnormal behavior as, essentially, deviations from what is considered normal or most prevalent in the sociocultural context. The underlying criteria for judging normality and abnormality may be a statistical average, a concept of ideal mental health, or a concept of cultural universality or specificity. In one form or another, they form the basis for diagnosing a mental disorder.

Statistical Deviation Statistical criteria equate normality with those behaviors that occur most frequently in the population. Abnormality is therefore defined in terms of those behaviors that occur least frequently. For example, data on IQ scores may be accumulated and an average calculated. Then IQ scores near that average are considered normal, and relatively large deviations from the norm (in either direction) are considered abnormal. In spite of the word

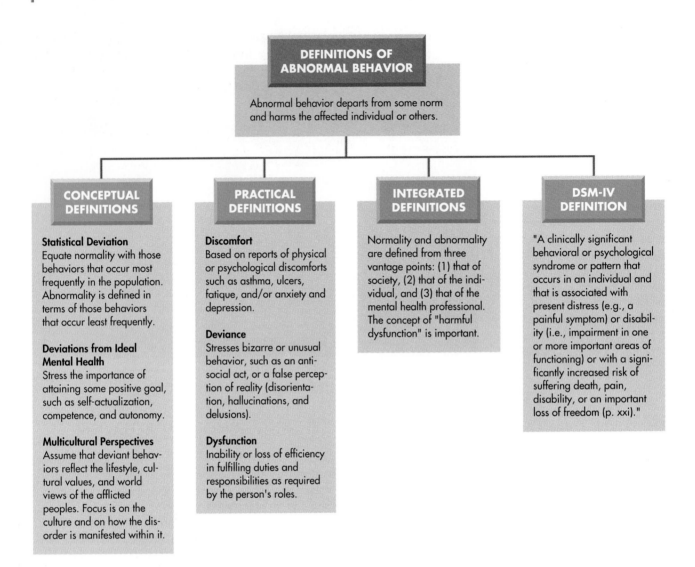

FIGURE 1.1 **Abnormal Behavior Defined** There are numerous definitions of abnormal behavior that have been used by mental health professionals. Some of the most current and widely used ones are briefly described here.

statistical, however, these criteria need not be quantitative in nature: People who talk to themselves incessantly, undress in public, or laugh uncontrollably for no apparent reason are considered abnormal according to statistical criteria simply because most people do not behave that way. Chung's behavior can certainly be considered a violation of a statistical norm.

Definitions based on statistical deviation may seem adequate in some specific instances, but they present many problems. One problem is that they fail to take into account differences in place, community standards, and cultural values. For example, some lifestyles that are acceptable in San Francisco and New York may be judged abnormal by community standards in other parts of the nation. Likewise, if deviations from the majority are considered abnormal,

then many ethnic and racial minorities that show strong subcultural differences from the majority must be classified as abnormal. When we use a statistical definition, the dominant or most powerful group generally determines what constitutes normality and abnormality.

In addition, the statistical criteria do not provide any basis for distinguishing between desirable and undesirable deviations from the norm. An IQ score of 100 is considered normal or average. But what constitutes an abnormal deviation from this average? More important, is abnormality defined in only one direction or in both? An IQ score of 55 is considered abnormal by most people; but should people with IQ scores of 145 or higher also be considered abnormal? How does one evaluate such personality traits as assertiveness and dependence in terms of statistical criteria?

Two other central problems also arise. First, people who strike out in new directions—artistically, politically, or intellectually—may be seen as candidates for psychotherapy simply because they do not conform to normative behavior. Second, statistical criteria may "define" quite widely distributed but undesirable characteristics, such as anxiety, as normal.

In spite of these weaknesses, statistical criteria remain among the most widely used determinants of normality and abnormality. Not only do they underlie the layperson's evaluation of behaviors, they are the most frequently used criteria in psychology. Many psychological tests and much diagnosis and classification of behavior disorders are based in part on statistical criteria.

Deviation from Ideal Mental Health

The concept of ideal mental health was proposed as a criterion of normality by humanistic psychologists Carl Rogers and Abraham Maslow. Deviations from the ideal are taken to indicate varying degrees of abnormality.

This type of definition stresses the importance of attaining some positive goal. For Maslow and his followers, the goal was *self-actualization* or *creativity*. Psychoanalytically oriented psychologists have used the concept of *consciousness* (awareness of motivations and behaviors) and *balance of psychic forces* as criteria for normality. Others have proposed aspects of maturity, such as *competence, autonomy,* and *resistance to stress*. But using any of these constructs as the sole criterion for defining normality leads to a number of problems.

First, which particular goal or ideal should be used? The answer depends largely on the particular theoretical frame of reference or values embraced by those proposing the criterion. Second, most of these goals are vague; they lack clarity and precision. If resistance to stress is the goal, are the only healthy persons those who can always adapt? Study of the experiences of prisoners of war indicates that many of them eventually break down under repeated stress. Should we label them as unhealthy? A third problem is that ideal criteria exclude too many people: Most persons would be considered mentally unhealthy by these definitions.

Multicultural Perspectives

The traditional view of abnormal psychology is based on the assumption that a fixed set of mental disorders exists, whose obvious manifestations cut across cultures (Draguns, 1985; D. W. Sue & D. Sue, 1990; Triandis, 1983). This psychiatric tradition dates back to Emil Kraepelin (discussed later in this chapter), who believed that depression, sociopathic behavior, and especially schizophrenia were universal disorders that appeared in all cultures and societies. Early research supported the belief that these disorders occurred worldwide, had similar processes, and were more similar than dissimilar (Howard, 1992; Wittkower & Rin, 1965). Such **cultural universality** has led to the belief that a disorder such as depression is similar in origin, process, and manifestation in Asian American, African American, Hispanic, or Euro-American clients. As a result, no modifications in diagnosis and treatment need be made; Western concepts of normality and abnormality can be considered universal and equally applicable across cultures.

At the other extreme were social scientists who stressed **cultural relativism,** the belief that lifestyles, cultural values, and world views affect the expression and determination of deviant behavior. This concept arose from the anthropological tradition and emphasized the importance of culture and diversity in the manifestation of abnormal symptoms. For example, a body of research supports the conclusion that "acting-out" behaviors associated with mental disorders are much higher in the United States than in Asia, and that even Asian Americans in the United States are less likely to express symptoms via "acting out" (Leong, 1986; Uba, 1994). Researchers have proposed that Asian cultural values (restraint of feelings, emphasis on self-control, and need for subtlety in approaching problems) all contribute to their restraint. Proponents of cultural relativism also point out that cultures vary in what they consider to be normal or abnormal behavior. In some societies and cultural groups, hallucinating is considered normal in specific situations. Yet in the United States, hallucinating (having false sensory impressions) is generally perceived to be a manifestation of a disorder.

Which of these views is correct? Are the criteria used to determine normality and abnormality culturally universal or specific? Few mental health professionals today embrace the extreme of either position, although most gravitate toward one or the other. Proponents of cultural universality focus on the disorder and minimize cultural factors, and proponents of cultural relativism focus on the culture and on how the disorder is manifested within it. Both views have validity. It is naive to believe that no disorders cut across different cultures and share universal characteristics. For example, even though hallucinating may be viewed as normal in some cultures, proponents of cultural universality argue that it still represents a breakdown in biological-cognitive processes. Likewise, it is equally naive to believe that the relative frequencies and manner of symptom formation for various disorders do not reflect dominant cultural values and the lifestyles of a society. A third point to

Cultural differences often lead to misunderstandings and misinterpretations. In a society that values technological conveniences and one whose holidays are shared by the majority of people in the United States, the lifestyles and cultural values of minority groups may be perceived as strange. The Amish, for example, continue to rely on traditional modes of transportation (horse and buggy), and many African Americans now celebrate Kwanzaa as a cultural expression rather than Christmas.

consider is that some common disorders, such as depression, are manifested similarly in different cultures.

A more fruitful approach to studying multicultural criteria of abnormality is to explore two questions. First, what is universal in human behavior that is also relevant to understanding psychopathology? Second, what is the relationship between cultural norms, values, and attitudes, and the incidence and manifestation of behavior disorders? These are important questions that we hope you will ask as we continue our journey into the field of abnormal psychology.

Practical Definitions

Practical definitions of abnormal behavior are based on pragmatic or clinical criteria concerning the effect of the behavior on the person exhibiting it or on others. These definitions are subject to many of the same criticisms discussed earlier. Nonetheless, according to Buss (1966), they are often the basis on which people who are labeled abnormal or unhealthy come to the attention of psychologists or other mental health specialists. Moreover, clinicians often must act primarily on the basis of pragmatic manifestations. The practical criteria for abnormality include subjective *discomfort*, *deviance* (bizarreness), and *dysfunction* (inefficiency in behavioral affective and/or cognitive domains).

Discomfort Most people who see clinicians are suffering physical or psychological discomfort. Many

physical reactions stem from a strong psychological component; among them are disorders such as asthma, hypertension, and ulcers as well as physical symptoms such as fatigue, nausea, pain, and heart palpitations. Discomfort can also be manifested in extreme or prolonged emotional reactions, of which anxiety and depression are the most prevalent and common. Of course, it is normal for a person to feel depressed after suffering a loss or a disappointment. But if the reaction is so intense, exaggerated, and prolonged that it interferes with the person's capacity to function adequately, it is likely to be considered abnormal.

Deviance As a practical criterion for abnormality, deviance is closely related to statistical criteria. Bizarre or unusual behavior is an abnormal deviation from an accepted standard of behavior (such as an antisocial act) or a false perception of reality (such as an hallucination). This criterion is extremely subjective; it depends on the individual being diagnosed, the diagnostician, and, as we have just seen, on the particular culture.

Certain sexual behaviors, delinquency, and homicide are examples of acts that our society considers abnormal. But social norms are far from static, and behavioral standards cannot be considered absolute. Changes in our attitudes toward human sexuality provide a prime example. During the Victorian era, women wore six to eight undergarments to make sure that every part of the body from the neck down was covered. Exposing an ankle was roughly equivalent to wearing a topless bathing suit today. Taboos against publicly recognizing sexuality dictated that words be chosen carefully to avoid any sexual connotation. Victorians said "limb" instead of "leg" because the word *leg* was considered too erotic. (Even pianos and tables were said to have limbs.) People who did not adhere to these strict codes of conduct were considered immoral or even perverted.

Nowadays, however, magazines and films openly exhibit the naked human body, and topless and bottomless nightclub entertainment is hardly newsworthy. Various sex acts are explicitly portrayed in X-rated movies. Women are freer to question traditional sex roles and to act more assertively in initiating sex. Such changes in behavior make it difficult to subscribe to absolute standards of normality.

Nevertheless, some behaviors can usually be judged abnormal in most situations. Among these are severe disorientation, hallucinations, and delusions. *Disorientation* is confusion with regard to identity, place, or time. People who are disoriented may not know who they are, where they are, or what historical era they are living in. *Hallucinations* are false impressions—either pleasant or unpleasant—that involve the senses. People who have hallucinations may hear, feel, or see things that are not really there, such as voices accusing them of vile deeds, insects crawling on their bodies, or monstrous apparitions. *Delusions* are false beliefs steadfastly held by the individual despite contradictory objective evidence. A delusion of grandeur is a belief that one is an exalted personage, such as Jesus Christ or Joan of Arc; a delusion of persecution is a belief that one is controlled by others or is the victim of a conspiracy.

Chung, for example, had delusions of persecution. He believed that his home country of Taiwan was engaged in a space war with the People's Republic of China, and that "the enemy" had planted electrodes in his head during one of his ECT sessions so that his thoughts could be read. Because China was able to read his mind and extract valuable data about Taiwan's battle plans, Chung believed he had been ordered to commit suicide for the sake of his country. His several suicide attempts were the result of these distorted beliefs.

Interestingly, Chung's attack on one of his authors arose from his belief that the author was a spy from China, getting ready to implant a more powerful mind-reading device in Chung's head. (He was due for another ECT session that afternoon.) In many respects, Chung's delusions seem to incorporate realistic aspects of his life: The intern was Chinese; China and Taiwan have historically been countries at odds with one another; and the ECT process involved attaching electrodes to Chung's head and body. In the patient's belief system, these facts were misconstrued and transformed into an image of a spy from China who would soon implant powerful electronic devices to read Chung's thoughts.

Dysfunction Dysfunctions in a person's biological, mental, and emotional states are often manifested in role performance. One way to assess dysfunction is to compare an individual's performance with the requirements of a role. In everyday life, people are expected to fulfill various roles—as students or teachers, as workers and caretakers, as parents, lovers, and

Societal norms often affect our definitions of normality and abnormality. When social norms begin to change, standards used to judge behaviors or roles also shift. Here we see two examples of role reversal: a woman working as a stonemason cutting limestone blocks and a "househusband" folding clothes.

marital partners. Emotional problems sometimes interfere with the performance of these roles, and the resulting role dysfunction may be used as an indicator of abnormality.

Another related way to assess dysfunction is to compare the individual's performance with his or her potential. An individual with an IQ score of 150 who is failing in school can be labeled inefficient. (The label *underachiever* is often hung on students who possess high intelligence but obtain poor grades in school.) Similarly, a productive worker who suddenly becomes unproductive may be experiencing emotional stress. The major weakness of this approach is that it is difficult to accurately assess potential. How do we know whether a person is performing at his or her peak? To answer such questions, psychologists, educators, and the business sector have relied heavily on testing. Tests of specific abilities and intelligence are attempts to assess potential and to predict performance in schools or jobs.

Integrated Definitions

Different definitions of abnormality carry different implications, and there is no easy consensus on a best definition. All the criteria we have discussed have shortcomings. Many of these deficiencies and their sociopolitical implications have been well articulated by Thomas Szasz (1961, 1987). In a radical departure from conventional beliefs, he has asserted that mental illness is a myth, a fictional creation by society used to control and change people. According to Szasz, people may suffer from "problems in living" not from "mental illness." His argument stems from three beliefs: that abnormal behavior is so labeled because it is different, not necessarily because it is a reflection of "illness"; that unusual belief systems are not necessarily wrong; and that abnormal behavior is frequently a reflection of something wrong with society rather than the individual. Individuals are labeled "mentally ill" because their behaviors violate the social order and their beliefs challenge the prevailing wisdom of the times. Szasz finds the concept of mental illness to be dangerous and a form of social control used by those in power. While few mental health professionals would take the extreme position advocated by Szasz, his arguments highlight an important area of concern. Those who diagnose behavior as abnormal must be sensitive not only to such variables as psychological orientation but also to individual value systems, societal norms and values, and potential sociopolitical ramifications.

Perhaps, then, definitions of abnormality should not be viewed from a single perspective or in accordance with a single criterion, but rather should be an integrated statement incorporating multiple perspectives. Two researchers (Strupp & Hadley, 1977) working together have proposed a three-part method that can be used to define normality and abnormality. They identify three vantage points from which to judge a person's mental health: (1) that of society, (2) that of the individual, and (3) that of the mental health professional. Each "judge" operates from a different perspective, perhaps using different criteria. At times, three people taking these viewpoints would agree that a person is either mentally disturbed or mentally healthy. At other times, they might disagree. Nonetheless, using an integrated set of criteria alleviates the problems inherent in imposing a single criterion to define behavior.

We must carefully consider two important points as we assess the value of the multiple-perspectives concept. First, a person who feels subjectively contented—mentally sound—may be perceived as unhealthy from a societal perspective. For example, people who commit antisocial acts such as rape, murder, or robbery may not feel remorseful but may be quite contented with their acts. Similarly, an artist living a very unconventional lifestyle may be judged maladapted from society's perspective; from that individual's perspective and the perspective of many health professionals, however, he or she is intact and sound. Second, a judgment must be recognized as stemming from one of the three vantage points. Otherwise, even greater confusion could result.

Another proposal for an integrated definition comes from Wakefield (1992), who has advocated defining the concept of mental disorder from the perspective of biological facts and social values. He argues that a mental disorder is a "harmful dysfunction," wherein the term *harmful* is based on social norms, and *dysfunction* is a scientific term referring to the "failure of a mental mechanism to perform a natural function for which it was designed by evolution." This definition considers the following points to be essential:

1. Understanding dysfunction requires identifying the natural functions of an organ or organ system; the function of the heart, for example, is to pump blood.

2. We must distinguish between functions and effects; the sound of a beating heart is an effect and not a function—thus a quiet heart is not a dysfunction.

3. We must ultimately look for our definition of disorder in the biological sciences.

4. Dysfunction must involve the harm requirement—seen from a social and cultural perspective—if it is to be considered a disorder.

This fourth point is an important one. Wakefield argues that dysfunctions must cause significant harm to the person according to current environmental and cultural standards. For example, a man whose aging mechanism suffers a dysfunction that slows the aging process would not be considered disordered but lucky! Thus albinism, reversal of heart position, or fused toes would not be considered a disorder even though each involves a breakdown of natural functions. Likewise, hallucinations may be a manifestation of a mental disorder because they represent a *dysfunction* of a normal biological process. Yet, a cultural group that values "visions" would not consider them harmful but would view them as a positive development.

A truly adequate understanding of mental illness and health can be reached through comprehensive evaluation from all points of view. It may not be enough to rely solely on the judgments of mental health professionals, who are not immune to biases and shortcomings.

The DSM-IV Definition

Thus we may define **abnormal behavior** as behavior that departs from some norm and that harms the affected individual or others. This definition encompasses—or at least allows room for—the various criteria and perspectives on behavior. It also accurately implies that no precise, universally acknowledged line delineates normal behavior from abnormal behavior. Somewhat more loosely, we will speak of *mentally disturbed people* as those individuals who display abnormal behavior. And by a *mental disorder* or *mental disturbance* we mean some recognizable pattern of abnormal behavior.

This definition is also consistent with the one used in the American Psychiatric Association's *Diagnostic and Statistical Manual of Mental Disorders* (DSM-IV): "a clinically significant behavioral or psychological syndrome or pattern that occurs in an individual and that is associated with present distress (e.g., a painful symptom) or disability (i.e., impairment in one or more important areas of functioning) or with a significantly increased risk of suffering death, pain, disability, or an important loss of freedom" (p. xxi).

THE INCIDENCE OF ABNORMAL BEHAVIOR

A student once asked one of the authors, "How crazy is this nation?" This question, put in somewhat more scientific terms, has occupied psychologists for some time. Psychiatric epidemiology provides insights into

By all appearances, this photo seems to depict a well-functioning group of people from all facets of life. Yet, studies reveal that approximately one in three persons suffer from at least one mental disorder.

factors that contribute to the occurrence of specific mental disorders. From this information, we can find out how frequently or infrequently various disturbances occur in the population; how the prevalence of disorders varies by ethnicity, gender, and age; and whether current mental health practices are sufficient and effective (Lopez, 1989; Watkins & Peterson, 1986).

Current Research into the Epidemiology of Mental Disorders

An early but highly regarded and frequently cited study, the Midtown Manhattan Study, was performed in 1950 (Srole et al., 1962). Fifteen hundred New Yorkers were interviewed and rated on their psychological health. The results were startling: Approximately 25 percent of those interviewed showed severe impairment, about 55 percent were mildly impaired, and only 20 percent (one in five) were rated unimpaired.

Some social commentators contend that our mental health has deteriorated since the Midtown Manhattan Study was conducted. They point to such "evidence" as the mushrooming of cults, a revival of belief in the supernatural, the increased incidence of mass and serial murders, and attempts at political assassination. To ascertain whether the population's mental health was deteriorating, a similar study was carried out in the 1970s (Srole & Fisher, 1980). Although the investigators found no support for this contention, neither did they find any evidence that the mental health of Americans had improved in the intervening decades!

A number of other studies have found equally disheartening tendencies (Dohrenwend & Dohrenwend, 1982; Dohrenwend et al., 1980; Mechanic, 1978; and Regier, Goldberg & Taube, 1978). These studies estimate that some 25 million to 40 million Americans, or approximately 15 percent of the population, suffer from serious emotional disorders. Counting both severe and milder disturbances, estimates are that 44 million Americans suffer from symptoms of depression, 20 million have drug-related problems, 4 million to 9 million have some form of phobic or anxiety disturbance, 6 million are mentally retarded, and 2 million suffer from schizophrenia. In addition, some 25,000 to 60,000 people commit suicide each year, and another 200,000 attempt it. These estimates do not include disorders such as child abuse, sexual dysfunctions, and pathological expressions of violence, which could increase the total substantially. For example, every year 20,000 murders are committed in the United States; an average of 10 out of every 100,000 Americans will be murdered (Thiers, 1988). Crime statistics also show that 456,000 acts of family violence are reported each year in the United States, and that figure probably grossly underestimates the number of acts committed because many such acts go unreported.

Perhaps the most thorough and comprehensive study of the incidence of mental disorders in the U.S. adult population (eighteen years and older) was conducted by the National Institute of Mental Health (NIMH, 1985; Eaton et al., 1984; Freedman, 1984; Myers et al., 1984; Regier et al., 1988; Robins et al., 1984; Robins, Locke & Regier, 1991). The NIMH epidemiological study included data collected in three major cities: New Haven, Baltimore, and St. Louis. The study had several features that distinguished it from others. It included a large sample of approximately 20,000 persons, and it used the categories in the *Diagnostic and Statistical Manual* of the American Psychiatric Association in the construction of the research instruments.

Like the previous studies cited, subjects reported a high rate of disorders. Approximately 29 to 38 percent (percentage range accounts for variations in the three cities) of the sample reported that they experienced at least one mental disorder! Schizophrenia, often one of the most severe mental disturbances, affects 1 percent of the population, or approximately 2.5 million Americans. Figure 1.2 presents one-year and lifetime prevalence rates of various mental disorders as percentages of the total U.S. population.

Researchers also found that although men and women were equally likely to suffer from mental disorders, they differ in the kinds of disorders they experience. For example, alcohol abuse or dependence occurs in 24 percent of men but in only 4 percent of women; drug abuse is more likely to occur in men; and depression and anxiety are more likely to occur in women. Age was also an important factor. Alcoholism and depression are most prominent in the 25- to 44-year-old age group; drug dependence in the 18- to 24-year-old age group; and cognitive impairment in people age 65 and older. Phobias, however, were equally represented at all ages. Studies on even the young (children and adolescents) suggest that nearly 17 percent suffer from a serious disorder (Kessler et al., 1994, Regier et al., 1993). Figure 1.3 summarizes the rates of psychiatric disorders in various demographic categories. Some of the findings are not surprising—for example, common sense might cause us to guess that financially dependent or less educated Americans would have higher rates of disorders. The relationship of disorders to other characteristics is more obscure, and sometimes downright baffling: How would you explain the fact that the lowest percentages are found for people 65 or older, or that rural dwellers have a lower rate than their urban counterparts? Such findings require critical analyses.

These epidemiological findings are troubling, to say the least. Clearly, mental disturbances are widespread, and many persons are currently suffering from them. What is even more troubling is that the study reveals that fewer than one-third of the people with mental disorders are receiving mental health services!

Stereotypes About the Mentally Disturbed

Americans tend to be suspicious of people with mental disorders. Are most of them really maniacs who at any moment may be seized by uncontrollable urges to murder, rape, or maim? Such portrayals seem to emerge from the news media and the entertainment industry, but they are rarely accurate. Like other minority groups in the United States, people with mental

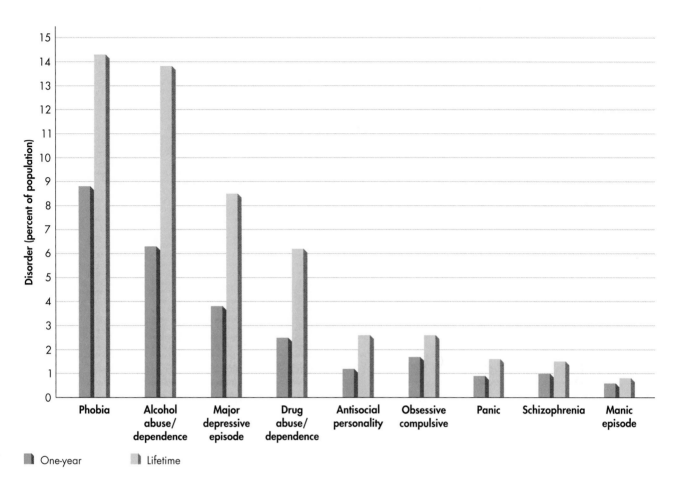

FIGURE 1.2 **Rates of Various Mental Disorders** This figure shows the one-year and lifetime prevalence of mental disorders as percentages of the population. It is clear that the most common mental disorders in the United States are phobias, followed by alcohol-related problems, anxiety, and depressive episodes.

Source: Data from Robins & Regier, 1991.

disturbances are the subject of rampant stereotyping and popular misconceptions. It is worthwhile at this point to dispel the most common of these misconceptions or myths.

Myth: "Mentally disturbed people can always be recognized by their consistently deviant abnormal behavior."

Reality: Mentally disturbed people are not always distinguishable from others on the basis of consistently unusual behavior. Even in an outpatient clinic or a psychiatric ward, distinguishing patients from staff on the basis of behavior alone is often difficult. There are two main reasons for this difficulty. First, as already noted, no sharp dividing line usually exists between "normal" and "abnormal" behaviors. Rather, the spectrum of behaviors is continuous, ranging from abnormal to normal. Depending on the situational context and the perspective of the person

judging the behavior, many behaviors could be considered either normal or deviant. Second, even when people are suffering from some form of emotional disturbance, that experience may not always be detectable in their behavior.

Myth: "The mentally disturbed have inherited their disorders. If one member of a family has an emotional breakdown, other members will probably suffer a similar fate."

Reality: The belief that insanity runs in certain families has caused misery and undue anxiety for many people. Although the data are far from conclusive, heredity does not seem to play a major role in most mental disorders, except for some cases of schizophrenia and depression, certain types of mental retardation, and the bipolar disorders. Evidence suggests that, even though heredity may predispose an individual to certain disorders, environmental factors

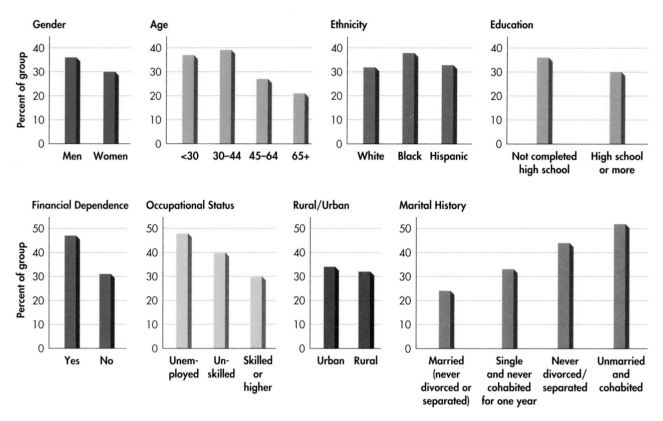

FIGURE 1.3 **Rates of Psychiatric Disorders in Particular Groups** Research indicates that psychiatric disorders are present in about one-third of the U.S. population. The bar graphs in this figure illustrate the extent to which any psychiatric disorder is found in combination with other characteristics of the population, such as gender, age, ethnicity, and marital status.

Source: Data from Robins & Regier, 1991.

are extremely important. When many family members suffer from mental disorders, a stress-producing environment is usually acting on the family predisposition. If the environment is benign, however, or if predisposed individuals modify a stressful environment, psychopathology may never occur.

Myth: "The mentally disturbed person can never be cured and will never be able to function normally or hold a job in the community."

Reality: This erroneous belief has caused great distress to many people who have at some time been labeled mentally ill. Former mental patients have endured social discrimination and have been denied employment because of the public perception that "once insane, always insane." Unfortunately, this myth may keep former mental patients or those currently experiencing emotional problems from seeking help. Although most people don't hesitate to consult a doctor, dentist, or lawyer for help, many who need mental health services are fearful and anxious about the social stigma attached to being labeled "mentally ill."

Nearly three-fourths of clients who are hospitalized with severe disorders will improve and go on to lead productive lives. Many recovered mental patients make excellent employees, and employers frequently report that they outperform other workers in attendance and punctuality. Some famous examples of persons who have recovered from mental disorders are President Abraham Lincoln, philosopher William James, Senator Thomas Eagleton, singer Rosemary Clooney, actress Patty Duke, and golfer Bert Yancy.

Myth: "People become mentally disturbed because they are weak-willed. To avoid emotional disorders or cure oneself of them, one need only exercise will power."

Reality: These statements show that the speaker does not understand the nature of mental disorders. Needing help to resolve difficulties does not indicate a lack of will power. In fact, recognizing one's own need for help may be a sign of strength rather than a sign of weakness. Many problems stem from situations that are not under the individual's immediate control, such as the death of a loved one or the loss of a job. Other problems stem from lifelong patterns of faulty learning; it is naive to expect that a simple exercise of will can override years of experience.

Myth: "Mental illness is always a deficit and the person suffering from it can never contribute anything of worth until cured."

Reality: Many persons who suffered from mental illness were never "cured," but they nevertheless made great contributions to humanity. Ernest Hemingway, who was one of the greatest writers of our time and who won the Nobel Prize for literature in 1954, suffered from lifelong depressions, alcoholism, and frequent hospitalizations. In 1961 he put a shotgun in his mouth and killed himself. The famous Dutch painter Vincent van Gogh produced great works of art despite the fact that he was severely disturbed. Not only did he lead an unhappy and tortured life, he frequently heard voices, cut off a piece of his left ear as a gift to a prostitute, and finally committed suicide. Others like Pablo Picasso and Edgar Allan Poe contributed major works to humanity while seriously disturbed. The point of these examples is not to illustrate that madness and genius go hand in hand, but that many who are less severely disturbed can continue to lead productive and worthwhile lives. Because people suffer from psychological problems does not mean that their ideas and contributions are less worthy of consideration.

Myth: "The mentally disturbed person is unstable and potentially dangerous."

Reality: This misconception has been perpetuated by the mass media. Many murderers on television are labeled "psychopathic," and the news media concentrate on the occasional mental patient who kills. But the thousands of mental patients who do not commit crimes, do not harm others, and do not get into trouble with the law are not news. An important study of the issue does not support the notion that mental patients are seriously dangerous (Rabkin, 1979). Unfortunately, the myth persists.

HISTORICAL PERSPECTIVE ON ABNORMAL BEHAVIOR

In this section and the next, we briefly review the historical development of Western thought concerning abnormal behavior. This task is extremely difficult for two reasons. First, we lack specific facts about the historical past and must piece them together. Until other information is uncovered, these gaps in our knowledge could lead us to mistaken conclusions. For ex-

ample, disagreements now exist over the psychiatric interpretation of witchcraft.

Second, historical interpretation depends on the perspective of the researcher. For example, an anthropological approach to the study of history may differ from a psychological one. Within each discipline, one's biases and point of view may affect how an interpretation is made. Even given these limitations, many current attitudes toward abnormal behavior, as well as modern ideas about its causes and treatment, appear to have been influenced by early beliefs. In fact, some psychologists contend that modern societies have, in essence, adopted more sophisticated versions of earlier concepts. For example, the use of electroconvulsive therapy to treat depression is in some ways similar to ancient practices of exorcism in which the body was physically assaulted. The Greek physician Hippocrates, 2,500 years ago, believed that many abnormal behaviors were caused by imbalances and disorders in the brain and the body, a belief shared by many contemporary psychologists.

Most ideas about abnormal behavior are firmly rooted in the system of beliefs that is operative in a given society at a given time. Perhaps for that reason, change—especially in the form of new ideas—does not come quickly or easily. People who dare to voice ideas that differ from the prevalent beliefs of their time are often made outcasts; in some periods, some were even executed. Yet in spite of the difficulties, we have evolved a humanistic and scientific explanation of abnormal behavior. It remains to be seen whether such an explanation will still be thought valid in decades to come. (Much of this history section is based on discussions of deviant behavior by Alexander & Selesnick, 1966; Hunter & Macalpine, 1963; Neugebauer, 1979; Spanos, 1978; and Zilboorg & Henry, 1941).

Prehistoric and Ancient Beliefs

Prehistoric societies some half a million years ago did not distinguish sharply between mental and physical disorders. Abnormal behaviors, from simple headaches to convulsive attacks, were attributed to evil spirits that inhabited or controlled the afflicted person's body. According to historians, these ancient peoples attributed many forms of illness to demonic possession, sorcery, or the behest of an offended ancestral spirit. Within this system of belief, called *demonology*, the victim was usually held at least partly responsible for the misfortune.

It has been suggested that Stone Age cave dwellers may have treated behavior disorders with a surgical method called **trephining,** in which part of the skull was chipped away to provide an opening through which the evil spirit could escape. People may have

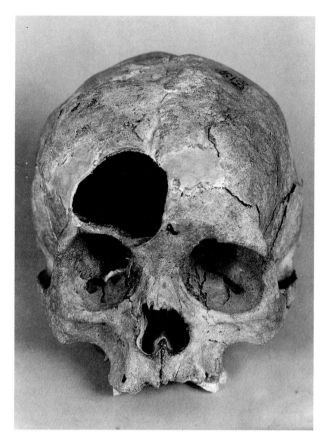

There are two theories about trephining. The most widely accepted postulates that trephining was a form of surgery that enabled an evil spirit to leave the body. The other theory rejects this idea, proposing instead that the holes were actually the result of wounds.

believed that when the evil spirit left, the person would return to his or her normal state. Surprisingly, some trephined skulls have been found to have healed over, indicating that some patients survived this extremely crude operation. As pointed out earlier, however, disputes often arise from the interpretation of historical data: A different explanation of trephining is that it was used to remove bone splinters and blood clots resulting from blows to the head in fights between men (Maher & Maher, 1985). This explanation is consistent with findings that most trephined skulls were of men and many had fractures (suggesting a vigorous blow).

Another treatment method used by the early Greeks, Chinese, Hebrews, and Egyptians was exorcism. In an **exorcism,** elaborate prayers, noises, emetics (drugs that induce vomiting), and extreme measures such as flogging and starvation were used to cast evil spirits out of an afflicted person's body.

Naturalistic Explanations (Greco-Roman Thought)

With the flowering of Greek civilization and its continuation into the era of Roman rule (500 B.C.–A.D. 500), naturalistic explanations gradually became distinct from supernatural ones. Early thinkers, such as Hippocrates (460–370 B.C.), a physician who is often called the father of medicine, actively questioned prevailing superstitious beliefs and proposed much more rational and scientific explanations for mental disorders.

The beliefs of many thinkers of this era were based on incorrect assumptions. They all relied heavily on observations and explanations, however, which form the foundation of the scientific method. Also, they denied the intervention of demons in the development of abnormality and instead stressed organic causes. Because of these factors, the treatment they prescribed for mental disorders tended to be more humane than previous treatments.

Hippocrates believed that, because the brain was the central organ of intellectual activity, deviant behavior was caused by **brain pathology**—that is, a dysfunction or disease of the brain. He also considered heredity and environment important factors in psychopathology. He classified mental illnesses into three categories—mania, melancholia, and phrenitis (brain fever)—and for each category gave detailed clinical descriptions of such disorders as paranoia, alcoholic delirium, and epilepsy. Many of his descriptions of symptoms are still used today, eloquent testimony to his keen powers of observation.

To treat melancholia, Hippocrates recommended tranquility, moderate exercise, a careful diet, abstinence from sexual activity, and bloodletting if necessary. His belief in environmental influences on behavior sometimes led him to separate disturbed patients from their families. He seems to have gained insight into a theory popular among psychologists today: that the family constellation often fosters deviant behavior in its own members.

Other thinkers who contributed to the organic explanation of behavior were the philosopher Plato and Greek physician Galen, who practiced in Rome. Plato (429–347 B.C.) carried on the thinking of Hippocrates; he insisted that the mentally disturbed were the responsibility of the family and should not be punished for their behavior. Galen (A.D. 129–199) made major contributions through his scientific examination of the nervous system and his explanation of the role of the brain and central nervous system in mental functioning. His greatest contribution may have been his codification of all medical knowledge from Hippocrates' time to his own.

During the Middle Ages, people suffering from a mental disorder were often perceived as being victims of a demonic possession. The most prevalent form of treatment was exorcism, usually conducted by religious leaders who used prayers, incantations, and sometimes torturous physical techniques to cast the evil spirit from the bodies of the afflicted.

Reversion to Superstition (the Middle Ages)

With the collapse of the Roman Empire and the rise of Christianity, rational and scientific thought gave way to a reemphasis on the supernatural. Religious dogma included the beliefs that nature was a reflection of divine will and beyond human reason, and that earthly life was a prelude to the "true" life (after death). Scientific inquiry—attempts to understand, classify, explain, and control nature—was less important than accepting nature as a manifestation of God's will.

The Dark Ages (Fifth Through Tenth Centuries)   Early Christianity did little to promote science and in many ways actively discouraged it. The church demanded uncompromising adherence to its tenets. Christian fervor brought with it the concepts of heresy and punishment; certain truths were deemed sacred, and those who challenged them were denounced as heretics. Scientific thought that was in conflict with church doctrine was not tolerated. Because of this atmosphere, rationalism and scholarly scientific works went underground for many years, preserved mainly by Arab scholars and European monks. Natural and supernatural explanations of illness were fused.

People came to believe that many illnesses were the result of supernatural forces, although they had natural causes. In many cases, the mentally ill were treated gently and with compassion in monasteries and at shrines where they were prayed over and allowed to rest. In other cases, treatment could be quite brutal, especially if illnesses were believed to be due to God's wrath. Because illness was then perceived to be punishment for sin, the sick person was assumed to be guilty of wrongdoing, and relief could come only through atonement or repentance.

During this period, treatment of the mentally ill sometimes consisted of torturous exorcistic procedures seen as appropriate to combat Satan and eject him from the possessed person's body. Prayers, curses, obscene epithets, and the sprinkling of holy water—as well as such drastic and painful "therapy" as flogging, starving, and immersion in hot water—were used to drive out the devil. The humane treatments that Hippocrates had advocated centuries earlier were challenged severely. A time of trouble for everyone, the Dark Ages were especially bleak for the mentally ill.

Mass Madness (Thirteenth Century)   Belief in the power of the supernatural became so prevalent and intense that it frequently affected whole populations. Beginning in Italy early in the thirteenth century, large numbers of people were affected by various forms of **mass madness,** or group hysteria, in which a great many people exhibit similar symptoms that have no apparent physical cause. One of the better known manifestations of this disorder was *tarantism,* a dance mania characterized by wild raving, jumping, dancing, and convulsions. The hysteria was most prevalent during the height of the summer and was attributed to the sting of a tarantula. A victim would leap up and run out into the street or marketplace, jumping and raving, to be joined by others who believed that they had also been bitten. The mania soon spread throughout the rest of Europe, where it became known as St. Vitus's Dance.

Another form of mass madness was *lycanthropy,* a mental disorder in which victims imagine themselves to be wolves and imitate wolves' actions. (Motion pictures about werewolves—people who assume the physical characteristics of wolves during the full moon—are modern reflections of this delusion.)

How can these phenomena be explained? Stress and fear are often associated with outbreaks of mass hysteria. During the thirteenth century, for example, there was enormous social unrest. The bubonic plague had decimated half the population of Europe. War, famine, and pestilence were rampant, and the social order of the times was crumbling.

A more recent example of mass hysteria apparently occurred in the small town of Berry, Alabama, where elementary school children became ill. A fifth-grader came to school with a rash and began scratching vigorously and uncontrollably. Other classmates began to scratch at an imaginary itch. The incident resulted in more than 150 schoolchildren afflicted with a frenzy of scratching, fainting, vomiting, numbness, crying, and screaming. Medical authorities concluded after months of study that the culprit could not be an infectious disease or food poisoning. Rather, the symptom pattern, onset, and manifestation suggested mass hysteria (Kramer, 1973).

Witchcraft (Fifteenth Through Seventeenth Centuries)
During the fifteenth and sixteenth centuries, the authority of the church was increasingly challenged by social and religious reformers. Reformers such as Martin Luther attacked the corruption and abuses of the clergy, precipitating the Protestant Reformation of the sixteenth century. Church officials viewed such protests as insurrections that threatened their power. According to the church, Satan himself fostered these attacks. By doing battle with Satan and with people supposedly influenced or possessed by Satan, the church actively endorsed an already popular belief in demonic possession and witches.

To counter the threat, Pope Innocent VIII issued a papal bull (decree) in 1484 calling on the clergy to identify and exterminate witches. This resulted in the 1486 publication of the extremely influential *Malleus Maleficarum* (The Witch's Hammer). The mere existence of this document acted to confirm the existence of witches, and it also outlined means of detecting them. For example, red spots on the skin (birthmarks) were supposedly made by the claw of the devil in sealing a blood pact and thus were damning evidence of a contract with Satan. Such birth defects as club foot and cleft palate also aroused suspicion.

The church initially recognized two forms of demonic possession: unwilling and willing. God let the devil seize an unwilling victim as punishment for a sinful life. A willing person, who made a blood pact with the devil in exchange for supernatural powers, was able to assume animal form and cause disasters such as floods, pestilence, storms, crop failures, and sexual impotence. Although unwilling victims of possession at first received more sympathetic treatment than that given those who willingly conspired with the devil, this distinction soon evaporated.

People whose actions were interpreted as peculiar were often suspected of witchcraft. It was acceptable to use torture to obtain confessions from suspected witches, and many victims confessed because they preferred death to prolonged agony. Thousands of innocent men, women, and even children were beheaded, burned alive, or mutilated.

Witch hunts occurred in both colonial America and Europe. The witchcraft trials of 1692 in Salem, Massachusetts, were infamous. Authorities there acted on statements taken from children who may have been influenced by the sensational stories told by an old West Indian servant. Several hundred people were accused, many were imprisoned and tortured, and twenty were killed. It has been estimated that some 20,000 people (mainly women) were killed as witches in Scotland alone, and that more than 100,000 throughout Europe were executed as witches during the middle of the fifteenth to the end of the seventeenth century.

It would seem reasonable to assume that the mentally ill would be especially prone to being perceived as witches. Indeed, most psychiatric historians argue that mental disorders were at the roots of witchcraft persecutions (Alexander & Selesnick, 1966; Deutsch, 1949; Zilboorg & Henry, 1941). Support for the belief that many accused witches were mentally ill was based on the following evidence: (1) some witches claimed that they could do impossible acts (such as fly and cause floods) and thus must have been deluded (schizophrenic); (2) they participated in sabbats (nocturnal orgies) and must have been psychopaths or nymphomaniacs; (3) they evidenced localized sensitivity to pain in various parts of their bodies and must have been hysterics; and (4) they evidenced symptoms associated with high suggestibility, delusions, or hallucinations. Spanos (1978), however, in a comprehensive critical analysis concluded that very little support could be found to indicate that accused witches were mentally ill.

Indeed, the lines of evidence just mentioned either have no basis in fact or were misinterpreted. Sabbats, for example, seem to have existed only in the imaginations of the witch-hunters. Claims of supernatural powers were obtained from the accused only after prolonged and painful torture, and trickery was often used to diminish body sensitivity. It appears that, while some accused witches may have been mentally ill, most were normal (Schoeneman, 1984).

The Rise of Humanism (the Renaissance)

A resurgence of rational and scientific inquiry during the Renaissance (fifteenth and seventeenth centuries) led to great advances in science and **humanism,** a philosophical movement that emphasizes human welfare and the worth and uniqueness of the individual. Until this time, most asylums were at best custodial centers where the mentally disturbed were chained, caged, starved, whipped, and even exhibited to the public for a small fee, much like animals in a zoo. But if people were "mentally ill" and not possessed, then they should be treated as though they were sick. A number of new methods for treating the mentally ill reflected this humanistic spirit.

In 1563 Johann Weyer (1515–1588), a German physician, published a revolutionary book that challenged the foundation of witchcraft. Weyer asserted that many people who were tortured, imprisoned, and burned as witches were mentally disturbed, not possessed by demons. The emotional agonies he was made to endure for committing this heresy are well documented. His book was severely criticized and banned by both church and state, but it proved to be a forerunner of the humanitarian perspective on mental illness. Others eventually followed his lead.

The Reform Movement (Eighteenth and Nineteenth Centuries)

In France, Philippe Pinel (1745–1826), a physician, was put in charge of La Bicêtre, a hospital for insane men in Paris. Pinel instituted what came to be known as the **moral treatment movement**—a shift to more humane treatment of the mentally disturbed. He ordered that inmates' chains be removed, replaced dungeons with sunny rooms, encouraged exercise outdoors on hospital grounds, and treated patients with kindness and reason. Surprising many disbelievers, the freed patients did not become violent; instead, this humane treatment seemed to foster recovery and improved behavior. Pinel later instituted similar equally successful reforms at La Salpêtrière, a large mental hospital for women in Paris.

In England William Tuke (1732–1822), a prominent Quaker tea merchant, established a retreat at York for the "moral treatment" of mental patients. At this pleasant country estate, the patients worked, prayed, rested, and talked out their problems—all in an atmosphere of kindness quite unlike that of the lunatic asylums of the time.

In the United States, three individuals—Benjamin Rush, Dorothea Dix, and Clifford Beers—made important contributions to the moral treatment movement. Benjamin Rush (1745–1813), widely acclaimed as the father of U.S. psychiatry, attempted to train physicians to treat mental patients and to introduce more humane treatment policies into mental hospitals. He insisted that patients be accorded respect and dignity and that they be gainfully employed while hospitalized, an idea that anticipated the modern concept of work therapy. Yet Rush was not unaffected by the established practices and beliefs of his times: His theories were influenced by astrology, and his remedies included bloodletting and purgatives.

Dorothea Dix (1802–1887), a New England schoolteacher, was the preeminent American social reformer of the nineteenth century. While teaching

Dorothea Dix was an exceptional contributor to the social reform movements of the nineteenth century—an era when women were discouraged from political participation.

Sunday school to female prisoners, she became familiar with the deplorable conditions in which jailed mental patients were forced to live. (Prisons and poorhouses were commonly used to incarcerate these patients.) For the next forty years, Dix worked tirelessly for the mentally ill. She campaigned for reform legislation and funds to establish suitable mental hospitals and asylums. She raised millions of dollars, established more than thirty modern mental hospitals, and greatly improved conditions in countless others. But the struggle for reform was far from over. Although the large hospitals that replaced jails and poorhouses had better physical facilities, the humanistic, personal concern of the moral treatment movement was lacking.

That movement was given further impetus in 1908 with the publication of *A Mind That Found Itself,* a book by Clifford Beers (1876–1943) about his own mental collapse. His book describes the terrible treatment he and other patients experienced in three mental institutions, where they were beaten, choked, spat on, and restrained with straitjackets. His vivid account aroused great public sympathy and attracted the interest and support of the psychiatric establishment, including such eminent figures as psychologist-philosopher William James. Beers founded the National Committee for Mental Hygiene (forerunner of the National Mental Health Association), an organization dedicated to educating the public about mental illness and about the need to treat the mentally ill rather than punish them for their unusual behaviors.

It would be naive to believe that these reforms have totally eliminated inhumane treatment of the mentally disturbed. Books like Mary Jane Ward's *The Snake Pit* (1946) and films like Frederick Wiseman's *Titicut Follies* (1967) continue to document harsh treatment of mental patients. Even the severest critic of the mental health system, however, would have to admit that conditions and treatment for the mentally ill have improved in this century.

CAUSES: EARLY VIEWPOINTS

Paralleling the rise of humanism in the treatment of mental illness was an inquiry into its causes. Two schools of thought emerged. The *organic viewpoint* holds that mental disorders are the result of physiological damage or disease; the *psychological viewpoint* stresses an emotional basis for mental illness. It is important to note that most people were not extreme adherents of one or the other. Rather, they tended to combine elements of both, which predated the biopsychosocial model widely used today.

The Organic Viewpoint

Hippocrates' suggestion of an organic explanation for abnormal behavior was ignored during the Middle Ages but revived after the Renaissance. Not until the nineteenth century, however, did the organic or **biogenic view**—the belief that mental disorders have a physical or physiological basis—become important. The ideas of Wilhelm Griesinger (1817–1868), a German psychiatrist who believed that all mental disorders had physiological causes, received considerable attention. Emil Kraepelin (1856–1926), a follower of Griesinger, observed that certain symptoms tend to occur regularly in clusters, called **syndromes.** Kraepelin believed that each cluster of symptoms represented a mental disorder with its own unique—and clearly specifiable—cause, course, and outcome. He attributed all disorders to one of four organic causes: metabolic disturbance, endocrine difficulty, brain disease, or heredity. In his *Textbook of Psychiatry* (1923 [1883]), Kraepelin outlined a system for classifying mental illnesses on the basis of their organic causes. That system was the original basis for the diagnostic categories in the *Diagnostic and Statistical Manual of Mental Disorders* (DSM), the classification system of the American Psychiatric Association.

The acceptance of an organic cause for mental disorders was accelerated by medical breakthroughs in the study of the nervous system. The effects of brain disorders, such as cerebral arteriosclerosis, on mental retardation and on senile and other psychoses led many scientists to suspect or advocate organic factors as the sole cause of all mental illness. And, as we will see in Chapter 2, the drug revolution of the 1950s made medication available for almost every disorder. The issue of their therapeutic effectiveness and how they work, however, is still hotly debated today.

The organic viewpoint gained even greater strength with the discovery of the organic basis of general paresis, a progressively degenerative and irreversible physical and mental disorder. Several breakthroughs had led scientists to suspect that the deterioration of mental and physical abilities exhibited by certain mental patients might actually be caused by an organic disease. The work of Louis Pasteur (1822–1895) established the germ theory of disease (invasion of the body by parasites). Then in 1897 Richard von Krafft-Ebing (1840–1902), a German neurologist, inoculated paretic patients with pus from syphilitic sores; when the patients failed to develop the secondary symptoms of syphilis, Krafft-Ebing concluded that the subjects had been previously infected by that disease. Finally, in 1905 a German zoologist, Fritz Schaudinn (1871–1906), isolated the microorganism that causes syphilis and thus paresis.

These discoveries convinced many scientists that every mental disorder might eventually be linked to an organic cause.

The Psychological Viewpoint

Some scientists noted, however, that certain types of emotional disorders were not associated with any organic disease in the patient. Such observations led to another view that stressed psychological factors rather than organic factors as the cause of many disorders. For example, the inability to attain personal goals and resolve interpersonal conflicts could lead to intense feelings of frustration, depression, failure, anger, and consequent disturbed behavior.

Mesmerism and Hypnotism   The unique and exotic techniques of Friedrich Anton Mesmer (1734–1815), an Austrian physician who practiced in Paris, presented an early challenge to the organic point of view. It is important to note, however, that Mesmer was really an anomaly and not part of mainstream scientific thinking. Mesmer developed a highly controversial treatment that came to be called *mesmerism* and that was the forerunner of the modern practice of hypnotism.

Mesmer performed his most miraculous cures in the treatment of *hysteria*—the appearance of symptoms such as blindness, deafness, loss of bodily feeling, and paralysis that seem to have no organic basis. According to Mesmer, hysteria was a manifestation of the body's need to redistribute the magnetic fluid that determined a person's mental and physical health. His techniques for curing this illness involved inducing a sleeplike state, during which his patients became highly susceptible to suggestion. During this state, their symptoms often disappeared.

Mesmer's dramatic and theatrical techniques earned him censure as well as fame. A committee of prominent thinkers, including U.S. ambassador Benjamin Franklin, investigated Mesmer and declared him a fraud. He was finally forced to leave Paris.

Although Mesmer's basic assumptions were discredited, the power of suggestion proved to be a strong therapeutic technique in the treatment of hysteria. The cures he effected stimulated scientific interest in and much bitter debate about the **psychogenic view**—the belief that mental disorders are caused by psychological and emotional factors, rather than organic factors.

An English physician, James Braid (1795–1860), renamed mesmerism *neurohypnotism* (later shortened to *hypnotism*) because he believed that the technique induced sleep by producing paralysis of the eyelid muscles. (The Latin word *hypnos* means "sleep.")

The work of Louis Pasteur (1822–1895) was considered instrumental in establishing the germ theory of disease leading to the organic view of mental illness.

Braid's trance-inducing technique of having a subject gaze steadily at an object has now become almost a standard procedure in hypnosis.

The Nancy School   About ten years after Mesmer died, a number of researchers began to experiment actively with hypnosis. Among them was Jean-Martin Charcot (1825–1893), a neurosurgeon at La Salpêtrière Hospital in Paris and the leading neurologist of his time. His initial experiments with hypnosis led him to abandon it in favor of more traditional methods of treating hysteria, which he claimed was caused by organic damage to the nervous system. Other experimenters had more positive results using hypnosis, however, which convinced him to try it again. His subsequent use of the technique in the study of hysteria did much to legitimize the application of hypnosis in medicine.

The experimenters most instrumental in Charcot's conversion were two physicians practicing in the city of Nancy, in eastern France. First working separately, Ambroise-Auguste Liébeault (1823–1904) and Hippolyte-Marie Bernheim (1840–1919) later came together to work as a team. As a result of their experiments, they hypothesized that hysteria was a form of self-hypnosis. The results they obtained in treating patients attracted other scientists, who collectively became known as the "Nancy School." In treating hysterical patients under hypnosis, they were often able to remove symptoms of paralysis, deafness, blindness, and anesthesia. They were also able to produce these symptoms in normal persons through hypnosis. Their work demonstrated impressively that suggestion could cause certain forms of mental illness; that is, symptoms of mental and physical disorders could have a psychological rather than an organic explanation. This conclusion represented a major breakthrough in the conceptualization of mental disorders.

Breuer and Freud The idea that psychological processes could produce mental and physical disturbances began to gain credence among several physicians who were using hypnosis. Among them was the Viennese doctor Josef Breuer (1842–1925). He discovered accidentally that, after one of his female patients spoke quite freely about her past traumatic experiences while in a trance, many of her symptoms abated or disappeared. He achieved even greater success when the patient recalled previously forgotten memories and relived their emotional aspects. This latter technique became known as the **cathartic method,** a therapeutic use of verbal expression to release pent-up emotional conflicts. It foreshadowed psychoanalysis, whose founder, Sigmund Freud (1856–1939), was influenced by Charcot and was a colleague of Breuer. Freud's theories have had a great and lasting influence in the field of abnormal psychology.

While psychoanalysis offered an intrapsychic explanation of abnormal behavior, another viewpoint that emerged during the latter part of this period was more firmly rooted in laboratory science: *behaviorism*. The behavioristic perspective stressed the importance of directly observable behavior and the conditions or stimuli that evoked, reinforced, and extinguished them. As we will see in Chapter 2, behaviorism not only offered an alternative explanation of the development of both normal and abnormal behavior, it also demonstrated a high degree of success in treating maladaptive behaviors.

CONTEMPORARY TRENDS IN ABNORMAL PSYCHOLOGY

Earlier, we made the statement that our current explanations of abnormal behavior have been heavily influenced by the beliefs of the past. Much has changed, however, in our understanding and treatment

of psychopathological disorders. Twentieth-century views of abnormality continue to evolve as they incorporate the effects of several major events and trends in the field: (1) the drug revolution in psychiatry, (2) diversity and the influence of multicultural psychology, (3) managed health care and proliferation of mental health professionals, and (4) increased appreciation for research in abnormal psychology.

The Drug Revolution

Many mental health professionals consider the introduction of psychiatric drugs in the 1950s as one of the great medical advances in the twentieth century (Andreasen, 1984; Lickey & Gordon, 1991). Although some might find such a statement excessive, it is difficult to overemphasize the impact that drug therapy has had. It started in 1949 when an Australian psychiatrist, John F. J. Cade, reported on his successful experiments with lithium (a drug currently used for persons with bipolar affective disorders) in radically calming manic patients who had been hospitalized for years. Several years later, French psychiatrists Jean Delay and Pierre Deniker discovered that the drug chlorpromazine (brand name, Thorazine) was extremely effective in treating agitated schizophrenics. Within a matter of years, drugs were developed to treat disorders such as depression, schizophrenia, phobias, obsessive-compulsive disorders, and anxiety. Large classes of drugs were developed for depression (antidepressant drugs), anxiety (antianxiety drugs), and grossly impaired thinking (antipsychotic drugs).

These drugs were considered revolutionary because they rapidly and dramatically decreased or eliminated troublesome symptoms experienced by patients. As a result, other forms of therapy became available to the mentally ill, who were now more able to focus their attention on their therapy. Their stays in mental hospitals were shortened and were more cost effective than prolonged hospitalizations. In addition, they were allowed to return home while receiving treatment. The new drug therapies were credited with the depopulation of mental hospitals, often referred to as deinstitutionalization (see discussion in Chapter 18).

Statistics on mental health care between 1905 and 1986 map the impact of drug therapy. The number of patients residing in mental institutions continued to rise steadily to a high of 550,000 in 1956. At that point, drugs were introduced and the upward trend was reversed. By 1986, only 111,000 patients remained hospitalized. This decline can be attributed not to a decrease in new admissions but rather to shorter stays and earlier releases (Lickey & Gordon, 1991; Manderscheid & Sonnenschein, 1992). To handle the large increase of patients returning to the community, outpatient treatment became the primary mode of service for the severely disturbed. In addition to changing the way therapy was dispensed, the introduction of psychiatric drugs revived strong belief in the biological bases of mental disorders.

Diversity and Multicultural Psychology

We are fast becoming a multicultural, multiracial, and multilingual society. U.S. Census figures support the fact that within several short decades, racial and ethnic minorities will become a numerical majority (Atkinson, Morten & Sue, 1993). These changes have been referred to as "the diversification of the United States" or literally the "changing complexion of society." Much of this is fueled by two major trends in the United States: the increased immigration of visible racial and ethnic minorities, and the differential birth rates among the various racial ethnic groups in our society. We know that the majority of new immigrants to the United States are of Asian origin (34 percent) or Hispanic/Latino origin (34 percent). It is people of color—visually identifiable racial and ethnic minority groups—who are coming to the United States in the largest numbers. At the same time, the average number of children born to racial and ethnic minorities is much higher than that of their White counterparts (Whites, 1.7; African Americans, 2.4; Mexican Americans, 2.9; Cambodian Hmongs, 11.9). Taken together, these two trends make it clear that European Americans will soon become a numerical minority.

Diversity has had a major impact on the mental health profession, creating a new field of study called **multicultural psychology**. As we saw earlier in this chapter, the multicultural approach stresses the importance of culture, race, ethnicity, gender, age, socioeconomic class, and other similar factors in its effort to understand and treat abnormal behavior. There is now recognition that mental health professionals need to (1) increase their cultural sensitivity, (2) acquire knowledge of the world views and lifestyles of a culturally diverse population, and (3) develop culturally relevant therapy approaches in working with different groups (APA, 1993; Sue, Arredondo & McDavis, 1992). Although issues of race, culture, ethnicity, and gender have traditionally been ignored or distorted in the mental health literature, there is now increasing recognition that these factors are powerful forces in influencing many aspects of normal and abnormal human development (D. W. Sue & D. Sue, 1990).

For example, gender differences are clear in findings like those cited earlier in this chapter—men are more likely to have higher rates of alcohol or drug abuse or dependence, whereas women are more likely to have higher rates of depressive and anxiety disorders (Regier et al., 1988). Some evidence exists that people in lower socioeconomic classes are likely to be identified as severely disturbed when they suffer an emotional disorder (Lopez, 1989). Some disorders are often found at higher-than-average rates among members of particular racial or ethnic minority groups. American Indians have higher rates of alcohol abuse and dependence than those found in the general population (Red Horse, 1982; Rhoades et al., 1980). Statistics also show inordinately high suicide rates in the American Indian population (Shore, 1988). Likewise, Hispanic Americans have been identified as suffering more severe cognitive impairment than European Americans and may somaticize (express psychological problems via bodily complaints) more (Lopez, 1989; Lopez & Hernandez, 1987).

What do these differences mean? Are they real or just artifacts that can be explained in other possible ways? Although these questions will no doubt continue to be debated, several tentative conclusions seem warranted. First, all groups appear to be equally susceptible to psychological distress. Furthermore, considerable evidence suggests that social conditioning, cultural factors, sociopolitical influences, and diagnostic bias may all affect the identification and manifestation of a behavior disorder. The First Person feature is one example of successful therapy based on sociocultural factors.

Social Conditioning How we are raised, what values are instilled in us, and how we are expected to behave in fulfilling our roles seem to have a major effect on the type of disorder we are most likely to exhibit. In the case of gender, for example, the roles we are expected to play and the traditional standards of appropriate or inappropriate gender-role behavior may account for some differences between men and women in mental disorders. In our culture, men are raised to fulfill the masculine role, to be independent, assertive, courageous, active, unsentimental, and objective. Women, in contrast, are raised to be dependent, helpful, fragile, self-abnegating, conforming, empathetic, and emotional. Some mental health professionals believe that, as a result, women are more likely to internalize their conflicts (resulting in anxiety and depression), whereas men are more likely to externalize and act out (resulting in drug or alcohol abuse and dependence). Although gender roles have begun to change, their effects continue to be widely felt.

Cultural Values and Influences Another heavily researched area of psychopathology is the way culture affects the manifestation of behavior disorders. Mental health professionals now recognize that types

FIRST PERSON

Patricia Arredondo

Over the years, I have had many opportunities to work with persons from different ethnic, linguistic, and racial backgrounds. Some of my first experiences were as a novice high school counselor. There were many new arrivals from Iran, Vietnam, the former Soviet Union, Hong Kong, and South America. I speak Spanish, which was helpful with students and their families from South America, but with others I had to use gestures, drawings, and a few basic English words. I can honestly say that there were many times that both the students and I felt frustrated and helpless. We wanted to communicate but were limited by language differences.

These experiences made me realize the importance of cultural and linguistic similarity between a counselor and a client. Even though I established good relationships with students from non-Latino backgrounds, they expressed real comfort with the resource persons who were more similar to them culturally. I also believe that my knowledge of issues of loss and grief typically experienced by immigrants enabled me to demonstrate understanding.

Currently, I am a licensed psychologist whose small clinical practice focuses on women. My work is twofold: providing seminars and psychoeducational groups on topics such as career transitions, enhancing personal empowerment, and managing stress; and providing psychotherapy. Most clients have weekly sessions.

I remember one client who was sent to me by an employee assistance program of a local hospital. Elsa, a woman in her fifties, was originally from Ecuador but had been in the United States for ten years. Elsa's supervisor was concerned about her withdrawn behavior. She thought it might indicate a personality problem with her co-workers, although Elsa had had no previous work problems.

Elsa came in looking very dejected. When I greeted her in Spanish, she broke into tears, saying that she was glad she could finally speak to someone who might understand her. Elsa continued to cry as she shared her story. Her husband had died two years after coming to Boston. Although her work at the hospital was not a problem, only one of her co-workers spoke Spanish. She could make small talk with others but could not share anything very personal.

Elsa's current sadness involved her son who had stayed in Ecua-

of mental disorders differ from country to country, and that major differences in cultural traditions among various racial and ethnic minority groups in the United States may influence their susceptibility to certain emotional disorders. Hispanic Americans are not alone in their tendency to somaticize. Among Asian Americans, experiencing physical complaints is a common and culturally accepted means of expressing psychological and emotional stress (S. Sue & Morishima, 1982; Uba, 1994). It is believed that physical problems cause emotional disturbances and that the emotional disturbances will disappear as soon as appropriate treatment for the physical illness is instituted. In addition, mental illness among Asians is seen as a source of shame and disgrace, although physical illness is acceptable. Asian values also emphasize restraint of strong feelings. Thus when stress is encountered, the mental health professional is likely to hear complaints involving headaches, fatigue, restlessness, and disturbances of sleep and appetite.

Sociopolitical Influences In response to a history of prejudice, discrimination, and racism, many minorities have adopted various behaviors (in particular, behaviors toward Whites) that have proved important for survival in a racist society (Grier & Cobbs, 1968; Ridley, 1995). Mental health professionals may define these behaviors as abnormal and deviant. Yet, from the minority group perspective, such behaviors may function as healthy survival mechanisms. For example, "playing it cool" has been identified as one means by which minorities may conceal their true thoughts and feelings. An African American who is experiencing conflict, anger, or even rage may be skillful at appearing serene and composed. This tactic is a survival mechanism aimed at reducing one's vulnerability to harm and exploitation in a hostile environment. Early personality studies of African Americans concluded that, as a group, they tend to appear more "suspicious," "mistrustful," and "paranoid" than their white counterparts. But are African Americans inher-

dor with an aunt and uncle, hoping to join her and her husband after they had settled economically. The years had passed, and with her husband's death the reunion had never taken place. Now, her son was about to graduate from dental school and Elsa was unable to make a visit to Ecuador for the special occasion. As a result, she was experiencing profound loss and grief. She talked about her dreams for her children and how sad and angry she felt at not being able to be with them. I listened to her story, empathizing with her separation from her family and the loneliness of living in a foreign culture. We spoke entirely in Spanish.

Elsa and I met on a weekly basis. I saw my role as helping Elsa clarify her feelings and develop coping strategies to deal with her situation. We talked about her options, and she kept a journal during this time. Since she had few people to speak with after work, I suggested that she transfer some of her thoughts and feelings to paper. She did so and reported this to be a very comforting activity.

Within a few weeks, Elsa reported feeling better and was making arrangements for her son to visit Boston. Elsa seemed to have relieved herself of many sad thoughts and loneliness, enabling her to be resourceful and involved with her job. She told me how much she appreciated my listening and communicating with her in Spanish.

I have thought about what might have happened to Elsa if the EAP had not sought out a Spanish speaking, Latina therapist. It is possible that Elsa may have had difficulty describing her grief in English. Most persons, I have found, prefer to use their native language when expressing feelings. A non-Latina therapist may also have inferred a culturally inappropriate explanation for Elsa's sadness. She may have been seen as overinvolved with her grown son and in a dependent relationship. Her emotional crying in the first sessions might have been interpreted as the behavior of a helpless, passive woman unable to deal with disappointment.

A person familiar with Latino culture, on the other hand, would appreciate the great emphasis placed on family interdependence and closeness, a mother's wish to be with her child at special events, and a child's wish to have his or her success be recognized by the family. A culturally aware therapist would likely recognize Elsa's case as situational rather than chronic depression, and avoid administering American-normed tests or prescribing drugs as the first step in treatment.

Based on my experiences, I believe that knowledge of culture is key to providing appropriate and relevant interventions. Learned cultural, linguistic, and counseling competencies are essential, but cultural and linguistic similarity between counselor and client are equally desirable.

Patricia Arredondo is director of Empowerment Workshops, a women-oriented private practice in Brookline, Massachusetts.

---

ently pathological, as studies suggest, or are they making healthy responses? Members of minority groups who have been victims of discrimination and oppression in a society not yet free of racism have good reason to be suspicious and distrustful of white society. The "paranoid orientation" may reflect not only survival skills but also *accurate reality testing.* We are pointing out that certain behaviors and characteristics need to be evaluated not only by an absolute standard, but by the sociopolitical context in which they arise.

Bias in Diagnosis and Classification Epidemiological studies reporting the distribution and types of mental disorders that occur in the population may be prone to bias on the part of the clinician and researcher. The mental health professional is not immune from inheriting the prejudicial attitudes, biases, and stereotypes of the larger society. Even the most enlightened and well-intentioned mental health professional may be the victim of race, gender, and social class bias. Several forms of bias also appear to be operative when clinicians are identifying certain disorders. One is the tendency to overpathologize—to exaggerate the severity of disorders—among clients from particular socieconomic, racial, or ethnic groups because their cultural values or lifestyles may differ markedly from the clinician's own. Overpathologizing disorders has been found to exist for African Americans, Hispanic Americans, and women (Lopez & Hernandez, 1986).

Equally disturbing is a second bias: underpathologizing a disorder. For example, some studies reveal a minimizing bias in the diagnosis of psychotic symptoms for mentally retarded individuals, stemming from an assumption that such symptoms are more "normal" for them (Reiss, Levitan & Szyszko, 1982). Women who present symptoms perceived to be related to their gender role (emotionality and depression) may be seen as less disturbed (Horwitz & White, 1987).

In evaluating normality and abnormality, it is important to consider the sociopolitical context in which thoughts, feelings, and behaviors arise. Many African Americans, for example, are more likely to consider the possibility of police misconduct due to prejudice and discrimination, as did the predominantly African American jury in the O. J. Simpson trial. Likewise, the growth of paramilitary groups reflects increased suspicion and distrust of government. Many consider this perception "healthy paranoia" rather than pathology.

A third instance of biases is linked to overdiagnosis and underdiagnosis of specific disorders. Being African American or Hispanic may increase a person's chances of being misdiagnosed as schizophrenic when in fact the patient has a bipolar disorder (Mukherjee et al., 1983).

Thus it is clear that one of the most powerful emerging trends in the mental health field is in increased interest, appreciation, and respect for multicultural psychology. Understanding abnormal behavior requires a realistic appraisal of the cultural context in which behavior occurs and an understanding of how culture influences the manifestations of abnormality.

Managed Health Care and Proliferation of Mental Health Care Professionals

The U.S. public spends increasing amounts each year in either direct or indirect expenses for mental health care. Some 20 years ago we spent $40 billion, of which nearly 40 percent went for direct care, including therapy and hospitalization (Levine & Willner, 1976). From 1974 to 1985 the number of psychologists in health care increased by more than 100 percent (Dorken, Stapp & VandenBos, 1986; Enright et al., 1990). A recent report of the National Behavioral Science Research Agenda Committee (Observer, 1992) indicates that when the costs of mental health problems are calculated to include decreased productivity in the workplace, educational problems, an aging society, drug and alcohol abuse, and health and violence in the United States, we are literally speaking about hundreds of billions of dollars.

Managed Health Care Managed health care is a term that refers to the industrialization of health care, whereby large organizations in the private sector control the delivery of services.

With mental health costs escalating at such a rapid rate in the 1980s, attempts were made to contain costs via "managed health care" or some form of health reform (Cummings, 1995; Hall, 1995).

In the past, psychotherapy was carried out primarily by individuals in solo offices or in small group practices. Some clients paid for services out of their own pockets. Others had health plans that covered treatment, generally with minimal restrictions on the number of sessions the client could attend, and usually with reimbursable treatment for a broad array of "psychological problems." The fees, number of sessions, and types of treatment were determined by the mental health practitioner.

As health-care costs escalated, however, the federal government passed legislation that enabled the private sector (insurance companies, large medical care groups, and other medical business organizations) to influence the dispensing of health care. Overnight, the managed health-care industry was launched, allowing these groups to develop comprehensive health-care systems (including mental health services) patterned after such large organizations as Kaiser and Blue Cross–Blue Shield.

The industrialization of health care has wrought major changes in the mental health profession:

■ Business interests are exerting increasing control over psychotherapy by determining reimbursable diagnoses, limiting the number of sessions psychologists may offer clients, and imposing other such restrictions.

■ Current business practices may depress the income of practitioners. Organizations may prefer hiring therapists with a degree at the master's level rather than the doctoral level, or they may reimburse at rates below those set by the therapist.

■ Psychologists may be asked to justify the use of their therapies on the basis of whether they are empirically validated—established treatments with research support.

This last point is especially important. For example, if research reveals that cognitive-behavioral forms of treatment are more successful than psychodynamic approaches for a certain form of phobia, then therapy using the latter approach might be denied by the insurance carrier.

These trends have alarmed many psychologists who fear that decisions will be made not so much for health reasons but for business ones, that the need for doctoral-level practitioners will decrease, and that the livelihood of clinicians will be threatened. No one can say with certainty whether these fears will be realized. The jury is still out on the effects of managed care.

The Growing Number of Mental Health Care Professionals The number and type of qualified helping professionals have grown along with the demand for mental health treatment. In the past, mental health

services were controlled primarily by psychiatrists, psychologists, and psychiatric social workers. The list of acceptable (licensed) providers in different fields has expanded rapidly. In 1968 there were 12,000 clinical psychologists in the United States; today there are more than 40,000. As Figure 1.4 illustrates, nearly 300,000 professional therapists now practice in the United States (primarily in clinical psychology, counseling psychology, psychiatry, psychoanalysis, social work, and marriage and family counseling). As one writer observed, there are more professional therapists than librarians, firefighters, or mail carriers, and there are twice as many therapists as dentists and pharmacists (Zilbergeld, 1983).

The qualifications, training, and functions of the people who work as mental health professionals are briefly described in Table 1.1. Today, students desiring to enter practice can choose from a variety of professional careers.

Appreciation for Research

Breakthroughs in neuroanatomy, identification of the role that neurotransmitters play in mental disorders, and increasing interest in exploring empirically validated forms of psychotherapy have produced another contemporary trend: a heightened appreciation for the role of research in the study of abnormal behavior. The success of psychopharmacology spawned renewed interest and research into brain-behavior relationships. Indeed, it appears that more and more researchers are now turning to an exploration of the biological bases (chemical and structural) of abnormal behavior. Within recent years, biological factors have been associated with depression, suicide, certain

The industrialization of health care has altered the therapy landscape. In order to contain rising mental health care costs, control of psychotherapy is increasingly being determined by business interests rather than by the medical community.

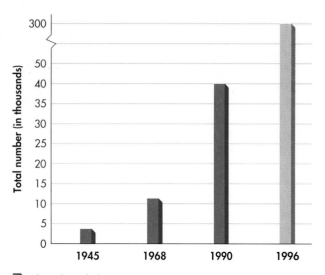

FIGURE 1.4 **Number of Professional Therapists in the United States** From 1945 to 1968 the number of clinical psychologists in the United States more than tripled; from that time until today, it quadrupled again. Clinical psychologists represent only a small portion of mental health professionals, who now approach nearly three hundred thousand. Professional therapists include psychiatrists, social workers, counseling psychologists, marriage and family counselors, and others.

forms of schizophrenia, learning disabilities, alcoholism, and Alzheimer's disease.

On another front, many researchers are focusing on aspects of mental illness that are primarily psychological rather than biological. As we shall see in Chapter 2, the behavioral school of thought and the recent interest and work in cognitive psychology have been instrumental not only in expressing this point of view but in advocating the use of scientific research in understanding human behavior (Hollon, DeRubeis & Seligman, 1992; Lipman & Kendall, 1992). Currently, insight into the most effective means of understanding and treating specific disorders is being sought in the comparison studies concerning the effectiveness of drug treatment versus cognitive treatment and in the development of empirically validated treatments (Chambless, 1993).

SOME CLOSING THOUGHTS

As you can see, the study of abnormal psychology is not only complex but also heavily influenced by the tenor of the times. As we begin our journey into at-

tempts to explain the causes of certain disorders, we encourage you not to become rigidly locked into one system or model. It is our contention that no one model is equally applicable to all situations, problems, and populations. All have something of worth to add. And, in reality, few contemporary psychologists or psychiatrists take the extreme of adhering just to one position. Indeed, most psychologists believe that mental illness probably springs not only from a combination of biological and psychological factors, but from societal and environmental influences as well. The realization that biological, psychological, and social factors must all be considered in explaining and treating mental disorders has been termed the **biopsychosocial approach.** It would be a serious oversight to neglect the powerful impact on mental health of family upbringing and influence, the stresses of modern society (unemployment, poverty, loss of a loved one, adapting to technological change, and so on), experiences of oppression (prejudice, discrimination, stereotyping), effects of natural disasters (earthquakes, floods, hurricanes), and human-made conflicts such as wars.

Finally, we would like to close this chapter with a word of caution. To be human is to encounter difficulties and problems in life. A course in abnormal psychology dwells on human problems—many familiar. As a result, we may be prone to the "medical student syndrome": reading about a disorder may lead us to suspect that we have the disorder or that a friend or relative has it (see Focus On on page 30). This reaction to the study of abnormal behavior is a common one, but one that we must all guard against.

SUMMARY

1. The objectives of abnormal psychology are to describe, explain, predict, and control behaviors that are strange or unusual. Four types of definitions are used to describe such behaviors and they differ in the criteria they apply. Conceptual definitions include statistical deviation, deviations from ideal mental health, and multicultural perspectives. Practical criteria consider the effect of the behavior on the person exhibiting it or on others. The third type involves an integrated approach in which behavior is judged from a number of different perspectives. And the fourth is the definition in the *Diagnostic and Statistical Manual of Mental Disorders* (DSM-IV). It may be that a single criterion or viewpoint is not sufficient but that abnormality should be defined from the combined vantage points of society, the individual, and the mental health professional.

TABLE 1.1 The Mental Health Professions

Clinical Psychology

Clinical psychology is the professional field concerned with the study, assessment, treatment, and prevention of abnormal behavior in disturbed individuals. Clinical psychologists must hold a Ph.D. degree from a university or a Psy.D. (doctor of psychology) degree, a more practitioner-oriented degree granted by several institutions. Their training includes coursework in psychopathology, personality, diagnosis, psychological testing, psychotherapy, and human physiology. Apart from these and other course requirements, there are two additional requirements for the Ph.D. degree. First, the candidate must complete a doctoral dissertation. Second, a practicum experience or internship, usually one year at a psychiatric hospital or mental health center, is also required.

Clinical psychologists work in a variety of settings, but most commonly they provide therapy to clients in hospitals and clinics and in private practice. Some choose to work in an academic setting where they can concentrate on teaching and research. Other clinical psychologists are hired by government or private organizations to do research.

Counseling Psychology

To a great extent, a description of clinical psychology applies to counseling psychology as well. The academic and internship requirements are similar, but the emphasis differs. Whereas clinical psychologists are trained to work specifically with a disturbed client population, counseling psychologists are usually more immediately concerned with the study of life problems in relatively normal people. Furthermore, counseling psychologists are more likely to be found in educational settings than in hospitals and clinics.

Psychiatry

Psychiatrists hold an M.D. degree. Their education includes the four years of medical school required for that degree, along with an additional three or four years of training in psychiatry. Of all the specialists involved in mental health care, only psychiatrists can prescribe drugs in the treatment of mental disorders.

Psychoanalysis

Psychoanalysis has been associated with medicine and psychiatry because its founder, Sigmund Freud, and his major disciples were physicians. But Freud was quite adamant in stating that one need not be medically trained to be a good psychoanalyst. Nevertheless, most psychoanalysts hold either the M.D. or the Ph.D. degree. In addition, psychoanalysts receive intensive training in the theory and practice of psychoanalysis at an institute devoted to the field. This training includes the individual's own analysis by an experienced analyst.

Psychiatric Social Work

Those entering psychiatric social work are trained in a school of social work, usually in a two-year graduate program leading to a master's degree. Included in this program is a one-year internship in a social-service agency, sometimes a mental health center. Some social workers go on to earn the D.S.W. (doctor of social work) degree. Traditionally, psychiatric social workers work in family counseling services or community agencies, where they specialize in intake (assessment and screening of clients), take psychiatric histories, and deal with other agencies.

Marriage and Family Counseling

Formerly, the counseling of married couples was usually performed by the clergy or by social workers in churches, public welfare agencies, and family-service organizations. Counseling and clinical psychologists may also work with couples and families. A specialty in marriage and family counseling has recently emerged, however, with its own professional organizations, journals, and state licensing requirements. Marriage and family counselors have varied professional backgrounds, but their training usually includes a master's degree in counseling and many hours of supervised clinical experience.

"I Have It, Too": The Medical Student Syndrome

Medical students probably caught it first. As they read about physical disorders and listened to lecturers describing illnesses, some students began to imagine that they themselves had one disorder or another. "Diarrhea? Fatigue? Trouble sleeping? That's me!" In this way, a cluster of symptoms—no matter how mild or how briefly experienced—can lead some people to suspect that they are very sick.

Students who take a course that examines psychopathology may be equally prone to believe that they have a mental disorder that is described in their text. It is possible, of course, that some students do suffer from a disorder and would benefit from counseling or therapy. Most, however, are merely experiencing an exaggerated sense of their susceptibility to disorders. In one study, it was found that one of every five individuals responded yes to the question "Have you ever felt that you were going to have a

nervous breakdown?" Of course, most of those people never suffered an actual breakdown (U.S. Department of Health, Education, and Welfare, 1971).

Two influences in particular may make us susceptible to these imagined disorders. One is the universality of the human experience. All of us have experienced misfortunes in life. We can all remember and relate to feelings of anxiety, unhappiness, guilt, lack of self-confidence, and even thoughts of suicide. In most cases, however, these feelings are normal reactions to stressful situations, not symptoms of disease. Depression following the loss of a loved one or anxiety before giving a speech to a large audience may be perfectly normal and appropriate. Another influence is our tendency to compare our own functioning with our perceptions of how other people are functioning. The outward behaviors of fellow students may

lead us to conclude that they experience few difficulties in life, are self-assured and confident, and are invulnerable to mental disturbance. If we were privy to their inner thoughts and feelings, however, we might be surprised to find that they share our apprehension and insecurities.

If you see yourself anywhere in the pages of this book, we hope you will take the time to discuss the matter with a friend or with one of your professors. You may be responding to pressures that you have not encountered before—a heavy course load, for example—and to which you have not yet adjusted. Other people can help point out these pressures to you. If your discussion supports your suspicion that you have a problem, however, then by all means consider getting help from your campus counseling and/or health clinic.

2. Mental health problems are widespread in the United States, and the human and economic costs are enormous. Among the many problems encountered by those suffering or who have suffered from a mental disturbance are the many myths and stereotypes that have plagued them.

3. Many of our current concepts of mental illness have their roots in past beliefs and practices. Ancient peoples believed in demonology and attributed abnormal behaviors to evil spirits that inhabited the victim's body. Treatment consisted of trephining, exorcism, and bodily assaults. Rational and scientific explanations of abnormality emerged during the Greco-Roman era. Especially influential was the thinking of Hippocrates, who believed that abnormal behavior

was due to organic causes, such as a dysfunction or disease of the brain. Treatment became more humane. With the collapse of the Roman Empire and the increased influence of the church and its emphasis on divine will and the hereafter, rationalist thought was suppressed and belief in the supernatural began to flourish again. During the Middle Ages, famine, pestilence, and dynastic wars caused enormous social upheaval. Forms of mass hysteria affected groups of people. In the fifteenth century, the church endorsed witch hunts, both in response to fear generated by social unrest and as a way to deal with those opposing the church's authority. Among the numerous men, women, and children who were tortured and killed as witches were some whom we would today call mentally ill. The Renaissance brought a return to rational and scientific inquiry along with a heightened interest in humanitarian methods of treating the mentally ill.

4. In the nineteenth and twentieth centuries, major medical breakthroughs fostered a belief in the organic roots of mental illness. The discovery of the microorganism that caused general paresis was especially important in this regard. Scientists believed that they would eventually find organic causes for all mental disorders. Mesmerism and later hypnosis supported another view, however. The uncovering of a relationship between hypnosis and hysteria corroborated the belief that psychological processes could produce emotional disturbances.

5. Four contemporary developments have had a major influence in the mental health professions: (a) the drug revolution in psychiatry, which not only allowed many of the more severely disturbed to be treated outside of a hospital setting, but lent credence to the organic viewpoint; (b) the increasing diversity of the United States, leading to renewed reliance on multicultural psychology; (c) the development of managed health care and the increasing proliferation of various mental health professionals; and (d) an increased appreciation for the role of research.

KEY TERMS

abnormal behavior Behavior that departs from some norm and that harms the affected individual or others

abnormal psychology The scientific study whose objectives are to describe, explain, predict, and control behaviors that are considered strange or unusual

biogenic view The belief that mental disorders have a physical or physiological basis

biopsychosocial approach The belief that biological, psychological, and social factors must all be considered in explaining and treating mental disorders

brain pathology Dysfunction or disease of the brain

cathartic method The therapeutic use of verbal expression to release pent-up emotional conflicts

cultural relativism The belief that what is judged to be normal or abnormal may vary from one culture to another

cultural universality The belief that the origin, process, and manifestation of disorders are equally applicable across all cultures

exorcism Ritual in which prayer, noise, emetics, and extreme measures such as flogging and starvation were used to cast evil spirits out of an afflicted person's body

humanism Philosophical movement that emphasizes human welfare and the worth and uniqueness of the individual

managed health care A term that refers to the industrialization of health care, whereby large organizations in the private sector control the delivery of services

mass madness Group hysteria, in which large numbers of people exhibit similar symptoms that have no apparent physical cause

moral treatment movement A shift to more humane treatment of the mentally disturbed; its initiation is generally attributed to Philippe Pinel

multicultural psychology A field of psychology that stresses the importance of culture, race, ethnicity, gender, age, socioeconomic class, and other similar factors in its efforts to understand and treat abnormal behavior

psychodiagnosis An attempt to describe, assess, and systematically draw inferences about an individual's psychological disorder

psychogenic view The belief or theory that mental disorders are caused by psychological and emotional factors, rather than organic factors

syndrome A cluster of symptoms that tend to occur together and that are believed to represent a particular disorder with its own unique cause, course, and outcome

therapy A program of systematic intervention whose purpose is to modify a client's behavioral, affective (emotional), or cognitive state

trephining An ancient surgical technique in which part of the skull was chipped away to provide an opening through which evil spirits could escape

CHAPTER 2

MODELS OF ABNORMAL BEHAVIOR

I n Chapter 1, we described the way the rise of humanism influenced society's attitude toward mental disorders. As rational thought replaced superstition in the eighteenth and nineteenth centuries, the mentally disturbed were increasingly regarded as unfortunate human beings who deserved respectful and humane treatment, not as monsters inhabited by the devil.

This humanistic view gave rise, in the late nineteenth and early twentieth centuries, to two different schools of thought about the causes of mental disorders. According to one group of thinkers, mental disorders are caused primarily by biological problems, and the disturbed individual is displaying symptoms of physical disease or damage. The second group of theorists believed that abnormal behavior is essentially psychosocial, rooted not in cells and tissues but in the invisible complexities of the human mind or in environmental forces.

In this chapter, we continue to trace the evolution of these two schools of thought and bring them up to date. We begin with the biological perspective and then examine several major psychosocial perspectives. A chart outlining these various approaches appears in Figure 2.1. The theories we examine in this chapter are by no means the only possible explanations of abnormal behavior. In the United States alone, over 130 such theories have been identified (Corey, 1991). Many are variants of the more basic theories discussed here; others have never gained widespread acceptance.

Let's begin by clarifying two terms you will encounter frequently. The first is **psychopathology,** which clinical psychologists use as a synonym for abnormal behavior. The second is **model,** a term that requires a more elaborate explanation.

MODELS IN THE STUDY OF PSYCHOPATHOLOGY

Scientists who need to discuss a phenomenon that is difficult to describe or explain often use an analogy, which enables them to liken the phenomenon to something more concrete. A *model* is such an analogy, and scientists most often use it to describe a phe-

nomenon or process that they cannot directly observe. In using an analogy, the scientist borrows terms, concepts, or principles from one field and applies them to another, as when a physician describes the eye as a camera.

Psychologists have used models extensively to help them conceptualize the causes of abnormal behavior, ask probing questions, determine what information and data are relevant, and interpret data. For example, when psychologists refer to their "patients" or speak of deviant behavior as "mental illness," they are borrowing the terminology of medicine and applying a *medical model* of abnormal behavior. They may also describe certain external symptoms as being visible signs of deep underlying conflict. Again, the medical analogy is clear: Just as fevers, rashes, perspiration, or infections may be symptoms of a bacterial or viral invasion of the body, bizarre behavior may be a symptom of a mind "invaded" by unresolved conflicts. Psychologists use a variety of such models, each embodying a particular theoretical approach. Hence we tend to use the terms *model, theory, viewpoint,* and *perspective* somewhat interchangeably. Most theorists realize that the models they construct will be limited and will not correspond in every respect to the phenomena they are studying. Because of the complexity of human behavior and our relatively shallow understanding of it, psychologists do not expect to develop *the* definitive model. Rather, they use the models to visualize psychopathology as if it truly worked in the manner described by the models.

To aid us in our analyses, we present the case of Steven V. We begin our discussion of each model with a thumbnail sketch of Steve's situation, as it might be seen by a clinician conceptualizing Steve's problems and recommending treatment within the parameters of the model being discussed.

Steven V., a 21-year-old college student, had been suffering from a crippling and severe bout of depression. Eighteen months earlier, Steve's woman friend, Linda, had broken off her relationship with him. However, it is important to note that Steve had a long psychiatric history, beginning well before he first sought help from the therapist at the university's psychological services center. Steve had actually been in and out of psychotherapy

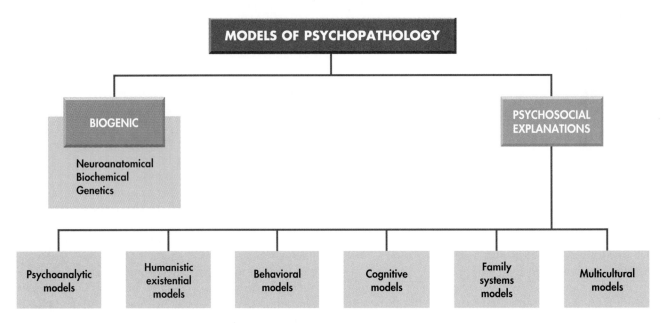

FIGURE 2.1 **The Major Models of Psychopathology** Attempts to explain abnormal behavior have resulted in more than a hundred explanations. The major models of psychopathology, however, are displayed here.

since kindergarten; while in high school, he was hospitalized twice for depression. His case records, nearly two inches thick, contained a number of diagnoses, including labels such as *schizoid personality, paranoid schizophrenia,* and *bipolar mood disorder.* Although his present therapist did not find these labels particularly helpful, Steve's clinical history did provide some clues to the causes of his problems.

Steven V. was born in a suburb of San Francisco, California, the only child of an extremely wealthy couple. His father, who is of Scottish descent, was a prominent businessman who worked long hours and traveled frequently. On those rare occasions when he was at home, Mr. V. was often preoccupied with business matters and held himself quite aloof from his son. The few interactions they had were characterized by his constant ridicule and criticism of Steve. Mr. V. was greatly disappointed that his son seemed so timid, weak, and withdrawn. Steve was extremely bright and did well in school, but Mr. V. felt that he lacked the "toughness" needed to survive and prosper in today's world. Once, when Steve was about ten years old, he came home from school with a bloody nose and bruised face, crying and complaining of being picked on by his schoolmates. His father showed no sympathy but instead berated Steve for losing the fight. In his father's presence, Steve usually felt worthless, humiliated, and fearful of doing or saying the wrong thing.

Mrs. V. was very active in civic and social affairs, and she, too, spent relatively little time with her son. Although she treated Steve more warmly and lovingly than his father did, she seldom came to Steve's defense when Mr. V. bullied him. She generally allowed her husband to make family decisions. In reality, Mrs. V. was quite lonely, feeling abandoned by Mr. V. She harbored a deep resentment toward him which she was frightened to express.

When Steve was a child, his mother at times had been quite affectionate. She had often allowed Steve to sleep with her in her bed when her husband was away on business trips. She usually dressed minimally on these occasions and was very demonstrative—holding, stroking, and kissing Steve. This behavior had continued until Steve was twelve, when his mother abruptly refused to let Steve into her bed. The sudden withdrawal of this privilege had confused and angered Steve, who was not certain what he had done wrong. He knew, though, that his mother had been quite upset when she awoke one night to find him masturbating next to her.

Most of the time, Steve's parents seemed to live separately from one another and from their son. Steve was raised, in effect, by a full-time maid. He rarely had playmates of his own age. His birthdays were celebrated with a cake and candles, but the only celebrants were Steve and his mother. By age ten, Steve had learned to keep himself occupied by playing "mind games," letting his imagination carry him off on flights of fantasy. He frequently imagined himself as a powerful figure—Superman or Batman. His fantasies were often extremely violent, and his foes were vanquished only after much blood had been spilled.

As Steve grew older, his fantasies and heroes became increasingly menacing and evil. When he was fifteen, he obtained a pornographic videotape that he viewed repeatedly on a video player in his room. Often, Steve would masturbate as he watched scenes of women being sexually violated. The more violent the acts against women, the more aroused he became. He was addicted to the *Nightmare on Elm Street* films, in which the villain, Freddie Kruger, disemboweled or slashed his victims to death with his razor-sharp glove. Steve now recalls that he spent much of his spare time between the ages of fifteen and seventeen watching X-rated videotapes or violent movies, his favorite being *The Texas Chainsaw Massacre,* in which a madman saws and hacks women to pieces. Steve always identified with the character perpetrating the outrage; at times, he imagined his parents as the victims.

At about age sixteen, Steve became convinced that external forces were controlling his mind and behavior and were drawing him into his fantasies. He was often filled with guilt and anxiety after one of his mind games. Although he was strongly attracted to his fantasy world, he also felt that something was wrong with it and with him. After seeing the movie *The Exorcist,* he became convinced that he was possessed by the devil.

THE BIOGENIC MODEL

Steven V. is a biological being, and the causes of his mental disorders are due to some form of biological malfunctioning. Environmental influences are important but probably secondary to the manifestation of psychopathology. I believe that the causes of Steve's problems reside in a possible genetic predisposition to mental disorders, an imbalance of brain chemistry, or, perhaps, in structural abnormalities in his neurological make-up. The fact that he suffers from paranoid schizophrenia and a bipolar affective disorder (disorders that have an increased probability of being present in blood relatives) seems to support such an explanation. The most effective way to treat this disorder is through drug therapy or some variation of somatic therapy.

Modern biological explanations of normal and abnormal behavior continue to share certain assumptions: (1) human thoughts, emotions, and behaviors are associated with nerve cell activities of the brain and spinal cord; (2) a change in thoughts, emotions, or behaviors will be associated with a change in activity or structure (or both) of the brain; (3) a mental disorder is highly correlated with some form of brain dysfunction; and (4) mental disorders can be treated by drugs or somatic intervention (P. R. Harris, 1980; Cottone, 1992).

The biological models have been heavily influenced by the neurosciences, a group of subfields that focus on brain structure, function, and disorder. Understanding biogenic explanations of human behavior requires knowledge about structure and function of the central nervous system (composed of the brain and spinal cord). Especially important is knowledge about how the brain is organized, how it works, and, especially, the chemical reactions that enhance or diminish normal brain actions.

The Human Brain

The brain is composed of billions of **neurons,** or nerve cells that transmit messages throughout the body. The brain is responsible for three very important and highly complicated functions. It receives information from the outside world, it uses the information to decide on a course of action, and it implements decisions by commanding muscles to move and glands to secrete. Weighing approximately three pounds, this relatively small organ continues to amaze and mystify biological researchers.

The brain is separated into two hemispheres. A disturbance in either one (such as by a tumor or by electrical stimulation with electrodes) may produce specific sensory or motor effects. Each hemisphere controls the opposite side of the body. For example, paralysis on the left side of the body indicates a dysfunction in the right hemisphere. In addition, the right hemisphere is associated with visual-spatial abilities and emotional behavior. The left hemisphere controls the language functions for nearly all right-handed people and for most left-handed ones (Golden & Vincente, 1983).

Viewed in cross section, the brain has three parts: forebrain, midbrain, and hindbrain. Although each part is vital for functioning and survival, the forebrain is probably the most relevant to a discussion of abnormality.

The Forebrain   The *forebrain* probably controls all the higher mental functions associated with human consciousness, learning, speech, thought, and memory. Within the forebrain are the thalamus, hypothalamus, reticular activating system, limbic system, and cerebrum (see Figure 2.2). The specific functions of these structures are still being debated, but we can discuss their more general functions with some confidence.

The *thalamus* appears to serve as a "relay station," transmitting nerve impulses from one part of the brain to another. The *hypothalamus* ("under the thalamus") regulates bodily drives (such as hunger, thirst, and sex) and body conditions such as temperature and hormone balance. The *reticular formation* is a network of nerve fibers that controls bodily states such as sleep, alertness, and attention. The *limbic system* is involved in experiencing and expressing emotions and motivation—pleasure, fear, aggressiveness, sexual arousal, and pain. The largest structure in the brain is the *cerebrum,* with its most visible part, the *cerebral cortex*, covering the midbrain and thalamus.

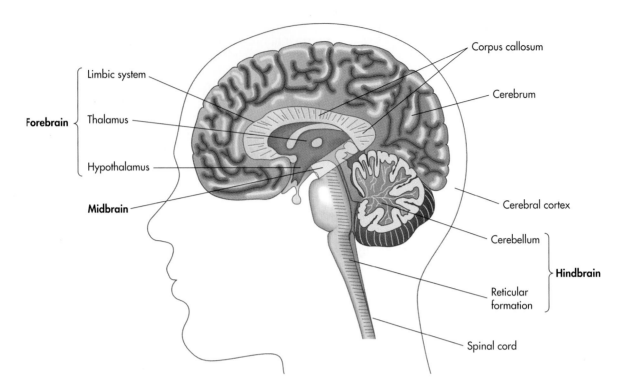

FIGURE 2.2   The Internal Structure of the Brain A cross-sectional view of the brain reveals the forebrain, midbrain, and hindbrain. Some of the important brain structures are identified within each of the divisions.

The Midbrain and Hindbrain   The other two regions of the brain also have distinct functions. The *midbrain* is involved in vision and hearing and—with the hindbrain—in the control of sleep, alertness, and pain. Of interest to mental health professionals is its role in the manufacture of certain chemicals: serotonin, norepinephrine, and dopamine, which have been implicated in certain mental disorders. The *hindbrain* also manufactures serotonin and appears to control vegetative functions such as heart rate, sleep, and respiration.

Because the brain controls all aspects of human functioning, it is not difficult to conclude that damage or interruption of normal brain function and activity could lead to observable mental disorders. There are, of course, many biological causes for psychological disorders. Damage to the nervous system is one: As Schaudinn demonstrated, general paresis results from brain damage caused by parasitic microorganisms. Tumors, strokes, excessive intake of alcohol or drugs, and external trauma (such as a blow to the head) have also been linked to cognitive, emotional, and behavioral disorders. Two specific biological sources—body chemistry and heredity—have given rise to important biogenic theories of psychopathology.

Biochemical Theories

The basic premise of the biochemical theories is that chemical imbalances underlie mental disorders. This premise relies on the fact that most physiological and mental processes, from sleeping and digestion to reading and thinking, involve chemical actions within the body. Support for these theories has been provided by research into anxiety disorders, mood disorders (both depression and bipolar disorder), and schizophrenia (Lickey & Gordon, 1991; McGeer & McGeer, 1980; Seiver, Davis & Gorman, 1991; Snyder, 1986). To see how biochemical imbalances in the brain can result in abnormal behavior, we need to understand how messages in the brain are transmitted from nerve cell to nerve cell.

Nerve cells (neurons) vary in function throughout the brain and may appear different, but they all share certain characteristics. Each neuron possesses a cell membrane that separates it from the outside environment and regulates the chemical contents within it. On one side of the cell body are **dendrites,** numerous short rootlike structures whose function is to receive signals from other neurons. At the other end is an **axon,** a much longer extension that sends signals to other neurons, some a considerable distance away. Under an electron microscope dendrites can be distinguished by their many short branches (see Figure 2.3).

Messages travel through the brain by electrical impulses via neurons: An incoming message is received by a neuron's dendrites and is sent down the axon to bulblike swellings called *axon terminals,* usually located near dendrites of another neuron. Note that neurons do not touch one another. A minute gap (the **synapse**) exists between the axon of the sending neuron and the dendrites of the receiving neuron. The electrical impulse crosses the synapse when the axon releases chemical substances called **neurotransmitters.** When the neurotransmitters reach the dendrites of the receiving neuron, they attach themselves to receptors and bind with them if their "shapes" correspond (see Figures 2.4 and 2.5). The binding of transmitters to receptors in the neuron triggers either a synaptic excitation (encouragement to produce other nerve impulses) or synaptic inhibition (prevents production of nerve impulses).

The human body has many different chemical transmitters, and their effect on neurons varies (see Table 2.1). An imbalance of certain neurotransmitters in the brain is believed to be implicated in mental disorders. As discussed in Chapter 1, the search for chemical causes and cures for mental problems accelerated tremendously in the early 1950s with the discovery of psychoactive drugs. The lines of evidence supporting this belief were very convincing. First, it was found that antipsychotic drugs have beneficial effects on schizophrenics, that lithium is useful in controlling affective disorders, and that tricyclic and monoamine oxidase inhibitors alleviate symptoms of severely depressed patients. Second, biochemical studies (Andreasen, 1984; Lickey & Gordon, 1991) indicate that these drugs seem to work by blocking or facilitating neurotransmitter activity at receptor sites. Most of the current psychiatric drugs seem to affect one of five different transmitters: norepinephrine, dopamine, serotonin, acetylcholine, and gamma aminobutyric acid (GABA).

Last, evidence began to accumulate that certain chemical imbalances were disorder-specific. For example, we have already discussed the finding that insufficient dopamine is a possible cause of Parkinson's disease. Ironically, an excess of dopamine has been implicated in the development of schizophrenia (Cooper, Bloom & Roth, 1986; Lickey & Gordon, 1991; Snyder, 1986). It is hypothesized that people with schizophrenia may have too many postsynaptic dopamine receptors (a structural explanation) or that their receptors may be supersensitive to dopamine. The effect of drug therapy on receptor sites has been shown with other disorders. Drugs used to treat de-

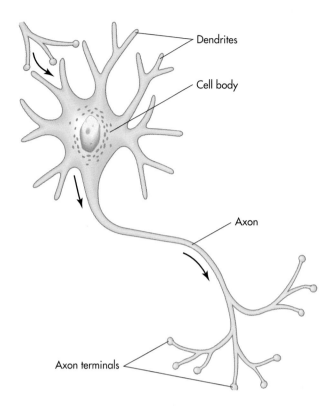

FIGURE 2.3 Major Parts of a Neuron The major parts of a neuron include dendrites, the cell body, the axon, and the axon terminals.

pression alter norepinephrine and serotonin sensitivity and receptivity at the receptor sites. Drugs used in the treatment of anxiety affect receptor reactivity to GABA.

Research into biochemical mechanisms holds great promise for our understanding and treatment of mental disorders. It appears unlikely, however, that biochemistry alone can provide completely satisfactory explanations of the biological bases of abnormal behavior. Researchers should instead expect to find hundreds—or perhaps even thousands—of pieces in the biogenic puzzle.

Genetic Explanations

A scientific highlight of the year 1993 was the discovery of the gene that determines the occurrence of Huntington's disease, which causes an irreversible degeneration of the nervous system. Medical experts believe that the link between gene and illness is very strong and may indicate an inevitable progression. Such a relationship is often cited as evidence of the power of heredity. A one-to-one correspondence like this one is, however, a rarity in behavioral genetics.

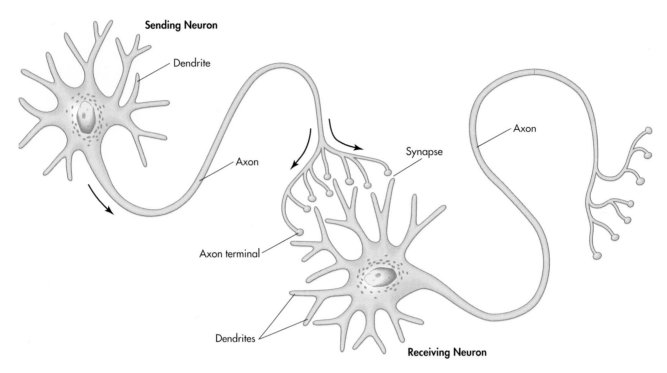

Sending Neuron

Dendrite

Axon

Axon terminal

Synapse

Axon

Dendrites

Receiving Neuron

FIGURE 2.4 **Synaptic Transmission** Messages travel via electrical impulses from one neuron to another. The impulse crosses the synapse in the form of chemicals called *neurotransmitters*. Note that the axon terminals and the receiving dendrites do not touch.

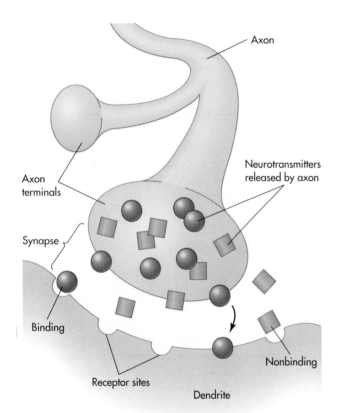

Axon

Neurotransmitters released by axon

Axon terminals

Synapse

Binding

Receptor sites

Dendrite

Nonbinding

FIGURE 2.5 **Neurotransmitter Binding** Neurotransmitters are released into the synapse and travel to the receiving dendrite. Each transmitter has a specific shape that corresponds to a receptor site. Like a jigsaw puzzle, binding occurs if the transmitter fits into the receptor site.

Research does indicate that genetics play an important role in the development of certain abnormal conditions. For instance, "nervousness" can be inherited in animals; this finding was demonstrated by breeding generations of dogs that were either fearful or friendly (Murphree & Dykman, 1965). There is evidence that autonomic nervous system (ANS) reactivity may be inherited in human beings as well; that is, a person may be born with an ANS that makes an unusually strong response to stimuli (Andreasen, 1984; Baker & Clark, 1990). Other studies (Cloninger et al., 1986; Gatz, 1990; Neale & Oltmanns, 1980; Paykel, 1982; Plonin, 1989) implicate heredity as a causal factor in alcoholism, schizophrenia, and depression. To show that a particular disorder is inherited, however, researchers must show that it could not be caused by environmental factors alone, that closer genetic relationships produce greater similarity of the disorder in human beings, and that people with these problems have similar biological and behavioral patterns (Siegel, 1990).

Biological inheritance is transmitted by genes. A person's genetic makeup is called his or her **genotype.** Interaction between the genotype and the environment results in the person's **phenotype,** or observable physical and behavioral characteristics. At times, however, it is difficult to determine whether genotype or environment is exerting a stronger influence. For example, characteristics such as eye color are determined solely by our genotype—that is, by the coding in our genes. But other physical characteristics, such as height, are determined partly by the genetic code and partly by environmental factors. Adults who were undernourished as children will be shorter than the height they were genetically capable of reaching, but even the most effective nutrition would not have caused them to grow taller than their "programmed" height limit. As is detailed more fully in Chapter 14, twin studies and correlational associations between genetics and certain mental disorders lend strong support to the behavioral genetics model.

Criticisms of the Biological Model

The biological model of abnormal behavior, which drifted out of favor when psychoanalysis was at the peak of its influence in the 1940s, has regained its popularity. Indeed, rarely does a week go by without news reports linking genetics to intelligence, homosexuality, obesity, alcohol abuse, learning disabilities, temperament, personality, or susceptibility to stress.

TABLE 2.1 Major Neurotransmitters and Their Effects

Neurotransmitter	Source and Function
Acetylcholine (ACh)	One of the most widespread neurotransmitters. Occurs in systems that control the muscles and in circuits related to attention and memory.
Dopamine	Concentrated in small areas of the brain, one of which is involved in the control of the muscles. In excess, dopamine can cause hallucinations.
Endorphins	Found in the brain and spinal cord. Suppresses pain.
Gamma amino-butyric acid (GABA)	Widely distributed in the brain. Works against other neurotransmitters, particularly dopamine.
Norepinephrine	Occurs widely in the central nervous system. Regulates moods and may increase arousal and alertness.
Serotonin	Occurs in the brain. Works more or less in opposition to norepinephrine, suppressing activity and causing sleep.

These two identical 5-year-old twins share not only physical similarities but many personality characteristics as well. Research reveals that genetics may play a powerful role in the development of many traits and in certain disorders.

Structural differences in the brain have been linked to schizophrenia, and new "miracle" drugs are being discovered for various disorders. But the biological model has some major shortcomings if viewed as the sole explanation for mental disorders.

First, one of its basic tenets is that abnormal behavior results from an underlying physical condition, such as damage to the brain or malfunction of neural processes. The model implies that treatment should be aimed at controlling the underlying disease by changing the individual's biochemistry or removing toxic substances. This approach does not adequately account for abnormal behavior for which no organic etiology, or cause, can be found. For example, some mental disorders, such as bipolar and unipolar psychotic mood states and schizophrenia, may have primary biological causes. Strong evidence exists, however, that other disorders, including phobias and eating disorders, have a predominantly social cause. Many disorders are probably a mix of predisposition and environment.

Second, the biological model implicitly assumes a correspondence between organic dysfunction and mental dysfunction, with only a minimal impact from environmental, social, or cultural influences. But rarely are the equations of human behavior so uncomplicated. More often there are a multitude of causes behind any human behavior, and environmental factors seem to play as important a role as any other. Increasingly, mental health research has focused on the diathesis-stress theory, originally proposed by Meehl (1962) and developed further by Rosenthal (1970). The **diathesis-stress theory** holds that it is not a particular abnormality that is inherited but rather a *predisposition to develop illness* (diathesis). Certain environmental forces, called *stressors,* may activate the predisposition, resulting in a disorder. Alternatively, in a benign and supportive environment, the abnormality may never materialize.

A third shortcoming, related to the preceding one, is revealed by our accumulating knowledge that biochemical changes often occur because of environmental forces. We know, for example, that stress-produced fear and anger cause the secretion of adrenalin and noradrenalin. Similarly, schizophrenia could cause the secretion of excess amounts of chemicals such as dopamine in persons with the disorder rather than result from the presence of the chemicals.

Last, wholesale adoption of the biological model could foster helplessness in the patient by eliminating patient responsibility in the treatment process. Patients might be seen—both by their therapists and by themselves—as passive participants, to be treated only with appropriate drugs and medical interventions. For patients who are already suffering from feelings of helplessness or loss of control, such an approach could be devastating.

THE PSYCHOANALYTIC MODEL

> At the core of Steve's problems are his early childhood experiences, his inability to confront his own intense feelings of hostility toward his father (fears of castration), his unresolved Oedipal longing toward his mother, and the unconscious symbolism he draws between his mother and former woman friend Linda. As a psychodynamically oriented therapist, I believe that, at crucial psychosexual stages, Steve did not receive the love and care a child needs to develop into a healthy adult. He was neglected, understimulated, and left on his own. As a result, he felt unloved and rejected. Therapy should be aimed at uncovering Steve's unconscious conflicts, letting him relive his early childhood traumas, and helping him to attain insight into his motivations and fears.

The **psychoanalytic model** of abnormal behavior has two main distinguishing features. First, it views disorders in adults as the result of childhood traumas or anxieties. Second, the psychoanalytic model holds that many of these childhood-based anxieties operate unconsciously; because they are too threatening for the adult to face, they are repressed through mental defense mechanisms. As a result, people exhibit symptoms they are unable to understand. To eliminate the symptoms, the therapist must make the patient aware of these unconscious anxieties or conflicts.

The early development of psychoanalytic theory is generally credited to Sigmund Freud (1938, 1949), a Viennese neurologist who gave up his practice to enter psychiatry. During his clinical work, Freud became convinced that powerful mental processes could remain hidden from consciousness and could cause abnormal behaviors. He believed that the therapist's role was to help the patient achieve insight into these unconscious processes. Although he originally relied on hypnosis for this purpose, Freud soon dropped it in favor of other techniques. He felt that cures were more likely to be permanent if patients became aware of their problems without the aid of hypnosis. This view eventually led Freud to his formulation of **psychoanalysis,** the therapy based on the view that unconscious conflicts must be aired and understood by the patient if abnormal behavior is to be eliminated.

Personality Structure

Freud believed that personality is composed of three major components—the *id,* the *ego,* and the *superego*—and that all behavior is a product of their interaction. The *id* is the original component of the personality; it is present at birth, and from it the ego and superego eventually develop. The id operates from the **pleasure principle**—the impulsive, pleasure-seeking aspect of our being—and it seeks immediate gratification of instinctual needs, regardless of moral or realistic concerns.

In contrast, the *ego* represents the realistic and rational part of the mind. It comes into existence because the human personality must be able to cope with the external world if it is to survive. The ego is influenced by the **reality principle**—an awareness of the demands of the environment and of the need to adjust behavior to meet these demands. The ego's decisions are dictated by realistic considerations rather than by moral judgments.

Moral judgments and moralistic considerations are the domain of the *superego;* they often represent society's ideals or values as interpreted by our parents. The superego is composed of the *conscience,* which instills guilt feelings about engaging in immoral or unethical behavior, and the ego *ideal,* which rewards altruistic or moral behavior with feelings of pride.

The energy system from which the personality operates occurs through the interplay of instincts. Instincts give rise to our thoughts and actions and fuel their expression. Freud emphasized sex and aggression as the dominant human instincts because he recognized that the society in which he lived placed strong prohibitions on these drives and that, as a result, people were taught to inhibit them. A profound need to express one's instincts is often frightening and can lead a person to deny their existence. Indeed, Freud felt that even though most impulses are hidden from one's consciousness, they nonetheless determine human actions.

Psychosexual Stages

According to psychoanalytic theory, human personality develops through a sequence of five **psychosexual stages,** each of which brings a unique challenge. If unfavorable circumstances prevail, the personality may be drastically affected. Because Freud stressed the importance of early childhood experiences, he saw the human personality as largely determined in the first five years of life—during the *oral* (first year of life), *anal* (around the second year of life), and *phallic* (beginning around the third or fourth years of life) stages. The last two psychosexual stages are the *latency* (approximately 6 to 12 years of age), and *genital* (beginning in puberty) stages.

The importance of each psychosexual stage for later development lies in how much fixation occurs during that stage. (*Fixation* is the arresting of emotional development at a particular psychosexual

Sigmund Freud (1856–1939) began his career as a neurologist. He became increasingly intrigued with the relationship between illness and mental processes when he worked with Josef Breuer, who successfully used hypnotism to treat hysterical patients.

stage.) If the infant is traumatized (harmed) in some way during the oral stage, for example, some of the infant's instinctual energy becomes trapped at that stage. Consequently, the personality of that person as an adult will retain strong features of the oral stage. Passivity, helplessness, obesity, chronic smoking, and alcoholism may all be characteristics of an oral personality. According to the psychodynamic model, each stage is characterized by distinct traits and, should fixation occur, by distinct conflicts.

Freud believed that a person who could transcend the various fixations would develop into a normal, healthy individual. Heterosexual interests, stability, vocational planning, marriage, and other social activities would become a person's prime concern during the genital stage.

Anxiety and Psychopathology

Anxiety is at the root of Freud's theory of psychopathology. Freud identified three types of anxiety (shown diagrammatically in Figure 2.6), arising from conflicts among the id, ego, and superego. *Realistic anxiety* occurs when there is potential danger from the external environment. For example, you smell smoke in a building and experience realistic anxiety

During the oral stage, the first stage of psychosexual development, the infant not only receives nourishment but also derives pleasure from sucking and being close to its mother. Later, during the anal stage, toilet training can be a time of intense emotional conflict between parent and child, or it can be a time of cooperation.

as your ego warns you to take action to protect yourself from physical harm. *Moralistic anxiety* results when someone does not live up to his or her own moral standards or engages in unethical conduct. In this case, the ego warns of possible retaliation from the superego. *Neurotic anxiety* often results when id impulses seem to be getting out of hand, bursting through ego controls. In all these cases, anxiety is a signal that something bad is about to happen and that appropriate steps should be taken to reduce it.

Although Freud studied and treated all three types of anxiety, he concentrated mainly on neurotic anxiety. We shall do the same, although much of our discussion applies to the other two types of anxiety as well. (Recent editions of the *Diagnostic and Statistical Manual of Mental Disorders*, including DSM-IV, have replaced the traditional subcategories of neurotic behavior with other, more refined concepts. We use the term *neurotic* here because of its importance to Freud's theory.)

Defense Mechanisms

Neurotic behavior develops from the threat of overwhelming anxiety, which may lead to full-scale panic. To forestall this panic, the ego often resorts to defense mechanisms, such as those in Table 2.2. **Defense mechanisms** share three characteristics: they protect

the individual from anxiety, they operate unconsciously, and they distort reality.

All individuals use some strategies to reduce anxiety. The defense mechanisms in Table 2.2 are considered maladaptive, however, when they are overused—that is, when they become the predominant means of coping with stress and when they interfere with one's ability to handle life's everyday demands. The difference is one of degree, not of kind.

Psychoanalytic Therapy

Psychoanalytic therapy, better known as psychoanalysis, attempts to rid people of maladaptive behaviors by inducing ego weakness. According to Freud, ego weakness occurs during the natural state of sleep and under conditions of excessive fatigue. Therapists—called *psychoanalysts*, or just *analysts*—attempt to induce this state through such techniques as hypnosis and *projective tests*, in which ambiguous stimuli such as ink blots, word associations, or pictures provoke revealing verbal responses. These techniques give the analyst some access to unconscious material, which is used to help patients achieve insight into their inner motivations and desires. The basic premise of psychoanalysis is that a cure can be effected only through this process. (Psychoanalytic methods are discussed further in Chapter 17.)

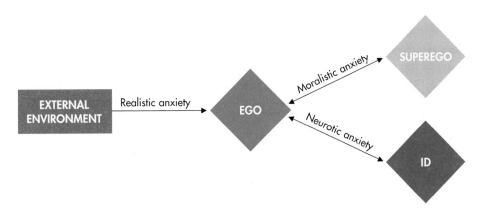

FIGURE 2.6 Three Types of Anxiety Freud believed that people suffer from three types of anxiety, arising from conflicts involving the id, ego, and superego. Each type of anxiety is, in essence, a signal of impending danger.

TABLE 2.2 Defense Mechanisms

Repression: The blocking of forbidden or dangerous desires and thoughts to keep them from entering one's consciousness; according to Freud, the most basic defense mechanism. *Example:* A soldier who witnesses the horrible death of his friend in combat may force the event out of consciousness because it symbolizes his own mortality.

Reaction Formation: Repression of dangerous impulses, followed by converting them to their direct opposite. *Example:* A woman who gives birth to an unwanted child may become an extremely overprotective mother who is afraid to let the child out of her sight and who showers the child with superficial attention.

Projection: Ridding oneself of threatening desires or thoughts by attributing them to others. *Example:* A worker may mask unpleasant feelings of inadequacy by blaming his poor performance on the incompetence of fellow workers or on a conspiracy in which enemies are disrupting his life.

Rationalization: Explaining one's behavior by giving well-thought-out and socially acceptable reasons that do not happen to be the real ones. *Example:* A student may explain flunking a test as follows: "I'm not interested in the course and don't really need it to graduate. Besides, I find the teacher extremely dull."

Displacement: Directing an emotion, such as hostility or anxiety, toward a substitute target. *Example:* A meek clerk who is constantly belittled by her boss builds up tremendous resentment and snaps at her family members instead of at her boss, who might fire her.

Undoing: A symbolic attempt, often ritualistic or repetitive, to right a wrong or negate some disapproved thought, impulse, or act. *Example:* In Shakespeare's play, Lady Macbeth goads her husband into slaying the king, and then tries to cleanse herself of sin by constantly going through the motions of washing her hands.

Regression: A retreat to an earlier developmental level—according to Freud, the person's most fixated stage—that demands less mature responses and aspirations. *Example:* A dignified college president drinks too much and sings old school songs at a reunion with college classmates.

Neo-Freudian Perspectives

Freud's psychoanalytic movement attracted many followers. Some of Freud's disciples, however, came to disagree with his insistence that the sex instinct is the major determinant of behavior. Many of his most gifted adherents broke away from him and formulated coherent psychological models of their own. These thinkers have since become known as **neo-Freudians** (or *post-Freudians*) because, despite their new ideas, they remained strongly influenced by Freud's constructs. For example, nearly all of them continued to believe in the power of the unconscious, in the use of "talking" methods of psychotherapy that rely heavily on the patient's introspection, in the three-part structure of personality, and in the one-to-one analyst-patient approach to therapy.

The major differences between the various neo-Freudian theories and psychoanalytic theory lie in the emphasis that the neo-Freudians placed on five areas: freedom of choice and future goals, ego autonomy, social forces, object relations (past interpersonal relations), and treatment of seriously disturbed people (see Table 2.3).

Criticisms of the Psychoanalytic Model

Psychoanalytic theory has had a tremendous impact on the field of psychology. Psychoanalysis and its variations are very widely employed. Nonetheless, three major criticisms, discussed below, are often leveled at psychoanalysis (Hall & Lindzey, 1970; Joseph, 1991).

First, the empirical procedures by which Freud validated his hypotheses have grave shortcomings. His observations about human behavior were often made under uncontrolled conditions (Edelson et al., 1985). For example, he relied heavily on case studies and on his own self-analysis as a basis for formulating theory. His patients, from whom he drew conclusions about universal aspects of personality dynamics and behavior, tended to represent a narrow spectrum of one society. Although case studies can be a rich source of clinical data, Freud's lack of verbatim notes means that his recollections were subject to distortions and omissions. Furthermore, he seldom submitted the material related by his patients to any form of external corroboration—statements from relatives or friends, test data, documents, or medical records. Using such private and uncontrolled methods of inquiry as a basis for theory is fraught with hazards.

Second, is a theory of human behavior adequate if it does not apply to more than one-half the population of the world? Freud's theory of female sexuality and personality has drawn heavy criticisms from feminists for many years. Phallic-stage dynamics, penis envy, unfavorable comparisons of the clitoris to the penis, the woman's need for a male child as a penis substitute, and the belief that penetration is necessary for a woman's sexual satisfaction all rest on assumptions that are biologically questionable and that fail to consider social forces shaping women's behavior. Such theories, at face value, seem to depreciate female sexuality and legitimize male sexuality (McBride, 1990; Schaef, 1981). "Since man is the measure of all things—man, literally, rather than human beings—we have all tended to measure ourselves by men" (Miller, 1976, p. 69).

A third criticism of psychoanalysis is that it cannot be applied to a wide range of disturbed people. Among them are individuals who have speech disturbances or are inarticulate (talking is important in therapy); people who have urgent, immediate problems (classical psychoanalysis requires much time); and people who are very young or old (Fenichel, 1945). Research studies have shown that psychoanalytic therapy is best suited to well-educated people of the middle and upper socioeconomic classes who exhibit anxiety disorders rather than psychotic behavior. It is more limited in therapeutic value with people of lower socioeconomic levels and with people who are less verbal, less intelligent, and more severely disturbed (Sloane et al., 1975).

HUMANISTIC AND EXISTENTIAL APPROACHES

Steve is a flesh-and-blood person, alive, organic, and moving, with thoughts, feelings, and emotions. I object to the use of *diagnosis* because labels serve only to pigeonhole people and act as barriers to the development of a therapeutic relationship. In my attempt to understand the subjective world of Steve's experience, it appears that he is feeling trapped, immobilized, and lonely and that he is externalizing his problems. In this way Steve may be evading responsibility for making his own choices and may be protecting himself by staying in the safe, known environment of his "illness." Steve needs to realize that he is responsible for his own actions, that he cannot find his identity in others, and that his life is not predetermined.

The humanistic and existential approaches evolved as a reaction to the determinism of early models of psychopathology. For example, many psychologists were disturbed that Freudian theory did not focus on the inner world of the client but rather categorized the client according to a set of preconceived diagnoses (May, 1967). Psychoanalysts, these critics said, described clients in terms of blocked instinctual forces

TABLE 2.3   Contributions of Neo-Freudians

Traditional psychoanalytic theory has changed over the years due to the work of neo-Freudians. While most of the individuals listed below accept many of the basic tenets of the theory, they have stressed different aspects of the human condition. Some differences are listed below.

1. **Freedom of Choice and Future Goals**   People are not just mechanistic beings. They have a high degree of free choice and are motivated toward future goals.

   Alfred Adler (1870–1937)   Stressed that people are not passive victims of biology, instincts, or unconscious forces. Stressed freedom of choice and goals directed by means of social drives.

   Carl Jung (1875–1965)   Believed in the collective unconscious as the foundation of creative functioning. Believed that humans were goal directed and future oriented.

2. **Ego Autonomy**   The ego is an autonomous entity and can operate independently from the id. It is creative, forward moving, and capable of continual growth.

   Anna Freud (1895–1982)   Emphasized the role, operation, and importance of the ego. Believed ego is an autonomous component of the personality and not at the mercy of the id.

   Erik Erikson (1902–)   Perhaps the most influential of the ego theorists. Formulated stages of ego development from infancy to late adulthood—one of the first true developmental theorists. Considers personality to be flexible and capable of growth and change throughout the adult years.

3. **Social Forces**   Interpersonal relationships are of primary importance in our psychological development. Especially influential are our primary social relationships.

   Karen Horney (1885–1952)   Often considered one of the first feminist psychologists who rejected Freud's notion of penis envy. Stressed that behavior disorders are due to disturbed interpersonal childhood relationships.

   Harry Stack Sullivan (1892–1949)   Major contribution was his interpersonal theory of psychological disorders. Believed that the individual's psychological functions could be understood only in the context of his or her social relationships.

4. **Object Relations**   The technical term *object relations* is roughly equivalent to "past interpersonal relations." It refers to how people develop patterns of living from their early relations with significant others.

   Heinz Kohut (1913–1981)   Felt it was especially important to study the mother-child relationship. Known for his work on the narcissistic personality.

   Otto Kernberg (1928–)   Known especially for his studies of the borderline personality. Especially interested in understanding how clients seem to have difficulty in forming stable relationships because of pathological objects in the past.

5. **Treatment of the Seriously Disturbed**   Freud believed that psychoanalysis could not be used with very seriously disturbed individuals because they were "analytically unfit." By this he meant that they did not have sufficient contact with reality to benefit from insight.

   Hyman Sponitz   Demonstrated that modern psychoanalysis could be used with severely disturbed clients. Associated with new treatment techniques that do not require clients to be intellectually capable of understanding interpretations. Techniques provide feedback that helps client resolve conflicts by experiencing them rather than understanding them.

and psychic complexes that made them victims of some mechanistic and deterministic personality structure.

It is important to note that the humanistic and existential perspectives represent many schools of thought. But they do share a set of assumptions that distinguish them from other approaches or viewpoints.

First, both perspectives view an individual's reality as a product of that person's unique experiences and perceptions of the world. Moreover, the subjective universe of this person—how he or she construes events—is more important than the events themselves. Hence, to understand why a person behaves as he or she does, the psychologist must reconstruct the world from that individual's vantage point. Second, both humanistic and existential theorists stress that individuals have the ability to make free choices and are responsible for their own decisions. Third, these theorists believe in the "wholeness" or integrity of the person. They view as pointless all attempts to reduce human beings to a set of formulas, to explain them simply by measuring responses to certain stimuli. And last, according to the humanistic and existential perspectives, people have the ability to become what they want, to fulfill their capacities, and to lead the lives best suited to themselves.

The Humanistic Perspective

One of the major contributions of the **humanistic perspective** has been its positive view of the individual. Carl Rogers (1902–1987) is perhaps the best known of the humanistic psychologists. Rogers's theory of personality (1959) reflects his concern with human welfare and his deep conviction that humanity is basically "good," forward-moving, and trustworthy.

Besides being concerned with treating the mentally ill, psychologists such as Rogers and Abraham Maslow (1908–1970) have focused on improving the mental health of the person who is considered normal (Rogers, 1961, 1980, 1987; Maslow, 1954). This focus has led humanistic psychologists and others to explore the characteristics of the healthy personality.

The Actualizing Tendency

Instead of concentrating exclusively on behavior disorders, the humanistic approach is concerned with helping people *actualize* their potential and with bettering the state of humanity. Humanistic psychological theory is based on the idea that people are motivated not only to satisfy their biological needs (for food, warmth, and sex) but also to cultivate, maintain, and enhance the self. The *self* is one's image of oneself, the part one refers to as "I" or "me."

The quintessence of this view is the concept of **self-actualization**—a term popularized by Maslow—which is an inherent tendency to strive toward the realization of one's full potential. As one psychologist has pointed out, the actualizing tendency can be viewed as fulfilling a grand design or a genetic blueprint (Maddi, 1972). This thrust of life that pushes people forward is manifested in such qualities as curiosity, creativity, and joy of discovery. According to Rogers (1961), this inherent force is common to all living organisms (Maslow, 1954; Rogers, 1959). How one views the self, how others relate to the self, and what values are attached to the self all contribute to one's **self-concept**—the individual's assessment of his or her own value and worth.

Development of Abnormal Behavior

Rogers believed that if people were left unencumbered by societal restrictions and were allowed to grow and develop freely, the result would be self-actualized, fully functioning people. In such a case, the self-concept and the actualizing tendency would be considered congruent.

However, society frequently imposes *conditions of worth* on its members, standards by which people determine whether they have worth. They are transmitted via *conditional positive regard*. That is, significant others (such as parents, peers, friends, and spouse) in a person's life accept some but not all of that person's actions, feelings, and attitudes. The person's self-concept becomes defined as having worth only when others approve. But this reliance on others forces the individual to develop a distorted self-concept that is inconsistent with his or her self-actualizing potential, inhibiting that person from being self-actualized. A state of disharmony or *incongruence* is said to exist between the person's inherent potential and his or her self-concept (as determined by significant others). According to Rogers, this state of incongruence forms the basis of abnormal behavior.

Rogers believed that fully functioning people have been *allowed to grow* toward their potential. The environmental condition most suitable for this growth is called *unconditional positive regard* (Rogers, 1951). In essence, people who are significant figures in someone's life value and respect that person *as a person*. Giving unconditional positive regard is valuing and loving regardless of behavior. People may disapprove of someone's actions, but they still respect, love, and care for that someone. The assumption that humans need unconditional positive regard has many implications for child rearing and psychotherapy. For parents, it means creating an open and accepting environment for the child. For the therapist, it means fostering conditions that will allow clients to grow

Carl Rogers (1902–1987) believed people need both positive regard from others and positive self-regard. According to Rogers, when positive regard is given unconditionally, a person can develop freely and become self-actualized.

Abraham Maslow (1908–1970) proposed that people are motivated toward self-actualization once basic needs are met. He formed his ideas by studying people he believed to be self-actualized–people such as Albert Einstein, Barach Spinoza (a seventeenth century philosopher), and Eleanor Roosevelt.

and fulfill their potential; this approach has become known as *nondirective* or *person-centered* therapy.

Person-Centered Therapy

Carl Rogers emphasized that therapist attitudes are more important than specific counseling techniques. The therapist needs to have a strong positive regard for the client's ability to deal constructively with all aspects of life. The more willing the therapist is to rely on the client's strengths and potential, the more likely the client is to discover such strengths and potential. The therapist cannot help the client by explaining the client's behavior or by prescribing actions to follow. Therapeutic techniques involve expressing and communicating respect, understanding, and acceptance.

The way a person-centered therapist most commonly communicates understanding of a client's subjective world is through *reflecting feelings*. In "saying back" to the client what he or she understood the client to say, the therapist provides a "mirror" for the client. The client can then actively evaluate thoughts and feelings with less distortion. Even in very strained situations, the person-centered therapist relies on reflection of feelings and on acceptance in working with the client. The following dialogue between client (*S*) and counselor (*C*), transcribed by Rogers (1951, pp. 211–213), illustrates the technique:

S: (Silent for two minutes. Then begins to talk in hard, flat voice, quite unlike her usual tone. Does not look at counselor. There is much repetition but the following excerpts give the major thoughts.) You feel

I want to come, but I don't! I'm not coming anymore. It doesn't do any good. I don't like you. I hate you! I wish you never were born.

C: You hate me very bitterly.

S: I think I'll throw you in the lake. I'll cut you up! You think people like you, but they don't.... I wish you were dead.

C: You detest me and you'd really like to get rid of me.

S: You think my father did bad things to me, but he didn't! You think he wasn't a good man, but he was. You think I want intercourse, but I don't.

C: You feel I absolutely misrepresent all your thoughts.

You might well sense a lack of direction here and wonder where this conversation is leading. The therapist, as you can see, is not steering this exchange but is using a standard technique of humanistic therapy, the understanding reflection of the client's feelings. It is the client who will ultimately move on his or her own in the direction of health; the client, that is, *wants* to be healthy.

The Existential Perspective

The **existential approach** is really not a systematized school of thought but a set of attitudes. It shares with humanistic psychology an emphasis on individual uniqueness, a quest for meaning in life and for freedom and responsibility, a phenomenological approach to understanding the person, and a belief that the

Existentialists contend that many of the problems encountered by people are due to the loss of their "connectedness" with the world. They believe that modern society has reduced people to "cogs in a machine," which has led to the questioning of old values and a search for meaning in life.

individual has positive attributes that will eventually be expressed unless they are distorted by the environment.

The existential and humanistic approaches differ in several dimensions. First, existentialism is less optimistic than humanism; it focuses on the irrationality, difficulties, and suffering all humans encounter in life. Although humanism allows the clear possibility of self-fulfillment and freedom, existentialism deals with human alienation from the social and spiritual structures that no longer provide meaning in an increasingly technological and impersonal world.

Second, humanists focus on the individual. Humanistic therapists attempt to reconstruct the subjective world of their clients through empathy. Although existentialists also stress phenomenology (understanding the person's subjective world of experience), their perspective is slightly different: The individual must be viewed within the context of the human condition, and moral, philosophical, and ethical considerations are part of that context. Last, humanism stresses individual responsibility; that is, the individual is ultimately responsible for what he or she becomes in this life. Existentialism also stresses individual responsibility, but it stresses responsibility to others as well. Self-fulfillment is not enough.

Criticisms of the Humanistic and Existential Approaches

Many psychologists have criticized the formulations of the humanistic and existential perspectives (Holt, 1962; Millon, 1973; Smith, 1950). Although these phenomenological approaches have been extremely creative in describing the human condition, they have been less successful in constructing theory. Moreover, they are not suited to scientific or experimental investigation. The emphasis on subjective understanding rather than prediction and control, on intuition and empathy rather than objective investigation, and on the individual rather than the more general category, all tend to hinder empirical study.

Carl Rogers has certainly expressed many of his ideas as researchable propositions, but it is difficult to verify scientifically the humanistic concept of people as rational, inherently good, and moving toward self-fulfillment. The existential perspective can be similarly criticized for its lack of scientific grounding because of its reliance on the unique subjective experiences of individuals to describe the inner world. Such data are difficult to quantify and test. Nevertheless, the existential concepts of freedom, choice, responsibility, being, and nonbeing have had a profound influence on contemporary thought beyond the field of psychology.

Another major criticism leveled at the humanistic and existential approaches is that they do not work well with severely disturbed clients. They seem to be most effective with intelligent, well-educated, and relatively "normal" individuals who may be suffering adjustment difficulties. In fact, Carl Rogers's person-centered counseling originated from his work with college students who were bright, articulate, and psychology-minded—what some psychologists describe as the "worried well." This limitation, along with the occasional vagueness of humanistic and existential thought, has made applying these ideas broadly to abnormal psychology difficult.

BEHAVIORAL MODELS OF PSYCHOPATHOLOGY

The roots of Steve's problems can be traced to his behavioral repertoire. Many of the behaviors he has learned are inappropriate and his repertoire lacks useful, productive behaviors. He has had little practice in social relationships, lacks good role models, and has difficulty distinguishing between appropriate and inappropriate behavior. Furthermore, his delusion that he is controlled by demonic forces and his continual thinking about satanism may be unwittingly reinforced by those around him. When Steve discusses or acts out these beliefs, he garners much attention from his parents, peers, and onlookers (perhaps a form of reinforcement). In sum, I recommend behavioral therapy that includes modeling and role playing to enhance Steve's social skills and a program to eliminate or control his delusional thoughts.

The **behavioral models** of psychopathology are concerned with the role of learning in abnormal behavior. The differences among them lie mainly in their explanations of how learning occurs. Although some models appear to disagree, they generally tend to complement one another. Each of the three learning models discussed here is, for the most part, applied to a different type of behavior.

The Classical Conditioning Model

Early in the twentieth century, Ivan Pavlov (1849–1936), a Russian physiologist, discovered a process known as **classical conditioning,** in which responses to new stimuli are learned through association. This process involves the involuntary responses (such as reflexes, emotional reactions, and sexual arousal), which are controlled by the autonomic nervous system.

Pavlov's discovery was accidental. He was measuring dogs' salivation as part of a study of their digestive processes when he noticed that the dogs began to salivate at the sight of an assistant carrying their food. This response puzzled Pavlov and led to his formulation of classical conditioning. He reasoned that food is an **unconditional stimulus (UCS)** which, in the mouth, automatically elicits salivation; this salivation is an unlearned or **unconditioned response (UCR)** to the food. Pavlov then presented a previously *neutral* stimulus (one that does not initially elicit salivation, such as the sound of a bell) to the dogs just before presenting the food. He found that, after a number of repetitions, the sound of the bell alone elicited salivation. This learning process is based on association: The neutral stimulus (the bell) acquires some of the properties of the unconditioned stimulus (the food) when they are repeatedly paired. When the bell alone can provoke the salivation, it becomes a **conditioned**

Ivan Pavlov (1849–1936), a Russian physiologist, discovered the associative learning process we know as classical conditioning, while he was studying salivation in dogs. Pavlov won the Nobel Prize in physiology and medicine in 1904 for his work on the principal digestive glands.

stimulus (CS). The salivation elicited by the bell is a **conditioned response (CR)**—a learned response to a previously neutral stimulus. Each time the conditioned stimulus is paired with the unconditioned stimulus, the conditioned response is said to be *reinforced,* or strengthened. Pavlov's conditioning process is illustrated in Figure 2.7.

Classical Conditioning in Psychopathology

Pavlov never fully explored the implications of classical conditioning for human behavior; John B. Watson is credited with recognizing the importance of associative learning in the explanation of abnormal behavior. In a classic and oft-cited experiment, Watson (Watson & Rayner, 1920), using classical conditioning principles, was able to demonstrate that the acquisition of a *phobia* (an exaggerated, seemingly illogical fear of a particular object or class of objects) could be explained by classical conditioning.

| **Stimulus:** | UCS (food) | UCS & CS (food & bell) | CS (bell alone) |
| **Response:** | UCR (salivation) | UCR (salivation) | CR (conditioned salivation) |

FIGURE 2.7   A Basic Classical Conditioning Process   Dogs normally salivate when food is provided (left drawing). With his laboratory dogs, Ivan Pavlov paired the ringing of a bell with the presentation of food (middle drawing). Eventually, the dogs would salivate to the ringing of the bell alone, when no food was near (right drawing).

In operant conditioning, positive consequences increase the likelihood and frequency of a desired response. This is particularly important in a classroom setting where a child knows that appropriate behavior will be rewarded and inappropriate behavior will be punished.

As we shall see in later chapters, classical conditioning has provided explanations not only for the acquisition of phobias but also for certain unusual sexual attractions and other extreme emotional reactions. It has also served as a basis for effective treatment techniques. Yet the "passive nature" of associative learning limited its usefulness as an explanatory and treatment tool. Most human behavior, both normal and abnormal, tends to be much more active and voluntary. To explain how these behaviors are acquired or eliminated necessitates an understanding of operant conditioning.

The Operant Conditioning Model

An **operant behavior** is a voluntary and controllable behavior, such as walking or thinking, that "operates" on an individual's environment. In an extremely warm room, for example, you would have difficulty consciously controlling your sweating—"willing" your body not to perspire. You could, however, simply walk out of the uncomfortably warm room—an operant behavior. Most human behavior is operant in nature.

Edward Thorndike (1874–1949) first formulated the concept of **operant conditioning,** which he called *instrumental conditioning.* This theory of learning holds that behaviors are controlled by the consequences that follow them. In working with cats, Thorndike observed that they would repeat certain behaviors that were followed by positive consequences and reduce behaviors followed by unpleasant consequences. This principle became known as the **law of effect.** Some fifty years later, B. F. Skinner

(1904–1990) started a revolution in the field by innovatively applying Thorndike's law of effect, which he renamed *reinforcement.*

Operant conditioning differs from classical conditioning primarily in two ways. First, classical conditioning is linked to the development of involuntary behaviors such as fear responses, whereas operant conditioning is related to voluntary behaviors.

Second, as we discussed earlier, behaviors based on *classical* conditioning are controlled by stimuli, or events *preceding* the response: Salivation occurs only when it is preceded by a UCS (food in the mouth) or a CS (the thought of a sizzling, juicy steak covered with mushrooms). In *operant* conditioning, however, behaviors are controlled by reinforcers—consequences that influence the frequency or magnitude of the event they follow. Positive consequences increase the likelihood and frequency of a response. But when the consequences are negative, the behavior is less likely to be repeated. For example, a student is likely to raise his or her hand in class often if the teacher recognizes the student, smiles, and seems genuinely interested in the student's comments.

Operant Conditioning in Psychopathology

Studies have demonstrated a relationship between environmental reinforcers and certain abnormal behaviors. For example, self-injurious behavior, such as head banging, is a dramatic form of psychopathology that is often reported in psychotic and mentally retarded children. It has been hypothesized that some forms of head banging may be linked to reinforcing features in the environment (Schaefer, 1970; Schaefer & Martin, 1969). To test this hypothesis, experimenters used bananas as reinforcement to shape a self-injurious behavior, head hitting, in two monkeys. The experimenters rewarded the monkeys for successive approximations of the behavior: first, for raising a paw; then for holding the paw over the head; and finally for bringing the paw down on the head. This sequence of behaviors was shaped in about sixteen minutes in both monkeys. Each time the investigators gave the reinforcement, they said, 'Poor boy! Don't do that! You'll hurt yourself.' Head hitting later occurred whenever these words were spoken. It seems clear from these findings that self-injurious behaviors can be developed and maintained through reinforcement.

Although positive reinforcement can account for some forms of self-injurious behaviors, in some instances other variables seem more important (Carr, 1977). Negative reinforcement (the removal of an aversive stimulus), for example, can also strengthen and maintain unhealthy behaviors. Consider a student who has enrolled in a class in which the instructor re-

B. F. Skinner (1904–1990) was a leader in the field of behaviorism. His research and work in operant conditioning started a revolution in applying the principles of learning to the psychology of human behavior. He was also a social philosopher and many of his ideas fueled debate about the nature of the human condition. These ideas were expressed in his books, *Walden II* and *Beyond Freedom and Dignity.*

quires oral reports. The thought of doing an oral presentation in front of a class produces feelings of anxiety, sweating, an upset stomach, and trembling in the student. Having these feelings is aversive. To stop the unpleasant reaction, the student switches to another section whose instructor does not require oral presentations. The student's behavior is reinforced by escape from aversive feelings, and such avoidance responses to situations involving "stage fright" will increase in frequency.

As in classical conditioning, operant conditioning principles have proven invaluable in the treatment of psychopathology. In many cases, the therapist must be ingenious in devising successful strategies. In later chapters on specific psychological disorders, and in Chapter 17 on treatment approaches, we discuss a variety of ways in which operant conditioning has been applied to the treatment of abnormal behaviors.

Observational learning is based on the theory that behavior can be learned by observing it. While much has been made of the relationship between violence and aggression viewed on television and movies, observational learning can have positive benefits as well.

The Observational Learning Model

The traditional behavioral theories of learning—classical conditioning and operant conditioning—require that the individual actually perform behaviors to learn them. **Observational learning theory** suggests that an individual can acquire new behaviors simply by watching other people perform them (Bandura, 1969; Bandura & Walters, 1963). The process of learning by observing models (and later imitating them) is called *vicarious conditioning* or **modeling.** Direct and tangible reinforcement (such as giving praise or other rewards) for imitation of the model is not necessary, although reinforcers are necessary to maintain behaviors learned in this manner. Observational learning can involve both respondent and operant behaviors, and its discovery has had such an impact in psychology that it has been proposed as a third form of learning.

Observational Learning in Psychopathology

Models that attribute psychopathology to observational learning assume—as do those emphasizing classical and operant conditioning—that abnormal behaviors are learned in the same manner as normal behaviors. More specifically, the assumption is that exposure to disturbed models is likely to produce disturbed behaviors. For example, when monkeys watched other monkeys respond with fear to an unfamiliar object, they learned to respond in a similar manner (Cook, Hodes & Lang, 1986). Observational learning can have four possible effects on an observer (Spiegler, 1983):

1. New behaviors can be acquired by watching the model.

2. The model may serve to elicit particular behaviors by providing the observer with cues to engage in those behaviors.

3. Behaviors formerly inhibited because of anxiety or other negative reactions may be performed after they have been observed.

4. A behavior may become inhibited if the observer sees that a similar behavior performed by the model resulted in aversive consequences.

Criticisms of the Behavioral Models

Behavioral approaches to psychopathology have had a tremendous impact in the areas of cause and therapy, and they are a strong force in psychology today (Franks, 1990; Liberman, Mueser & DeRisi, 1989). The contributions of behaviorist perspectives include (1) questioning the adequacy of the organic model of psychological disorders, (2) stressing the importance of external influences on behavior, (3) requiring strict adherence to scientific methods, and (4) encouraging continuing evaluation of the techniques employed by psychologists. These features endow behaviorism with a degree of effectiveness and accountability that is lacking in the insight-oriented perspectives.

A behavioral orientation may often, however, neglect or place low importance on the inner determinants of behavior. This exclusion has been criticized, as has the behaviorists' extension to human beings of results obtained from animal studies. A lack of attention to human values in relation to behavior has also led to the charge that the behaviorist perspective is mechanistic, viewing people as "empty organisms" (Hayes & Zettle, 1979, p. 5). Some critics also complain that behaviorists are not open minded and that they tend to dismiss out of hand the advances and data accumulated by other approaches to therapy (Hayes & Zettle, 1979; Lazarus, 1977). Criticism that behavioral approaches ignore the person's inner life are less applicable to proponents of modeling. As you will see in the next section of this chapter, a recent trend among behaviorists is to place increasing importance on cognitive processes and to deemphasize the importance of intrapsychic dynamics. This has led to the development of cognitive models. Many theorists and practitioners, however, find it hard to believe that clients can help themselves by simply changing their thinking.

COGNITIVE MODELS OF PSYCHOPATHOLOGY

Steve is a "thinking being." The psychological problems he is experiencing derive from two main cognitive sources: his irrational thoughts or belief system about himself and others, and his distorted thought processes, which lead him to misinterpret events. Steve's tendency to interpret all events to his disadvantage is obvious. For example, because his father constantly criticized and belittled him, Steve believes he is a "worthless" person and will always be "worthless." A cognitive approach to Steve would be highly didactic (analytical), cognitive, and behavior-oriented. As a therapist in this tradition, I would recommend a program that would emphasize three points. First, Steve needs to recognize the role thinking and belief systems play in his problems. Second, he must learn to identify self-statements, belief systems, or assumptions that are irrational and maladaptive, and to respond to them by rationally disputing them. Finally, he must learn to replace irrational self-statements with productive ones.

The **cognitive model** is based on the assumption that conscious thought mediates, or modifies, an individual's emotional state and/or behavior in response to a stimulus. According to this model, people actually create their own problems (and symptoms) by the way they interpret events and situations. For example, one person who fails to be hired for a job may become severely depressed, blaming himself for the failure. Another might become only mildly irritated, believing that failure to get the job had nothing to do with personal inadequacy. How does it happen that events (not being hired for a job) are identical for both people, but the responses are very different? To explain this phenomenon, we have to look at *mediating processes*—the thoughts, perceptions, and self-evaluations that determine our reactions and behaviors.

Cognitive theories argue that modifying thoughts and feelings is essential to changing behavior. How people label a situation and how they interpret events profoundly affect their emotional reactions and behavior. How a person interprets events is a function of his or her **schema**—a set of underlying assumptions heavily influenced by a person's experiences, values, and perceived capabilities. Cognitive psychologists usually search for the causes of psychopathology in one of two processes: in the actual irrational and maladaptive assumptions and thoughts or in distortions of the actual thought process. Although many theorists have contributed greatly to this area, we will concentrate primarily on the contributions of Albert Ellis and Aaron Beck.

Irrational and Maladaptive Assumptions and Thoughts

Almost all cognitive theorists stress heavily that disturbed individuals have both irrational and maladaptive thoughts. Ellis (1962, 1984, 1987) labels these "irrational" assumptions; Beck (1976, 1991) calls them dysfunctional "automatic thoughts"; and Meichenbaum (1977, 1986) refers to them as counterproductive "self-statements." As a practicing therapist for many years, Beck became interested in the way many of his clients would engage in an almost rigid, inflexible, and automatic interpretation of events they had experienced. These negative thoughts seemed to "just happen" as if by reflex, even in the face of objective contrary evidence. For example, Beck believes that depression revolves around firmly entrenched "negative views of self, experience and the future" and that the paranoid individual persists in assuming that other people are deliberately abusive, interfering, or critical (Beck & Weishaar, 1989).

In working with his clients, Beck concluded that cognitive content is organized in a hierarchy, along three levels. At the first level are our most accessible and least stable cognitions, the voluntary thoughts that we have the greatest ability to control and summon at will. Clients suffering from an anxiety disorder, for example, are readily able to describe their symptoms and to offer superficial causes and solutions for them. Most people do not, however, have such ready access to the second level of cognitions, the automatic thoughts that occur spontaneously. The cognitions at this second level are triggered by circumstances and intercede between an event or stimulus and the individual's emotional and behavioral reactions. A student who must make an oral presentation in class may think that "everyone will see I'm nervous." Such thoughts are given credibility without being challenged and usually derive from the third level of cognitions: underlying assumptions about ourselves and the world around us. For example, the belief that one is a failure and an ineffectual person in all aspects of life moderates interpretation of all events. These assumptions are quite stable and almost always outside of the person's awareness.

One of the most prominent psychologists associated with implicating the role of irrational beliefs and assumptions in maladaptive emotions and behaviors is Albert Ellis (Dryden, 1989; Ellis, 1979, 1989). According to Ellis, psychological problems are produced by irrational thought patterns that stem from the individual's belief system. Unpleasant emotional responses that lead to anger, unhappiness, depression, fear, and anxiety result from the *thoughts* about an event rather than from the *event itself*. These irrational thoughts have been conditioned through early childhood, but we also add to the difficulty by reinstilling these false beliefs in ourselves by autosuggestion and self-repetition. Ellis hypothesized that irrational thinking operates from dogmatic, absolutist "shoulds," "musts," and "oughts." Some examples are self-statements such as "I must be loved by my mother or father," "I ought to be able to succeed in everything," and "If I don't get what I want, it will be awful." Cynically, Ellis has referred to the many "musts" that cause human misery as "musturbatory activities."

Although being accepted and loved by everyone is desirable, it is an unrealistic and irrational idea, and as such creates dysfunctional feelings and behaviors. Consider a student who becomes depressed after an unsuccessful date. An appropriate emotional response in such an unsuccessful dating situation might be frustration and temporary disappointment. A more severe depression will develop only if the student adds irrational thoughts, such as "Because this person turned me down, I am worthless.... I will never succeed with anyone of the opposite sex.... I am a total failure."

Distortions of Thought Processes

The study of cognitions as a cause of psychopathology has led many therapists to concentrate on the process (as opposed to the content) of thinking that characterizes both normal and abnormal individuals. Ellis (1962, 1971, 1973) believed that human beings are born with the potential for rational and irrational thinking. Ellis described the process by which an individual acquires irrational thoughts through interactions with significant others, and he called it the *A-B-C theory of personality. A* is an event, a fact, or the individual's behavior or attitude. *C* is the person's emotional or behavioral reaction. The activating event *A* never causes the emotional or behavioral consequence *C*. Instead, *B*, the person's beliefs about *A*, causes *C*.

Think back to the two job hunters. Job hunter 1, whose activating event *A* was being turned down for the position, may think to himself (irrational beliefs *B*), "How awful to be rejected! I must be worthless. I'm no good." Thus he may become depressed and withdraw (emotional and behavioral consequence *C*). Job hunter 2, on the other hand, reacts to the activating event *A* by saying (rational beliefs *B*), "How unfortunate to get rejected. It's frustrating and irritable. I'll have to try harder" (healthy consequence *C*). The two sets of assumptions and expectations are very different. Job hunter 1 blamed himself and was overcome with feelings of worthlessness; job hunter 2 recognized that not every person is right for every job (or vice versa), and left the situation with self-esteem intact. Job hunter 1 interprets the rejection as "awful and catastrophic" and, as a result, reacts with depression and may cease looking for a job. Job hunter 2 does not interpret the rejection personally, reacts with mild irritation and annoyance, and redoubles his efforts to seek employment. Figure 2.8 illustrates the *A-B-C* relationship and suggests a possible path for a cognitive approach to treatment.

Although the cognitive model proposed by Ellis applies to both rational and irrational thinking, interest has focused on identifying the types of cognitive distortions that lead to abnormal functioning. Aaron Beck has proposed six types of faulty thinking (Beck, Kovacs & Weissman, 1979; Beck & Weishaar, 1989), which are described in Table 2.4.

Cognitive Approaches to Therapy

Certain commonalities characterize almost all cognitive approaches to psychotherapy. These have been summarized by Beck and Weishaar (1989):

> Cognitive therapy consists of highly specific learning experiences designed to teach patients (1) to monitor their negative, automatic thoughts (cognitions); (2) to recognize the connections between cognition, affect, and behavior; (3) to examine the evidence for and against distorted automatic thoughts; (4) to substitute more reality-oriented interpretations for these biased cognitions; and (5) to learn to identify and alter the beliefs that predispose them to distort their experiences. (p. 308)

IRRATIONAL COGNITIVE PROCESS

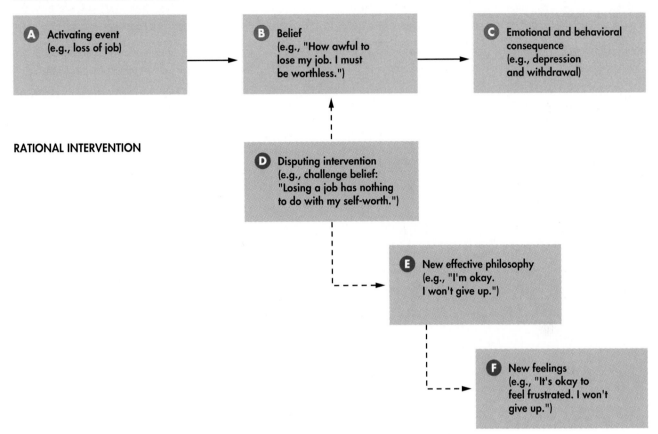

RATIONAL INTERVENTION

FIGURE 2.8   Ellis's A-B-C Theory of Personality The development of emotional and behavioral problems is often linked to a dysfunctional thinking process. The cognitive psychologist is likely to attack these problematic beliefs using a rational intervention process, resulting in a change in beliefs and feelings.

Criticisms of the Cognitive Models

In many respects, the cognitive model shares many characteristics of the traditional behavioral models. It emphasizes learned cognitions that occur within people as they interact with internally generated stimuli and external events. Both types of model stress the altering of behavior and both deemphasize childhood experiences; neither considers insight into a problem necessary to alleviate it (Beck, 1970; Rimm & Masters, 1979). In addition, successful treatment is measured by changes in overt behavior, and therapists rely on experimental methods to validate techniques.

Yet some behaviorists remain quite skeptical of the cognitive schools. Just before his death, Skinner (1990) warned that cognitions were not observable phenomena and could not form the foundations of empiricism. In this context, he echoed the historical beliefs of John B. Watson, who stated that the science of psychology was observable behaviors, not "mentalistic concepts." Although Watson's reference was to the intrapsychic dynamics of the mind postulated by Freud, Watson might have viewed cognitions in the same manner.

Cognitive theories have also been attacked by more humanistically oriented psychologists who believe that human behavior is more than thoughts and beliefs (Corey, 1991). They object to the mechanistic manner by which human beings are reduced to the sum of their cognitive parts. Do thoughts and beliefs really cause disturbances, or do the disturbances themselves distort thinking?

Criticisms have also been leveled at the therapeutic approach taken by cognitive therapists. The nature of

TABLE 2.4 Beck's Six Types of Faulty Thinking

1. **Arbitrary Inference** Drawing conclusions about oneself or the world without sufficient and relevant information. *Example:* A man not hired by a potential employer perceives himself as "totally worthless" and believes he probably will never find employment of any sort.

2. **Selective Abstraction** Drawing conclusions from very isolated details and events without considering the larger context or picture. *Example:* A student who receives a C on an exam becomes depressed and stops attending classes even though he has A's and B's in his other courses. The student measures his worth by failures, errors, and weaknesses rather than by successes or strengths.

3. **Overgeneralization** Holding extreme beliefs on the basis of a single incident and applying it to a different or dissimilar and inappropriate situation. *Example:* A depressed woman who has relationship problems with her boss may believe she is a failure in all other types of relationships.

4. **Magnification and Exaggeration** The process of overestimating the significance of negative events. *Example:* A runner experiences shortness of breath and interprets it as a major health problem, possibly even an indication of imminent death.

5. **Personalization** Relating external events to one another when no objective basis for such a connection is apparent. *Example:* A student who raises his hand in class and is not called on by the professor believes that the instructor dislikes or is biased against him.

6. **Polarized Thinking** An "all-or-nothing," "good or bad," and "either-or" approach to viewing the world. *Example:* At one extreme, a woman who perceives herself as "perfect" and immune from making mistakes; at the other extreme, a woman who believes she is a total incompetent.

the approach makes the therapist a teacher, expert, and authority figure. The therapist is quite direct and confrontive in identifying and attacking irrational beliefs and processes. In such interactions, clients can readily be intimidated into acquiescing to the therapist's power and authority. Thus the therapist may misidentify the client's disorder, and the client may be hesitant to challenge the therapist's beliefs.

Although more evaluative research must be conducted before the cognitive learning approach can be evaluated, this approach, with its emphasis on the powerful influence of internal mediating processes, seems to offer an exciting new direction for behaviorists. It is clear that psychology has undergone a "revolution" in that cognitive and behavioral approaches have been integrated into mainstream psychological thought (Mahoney, 1977).

THE FAMILY SYSTEMS MODEL OF PSYCHOPATHOLOGY

Steve's problem is not an isolated phenomenon. It resides in the family system, which should be the primary unit of treatment. Although Steve is manifesting the dis-

orders, his father and mother are also suffering, and their pathological symptoms are reflected in Steve. Attempts to help Steve must therefore focus on the entire family. It is obvious that the relationships between Steve and his father, between Steve and his mother, and between his father and mother are unhealthy.

Furthermore, Mr. and Mrs. V's. relationship can be characterized as isolative. Each seems to live a separate life, even when they are together in the same house. Each has unfulfilled needs, and each denies and avoids interactions and conflicts with the other. As long as Steve is the "identified patient" and is seen as "the problem," Mr. and Mrs. V. can continue in their mutual self-deception that all is well between them. I recommend that Steve's entire family be included in a program of therapy.

Almost all of the theories of psychopathology discussed so far in this chapter have focused on the individual. Given the emphasis in the United States on individual achievement and responsibility—on "rugged individualism"—it is not surprising that these approaches have been very popular in the United States.

In contrast, the **family systems model** emphasizes the family's influence on individual behavior. This viewpoint holds that all members of a family are enmeshed in a network of interdependent roles,

"*What's wrong with us, Fred? We never FIGHT anymore.*"

Family system approaches tend to avoid focusing on individuals or couples like the one in this cartoon. Rather, they see the entire family as the unit of treatment. Treating only one member of a family leads to failure because it is the family dynamics, not just the individuals within a family, that need to be altered.

statuses, values, and norms. The behavior of one member directly affects the entire family system. Correspondingly, people typically behave in ways that reflect family influences.

We can identify three distinct characteristics of the family systems approach (Goldenberg & Goldenberg, 1995; Foley, 1989). First, personality development is ruled largely by the attributes of the family, especially the way parents behave toward and around their children. Second, abnormal behavior in the individual is usually a reflection or "symptom" of unhealthy family dynamics and, more specifically, of poor communication among family members. Third, the therapist must focus on the family system, not solely on the individual, and must strive to involve the entire family in therapy. As a result, the locus of disorder is seen to reside not within the individual, but within the family system.

Development of Personality and Identity Within the Family

One of the earliest individuals to emphasize the importance of family influences was American psychiatrist Harry Stack Sullivan (1892–1949). Sullivan started out with a strong psychoanalytic orientation but eventually broadened his focus to include interpersonal relations. He proposed that our concepts of self, identity, and self-esteem are formed through our interactions with "significant others," typically parents, siblings, and peers (Sullivan, 1953). Parents, of course, have the major share of responsibility for socializing the child. If parents behave toward the child as though he or she is worthwhile, the child is likely

to develop a positive self-image and sense of self-worth. This sense of self, in turn, provides the emotional resilience that all people need if they are to persevere through defeats, conflicts, and the many other stressors of day-to-day life. Those parents who do not see their child as a worthwhile person and who belittle or antagonize the child may cause the child to develop a negative self-image. This negative self-image can lead to the child's making self-statements such as "I am worthless" and "If I try, I'll only fail."

Another neo-Freudian, Erik Erikson, also stressed child-parent relationships. He pointed out the importance of parental love and attention for a child's development of a sense of trust (Erikson, 1968). We all need a few people on whom we can rely and in whom we can confide with confidence. Without this trust, we are likely to see the world as dangerous, hostile, and threatening. As a result, we may shun close personal relationships and avoid even casual social interactions. How trust develops in a child depends very much on the parents.

Family Dynamics

By **family dynamics** we mean the day-to-day "operation" of the family system, including communication among its members. Inconsistent communication or distorted patterns of operation can cause children to develop a misconception of reality.

Early theorists proposed that psychopathology (especially schizophrenia) was the result of inconsistency in family communications (Bateson et al., 1956; Weakland, 1960). Most communications occur at two

Family interaction patterns can exert tremendous influence on a child's personality development, determining the child's sense of self-worth and the acquisition of appropriate social skills. This picture shows an Inuit (Eskimo) family in Kotzebue, Alaska, during a meal. Notice the attentiveness of the parents toward their children (communicating a sense of importance to them) and how every family member is present during the meal (emphasizing family cohesion and belonging).

levels—verbal and nonverbal. The verbal content of a message can be enhanced or negated by its nonverbal content. For example, a father who insists, "I'm not angry!"—while raising his voice, clenching his fists, and pounding the table—is physically contradicting his verbal message. Another form of inconsistency occurs when family members continually disqualify one another's messages. For example, a mother's message to her child may be negated by the father: "Your mother doesn't know what she's talking about." Such contradictions create a *double bind* within the child, which may result in an inability to communicate, social withdrawal, and eventually schizophrenia (Abels, 1975, 1976; Bateson, 1978; Nichols, 1984; Smith, 1982). The process is discussed in greater detail in Chapter 14.

The double-bind theory was very popular in the 1950s and 1960s, but it has since fallen into disrepute. As a specific explanation of schizophrenia, it has been found seriously lacking. Nevertheless, faulty and distorted communications continue to be strongly emphasized in family system approaches.

Family Treatment Approaches

The family therapy movement has spawned a number of approaches to treatment. Three of the major ones are the communications, strategic, and structural approaches.

Among those who have emphasized the importance of clear and direct *communications* for healthy family system development is Virginia Satir (Bandler & Grinder, 1979; Satir, 1967). Her *conjoint family therapeutic approach* stresses the importance of teaching message-sending and message-receiving skills to family members. Like other family therapists, Satir believes that the identified patient is really a reflection of the family system gone awry.

The term *strategic* as applied to family therapy grew out of the ideas of Don Jackson and Jay Haley (Haley, 1963, 1977, 1987). Therapy is conceived as a power struggle between client and therapist. According to this viewpoint, the identified patient is in control, making other family members feel helpless. To shift the balance of power, the therapist must devise strategies (hence the term *strategic*) to effect change.

In the *structural family approach* advocated by Salvatore Minuchin (1974), disorder is seen simply as a result of a system of relationships that need to be basically modified or restructured. Most family problems arise because members are either too involved or too little involved with one another.

All three of these approaches focus on communications, unbalanced power relationships among family members, and the need to restructure the troubled family system.

Criticisms of the Family Systems Model

There is no denying that we are social creatures, and by concentrating on this aspect of human behavior, the family systems approach has added an important social dimension to our understanding of abnormal behavior. In fact, much evidence shows that unhealthy family relationships can contribute to the development of disorders. But the family systems model is subject to a number of criticisms. For one thing, the definition of *family* used by these models may be culture bound (see Focus On). Also, the basic tenets and specific applications of this approach are difficult to study and quantify.

As we have stated frequently, a psychologist who places too much emphasis on any one model may overlook the influence of factors that are not included in that model. But exclusive emphasis on the family systems model may have particularly unpleasant consequences. Too often, psychologists have pointed an accusing finger at the parents of children who suffer from certain disorders, despite an abundance of evidence that parental influence may not be a factor in those disorders. The parents are then burdened with unnecessary guilt over a situation they could not have otherwise controlled.

Perhaps the most credible attack on family systems theory, however, comes from the feminist perspective (Cottone, 1992). Bolgrad (1984, 1986) uses the issue of wife-battering and incest as examples of subtle biases against women in the family systems approach. This bias can be found in the language and assumptions of the systems approach. These assumptions are that (1) sexual and physical abuse serves a functional role in the family; (2) all members actively participate in perpetuating the dysfunctional system; and (3) the abused wife or sexually molested daughter is viewed as a symptom of a sick system. In essence, the family systems approach, with its emphasis on the interrelationship of parts to the whole and its belief in balance (homeostasis), may inadvertently minimize acts of violence against women. Bolgrad (1984) stated the following:

> Feminist values are clear regarding the allocation of responsibility for wife battering incidents: (1) no woman deserves to be beaten; (2) men are solely responsible for their actions.... From a feminist perspective, a systemic formulation is biased if it can be employed to implicate the battered woman or to excuse the abusive man. (pp. 560–561)

Such reasoning necessitates a straightforward cause-effect analysis: Abusive men are to be blamed for abusive incidents, and women should not be blamed. Bolgrad believes that the premise of causality in family systems theory breaks down in this case, especially when applied to a two- or three-year-old who is sexually abused. To even suggest that young children may have contributed to their own sodomy or rape is to truly blame the victim.

MODELS OF DIVERSITY AND PSYCHOPATHOLOGY

Steven V. is not only a biological, feeling, behaving, thinking, and social being, but a person with a culture. The cultural context in which his problems arise must be considered in understanding Steve's dilemma. He is a European American of Scottish descent, born to an extremely wealthy family in the upper socioeconomic class. He is a male, raised in a cultural context that values individual achievement. All of these characteristics mean that many of his experiences are likely to be very different from those of a person who is a member of a minority group, economically indigent, or of female gender. One might argue, for example, that Steve's father values American individualistic competitiveness and achievement in the extreme. He has succeeded by his own efforts but, unfortunately, his success has come at the emotional cost of his family. To truly understand Steve, we must recognize that the many multicultural variables—race, culture, ethnicity, gender, religion, sexual orientation, and so on—are powerful factors. As such, they influence the types of social-psychological stressors Steve is likely to experience, the ways he will manifest disorders, and the types of therapeutic approaches most likely to be effective.

Minority groups have always expressed dissatisfaction with European American standards of mental health, but this dissatisfaction assumed a more specific form during the 1960s, with the Civil Rights movement. At that point, the models of psychopathology came under systematic criticism by minority mental health professionals (Mackler & Giddings, 1965; Baratz & Baratz, 1970; Grier & Cobb, 1968; Thomas & Sillen, 1972). The cry for the development of multicultural models of psychology has been fueled by a rapid increase in U.S. racial and ethnic minority populations. The 1990 U.S. Census revealed that the United States is undergoing some rapid and radical demographic changes, which can be referred to as the "diversification of the United States." Projections indicate that by the year 2000, more than one-third of the population will be members of racial or ethnic minorities, and that within several short decades, European Americans will constitute a numerical minority. The reality of cultural diversity in the United States has already had tremendous impact on educational, political, economic, and social systems. The mental health professions and the traditional models used to explain both normal and abnormal behavior are also experiencing a major revolution (Sue, 1995; Sue, Ivey & Pedersen, 1996).

Multicultural psychology encompasses more than racial and ethnic minorities; it also focuses on issues

Cultural Definitions of the Family

Increasingly, family system advocates have had to work with culturally different families. Most of the concepts, principles, and techniques of family system approaches, however, have been derived from white middle-class norms. For example, we need only look at our concept of the family structure to ascertain that middle-class European Americans define the family as being composed of the biological mother, father, and children (the nuclear family). Yet almost all other minority groups have traditionally operated from an extended family system (Ho, 1987; McGoldrick, Pearce & Giordano, 1982; Sue & Sue, 1990). Hispanic families consider godparents to be an intimate part of the family, responsible for the child's moral, ethical, and religious upbringing. African Americans have a family structure that may include aunts, uncles, and male and female friends. Asian Americans operate from an extended family system that may include ancestor worship. American Indians may subscribe to a communal family system. As a result, people in these family structures view transferring children from one nuclear family to another within the extended system as a common practice. White therapists may not understand this viewpoint and may consider the practice a form of child abuse or neglect.

Ho (1987) reported just such a case, in which an American Indian child was taken away from the parents on the recommendation of a social worker. The social worker had observed that the parents "were negligent in raising their child and did not provide proper food and shelter." The basis for this conclusion was a very common tribal practice in which the child had spent one week with one family and several weeks with another. In American Indian culture and custom, this was considered acceptable.

To accurately assess and understand a minority family system, mental health professionals must be aware that there are a number of major cultural differences between European American family values and those of other ethnic groups. These cultural values are often very difficult for European Americans to understand, and they can cause major difficulties in family system analysis and treatment.

1. Studies indicate that ethnic minority extended family ties are more cohesive and exten-

concerning sexual orientation, religious preference, socioeconomic status, gender, physical disabilities, and other such factors. In the following discussion, however, we will use racial and ethnic minority groups to illustrate the major premises of the multicultural models.

A number of multicultural experts (White & Parham, 1990; Ponterotto & Casas, 1991; Sue & Sue, 1990) have identified three primary models in the mental health field that are used to explain differences between various minority groups and their white counterparts: (1) the inferiority model, (2) the deprivations/deficit model, and (3) the multicultural model. Each tends to view minority characteristics from a different perspective.

Early Models

The Inferiority Model The inferiority model generally contends that racial and ethnic minorities are inferior in some respect to the majority population. Low academic achievement and higher unemployment rates among African Americans and Latino Americans are attributed to heredity. For example, de Gobineau's (1915) *Essay on the Inequality of the Human Races* and Darwin's (1859) *On the Origin of Species by Means of Natural Selection* were used to support the genetic intellectual superiority of whites and the genetic inferiority of the "lower races."

The assertions of racial inferiority continued well into the 1900s and were promoted by leading psychologists. For example, Cyril Burt, an eminent British psychologist, believed that intelligence is inherited and that African Americans have inherited inferior brains. Although his data were later found to have been fabricated (Dorfman, 1978; Gillie, 1977) and questions were raised regarding his integrity, many other psychologists (Herrnstein, 1971; Jensen, 1969; Shockley, 1972; Shuey, 1966) have voiced similar beliefs. These same assertions have recently surfaced in the controversial book *The Bell Curve* (Herrnstein & Murray, 1994).

sive than kinship relationships among European Americans. Most middle-class European Americans stress individual autonomy. Ethnic minorities stress collectivity and primary allegiance to the family, and they downplay individual autonomy and identity for the good of the family unit. In this context, a traditional Asian American college student who desires to consult with parents before making a vocational choice may not be manifesting dependency or immaturity.

2. Many ethnic minority families are patriarchal. That is, the male partner is the primary decision maker and the female partner is relegated to a lesser role. This is particularly true of traditional Hispanic, Asian American, and American Indian cultures; it is less true for African Americans. European Americans prefer an egalitarian relationship that minority couples may not desire.

3. Communication patterns between parent and child in traditional white society tend to be more egalitarian than those found in many minority groups. In Asian and Hispanic groups, for example, communication may be more rigidly hierarchical (parent to child). In such cultures, a child speaks when spoken to and is discouraged from initiating conversations. Conjoint family therapy, whose sessions are characterized by free and open expression, may be a violation of cultural norms.

4. Sibling relationships in minority families may also differ radically from their white counterparts. Traditional Asian and Hispanic cultures, for example, have firm hierarchial standards determined by age and sex. The older the sibling, the more status, responsibility, and influence he or she possesses. Also, gender is an important determinant of status. Historically,

male children are more valued than female children.

Other cultural differences exist, such as how various ethnic groups view divorce and intermarriage. The mental health professional who is unaware of cultural differences may actually view these differences as pathological and deviant. It may not be that the techniques and methods of family approaches are culturally biased, so much as they are inappropriately applied. For example, Minuchin's (1974) structural approach has been used effectively with African American families. This success may stem from his recognition that cultures have different patterns of what they consider "close" and "too close" (enmeshed). His approach handles the issue of restructuring differently, depending on the pattern.

Deprivations/Deficit Model The deprivations/deficit model arose during the 1950s and 1960s when well-meaning social scientists began actively to question whether the existing differences between blacks and whites were encoded in their genes or whether environmental factors could account for them. One explanation put forward was that years of racism and discrimination had deprived minorities of the opportunity to develop a positive self-esteem. Related to this explanation was the belief that the deficits observed in African Americans, for example, were the result of "cultural deprivation." Reissman's (1962) widely read book *The Culturally Deprived Child* indicated that minority groups performed poorly on tests or exhibited deviant characteristics because they were "culturally impoverished."

Although Reissman meant his concept to add balance to understanding minority groups and, ultimately, to improve their conditions, it was conceptually inaccurate. First, the term *culturally deprived* means to lack a cultural background (which concep-

tually means Africans arrived in America without a culture!), but everyone inherits a culture. Second, such terms cause conceptual and theoretical confusion because they imply that white middle-class values are superior and that a "transfusion" of them would solve the problems of minority groups. Third, these deviations in values become equated with disorder because one group's cultural values are seen as pathological. In some respects, the deprivations/deficit model, instead of blaming the genes, blamed the lifestyles and values of various ethnic groups.

The Multicultural Model During the late 1980s and early 1990s, a new and conceptually different model emerged in the literature. Often referred to as the "multicultural model" (Johnson, 1990; White & Parham, 1990), "culturally different model" (Katz, 1985; Sue, 1981), "culturally pluralistic model or culturally diverse model" (Ponterotto & Casas, 1991), the new model emphasizes that to be culturally different does not equal deviancy, pathology, or inferiority.

The model recognizes that each culture has strengths and limitations and that differences are inevitable. Behaviors must be evaluated from the perspective of a group's value system as well as other standards used in determining normality and abnormality. Several major assumptions are made (Sue, 1995; Sue, Ivey & Pedersen, 1996):

1. Culture is central to all theories of pathology and failure to acknowledge this fact leads to inaccurate diagnosis and treatment.

2. European American conceptions of mental health must be balanced by non-Western perspectives.

3. Human development is embedded in multiple levels of experiences—individual, group, and universal—and in multiple contexts, including individual, family, and cultural milieu.

4. A metatheoretical approach (a theory about theories) to models of pathology may yield the most fruitful results (Sue, 1995; Sue, Ivey & Pedersen, 1996).

The influence of the multicultural movement is most clearly seen in the latest revision of the *Diagnostic and Statistical Manual of Mental Disorders* (DSM-IV; APA, 1994), the major nomenclature used to diagnose mental disorders. For the first time since the inception of this manual in 1952, DSM-IV acknowledges ethnic and cultural considerations. It does so in the following three ways:

■ It attempts to present information related to cultural variations in the clinical presentation of disorders.

■ It contains an appendix of culture-bound syndromes—disorders seemingly unique to a particular culture or society.

■ It offers a suggested outline to aid clinicians in understanding the impact of an individual's cultural context.

Multicultural Explanations of Psychopathology

As noted earlier, the multicultural model makes an explicit assumption that all theories of human development arise from a particular cultural context (Sue & Sue, 1990; White & Parham, 1990; Pedersen, 1987). Thus, many traditional European American models of psychopathology are culture bound, evaluating and viewing events and processes from a world view not experienced or shared by other cultural groups. For example, individualism and autonomy are highly valued in the United States and are equated with healthy

functioning. Most European American children are raised to become increasingly independent, to be able to make decisions on their own, and to "stand on their own two feet." In contrast, many traditional Asians and Asian Americans place an equally high value on "collectivity," in which the psychosocial unit of identity is the family, not the individual (Sue, 1995). Similarly, while European Americans fear the loss of "individuality," members of traditional Asian groups fear the loss of "belonging."

Such different experiences and values may lead unenlightened mental health professionals to make biased assumptions about human behavior. In some instances, these assumptions influence their judgments of normality and abnormality among various racial and ethnic minorities. For example, a mental health professional who did not understand that Asian Americans value a collectivistic identity could see them as overly dependent, immature, and unable to make decisions on their own. Likewise, such a person might perceive "restraint of strong feelings"—a valued characteristic among some Asian groups—as evidence of "being inhibited," "unable to express emotions," or "repressed."

The multicultural model suggests that European American perspectives of pathology place too much emphasis on locating the problems within the person (intrapsychic). Although these perspectives do not deny that problems may originate from within the individual, they are likely to consider external or system forces equally important for all individuals, regardless of social or ethnic group (Sue & Sue, 1990). The multicultural model suggests that problems are often located in the social system rather than in the person. Minority group members, for example, may have to deal with greater and more unique stressors than those of their white counterparts. Racism, bias, discrimination, economic hardships, and culture conflicts are just a few of the sociopolitical realities that racial and ethnic minorities must contend with. As a result, the role of therapist may be better served by ameliorating oppressive or detrimental social conditions than by attempting therapy aimed at changing the individual. Appropriate individual therapy may, however, be directed at teaching clients self-help skills and strategies focused on influencing their immediate social situation.

Criticisms of the Multicultural Model

In many respects, the multicultural model operates from a relativistic framework, that is, normal and abnormal behavior must be evaluated from a cultural perspective. The reasoning is that disordered behavior in one context might not be so considered in another.

As diversification in the United States has increased and as the nation has become more global in perspective, multicultural psychology has become increasingly important. In China, children are taught to value group harmony over individual competitiveness. Likewise, racial and ethnic minorities in the United States seem to possess a more collectivistic source of identity. Multicultural models of human behavior regard race, culture, and ethnicity as central to the understanding of normality and abnormality.

As indicated in DSM-IV, some religious practices and beliefs consider it normal to hear or see the deceased relative during bereavement. In addition, there are certain groups, including some American Indian and Hispanic/Latino groups, that may perceive "hallucinations" as positive events.

Some critics of the multicultural model argue that "a disorder is a disorder," regardless of the cultural context in which it is considered. For example, a person suffering from schizophrenia and actively hallucinating is evidencing a malfunctioning of the senses (seeing, hearing, or feeling things that are not there) and a lack of contact with reality. Regardless of whether *the person* judges the occurrence to be desirable or undesirable, it nevertheless represents a disorder (biological dysfunction), according to this viewpoint.

Another criticism leveled at the multicultural model is its lack of empirical validation concerning many of the concepts and assumptions they pose. The field of multicultural counseling and therapy, for example, has been accused of not being solidly grounded in research (Ponterotto & Casas, 1991). Most of the underlying concepts of the multicultural model are based on conceptual critiques or formulations that have not been subjected to formal testing methodology. There is generally heavy reliance on case studies, ethnographic analyses, and investigations of a more qualitative type.

In all fairness, however, such criticisms are based on a Western world view that emphasizes precision and empirical definitions. Multicultural psychologists point out that there is more than one way to ask and answer questions about the human condition.

A FINAL NOTE ABOUT THE MODELS OF PSYCHOPATHOLOGY

Table 2.5 compares the models of psychopathology that we have discussed in this chapter. (You can also review the models by applying them to the hypothetical case of Bill in the Critical Thinking feature.) Each model has devout supporters who, in turn, are influenced by the model they support. But even though theory building and the testing of hypotheses are critical to psychology as a science, it seems evident that we can best understand abnormal behavior only by integrating the various approaches. There is, in fact, a movement among some therapists to seek the best ideas and techniques from all the psychotherapies. For example, some psychologists believe that psychoanalysts and behavior therapists could offer a more complete form of psychotherapy if they listened more carefully to one another and borrowed useful ideas from one another (Wachtel, 1977). Cognitive learning theorists stress the importance of internal mediating processes (the individual's perception of events), which have also been emphasized by humanistic psychologists.

It is clear from recent writings and research publications that a major evolution, or revolution, is occurring in the field. This movement may lead to an

TABLE 2.5 A Comparison of the Most Influential Models of Psychopathology

	Biogenic	Psychoanalytic	Humanistic
Motivation for Behavior	State of biological integrity and health	Unconscious influences	Self-actualization
Basis for Assessment	Medical tests, self-reports, and observable behaviors	Indirect data, oral self-reports	Subjective data, oral self-reports
Theoretical Foundation	Animal and human research, case studies, and other research methods	Case studies, correlational methods	Case studies, correlational and experimental methods
Source of Abnormal Behavior	Biological trauma, heredity, biochemical imbalances	Internal: early childhood experiences	Internal: incongruence between self and experiences
Treatment	Biological interventions (drugs, ECT, surgery, diet)	Dream analysis, free association, transference; locating unconscious conflict from early childhood; resolving the problem and reintegrating the personality	Nondirective reflection, no interpretation; providing unconditional positive regard; increasing congruence between self and experience

integration of some of the currently contrasting views on treatment and psychopathology, in line with a more eclectic approach. Such theoretical integration is a long way off, and there are still a number of strong fundamental differences among the major schools of psychotherapy.

On a treatment level, however, few practicing clinicians adhere rigidly to any one model of psychopathology. Most remain open to more than one perspective not only because there is no single "true" model of abnormal behavior but also because they see considerable value in an eclectic approach. They recognize that the different models do not completely contradict one another on every point. Rather, the elements of various models can complement one another

to produce a broad and detailed explanation of a person's condition (Corey, 1995). We are all biological, psychological, social, and cultural beings. To neglect any one of these aspects of human life would be to deny an important part of our existence.

SUMMARY

1. Psychologists use theories, or models, to explain behavior. Each model is built around its own set of assumptions. The model one adopts determines not only how the therapist explains abnormal behavior but also what treatment methods he or she is likely to use.

TABLE 2.5 A Comparison of the Most Influential Models of Psychopathology *(cont.)*				
Existential	**Behavioral**	**Cognitive**	**Family systems**	**Multicultural**
Capacity for self-awareness; freedom to decide one's fate; search for meaning in a meaningless world	External influences	Interaction of external and cognitive influences	Interaction with significant others	Cultural values and norms (race, culture, ethnicity, socioeconomic status, gender, sexual orientation, religious preference, physical disabilities, and so on)
Subjective data, oral self-reports, experiential encounter	Observable, objective data, overt behaviors	Self-statements, alterations in overt behaviors	Observation of family dynamics	Study of group norms and behaviors; understanding of societal values and interplay of minority and dominant group relations
An approach to understanding the human condition rather than a firm theoretical model	Animal research, case studies, experimental methods	Human research, case studies, experimental methods	Case studies, social psychological studies, experimental methods	Study of cultural groups; data from anthropology, sociology, and political science
Failure to actualize human potential; avoidance of choice and responsibility	External: learning maladaptive responses or not acquiring appropriate responses	Internal: learned pattern of irrational or negative self-statements	External: faulty family interactions (family pathology and inconsistent communication patterns)	Culture conflicts and oppression
Provide conditions for maximizing self-awareness and growth, to enable clients to be free and responsible	Direct modification of the problem behavior; analysis of the environmental factors controlling the behavior and alteration of the contingencies	Understanding relationship between self-statements and problem behavior; modification of internal dialogue	Family therapy involving strategies aimed at treating the entire family, not just the identified patient	Understanding of minority group experiences; social system intervention

2. Biogenic models cite various organic causes of psychopathology. Damage to the nervous system is one such cause. Another is biochemical imbalances. Several types of psychological disturbances have been found to respond to drugs. In addition, a good deal of biochemical research has focused on identifying the role of neurotransmitters in abnormal behavior. Still another biological explanation looks at heredity in mental disorders. Researchers have found correlations between genetic inheritance and certain psychopathologies. Mental health research increasingly focuses on the diathesis-stress theory—the idea that a predispositon to a disorder, not the disorder itself, may be inherited.

3. The psychoanalytic model emphasizes childhood experiences and the role of the unconscious in determining adult behavior. Sigmund Freud, the founder of psychoanalysis, believed that personality has three components: the id, which represents the impulsive, selfish, pleasure-seeking part of the person; the ego, which represents the rational part; and the superego, which represents society's values and ideals. Each component checks and balances the others. The instincts are the energy system from which the personality operates. These instincts manifest themselves in various ways during the five different periods of life, or psychosexual stages, through which people pass: the oral, anal, phallic, latency, and genital

Applying the Models of Psychopathology

A useful learning exercise to evaluate your mastery of the various models is to apply them to a case study. We invite you to try your hand at explaining the behavior of a hypothetical client—Bill. The following hints may help you in your efforts.

1. Consider what each theory proposes as the basis for the development of a mental disorder.

2. Consider the type of data that each perspective considers most important.

3. Compare and contrast the models.

4. Because there are eight models represented, you might wish to do a comparison only between selected models (psychoanalytic, humanistic, and behavioral, for example).

Notice how the adoption of a particular framework influences the type of data you will consider important. Is it possible that all the models hold some semblance of truth? Are their positions necessarily contradictory? Is it possible to integrate them into a unified explanation of Bill? You might wish to use Table 2.5 to aid you on your task.

Bill was born in Indiana to extremely religious parents who raised him in a rather strict moralistic manner. His father, a Baptist minister, often told him and his two sisters to "keep your mind clean, heart pure, and body in control." He forbade Bill's sisters to date at all while they lived at home. Bill's own social life and contacts were extremely limited, and he recalls how anxious he became around girls.

Bill's memories of his father always included feelings of fear and intimidation. No one in the family dared disagree with the father openly, lest they be punished and ridiculed. The father appeared to be hardest on Bill's two sisters, especially when they expressed any interest in boys. The arguments and conflicts between father and daughters were often loud and extreme, disrupting the typical quietness of the home. Although it was never spoken of, Bill was aware that one of his sisters suffered from depression, as did his mother; his sister had twice attempted suicide.

Bill's recollections of his mother were unclear, except that she was always sick with what his father referred to as "the dark cloud," which seemed to visit her periodically. His relationships with his sisters, who were several years older, were uncomfortable.

stages. Each stage poses unique challenges that, if not adequately resolved, can result in maladaptive adult behaviors.

4. According to Freud, abnormal behavior results from neurotic anxiety and the threat that unconscious thoughts will attain consciousness. To repress forbidden thoughts and impulses, the ego uses defense mechanisms. Psychoanalytic therapy attempts to help the patient achieve insight into his or her unconscious.

5. Neo-Freudians have adapted traditional psychoanalytic theory. While accepting basic psychodynamic tenets, they differ from strict Freudian theorists along five dimensions: freedom of choice and future goals, ego autonomy, the influence of social forces, the importance of object relations, and treatment of seriously disturbed people.

6. Critics of psychoanalytic theory point out that it lacks scientific rigor and is difficult to validate empirically. Second, gender bias is clearly evident in how it conceptualizes female sexuality and personality. Third, psychoanalytic theory appears to be less effective with people who are experiencing pressing, immediate problems; those who are less verbal; those who are very young or very old; and those who are psychotic as opposed to less severely disturbed.

7. The humanistic perspective actually represents many perspectives and shares many basic assumptions with the existential perspective. Both view an individual's reality as a product of personal perception and experience. Both see people as capable of making free choices and fulfilling their potential. Both emphasize the whole person and the individual's ability to fulfill

When Bill was a young child, they had teased him mercilessly, and when he reached adolescence, they seemed to take sadistic delight in arousing his raging hormones by flaunting their partially exposed bodies. The result was that Bill became obsessed with having sex with one of his sisters, and he tended to masturbate compulsively. Throughout his adolescence and early adulthood he was tortured by feelings of guilt and believed himself to be, as his father put it, "an unclean and damned sinner."

By all external standards, Bill was a quiet, obedient, and well-behaved child. He did well in school, attended Sunday School without fail, never argued or spoke against his parents, and seldom ventured outside of the home. Although he did exceptionally well in high school—obtaining nearly straight *A*'s—some of his teachers were concerned about his introverted behavior and occasional bouts of depression. When they brought Bill's depression to the attention of his father, however, Mr. M. seemed unconcerned and dismissed it as

no reason to worry. Indeed, Mr. M. complimented Bill on his good grades and unobtrusive behavior, rewarding him occasionally with small privileges, such as a larger portion of dessert or the choice of a television program. To some degree of awareness, Bill felt that his worth as a person was dependent only on "getting good grades" and "staying out of trouble."

As a young child, Bill had exhibited excellent artistic potential, and his teachers tried to encourage him in that direction. In elementary school he won several awards with his drawings and teachers frequently asked him to paint murals in their classrooms or to draw and design flyers and posters for school events. His artistic interests continued into high school, where his art instructor entered one of Bill's drawings in a state contest. His entry won first prize. Unfortunately, Mr. M. discouraged Bill from his interests and talents and told him that "God calls you in another direction." Attempting to please his father, Bill became less involved in art during his ju-

nior and senior years and concentrated more on math and the sciences. He did exceptionally well in these subjects, obtaining nearly straight A's at the finish of his high school years.

When Bill entered college, his prime objective was to remain a straight-A student. Although he had originally loved the excitement of learning, achieving, and mastering new knowledge, he now became cautious and obsessed with "safety"; he was fearful of upsetting his father. As his string of perfect grades became longer and longer, safety (not risking a B grade) became more and more important. He began to choose safe and easy topics for essays, to enroll in very easy courses, and to take incompletes or withdrawals when courses appeared tough.

Toward the end of his sophomore year, Bill suffered a mental breakdown characterized by pessimism and hopelessness. He became very depressed and was subsequently hospitalized after he tried to take his own life.

his or her capacities. The best-known humanistic formulation is Carl Rogers's person-centered approach, which has as a strong tenet the belief that humanity is basically good. Rogers believed that people are motivated not only to meet their biological needs but also to grow and to enhance the self, to become actualized or fulfilled. If the actualizing tendency is thwarted, behavior disorders may result. In person-centered therapy, the therapist projects a strong belief in the client's ability to deal with life, to grow, and to reach his or her potential.

8. As noted, the existential perspective shares similarities with its humanistic counterpart but is generally less optimistic. It focuses on the irrational, on human alienation, on the search for meaning, and on the individual's responsibility to others as well as to oneself.

9. Humanistic and existential perspectives have been characterized as vague, too subjective, and not open to empirical investigation. In addition, these approaches may not work well with severely disturbed clients.

10. Behavioral models of psychopathology focus on the role of learning in abnormal behavior. The approach dates to Pavlov's classical conditioning and the work of John B. Watson, who proposed that psychology's goal should be the prediction and control of human behavior and that, as a science, psychology should be limited to observable and measurable events.

11. The traditional behavioral models of psychopathology hold that abnormal behaviors are acquired through association (classical conditioning) or

reinforcement (operant conditioning). Negative emotional responses such as anxiety can be learned through classical conditioning: A formerly neutral stimulus evokes a negative response after it has been presented along with a stimulus that already evokes that response. Negative voluntary behaviors may be learned through operant conditioning if those behaviors are reinforced (rewarded) when they occur.

12. Some psychologists assert that the acquisition of many complex behaviors cannot be explained solely by classical or operant conditioning. These behaviors may, however, be acquired through observational learning, in which a person learns behaviors by observing them in other people, who act as models, and then imitating them. Pathological behavior results when the imitated behavior is inappropriate or inappropriately applied.

13. Cognitive models developed partly as a reaction to the criticism that traditional behaviorists ignore the influence of thought processes on behavior. According to the cognitive model, perceptions of events are mediated by thoughts and feelings, and the perception may have a greater influence on behavior than the event itself. Despite this emphasis on cognition, the cognitive perspective shares many characteristics with the traditional behavioral models. Cognitive therapeutic approaches are generally aimed at normalizing the client's perception of events. Critics of cognitive models vary. Some behaviorists state that cognitions are not observable and therefore not open to study. Some humanists believe the approach is too mechanistic. Some critics believe the approach places too much emphasis on the therapist as expert.

14. The family systems model asserts that family interactions guide an individual's development of personal identity as well as his or her sense of reality. Abnormal behavior is viewed as the result of distortion or faulty communication or unbalanced structural relationships within the family. Children who receive faulty messages from parents, or who are subjected to structurally abnormal family constellations, may develop behavioral and emotional problems. Therapeutic techniques generally focus on the family as a whole, rather than on one disturbed individual.

15. With an increase in racial and ethnic minority populations, interest in multicultural models of psychology has been renewed. Proponents of this approach believe that race, culture, ethnicity, gender, sexual orientation, religious preference, socioeconomic status, physical disabilities, and other variables are powerful influences in determining how mental health professionals perceive a disorder, how it may be manifested by specific cultural groups, and how it is best treated.

16. Cultural differences have been perceived in three ways: (a) the inferiority model, in which differences are attributed to the interplay of undesirable elements in a person's biological makeup, (b) the deprivations/deficit model, in which differences in traits or behaviors are blamed on not having the "right culture," and (c) the new multicultural model, which recognizes that differences do not equate with deviance. The multicultural model has been criticized for its stand on cultural relativism and for the lack of empirical research supporting its basic tenets.

KEY TERMS

axon At the end of a neuron, a long, thin extension that sends signals to other neurons

behavioral models Theories of psychopathology that are concerned with the role of learning in abnormal behavior

classical conditioning A principle of learning in which involuntary responses to stimuli are learned through association

cognitive model A principle of learning holding that conscious thought mediates, or modifies, an individual's emotional state and/or behavior in response to a stimulus

conditioned response (CR) In classical conditioning, the learned response made to a previously neutral stimulus that has acquired some of the properties of another stimulus with which it has been paired

conditioned stimulus (CS) In classical conditioning, a previously neutral stimulus that has acquired some of the properties of another stimulus with which it has been paired

defense mechanisms In psychoanalytic theory, ego-protection strategies that shelter the individual from anxiety, operate unconsciously, and distort reality

dendrites Rootlike structures that are attached to the body of the neuron and that receive signals from other neurons

diathesis-stress theory The theory that a predisposition to develop mental illness—not mental illness itself—is inherited and that this predisposition may or may not be activated by environmental forces

existential approach A set of attitudes that has many commonalities with humanism but is less optimistic, focusing (1) on human alienation in an increasingly technological and impersonal world, (2) on the individual in the context of the human condition, and (3) on responsibility to others as well as to oneself

family dynamics The day-to-day "operation" of the family system, including communication among its members

family systems model A model of psychopathology that emphasizes the family's influence on individual behavior

genotype A person's genetic makeup

humanistic perspective The optimistic viewpoint that people are born with the ability to fulfill their potential and that abnormal behavior results from disharmony between the person's potential and his or her self-concept

law of effect The principle that behaviors associated with positive consequences will be repeated and behaviors associated with unpleasant consequences will be reduced

model An analogy used by scientists, usually to describe or explain a phenomenon or process that they cannot directly observe

modeling The process of learning by observing models and later imitating them; also known as *vicarious conditioning*

neo-Freudians Theorists who broke away from Freud and formulated psychological models whose ideas were strongly influenced by Freud's psychoanalytic model; also called *post-Freudians*

neurons Nerve cells that transmit messages throughout the body

neurotransmitters Chemical substances released by the axons of sending neurons involved in the transmission of neural impulses to the dendrites of receiving neurons

observational learning theory A theory of learning that holds that an individual can acquire new behaviors simply by watching other people perform them

operant behavior A voluntary and controllable behavior that "operates" on an individual's environment

operant conditioning A theory of learning, applying primarily to voluntary behaviors, that holds that these behaviors are controlled by the consequences that follow them

phenotype The observable results of the interaction of a person's genotype and the environment

pleasure principle Usually associated with the id in Freudian theory; the impulsive, pleasure-seeking aspect of our being that seeks immediate gratification of instinctual needs, regardless of moral or realistic concerns

psychoanalysis Therapy based on the Freudian view that unconscious conflicts must be aired and understood by the patient if abnormal behavior is to be eliminated

psychoanalytic model The view that adult disorders arise from traumas or anxieties originally experienced in childhood but later repressed because they are too threatening for the adult to face

psychopathology Clinical term meaning abnormal behavior

psychosexual stages In psychoanalytic theory, the sequence of stages—oral, anal, phallic, latency, and genital—through which human personality develops

reality principle Usually associated with the ego in Freudian theory; an awareness of the demands of the environment and of the need to adjust behavior to meet these demands

schema The set of underlying assumptions that is heavily influenced by a person's experiences, values, and perceived capabilities and that influences how he or she interprets events

self-actualization An inherent tendency to strive toward the realization of one's full potential

self-concept An individual's assessment of his or her own value and worth

synapse A minute gap between the axon of the sending neuron and the dendrites of the receiving neuron

unconditioned response (UCR) In classical conditioning, the unlearned response made to an unconditioned stimulus

unconditioned stimulus (UCS) In classical conditioning, the stimulus that elicits an unconditioned response

CHAPTER 3

ASSESSMENT AND CLASSIFICATION OF ABNORMAL BEHAVIOR

A mong the most important tasks in the mental health field are to find the nature and rate of mental disorders, the factors that cause or affect mental disorders, and an effective means of treating and preventing disorders. To accomplish these tasks, therapists must collect information on the well-being of individuals and organize information about a person's condition. Among the assessment tools available to the clinician are observations, conversations and interviews, a variety of psychological and neurological tests, and the reports of the patient and his or her relatives and friends. When the data gathered from all sources are combined and analyzed, the therapist can gain a good picture of the patient's behavior and mental state.

As noted in Chapter 1, the evaluation of the information leads to a *psychodiagnosis,* which involves describing and drawing inferences about an individual's psychological state. Psychodiagnosis is often an early step in the treatment process. It is for many psychotherapists the basis on which a program of therapy is first formulated.

To arrive at a psychodiagnosis, the therapist attempts to obtain a clear description of the client's behavioral patterns and to classify or group them, based on the symptom picture that emerges. This classification performs several functions. First, it helps clarify the therapist's "picture" of the client's mental state; once the data are organized, they are easier to analyze. Second, if the classification scheme is an effective one, it can lead the therapist to possible treatment programs. Third, the names of the categories within a classification scheme provide concise descriptions of, or referents to, symptoms and disorders; these descriptions facilitate communication among psychologists who try to use the same categories to convey information about clients. Finally, using a classification scheme standardizes psychological assessment procedures. That is, if particular information is required for classification, therapists will tend to use the assessment techniques that provide that information. Thus classification may affect the entire psychodiagnostic process as well as the therapy that follows it. Classification is at the heart of science (Barlow, 1991).

RELIABILITY AND VALIDITY

To be useful, assessment tools and classification systems must demonstrate reliability and validity. **Reliability** is the degree to which a procedure or test—such as an evaluation tool or classification scheme—will yield the same results repeatedly, under the same circumstances. There are many types of reliability (Robinson, Shaver & Wrightsman, 1991).

Test-retest reliability determines whether a measure yields the same results when given to an individual at two different points in time. For example, if we administer a measure of anxiety to an individual in the morning and then readminister the measure later in the day, the measure is reliable if the results show consistency or stability (that is, the results are the same) from one point in time to another.

In reliability involving *internal consistency,* a measure is considered reliable if various parts of the measure yield similar results. For example, if responses to different items on a measure of anxiety are not related to one another, the items may be measuring different things and not just anxiety.

Finally, *interrater reliability* determines consistency of responses when different judges or raters administer the measure. For instance, let us imagine that two clinicians are trained to diagnose individuals according to a certain classification scheme. Yet, one clinician diagnoses a patient as schizophrenic and the other diagnoses mental retardation. There is a reliability problem here, either in the raters' judgment or in the classification scheme. The problem may be interrater reliability; one clinician may simply be a poor judge. Or in test-retest reliability, inconsistent results may reflect real changes in the behavior of the individual. Nevertheless, in such circumstances, the reliability of the classification scheme or measurement instrument is open to question.

Validity is the extent to which a test or procedure actually performs the function it was designed to perform. If a measure that is intended to assess depression instead assesses anxiety, the measure demonstrates poor validity for depression. As in the case of reliability, there are several ways to determine validity. The most important ways are predictive, criterion-related, construct, and content.

Predictive validity refers to the ability of a test or measure to predict or foretell how a person will behave, respond, or perform. Colleges and universities often use applicants' high school achievement test scores to predict their future college grades. If the test scores have good predictive validity, they should be able to differentiate students who will perform well from those who will perform poorly in college. *Criterion-related validity* determines whether a measure is related to the phenomenon in question. Assume, for example, that we devise a measure that is intended to tell us whether recovering alcoholics are likely to return to drinking. If we find that those who score high on the measure start drinking again, and those who score low do not, then the measure is valid.

Determining *construct validity* is actually a series of tasks with one common theme: all are designed to test whether a measure is related to certain phenomena that are empirically or theoretically thought to be related to that measure. Let us say that a researcher has developed a questionnaire to measure anxiety. To determine construct validity, the researcher should show that the questionnaire is correlated with other measures, such as existing tests of anxiety. Furthermore, we would have increased confidence that the questionnaire is measuring anxiety if it is related to other phenomena that (based on our theory of anxiety) appear in anxious people, such as muscle tension, sweating, tremors, and startle responses. The questionnaire should also be unrelated to characteristics that are not consistently associated with anxiety, such as paranoia.

Finally, *content validity* refers to the degree to which a measure is representative of the phenomenon being measured. For example, we know that depression involves cognitive, emotional, behavioral, and physiological features. If a self-report measure of depression contains items that assess only cognitive features, such as items indicating pessimism, then the measure has poor content validity because it fails to assess three of the four known components of the disorder.

Reliability and validity are also influenced by the conditions in which a test or measure is administered. Standard administration requires that those who administer a test strictly follow common rules or procedures. If an instructor creates a tense and hostile environment for some students who are taking final exams for a course but not for others, for example, the students' test scores may vary simply because the instructor is not treating all students in a similar or standard fashion. An additional concern is the standardization sample—a group of people who have taken the measure and whose performance can be used as a standard or norm. The performance of another person can therefore be interpreted against this norm. However, the standardization sample must be appropriate to the person being evaluated. Our interpretations may not be valid if we compare the test score of a twenty-year-old African American woman with the scores of forty-year-old white American males in a standardization sample.

Questions of reliability and validity are essential to address in assessment tools and in any diagnostic system. In this chapter, we examine assessment methods and clinicians' use of assessment tools. We also discuss the most widely employed diagnostic classification system, DSM-IV, as well as the issues of reliability and validity.

THE ASSESSMENT OF ABNORMAL BEHAVIOR

Assessment is the process of gathering information and drawing conclusions about the traits, skills, abilities, emotional functioning, and psychological problems of the individual, generally for use in developing a diagnosis. Assessment tools are necessary to the study and practice of mental health. Without them, data could not be collected, and psychologists could not conduct meaningful research, develop theories, or engage in psychotherapy. Data collection necessarily involves the use of tools to systematically record the observations, behaviors, or self-reports of individuals. Four principal means of assessment are available to clinicians: observations, interviews, psychological tests and inventories, and neurological tests. These assessment techniques and some specific tools for conducting them are discussed in the following pages and are summarized in Table 3.1.

Observations

Observations of overt behavior provide the most basic method of assessing abnormal behavior; indeed, behavioral observation is the most basic tool in all of science. Research methods are examined in Chapter 4; we concentrate here on clinical observations, which can be either controlled or naturalistic. *Controlled observations* are made in a laboratory, clinic, or other contrived setting. *Naturalistic observations,* which are much more characteristic of the clinician's work, are made in a natural setting—a schoolroom, an office, a hospital ward, or a home—rather than in a laboratory. Although we focus our discussion primarily on observing a client alone, interpersonal interactions, such as those between client and family, also offer important insights for determining the factors that pro-

---

TABLE 3.1 Assessment Techniques

Observation Controlled observations; naturalistic observations

Interviews Clinical interview; mental status examination

Psychological Tests and Inventories

    Projective Personality Tests Rorschach technique; Thematic Apperception Test; sentence-completion tests; draw-a-person tests

    Self-Report Inventories Minnesota Multiphasic Personality Inventory; Beck Depression Inventory

    Intelligence Tests Wechsler Adult Intelligence Scale; Stanford-Binet Intelligence Scale; Wechsler Intelligence Scale for Children; Wechsler Preschool and Primary Scale of Intelligence; Kaufman Assessment Battery for Children

    Tests for Cognitive Impairment Bender-Gestalt Visual Motor Test; Halstead-Reitan Neuropsychological Test Battery; Luria-Nebraska Neuro-psychological Battery

    Neurological Tests Computerized axial tomography; positron emission tomography; electroencephalograph; magnetic resonance imaging

---

duce and maintain disturbed behaviors (Guerin & Chabot, 1992). Observations can be highly structured and specific, as when an observer notes the frequency of stuttering and the circumstances under which stuttering occurs in a client. On other occasions, an observer may be less formal and specific, simply looking for any unusual behaviors on the part of a client. In such a situation, the observations and interpretations of the behaviors may be subjective in nature. Leichtman (1995) believes that this subjectivity has certain advantages in fully understanding clients and their circumstances.

Observations of behavior are usually made in conjunction with an interview, although verbal interaction is not necessary. A trained clinical psychologist watches for external signs or cues and expressive behaviors that may have diagnostic significance (Kleinmuntz, 1967). The client's general mode of dress (neat, conventional, sloppy, flashy), significant scars or tattoos, and even the choice of jewelry may be correlated with personality traits or, perhaps, with disorder. Likewise, other expressive behaviors, such as posture, facial expression, language and verbal patterns, handwriting, and self-expression through graphic art, may all reveal certain characteristics of the client's life. Here is an example of some typical observations.

Margaret is a 37-year-old depressive patient who was seen by one of the authors in a hospital psychiatric ward. She had recently been admitted for treatment. It was obvious from even a casual glance that Margaret had not taken care of herself for weeks. Her face and hands were dirty. Her long hair, which had originally been done up in a bun, had shaken partially loose on one side of her head and now hung down her left shoulder. Her beat-up tennis shoes were only halfway on her stockingless feet. Her unkempt and disheveled appearance and her stooped body posture would lead one to believe she was much older than her actual age.

When first interviewed, Margaret sat as though she did not have the strength to straighten her body. She avoided eye contact with the interviewer and stared at the floor. When asked questions, she usually responded in short phrases: "Yes," "No," "I don't know," "I don't care." There were long pauses between the questions and her answers. Each response seemingly took great effort on her part.

Some psychologists rely on trained raters or on parents, teachers, or other third parties to make the observations and gather information for assessment and evaluation. Others prefer their own observations to those of a third party. Regardless of who conducts the observation, two problems may occur (Sundberg, Taplin & Tyler, 1983). First, observers must check the validity of their own interpretations of the patient's behaviors. This is particularly important when the patient is from a culture different from that of the observer. Second, a person who is aware of being observed or assessed may change the way he or she

Naturalistic observations are made in settings that occur naturally in one's environment. Here, on the left, a rater, sitting behind a one-way mirror, observes interactions among children in a day-care setting. Controlled observations, on the other hand, are made in a laboratory or in a contrived setting that allows researchers or clinicians to regulate many of the events that occur. In the clinic laboratory on the right, a researcher at the Child Development Center at the University of California, Berkeley, gives a three-year-old boy, sitting behind a one-way screen, a task to perform.

usually responds, a phenomenon called **reactivity.** Observers must try to minimize the impact of their observation on the patient's behaviors.

Interviews

The clinical interview is a time-honored tradition as a means of psychological assessment. It lets the therapist observe the client and collect data about the person's life situation and personality. Verbal and nonverbal behaviors, as well as the content (what the client is saying) and process (how the client is communicating—with anxiety, hesitation, or anger) of communications are important to analyze (Reiser, 1988).

Depending on the particular disciplinary training of the interviewer, the interview's frame of reference and its emphasis may vary considerably. (This variability has been a source of inconsistency and error in the assessment of clients.) Psychiatrists, being trained in medicine, may be much more interested in biological or physical variables. Social workers may be more concerned with life history data and the socioeconomic environment of the client. Clinical psychologists may be most interested in establishing rapport with clients as a form of therapy.

Likewise, variations in therapeutic orientation within the discipline of psychology can affect the interview. Because of their strong belief in the unconscious origin of behavior, psychoanalysts may be more interested in psychodynamic processes than in the surface content of the client's words. They are also more likely to pay particular attention to life history variables and dreams. Behaviorists are more likely to concentrate on current environmental conditions related to the client's behavior. In practice, however, mental health practitioners with different therapeutic orientations can also exhibit a great deal of similarity in psychotherapeutic style.

Standardization   As mentioned in the earlier discussion of reliability and validity, standard administration means that common rules or procedures must be strictly followed. Interviews can vary in the degree to which they are structured, the manner in which they are conducted, and the degree of freedom of response on the part of the client. In some interviews, the client is given considerable freedom about what to say and when to say it. The clinician does little to interfere with conversation or to direct its flow. Psychoanalysts, who use free association, and Rogerians, who carry on nondirective therapy, tend to conduct highly unstructured interviews. Behaviorists tend to use more structured interviews.

The most highly structured interview is the *formal standardized interview.* The questions are usually arranged as a checklist, complete with scales for rating answers. The interviewer uses the checklist to ask each interviewee the same set of questions, so that errors are minimized. One widely used structured interview is the Composite International Diagnostic Interview. The purpose of an interview is to enable a trained interviewer to arrive at a diagnosis. The interviewer asks questions, makes clinical judgments, and, depending on the interviewee's previous responses, may ask follow-up questions (Kessler et al., 1994).

A less structured but also widely used interview procedure is the *mental status examination*. The intent of this examination is to determine a client's cognitive, psychological, and behavioral functioning by means of questions, observations, and tasks posed to the client (Othmer & Othmer, 1994). The clinician notes the appropriateness and quality of the client's responses (behaviors, speech, emotions, intellectual functioning) and then attempts to render provisional evaluations of the diagnosis, prognosis, client dynamics, and treatment issues.

Errors In the field of mental health, straightforward questions do not always yield usable or accurate information. Believing personal information to be private, patients may refuse to reveal it, may distort it, or may lie about themselves. Furthermore, many patients may be unable to articulate their inner thoughts and feelings. An interview should therefore be considered a measurement device that is fallible and subject to error (Wiens, 1983).

Three sources of interviewing errors were summarized by Kleinmutz (1967). One is the interview process itself and the relationship between the interviewer and interviewee. Information exchange may be blocked if either the client or the clinician fails to respect the other or if one or the other is not feeling well. A second source of error may be intense anxiety or preoccupation on the part of the interviewee; his or her revelations may be inconsistent or inaccurate. Third, the interviewer may be a source of error. A clinician's unique style, degree of experience, and theoretical orientation definitely will affect the interview.

Psychological Tests and Inventories

Psychological tests and inventories are a variety of standardized instruments that have been used to assess personality, maladaptive behavior, development of social skills, intellectual abilities, vocational interests, and cognitive impairment. Tests have also been developed for the purpose of understanding personality dynamics and conflicts. They vary in form (that is, they may be oral or written and may be administered to groups or to individuals), structure, degree of objectivity, and content. To varying degrees (less so in the case of projective personality tests), they share two characteristics involving standard administration and use of a standardization sample. First, they provide a standard situation in which certain kinds of responses are elicited. The same instructions are given to all who take the same test, the same scoring is applied, and similar environmental conditions are maintained to ensure that the responses are due to each test taker's unique attributes rather than to differences in situations. Second, by comparing an individual test taker's responses with norms, established by the standardization sample, the therapist can make inferences about the underlying traits of the person. For instance, the test taker may answer yes to questions such as "Is someone trying to control your mind?" more frequently than is the norm. The therapist might infer that this pattern of response is similar to that of diagnosed paranoids.

In the remainder of this section, we examine two different types of personality tests and measures (projective and self-report inventories) and tests of intelligence and cognitive impairment.

Projective Personality Tests In a **projective personality test**, the test taker is presented with ambiguous stimuli, such as inkblots, pictures, or incomplete sentences, and asked to respond to them in some way. The stimuli are generally novel, and the test is relatively unstructured. Conventional or stereotyped patterns of response usually do not fit the stimuli. The person must "project" his or her attitudes, motives, and other personality characteristics into the situation. The nature of the appraisal is generally well disguised: subjects are often unaware of the true nature or purpose of the test and usually do not recognize the significance of their responses. Based largely on a psychoanalytic perspective, projective tests presumably tap into the individual's unconscious needs and motivations.

No matter which form of test is used, the goal of projective testing is to get a multifaceted view of the total functioning person, rather than a view of a single facet or dimension of personality. We will concentrate on inkblot descriptions and storytelling because they are both popular and typical of projective tests.

The *Rorschach technique* was devised by Swiss psychiatrist Hermann Rorschach in 1921 for personality appraisal. A Rorschach test consists of ten cards displaying symmetrical inkblot designs. The cards are presented one at a time to subjects, who are asked (1) what they see in the blots and (2) what characteristics of the blots make them see that. Inkblots are considered appropriate stimuli because they are ambiguous, are nonthreatening, and do not elicit learned responses.

What people see in the blots, whether they attend to large areas or details, whether they respond to color, and whether their perceptions suggest movement are assumed to be symbolic of inner promptings, motivations, and conflicts. Test takers react in a personal and "unlearned" fashion because there are no right or wrong answers. The psychologist then interprets the individual's reactions. Both the basic premise of the Rorschach test and the psychologist's interpretation of the symbolism within the patient's responses are strongly psychoanalytic. For example, seeing eyes or buttocks may imply paranoid tendencies; fierce animals may imply aggressive tendencies; blood may imply strong uncontrolled emotions; food may imply dependency needs; and masks may imply avoidance of personal exposure (Klopfer & Davidson, 1962).

There are actually a variety of approaches to interpreting and scoring Rorschach responses. The most extensive and recent is that of Exner (1983, 1990), whose scoring system is based on reviews of research findings and studies of the Rorschach technique. Exner thinks of the Rorschach technique as a problem-solving task; test takers are presented with ambiguous stimuli that they interpret according to their preferred mode of perceptual-cognitive processing. Exner's system has also yielded indexes of specific disorders such as depression, although the adequacy of the Rorschach technique in assessing specific disorders is a matter of continuing research (Ball et al., 1991). Because it relies on research findings and normative data, Exner's system is becoming the standard for scoring the Rorschach test (Weiss, 1988). It should be noted that use of the Rorschach is not con-

fined solely to the evaluation of psychopathology. Lerner (1995) has developed a means to analyze the adaptive capacities of individuals.

The *Thematic Apperception Test (TAT)* was first developed by Henry Murray in 1935 (Murray & Morgan, 1938). It consists of thirty picture cards, each typically depicting two human figures. Their poses and actions are vague and ambiguous enough to be open to different interpretations. Some cards are designated for specific age levels or for a single gender, and some are appropriate for all groups. Like the Rorschach technique, the TAT relies on projection to tap underlying motives, drives, and personality processes. Most clinicians agree, however, that the TAT is best when it is used to uncover aspects of interpersonal relationships.

Generally, twenty TAT cards are shown to the subject, one at a time, with instructions to tell a story about each picture. Typically, the tester says, "I am going to show you some pictures. Tell me a story about what is going on in each one, what led up to it, and what its outcome will be." The entire story is recorded verbatim. There is usually no limit on time or the length of the stories.

A trained clinician interprets the subject's responses, either subjectively or by using a formal scoring system. Both interpretations usually take into account the style of the story (length, organization, and so on); recurring themes, such as retribution, fail-

The Rorschach technique uses a number of cards, with each showing a symmetrical inkblot design. The earlier cards in the set are black and white, while the later cards are more colorful. A client's responses to the inkblots are interpreted according to assessment guidelines and can be compared by the therapist to the responses that other clients have made.

ure, parental domination, aggression, and sexual concerns; the outcome of the story in relationship to the plot; primary and secondary identification (the choice of hero or secondary person of importance); and the handling of authority figures and sexual relationships. The purpose is to gain insight into the subject's conflicts and worries as well as clues about his or her core personality structure.

Other types of projective tests include sentence-completion and draw-a-person tests. In the *sentence-completion test,* the subject is given a list of partial sentences and is asked to complete each of them. Typical partial sentences are "My ambition," "My mother was always," and "I can remember." Clinicians try to interpret the meaning of the subject's responses. In *draw-a-person tests,* such as the Machover D-A-P (Machover, 1949), the subject is actually asked to draw a person. Then he or she may be asked to draw a person of the opposite sex. Finally, the subject may be instructed to make up a story about the characters that were drawn or to describe the first character's background. Many clinicians analyze these drawings for size, position, detail, and so on, assuming that the drawings provide diagnostic clues. For example, persons suffering from brain impairments may draw disproportionately large heads. The validity of such assumptions is open to question, and well-controlled studies cast doubt on diagnostic interpretations (Anastasi, 1982).

The analysis and interpretation of responses to projective tests are subject to wide variation. Clinicians given the same data frequently disagree with one another about scoring. Much of this disparity is caused by differences in clinicians' orientation, skills, and personal style. But, as noted earlier, the demonstrably low reliability and validity of these instruments means that they should be used with caution and in conjunction with other assessment measures (Weiss, 1988). And even when projective tests exhibit reliability, they may still have low validity. For example, many clinicians agree that certain specific responses to the Rorschach inkblots indicate repressed anger. The fact that many clinicians agree makes the test reliable, but those specific responses could indicate something other than repressed anger. Illusory correlations may exist, and clinicians may erroneously link a patient's response to the existence of a syndrome (Chapman & Chapman, 1967). In general, projective tests may yield important information when they are interpreted by clinicians who are highly skilled and insightful in their use. Because many projective tests are subjectively interpreted by clinicians in accordance with their intuition, however, overall validity of the tests is low. Exner's (1990) work in developing norms and in using empirical research in the

In the Thematic Apperception Test, clients tell a story about each of a series of pictures they are shown. These pictures—often depicting one, two, or three people doing something—are less ambiguous than Rorschach inkblots.

Rorschach scoring system is a major step in reducing the subjectivity problems.

Self-Report Inventories Unlike projective tests, **self-report inventories** require test takers to answer specific written questions or to select specific responses from a list of alternatives—usually self-descriptive statements. Subjects are asked to either agree or disagree with the statement or to indicate the extent of their agreement or disagreement. Because a predetermined score is assigned to each possible answer, human judgmental factors in scoring and interpretation are minimized. In addition, subjects' responses and scores can be compared readily with a standardization sample.

Perhaps the most widely used self-report personality inventory is the *Minnesota Multiphasic Personality Inventory,* or *MMPI* (Hathaway & McKinley, 1943). The MMPI was recently revised by Butcher and colleagues into the MMPI-2 (see Butcher, 1990; Graham, 1990; Greene, 1991). The revisions were intended to restandardize the inventory, refine the wording of certain items, eliminate items that were considered outdated, and include appropriate representations of ethnic minority groups. The MMPI-2 consists of 567 statements; subjects are asked to indicate whether each statement is true or false as it applies to them. There is also a "cannot say" alternative, but clients are strongly discouraged from using this category because too many such responses can invalidate the test.

The test taker's MMPI-2 results are rated on ten clinical scales and three validity scales. The ten clinical scales were originally constructed by analyzing the responses of diagnosed psychiatric patients (and the responses of normal subjects) to the 567 test items. These analyses allowed researchers to determine what kinds of responses each of the various types of psychiatric patients usually made, in contrast to those of normal subjects. The three validity scales, which assess the degree of candor, confusion, and falsification, help the clinician detect potential faking or special circumstances that may affect the outcome of other scales. Figure 3.1 shows the possible responses to ten sample MMPI-2 items and the kinds of responses that contribute to a high rating on the ten MMPI clinical scales.

A basic assumption of the original version of the MMPI was that a person whose MMPI answers are similar to those of diagnosed patients is likely to behave similarly to those patients. However, single-scale interpretations are fraught with hazards. Although a person with a high rating on Scale 6 may be labeled paranoid, many persons with paranoia are not detected by this scale. Interpretation of the MMPI-2 scales can be quite complicated and requires special training. Generally, multiple-scale interpretations (pattern analysis) and characteristics associated with the patterns are examined. Butcher (1995) has noted that although the MMPIs of clients are subjected to pattern and statistical analyses, client responses can also be viewed as direct communications of important content—information about the client's symptoms, attitudes, and behaviors. The MMPI-2 should be used by clinicians who have mastered its intricacies, understand relevant statistical concepts, and can interpret the client's responses (Butcher, 1995; Graham, 1990; Newmark, 1985).

Whereas the MMPI-2 assesses a number of different personality characteristics of a person, some self-report inventories or questionnaires focus on only certain kinds of personality traits or emotional problems, such as depression or anxiety. For example, the *Beck Depression Inventory* (BDI) is composed of 21 items that measure various aspects of depression, such as mood, appetite, functioning at work, suicide ideas, and sleeping patterns (Beck et al., 1961).

Though widely used, personality inventories have limitations. First, the fixed number of alternatives can hinder individuals from presenting an accurate picture of themselves. Being asked to answer true or false to the statement "I am suspicious of people" does not permit an individual to qualify the item in any way. Second, a person may have a unique response style or response set (a tendency to respond to test items in a certain way regardless of content) that may distort the results. For example, many people have a need to present themselves in a favorable light, and this can cause them to give answers that are socially acceptable but inaccurate. Some individuals may fake having a disorder or try to avoid appearing deviant. Third, interpretations of responses of people from different cultural groups may be inaccurate if norms for these groups have not been developed.

Despite these potential problems, personality inventories are widely used. Some, like the MMPI-2, have been extensively researched, and in many cases their validity has been established. Sophisticated means have also been found to control for response sets and for faking, and, as noted earlier, attempts have been made to establish the cross-cultural validity of instruments such as the MMPI-2. In general, inventories are inexpensive and more easily administered and scored than are projective tests. (In fact, many inventories are scored and interpreted by computer.) These features make the use of self-report inventories desirable, especially in the busy clinic or hospital environment.

Moreover, although progress has been slow, the predictive ability and validity of personality assessment have been improved. **Psychometrics**—mental measurement, including its study and techniques—is becoming increasingly sophisticated. Further refinement will be achieved when situational variables that help determine behaviors can be taken into account and when fluctuations in mood and other more stable personality processes can be measured.

Intelligence Tests Intelligence testing has two primary diagnostic functions and one secondary function. The first one is to obtain an estimate of a person's current level of cognitive functioning, called the *intelligence quotient* (IQ). An IQ score indicates an individual's level of performance relative to that of other people of the same age. As such, an IQ score is an important aid in predicting school performance and detecting mental retardation. (Through statistical procedures, IQ test results are converted into numbers, with 100 representing the mean, or average, score. An IQ score of about 130 indicates performance exceeding that of 95 percent of all same-age peers.) The second diagnostic function of intelligence testing is assessing intellectual deterioration in organic

FIGURE 3.1   The Ten MMPI-2 Clinical Scales and Sample MMPI-2 Test Items

Shown here are the MMPI-2 clinical scales and a few of the items that appear on them. As an example, answering "no" or "false" (rather than "yes" or "true") to the item "I have a good appetite" would result in a higher scale score for hypochondriasis, depression, and hysteria.

SAMPLE ITEMS

TEN MMPI CLINICAL SCALES WITH SIMPLIFIED DESCRIPTIONS	I like mechanics magazines.	I have a good appetite.	I wake up fresh and rested most mornings.	I think I would like the work of a librarian.	I am easily awakened by noise.	I like to read newspaper articles on crime.	My hands and feet are usually warm enough.	My daily life is full of things that keep me interested.	I am about as able to work as I ever was.	There seems to be a lump in my throat much of the time.
1. **Hypochondriasis (Hs)**—Individuals showing excessive worry about health with reports of obscure pains.		NO	NO				NO		NO	
2. **Depression (D)**—People suffering from chronic depression, feelings of uselessness, and inability to face the future.		NO		YES				NO	NO	
3. **Hysteria (Hy)**—Individuals who react to stress by developing physical symptoms (paralysis, cramps, headaches, etc.)		NO	NO			NO	NO	NO	NO	YES
4. **Psychopathic Deviate (Pd)**—People who show irresponsibility, disregard social conventions, and lack deep emotional responses.								NO		
5. **Masculinity-Femininity (Mf)**—People tending to identify with the opposite sex rather than their own.	NO		YES							
6. **Paranoia (Pa)**—People who are suspicious, sensitive, and feel persecuted.										
7. **Psychasthenia (Pt)**—People troubled with fears (phobias) and compulsive tendencies.			NO					NO		YES
8. **Schizophrenia (Sc)**—People with bizarre and unusual thoughts or behavior.								NO		
9. **Hypomania (Ma)**—People who are physically and mentally overactive and who shift rapidly in ideas and actions.										
10. **Social Introversion (Si)**—People who tend to withdraw from social contacts and responsibilities.										

Note: Item 5 illustrates a male's response.

Source: Adapted from Dahlstrom & Welsh, 1965.

Intelligence tests provide valuable information about intellectual functioning and can help psychologists to assess mental retardation and intellectual deterioration. Although many of these tests have been severely criticized as being culturally biased, they can be beneficial tools, if used appropriately. Here, an eight-year-old boy is taking a WISC test.

or functional psychotic disorders. And, finally, an individually administered intelligence test may yield additional useful data for the clinician. The therapist may find important observations of how the subject approached the task (systematic versus disorganized), handled failure (depression, frustration, or anger), and persisted in (or gave up) the task.

The two most widely used intelligence tests are the Wechsler Scales (Wechsler, 1981b) and the Stanford-Binet Scales (Terman & Merrill, 1960; Thorndike, Hagen & Sattler, 1986). The *Wechsler Adult Intelligence Scale* (the WAIS and its revised version WAIS-R) is administered to persons aged sixteen and older. Two other forms are appropriate for children aged six to sixteen (the *Wechsler Intelligence Scale for Children,* or WISC-R) and four to six (the *Wechsler Preschool and Primary Scale of Intelligence,* or WPPSI-R). The WAIS-R consists of six verbal and five

performance scales, which yield verbal and performance IQ scores. These scores are combined to present a total IQ score. Table 3.2 shows subtest items similar to those used in the WAIS-R.

The *Stanford-Binet Intelligence Scale* is used for people aged two and older. Much more complicated in administration and scoring, and not standardized on an adult population, the Stanford-Binet requires considerable skill in its use. The test procedure is designed to establish a basal age (the subject passes all subtests for that age) and a ceiling age (the subject fails all subtests for that age), from which an IQ score is calculated. In general, the WISC-R is preferred over the Stanford-Binet for school-age children (LaGreca & Stringer, 1985). It is easier to administer and yields scores on different cognitive skills (such as verbal and performance subtests).

Some interesting research has been conducted on possible physiological measures of intelligence. When individuals are exposed to an auditory stimulus, brain reactions to the stimulus can be monitored by electroencephalograph (EEG) recordings of the brain waves. Matarazzo (1992) has noted that brain wave patterns have been found to be strongly correlated with IQ scores on the WAIS. Moreover, his review of research also showed that measures of intellectual functioning were related to the rate of glucose metabolism in certain brain regions, as revealed by positron emission tomography (a technique described later in this chapter). Even if the findings prove to be valid, such results are difficult to interpret. We cannot assume that as indicators of intelligence, physiological measures are somehow "superior" to performance on the WAIS-R.

There are four major critiques of the use of IQ tests. First, some investigators believe that IQ tests have been popularized as a means of measuring innate intelligence, when in truth the tests largely reflect cultural and social factors (Garcia, 1981; Williams, 1974). The issue of racial differences in innate intelligence has a long history of debate, but the publication of *The Bell Curve*, a book by Herrnstein and Murray (1994) has refocused attention on this issue. The authors propose that racial differences in IQ scores are determined by heredity, and that social and status differences between intellectually different classes are therefore difficult to overcome (see Figure 3.2).

Gould (1994) has attacked this position, stating that the basic premises of Herrnstein and Murray's book are faulty. Many ethnic groups have attacked the use of IQ testing (and some other standardized testing) over the years, arguing that it raises these issues and others covered by the second critique. The second major critique of IQ testing focuses on the

TABLE 3.2 Simulated Items for the Wechsler Adult Intelligence Scale—Revised (WAIS—R)

Information

1. How many nickels make a dime?
2. What is steam made of?
3. What is pepper?

Comprehension

1. Why do some people save sales receipts?
2. Why is copper often used in electrical wire?

Arithmetic (all calculated "in the head")

1. Sue had 2 pieces of candy and Joe gave her 4 more. How many pieces of candy did Sue have altogether?
2. If 2 pencils cost 15¢, how much will a dozen pencils cost?

Similarities

In what way are the following alike?

1. lion/tiger
2. saw/hammer
3. circle/square

Vocabulary

What is the meaning of the following words?

1. chair   5. foreboding
2. mountain   6. prevaricate
3. guilt   7. plethora
4. building

issue of the predictive validity of IQ tests. That is, do IQ test scores accurately predict the future behaviors or achievements of different cultural groups? Proponents and critics disagree on this point (Anastasi, 1982). Third, investigators have disagreed over criterion variables (in essence, what is actually being predicted by IQ tests). For example, two investigators may be interested in the ability of IQ tests to predict future success. The first may try to find a correlation between test scores and grades subsequently received in school. The second investigator may argue that grades are a poor indicator of success—that leadership skills and the ability to work with people are better indicators of success. Fourth, some researchers have questioned whether our current conceptions of IQ tests and intelligence are adequate. A number of researchers have proposed that intelligence is a multidimensional attribute. Taylor (1990) stated that an important aspect of intelligence, and one that cannot be adequately assessed using IQ tests, is social intelligence or competency. Social skills may be important in such areas as problem solving, adaptation to life, social knowledge, and the ability to use resources effectively.

The controversies over the validity and usefulness of IQ testing may never fully subside. Some continue to claim that IQ tests demonstrate predictive validity for many important attributes, including future success (Barrett & Depinet, 1991). Others maintain that

FIGURE 3.2 **A Bell Curve, Showing Standard Deviations** The *bell curve* refers to the fact that the distribution of IQ scores in a population resembles the shape of a bell, with most scores hovering over the mean and fewer scores falling in the outlying areas of the distribution. IQ scores are transformed so that the mean equals 100, and deviations from the mean are expressed in terms of standard deviations. One standard deviation from the mean (about 15 IQ points above or below the mean, or IQ scores between 85 and 115) represent about 68 percent of the scores. Two standard deviations (about 30 IQ points above or below the mean, or IQs between 70 and 130) account for over 95 percent of the scores.

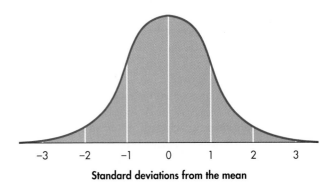

Standard deviations from the mean

such tests are biased and limited (Helms, 1992). Reliance on IQ scores has resulted in discriminatory actions. In California, for example, African American children were in the past disproportionately assigned to classes for the educable mentally retarded on the basis of IQ results. Mercer (1979) has argued that all cultural groups have the same average intellectual potential and that members of a cultural minority may score low on a given IQ test because they are less familiar with the tasks required on such tests, not because of mental retardation. She developed the System of Multicultural Pluralistic Assessment, an assessment procedure that compares a person's performance on the WISC-R with that of groups of people who have similar social and cultural backgrounds, rather than with others from different backgrounds. This procedure results in fewer children who represent ethnic minorities being assigned to classes for the mentally retarded.

The Kaufman Assessment Battery for Children (K-ABC)

An increasingly popular means of evaluating the intelligence and achievement of children aged two-and-a-half to twelve-and-a-half years is the *Kaufman Assessment Battery for Children (K-ABC)*. Based on theories of mental processing developed by neuropsychologists and cognitive psychologists, the K-ABC is intended for use with both the general and special populations. For example, the assessment battery has been used with children who have hearing or speech impairments and with those who have learning disabilities. Because of its reliance on visual stimuli, the K-ABC is unsuitable for visually impaired individuals (Kaufman, Kamphaus & Kaufman, 1985).

The K-ABC can be used with exceptional children and members of ethnic minority groups. Its applicability to diverse groups has been attributed to measures that (1) are less culturally dependent than those found on traditional tests and (2) focus on the process used to solve problems rather than on the specific content of test items. Children are administered a wide variety of tasks, such as copying a sequence of hand movements performed by the examiner, recalling numbers, assembling triangles to match a model, and demonstrating reading comprehension. Their verbal performance and nonverbal performance are then assessed. For certain language-disordered children or those who do not speak English, nonverbal performance can be used to estimate intellectual functioning.

A Spanish-language version of the K-ABC is available, and norms for African American and Hispanic children have been developed. Interestingly, differences in performance between white and ethnic minority children are much lower on the K-ABC than on traditional IQ tests. Kaufman and Kaufman (1983)

and Kaufman, Kamphaus, and Kaufman (1985) reported that the K-ABC has high reliability and validity. Reynolds, Kamphaus, and Rosenthal (1989) proposed that the K-ABC will continue to provide a comprehensive, unique, and useful assessment tool for children. This approach offers promise in the effort to devise more culturally unbiased tests of intelligence. Taylor (1990) also believes that the K-ABC is more likely than traditional IQ tests to assess social intelligence because many of the subscales measure performance using social information.

Tests for Cognitive Impairment Clinical psychologists, especially those who work in a hospital setting, are concerned with detecting and assessing **organicity** (an older term referring to damage or deterioration in the central nervous system) or cognitive impairments due to brain damage. The use of individual intelligence tests such as the WAIS-R can sometimes identify such impairments. For example, a difference of twenty points between verbal and performance scores on the WAIS-R may indicate the possibility of brain damage. Certain patterns of scores on the individual subtests, such as those that measure verbal concept formation or abstracting ability (comparison and comprehension) can also reveal brain damage. Because impaired abstract thinking may be characteristic of brain damage, a lower score on this scale (when accompanied by other signs) must be investigated.

One of the routine means of assessing cognitive impairment is the *Bender-Gestalt Visual-Motor Test,* developed by Bender (1938) and shown in Figure 3.3. Nine geometric designs, each drawn in black on a piece of white cardboard, are presented one at a time to the subject, who is asked to copy them on a piece of paper. Certain errors in the copies are characteristic of neurological impairment. Among these are rotation of figures, perseveration (continuation of a pattern to an exceptional degree), fragmentation, oversimplification, inability to copy angles, and reversals.

The *Halstead-Reitan Neuropsychological Test Battery,* developed by Reitan from the earlier work of Halstead, has been used successfully to differentiate patients with brain damage from those without brain damage and to provide valuable information about the type and location of the damage (Boll, 1983). The full battery consists of eleven tests, although several are often omitted. Clients are presented with a series of tasks that assess sensorimotor, cognitive, and perceptual functioning, including abstract concept formation, memory and attention, and auditory perception. The full battery takes more than six hours to administer, so it is a relatively expensive and time-consuming assessment tool. Versions of the Halstead-Reitan Battery are available for children age five and

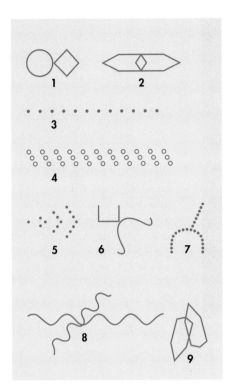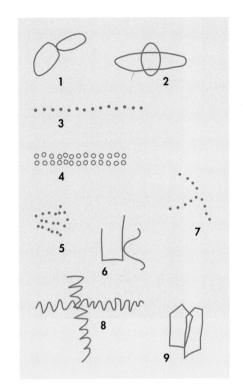

FIGURE 3.3   The Nine Bender Designs The figures presented to subjects are shown on the left. The distorted figures drawn by subjects are possibly indicative of organicity (brain damage) and are shown on the right.

Source: The American Orthopsychiatric Association, 1938.

older (Nussbaum & Bigler, 1989), and normative data for children have been collected.

A less costly test for cognitive impairment is the *Luria-Nebraska Neuropsychological Battery,* which requires about $2\frac{1}{2}$ hours to administer and is more standardized in content, administration, and scoring than is the Halstead-Reitan Battery. Developed by Golden and colleagues (1981), this battery includes twelve scales that assess motor functions, rhythm, tactile functions, visual functions, receptive and expressive speech, memory, writing, intellectual processes, and other functions. Validation data indicate that the battery is highly successful in screening for brain damage and quite accurate in pinpointing damaged areas (Anastasi, 1982). A children's version has been developed (Golden, 1989). Although the battery has been shown to differentiate brain-damaged children from normal children, its ability to discriminate between different types of learning disabilities has been questioned (Morgan & Brown, 1988). Golden (1989) suggested that other tests be used in conjunction with the Luria-Nebraska when clinicians must make detailed analyses of specific diagnostic decisions.

Neurological Tests

In addition to psychological tests, a variety of neurological medical procedures are available for diagnosing cognitive impairments due to brain damage or abnormal brain functioning. For example, x-ray studies can often detect brain tumors. A more sophisticated procedure, *computerized axial tomography (CAT) scan,* involves repeatedly scanning different areas of the brain with beams of x-rays. With the assistance of a computer, a three-dimensional image of the structure of the brain emerges, and the results of the CAT scan provide a detailed view of brain deterioration or abnormality. In addition to the study of brain damage, CAT scans have also been used to study brain tissue abnormalities among patients diagnosed with schizophrenia, affective disorders, Alzheimer's disease, and alcoholism (Coffman, 1989). More recently, *positron emission tomography (PET) scan* has been developed to study the physiological and biochemical processes of the brain, rather than the anatomical structures seen in the CAT scan. In PET scans, a radioactive substance is injected into the

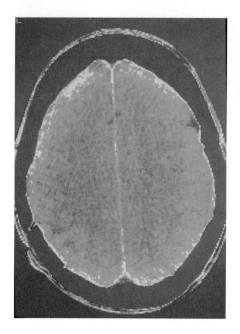

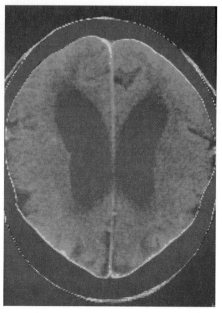

Neurological tests, such as CAT scans, MRIs, and PET scans, have dramatically improved our ability to study the brain and to assess brain damage. On the left is a normal CAT scan; on the right, a CAT scan showing the enlarged ventricals (butterfly shape in the center) of a person with senile dimentia.

patient's bloodstream. The scanner detects the substance as it is metabolized in the brain, yielding information about brain functioning. PET scans, like CAT scans, have been used to study a variety of mental disorders and brain diseases. Characteristic metabolic patterns have been observed in many of these disorders (Holcomb et al., 1989). A widely used examina-

This PET scan reveals increased brain activity as a function of visual stimulation. The areas in red show the most intense stimulation, and as you can see, the more complex the information being processed, the more active the brain is.

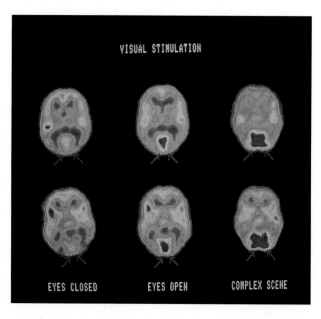

tion involves the *electroencephalograph*, in which electrodes are attached to the skull. The electrical activity (brain waves) is recorded from the electrodes, and abnormalities in the activity can provide information as to the presence of tumors or other brain conditions. Finally, by creating a magnetic field around the patient and using radio waves to detect abnormalities, *magnetic resonance imaging (MRI)* can produce an amazingly clear "picture" of the brain and its tissues. Because of its superior clear pictures, which are reminiscent of postmortem brain slices, MRI may eventually supplant CAT scans (Andreasen, 1989).

These neurological techniques, coupled with psychological tests, are increasing our diagnostic accuracy and understanding of brain functioning and disorders. Matarazzo (1992) has predicted that in the future such techniques will allow therapists to make more precise diagnoses and to pinpoint precise areas of the brain that are affected by disorders such as Alzheimer's and Huntington's diseases.

The Ethics of Assessment

Over the years, a strong antitesting movement has developed in the United States. Issues such as the confidentiality of a client's records, invasion of privacy, client welfare, cultural bias, and unethical practices have increasingly been raised (Bersoff, 1981; Weiner, 1995). In assessing and treating emotionally disturbed people, the clinical psychologist must often ask embarrassing questions or use tests that may be construed as invasions of privacy. In many cases, the clinician may not know beforehand whether the results of the tests will prove beneficial to the client. Yet to exclude testing because it may offend the client or place him or her in an uncomfortable position could ultimately deprive the client of the test's long-range benefits.

Some people strongly criticize tests on the grounds that they can have undesirable social consequences. They ask, "Who will use the test results, and for what purpose is the test employed?" Test results may be used to the client's detriment in some instances. Tests may also be inaccurate, causing serious misdiagnosis and its consequences. Note the fears and concerns over the possible widespread use of tests to detect antibodies to the HIV virus (AIDS) and drug abuse, as well as the use of the polygraph in job settings.

Another interesting development is the increased role of computers in assessment. For decades, computers have been used to score the test results of clients and to provide psychological profiles of clients. More recently, computer programs have become available to administer clinical interviews, IQ tests, personality inventories, and projective tests. They may also interpret responses of clients or other persons, such as applicants for jobs. The computers are programmed, for example, to simulate a structured clinical interview. Individuals who are being assessed sit before a keyboard and answer questions shown on the computer screen.

Computer assessment has some advantages over face-to-face assessment. First, with the rising costs of mental health care, this technique can free up the time of clinicians and other personnel who have traditionally administered the interviews or tests. Scoring and interpretation can be easily performed by the computer. Second, the motivation and attention of clients may be increased because clients often enjoy using a computer. Third, because clinicians often differ in interviewing styles and backgrounds, computer assessment may provide superior standardization of procedures. But two important questions remain: how valid are computer assessments, and can they be a substitute for face-to-face assessment between client and clinician?

Some studies of computer assessment have yielded encouraging results. Farrell, Stiles-Camplair, and McCullough (1987) evaluated the ability of a computer interview to assess the target complaints of clients. The clients completed a computer interview in which they were told to answer a series of questions by pressing the appropriate keyboard selections that corresponded to their feelings. Depending on their answers, further programmed questions were asked to refine their responses. Clients were also given a traditional clinical interview and psychological tests so that the results of the computer interview could be

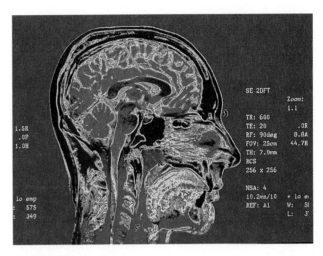

In magnetic resonance imaging, radio waves are used to produce detailed pictures of the brain.

compared with the results of the traditional forms of assessment. The computer interview findings generally agreed with those of the traditional clinical interview and test results. However, most of the clients preferred being interviewed by the clinician.

Although some studies have provided positive results, critics of computer assessment are concerned about the proliferation of computer assessment techniques, the paucity of research studies that have established their validity, and the unwarranted impression that computerized assessments are scientifically precise (Butcher, 1995; Matarazzo, 1986). Also, as computer assessment becomes more popular, there is a risk that untrained individuals, or even clients themselves, may not be aware of the limits of this form of assessment and may misinterpret the meaning of the findings. Computer assessment research should therefore address issues involving validity, use and abuse of test results, and ethical concerns, such as privacy.

Psychological testing has ethical, legal, and societal implications that go beyond the field of psychology. Psychologists should be aware of these implications and should guard against the misuse of test results. They should also carefully weigh the consequences of permitting such considerations to interfere with devising, improving, and applying tests that will benefit their patients. The mental health professions and the general public are increasingly aware of the need to guard against possible abuses and to continually refine and improve classification systems and assessment procedures.

A final problem relates to the use of psychological tests or assessment procedures to assess the status of individuals from different cultures. Evidence exists that biases often occur in the assessment of individuals from different cultures and that therapists of different ethnicities evaluate the same client behaviors differently (Okazaki & Sue, 1995). In one study, Li-Repac (1980) had five Chinese American and five European American male therapists rate Chinese American and European American male clients who appeared on a videotaped interview. The results revealed that therapists evaluate clients of other ethnicities more negatively than they evaluate clients of their own ethnicities. European American therapists rated Chinese American clients as anxious, awkward, confused, and nervous, while Chinese American therapists perceived the same clients as alert, ambitious, adaptable, honest, and friendly. The European American clients, who were deemed active, aggressive, rebellious, and outspoken by Chinese American therapists, were seen as affectionate, adventurous, sincere, and easy-going by European American therapists. In addition, European American therapists rated Chinese American clients as more depressed, more inhibited, less socially poised, and having a lower capacity for interpersonal relationships than did Chinese American therapists. Similarly, Chinese American therapists rated European American clients as more severely disturbed than did European American therapists. These findings suggest that judgments about psychological functioning depend at least in part on whether therapists are of the same ethnic background as their clients. Because tests or procedures may not be normed, standardized, or widely used on individuals from different cultural groups or because of cultural biases, clinicians should consider some of the issues discussed in Critical Thinking.

THE CLASSIFICATION OF ABNORMAL BEHAVIOR

The goal of having a **classification system** for abnormal behaviors is to provide distinct categories, indicators, and nomenclature for different patterns of behavior, thought processes, and emotional disturbances. Thus the pattern of behavior that is classified as *paranoid schizophrenia* should be clearly different from the pattern named *borderline personality*. At the same time, the categories should be constructed in such a way as to accommodate wide variation in these patterns. That is, the clinician should be able to categorize paranoid schizophrenic behavior as such, even when the patient does not show the "perfect" or "textbook" paranoid schizophrenic pattern.

Problems with Early Diagnostic Classification Systems

As indicated in Chapter 1, the first effective classification scheme for mental disorders was devised by Emil Kraepelin toward the end of the nineteenth century. Kraepelin held the organic view of psychopathology, and his system had a distinctly biogenic slant. Classification was based on the patient's symptoms, as in medicine. It was hoped that disorders (similar groups of symptoms) would have a common **etiology** (cause or origin), would require similar treatments, would respond to those treatments similarly, and would progress similarly if left untreated.

Many of these same expectations were held for the first edition of the Diagnostic and Statistical Manual of Mental Disorders (DSM-I), published by the American Psychiatric Association in 1952 and based on Kraepelin's system. These expectations, however, were not realized in DSM-I. The DSM was revised in 1968 (DSM-II), 1980 (DSM-III), 1987 (DSM-III-R), and 1994 (DSM-IV). Each revision was made to increase the reliability, validity, and usefulness of the classification scheme (Spitzer & Williams, 1987). As mentioned previously, reliability and validity are cru-

In an 1883 publication, the psychiatrist Emil Kraepelin (1856–1926) proposed that mental disorders could be directly linked to organic brain disorders, and further proposed a diagnostic classification system for all disorders. Kraepelin is also noted for being a pioneer in experimental abnormal psychology. He established his own laboratory where he conducted research on mental illness.

CRITICAL THINKING

Can We Accurately Assess the Status of Members of Different Cultural Groups?

We often have a difficult time evaluating the behaviors of people from other cultures. Cultural groups differ in many aspects, including dietary practices, type of clothing, religious rituals, and social interactions. How do we decide whether an individual from a different culture is behaving in a certain way because of a mental disorder or because of cultural practices? What signs or clues indicate that someone is truly mentally and emotionally disturbed? Can we use assessment measures standardized in the United States with people from other countries?

These questions are only a sampling of the kinds of issues clinicians must consider when trying to assess members of ethnic minority groups or individuals from different cultures. Brislin (1993) has identified several major problems, including the equivalence of concepts and scales.

First, certain concepts may not be equivalent across cultures. For instance, Americans living in the United States and the Baganda living in East Africa have different concepts of intelligent behavior. In the United States, one indicator of intelligence is quickness in mental reasoning; among the Baganda, slow, deliberate thought is considered a mark of intelligence. Obviously, tests of intelligence devised in the two cultures would differ. Individuals taking the tests could be considered intelligent on one culture's measure but not on the other.

The second major problem is whether scores on assessment instruments are really equivalent in cross-cultural research. For example, many universities use the Scholastic Aptitude Test (SAT), which has a verbal and quantitative component, as a criterion for admissions. Do the test scores mean the same thing for different groups in terms of assessing academic potential, achievements, and ability to succeed? SAT scores do tend to be moderately successful predictors of subsequent university grades. Sue and Abe (1988), however, found that the SAT score's ability to predict success varies according to ethnicity and the components of the SAT. Whereas the SAT verbal component was a good predictor of university grades for White American students, the SAT quantitative portion was a good predictor of grades for Asian American students. Thus, Asian American and White American students with the same overall SAT scores may receive very different grades in individual courses.

What are the implications of these findings? Should we abolish measures of performance for members of groups that have not been part of the standardization process? If so, how can we evaluate them? These are only a few of the dilemmas involved in assessment.

---

cial to any diagnostic scheme and, in fact, to any scientific construct.

Reliability Early studies of the DSM that compared the diagnoses of pairs of clinicians found poor agreement (interrater reliability) between the members of each pair (Ash, 1949; Schmidt & Fonda, 1956). The greatest disagreement was found in specific categories. In about 80 percent of the pairs, both clinicians agreed on the general category (organic, psychotic, or personality disturbance) in which a particular disorder belonged. As a rule, reliability is higher for broad distinctions than it is for fine distinctions (Phares, 1984). A fine distinction, for example, would focus on the precise type of personality disturbance or disorder.

In other reliability studies, the same information was presented to clinicians on two occasions or at different times (test-retest reliability). These studies showed that the clinicians' later diagnoses often did not agree with their earlier ones (Beck, 1962; Wilson & Meyer, 1962). Thus even a single clinician's diagnosis was not very reliable over time.

Much unreliability of early DSM editions can be attributed to the diagnostic categories themselves. Three sources of diagnostic error have been identified: of the errors, 5 percent were attributable to the patients, who gave different material to different interviewers. Nearly one-third (32.5 percent) of the errors were due to inconsistencies among diagnosticians in interview techniques, in interpreting similar data, and in judging the importance of symptoms. Most significantly, however, 62.5 percent of the errors derived from inadequacies of the diagnostic system (Ward et al., 1962). It was simply not clear which behavior patterns belonged in which categories.

In view of these problems, DSM-III and DSM-III-R were developed to have greater interrater reliability. Results of field trials indicated that good to excellent interrater reliability could be obtained for many, but not all, of the major classes of disorders (Widiger et al., 1991).

Validity   Many critics questioned the validity and usefulness of psychiatric classification (Ferster, 1965; Kanfer & Phillips, 1969; Ullmann & Krasner, 1965). They claimed that DSM did not adequately convey information about underlying causes, processes, treatment, and prognosis. (A **prognosis** is a prediction of the future course of a particular disorder.) The problem arose because early versions of DSM were strongly influenced by the biogenic model of mental illness, in which cause is supposed to be a basis of classification. With the exception of the categories involving brain damage, which may parallel diseases, most DSM categories were purely descriptive. In addition, a prerequisite for high validity is high reliability. Because the reliability of early versions of DSM was questionable, the validity of the DSM was also limited. Indeed, it is difficult to talk about the validity of the entire diagnostic system because reliability and validity vary from one category to another. Carson (1991) noted that empirical tests of the construct validity of DSM have been largely absent.

DSM-III-R tried to respond to new research findings (Spitzer & Williams, 1987). Although Kraepelin's concepts still formed the basis for some of its categories, DSM-III-R contained substantial revisions. For example, to improve reliability, DSM-III-R specified the exact criteria clinicians should use in making a diagnosis. Clinical usefulness and suitability for research studies were also considered. DSM-III-R was intended to be atheoretical and descriptive, making it more useful to clinicians of varying orientations. In a survey of use and attitudes among mental health professionals in forty-two countries, DSM-III-R was widely used and considered useful, although certain diagnostic categories such as personality disorders were felt to be very problematic (Maser, Kaelber & Weise, 1991).

The Current System: DSM-IV

DSM-IV (American Psychiatric Association, 1994) is a revision of DSM-III-R that takes into account the accumulating research on psychopathology and diagnosis. The adequacy of DSM-IV has been under investigation. Particularly important is the large-scale research being conducted on thousands of clinicians and clients. In this research, videotapes are made of interviews of clients with different disorders. Clinicians are asked to evaluate and diagnose the clients. Factors (such as degree of training with DSM-IV among clinicians and type of symptoms shown by the clients) that may affect the ability to make a reliable diagnosis are being studied (Nelson-Gray, 1991). Other field trials or studies are being conducted on certain diagnostic categories (Kline et al., 1993), and the results are only now being analyzed.

DSM-IV recommends that the clinician examine and evaluate the individual's mental state with regard to five factors or dimensions (called axes in the manual). Axes I, II, and III adddress the individual's present mental and medical condition. Axes IV and V provide additional information about the person's life situation and functioning. Together, the five axes are intended to provide comprehensive and useful information.

Axis I—Clinical syndromes and other conditions that may be a focus of clinical attention   Any mental disorder listed in the manual (except those included on Axis II) is indicated on Axis I—clinical syndromes. If an individual has more than one mental disorder, they are all listed. The principal disorder is listed first.

Axis II—Personality disorders and mental retardation   Personality disorders, as well as prominent maladaptive personality features, are listed on Axis II. Personality disorders may be present in combination with a mental disorder from Axis I or alone. If more than one personality disorder is present, they are all listed. Also included on Axis II is mental retardation.

Axis III—General medical conditions   Listed on Axis III are any medical conditions that are potentially relevant to understanding and treating the person.

Axis IV—Psychosocial and environmental problems   These problems may affect the diagnosis, treatment, and prognosis of mental disorders. For example, the client may be experiencing the death of a family member, social isolation, homelessness, extreme poverty, and inadequate health services. The clinician lists these problems if they have been present during the year preceding the current evaluation or if they occurred before the previous year and are clearly contributory to the disorder or have become a focus of treatment. The clinician has various categories in which to classify the type of problems.

Axis V—Global assessment of functioning   The clinician provides a rating of the psychological, social, and occupational functioning of the person. Nor-

An Example of Classification Using DSM-IV

The client: Mark is a 56-year-old machine operator who was referred for treatment by his supervisor. The supervisor noted that Mark's performance at work had deteriorated during the past four months. Mark was frequently absent from work, had difficulty getting along with others, and often had a strong odor of liquor on his breath after his lunch break. The supervisor knew Mark was a heavy drinker and suspected that Mark's performance was affected by alcohol consumption. In truth, Mark could not stay away from drinking. He consumed alcohol every day; during weekends, he averaged about 16 ounces of Scotch per day. Although he had been a heavy drinker for thirty years, his consumption had increased after his wife divorced him six months ago. She claimed she could no longer tolerate his drinking, extreme jealousy, and unwarranted suspicions concerning her marital fidelity.

Co-workers avoided Mark because he was a cold, unemotional person who distrusted others.

During interviews with the therapist, Mark revealed very little about himself. He blamed others for his drinking problems: if his wife had been faithful or if others were not out to get him, he would drink less. Mark appeared to overreact to any perceived criticisms of himself. A medical examination revealed that Mark was developing cirrhosis of the liver as a result of his chronic and heavy drinking.

The evaluation: Mark's heavy use of alcohol, which interfered with his functioning, resulted in an alcohol abuse diagnosis on Axis I. Mark also exhibited a personality disorder, which was diagnosed as paranoid personality on Axis II because of his suspiciousness, hypervigilance, and other behaviors. Cirrhosis of the liver was noted on Axis III. The clinician noted

Mark's divorce and difficulties in his job on Axis IV. Finally, Mark was given a 54 on the Global Assessment of Functioning scale (GAF), used in Axis V to rate his current level of functioning, mainly because he was exhibiting moderate difficulty at work and in his social relationships. Mark's diagnosis, then, was as follows:

Axis I—Clinical syndrome: alcohol abuse

Axis II—Personality disorder: paranoid personality

Axis III—Physical disorder: cirrhosis

Axis IV—Psychosocial and environmental problems: (1) Problems with primary support group (divorce), (2) occupational problems

Axis V—Current GAF, 54

---

mally, the rating is made for the level of functioning at the time of the evaluation. The clinician uses a 100-point scale in which 1 indicates severe impairment in functioning (for example, the individual is in persistent danger of severely hurting self or others or is unable to maintain minimal personal hygiene) and 100 refers to superior functioning with no symptoms.

The disorders (categories) for Axes I and II that are included in DSM-IV are shown on the inside covers of this book. Focus On provides an example of the classifications that result from the five-axis evaluation.

DSM-IV Mental Disorders

The task of making a diagnosis of mental disorder involves classifying individuals on Axes I and II. Most disorders found in clients are listed under either Axis I or Axis II, but some clients may have disorders on

both axes or more than one on each axis. The following are the broad categories of mental disorders, most of which are discussed in this book:

Disorders usually first diagnosed in infancy, childhood, or adolescence A variety of problems are included in the category of disorders that begin before maturity. The problems include impairment in cognitive and intellectual functioning, language or motor deficiencies, disruptive behaviors, poor social skills, anxiety, eating disorders, and so on (see Chapter 16). Although mental retardation is listed under Axis II, it is described in this category.

Delirium, dementia, amnestic, and other cognitive disorders The essential feature of the cognitive impairment disorders is a psychological or behavioral abnormality that is associated with a transient or permanent, identifiable dysfunction of the brain. Included in this category are cognitive, emotional, and

There is a fine line between mental disorders and extreme but normal behavior. Shy children could easily be diagnosed as disordered, when instead their social development may simply be delayed.

behavioral problems that arise from head injuries, ingestion of toxic or intoxicating substances, brain degeneration or disease, and so on (see Chapter 15).

Mental disorders due to a general medical condition Medical conditions can be an important cause of mental disorders. When there is evidence that general medical conditions are causally related to and explain a disorder, the client is considered to have a mental disorder due to a general medical condition. For example, hypothyroidism can be a direct cause of major depressive disorder. In that case, the diagnosis would be "major depressive disorder due to a general medical condition (hypothyroidism)." Many of the major diagnostic categories (mood disorders or anxiety disorders) have specific categories that include disorders caused by medical conditions.

Substance-related disorders Psychoactive substances, such as alcohol, amphetamines, marijuana, cocaine, and nicotine, are those that affect the central nervous system. Whenever use of these substances continues despite social, occupational, psychological, or physical problems, it is considered a mental disorder. Individuals with substance use disorders are often unable to control intake and have a persistent desire to use the substance (see Chapter 9). Some disorders (anxiety or mood) occur because of the ingestion of substances. In these cases, they are considered substance-induced disorders and are listed by DSM-IV not in the section on substance-related disorders but in the section for those disorders that share the same symptoms. (For example, substance-induced major depressive disorder would be classified under mood disorders.)

Schizophrenia and other psychotic disorders The disorder known as schizophrenia is marked by severe impairment in thinking and perception. Speech may be incoherent, and the person often has delusions (false belief systems), hallucinations (such as hearing imaginary voices), and inappropriate affect. Schizophrenia as well as other psychotic disorders seriously disrupts social, occupational, and recreational functioning (see Chapters 13 and 14).

Mood disorders A separate class of disorders is composed of disturbances in mood or affect. The mood may be one of serious depression, in which the person shows marked sadness, diminished interest, and loss of energy. Extreme elation or mania is also included in these disorders. People with mania frequently have grandiosity, decreased need for sleep, flight of ideas, and impairment in functioning. Severity of mood disorders can vary, and sometimes, in bipolar conditions, both depression and mania are exhibited (see Chapter 11).

Anxiety disorders Anxiety is the predominant symptom in anxiety disorders, and avoidance behaviors are almost always present. For example, people with phobias fear an object or situation and avoid encountering the feared object. People with other anxiety disorders may not know the reasons for their extreme feelings of anxiety or may exhibit obsessions (recurrent thoughts) or compulsions (repetitive behaviors), which, when not performed, cause marked distress (see Chapter 5).

Somatoform disorders Symptoms of a physical disorder that cannot be fully explained by a known general medical condition are usually classified as somatoform disorders. Individuals with these disorders usually complain of bodily problems or dysfunctions, are preoccupied with beliefs of having a disease or health problem, or experience pain. Yet the symptoms may be inconsistent with anatomical structures, and the discrepancy suggests a psychological basis for the symptoms (see Chapter 6).

Factitious disorders In factitious disorders, there is intentional feigning of physical or psychological symptoms. The individual with this disorder is motivated not by external incentives, such as economic gain or avoiding legal responsibility, but by the assumption of a sick role.

Dissociative disorders The essential feature of these disorders is a disturbance or alteration in memory, identity, or consciousness. The disturbance may be reflected in people who cannot remember who they are, who assume new identities, who have two or more distinct personalities, or who experience feelings of depersonalization in which the sense of reality is lost (see Chapter 6).

Sexual and gender identity disorders Two main groups of disturbances are included in sexual disorders: paraphilias and sexual dysfunctions. Paraphilias are characterized by intense sexual arousal and fantasies involving nonhuman objects, suffering or humiliation of oneself or one's partner, or children or nonconsenting people. Paraphilias are considered disorders only if the person has acted on the fantasies or is markedly distressed by them. Sexual dysfunctions may involve inhibitions in sexual desires, inhibited orgasms, premature ejaculations among males, or recurrent pain during the process of sexual intercourse. In gender identity disorders, there is a strong cross-gender identification and a desire to be the other sex coupled with a persistent discomfort with one's own sex (see Chapter 10).

Eating disorders Included in this category are such disorders as refusal to maintain body weight above a minimally normal weight, and binge eating and purging (that is, eating excessively and then intentionally vomiting).

Sleep disorders The primary symptoms in these disorders involve sleeping difficulties: problems in initiating or maintaining sleep, excessive sleepiness, sleep disruptions, repeated awakening from sleep associated with extremely frightening nightmares, sleepwalking, and so on.

Impulse control disorders not elsewhere classified A separate class of disorders involves the failure to resist an impulse or temptation to perform some act that is harmful to oneself or to others. Included are disorders involving loss of control of impulses over aggression, stealing, gambling, setting fires, and pulling hair. Disorders of impulse control that are listed under other disorders (such as drug use or paraphilias) are not classified in this group of disorders (see Chapter 8).

Adjustment disorders These disorders are characterized by marked and excessive distress, or significant impairment in social, occupational, or academic functioning because of a recent stressor. The symptoms do not meet the criteria for Axis I or II disorders and do not include bereavement.

Personality disorders Whenever personality traits are inflexible and maladaptive and notably impair functioning or cause subjective distress, a diagnosis of personality disorder is likely. The patterns of these disorders are usually evident by adolescence. They typically involve odd or eccentric behaviors, excessive dramatic and emotional behaviors, or anxious and fearful behaviors (see Chapter 8).

Throughout DSM-IV, there are categories entitled "Not Otherwise Specified." The categories are intended to include disorders that do not fully meet the criteria for a particular disorder. For example, a disorder that is cognitive in nature but does not meet all of the criteria for delirium, demential, amnestic, or other specified cognitive disorders would be considered a "cognitive disorder, not otherwise specified." Furthermore, after each diagnosed disorder, clinicians can use specifiers that indicate severity and remission status. Severity is rated as mild, moderate, or severe, depending on the symptoms and degree of impairment. *Remission* refers to a disorder in which the full criteria for making the diagnosis were met at one time but the current symptoms or signs of the disorder are only partially apparent (partial remission) or no longer remain (full remission).

Figure 3.4 shows the prevalence rate (the percentage of the population with the disorder) of certain disorders, as determined by the largest epidemiologic investigation (the study of the rate and distribution of disorders) ever conducted in the United States.

＊ Finally, DSM-IV emphasizes cross-cultural assessment issues far more than previous versions of DSM. It has an introductory section that places diagnosis within a cultural context. It provides a description of pertinent culture, age, and gender features for each disorder, and it supplies guidelines for addressing the cultural background of the client and the context for evaluating the client. DSM-IV also contains an outline of culture-bound syndromes (disorders unique to a particular cultural group). These improvements make DSM-IV far more culturally sensitive than were the previous editions.

Evaluation of the DSM Classification System

It is still too soon to provide a comprehensive evaluation of DSM-IV because it was so recently developed. Extensive research needs to be conducted on its reliability and validity with different populations; the social and research consequences of its use need to be

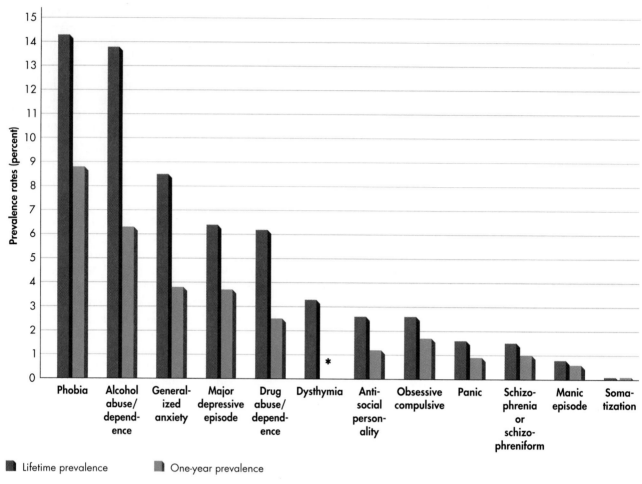

Lifetime prevalence   One-year prevalence

*Not ascertained.

FIGURE 3.4 **Lifetime and One-Year Prevalence Rates for Mental Disorders, as Percentage of U.S. Population** As this graph shows, anxiety, alcohol abuse, and depressive disorders are among the most common.

Source: Data from Robins, Locke & Regier, 1991.

studied as well. Many sections of DSM-IV are basically unchanged from those of DSM-III-R. Because research findings helped to shape DSM-IV, it is likely that reliability and validity are stronger than in the previous versions.

Most objections have been directed to DSM in general, and many are applicable to DSM-IV. For example, some clinicians and researchers believe that DSM has a strong medical orientation, even though more than one-half of the disorders listed are not attributable to known or presumed organic causes and should not be considered biogenic in nature (Nelson-Gray, 1991; Schacht, 1985; Schacht & Nathan, 1977). Some psychologists believe that the medical emphasis of DSM is in part a response to psychiatrists' need to define abnormality more strongly within their profession. A survey of psychotherapists

who are psychologists rather than psychiatrists indicated that there was little enthusiasm for DSM (Smith & Kraft, 1983). Most of the respondents rejected the notion that mental disorders form a subset of medical disorders. They preferred a social and interpersonal, rather than a medical, approach to mental disorder. However, no such alternative to DSM enjoys widespread use at present.

Other psychologists question the usefulness of the DSM classification scheme for research. Some of the categories were created out of compromises between conflicting views or were rooted in practical considerations, such as ease of application and acceptability to practitioners. Schacht (1985) believes that political and practical aspects of DSM are inseparable from scientific considerations. For example, certain diagnostic categories in DSM have been characterized as being sexist. In other words, specific behaviors sometimes seen among women may be inappropriately interpreted as signs of mental disorders (D. Franklin, 1987; M. Kaplan, 1983; and see Critical Thinking in Chapter 8).

One example of this controversy is the continuing discussion of whether to establish premenstrual dysphoric disorder as a DSM diagnostic category. Premenstrual dysphoric disorder, many times associated with women experiencing premenstrual syndrome (PMS), has been a hotly debated category (Tavris, 1991). According to DSM-IV, the symptoms include marked changes in mood, persistent anger, depression, or anxiety, often accompanied by complaints of breast tenderness and bodily aches. There is often an increase in interpersonal conflicts and a marked interference with work or social activities and relationships. These symptoms occur in a cyclical pattern a week before menses and remit a few days afterward. Although critics of this category acknowledge that many women have some of these symptoms, they believe the disorder should be treated as a strictly physical or gynecological disorder. Labeling it as a psychiatric disorder stigmatizes women as being emotional and controlled by "raging hormones." It also suggests that being a woman is per se a risk factor in developing psychiatric disorders (Holden, 1986). In recognition of the controversy, DSM-IV considers premenstrual dysphoric disorder to be a proposed condition requiring further study rather than a new disorder category.

Some researchers (Persons, 1986) have argued that the study of the symptoms of a disorder is more valuable than research on diagnosed disorders because many patients may be misdiagnosed. Furthermore, by placing patients in diagnosed categories, important information regarding the severity of symptoms is lost. Carson (1991) questioned whether a diagnostic system that uses categories for disorders is appropriate. He prefers a model that views disorders on dimensions (that is, having more or less of certain characteristics) rather than one that categorizes disorders. For these reasons, the DSM (in any revision) may be difficult to use for scientific purposes.

Millon (1983) tried to clarify the intent of DSM and respond to its critics. He noted that the classification system was not intended to imply that all mental disorders have an organic basis. To Millon, the important question is whether the DSM revised editions are a substantial improvement over past systems. He believes they are. Millon also pointed out that constructing a diagnostic classification system is an ongoing process, requiring continual revision and improvement. The limitations in the usefulness of DSM may therefore partly reflect holes in our knowledge of psychopathology (Goldman & Foreman, 1988). It should

also be noted that nosological or classification systems such as DSM-IV are constructed by people. This means that the philosophical and scientific orientation and cultural beliefs of the developers of a nosological system are important issues to examine. One can imagine that a group of individuals who believe that spiritual forces influence human behavior would devise a nosological system that would be completely different from DSM-IV. Even within DSM-IV, according to some critics, the psychopathology found in non-Western societies may not be easily classified. This points to the need to continually attend to issues of cross-cultural usefulness (Frances et al., 1991).

The debates over the usefulness of the DSM system have been valuable in suggesting new research directions, increasing the role of research in developing the system, and stimulating the examination of conceptual, methodological, philosophical, and clinical assumptions in the classification of mental disorders. Future research, particularly research that examines the construct validity of DSM, is essential to evaluating the usefulness of the system.

Alternatives to DSM classification are available, such as a behavioral classification scheme developed by Goldfried and Davison (1976). In the scheme, deviant behaviors are classified according to the variables that are maintaining the behaviors. For example, a child may learn to be physically aggressive while playing football and then bring such behavior into the classroom (inappropriate behavior). The inappropriate behavior is classified as a stimulus control problem. Stimulus control is defective because the behavior does not conform to the appropriate stimulus (the child should be physically nonaggressive in the classroom). The change of stimuli (playing field to classroom) fails to change the child's behavior. Because this classification scheme emphasizes the variables that maintain behavioral patterns, it lets the therapist isolate those variables for treatment purposes (Goldfried & Davison, 1976). The behavioral classification approach also tends to be superior to DSM in reliability and validity (Bellack & Hersen, 1980). However, DSM continues to be the dominant diagnostic system.

Objections to Classification and Labeling

Classification schemes can be of immense aid in categorizing disorders and in communicating information about them and conducting research on them. They have nevertheless been criticized on the grounds that classifcation schemes foster belief in an erroneous all-or-nothing quality of psychopathology. As we noted in Chapter 1, behaviors lie on a spectrum from normality to abnormality. To place a diagnostic label on someone categorizes that person as "abnormal" and

"How long have you had this feeling that you're Orville Wright"

implies that he or she is qualitatively different from normal. Many psychologists now perceive that, for many disorders, the differences between normal and abnormal are differences of degree, not of kind (Persons, 1986).

In Chapter 1, we also touched on two problems that can arise when a diagnosis becomes a label. Here are four more:

1. *A label can predispose people to interpret all activities of the affected individual as pathological.* An exellent example of this occurred when a young psychology intern, training in the psychiatric ward of a VA hospital, talked very openly about his feelings of inadequacy. Most people have such feelings, but his openness gave him the reputation of being anxious. On the basis of this prejudgment and label, his supervisor became concerned about the young intern's competence and watched him very closely. One of the supervisor's chief complaints about the intern was that his anxiety prevented him from acquiring sufficient information during interviews with patients. Frustrated by his inability to shake this impression from the supervisor's mind, the intern took copious notes on all his patients. When he was next scheduled to present a case to his supervisor, the young intern prepared thoroughly and memorized details of the patient's life. He displayed a remarkable knowledge of the patient's life history to his supervisor that day, but

the supervisor's response was not at all what he expected. The supervisor felt that the intern's anxiety had caused him to become so compulsive in obtaining information from patients that he was not listening to their feelings! Thus a label or first impression can predispose the observer to distort even contradictory evidence to fit into the suggested frame of reference.

2. *A label may lead others to treat a person differently.* A study by Rosenthal and Jacobson (1968) showed how responses to a label can cause differential treatment. They tested school children and then randomly assigned them to either of two groups. Teachers were told that tests of one group indicated that they were potential intellectual "bloomers" (gaining in competence and maturity); the other group was not given this label. After a one-year interval, children from both groups were retested. Children identified as bloomers showed dramatic gains in IQ scores. How did this occur? Many have speculated that the label led teachers to have higher intellectual expectations for the bloomers and thus to treat them differently. Even though there was no significant difference in IQ levels between the two groups to begin with, differences were present by the end of the year. The Rosenthal and Jacobson study has been criticized on the basis of its methodology and statistical analysis. Nevertheless, other studies have yielded similar results (Rappaport & Cleary, 1980).

3. *A label may lead those who are labeled to believe that they do indeed possess such characteristics.* In these cases, the label becomes a self-fulfilling prophecy. In the Rosenthal and Jacobson study just cited, the label not only caused teachers to behave differently but also affected the children. It is possible that when people are constantly told by others that they are stupid or smart, they may come to believe such labels. For example, if people ascribe certain stereotypical traits to a racial minority or an ethnic group, then it is reasonable to believe that they will behave differently toward that group and cause cognitive and behavioral changes among members of that group. Rosenhan (1973) showed how people labeled mentally ill can become trapped by this label. Rosenhan's most renowned research study is discussed in Focus On. Another case of labeling is presented in this chapter's First Person narrative. The narrative raises the question of what would have happened to a boy's self-image had the initial labels concerning his intellectual and social impairment persisted. The effect of labeling may be pronounced among children who are forming their self-identities and self-concepts. Reschly (1992) noted that labeling a child as mentally retarded is not only demeaning but problematic. Many people believe that mental retardation is a biological anomaly, a permanent disability, and a gross

Normal or Abnormal: The Consequences of Labeling

Can "normal" people be diagnosed as disturbed? To find out, psychologist D. L. Rosenhan (1973) sent eight experimenters as pseudopatients to different psychiatric hospitals. Their assignment was first to simulate psychiatric symptoms to gain admission into psychiatric wards and, once there, to behave in a normal manner. Rosenhan wanted the pseudopatients to record their experiences as patients without hospital staff members becoming aware of the experiment.

Several interesting and provocative findings emerged. First, no one on the ward staff in the hospitals ever detected that the pseudopatients were normal—despite the fact that many *patients* suspected the pseudopatients were not ab-

normal but were merely "checking up on the hospital." In fact, the pseudopatients' length of hospitalization ranged from seven to fifty-two days. Second, nearly all pseudopatients were initially diagnosed as schizophrenic. And many of their normal behaviors on the ward were subsequently interpreted as manifestations of schizophrenia; one example was "excessive note-taking." Third, the staff failed to interact much with patients, who were treated as powerless, irresponsible individuals.

Rosenhan concluded that it is difficult to distinguish normal and disturbed behaviors in persons in mental hospitals, that the labels applied to patients often outlive their usefulness, and that the hospital environment is harsh and fre-

quently maintains maladaptive behaviors. His study has generated a great deal of controversy (Millon, 1975; Weiner, 1975). One critic argued that, because patients did report abnormal symptoms at the time of hospital admission, it is understandable that they were hospitalized (Spitzer, 1975). And, although the pseudopatients were not detected by the staff, they were all released within sixty days. All were said to be "in remission."

Of course, over the past 25 years, improvements have been made in our assessment procedures and hospitalization practices. Rosenhan's study served as a stimulus to examine and reform such practices.

intellectual handicap. Such beliefs and the accompanying reactions can have a profound effect on a child's self-image.

✱ 4. *A label may not provide the precise, functional information that is needed.* Today, many forms of managed-care organizations (MCOs)—such as health-maintenance organizations like Kaiser Permanente, preferred-provider organizations, and others—are gaining popularity in the provision of health and mental health care (Pallack, 1995). MCOs are less concerned about classifying or labeling clients' mental disorders than about finding a more precise means of measuring client functioning. The assessment of functioning at work, home, school, and elsewhere may be of greater interest than the validity of the clinician's diagnosis of schizophrenia or another disorder.

SUMMARY

1. Assessment and classification of disorders are essential in the mental health field. In developing assessment tools and useful classification schemes, re-

searchers and clinicians have been concerned with issues regarding reliability and validity.

2. Clinicians primarily use four methods of assessment: observations, interviews, psychological tests and inventories, and neurological tests. Observations of external signs and expressive behaviors are often made during an interview and can have diagnostic significance. Interviews, the oldest form of psychological assessment, involve a face-to-face conversation after which the interviewer differentially weighs and interprets verbal information obtained from the interviewee. Psychological tests and inventories provide a more formalized means of obtaining information. Most testing situations have two characteristics in common. They provide a standard situation in which certain responses are elicited, and responses from subjects are measured and used to make inferences about underlying traits. In personality testing, projective techniques or self-report inventories may be used. In the former, the stimuli are ambiguous; in the latter, the stimuli are much more structured. Two of the most widely used projective techniques are the Rorschach inkblot technique and the Thematic

FIRST PERSON

Eddy Regnier

Early in my training, when I was learning about psychological assessment tools, diagnostic criteria, and nomenclature, I became aware of the limitations of methodology. This discovery occurred because of a case I had as a graduate student. During my training, I worked with a ten-year-old boy who as an infant and a child had been through the most horrendous experiences. He had, perhaps for years, been sexually assaulted by his father in a dark, confined space. Further, he had watched an older sibling being similarly abused.

I met Steven (not his real name) after he had been hospitalized for a year. When I was assigned to be his primary therapist, he had already undergone a variety of psychological tests, that included behavioral observations, intelligence tests, and projectives, such as the Rorschach, Thematic Apperception, and Harris-Goodenough draw-a-person tests. The results of these tests suggested that Steven

was intellectually below average and functioning emotionally in the pervasive developmental disorder range, which is characterized by impaired social interactions and communication skills. My supervisors cautioned me against getting too attached to Steven, probably because they thought he was unlikely ever to improve. He had not shown any social response during the year he had been hospitalized and held himself aloof from everyday affairs. Although he ate and slept, he refused all overtures of friendship by the staff and the other boys on the ward. Their attempts to involve him in games and activities actually seemed to frighten him. He had an odd quality about him, which drove most people away. At our first meeting, I was immediately drawn to his eyes: they had the distant, faraway expression of a person who had been in hell. I believe he thought that at any moment he would be returned to the fiendish world he had come from. My first goal was to reevaluate his intellectual and emotional functioning, but I didn't know how to engage him sufficiently to get a true sample of his abilities. Usually a psychologist has only a limited amount of time to complete such an evaluation. In this instance, because I was a student and also seeing Steven for therapy, that time was extended.

I thought how frightening it must be for a baby to be born into a violent world of bright lights, sensations, and rapid change, and I wondered whether it was equally difficult for Steven to re-engage in our world. I spent as much time with him as I could, and slowly he began to trust me. As he opened up to me, we started to communicate through a game we devel-

oped, which can be described as "Draw what you are feeling." This game consisted of his drawing a picture, usually a family scene; I would then try to guess what was happening in it. To shape his drawings to more closely approximate the themes (sexual and physical abuse) I thought he was trying to convey, I made wild guesses about what was going on in his pictures to encourage him to reveal much more of what he had experienced. Responding to my incorrect guesses, Steven added more detail to his pictures, thus clarifying his experiences. I was eventually able to complete an evaluation using standard psychological tools, and I discovered that Steven had above-normal intellectual functioning.

By today's standards, Steven would have been diagnosed as having posttraumatic stress disorder because his traumatic experiences were so far outside the range of usual human experience. A person experiencing extremely traumatic events may show such symptoms as depression and anxiety, poor social interactions, and somatic changes. So it isn't hard to understand how Steven could have been misdiagnosed.

Once Steven was correctly diagnosed and given appropriate therapy, he began to get better. I have watched him grow from a terrified little boy into a wonderful, bright adolescent. He's lost that sad look in his eyes, and I'm grateful that I've had the chance to play a small part in his development.

Eddy Regnier is director of the day treatment program at the Fuller Mental Health Center in Boston, Massachusetts.

Apperception Test (TAT). Unlike projective tests, self-report personality inventories, such as the MMPI-2, supply the test taker with a list of alternatives from which to select an answer. Intelligence tests can be used to obtain an estimate of a person's current level of cognitive functioning and to assess intellectual deterioration. Behavioral observations of how a person takes the test are additional sources of information about personality attributes. The WAIS, Stanford-Binet, and Bender-Gestalt tests can be used to assess brain damage. The Halstead-Reitan and Luria-Nebraska test batteries specifically assess brain dysfunction. Neurological medical procedures, including x-rays, CAT and PET scans, EEG, and MRI have added highly important and sophisticated means to detect brain damage.

3. The first edition of DSM was based to a large extent on the biogenic model of mental illness. It assumed that people classified in a psychodiagnostic category would show similar symptoms that stem from a common cause, should be treated in a certain manner, would respond similarly, and would have similar prognoses. Critics questioned the reliability and validity of earlier versions of DSM. The current version, DSM-IV, contains detailed diagnostic criteria; research findings and expert judgments were used to help construct this latest version. As a result, its reliability appears to be higher than that of the previous manuals. Furthermore, data are collected on five axes so that much more information about the patient is systematically examined. General objections to classification are based primarily on the problems involved in labeling.

4. In addition to issues involving reliability and validity, a number of ethical questions have been raised about classifying and assessing people through tests. These include questions about confidentiality, privacy, and cultural bias. Concerned with these issues, psychologists have sought to improve classification and assessment procedures and to define the appropriate conditions for testing and diagnosis. In spite of the problems and criticisms, classification and assessment are necessary to psychological research and practice.

KEY TERMS

assessment With regard to psychopathology, the process of gathering information and drawing conclusions about the traits, skills, abilities, emotional functioning, and psychological problems of an individual

classification system With regard to psychopathology, a system of distinct categories, indicators, and nomenclature for different patterns of behavior, thought processes, and emotional disturbances

etiology The causes or origins of a disorder

organicity Damage or deterioration in the central nervous system

prognosis A prediction of the future course of a particular disorder

projective personality test A personality assessment technique in which the test taker is presented with ambiguous stimuli and is asked to respond to them in some way

psychological tests and inventories A variety of standardized test instruments used to assess personality, maladaptive behavior, development of social skills, intellectual abilities, vocational interests, and cognitive impairment

psychometrics Mental measurement, including its study and techniques

reactivity Change in the way a person usually responds, triggered by the person's knowledge that he or she is being observed or assessed

reliability The degree to which a procedure or test will yield the same results repeatedly, under the same circumstances

self-report inventories An assessment tool that requires test takers to answer specific written questions or to select specific responses from a list of alternative self-descriptive statements; standardization helps reduce subjective responses by the test giver

validity The extent to which a test or procedure actually performs the function it was designed to perform

CHAPTER 4

THE SCIENTIFIC METHOD IN ABNORMAL PSYCHOLOGY

like the way you read to me at night. I know how to read too, but I like to hear you laught [sic] at the stories. I wish you and Mom could geyt [sic] God in your friendship. My house is fairly happy with you and Mom. (Bligh & Kupperman, 1993)

Could this note have been typed by a ten-year-old girl with severe mental retardation, who is legally blind, has only a few words in her vocabulary, and communicates by screaming? According to her teacher, the girl could and did type it, through facilitated communication (Bilken, 1990). Thousands of teachers and others have been trained as facilitators in the use of this technique, which is purported to help cognitively disabled individuals communicate their innermost thoughts. The facilitator "assists" the individual who is typing or pointing at letters by supporting the person's arm or hand. Although amazing stories of the success of facilitated communication have been reported (Whittenmore, 1992), questions have also been raised about its effectiveness. Determining the validity of this technique became especially important when the ten-year-old girl later typed that she was being abused by her mother's fiancé.

Two researchers, Sally Bligh and Phyllis Kupperman, viewed a videotaped session in which the child and her teacher were engaged in facilitated communication. As they watched, the researchers noted certain discrepancies: (1) reading the small print from the computer screen appeared to be beyond the capability of a legally blind child; (2) the thoughts, expression, and punctuation skills appeared to be beyond the level expected of a ten-year-old child; and (3) the child answered correctly even when she was not attending to the question on the screen. The researchers also observed that, unlike the child, the facilitator was looking very intently at the keyboard.

To eliminate the possibility that the teacher was actually answering the questions, the researchers varied the conditions in which the communication took place. They found that an intelligible response occurred only when the facilitator was allowed to look at the keyboard. Also, a correct answer was given only when the facilitator could see the question and knew the answer. If the questions were shown only to the child, no correct response was obtained. The re-

sults clearly demonstrated that the "communication" was coming from the facilitator. As a result, all charges were dropped against the mother and her fiancé. Other studies also have found that the communication comes from the facilitators and not from the cognitively impaired individuals (Eberlin et al., 1993; Moore et al., 1993; Moore, Donovan & Hudson, 1993).

Interestingly, the teacher involved in the test case remained firmly convinced of the validity of the approach, and she continued to use it with students in her classroom. Equally fascinating is the finding that facilitators appear to be unaware that they are furnishing the "communication." How can the belief in a technique be maintained despite contradictory evidence, and how can the facilitators be unaware that they are providing the answers for their clients? When opinions differ on clinical or research findings, the scientific method can offer important insights.

Scientists are often described as skeptics. Rather than accept the conclusions from a single study, scientists demand that the results be *replicated*, or repeated by other researchers. Replication lessens the chance that the findings were due to experimenter bias, methodological flaws, or sampling errors. The following list gives some examples of findings that were initially reported as "conclusive" by the mass media and describes their current status after further investigation:

■ Taraxein, a substance found in the blood of people with schizophrenia, is responsible for this disorder. Heath and associates (1970) reported that when this substance was injected into volunteers who do not have the disorder, they displayed schizophrenic behaviors. *Status:* Other researchers were unable to replicate the findings.

■ Autism is related to an underdevelopment of the cerebellum region known as the vermis (Courchesne et al., 1988). *Status:* Unclear. Another researcher reported finding no differences between autistic individuals and controls in that brain region.

■ Hyperactivity in children is due to reactions to specific food groups or food additives. *Status:* Probably not supported. In general, experimental studies using biological challenge or double-blind methods (described later in this chapter) have reported no change in behavior as a result of food or additives.

■ An individual's attitude or personality can influence both the development and course of diseases such as cancer. *Status:* Unresolved. Little evidence exists that attitude or personality influences the development of cancer.

■ Specific negative family communication patterns may be responsible for the development of schizophrenia. *Status:* Little support exists for this view, although a negative family environment might be associated with relapses and increased stress for a number of disorders.

■ Childhood sexual abuse is a major causal factor in the development of eating disorders. *Status:* When methodological problems are controlled for, there is little support for this position (Conners &

Morse, 1993; Pope & Hudson, 1992; Pope et al., 1994).

As you can see, the search for "truth" is a long and torturous journey. Answers to the causes of abnormal behavior have come and gone. In this chapter, we will discuss the components of the scientific method. Understanding different research designs and their shortcomings is necessary to be able to critically evaluate reported findings in abnormal psychology. For a fuller example of a scientific investigation by researchers, see Focus On.

THE SCIENTIFIC METHOD IN CLINICAL RESEARCH

The **scientific method** is a method of inquiry that provides for the systematic collection of data through controlled observation and for the testing of hypotheses. A **hypothesis** is a conjectural statement, usually describing a relationship between two variables. Different theories may result in different hypotheses for the same phenomenon. A **theory** is a group of principles and hypotheses that together explain some aspect of a particular area of inquiry. For example, hypothesized reasons for eating disorders have included biological or neurochemical causes, fear of sexual maturity, societal demands for thinness in women, and pathological family relationships. Each of these hypotheses reflects a different theory.

Characteristics of Clinical Research

Clinical research can proceed only when the relationship expressed in a hypothesis is clearly and systematically stated and when the variables of concern are measurable and defined. We need to define clearly what we are studying and make sure that the variables are measured with reliable and valid instruments. Clinical research relies on these characteristics of the scientific method—the potential for self-correction, the hypothesizing of relationships, the use of operational definitions, the consideration of reliability and validity, and the acknowledgment of base rates.

Potential for Self-Correction Perhaps the unique and most general characteristic of the scientific method is its *potential for self-correction.* Under ideal conditions, data and conclusions are freely exchanged and experiments are replicable (reproducible), so that all are subject to discussion, testing, verification, and modification. The knowledge developed under these conditions is as free as possible from the scientist's

During facilitated communication, the facilitator is merely supposed to support the hand or arm of the child. Research seems to indicate, however, that it is not the child who is "communicating" but the facilitator.

The scientific method involves the collection of data through controlled observations. Here, the child's responses are videotaped through a one-way mirror.

personal beliefs, perceptions, biases, values, attitudes, and emotions.

Hypothesizing Relationships   Another characteristic of the scientific method is that it attempts to identify and explain (hypothesize) the relationship between variables. Examples of hypotheses are statements such as "Some seasonal forms of depression may be due to decreases in light," "Autism (a severe disorder beginning in childhood) is a result of poor parenting," and "Eating disorders are a result of specific family interaction patterns."

Operational Definitions   **Operational definitions** are definitions of the variables that are being studied. For example, an operational definition of depression could be a score representing some pattern of responses to a self-report questionnaire on a depression inventory, a rating assigned by an observer using a depression checklist, or a laboratory identification of specific neurochemical changes. Operational definitions are important because they force an experimenter to clearly define what he or she means by the variable. This allows others to agree or disagree with the way the variable was defined. When operational definitions of a phenomenon differ, comparing research is problematic and conclusions can be faulty.

Let us consider the recent studies or reports linking child sexual abuse with panic disorder, phobias, depression, alcohol and substance abuse, multiple personality and dissociative disorders, and bulimia and anorexia nervosa (Briere, 1992; Pribor & Dinwiddie,

1992; Terr, 1991). Unfortunately, these studies employ different operational definitions. Consider the following different definitions of *child sexual abuse:*

> Any sexual activity, overt or covert, between a child and an adult (or older child), where the younger child's participation is obtained through seduction or coercion. (Ratican, 1992, p. 33)

> Any self-reported contact—ranging from fondling to sexual intercourse—experienced by a patient on or before age 18 and initiated by someone 5 or more years senior or by a family member at least 2 years senior. (Brown & Anderson, 1991, p. 56)

Other definitions of child sexual abuse include "any unwanted sexual experience before 14," "any attempted or completed rape before 18 years," and "contact between someone under 15 and another person 5 years older" (Briere, 1992, p. 198). The use of so many different definitions of child sexual abuse makes any general conclusions difficult (Conners & Morse, 1993; Mallinckrodt, McCreary & Robertson, 1995; Pope & Hudson, 1992; Pope et al., 1994).

Operational definitions need to be clear and precise. How should "any unwanted sexual experience before 14" be interpreted? What behaviors can this definition include? It is no wonder that the reported rate of sexual abuse in different studies ranges from 6 to 62 percent for females and from 3 to 31 percent for males (Watkins & Bentovim, 1992). In evaluating or comparing research, the operational definition of the phenomenon must be considered.

Have We Found the Gene That Causes Alcoholism?

An article appeared in the *New York Times* stating the following:

> The biological approach took a big step forward in April, when researchers reported the identification of a specific gene that may play a key role in some forms of alcoholism, as well as other addictions.... The discovery, announced by researchers at the University of Texas and the University of California at Los Angeles, is a gene linked to the receptors for dopamine, a brain chemical involved in the sensation of pleasure. (Goldman, 1990, p. 5)

This article was based in part on a study by Blum and colleagues (1990), who were looking for specific genetic characteristics in alcoholics. They believed that the genetic link involved the A1 allele of DRD2. In their study, twenty-four (69 percent) of thirty-five alcoholics were found to carry this genetic characteristic, as compared with only seven (20 percent) of thirty-five nonalcoholics. The researchers based their analysis on an examination of the brain tissue of deceased individuals. The alcoholics were characterized as being treatment failures and had died of alcoholic-related problems.

Had these researchers found the gene responsible for alcoholism? Any conclusions have to be interpreted cautiously. First, 31 percent of the alcoholics did not show this genetic characteristic, and 20 percent of nonalcoholics did. Thus causes other than the identified genetic characteristic have to be involved. Second, because the study's sample sizes are small, its findings must be considered preliminary until larger samples can be assessed. Third, the characteristics (treatment failures and death from alcohol-related problems) of the thirty-five alcoholics in the study may not be representative of alcoholics in general. Fourth, although a normal control group was included, we need to determine whether the gene is specific (pathognomonic) to alcoholism. If it is also found in combination with other disorders,

Reliability and Validity of Measures and Observations

The scientific method requires that the measures we use be reliable or consistent. *Reliability* refers to the degree to which a measure or procedure will yield the same results repeatedly (see Chapter 3). Consider, for example, an individual who has been diagnosed, by means of a questionnaire, as having an antisocial personality. If the questionnaire is reliable, the individual should receive the same diagnosis after taking the questionnaire again. Results must be consistent if we are to have any faith in them. Diagnostic reliability is low for many of the childhood disorders and some of the personality disorders.

Even if consistent results are obtained, questions can arise over the *validity* of a measure (see Chapter 3). Does the testing instrument really measure what it was developed to measure? If we claim to have developed a test that identifies multiple personality disorder, we have to demonstrate that it can accomplish this task. Many of the clinical tests used in studies have not been evaluated to determine their validity. We return to this topic later in this chapter.

Base Rates

A **base rate** is a phenomenon's natural occurrence in the population studied. When the base rate is not known or considered, research findings can be misinterpreted. For example, both unwanted sexual events and eating problems are reported by a high percentage of females (Conners & Morse, 1993; Pope & Hudson, 1992). As a result, clinicians may find that the majority of individuals treated for eating problems report a history of sexual abuse. An investigator, not recognizing that these are both high-frequency behaviors (high base rates), may mistakenly conclude that one is the cause of the other. Lack of information in the past about the base rate of masturbation caused it to be viewed as a relatively rare and harmful behavior. Survey data showing that the majority of both sexes engage in this behavior forced a change in how it was viewed.

The importance of base rates in clinical research can be seen in the responses of a control group to a psychotic traits questionnaire. Persons with severe mental disorders are thought to have "unusual" thoughts or reactions. On a psychotic traits questionnaire, however, a large percentage of a control group gave positive answers to the questions in Figure 4.1.

Although individuals with schizophrenia are twice as likely as normal persons to endorse such statements (Jackson & Claridge, 1991), "normal" individ-

the relationship between the gene and alcoholism would be weakened. To address these concerns, replication of the study was necessary.

Conflicting findings were soon reported. Gelernter and associates (1991a) found no difference in the prevalence of the A1 allele in controls and alcoholics in their sample. They suggested that the significant differences presented in the earlier study were due to "falsely low estimates" of its prevalence in control groups. In a review of six studies on the A1 allele, Cloninger (1991) did find the A1 allele in a larger percentage of alcoholics (45 percent) than in members of control groups (26 percent). There is evidence, therefore, that the A1 allele is found in nearly one-half of the alcoholics studied; it is also found in more than one-fourth of the persons in the control groups.

Is the genetic characteristic also found in other psychiatric populations? Comings and co-workers (1991)—who found the A1 allele among 42.3 percent of alcoholics they studied—reported the same genetic characteristic in the following groups: controls (24.5 percent); Tourette's syndrome (44.9 percent); attention-deficit hyperactive disorder (46.2 percent); autistic disorder (54.5 percent); and posttraumatic stress disorder (45.7 percent).

It is clear from a review of the research that the A1 allele is neither sufficient nor necessary for the development of alcoholism. Fewer than 50 percent of alcoholics carry this genetic characteristic. This characteristic is also not specific or pathognomonic to alcoholism because it is associated with a number of different behav-

ior disorders. The A1 allele may act as a modifying influence, perhaps making a number of disorders worse. But even this is only speculation; the influence of the A1 allele, if any, must be determined by further research.

These research findings do not mean that an alcoholism-related gene will never be found. As Cloninger observed, however, "It was surprising that a single gene could be so strongly associated with a common disorder that is known to be developmentally complex and genetically heterogeneous" (p. 1833). These studies demonstrate the self-corrective feature of the scientific method—the demand for replication of original findings.

FIGURE 4.1   Responses to Psychotic Traits Questionnaire This figure on the right shows the percentage of "normal" individuals endorsing items on a questionnaire used to identify psychotic thinking and beliefs.

uals in control groups also report disturbing thoughts and urges, "paranoid ideation," and "magical thinking." That an individual or client reports having odd or bizarre thoughts of sex or being bothered by the feeling of being watched may therefore not be indicative of a disorder.

Statistical Versus Clinical Significance The scientific method also requires that research findings be evaluated in terms of their *statistical significance*—the likelihood that the relationship could be due to chance alone. Even a statistically significant finding may have little practical significance in a clinical setting, however. For example, various articles based on a study by Phillips, Van Voorhees, and Ruth (1992) have stated that women are more likely to die the week after their birthday than in any other week of the year. This seemed to show that psychological factors

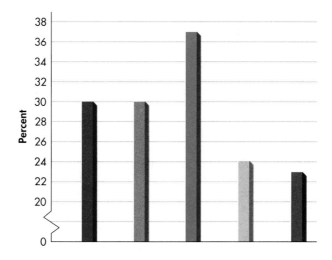

Percent

■ Bothered by the feeling that others are watching you

■ Thought that people were talking when it was only a noise

■ Believed that you were communicating with others through telepathy

■ Felt urge to injure yourself

■ Have odd and bizarre thoughts about sex

Source: Data from Jackson & Claridge, 1991.

have a powerful effect on biological processes. The study involved 2,745,149 persons, and the findings were statistically significant (not due to chance). The excess in deaths for the week after the birthday, however, was only 3.03 percent higher than would be expected in any other week. Thus psychological factors associated with deaths and birthdays, although statistically significant, play a relatively small role in deaths among women. When evaluating research, you must determine if the statistical significance reported is really "clinically" significant. This problem is most likely to occur in studies with large sample sizes.

EXPERIMENTS

The **experiment** is perhaps the best tool for testing cause-and-effect relationships. In its simplest form, the experiment involves the following:

1. An **experimental hypothesis,** which is the prediction concerning how an independent variable affects a dependent variable in an experiment

2. An **independent variable** (the possible cause), which the experimenter manipulates to determine its effect on a dependent variable

3. A **dependent variable** that is expected to change as a result of changes in the independent variable

As we noted, the experimenter is also concerned with controlling extraneous variables. Let us clarify these concepts by examining their use in an actual research study.

> Melinda N. was a nineteen-year-old sophomore who sought help from a university psychology clinic for panic attacks. At least four times a month she had severe bouts of anxiety during which she felt that she was dying. Although she could never predict when the attacks would occur, she always became highly anxious before and during class examinations. Fear of having panic attacks interfered with her ability to perform. The therapist had heard that an antidepressant, alprazolam, and psychological methods (relaxation training and changing thoughts about the attacks) were both successful in treating this disorder. Before deciding which treatment to use, the therapist searched the research literature to determine whether studies had compared the effectiveness of approaches.
>
> A study by Janet Klosko and her colleagues (1990) seemed to provide an answer. That study included fifty-seven individuals who were diagnosed as suffering from a panic disorder according to the Anxiety Disorders Interview Schedule-Revised (ADIS-R) and DSM-III. These subjects were randomly assigned to one of the following groups: (1) alprazolam, (2) behavior therapy, (3) placebo treatment, and (4) waiting list control.

The Experimental Group

An *experimental group* is the group that is subjected to the independent variable. In their study, Klosko and her colleagues created two experimental groups: one exposed to alprazolam for fifteen weeks, and the other exposed to behavioral treatment for fifteen weeks. The behavioral treatment included cognitive, relaxation, and breathing training.

Because the investigators were interested in how treatment affects level of anxiety and reports of panic attacks, the dependent variables were measured in two ways. In the first, self-monitoring, subjects kept a daily record of each episode of anxiety above a certain level and indicated whether they thought it was a panic attack. The second measurement was a rating by clinicians on anxiety and frequency of panic attacks. Pretesting occurred before treatment, and posttesting occurred after fifteen weeks. These two sets of measurements enabled the investigators to evaluate how much improvement was made after treatment.

The Control Group

If the subjects in the two experimental groups in the study by Klosko and her colleagues showed a reduction of anxiety and panic attacks on the outcome measures from pretesting to posttesting, could the researchers conclude that the treatments were effective forms of therapy? The answer would be no. Students may have shown less anxiety and fewer panic attacks merely as a result of the passage of time or as a function of completing the assessment measures. The use of a control group enables one to eliminate such possibilities.

A *control group* is a group that is similar in every way to the experimental group except for the manipulation of the independent variable. In the study by Klosko and colleagues, the control group also took the pretest measures, were placed on a fifteen-week waiting list for treatment, and took the posttest measures. They did not receive any of the experimental treatments.

The Placebo Group

You should note that the results of the experiment may also be challenged for another reason. For example, what if the subjects in the treated, experimental groups improved not because of the treatment but because they had faith or an expectancy that they would improve? Some researchers have found that if subjects expect to improve from treatment, this expectancy—

"If this doesn't help you, don't worry, it's a placebo."

rather than specific treatment—is responsible for the outcome.

One method to induce an expectancy in students without using the specific treatment is to have a placebo control group, which was the second control group in the study by Klosko and her co-workers. Participants in the placebo control group were told that they were taking a medication for anxiety, but they were actually given an inert drug (a placebo) that could have no chemical impact on their anxiety. If the therapy groups improved more than the placebo control group, then one could be more confident that therapy, rather than expectancy, was responsible for the results. As Figure 4.2 shows, the percentage of individuals who were free from panic attacks was higher in both experimental groups than in either the waiting-list control or the placebo control group. The behavior therapy package was more effective than alprazolam in reducing anxiety and specific panic symptoms. These results indicated that the therapist could choose either of the two effective treatments in working with her client with panic disorder.

Additional Concerns in Clinical Research

Although researchers hope to control expectations of outcome through the use of a placebo control group, two types of problems can occur. First, the placebo control group may also report significant improvements. In one study of a group of fifty patients with mild depression, all reported that they were "much or very much" improved after taking a placebo (Rabkin et al., 1990). This finding would make it difficult to separate treatment from expectancy effects. Second, subjects may "guess" correctly that they are receiving a placebo, thereby reducing any expectancy effects.

Experimenter expectations can also influence diagnosis and the outcome of a study. In genetic studies, interviews or diagnoses are often made with the patients' relatives to determine if they have the same or related disorders. When clinicians are aware that they are interviewing the patient's relatives, they report higher rates of psychopathology than when they are not aware of the family connections (Gottesman & Shields, 1982). To control for experimenter expectations, the researcher may use a *blind design,* in which the clinicians doing the interviewing are not aware of the purpose of the study. Even in this case we may not be totally satisfied that clinician ratings are not influenced in some way. In family history studies, relatives are often contacted by the researcher or the patient (Alexander, Lerer & Baron, 1992). The knowledge that they are participating in a genetic study could cause the relatives of the patients to behave differently than a control subject during the interview. These behavioral differences may be picked up by the clinician and influence diagnostic decisions.

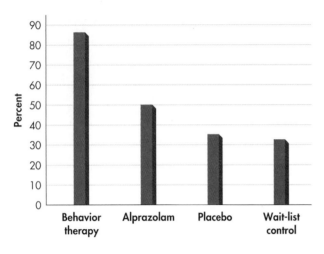

FIGURE 4.2 **Results of Klosko Study on Anxiety and Panic Attacks** This figure shows the percentage of individuals who were panic-free after the Klosko study, by experimental condition. Behavior therapy was clearly the most effective procedure. Note that about one-third of clients "recover," even without treatment.

Source: Data from Klosko et al., 1990.

A method to reduce the impact of both experimenter and subject expectations is the *double-blind design.* In this procedure, neither the individual working directly with the subject nor the subject is aware of the experimental conditions. However, the effectiveness of this design is dependent on the "blindness" of the participants, which may not always be ensured. In a randomized, double-blind study (Margraf et al.,

In a double-blind design, neither the subject nor the experimenter is aware of the type of drug or placebo that is to be administered. The purpose of this is to prevent expectations about the drug being tested from affecting the outcome of the study.

1991), patients with panic disorder were given one of two antidepressants (alprazolam or imipramine) or a placebo. All of the substances were dispensed in identical capsules. Were the patients and physicians "blind" to the conditions? Apparently not. The great majority of patients and physicians were able to assess the physiological responses and accurately rate whether the patient was taking an antidepressant. Further, the physicians were able to distinguish between the two types of active drugs based on the reaction of the patients. These findings indicate the need to modify experimental designs so the degree of "blindness" is increased. Otherwise, the results may be influenced by both client and experimenter expectations.

CORRELATIONS

A **correlation** is the extent to which variations in one variable are accompanied by increases or decreases in a second variable. The variables in a correlation, unlike those in an experiment, are not manipulated. Instead, a statistical analysis is performed to determine if increases in one variable are accompanied by increases or decreases in the other. The relationship is expressed as a statistically derived *correlation coefficient,* symbolized by the symbol *r,* which has a numerical value between -1 and $+1$. In a positive correlation, an increase in one variable is accompanied by an increase in the other. When an increase in one variable is accompanied by a decrease in the other variable, it is a negative correlation. The greater the value of *r,* positive or negative, the stronger the relationship. See Figure 4.3 for examples of correlations.

Correlations indicate the degree to which two variables are related, but not the reason for the relationship. Consider a study reported in the *American Journal of Psychiatry,* "Dissociation and Childhood Trauma in Psychologically Disturbed Adolescents." The researchers (Sanders & Giolas, 1991) hypothesized that dissociation (disturbance or change in function of identity, memory, or consciousness) during adolescence is positively correlated with childhood stress and abuse. Their subjects were a group of institutionalized adolescents (thirty-five females and twelve males) between the ages of thirteen and seventeen. They completed the Dissociative Experiences Scale and a questionnaire on child abuse and trauma. Statistically significant correlations were obtained between these measures ($r = 0.38$, $p > 0.01$). A correlation this high is likely to occur by chance less than one time out of a hundred. The researchers concluded that "these findings support the view that

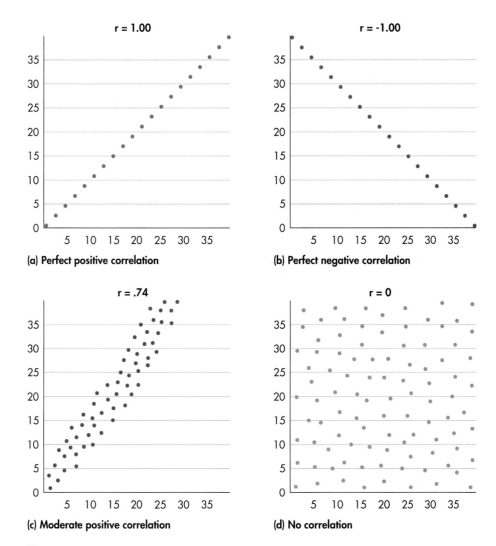

FIGURE 4.3 **Possible Correlation Between Two Variables** The more closely the data points approximate a straight line, the greater the magnitude of the correlation coefficient *r*. The slope of the regression line rising from left to right in example (a) indicates a perfect positive correlation between two variables, whereas example (b) reveals a perfect negative correlation. Example (c) shows a lower positive correlation. Example (d) shows no relationship whatsoever.

dissociation represents a reaction to early negative experience."

If we adopt the scientific method, what questions might we raise about this study? We must first remember that correlations do not necessarily imply a cause-and-effect relationship. Many alternative reasons for the relationship may exist. A third variable, such as environmental stress, might make it more likely for parents to physically abuse the child and for the child to develop a range of problem behaviors. Poverty or poor living conditions may cause both the dissociation in the adolescent and the abusive behavior on the part of the parents. Such third-variable possibilities in correlations are numerous. Consider the

following actual observations. What third-variable explanations can you suggest for them?

The number of storks nesting on rooftops in certain New England communities is positively correlated with the human birthrate.

The number of violent crimes committed in a community is positively correlated with the number of churches in the community.

In correlations, it is also often difficult to determine the direction of the causation. If we accept the findings of Sanders and Giolas, we must then determine whether the physical abuse caused dissociation

Identical twins are often used in correlational studies in an attempt to determine the influence of genetic factors on psychopathology because twins share an identical genetic makeup. The probability that one member of a twin pair will develop a disorder manifested in the other can be determined by studying a large number of identical twins. For schizophrenia, the probability that both twins will develop the disorder if one does is about 50 percent.

or the child's early dissociative behaviors produced more negative parenting.

This study also raises other issues. Do we agree or disagree with the operational definitions used in the study? How were *child abuse* and *trauma* defined and measured? Because the questionnaire devised by Sanders and Giolas did not appear to undergo validation procedures, we cannot be certain that the questionnaire actually measured the variable the researchers intended to measure (child abuse and trauma). Consider, for example, these sample questions from their questionnaire:

Do you feel safe living at home?

Were your parents unwilling to attend any of your school-related activities?

Were you physically mistreated as a child or teenager?

When you didn't follow the rules of the house, how often were you severely punished?

Did your parents ridicule you?

Were there traumatic or upsetting sexual experiences when you were a child or teenager that you couldn't speak to adults about?

As a child did you feel unwanted or emotionally neglected?

Did you ever think you wanted to leave your family and live with another family?

Do these questions measure "child abuse and trauma" exclusively, or could they measure something else? Would other groups of adolescents give similar or different answers to these questions? Might institutionalized adolescents describe their home situation inaccurately? As one researcher pointed out, "One could undoubtedly question these adolescents about a good many things and produce interesting correlations and comparisons to others whose mind set is more objective" (Furlong, 1991, p. 1423). We would be more certain about the validity of the child abuse trauma questionnaire if we had some independent verification of the severity of actual abuse suffered by the adolescents. Unfortunately, in the Sanders and Giolas study, responses on their questionnaire were not even related to abuse ratings obtained by clinicians at the institution.

Even if we accepted the operational definitions in this study, we could not say that child abuse is specifically related to dissociation. We would have to give both questionnaires to control groups and to other psychiatric populations to determine how they would respond.

In summary, a correlation indicates the degree to which two variables are related. It is a very important method of scientific inquiry because we cannot control many variables, such as genetic makeup, gender, and socioeconomic status. Manipulating other variables that we might be able to control, such as exposing a child to trauma or abuse, would be unethical. Correlations can tell us how likely it is that two variables can occur together. Even when the variables are highly related, however, we must exercise caution in interpreting causality. The two variables may not be causally related, or both may be influenced by a third variable. Even if they are causally related, the direction of causality may be unclear.

ANALOGUE STUDIES

As we have noted, ethical, moral, or legal standards may prevent researchers from devising certain studies on mental disorders or on the effect of treatment. In other situations, studying real-life situations is not feasible because researchers would have a difficult time controlling all the variables. In such cases, researchers may resort to an **analogue study**—an investigation that attempts to replicate or simulate, under controlled conditions, a situation that occurs in real life (Noble & McConkey, 1995). The advantage of this type of investigation is that it allows us to study phenomenon using experimental designs which are not possible with correlational studies. Here are some examples of analogue studies:

1. To study the possible effects of a new form of treatment on patients with anxiety disorders, the researcher may use students who have high test anxiety rather than patients with anxiety disorders.

2. To test the hypothesis that human depression is caused by continual encounters with events that one cannot control, the researcher exposes rats to uncontrollable aversive stimuli and examines the increase of depressivelike behaviors (such as lack of motivation, inability to learn, and general apathy) in these animals.

3. To test the hypothesis that sexual sadism is influenced by watching sexually violent films and television programs, an experimenter exposes normal subjects to either violent or nonviolent sexual programs. The subjects then complete a questionnaire assessing their attitudes and values toward women and their likelihood of engaging in violent behaviors with women.

Obviously, each example is only an approximation of real life. Students with high test anxiety may not be equivalent to individuals with anxiety disorders. Findings based on rats may not be applicable to human beings. And exposure to one violent sexual film and the use of a questionnaire may not be sufficient to allow a researcher to draw the conclusion that sexual sadism is caused by long-term exposure to such films. However, analogue studies give researchers insight into the processes that might be involved in abnormal behaviors and treatment.

Depression is often inversely related to activity level. The more depressed a person is, the less likely he or she is to engage in any activities, particularly physical ones. It is not surprising then that research continues to show that jogging or other aerobic activity helps to reduce depression.

FIELD STUDIES

In some cases, analogue studies would be too contrived to be accurate representations of the real-life situation. Investigators may then resort to the **field study,** in which behaviors and events are observed and recorded in their natural environment. The subjects of a field study are most often members of a given social unit—a group, an institution, or a community. However, the investigation may also be limited to a single individual; single-subject studies are discussed in the next section.

Field studies sometimes employ data collection techniques, such as questionnaires, interviews, and the analysis of existing records, but the primary technique is observation. The observers must be highly trained and have enough self-discipline to avoid disrupting or modifying the behavior processes they are observing and recording.

A field study may be used to examine mass behavior after events of major consequence, such as wars, floods, and earthquakes. It may also be applied to the study of personal crises, as in military combat, major surgery, terminal disease, or the loss of loved ones. An example of a field study is the recordings made by mental health personnel of the emotional reactions of people in the aftermath of an earthquake in Mexico. More than 50 percent of the victims displayed generalized anxiety, agitation, and trembling and had difficulty concentrating (De La Fuente, 1990).

Although field studies offer a more realistic investigative environment than other types of research, they suffer from certain limitations. First, as with other nonexperimental research, determining the direction of causality is difficult in field studies because the data are correlational. Second, so many variables are at work in real-life situations that it is impossible to control—and sometimes even distinguish—them all. As a result, they may contaminate the findings. Third, observers can never be absolutely sure that their presence did not influence the interactions they observed.

SINGLE-SUBJECT STUDIES

Most scientists advocate the study of large groups of people to uncover the basic principles governing behavior. This approach, called the *nomothetic orientation,* is concerned with formulating general laws or principles while deemphasizing individual variations or differences. Experiments and correlational studies are nomothetic. Other scientists advocate the in-depth study of one person. This approach, exemplified by the single-subject study, has been called the *idiographic orientation.* There has been much debate over which method is more fruitful in studying psychopathology.

Although the idiographic method has many limitations, especially its lack of generality, it has proved very valuable in applied clinical work. Furthermore, the argument over which method is more fruitful is not productive because both approaches are needed to study abnormal behavior. The nomothetic approach seems appropriate for laboratory scientists, whereas the idiographic approach seems appropriate

Parts of Florida were severely damaged by Hurricane Andrew in 1992. Such a disaster provides a unique opportunity for social scientists to use field study techniques to study the psychological and social effects that a major disaster can have on a population.

for their clinical counterparts, the psychotherapists, who daily face the pressures of treating disturbed individuals.

There are two types of single-subject studies: the case study and the single-subject experiment. Both techniques may be used to examine a rare or an unusual phenomenon, to demonstrate a novel diagnostic or treatment procedure, to test an assumption, to generate future hypotheses on which to base controlled research, and to collect comprehensive information for a better understanding of the individual. Only the single-subject experiment, however, can determine cause-effect relationships.

The Case Study

Physicians have used the case study extensively in describing and treating medical disease. In psychology, a **case study** is an intensive study of one individual that relies on clinical data, such as observations, psychological tests, and historical and biographical information. A case study thus lacks the control and objectivity of many other methods. It serves as the primary source of data where systematic experimental procedures are not feasible. It is especially valuable for studying rare or unusual phenomena. Hatcher (1989), for example, reported a case in which a fourteen-year-old boy would "scream with terror" when seeing a doll with mobile eyes or with the roots of the hair showing. The origin of such a specific fear can be investigated by examining historical data. Case studies can also be helpful in determining diagnosis, characteristics, course, and outcome of a disorder. (They cannot, however, be used to demonstrate cause-and-effect relationships.) An example of a case study follows:

> Mr. P., a 28-year-old medical student, presented for treatment with a several-year history of recurrent and intrusive thoughts about losing his hair. He stated that he had been concerned with his appearance for as long as he could remember and had never been happy with the way his hair looked. In college, as his hair began to thin he began to use treatments to thicken his hair. During this time, he became a marathon runner, stating that "even if his hair wasn't right, he could make his body perfect." He began to have trouble looking in the mirror or at pictures of himself because of his defect. He developed a ritual way of fondling his hair in a certain way to relieve his anxiety over hair loss. At the time he entered treatment, the thoughts and ritualistic behaviors were interfering with his ability to perform in school. (Brady, Austin & Lydiard, 1991, p. 538)

Case studies are useful in helping clinicians formulate hypotheses that can be tested later in research. The clinicians treating Mr. P., for example, had observed certain patterns among their clients with body dysmorphic disorder (exaggerated preoccupation with an imagined defect in a normal-appearing individual). All of these clients showed behaviors that were consistent with obsessive-compulsive disorder (intrusive and recurrent thoughts, ritualistic behaviors, or both). The clinicians hypothesized that body dysmorphic disorder and obsessive-compulsive disorder may stem from the same biological cause. They based this view on the findings that both disorders show the same pharmacological response to the same medication.

Other clinicians have also proposed hypotheses based on their work with clients. Goldman and Gutheil (1991) reported in the *American Journal of Psychiatry* that *bruxism* (clenching and grinding of teeth, especially during sleep) may be associated with sexual abuse. They base this preliminary observation on their work with five patients in whom this relationship was found. From their work with three patients, Coons and Bowman (1993) believe that psychiatric patients who are unable to lose weight from dieting may suffer from dissociation. (Remember that these are hypothesized relationships that have to be verified in more rigorous studies.)

The Single-Subject Experiment

The **single-subject experiment** differs from the case study in that the former is actually an experiment in which some aspect of the person's own behavior is used as a control or baseline for comparison with future behaviors. To determine the effectiveness of a treatment, for example, the experimenter begins by plotting a baseline to show the frequency of a behavior before intervention. Then the treatment is introduced and the person's behavior is observed. If the behavior changes, the treatment is withdrawn. If after the withdrawal of treatment the person's behavior again resembles that observed during the baseline condition, we can be fairly certain that the treatment was responsible for the behavior changes observed earlier. In the final step, the treatment is reinstated.

Kohler and his colleagues (1995) used this design to gauge success in a program to increase social interaction in a four-year-old boy with autism. Before participating in the program, the child, named Bert, rarely interacted with other children, and he behaved in bizarre and inappropriate ways, such as constantly repeating words and being preoccupied with objects. The progam paired three preschoolers—Bert and two socially competent peers who did not have autism—in regularly scheduled play sessions. The children had been taught to interact with one another by sharing, assisting, complimenting, and demonstrating affection.

In the initial sessions, the two peers showed appropriate social interactions, but—as you can see from

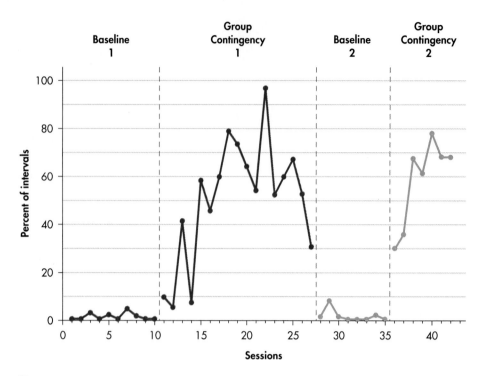

FIGURE 4.4 **A Single-Subject Experimental Design** Bert was rewarded for social interactions during Treatments 1 and 2 and not during Baselines 1 and 2. It was clearly demonstrated that social interactions are dependent on reinforcements.

Source: Adapted from Kohler et al., 1995.

Figure 4.4, Baseline 1—Bert was nonresponsive. To determinine whether a reward for social interactions would change Bert's behavior, the investigator began the Treatment 1 phase, in which rewards were given only when all members of the group interacted with one another. The interaction had to include a number of responses, such as complimenting one another, sharing, or making a request of another. During this phase, Bert's social interactions jumped to over 50 percent, as shown in Figure 4.4, Treatment 1.

To determine whether the group reward was responsible for this increase, the investigators initiated Baseline 2, in which they no longer rewarded social interactions. As you can see, Bert's level of social responding dropped dramatically. Rewards were reestablished in the Treatment 2 phase, and Bert again showed social interactions about 50 percent of the time. Because Bert's behavior varied according to the baseline or treatment conditions, we can be fairly certain that the rewards were the influencing variable.

Biological Research Strategies

More and more research is being performed in the biological area on the causes and treatment of mental disorders. Some of these research strategies are applicable to psychological research.

Genetic Linkage Studies **Genetic linkage studies** attempt to determine whether a disorder follows a genetic pattern. If a disorder is genetically linked, individuals closely related to the person with the disorder (who is called the *proband*) should be more likely to display that disorder or a related one. Genetic studies of psychiatric disorders often employ the following procedure (Alexander, Lerer & Baron, 1992):

1. The proband and his or her family members are identified.

2. The proband is asked for the psychiatric history of specific family members.

3. These members are contacted and given some type of assessment to determine if they have the same or a "related" disorder.

4. Assessment of the proband and family members may include psychological tests, brain scans, and neuropsychological examinations.

This research strategy depends on the accurate diagnosis of both the proband and the relatives. One complication is that the criteria for specific disorders have changed with each new edition of the *Diagnostic and Statistical Manual of Mental Disorders* (DSM). Are the findings based on the DSM-IV categories applicable to their counterparts in DSM-II, DSM-III, or DSM III-R? Kendler, Silberg, and colleagues (1991) have pointed out another possible source of error. In the family history interview method, the proband is asked if relatives also have the same disorder. Kendler and colleagues used this method in a study of female twin pairs who were discordant for major depression, generalized anxiety disorder, and alcoholism—that is, in each pair, one twin had the disorder, the other did not. When asked if her parents also had the disorder, the "sick" twin was more likely than the "well" twin to report that they did. As this study indicates, caution must be used in employing the family history method in genetic linkage studies. An individual's psychiatric status ("sick" or "well") may influence the accuracy of his or her assessment of the mental health of relatives. This bias in reporting may be reduced by using multiple informants or assessing the family members directly.

Biological Markers Genetic studies may attempt to identify **biological markers** (biological indicators of a disorder that may or may not be causal) for specific disorders. Indicators that have been noted in these studies include differences in variables such as cerebral blood-flow patterns, responses to specific medications, and brain structure differences. Some researchers believe that for schizophrenia, for example, differences in eye movement pursuit, attention and information-processing deficits, and reduced brain size are biological markers. Although some of these biological markers have been reported in close relatives of the patients, they have also been seen in populations that do not have the disorder. Several researchers concluded, "No definite 'biological marker' for schizophrenia or related spectrum conditions has been identified" (Szymanski, Kane & Lieberman, 1991, p. 106). They based their view on the criteria needed for a biological marker: (1) it is distributed differently in the patient group than in control populations; (2) it is stable over time; (3) it appears more frequently in relatives of the patients than in the general population; and (4) it is associated with and precedes the development of the disorder in high-risk children. Many psychologists hoped that biological markers could be included in DSM-IV's diagnostic criteria, but this has not been possible. Mass media constantly report that some biological marker has been found that either causes or is diagnostic of mental disorders. Unfortunately, most of these have not been supported with subsequent research.

Other Concepts in Biological Research **Iatrogenic** refers to the unintended effects of therapy—in psychology, a change in behavior resulting from a med-

ication prescribed or a psychological technique employed by the therapist. The therapist may not recognize the behavior change as a side effect of the medication or technique and may treat it as a separate disorder. For example, therapists have mistakenly diagnosed memory losses—which can be side effects from antidepressant medication—as Alzheimer's disease or other organic conditions (Heston & White, 1991).

Psychological interventions or techniques may also produce unexpected results. Researchers and therapists believe that some cases of multiple personality disorder may be inadvertently produced by hypnotism, the very method used to investigate it (Coons, 1988; Merskey, 1995; Ofshe, 1992). Hypnotism has been used to retrieve memories reported by the different personalities, and clinicians often believe that the information obtained in this manner is accurate. The Council on Scientific Affairs (1985), however, concluded the following in its investigation of hypnosis:

Here, a researcher studies genetic patterns in an attempt to determine which genes are responsible for specific forms of pathology.

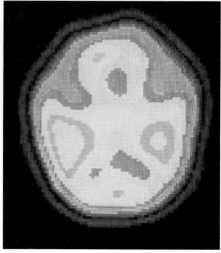

PET scans reveal the metabolism of different parts of the brain. Differences have been found between those with schizophrenia (photo on the left) and those without the disorder (photo on the right).

1. Traumatic memories retrieved may reflect an emotional reality rather than an accurate recollection.

2. Hypnosis produces a state in which an individual is more vulnerable to subtle cues and suggestions that often distort recollections.

3. Hypnosis increases both accurate and inaccurate information.

4. Without independent verification, neither the hypnotist nor the subject can distinguish between accurate and inaccurate information.

5. Hypnosis can "increase the subject's confidence in his memories without affecting accuracy and...increase errors while also falsely increasing confidence" (p. 1921).

6. In general, recollections obtained during nonhypnotic recall are more accurate than those obtained during hypnosis.

These conclusions indicate the need to question material obtained during a hypnotic state. Compare your

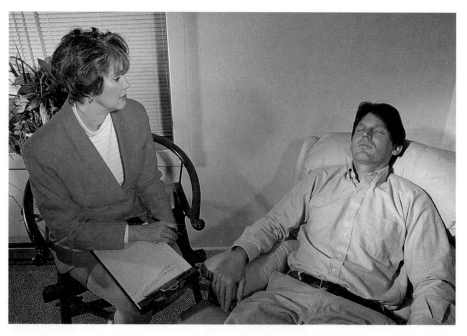

It was once thought that memories retrieved through hypnosis were accurate. We now know that they are often distorted. Without independent verification of memories recalled during hypnosis, we cannot rely on their veracity.

CRITICAL THINKING

Can Memories Be Recovered During Hypnosis?

Which of the following questions do you believe are accurate?

1. People cannot lie under hypnosis.

2. Psychotherapists have greater faith in the details of a traumatic event when they are obtained hypnotically.

3. If someone has memory of a trauma when under hypnosis, the memory must have actually occurred.

4. Hypnosis can be used to recover memories of actual events as far back as birth.

5. Hypnosis can be used to recover accurate memories of past lives.

Clinical practice and beliefs should be grounded in research. When Yapko (1994) surveyed over 860 therapists to determine the accuracy of their knowledge regarding hypnosis and memory, the following percentage of therapists agreed with the five questions:

Question	Percentage
1	15 percent
2	47 percent
3	31 percent
4	51 percent
5	28 percent

In reality, not one is supported by controlled research studies. Especially troublesome are the 51 percent who endorsed the belief that memories from as early as birth can be recovered and the 28 percent who believed that memories of past lives can be retrieved. As Elizabeth Loftus and her colleagues (1994) have observed, the misconceptions "persist in the face of no clear evidence…or overwhelming evidence to the contrary" (p. 178). The recollection of memories does not appear much earlier than about three years of age.

The conclusions on hypnosis published over ten years ago still hold: "Recollections obtained during hypnosis can involve confabulations and pseudomemories and not only fail to be more accurate, but actually appear to be less reliable than nonhypnotic recall" (Council on Scientific Affairs, 1985, p. 1918). In addition, this report noted that no controlled study supported the accuracy of recall in hypnotic age regression.

Assuming that the therapists in Yapko's survey had taken courses in abnormal psychology and had some knowledge of research, why do you think so many held mistaken beliefs? How could the courses be changed so that more critical thinking was stressed? How important do you think it is that therapists remain up to date with published research? Would individuals from fields other than therapy be less likely to endorse the misconceptions? Which of the above questions did you believe to be true? What did you base your belief on? Under what conditions would you give up this belief?

---

own ideas about hypnosis with the beliefs of therapists in the Critical Thinking feature.

Penetrance refers to the degree to which a genetic characteristic is manifested by individuals carrying a specific gene or genes associated with it. Complete penetrance occurs when a carrier always manifests the characteristic associated with the gene or genes. In mental disorders, incomplete penetrance is the rule. Even in cases of schizophrenia, only about half of the identical twins of the proband develop this disorder, even though their status as identical twins means that they carry the same genes.

Pathognomonic refers to a biological or psychological symptom or characteristic on which a diagnosis can be made. A great deal of research has been directed to discovering a symptom that is specifically distinctive of a disorder.

Biological challenge tests are often used to determine the effect of a substance on behavior. If we believe that a specific additive or food is responsible for hyperactivity in a child, we might observe the child's behavior when given food with the additive (the "challenge" phase) and the behavior when given food without the additive. If the additive and disruptive be-

Historical Research: Minorities and Pathology

When we study past "scientific" literature relating to people who are culturally different from the dominant social group, we are immediately impressed with how often minority groups and pathology are implicitly equated (Garretson, 1993; Sue & Sue, 1990). For example, the historical use of science in the investigation of racial differences seems to be linked with white supremacist notions.

Thomas and Sillen (1972) referred to this as "scientific racism" and cited several historical examples to support their contention:

1. In 1840, fabricated census figures were used to support the notion that black people living under "unnatural" conditions of freedom were prone to anxiety.
2. Mental health for blacks was taken to consist of contentment with subservience.
3. It was assumed that psychologically normal blacks were faithful to their "masters," and happy-go-lucky.
4. Influential medical journals presented as facts what were really fantasies supporting the belief that the anatomical, neurological, or endocrinological attributes of blacks were always inferior to those of whites.
5. A black person's brain was assumed to be smaller and less developed than that of a white person.

6. Blacks were thought to be less prone to mental illness "because their minds were so simple."
7. The dreams of blacks were judged juvenile in character and not as complex as those of whites.

Furthermore, the belief that various human groups exist at different stages of biological evolution was accepted by the respected psychologist G. Stanley Hall (1904). He explicitly stated that Africans, Indians, and Chinese were members of "adolescent races" and in a stage of incomplete development. In most studies, the evidence used to support such conclusions was fabricated, extremely

Historical researchers spend hours poring over original documents and records, systematically reconstructing some moment in the past in a detailed and accurate manner. Usually, the researcher is trying to prove some hypothesis, so any conclusions reached must be defensible.

havior are linked, the behavior should be present during the challenge phase and absent during the other phase.

We now examine the major techniques of clinical research. They vary in their adherence to the scientific method.

EPIDEMIOLOGICAL AND OTHER FORMS OF RESEARCH

In the field of abnormal and clinical psychology, investigators may employ experimental, correlational, case study, or field observation strategies in their research. The following strategies are important sources of information about disorders and their treatment.

Survey research Collecting data from all or part of a population to assess the relative prevalence, distribution, and interrelationships of naturally occurring phenomena.

Longitudinal research Observing and evaluating people's behaviors over a long period of time so

flimsy, or distorted to fit the belief in nonwhite inferiority (Thomas & Sillen, 1972). For example, Gossett (1963) reported how, when one particular study in 1895 revealed that the sensory perception of American Indians was superior to that of blacks, and that of blacks to that of whites, the results were used to support a belief in the mental superiority of whites. "Their reactions were slower because they belonged to a more deliberate and reflective race than did the members of the other two groups" (p. 364). The belief that blacks are "born athletes" (as opposed, for example, to being "born" scientists or heads of state) derives from this tradition. The fact that Hall was a well-respected psychologist, often referred to as "the father of child study," and was first president of the American Psychological Association did not prevent him from inheriting the racial biases of his times.

In psychological literature, the portrayal of the culturally different has generally taken the form of stereotyping them as "deficient" in certain "desirable" attributes. For example, de Gobineau's *Essay on the Inequality of the Human Races* (1915) and Darwin's *On the Origin of the Species by Means of Natural Selection* (1859) were used to support the genetic intellectual superiority of whites and the genetic inferiority of the "lower races." Galton (1869, p.14) wrote explicitly that African "Negroes" were "half-witted men" who made "childish, stupid and simpleton-like mistakes," and Jews were deemed inferior physically and mentally and fit only for a parasitical existence on other nations. Using the Binet scales in testing Spanish, Indian, Mexican American, and African American families, Terman (1916) concluded from the results that these people were uneducable.

That the genetic deficiency model still exists can be seen in the writings of Shuey (1966), Jensen (1969), Herrnstein and Murray (1994), and Shockley (1972). These writers adopted the position that genes play a predominant role in the determination of intelligence. While heredity plays a role in intelligence, the central issues are whether racial differences or IQ scores can be attributed to heredity and what policy implications are proposed. For example, Shockley (1972) expressed fears that the accumulation of genes for weak or low intelligence in the black population would seriously affect overall intelligence in the general population. Thus he advocated that people with low IQ scores should not be allowed to bear children and that they should be sterilized. Such ideas have generated considerable anger and controversy.

that the course of a disorder or the effects of some factor such as a prevention program can be assessed over time.

Historical research Reconstructing the past by reviewing and evaluating evidence available from historical documents. (See Focus On for a revealing look at some of this research.)

Twin studies Focusing on twins as a population of interest because twins are genetically similar. Twin studies are often used to evaluate the influence of heredity and environment.

Treatment outcome studies Evaluating the effectiveness of treatment in alleviating mental disorders. Outcome is concerned with answering the question of whether treatment is effective.

Treatment process studies Analyzing how therapist, client, or situational factors influence one another during the course of treatment. Process research focuses on how or why treatment is effective.

Program evaluation Analyzing the effectiveness of intervention or prevention programs.

The reliance on experimental, correlational, and single-subject methods varies with the research strategy. For instance, survey researchers often collect data and then correlate certain variables, such as social class and adjustment, to discover whether they are related. Researchers may also combine elements of different methods in their research. For example, an investigator conducting treatment outcome studies may use surveys and longitudinal studies.

Surveys are frequently used in **epidemiological research,** which examines the rate and distribution of mental disorders in a population. This important type of research is used to determine the extent of mental disturbance found in a targeted population and the factors influencing the rate of mental disturbance. Two terms, *prevalence* and *incidence,* are used to describe the rates. The *prevalence rate* tells us how many individuals in a targeted population have a particular disorder. This figure is determined for a specified time period. Determining the prevalence rate is

Research involving animals has yielded important information. The APA's 1992 ethical standards require that animals be treated "humanely" and that any procedure that subjects them to stress or pain be carefully evaluated.

vital for planning treatment services because mental health workers need to know the percentage of people who are likely to be afflicted with disorders.

The *incidence rate* tells us how many *new* cases of a disorder appear in an identified population within a specified time period. The incidence rate is likely to be lower than the prevalence rate because incidence involves only new cases, and prevalence includes new and existing cases during the specified time period. Incidence rates are important for examining hypotheses about the causes or origins of a disorder. For example, if we find that new cases of a disorder are more likely to appear in a population exposed to a particular stressor than in another population not exposed to the stressor, we can hypothesize that the stress causes the disorder. Epidemiological research, then, is important not only in describing the distribution of disorders but also in analyzing the possible factors that contribute to disorders. Focus On compares the prevalence rates of disorders in the United States and China and describes some problems that researchers must consider when conducting epidemiological studies.

ETHICAL ISSUES IN RESEARCH

Although research is primarily a scientific endeavor, it also raises ethical issues. Consider the following examples:

1. To study the effects of a new drug in treating schizophrenia, a researcher needs an experimental group that receives the drug treatment and a control group that receives no treatment. Is it ethical to withhold treatment from a control group of schizophrenics, who need treatment, to test the effectiveness of the drug?

2. To study the way depressed individuals respond to negative feedback, an investigator deceives depressed people into believing they performed poorly on a task. Is the deception ethical?

3. A researcher is interested in developing a new assessment tool to uncover personal conflicts. The assessment tool asks people to disclose information about their sexual conduct and private thoughts and feelings—information that may cause embarrassment and discomfort. Does the assessment measure invade the subjects' privacy?

4. A researcher hypothesizes that alcoholics cannot stop drinking after having one alcoholic drink. He arranges for alcoholic patients to have one drink and then examines how strongly they are motivated to receive additional drinks. Is it ethical and detrimental for alcoholics to be given alcohol as a part of an experiment?

5. An investigator believes that people who are exposed to inescapable stress are likely to develop feelings of helplessness and depression. Because the investigator does not want to subject human beings to inescapable stress, the experiment is conducted with dogs, which are given painful and inescapable electric shocks. Is it ethical to cause pain to animals as part of a study?

Are Americans More Prone to Mental Disturbance Than Chinese Are?

The prevalence rate of mental disorders in the mainland of China appears to be much lower than in the United States. A major epidemiological study of mental disorders in China was conducted with the assistance of U.S. investigators, including the director of mental health for the World Health Organization. The results revealed that the prevalence rate of most disorders was much lower in China than in the United States. For example, nearly 1 percent of the U.S. population was diagnosed as having schizophrenia (Myers et al., 1984), about twice the proportion in China. Americans were also far more likely than the Chinese to have other forms of mental disturbance. Do the findings mean that Americans are more disturbed?

Americans may in fact be more prone to mental illness, but an alternative explanation is that the different prevalence rates are the result of methodological and conceptual differences between the two studies that yielded the different results. Bromet (1984) suggested that two major sources of error—sample characteristics and case identification—must be controlled in epidemiological studies, especially in studies that include cross-cultural comparisons.

■ *Sample characteristics:* Rates could differ because samples from the two populations are not comparable. For example, the Chinese study included people fifteen years of age and older, while the U.S. sample targeted people aged eighteen and older. Social class and rural-urban differences were also apparent.

■ *Case identification:* Correctly identifying cases of a disorder is extremely difficult in cross-cultural or cross-national research. We do not know if the two studies employed the same procedures and assumptions, or if they used the same criteria to define whether a person had a particular mental disorder. Furthermore, respondents might have differed in their willingness to report or show symptoms of mental disorders. Some studies have shown that Chinese may not report psychological symptoms as readily as Americans do (Sue & Morishima, 1982). Even more problematic is the possibility that different cultures express the same mental disorders in different ways. For example, Chinese are more likely than Americans to show somatic complaints when they are depressed.

These factors are important to consider before the conclusion can be drawn that one population is more disturbed than another. Although it may be true that Chinese are less prone to mental disturbance, much more research needs to be conducted before this conclusion can be accepted.

These examples raise a number of ethical concerns about how research is conducted and whether it has, or should have, limits. How can the rights of human beings (or even of other animals) be protected without impeding valuable experimentation? There is no question that to understand psychopathology and to devise effective treatment and prevention interventions, experimenters occasionally may have to devise investigations that cause pain and involve deception. To study human behavior, pain may be inflicted (for example, surgical implants may cause pain, or shocks may be used to induce stress), and deception is sometimes necessary to conceal the true nature of a study. The research must be consistent with certain principles of conduct, however, and intended to protect participants as well as to enable researchers to contribute to the long-term welfare of human beings (and other animals).

The American Psychological Association (APA, 1992) has adopted the principle that the prospective scientific, applied, or educational value of the proposed research must outweigh the risk or discomfort to its subjects. APA guidelines set up to protect participants state that participants should be fully informed of the procedures and risks involved in the research and should give their consent to participate. Researchers may use deception only when alternative means are not possible, and they should provide participants with a sufficient explanation of the study as soon as possible. Participants should be free to with-

The prevalence and expression of psychopathology differ among ethnic groups. As a result, the American Psychological Association published guidelines in 1993 for working with culturally diverse populations.

draw from a study at any time. Furthermore, all participants must be treated with dignity, and research procedures must minimize pain, discomfort, embarrassment, and so on. If undesirable consequences to participants are found, the researcher has the responsibility to detect the extent of these consequences and to remedy them. Finally, unless otherwise agreed on in advance, information obtained from participants is confidential.

The American Psychological Association (1993) has also published guidelines for those working with culturally diverse populations. The guidelines indicate the need for researchers to (1) consider the impact of sociopolitical factors, (2) become aware of how their own cultural background might affect their perception, and (3) consider the validity of instruments used in research in a cross-cultural context.

SUMMARY

1. The scientific method provides for the systematic and controlled collection of data through controlled observation and for the testing of hypotheses. The characteristics of the scientific method include the potential for self-correction, the testing of hypotheses, the use of operational definitions, a consideration of reliability and validity, and an acknowledgment of base rates.

2. The experiment is the most powerful research tool we have for determining and testing cause-and-effect relationships. In its simplest form, an experiment involves an experimental hypothesis, an independent variable, and a dependent variable. The investigator manipulates the independent variable and measures the effect on the dependent variable. The experimental group is the group subjected to the independent variable. The control group is similar in every way to the experimental group except for the manipulation of the independent variable. Additional concerns include expectancy effects on the part of the participants and the investigator.

3. A correlation is a measure of the degree to which two variables are related. It is expressed as a correlation coefficient, a numerical value between -1 and $+1$, symbolized by r. Correlational techniques provide less precision, control, and generality than experiments, and they cannot be taken to imply cause-and-effect relationships.

4. In the study of abnormal behavior, an analogue study is used to create a situation as close to real life as possible. It permits the study of phenomena under controlled conditions when such study might otherwise be ethically, normally, legally, or practically impossible.

5. The field study relies primarily on naturalistic observations. In this technique, the psychologist enters a situation as unobtrusively as possible to observe and record behavior as it occurs naturally.

6. Rather than studying large groups of people, many scientists study one individual in depth. Two types of single-subject techniques are the case study and the single-subject experiment. The case study is

especially appropriate when a phenomenon is so rare that it is impractical to try to study more than one instance of it. Single-subject experiments differ from case studies in that they rely on experimental procedures; some aspect of the person's own behavior is taken as a control or baseline for comparison with future behaviors.

7. Biological research strategies have involved genetic linkage studies and have attempted to identify biological markers or indications of a disorder. Iatrogenic effects are side effects resulting from the activity of the therapist.

8. A particularly important type of research in abnormal psychology is epidemiological research, which examines the rate and distribution of mental disorders in a population. It can also provide insight into what groups are at risk for mental disturbance and what factors may influence disturbance.

9. The scientific method has weaknesses and limitations. Like other tools, it is subject to misuse and misunderstanding, both of which can give rise to moral and ethical concerns. Such concerns have led the American Psychological Association (APA) to develop guidelines for ethical conduct and to establish ways for dealing with violations within the mental health professions. The APA has also published guidelines for those working with culturally diverse populations.

KEY TERMS

analogue study An investigation that attempts to replicate or simulate, under controlled conditions, a situation that occurs in real life

base rate A phenomenon's natural occurrence in the population studied

biological markers Biological indicators of a disorder that may or may not be causal

case study Intensive study of one individual that relies on observation, psychological tests, and historical and biological data

correlation The extent to which variations in one variable are accompanied by increases or decreases in a second variable

dependent variable A variable that is expected to change when an independent variable is manipulated in a psychological experiment

epidemiological research The study of the rate and distribution of mental disorders in a population

experiment A technique of scientific inquiry in which a prediction—an experimental hypothesis—is made about two variables; the independent variable is then manipulated in a controlled situation, and changes in the dependent variable are measured

experimental hypothesis A prediction concerning how an independent variable affects a dependent variable in an experiment

field study An investigative technique in which behaviors and events are observed and recorded in their natural environment

genetic linkage studies Studies that attempt to determine whether a disorder follows a genetic pattern

hypothesis A conjectural statement, usually describing a relationship between two variables

iatrogenic Unintended effects of therapy; a change in behavior resulting from a medication prescribed or a psychological technique employed by the therapist

independent variable A variable or condition that an experimenter manipulates to determine its effect on a dependent variable

operational definitions Definitions of the variables under study

scientific method A method of inquiry that provides for the systematic collection of data through controlled observation and for the testing of hypotheses

single-subject experiment An experiment performed on a single individual in which some aspect of the person's own behavior is used as a control or baseline for comparison with future behaviors

theory A group of principles and hypotheses that together explain some aspect of a particular area of inquiry

CHAPTER 5

ANXIETY DISORDERS

The disorders discussed in this chapter are all characterized by **anxiety,** or feelings of fear and apprehension. These disorders can produce seemingly illogical—and often restrictive—patterns of behavior, as illustrated in the following examples:

> A woman reports, "All of a sudden, I felt a tremendous wave of fear for no reason at all. My heart was pounding, my chest hurt, and it was getting harder to breathe. I thought I was going to die." (National Institute of Mental Health, 1991, p. 1)

> A male college student displayed extreme nervousness and anxiety in social situations with females. He would cross the street to avoid having to interact with female classmates. Thoughts of asking them out produced such anxiety that he had only once tried to ask a woman for a date. (Author's file)

> The patient was a 35-year-old woman who experienced a panic attack while driving to her home in a suburb of Albany, New York, during the first cold and snowy night of winter. She reported that her heart suddenly began to beat wildly as she struggled to breathe. . . . She stopped her car in the middle of the road, got out, and started running down the highway. . . . She felt that she was going to die. (Ley, 1992, pp. 349–350)

> Jane was a twelve-year-old Caucasian girl who presented for treatment with a five-year history of severe obsessions and compulsions. Obsessions centered around fear of contamination, fear that harm would come to her family, and fear that saying certain words (such as *never* and *goodbye*) would make her family disappear. Compulsions included washing rituals, avoidance of contaminants, elaborate praying rituals, and saying goodbye with an invented word. In addition, Jane called her mother at work approximately six times a day to check on her safety. (Piacentini et al., 1994, p. 283)

Anxiety is a fundamental human emotion that was recognized as long as five thousand years ago. Everyone has experienced it, and we will continue to experience it throughout our lives. Many observers regard anxiety as a basic condition of modern existence. The British poet W. H. Auden called the twentieth century "the age of anxiety." Yet "reasonable doses" of anxiety act as a safeguard to keep us from ignoring danger, and anxiety appears to have an adaptive function. Something would be wrong if an individual did not feel some anxiety in facing day-to-day stressors. For example, many persons report anxiety in terms of overload at home, work, or school; family demands; financial concerns; and interpersonal conflicts (Bolger & Schilling, 1991). When facing these stressors, individuals without a disorder are likely to handle the situation by facing it. They use strategies such as relaxation and problem solving to reduce stress (Genest et al., 1990). For others, however, overwhelming anxiety can disrupt social or occupational functioning or produce significant distress, as illustrated in the following case.

> I've always been tense from as far back as I can remember. But lately it's getting worse. Sometimes I think I'm going crazy—especially at . . . night. I can't sleep for fear of what has to be done the next day. Should I go to my psych class tomorrow, or skip it and study for my stat exam? If I skip it, maybe the prof will throw a pop quiz. He's known for that, you know. These attacks are frightful. I had another one last week. It was horrible. I thought I would die. My roommate didn't know what to do. By the time it was over, my blouse was completely drenched. My roommate was so scared she called you. I was so embarrassed afterward. I think she [the roommate] wants to move out. I don't blame her. (Author's file)

The person describing herself here suffers from an **anxiety disorder,** which, according to the current definition, is a disorder that meets one of the following criteria:

■ The anxiety itself is the major disturbance.

■ The anxiety is manifested only in particular situations.

■ The anxiety results from an attempt to master other symptoms.

Anxiety disorders can be quite debilitating for some individuals and quite costly for society. They account for over one-third of the costs for mental disorders (Norton et al., 1995). Anxiety can be manifested in three ways.

1. *Cognitive manifestations* of anxiety take place in a person's thoughts. They may range from mild worry to panic. Severe forms can bring a conviction

of impending doom (the end of the world or death), a preoccupation with unknown dangers, or fears of losing control over bodily functions.

2. *Behavioral manifestations* of anxiety occur in a person's actions. They may take the form of avoiding anxiety-provoking situations. A student with an extreme fear of public speaking, for example, may avoid classes in which oral presentations are necessary. Individuals who experience extreme anxiety in public may stay at home rather than risk the possibility of experiencing an attack.

3. *Somatic manifestations* are changes in a person's physiological or biological reactions. They include shallow breathing, mouth dryness, cold hands and feet, diarrhea, frequent urination, fainting, heart palpitations, elevated blood pressure, increased perspiration, muscular tenseness (especially in the head, neck, shoulders, and chest), and indigestion.

The anxiety disorders do not involve a loss of contact with reality: People suffering from them can usually go about most of the day-to-day business of living. Although these people are aware of the illogical and self-defeating nature of some of their behaviors, they seem incapable of controlling them. In severe cases, the disturbed individuals may spend great amounts of time dealing with their debilitating

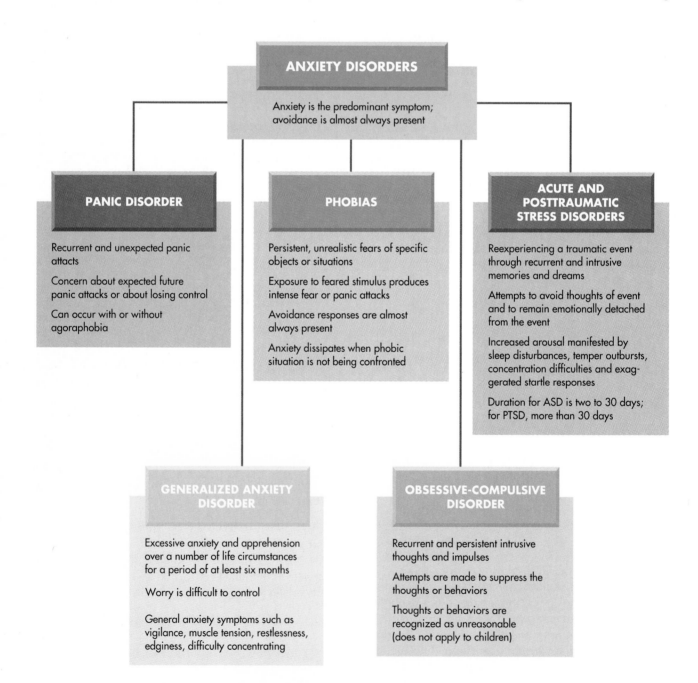

TABLE 5.1 Anxiety Disorders: Their Prevalence, Onset, and Course

Disorder	Lifetime Prevalence (%)		Age of Onset	Course
	Females	Males		
Panic Disorder	5	2.3	Late adolescence and mid-30s	Chronic; waxing and waning
Generalized Anxiety Disorder	6.6	3.6	Usually childhood or adolescence	Chronic; fluctuating; worsens during stress
Agoraphobia	7	3.5	20s to 40s	Chronic
Social Phobias	15.5	11.1	Midteens	Often continuous; may attenuate in adulthood
PTSD	1–14 (for both males and females) depending on stressor and population sampled		Any age	Variable; approximately half recover within 3 months
Specific Phobia	14.4	7.8	Childhood to mid-20s	Varied; often remits
Obsessive-Compulsive Disorder	2.8	2.4	Usually adolescence or early adulthood	Waxing and waning

Source: Based on data from American Psychiatric Association, 1994; Kessler et al., 1994; Regier et al., 1993; Robbins, Locke & Regier, 1991; Karno & Golding, 1991.

fears—but to no avail. This preoccupation may, in turn, lead to emotional stress and turmoil, maladaptive behaviors, and disruptions in interpersonal relationships.

In this chapter, we discuss five major groups of anxiety disorders—panic disorder, generalized anxiety disorder, phobias, obsessive-compulsive disorder, and acute and posttraumatic stress disorders. These are shown in the disorders chart on page 124. Table 5.1 compares the prevalence, onset, and course of some anxiety disorders.

In each of the anxiety disorders, the person can experience *panic attacks,* intense fear accompanied by symptoms such as a pounding heart, trembling, shortness of breath, or fear of losing control or dying. DSM-IV recognizes three types of panic attacks: (1) situationally bound—those that occur before or during exposure to the feared stimulus; (2) situationally predisposed—those that occur usually but not always in the presence of the feared stimulus; and (3) unexpected or uncued—those that occur "spontaneously" and without warning. Persons with obsessive-compulsive disorder and social and specific phobias generally report that their panic attacks are triggered by specific situations (situationally bound). An individual's panic when facing a feared situation—as occurs in types 1 and 2—is not considered unusual. What has

generated much controversy and research is the question of unexpected or "spontaneous" panic attacks. Why do some persons experience panic when no identifiable fearful stimulus is present? To gain insight into this question, we begin our discussion with a closer look at panic disorder. Individuals with panic disorder can have both unexpected and situation-specific panic attacks (Craske, Glover & DeCola, 1995).

PANIC DISORDER AND GENERALIZED ANXIETY DISORDER

The predominant characteristic of both panic disorder and generalized anxiety disorder is unfocused, or *free-floating,* anxiety. That is, the affected individual is fearful and apprehensive but often does not know exactly what he or she is afraid of. Patients suffering from panic disorder often have terrifying cognitions such as dying of suffocation or having some catastrophe befall a family member. Individuals with generalized anxiety disorder tend to have milder anxiety-evoking thoughts dealing with themes such as misfortune, financial concerns, academic and social performance, and rejection. This disorder can be characterized by "chronic pathological worry" (Starcevic, Fallon & Uhlenhuth, 1994).

Panic Disorder

Anxiety itself is the major disturbance in **panic disorder,** which is characterized by severe and frightening episodes of apprehension and feelings of impending doom. These episodes are often described as horrible and can last from a few minutes to several hours. The anxiety associated with panic disorder is much greater than that found in generalized anxiety disorder. According to DSM-IV, a diagnosis of panic disorder includes recurrent unexpected panic attacks and at least one month of apprehension over having another attack or worrying about the consequences of an attack. Individuals with panic disorder report intense panic attacks alternating with periods of somewhat low anxiety, during which they may be apprehensive about having another panic attack. One 25-year-old woman described her feelings this way: "It could not be worse if I were hanging by my fingertips from the wing of an airplane in flight. The feeling of impending doom was just as real and frightening" (Fishman & Sheehan, 1985, p. 26). The attacks are especially feared because they often occur unpredictably and without warning. "They would start just out of nowhere with this explosive anxiety or panic, fast heartbeat—just uncontrollable shaking and wanting to clutch up and not move" (Pasnau, 1984, p. 7).

During the attacks, people report a variety of physical symptoms, such as breathlessness, sweating, choking, nausea, and heart palpitations (Antony, Brown & Barlow, 1992). Some people also develop *agoraphobia,* or anxiety about leaving the home, which is caused by fear of having an attack in a public place. Such cases are diagnosed as panic disorder with agoraphobia. The following case seems typical:

> Lois R. was sixteen when she had her first panic attack. She felt as if she were going to die. "My heart was beating so fast that I thought I was having a heart attack, my mouth was very dry, I couldn't think."
>
> That was only the start. At school she began running to the nurse's office several times a week, in terror and asking for help. She lived in fear of attacks and of being where she could not cope with them. She stopped riding in elevators. She was afraid to go anywhere in a car. Open spaces seemed threatening, especially if she was alone.
>
> For the next thirty-nine years fear plagued her. It sometimes waned but never left. She saw many doctors: a family physician who thought she was having a nervous breakdown and tried to cure her by making her sleep for a week; a psychiatrist who prescribed Valium and other tranquilizers, plus sleeping pills, over a ten-year period; a psychologist who hypnotized her to return her to her childhood. "It was expensive," she says, "and it didn't help." (*Novato* [California] *Independent Journal,* July 6, 1984, p. C3)

Some factors seem to be associated with an increased risk of developing panic disorder. Many patients report a disturbed childhood environment that involved anxiety over separation from parents, family conflicts, or school problems (Laraia et al., 1994). Others indicate that they first experienced panic attacks after some form of separation, such as leaving home, or after the loss or threatened loss of a loved one (Raskin et al., 1982; Roy-Byrne, Geraci & Uhde, 1986; Wittchen et al., 1994). Exposure to stressors may also contribute. Individuals who report having panic attacks indicate that they faced more major life changes just before the attacks began (Pollard, Pollard & Corn, 1989).

The *lifetime prevalence rate* (in a sample, the proportion of individuals who have ever had the disorder) for panic disorder is approximately 3.8 percent (Katerndahl & Realini, 1993; Kessler et al., 1994). Women are two to three times more likely to be diagnosed with this disorder than are men. It is somewhat less prevalent a problem among Mexican Americans (Eaton, Dryman & Weissman, 1991). Future studies will probably report a higher prevalence of the disorder because the category of panic disorder has been expanded to encompass most cases of agoraphobia.

Although panic disorder is diagnosed only in a small percentage of individuals, panic attacks appear to be fairly common. Among college students, one-fourth to one-third reported having had a panic attack during a one-year period (Asmundson & Norton, 1993; Brown & Cash, 1990). Women are more likely to report panic symptoms. Nearly 45 percent of college coeds had one panic attack or more within the past year (Whittal, Suchday & Goetsch, 1994). Similarly, 43 percent of adolescents in one sample reported having had a panic attack (King et al., 1993). Most of these panic attacks are associated with an identifiable stimulus. However, more than 12 percent reported unexpected panic attacks (Telch, Lucas & Nelson, 1989). Although panic attacks appear common, few persons who have them will develop a panic disorder.

Generalized Anxiety Disorder

Generalized anxiety disorder (GAD) is characterized by persistent high levels of anxiety and excessive worry over many life circumstances. These concerns are accompanied by physiological responses such as heart palpitations, muscle tension, restlessness, trembling, sleep difficulties, poor concentration, and persistent apprehension and nervousness. Afflicted people are easily startled and are continually "on edge" (Starcevic, Fallon & Uhlenhuth, 1994). Because they are unable to discover the "real" source of their fears, they remain anxious and occasionally experience even more acute attacks of anxiety.

Such people often feel apprehension or worry over life situations (such as the ability to do well in a job or in school, acceptance by others, or worry over misfortune befalling someone loved). Individuals with GAD, in contrast with those with panic disorder, are as likely to worry over minor events as over major events. Their physiological reactions are also less extreme than those of people with panic disorder, but they tend to be more persistent (Gross & Eifert, 1990). Generalized anxiety disorder appears to be a cognitive problem involving worry or apprehension. As opposed to individuals without the disorder, those with GAD are more likely to engage in more thinking during relaxation and to engage in more negative thoughts during a period of induced worry (Pruzinsky & Borkovec, 1990), as in the following case:

> Joanne W. was known by her college friends as a worrier. She was apprehensive about anything and everything: failing in school, making friends, eating the right foods, maintaining her health, and being liked. Because of her concerns, Joanne was constantly tense. She often felt short of breath, which was accompanied by a fast heart rate and trembling. Joanne also had difficulty making decisions. Her insecurity was so great that even the most common decisions—what clothes to wear, what to order at a restaurant, which movies to see—became major problems. Every night Joanne reviewed and re-reviewed every real and imaginary mistake she had made during the day or might make in the future. This produced another problem, sleeplessness.

To meet DSM-IV's criteria for a diagnosis of generalized anxiety disorder, symptoms must be present for six months. The estimated lifetime prevalence of the disorder in the United States is 6.6 percent in females and 3.6 percent in males (Kessler et al., 1994). Risk factors that are significantly correlated with GAD are being older, separated, widowed, divorced, or unemployed (Wittchen et al., 1994).

Etiology of Panic Disorder and Generalized Anxiety Disorder

In our discussions of the causes and origins of mental disorders in this chapter and ensuing chapters, we must distinguish among the viewpoints that derive from the various models of psychopathology. Here we examine the etiology of unfocused anxiety disorders from the psychoanalytic, behavioral, and biological perspectives. Research has been directed toward explaining the reason for unexpected panic attacks.

Psychoanalytic Perspective The psychoanalytic view stresses the importance of internal conflicts (rather than external stimuli) in the origin of panic disorder and generalized anxiety disorder. Because the problem originates in sexual and aggressive impulses that are seeking expression, anxiety is always present. When a forbidden impulse threatens to disturb the ego's integrity, an intense anxiety reaction occurs. Because this conflict is unconscious, the individual does not know the source of the anxiety.

A person's defense against unfocused anxiety is generally considered poorly organized and less effective than defenses mounted against other anxiety disorders. In a phobia, for example, the conflict between id impulses and ego is displaced onto a specific external stimulus that can be controlled simply through avoidance. But the person with generalized anxiety disorder has only one defense—to try to repress the

The daily demands of each person's life can be very stressful. Juggling parenthood and career, as this woman is doing, caring for elderly parents, and dealing with financial concerns and relationships are just some of the areas that pull and tug at individuals, creating stress and, oftentimes, anxiety.

If what happened on your inside happened on your outside, would you still smoke?

JOIN THE GREAT AMERICAN SMOKEOUT.®

Evidence suggests that anxiety may serve an adaptive purpose and that moderate levels of fear about realistic threats may play a role in the development of coping behaviors. Functional fear appeals have been used in advertising campaigns to encourage people to use seat belts, to think about the effects of drinking and driving, and as shown in this photo, to stop smoking.

impulses. When that defense weakens, panic attacks may occur.

Cognitive Behavioral Perspective   Cognitive behavioral theorists emphasize that cognitions and conditioning are major factors in the development of anxiety disorders. Because an external source of anxiety often cannot be identified, it is possible that catastrophic thoughts and overattentiveness to internal bodily sensations may function as *internal triggers* for panic attacks (Belfer & Glass, 1992). Some theorists (Clark, 1986; Hibbert, 1984) believe that the cognitions and somatic symptoms can best be viewed as a positive feedback loop that results in increasingly

higher levels of anxiety. In other words, after an external or internal stressor, a person may become aware of a bodily sensation, such as a racing heart. Anxiety develops when the person interprets the sensation as a signal of a dreadful event. This belief then produces even greater physical reactions. Figure 5.1 illustrates this pattern. If the positive feedback loop continues, a panic attack may follow.

In one study supporting the positive feedback loop hypothesis, twenty-eight subjects with panic disorder and twenty healthy controls wore portable ECGs so that their heart rate during a 24-hour period could be recorded. Both groups noticed changes in cardiac activity. But after observing these changes, only the clients with panic disorder showed an acceleration of their heart rate and reported feelings of anxiety (Pauli et al., 1991). Although this study highlighted the importance of the perception of bodily sensations, some research has also suggested that panic attacks may begin with anxiety-provoking thoughts.

To support this hypothesized relationship between cognitions and anxiety, a researcher must be able, first, to find that thoughts precede or contribute to panic attacks and, second, to show that cognitions influence the severity of somatic symptoms. Some research supports the cognitive hypothesis. Cognitions preceding or accompanying panic attacks in patients have been reported by George and colleagues (1987) and by Rachman and colleagues (1988). The cognitions included thoughts of being "out of control," "passing out," or "acting foolish." These thoughts resulted in increased anxiety.

Cognitions or appraisal (interpretation) can have an influence on somatic symptoms. Significant increases in cardiovascular activity were found in a group of college students who were asked to focus on negative thoughts such as "My mind is racing" or "I'm so worried I can't concentrate on anything" or "It's frightening how tense I feel." In contrast, concentrating on neutral statements had little effect on somatic responses (York et al., 1987).

Although disturbing thoughts can increase cardiovascular activity, can they precipitate a panic attack? The answer is yes, at least some of the time. In one study, a 25-year-old woman with a nine-year history of panic attacks received two types of feedback, accurate and false. When she received accurate feedback of her resting heart rate, no changes were observed in her physiological functioning. Twenty seconds after the woman received inaccurate feedback showing that her heart rate had increased, however, her heart rate really did increase—to fifty beats per minute over baseline (see Figure 5.2). During this period, the patient reported that she was having a severe panic attack (Margraf, Ehlers & Roth, 1987). Similar results were found in another group of patients with panic

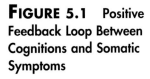

FIGURE 5.1 Positive Feedback Loop Between Cognitions and Somatic Symptoms

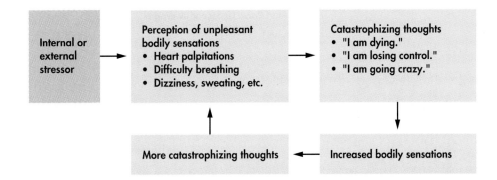

disorder. Of particular interest is the finding that feedback falsely suggesting arousal produced significantly greater increases in physiological measures in people who had histories of panic attacks than in people who lacked such a history (Ehlers et al., 1988).

The search for cognitive factors, although promising, leaves some questions unanswered. First, although most patients report that their panic attacks are accompanied by cognitions, a substantial percentage report they are not aware of any thoughts during these episodes (Rachman, Lopatka & Levitt, 1987). However, there is some evidence that catastrophic thoughts may occur so quickly and automatically that the individual is not consciously aware of them (Cloitre et al., 1994). Second, it is unclear why individuals with GAD and panic disorder are so prone to having thoughts of catastrophe. It must be remembered that the cognitive approach does not preclude the possible impact of biological factors in the cause of panic disorders.

Biogenic Perspective Biological factors associated with GAD have not been widely investigated. Panic disorder, however, has received much attention. Although the precise biologic mechanism triggering panic disorder has not been identified, several explanations have been offered. Papp and colleagues (1993) believe that people who experience panic have a specific biological dysfunction that predisposes them to this disorder. They hypothesize the dysfunction involves receptors that monitor the amount of oxygen in the blood. The receptors give the incorrect message that oxygen is insufficient, triggering fears of suffocation and resulting in hyperventilation. George and Ballenger (1992) hypothesized that panic disorders may be associated with a dysfunction of the *locus ceruleus*, which is part of the central anxiety system in the brain (see Figure 5.3). The increased sensitivity of the anxiety network can be activated by anything that increases anxiety, such as thoughts or anxiogenic agents like cocaine and caffeine.

The search for biological factors that may contribute to panic disorder has taken several forms. Two

of the most important are biological challenge tests and genetic studies. To determine if some people have a predisposition to panic attacks, researchers have designed *biological challenge tests*. In these tests, researchers administer a biological agent such as sodium lactate or carbon dioxide to people who have panic attacks and to others who do not have such attacks. The assumption is that a biological sensitivity

The Scream, by Edvard Munch, depicts some of the symptoms that accompany anxiety. The swirling colors of the background evoke a feeling of uncontrollable disorder that cannot be escaped. The subject, clutching his head, seems terrorized by something, which must be in his own mind, for the scene is otherwise peaceful.

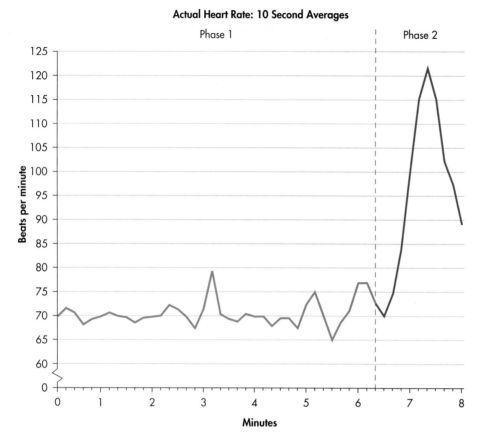

Actual Heart Rate: 10 Second Averages

FIGURE 5.2 **Actual Heart Rate of a Woman with Panic Disorder** During Phase 1, the client received accurate feedback on her heart rate. During Phase 2, after receiving inaccurate feedback that her heart rate increased, the woman's heart rate actually did increase, and at the seven-minute mark she reported having a panic attack.

Source: Adapted from Margraf, Ehlers & Roth, 1987.

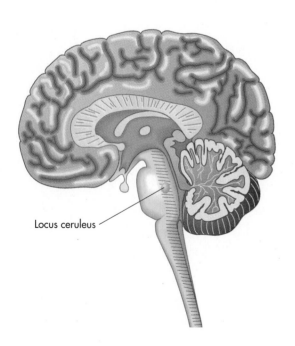

Locus ceruleus

to lactate or carbon dioxide produces feelings of alarm, and only people who are biologically susceptible should show panic symptoms. Most people with panic disorder do have a panic attack when given sodium lactate (Papp et al., 1993) or carbon dioxide (Carter et al., 1995). Antidepressants have been found to block both spontaneous and lactate-induced panic attacks (Aronson, 1987). Presumably, medication raises the threshold for attacks in individuals who are susceptible.

Although these results support a biological model, some findings are contradictory. For example, some "normal" subjects infused with sodium lactate also experience panic attacks (Balon et al., 1988). Individuals who have a panic attack after infusion of sodium lactate may no longer respond to the sodium

FIGURE 5.3 **Locus Ceruleus** Dysfunctions or oversensitivity of the locus ceruleus, a part of the brain involved in emotional reactions, may trigger panic attacks.

lactate after going through desensitization treatment (Guttmacher & Nelles, 1984) or cognitive-behavioral therapy (Shear et al., 1991). An individual's expectations may also affect the results of biological challenge tests. For example, instructions given before lactate infusion seem to influence the way participants respond to the substance. Those who expect pleasant sensations show less anxiety than those who expect unpleasant bodily sensations (Van Der Molen et al., 1986). Also, an individual's reactions can be influenced by the presence of another person with whom he or she feels safe. Panic disorder patients accompanied by a "safe" person reported fewer catastrophic thoughts and showed less physiological arousal when inhaling carbon dioxide than did those without a safe person present (Carter et al., 1995).

Thus psychological factors may influence panic attacks by changing the threshold for this response. Although the research seems to support a biological mechanism in panic disorder, cognitive factors can also influence the emotional and physiological reactivity (Rapee, 1995).

Genetic studies offer researchers another avenue in their search for a biological mechanism. Adoption studies have not been reported for anxiety disorders, so environmental influences cannot be eliminated. We must be careful in interpreting studies because the possible impact of modeling has not been eliminated. Nevertheless, several studies seem to support a genetic influence for panic disorder. Higher concordance rates (percentages of relatives sharing the same disorder) for panic disorder have been found for monozygotic (MZ) twins versus dizygotic (DZ) twins (Torgersen, 1983). A lifetime risk of 41 percent has been found in first-degree relatives (parents and siblings) of individuals with panic disorder (Crowe et al., 1983). In general, available data support a genetic predisposition for panic disorder.

Fewer genetic studies have been done on generalized anxiety disorder than on panic disorder. The strategy used to study GAD has been to examine the distribution of anxiety disorders among family members of people with the disorder and compare it with control group members. This strategy yields less support for the role of genetic factors in generalized anxiety disorder than in panic disorder (Crowe et al., 1983; Last et al., 1991; Torgersen, 1983).

Treatment of Panic Disorder and Generalized Anxiety Disorder

Treatments for panic disorder and GAD can generally be divided into two approaches: biochemical (via medication) and psychotherapeutic. The latter tend to take the form of behavioral approaches, including cognitive behavioral therapy.

Biochemical Treatment Both antidepressants and antianxiety medications have been used to treat panic disorder. Although there is considerable controversy about how antidepressants work against panic attacks, these drugs do seem to reduce not only depression but also extreme fears. Some success has been reported in treating panic disorder with a particular antidepressant, imipramine (Poling, Gadow & Cleary, 1991). Antidepressants may be successful because they make it easier for patients to confront fearful stimuli. Aronson (1987) concluded that imipramine only blocks panic attacks and that patients still must learn to overcome avoidance responses through exposure.

Other medications, such as alprazolam (Fyer et al., 1987) and verapamil (Klein & Uhde, 1988), have also been somewhat effective in treating panic disorder. That so many different medications have been used successfully raises questions about the specificity of the biological nature of panic disorder. It is possible that there are several different forms of the disorder,

The anxiety over having a panic attack in public can cause individuals to become prisoners in their own home.

which would help explain the success of so many different medications. In general, medications have been useful in treating anxiety disorders. However, in one large-scale study, only 24 percent of patients with panic disorder were panic-free one year after treatment with either imipramine or alprazolam (Katschnig & Amering, 1994). Relapse rates after cessation of drug therapy appear to be quite high.

Benzodiazepines (Valium and Librium) have been used to treat generalized anxiety disorder, but tolerance and dependence are a problem. Lindsay and associates (1987) compared the relative effectiveness of anxiety management training to treatment with benzodiazepines for a group of patients with GAD. At first, the benzodiazepines seemed more effective, but as the study progressed the anxiety management group began to show more improvement. In general, medication appears to help reduce anxiety in people who have GAD, but psychological intervention nevertheless seems to be necessary to reduce their avoidance responses.

Behavioral Treatment   Michelson and Marchione (1991) found higher success rates and lower relapse rates for behavioral approaches than for medications. Sometimes, clients who discontinued medication suffered rebound panic attacks that were worse than those they had originally experienced. A review of cognitive behavioral treatments for panic disorder found that 80 percent or more of clients achieved and maintained panic-free status. The reviewers (Margraf et al., 1993) concluded that "cognitive-behavioral treatments rest on firm experimental evidence that justifies their application in everyday practice" (p. 6). Another follow-up study of behavioral treatments involving exposure for panic disorder (Fava et al., 1995) found promising remission rates: 96 percent remained in remission for at least two years; 78 percent for at least five years; and 67 percent for at least seven years. It would appear that cognitive, exposure, and other behavioral approaches are effective treatments (Öst & Westling, 1995). How do clients feel about therapy that involves exposure to anxiety-provoking situations? Most rated it as not well-liked but very useful—a sort of "bitter medicine" (Cox, Fergus & Swinson, 1994). In general, this "medicine" for panic disorders comprised the following steps (Cox, Fergus & Swinson, 1994; Öst & Westling, 1995; Bourne, 1990):

1. Educating the client about panic disorder and symptoms.

2. Training the client in muscle-relaxation techniques.

3. Helping the client identify and change unrealistic thoughts—for example, the therapist might comment, "Maybe you are attributing danger to what is going on in your body," or "A panic attack will not stop your breathing."

4. Encouraging the client to face the symptoms, both within the session and in the outside world, using such statements as, "Allow your body to have its reactions and let the reactions pass."

5. Providing coping statements: "This feeling is not pleasant, but I can handle it."

6. Teaching the client to identify the antecedents of the panic: "What stresses are you under?"

7. Helping the client to learn to use coping strategies, such as relaxation and cognitive restructuring (interpreting events more positively), to handle stress.

Psychological treatment for generalized anxiety disorder is similar to that for panic disorder. Treatment that deals with the three response systems (cognitive, physiological, and behavioral) is more effective in treating GAD than therapy relying on only a single technique such as relaxation training. Butler and colleagues (1987) reported a highly effective treatment that includes identifying and altering anxiety-evoking thoughts, developing coping strategies, teaching relaxation training, and gradually exposing the client to anxiety-evoking situations. Highly significant changes were reported in anxiety, depression, and avoidance responses. In a study that compared behavior therapy (relaxation and graded exposure) and cognitive behavior therapy (identification and examination of unrealistic thoughts and behavioral assignments), the researchers (Butler et al., 1991) found that the latter was clearly superior. This makes sense if GAD is seen as primarily a cognitive disturbance.

PHOBIAS

The word *phobia* comes from the Greek word that means *fear*. A **phobia** is a strong, persistent, and unwarranted fear of some specific object or situation. An individual with a phobia often experiences extreme anxiety or panic attacks when he or she encounters the phobic stimulus (Craske, 1991). Attempts to avoid the object or situation notably interfere with the individual's life. Adults with this disorder realize that their fear is excessive, though children may not. Nearly anything can become the focus of this intense fear. In fact, there is even a fear of phobias, called *phobophobia* (see Table 5.2). Phobias are the most common mental disorder in the United States. DSM-IV includes three subcategories of pho-

TABLE 5.2 Phobias and Their Objects

Acrophobia: fear of heights	*Microphobia:* fear of germs
Agoraphobia: fear of open spaces	*Monophobia:* fear of being alone
Ailurophobia: fear of cats	*Mysophobia:* fear of contamination or germs
Algophobia: fear of pain	*Nyctophobia:* fear of the dark
Arachnophobia: fear of spiders	*Ochlophobia:* fear of crowds
Astrapophobia: fear of storms, thunder, and lightning	*Pathophobia:* fear of disease
Aviophobia: fear of airplanes	*Phobophobia:* fear of phobias
Brontophobia: fear of thunder	*Pyrophobia:* fear of fire
Claustrophobia: fear of closed spaces	*Syphilophobia:* fear of syphilis
Dementophobia: fear of insanity	*Topophobia:* fear of performing
Genitophobia: fear of genitals	*Xenophobia:* fear of strangers
Hematophobia: fear of blood	*Zoophobia:* fear of animals or some particular animal

bias: agoraphobia, the social phobias, and the specific phobias. Figure 5.4 illustrates ages at which different phobias typically begin.

Agoraphobia

Agoraphobia is an intense fear of being in public places where escape or help may not be readily available. It arises from a fear that panic-like symptoms will occur and incapacitate the person or cause him or her to behave in an embarrassing manner, such as fainting, losing control over bodily functions, or displaying excessive fear in public. Anxiety over showing these symptoms can prevent people from leaving their homes. If the individual has a history of unexpected panic attacks, a more appropriate diagnosis might be panic disorder with agoraphobia. Agoraphobia has a lifetime prevalence rate of approximately 3.5 percent

FIGURE 5.4 Phobia Onset This graph illustrates the average ages at which 370 patients said their phobias began. Animal phobias began during childhood, while the onset of agoraphobia did not occur until the individuals were in their late twenties.

Source: Data from Öst, 1987a.

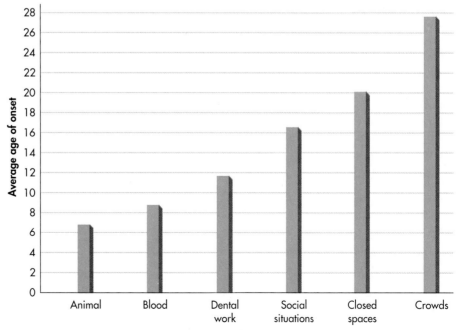

for males and 7 percent for females (Horwath, Johnson & Horning, 1993; Kessler et al., 1994). Although this is not the most common phobia, people who have this disorder account for the majority of phobics who are seen for treatment.

Many people report having panic attacks before developing agoraphobia, as illustrated in the following case:

> The patient was a 28 year-old woman whose attacks of anxiety were triggered by the terrifying sensation of impending death. This feeling was so horrifying that she would clutch passers-by and beg them for help. These episodes were acutely embarrassing to her, because no physical illness could be found. In an interview, it was discovered that her anxiety attacks occurred in situations where she felt trapped, such as in crowded restaurant. Finally, her fear of experiencing these symptoms in public reached the point where she was unwilling to leave her home unless accompanied by her husband.

A nationwide survey of more than nine hundred persons with agoraphobia revealed that nearly 75 percent of those surveyed could recall some event that had precipitated the disorder. In 38 percent of the persons, this event was a traumatic experience; in 23 percent, it was the death of a family member or friend; in 13 percent, it was a personal illness; in 8 percent, it was giving birth; and in 4 percent, it was marital difficulties. The situations most likely to produce attacks were being trapped, having to wait in line, being far away from home, and having domestic arguments. But most of those surveyed felt less anxious when they were accompanied by a spouse or friend or when they had easy access to an exit (Thorpe & Burns, 1983).

Interest in examining the role of cognitions in agoraphobia is increasing. Like depressed clients, people with panic disorders or agoraphobia display perception of personal helplessness (Ganellen, 1988). It is possible that agoraphobics misinterpret events or elevate them to catastrophes. In a study of sixty patients with agoraphobia, J. A. Franklin (1987) found the following pattern:

- Some physical or psychological stressor

- Altered physical sensations, such as increased heart rate and overbreathing

- Faulty appraisal, such as incorrectly interpreting the symptoms as representing a severe physical problem—a heart attack or loss of control

- Avoidance of the situation associated with the fear. Although the attacks were described as highly aversive, believing that they represented a pathological outcome intensified the fear. This led to avoidance.

Not everyone who experiences altered physical sensations develops anxiety attacks. Reiss and coworkers (1986) contended that people react differently to physical symptoms or sensations. They developed the Anxiety Sensitivity Inventory (ASI) to investigate this phenomenon. The ASI measures a person's reaction to anxiety symptoms. People who score high on the test agreed with such statements as "When I notice that my heart is beating rapidly, I worry that I might be having a heart attack." People with low anxiety sensitivity interpreted the sensation as only being unpleasant. Reiss and colleagues did find that agoraphobics scored higher on the ASI than did people with other anxiety disorders. Similar results were obtained by Asmundson and Norton (1993). It is too early to tell whether anxiety sensitivity or faulty appraisal act as predisposing factors in the development of panic disorders and agoraphobia, or whether both are the result of having the disorders. However, there is increasing support for the role of cognitions in the cause of anxiety disorders.

Social Phobias

A **social phobia** is an intense, excessive fear of being scrutinized in one or more social situations. An individual with a social phobia avoids or endures these situations, which often lead to intense anxiety reactions or panic attacks. The person's fear stems from anxiety that, when in the company of others, he or she will perform one or more activities in a way that is embarrassing or humiliating. There is no such fear when the person engages in any of these activities in private. The following case example describes a typical fear:

> Mr. B. was a 37-year-old divorced male who reported being unable to urinate in the presence of other people since the age of 12.... Mr. B. would typically avoid restrooms if they were occupied and... had waited 4 to 5 hours for privacy.... He reported feeling very anxious when he had to urinate in the presence of others. (McCracken & Larkin, 1991, p. 58)

Like other phobics, socially phobic people usually realize that their behavior and fears are irrational, but this understanding does not reduce the distress they feel. Individuals with high social anxiety tend to be biased in the direction of identifying other people's emotions toward them as negative (Winton, Clark & Edelmann, 1995). Social phobias can be divided into three types: (1) *performance* (excessive anxiety over activities such as playing a musical instrument, public speaking, eating in a restaurant, using public restrooms); (2) *limited interactional* (excessive fear only in specific social situations, such as going out on a date or interacting with an authority figure); and (3)

One type of social phobia is performance anxiety. Although the excessive nature of the anxiety is realized by the person, afflicted individuals are concerned that others will notice their nervousness or be critical of their performance.

generalized (extreme anxiety displayed in most social situations).

Although these distinctions are useful in conceptualizing differences in social phobias, the generalized type has come under much criticism. Several researchers (Herbert, Hope & Bellack, 1992; Turner, Beidel & Townsley, 1992) have reported a great overlap (100 percent in one study) between two diagnostic categories—generalized social phobia and avoidant personality disorder. Such an overlap between distinct categories raises questions about whether two separate disorders exist or whether they are variations of the same disorder. Anxiety in social situations is relatively common. How extreme does it have to be before it is considered a phobia? Focus On discusses this issue. The lifetime prevalence rate for social phobias is approximately 11.1 percent for males and 15.5 percent for females (Kessler et al., 1994). Social phobias tend to begin during adolescence, and they appear to be more common in families who use shame as a method of control and who stress the importance of the opinions of others (Bruch & Heimberg, 1994). These are common child-rearing practices in Asian families, and social evaluative fears tend to be more common in Chinese children and adolescents than in Western comparison groups (Dong, Yang & Ollendick, 1994).

Specific Phobias

A **specific phobia** is an extreme fear of a specific object (such as snakes) or situation (such as being in an enclosed place). Exposure to the stimulus nearly always produces intense anxiety or a panic attack. The specific phobias provide a catch-all category for irrational fears that are neither agoraphobia nor social phobias. The only similarity among the various specific phobias is the existence of an irrational fear. To produce some organizational framework, DSM-IV divides specific phobias into five types:

1. Animal

2. Natural environmental (such as earthquakes, thunder, water)

3. Blood/injections or injury; individuals with this type of phobia, as opposed to other phobias, are likely to have a history of fainting in the phobic situation (Öst, 1992)

4. Situational (includes fear of traveling in cars, planes, and elevators and fear of heights, tunnels, and bridges)

5. Other (phobic avoidance of situations that may lead to choking, vomiting, or contracting an illness)

The most common specific fears are of small animals, heights, the dark, and lightning; others involve death, exams, deep water, and being mentally ill (Kirkpatrick, 1984). Phobic reactions have also been described for organisms such as slugs, cockroaches, and worms (Davey, Forster & Mayhew, 1993). Unusual and uncommon specific phobias have focused on bath water running down the drain (after pulling out the plug, the affected person would dash out of the bathroom with great anxiety); snow (the

Anxiety and Fear: When Is a Fear a Phobia?

Social fears are common, especially in the areas of public speaking or musical performance (Cox & Kenardy, 1993). This apprehension is reflected in excessive self-consciousness and concern about what others think, along with such physiological reactions as increased pulse rate, blushing, and perspiration.

But when is a fear extreme enough to be considered a phobia? According to DSM-IV, only when three elements are present: (1) a persistent and irrational fear with a compelling desire to avoid the situation, (2) anxiety in the presence of the phobic stimulus, and (3) significant distress because the person recognizes that the fear is excessive.

Are these criteria fulfilled in the case of a student with public speaking anxiety who drops out of classes where oral participation is required, or in the case of a student with heterosexual anxiety who will not talk to people of the opposite gender even when he or she strongly wants to do so? The subjective nature of the DSM-IV criteria makes that question difficult to answer. Exactly how "compelling" must the desire to avoid the situation be? How much distress is "significant"? When does a "normal" fear become "irrational"?

---

fear developed after the man got stuck in a snowstorm and arrived too late to talk to his dying father); and three-legged stools (Adler et al., 1984). One boy who displayed a phobia of dolls reacted with greatest fear to plastic dolls with mobile eyes or dolls with the roots of their hair visible on the scalp (Hatcher, 1989).

The following is a report of a fairly common specific phobia:

> Ms. B, a 23-year-old woman, complained of a phobia of spiders that had not changed for as long as she could re-

The extreme fear of spiders is a specific phobia. An individual with this fear may believe that the spider is malevolent and has targeted him or her for attack.

member. She had no history of any other psychiatric symptoms. In treatment, when initially approached with a closed glass jar containing spiders, she breathed heavily, wept tears, and rated her subjective distress as 70 to 80. She suddenly began scratching the back of her hand, stating she felt as though spiders were crawling under her skin, although she knew this was not the case. The sensation lasted only a few seconds and did not recur. Her total treatment consisted of four 1-hour sessions distributed over the span of a month. At completion she had lost all fear of spiders and was able to let them crawl freely about her arms, legs, and face as well as inside her clothing with no distress whatever. She remained free of fear at one-year follow-up, expressing disbelief that she had allowed such a "silly fear" to dominate her life for so long. (Curtis, 1981, p. 1095)

Specific phobias are about twice as prevalent in women than in men (see Table 5.1, p. 125 and Critical Thinking) and are rarely incapacitating. The degree to which they interfere with daily life depends on how easy it is to avoid the feared object or situation. These phobias often begin during childhood. In a study of 370 patients with phobias (Öst, 1987a), retrospective data revealed that animal phobias tended to have the earliest onset age (seven years), followed by blood phobia (nine years), dental phobia (twelve years), and claustrophobia (twenty years).

Fears are common in children and involve themes such as injury and death, being in the dark, traffic accidents, not being able to breathe, and falling from high places (Ollendick & King, 1991). These fears

Over 25 million individuals fear flying. This photo shows an airplane captain talking to individuals as part of an anxiety reduction program. The participants are shown different parts of the airplane and learn to use relaxation to combat their fear during actual flights.

very seldom remain to become phobias; most are lost as the child gets older. Most children with phobias recover without treatment, although phobias that begin during later adolescence or adulthood tend to persist if they are not treated.

Etiology of Phobias

How do such strong and "irrational" fears develop? Both psychological and biological explanations have been proposed. In this section, we will examine the psychoanalytic, behavioral, and biogenic views of the etiology of phobias.

Psychoanalytic Perspective According to the psychoanalytic viewpoint, phobias are "expressions of wishes, fears and fantasies that are unacceptable to the patient" (Barber & Luborsky, 1991). These unconscious conflicts are displaced (or shifted) from their original internal source to an external object or situation. The phobia is less threatening to the person than is recognition of the underlying unconscious impulse. A fear of knives, for example, may represent castration fears produced by an unresolved Oedipus complex or aggressive conflicts. Agoraphobics may develop their fear of leaving home because they unconsciously fear that they may act out unacceptable sexual desires. The presence of a friend or spouse lowers anxiety because it provides some protection against the agoraphobic's impulses. In this sense, phobias represent a compromise between the ego and the impulses that seek gratification. The person blocks from consciousness the real source of anxiety and is

able to avoid the dangerous impulse that the phobia represents.

Psychoanalysts believe that the level of phobic fear shows the strength of the underlying conflict. This formulation, presented by Freud in 1909, was based on his analysis of a fear of horses displayed by a five-year-old boy named Hans (Freud, 1909/1959). Freud believed that the phobia represented a symptomatic or displaced fear arising from the Oedipus complex. The factors involved were the boy's incestuous attraction to his mother, hostility toward his father because of the father's sexual privileges, and castration fear (fear of retribution by his father). Freud became convinced that these elements were present in the phobic boy.

At the age of three, Hans had displayed an interest in his penis (which he called his "widdler"); he would examine both animate and inanimate objects for the presence of a penis. One day as he was fondling himself, his mother threatened to have a physician cut off his penis. "And then what will you widdle with?" (Freud 1909/1959, p. 151). Hans enjoyed having his mother bathe him and especially wanted her to touch his penis. Freud interpreted these events to suggest that Hans was aware of pleasurable sensations in his penis and that he knew it could be "cut off" if he did not behave. Wanting his mother to handle his genitals showed Hans's increasing sexual interest in her.

Hans's fear that horses would bite him developed after he saw a horse-drawn van overturn. According to Freud, little Hans's sexual jealousy of his father and the hostility it aroused produced anxiety. He believed that his father could retaliate by castrating him.

CRITICAL THINKING

Do Men Lie About Fear?

In general, men are thought to have fewer problems with specific fears and anxiety than women. The reason for this difference is not clear, but several explanations have been offered.

1. Women may be more predisposed to the development of fears because of genetic or sociocultural factors. If this is true, women may actually *show* more fears and phobias than men do.

2. Women may overreport and men may underreport specific fears. This explanation focuses on responding in a socially desirable manner. Women may be subject to less stigma for acknowledging their fears than men are.

3. Men may be less likely to have specific fears because those fears have been put through a process of extinction. This ex-

planation indicates that because men are more likely to be expected to face phobic items such as snakes and other animals, their fears become extinguished.

In a study titled "Do Men Lie on Fear Surveys?" Pierce and Kirkpatrick (1992) had thirty female and twenty-six male college students take a survey of specific fears (condition 1). One month later, the same students took a shorter survey that contained fourteen items from the first survey. During the short survey, the students were hooked up to a heart-rate sensor and told that it was often used in "a lie detector test" (condition 2). Under this condition, the male students rated the items of specific fears significantly higher than they did during the earlier session. Women showed no change of ratings from the first to

second session. Although the men acknowledged greater anxiety the second time around, they still showed significantly lower anxiety on the items than did the women.

Considering the results of this study, which of the three hypotheses do you believe has the greatest experimental support for the gender differences in ratings of specific fears? Is it possible that the men still underreport their fears in condition 2? How might you set up an experiment to test this possibility? If you believe gender roles influence reports of anxiety, which fears do you think should be the most exaggerated between men and women?

Women are overrepresented among the anxiety disorders with the exception of obsessive-compulsive disorder. Which hypothesis could account for this, and why is the gender difference not observed in obsessive-compulsive disorder?

This unconscious threat was so unbearable that the fear was displaced to the idea that horses "will bite me." Freud concluded that phobias were adaptive because they prevented the surfacing of traumatic unconscious conflicts.

Although Freud's formulation has clinical appeal, it has problems. According to the psychoanalytic perspective, if the phobia is only a symptom of an underlying unconscious conflict, treatment directed to that symptom—the feared object or situation—should be ineffective, leave the patient defenseless and subject to overwhelming anxiety, or lead to the development of a new symptom. But the evidence does not support the view that eliminating the symptom is ineffective.

Behavioral Perspective Behaviorists have examined three possible processes—classical conditioning, mod-

eling, and cognitive/negative information—in their attempt to explain the etiology of phobias. Different phobias seem to be the result of different processes.

Classical Conditioning Perspective The view that phobias are conditioned responses is based primarily on Watson's conditioning experiment with Little Albert. There is some evidence that emotional reactions can be conditioned. Before undergoing chemotherapy for breast cancer, women were given lemon-lime Kool-Aid in a container with a bright orange lid. After repeated pairings of the drink and the chemotherapy, the women indicated emotional distress and nausea when presented with the container (Jacobsen et al., 1995). Phobias related to driving have also developed in individuals involved in automobile accidents (Kuch et al., 1994).

"Glad to hear you have your fear of contracting infectious diseases under control."

More clients attributed their phobias to direct (classical) conditioning experiences than to any other factor (Öst, 1987a; Öst & Hugdahl, 1981; Rimm et al., 1977). Öst and Hugdahl (1981) found that people with agoraphobia were most likely to attribute their disorder to direct conditioning experiences, followed by those with claustrophobia and dental phobia.

In general, retrospective reports seem to indicate that conditioning experiences play a role in the development of phobias for most clients seeking therapy and that this process may be more important for some types of phobias than for others. However, a substantial percentage of surveyed patients report something other than a direct conditioning experience as the "key" to their phobias. Also, the classical conditioning perspective does not explain why only some people exposed to potential conditioning experiences actually develop phobias.

Observational Learning Perspective Emotional conditioning can be developed through observational learning, or modeling. An observer who watched while a model exhibited pain cues in response to an auditory stimulus (a buzzer) gradually developed an emotional reaction to the sound (Bandura & Rosenthal, 1966). The buzzer, formerly a neutral stimulus, became a conditioned stimulus for the observer. In a clinical (rather than an experimental) example involving modeling, several people who had seen the horror film *The Exorcist* had to be treated for a variety of anxiety reactions (Bozzuto, 1975). In another study, Ollendick and King (1991) found that only 36 percent of the children in the study reported a direct conditioning experience, whereas negative in-

formation accounted for 89 percent and modeling accounted for 56 percent (more than one source could be chosen) of the source of their fears. It appears that strong fears can be produced through exposure to informational sources such as parents or television programs. But it is not clear whether negative information is sufficient to produce a phobia.

The role of modeling may depend on the type of phobia. Among individuals with speech phobia, none attributed his or her fear to "observing others who are afraid of speaking" or "seeing someone else experience an extremely unpleasant event" (Hofmann, Ehlers & Roth, 1995). The data from these studies, however, are based on patients' recollections of past events, and such data are subject to a variety of errors. The observational learning perspective seems to share a problem with the classical conditioning approach: Neither, by itself, can explain why only some people develop phobias after exposure to a vicarious experience.

Cognitive-Behavioral Perspective Why do individuals with spider phobia react with such terror at the sight of a spider? Some researchers believe cognitive distortions and catastrophic thoughts may cause such strong fears to develop. For example, people with spider phobia believe that spiders single them out for attack and that they will move rapidly and aggressively toward them (Riskind, Moore & Bowley, 1995). Similarly, negative thoughts such as "I will be trapped," "I will suffocate," or "I will lose control" have been reported by individuals with claustrophobia. Removal of these thoughts was associated with dramatic decreases in their fear (Shafran, Booth &

Rachman, 1993). Individuals with high social anxiety tend to interpret other people's reactions more negatively than those without as much anxiety (Winton, Clark & Edelmann, 1995). Studies indicate that a person with a phobia is more likely to overestimate the odds of an unpleasant event occurring. Patients with acrophobia (fear of heights) overestimate not only the probability of falling but also the probability of being injured (Menzies & Clarke, 1995). These studies seem to indicate that cognitions involving catastrophic or distorted thinking are causal or contributing factors for phobias.

Operant Conditioning Perspective Some theorists have suggested that phobias may be learned through reinforcement (operant conditioning). For example, a child who is reinforced—perhaps by being held and comforted—after making statements about fears often increases such verbalizations of fears. Considering the aversive nature of phobias and the distress they produce, however, such reinforcement is not likely to be a major factor in their development.

Biogenic Perspective You may recall that genetic factors may be implicated in the development of a disorder if a higher-than-average prevalence of the disorder is found in close relatives, or if identical twins (who share the same genetic makeup) show a higher concordance rate for the disorder than that found among fraternal twins (who have different genetic makeups). Harris and her colleagues (1983) found that the prevalence of reported anxiety disorders for *first-degree relatives* (parents and siblings) of patients with agoraphobia was more than twice that for first-degree relatives of a control group (32 percent versus 15 percent). Last and colleagues (1991) reported similar results for the first-degree relatives of individuals with social phobia (8.7 percent versus 3.4 percent) and specific phobia (11.7 percent versus 4.3 percent). These findings can be interpreted as supporting the view that agoraphobia is a familial disorder, although an alternative explanation could point to modeling.

Evidence for the direct genetic transmission of specific anxiety disorders is not strong. In a study of the influence of heredity on agoraphobia, social phobia, and specific phobias in women, Kendler and associates (1992b) concluded that genetic influences are modest and that they vary among the subtypes of phobias. Specific phobias appear to be a result of a modest genetic vulnerability and conditioning experiences, whereas agoraphobia has a slightly stronger genetic influence and involves an exposure to negative environmental experiences.

More support exists for the view that constitutional or physiological factors may *predispose* indi-

viduals to develop fear reactions. It is possible that a certain level of autonomic nervous system (ANS) reactivity is inherited; people born with high ANS reactivity respond more strongly to stimuli, and their chances of developing an anxiety disorder are increased. In support of this possibility, researchers found that people who had high resting arousal levels showed easier conditioning to certain stimuli than did people with low resting arousal levels (Hugdahl, Frederickson & Ohman, 1977).

A different biological approach to the development of fear reactions is that of *preparedness* (Seligman, 1971). Proponents of this position argue that fears do not develop randomly. In particular, they believe that it is easier for human beings to learn fears to which we are physiologically predisposed. Such quickly aroused (or "prepared") fears may have been necessary to the survival of pretechnological humanity in the natural environment.

Several predictions can be made from the preparedness hypothesis:

1. Certain classes of stimuli (those dangerous to pretechnical humans, such as snakes and other animals) should be more easily conditioned.

2. Onset of phobias should be sudden rather than gradual because the organism is biologically prepared to respond to certain stimuli.

3. The phobia should be resistant to extinction.

One proponent of this view noted that it is rare to encounter phobias about automobiles or electrical appliances, presumably because pretechnical human beings did not have an innate phobic response to these items (McConaghy, 1983). Ohman and Soares (1993) believe that the conditioning for prepared fears occurs at the subcortical level and is therefore not under conscious control. DeSilva (1988) wanted to see whether the preparedness theory applied to non-Western populations. Records of eighty-eight patients with phobias treated in Sri Lanka were examined and rated in terms of "preparedness" (objects or situations dangerous to pretechnical humanity under most circumstances). Most of the phobias were rated as "prepared." In conflict with the preparedness theory, however, no association was found between the type of phobias and sudden or gradual onset. Matchett and Davey (1991) believe that Seligman's theory is incomplete and does not sufficiently explain phobias involving harmless animals such as cockroaches, maggots, and slugs. They believe that these fears are produced more by disgust and contamination concerns than by prepared fears of being physically harmed.

The combination of classical conditioning and prepared learning is a promising area for further research. But it is difficult to believe that many (or even most) phobias stem from prepared fears, simply because they just do not fit into that model. It would be difficult, for example, to explain the survival value of social phobias as the fear of using public restrooms and of eating in public, of agoraphobia, and of many specific phobias. In addition, prepared fears appear to have variable age of onset and are among the most easy to eliminate.

Treatment of Phobias

Specific and social phobias are treated primarily by behavioral methods, although anxiety-reducing drugs are sometimes prescribed. There have been some reports of the use of a beta blocker (Atenolol) for treatment of social phobias. This drug interferes with sympathetic nervous system functions and reduces heart rate, trembling, and other symptoms associated with anxiety. Atenolol was much less effective than exposure therapy in one study of people with social phobia (Turner, Beidel & Jacob, 1994). The disorder on which most treatment effort has been focused has been agoraphobia.

Biochemical Treatments　Several studies have shown that antidepressants such as imipramine and clomipramine help reduce not only depression but also the extreme fear displayed by those with agoraphobia (Gloger et al., 1989; Mavissakalian, Michelson & Dealy, 1983). But less positive results were reported when imipramine was compared with a placebo and exposure to the feared object; these researchers concluded that the effective component was exposure (Lelliott et al., 1987; Marks et al., 1983). Significant improvement was also found in twenty patients with agoraphobia who received a placebo rather than imipramine (Mavissakalian, 1987b).

Methodological flaws tend to hamper the evaluation of drugs in treating agoraphobia for three reasons. First, most studies rely only on self-reports as measures of success. Second, few studies employ control groups. And third, the treatment conditions often encourage patients to expose themselves to the fear-producing situation while they receive medication. Having patients confront fear-producing situations in an attempt to reduce this fear is a basic part of behavioral therapy. When biochemical treatment studies do not control for this effect, results are difficult to interpret.

One study was designed specifically to separate and compare the contributions of drugs and exposure in the treatment of agoraphobia. The patients were randomly assigned to treatment with imipramine alone, imipramine plus exposure, or placebo plus exposure. An important element in the study was control of the possible effects of exposure on the drug-only group: Patients in this group were told not to enter fear-arousing situations until the medication had a chance to build up (some six or eight weeks). Results were measured with self-reports and behavioral and physiological scales. Both exposure groups showed significant improvement according to all three measures. The imipramine-only patients showed no improvement on any of the measures, although they did show a significant reduction of depressed mood. Imipramine plus exposure showed a slight advantage over placebo plus exposure in reducing phobic anxiety (Telch, Tearnan & Taylor, 1983).

Behavioral Treatments　Individuals with agoraphobia who are treated with imipramine appear also to require behavioral treatment to reduce anxiety and avoidance of the feared situation. Because 60 to 70 percent of these patients can be treated successfully by exposure methods alone, medication is usually not a necessary part of treatment for this disorder (Mavissakalian, Michelson & Dealy, 1983).

The behavioral treatment of agoraphobia (and other phobias) has centered on **exposure therapy.** In this technique, the patient is gradually introduced to increasingly difficult encounters with the feared situation (Ghosh & Marks, 1987). Initially, the therapist may ask the patient only to visualize, or imagine the encounter. Then the person would be asked, for example, to take longer and longer walks outside the home with the therapist. After the fear has been reduced, the therapist conducts relapse training to help the patient anticipate possible setbacks and learn to deal with them.

Exposure, especially with appropriate modifications, has significantly reduced fears and panic attacks in people with agoraphobia, and it seems a viable treatment for this disorder. Follow-up studies at periods ranging from four to seven years after exposure treatment show little evidence of relapse (Marks, 1987). Though significant improvements occur, however, most patients retain mild to moderate symptoms (Michelson, Mavissakalian & Marchione, 1988).

To increase the effectiveness of behavioral treatment of agoraphobia, therapists increasingly emphasize multiple treatment methods, including cognitive therapy. Although exposure treatment has traditionally ignored the cognitive aspects of phobias, some studies show that cognitions and expectations are important in such treatment. Individuals with agoraphobia who were told that a treatment was effective were able to travel about twice as far from home as those who were told the procedure was merely for the purposes of assessment (Southworth & Kirsch, 1988).

Both groups had received ten in vivo exposure sessions. Thus expectancy may mediate or increase the effectiveness of exposure to feared situations.

Marchione and colleagues (1987) also contended that adding cognitive therapy to exposure therapy can increase the effectiveness of both types of therapy. They assigned patients with agoraphobia to (1) a gradual-exposure–only group or (2) a gradual-exposure-plus-cognitive-therapy group. Cognitive therapy included the monitoring and recording of automatic thoughts, understanding their relationship to phobic behavior, generating alternative rational responses, developing problem-solving skills, and learning relapse prevention. Both approaches were successful in treating agoraphobia, but including cognitive therapy increased the potency of the exposure treatment. More researchers are stressing the importance of assessing and directly altering different response systems to increase the effectiveness of treating agoraphobia.

The treatment of choice for the social and specific phobias is also behavioral, but a number of different behavioral techniques appear to be beneficial. One such technique is **systematic desensitization**—in which relaxation is used to eliminate the anxiety associated with phobias and other fear-evoking situations. Wolpe (1958, 1973), who introduced the treatment, taught patients a relaxation response that is incompatible with fear, and he repeatedly paired relaxation with visualizations of the feared stimulus. This procedure was adopted for Mr. B., who had a fear of urinating in restrooms when others were present. He was trained in muscle relaxation and, while relaxed, learned to urinate under the following conditions: no one in the bathroom, therapist in the stall, therapist washing hands, therapist at adjacent urinal, therapist waiting behind client. These conditions were arranged in ascending difficulty. The easier items were practiced first until anxiety was sufficiently reduced. Over a period of seventeen weeks, the anxiety diminished completely, and the gains were maintained in a 7.5-month follow-up (McCracken & Larkin, 1991). Systematic desensitization has been shown to be effective with both specific and social phobias (Hekmat, Lubitz & Deal, 1984).

Modeling therapy procedures have also been highly effective in treating certain phobias. When modeling is used as therapy, the person with the phobia observes a model in the act of coping with, or responding appropriately in, the fear-producing situation. Some researchers believe that modeling is a unique therapeutic approach in its own right, whereas others believe that it is a type of exposure treatment.

Exposure therapy has been used successfully to treat a variety of phobias such as fear of spiders (Muris, Merckelbach & de Jong, 1995), fear of heights (Marshall, 1988), claustrophobia (Booth & Rachman, 1992), and fear of flying (Walder et al., 1987). With these phobias, as with agoraphobia, gradual exposure appears to be more effective when combined with other techniques such as coping skills and anxiety management (Butler et al., 1984).

Other researchers are focusing on increasing assessing cognitions and using cognitive treatment strategies. Walder and colleagues (1987) found that people with dental phobias had anxiety-provoking thoughts, such as "The dentist is going to hit a nerve." These feelings of anxiety were related to thoughts of losing control. These researchers suggested that treatment procedures be developed to enhance control over both behavior and cognitions.

The behavioral approaches discussed here have all demonstrated reasonably good results in treating a variety of phobias. McCann, Woofolk, and Lehrer (1987) compared the effectiveness of systematic desensitization, behavioral rehearsal (exposure and practice), and cognitive restructuring (identifying anxiety-inducing thoughts and replacing them with positive coping statements) in treating individuals with severe interpersonal anxiety. All the treatments successfully reduced social fears. Although few differences appeared among the three treatment groups, cognitive restructuring had a more significant impact on the cognitive measures of anxiety, whereas behavioral rehearsal had greater impact on behavioral measures. The researchers believe the results are consistent with the three-part model of anxiety, in which there is some overlap but also some independence among the three dimensions (cognitive, behavioral, and biological). A multimodal treatment strategy seems the most effective (Mattick & Peters, 1988).

Although cognitive-behavioral approaches are effective in treating phobias, interpersonal factors such as positive regard are also important. In one study, persons with phobias received treatment involving both exposure and cognitive intervention. Everyone improved, but those who rated their therapist more favorably during the initial session reported more improvement. Bennun and Schindler (1988) believe that increased attention to interpersonal variables could improve the effectiveness of behavior therapy.

OBSESSIVE-COMPULSIVE DISORDER

Obsessive-compulsive disorder is characterized by **obsessions** (intrusive, repetitive thoughts or images that produce anxiety) or **compulsions** (the need to perform acts or to dwell on thoughts to reduce anxiety). Obsessions and compulsions may occur together. One woman, for example, had the obsession that she might have thrown away important pieces of paper. These thoughts produced great anxiety, which was

Modeling therapy has proven effective in treating both specific and social phobias. Watching a fear-producing act being performed successfully (like the man handling the snake) can help people overcome their own fear.

temporarily reduced when she repeatedly checked the contents of garbage cans and retrieved any paper she saw outside (Drummond & Mathews, 1988). The woman realized her concern was irrational but was unable to control the doubts or resist the compulsions.

The symptoms of obsessive-compulsive disorder are described as *ego-dystonic*—that is, the afflicted individual considers the thoughts and actions alien and not subject to his or her voluntary control. The inability to resist or rid oneself of uncontrollable, alien, and often unacceptable thoughts or to keep from performing ritualistic acts over and over again arouses intense anxiety. These thoughts and impulses are recognized as being unreasonable (this latter characteristic may not apply to children). Failure to engage in ritual acts often results in mounting anxiety and tension.

Some features of obsessive-compulsive disorder are obvious in the following case:

A 24-year-old single man felt compelled to ruminate practically all his waking hours. He had a seven-year history of obsessional ruminations, had been out of work for three years, and was living with his parents. Ruminations usually involved worrying in case he had made a mistake in the course of performing some quite trivial action. Anxiety and doubt would be evoked by mundane activities, such as turning a light switch, changing direction when walking, or going from one room to another. For example, when driving his car and taking a right turn at a traffic light, he would start thinking, "What would happen if I had turned left?" His ruminations would only come to an end once he had gone through all the possible alternative routes in his head. The degree of doubt felt by this patient was so strong

that at times, when switching on a light, he would not trust his perception, and wondering if he had made a mistake, he would attempt to trace the wiring behind the wall in order to try to follow where the current went back to the switch, thus convincing himself that the bulb was actually illuminated.... At the time of his admission to hospital, he was thinking of hypothetical solutions to hypothetical errors following almost every activity he did. (Robertson, Wendiggensen & Kaplan, 1983, p. 352)

Obsessive-compulsive disorder was once thought to be relatively rare. Individuals with the disorder, however, may now be more willing to be identified as having the problem. In an epidemiological study of obsessive-compulsive disorder, Karno and Golding (1991) reported that the lifetime prevalence rate for the disorder is between 2 and 3 percent. They found that the disorder is about equally common in males and females but is less common in African Americans and Mexican Americans. It is more common among the young and among individuals who are divorced, separated, or unemployed. Most have both obsessions and behavioral or mental compulsions (Foa & Kozak, 1995). See Figure 5.5 for some of the more common obsessions and compulsions.

Obsessions

As mentioned earlier, an obsession is an intrusive and repetitive anxiety-arousing thought or image. The person may realize that the thought is irrational, but he or she cannot keep it from arising over and over again. Among a sample of children and adolescents,

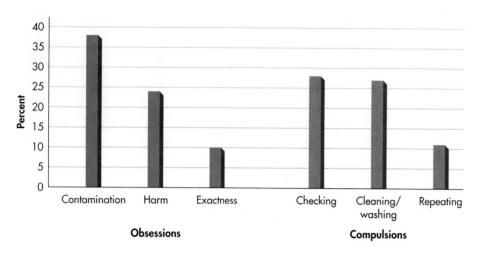

FIGURE 5.5 **Common Obsessions and Compulsions** About half of the patients reported both obsessions and compulsions. Twenty-five percent believed that their symptoms were reasonable.

Source: Data from Foa & Kozaky, 1995.

The individual who wrapped this chair had an obsessive fear of dust that reached psychotic proportions.

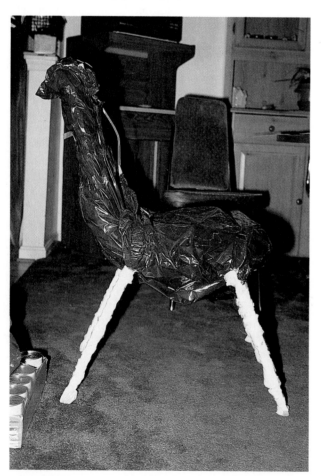

the most common obsessions involved dirt or germs, disease and death, or danger to self or loved ones (Swedo et al., 1989). Obsessions common to adults involve bodily wastes or secretions, dirt or germs, and environmental contamination (George et al., 1993).

Although most of us have experienced persistent thoughts—for instance, a song or tune that keeps running through one's mind—clinical forms are stronger and more intrusive. They create great distress or interfere with social or occupational activities. Many people who suffer from this disorder become partially incapacitated. Howard Hughes, a spectacularly successful businessman, pilot, and movie producer, withdrew so completely from the public eye that his only communication with the outside world was through telephones and intermediaries. His seclusiveness was connected to his obsessional fear of being contaminated by germs.

> He took to refusing to shake hands with people and covering his hands with the ubiquitous sheets of Kleenex when he had to hold a glass or open a door. He forbade aides to eat onions, garlic, Roquefort dressing or other "breath destroyers." He considered air conditioners deadly germ collectors; he is said to have taken to sitting naked in darkened, sweltering hotel rooms, surrounded by crinkled Kleenex and covered only with a few sheets over his privates. (*Newsweek*, April 19, 1976, p. 31)

Covering his hands with Kleenex as a defense against germs suggests that Hughes had also developed compulsions. In addition, he was preoccupied with the care of women's breasts. If women were passengers in his car, he would instruct his chauffeur to slow down when going over bumps in the road. Otherwise, he felt, the stress on the breasts would cause tissue breakdown and sagging; he was very concerned about preventing this.

Do "normal" people have intrusive, unacceptable thoughts and impulses? Several studies (Edwards & Dickerson, 1987; Freeston & Ladouceur, 1993; Salkovskis & Harrison, 1984; Sanavio, 1988) have found that more than 80 percent of normal samples report the existence of unpleasant intrusive thoughts and impulses. Apparently, a considerable majority of the "normal" population have obsessive symptoms. But are obsessions reported by patients different from those reported by normal individuals?

Rachman and DeSilva (1987) printed the obsessions of individuals with and without obsessive-compulsive disorder on cards, mixed them up, and gave them to six expert judges to re-sort into normal and clinical obsessional thoughts. On the whole, the judges were not very accurate in identifying the clinical obsessions. They were somewhat more successful in identifying "normal" obsessions or impulses (such as the impulse to buy unwanted things). Obsessions reported by obsessive-compulsive patients and by normal populations overlap considerably. But Rachman and DeSilva did find some differences. Obsessive patients reported that their obsessions lasted longer, were more intense, produced more discomfort, and were more difficult to dismiss. The mere existence of obsessive-compulsive symptoms may not be very meaningful for diagnostic purposes because these symptoms are also reported in the general population.

Compulsions

A compulsion is the need to perform acts or to dwell on thoughts to reduce anxiety. Distress or anxiety occurs if the behavior is not performed or if it is not done "correctly." Compulsions are often, but not always, associated with obsessions. Mild forms include behaviors such as refusing to walk under a ladder or step on cracks in sidewalks, throwing salt over one's shoulder, and knocking on wood. The three most common compulsions among a sample of children and adolescents involved excessive or ritualized washing, repeating rituals (such as going in and out of a door, and getting up and down from a chair), and checking behaviors (doors and appliances). Changes in patterns or type of compulsion were common (Swedo et al., 1989).

In the severe compulsive state, the behaviors become stereotyped and rigid; if they are not performed in a certain manner or a specific number of times, the compulsive individual is flooded with anxiety. To the person performing them, these compulsive behaviors often seem to have magical qualities, as though their correct performance wards off danger. The following case, treated by one of the authors, is fairly typical:

> A fifteen-year-old boy had a two-year history of compulsive behaviors involving sixteen repetitions of the following behaviors: opening and closing a door, touching glasses before drinking from them, walking around each tree in front of his house before going to school. These compulsive acts produced much discomfort in the boy. His schoolmates ridiculed him, and his parents were upset because his rituals prevented him from reaching school at the appropriate time. An interview with the boy revealed that his compulsive behaviors were associated with the onset of masturbation, an act that the boy considered "dirty," although he was unable to refrain from it. It was when he began to masturbate that the first of his compulsive behaviors (touching a glass sixteen times before drinking from it) developed.

Table 5.3 contains additional examples of obsessions and compulsions.

Etiology of Obsessive-Compulsive Disorder

The causes of obsessive-compulsive disorder remain speculative, although increased attention has recently been paid to biogenic explanations. We'll examine the cause of this disorder from the perspectives of the psychoanalytic, behavioral, and biogenic models.

Psychoanalytic Perspective Freud (1949) believed that obsessions represent the substitution or replacement of an original conflict (usually sexual in nature) with an associated idea that is less threatening. He found support for his notion in the case histories of some of his patients. One patient, a girl, had disturbing obsessions about stealing or counterfeiting money; these thoughts were absurd and untrue. During analysis, Freud discovered that these obsessions reflected anxiety that stemmed from guilt about masturbation. When the patient was kept under constant observation, which prevented her from masturbating, the obsessional thoughts (or perhaps, the reports of the thoughts) ceased.

The dynamics of obsession have been described as involving "the intrusion of the unwelcome thought [that] 'seeks' to prevent anxiety by serving as a more tolerable substitute for a subjectively less welcome thought or impulse" (Laughlin, 1967, p. 311). Freud's patient found thoughts involving stealing less disturbing than masturbation. Her displacement of that feeling to a *substitute* action prevented her ego defenses from being overwhelmed.

TABLE 5.3 Clinical Examples of Obsessions and Compulsions

Patient		Duration of Obsession in Years	Content of Obsession
Age	Gender		
21	M	6	Teeth are decaying, particles between teeth
42	M	16	Women's buttocks, own eye movements
55	F	35	Fetuses lying in the street, killing babies, people buried alive
24	M	16	Worry about whether he has touched vomit
21	F	9	Strangling people
52	F	18	Contracting venereal disease

Patient		Duration of Compulsion in Years	Compulsive Rituals
Age	Gender		
47	F	23	Handwashing and housecleaning; contact with dirt, toilet, or floor triggers about 100 handwashings per day
20	F	13	Severe checking ritual; checks 160 times to see if window is closed; also compelled to read the license numbers of cars and the numbers on manhole covers
21	M	2	Intense fear of contamination after touching library books, money; washes hands 25 times a day and ruminates about how people have handled the objects before him
7	M	4	Walking only on the edges of floor tiles
9	M	4	Going back and forth through doorways 500 times

Source: Based on data from Boersma et al., 1976; Rachman, Marks & Hodgson, 1973; Roper, Rachman & Marks, 1975; Shahar & Marks, 1980; Stern, Lipsedge & Marks, 1973; and Swedo et al., 1989.

Several other psychoanalytic defense mechanisms are considered prominent in obsessive-compulsive behaviors. For example, *undoing* is canceling or atoning for forbidden impulses by engaging in repetitive, ritualistic activities. Washing one's hands may symbolically represent cleansing oneself of unconscious wishes. Because the original conflict remains, however, one is compelled to perform the act of atonement over and over again. *Reaction formation* provides a degree of comfort because it counterbalances forbidden desires with diametrically opposed behaviors. To negate problems stemming from the anal psychosexual stage (characteristic of obsessive-compulsives) such as the impulse to be messy, patients tend toward excessive cleanliness and orderliness.

Obsessive-compulsives may also employ the defense of *isolation*, which allows the separation of a thought or action from its effect. Aloofness, intellectualization, and detachment reduce the anxiety produced by patently aggressive or sexual thoughts.

Behavioral Perspective Proponents of the behavioral perspective maintain that obsessive-compulsive behaviors develop because they reduce anxiety. A distracting thought or action recurs more often if it reduces anxiety. For example, many college students may develop mild forms of compulsive behavior during intense exam periods, such as final examinations. During this stressful and anxiety-filled time, students may find themselves engaging in escape activities such as daydreaming, straightening up their rooms, or eating five or more times a day, all of which serve to shield them from thoughts of the upcoming tests. If the stress lasts a long time, a compulsive behavior may develop.

Although the *anxiety-reduction hypothesis* is popular among learning theorists, it has not been very helpful in explaining how a behavior, such as handwashing that goes on for hours, can originate. Maher (1966) suggested that a compulsion is acquired through operant conditioning. For example, a person who has developed a compulsion for handwashing might have been reinforced in the past by parents for cleanliness, and therefore he or she considers handwashing desirable. When a transgression occurs, performing a socially learned anxiety-reducing response reduces the transgressor's feeling of guilt. Because this response is reinforcing, the person uses it whenever he or she feels anxiety or another negative emotion. Unfortunately, this formulation does not explain why some adults display anxiety-reducing behaviors and others do not. Neither does it explain why some people with compulsions perform acts that certainly were not endorsed or socially reinforced by parents or others—for example, walking around every tree in the back yard before performing a task.

Researchers have sought support for the anxiety-reduction hypothesis with a specific sample of patients: obsessive washers and checkers. If the hypothesis is correct, touching a contaminated item should increase anxiety, and performing the compulsive act should reduce anxiety (Carr, 1974; Hodgson & Rachman, 1972; Roper & Rachman, 1976). Carr found that compulsive acts were performed when there were high levels of autonomic activity and that the performance of these acts reduced the person's arousal levels to those of a resting state.

Sometimes, it does appear that the compulsive acts may continue because they reduce anxiety. However, the anxiety-reduction hypothesis does not explain how these behaviors originate. In addition, many obsessional ruminations involve disease, insanity, mutilation, or death—events that one would expect to elevate anxiety. Yet we can only speculate about the reinforcements associated with them.

Biogenic Perspective   Biological explanations of obsessive-compulsive behaviors are based on data relating to brain structure, genetic studies, and biochemical abnormalities. Positron emission tomography (PET) has enabled us to observe metabolic reactions in the brain. These reactions have been found to differ among people with obsessive-compulsive disorder, severe depression, and control groups with no evidence of psychiatric disorders. Obsessive-compulsives

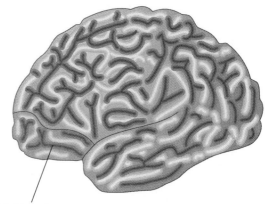

Orbital frontal cortex

FIGURE 5.6   Orbital Frontal Cortex   Untreated patients with obsessive compulsive disorder show a high metabolism rate in this area of the brain. This rate is reduced to "normal" levels by certain medications, which also produce a reduction in obsessive-compulsive symptoms.

show increased metabolic activity in the frontal lobe of the left hemisphere. Perhaps this area of the brain, the orbital frontal cortex, is associated with obsessive-compulsive behaviors (Rauch et al., 1994) (see Figure 5.6). Heightened glucose metabolism in the frontal lobes has also been found in individuals with obsessive-compulsive disorder. Of special interest is the fact that when these individuals were given fluoxetine, the cerebral blood flow to the frontal lobes was decreased to values found in individuals without the disorder and there was a reported reduction in symptoms (Hoehn-Saric et al., 1991). PET scans offer therapists a fascinating opportunity to observe metabolic differences and changes in the brain in response to therapy, which could lead to a new way of evaluating the effectiveness of therapies. It is not clear, however, whether metabolic changes reflect the cause of obsessive-compulsive disorder, its effects, or some combination of the two.

The search for the cause of obsessive-compulsive disorder has led two prominent researchers, Steketee and White (1990), to examine its relationship to the neurotransmitter serotonin. Medications such as clomipramine and fluoxetine increase the amount of available serotonin in the brain, and these medications have been effective in treating some individuals with obsessive-compulsive disorder. As a result, researchers have hypothesized that the disorder is the result of a serotonin deficiency (Jenike et al., 1989; Perse et al., 1987; Tollefson et al., 1994). Drugs that have less effect on raising serotonin availability have been less effective in treating this disorder. Although most studies of medication have methodological flaws—including reliance on clinical reports, small sample size, failure to include control and placebo groups, and differences in dosage levels—a small body of methodologically sound literature supports the hypothesis that serotonin is involved in obsessive-compulsive disorder.

Some researchers (Comings & Comings, 1987) believe that some obsessive-compulsive behaviors are caused by genetic factors. Family and twin studies offer some support for this theory. First-degree relatives of individuals with obsessive-compulsive disorder are more likely to have an anxiety disorder than are first-degree relatives of psychiatrically normal controls (Black et al., 1992). In a carefully controlled study, McKeon and Murray (1987) found that the relatives of people with obsessive-compulsive disorder were twice as likely to have an anxiety or emotional disorder than were relatives of the matched control group. However, both groups had a similar number of relatives with obsessive-compulsive disorder. These studies seem to suggest that "over-reactive tendency" or vulnerability to developing an anxiety disorder may be inherited and that the actual development of an obsessive-compulsive disorder may depend on life events or personality factors.

Treatment of Obsessive-Compulsive Disorder

The primary modes of treatment for obsessive-compulsive disorder are either biological or behavioral in nature. Behavioral therapies have been used successfully for many years, but treatment with medication has recently enjoyed increased attention.

Biological Treatments   Because obsessive-compulsive disorder is classified as an anxiety disorder, minor tranquilizers might be thought helpful. However, these drugs have not proven capable of decreasing to any extent the frequency of patients' obsessive thoughts or compulsive rituals.

Antidepressant drugs have also been tried with mixed results. A review of nineteen studies led to the conclusion that antidepressants were a beneficial part of the treatment for obsessive-compulsive disorder if the patient showed signs of depression. In these cases, the drugs not only alleviated depression but also decreased ritualistic behavior (Marks, 1983). As mentioned earlier, fluoxetine and clomipramine, which increase the serotonin level in the brain, have been reported to successfully treat patients with obsessive-compulsive disorder (Jenike et al., 1989; Tollefson et al., 1994). However, only 60 to 80 percent of persons with obsessive-compulsive disorder respond to these medications, and often the relief is only partial (Pigott

& Murphy, 1991). Many clients also report adverse side reactions to medications and drop out of treatment (Clomipramine Collaborative Study Group, 1991). In addition, there is a rapid return of symptoms and relapse occurs within months of stopping the medication (Stanley & Turner, 1995).

Behavioral Treatments   The treatment of choice for obsessive-compulsive disorder is the combination of flooding and response prevention. The results of this two-stage approach have been consistently impressive, and fewer therapy sessions are typically required than in systematic desensitization (Calamari et al., 1994; Steketee & White, 1990). **Flooding** is a technique that involves continued actual or imagined exposure to a highly fear-arousing situation. In the flooding segment of treatment, clients are repeatedly exposed to the anxiety-producing stimulus; in the response-prevention stage, they are prevented from performing rituals.

As an example, consider a man who fears that he will develop a fatal infection from contact with germs. In the flooding stage, this patient would be exposed to something he perceives as containing deadly germs—perhaps dirt, a newspaper, or leftover food. He would be required initially to touch the items and, later, to smear them over his body. Once he was properly "contaminated," the response-prevention stage would begin and the client would not be allowed to cleanse himself by engaging in his compulsive ritual, repeated handwashing. Instead, he would be required to remain "contaminated" until his anxiety had been extinguished. Flooding is used to extinguish anxiety as a response to the conditioned stimulus, and response prevention further extinguishes anxiety and helps eliminate the avoidance behavior (the ritual).

Follow-up studies that range from one to six years indicate that from 55 to 79 percent of individuals treated with behavior therapy maintain their improvement. Some, however, required additional treatments during the follow-up period (Stanley & Turner, 1995).

A promising approach is cognitive therapy that attempts to identify and modify clients' irrational thoughts. This technique may be as effective as exposure alone in reducing symptoms of the disorder (Emmelkamp & Beens, 1991; Van Oppen et al., 1995). Some therapists report success in combining cognitive strategies with exposure and response prevention, as in the following case.

A 24-year-old woman reported having intrusive thoughts of stabbing her mother and sister with a large knife. She was very fearful that she would harm them. These thoughts had first occurred at the age of 16 after she read a murder mystery. Later, she also had obses-

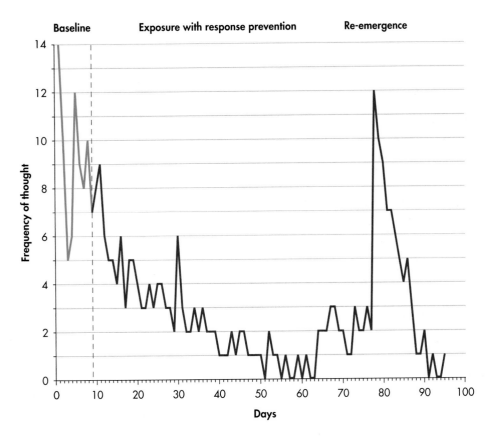

FIGURE 5.7   Frequency of Intrusive Eye-Gouging Thought   One patient's obsessive thought of gouging out her own eyes declined during cognitive therapy. One relapse occurred when she viewed another individual's reaction to a blood test, but the patient was able to recover from that situation when cognitive training focused on perceived loss of control.

Source: O'Kearney, 1993, p. 360.

sions about gouging out her own eyes, thrusting her face into an operating fan, and driving her car off a bridge. (O'Kearney, 1993)

To eliminate the obsessive-compulsive disorder, the woman's therapist employed both exposure with response-prevention and cognitive therapy. The woman monitored the frequency of her obsessive thoughts, recorded them on tape, and listened to them at home. She also identified illogical and catastrophizing thoughts and generated new and more realistic thoughts. These approaches were successful in reducing the obsessive thoughts. She had one relapse when she observed a woman patient reacting hysterically to a blood test; during this relapse, thoughts of gouging out her own eyes returned. (Figure 5.7 shows the changes in the frequency of her obsessional thoughts.) This was successfully treated when therapy focused on the theme of loss of control. The addition of cognitive strategies to combined exposure and response

prevention may be more effective than either treatment alone.

ACUTE AND POSTTRAUMATIC STRESS DISORDERS

Acute and posttraumatic stress disorders are anxiety disorders that develop in response to an extreme psychological or physical trauma. **Acute stress disorder** results from exposure to a traumatic stressor that results in dissociation, reliving the experience, and attempts to avoid reminders of the event; this disorder lasts for more than two and less than thirty days and occurs within four weeks of exposure to the stressor. **Posttraumatic stress disorder (PTSD)** lasts for more than thirty days, develops in response to a specific extreme stressor, and is characterized by intrusive memories of the traumatic event, emotional withdrawal,

Refugees escaping from combat situations often suffer from acute stress or posttraumatic stress disorder. Here Muslim refugees are forced to live in a makeshift camp in Bosnia.

and heightened autonomic arousal. The events that trigger these disorders may involve a threat to one's life or to a spouse or family member. Examples include combat experiences (King et al., 1995; Orr et al., 1995); being abducted and threatened (Saigh, 1987); automobile accidents (Blanchard et al., 1995); natural disasters (Joseph et al., 1993); rape and incest (Kilpatrick, Veronen & Best, 1985); concentration camp experiences (Kinzie et al., 1984); refugee status (Hauff & Vaglum, 1994); child abuse (Eth & Pynoos, 1985); and the battered woman syndrome (Astin et al., 1995; Walker, 1991). These and similar events produce feelings of terror and helplessness. (See the First Person narrative for an account of PTSD.)

Since acute stress disorder is new to DSM-IV, little has been written about it. We therefore limit our discussion to posttraumatic stress disorder. The following case illustrates the features and origin of PTSD.

Ms. A. is a 36-year-old woman who was admitted to the hospital for depression, suicidal ideation, anxiety attacks, dissociative episodes, hypervigilance, intrusive thoughts, and nightmares. These symptoms began after an experience seventeen years before admission, when she was picked up hitchhiking by a group of motorcyclists. For three days she was tortured, raped, beaten, burned, and threatened with sudden death by, for instance, Russian roulette. When she came home, she withdrew to her room, depressed and numbed, for 6 months. . . . Shortly thereafter, she began to reexperience the traumatic events through daytime flashbacks and nightmares. (Hudson et al., 1991, p. 572)

Diagnosis of Posttraumatic Stress Disorder

Experiencing a specific extreme stressor is an essential criterion for the diagnosis of posttraumatic stress disorder. Not everyone who is exposed to an extreme stressor develops PTSD, however.

DSM-IV Criteria As noted earlier, the following additional symptoms are necessary for the diagnosis. Let's examine them in more detail.

1. *Reexperiencing the event in dreams or intrusive memories* For Ms. A., these symptoms were displayed in flashbacks and nightmares of the event: "Different scenes came back, replays of exactly what happened, only the time is drawn out. . . . It seems to take forever for the gun to reach my head" (Hudson et al., 1991, p. 572). One veteran with PTSD reported continued disturbing thoughts of a Viet Cong soldier whom he had taken prisoner. Later, he saw the prisoner pushed out of a helicopter in flight. Because Mr. B. had captured the prisoner, he felt responsible for the death (Hendin et al., 1981) and continued to reex-

perience this episode. Many rape victims report intrusive memories of the attack (Kilpatrick et al., 1985).

2. *Emotional numbing, or avoiding stimuli associated with the trauma* As a defense against intrusive thoughts, people may withdraw emotionally and may avoid anything that might remind them of the events. Ms. A. reported emotional numbing and dissociative episodes. Concentration camp survivors who developed posttraumatic stress disorder often displayed emotional numbness and avoided talking about their experiences in the camp. One man said flatly, "What is there to say? There was just killing and death" (Kinzie et al., 1984, p. 646). Avoidance is only partially successful, however. Certain stimuli, such as the sound or sight of helicopters for combat veterans, can bring back the intrusive memories (Mooney, 1988).

3. *Heightened autonomic arousal* This reaction can include symptoms such as sleep disturbance, hypervigilance, and loss of control over aggression. Ms. A. reported anxiety attacks and difficulty falling asleep or staying awake. Combat veterans with PTSD show an exaggerated startle response (Orr et al., 1995).

The Therapist's Subjective Judgment Although posttraumatic stress disorder clearly exists, many questions regarding its diagnosis, etiology, and treatment remain unanswered. In diagnosing the disorder, the therapist's subjective judgment still plays a big role. For example, what constitutes a "psychologically traumatic event"? Although examples are given in DSM-IV, it is not clear what specific situations can produce the disorder. Defining the criterion stressor is of vital importance in the diagnosis of PTSD because it acts as a gatekeeper. Unless a specific stressor occurs, the diagnosis is not given, regardless of other symptoms that may be present, such as reliving the experience, emotional numbing, and emotional reactivity.

Certainly the magnitude of the stressor may be very important in the development of PTSD. In a study of Cambodian refugees living in the United States for four to six years who had experienced multiple stressors such as the death of family members, torture, extreme fear, and deprivation during their escape, 86 percent met the criteria for PTSD (Carlson & Rosser-Hogan, 1991). Rape is also clearly a traumatic event. Immediately after a sexual assault, 94 percent of the victims met the criteria for acute stress disorder and, after three months, 47 percent of the sample met the criteria for PTSD (Rothbaum et al., 1990). This supports the contention that some extreme stressors may produce PTSD in almost every-

one (Carlson & Rosser-Hogan, 1991). (See Figure 5.8 for PTSD associated with specific stressors.)

Davidson and Foa (1991) raised additional questions about the criterion stressor. Whether a stressor is regarded as outside the range of normal human experience or "exceptional" may differ from person to person. In certain urban areas, killings and physical assaults may occur so frequently that they may not be considered exceptional. There is also evidence that PTSD symptoms can develop in individuals faced with repeated subtraumatic stressors, such as employment problems or marital distress (Astin et al., 1995; Scott & Stradling, 1994). If such cases fulfill all the criteria for PTSD with the exception of a specific traumatic stressor, how should they be diagnosed? More work needs to be done to define more clearly the nature of a traumatic stressor in PTSD and to determine its necessity in the diagnosis of the disorder.

Posttraumatic stress disorder is not isolated to combat situations. Women who have been battered or have suffered sexual assaults often report high rates of acute stress or posttraumatic disorder. Here, two women living in a shelter for battered women share their experiences in a counseling session.

FIRST PERSON

Beverly A. Brauer

When thinking of posttraumatic stress disorder, one generally does not first consider women. Yet, while studying anxiety disorders during my graduate program, it slowly occurred to me that I had experienced my own posttraumatic stress reaction. I had been a young, inexperienced army nurse when I went to Vietnam in August 1972. I did not experience a combat situation, yet the tension of being in a war zone and the uncertainty of what could and did happen around me (the beating of a corpsman within sight of the hospital compound, the windows being blown out of the hospital by the shelling of nearby headquarters, treatment of the sick and of those injured by the war) had a major impact. These experiences helped me understand that women are also damaged by the threat and the reality of violence. Although women may experience violence in a military setting as I did, violence most frequently takes place in the woman's own home.

When I first started working with battered women, I found it striking to see the psychological similarities between veterans and these women. The tension of never knowing when the abuse will occur, of being fearful for one's own life, and of feeling responsible for every situation with no escape, is very similar to a war situation. There is no sense of safety anywhere—especially not at home.

For example, Sally (not her real name), one of the women I worked with, came to the shelter in shock and with nothing but the clothes she was wearing. When Sally married, she had considered her husband a caring, loving man. She was shocked when he began to abuse her after several years of marriage. She kept hoping things would get better, but her situation was bleak. She lived in another state, isolated from her family. Her

FIGURE 5.8   Percentage of Individuals Diagnosed with PTSD Extreme stressors may produce posttraumatic stress disorder in almost anyone. For example, 80 percent of sexual assault victims were diagnosed with PTSD symptoms in one study.

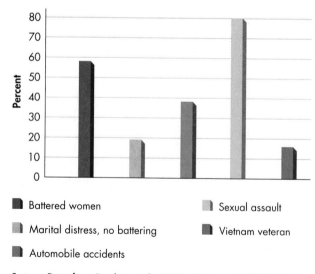

■ Battered women
■ Marital distress, no battering
■ Automobile accidents
□ Sexual assault
■ Vietnam veteran

Source: Data from Breslau et al., 1991; Astin et al., 1995; King et al., 1995.

The Individual's Perception of the Event   Little is also said about the individual's subjective perception of the event. The degree of trauma often depends on the way the individual views the event (King et al., 1995). There is little emphasis on individual differences in reaction to extreme stressors in DSM-IV. More than a decade ago, Figley (1985) posed the following questions, which still have to be answered for PTSD:

■ When people are exposed to a psychologically traumatic event, which ones will develop posttraumatic stress disorder?

■ Is this condition lifelong or curable?

■ Among those who develop PTSD, how many will show the reaction immediately and how many after a period of time?

■ Can we determine who has PTSD and who is malingering?

Breslau and associates (1991) studied PTSD in a random sample of 1,007 young adults living in Detroit, Michigan. They were specifically interested in the percentage of individuals exposed to extreme stressors, using the DSM-III-R definitions. In this

husband tolerated no social contacts and she would be beaten if he even thought she had talked to the neighbors. He demanded that she account for every minute of her commuting time to and from work. If she was late, she'd be beaten and tyrannized with a derogatory, demeaning lecture on her worthlessness.

Sally lived in constant terror that she would be killed if she made any efforts to leave. When her husband physically threatened her young son, she borrowed money to escape while her husband was not at home. She was able to utilize the support of the shelter to establish a safe home away from her abusive spouse.

When her basic needs (food, clothing, an apartment, and a job to support her son and herself) were met, Sally began to show increased symptoms of her PTSD.

She felt very guilty at leaving her husband, yet highly fearful and anxious that he might find and hurt her, as he had threatened to do. She was hypervigilant to any stimulus that reminded her of the abuse, and she experienced recurrent, intrusive dreams. Sally isolated herself in her home and had little interest in normal family or social activities. She became more depressed and suicidal. Sally tried to ignore the past and minimize the effect her abusive marriage had on her.

In her individual therapy with me, Sally learned to tolerate addressing her memories, anger, feelings of helplessness, and fear. Sally worked cognitively to improve her self-esteem and to recognize options open to her (that is, that she was no longer trapped). She began to work on developing a network of support. Sally continues to

work on building her self-esteem and confidence in her ability to make choices that will protect herself and her son.

As with all trauma survivors, Sally will have the memories—the "scars"—to live with the rest of her life. I find it very rewarding to work with these women to witness their courage to face their fears and to make a future for themselves despite the traumas they have experienced. It's a constant reminder for me of the human spirit's ability to survive in the face of adversity.

Beverly A. Brauer is a psychiatric nurse in group practice in Aurora, Colorado. She does pro-bono work at the Safehouse for Battered Women, Inc., in Denver, Colorado.

---

sample, the lifetime prevalence rate was 39.1 percent for exposure to one or more of the following stressors: sudden injury or serious accident, physical assault, seeing someone seriously hurt or killed, news of sudden death or injury of close relative or friend, narrow escape, threat to one's life, rape, robbery, childhood physical or sexual abuse, and natural disaster. Of the individuals exposed to one of these conditions, 23.6 percent met the criteria for PTSD, showing a lifetime prevalence rate of 9.2 percent for the disorder.

Breslau and his colleagues also found that women were more likely than men to suffer from PTSD, even though men were more likely to be exposed to traumatic situations. Most women, like most men, did not develop PTSD after experiencing a trauma. The one exception was rape, in which 80 percent of the women developed PTSD. In an attempt to find differences between those who did or did not develop PTSD after being exposed to a stressor, the researchers compared the two groups. Of those who developed PTSD, 75.3 percent either had a preexisting anxiety disorder or a family history of anxiety symptoms. Among the unaffected, only 50 percent had the preexisting disorder or family history of symptoms.

Interestingly, the researchers found only one case of delayed-onset PTSD, so it may not be as common as many have thought.

Etiology and Treatment of Posttraumatic Stress Disorder

Because a traumatic event precipitates the disorder, several researchers (Keane et al., 1985; Kilpatrick et al., 1985; Kolb, 1987) believe that classical conditioning is involved. People who have PTSD often show reactions to stimuli present at the time of the trauma (darkness, time of day, smell of diesel fuel, propeller noises, and so on). According to this perspective, the reason extinction does not occur is that the individual avoids thinking about the situation. As we indicated in our discussion of phobias, however, the classical conditioning model falls short of a full explanation. Not everyone who is exposed to a traumatic event develops acute or posttraumatic stress disorder. Other factors—such as the person's individual characteristics, his or her perception of the event, and the existence of support groups—also have an influence.

According to the model shown in Figure 5.9, the degree of trauma is one variable in developing PTSD,

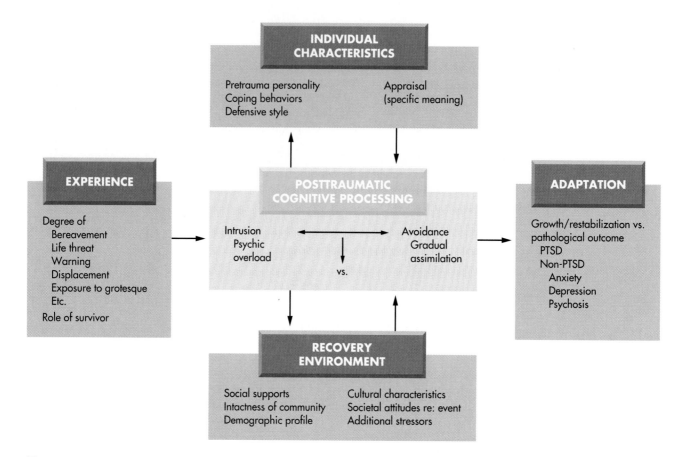

FIGURE 5.9   **Processing a Catastrophic Event: A Working Model**   Factors such as the coping style and characteristics of the individual, the way traumatic events are processed, and whether or not social supports are available have an impact on whether PTSD develops.

Source: From Green, Wilson & Lindy, 1985.

but the person's own coping styles and a supportive recovery environment can reduce its effects. One study showed that war veterans who developed PTSD were more likely to have sustained injuries, came closer to their own death, felt more guilty about their role in the event, and perceived less support from their families (Solkoff, Gray & Keill, 1986). Negative childhood experiences (Bremner et al., 1993) and being more withdrawn and inhibited (Schnurr, Friedman & Rosenberg, 1993) are also associated with an increased risk of developing PTSD. Among the general population, people with less education, those who scored high on neuroticism, and those who are African American were more likely to be exposed to traumatic events and were therefore at a higher risk for developing PTSD (Breslau, Davis & Andreski, 1995).

Incest victims who were able to "make sense" of their victimization showed better adjustment than those who were unable to redefine the event (Janoff-Bulman, 1985). Victims of trauma whose experience leads them into developing a generalized perceived loss of control are likely to develop the most severe symptoms of PTSD (Kushner et al., 1992). It appears that a variety of individual experiences or characteristics of a supportive environment can moderate the impact of a traumatic stressor.

Treatments for PTSD have varied, from crisis intervention approaches for individuals suffering from the recent impact of a stressor, to psychoanalytic and cognitive behavioral approaches for more chronic forms of PTSD. Because anxiety symptoms are common in this disorder, therapy often includes antianxiety medications. In working with Vietnam veterans with PTSD, Embry (1990) recommended the following steps:

1. Build rapport by understanding the meaning of the trauma for the individual.

2. Allow the individual to have "permission" to express his emotions.

The intense terror and fear associated with combat may result in posttraumatic stress disorder. Here a group of Vietnam veterans are undergoing group therapy to deal with symptoms such as recurrent and disturbing recollections of traumatic events.

3. Help the individual learn to give up the "sick" role.

4. Focus on here-and-now problems as well as on the earlier trauma.

Extinction procedures have also been successful. A six-year-old boy who developed PTSD after being involved in a bomb blast and seeing injured people was successfully treated through relaxation techniques and imaginal flooding. The boy was asked to imagine scenes of injured people, the smell of smoke, and shouts of individuals. This procedure markedly reduced his symptoms (Saigh, 1987). Among rape victims, prolonged exposure (continued imagination of the rape scene) was more effective in reducing PTSD symptoms, rape-related distress, and general anxiety than was stress inoculation training (learning coping skills, relaxation, and cognitive restructuring) or supportive counseling. The authors (Foa et al., 1991) believe that a major therapeutic component in exposure was in confronting the anxiety situation directly so that a positive change occurred in the rape memory.

A recent and promising treatment for PTSD called *eye movement desensitization* has been developed by Shapiro (1989). It involves asking the client to visualize the disturbing imagery and then to describe it, using all sensory modalities. After the image is clear, the client holds his or her head immobile and visually tracks the lateral movements of the clinician's finger or pencil. These movements are repeated twenty to thirty times, about one second apart. This procedure appears to result in a very rapid diminishing of distress and eliminates symptoms such as nightmares and flashbacks; few cases of relapse have been reported (Forbes, Creamer & Rycroft, 1994; Montgomery & Ayllon, 1994; Wolpe & Abrams, 1991). Although the initial findings are impressive, the reason that eye movements are effective is not clear. As Marquis (1991) pointed out in his review of this approach, "It is necessary to show beyond doubt that eye movements are essential to the deconditioning, and that not just any simultaneous activity will do— such as waving arms, repeating nonsense syllables, smelling roses, or sitting on a block of ice" (p. 192). Even if eye movements are shown to be essential to this procedure, we still need to find the mechanism that accounts for its success. Some studies are already raising questions about both its effectiveness (Acierno et al., 1994; Bauman, 1994) and its theoretical foundation (Renfrey & Spates, 1994).

SUMMARY

1. Anxiety is an emotion we all experience. It appears in our cognitions or thoughts, in our behaviors, and in our physiological or biological reactions.

2. The anxiety disorders are all characterized by anxiety—by feelings of fear and apprehension. The anxiety may be the major disturbance (as it is in panic disorder and generalized anxiety disorder), may arise when the individual confronts a feared object or situation (as in the phobias), may result from an attempt to master the symptoms (as in obsessive-compulsive disorder), or may occur during intrusive memories of a traumatic event (as in posttraumatic stress disor-

der). An individual with any of these disorders may experience panic attacks.

3. Panic disorder and generalized anxiety disorder (GAD) are characterized by direct and unfocused anxiety. Panic disorder is marked by episodes of extreme anxiety and feelings of impending doom. Generalized anxiety disorder involves chronically high levels of anxiety and excessive worry that is present for six months or more. Psychoanalysts believe these disorders are unfocused because they stem from internal conflicts that remain in the person's unconscious. Cognitive behavioral theorists emphasize cognitions and conditioning in the development of these disorders. According to the biogenic perspective, a specific biological dysfunction may predispose some people to panic disorder. Drug therapy, behavioral therapies, and psychoanalysis have been used to treat these disorders.

4. Phobias are strong fears that exceed the demands of the situation. Agoraphobia is an intense fear of being in public places; it can keep afflicted people from leaving home because attempts to do so may produce panic attacks. Social phobias are irrational fears about situations in which the person can be observed by others. The anxiety generally stems from the possibility of appearing foolish or making mistakes in public. Specific phobias include all the irrational fears that are not classed as social phobias or agoraphobia. Commonly feared objects in specific phobias include small animals, heights, and the dark. In the psychoanalytic view, phobias represent unconscious conflicts that are displaced onto an external object. Behavioral explanations include the classical conditioning view, in which phobias are based on an association between some aversive event and a conditioned stimulus; conditioning through observational learning; the role of thoughts that are distorted and frightening; and reinforcement for fear behaviors. Biogenic explanations are based on studies of the influence of genetic, biochemical, and neurological factors or on the idea that humans are prepared to develop certain fears. The most effective treatments for phobias seem to be biochemical (via antidepressants) and, primarily, behavioral (via exposure, and flooding, systematic desensitization, modeling, and graduated exposure).

5. Obsessive-compulsive disorder involves thoughts or actions that are involuntary, intrusive, repetitive, and uncontrollable. Most persons with obsessive-compulsive disorder are aware that their distressing behaviors are irrational. Obsessions (which involve thoughts or images) and compulsions (which involve actions or thoughts) may occur together or separately. Freud believed that this disorder represented the sub-

stitution of a threatening conflict with a behavior or thought that was less threatening. According to the anxiety-reduction hypothesis, a behavioral explanation, obsessions and compulsions develop because they reduce anxiety. Proponents of operant conditioning suggest the disorder stems from the chance association of a behavior with a reinforcer, but this view fails to explain some aspects of the disorder. Positron emission tomography has opened new avenues of research for those using the biogenic approach. The most commonly used treatments are either biological or behavioral. The treatment of choice is a combination of flooding and response prevention, sometimes combined with cognitive therapy.

6. Posttraumatic and acute stress disorders involve exposure to a traumatic event resulting in intrusive memories of the occurrence, attempts to forget or repress the memories, emotional withdrawal, and increased arousal. Classical conditioning principles have been used to both explain and treat the condition.

KEY TERMS

acute stress disorder Exposure to a traumatic stressor that results in dissociation, reliving the experience, and attempts to avoid reminders of the event and that lasts for more than two and less than thirty days

agoraphobia An intense fear of being in public places where escape or help may not be readily available; in extreme cases, a fear of leaving one's home

anxiety Feelings of fear and apprehension

anxiety disorder A disorder that meets one of three criteria: the anxiety itself is the major disturbance, the anxiety is manifested only in particular situations, or the anxiety results from an attempt to master other symptoms

compulsion The need to perform acts or to dwell on thoughts to reduce anxiety

exposure therapy A therapy technique in which the patient is introduced to encounters (gradual or rapid) with the feared situation

flooding A therapeutic technique that involves continued *in vivo* (actual) or imagined exposure to a highly fear-arousing situation; a form of exposure therapy

generalized anxiety disorder (GAD) Disorder characterized by persistent high levels of anxiety and excessive worry over many life circumstances

modeling therapy A therapeutic approach to phobias in which the person with the phobia observes a model in the act of coping with, or responding appropriately in, the fear-producing situation

obsession An intrusive and repetitive thought or image that produces anxiety

obsessive-compulsive disorder Disorder characterized by intrusive and repetitive thoughts or images or by the need to perform acts to reduce anxiety or to dwell on thoughts

panic disorder Anxiety disorder characterized by severe and frightening episodes of apprehension and feelings of impending doom

phobia A strong, persistent, and unwarranted fear of some specific object or situation

posttraumatic stress disorder (PTSD) An anxiety disorder that lasts for more than thirty days, develops in response to a specific extreme stressor, and is characterized by intrusive memories of the traumatic event, emotional withdrawal, and heightened autonomic arousal

social phobia An intense, excessive fear of being scrutinized in one or more social situations

specific phobia An extreme fear of a specific object or situation; a phobia that is not classified as either agoraphobia or a social phobia

systematic desensitization A behavioral therapy technique in which relaxation is used to eliminate the anxiety associated with phobias and other fear-evoking situations

CHAPTER 6

DISSOCIATIVE DISORDERS AND SOMATOFORM DISORDERS

he two cases below illustrate characteristics found in the four **dissociative disorders**—mental disorders in which a person's identity, memory, and consciousness are altered or disrupted.

> A man was found severely dehydrated, wandering in the desert. It was estimated that he had been without water for at least three days. He claimed to have no memories of the past but retained many skills. For example, he demonstrated the ability to fly a plane. He appeared on the television program "Unsolved Mysteries" to ask the help of others to identify him.

> A woman came in for therapy because of several puzzling events. She had been told that she had been dancing and flirting in a bar, an event that she could not remember and that was against her moral standards. She had also awakened in a hospital after an overdose and had not remembered being suicidal. Under hypnosis thirteen different personalities were revealed. (Shapiro, 1991)

In this chapter, we examine these disorders and the **somatoform disorders,** which involve physical symptoms or complaints that have no physiological basis. Both groups of disorders occur because of some psychological conflict or need.

The symptoms of the dissociative disorders and the somatoform disorders, such as memory disturbance or hysterical blindness, generally become known through self-reports. There is, then, the possibility of faking. The man found wandering in the desert was identified as Arthur Beal after his appearance on television. But he was soon arrested by the police for stealing a shipment of food just before his disappearance. The police believed that he was feigning the disorder. In addition to the possibility of faking, other questions have been raised about several of the dissociative disorders. For example, some researchers are concerned about the sudden increases in reports of multiple personalities and dissociative amnesia. They believe that counselors and therapists or clients may be inadvertently "creating" these disorders.

Physical complaints from individuals with somatoform disorders are also difficult to evaluate when no organic basis seems to exist for the physical symptoms. Yet the fact remains that in genuine cases of dissociative and somatoform disorders, the symptoms are produced "involuntarily" or unconsciously. Affected individuals actually are puzzled by their memory loss and behavioral changes or suffer from their physical pain or disability. This situation leads to a paradox: A person *does* suffer memory disturbance in psychogenic amnesia, yet that memory must exist somewhere in the neurons and synapses of the brain. Similarly, a person *does* "lose" his or her sight in hysterical blindness, yet physiologically the eyes are perfectly capable of seeing. What exactly happens in these cases? The dissociative disorders and the somatoform disorders are among the most puzzling of all disorders.

DISSOCIATIVE DISORDERS

The dissociative disorders—*dissociative amnesia, dissociative fugue, dissociative identity disorder (multiple personality),* and *depersonalization disorder*—are shown in the disorders chart on page 160. Each disorder involves some sort of dissociation, or separation, of a part of the person's consciousness, memory, or identity. Table 6.1 summarizes some of the other characteristics of dissociative disorders.

The dissociative disorders are highly publicized and sensationalized and, except for depersonalization disorder, were considered relatively rare. But reports of one of these disorders—dissociative identity disorder, or multiple-personality disorder, as it is commonly known—have increased dramatically. It is now estimated that approximately 5 percent of patients on adult psychiatric units have this disorder (Ross et al., 1991). (Reasons for this increase are discussed later in the chapter.) Interestingly, this disorder is rarely diagnosed in Japan or Britain (Merskey, 1992).

Corresponding to this increase is a complex legal debate about acts that are committed and that the individual is amnesic for:

■ Billy Milligan was acquitted of the crime of rape because it was committed by another personality (Keyes, 1981).

■ A man was charged with the rape of a woman with multiple personalities when the nonconsenting personalities brought up the charge.

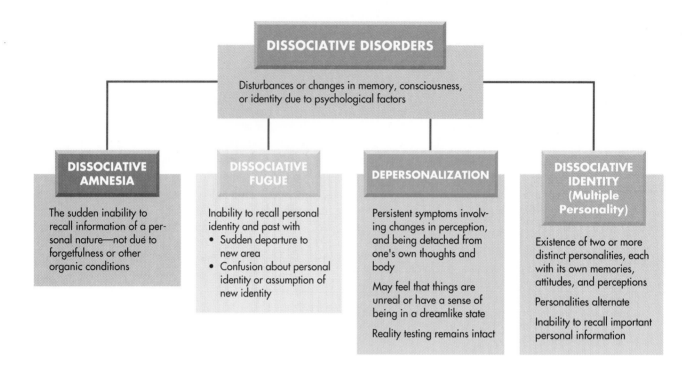

DISSOCIATIVE DISORDERS

Disturbances or changes in memory, consciousness, or identity due to psychological factors

DISSOCIATIVE AMNESIA

The sudden inability to recall information of a personal nature—not due to forgetfulness or other organic conditions

DISSOCIATIVE FUGUE

Inability to recall personal identity and past with
- Sudden departure to new area
- Confusion about personal identity or assumption of new identity

DEPERSONALIZATION

Persistent symptoms involving changes in perception, and being detached from one's own thoughts and body

May feel that things are unreal or have a sense of being in a dreamlike state

Reality testing remains intact

DISSOCIATIVE IDENTITY (Multiple Personality)

Existence of two or more distinct personalities, each with its own memories, attitudes, and perceptions

Personalities alternate

Inability to recall important personal information

■ A woman with twenty-one personalities asked for alimony payments, claiming that she did not commit adultery and that she had tried to stop the responsible personality "Rosie." (In South Carolina, adultery is grounds for barring alimony payments.)

These issues raise troubling questions regarding responsibility in these disorders. Does a diagnosis of dissociative identity disorder or dissociative amnesia constitute mitigating circumstances and "diminished capacity"? (See Chapter 18 for a discussion of legal issues.)

Dissociative Amnesia

Dissociative amnesia is the partial or total loss of important personal information, sometimes occurring suddenly after a stressful or traumatic event. The disturbed person may be unable to recall information such as his or her name, address, friends, and relatives but does remember the necessities of daily life—how to read, write, and drive.

There are four types of dissociative amnesia—localized, selective, generalized, and continuous—and they vary in terms of the degree and type of memory

Dissociative amnesia generally occurs after a traumatic event. Here a man is trying to remember his past by examining photographs of his wife and children.

TABLE 6.1 Dissociative Disorders: Their Prevalence, Onset, and Course

Dissociative Disorder	Prevalence	Age of Onset	Course
Dissociative amnesia	Recent increase involving forgotten early childhood trauma	Any age group	Acute forms may remit spontaneously—others are chronic; usually related to trauma or stress
Dissociative fugue	0.2 percent	Usually adulthood	Related to stress or trauma; recovery is generally rapid
Depersonalization disorder	Unknown; 50 percent of adults may experience brief episodes of stress-related depersonalization	Adolescence or adulthood	May be short lived or chronic
Dissociative identity disorder	Sharp rise in recently reported cases; up to nine times more frequent in women	Usually adulthood, but misdiagnosis may result in underreporting	Fluctuates; tends to be chronic and recurrent

Source: Data from DSM-IV.

that is lost. The most common, **localized amnesia,** is a failure to recall all the events that happened in a specific short period, often centered on some highly painful or disturbing event. The following cases are typical of localized amnesia.

> A 38-year-old mother had no memory of being molested by her father until she underwent therapy at the age of thirty-three.

> An eighteen-year-old woman who survived a dramatic fire claimed not to remember it or the death of her child and husband in the fire. She claimed her relatives were lying about the fire. She became extremely agitated and emotional several hours later, when her memory abruptly returned.

> A four-year-old boy whose mother was murdered in his presence was found mopping up her blood. During interviews with a psychiatrist, however, he denied any memory of the incident.

Selective amnesia is an inability to remember certain details of an incident. For example, a man remembered having an automobile accident but could not recall that his child had died in the crash. Selective amnesia is often claimed by people accused of violent criminal offenses. Many murderers report that they remember arguments but do not remember killing anyone. In fact, 30 to 65 percent of individuals who are charged or convicted of homicide claim amnesia as a defense (Schacter, 1986).

In contrast, **generalized amnesia** is an inability to remember anything about one's past life. Arthur Beal, who appeared on the program "Unsolved Mysteries," was given this diagnosis. After talking to and meeting his mother, he still claimed not to remember her or who he was. The following case illustrates some of the psychological events associated with generalized amnesia:

> Mr. X. was brought to the admission ward of a psychiatric hospital at the end of February 1988.... He could not give any information about himself apart from vague recollections from the immediate past. He had no money or identification on him on admission.... He mainly expressed concern that he might have left a wife who might be looking for him.... We contacted the pastor of the church mentioned in the leaflet Mr. X. had had on him on admission. The pastor led us to a woman who recognized and identified Mr. X.... He suddenly remembered that his wife had died and that he had promised her he would kill himself as he felt he could not live without her.... He explained in his own words: "I must have lost my memory because otherwise I might have killed myself." (Domb & Beaman, 1991, pp. 424–425)

Finally, **continuous amnesia,** the fourth and least common form of dissociative amnesia, is an inability to recall any events that have occurred between a specific time in the past and the present time. The individual remains alert and attentive but forgets each successive event after it occurs.

CRITICAL THINKING

How Valid Are Repressed Memories?

In May 1990, George Franklin was brought to trial for raping and killing a child twenty years previously. This case was one of the first to rely heavily on repressed memories. The man's daughter, twenty years after the incident, remembered the killing of her friend in flashes of memory. She was playing with her friend in the back of the family van when the attack took place. She also retrieved memories of being sexually abused by her father. Three of her sisters

also related being sexually abused. George Franklin was convicted and sent to prison. (Questions about the testimony's validity led to his recent release, although he may be retried.)

In the past few years, many individuals have reported repressed memories. For example, after her former husband related an instance of sexual abuse that he suffered as a child, Roseanne, the television celebrity, remembered being abused by her father thirty-

six years ago. And in a sample of psychologists who had experienced childhood abuse, 40 percent reported a period of forgetting some or all of the abuse. In 56 percent of the cases, the memory returned during therapy (Feldman-Summers & Pope, 1994).

Although survey data show that childhood sexual abuse and incest are more prevalent than had previously been estimated, controversy arises over the accuracy and validity of repressed memories. Some

In generalized amnesia, the individual "loses" memory of personal information for his or her entire life. This woman talking to television host David Hartmann was found wandering alone naked and near death in a Florida state park. She was later identified as the daughter of a suburban Chicago couple.

clinicians would prefer to err on the side of the victim. Bass and Davis (1988), authors of the book *Courage to Heal,* which deals with sexual abuse, wrote, "If you are unable to remember any specific instances, but still have a feeling that something happened to you, it probably did." Psychologist Elizabeth Loftus, however, believes that for some individuals, the "memory" may be inaccurate and may result from imagination or suggestion or may function as a means of explaining unhappiness in life (Loftus, 1993). Determining the authenticity of the memories, especially those dating to very early ages, is difficult. One therapist indicated that some of his patients report that they remember incidents that occurred before speech had developed or even while in the womb (Laker, 1992).

Parents who believe they have been falsely accused of child abuse have formed a nationwide support group, the False Memory Syndrome Foundation. They claim that the "memories" are often a product of the therapist's approach or perspective or their children's attempt to blame them for their problems. Although sexual abuse of children does exist and some victims do repress the memory of the event, controversy remains over the accuracy and acceptability of the reports.

As a scientist, how could you determine whether any "repressed memories" are accurate representations of the past? How could you separate "true" from "false" memories, knowing that information obtained through hypnosis may be unreliable? Can counselors inadvertently produce false memories in their clients? In cases of suspected sexual abuse, some clinicians say they will believe what the client says no matter how bad the details. But, as Loftus, Garry, and Feldman (1994) have pointed out, people also forget automobile accidents, the death of family members, or being hospitalized. Have these memories been repressed or merely forgotten? How can you distinguish between these two processes? How might you interpret a statement from a client who says that she has no clear memory of her childhood before the age of five? Before trying to answer these questions, you may want to read the First Person narrative by Elizabeth Loftus on page 164.

Psychologists are uncertain about the processes involved in dissociative amnesia. They believe it results from the person's repression of a traumatic event or from some process closely related to repression. For example, **posthypnotic amnesia,** in which the subject cannot recall events that occurred during hypnosis, is somewhat similar to dissociative amnesia. In both cases, the lost material can sometimes be retrieved with professional help. There is, however, one important difference. In posthypnotic amnesia, the hypnotist suggests what is to be forgotten, whereas in dissociative amnesia, both the source and the content of the amnesia are unknown (Sarbin & Cole, 1979). Because of this difference, experiments to study amnesia are difficult to design. Therefore, information on dissociative amnesia has been gathered primarily through case studies.

An increasing number of cases of dissociative amnesia involving sexual abuse have recently been reported (Shapiro et al., 1993). Some researchers now question whether the memories reported in some of these cases may be caused by therapists' suggestions and clients' attempts to explain their problems (see Critical Thinking and the First Person narrative).

Dissociative Fugue

Dissociative fugue (also called *fugue state*) is confusion over personal identity (often involves the partial or complete assumption of a new identity) accompanied by unexpected travel away from home. Most cases involve only short periods away from home and an incomplete change of identity. However, there are exceptions:

> A 38-year-old man who had been missing for a year was living in another state when relatives saw his photograph printed in a newspaper. The man had established a new identity and was spearheading a charitable drive in his new home state; the newspaper article praised him for his energy and leadership. When confronted by his relatives, the man initially denied knowing them. The relatives were certain of their identification but also puzzled by his outgoing personality. The person they knew had always been shy and retiring.

Sometimes, a patient reports multiple fugue episodes, as here:

> E. F. was a 46-year-old man who described twelve to fifteen episodes of "going blank" during the previous five

FIRST PERSON

Elizabeth Loftus

Since the mid-1970s, I and other researchers have been conducting investigations into the creation of false memories through exposure to misleading information. Now, nearly two decades later, we have completed hundreds of studies that support a high degree of memory distortion. People have recalled nonexistent broken glass and tape recorders, a clean-shaven man as having a mustache, straight hair as curly, and even something as large and conspicuous as a barn in a bucolic scene that actually contained no buildings at all. This growing body of research shows that new, postevent information is often incorporated into memory, supplementing and altering a person's recollections. Like the Trojan horse, the new information invades us precisely because we do not detect its influence.

My own recent research on false memories shows that it is even possible to inject into the mind of someone an entire memory of a childhood event that never happened. In this instance, implantation is accomplished by a small suggestion by a trusted family member. Consider what happened when Jim Coan, the chief research assistant on a project, tried to convince his younger brother Chris that Chris had been lost in a shopping mall at age five when he was out with his mother and brother. Jim told Chris this story as if it were the truth:

It was 1981 or 1982. I remember that Chris was five. We had gone shopping at the University City shopping mall in Spokane. After some panic, we found Chris being led down the mall by a tall, older man. (I think he was wearing a flannel shirt.) Chris was crying and holding the man's hand. The man explained that he had found Chris walking around crying his eyes out just a few moments before and was trying to help him find his parents.

Just two days later, Chris recalled his feelings about being lost: "That day I was so scared that I would never see my family again. I knew that I was in trouble." On day 3, he recalled a conversation with his mother: "I remember Mom telling never to do that again." On day 4: "I also remember the stores." In his last recollection, he could even remember a conversation with the man who found him: "I remember the man asking me if I was lost."

A couple of weeks later, when Chris was reinterviewed about the false memory, he characterized his

---

years. He said that these episodes lasted two to thirty-six hours, and that, in "coming round," his feet were often sore, he was a long way from home, and he had no idea of the time or what had been happening during the previous hours. For example, he found himself on one occasion near the Thames, ten miles from his home, with his clothes sopping wet. Marital and legal difficulties were believed to be contributing factors in the episodes of fugue. (Kopelman, 1987, p. 438)

As with dissociative amnesia, recovery from fugue state is often abrupt and complete, although the gradual return of bits of information has also been found.

Depersonalization Disorder

Depersonalization disorder is perhaps the most common dissociative disorder. It is characterized by feelings of unreality concerning the self and the environment. This diagnosis is given only when the feeling of unreality and detachment cause major impairment in social or occupational functioning. At one time or another, most young adults have experienced some symptoms typical of depersonalization disorder: Perceptions that the body is distorted or that the environment has somehow changed, feelings of living out a dream, or minor losses of control. But episodes of depersonalization can be fairly intense, and they can produce great anxiety because the people who suffer from them consider them unnatural, as the following case illustrates.

A twenty-year-old college student became alarmed when she suddenly perceived subtle changes in her appearance. The reflection she saw in mirrors did not seem to be hers. She became even more disturbed when her room, her friends, and the campus also seemed to take on a slightly distorted appearance. The world around her felt unreal and was no longer predictable. During the day before the sudden appearance of the symptoms, the woman had been greatly distressed by the low grades she received on several important exams. When she fi-

memory as reasonably clear and vivid, and he greatly expanded on it:

> I was with you guys for a second and I think I went over to look at the toy store, the Kaybee toy and, uh, we got lost and I was looking around and I thought, "Uh-oh. I'm in trouble now."

> I was really scared, you know. And then this old man, I think he was wearing blue flannel, came up to me. . . . He was kind of old. He was kind of bald on top. . . . He had like a ring of gray hair . . . and he had glasses.

Then Chris was debriefed. When told that his "getting lost" memory was made up, he clung to it. "Really? I thought I remembered being lost . . . and looking around for you guys. I do remember that. And then crying. And Mom coming up and saying 'Where were you? Don't you . . . don't you ever do that again.'"

Chris, as well as others, had been led to develop false "memories" for something that never hap-pened—a specific episode of being lost. Did Chris truly believe that his false memory was genuine? If the willingness to expand on the memory and to provide details that were not initially suggested is an indication of genuine belief in memory, then the answer is yes. Chris embellished his memory with conversation, flannel shirts, and balding bespectacled rescuers. These confidently held and richly detailed false memories do not of course prove that repressed memories of abuse that are later recalled are false. But they do demonstrate a mechanism by which false memories can be created by suggestion. And they help us understand how someone could believe they had a memory for something that happened at six months of age, when in fact they did not.

Understanding how we can become tricked by revised data about our past is central to understanding how a person could unwittingly develop a false memory about his or her past. Therapists might want to consider whether it is really wise to "suggest" to their patients, as some do, that child-hood trauma happened. Additionally, uncritical acceptance of un-corroborated trauma memories by therapists, social agencies, and law enforcement personnel have fueled public accusations by alleged "sur-vivors." We do not yet have the tools for reliably distinguishing the signal of true repressed memories from the noise of false ones. Until we gain those tools, it seems prudent to urge care in how a possible amnesiac barrier is probed.

There is one last tragic risk of uncritical acceptance of every single claim of sexual abuse, no matter how dubious. These activities are bound to trivialize the ruthless cases of abuse and to increase the suffering of genuine victims.

Elizabeth Loftus is a professor of psychology at the University of Washington in Seattle. In addition to her teaching, she is also a leading researcher in cognitive psychology.

In depersonalization disorder, an individual may feel like an automaton—mechanical and robot-like. This painting, "The Subway" (ca. 1950), by George Tooker captures this feeling.

nally sought help at the university clinic, her major concern was that she was going insane.

Like other dissociative disorders, depersonalization can be precipitated by physical or psychological stress.

Dissociative Identity Disorder (Multiple-Personality Disorder)

Dissociative identity disorder, formerly known as *multiple-personality disorder,* is a dramatic condition in which two or more relatively independent personalities appear to exist in one person. The relationships among the personalities are often complex. Only one personality is evident at any one time, and the alternation of personalities usually produces periods of amnesia in the personality that has been displaced. However, one or several personalities may be aware of the existence of the others. The personalities usually differ from one another and sometimes are direct opposites, as the following case illustrates.

A 28-year-old female has a total of sixteen personalities. Three major personalities are usually present sometime during each day.

Billy Milligan, a 23-year-old drifter, was the first person in the United States to be acquitted of a major crime (rape) as a result of having multiple-personality disorder. Psychologists ascertained that Billy had ten personalities—eight male and two female—and that it was Adelena, his 19-year-old lesbian personality who had committed the rapes.

Margaret is the core personality and is described as having good social skills but tends not to be assertive. She has a good sense of humor and puts on a "good front" to prevent the detection of the other personalities. She is left-handed.

Rachel is sixteen years old. She engages in antisocial behaviors involving activities such as prostitution and aggression. She has a sarcastic sense of humor and appears when there is a need to fight back. She is right-handed.

Dee is eight years old. She speaks and behaves like a child. She appears to have "taken the pain" whenever the personalities have been abused. She holds the memories of sexual abuse. She is ambidextrous. (Dick-Barnes, Nelson & Aine, 1987)

In cases where one personality is that of a child (like Dee), that part of the personality may be aware only of events that took place at an early age. For example, one woman's "child" personality was confused about being in an adult body and had never heard of "Sesame Street," Burger King, or Sprite, which did not exist when she was a child. She wanted to see her childhood friends and return to elementary school (Davidson, Allen & Smith, 1987).

Dissociative identity disorder is much more prevalent in women, who often report having experienced childhood physical or sexual abuse (Boon & Draijer, 1993; Coons, 1994; Kluft, 1987a). No gender differences in the prevalence of the disorder, however, were found in Switzerland (Modestin, 1992). *Conversion symptoms* (loss of physical or sensory function with no physical basis), depression, and anxiety are common in people with the disorder (Bliss, 1980; Coons, 1986). The characteristics of this disorder have changed over time. Goff and Simms (1993) compared case reports between 1800 and 1965 with those from the 1980s. The earlier cases involved fewer personalities (three versus twelve), a later age of onset of first dissociation (age 20 as opposed to age 11 in the 1980s), a greater proportion of males, and a lower incidence of a history of child abuse (see Figure 6.1). Goff and Simms believe that this disorder is a "culturally determined disorder that occurs in highly suggestible patients."

Psychological and physiological tests have been used to try to confirm the existence of distinct personalities in dissociative identity disorders. Current attempts to identify this disorder through the use of electroencephalograms (EEGs), cerebral blood flow, galvanic skin response, and other physiological measures have produced contradictory and conflicting findings (Miller & Triggiano, 1992).

Diagnostic Controversy We noted earlier that dissociative identity disorder is among the less common dissociative disorders, but there is some question about how rare it really is. Hundreds of cases of multiple personalities have been reported in recent years (Fagan & McMahon, 1984); one clinician alone reported more than 130 cases (Kluft, 1982). The identification of this disorder in children has also increased. Fagan and McMahon (1984) diagnosed eleven childhood cases over a period of eighteen months and believe that thousands of children may have dissociative identity disorder.

Fagan and McMahon believe that parents, teachers, and mental health professionals should be aware of the signs of multiple personalities in children. These include trance states; confusion about time, place, or person; responding to more than one name; marked and rapid shifts in personality; forgetting recent events; extreme or odd variation in artistic abilities, handwriting and other skills, and food preferences; varying responses to discipline; self-injurious behavior; multiple physical complaints; hysteric symptoms such as sleepwalking, sudden blindness, or loss of sensation; and reports of hearing voices, losing track of time, or being innocent when punished. The more such symptoms the child displays, the more likely that a diagnosis of incipient dissociative identity disorder is appropriate.

Some clinicians believe that dissociative identity disorder is relatively common but that the condition is underreported because of misdiagnosis (Ellason & Ross, 1995). For example, in a study of one hundred persons diagnosed with this disorder, Putnam, Guroff & Silberman (1986) found that nearly seven years elapsed from the initial assessment of symptoms before an accurate diagnosis was made. The patients received an average of four prior psychiatric or neurological diagnoses.

Misdiagnosis is illustrated in the case of a 37-year-old man who reported having experienced symptoms of dissociation since age six. He reported a history of blackouts, amnesia for certain acts, and behavior and personality changes. He received several diagnoses, including undifferentiated schizophrenia, organic brain syndrome, schizoid personality, and seizure disorder (Salley, 1988). People with multiple personality have also been diagnosed as having bipolar disorder and major depression with psychotic features. They commonly complained about "hearing voices arguing," "hearing voices commenting on my actions," "experiencing feelings that don't seem to be coming from me," and feelings of depression (Kluft, 1987b). Because changes in mood and memory and hearing voices are symptoms of dissociative identity disorder as well as schizophrenia, diagnosis may be difficult.

Of course, misdiagnosis works both ways: Other disorders may be diagnosed as dissociative identity. In addition, it is possible that, in their enthusiasm, some researchers and therapists are labeling people as having multiple personalities when they do not *(false pos-*

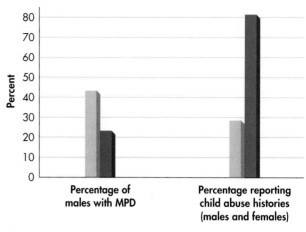

Between 1800 and 1965

1980s

FIGURE 6.1 **Comparison of Characteristics of Reported Cases of Dissociative Identity Disorder (Multiple-Personality Disorder)** This graph illustrates characteristics of MPD cases reported in the 1980s versus those reported between 1800 and 1965. What could account for these differences?

Source: Data from Goff & Simms, 1993.

itives). For example, Bliss and co-workers (1983) found evidence of multiple personalities in approximately 60 percent of a group of persons with schizophrenia who had auditory hallucinations. It is difficult to believe that such a large percentage could be misdiagnosed, and the results of this study may reflect the researchers' bias. Other researchers have suggested that the sudden increase in reports of dissociative identity disorder may be an artifact of the procedures used in investigating this disorder and that it is a "fashionable" diagnosis.

Dissociative identity or multiple-personality disorder is rarely diagnosed outside the United States and Canada (Merskey, 1995). In a study of this disorder in Switzerland, Modestin (1992) concluded that it is relatively rare and estimated its prevalence rate to be .05 percent to .1 percent of patients. He also found that three psychiatrists accounted for more than 50 percent of the patients given this diagnosis. Why is it that some psychiatrists report treating many patients with multiple personalities whereas the majority do not? One prominent psychiatrist indicated that in forty years of practice he had encountered only one "doubtful case" of the disorder and wondered why he and his colleagues had seen so few cases of multiple-personality disorder" (Chodoff, 1987). The psychiatrists who treated Eve, a well-known case, received tens of thousands of referrals and found only one genuine case of multiple personalities (Thigpen & Cleckley, 1984). Another therapist characterized the disorder as a "psychiatric growth industry" (Weissberg, 1993).

In a study of patients with reported multiple-personality disorder, Merskey (1992) believed that the "personalities" represent differences in mood, memory, or attention and that "they" are developed by unwitting therapists through expectation, suggestion, and social reinforcement. Cases of dissociated states and multiple personalities produced through hypnosis or suggestion have been reported (Coons, 1988; Ofshe, 1992). Dissociation experiences are common in the face of stress (Freinkel, Koopman & Spiegel, 1994) and are found in many different disorders. Many individuals developed dissociative symptoms in the aftermath of the San Francisco earthquake in 1989. They reported alterations in memory and thoughts, alterations of time perception, changes in reality, and depersonalization (feeling detached or numb). These symptoms abated over time (Cardena & Spiegel, 1993). Some clinicians could interpret these symptoms of stress as multiple personalities.

Because this disorder is difficult to diagnose, some clinicians have developed questionnaires to assess dissociation. The following questions are used to determine if some type of dissociation is occurring in children (M. K. Shapiro, 1991):

"Do you ever kinda space out, and lose track of what's going on around you?" (decreased awareness of the environment)

"Do you have any problems with forgetting things?" (amnesia)

"Does it ever happen that time goes by, and then you can't really remember what you were doing during that time?" (fugue state)

"Does it ever seem like things aren't real, like everything is just a dream?" (feelings of unreality)

"Does it ever happen that you do things that surprise you, and afterwards you stop and say to yourself, 'Why did I do that?'?" (multiple personalities)

These questions direct the clinician to investigate possible dissociation disorders. Some researchers, however, doubt the validity of scales purporting to measure this phenomenon (Fischer & Elnitsky, 1990). Many children, adolescents, and adults may answer yes to these questions without having a dissociative disorder. Interpretations are difficult to make without appropriate comparison groups. Whether the increase in cases of dissociative identity disorder is the result of more accurate diagnosis, false positives, an artifact, or an actual increase in the incidence of the disorder is still being debated.

Etiology of Dissociative Disorders

The diagnosis and causes of dissociative disorders are subject to much conjecture. Because diagnosis depends heavily on patients' self-reports, feigning or faking is always a possibility. One man charged with driving under the influence of alcohol said he had been in a fugue state. In a study of accused murderers who claimed amnesia for the act, almost all who submitted to polygraph tests or sodium amytal appeared to be lying (Bradford & Smith, 1979). Coons and Bradley (1985) discovered that a person diagnosed as having multiple personalities was feigning the disorder. Differentiating between genuine cases of dissociative disorders and faked ones is difficult. Even expert judges cannot distinguish between genuine inability to recall and subjects who simulate amnesia (Schacter, 1986). Researchers have found that recollections obtained under hypnosis are often inaccurate and distorted and that the retrieved information can alter waking memories (Nash et al., 1986; Sheehan, Grigg & McCann, 1984).

Some researchers hoped that objective measures such as EEG readings could show the presence of multiple personalities. Researchers later concluded, however, that EEG differences among the different personalities in individuals with multiple-personality disorder reflected differences mainly in concentration, mood changes, and degree of muscle tension (Coons, Milstein & Marley, 1982). Although clinical evidence supports the existence of dissociative disorders, reliable methods of determining their validity do not currently exist.

We will examine the causes of dissociative disorders from the psychoanalytic and learning perspectives and we also examine the possible influence of the clinician. It is important to realize that none of these approaches provides completely satisfactory explanations. As we indicated earlier, the dissociative disorders are not well understood.

Psychoanalytic Perspective Psychoanalytic theory views the dissociative disorders as a result of the person's use of repression to block from consciousness unpleasant or traumatic events (Kopelman, 1987). When complete repression of these impulses is not possible because of the strength of the impulses or the weakness of the ego, dissociation or separation of certain mental processes may occur. In dissociative amnesia and fugue, for example, large parts of the individual's personal identity are no longer available to conscious awareness. This process protects the individual from painful memories or conflicts (Paley, 1988).

> A 27-year-old man found lying in the middle of a busy intersection was brought to a hospital. He appeared agitated and said, "I wanted to get run over." He claimed not to know his personal identity or anything about his past. He only remembered being brought to the hospital by the police. The inability to remember was highly distressful to him. Psychological tests using the TAT [Thematic Apperception Test] and the Rorschach inkblot test revealed primarily anxiety-arousing, violent, and sexual themes. The clinician hypothesized that a violent incident involving sex might underlie the amnesia. Under hypnosis the patient's memory returned, and he remembered being severely assaulted. He had repressed the painful experience. (Kaszniak et al., 1988)

The dissociation process is carried to an extreme in dissociative identity disorder. Here, the splits in mental processes become so extreme that more or less independent identities are formed, each with its own unique set of memories. Conflicts within the personality structure are responsible for this process. Equally strong and opposing personality components (stemming from the superego and the id) render the ego incapable of controlling all incompatible elements. A compromise solution is then reached in which the different parts of the personality are alternately allowed expression and repressed. Because intense anxiety and disorganization would occur if these personality factions were allowed to coexist, each is sealed off from the others.

The split in personality may develop because of traumatic early experiences combined with an inability to escape them. Some researchers believe that one or more personalities take on the "pain" to shield the other personalities (Shapiro, 1991). From case histories, we have learned that some conditions may produce a dissociative reaction. In the case of Sybil, for example, Sybil's mother severely abused her. Dr. Wilbur, Sybil's psychiatrist, speculated that "by dividing into different selves [which were] defenses against an intolerable and dangerous reality, Sybil had found a [design] for survival" (Schreiber, 1973, p. 158).

Most people with multiple personalities do report a history of physical or sexual abuse during childhood (Boon & Draijer, 1993; Fagan & McMahon, 1984). Besides traumatic childhood events, the person must have the capacity to dissociate—or separate—certain memories or mental processes. A person's susceptibility to hypnotism may be a characteristic of the dissociation process, and, in fact, people who have multiple personalities appear to be very receptive to hypnotic suggestion (Frischholz et al., 1992). Those people might escape unpleasant experiences through self-hypnosis—by entering a hypnotic state. According

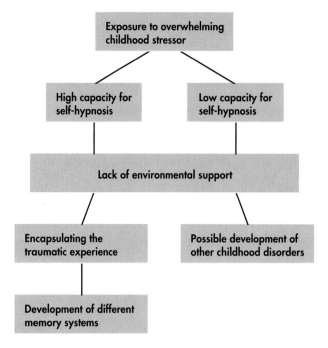

FIGURE 6.2 Psychoanalytic Model for Dissociative Identity Disorder Note the importance of the capacity for self-hypnosis in the development of multiple-personality disorder.

Source: Adapted from Kluft, 1987a.

to Kluft (1987a), the four factors necessary in the development of multiple personalities are

1. The capacity to dissociate (whether this is produced by traumatic events or is innate is not known)

2. Exposure to overwhelming stress, such as physical or sexual abuse

3. Encapsulating or walling off the experience

4. Developing different memory systems

If a supportive environment does not develop, multiple personality results from these factors (see Figure 6.2).

Behavioral Perspective Behavioral theorists suggest that the avoidance of stress by indirect means is the main factor to consider in explaining dissociative disorders. For example, patients with dissociative amnesia and fugue are often ill-equipped to handle emotional conflicts. Their way of fleeing stressful situations is either to forget them or to block out the disturbing thoughts. These people typically have much to gain and little to lose from their dissociative symptoms.

Behavioral explanations of dissociative identity disorder include the additional factors of role playing and selective attention. Each of us exhibits a variety of behaviors, moods, and emotions. For example, people wear different clothes, display different styles or mannerisms, and experience different emotional states depending on whether they are scrubbing a floor, thinking about something sad or happy, going shopping, working, or socializing. In persons with dissociative identity disorder, role playing may be combined with selective attention to certain cues. The person responds only to certain environmental stimuli and then behaves in a way that would be appropriate if only those stimuli were present. If that person seeks counseling, a clinician may mistake these changes in mood, attention, and behavior as different personalities and inadvertently create the disorder.

The Iatrogenic, or Therapist-Produced, Perspective
The term *iatrogenic* refers to an unintended effect of therapy—a condition or disorder produced by a physician or therapist through such mechanisms as selective attention, suggestion, reinforcement, and expectations that are placed on the client. Could some or even most cases of dissociative identity disorder be the result of these factors? A number of researchers and clinicians say yes. They believe that many of the "cases" of multiple personalities and of dissociative amnesia have unwittingly been produced by therapists, self-help books, and the mass media (Aldridge-Morris, 1989; Chodoff, 1987; Goff & Simms, 1993; Loftus, Garry & Feldman, 1994; Merskey, 1995; Ofshe, 1992; Weissberg, 1993). Interestingly, Goff and Simms (1993) observed that early cases of multiple-personality disorder averaged about three different personalities. After the publication of *Sybil* in 1973, a novel about a woman with sixteen personalities, the mean number of personalities rose to twelve.

Lynn and Nash (1994) point out that therapists hold implicit theories regarding the cause of mental disorders and that they may convey these theories to their clients. Therapists may insist, for example, that clients with eating disorders "remember" incidents of abuse and may treat clients' denials as indications of defense (Esman, 1994). Roland (1993) believes that repressed memories have to be uncovered through "memory reconstruction" procedures, such as visualization.

Although iatrogenic influences can be found in any disorder, dissociative disorders may be especially vulnerable, in part because of high levels of hypnotizability and suggestibility found in people with dissociative disorders. As Goff (1993) states, it is "no coincidence that the field of [multiple-personality disorder] studies in the United States largely originated among practitioners of hypnosis" (p. 604). Hypnosis and other memory retrieval methods may create rather than uncover personalities in suggestible clients. Spanos and his colleagues (1985) found that suggestions and hypnosis could induce students to report having different personalities. Interestingly, the "personalities" showed different patterns of responses on personality tests. In a later study, Spanos and colleagues (1991) found that the characteristics of the personalities and the reports of child abuse were also influenced by the instructions or expectations of the hypnotists. Although some cases of dissociative identity disorder probably are therapist produced, we do not know to what extent iatrogenic influences can account for this disorder.

Treatment of Dissociative Disorders

A variety of treatments for the dissociative disorders have been developed, including supportive counseling and the use of hypnosis and personality reconstruction.

Dissociative Amnesia and Dissociative Fugue The symptoms of dissociative amnesia and fugue tend to remit, or abate, spontaneously. Moreover, patients typically complain of psychological symptoms other than the amnesia, perhaps because the amnesia interferes only minimally with their day-to-day functioning. As a result, therapeutic intervention is often not directed specifically toward the amnesia. Instead, therapists provide supportive counseling for clients with amnesia.

It has been noted, however, that depression is often associated with the fugue state and that stress is often associated with both fugue and dissociative amnesia (Sackeim & Vingiano, 1984). A reasonable therapeutic approach is then to treat these dissociative disorders indirectly by alleviating the depression (with antidepressants or cognitive behavior therapy) and the stress (through stress-management techniques).

Depersonalization Disorder Depersonalization disorder is also subject to spontaneous remission, but at a much slower rate than that of dissociative amnesia and fugue. Treatment generally concentrates on alleviating the feelings of anxiety or depression or the fear of going insane. Occasionally a behavioral approach has been tried. For example, behavior therapy was successfully used to treat depersonalization disorder in a fifteen-year-old girl who had blackouts that she described as "floating in and out." These episodes were associated with headaches and feelings of detachment, but neurological and physical examinations revealed no organic cause. Treatment involved getting increased attention from her family and reinforcement from them when the frequency of blackouts was reduced, training in appropriate responses to stressful situations, and self-reinforcement (Dollinger, 1983).

Dissociative Identity Disorder

The mental health literature contains more information on the treatment of dissociative identity (multiple-personality) disorder than on the other three dissociative disorders combined. Treatment for this disorder is not always successful. Chris Sizemore (of *The Three Faces of Eve*) developed additional personalities after therapy but has now recovered. She is a writer, lecturer, and artist. Sybil also recovered—she has become a college professor. Success, however, may be difficult to achieve. Coons (1986) conducted a follow-up study of twenty patients with multiple personalities. Each patient was studied for about thirty-nine months after his or her initial assessment. Nine patients obtained partial or full recovery but only five patients maintained it—the others dissociated again. More than one-third were unable to work because of their disorder.

Patients with dissociative identity disorder are difficult to work with. Coons (1986) found that 75 percent of the therapists indicated they had feelings of exasperation, 58 percent anger, and 50 percent emotional exhaustion during therapy. One or more of the personalities might resist treatment. A thirty-year-old physician abruptly got up in the middle of a session and remarked, "You can analyze HER, but I'm leaving" (p. 723). More positive outcomes have been reported when therapists are experienced in working with multiple personalities and when therapy contin-

ues even after the personality has become fused (Kluft, 1987b).

The most widely reported approaches to treating dissociative identity disorder combine psychotherapy and hypnosis. One suggested procedure begins with hypnosis. With the patient in a hypnotic state, the different personalities are asked to emerge and introduce themselves to the patient, to make the patient aware of their existence. Then the personalities are asked to help the patient recall the traumatic experiences or memories that originally triggered the development of new personalities. An important part of this recalling step is to enable the patient to experience the emotions associated with the traumatic memories. The therapist then explains to the patient that these additional personalities used to serve a purpose, but that alternative coping strategies are available now. The final steps involve piecing together the events and memories of the personalities, integrating them, and continuing therapy to help the patient adjust to the new self (Bliss, 1980; Sakheim, Hess & Chivas, 1988).

Behavioral therapy has also been used successfully in some cases of multiple personalities. Here is an example:

> A 51-year-old male, diagnosed as a schizophrenic with multiple personalities, was treated through selective reinforcement. The reinforcement consisted of material and social rewards; the patient received reinforcement only when he displayed his "healthiest" personality. Eventually his other two personalities were eliminated, and the patient was discharged. (Kohlenberg, 1973)

The different personalities in multiple-personality disorder often show contrasting interests. Here Chris Sizemore ("three faces of Eve") is surrounded by some of the paintings created by her personalities.

Family therapy and play therapy are two treatments advocated for children with multiple personality. The most important aspect of play therapy seems to be a supportive, nonthreatening environment in which the child can explore all of his or her personalities.

As this case illustrates, reinforcement can dramatically increase the frequency with which a specific personality appears.

Some clinicians advocate the use of family therapy in treating multiple personalities. In one case, the therapist regarded a female client's symptoms as signifying an imbalanced family situation; he found an unusually strong, dependent, and emotional attachment between the client and her mother. He believed that the girl was part of an emotional triangle with her mother and father, and he interpreted her transformations to different personalities as an attempt to include her father into the life of the family. As treatment continued and the client gradually became somewhat detached from her mother, her relationship with her father improved and the family system became more balanced. The multiple personalities appeared less frequently as the client accepted more responsibility for her actions (Beal, 1978).

Fagan and McMahon (1984) also recommended family therapy for children displaying multiple personalities. In addition, for the child client they suggested play therapy, in which games and fantasy are used to explore the child's other personalities in a nonthreatening manner. Particularly intriguing is their method of fusing the child's different personalities by having them hug each other repeatedly, a little harder each time, until they become one.

SOMATOFORM DISORDERS

The somatoform disorders, shown in the disorders chart on page 174, involve complaints of physical symptoms that closely mimic authentic medical conditions. Although no actual physiological basis exists for the complaints, the symptoms are not considered voluntary or under conscious control. The patient believes the symptoms are real and are indications of a physical problem. The somatoform disorders include somatization disorder, conversion disorder, pain disorder, hypochondriasis, and body dysmorphic disorder. Table 6.2 summarizes their prevalence, onset, and course.

Before we discuss the somatoform disorders individually, we should note that they are wholly different from either **malingering**—faking a disorder to achieve some goal, such as an insurance settlement—or the factitious disorders. **Factitious disorders** are mental disorders in which the symptoms of physical or mental illnesses are deliberately induced or simulated with no apparent incentive (see Focus On). In contrast with both of these conditions, individuals with somatoform disorders believe that a physical condition actually exists.

Cultural factors can influence the frequency, expression, and interpretation of somatic complaints. Physical complaints often occur in reaction to stress

TABLE 6.2 Somatoform Disorders: Their Prevalence, Onset, and Course

Somatoform Disorder	Prevalence	Age of Onset	Course
Somatization disorder	Up to 2 percent; mostly women with less education; high rates also found among African Americans	Often by adolescence; menstrual complaints are frequently first symptom in women	Chronic and fluctuating; rarely remits
Conversion disorder	Relatively rare; only 1 to 3 percent of referrals to mental health clinics; more women, lower socioeconomic status	Late childhood to early adulthood; onset usually acute	Mixed; if of sudden onset, with identifiable stressor, prognosis is better
Pain disorder	Relatively common; gender ratio is unknown—depends on type of pain	Can occur at any age	Most resolve with treatment
Hypochondriasis	Equally common in males and females; from 4 to 9 percent of all medical-practice patients	Any age, but most often in early adulthood	Usually chronic, with waxing and waning
Body dysmorphic disorder	Equally common in males and females	Early adolescence to twenties; onset may be sudden or gradual	Fairly continuous

Sources: Data from Phillips, 1993; Swartz et al., 1991; and DSM-IV.

Dissociative trance states can be entered voluntarily as part of certain cultural or religious practices as demonstrated by this woman during a voodoo ritual. Such cross-cultural phenomena are common.

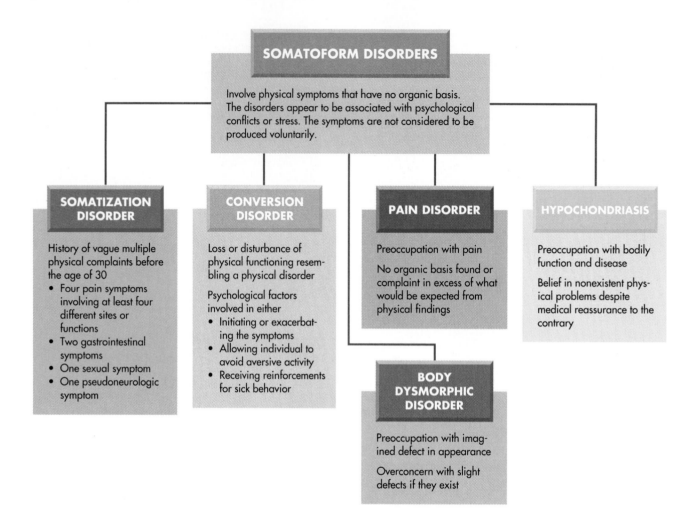

among Asian Americans (Sue & Sue, 1990). In fact, Asian Indian children who were referred for psychiatric services had three times as many somatoform disorders as their counterparts in a control sample of white children (Jawed, 1991). Among some African groups, somatic complaints (feelings of heat, peppery and crawling sensations, and numbness) differ from those expressed in Western cultures (Ohaeri & Odejide, 1994).

Differences like those just described may reflect different cultural views of the relationship between mind and body. The dominant view in Western culture is the *psychosomatic* perspective, in which psychological conflicts are expressed in physical complaints. But many other cultures have a *somatopsychic* perspective, in which physical problems produce psychological and emotional symptoms. Although we probably believe that our psychosomatic view is the "correct" one, the somatopsychic view may be the dominant perspective in most cultures. As White (1982) claimed, "It is rather the more psychological and psychosomatic mode of reasoning found in Western cultures which appears unusual among the world's

popular and traditional system of belief" (p. 1520). Physical complaints expressed by persons of ethnic minorities may have to be interpreted differently than similar complaints made by members of the majority culture.

Somatization Disorder

An individual with **somatization disorder** chronically complains of bodily symptoms that have no physical basis. According to DSM-IV, the following are necessary for a diagnosis of somatization disorder:

■ A history of complaints that involve at least four pain symptoms in different sites, such as the back, head, and extremities

■ Two gastrointestinal symptoms, such as nausea, diarrhea, and bloating

■ One sexual symptom, such as sexual indifference, irregular menses, or erectile dysfunction

■ One pseudoneurologic symptom, such as conversion symptoms, amnesia, or breathing difficulties

Factitious Disorders

A most remarkable type of mental disorder is illustrated in the following cases:

> A hidden camera at a children's hospital captured the image of a mother suffocating the baby she had brought in for treatment of breathing problems. In another case, a child was brought in for treatment of ulcerations on his back; hospital staff discovered the mother had been rubbing oven cleaner on his skin. A "sick" infant had been fed laxatives for nearly four months (Wartik, 1994). In each of these cases, no apparent incentive was found other than the attention the parent received from the hospital staff who cared for the child's "illness."

> [A] woman had an FUO [fever of unknown origin] and nothing seemed to help. For two-and-a-half months, specialists at two hospitals studied her x-rays and blood tests, prescribed penicillin and a variety of other antibiotics, and had no success at all—until doctors at Massachusetts General tried a massive dose of skepticism. She was whisked off for x-rays and her belongings searched, and in her purse was found the source of her baffling sickness: three used syringes and a cup with traces of spittle. She had been injecting herself with traces of spittle. (Adler & Gosnell, 1979, p. 65)

> A survey by the National Institute of Health suggests that the problem deserves more attention. Of 343 persons with a fever of unknown origin recorded over sixteen years, thirty-two patients (nearly 10 percent) were found to be faking their fevers. Among them was a 25-year-old practical nurse who underwent exploratory surgery four times before it was discovered that she was injecting herself with fecal matter (Adler & Gosnell, 1979). Others have "[spat] up blood from a rubber pouch hidden in the mouth, caused genital bleeding by use of sharp objects, [and] injected themselves with insulin, sputum, or bacteria" (Lipsitt, 1983).

These cases illustrate a group of mental disorders, termed *factitious disorders* in DSM-IV, in which people voluntarily simulate physical or mental conditions or voluntarily induce an actual physical condition. (This practice differs from *malingering*, which involves simulating a disorder to achieve some goal—such as feigning sickness to collect insurance.) In factitious disorders, the purpose of the simulated or induced illness is much less apparent, and complex psychological variables are assumed to be involved. The person's behavior is not motivated by incentives such as monetary gain, health improvement, or avoiding legal responsibilities. The individual displays a compulsive quality in the need to simulate illness. If an individual deliberately feigns or induces an illness in another person, the diagnosis is *factitious disorder by proxy*. In the cases above, the mothers produced symptoms in their children to indirectly assume the sick role. Because this diagnostic category is somewhat new, little information is available on prevalence, age of onset, or familial pattern.

Typically, the individual also expresses a number of psychological complaints (Wetzel et al., 1994). The following case illustrates several of these characteristics.

> An internist was examining a woman who made jerky and contorted movements. She complained of seizures in her spine as well as nausea, abdominal cramps, and pain in her hands and feet. She's had these problems since the age of seventeen. The abdominal complaints were investigated during exploratory surgery, and no specific cause for the discomfort could be found. A hysterectomy was also performed to treat problems with a "tipped uterus." She's experienced "dizziness" and "blackouts" since the age of forty. In addition, symptoms involving weakness, blurred vision, and problems urinating were present. Medical assessments were made for the possibility of a hiatal hernia because of complaints of bloating and problems in digesting food. Exhaustive neurological, hypertensive and other workups were made. All examinations failed to reveal an organic basis for the physical complaints. The patient is divorced and lives with an adult son. She also indicated indifference to sex. The internist referred the client to a psychiatrist. (Spitzer et al., 1981)

People who have somatization disorder tend to constantly "shop around" for doctors and often have unnecessary operations. Psychiatric interviews typically reveal psychological conflicts that may be involved in the disorder. Anxiety and depression and other psychiatric disorders are common complications of somatization disorder (Stern, Murphy & Bass, 1993).

Physical complaints are common, but somatization disorder (or *hysteria,* as it was formerly called) is relatively rare, with an overall prevalence rate of 2 percent. It is much more prevalent in females and African Americans and twice as likely among those with less than a high school education (Swartz et al., 1991). Accurate data on its prevalence are difficult to obtain, however, because until DSM-III was published, somatization disorder and conversion disorder were combined in prevalence studies. Although this disorder is rarely diagnosed in men, more than one-third of men who had been referred because of multiple unexplained somatic complaints met the criteria for somatization disorder (Golding, Smith & Kashner, 1991).

Conversion Disorder

Conversion disorder is one of the more puzzling disorders. The term *conversion neurosis* comes from Freud, who believed that an unconscious sexual or aggressive conflict was "converted" into a physical problem. An individual with **conversion disorder** will complain of physical problems or impairments of sensory or motor functions controlled by the voluntary nervous system—such as paralysis, loss of feeling, and impairment in sight or hearing—all suggesting a neurological disorder but with no underlying organic cause. Although they are rare, complaints may also include memory loss or "cognitive or intellectual impairment" that resembles dementia but is reversible (Liberini et al., 1993). Individuals with conversion disorder are not consciously faking symptoms, as are those who have a factitious disorder or who are malingering. A person with conversion disorder actually believes that there is a genuine physical problem, and it produces notable distress or impairment in social or occupational functioning. As discussed in Chapter 1, it was known earlier as *hysteria,* and Mesmer was able to effect cures of individuals with these complaints. A case of a visual conversion disorder follows:

> D.B. was a 33-year-old, single white male who was employed in a clerical job and who lived with his parents. . . . D.B.'s visual disorder began. . . . when he was hit in the right eye with a rifle butt during military training. D.B. reported pain and impaired vision in his right eye and was hospitalized for three weeks. He reported seeing only "shapes and silhouettes of objects" and "cones of white rings" in his right eye. Toward the end of this period, D.B. reported that he could not see anything with his right eye. . . . D.B. then received intensive ophthalmological and neuropsychological assessment.

Although there is nothing physically wrong with the eyes of this Cambodian woman, she claims to be blind. It is thought that trauma suffered in Cambodian prison camps, due to the brutality of the Khmer Rouge, produced such horror that her eyesight "shut down" psychologically. Hysterical blindness is a very rare conversion disorder in the United States but is quite high among Cambodian refugees. Approximately 150 individuals (mostly women) from a Cambodian community of 85,000 people in Long Beach, California, suffer from this disorder.

None of these assessments revealed any apparent physical basis for his visual disorder. (Bryant & McConkey, 1989, pp. 326–327)

One intriguing factor in this case is D.B.'s clear use of visual information. Although he claimed to be unable to see, D.B. did do better on tasks where visual cues were present than on those with no visual cues. Yet he was not aware of this ability. This finding produces a contradiction between the belief that conversion disorders are involuntary and the evidence that on some level, D.B. could "see." The dynamic underlying this process is not clear, although psychological factors are considered important in conversion disorder, in either the initiation or exacerbation of the problem, as illustrated in the following case:

The patient, a 42-year-old white, married male, was admitted in a wheelchair to the Psychiatry Service of the Veterans Administration Center, Jackson, Mississippi. When admitted, he was bent forward at the waist (45-degree angle) and unable to straighten his body or move his legs. For the past fifteen years, he had consistently complained of lumbosacral [lower back] pain. On two occasions (twelve and five years prior to admission) he underwent orthopedic surgery; however, complaints of pain persisted. In the last five years the patient had numerous episodes of being totally unable to walk. These episodes, referred to by the patient as "drawing over," typically lasted ten to fourteen days and occurred every four to six weeks. The patient was frequently hospitalized and treated with heat applications and muscle relaxants. Five years prior to this admission the patient had retired on Social Security benefits and assumed all household duties, as his wife was compelled to support the family.

Orthopedic and neurological examinations failed to reveal contributory causes. An assessment of the patient's family life revealed that there were numerous stresses coinciding with the onset of "drawing over" episodes. Included were the patient's recent discharge from the National Guard after twenty years of service, difficulties with his son and youngest daughter, and "guilt" feelings about the role reversal he and his wife had assumed. Moreover, it was clear that the patient received considerable social reinforcement from family members when he presented symptoms of "illness" (e.g., receiving breakfast in bed and being relieved of household chores). (Kallman, Hersen & O'Toole, 1975, pp. 411–412)

One study of the prevalence and type of conversion symptoms in forty male patients at a Veterans Administration (VA) hospital found that the most common symptoms were paresis (muscle paralysis), anesthesia (loss of bodily sensation), paresthesia (prickling or tingling sensations), and dizziness (Watson & Buranen, 1979). Conversion reactions were also diagnosed in fifteen children, of whom nine were girls.

Their most common problems involved the function of the legs (paralysis and flexing or walking difficulties), whereas problems involving vision and speech were found in only three children. Twelve of the fifteen children had experienced psychological problems in the past (Regan & LaBarbera, 1984).

It is often difficult to distinguish between actual physical disorders and conversion reactions. Conversion disorder usually involves either the senses or motor functions that are controlled by the voluntary (rather than the autonomic) nervous system, however, and there is seldom any actual organic damage. For example, a person with hysterical paralysis of the legs rarely shows the atrophy of the lower limbs that occurs when there is an underlying organic cause (though in some persistent cases, disuse *can* result in atrophy).

Some symptoms, such as glove anesthesia (the loss of feeling in the hand, ending in a straight line at the wrist) are easily diagnosed as conversion disorder because the area of sensory loss does not correspond to the distribution of nerves in the body (see Figure 6.3). Other symptoms may require extensive neurological and physical examinations to rule out a true medical disorder before a diagnosis of conversion disorder can

FIGURE 6.3 Glove Anesthesia In glove anesthesia, the lack of feeling covers the hand in a glove-like shape. It does not correspond to the distribution of nerve pathways. This discrepancy leads to a diagnosis of conversion disorder.

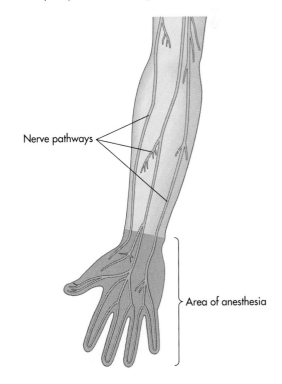

Nerve pathways

Area of anesthesia

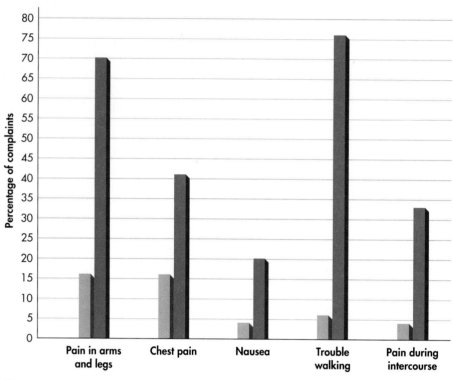

Healthy Controls

Patients

FIGURE 6.4 **Physical Complaints: A Comparison of Individuals with Pain Disorder Versus Healthy Controls** Individuals with somatoform disorders have numerous physical complaints. This graph illustrates the percentage of complaints expressed by a group of individuals with pain disorders.

Source: Data from Bacon et al., 1994.

be made. Discriminating between people who are faking and those with conversion disorder is difficult. For example, subjects asked to simulate a hearing loss can produce response patterns highly similar to individuals with hearing loss from conversion disorder (Aplin & Kane, 1985).

Pain Disorder

Pain disorder is characterized by reports of severe pain that may (1) have no physiological or neurological basis, (2) be greatly in excess of that expected with an existing physical condition, or (3) linger long after a physical injury has healed (Fordyce, 1988). As with the other somatoform disorders, psychological conflicts are involved. People who have pain disorder make frequent visits to physicians and may become drug or medication abusers. Most individuals with pain disorder have numerous physical complaints (see Figure 6.4).

Avoidance behavior can play a role in sustaining pain. Pain is an extremely complex phenomenon involving both psychological and physiological factors (Elliot & Jay, 1987). Typically, pain results from *nocioception* (sensations from pain receptors) and from cognitive factors, including the expectation of experiencing pain while engaging in certain activities, such as exercising or working. If one expects a painful experience, one attempts fewer activities (Fordyce, 1988). As Figure 6.5 indicates, whether avoidance is exhibited depends on several factors (Philips, 1987):

1. The current pain level, which fluctuates

2. Environmental rewards for avoidance

3. Cognitions involving expectations, memories, and *self-efficacy beliefs,* the view that one can successfully perform a certain activity

Avoidance reduces feelings of self-control and increases expectancies of pain. This "self-defeating

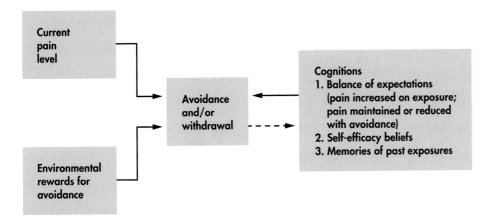

FIGURE 6.5   Avoidance Behavior and Its Role in Sustaining Chronic Pain
Whether avoidance occurs in reaction to pain is dependent on the current level of pain, environmental reinforcers, and individuals' beliefs in their ability to deal with pain.
Source: Adapted from Phillips, 1987.

cycle" between behavior and cognitions may play the greatest role in maintaining avoidance.

Hypochondriasis

The primary characteristic of **hypochondriasis** is a persistent preoccupation with one's health and physical condition, even in the face of physical evaluations that reveal no organic problems. The disorder is a complex phenomenon that includes a fear of having a disease, fear of death or illness, a tendency toward self-observation, and oversensitivity to bodily sensations (Kellner, Hernandez & Pathak, 1992). People with this disorder are hypersensitive to bodily functioning and processes. They regard symptoms such as chest pain or headaches as evidence of an underlying disease, and they seek repeated reassurance from medical professionals, friends, and family members. An estimated 4 to 9 percent of general medical patients have this disorder (Barsky, Wyshak & Klerman, 1992; DSM-IV).

> Mr. B. is a 26-year-old married manual worker. He developed headaches while on holiday abroad, probably due to excess exposure to direct sunlight. These persisted, and he also developed precordial [chest] pain associated with a range of other bodily symptoms, particularly dizziness, breathlessness, and weakness. Physical investigations by a number of physicians including cardiologists and neurologists revealed no physical basis for his symptoms, and he was referred to the department of clinical psychology after a further series of tests (including brain scans), which were carried out with the explicit purpose of reassuring him. He was on sick leave from work, spent much of his time in a prone position, and frequently called the emergency services. He also asked

Hypochondriasis involves a preoccupation with physical symptoms and frequent visits to the doctor in an effort to identify a physical problem. If no readily discernible cause for the physical complaint can be found, a diagnosis of hypochondriasis may be made.

*"You're not really a hypochondriac,
you only think you're a hypochondriac."*

his wife constantly for reassurance, to take his pulse and not to leave him alone in the house. At referral he complained that the doctors were missing something and was eager for more tests to be carried out. The most probable causes of his symptoms were identified by the patient as heart disease, a brain tumor or some other cancer. (Salkovskis & Warwick, 1986, p. 599)

A study of forty-five hypochondriacs (twenty-eight females and seventeen males) found that fear, anxiety, and depression were common complaints. Like Mr. B., each patient feared that he or she had an undetected physical illness. Their anxiety was increased by the expectation that the disorder was progressive and terminal. As a group, the patients also believed that previous physical examinations had been inaccurate (Kellner, 1982).

In his review of hypochondriacs, Kellner (1985) found several predisposing factors. These factors included a history of physical illness, parental attention to somatic symptoms, low pain threshold, or greater sensitivity to somatic cues. Hypochondriasis, therefore, might develop in predisposed people in the following manner: An anxiety- or stress-arousing event, the perception of somatic symptoms, and the fear that sensations reflect a disease process, resulting in even greater attention to somatic cues. Kellner believes that reassurance by physicians reduces anxiety only temporarily because the patients continue to experience bodily symptoms that they interpret as symptoms of an undiagnosed condition.

Body Dysmorphic Disorder

According to DSM-IV, **body dysmorphic disorder** involves a preoccupation with some imagined defect in appearance in a normal-appearing person, or an excessive concern with a slight physical defect. The preoccupation produces marked clinical distress.

Mr. F., a 27-year-old lawyer, was referred for treatment of severe anxiety and depression. At age fourteen, he developed a large acneform blemish on his face over which he developed tremendous concern. This blemish resolved in a rather natural fashion over the course of several weeks, but the patient remained convinced that it was visible and visited several physicians including a dermatologist, requesting help. Thirteen years later, he remained convinced that the blemish was visible, although he acknowledged that it was his perception and no one else's. (Brady, Austin & Lydiard, 1991, p. 539)

Concern commonly focuses on bodily features such as excessive hair or lack of hair and the size or shape of the nose, face, or eyes (see Figure 6.6). Individuals with this disorder often engage in frequent mirror checking, regard their "defect" with embarrassment and loathing, and are concerned that others may be looking at or thinking about their defect (Myers, 1992; Phillips, 1991; Phillips et al., 1993). People with body dysmorphic disorder show evidence of emotional problems, have a minimal degree of "disfigurement," and make frequent requests for addi-

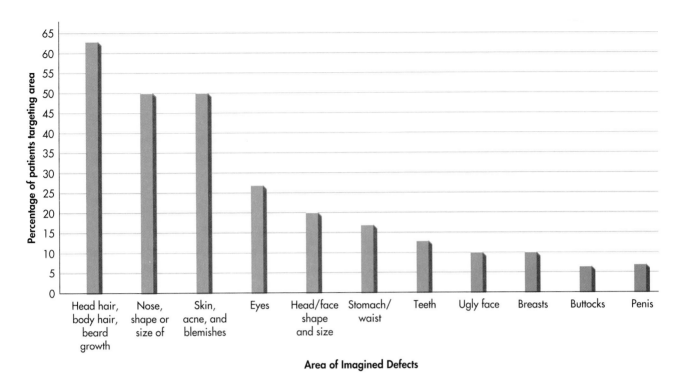

FIGURE 6.6 **Imagined Defects in Patients with Body Dysmorphic Disorder**
This graph illustrates the percentage of thirty patients who targeted different areas of their body as having "defects." Many of the patients selected more than one body region.

Source: From Phillips et al., 1993.

tional operations despite the outcome of previous treatment. They may have a body image disorder similar to that found in anorexia. Most have more than one concern (Phillips et al., 1993). As with the other somatoform disorders, individuals with body dysmorphic disorder seek medical attention—often from dermatologists or plastic surgeons. They are also likely to undergo multiple medical procedures. One patient had surgery to increase the size of her breasts, later had them reduced because they were "too large," and then requested a change in her breast size again (Turner, Jacob & Morrison, 1984).

Researchers have raised several issues regarding body dysmorphic disorder. First, the other somatoform disorders deal with physical disease or dysfunction. Does concern over appearance fit best in this category? Second, how easy is it to figure out where the boundary lies between those with the disorder and individuals who have "normal" concerns over their appearance or those who seek cosmetic surgery? In one study of college students, 70 percent indicated some dissatisfaction and 46 percent had some preoccupation with their appearance (Fitts et al., 1989). Third, what is the relationship between body dysmorphic disorder and obsessive-compulsive disorder or

This individual with body dysmorphic disorder is preoccupied with an imagined "defect" in his appearance.

delusional disorder, somatic type (a psychotic disorder characterized by delusions that the person has a physical defect)? The preoccupation with the imagined defect in body dysmorphic disorder is very similar to obsessive-compulsive disorder. Some with body dysmorphic disorder have been successfully treated with fluoxetine, a serotonin uptake inhibitor, which is also used to treat obsessive-compulsive disorder (Lydiard, Brady & Austin, 1994). The precise relationship between obsessive-compulsive disorder and delusional disorder is still not known. If imagined defects qualify as delusions, then delusional disorder, somatic type, may be an extreme form of body dysmorphic disorder, as Phillips and others have suggested (1994).

Etiology of Somatoform Disorders

Most etiological theories tend to focus on what they consider to be the "primary" cause of somatoform disorders. Diathesis-stress models, however, point to multiple contributing factors. For example, Barsky and Wyshak (1990) believe that a predisposition may develop either through learning or may be "hard wired" into the central nervous system. They believe the predisposition involves (1) hypervigilance or exaggerated focus on bodily sensation, (2) increased sensitivity to weak bodily sensations, and (3) a disposition to react to somatic sensations with alarm. The predisposition becomes a fully developed disorder only when a trauma or stressor occurs that the individual cannot deal with. An even broader diathesis-stress model is presented by Kellner, who includes other variables, such as social and cultural components, personality, and maintaining factors (see Figure 6.7). As you read the following etiological theories, consider the possible advantages of a diathesis-stress model over the single-focus explanations.

Psychoanalytic Perspective Sigmund Freud believed that hysterical reactions (psychogenic complaints of pain, illness, or loss of physical function) were caused by the repression of some type of conflict, usually sexual in nature. To protect the individual from intense anxiety, this conflict is converted into some physical symptom (Breuer & Freud, 1895/1957). For example, in the case of a 31-year-old woman who developed visual problems with no physical basis, therapy revealed the woman had, as a child, witnessed her parents engaging in sexual intercourse. The severe anxiety associated with this traumatic scene was later converted into visual difficulties (Grinker & Robbins, 1954).

The psychoanalytic view suggests that two mechanisms produce and then sustain somatoform symptoms. The first provides a *primary gain* for the person by protecting him or her from the anxiety associated with the unacceptable desire or conflict; the need for protection gives rise to the physical symptoms. This focus on the body keeps the patient from an awareness of the underlying conflict (Simon & Vonkorff, 1991). Then a *secondary gain* accrues when the person's dependency needs are fulfilled through attention and sympathy. Consider the case of an 82-year-old man who reported the sudden onset of diffuse right abdominal pain in March 1977. No abnormal signs were found at that time. In August 1977, he was rehospitalized for the same complaint. Again nothing physical was found. In an analysis of the case, Weddington (1979) noted that the patient's symptom first developed near the twelfth anniversary of his wife's death. His second hospitalization took place near the anniversary of his mother's death, which had occurred when he was twelve. Weddington hypothesized that the painful memories were converted to a physical symptom and that the care and attention bestowed by the hospital staff fulfilled the patient's dependency needs.

Behavioral Perspective Behavioral theorists generally contend that people with somatoform disorders assume the "sick role" because it is reinforcing and because it allows them to escape unpleasant circumstances or avoid responsibilities (Schwartz, Slater & Birchler, 1994). Among 180 subjects, Moss (1986) found that parental modeling and reinforcement of illness behaviors were influential in determining people's current reactions to illness. Having parental models with chronic physical illnesses was prevalent in individuals with somatoform disorders (Craig et al., 1993). They were also more likely to report missing school for health reasons and having childhood illnesses (Barsky et al., 1995).

Fordyce (1982, 1988) analyzed psychogenic pain from the operant perspective. He pointed out that the only available data concerning the pain (or any other somatoform symptoms) are the subjective reports from the afflicted people. Physicians and nurses are trained to be attentive and responsive to reports of pain. Medication is given quickly to patients suffering pain. In addition, exercise and physical therapy programs are set up so that exertion continues only until pain or fatigue is felt. These practices serve to reinforce reports of pain.

Fordyce says that psychogenic pain is often under the influence of these and other external (or environmental) variables. He cited several studies that support his contention. For example, when patients with chronic pain were asked to perform physical therapy exercises until "the pain becomes too great," approxi-

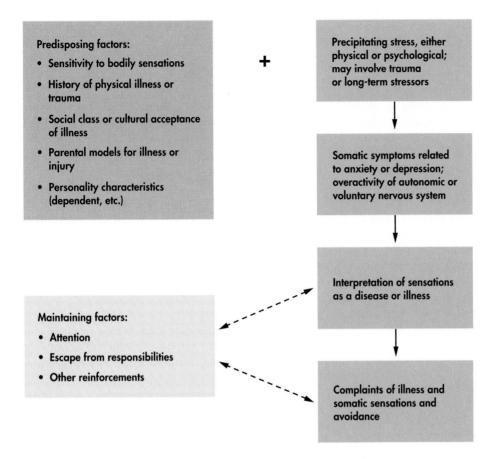

FIGURE 6.7 **Diathesis-Stress Model for Somatoform Disorders** This chart illustrates a diathesis-stress model for somatoform disorder that considers a number of predisposing factors, stressors, and maintaining variables.

Source: Adapted from Kellner, 1985.

mately half the time they stopped after multiples of five exercises! This led to the suspicion that something other than pain was controlling their behavior. When patients in pain exercised on bicycles arranged so that they received no feedback regarding their performance, their tolerance for exercise did not differ from that of patients not in pain. But when performance feedback was available, the pain patients performed significantly worse. Clearly, their tolerance depended on more than their internal bodily sensations.

The importance of reinforcement was shown in a study of male pain patients. Men with supportive wives (attentive to pain cues) reported significantly greater pain when their wives were present than when the wives were absent. The reverse was true of patients whose wives were nonsupportive: Reports of pain were greater when their wives were absent.

Sociocultural Perspective Hysteria, now known as conversion disorder, was originally perceived as a problem that afflicted only women and in fact derived its name from *hystera*, the ancient Greek word for uterus. Hippocrates believed that a shift or movement of the uterus resulted in complaints of breathing difficulties, anesthesia, and seizures. He presumed that the movement was due to the uterus "wanting a child." Although Freud was among the first to suggest that hysteria could also occur in men, most of his patients were women. Satow (1979) argued that hysteria was more prevalent in women when social mores did not provide them with appropriate channels for the expression of aggression or sexuality. Hollender (1980) also stressed the importance of societal restrictions in producing hysterical symptoms in women and suggested the case of Anna O. as an example.

Anna O., a patient of Freud and Breuer, was a twenty-year-old woman who developed a variety of symptoms including dissociation, muscle rigidity, and insensitivity to feeling. Freud and Breuer both believed that these symptoms were the result of intrapsychic conflicts. They did not consider the impact of social roles on abnormal behavior.

According to Hollender, Anna O. was highly intelligent, but her educational and intellectual opportunities were severely restricted because she was a woman. Breuer described her as "bubbling over with intellectual vitality." As Hollender pointed out, "Not only was Anna O., as a female, relegated to an inferior position in her family with future prospects limited to that of becoming a wife and mother, but at the age of twenty-one she was suddenly called on to assume the onerous chore of nursing her father" (Hollender, 1980, p. 798). He suggested that many of her symptoms were produced to relieve the guilt she felt because of her resentment of this duty—as well as to maintain her intellectually stimulating contact with Breuer. After treatment, Anna was supposedly cured. However, Anna O. remained severely disturbed and received additional treatment at an institution. Later, she headed a home for orphans, was involved in social work, and became recognized as a feminist leader. Interestingly, Ellenberger (1972) believes that the cathartic treatment was unsuccessful and that Anna O. is a poor case study on which to build the psychoanalytic foundation.

Satow believes that, as societal restrictions on women are loosened, the incidence of somatoform disorders among women should decline. Yet, the diagnostic criteria involved in some of these disorders tend to ensure the overrepresentation of women.

Biological Perspective Some physical complaints may have more than a merely imaginary basis. Researchers have found that hypochondriac patients were more sensitive to bodily sensations than other people (Barsky et al., 1993); they were better at estimating their heart rates when exposed to short films than were individuals with phobias (Tyrer, Lee & Alexander, 1980). It has been hypothesized that "people who continually report being bothered by pain and bodily sensations [hypochondriacs] may have a higher-than-normal arousal level, which results in increased perception of internal stimuli" (Hanback & Revelle, 1978, p. 523). College students who are predisposed to attending to somatic symptoms rate the sensations they experience more negatively than those who attend less to bodily symptoms (Ahles, Cassens & Stalling, 1987). Innate factors may account for greater sensitivity to pain and bodily functions.

Treatment of Somatoform Disorders

Somatoform disorders have been treated with psychoanalytic approaches, cognitive and operant techniques, and family therapy. The behavioral approaches have received the greatest amount of attention.

Psychoanalytic Treatment The earliest treatment for somatoform disorders was psychoanalysis. Over the years Freud (1905) and Freud and Breuer (1895) reported many cases of "hysterical" patients who, like Anna O., would probably now be classified as showing a conversion reaction or a somatization disorder. Freud believed that the crucial element in treating hysterical patients with psychoanalysis was to help them *relive* the actual feelings associated with the repressed traumatic event—and not simply to help them remember the details of the experience. Once the emotions connected with the traumatic situation were experienced, the symptoms would disappear.

Although Freud eventually dropped hypnosis from his psychoanalytic repertoire, many of his disciples continued to find it beneficial, and variations of it became known as *hypnotherapy*. Bliss (1984) was a modern advocate of hypnotherapy as treatment for somatization disorder and conversion symptoms. Bliss

Anna O., whose real name was Bertha Pappenheim, was diagnosed as being severely disturbed, even though her later years were extremely productive. Was her condition a product of societal restrictions on the role of women or her inability to conform to that role? Or was it something totally different?

Freud dropped hypnosis as a treatment for hysteria because he believed the patient must reexperience the traumatic event, and that hypnosis actually prevented this reliving. Some modern treatments for somatization and conversion disorders are beginning to rely on hypnosis once again, based upon the belief that these disorders are induced by self-hypnosis.

argued that people afflicted with a somatoform disorder engage in involuntary self-hypnosis as a defense, much the same way that patients with multiple-personality disorders do. Hypnotherapy involves bringing repressed conflicts to consciousness, mastering these traumas, and developing coping skills that are more adaptive than self-hypnosis.

Behavioral Treatment   Although psychoanalytic treatments are most often associated with certain somatoform disorders, several behavioral methods appear worth investigating. Individuals with hypochondriasis have been treated with a variety of approaches, including exposure and response prevention. The approach generally involves extinction and nonreinforcement of complaints of bodily symptoms. For example, in one study, seventeen patients were forced to confront their health fears by visiting hospitals, reading literature about their feared illness, and writing down extensive information about the illness. Some were asked to try to "bring forth a heart attack." Reassurance seeking was banned, and relatives were taught not to reinforce the behavior. If a patient said, "My heart has a pain. I think it might be a heart attack," relatives were instructed to ignore the statements. Under this program, the patients improved significantly. However, seven of the patients were found to still have concerns about illness or disease at a five-year follow-up (Warwick & Marks, 1988).

Some researchers have suggested that a cognitive-behavioral approach might be valuable in dealing with somatoform disorders. Salkovskis and Warwick

(1986) compared the effectiveness of operant and cognitive treatments. Eighty-one patients with chronic low back pain were randomly assigned to one of three groups:

1. An operant-behavioral group that focused on changing social and environmental reinforcers (in which patients' spouses were instructed to reinforce exercising and well behaviors and to ignore complaints of pain)

2. A cognitive-behavioral group that focused on modifying patients' cognitions about pain (in which patients identified negative thoughts associated with pain and practiced more adaptive ones)

3. A waiting-list control group (a list of people to be treated at a later time)

Both the operant-behavioral and cognitive-behavioral treatments significantly reduced physical and psychosocial disability. The operant-behavioral approach showed the greatest improvement, however. Interestingly, a twelve-month follow-up revealed that the cognitive-behavioral group eventually improved as much as the operant-behavioral group. Patients in the cognitive-behavioral group were more satisfied with their treatment. They rated the therapy as more helpful and the therapist as warmer (Turner & Clancy, 1988). A two-year follow-up of individuals with chronic pain treated with cognitive-behavioral therapy revealed that, although important gains were maintained, the majority still reported notable levels of pain (Spence, 1991). Cognitive-behavioral treatment has also been effective in treating body dysmorphic disorder (Rosen, Reiter & Orosan, 1995).

Future behavioral treatments probably will include more complete treatment packages. Most somatoform disorders are characterized by sensitivity to somatic symptoms, reinforcement for "sick" behaviors, and concern about disease and the inability to perform activities. Use of operant or cognitive approaches alone may not be enough. A combination of relaxation training to reduce somatic sensations, changing environmental rewards, and altering cognitions may be most successful in treating somatoform disorders.

Family Systems Treatment   The role of the family in maintaining somatoform symptoms has also been recognized by promoters of family therapy for the disorder. Chronic pain is often used to gain rewards (such as attention) and to disclaim responsibility for certain behaviors (such as anger) within the family system. Thus family therapy is recommended as an important part of the treatment for somatoform disorders (Hudgens, 1979).

Research indicates that, in families of patients with somatization disorder, a disproportionately high number of female relatives also have somatization disorder, and many male relatives are labeled either antisocial personalities or alcoholics (Arkonac & Guze, 1963; Bohman et al., 1984). It is certainly not necessary to have multiple cases of psychiatric disorders in a family before considering family therapy, but these research findings strongly suggest that the entire family be drawn into the treatment process. The therapy could then be used to place the identified patient's disorder in proper perspective, to teach the family adaptive ways of supporting one another, and to prepare family members to deal with anticipated and predicted problems.

SUMMARY

1. The dissociative disorders (which are considered relatively rare) involve a dissociation, or separation, of the person's memory, identity, or consciousness. Dissociative amnesia and dissociative fugue involve a selective form of forgetting in which the person loses memory of information that is of personal significance. Depersonalization disorder is characterized by feelings of unreality—distorted perceptions of oneself and one's environment. Multiple personality involves the alternation of two or more relatively independent personalities in one individual.

2. Psychoanalytic perspectives on the etiology of dissociative disorders attribute them to the repression

of certain impulses that are seeking expression. Behavioral explanations suggest that avoiding stress by indirect means is the main causal factor. Dissociative amnesia and dissociative fugue tend to be short-lived and to remit spontaneously; behavioral therapy has also been used successfully. Multiple personality has most often been treated with a combination of psychotherapy and hypnosis, as well as with behavioral and family therapies. In most cases, the therapist attempts to fuse the several personalities.

3. Somatoform disorders involve complaints about physical symptoms that mimic actual medical conditions but for which no organic basis can be found. Instead, psychological factors are directly involved in the initiation and exacerbation of the problem. Somatization disorder is characterized by chronic multiple complaints and early onset. Conversion disorder involves such problems as the loss of sight, paralysis, or another physical impairment with no organic cause. Pain disorder is a condition in which reported severe pain has a psychological rather than a physical basis. Hypochondriasis involves a persistent preoccupation with bodily functioning and disease. Body dysmorphic disorder is preoccupation with an imagined bodily defect in a normal-appearing individual.

4. The psychoanalytic perspective holds that somatoform disorders are caused by the repression of sexual conflicts and their conversion into physical symptoms. Behavioral theorists contend that the role of "being sick" is reinforcing and allows the individual to escape from unpleasant circumstances or avoid responsibilities. Furthermore, psychogenic pain is often reinforced by the external environment. From the sociocultural perspective, the somatoform disorders are seen to result from the societal restrictions placed on women, who are affected to a much greater degree than men by these disorders. Psychoanalytic treatment emphasizes reliving the emotions associated with the repressed traumatic event. Other treatment approaches involve reinforcing only "healthy" behaviors rather than the pain or disability. If possible, treatment is administered within the family system.

KEY TERMS

body dysmorphic disorder A somatoform disorder that involves preoccupation with an imagined defect in a normal-appearing person, or an excessive concern with a slight physical defect

continuous amnesia An inability to recall any events that have occurred between a specific time in the past and the present time; the least common form of psychogenic amnesia

conversion disorder A somatoform disorder in which there are complaints of physical problems or impairments of sensory or motor functions controlled by the voluntary nervous system, all suggesting a neurological disorder but with no underlying cause

depersonalization disorder A dissociative disorder in which feelings of unreality concerning the self or the environment cause major impairment in social or occupational functioning

dissociative amnesia A dissociative disorder characterized by the partial or total loss of important personal information, sometimes occurring suddenly after a stressful or traumatic event

dissociative disorders Mental disorders in which a person's identity, memory, or consciousness is altered or disrupted; include dissociative amnesia, dissociative fugue, dissociative identity disorder (multiple-personality disorder), and depersonalization disorder

dissociative fugue Confusion over personal identity accompanied by unexpected travel away from home; also called *fugue state*

dissociative identity disorder A dissociative disorder in which two or more relatively independent personalities appear to exist in one person; formerly known as *multiple-personality disorder*

factitious disorders Disorders in which symptoms of physical or mental illnesses are deliberately induced or simulated with no apparent incentive

generalized amnesia An inability to remember anything about one's past life

hypochondriasis A somatoform disorder characterized by a persistent preoccupation with one's health and physical condition, even in the face of physical evaluations that reveal no organic problems

iatrogenic Conditions or disorders produced by the therapist

localized amnesia The most common type of amnesia; an inability to recall all the events that happened during a specific short period, often centered on some highly painful or disturbing event

malingering Faking a disorder to achieve some goal, such as an insurance settlement

pain disorder A somatoform disorder characterized by reports of severe pain that has no physiological or neurological basis, is greatly in excess of that expected with an existing physical condition, or lingers long after a physical injury has healed

posthypnotic amnesia An inability to recall events that occurred during amnesia

selective amnesia An inability to remember certain details of an incident

somatization disorder A somatoform disorder in which the person chronically complains of a number of bodily symptoms that have no physiological basis; complaints include at least four symptoms in different sites, two gastrointestinal symptoms, one sexual symptom, and one pseudoneurologic symptom

somatoform disorders Mental disorders that involve physical symptoms or complaints that have no physiological basis; include somatization disorder, conversion disorder, pain disorder, hypochondriasis, and body dysmorphic disorder

CHAPTER 7

PSYCHOLOGICAL FACTORS AFFECTING MEDICAL CONDITIONS

R ob Anderson has been infected with HIV since 1979, is still healthy, and has this to say:

I feel it all goes back to my attitude. . . . I won't let this make me ill. I've watched quite a number of friends go from being relatively healthy to sick and dead in very short periods of time. In every case, they all bought into the idea that you have to die from AIDS if you have HIV. I just simply don't agree with that. (Associated Press, 1994)

Why is it that some individuals succumb and develop AIDS (acquired immune deficiency syndrome) rapidly and others such as Rob are able to resist the disease? Rob attributes survival to his attitude, but it may be that a less virulent strain of HIV is involved or that he has a genetically superior immune system. Such factors must be eliminated before we can assess the importance of a positive attitude in delaying the appearance of AIDS.

But in some cases, attitudes do appear to influence the course of an illness. What other biological effects might attitudes have? Can people "worry or scare themselves to death"? Medical evidence suggests that they can. Stress and anxiety appear to have at least some role in what is called the **sudden death syndrome**—unexpected, abrupt death that often seems to have no specific physical basis.

Sudden death is the leading cause of death in industrialized countries. Each year, about half a million people in the United States wake up feeling fine but collapse and die later in the day. Most people who die this way are discovered to have coronary heart disease, such as narrowing of the arteries or evidence of past heart attacks. Occasionally, some who succumb have normal hearts and cardiac vessels. Sudden death may involve the physiological changes that occur with stress (Kamarck & Jenning, 1991), which include the following:

1. Blood tends to clot more easily, and the risk of blockage in the coronary arteries rises.

2. Blood pressure rises and may result in fat deposits being torn loose and blocking cardiac vessels.

3. Changes in heart rhythm occur, such as *ventricular fibrillation* (rapid, ineffective contractions of the

heart), *bradycardia* (slowing of the heartbeat), *tachycardia* (speeding up of the heartbeat), or *arrhythmia* (irregular heartbeat).

Death from bradycardia in particular may result from feelings of helplessness. The following case shows the impact of this emotion on heart rate:

The patient was lying very stiffly in bed, staring at the ceiling. He was a 56-year-old man who had suffered an anterior myocardial infarction [heart attack] some $2\frac{1}{2}$ days ago. He lay there with bloodshot eyes, unshaven, and as we walked into the room, he made eye contact first with me and then with the intern who had just left his side. The terror in his eyes was reflected in those of the intern. The patient had a heart rate of forty-eight that was clearly a sinus bradycardia. I put my hands on his wrist, which had the effect of both confirming the pulse and making some physical contact with him, and I asked what was wrong.

"I am very tired," he said. "I haven't slept in two and one-half days, because I'm sure that if I fall asleep, I won't wake up."

I discussed with him the fact that we had been at fault for not making it clear that he was being very carefully monitored, so that we would be aware of any problem that might develop. I informed him further that his prognosis was improving rapidly. As I spoke, his pulse became fuller. (Shine, 1984, p. 27)

Here, the patient's physiological response was counteracted by the physician's assurance that his situation was not hopeless—in essence, by removing the source of stress.

Certainly, the sudden death syndrome is an extreme example of the power of anxiety and stress to affect physiological processes. (See Focus On for another example of a similar phenomenon.) Most researchers now acknowledge that attitudes and emotional states can have an impact on physical well-being. In DSM-I and DSM-II, physical disorders such as asthma, ulcers, hypertension, and headaches that stem from psychological problems were called *psychosomatic disorders*. The use of this term was meant to distinguish disorders from conditions considered strictly organic in nature. Mental health professionals now recognize, however, that almost any physical disorder can have a strong psychological component or basis.

The Hmong Sudden Death Syndrome

Vang Xiong is a former Hmong (Laotian) soldier who, with his wife and child, was resettled in Chicago in 1980. The change from his familiar rural surroundings and farm life to an unfamiliar urban area must have produced a severe culture shock. In addition, Vang vividly remembered seeing people killed during his escape from Laos, and he expressed feelings of guilt about having to leave his brothers and sisters behind in that country. He reported having problems almost immediately.

[He] could not sleep the first night in the apartment, nor the second, nor the third. After three nights of sleeping very little, Vang came to see his resettlement worker, a bilingual Hmong man named Moua Lee. Vang told Moua that the first night he woke suddenly, short of breath, from a dream in which a cat was sitting on his chest. The second night, the room suddenly grew darker, and a figure, like a large black dog, came to his bed and sat on

his chest. He could not push the dog off, and he grew quickly and dangerously short of breath. The third night, a tall, white-skinned female spirit came into his bedroom from the kitchen and lay on top of him. Her weight made it increasingly difficult for him to breathe, and as he grew frantic and tried to call out he could manage but a whisper. He attempted to turn onto his side, but found he was pinned down. After fifteen minutes, the spirit left him, and he awoke, screaming. (Tobin & Friedman, 1983, p. 440)

As of 1993, 150 cases of sudden death among Southeast Asian refugees had been reported. Almost all were men, with the possible exception of one or two women; most occurred within the first two years of residence in the United States. Autopsies produced no identifiable cause for the deaths. Some cases of sudden unexplained deaths have also been reported in Asian countries. Although the

number of cases is declining, these deaths remain a most puzzling phenomenon (Gib Parrish, Center for Disease Control, personal communication, 1993). All the reports were the same: A person in apparently good health went to sleep and died in his or her sleep. Often, the victim displayed labored breathing, screams, and frantic movements just before death. Some consider the deaths to represent an extreme and very specific example of the impact of psychological stress on physical health.

Vang was one of the lucky victims of the syndrome—he survived it. He went for treatment to a Hmong woman, Mrs. Thor, who is highly respected in Chicago's Hmong community as a shaman. She interpreted his problem as being caused by unhappy spirits and performed the ceremonies that are required to release them. After that, Vang reported, he had no more problems with nightmares or with his breathing during sleep.

Although the psychosomatic disorders were previously considered a separate class of disorders, DSM-IV does not categorize them as such. Instead, it contains the category "Psychological Factors Affecting Medical Condition." The physical disorders themselves are listed on Axis III. This classification method acknowledges the belief that both physical and psychological factors are involved in all human processes. And the term *psychosomatic disorder* has been replaced with **psychophysiological disorder,** meaning any physical disorder that has a strong psychological basis or component.

The psychophysiological disorders should not be confused with the conversion disorders discussed in Chapter 6. The conversion disorders do involve reported physical symptoms, such as loss of feeling,

blindness, and paralysis, but they do not involve any physical disorder or process. They are considered essentially psychological in nature. By contrast, most psychophysiological disorders involve actual tissue damage (such as an ulcer) or physiological dysfunction (as in asthma or migraine headaches). Both medical treatment and psychotherapy are usually required.

A DSM-IV diagnosis of psychological factors affecting medical condition requires both the presence of a medical condition and the presence of one of the following:

■ A temporal relationship between psychological factors and the onset, exacerbation, or delay in recovery with a medical condition

High-pressure jobs, like that of a stockbroker, are likely to be stressful. But the amount of stress needed to negatively affect an individual varies from person to person. In fact, some people seem to deal efficiently with a great deal of stress, while others find it difficult to cope with even small amounts.

- A psychological factor that interferes with treatment

- Psychological factors that constitute additional health-risk factors in the individual

The relative contributions of physical and psychological factors in a physical disorder may vary greatly. Although psychological events are often difficult to detect, repeated association between stressors and the disorder or its symptoms should increase the suspicion that a psychological component is involved.

In this chapter, we first consider three models that help explain the impact of stress on physical health. Second, we examine the evidence suggesting a connection between stress and how decreased immunological function can contribute to the onset and course of cancer. Finally, we discuss several of the more prevalent psychophysiological disorders: coronary heart disease, hypertension (high blood pressure), ulcers, headaches, and asthma.

MODELS FOR UNDERSTANDING STRESS

A **stressor** is an external event or situation that places a physical or psychological demand on a person. **Stress** is an internal response to a stressor. But something that disturbs one person doesn't necessarily disturb someone else, and two people who react to the same stressor may do so in different ways. Many people who are exposed to stressors, even traumatic ones, eventually get on with their lives. Other people show intense and somewhat long-lasting psychological symptoms.

This section discusses three stress models—the general adaptation, the life-change, and the transaction models—each seeking to explain this difference. To do so, they examine

1. the development and differential effects of stress.

2. the apparent ability of relatively weak stressors to result in strong stress reactions.

3. the ability some people have to cope more "easily" with stress.

The General Adaptation Model

Being alive means that you are constantly exposed to stressors: relationship problems, illness, marriage, divorce, the death of someone you love, seeking a job, aging, retiring, even schoolwork. Most people can cope with the stressors they encounter, provided those stressors are not excessively severe and do not "gang up" on the individual. But when someone is confronted with excessive external demands, coping behaviors may fail, and he or she may resort to inappropriate means of dealing with them. The result may be psychophysiological symptoms, apathy, anxiety, panic, depression, violence, and even death.

There are, in general, three kinds of stressors:

- *Biological stressors* such as infection, physical trauma, disease, malnutrition, and fatigue

■ *Psychological stressors* such as threats of physical harm, attacks on self-esteem, and guilt-inducing attacks on one's belief system

■ *Social stressors* such as crowding, excessive noise, economic pressures, and war

Hans Selye (1956, 1982) proposed a helpful model for understanding the body's physical reaction to biological stressors. He put forth a three-stage model, which he called the **general adaptation syndrome (GAS),** for understanding the body's physical and psychological reaction to biological stressors. The stages are alarm, resistance, and exhaustion.

Selye describes the *alarm stage* as a "call to arms" of the body's defenses when it is invaded or assaulted biologically. During this first stage, the body reacts immediately to the assault, with rapid heartbeat, loss of muscle tone, and decreased temperature and blood pressure. A rebound reaction follows as the adrenal cortex enlarges and the adrenal glands secrete corticoid hormones.

If exposure to the stressor continues, the *adaptation or resistance stage* follows. Now the body mobilizes itself to defend, destroy, or coexist with the injury or disease. The symptoms of illness may disappear. With HIV, for example, the immune system reacts by producing nearly a billion lymphocytes a day to combat the virus. Over time, the immune system gradually weakens and is overcome (Ho et al., 1995). The decrease in the body's resistance increases its susceptibility to other infections or illnesses.

If the stressor continues to tax the body's finite resistive resources, the symptoms may reappear as exhaustion sets in (therefore the name *exhaustion stage*). If stress continues unabated, death may result.

Biological Consequences of Stress Although Selye developed his model for describing physical responses to biological stressors, continuing research now suggests that psychological and social stressors have similar effects. In fact, sustained stress—resulting from psychological or social stressors—not only may make a person more susceptible to illness but may actually alter the course of a disease. For example, it has been documented that recently bereaved widows are three to twelve times more likely to die than are married women; that tax accountants are most susceptible to heart attacks around April 15; that people living in high-noise areas near airports have more hypertension and medical complaints than other people; and that air traffic controllers suffer four times as much hypertension as the general population (Wilding, 1984). The common factor in these groups is *stress.*

For years scientists were skeptical about the supposed effects of stress on the body and dismissed any

relationship between the two as folklore. We now know, however, that stress affects the immune system, heart function, hormone levels, the nervous system, and metabolic rates. Bodily "wear and tear" owing to stress can contribute to diseases such as hypertension, ulcers, chronic pain, heart attacks, cancer, and the common cold.

Psychological Consequences of Stress Most of us maintain certain levels of psychological adjustment that vary little over time. When we encounter a crisis that cannot be resolved through our customary method of coping, our behaviors can become disorganized and ineffective in solving problems.

De La Fuente (1990) proposed an alternative model after interviewing survivors of an earthquake. He described three stages in crisis decompensation, which parallel the three stages of Selye's general adaptation syndrome. **Decompensation** is the loss of the ability to deal successfully with stress, resulting in more primitive means of coping. De La Fuente's three stages are impact, attempted resolution, and decompensated adjustment. More than 90 percent of the survivors interviewed had suffered either a total or partial loss of home. Some 28 percent had lost friends or family members, and 8 percent had been trapped under rubble.

During the *impact* of the crisis (the first stage), the person experiences a sense of confusion and is upset. He or she is bewildered and wonders what is happening, why it is happening, and how a situation so far beyond one's experience can be resolved. Nearly 32 percent of those interviewed showed symptoms of posttraumatic stress disorder (PTSD). Another 19 percent displayed symptoms of generalized anxiety; 13 percent indicated evidence of depression. Many showed decompensated responses such as panic, weeping, hysteria, and dissociation. Guilt and anger were common.

The disequilibrium of the first stage is followed by a period of *attempted resolution,* during which all resources are mobilized to deal with the situation. In the case of a disaster, the person may selectively perceive the situation in a more favorable light. ("We've lost our home and all our possessions, but we're lucky to be alive. We can always rebuild.") Within days or weeks, most of the victims were adapting. When people cope successfully, they tend to resume functioning again at their precrisis level and, in some cases, move into a growth adjustment phase.

If coping is ineffective, the person is likely to move into a *decompensated adjustment phase* (the third stage). This phase may be characterized by withdrawal, depression, guilt, apathy, anxiety, anger, or any number of physical illnesses. As many as 20 percent of the victims required continued specialized help.

The Life-Change Model

As several researchers (Holmes & Holmes, 1970; Rahe, 1994) have noted, events that lead to stress reactions need not be of crisis proportions. Seemingly small, everyday events can also create stress, and any life change, even positive ones, can have a detrimental impact on health. These researchers' work led to the formulation of the **life-change model,** which assumes that all changes in a person's life—large or small, desirable or undesirable—can act as stressors and that the accumulation of small changes can be as powerful as one major stressor. Consider the following case:

> Janet M., a college freshman, had always been a top-notch student in her small-town high school and had been valedictorian of her graduating class. Her SAT test scores placed her in the ninety-fifth percentile of all students taking the exam. Her social life was in high gear from the moment she arrived on the Berkeley campus. Yet Janet was suffering. It started with a cold that she seemed unable to shake. During her first quarter, she was hospitalized once with the "flu" and then three weeks later for "exhaustion." In high school Janet ap-

peared vivacious, outgoing, and relaxed; at Berkeley she became increasingly tense, anxious, and depressed.

In Janet's case, all the classic symptoms of stress were present. No single stressor was responsible; rather, a series of life changes had a cumulative impact. An examination of Janet's intake interview notes at her university's counseling center revealed the following stressors:

1. Change from a somewhat conservative small-town environment to a more permissive atmosphere on a liberal campus

2. Change from being the top student in her high school class to being slightly above average at Berkeley

3. Change in living accommodations, from a home with a private room to a dormitory with a roommate

4. Change from being completely dependent on family finances to having to work part time for her education

5. Change from having a steady boyfriend in her home town to being unpaired

Even relatively minor changes such as leaving home to enter school can produce stress reactions that can lead to illness.

Changes in a person's life can be stressful. Research has found, however, that undesirable life changes, such as loss of a spouse, are more likely to produce anxiety, depression, and physical symptoms in people than are positive life changes, such as graduating from college and beginning a new phase in life.

6. Change in family stability (her father recently lost his job, and her parents seem headed for divorce)

7. Change in food intake from home-cooked meals to dormitory food and quick snacks

Although each of these changes may seem small, their cumulative impact was anything but insignificant. And what happened to Janet is seen, to various degrees, among many entering college students. Going to college is a major life change. Most students can cope with the demands, but others need direct help dealing with stress.

To measure the impact of life changes, Holmes and Rahe (1967) devised the *Social Readjustment Rating Scale* (SRRS), in which they asked people to rate forty-three events in terms of the amount of readjustment that would be required. For example, participants rated the death of a spouse as requiring the greatest adjustment, whereas a minor law violation required the least. For each life event, researchers assigned a numerical value that corresponded to its strength as a stressor (Wyler, Masuda & Holmes, 1971). These "stress potential" values are referred to as *life change units* (LCUs). The investigators found that 93 percent of health problems (infections, allergies, bone and muscle injuries, and psychosomatic illness) affected patients who, during the previous year, had been exposed to events whose LCU values totaled 150 or more. Although a minor life change was not sufficient to constitute a serious stressor, the cumulative impact of many events could be considered a crisis. Particularly revealing was the finding that exposure to a greater number of LCUs increased the chances of illness. Of those exposed to mild crises

(150 to 199 LCUs), 37 percent reported illness; to moderate crises (200 to 299 LCUs), 51 percent; and to major crises (more than 300 LCUs), 79 percent.

Further research shows that different populations and cultures vary in the way they rank stressors. In one study, mainland Chinese ranked divorce fourth in severity of impact, whereas American samples ranked it second. The Chinese participants gave death and serious illness in a close family member second and third ratings. This may reflect the greater importance of the family of origin in Chinese culture. Both groups, however, rated the death of a spouse as the greatest stressor (Zheng & Lin, 1994). See Table 7.1 for ratings of stressors among U.S. undergraduates.

Clearly, stressful life events do play some part in producing physical and psychological illnesses for many people. Yet it is too soon to say that stress causes these illnesses. Most studies cited here are retrospective—they search for influences after the illness is diagnosed. And they are also correlational in nature, so no cause-and-effect relationship can be inferred. In addition, the data used in the studies depend on (1) people's perceptions of health and illness, (2) their recollections and reports of illness (both psychological and physical; sick individuals may recall more events than healthy ones), and (3) their health histories over a defined period (Levenstein et al., 1993). Furthermore, the illnesses of many people do not seem to be preceded by identifiable stressors, and some who undergo stress do not seem to get sick. Finally, evidence now shows that positive and negative life events do not have equal effects. Undesirable life changes seem to be more detrimental than positive life changes (Sarason, Johnson & Siegel, 1978). Also, personal interpretations or characteristics modify the impact of life changes (Lazarus, 1983; Kobasa, Hilker & Maddi, 1979; Sarason, Johnson & Siegel, 1978). Obviously, further investigation of the relationship between life changes and illness is needed.

The Transaction Model

The GAS model is concerned with the process by which the body reacts to stressors, and the life-change model is concerned with external events that cause stress as a response. But neither model considers the person's subjective definition or interpretation of stressful events or life changes. Several processes intervene between the stressor and the development of stress. In particular, the thoughts and interpretations we have about impending threats (stressors), the emotions we attach to them, and the actions we take to avoid them can either increase or decrease the impact of stressors (Levenstein et al., 1993). In his classic book *Psychological Stress and the Coping Process* (1969), Lazarus formulated a **transaction model of stress.** He noted that stress resides neither in the person alone nor in the situation alone, but rather in a transaction between the two. An example can illustrate this point:

> On the morning of August 16, 1992, Mrs. Mavis C. discovered a small lump on her left breast. She immediately contacted her doctor and made an appointment to see him. After examining her, the physician stated that the lump could be a cyst or tumor and recommended a biopsy. The results revealed that the tumor was malignant.
>
> Mrs. C. accepted the news with some trepidation but went about her life with minimal disruption. When she was questioned about the way in which she was handling the situation, she replied that there was no denying that this was a serious problem, and there is great ambiguity about the prognosis, but people are successfully treated for cancer. She planned to undergo treatment and would not give up.

Unlike Mrs. C., many patients would have been horrified at even the thought of having cancer. They might have viewed the news that the tumor was malignant as a catastrophe and focused on thoughts of dying, abandoning all hope. This reaction differs from Mrs. C.'s, who coped with the stressor through internal processes.

The impact of stressors can be reduced or increased depending on the way the situation is interpreted. A person who can adapt cognitively may reduce susceptibility to illness or limit its course. Individuals who deny any negative effects of a stressor or disease, however, do more poorly than those who attempt to cope (King et al., 1990).

TABLE 7.1 Sample Stressors Generated and Ranked by College Undergraduates

Item	Severity	Frequency
Death of family member or friend	3.97	1.89
Had lots of tests	3.62	4.39
Finals week	3.62	3.64
Breaking up a relationship	3.45	2.21
Property stolen	3.41	1.96
Having roommate conflicts	3.10	2.68
Lack of money	3.07	3.36
Arguments with friends	2.97	2.43
Trying to decide on a major	2.79	3.25
Sat through boring class	1.66	4.07

Note: Event severity was rated on a four-point scale, ranging from "none" to "a lot." Event frequency was rated on a five-point scale, ranging from "never" to "always."
Source: Data from Crandall, Preisler & Aussprung, 1992.

One dominant theme threads its way through each of the models discussed: No one factor is enough to cause illness. Rather, as Figure 7.1 indicates, illness results from a complex interaction of psychosocial, physiological, and cognitive stressors.

STRESS AND THE IMMUNE SYSTEM

We have already suggested a relationship between stress and illness. How do emotional and psychological states influence the disease process? Consider the following case:

> Anne was an unhappy and passive individual who always acceded to the wishes and demands of her husband. She had difficulty expressing strong emotions, especially anger, and often repressed her feelings. She had few friends and, other than her husband, had no one to talk to. She was also depressed and felt a pervasive sense of hopelessness. During a routine physical exam, her doctor discovered a lump in her breast. The results of a biopsy revealed that the tumor was malignant.

Could Anne's personality or emotional state have contributed to the formation or the growth of the malignant tumor? If so, how? Could she now alter the

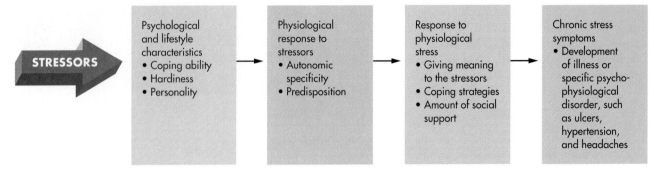

FIGURE 7.1   Interaction Among Psychosocial, Physiological, and Cognitive
Stressors   Stage 4 occurs only if the person has been unable to respond successfully
to stressors.

Source: Adapted from Rahe & Arthur, 1978.

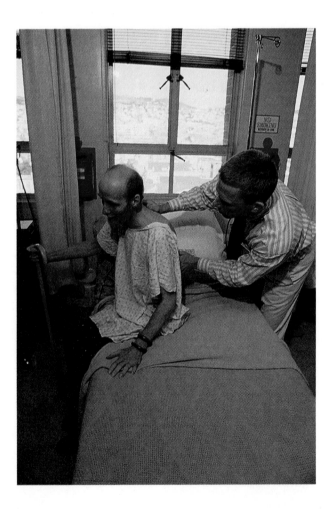

Some AIDS patients live longer than others. It is not certain if it is because some strains of HIV are less virulent than others or if psychological and social factors influence the course of the disease. Perhaps the answer lies in the lower levels of stress experienced by those with greater support. Here, a man is being treated at an outpatient clinic at San Francisco General Hospital.

course of her disease by changing her emotional state? That such questions are being asked represents a profound change in the way in which physical illness is being conceptualized.

The view that diseases other than traditional psychophysiological disorders are strictly organic appears too simplistic. Many theorists now believe that most diseases are caused by an interaction of social, psychological, and biological factors. This relationship has been found in many diseases. King and Wilson (1991), for example, found that interpersonal stress and depression were significantly related to dermatitis. The researchers pointed out, however, that although it is possible to speculate that interpersonal stress caused the skin symptoms, it is also possible that increases in itchiness or unsightliness from the skin condition produced interpersonal stress. The recurrence of herpes symptoms also appears to be influenced by emotional factors. A study by McLarnon and Kaloupek (1988) appears to support the stress-causes-symptom view. People with herpes reported their moods and thoughts daily on a questionnaire. New lesions developed in participants who reported higher anxiety four days before lesions appeared. This held true even when physical symptoms such as tingling and itchiness were controlled. Here the emotional state clearly preceded the physical sensations. Stress has also been implicated in the cause and course of upper respiratory infections and bacterial infections (Cohen & Williamson, 1991). Possible ways in which stress may increase susceptibility to infectious diseases involve (1) altering resistance to infections, (2) initiating or triggering a process that allows the expression of an already present pathogen, and (3) contributing to the maintenance of the disease process.

Even in a disease process such as AIDS, great variations are found in the clinical course of the disease (see Figure 7.2). Some researchers believe these variations may be due partly to psychological variables (Solano et al., 1993). Theorell and colleagues (1995), for example, reported that individuals with HIV who had fewer sources of emotional support showed more rapid deterioration of immune functioning. Such findings could have important treatment implications. An estimated 1.5 million Americans are currently infected with HIV, and this number is expected to total over 30 million worldwide by the year 2000 (Chesney, 1993).

Yet the evidence supporting the importance of psychosocial stressors on the development and progress of AIDS is mixed. One study that found no support for this hypothesis was conducted by Rabkin and her colleagues (1991). The ongoing five-year study followed 124 men who tested HIV-positive but had not developed AIDS. The researchers focused on the following questions: (1) Do HIV-positive persons who are currently depressed have lower immune functioning than those who are not depressed? (2) Is psychological distress related to immune functioning? (3) Do men with current depressive disorders have more symptoms of HIV infection than men without such disorders? After examining the patients who participated in the study for six months, the researchers came up with some tentative findings. HIV-positive men who were depressed or who reported more life stressors showed no more immunosuppression or advanced illness than the other men in the study. In a review of studies examining the impact of psychosocial variables such as depression on the immune function of individuals with HIV, Stein, Miller, and Trestman (1991) concluded that "psychosocial factors, such as depression or stress, do not have a measurable or substantial effect on the immune system in relation to physical disorders, such as AIDS" (p. 171).

It is possible that the duration of studies reviewed was too short for the impact of depression to be fully assessed. Burack and colleagues (1992) found that immune functioning tended to drop drastically after about three years for depressed HIV-positive men versus five years for their nondepressed counterparts. These researchers believe life can be prolonged by treating depression early in HIV-positive persons. In fact, Antoni and colleagues (1991) found that, compared with an assessment-only control group, a stress management group of HIV-positive men showed higher levels of immune functioning.

Factors that may contribute to the contradictory findings include differences in the prior health of the individual, drug abuse history, age, gender, health behaviors, and the stage of the disease process (Kiecolt-Glaser & Glaser, 1995). At this point, it is still unclear how much impact on immune function

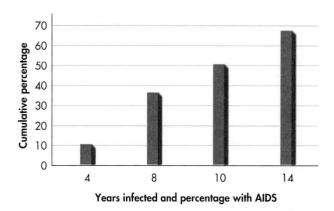

FIGURE 7.2 **Percentage of People Who Develop AIDS After Contracting HIV** A puzzling aspect of AIDS is why it appears so quickly in some HIV-positive individuals and so slowly, if at all, in others. It is possible that 10 to 17 percent of those with HIV will remain free of AIDS even after twenty years.

Source: Data from Curnan et al., 1990.

psychological factors have on a disease such as AIDS. Nevertheless, psychological treatments can at the very least improve the mental well-being of clients.

The Immune System

We know that stress is related to illness, but what is the precise relationship between the two? How does stress affect health? Stress itself does not appear to cause infections, but it may decrease the immune system's efficiency, thereby increasing a person's susceptibility to disease. This connection has received the greatest amount of attention.

The white blood cells in the immune system help maintain health by recognizing and destroying pathogens such as bacteria, viruses, fungi, and tumors. In an intact system, over 1,000 billion white blood cells are based in the lymph system or circulate through the bloodstream. Two major classes of white blood cells are lymphocytes and phagocytes. *Lymphocytes* comprise B-cells (which produce antibodies against invaders), T-cells (which detect and destroy foreign cells), and natural killer (NK) cells (which act as an early detection system to prevent the growth of tumors). *Phagocytes* are also attracted to and destroy invaders (Kiecolt-Glaser & Glaser, 1993).

As mentioned earlier, stress produces physiological changes in the body. Part of the stress response involves the release of several neurohormones (catecholamines, corticosteroids, and endorphins). These

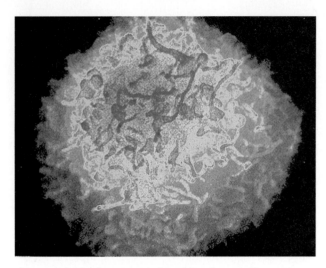

This is a photo of an AIDS-infected T-cell. A T-cell is a white blood cell, which matures in the thymus. T-cells generally kill other cells, but in this case, the T-cell is being destroyed by the AIDS virus.

substances impair immune functioning. *Corticosteroids*, for example, have very strong immunosuppressive actions and are often used to suppress immunity caused by allergic reactions. *Endorphins* also appear to decrease natural killer cells' tumor-fighting ability (Holland & Lewis, 1993). A deficient immune system may fail to detect invaders or produce antibodies. Its killing ability may be impaired, or its blood cells may be unable to multiply. Because of the weakening in defenses, infections and diseases are more likely to develop or worsen.

Decreased Immunological Functioning as a Function of Stress Impaired immunological functioning has been associated with a variety of social and psychological stressors. The spouses of dementia victims showed lower immune functioning than that found among controls, and spouses who reported lower levels of social support showed the greatest drop (Kiecolt-Glaser et al., 1991). Divorced or separated men tend to have poorer immunological functioning than their married counterparts. And happily married men tend to have stronger immune systems than men who are experiencing marital problems (Kiecolt-Glaser et al., 1987). The quality of social relationships may affect our vulnerability to illnesses.

Bereavement (loss of a spouse) has also been found to weaken the immune system. The lymphocyte responsiveness of men married to women with terminal breast cancer was measured approximately one month before their wives' death and again afterward. The second measurement showed a drop in immune response. The decrease in efficiency continued for approximately two months, after which the immune functioning gradually increased (Schleifer et al., 1983). Similar results have been reported in recently widowed women. Women whose husbands had died showed lower NK cell responsiveness than did a group of nonbereaved women (Irwin et al., 1987). Although these stressors are associated with a decrease in immune response, not everyone was equally affected. As indicated in our discussion of the transaction model, the person's perception or interpretation of the event is important. Separated and divorced men who were preoccupied with thoughts of their former partner showed a lower level of immune functioning (Kiecolt-Glaser et al., 1987). How a person interprets an event can influence its impact.

Although our discussion has focused on stress's direct impact on the immune system, indirect pathways must also be considered. For example, an individual who is depressed or facing many different stressors may deteriorate in health practices. He or she may sleep less, drink alcoholic beverages, neglect physical care, or eat fewer nutritious meals. Such changes in health practices can also decrease immune functioning (Kiecolt-Glaser & Glaser, 1988). Thus decreased resistance to disease might be due to changes in behavioral or nutritional patterns as a function of being depressed or stressed. (See Critical Thinking for a discussion of this problem.) It is possible that bereaved persons may show lowered immune functioning because of a decrease in health care practices. Research that attempts to link changes in immune functioning directly with stressors or psychological states must control for these variables.

Mediating the Effects of Stressors

As we have seen, not everyone who faces stressful events develops an illness; this suggests that intervening factors can mediate the effects of a stressor. In this section, we explore some of those factors.

Helplessness or Control Control and the perception of control over the environment and its stressors appear to mitigate the effects of stress. One study of nursing home residents examined the impact of control on the residents' health and emotional states. In the "responsibility induced" group, residents were allowed to make certain decisions, such as how to arrange their rooms, when to see movies, whether to accept visitors, and whether to have plants in their room. The "traditional" group was not offered these choices. Movies were seen when scheduled. Nurses arranged rooms and chose and cared for residents' plants.

Illness: Are Psychological or Physical Factors More Important?

When we talk about psychophysiological disorders, we generally mean that certain psychological states such as depression, feelings of helplessness, and other emotional conditions can cause diseases such as cancer. Much of the research in this area has been developed to identify emotional states and personality variables that may contribute to physical illnesses. This approach has been especially strong in Western countries.

However, other cultural groups focus more on the direct influence of external stresses (loss of job, arguments, bad weather) on illness and place little value on the intervening psychological states such as emotions. There is little acknowledgment or discussion of intervening personality characteristics or emotional states in the etiology of illnesses. In fact, instead of seeing depression as the cause of an illness or disease, they might see depression as a direct result of having a disease such as cancer or hypertension. Western countries see stressors as leading to *psychological states*, which in turn lead to illness. Non-Western cultures, on the other hand, see stressors as leading to *physical behaviors*, which in turn lead to illness.

What advantages or disadvantages do you see in each perspective? When there are cultural differences in perception, how do you determine which view is the most accurate? What are the implications of treatment strategies with each approach? Why do you think Western countries have tended to stress individual-centered (emotional) explanations for illnesses while other countries have not?

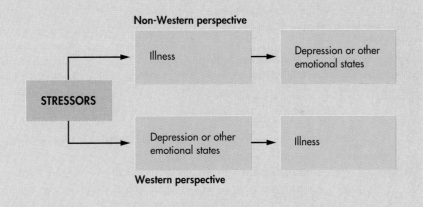

Within a short period, the nurses rated 71 percent of the traditional group as more debilitated and 93 percent of the responsibility-induced group as improved. Self-report questionnaires revealed that the responsibility-induced group rated themselves as more active and happier. Mortality rates also differed between the two groups. After eighteen months, 15 percent (7 of 47) of those in the responsibility-induced group had died, versus 30 percent (13 of 44) in the traditional group. The reason for the differences in mortality rates is unclear. Some deaths, however, might be associated with a less-efficient immune system (Langer & Rodin, 1976; Rodin & Langer, 1977).

A direct relationship between control and the immune system has been found in several studies. In one study, ten subjects were placed in two stress situations. In the first situation, subjects could control the noise level by pressing buttons in a simple sequence. In the other, subjects could not control the noise level. Blood samples were obtained and analyzed after each session. The level of epinephrine (a hormone released during stress) in the uncontrollable stress situation was significantly higher than that found in the controllable one. The subjects also reported a greater sense of helplessness, higher tension, anxiety, and depression while in the uncontrollable stress situation (Breier et al., 1987). Although changes in physical functioning occur with stress, can we show experimentally that lack of control is related to disease?

A study directly measured the effect of the ability to "control" immune functioning. Rats were injected with cancer cells and assigned to one of three groups:

Control or the perception of control over one's environment and its stressors appears to lessen the effects of stress. People in low-stress, low-control jobs may experience greater levels of stress than do people in high-stress, high-control jobs. For example, the manager in this photo probably feels less stress than his employee.

(1) a controllable shock (pressing a bar would end the shock), (2) a yoked control (rats in this group would receive the same pattern of shocks as in the escapable condition but would have no control over it), or (3) a no-shock control group. Sixty-five percent of the rats in the controllable shock group rejected the cancer cells, as opposed to only 27 percent in the yoked control group and 55 percent in the no-shock control group. The inability to control a stressor seems to decrease immune system efficiency (Laudenslager et al., 1983; Visintainer, Volpicelli & Seligman, 1982).

Hardiness: Personality Characteristics and Mood State

Maddi (1972) believes that "hardy" people are more resistant to illnesses. Kobasa and her colleagues (1979) conducted large-scale research on highly stressed executives in various occupations, seeking to identify the traits that distinguish those who handle stress well from those who do not. They found that high-stress executives who reported few illnesses showed three kinds of **hardiness,** or ability to deal well with stress. In their attitudes toward life, these stress-resistant executives showed an *openness to*

change, a feeling of *involvement* or *commitment,* and a *sense of control* over their lives. The most important protective factor correlated with health was attitude toward change (or *challenge*). Those who are open to change seem likely to interpret events to their advantage and to reduce their level of stress.

Suppose, for example, that two people lose their jobs. The person who is open to change may view this situation as an opportunity to find a new career better suited to his or her abilities. The person who is not open to change is likely to see the job loss as a devastating event and to suffer the emotional and physical consequences of this perception. Although the idea that hardiness may buffer the impact of stressors makes sense, the construct has been difficult to define and assess (Funk, 1992).

What can we conclude about stress and its impact on the immune system? The results of many studies consistently show that both short-term stressors (exams, loss of sleep, emotional state) and long-term stressors (marital problems, divorce, bereavement, care for the chronically ill) impair immune system function. Although there is some evidence that certain psychological states such as depression can directly affect the immune system, changes in health practices also have an impact on immune functioning. Stress also seems to aggravate and prolong some viral or bacterial infections.

Evidence suggests, however, that the reduction in immune system efficiency from psychological factors is often relatively small and may account for only about 10 percent of the variance in predicting disease occurrence (Rabkin et al., 1991). As Kiecolt-Glaser and Glaser (1992) point out, "It is sometimes erroneously assumed that changes in immune function translate directly into changes in health. In fact, whether interventions that produce relatively small immunological changes can actually affect the incidence, severity, or duration of infections or malignant disease is not known" (p. 573). And, as we have seen, attitudes and perceptions can influence the impact of stress.

Personality, Mood States, and Cancer

Are certain emotions or personality characteristics involved in either the cause or the course of cancers? Certain researchers believe so. Demonstrating such a link would have important implications in treatment and prevention. In 1993, approximately 526,000 Americans died of this disease and it is estimated that about one in three or 85 million Americans living today will eventually develop cancer (American Cancer Society, 1993).

Bahnson (1981) hypothesized that persons who were sad and depressed but coped by denial and repression of emotions were at greater risk for developing cancer. In the same vein, Simonton and colleagues (1978) hypothesized that certain emotions could inhibit immune system functioning, allowing malignant cells to form. The inability to express emotions or to form lasting interpersonal relationships is believed to be associated with cancer. According to Simonton and colleagues, positive emotions can enhance immune functioning. Meares (1979) agreed and said that physicians should take "the big step of attempting to influence cancer growth by psychological means" (p. 978). Many cancer patients also believe that they can control the course, outcome, and recurrence of the cancer. One patient put it this way: "I think that if you feel you are in control of it [cancer], you can control it up to a point. I absolutely refuse to have any more cancer" (Taylor, 1983, p. 1163). This patient clearly believed that her attitude would have an effect on her cancer. This interpretation, however, is still a subject of controversy (see Focus On).

Several problems exist in research investigating the relationship between moods and personality on cancer. First, *cancer* is a general name for a variety of disease processes, each of which may have a varying susceptibility to emotions. Second, cancer develops over a relatively long period of time. Determining a temporal relationship between its occurrence and a specific mood or personality is not possible. Third, most studies examining the relationship between psychological variables and cancer have been retrospective—that is, personality or mood states were assessed after the cancer was diagnosed. The discovery that one has a life-threatening disease can produce a variety of emotions. Women who received the life-threatening diagnosis of cancer responded with depression, anxiety, and confusion. Thus instead of being a cause, negative emotions may be a result of the knowledge of having a life-threatening disease. Fourth, although it has been shown that injected malignant cells are more likely to grow in stressed versus unstressed mice, the findings do not address the development of "spontaneous" cancers. Would the stressed mice be more likely to develop cancer anyway, without being injected with malignant cells?

The relationship between personality characteristics and cancer is difficult to demonstrate even with well-designed research. Consider the following study: One-hundred-and-sixty women with breast tumors were given a battery of personality tests before being told the results of their biopsies. This was done to control for effects that knowledge of the malignancy would create. Of the women, sixty-nine were found to have a malignant tumor. According to personality measures, the women in this group tended to display extremes in dealing with anger—some were very controlled, and others had frequent outbursts (Greer &

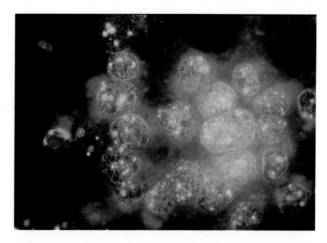

Cancer is produced by the uncontrolled growth of malignant cells. Whether psychological or social factors influence its development or course is a subject of controversy. This photograph shows breast cancer cells.

Morris, 1975). Although this study appeared to control for the impact of knowledge of having a disease on the emotional state, perhaps it did not. Could some women in this study have guessed correctly about the results of their biopsies? And if so, how could they have guessed?

Schwartz and Geyer (1984) found that many patients are aware that they have cancer before a formal diagnosis is made. How do they know? Patients may be very attentive to their physicians' reactions during the examination; physicians may "unwittingly" convey cues that reflect their opinion. These cues may account for the fact that 75 percent of the women in the study were accurate in predicting whether they had the disease before they received their biopsy results. Schwartz and Geyer suggested that emotional expressions such as anger, depression, denial, and hopelessness may reflect the patient's reaction to the anticipated negative diagnosis. Because it is difficult to eliminate patient expectations, the precise relationship between personality and cancer is still unclear.

Specific emotional states have been suspected of influencing the onset and course of cancer. Depression (measured by the MMPI) was positively associated with a twenty-year incidence of mortality from cancer (Persky, Kempthorne-Rawson & Shekelle, 1987). People with high depression scores were more than one-third more likely to develop cancer and almost twice as likely to die of cancer, compared with those rated low in depression. This was true even when risk factors such as age, smoking, alcohol intake, occupational status, family history of cancer, and serum cholesterol levels were considered. Because the study was prospective (begun before the cancer cases were diagnosed), the possibility that depression resulted from

Do Psychological and Social Factors Contribute to the Development of Cancer?

Are cancers caused by psychological factors, and if so, can they be cured by psychological means? To examine the impact of social and psychological factors on patients' ability to fight their disease, Cassileth and colleagues (1985) studied a group of 204 men and women with advanced cancer and a group of 155 women with breast cancer. The variables they examined included social ties and marital history, job satisfaction, general life satisfaction, and degree of hopelessness and helplessness. These variables were selected because they were considered factors that might influence immune functioning. But no relationship was found between disease recurrence or length of survival and any of the social or psychological variables. Cassileth and colleagues concluded that in cases of advanced cancer, "the inherent biology of the disease alone determines the prognosis" (p. 1555).

In an editorial accompanying the Cassileth study, deputy editor of the *New England Journal of Medicine* Marcia Angell (1985, p. 1570) asked, "Is cancer more likely in unhappy people? Can people who have cancer improve their chances of survival by learning to enjoy life and to think optimistically?" Angell answered these questions with a resounding "No!" She pointed out that most reports suggesting the influence of psychological factors on diseases are anecdotal and that few of the studies are "scientifically sound." In addition, the view that psychological states can influence the development of cancer serves to blame the victim and to further burden them. She concluded by stating that "it is time to acknowledge that our belief in disease as a direct reflection of mental states is largely folklore" (p. 1572).

Angell's comments produced a flurry of letters to the *New England Journal of Medicine*. Wil-

knowledge of having a cancer was eliminated. Depression was assessed only at the beginning of the study, however. To demonstrate a relationship of this emotion with cancer, we would have to show that it was a long-term disorder in these people.

Do stress, emotional difficulties, or personality characteristics increase the chance that a person will develop cancer or increase the cancer's severity if it does occur? Certain emotions and stressors have been associated with a less-efficient immune system, and under these conditions cancer might be more likely to gain a foothold. Nevertheless, the connection between stress and naturally occurring cancers remains to be shown. Maybe only certain cancers, at a certain level of development, are influenced by emotional states. Researchers are currently investigating this possibility.

PSYCHOLOGICAL INVOLVEMENT IN SPECIFIC PHYSICAL DISORDERS

Although most research studying the impact of psychological factors on immune function is fairly recent, the mind-body connection between some physical disorders has been extensively studied. In many instances, a relationship has been found between psychological or social factors and the origin and exacerbation of these conditions. In addition, particularly stressful occupations have also been linked to the development of certain disorders. The First Person narrative in this chapter examines some of the more stressful aspects of police work.

Coronary Heart Disease

In 1990, nearly 500,000 people died of coronary heart disease in the United States; more than one-third of them were younger than age 65 (American Heart Association, 1993). **Coronary heart disease (CHD)** is a narrowing of the arteries in or to the heart, resulting in the restriction or partial blockage of the flow of blood and oxygen to the heart. Symptoms of CHD may include chest pain (*angina pectoris*), heart attack, or, in severe cases, cardiac arrest. The incidence of coronary heart disease has diminished in recent years because of changes in smoking, diet, exercise, and treatment of hypertension (Rothenberg & Aubert, 1990). Although cigarette smoking, obesity, physical inactivity, hypertension, and elevated serum cholesterol are known to increase the risk of CHD, they do not by themselves seem to be sufficient to cause the disease. Studies suggest that psychological and social variables may be contribu-

liams, Benson, and Follick (1985), each of whom has served as the president of the Society of Behavioral Medicine, commented that the Cassileth study did not rule out the possibility that psychological factors were involved in the initiation of cancer and warned that accepting Angell's views could eliminate research into the biological correlates of mental states. Livnat and Felton (1985) pointed out that a growing body of scientific literature showed that psychological factors influence many physiologic functions. They argued that "Angell urges us to throw out the baby with the bath water" (p. 1357). The American Psychological Association sent a letter to the *New England Journal of Medicine* characterizing Angell's

editorial as "inaccurate" (Abels, 1986).

Debate will continue on the role of psychological factors in the cause and treatment of this disease. Ramirez and colleagues (1989) reported a tentative relationship between severe life stressors and the recurrence of breast cancer in women. In a meta-analysis of studies involving adult cancer patients, Meyer and Mark (1995) concluded that psychosocial interventions had a "small" or modest positive effect on emotional and functional adjustment but had little effect on the progression of the disease itself. The discrepant findings are confusing and represent the complexities of research in this area.

To make progress in determin-

ing the link between psychological state and cancer, we must first decide what psychological or social variables may be important. We then need to develop valid instruments to measure these dimensions. Third, we have to decide which of the many types of cancer we are interested in studying and the stage of development at which we would study them. Finally, even if we found a relationship, how could we be certain of the direction of causality? That is, how would we know that the physiology of the cancer or the patient's knowledge of having cancer is not causing the psychological state, rather than the other way around?

tory factors that produce certain pathogenic physiological changes.

For example, women who reported high job stress or perceived their relationship with their boss to be poor had higher fibrinogen levels than those found among other female employees. Fibrinogen, a blood-clotting compound, may contribute to coronary heart disease by contributing to atherosclerosis and by participating in the formation of blood clots (Davis et al., 1995). Thus, emotional states may increase susceptibility to developing CHD. There is also some evidence that high levels of anxiety may be related to incidents of fatal heart attacks. In a 32-year prospective study on 2,280 men with or without coronary heart disease, those with anxiety symptoms, as measured by a five-item questionnaire, were more than three times more likely to eventually die of sudden cardiac arrest. (See Table 7.2 for questions used in the anxiety questionnaire.) It is possible that anxiety may hasten the development of coronary heart disease and may produce coronary spasms or ventricular arrhythmias leading to fatal cardiac arrest (Kawachi et al., 1994).

Type A and Type B Personality Patterns   Friedman and Rosenman (1974) identified a behavior pattern, called Type A behavior, that they believed was associated with increased risk of heart attack. The pattern

involves aggressiveness, competitiveness, hostility, time pressure, and constant striving for achievement. In self-reports, Type A people indicate that they are easily aroused to anger and that they experience this emotion intensely and frequently (Levenkron et al., 1983; Stevens et al., 1984). Coronary heart disease is

Stress may contribute to coronary heart disease by producing physiological changes that help plaque build up on the wall of the coronary artery. In this picture, the artery is almost entirely blocked.

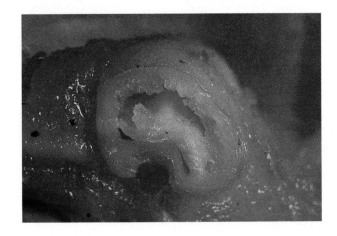

FIRST PERSON

Leslie Sue

Stress and police work go hand in hand. In fact, very few careers cause as much stress as law enforcement. Research shows that police officers spend more time maintaining order than making arrests. Nevertheless, at any moment in an otherwise routine day, an officer may confront a life-and-death situation. An officer who stops a vehicle for speeding, for example, has no idea what to expect. The occupant could be a newly licensed teenager, a bank executive hurrying to get home, or a psychopath who has just robbed a local convenience store at gunpoint! It is the uncertainty of what lies ahead and the need to respond to it immediately that leads to stress and its symptoms.

I recall one incident that occurred in 1983. While assigned to the Selma resident agency of the Mobile, Alabama, FBI field office as a special agent, I was called to a scene where an armed robbery had just occurred. When I got there, the police had already cordoned off a heavily forested area where the suspect was thought to be hiding. We knew he was armed, but the area had to be searched anyway. It was a stressful situation, and I'm sure every officer there was as apprehensive as I was because we knew we could be wounded or killed. And in fact, during the early morning hours, the suspect was killed in an exchange of gunfire that began when he resisted arrest.

Police officers must always be mentally and physically prepared to respond quickly to threatening situations. Their lives and the lives of others often depend on quick response. It's not surprising, then, that the stress this causes often manifests itself in a high prevalence of cardiovascular disease, suicide, marital conflict and divorce, alcoholism and drug dependency, and stomach ailments.

In recent years, researchers have identified stress as a major hazard in this occupation. Some of the more progressive police agencies have even designed programs to help officers improve their diet and learn stress-reduction techniques such as meditation and relaxation. Many organizations also provide counseling services. These efforts have had a positive impact on reducing job stress and burnout, resulting in increased use of such programs. However, stress on the job continues to be a major debilitator in police work.

Leslie Sue is the chairman of the law enforcement program at Tacoma Community College. He was formerly a special agent with the FBI and a police officer.

Japanese living in America who maintain traditional lifestyles have a lower rate of coronary heart disease than acculturated Japanese. The difference is not accounted for by diet or other risk factors.

more likely in Type A than in Type B people. Among middle-aged men with coronary heart disease, 70 percent were Type A; in healthy men, only 46 percent were Type A (Miller et al., 1991). A second behavior pattern, Type B, is characterized as relaxed and not subject to time pressure. These two behavior patterns appear to be relatively stable.

Questioning the Type A Hypothesis   Although evidence initially suggested that the Type A personality was related to coronary heart disease, recent research suggests something different. Researchers are reexamining the picture of a harried businessperson, competitive, hostile, under strict time constraints, and doing several things at once. Julkunen and colleagues (1993) reviewed the qualities for CHD related to the Type A personality and found that the only significant risk factor was irritability and hostility, either openly expressed or suppressed. Similar conclusions have been reached by Williams and associates (1988) and Wood (1986). The Type A behavior pattern apparently includes both benign factors and others that place individuals at risk. If hostility is the important element, programs that focus on benign factors, such as helping people slow down and enjoy life, may not be helpful in averting the risk of CHD.

Stress and Hypertension

> October 19, 1987, has become known as "Black Monday," the day the stock market dropped 508 points. On that day, a 48-year-old stockbroker was wearing a device that measured stress related to the work environment. The instrument measured his pulse every fifteen minutes. At the beginning of the day, his pulse was sixty-four beats per minute and blood pressure was 132 over 87 (both rates within the normal range). As stock prices fell dramatically, the man's physiological system surged in the other direction. His heart rate increased to eighty-four beats per minute and blood pressure hit a dangerous 181 over 105. His pulse was "pumping adrenalin, flooding his arteries, and maybe slowly killing himself in the process." (Tierney, 1988)

This case illustrates the impact of a stressor on blood pressure. This physiological response is found in all of us. In some people, however, it develops into a chronic condition called **essential hypertension,** or high blood pressure of 140 over 90 or higher. Blood pressure is a measurement of the force of blood against the walls of the arteries and veins. Essential hypertension is found in nearly 28 percent of the U.S. population, which makes it the most common disease in the United States (Burt et al., 1995). In 90 percent of persons with this diagnosis, no organic cause can be determined. Figure 7.3 shows some gender and ethnic comparisons of hypertension among adults.

TABLE 7.2   Anxiety Questionnaire Items That Correlated with Eventual Onset of Fatal Heart Attacks
Do strange people or places make you afraid?
Are you considered a nervous person?
Are you constantly keyed up and jittery?
Do you often become suddenly scared for no good reason?
Do you often break out in a cold sweat?

Source: Kawachi et al. (1994).

Participants who checked yes for two or more of these questions were more than three times more likely to develop fatal coronary heart disease than were those who answered no.

Although sensitivity to time pressure, hostility, competitiveness, and the inability to relax are some characteristics of Type A personalities, only hostility has been directly related to coronary heart disease.

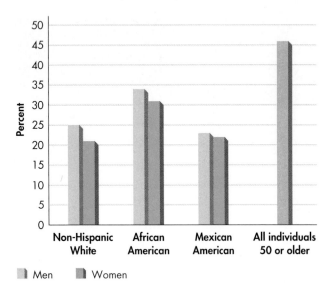

Men   Women

FIGURE 7.3 **Gender and Ethnic Differences in Hypertension Among U.S. Adults** The highest prevalence (percentage) of chronic high blood pressure occurs most frequently among African Americans and among all individuals over the age of 50. Women tend to score somewhat lower than other groups. Biological, lifestyle, and psychological factors have been implicated in the gender and ethnic differences in hypertension.

Source: Data from Burt et al., 1995.

Chronic hypertension may lead to arteriosclerosis (narrowing of arteries) and increased risk of strokes and heart attacks (Waldstein et al., 1991).

A number of studies suggest that stressors and hypertension may be related. Living in crowded neighborhoods and being in a stressful occupation are both associated with high blood pressure (Ely & Mostardi, 1986; Fleming et al., 1987). Increases in blood pressure have been observed in persons exposed to stressors (Patterson et al., 1995). A familial component may also be involved. Men who have both a family history of hypertension and normal blood pressure showed exaggerated cardiovascular responses to stressors (Semenchuk & Larkin, 1993).

In addition to studies that link the presence of stressors to the presence of hypertension, others have shown a connection between reducing stress and lowering blood pressure. Reducing stress by relaxing, both at home and at work, significantly lowers blood pressure. Having social support also reduces the impact of stressors (Gerin et al., 1992). Taken together, the two types of studies indicate that stress has a definite impact on blood pressure, and they support the contention that people who suffer from chronic stress may be at risk for developing hypertension.

Along with exposure to stressors, emotional reactions may also contribute to hypertension. Blood pressure tends to be temporarily higher when people are angry or anxious than when they are relaxed and contented (James et al., 1986). Researchers are trying to identify emotional patterns that produce a chronic elevation. As with other disorders, there is evidence that angry cognitions or thoughts play a role in hypertension (Davison et al., 1991). Conversely, psychological factors such as social support can act as a buffer to reduce blood pressure increases in individuals facing stressors (Gerin et al., 1995).

Gender may also play a role in the development of hypertension. In a study by Lai and Linden (1992), men and women were evaluated on emotional expressiveness and classified as either "anger in" (suppressing anger) or "anger out" (expressing anger). They were then exposed to verbal harassment and either allowed to release their anger or inhibited from doing so. Men displayed greater cardiovascular reactivity to the harassment than did women. The opportunity to release anger facilitated heart rate and diastolic (blood pressure when the heart is at rest) recovery in men but not in women. Women with "anger in" tendencies showed better systolic (blood pressure when the heart is contracting) recovery than women with "anger out" tendencies, regardless of whether they had an opportunity to express anger. Holding in anger did not produce the strong negative physiological reactions in women that it did in men. The researchers hypothesized that these differences in recovery patterns may be due to the differential socialization of males and females.

Certain individuals may be more susceptible to stress on the job. Light et al. (1995) found that two variables—a high-status job and the belief in hard work to achieve success—are related to higher blood pressure in women and in African American men. A high-status job alone was not related to higher blood pressure. The correlation appeared only when it was combined with the belief that great effort was necessary for success. Interestingly, white males with the same characteristics did not show elevated blood pressure. It may be that women and black men in this study believe that they must overcome barriers and hostility to maintain their high-status positions.

Ethnic Factors in Hypertension That African Americans have higher mean blood pressure levels and higher rates of hypertension than their white counterparts has been taken as evidence of genetic influence. Black men show greater increases in systolic and diastolic blood pressure in reaction to cold stimulation than white men do. This finding has been used as an indication that there may be differences in sympathetic nervous system activity between the two

TABLE 7.3 Some Differences Between Duodenal and Gastric Ulcers

Duodenal Ulcer	Gastric Ulcer
1. More frequent in young people	More frequent in older people
2. Associated with oversecretion of stomach acid	Associated with normal amounts of stomach acid
3. Occurs in members of higher social classes	Usually occurs in members of lower social classes
4. Associated with intellectually demanding jobs	Associated with jobs involving heavy manual labor
5. Eating relieves symptoms	Eating causes discomfort
6. Occurs mainly in males	Somewhat more common in males than in females

Source: Adapted from Eisenberg, 1989.

groups. Increased awareness of the disorder and better treatment for it have substantially reduced hypertension among African Americans and have slightly reduced rates for white women (Foreyt, 1987). However, hypertension is still more prevalent among black Americans than among white Americans (Treiber et al., 1993). Asian Americans show lower rates of hypertension than are found in the general population (Stavig, Igra & Leonard, 1988).

Social factors are also involved. Dressler, Dos Santos, and Vitere (1986) found that the availability of psychosocial resources modified black-white differences in blood pressure. The highest blood pressure was found among African Americans with the lowest psychosocial resources, a finding that suggests the impact of environmental factors. The degree of genetic contribution to hypertension remains an unanswered question.

Peptic Ulcers

Peptic ulcers, which are essentially open sores within the digestive system, cause 10,000 deaths each year in the United States. One of every ten persons is afflicted by this disorder at some point in his or her life (Weiner, 1991).

Tony L. is a hard-working and competitive student. For a period of about a year, he felt a burning sensation in his stomach. On the day before he was to take his graduate record examinations, he felt an overwhelming pain in his abdomen. He collapsed and was taken to a hospital, where examination revealed that he had a duodenal ulcer.

The most common site for ulcers is the small intestine; ulcers located there are called *duodenal ulcers.* A somewhat less-common site is the stomach, where

they are called *gastric ulcers.* (See Table 7.3 for differences between the two types.) Duodenal ulcers are associated with excessive hydrochloric acid secretion. The pain tends to be rhythmic, occurring when the stomach is empty and diminishing after eating. Gastric ulcers seem to occur more frequently in older people, and eating causes discomfort.

It was once thought that ulcers were the result of factors such as excessive secretion of stomach acid, insufficient secretion of the mucous that coats and protects the walls of the stomach, or inadequate regeneration of the stomach lining (Whitehead, 1993). Evidence is accumulating, however, that a specific form of bacteria, **H pylori** (helicobacter pylori) is the cause of peptic ulcers. Beam (1995) indicates the reasoning behind this conclusion. First, although antisecretory agents can help ulcers heal, rates of recurrence are very high. Second, H pylori has been found in nearly every patient with ulcers. Third, once the ulcers are healed and H pylori has been eliminated, recurrence is rare.

Although H pylori appears to cause peptic ulcers, psychological stress may play a role in making an individual more susceptible to the presence of the bacteria or may exacerbate an ulcer once it is present. Ulcer patients often report that emotional events preceded the onset of pain (Salim, 1987).

Migraine, Tension, and Cluster Headaches

Headaches are among the most common psychophysiological complaints, accounting for over 18 million visits to medical practitioners each year (Jones, 1995). The pain of a headache can vary in intensity from dull to excruciating. It is unclear whether the different forms of headaches (migraine, tension, and cluster)

"I'd say the sales chart is the ulcer, the phone is the hypertension, the paperwork is the migraine..."

several days and often accompanied by nausea and vomiting. A nationwide survey (Stewart et al., 1995) revealed that migraine headaches were common among women and people with lower incomes (see Figure 7.5). They are less common among African Americans than among white Americans.

Migraine headaches are of two general types: classic and common. The *classic* type begins with an intense constriction of the blood vessels in the brain, dramatically diminishing the supply of blood. Depending on which part of the brain is affected most, the person may show various neurological symptoms, such as distortion of vision, numbness of parts of the body, or speech and coordination problems. When the blood vessels then become distended to compensate for the diminished blood supply, severe pain occurs. The nerves become so sensitive that the blood, as it courses through the vessels with each heartbeat, produces a characteristic pulsating or throbbing pain (Goleman, 1976; Walen et al., 1977). With *common* migraine headaches, the first phase is less severe, and neurological symptoms may not be evident. The pain also is less intense than in classic migraine headaches. Although stress is a factor, sufferers may be congenitally predisposed to migraines (Messinger et al., 1991).

Tension Headaches Tension headaches were once thought to be produced by prolonged contraction of the scalp and neck muscles, resulting in vascular constriction and steady pain. Some studies, however, have found a lack of correspondence between reports of pain and muscle tension among people who have tension headaches. Many people showed no detectable muscle tension but still reported headaches (Philips, 1983). Friedman (1979) listed some complaints of 1,420 persons who experienced tension headaches:

"Feeling as if my head is being squeezed in a vise"

"A tight headband that keeps getting tighter"

"Top of the head is blown off"

Psychological factors precipitated the headaches in 77 percent of the patients, most of whom were women. Tension headaches are generally not as severe as migraine headaches, and they can usually be relieved with aspirin or other analgesics.

Cluster Headaches Cluster headaches are often described as excruciating, and they tend to occur on one side of the head near the eye, producing tears and a blocked nose. The pain is so great that sufferers may commit violent acts such as banging their heads against the wall (Clark et al., 1988). Little research has been conducted on cluster headaches.

are produced by different psychophysiological mechanisms or whether they merely differ in severity. Compared with people who are headache free, individuals with headaches show greater sensitivity to pain in body areas other than the head (Marlowe, 1992). One factor, stress, appears to contribute to the initiation of headaches.

Although we discuss migraine, tension, and cluster headaches separately, the same person can be susceptible to more than one type of headache. Furthermore, Blanchard and Andrasik (1982), who analyzed well-designed research studies comparing the different forms of headaches, concluded that, in spite of some apparent differences, there is little support for the view that the forms can be easily distinguished from one another. (Figure 7.4 illustrates some differences among the three types of headaches.)

Migraine Headaches Constriction of cranial arteries, followed by dilation of the cerebral blood vessels resulting in moderate to severe pain, are the distinguishing features of **migraine headache.** Anything that affects the size of these blood vessels, which are connected to sensitive nerves, can produce a headache. Thus certain chemicals, such as sodium nitrate (found in hot dogs), monosodium glutamate, and tyramine (found in red wines), can produce headaches by distending blood vessels in certain people. Although pain from a migraine headache may be moderate, as noted earlier, it is usually severe, lasting from a few hours to

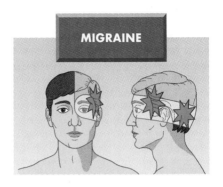

MIGRAINE	**TENSION**	**CLUSTER**

SYMPTOMS

Throbbing pain (most severe in red) on one side of the head. Often preceded by an "aura," with glowing spots before the eyes. May cause nausea and aversion to lights, sounds. Often associated with menstruation. Lasts four hours to two days.

SYMPTOMS

Dull, constricting ache on both sides of head rather than piercing pain. Often concentrated in "hatband" region or running into neck and shoulders. Can be intermittent or chronic.

SYMPTOMS

Intense pain, always on the same side of the head. Eye often teary, nose clogged. Lasts 20 minutes to two hours. Occurs at least once a day for two weeks or months, then stops for months or years before recurring.

TREATMENT

During attacks: rest in a quiet, dark place. Medications include ergot compounds and nonnarcotic and anti-inflammatory pain relievers. To prevent attacks: beta blockers, tricyclic antidepressants, and anti-inflammatories.

TREATMENT

During attacks: nonnarcotic pain relievers and muscle relaxants. To prevent attacks: biofeedback, relaxation exercises, and tricyclic antidepressants.

TREATMENT

During attacks: ergotlike compounds, oxygen. To prevent attacks: calcium channel blockers, ergotlike compounds, lithium, and steroids.

FIGURE 7.4 Three Types of Headaches

Source: From *Newsweek on Health,* Spring 1988.

Headaches appear to involve a biological predisposition such as greater reactivity of the blood vessels in the brain that respond to physical and psychological stressors. The precise mechanism involved, however, is not known. Headache pain is being perceived as more than a function of a physiological factor (muscle tension, dilation of cranial arteries). Several psychological interventions such as relaxation, cognitive therapy, and biofeedback show promise in treating headaches (Blanchard, 1992). We explore these interventions in more detail later in this chapter.

Asthma

Asthma is a respiratory disorder that results from constriction of the airways in the lungs owing to muscle tone changes in the airways, excessive mucus secretion, edema, or inflammation. During asthma attacks, breathing becomes very difficult and produces a wheezing sound. The person struggles for breath and may develop acute anxiety, which aggravates the condition. Between 1980 and 1989, the death rate from asthma increased 46 percent; it rose disproportionately among women of any race (Rollason, 1995). The death of model Krissy Taylor in 1995 was attributed to undiagnosed asthma. The reason for the increase in mortality among asthma sufferers is unknown.

Asthma appears to have a diurnal variation: Symptoms often are worse during the night and early morning. Persons with asthma may report nightmares involving strangling or drowning (Monday, Montplaisir & Malo, 1987). The prevalence of asthma is estimated to be about 7 percent of the population, occurring mostly in persons younger than 17 years of age. As many as 80 percent show substantial or complete remission of symptoms as they grow older (Mrazek, 1993).

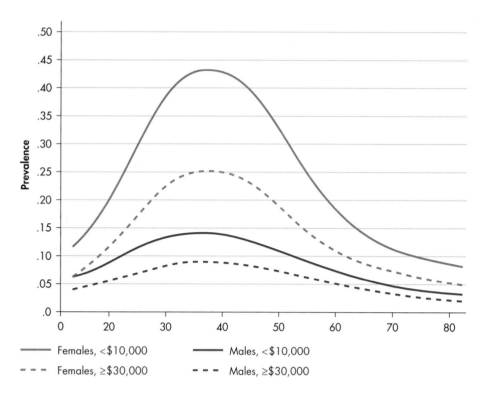

FIGURE 7.5 **Prevalence of Migraine Headaches** The prevalence of migraine headaches appears to peak between the ages of 35 and 40, is about two times more common in women than in men, and is more frequently reported by those with lower incomes.

Source: Adapted from Stewart et al., 1992.

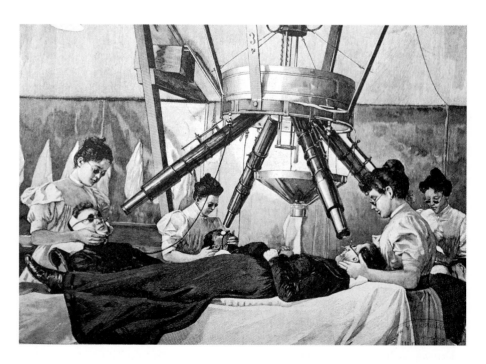

People suffering from headaches treat the condition in a number of ways—with over-the-counter remedies, biofeedback and relaxation techniques, exercise, and meditation. This 1898 engraving illustrates another method once tried—sunlight magnified and focused on individuals wearing sunglasses to protect their eyes.

Pollens or other substances to which a person with asthma is allergic can produce attacks, but sometimes psychological factors seem more important. Emotional arousal has been found to be associated with decreased size of the airways of the lung (Isenberg, Lehrer & Hochron, 1992). In one study (Fritz, Rubenstein & Lewiston, 1987), psychological factors such as depression and family conflicts were found to be the main causes in 18 percent of individuals with this disorder. Deaths among children with asthma have been associated with family dysfunction, poor adherence to medication, and poor self-care (Lehrer, Sargunaraj & Hochron, 1992). Infections can also play a major role in asthma. In most cases, however, physical and psychological causes interact, as in the following case. Here, a teenager with asthma used her attacks to influence family members, in an intricate interplay of physical and psychological factors.

> Kathy was a 15-year-old girl whose asthma was diagnosed at age six. . . . Early on, emotional reactions were identified as important triggers to her episodes, along with exercise and infections. . . . Her biologic parents had a stormy relationship that included the father's physical abuse of the mother during their frequent drinking bouts, numerous separations, and financial insecurity. . . . Her asthma also served to interrupt parental fights, and Kathy consciously used her asthma in her role as a peacemaker. . . . The asthmatic symptoms were . . . associated with helplessness and extreme anxiety. (Fritz, Rubenstein & Lewiston, 1987, pp. 253–254)

Self-management procedures can be effective in treating asthma. Vazquez and Buceta (1993) devised a program in which the client and family members receive information about the disease to help them identify and avoid situations associated with the attacks; they also receive training in relaxation.

Perspectives on Etiology

Why does stress produce a physical disorder in some people but not in others? If a disorder does develop in someone experiencing emotional duress, what determines what the psychophysiological illness will be? Innate, developmental, and acquired characteristics certainly interact, but the nature and contribution of each are not well understood. In this section we discuss different perspectives on cause—none of which adequately accounts for all the factors involved.

Psychodynamic Perspective Psychoanalysts have developed several formulations to explain physical disorders associated with psychological factors. According to these formulations, each type of psy-

Mysteriously, the death rate from asthma in young women has increased dramatically in recent years. Model Krissy Taylor died at the age of 17 of an asthmatic attack.

chophysiological disorder is produced by a specific form of unconscious conflict.

Alexander (1950) believed that an early unresolved childhood conflict produces an emotional response that is reactivated in adulthood. For example, the inhibition of aggressive feelings may produce hypertension or other cardiovascular disorders. According to this hypothesis, aggression and dependency needs are the basis for most of the psychophysiological disorders. The expression of dependency needs increases activity of the parasympathetic division of the autonomic nervous system. Chronic activation of this division produces such disorders as peptic ulcers, diarrhea, and colitis. If feelings of anger predominate, the energy-expending sympathetic nervous system is activated, which may result in hypertension, migraine headaches, or arthritis.

A list of the unconscious complexes associated with various disorders is given in Table 7.4. Although

TABLE 7.4 A Psychodynamic Etiology: The Unconscious Correlates to Certain Physical Disorders

Disorder	Unconscious Correlates
Peptic ulcer	A conflict over dependency needs produces guilt and hostility. The person unsuccessfully attempts to sublimate these aggressive tendencies through achievement. Unsatisfied oral needs produce overactivity of gastrointestinal function, which produces an ulcer.
Asthma	The person has an unresolved dependency on his or her mother, who is perceived as cold; fears separation; or needs to be protected. The person feels guilty about the dependency needs. Instead of crying, he or she develops a wheeze that can develop into respiratory disorder.
Hypertension	The person experiences a struggle against unconscious hostile impulses and fluctuates from excessive control to outbursts of aggression. Repressing these hostile feelings leads to chronic blood pressure elevation.
Arthritis	The person inhibits hostile impulses or has experienced parental restrictions of freedom of movement. Developing arthritis allows this individual to avoid physically expressing aggression.

Source: Adapted from Alexander, 1950.

Alexander's theory is impressive in breadth and specificity, his propositions have not been experimentally supported.

Biological Perspective Some evidence points to a genetic base for the development of psychophysiological disorders. For example, ulcers are twice as common in siblings of ulcer patients as in siblings of nonpatients. Additionally, people with type O blood are more likely to develop duodenal ulcers than are people with type A, B, or AB blood (Eisenberg, 1978). A modest significant correlation on cardiovascular reactivity has been found between monozygotic (identical) twins. Presumably a greater reactivity could contribute to the development of hypertension and coronary heart disease (Smith et al., 1987). Children with one asthmatic parent have a 20 percent chance of developing asthma. The probability increases to 50 percent with two asthmatic parents (Mrazek, 1993).

In addition, three other biological explanations for psychophysiological disorders have been suggested: somatic weakness, autonomic response specificity, and general adaptation syndrome.

The *somatic weakness hypothesis* is a common-sense explanation for the development of particular psychophysiological disorders. This view suggests that congenital factors or a vulnerability acquired through physical trauma or illness may predispose a particular organ to develop irregularities or become weakened structurally by stressors. Therefore, which particular physiological disorder develops is determined by which system is the "weakest link" in the body (Hovanitz & Wander, 1990). For example, 80 percent of the asthmatics in one study had experienced previous respiratory infections, compared with only 30 percent of the nonasthmatic controls (Rees, 1964). The infection may have weakened the respiratory system and made it more vulnerable to the development of asthma. Logical as it seems, the somatic weakness hypothesis is difficult to validate because it is not yet possible to measure the relative strengths of the different physical systems in the human body before an organ weakness appears.

Closely related to the somatic weakness hypothesis is the concept of *autonomic response specificity*—the hypothesis that each person has a unique physiological reaction to all types of stressful situations. This specific response is believed to be largely inherited but able to be affected by a previously acquired vulnerability (Steptoe, 1991). Autonomic response specificity has been demonstrated experimentally. College students subjected to a variety of stressors (from cold water to tough mathematics problems) tended to show stable and consistent idiosyncratic patterns of autonomic activity in the different stress-producing conditions. That is, a person who showed a rise in blood pressure when reacting to one type of stressor showed a similar reaction to other types of stressors (Lacey, Bateman & Van Lehn, 1953). Similar consistency was found in people who suffered migraine headaches, but not in a control group of people who did not get migraines (Cohen, Richels & McArthur, 1978). The suggestion that these physiological responses are innate is supported by researchers who observed that distinctive autonomic behavior patterns in infants tended to persist throughout early childhood (Thomas, Chess & Birch, 1968).

The general adaptation syndrome, consisting of an alarm stage, a resistance stage, and an exhaustion stage, was discussed earlier in the chapter. According to Selye (1956), continued stress after the final stage may result in diseases of adaptation such as ulcers or hypertension. Unfortunately, this formulation is very general and does not explain why these diseases do not occur in all people experiencing long-term stress. Nor does it specify which psychophysiological disorder will develop. Combining this theory with the somatic weakness or autonomic response specificity hypotheses may be one way to deal with such conceptual problems.

The Behavioral Perspective   As noted, classical conditioning may be involved in the psychophysiological disorders. The conditioning of neutral stimuli can elicit or activate a physiological response through generalization, as discussed in Chapter 3. Probably, the greater the number of stimuli that can produce a specific physical reaction, the more likely a chronic condition will develop.

Psychophysiological reactions can generalize to words or thoughts. In one study, the bronchial reactions of forty patients with asthma were compared with those of a normal control group. The patients were told they were being exposed to different concentrations of substances to which they were allergic: in fact, they were exposed only to neutral saline solution. Nearly half (nineteen) of the patients with asthma displayed bronchial constriction (a symptom of asthmatic attacks), and twelve developed full-blown asthma attacks. None of the participants in the control group showed any of these symptoms (Luparello et al., 1968). The experimenters hypothesized that principles of classical conditioning could account for their finding. The thought of inhaling an allergic substance had become a conditioned stimulus capable of inducing asthmatic symptoms or attacks. In a review of twenty studies involving 427 persons with asthma, more than one-third of the persons with asthma were found to be "reactors," that is, they showed significant bronchial effects following suggestion (Isenberg, Lehrer & Hochron, 1992).

The classical conditioning position alone cannot, however, account for the cause of the disorders discussed in this section. Physiological reactions must occur before other stimuli can be conditioned to them and before generalization can occur. Hence classical conditioning may explain the continuation or increased severity of a disorder, but not its origin.

Although theorists first believed that the autonomic nervous system is not under operant control, later findings demonstrated that involuntary processes such as heart rate, blood pressure, and a variety of other functions can be influenced by reinforcement. These findings have important implications for the origin and treatment of psychophysiological disorders.

Evidence that operant learning influences visceral (digestive tract) responses supports the possibility that disorders involving the autonomic nervous system can be learned (Miller, 1974). A child who fears school, for example, may show a variety of physiological responses (increase in heart rate, changes in blood pressure, constriction of the bronchioles, and increased gastrointestinal activity). Parental attention to a particular physical symptom can reinforce it's appearance. Thus expressing sympathy or allowing a child to stay home to recover from a stomachache might contribute to the development of gastrointestinal disorders such as ulcers, colitis, or diarrhea.

The precise role of operant conditioning in the cause of the disorders discussed here is still not clear. There is support for the contention that autonomic processes can be altered through reinforcement. But there is also controversy about the magnitude of the changes that are possible.

Sociocultural Perspectives   In a study of Japanese persons living in Japan, Hawaii, and California, researchers found the highest mortality rate from coronary heart disease among those living in California and the lowest among those living in Japan. This difference was not accounted for by differences in the risk factors for CHD discussed earlier. In trying to decide what was responsible for the variation in mortality rates, the researchers compared Japanese immigrants who had maintained a traditional lifestyle with those who had acculturated (adopted the habits and attitudes prevalent in their new home). The CHD rate for acculturated Japanese individuals was five times greater than that for those who had retained their traditional values (Marmot & Syme, 1976). Perhaps breaking close social and community ties, which is part of the acculturation process, promoted a greater vulnerability to the disease.

TREATMENT OF PSYCHO-PHYSIOLOGICAL DISORDERS

Treatment programs for psychophysiological disorders generally consist of both medical treatment for the physical symptoms and conditions and psychological therapy to eliminate stress and anxiety. **Behavioral medicine** comprises a number of disciplines that study social, psychological, and lifestyle influences on health. This combined approach provides a wide array of approaches to these disorders, with mainly positive results. Two of the dominant psychological approaches are stress management and anxiety management programs, which usually include either relaxation training or biofeedback. The concept of combined therapies is illustrated in the following case:

> Jerry R. is a 33-year-old male who has always taken pride in the vigor with which he attacks everything he does. He worries about keeping slim, so he exercises at a health spa three nights a week. He was shocked to discover, during a routine physical exam, that he has borderline high blood pressure.
>
> His physician recommended that he take steps to lower his blood pressure by reducing his intake of salt, caffeine, and alcohol. Because coronary heart disease runs in Jerry's family, the physician also recommended that Jerry decrease his cholesterol intake by reducing the amount of eggs, saturated fats, and whole milk in his diet. He commended Jerry for having given up smoking five months ago.
>
> Finally, Jerry was urged to become active in a stress management program geared toward lowering his blood pressure and preventing coronary heart disease. Although the effectiveness of these programs is somewhat controversial, Jerry's physician believes Jerry has more to gain than to lose by participating in a course of biofeedback and relaxation training.

The success of combined treatment programs suggests that the psychological approach to the treatment of certain physical disorders is more than a passing fad (Bennett & Carroll, 1990; Bennett et al., 1991; Davison et al., 1991; Shahidi & Salmon, 1992).

Relaxation training, biofeedback, and cognitive-behavioral interventions are emerging as the primary stress management techniques of behavioral medicine. They are used in treating all the psychophysiological disorders described in this chapter.

Relaxation Training

Relaxation training is a therapeutic technique in which a person acquires the ability to relax the muscles of the body in almost any circumstance. Current programs are typically modeled after Jacobson's (1938, 1967) progressive relaxation training. Imagine that you are a patient who is beginning the training. You are instructed to concentrate on one set of muscles at a time—first tensing them and then relaxing them. First you clench your fists as tightly as possible for approximately ten seconds, then you release them. As you release your tightened muscles, you are asked to focus on the sensation of warmth and looseness in your hands. You practice this tightening and relaxing cycle several times before proceeding to the next muscle group in your lower arms. After each muscle group has received individual attention in tensing and relaxing, the trainer asks you to tighten and then relax your entire body. The emphasis throughout the procedure is on the contrast between the feelings pro-

duced during tensing and those produced during relaxing. For a novice, the entire exercise lasts about thirty minutes.

With practice, you eventually learn to relax the muscles without first having to tense them. You can then use the technique to relax at almost any time during the day, even when only a few moments are available for the exercise.

Biofeedback

In **biofeedback training,** the client is taught to *voluntarily* control some physiological function, such as heart rate or blood pressure. During training, the client receives second-by-second information (feedback) regarding the activity of the organ or function of interest. For someone attempting to lower high blood pressure, for example, the feedback might be actual blood pressure readings, which might be presented visually on a screen or as some auditory signal transmitted through a set of headphones. The biofeedback device enables the patient to learn his or her own idiosyncratic method for controlling the particular physiological function. Eventually the patient learns to use that method without benefit of the feedback device.

> A 23-year-old male patient was found to have a resting heart rate that varied between 95 and 120 beats per minute. He reported that his symptoms first appeared during his last year in high school, when his episodes of tachycardia were associated with apprehension over exams. The patient came into treatment concerned that his high heart rate might lead to a serious cardiac condition.
>
> The treatment consisted of eight sessions of biofeedback training. The patient's heart rate was monitored, and he was provided with both a visual and an auditory feedback signal. After the treatment period, his heart rate had stabilized and was within normal limits. One year later, his heart rate averaged 73 beats per minute. The patient reported that he had learned to control his heart rate during stressful situations such as going for a job interview, both relaxing and concentrating on reducing the heart rate. (Janssen, 1983)

Biofeedback is essentially an operant conditioning technique in which the feedback serves as reinforcement. It has been used to help people lower their heart rate and decrease their blood pressure (Shahidi & Salmon, 1992), treat tension headaches (Hovanitz & Wander, 1990), reduce muscle tension (Gamble & Elder, 1983), and redirect blood flow (Reading & Mohr, 1976). Patients with duodenal ulcers have been taught to decrease the level of gastric acid secretion after receiving feedback on stomach acidity (Welgan, 1974). Biofeedback and verbal reinforcement were used to help children with asthma control their respiratory functioning (Kahn, Staerk & Bonk, 1974). In an interesting marriage of operant and classical conditioning techniques, the children were also trained to control bronchial constriction by dilating their bronchi when exposed to previously conditioned stimuli.

Cognitive-Behavioral Interventions

An increasing number of stress management programs are also including a cognitive-behavioral component, often in the form of self-instructional techniques and cognitive restructuring. In one study (Bennett et al., 1991), Type A persons with hypertension were taught to evaluate and change the impact of stressors and to understand how their Type A behavior contributes to hypertension. They learned to change their thoughts to reduce their emotional reactions. This approach seems to augment the effectiveness of other components in stress management in dealing with hypertension (Davison et al., 1991).

Certainly both psychological and biological processes are involved in all diseases. In some disorders and in some people, biological factors have the primary influence, whereas in others, psychological factors predominate. Because so many variables are involved, science cannot predict which person will develop a psychophysiological disorder and under what conditions.

Although much is known about the psychophysiological disorders, a great deal is still to be learned. Psychologists in behavioral medicine are seeking to decrease a person's vulnerability to physical problems by suggesting changes in lifestyle, attitudes, and perceptions. Attention is also directed toward altering the course of an illness after it has occurred. The field of behavioral medicine will continue to receive greater attention from psychologists. We are only beginning to understand the relationship between psychological factors and physical illnesses.

In biofeedback training, clients can get instant-by-instant information about their heart rate, blood pressure, gastrointestinal activity, muscle tension, and other physical functions. Through operant conditioning techniques, they learn to control their physiological functions.

SUMMARY

1. The sudden death syndrome is an extreme example of the effect of psychological factors on physical health. In sudden death, stress is thought to kill susceptible people by producing clotting and blockage of arteries, alterations in blood pressure and dislodging of fat deposits, and variations and irregularities in heart rhythm.

2. Formerly, the term *psychosomatic* was used to categorize a number of specific physical disorders that stem from psychological problems. This usage fostered the incorrect view that only certain physical conditions have significant psychological components. Now, the DSM-IV category of *psychophysiological disorder* recognizes the belief that both physical and psychological factors may be involved in any illness.

3. Models explaining the impact of stress include the general adaptation syndrome, which examines the impact of stressors on physical functioning; the life-change model, which is based on the view that life changes have a detrimental impact on health; and the transaction model, which stresses the importance of subjective interpretation and stress.

4. Immunological functioning seems to be affected by physical and psychological stress, both short term and long term. A variety of factors such as anxiety,

divorce, and bereavement can produce poor immunological responses. The causal direction of this relationship is unclear. Some research supports the suggestion that psychological stress can influence the initiation and course of certain infectious diseases. Other research, particularly that focusing on AIDS, only offers limited support. Although stress decreases the ability of animals to reject injected cancer cells, whether psychological variables can influence the development of cancer in human beings is not known. *Cancer* is a term describing a variety of disease processes, which may vary in their susceptibility to emotions. Most studies are short term and retrospective, and they do not address the development of spontaneous cancer.

5. Coronary heart disease (CHD) and essential hypertension are the most pervasive cardiovascular disorders. The incidence of CHD is influenced by social factors, personality, and lifestyle as well as such risk factors as smoking, obesity, inactivity, hypertension, and cholesterol levels. Hypertension is related to the emotions and how they are expressed, especially anger. There are gender and ethnic differences in the incidence of hypertension.

6. Peptic ulcers—duodenal or gastric—afflict 10 percent of all people at some point in their lives. It is now believed that a form of bacteria, H pylori, is the cause of ulcers, although emotional stressors can exacerbate the condition.

7. Headaches are among the most common psychophysiological complaints. Migraine headaches involve the constriction and then the dilation of blood vessels in the brain. Tension headaches are thought to be caused by contraction of the neck and scalp muscles, which results in vascular constriction. These headaches can also occur in the absence of detectable tension. Cluster headaches are excruciating and occur on one side of the head near the eye.

8. Asthma attacks result from constriction of the airways in the lungs. Breathing is extremely difficult during the attacks, and acute anxiety may worsen the situation. In most cases, physical and psychological causes interact.

9. Etiological theories must be able to explain why some people develop a physical disorder under stress, whereas others do not, and what determines which psychophysiological illness develops. At present, none of the traditional perspectives does this in a satisfactory way. According to the psychodynamic perspective, the particular illness that is manifested depends on the stage of psychosexual development and the type of unresolved unconscious conflict involved. Biological explanations focus on somatic weakness and response specificity. The behavioral perspective emphasizes the importance of classical and operant conditioning in acquiring or maintaining these disorders.

10. Behavioral medicine combines a number of approaches to psychophysiological disorders. Generally, these disorders are treated through stress management or anxiety management programs, combined with medical treatment for physical symptoms or conditions. Relaxation training and biofeedback training, which help the client learn to control muscular or organic functioning, are usually a part of such programs. Cognitive-behavioral interventions, which involve changing anxiety-arousing thoughts, have also been useful.

KEY TERMS

asthma A respiratory disorder that results from constriction of the airways in the lungs owing to muscle tone changes in the airways, excessive mucous secretion, edema, or inflammation

behavioral medicine A number of disciplines that study social, psychological, and lifestyle influences on health

biofeedback training A therapeutic technique in which the person is taught to voluntarily control a particular physiological function such as heart rate or blood pressure

cluster headache Excruciating headache that tends to occur on one side of the head near the eye, producing tears and a blocked nose

coronary heart disease (CHD) A narrowing of the arteries in or near the heart, resulting in the restriction or partial blockage of the flow of blood and oxygen to the heart

decompensation Loss of the ability to deal successfully with stress, resulting in more primitive means of coping

essential hypertension Chronic high blood pressure, usually with no known organic cause; the most common disease in the United States

general adaptation syndrome (GAS) A three-stage model for understanding the body's physical and psychological reaction to biological stressors

H pylori Helicobacter pylori, the form of bacteria believed to be the cause of peptic ulcers

hardiness A concept developed by Kobasa and Maddi that refers to a person's ability to deal well with stress

life-change model An explanation of stress that assumes that all changes in a person's life—large or small, desirable or undesirable—can act as stressors and that the accumulation of small changes can be as powerful as one major stressor

migraine headache Severe headache characterized by constriction of cranial arteries, followed by dilation of the cerebral blood vessels, resulting in moderate to severe pain

peptic ulcer An open sore within the digestive system

psychophysiological disorder Any physical disorder that has a strong psychological basis or component

relaxation training A therapeutic technique in which the person acquires the ability to relax the muscles of the body in almost any circumstance

stress An internal response to a stressor

stressor An external event or situation that places a physical or psychological demand on a person

sudden death syndrome Unexpected abrupt death that seems to have no specific physical basis

tension headache A headache thought to be produced by prolonged contraction of the scalp and neck muscles resulting in vascular constriction

transaction model of stress Explanation of stress that states that stress resides neither in the person alone nor in the situation alone, but rather in a transaction between the two

CHAPTER 8

PERSONALITY DISORDERS AND IMPULSE CONTROL DISORDERS

The Personality Disorders
Etiological and Treatment Considerations for Personality
    Disorders
Disorders Characterized by Odd or Eccentric Behaviors
Disorders Characterized by Dramatic, Emotional, or
    Erratic Behaviors
Disorders Characterized by Anxious or Fearful Behaviors

Antisocial Personality Disorder
Explanations of Antisocial Personality Disorder
Treatment of Antisocial Personality Disorder

Disorders of Impulse Control
Intermittent Explosive Disorder
Kleptomania
Pathological Gambling
Pyromania
Trichotillomania
Etiology and Treatment of Impulse Control Disorders

Althoough this chapter discusses both personality disorders and impulse control disorders, the two are separate and distinct categories in DSM-IV. We are discussing them together for convenience rather than because of any relationship between these two categories of disorders. As in other disorders, those involving personality or impulse control are associated with a person's subjective distress or impaired functioning. Some of these disorders (such as antisocial personality and pyromania) may have detrimental consequences for society.

THE PERSONALITY DISORDERS

Personality disorders are characterized by inflexible, longstanding, and maladaptive personality traits that cause significant functional impairment or subjective distress for the individual. In addition to personal and social difficulties, these people also have temperamental deficiencies or aberrations, rigidity in dealing with life problems, and defective perceptions of self and others.

In spite of all this, people with personality disorders often function well enough to get along without aid from others. For this reason, and because these people rarely seek help from mental health professionals, the incidence of personality disorders has been difficult to ascertain. Available statistics indicate that personality disorders account for about 5 to 15 percent of admissions to hospitals and outpatient clinics. The overall lifetime prevalence of personality disorders is 10 to 13 percent (Weissman, 1993).

The gender distribution varies from disorder to disorder. Men are more likely than women to be diagnosed as having paranoid, obsessive-compulsive, and antisocial personality disorders, whereas women more often receive a diagnosis of borderline, dependent, and histrionic personality disorder (Reich, 1987; Widiger & Spitzer, 1991). The existence of gender differences in the diagnosis of certain personality disorders is widely accepted. It raises some important issues, discussed in Critical Thinking. Are gender differences real or a product of biased diagnoses?

Not surprisingly, one's culture shapes habits, customs, values, and personality characteristics so that expressions of personality in one culture may differ from those in another culture. For example, Asians are more likely to exhibit shyness and collectivism, whereas Americans are more likely to show assertiveness and individualism. An individual's cultural, ethnic, and social background must be considered by anyone making judgments about personality functioning and disturbance (American Psychiatric Association, 1994).

The signs of a personality disorder usually become evident during adolescence. In some cases, a person with a personality disorder may have had a similar childhood disorder. For example, it is common to find that a person diagnosed as having schizoid personality disorder was previously diagnosed as having schizoid disorder of childhood. When the features of certain childhood disorders persist into adulthood (that is, beyond age eighteen), the diagnosis may be changed to a personality disorder.

In the diagnostic scheme of DSM-IV, personality disorders are recorded on Axis II. A person may receive diagnoses on both Axis I and Axis II. For example, a person with a personality disorder may also be diagnosed as schizophrenic or as alcohol dependent (Axis I disorders). Usually, people with personality disorders are hospitalized only when a second, superimposed disorder so impairs social functioning that they require inpatient care. The rationale for having two axes for mental disorders is that Axis II disorders generally begin in childhood or adolescence and persist in a stable form into adulthood. Axis I disorders usually fail to show these characteristics.

Diagnosing personality disorders is difficult for three primary reasons. First, to varying degrees and at various times, we all exhibit some of the traits that characterize personality disorders—for example, suspiciousness, dependency, sensitivity to rejection, or compulsiveness. For this reason, many investigators (such as Livesley and colleagues [1994]) prefer to view personality disorders as the extremes of underlying dimensions of normal personality traits. They argue that dimensions such as extraversion (sociability), agreeableness (nurturance), neuroticism, conscientiousness, and openness to experience may be used to describe personality disorders. Because people differ in the extent to which they possess a trait, a clinician may have trouble deciding when a client exhibits

CRITICAL THINKING

Is There Gender Bias in Diagnosing Mental Disorders?

We know that gender differences exist in the diagnosed prevalence of mental disorders such as depression, which has been found to be higher among women than among men (see Chapter 11). For personality disorders, men have been found to have a higher rate of antisocial, paranoid, and obsessive personality disorders, whereas women have a higher rate of borderline, dependent, and histrionic personality disorders (Reich, 1987; Widiger & Spitzer, 1991). But are these real differences in the way these disorders affect men and women, or do the statistics reflect the influence of other factors, such as gender biases?

Gender bias in the diagnostic system occurs when diagnostic categories are not valid and when they have a different impact on men and women. Note that the mere fact that men and women have different prevalence rates for a particular disorder is not sufficient to prove gender bias. Rates may differ because of actual biological conditions (for example, a genetic predisposition) or social

conditions (stressors) that affect one gender more than another. For the diagnostic system itself to be biased, the differences must be attributable to errors or problems in the categories or diagnostic criteria. Widiger and Spitzer (1991) attempted to enumerate the sources of biases, in addition to biases in the diagnostic system. Try your hand at this task by examining the following sources of potential bias and indicating areas in which you believe bias can occur.

1. In what ways can clinicians themselves be biased when evaluating others or when making a diagnosis? For example, might a clinician evaluate the same behavior (for example, aggressiveness) differently, depending on whether a man or a woman displays it?

2. How might a clinical assessment instrument be biased? Can you think of characteristics that Western culture considers desirable and healthy, that are associated more with one gender than the other, and

that could be used in a questionnaire? Tavris (1991) has argued that characteristics associated with women are more likely to be considered deviant or undesirable than are those associated with men. She attributed this to a male norm that tends to define characteristics found primarily in women as negative.

3. Can you think of a situation in which sampling bias could distort the findings in a study of the prevalence of depression in women? *Sampling bias* occurs when one gender with a particular disorder is more likely than the other gender to be present in a particular setting and the research is conducted in that setting.

4. Given that gender bias can occur, what can a clinician do to guard against such bias in his or her work? This final question is, perhaps, the most important to address.

---

a trait to a degree that could be considered a symptom of a disorder (Millon, 1994). DSM-IV criteria for diagnosing disorders are based on a categorical model in which a disorder is present if "enough of" certain symptoms or traits are exhibited and is not present if "not enough of" the symptoms are demonstrated (American Psychiatric Association, 1994). Thus, according to DSM, people are classified as either having or not having a disorder. In reality, people may "have" a personality disorder to varying degrees. In

addition, personality patterns may not be stable. Many investigators have consistently argued that personality characteristics exhibited in one situation may vary or be unstable across situations (Mischel, 1968).

The second reason diagnosis is difficult is that symptoms of one personality disorder may also be symptoms of other disorders. Morey (1988) found that many people diagnosed as having one type of personality disorder also met the criteria for other personality disorders. Moreover, people can have more than one type of personality disorder, so the problems in diagnosing these disorders are formidable. Investigators (Widiger & Shea, 1991) have also found that although the distinction between personality disorders and other disorders is valid, many individuals have symptoms that do not neatly fall into a particular disorder and that overlap with different disorders.

Third, clinicians rendering a diagnosis may not adhere to diagnostic criteria. In one study, clinicians were asked to indicate the symptoms exhibited by their clients who had been diagnosed with personality disorders. In many cases, the clinicians' diagnoses were incongruent with the symptom patterns DSM requires for diagnosing the personality disorders (Morey & Ochoa, 1989).

DSM-IV asserts that a number of traits, not just one, must be considered in determining whether a disorder exists. For example, to diagnose dependent personality disorder, the clinician must find a constellation of characteristics (such as the inability to make decisions independently and the subordination of one's own needs). The clinician must also consider other criteria or factors. For example, the personality pattern (1) must characterize the person's current as well as long-term functioning, (2) must not be limited to episodes of illness, and (3) either must notably impair social or occupational functioning or must cause subjective distress. Thus a person who is temporarily dependent because of an illness would not be diagnosed as having a dependent personality. Focus On suggests some questions for thought about personality patterns as disorders.

Researchers are still debating the importance of personality versus situational determinants in behaviors. Are symptoms or behaviors really reflections of one's personality, or do they appear only in specific situations? Finally, while psychodynamic perspectives have guided the formulation of these disorders, the causes of the disorders are open to many interpretations. Genetic, biological, learning, cognitive, humanistic, and family systems approaches have all been advanced as important frameworks for understanding these disorders.

Etiological and Treatment Considerations for Personality Disorders

Although personality disorders have generated rich clinical examples and speculation, not much empirical research has been conducted to provide definitive insights into the causes of the disorders. Many researchers have found that personality patterns can be described by the five-factor model (FFM) of personality, in which the five factors are as follows: *neuroti-*

cism (emotional adjustment and stability), *extraversion* (preference for interpersonal interactions, fun loving, and active), *openness* to experience (curious, willing to entertain new ideas and values, and emotionally responsive), *agreeableness* (good natured, helpful, forgiving, and responsive), and *conscientiousness* (organized, persistent, punctual, and self-directed). Individuals vary in the extent to which they exhibit any of these factors. Widiger and his colleagues (1994) found that personality disorders can be translated as maladaptively extreme variants of the five basic factors of personality (Widiger et al., 1994). For example, in terms of deliberation (the factor of conscientiousness), antisocial personality disorder would score low, whereas obsessive-compulsive personality disorder would score high. The FFM allows researchers and clinicians to assess personality disorders as a particular set of personality characteristics and to compare different disorders. It also views the etiology of personality disorders as a matter of discovering determinants of personality in general.

Biogenic, behavioral, and cognitive factors have been proposed to explain the development of personality disorders. The fact that the disorders deal with *personality* means that research on the determinants of personality characteristics is germane. Socialization and family upbringing, learning and modeling, development of cognitions, and culture all contribute to personality.

Some interesting research has examined the role of heredity in personality development. Scarr and her colleagues (1981) studied the personality characteristics of biologically related and adoptive families. If heredity is important, biologically related parents, children, and siblings should show similar personality charac-teristics. If learning and environment are important, similarity should be shown between the adoptive family and those who were adopted. Although the results indicated that genetic as well as environmental factors are important in personality traits, neither could fully explain the development of personality characteristics. Individual differences between family members may be influential in personality. That is, certain genetic characteristics of individual children may determine much of the environment they experience, so that the contributions of heredity and environment may be quite complex.

Tellegen and colleagues (1988) reported on an interesting study of the personality characteristics of monozygotic and dizygotic twins reared apart or together. Monozygotic twins are genetically identical, and dizygotic twins share about 50 percent of each other's genes. This difference helps the researcher to sort out the effects of genetic and environmental similarity on personality and to study them. Results indicated that heredity is important in personality

Personality Patterns as Disorders: Questions for Thought

From time to time, new personality disorders are added to DSM. After all, isn't it possible to view almost any personality characteristic (or constellation of characteristics) as being a disorder if that characteristic is exhibited to an extreme degree? For example, can't chronically hostile and angry persons be diagnosed as having an "angry personality disorder," overly trusting individuals as having a "naive personality disorder," and extremely happy and idealistic persons as having a "pollyanna personality disorder"? What determines the personality characteristics that constitute a disorder?

DSM-IV does have a personality disorder category of "not otherwise specified" for disorders of personality functioning that cannot be classified as one of those identified by DSM. To be assigned to this category, the disorder must cause significant impairment in social or occupational functioning or subjective distress and must meet general guidelines for personality disorders. That is, the traits must be inflexible, maladaptive, generally recognizable by adolescence, and not reflect another disorder, such as schizophrenia. Given the

general guidelines, extreme happiness may not be a personality disorder unless the trait is maladaptive and causes significant impairment. But one can still ask why some personality disorders are included as specific disorders and why others are considered in the category of "not otherwise specified."

The creation of a specific personality disorder is probably influenced by many factors, such as the observed frequency of the constellation of personality traits, the degree of impairment and distress, and the consequence for society. If one personality pattern affects relatively more people, causes greater impairment and distress, and has more negative consequences for society than does another personality pattern, the chances are increased that it will be listed as a specified disorder. Furthermore, characteristics having a "history" of being discussed in the theoretical, empirical, and clinical literature stand a better chance of being specified as a disorder than those without such a history.

The final question that we would like to raise concerns the cross-cultural validity of the DSM-

IV personality disorders. People from different cultures and societies exhibit different personality characteristics and may disagree as to the traits they consider maladaptive. Given this fact, are the DSM-defined personality disorders universally valid and applicable? DSM categories are highly similar to those in the *International Classification of Diseases*, a classification scheme developed for the World Health Organization by leading experts from different countries. Nevertheless, cross-cultural mental health researchers, such as Mezzich and Good (1991), have maintained that definitions of "normal" personality may vary across societies and ethnic groups and that behaviors considered highly deviant in one context (such as forms of drug use or sexual behavior or modes of expressing emotion) may fall within the norm of another. They also note that to date, little evidence either confirms or disconfirms the universality of specific personality disorders.

development. Environment is also critical, but the investigators found that a shared environment—twin pairs living in the same family environment—was not strongly related to personality similarity. Environmental influences can be shared or unshared. Although it is popularly believed that shared environmental influences explain personality similarity, it is possible that a person's unique, unshared experiences are crucial. All of these studies indicate the complexities researchers confront in trying to find determinants of personality in general and of personality disorders in particular.

The treatment approaches to personality disorders are as varied as the many different theories about how personality characteristics develop and change. Many of these approaches are illustrated in the discussion of antisocial personality, which is the most studied personality disorder, and which is covered in depth later in this chapter. Unfortunately, data on the treatment of the full range of personality disorders is limited (Sanderson & Clarkin, 1994). In general, many people with these disorders do not seek treatment, often because they do not believe they need it. Many can function in society despite their adjustment

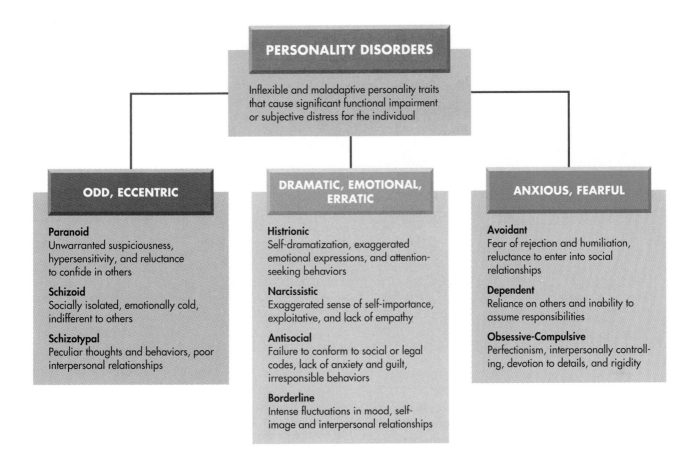

PERSONALITY DISORDERS

Inflexible and maladaptive personality traits that cause significant functional impairment or subjective distress for the individual

ODD, ECCENTRIC

Paranoid
Unwarranted suspiciousness, hypersensitivity, and reluctance to confide in others

Schizoid
Socially isolated, emotionally cold, indifferent to others

Schizotypal
Peculiar thoughts and behaviors, poor interpersonal relationships

DRAMATIC, EMOTIONAL, ERRATIC

Histrionic
Self-dramatization, exaggerated emotional expressions, and attention-seeking behaviors

Narcissistic
Exaggerated sense of self-importance, exploitative, and lack of empathy

Antisocial
Failure to conform to social or legal codes, lack of anxiety and guilt, irresponsible behaviors

Borderline
Intense fluctuations in mood, self-image and interpersonal relationships

ANXIOUS, FEARFUL

Avoidant
Fear of rejection and humiliation, reluctance to enter into social relationships

Dependent
Reliance on others and inability to assume responsibilities

Obsessive-Compulsive
Perfectionism, interpersonally controlling, devotion to details, and rigidity

problems, so their motivation to change may be weak. Also, the long-term and inflexible personality traits characterizing these disorders are not easily modified. Proponents of the five-factor model believe that by delineating core personality characteristics in personality disorders, treatment can be enhanced. There is evidence that individuals with different personality traits respond differently to therapy and treatment (McCrae, 1994). MacKenzie (1994) has tried to outline ways of treating individuals with high or low FFM characteristics. Although such approaches seem to make sense, research is needed to verify their efficacy.

As the personality disorders chart above illustrates, DSM-IV lists ten specific personality disorders and groups them into three clusters, depending on whether they are characterized by odd or eccentric behaviors; dramatic, emotional, or erratic behaviors; or anxious or fearful behaviors. The clustering of these disorders is based more on convenience than on actual similarity of symptoms or cause. Clustering and categorizing the disorders also mask dimensional aspects. That is, the task of categorizing often fails to reveal differences in the degree to which people possess certain characteristics. In any event, we begin by discussing each of the ten personality disorders rather briefly. Then we focus

on one of them—the *antisocial personality disorder*—in more detail, primarily because more information is available for this disorder.

Disorders Characterized by Odd or Eccentric Behaviors

Three personality disorders are included in this cluster: paranoid personality, schizoid personality, and schizotypal personality.

Paranoid Personality Disorder   People with **paranoid personality disorder** show unwarranted suspiciousness, hypersensitivity, and reluctance to trust others. They interpret others' motives as being malevolent, question their loyalty or trustworthiness, persistently bear grudges, or are suspicious of the fidelity of their spouse. They may demonstrate restricted affect (that is, aloofness and lack of emotion), and they tend to be rigid and preoccupied with unfounded beliefs that stem from their suspicions and sensitivity. These beliefs are extremely resistant to change.

Certain groups, such as refugees and members of minority groups, may display guarded or defensive behaviors because of their unfamiliarity with majority

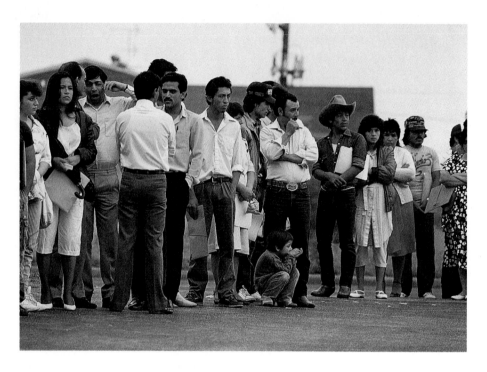

Symptoms such as chronic distrust and suspiciousness must be evaluated within the context of an individual's life before making a judgment as to whether the symptoms the person is experiencing are indicative of paranoid personality. These illegal immigrants applying for amnesty at an Immigration and Naturalization Service office may be distrustful and suspicious but understandably so.

society or because of their minority group status, not because of a disorder. To avoid misinterpreting the clinical significance of behaviors, clinicians assessing members of these groups must do so cautiously.

DSM-IV estimates the prevalence of paranoid personality disorder to be about 0.5 to 2.5 percent of the population, and probably somewhat higher among males. (Figure 8.1 shows the prevalence of this disorder and others.) Here is an example of paranoid personality disorder:

Ralph and Ann married after knowing each other for two months. The first year of their marriage was relatively happy, although Ralph tended to be domineering and very protective of his wife. Ann had always known that Ralph was a jealous person who demanded a great deal of attention. She was initially pleased that her husband was concerned about how other men looked at her; she felt that it showed Ralph really cared for her. It soon became clear, however, that his jealousy was excessive. One day when she came home from shopping later than usual, Ralph exploded. He demanded an explanation but did not accept Ann's, which was that she stopped to talk with a neighbor. Ralph told her that he wanted her to be home when he returned from work—always. Believing him to be in a bad mood, Ann said nothing. Later, she found out that Ralph had called the neighbor to confirm her story.

The situation progressively worsened. Ralph began to leave work early to be with his wife. He said that business was slow, and they could spend more time together. Whenever the phone rang, Ralph insisted on answering it himself. Wrong numbers and male callers took on special significance for him; he felt they must be trying to

call Ann. Ann found it difficult to discuss the matter with Ralph. He was always quick to take the offensive, and he expressed very little sympathy or understanding toward her.

Ralph's suspicions regarding his wife's fidelity were obviously unjustified. Nothing that Ann did implicated her with other men. Yet Ralph persisted in his pathological jealousy and suspiciousness, and he took the offensive when she suggested that he was wrong in distrusting her. This behavior pattern, along with Ralph's absence of warmth and tenderness, indicates paranoid personality disorder.

Follow-up: After several weeks of treatment, Ann began to feel stronger in her relationship with Ralph. During one confrontation, in which Ralph objected to her seeing the therapist, Ann asserted that she would continue the treatment. She said that she had always been faithful to him and that his jealousy was driving their marriage apart. In a rare moment, Ralph broke down and started crying. He said that he needed her and begged her not to leave him. At this time, Ralph and Ann are each seeing a therapist for marital therapy.

Some psychodynamic explanations propose that persons with paranoid personality disorder engage in the defense mechanism of projection, denying their unacceptable impulses and attributing them to others ("I am not hostile; they are"). Vaillant (1994) has shown that paranoid personality is associated with projection to a striking degree.

Schizoid Personality Disorder **Schizoid personality disorder** is marked primarily by social isolation, emotional coldness, and indifference to others. People

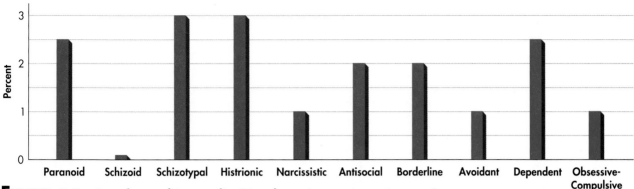

FIGURE 8.1 **Prevalence of Personality Disorders** The prevalence of personality disorders ranges from 0.5 to 3 percent, depending on the disorder. Schizotypal, histrionic, and dependent personality are the three most prevalent personality disorders.

Notes: (1) This graph illustrates the top of each range for each disorder. (2) Schizoid personality disorder occurs less than 0.5 percent in the general population.
Source: Estimates based on American Psychiatric Association (1994) except for dependent personality disorder, which is based on Marmar (1988).

with this disorder have a long history of impairment of social functioning. They are often described as being reclusive and withdrawn (Siever, 1981). Many live alone in apartments or furnished rooms and engage in solitary recreational activities such as watching television, reading, or taking walks. They tend to neither desire nor enjoy close relationships; they have few activities that provide pleasure. Because of a lack of capacity or desire to form social relationships, people with schizoid disorder are perceived by others as peculiar and aloof and therefore inadequate as dating or marital partners. The disorder appears to be uncommon, and slightly more males are diagnosed with it, according to DSM-IV. Members of different cultures do vary as to social behaviors, so that attention must be paid to the cultural background of individuals who show schizoid symptoms.

People with schizoid disorder may have to relate to others in the workplace and similar situations, but these relationships are superficial and frequently awkward. In such situations, people with this disorder tend to comply with the requests or feelings of others, perhaps in an attempt to avoid extensive involvements, conflicts, and expressions of hostility. Social isolation can be found even in their marital relationships. Spitzer and coworkers (1981) describe the case of a man who had married primarily to please his parents. After a while, his wife literally forced him to see a therapist because he was unaffectionate, lacked interest in sex, and was unwilling to participate in family activities. He was as emotionally unresponsive to members of his family as he was to his colleagues at work.

The relationship between this disorder and schizophrenia (described in Chapter 14) is unclear. One view is that schizoid personality disorder is a beginning stage of schizophrenia. Another is that schizophrenia may develop as a complication of the schizoid personality disorder. Some studies have shown that schizoid personality disorder is associated with a cold, unempathic, and emotionally impoverished childhood (Marmar, 1988). It is not clear if there is a genetic predisposition to the disorder.

"I can remember when paranoia was unusual."

Schizotypal Personality Disorder   People who have **schizotypal personality disorder** manifest peculiar thoughts and behaviors and have poor interpersonal relationships. Many believe they possess magical thinking abilities or special powers ("I can predict what people will say before they say it"), and some are subject to recurrent illusions ("I feel that my dead father is watching me"). Speech oddities, such as frequent digression or vagueness in conversation, are often present. The disorder occurs in approximately 3 percent of the population, and gender differences in prevalence are unclear (American Psychiatric Association, 1994).

Again, the evaluation of individuals must take into account their cultural milieu. Superstitious beliefs, delusions, and hallucinations may also occur in certain religious ceremonies or other cultures.

The peculiarities seen in schizotypal personality disorder stem from distortions or difficulties in cognition (Siever, 1981). That is, these people seem to have problems in thinking and perceiving. People with this disorder often show social isolation, hypersensitivity, and inappropriate affect (emotions). The prevailing belief is that the disorder is defined primarily by cognitive distortions, however, and that affective and interpersonal problems are secondary.

The woman described in the following case was diagnosed as having schizotypal personality disorder:

> The patient is a 32-year-old unmarried, unemployed woman on welfare who complains that she feels "spacey." Her feelings of detachment have gradually become stronger and more uncomfortable. For many hours each day she feels as if she were unreal. She feels especially strange when she looks into a mirror. For many years she has felt able to read people's minds by a "kind of clairvoyance I don't understand." According to her, several people in her family apparently also have this ability. She is preoccupied by the thought that she has some special mission in life, but is not sure what it is; she is not particularly religious. She is very self-conscious in public, often feels that people are paying special attention to her, and sometimes thinks that strangers cross the street to avoid her. She is lonely and isolated and spends much of each day lost in fantasies or watching TV soap operas. She speaks in a vague, abstract, digressive manner, generally just missing the point, but she is never incoherent. She seems shy, suspicious, and afraid she will be criticized. She has no gross loss of reality testing, such as hallucinations or delusions. She has never had treatment for emotional problems. She has had occasional jobs, but drifts away from them because of lack of interest. (Spitzer et al., 1981, pp. 95–96)

As peculiar as this patient's behaviors may seem, they are not serious enough to warrant a diagnosis of schizophrenia. Her belief that she is clairvoyant does not appear to be delusional: It is not firmly held (she admits to being confused about it), and there is no

gross loss of contact with reality. Moreover, she had no previous history of psychosis. All these factors point to a personality disorder.

As is true of schizoid personality, many characteristics of schizotypal personality disorder resemble those of schizophrenia, although in less serious form. For example, people with schizophrenia exhibit problems in personality characteristics, psychophysiological responses, and information processing—deficits that have also been observed among persons with schizotypal personality disorder (Grove et al., 1991; Lenzenweger, Cornblatt & Putnick, 1991). Some evidence is consistent with a genetic interpretation of the link between the two disorders. Kendler (1988) found a higher risk of schizotypal personality disorder among relatives of people diagnosed with schizophrenia than among members of a control group. In general, family, twin, and adoption studies support the genetic relationship between schizophrenia and schizotypal personality disorder.

Disorders Characterized by Dramatic, Emotional, or Erratic Behaviors

The group of disorders characterized by dramatic, emotional, or erratic behaviors includes four personality disorders: histrionic, narcissistic, antisocial, and borderline.

Histrionic Personality Disorder   People with **histrionic personality disorder** engage in self-dramatization, exaggerated expression of emotions, and attention-seeking behaviors. Despite superficial warmth and charm, the histrionic person is typically shallow and egocentric. Individuals from different cultures vary in the extent to which they display their emotions, but the histrionic person goes well beyond cultural norms. In the United States, about 2 to 3 percent of the population may have this disorder. Gender differences are unclear, although some studies reveal higher rates among women. Histrionic behaviors were evident in a woman client seen by one of the authors:

> The woman was a 33-year-old real estate agent who entered treatment for problems involving severe depression. She had recently been told by her boyfriend that she was a self-centered and phony person. He found out that she had been dating other men, despite their understanding that neither would go out with others. The woman claimed that she never considered "going out with other men" as actual dating. Once their relationship was broken, her boyfriend refused to communicate with her. The woman then angrily called the boyfriend's employer and told him that unless the boyfriend contacted her, she would commit suicide. He never did call, but instead of attempting suicide she decided to seek psychotherapy.

The woman was attractively dressed for her first therapy session. She wore a tight and clinging sweater. Several times during the session she raised her arms, supposedly to fix her hair, in a very seductive manner. Her conversation was animated and intense: When she was describing the breakup with her boyfriend, she was tearful; later, she raged over the boyfriend's failure to call her and, at one point, called him a "son of a bitch." Near the end of the session, she seemed upbeat and cheerful, commenting that the best therapy might be for the therapist to arrange a date for her.

None of the behaviors exhibited by this client alone warrants a diagnosis of histrionic personality disorder. In combination, however, her self-dramatization, incessant drawing of attention to herself via seductive movements, angry outbursts, manipulative suicide gesture, and lack of genuineness point to this disorder. Millon and Everly (1985) believe that important influences in the development of this disorder are biogenic factors such as autonomic or emotional excitability and environmental factors such as parental reinforcement of a child's attention-seeking behaviors and the existence of histrionic parental models.

Narcissistic Personality Disorder   The clinical characteristics of **narcissistic personality disorder** are an exaggerated sense of self-importance, an exploitative attitude, and a lack of empathy. People with this disorder require attention and admiration and have difficulty accepting personal criticism. In conversations, they talk mainly about themselves and show a lack of interest in others. Many have fantasies about power or influence, and they constantly overestimate their talents and importance. Owing to their sense of self-importance, people with narcissistic personality disorder expect to be the superior participants in all relationships. For example, they may be impatient and irate if others arrive late for a meeting but may frequently be late themselves and think nothing of it.

One narcissistic client reported, "I was denied promotion to chief executive by my board of directors, although my work was good, because they felt I had poor relations with my employees. When I complained to my wife, she agreed with the board, saying my relations with her and the children were equally bad. I don't understand. I know I'm more competent than all these people" (Masterson, 1981, p. ix). The client was depressed and angry about not being promoted and about the suggestion that he had difficulty in forming social relationships. His wife's confirmation of his problems further enraged him. During therapy, he was competitive and sought to devalue the observations of the therapist.

In a study that evaluated the kinds of defense mechanisms used by individuals with different personality disorders, narcissistic personality disorder

Entertainers, such as Michael Jackson, often exhibit self-dramatization, exaggerated expression of emotions, and attention-seeking behaviors while performing. If these characteristics, along with shallowness and egocentricity, are typical of one's personality, a diagnosis of histrionic personality disorder may be warranted.

was strongly associated with the use of dissociation as a defense mechanism (Vaillant, 1994). People with this disorder may use denial and dissociation to ward off feelings of inferiority developed from early childhood (Kernberg, 1975; Marmar, 1988), and they may attempt to maintain their inflated self-concept by devaluing others (Kernberg, 1975).

Narcissistic traits are common among adolescents and do not necessarily imply that a teenager has the disorder (American Psychiatric Association, 1994). The prevalence of the disorder is about 1 percent, with more males than females given the diagnosis.

Antisocial Personality Disorder   Chronic antisocial behavioral patterns such as a failure to conform to social or legal codes, a lack of anxiety and guilt, and irresponsible behaviors indicate **antisocial personality disorder.** People with this disorder show little guilt for

Blanche Dubois, a character in the film "A Street Car Named Desire" illustrates many of the symptoms of narcissistic personality disorder including an exaggerated sense of self-importance, an excessive need for admiration, and an inability to accept criticism or rejection.

their wrongdoing, which may include lying, using other people, and aggressive sexual acts. Their relationships with others are superficial and fleeting, and little loyalty is involved. Antisocial personality disorder, which is far more prevalent among men than among women, is discussed in greater detail later in this chapter.

Borderline Personality Disorder **Borderline personality disorder** is characterized by intense fluctuations in mood, self-image, and interpersonal relationships. Persons with this disorder are impulsive and often have chronic feelings of emptiness, recurrent suicidal behaviors or gestures, and unstable and intense interpersonal relationships. They may be quite friendly one day and quite hostile the next. Many perceive their early childhood as having malevolent others—

others who were hostile or physically violent (Nigg et al., 1992). Although no single feature defines the disorder, its true essence can be captured in the capriciousness of behaviors and the lability of moods (Millon & Everly, 1985).

According to DSM-IV, the prevalence is about 2 percent of the population, with females three times more likely to receive the diagnosis than men are. This is the most commonly diagnosed personality disorder in both inpatient and outpatient settings (Trull, 1995). Some researchers believe that the prevalence of the disorder is increasing because our society makes it difficult for people to maintain stable relationships and a sense of identity.

The First Person narrative in this chapter and the following example illustrate the many facets of borderline personality disorder.

> Bryan was a 23-year-old graduate student majoring in sociology at a prestigious university. He was active in student government and was viewed as charismatic, articulate, and sociable. When he met other students for the first time, he could often convince them to participate in the campus activities that interested him. Women were quite attracted to him because of his charm and self-disclosing nature. They described him as being exciting, intense, and different from other men. Bryan could form close relationships with others very quickly.
>
> Bryan could not, however, maintain his social relationships. Sometimes he would have a brief but intense affair with a woman and then abruptly and angrily ask himself what he ever saw in her. At other times, the woman would reject him after a few dates, because she thought Bryan was moody, self-centered, and demanding. He often called his friends after midnight because he felt lonesome, empty, bored, and wanted to talk. Several times he threatened to commit suicide. He gave little thought to the inconvenience he was causing. Once he organized a group of students to protest the inadequate student parking the university provided. The morning of the planned protest demonstration, he announced that he no longer supported the effort. He said he was not in the right mood for the protest, much to the consternation of his followers, who had spent weeks preparing for the event. Bryan's intense but brief relationships, the marked and continual shifts in moods, and boredom with others in spite of his need for social contacts all point to borderline personality.

Masterson (1981) believes that many clients with borderline personality disorder lack purposefulness. For example, one of his clients reported, "I have such a poor self-image and so little confidence in myself that I can't decide what I want, and when I do decide, I have even more difficulty doing it" (p. ix). Masterson sees this lack as a deficiency in the borderline personality–affected person's emotional investment in the self—a lack of directedness in long-term goals.

People who have borderline personality disorder may exhibit psychotic symptoms, such as auditory hallucinations (for example, hearing imaginary voices that tell them to commit suicide), but the symptoms are usually transient. They also usually have an ego-dystonic reaction to their hallucinations (Spitzer et al., 1981). That is, they recognize their imaginary voices or other hallucinations as being unacceptable, alien, and distressful. By contrast, a person with a psychotic disorder may not realize that his or her hallucinations are pathological. Trull (1995) found that individuals with borderline personality features were more likely to show dysfunctional moods, interpersonal problems, poor coping, and cognitive distortions than were people without borderline personality characteristics.

Different models have been used to conceptualize borderline personality disorder. Most of the literature on the disorder comes from those with psychodynamic perspectives. For example, Kernberg (1976) proposed the concept of object splitting—that people with borderline personality disorder perceive others as all good or all bad at different times. This split results in emotional fluctuations toward others.

Another perspective looks at the disorder from a social learning viewpoint: Millon (1981) argued that borderline personality is caused by a faulty self-identity, which affects the development of consistent goals and accomplishments. As a result, persons with this disorder have difficulty coping with their own emotions and with life in general. They then develop a conflict between the need to depend on others and the need to assert themselves. Fluctuations in emotions or dysfunctions in emotional regulation are at the core of the disorder, according to Linehan (1987), who adopted a behavioral perspective. Interestingly, she speculated that biological factors may be responsible for the emotional dysregulation among individuals with borderline personality disorder.

Cognitive-oriented approaches have also been used. Westen (1991) defined two core aspects of borderline personality: difficulties in regulating emotions and unstable and intense interpersonal relationships. According to this approach, these two aspects are affected by distorted or inaccurate attributions (explanations for others' behaviors or attitudes). Westen's cognitive-behavioral therapy for borderline personality disorders therefore involves changing the way clients think about and approach interpersonal situations. Another cognitive theorist, Beck, assumed that an individual's basic assumptions (that is, thoughts) play a central role in influencing perceptions, interpretations, and behavioral and emotional responses (Beck et al., 1990). Individuals with borderline personality disorder seem to have three basic assumptions: (1) "The world is dangerous and malevolent,"

In the film "Fatal Attraction," the character Alex Forrest exhibits many of the traits of borderline personality disorder: impulsiveness, marked fluctuations in mood, chronic feelings of emptiness, and unstable and intense interpersonal relationships.

(2) "I am powerless and vulnerable," and (3) "I am inherently unacceptable." Belief in these assumptions makes individuals with this disorder fearful, vigilant, guarded, and defensive.

These diverse theoretical perspectives on this disorder reflect the current strong interest in borderline personality. In contrast to the theoretical contributions, empirical research is sparse. Some investigators have found that individuals with the disorder have a history of chaotic family environments, including physical and sexual abuse (Clarkin, Marziali & Munroe-Blum, 1991). Such family experiences may affect perceptions of self and others. Benjamin and Wonderlich (1994) found in one study that borderline individuals viewed their mothers and others in their environment as more hostile than did a comparable group of people with mood disorders.

FIRST PERSON

Edward Spauster

Growing up, I was always fascinated by the characters I encountered in literature, film, and television. Many seem to live exciting, enviable lives, and all were distinct individuals. Consider Scarlett O'Hara and *Dynasty*'s Alexis Carrington-Colby. Their dramatic, seductive, attention-seeking behaviors (*histrionic* is the clinical term) draw us to them; their lies, exploitation, and lack of true warmth or remorse (antisocial traits) arouse our dislike. Similarly, successful comedy often depends on humorous portrayals of personality extremes. Fonzie's narcissism, Felix Unger's compulsiveness, and Walter Mitty's flights into schizoidal fantasy are all enduring personality traits that actually define the characters who possess them.

As an adult, I continue to be intrigued by personality characteristics and, as a psychologist, I work with many patients who are considered personality disordered. They are usually quite distinct, occasionally exciting—but rarely enviable. Unable to change their behavior patterns, they repeatedly suffer the painful consequences that these patterns produce.

This situation is most evident in borderline personality disorder, which is perhaps the most disturbing and most commonly treated character disorder. The following case is fairly typical.

Yolanda was transferred to the acute psychiatric unit after two days in intensive care, where she had been medically treated for an overdose of her antidepressant medication. The history gathered by the treatment team included several years of physical abuse by her parents; three prior suicide attempts; dozens of full- and part-time jobs; one marriage and three engagements; two abortions; and a cocaine habit that at times she supported by providing sex to dealers. Yolanda was twenty-four years old. During her hospitalization, she showed many sides of herself. Sometimes she was gregarious and quickly made friends with other patients. On

---

Again, mood changes, intense and unstable interpersonal relationships, identity problems, and other characteristics associated with borderline personality disorder can be observed in all persons to a greater or lesser extent. As is the case with other personality disorders, diagnosis is difficult and formulations about the causes of the disorder must rely on what we know about personality development in general. We return to that topic later in this chapter.

Disorders Characterized by Anxious or Fearful Behaviors

Another cluster of personality disorders is characterized by anxious or fearful behaviors. This category includes the avoidant, dependent, and obsessive-compulsive personality disorders.

Avoidant Personality Disorder   The essential features of **avoidant personality disorder** are a fear of rejection and humiliation, and a reluctance to enter into social relationships. Persons with this disorder tend to have low self-esteem and to avoid social relationships without a guarantee of uncritical acceptance by others.

Unlike persons with schizoid personalities who avoid others because they lack interest, and unlike persons who are shy because of their cultural background, people with avoidant personality disorder do not desire to be alone. On the contrary, they crave affection and an active social life. They want—but fear—social contacts, and this ambivalence may be reflected in different ways. For example, many people with this disorder engage in intellectual pursuits, wear fine clothes, or are active in the artistic community (Millon, 1981). Their need for contact and relationships is often woven into their activities. Thus an avoidant person may write poems expressing the plight of the lonely or the need for human intimacy. A primary defense mechanism is fantasy, whereby wishes are fulfilled to an excessive degree in the person's imagination (Millon & Everly, 1985).

Avoidant personality disorder occurs in less than 1 percent of the population, and no gender differences are apparent (American Psychiatric Association, 1994). People with this disorder are caught in a vicious cycle: Because they are preoccupied with rejection, they are constantly alert to signs of derogation or ridicule. This concern leads to many perceived in-

other occasions, she grew furious with staff and patients and sought solitude. Once, after a bitter phone conversation with her family, attendants found her in the bathroom scratching her wrists with an opened paper clip. Her emotions were so intense that she felt lost in them and unbearably empty. In this state, she found physical pain a relief because it reassured her of her existence.

Yolanda's constellation of symptoms, especially the mood instability, identity disturbance, uncontrolled anger, and self-destructive behaviors are typical of borderline personality disorder. It's often frightening. The reality of Yolanda's life is that she often considers suicide. Because she depends on others to provide boundaries for her emotions and behavior, she is extremely sensitive to the slightest shift in others, including me, her therapist. Her anger, fueled by years of abuse, is always expressed as rage, and frightens both her and others. I've been its target more than once.

At other times, her attachment to me is so strong that she finds her own fragile boundaries breaking down. Soon after revealing to me that she had been sexually abused fifteen years earlier, Yolanda became afraid that I would be killed by her uncle, the abuser. He had silenced Yolanda by threatening to hurt her parents if she told anyone about the abuse. The fear produced by her disclosure was as real in our sessions as it was years ago. She found it very difficult to believe that my bout of flu was not some repercussion for her telling me about the abuse.

Although challenging and exciting, working with borderlines is also tiring. I function best when I limit the number of borderline clients in my practice and have a colleague available for consultation. Maintaining an accepting and consistent therapeutic stance in the face of borderline chaos is not easy, but necessary. A therapeutic relationship that is stable, sets appropriate boundaries, survives in spite of intense emotions, and fosters hope becomes, in a very small way, a break in the pattern. And for disorders of personality, changing patterns is the only way out.

Edward Spauster is a staff psychologist on the Adult Services Unit at the Hollywood Hospital, a private psychiatric hospital in Queens, New York.

stances of rejection, which cause them to avoid others. Their social skills may then become deficient and invite criticism from others. In other words, their very fear of criticism may lead to criticism. Avoidants often feel depressed, anxious, angry at themselves, inferior, and inadequate.

Jenny L., an unmarried 27-year-old bank teller, shows several features of avoidant personality disorder. Although she functions adequately at work, Jenny is extremely shy, sensitive, and quiet with fellow employees. She perceives others as being insensitive and gross. If the bank manager jokes with other tellers, she feels that the manager prefers them to her.

Jenny has very few hobbies. A great deal of her time is spent watching television and eating chocolates. (As a result, she is about 40 pounds overweight.) Television romances are her favorite programs; after watching one, she tends to daydream about having an intense romantic relationship. Jenny L. eventually sought treatment for her depression and loneliness.

Little research has been conducted on the etiology of avoidant personality disorder. A complex interaction of early childhood environmental experiences and innate temperament has been advanced as causes for the disorder (Marmar, 1988).

Dependent Personality Disorder   People who rely on others and are unwilling to assume responsibility show **dependent personality disorder**. These people lack self-confidence, and they subordinate their needs to those of the people on whom they depend. Nevertheless, casual observers may fail to recognize or may misinterpret their dependency and inability to make decisions. Friends may perceive dependent personalities as understanding and tolerant, without realizing that they are fearful of taking the initiative because they are afraid of disrupting the relationship. In addition, a dependent personality may allow his or her spouse to be dominant or abusive for fear that the spouse will otherwise leave. Beck and associates (1990) believe that the dependency is not simply a matter of being passive and unassertive, which can be treated with assertiveness training. Rather, dependent personalities have two deeply ingrained assumptions that affect their thoughts, perceptions, and behaviors. First, they see themselves as inherently inadequate and unable to cope. Second, they conclude that their course of action should be to find someone who can take care of them. Depression, helplessness, and suppressed anger are often a part of dependent personality disorder.

The socializing process that trains people to be independent, assertive, and individual rather than group oriented is not equally valued in all cultures. Nor is it manifested by all people all the time in the cultures that do value it. Some individuals, such as hospitalized patients, typically develop some degree of dependency during confinement. Thus, the individual's environment must be considered before rendering a diagnosis. The prevalence of the disorder is about 2.5 percent, and gender differences are unclear. The following case illustrates a dependent personality disorder that cannot be attributed to cultural or situational factors.

> Jim is 56, a single man who was living with his 78-year-old widowed mother. When his mother was recently hospitalized for cancer, Jim decided to see a therapist. He was distraught and depressed over his mother's condition. Jim indicated that he did not know what to do. His mother had always taken care of him, and, in his view, she always knew best. Even when he was young, his mother had "worn the pants" in the family. The only time that he was away from his family was during his six years of military service. He was wounded in the Korean War, was returned to the United States, and spent a few months in a Veterans' Administration hospital. He then went to live with his mother. Because of his service-connected injury, Jim was unable to work full time. His mother welcomed him home, and she structured all his activities.
>
> At one point, Jim met and fell in love with a woman, but his mother disapproved of her. During a confrontation between the mother and Jim's woman friend, each demanded that Jim make a commitment to her. This was quite traumatic for Jim. His mother finally grabbed him and yelled that he must tell the other woman to go. Jim tearfully told the woman that he was sorry but she must go, and the woman angrily left.
>
> While Jim was relating his story, it was clear to the therapist that Jim harbored some anger toward his mother, though he overtly denied any feelings of hostility. Also clear were his dependency and his inability to take responsibility. His life had always been structured, first by his mother and then by the military. His mother's illness meant that his structured world might crumble.

People clearly differ in the degree to which they are dependent or submissive. How dependency is explained varies according to theoretical perspective. For psychoanalysts, it occurs because of maternal deprivation, which causes fixation at the oral stage of development (Marmar, 1988). Behavioral learning theorists believe that a family or social environment that rewards dependent behaviors and punishes inde-

pendence may promote dependency. Some cognitive theorists attribute dependent personality disorder to the development of distorted beliefs about one's inadequacies and helplessness that discourage independence.

Obsessive-Compulsive Personality Disorder The characteristics of **obsessive-compulsive personality disorder** are perfectionism, a tendency to be interpersonally controlling, devotion to details, and rigidity. Many of these traits are found in normal people. Unlike normal people, however, individuals with obsessive-compulsive personality disorder show marked impairment in occupational or social functioning. Further, the extent of the character rigidity is greater among people who have this disorder (Weintraub, 1981). Unlike obsessive-compulsive disorder, in which there are the recurrent thoughts or repetitive behaviors (chapter 5), obsessive-compulsive personality involves general traits of perfectionism, inflexibility, and attention to details.

Coworkers may find the individual with this disorder too demanding, inflexible, miserly, and perfectionistic. He or she may actually be ineffective on the job, despite long hours of devotion. The preoccupation with details, rules, and possible errors leads to indecision and an inability to see "the big picture." The disorder occurs in about 1 percent of the population and is more prevalent among males than females, according to DSM-IV.

> Cecil, a third-year medical student, was referred for therapy by his graduate adviser. The adviser told the therapist that Cecil was in danger of being expelled from medical school because of his inability to get along with patients and with other students. Cecil often berated patients for failing to follow his advice. In one instance, he told a patient with a lung condition to stop smoking. When the patient indicated he was unable to stop, Cecil angrily told the patient to go for medical treatment elsewhere—that the medical center had no place for such a "weak-willed fool." Cecil's relationships with others were similarly strained. He considered many members of the faculty to be "incompetent old deadwood," and he characterized fellow graduate students as "party-goers."
>
> The graduate adviser told the therapist that Cecil had not been expelled only because several faculty members thought that he was brilliant. Cecil studied and worked sixteen hours a day. He was extremely well read and had an extensive knowledge of medical disorders. Although he was always able to provide a careful and detailed analysis of a patient's condition, it took him a great deal of time to do so. His diagnoses tended to cover every disorder that each patient could conceivably have, on the basis of all possible combinations of symptoms.

We turn now to the etiology and treatment of antisocial personality disorder, which we touched on

In "Remains of the Day," actor Anthony Hopkins (right) portrays a butler with excessive perfectionism, stubbornness, and devotion to detail—all obsessive-compulsive traits.

lightly earlier in this chapter. Research on the other personality disorders has been quite limited. By discussing antisocial personality disorder at greater length, we hope to give you a broader view and an appreciation of the wide range of explanatory views that can be proposed for the personality disorders in general.

ANTISOCIAL PERSONALITY DISORDER

The following case presents an example of antisocial personality disorder:

Roy W. is an eighteen-year-old high school senior who was referred by juvenile court for diagnosis and evaluation. He was arrested for stealing an automobile, something he had also done on several other occasions. The court agreed with Roy's mother that he needed evaluation and perhaps psychotherapy.

During his interview with the psychologist, Roy was articulate, relaxed, and even witty. He said that stealing was wrong but that none of the cars he stole was ever damaged. The last theft occurred because he needed transportation to a beer party (which was located only a mile from his home) and his leg was sore from playing basketball. When the psychologist asked Roy how he got along with girls, he grinned and said that he was very outgoing and could easily "hustle" girls. He then related the following incident:

"About three months ago, I was pulling out of the school parking lot real fast and accidentally sideswiped this other car. The girl who was driving it started to scream at me. God, there was only a small dent on her fender! Anyway, we exchanged names and addresses and I apologized for the accident. When I filled out the accident report later, I said that it was her car that pulled out from the other side and hit my car. How do you like that? Anyway, when she heard about my claim that it was her fault, she had her old man call me. He said that his daughter had witnesses to the accident and that I could be arrested. Bull, he was just trying to bluff me. But I gave him a sob story—about how my parents were ready to get a divorce, how poor we were, and the trouble I would get into if they found out about the accident. I apologized for lying and told him I could fix the dent. Luckily he never checked with my folks for the real story. Anyway, I went over to look at the girl's car. I really didn't have any idea of how to fix that old heap so I said I had to wait a couple of weeks to get some tools for the repair job.

"Meanwhile, I started to talk to the girl. Gave her my sob story, told her how nice I thought her folks and home were. We started to date and I took her out three times. Then one night I laid her. The crummy thing was that she told her folks about it. Can you imagine that? Anyway, her old man called and told me never to get near his precious little thing again. She's actually a slut.

"At least I didn't have to fix her old heap. I know I shouldn't lie but can you blame me? People make such a big thing out of nothing."

The irresponsibility, disregard for others, and disregard for societal rules and morals evident in this interview indicated to the psychologist that Roy has antisocial personality disorder. Historically, the terms *moral insanity, moral imbecility, moral defect,* and *psychopathic inferiority* have been attached to this condition. An early nineteenth-century British psychiatrist, J. C. Prichard (1837), described it this way:

> The moral and active principles of the mind are strongly perverted or depraved; the power of self-government is lost or greatly impaired; and the individual is found to be incapable, not of talking or reasoning upon any subject proposed to him...but of conducting himself with decency and propriety in the business of life. (p. 15)

Prichard believed that the disorder was reflected not in a loss of intellectual skills but in gross violations of moral and ethical standards.

The diagnosis of antisocial personality (also referred to as *sociopathic* or *psychopathic* personality) has now lost some of its original moral overtones. Nevertheless, people with antisocial personalities do show a disregard for conventional societal rules and morals.

Cleckley's (1976) classic description of the disorder included the following characteristics:

1. *Superficial charm and good intelligence* Persons with antisocial personalities are often capable in social activities and adept at manipulating others.

2. *Shallow emotions and lack of empathy, guilt, or remorse* Absent are genuine feelings of love and loyalty toward others and of concern over the detrimental consequences of their behaviors.

3. *Behaviors indicative of little life plan or order* The actions of antisocial personalities are not well planned and are often difficult to understand or predict.

4. *Failure to learn from experiences and absence of anxiety* Although the behaviors may be punished, people with antisocial personality may repeat the same behaviors, and they frequently show little anxiety.

5. *Unreliability, insincerity, and untruthfulness* Persons with antisocial personalities are irresponsible and may lie or feign emotional feelings to callously manipulate others; their social relationships are usually unstable and short-lived.

Some of these characteristics are apparent in Roy's case. For example, he felt no guilt for his actions or for manipulating the girl and her family. In fact, he was quite proud of his ability to seduce the girl and avoid responsibility for the automobile repair. The ease with which Roy related his story to the psychologist demonstrated his lack of concern for those who were hurt by his behaviors. Roy showed no anxiety during the interview.

DSM-IV criteria for the disorder differ somewhat from Cleckley's description, which is based on clinical observations of various cases. For example, DSM-IV criteria do not include lack of anxiety, shallow emo-

Antisocial personality disorder, or psychopathy, involves characteristics such as criminal behavior, irritability, aggressiveness, impulsivity, lack of remorse, and deceitfulness. Many of these characteristics were exhibited by serial murderer Ted Bundy. Here, Bundy is shown waving to television cameras after his indictment for the murders of two Florida State University women.

Individuals who engage in social protest or civil disobedience are rarely regarded as having an antisocial personality disorder. Although some may break the law, the other features of antisocial personality disorder—chronic lack of remorse and deceitfulness, for example—are usually absent. In this photo, a group of deaf students demonstrate at a rally held to gather support for the removal of a school administrator.

tions, failure to learn from past experiences, and superficial charm. They do include a history before age fifteen of failing to conform to social norms with respect to lawful behaviors, irritability and aggressiveness, impulsivity, lack of remorse, and deceitfulness. For the diagnosis to be made, the individual must be at least eighteen years old. DSM-IV criteria, however, fail to convey the conceptual sense of the disorder that was conveyed in Cleckley's original description.

Hare and colleagues (Harpur, Hare & Hakstian, 1989; Hart & Hare, 1989) constructed a measure, the *Psychopathy Checklist—Revised (PCL-R)*, that captures some of the elements of Cleckley's description as well as those of DSM-IV. In an analysis of the features of the PCL-R, Hare, Hart, and Harpur (1991) found two factors underlying the measure. Factor 1 reflects a set of interpersonal and affective characteristics, such as egocentricity, lack of remorse, and callousness, similar to those proposed by Cleckley. Factor 2 reflects characteristics consistent with DSM-IV criteria—namely, impulsivity, antisocial and unstable lifestyle, and irresponsibility.

The distinction between Cleckley's conceptualization and DSM-IV criteria is important because sole use of DSM-IV may not capture the "personality" aspect or the underlying construct of the disorder. DSM-IV may overemphasize behavioral manifestations and criminality. Although this emphasis makes it easier and more reliable to render a diagnosis, it may fail to capture the essence of the disorder. The distinction between the two factors is also apparent from research findings on age. Factor 1 was found to

be fairly stable across different age spans among psychopathic prisoners. However, Factor 2 declined with age (Harpur & Hare, 1994).

In the United States, the incidence of antisocial personality disorder is estimated to be overall about 2 percent, with different rates by gender: 3 percent for men and less than 1 percent for women (American Psychiatric Association, 1994). Overall estimates vary, however, from study to study, which may be due to differences in sampling, diagnostic, and methodological procedures. Goodwin and Guze (1984) concluded that antisocial personality is fairly common, and probably increasingly so. It is much more frequent in urban environments than in rural ones, and in lower socioeconomic groups than in higher ones. Robins, Tipp, and Przybeck (1991) found comparable rates of antisocial personality disorder among Whites, African Americans, and Latinos. Although African Americans had a higher rate of incarceration for crimes, their rate of antisocial personality disorder was no different from the other groups.

The behavior patterns associated with antisocial personality disorder are different and distinct from behaviors involving social protest or criminal lifestyles. People who engage in civil disobedience or violate the conventions of society or its laws as a form of protest are not as a rule persons with antisocial personalities. Such people can be quite capable of forming meaningful interpersonal relationships and of experiencing guilt. They may perceive their violations of rules and norms as acts performed for the greater good. Similarly, engaging in delinquent or adult criminal behavior is not a necessary or sufficient condition for diagnosing antisocial personality. Although many convicted criminals have been found to have antisocial characteristics, many others do not. They may come from a subculture that encourages and reinforces criminal activity; hence, in perpetrating such acts they are adhering to group mores and codes of conduct. As mentioned earlier, DSM-IV criteria tend to emphasize criminality but the appropriateness of this emphasis is being questioned.

Finally, researchers often make a distinction between primary and secondary psychopaths. A *primary psychopath* apparently lacks anxiety or guilt over antisocial behaviors, but a *secondary psychopath* reports guilt over such behaviors.

People with antisocial personalities are a difficult population to study because they do not voluntarily seek treatment. Consequently, researchers often seek psychopathic subjects in prison populations, which presumably harbor a relatively large proportion of psychopaths. But now a different problem arises: Researchers cannot know whether the psychopaths in prison are representative of the nonprison psychopathic population as well.

Using an ingenious research approach, Widom (1977) tried to find a number of noninstitutionalized psychopaths to discover whether their characteristics matched those of psychopaths typically found in prison groups. She placed the following advertisement in a major Boston counterculture newspaper:

> *Are You Adventurous?* Psychologist studying adventurous, carefree people who've led exciting, impulsive lives. If you're the kind of person who'd do almost anything for a dare and want to participate in a paid experiment, send name, address, phone, and short biography proving how interesting you are.

Widom reasoned that such an ad might appeal to individuals with antisocial personalities. Of the seventy-three people who responded, twenty-eight met her criteria for antisocial personality and were studied further. On the basis of psychological tests and interviews, Widom concluded that the noninstitutionalized people she studied did have characteristics similar to those associated with antisocial personality among prisoners. But her respondents tended to have a higher level of education and, although often arrested, they were infrequently convicted of crimes.

Explanations of Antisocial Personality Disorder

People with antisocial personality disorder are apparently unable to learn from past experience. They continue to engage in antisocial behaviors despite criticism and scorn from others, the disruption of close personal relationships, and frequent encounters with legal authorities. They often sincerely promise to change their lives and make amends, only to return to antisocial behavior soon after. A variety of theories emphasize the inability of persons with antisocial personalities to learn appropriate social and ethical behaviors. The reasons given for this defect, however, are quite diverse.

Theories of the etiology of this disorder vary with theoretical orientation and with the theorist's definition of *antisocial personality*. We examine a number of the most frequently cited constructs from the psychoanalytic, family and socialization, biogenic, and anxiety-arousal-behavioral perspectives.

Psychoanalytic Perspective   According to one psychoanalytic approach, the psychopath's absence of guilt and frequent violation of moral and ethical standards are the result of faulty superego development (Fenichel, 1945). Id impulses are more likely to be expressed when the weakened superego cannot exert very much influence. People exhibiting antisocial behavior patterns presumably did not adequately identify with their parents. Frustration, rejection, or inconsistent discipline resulted in fixation at an early stage of development.

Family and Socialization Perspectives   Some theorists believe that relationships within the family—the primary agent of socialization—are paramount in the development of antisocial patterns (McCord & McCord, 1964). In a review of factors that predict delinquency and antisocial behaviors in children, Loeber (1990) found that a family's socioeconomic status was a weak predictor, whereas other family characteristics, such as poor parental supervision and involvement, were good predictors. Rejection or deprivation by one or both parents may mean that the child has little opportunity to learn socially appropriate behaviors or that the value of people as socially reinforcing agents is diminished. Parental separation has been correlated with antisocial personality. Children may have been traumatized or subjected to a hostile environment during the parental separation (Vaillant & Perry, 1985). Millon and Everly (1985) believe that hostility in such families may result in interpersonal hostility among the children. Hence psychopaths may find little satisfaction in close or meaningful relationships with others. Psychopaths do show a significant amount of misperception about people in general (Widom, 1976). The inability to perceive another's viewpoint can create problems in personal interactions.

People with antisocial personality disorder can learn and use social skills very effectively (Ullmann & Krasner, 1975), as shown in their adeptness at manipulation, lying, and cheating, and their ease at being charming and sociable. The difficulty is that, in many areas of learning, these individuals do not pay attention to social stimuli, and their schedules of reinforcement differ from those of most other people. Perhaps this relatively diminished attention stems from inconsistent reinforcement from parents or inadequate feedback for behaviors.

Another explanation is that the child may have modeled the behaviors of a parent who had antisocial tendencies. In one study, researchers examined the past records and statuses of nearly 500 adults who had been seen about thirty years earlier as children in a child guidance clinic. More than 90 of the adults exhibited antisocial tendencies. These persons were compared with a group of 100 adults who, as children, had lived in the same geographic area but had never been referred to the clinic. The researchers found the following (Robins, 1966):

1. There was little relationship between having antisocial personality disorder as an adult and participating in gangs as a youth.

2. Antisocial behavior (theft, aggression, juvenile delinquency, lying) in childhood was a predictor of antisocial behaviors in adults.

3. The adjustment level of fathers, but not that of mothers, was significant—having a father who was antisocial was related to adult antisocial characteristics.

4. Growing up in a single-parent home was not related to psychopathy.

The study seemed to indicate that antisocial behavior is probably influenced by the presence of an antisocial father who either serves as a model for such behavior or provides inadequate supervision, inconsistent discipline, or family conflict. The father's influence on antisocial behaviors in children may be a result of traditional gender role training. Males have traditionally received more encouragement to engage in aggressive behaviors than females have, and antisocial patterns are more prevalent among men than among women. If traditional gender roles change, one might reasonably expect that antisocial tendencies will increase among females and that mothers will play a greater role in the development of antisocial behaviors in children.

Another study also found that parental antisocial patterns, especially among fathers, were strongly associated with child conduct disorder (Lahey et al., 1988). Interestingly, results also indicated that divorce among parents was not related to having children with conduct disorder, once parental antisocial background was controlled. That is, although some re-

searchers have speculated that divorce of parents is associated with antisocial conduct problems among children, this study found that the association was caused primarily by the fact that divorced parents were more likely to be antisocial than were married parents. It is unclear, however, whether the effects of having a psychopathic parent are genetic (parents transmitting a certain genetic makeup to children) or environmental (parents providing an antisocial role model).

A disturbed family background or disturbed parental model is neither a necessary nor a sufficient condition for the development of antisocial personality. Indeed, antisocial personality probably has multiple causes.

Biogenic Perspectives   Throughout history, many people have speculated that some individuals are "born to raise hell." These speculations are difficult to test because of the problems involved in distinguishing between the influences of environment and heredity on behavior. For example, antisocial personality disorder is five times more common among first-degree biologic relatives of males and ten times more common among first-degree biologic relatives of females with this disorder than among the general population (American Psychiatric Association, 1987; 1994). These findings can be used to support either an environmental or a genetic hypothesis. Within the last decade, however, some interesting research has been conducted on genetic influences in antisocial personality disorder.

One strategy has been to compare concordance rates for identical, or monozygotic (MZ), twins with those for fraternal, or dizygotic (DZ), twins. Recall from Chapter 2 that MZ twins share exactly the same genes. But DZ twins share about 50 percent of the same genes; they are genetically no more alike than any two siblings. Most studies show that MZ twins do tend to have a higher concordance rate than DZ twins for antisocial tendencies, delinquency, and criminality (Mednick & Christiansen, 1977); this finding tends to support a genetic basis for these behavior patterns. Nevertheless, some caution must be exercised in drawing firm conclusions. Twin pairs can influence each other's behavior, and if MZ twins influence each other more than do DZ twins, the higher concordance rate may be caused at least in part by this influence. Carey (1992) found that twin interaction is important and believes that both heredity and sibling interaction contribute to antisocial behavior.

Another strategy for studying genetic influence is to note the rate of antisocial personality among adopted people with antisocial biological parents. Because these adoptees were separated from their biological parents early in life, learning antisocial behaviors from their parents would have been difficult. Results have generally shown that adoptees whose biological parents exhibited antisocial behaviors have a higher rate of antisocial characteristics than that found among adoptees whose biological parents did *not* exhibit antisocial behaviors (Cadoret & Cain, 1981). Even Robins' study (1966), in which the development of antisocial personality was associated with having antisocial fathers, revealed that the association existed even when the people were not raised in the presence of their fathers.

Do adoptive parents' antisocial patterns influence their psychopathic adoptees? If so, this would be evidence of environmental influence. Research results show, however, that the rate of criminality or antisocial tendencies is higher among the biological parents than among the adoptive parents of such individuals (Hutchings & Mednick, 1977; Mednick & Kandel, 1988; Schulsinger, 1972). Again the evidence suggests that antisocial personality patterns are influenced by heredity (Goodwin & Guze, 1984).

Although this body of evidence seems to show a strong casual pattern, it should be examined carefully, for several reasons. First, many of the studies fail to clearly distinguish between antisocial personalities and criminals; as we noted earlier, they may draw subjects only from criminal populations. Truly representative samples of people with antisocial personality disorder should be investigated. Second, evidence that supports a genetic basis for antisocial tendencies does not preclude the environment as a factor. Antisocial personality is undoubtedly caused by environmental as well as genetic influences. The relative contribution of each factor, as well as the interaction between heredity and environment, should be investigated (Marmar, 1988). Third, studies indicating that genetic factors are important do not provide much insight into how antisocial personality is inherited. What exactly is transmitted genetically? We need to understand more thoroughly the process that leads to the disorder.

Central Nervous System Abnormality Some early investigators suggested that people with antisocial personalities tend to have abnormal brain wave activity (Hill & Watterson, 1942; Knott et al., 1953). In these studies, the measurement of the brain waves, or electroencephalograms (EEGs), of psychopaths were sometimes found to be similar to those of normal young children. According to one survey, most studies revealed that between 31 and 58 percent of people with antisocial personality showed some EEG abnormality, frequently in the form of slow-wave, theta activity (Ellingson, 1954). Perhaps these abnormalities indicate brain pathology. Such pathology could in-

hibit the capacity of those with antisocial personalities to learn how to avoid punishment and render them unable to learn from experience (Hare, 1970). This explanation is plausible, but there simply is not enough evidence to support its acceptance. Many persons diagnosed with antisocial personality disorder do not show EEG abnormalities, and individuals who do not have the disorder may also exhibit theta-wave activity (Milstein, 1988). In addition, the EEG is an imprecise diagnostic device, and abnormal brain wave activity in people with antisocial personalities may simply be correlated with, rather than a cause of, disturbed behavior. For example, psychopathic personalities may simply be less anxious or more bored than are nonpsychopaths, which may account for slow-wave EEGs.

Autonomic Nervous System Abnormalities Other interesting and promising research points to the involvement of the autonomic nervous system (ANS) in the prominent features of antisocial personality disorder: the inability to learn from experience, the absence of anxiety, and the tendency to engage in thrill-seeking behaviors. Two lines of investigation can be identified, both based on the assumption that people with antisocial personality disorder have ANS deficiencies or abnormalities. The first is based on the premise that ANS abnormalities make antisocial personalities less susceptible to anxiety and therefore less likely to learn from their experiences in situations where aversive stimuli (or punishment) are involved. The second line of research focuses on the premise that ANS abnormalities could keep antisocial people emotionally underaroused. To achieve an optimal level of arousal or to avoid boredom, underaroused individuals might seek excitement and thrills and fail to conform to conventional behavioral standards. The two premises—lack of anxiety and underarousal—may, of course, be related, because underarousal could include underaroused anxiety.

Although Eysenck (Eysenck, 1957; Eysenck & Rachman, 1965) is considered a behaviorist, he was among the first to clearly argue the relevance of the ANS in antisocial personality. He believed that temperamental characteristics—or personality dimensions—could help explain why antisocial personalities fail to become adequately socialized to the rules and norms of society. Eysenck focused on two temperamental characteristics: neuroticism and introversion-extraversion. *Neuroticism* is autonomic instability or emotionality. Very neurotic people have an easily aroused and overactive autonomic nervous system. People who are not neurotic show the opposite characteristics—little anxiety or emotionality. The second personality dimension is *introversion-extraversion.*

Heroes and Psychopaths

Lykken (1982) argued that heroes and psychopaths are two sides of the same coin. For example, Lykken noted that Chuck Yeager, a heroic test pilot, once concealed broken ribs that he had suffered in a wild midnight horseback ride so that he could go aloft in the belly of a B-29, wedge himself in the tiny cockpit of the X-1 rocket plane, and let himself be jettisoned at an altitude of 26,000 feet to become the first person to travel faster than the speed of sound. And Ted Bundy was a charming, intelligent, and articulate psychopath who left a coast-to-coast trail of brutal and sadistic murders of young women. Lykken believes that heroes and psychopaths share one characteristic—namely, fearlessness. In an attempt to measure fearlessness, he developed the Activity Preference Questionnaire. The questionnaire instructs respondents to pretend that one or the other situation described must occur, and asks respondents to choose the situation that is the lesser of two evils. Here are some of the items:

1. a. Cleaning up your house after floodwaters have left it filled with mud
   b. Making a parachute jump
2. a. Spending hours fixing a fancy barbecue for some guests, who then eat very little and seem not to like it
   b. Distributing 1,000 handbills in mailboxes from door to door
3. a. Having to walk around all day on a blistered foot
   b. Sleeping out on a camping trip in an area where rattlesnakes have been reported
4. a. Washing a car
   b. Driving a car at 95 miles an hour

The questionnaire items present a frightening or embarrassing situation paired with a situation that is merely onerous. People who are relatively fearless, such as heroes and psychopaths, may have a greater tendency to choose the frightening or embarrassing alternative than do fearful people.

What factors influence the probability of becoming a hero rather than a psychopath among those who are relatively fearless? Although very fearless children are difficult to bring up, circumstances and family environment may play crucial roles. Those who have the opportunity to channel their fearlessness into socially approved activities (such as being a test pilot) and who are socialized in families that emphasize warm and loving relationships rather than punishment techniques may be less likely to become psychopaths.

Introverts are inhibited, less sociable, and quick to learn. Extraverts tend to be impulsive, sociable, uninhibited, and slow to learn.

Eysenck hypothesized that temperamental characteristics are inherited and that primary psychopaths are neurotic and extraverted. The combination of these two temperaments result in impulsivity and a lack of inhibitions. They learn slowly, quickly develop reactive inhibition (fatigue in learning), and slowly dissipate that reactive inhibition. The difficulty in learning becomes a handicap in developing normal social patterns.

Eysenck argued that psychopaths can learn but that they require more trials or repetitive experiences than others do. Hence antisocial patterns are seen primarily in youth or in young adults who have not yet been exposed to enough experiences to learn to control their behaviors.

Fearlessness or Lack of Anxiety   Lykken (1982) maintained that because of genetic predisposition, people vary in their level of fearlessness. Antisocial personality develops because of fearlessness or low anxiety levels. People who have high levels of fear avoid risks, stress, and strong stimulation; relatively fearless people seek thrills and adventures. Fearlessness is associated with heroes (such as volunteering for dangerous military action or risking one's life to save others) as well as with individuals with antisocial personalities, who may engage in risky criminal activities or impulsively violate norms and rules (see Focus On).

Lykken's classic research (1957) focused on behaviors of prisoners judged to be primary psychopaths, of prisoners judged to be nonpsychopathic, and of students matched with the prisoners in socioeconomic background, age, and intelligence. He hypothesized that the psychopathic group would show less anxiety and greater deficiencies in avoidance learning. His results generally confirmed these hypotheses. In a classical conditioning procedure wherein a buzzer (conditioned stimulus, or CS) was paired with a shock (unconditioned stimulus, or US), psychopaths showed less galvanic skin response than did the nonpsychopathic prisoners and the students. (Galvanic skin response measures sweating, which is presumed to indicate emotional reaction or anxiety.) On the Activities Preference Questionnaire that Lykken devised, the psychopaths exhibited less aversion to frightening social and physical situations, perhaps reflecting their low anxiety in such situations. In an avoidance learning task, in which errors could produce an electric shock, psychopaths made more errors than nonpsychopathic prisoners, who in turn made more errors than the students. Lykken's work suggested that, because psychopaths do not become conditioned to

Lykken theorized that people with low anxiety levels are often thrill seekers. The difference between the psychopath who takes risks and the adventurer may largely be a matter of whether the thrill-seeking behaviors are channeled into destructive or constructive acts.

aversive stimuli as readily as nonpsychopaths, they fail to acquire avoidance behaviors, experience little anticipatory anxiety, and consequently have fewer inhibitions about engaging in antisocial behavior.

Arousal, Sensation-Seeking, and Behavioral Perspectives Lykken's work suggested that antisocial personalities may have deficiencies in learning because of lower anxiety. As mentioned earlier, there is a second view—that antisocial personalities simply have lower levels of ANS reactivity and are underaroused. According to this view, the sensitivity of individuals' reticular cortical system varies, although there is an optimal level for each person. The system regulates the tonic level of arousal in the cortex, so that some people have high, and some have low, levels of arousal. Those with low sensitivity need more stimulation to reach an optimal level of arousal (Goma, Perez & Torrubia, 1988). If psychopaths are underaroused, it may take a more intense stimulus to elicit a reaction in them than in nonpsychopaths. The lowered levels of reactivity may cause psychopaths to show impulsive, stimulus-seeking behaviors to avoid boredom (Quay, 1965).

In a hypothesis similar to Lykken's concept of fearlessness, Farley (1986) proposed that people vary in their degree of thrill-seeking behaviors. Those at one end of the thrill-seeking continuum—the "Big T's"—are risk takers and adventurers who seek excitement and stimulation. Because of their low levels of central nervous system or autonomic nervous system arousal, they need stimulation to maintain an optimal level of arousal. On the other end of the continuum are "Little t's"—people with high arousal who seek low levels of stimulation to calm their hyped-up nervous systems. In contrast to Big T's, Little t's prefer certainty, predictability, low risk, familiarity, clarity, simplicity, low conflict, and low intensity.

Farley speculated that Big T characteristics can lead to both constructive or destructive behaviors in mental and physical domains. In the constructive-mental domain, Big T's include artists, scientists, and entertainers because they channel their thrill-seeking tendencies into creative mental contributions. Criminal masterminds, schemers, and con artists are Big T's who make destructive mental contributions to society. In the constructive-physical domain, Big T's become adventurers and physical risk-takers. Big T characteristics can also result in the antisocial, destructive behaviors exhibited by violent delinquents and criminals. Farley (1986) reported that juvenile delinquents are more likely than nondelinquents to be Big T's. In a study of delinquents in prison, Big T's were more likely than Little t's to fight, disobey supervisors, and attempt to escape. Farley believes that we need to direct stimulation-hungry Big T's into constructive, rather than destructive, mental and physical activities.

Other researchers have found evidence of underarousal as well as lowered levels of anxiety among those with antisocial personality. A study by Hare (1968) focused on the intensity of the stimulus needed to elicit a reaction in psychopaths and in nonpsychopaths. The study assessed the resting state reactivity and the stress-produced reactivity of primary psychopaths, secondary psychopaths, and nonpsychopaths, using cardiac, galvanic skin response, and respiratory measures. Hare found that psychopaths required a more intense stimulus, in both the resting state and in response to stressors, than did nonpsychopaths. As mentioned earlier, Quay (1965) felt that psychopaths exhibited lowered levels of reactivity so that they engage in impulsive, stimulus-seeking behaviors to avoid boredom. In one study, antisocial preadolescent children did show stimulus-seeking behaviors, a finding that tends to support this hypothesis (Whitehill, DeMeyer-Gapin & Scott, 1976).

If learning deficiencies among individuals with antisocial personality are caused by the absence of anxiety and by lowered autonomic reactivity, is it possible to improve their learning by increasing their anxiety or arousal ability? Researchers tested the ability of psychopaths and nonpsychopaths to perform an avoidance learning task with electric shock as the unconditioned stimulus, under two conditions. Under one condition, participants were injected with adrenalin, which presumably increases arousal; under the other, they were injected with a placebo. Psychopaths receiving the placebo made more errors in avoiding the shocks than nonpsychopaths did; psychopaths receiving adrenalin, however, tended to perform better than nonpsychopaths (see Figure 8.2). These findings imply that psychopaths do not react to the same amount of anxiety as do nonpsychopaths and that their learning improves when their anxiety is increased (Schachter & Latané, 1964).

The kind of punishment used in avoidance learning is also an important consideration in evaluating psychopaths' learning deficiencies (Schmauk, 1970). Whereas psychopaths may show learning deficits when faced with physical (electric shock) or social (verbal feedback) punishments, they learn as well as nonpsychopaths when the punishment is material (losing money for an incorrect response). Figure 8.3 charts the results of Schmauk's study of convicted psychopaths.

The certainty of punishment may also influence the responsiveness of antisocial personalities to punishment. Psychopaths and nonpsychopaths do not seem to differ in responding when punishment is a near certainty (Siegel, 1978). When the probability of punishment is highly uncertain, however, psychopaths do not suppress their behaviors. Threats of punishment by themselves do not seem to be sufficient to discourage psychopaths.

Normal people respond to physical, social, or material punishment, and they are influenced by uncertain as well as certain punishment. The work of Schmauk and Siegel suggested that psychopaths do not respond to the same range of aversive conditions. Hare (1975) proposed a psychophysiological model for this lack of responsiveness. He believes that psychopaths tend to lack anxiety, which makes learning difficult for them, and speculated that this lack of anxiety results from a defensive mechanism that reduces the aversiveness of painful stimuli. In other words, psychopaths may develop a psychophysiological ability to reduce the emotional impact (or anxiety-producing effect) of situations—a defense against anxiety and pain.

Taking a somewhat different perspective, Patrick, Cuthbert, and Lang (1994) argue that psychopaths may have an emotional imagery deficit. This deficit

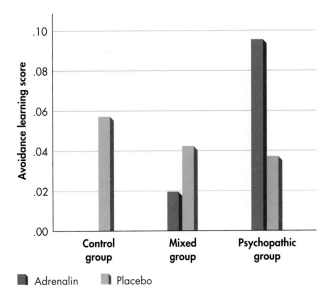

FIGURE 8.2 **Anxiety and Avoidance Learning Among Psychopaths and Others** When psychopaths, a group with mixed characteristics, and a control group were injected with a placebo, the psychopathic group performed least well on an avoidance learning task. However, when injected with adrenalin which increases arousal, the psychopaths outperformed the mixed group, indicating that arousal may facilitate learning in psychopaths.

Source: 1964 Nebraska Symposium on Motivation.

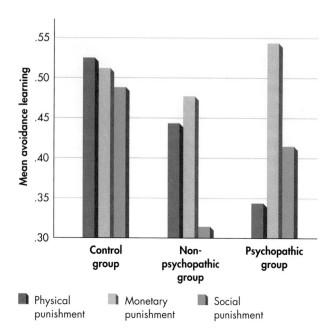

FIGURE 8.3 **Effect of Type of Punishment on Psychopaths and Others** The effects of three different types of punishment on an avoidance learning task are shown for three groups of subjects. Although physical or social punishment had little impact on psychopaths' learning, monetary punishment was quite effective.

Source: Schmauk, 1970.

takes the form of a weak or absent association between perceptual or semantic elements in memory and responding. That is, antisocial personality disorder may be characterized by a deficiency in the ability to respond physiologically to fear stimuli because the association between perception and responding is weakened. The investigators compared two groups—one of individuals who scored high on psychopathy and another who scored low on psychopathy. Even though both groups had similar ratings of fearfulness, the high-psychopathy group did not respond physiologically as strongly as did the other group. The study further demonstrates the consistency of the findings of reduced-anxiety responses among psychopaths, even though researchers continue to debate the reasons for the findings.

Reid (1981) agreed that psychophysiological factors may be involved in antisocial personality disorder. He viewed antisocial personality as a heterogeneous condition that has many causes. Familial, biological, social, and developmental factors may converge and provide a coherent picture in explaining the disorder.

Treatment of Antisocial Personality Disorder

As you have seen, evidence is growing that low anxiety and low autonomic reactivity characterize antisocial personalities. But we still do not know whether the low anxiety and autonomic underreactivity are due to inherited temperament, an acquired congenital defect, or social and environmental experiences that occur during childhood. The theory that psychopaths have developed a defense against anxiety is intriguing, but the factors behind the development of such a defense have not been pinpointed.

Because people with antisocial personalities feel little anxiety, they are poorly motivated to change themselves; they are also unlikely to see their behaviors as "bad." Thus traditional treatment approaches, which require the cooperation of the client, have not been very effective for antisocial personality disorder. For the same reason, relatively little research has been conducted on the efficacy of various treatment approaches. In some cases, drugs with tranquilizing effects (phenothiazines and Dilantin) have been helpful in reducing antisocial behavior (Meyer & Osborne, 1982). People with antisocial personalities, however, are not likely to follow through with self-medication. Moreover, drug treatment is effective in only a few cases, and it can result in side effects such as blurred vision, lethargy, and neurological disorders.

It may be that successful treatment can occur only in a setting where behavior can be controlled (Vaillant, 1975). That is, treatment programs may need to provide enough control so that those with antisocial personalities cannot avoid confronting their inability to form close and intimate relationships and the effect of their behaviors on others. Such control is sometimes possible for psychopaths who are imprisoned for crimes or who, for one reason or another, are hospitalized. Intensive group therapy may then be initiated to help clients with antisocial personalities in the required confrontation.

Some behavior modification programs have been tried, especially with delinquents who behave in antisocial ways. Money and tokens that can be used to purchase items have been used as rewards for young people who show appropriate behaviors (discussion of personal problems, good study habits, punctuality, and prosocial and nondisruptive behaviors). This use of material rewards has been fairly effective in changing antisocial behaviors (Van Evra, 1983). Once the young people leave the treatment programs, however, they are likely to revert to antisocial behavior unless their families and peers help them maintain the appropriate behaviors.

Peers and family are critically important in the treatment of antisocial youths and in maintaining progress made in treatment. Here, a group led by a peer counselor is exploring some of the issues troubling these young people.

Cognitive approaches have also been used. Because individuals with antisocial personalities may be influenced by dysfunctional beliefs about themselves, the world, and the future, they vary in skills for anticipating and acting on possible negative outcomes for their behaviors. Beck and colleagues (1990) have advocated that the therapist build rapport with the client, attempting to guide the patient away from thinking only in terms of self-interest and immediate gratification and toward higher levels of thinking. These higher levels would include, for example, recognizing the effects of one's behaviors on others and developing a sense of responsibility.

Kazdin (1987) noted that because current treatment programs do not seem very effective, new strategies must be used. These strategies should focus treatment on antisocial youth who seem amenable to treatment, and should broaden the base of intervention so that the programs involve the young clients, their families, and peers. Farley (1986) believes that because people with antisocial personality disorder may seek thrills (Big T's), they may respond to intervention programs that provide the physical and mental stimulation they need.

DISORDERS OF IMPULSE CONTROL

Most people have seen films and television programs that depict pathological gamblers, fire setters, or impulsive thieves. Such behaviors are characteristic of **impulse control disorders.** This residual category comprises disorders in which the person fails to resist an impulse or temptation to perform some act that is harmful to the person or others. The person feels tension before the act and release after it. Disorders in this category, including intermittent explosive disorder, kleptomania, pathological gambling, pyromania, and trichotillomania, are not classified elsewhere. The category does not include impulse control behaviors related to sexual conduct or compulsive ingestion of drugs or alcohol, for example, which are usually classified under the paraphilias and substance-use disorders, respectively.

Although not much is known about the cause of the impulse control disorders discussed here, people with these disorders tend to share three characteristics. First, they fail to resist an impulse or temptation to perform some act, although they know the act is considered wrong by society or is harmful to them.

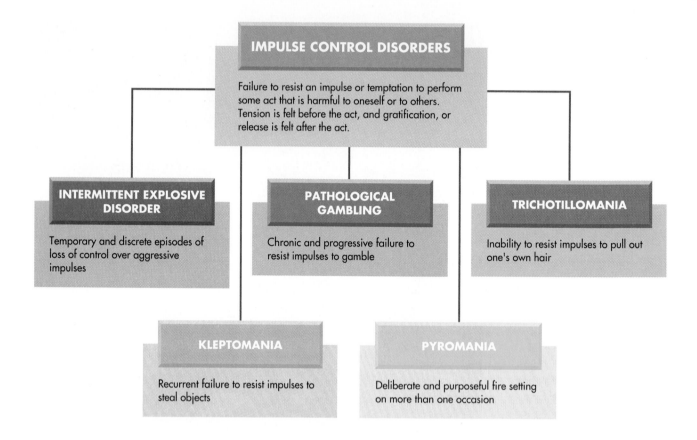

Second, they experience tension or arousal before the act. Third, after committing the act, they feel a sense of excitement, gratification, or release. Guilt or regret may or may not follow. The core feature of the disorder is the repeated expression of impulsive acts that lead to physical or financial damage to the individual or another person, often resulting in a sense of relief or release of tension (Fauman, 1994). Let's briefly examine the five specified disorders, which are shown on the impulse disorders chart above.

Intermittent Explosive Disorder

People with **intermittent explosive disorder** experience separate and discrete episodes of loss of control over their aggressive impulses, resulting in serious assaults on others or the destruction of property. The aggressiveness is grossly out of proportion to any precipitating stress that may have occurred. People with this disorder show no signs of general aggressiveness between episodes and may genuinely feel remorse for their actions. However, some believe that individuals with this disorder harbor a good deal of suppressed anger (Meyer, 1989). The disorder is apparently rare and believed to be more common among males than females. A patient diagnosed with intermittent explosive disorder described the following incident:

I'm usually a good and safe driver. I'm married and a very successful businessman. My colleagues say that I am a kind and happy-go-lucky person. That's why it's so strange that I lose control of my temper while driving my car. Last week an elderly woman was driving her car very slowly in front of me. I wanted her to speed up so I honked at her. She kept on moving slowly. I became so irritated that I rammed the back of her car and then drove off. Her car was severely damaged—and so was mine—and I could have killed her. After driving for several miles, I was overwhelmed with guilt and disgust with myself. I tried to find the woman, to apologize and pay for damages. But I couldn't find her. There's something wrong with me. Why do I do these things? I've run several people off the road and tried to ram others if they honk or cut in front of my car. I get so overwhelmed with rage I become a different person. Maybe I should turn myself into the police.

Kleptomania

Kleptomania is characterized by a recurrent failure to resist impulses to steal objects. The objects are not needed for personal use and are not stolen for their monetary value; indeed, people with this disorder usually have enough money to buy the objects, which are typically discarded, given away, or surreptitiously returned. They feel irresistible urges and tension before stealing or shoplifting and then an intense feeling of relief or gratification after the theft. The stealing is not committed to express anger or vengeance and is not in response to a delusion or hallucination. Although theft is common, only a small percentage of thieves (perhaps fewer than 5 percent) fit the criteria for kleptomania, which is believed to be a rare disorder (American Psychiatric Association, 1994). The disorder appears to be more common among females than among males (Spitzer et al., 1994). The woman in the following case relates feelings and behaviors that are typical for this disorder.

> The patient . . . described a special problem that worried her and that she had never disclosed to her husband. Periodically she experienced the urge to walk into one of the more elegant department stores in the city and steal an article of clothing. Over the course of the previous three or four years, she had stolen several blouses, a couple of sweaters, and a skirt. Since her husband's income was over $150,000 a year and her investments worth many times that, she recognized the "absurdity" of her acts. She also indicated that what she stole was rarely very expensive and sometimes not even enough to her liking for her to wear. She would become aware of the desire to steal something several days before she actually did it. The thoughts would increasingly occupy her mind until, on impulse, she walked into the store, plucked an item off the rack, and stuffed it into a bag she happened to be carrying or under her coat. Once out the door she felt a sense of relaxation and satisfaction; but at home she experienced anxiety and guilt. (Spitzer et al., 1981, p. 80)

Pathological Gambling

The essential feature of **pathological gambling** is a chronic and progressive failure to resist impulses to gamble. The gambling occurs despite the detrimental consequences that often accompany the behavior, such as financial ruin, turning to illegal activities to support gambling, disruptions of family or interpersonal relationships, and sacrificing obligations and responsibilities. Gambling is big business. About $166.5 billion was legally wagered in 1986, and about 80 percent of the U.S. population gambles (Lesieur, 1989). Those afflicted with pathological gambling constitute about 1 to 3 percent of adults, with the disorder more common among men than among women (American Psychiatric Association, 1994).

Unlike social gamblers who may place limits on the amount of money that may be lost or who can avoid gambling, a pathological gambler is preoccupied with gambling for its own sake and usually feels tension or restlessness if he or she is unable to gamble. There is a tendency to gamble with increasing amounts of money to achieve the desired excitement and, at

People with kleptomania have an irresistible urge to steal, even though the stolen objects may not be personally needed or taken because of financial constraints.

times, to use gambling as a way to relieve dysphoric moods. The person may constantly borrow money or engage in illegal activities (such as forgery or theft) to continue. Although antisocial, the activities are limited to obtaining money for gambling, and there is usually no childhood history of antisocial behavior (Spitzer et al., 1994).

Winning streaks are often occasions for manic behaviors and a heightened sense of excitement, but depression usually follows the frequent gambling losses. At such times, the person may try to borrow more money, rationalizing that the "big win" is about to happen, as in the following case:

> Jason L. was a 29-year-old married salesman. His wife of two years came from a well-to-do family, and Jason increasingly asked his wife's family to help subsidize his business ventures. She was initially impressed with Jason's dreams to "make it big" in his business ventures. Unknown to his wife, however, Jason actually needed the money to continue his habit of gambling at a local

In pathological gambling, a person is unable to resist urges to gamble, despite financial and interpersonal conflicts that may arise. The person may show hyperactivity and manic behaviors while gambling and then experience depression after losing money and having to find more money to support his or her urge to gamble.

card house. He was unable to stay away from gambling. When he won, he was ecstatic and would tell his wife that his business ventures were succeeding. Jason would then celebrate by taking her out to the finest restaurants. Unfortunately, he lost money most of the time. He would then beg his wife and her family for more money.

After a while, Jason's wife found out that he had no business ventures and that he was simply using the money to continue gambling. She threatened to divorce him if he did not stop gambling. At this point, Jason became infuriated. He claimed that her family looked down on him, so he was gambling in an attempt to get one big win that would let them live in luxury. He also said that he owed thousands of dollars in debts to the card house. Jason's wife indicated that she would take care of the debts but that he must stop gambling. After she gave him the money, Jason promptly lost the money playing cards. His wife then threatened to divorce him unless he entered psychotherapy and ceased his gambling habit. The therapist who saw Jason diagnosed him as a pathological gambler. Although Jason showed some antisocial behaviors, they were confined to his gambling and attempts to get money for gambling.

Pyromania

Pyromania is characterized by deliberate and purposeful fire setting on more than one occasion. People with this disorder are fascinated by fire and burning objects. They get intense pleasure or relief from setting the fires, watching things burn, or observing firefighters and their efforts to put out fires. Their fire-setting impulses are driven by this fascination rather

than by motives involving revenge, sabotage, or financial gains.

The history of fire setting usually begins in childhood. Gaynor and Hatcher (1987) believe that many children first start fires out of curiosity, exploration, or accident. The persistence of fire-setting behavior is associated with certain individual characteristics (young male, experience of overwhelming anger, and conduct or personality disorder), social circumstances (poor family environment and interpersonal maladjustment), and environmental conditions (stressful life events). Others have also found that fire-setting children have higher levels of behavioral dysfunction, hostility, and impulsivity than those found among other children (Kolko & Kazdin, 1991). Although many children may play with fire, they do so without the intense pleasure, lack of concern over the destruction caused by fires, and inability to control the impulse that is seen among people with pyromania.

The prevalence of pyromania is unknown, although it is probably rare and is diagnosed far more frequently among males than females. The case of Kevin, a fourteen-year-old boy, illustrates some of the characteristics associated with this disorder.

Kevin was arrested for the crime of arson in which he had allegedly set a fire that resulted in the destruction of some houses being constructed. Kevin was watching the fire when a witness told firefighters that she had seen Kevin with a gasoline can at the construction site just before the nighttime fire. After arson investigators found the gasoline can (which was later found to have Kevin's fingerprints) and questioned Kevin and his parents, he confessed to the crime. Kevin had a long history of setting fires. When he was about six years of age, he used his father's lighter to burn his sister's doll, which then ignited the window curtain. At age eight, he burned some bushes while he was camping with his family. Kevin was always playing with matches and lighters. He was also caught setting off a fire alarm at an office building. Kevin's parents reported that he always became quite excited when hearing the sirens of fire engines. He often asked his parents to follow the fire engines just to see the fires. Although the parents had punished Kevin for playing with fire, he continued, without his parents' knowledge, to burn items. Outside of setting fires, Kevin had few problems. He was an average student who was quiet and fairly well behaved.

Trichotillomania

Trichotillomania is a disorder characterized by an inability to resist impulses to pull out one's own hair. Although trichotillomania principally involves the hairs in the scalp, a person with this disorder may pull hair from other parts of the body, such as eyelashes, beard, or eyebrows. The hair pulling is not provoked by skin inflammation, itch, or other physical conditions. Rather, the person simply cannot resist the impulse, which begins with a feeling of tension, which is later replaced by a feeling of release or gratification after the act. Initially, the hair pulling may not disturb the follicles, and new hair will grow. In severe cases, new growth is compromised and permanent balding results. One 35-year-old woman entered therapy with one of the authors of this book. She said that she had a compulsion to pull the hairs from her head. When asked to reveal the extent of her hair pulling, the woman took off her wig. She was completely bald except for a few strands of hair at the back of her head.

There is no information on the prevalence of trichotillomania, although it is probably more common than currently believed and more common among women than men (Meyer, 1989). About 1 to 2 percent of college students appear to have a past or current history of this disorder (American Psychiatric Association, 1994).

Etiology and Treatment of Impulse Control Disorders

Although some of the impulse control disorders, such as pathological gambling and pyromania, have gained much public attention, we know very little about their specific causes. Furthermore, the characteristics of impulse control disorders seem similar to those found in other disorders in at least three ways: first, the disorders have an obsessive-compulsive quality, in that the person feels a compulsion to perform certain acts. In obsessive-compulsive disorders, however, the repetitive behaviors seem more purposeful and serve to prevent or produce some future event or situation. Second, the impulse control disorders also have a compulsive feature that is found in substance abusers or addicts who must maintain their habits. Substance use, however, has more clear physiological involve-

Pyromaniacs get intense pleasure or feel a sense of relief from setting fires, seeing burning objects or structures, or watching firefighters extinguish fires. Pyromaniacs are far more likely to be male than female.

ment. Third, to some extent, the behaviors of people with impulse control disorders resemble those of people with sexual disorders (such as exhibitionism and fetishism) in that tension, fascination, and release may precede or follow the acts. Indeed, some psychoanalysts link pyromania to sexual release and gratification. The problem is that orgasm and many sexual activities are intrinsically pleasurable or reinforcing, whereas trichotillomania and fire setting are not. Interestingly, the five impulse control disorders are so different from one another that it is impossible to confuse them diagnostically (Fauman, 1994).

Given the diverse disorders included in the impulse control category, it is not surprising that psychoanalytic explanations for impulse control disorders have been quite varied (see Booth, 1988). Pathological gambling has been likened to masturbation in that masturbation and gambling are both driven by built-up tension and a need to release the tension. Alternatively, it has been attributed to an unconscious need to lose because of underlying guilt. Kleptomania has been seen as an attempt to gain esteem, nourishment, or sexual gratification through stealing. Pyromania has been associated with sexual gratification, attempts to overcome feelings of impotence and inferiority, or unconscious anger toward a parental figure. And trichotillomania has been described as a response to unhealthy parent-child relationships. These psychoanalytic or psychodynamic formulations have been based primarily on clinical case studies rather than on empirical research.

Behaviorists tend to explain impulse control disorders through learning principles such as operant conditioning, classical conditioning, and modeling. For example, pathological gambling has been viewed as being influenced by reinforcement schedules. Researchers know that high rates of responding occur when a positive reinforcement schedule is variable rather than continuous. In the context of gambling, this could mean that initial wins may attract the person to gamble, and then, as wins become less frequent and are quite variable, a high rate of responding is likely. Learning principles can also be used to conceptualize the other disorders.

Some researchers have even speculated on the role of physiological factors. Roy and colleagues (1988) found that compulsive gamblers were more likely than nongamblers to have abnormalities in their noradrenergic system (affecting heart rate and blood pressure), which may indicate a greater sensation-seeking or thrill-seeking drive among pathological gamblers.

Lesieur (1989) noted the existence of two explanatory "camps." (Although he applied his analysis to pathological gambling, the same analysis can be applied to other impulse control disorders.) The first camp holds that impulse control ranges on a continuum from problem-free to troubled. Behavioral, cognitive, and sociological perspectives would probably be included in this first camp. The second camp holds that impulse control disorders are diseaselike—one either has the disorder or does not. Psychodynamic and physiologically based theories could, perhaps, fall into this second orientation. The diversity of explanations and the lack of empirical research on impulse control disorders reflect the fact that, although these disorders have fascinated mental health professionals, their prevalence is sufficiently low that researchers have difficulty studying them. Furthermore, it is likely that impulse control disorders may share similar symptoms (inability to resist an impulse, for example) but lack a common specific cause. That is, different types of disorders, such as intermittent explosive disorder and kleptomania, may be influenced by quite different factors.

Booth (1988) has noted the wide variety of treatment approaches used for impulse control disorders. In many of the disorders, behavioral and cognitive behavioral methods have been moderately successful. Some patients have been taught to recognize tension states that lead to the unacceptable behavior and to make self-statements, such as "I feel like stealing the item but I'd better not." Some therapists have patients rehearse alternative responses, such as having a person with intermittent explosive disorder take a deep breath and relax when tension exists. Other patients have been taught to associate their behavior with aversive consequences through aversive conditioning.

McCormick and Taber (1988) believe that changing the cognitive styles of people with impulse control problems may be beneficial. In a study of pathological gamblers undergoing treatment, these researchers found that attributional style (that is, their way of thinking about the causes of negative experiences; see Chapter 11) was related to failure to abstain from gambling after treatment. The implication is that a cognitive approach in treatment may be beneficial in helping change the way gamblers think about events. Some insight-oriented approaches have been helpful in treating kleptomania, especially with people who feel guilty over the theft. In treating intermittent explosive disorder, Meyer (1989) recommended awareness techniques, such as those found in gestalt therapy, which attempt to put clients in touch with their anger. Teaching ways to deal with anger in a productive fashion is also recommended. Multimodal approaches (combining techniques) involving family and friends and even organizations (such as Gamblers Anonymous for pathological gamblers) may also be beneficial.

SUMMARY

1. The personality disorders include a diversity of behavioral patterns in people who are typically perceived as being odd or eccentric; dramatic, emotional, and erratic; or anxious and fearful. DSM-IV lists ten specific personality disorders; each causes notable impairment of social or occupational functioning or subjective distress for the person. They are usually manifested in adolescence, continue into adulthood, and involve disturbances in personality characteristics. Because personality is at the core of the disorders, etiological explanations focus on factors that influence personality, such as heredity, family environment, self-identity, and others. The five-factor model of personality has been used to conceptualize personality disorders.

2. The main characteristics of antisocial (or psychopathic) personality are selfishness, irresponsibility, lack of guilt and anxiety, failure to learn from experience, superficiality, and impulsiveness. People with antisocial personalities frequently violate the rules, conventions, or laws of society. Most explanations of antisocial personality attribute its development to family and socialization factors, heredity, or autonomic nervous system abnormalities that result in lowered anxiety or underarousal. Traditional treatment approaches are not particularly effective with antisocial personalities.

3. The impulse control disorders involve the person's failure to resist a temptation to perform an act. People with such disorders experience tension before the act and a sense of gratification or release afterward. DSM-IV lists five impulse control disorders: kleptomania, intermittent explosive disorder, pathological gambling, pyromania, and trichotillomania. Although little is known about cause and effective treatment, the disorders have gained much public attention because of mass media dramatizations of kleptomania, pathological gambling, and pyromania.

KEY TERMS

antisocial personality disorder A personality disorder characterized by a failure to conform to social and legal codes, a lack of anxiety and guilt, and irresponsible behaviors

avoidant personality disorder A personality disorder characterized by a fear of rejection and humiliation and a reluctance to enter into social relationships

borderline personality disorder A personality disorder characterized by intense fluctuations in mood, self-image, and interpersonal relationships

dependent personality disorder A personality disorder characterized by reliance on others and an unwillingness to assume responsibility

histrionic personality disorder A personality disorder characterized by self-dramatization, the exaggerated expression of emotions, and attention-seeking behaviors

impulse control disorder A disorder in which the person fails to resist an impulse or temptation to perform some act that is harmful to the person or to others; the person feels tensions before the act and release after it

intermittent explosive disorder Impulse control disorder characterized by separate and discrete episodes of loss of control over aggressive impulses, resulting in serious assaults on others or destruction of property

kleptomania An impulse control disorder characterized by a recurrent failure to resist impulses to steal objects

narcissistic personality disorder A personality disorder characterized by an exaggerated sense of self-importance, an exploitative attitude, and a lack of empathy

obsessive-compulsive personality disorder A personality disorder characterized by perfectionism, a tendency to be interpersonally controlling, devotion to details, and rigidity

paranoid personality disorder A personality disorder characterized by unwarranted suspiciousness, hypersensitivity, and a reluctance to confide in others

pathological gambling An impulse control disorder in which the essential feature is a chronic and progressive failure to resist impulses to gamble

personality disorder A disorder characterized by inflexible and maladaptive personality traits that cause significant functional impairment or subjective distress for the individual

pyromania An impulse control disorder having as its main feature deliberate and purposeful fire setting on more than one occasion

schizoid personality disorder A personality disorder characterized by social isolation, emotional coldness, and indifference to others

schizotypal personality disorder A personality disorder characterized by peculiar thoughts and behaviors and by poor interpersonal relationships

trichotillomania An impulse control disorder characterized by an inability to resist impulses to pull out one's own hair

CHAPTER 9

SUBSTANCE-RELATED DISORDERS

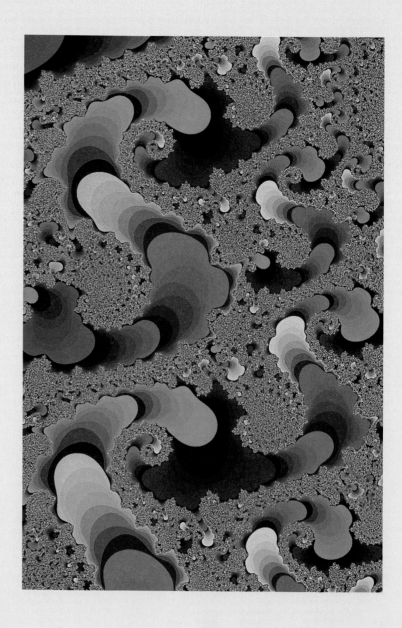

Throughout history, people have swallowed, sniffed, smoked, or otherwise taken into their bodies a variety of chemical substances for the purpose of altering their moods, levels of consciousness, or behaviors. The widespread use of drugs in our society today is readily apparent in our vast consumption of alcohol, tobacco, coffee, medically prescribed tranquilizers, and illegal drugs such as cocaine, marijuana, and heroin. Compared with other societies, our society is generally permissive with regard to the use of these substances. As indicated in Figure 9.1, many people have tried substances at some time in their lives, especially alcohol. The substances or drugs are psychoactive in that they alter moods, thought processes, or other psychological states.

Our society becomes less permissive and more concerned when a person's ingestion of drugs results in

- impairment of social or occupational functioning.

- an inability to abstain from using the drug despite its harmful effects on the body.

- the user's becoming a danger to others.

- criminal activities, such as the sale of illegal drugs or robbery, to support a drug habit.

The first two of these problems are directly involved in **substance-related disorders,** which result from the use of psychoactive substances that affect the central nervous system, causing significant social, occupational, or physical problems, and that sometimes result in abuse or dependence. The other two problems arise in connection with such use.

Yet another concern is that use of one substance may lead to use of other substances. In a longitudinal study of drug use among youths, Ellickson, Hays, and Bell (1992) found that involvement with "legal" drugs such as alcohol and cigarettes tended to precede the use of illicit drugs such as marijuana and "hard" drugs. Furthermore, alcohol or drug-related disorders are often part of a dual diagnosis, in which the individual has some other mental disorder. For example, antisocial personality, mania, and schizophrenia are diagnosed in combination with substance-related disorders relatively often (Anthony & Helzer, 1991).

DSM-IV divides substance-related disorders into two categories: substance-use disorders that involve dependence and abuse, and substance-induced disorders, such as withdrawal and substance-induced delirium. The discussion in this chapter is primarily concerned with the substance-use disorders, which are represented in the disorders chart on page 253. Substance-induced cognitive disorders are discussed in Chapter 15.

DSM-IV differentiates the substance-use disorders in two ways: (1) by the actual substance used and (2) by whether the disorder pattern is that of substance abuse or substance dependence. Regardless of the substance involved, the general characteristics of the abuse or dependence are the same. **Substance abuse** is a maladaptive pattern of recurrent use that extends over a period of twelve months; leads to notable impairment or distress; and continues despite social, occupational, psychological, physical, or safety problems. The abuse may cause legal problems or jeopardize the safety of the user or others (as in driving while intoxicated). It may impair the user's ability to maintain meaningful social relationships or fulfill major role obligations at work, school, or home. And need for the substance may lead to a preoccupation with its acquisition and use.

To make the diagnosis of **substance dependence,** a therapist must find that the client exhibits several of the following symptoms over a twelve-month period:

1. The user is unable to cut down or control use of the substance, despite knowledge of its harmful physical, psychological, or interpersonal effects.

2. The user takes increasingly larger amounts of the substance or continues to use it over a longer period than he or she intended.

3. The user devotes considerable time to activities necessary to obtain the substance, even though those activities mean important social, occupational, and recreational activities must be sacrificed.

4. The user exhibits evidence of **tolerance:** increasing doses of the substance are necessary to achieve the desired effect, such as a "high."

5. The user shows evidence of **withdrawal:** distress or impairment in social, occupational, or other areas

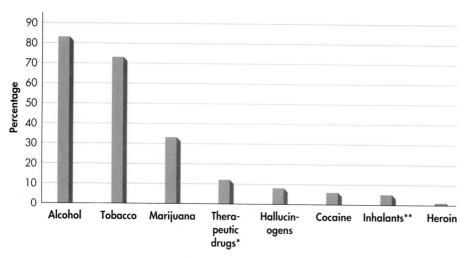

*Nonmedical use.
**Substances that are inhaled, such as glue.

FIGURE 9.1 **Percentage of Persons Who Reported Using Specific Substances at Any Time During Their Lives (Age 12 and Over)** As you can see, the vast majority of Americans have used psychoactive substances, particularly alcohol and tobacco.

Source: Data from National Institute of Drug Abuse, 1991.

of functioning, or physical or emotional symptoms such as shaking, irritability, and inability to concentrate after reducing or ceasing intake of the substance.

In diagnosing substance dependence, the clinician also specifies whether the dependence is physiological; evidence of either tolerance or withdrawal indicates physiological dependence.

Although intoxication and withdrawal are considered substance-induced disorders, and therefore outside the primary topic of this chapter, we discuss them here because they are necessary for an understanding of the substance-use disorders. **Intoxication** is a condition in which a substance affecting the central nervous system has been ingested and certain maladaptive behaviors or psychological changes, such as belligerence and impaired judgment and functioning, are evident. The effects of intoxication and withdrawal vary according to the substance, but they generally cause significant distress or impairment in social, occupational, or other important areas of functioning.

As can be readily noted, the criteria for substance dependence include those for abuse and withdrawal. Because dependence is considered the more severe disorder, people who meet the criteria for both dependence and abuse for a particular substance are diagnosed only as dependent, not as abusing. Although the two categories have some overlap in criteria and

both have biopsychosocial effects, research has indicated that distinguishing between dependence and abuse is meaningful and can differentially predict severity of disorder and treatment outcome (Nathan, 1991). Diagnosis of withdrawal or intoxication may be made when the major symptoms at the time of diagnosis are those of withdrawal or intoxication. In cases such as these, the client may also be substance dependent. Finally, some clients may be substance dependent or substance abusers, but they may not show certain psychological characteristics, such as intentional drug use. These persons may have substance-induced conditions as a result of unintentional exposure to substances or of side effects of medication.

In this chapter, we first examine substance-use disorders, including the effects of the abuse of alcohol and various drugs. We also examine the degree to which different theories may increase our understanding of the causes and treatment of the abuse of alcohol and other substances.

SUBSTANCE-USE DISORDERS

A number of substances can result in abuse, dependence, intoxication, and withdrawal. Among them are prescription drugs such as Valium; legal substances such as alcohol and cigarettes; and illegal substances such as LSD (lysergic acid diethylamine), cocaine, and

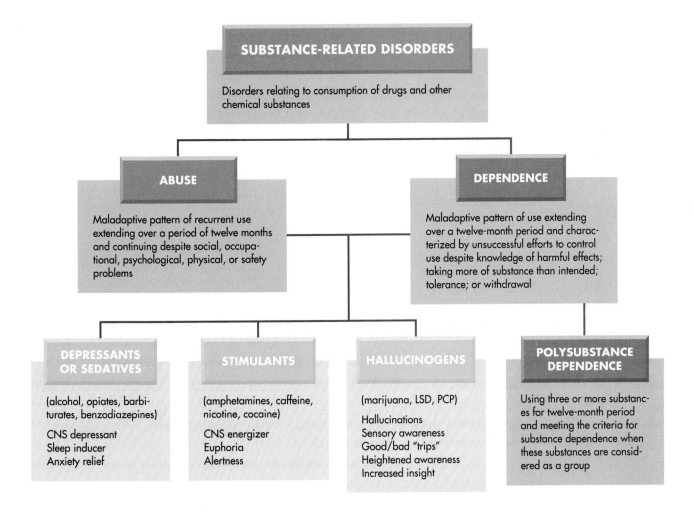

SUBSTANCE-RELATED DISORDERS

Disorders relating to consumption of drugs and other chemical substances

ABUSE

Maladaptive pattern of recurrent use extending over a period of twelve months and continuing despite social, occupational, psychological, physical, or safety problems

DEPENDENCE

Maladaptive pattern of use extending over a twelve-month period and characterized by unsuccessful efforts to control use despite knowledge of harmful effects; taking more of substance than intended; tolerance; or withdrawal

DEPRESSANTS OR SEDATIVES

(alcohol, opiates, barbiturates, benzodiazepines)

CNS depressant
Sleep inducer
Anxiety relief

STIMULANTS

(amphetamines, caffeine, nicotine, cocaine)

CNS energizer
Euphoria
Alertness

HALLUCINOGENS

(marijuana, LSD, PCP)

Hallucinations
Sensory awareness
Good/bad "trips"
Heightened awareness
Increased insight

POLYSUBSTANCE DEPENDENCE

Using three or more substances for twelve-month period and meeting the criteria for substance dependence when these substances are considered as a group

heroin. Table 9.1 shows the prevalence of various drug abuse/dependent disorders (not including alcohol) found in the Epidemiological Catchment Area (ECA) study—the most comprehensive survey ever conducted of the mental health of adult Americans.

Substance-related disorders are most prevalent among youths and young adults. A 1994 national survey of high school students found that among seniors, 31 percent said they had used marijuana during the past year and 46 percent reported they had used an illicit drug at least once in their lifetime. The use of cocaine, hallucinogens, and heroin appears to have increased during the past several years among high school students. Alcohol use remained stable, but it is still high, with 25 percent of eighth graders and 40 percent of tenth graders reporting that they had used the substance in the past month (SAMHSA, 1995). In terms of all drug abuse/dependence, the ECA study found the adult lifetime prevalence to be 6.2 percent, as indicated in Table 9.1. Abuse/dependence was greatest for marijuana.

Figure 9.2 shows the ECA findings with respect to gender and selected ethnic groups. Women are much

The prevalence of drug use is high. In many communities, drugs are openly sold. The graffiti on this building wall seems to attest to that.

TABLE 9.1 Prevalence of Specific Drug Abuse/Dependence Disorders

	Drug of Abuse/Dependence						
	Any Drug	*Cannabis*	*Opioids*	*Stimulants*	*Sedatives*	*Cocaine**	*Hallucinogens**
Lifetime prevalence of abuse/dependence	6.2%	4.4%	0.7%	1.7%	1.2%	0.2%	0.4%
Number of abuse/ dependence cases	1,316	837	364	314	289	101	97
Usage							
Used drug in prior month	22%	47%	18%	10%	18%	17%	8%
Used drug in prior year	30%	67%	60%	29%	41%	60%	44%
Problem with drug in prior year	24%	38%	42%	16%	18%	46%	30%

* Diagnosis of abuse only, in accord with DSM-III categories of disorder.

Source: Adapted from Anthony & Helzer, 1991.

Shown are the lifetime prevalence rates for individuals having drug abuse or dependency, according to the type of drug. The overall abuse/dependency rate for any drug is over 6 percent. It should be noted that actual use of drugs among those who show abuse/dependence is quite high both in the prior month and year.

FIGURE 9.2 Prevalence of Drug Abuse or Dependence by Gender and Selected Ethnic Groups   The one-month, one-year, and lifetime prevalence rates for drug abuse/dependence are shown for Whites, Blacks, and Hispanics by gender. Women consistently show lower rates of drug abuse/dependence than do men. Among men, Whites showed slightly higher one-year and lifetime rates than did other ethnic group individuals.

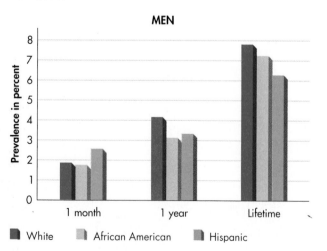

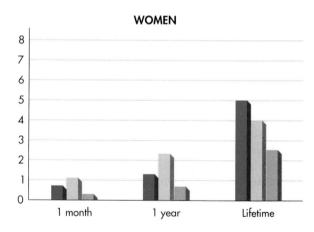

■ White   African American   ■ Hispanic

Source: Data from Anthony & Helzer, 1991.

TABLE 9.2 Characteristics of Various Psychoactive Substances

Drugs	Short-Term Effects*	Potential for Dependency
Sedatives		
Alcohol	Central nervous system (CNS) depressant, loss of inhibitions	Moderate
Narcotics (codeine, morphine, heroin, opium, methadone)	CNS depressant, pain relief	High
Barbiturates (amytal, nembutal, seconal)	CNS depressant, sleep inducer	Moderate to High
Benzodiazepines (Valium)	CNS depressant, anxiety relief	Low
Stimulants		
Amphetamines (Benzedrine, Dexedrine, Methedrine)	CNS energizer, euphoria	High
Caffeine	CNS energizer, alertness	Low
Nicotine	CNS energizer	High
Cocaine and crack	CNS energizer, euphoria	High
Hallucinogens		
Marijuana, hashish	Relaxant, euphoria	Moderate
LSD	Hallucinatory agent	Low
PCP	Hallucinatory agent	Moderate

*Specific effects often depend on the quality and dosage of the drug as well as on the experience, expectancy, personality, and the situation of the person using the drug.

less likely to take drugs than are men. White Americans have higher lifetime prevalence rates for drug abuse/dependence than do African Americans and Hispanic Americans.

Each of the drugs discussed in this chapter can result in an abuse disorder or a dependence disorder. Many are also associated with legal problems, for their use is expressly prohibited except under strict medical supervision. We discuss general categories of substances, depressants, stimulants, and hallucinogens, which contain many specific drugs, such as alcohol, narcotics, barbiturates, benzodiazepines, amphetamines, caffeine, nicotine, cocaine and crack, marijuana, LSD, and PCP. Table 9.2 lists these substances, their effects, and their potential for dependency. In practice, some substances are not easily classified because they may have multiple effects.

Depressants or Sedatives

Depressants or sedatives cause generalized depression of the central nervous system and a slowing down of responses. People taking such substances feel calm and relaxed. They may also become sociable and open because of lowered interpersonal inhibitions. Let us examine in more detail one of the most widely used depressants—alcohol—and then discuss other depressants such as narcotics, barbiturates, and benzodiazepines.

Alcohol-Use Disorders Alcohol abuse and alcohol dependence are, of course, substance abuse and dependence, in which the substance is alcohol. People who have either of these alcohol-related disorders are popularly referred to as **alcoholics,** and their disorder as **alcoholism.** Drinking problems can be exhibited in two major ways. First, the person may need to use alcohol daily to function; that is, he or she may be unable to abstain. Second, the person may be able to abstain from consuming alcohol for certain periods of time but unable to control or moderate intake once he or she resumes drinking. This person is a "binge" drinker. Both patterns of drinking can result in deteriorating relationships, job loss, family conflicts, and violent behavior while intoxicated. The following case is typical.

Jim is a 54-year-old alcoholic. He is well educated, having received a bachelor's degree in engineering and a master's degree in management. Until recently, he was employed as a middle manager in an aerospace firm. Because of federal defense industry budget cuts and because of his absenteeism from work caused by drinking, Jim lost his job. He decided to enter treatment.

His drinking history was long. Jim clearly recalled the first time that he drank. At age fifteen, he attended a party at his friend's house. Alcohol was freely served. Jim took a drink, and despite the fact that alcohol "tasted so bad," he forced himself to drink. Indeed, he became drunk and had a terrible hangover the next day. He swore that he would never drink again, but two weeks later he drank again at his friend's house. Over the next several years, Jim acquired the ability to consume large amounts of alcohol and was proud of his drinking capacity. At social gatherings, he was uninhibited and the "life of the party." His drinking continued during college, but it was confined primarily to his fraternity weekend parties. He was considered a very heavy drinker in the fraternity, but the drinking did not seem to affect his academic performance. He frequently drove his car during weekend binges, however, and was once caught and convicted of drunken driving.

After graduate school, he got married and took a position in an aerospace firm. Katie, Jim's wife, also drank but never as heavily as Jim. Although his drinking had been largely confined to weekends, Jim started drinking throughout the week. He attributed his increased drinking to pressures at work, company-sponsored receptions in which alcohol was served, and a desire to feel "free and comfortable" in front of company executives during the receptions. The drinking continued despite frequent arguments with Katie over his drinking and a physician's warning, after a routine physical examination, that alcohol had probably caused the abnormal results of Jim's liver-functioning tests. He could not control his alcohol consumption.

Katie noticed that Jim was getting more and more angry from his work assignments. Jim felt that deadlines for him to complete assignments were unrealistic. She felt that he was increasingly difficult to be around. He drank now daily, usually in his office at the end of the workday. His colleagues knew Jim had a drinking problem but because he was still functioning well at work, they kidded him about drinking rather than counseled him against consuming alcohol. They were, however, concerned about his absenteeism, frequent tardiness, and inability to get started in the morning, which were caused by his drinking.

Over the years, Katie simply fell out of love with Jim. The arguments, Jim's drinking, and his unwillingness to communicate with her finally led to a divorce. He was quite bitter over the divorce, although Katie could not see how he was getting anything out of the marriage.

When awards for defense contracts had diminished, Jim's company started to lay off workers. Jim was among the first to be asked to leave.

Problem drinking can develop in many different ways and can begin at almost any age. However, Jim's history is typical in several respects. First, as is true of most people, he initially found the taste of alcohol unpleasant, and, after his first bout of drunkenness, he swore that he would never drink again. Nevertheless, he did return to drinking. Second, heavy drinking served a purpose: It reduced his anxiety, particularly at work. Third, consumption continued despite the obvious negative consequences. Finally, a preoccupation with alcohol consumption and the deterioration of social and occupational functioning are also characteristic of the problem drinker.

Alcohol Consumption in the United States People drink considerable amounts of alcohol in the United States. About 11 percent of adults consume one ounce or more of alcohol a day, 55 percent drink fewer than three alcoholic drinks a week, and 35 percent abstain completely (American Psychiatric Association, 1987). Most of the alcohol is consumed by a small percentage of people; 50 percent of the total alcohol consumed is drunk by only 10 percent of drinkers. Drinking is widespread among young people. Heavy drinking is most common among those between 18 and 25 years of age (National Institute of Drug Abuse, 1991). And, as we have seen, one national survey found that almost 40 percent of tenth graders had tried alcohol in the past month (SAMHSA, 1995). Another study of adults revealed that 14 percent had alcohol dependence at some time in their lives, and approximately 7 percent had alcohol dependence during the past year (American Psychiatric Association, 1994). Men drink two to five times as much as women.

Alcohol consumption varies according to the cultural traditions of various societies. For example, in Italy and some other countries, individuals tend to drink with meals throughout the day. In most societies, females tend to consume less alcohol than do males, and in Asian countries, the male-to-female rate of consumption is particularly high (American Psychiatric Association, 1994). In general, drinking alcohol is less common in some Asian countries than in

Societies differ not only in the extent to which alcohol is consumed but also in the pattern of use. In many European countries, alcohol is freely used with meals throughout the day. Wine drinking is relatively high.

Europe or the United States. Within the United States, alcohol use and dependence varies among different groups (see Figure 9.3). The rates are somewhat higher among African Americans and Hispanic Americans than among non-Hispanic Whites at the later ages (Helzer, Burnam & McEvoy, 1991).

Problems associated with alcohol consumption in the United States are apparent in terms of social, medical, physical, and financial costs. Alcohol consumption and alcoholism are associated with up to 15 percent of the nation's health-care costs; lowered productivity on the job; shortened life expectancy (by about 10 to 12 years); and high rates of suicide, automobile accidents, spousal abuse, and divorce (Office of Technical Assessment, 1983; Office for Substance Abuse Prevention, 1990). Concern has also developed

FIGURE 9.3 **Gender, Ethnic, and Age Differences in Alcohol Abuse and Dependence** Striking gender, ethnic, and age differences are shown in the prevalence of alcohol abuse and dependence. Men have much higher rates than women. Ethnicity and age interacted such that higher rates occur for Whites and Hispanics at younger age levels, while Blacks had higher rates at relatively older age levels.

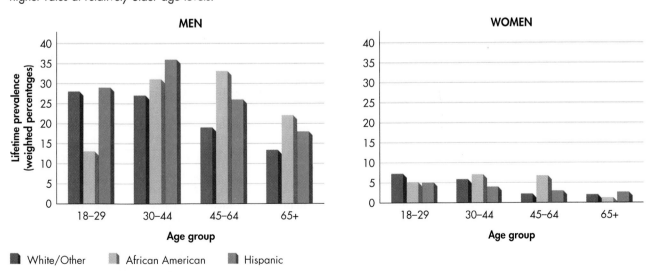

Source: Data from Helzer, Burnam & McEvoy, 1991.

MADD
(MOTHERS AGAINST DRUNK DRIVERS)

City of New York
Parks & Recreation

DRUNK DRIVE

Mothers Against Drunk Drivers (MADD) is an organization started by Candy Lightner, a mother whose daughter was killed by a drunk driver. MADD's goal is to prevent drunk people from driving and to assist the victims of drunk drivers and victims' families. Well over half-a-million individuals are involved in MADD.

over the children of alcoholic parents, who are at risk for social maladjustment, self-depreciation, lower self-esteem, and alcoholism (Berkowitz & Perkins, 1988; Cooper & McCormack, 1992).

In view of the problems associated with alcohol use, why do people continue drinking? Particularly ironic is the fact that, like Jim in the earlier case, most people consuming alcoholic beverages for the first time find the taste unpleasant. To better understand this puzzle, let's consider the physiological and psychological effects of alcohol.

The Effects of Alcohol Alcohol has both physiological and psychological effects, which can be further broken down into short-term and long-term effects. We consider short-term effects first. Once swallowed, alcohol is absorbed into the blood without digestion. When it reaches the brain, its short-term physiological effect is to depress central nervous system functioning. When the alcohol content in the bloodstream (the blood alcohol level) is about 0.1 percent (the equivalent of drinking 5 ounces of whiskey or 5 glasses of beer), muscular coordination is impaired. The drinker may have trouble walking a straight line or pronouncing certain words. At the 0.5 percent blood alcohol level, the person may lose consciousness or even die.

The short-term physiological effects of alcohol on a specific person are determined by the individual's body weight, the amount of food present in the stomach, the drinking rate over time, prior drinking experience, heredity, personality factors, and the environment and culture of the drinker. Table 9.3 shows the

effect of alcohol intake on blood alcohol level as a function of body weight.

The short-term psychological effects of alcohol often include feelings of happiness, loss of inhibitions (because alcohol depresses the inhibitory brain centers), poor judgment, and reduced concentration. Depending on the situation or context in which drinking occurs, other effects, such as negative moods and anger, may also be experienced. Reactions also depend on the expectancy that individuals have developed with respect to alcohol (Hull & Bond, 1986). Some people behave differently in the presence of others because of their perception that they have been drinking, not because of alcohol's effects (as, for example, when an individual has only a few sips of beer and begins to act hostile). Heavy and prolonged drinking often impairs sexual performance and produces a hangover. Ironically, because of the loss of inhibition, people mistakenly believe that alcohol is a stimulant rather than a depressant.

The long-term psychological effects of heavy drinking are more serious. Although there is no single type of alcoholic, Jellinek (1971) observed certain patterns in the course of individuals who develop alcohol dependence. Most people begin to drink in social situations. Because the alcohol relieves tension, the drinkers tend to drink more and to drink more frequently. Tolerance levels may increase over a period of months or years.

Because of stress, inability to adequately cope, or biological predisposition to alcoholism, some drinkers become preoccupied with thoughts of alcohol. They

TABLE 9.3   Blood Alcohol Level as a Function of Number of Drinks Consumed and Body Weight

Body Weight, Pounds	Number of Drinks Consumed*						
	1	*2*	*3*	*4*	*5*	*6*	*7*
100	.020	.055	.095	.130	.165	.200	.245
120	.015	.045	.075	.105	.135	.165	.195
140	.010	.035	.060	.085	.115	.140	.165
160	.005	.030	.050	.075	.095	.120	.145
180	.0	.025	.045	.065	.085	.105	.125
200	.0	.020	.040	.055	.075	.085	.110
220	.0	.020	.035	.050	.065	.085	.100
240	.0	.015	.035	.045	.060	.075	.090

*The given blood alcohol levels are those that would exist 1 hour after the start of drinking. Because alcohol is metabolized over time, subtract 0.015 from the given level for each additional hour. For example, a 100-pound person consuming 2 drinks would, after 2 hours, have a blood alcohol level of 0.055 minus 0.015, or 0.040. One drink equals 12 ounces of beer, 4 ounces of wine, and 1.25 ounces of liquor.

Source: Adapted from Vogler & Bartz, 1983.

may worry about whether there will be enough alcohol at a party; they may try to drink inconspicuously or furtively. They begin to consume large amounts and may "gulp" their drinks. Such drinkers frequently feel guilty; they are somewhat aware that their drinking is excessive. Heavy, sustained drinking may lead to blackouts, periods of time for which drinkers have no memory of their activities. Jellinek believed that sustained drinking could then lead to a loss of control over alcoholic intake and to frequent periods of intoxication. Individuals may then drink only to become intoxicated.

It should be noted that most investigators have formulated their ideas based on research with male alcoholics. Although relatively few studies have examined female alcoholics, the available evidence suggests that gender differences exist. For example, alcoholic women report more childhood problems such as alcoholic parents, unhappy childhoods, and broken homes than do alcoholic men. Furthermore, women become problem drinkers at a later age than men (Perodeau, 1984). These findings suggest that perspectives based on research with alcoholic men should be carefully scrutinized for their applicability to women.

The long-term physiological effects of alcohol consumption include an increase in tolerance as the person becomes used to alcohol, physical discomfort, anxiety, and hallucinations. Chronic alcoholism destroys brain cells and is often accompanied by poor nutritional habits and physical deterioration. Thus the left brain hemispheres of alcoholics have been found to be less dense than those of a control group of nonalcoholics (Golden et al., 1981). Other direct or indirect consequences generally attributed to chronic alcoholism are liver diseases such as *cirrhosis*, in which an excessive amount of fibrous tissue develops and impedes the circulation of blood; heart failure; hemorrhages of capillaries, particularly those on the sides of the nose; and cancers of the mouth and throat. Alcohol consumption in pregnant women may affect their unborn children: Children who suffer fetal alcohol syndrome are born mentally retarded and physically deformed.

Interestingly, the moderate use of alcohol (one or two drinks a day) in adults has been associated in some studies with lowered risk of heart disease. The precise reasons for this effect are unknown. What is clear, though, is that chronic heavy consumption has serious negative consequences, both for the drinker and sometimes for society at large, as the Focus On feature points out.

Narcotics (Opiates)   Like alcohol, the organic **narcotics**, which include opium and its derivatives morphine, heroin, and codeine, depress the central nervous system; act as sedatives to provide relief from pain, anxiety, and tension; and are addictive. Feelings of euphoria and well-being (and sometimes negative

MADD (Mothers Against Drunk Driving)

On May 3, 1980, a thirteen-year-old girl was walking to a church carnival in Fair Oaks, California. A car suddenly swerved out of control and killed her. Police arrested the vehicle's driver, who was intoxicated. A check of the driver's record revealed that he had a long history of arrests for drunk driving. Only the week before, he had been bailed out of jail after being charged with hit-and-run drunk driving.

Candy Lightner, the mother of the girl, was furious over the death of her daughter and concerned that the driver might not be sent to prison for the crime. At that time the penalties for drunk driving were frequently light, even when someone was injured or killed. Lightner wanted to find ways to keep drunk people from driving and to help the victims of drunk drivers and victims' families. She decided to form an organization called Mothers Against Drunk Drivers (MADD).

Initially Lightner was unsuccessful. She wanted to meet with then California Governor Jerry Brown to find a means of dealing with drunk drivers, but the governor declined to see her. Finally, after Lightner began to show up at his office day after day and succeeded in obtaining newspaper publicity for her crusade, Brown took action. He appointed a task force to deal with drunk driving and named her a member.

As a result of the efforts of Lightner and the task force, California eventually passed tough new laws against drunk driving. Lightner's organization has grown as well; MADD now has 320 chapters nationwide and 600,000 volunteers and donors. They have convinced most states to enact more severe penalties for drunk driving. In addition, MADD was the most aggressive group lobbying Congress for a law that would force every state to set its minimum drinking age at twenty-one or higher. Such a law was passed by Congress and signed by President Reagan in the summer of 1984, specifying that any state that did not comply by a certain fixed date could lose millions of dollars in federal highway funds.

Incidentally, the driver who was responsible for the death of Lightner's daughter did eventually serve twenty-one months in jail (Friedrich, 1985).

In view of the dangers associated with drunken driving, every person should address several questions: Have you ever driven after having several drinks? If so, did you feel that you were proficient as a driver? At a party where there is alcohol consumption, do you encourage others to drink to intoxication? What should you do if a friend who has driven to the party has had too much to drink? These questions are important to address ahead of time. After consuming alcohol, judgment may be impaired so that one may believe that safe driving is simply a matter of being careful. Safe driving is also a matter of being sober, and we must all plan strategies for handling situations in which we or others become intoxicated.

reactions such as nausea) often accompany narcotics use. Opium and its derivatives (especially heroin) result in dependency. Tolerance for narcotics builds rapidly, and withdrawal symptoms are severe. Opiates such as heroin are usually administered intravenously, causing puncture marks on the extremities of the body and spreading diseases such as AIDS, which can be transmitted through needle sharing (Smith & Landry, 1988).

About 0.7 percent of the adult population has had opioid abuse or dependence at some time during their lives. The prevalence of addiction decreases with age, and males are more affected than females, by a ratio of four to one (American Psychiatric Association, 1994).

Because dependency is likely to occur after repeated use, narcotics addicts are usually unable to maintain normal relationships with family and friends or to pursue legitimate careers. They live to obtain the drug through any possible means. Nonmedical use of narcotics is illegal, and many addicts have little choice but to turn to criminal activities to obtain the drug and to support their expensive habits.

Barbiturates Synthetic **barbiturates,** or "downers," are powerful depressants of the central nervous system and are commonly used to induce relaxation and sleep. Next to the narcotics, they represent the largest category of illegal drugs, and they are quite dangerous for several reasons. First, psychological and physical dependence can develop. Second, although their legal use is severely restricted, widespread availability of the drugs makes it difficult to control misuse or abuse. More than 1 million individuals—primarily middle-aged and older people—are now estimated to be barbiturate addicts. Third, users often experience harmful physical effects. Excessive use of either barbiturates or heroin can be fatal, but barbiturates are the more lethal. Constant heroin use increases the amount of the drug required for a lethal dosage. The lethal dosage of barbiturates does not increase with prolonged use, so accidental overdose and death can easily occur. And combining alcohol with barbiturates can be especially dangerous because alcohol compounds the depressant effects of the barbiturates, as it did in the following case.

> Kelly M., a seventeen-year-old girl from an upper-middle-class background, lived with her divorced mother. Kelly was hospitalized after her mother found her unconscious from an overdose of barbiturates consumed together with alcohol. She survived the overdose and later told the therapist that she had regularly used barbiturates for the past year and a half. The overdose was apparently accidental and not suicidal.
>
> For several weeks following the overdose, Kelly openly discussed her use of barbiturates with the therapist. She had been introduced to the drugs by a boy in school who told her they would help her relax. Kelly was apparently unhappy over her parents' divorce. She felt that her mother did not want her, especially because her mother spent a lot of time away from home building a real estate agency. And, although she enjoyed her occasional visits with her father, Kelly felt extremely uncomfortable in the presence of the woman who lived with him. The barbiturates helped her relax and relieved her tensions. Arguments with her mother would precipitate heavy use of the drugs. Eventually she became dependent on barbiturates and always spent her allowance to buy them. Her mother reported that she had no knowledge of her daughter's drug use. She did notice, though, that Kelly was increasingly isolated and sleepy.
>
> The therapist informed Kelly of the dangers of barbiturates and of combining them with alcohol. Kelly agreed to undergo treatment, which included the gradual reduction of barbiturate use, and psychotherapy with her mother.

Kelly's practice of *polysubstance use,* or the use of more than one chemical substance at the same time, can be extremely dangerous. For example, heavy smokers who consume a great deal of alcohol run an increased risk of esophageal cancer. Chemicals taken simultaneously may exhibit a synergistic effect, interacting to multiply one another's effects. For example, when a large dose of barbiturate is taken along with alcohol, death may occur because of a synergistic effect that depresses the central nervous system. Furthermore, one of the substances (such as alcohol) may reduce the person's judgment, resulting in excessive (or lethal) use of the other drug. Equally dangerous is the use of one drug to counteract the effect of another. For instance, a person who has taken a stimulant to feel euphoric may later take an excessive amount of a depressant (such as a barbiturate) in an attempt to get some sleep. The result can be an exceedingly harmful physiological reaction.

According to DSM-IV, **polysubstance dependence** may be diagnosed when a person has used at least three substances (not including nicotine and caffeine) for a period of twelve months, and, during this period, the person meets the criteria for substance dependence for the substances considered as a group but not for any single specific substance.

Benzodiazepines   One member of this category of drugs is Valium, which is one of the most widely prescribed drugs in the United States today. Like the other sedatives, Valium is a central nervous system

Polydrug use is the consumption of more than one psychoactive chemical substance. The practice is considered very dangerous. Actor River Phoenix died as a result of polydrug use. He was twenty-three years old.

depressant; it is often used to reduce anxiety and muscle tension. People who take the drug seem less concerned with and less affected by their problems. Some side effects may occur, such as drowsiness, skin rash, nausea, and depression, but the greatest danger in using Valium is its abuse. Because life stressors are unavoidable, many people use Valium as their sole means of dealing with stress; then, as tolerance develops, dependence on the drug may also grow.

Stimulants

A **stimulant** is a substance that is a central nervous system energizer, inducing elation, grandiosity, hyperactivity, agitation, and appetite suppression. Commonly used stimulants are the amphetamines, caffeine, nicotine, and cocaine and crack.

Amphetamines The **amphetamines,** also known as "uppers," speed up central nervous system activity and bestow on users increased alertness, energy, and sometimes feelings of euphoria and confidence. They increase the concentration of the neurotransmitter dopamine in synapses, which exposes the postsynaptic cells to high levels of dopamine. Increased concentration of dopamine may amplify nerve impulses in the brain that are associated with pleasure (Wise, 1988). Amphetamines inhibit appetite and sleep, and some are used as appetite suppressants or diet pills. These stimulants may be physically addictive and become habit forming with a rapid increase in tolerance. They are taken orally, intravenously, or nasally ("snorting"). "Speed freaks" inject amphetamines into their blood vessels and become extremely hyperactive and euphoric for days. Another immediate and powerful effect is obtained by smoking a pure, crystalline form ("ice") of the substance (American Psychiatric Association, 1994). Assaultive, homicidal, and suicidal behaviors can occur during this time. Heavy doses may trigger delusions of persecution, similar to those seen among paranoid schizophrenics. Overdoses are fatal, and brain damage has been observed among chronic abusers.

About 2 percent of U.S. adults have suffered from amphetamine abuse or dependence at some time during their lives. It is more common among persons from lower socioeconomic groups and among men than women by a ratio of four to one.

Caffeine *Caffeine* is a widely used legal stimulant ingested primarily in coffee, chocolate, tea, and cola drinks. It is considered intoxicating when, after the recent ingestion of 250 milligrams (about two cups of coffee) or more of caffeine, a person shows several of the following symptoms: restlessness, nervousness, excitement, insomnia, flushed face, gastrointestinal disturbance, rambling speech, and cardiac arrhythmia. The consequences of caffeine intoxication are usually transitory and relatively minor. In some cases, however, the intoxication is chronic and seriously affects the gastrointestinal or circulatory system.

Nicotine *Nicotine* is another widely used legal stimulant and dependence on it is most commonly associated with cigarette smoking. Recent media campaigns have immersed the public in warnings that cigarette smoking is harmful to the body. A U.S. surgeon general's report has indicated that cigarette smoking accounts for one-sixth of the deaths in the United States and is the single most preventable cause of death. The prevalence of smoking is decreasing slightly in most industrialized nations, but it is rising in developing areas. About 45 percent of the U.S. population have never smoked, 25 percent are ex-smokers, 30 percent are current smokers, 4 percent smoke pipes, and 3 percent use smokeless tobacco (American Psychiatric Association, 1994).

The following symptoms are characteristic of nicotine dependence:

- Attempts to stop or reduce tobacco use on a permanent basis have been unsuccessful.

- Attempts to stop smoking have led to withdrawal symptoms such as a craving for tobacco, irritability, difficulty in concentrating, sleep difficulties, and restlessness.

- Tobacco use continues despite a serious physical disorder, such as emphysema, that the smoker knows is exacerbated by tobacco use.

Cocaine and Crack A great deal of publicity and concern have been devoted to the use of **cocaine,** a substance that is extracted from the coca plant and that induces feelings of euphoria and self-confidence in users. A number of major-league baseball players, film stars, political figures, and other notables use this drug regularly. Indeed, its use is expanding. Cocaine is a fashionable drug, especially among middle-class and upper-class professionals, and is equally distributed between males and females. From one to three million cocaine abusers are in need of treatment, many times higher than the number of heroin addicts (Gawin, 1991).

In the late 1800s, cocaine was heralded as a wonder drug for remedying depression, indigestion, headaches, pain, and other ailments. It was often included in medicines, tonics, and wines; it was even used in cola drinks such as Coca-Cola. In the early 1900s, however, its use was controlled, and the possession of cocaine is now illegal.

Cocaine can be eaten, injected intravenously, or smoked, but it is usually "snorted" (inhaled). Eating

Even though the harmful effects of smoking are well known, cigarette advertisers still like to perpetuate the idea that smoking is "cool." The American Cancer Society, on the other hand, takes a different advertising approach.

does not produce rapid effects, and intravenous use requires injection with a needle, which leaves needle marks and introduces the possibility of infection. When cocaine is inhaled into the nasal cavity, however, the person quickly feels euphoric, stimulated, and confident. Heart rate and blood pressure increase, and (according to users) fatigue and appetite are reduced. As in the case of amphetamines, cocaine appears to increase synaptic dopamine levels in the brain by inhibiting the reuptake of the dopamine. Wise (1988) believes that these actions make the drug reinforcing and stimulating.

Users may become dependent on cocaine. That is, a user can develop an addiction and be unable to stop using it, sometimes after only a short period of time (American Psychiatric Association, 1994). Although users do not show gross physiological withdrawal symptoms, Gawin (1991) noted that the distinction between psychological and physical addiction is difficult to make and that chronic abuse of cocaine can produce neurophysiological changes in the central nervous system. The constant desire for cocaine can impair social and occupational functioning, and the

high cost of the substance can cause users to resort to crime to feed their habit. In addition, side effects can occur. Feelings of depression and gloom may be produced when a cocaine high wears off. Heavy users sometimes report weight loss, paranoia, nervousness, fatigue, and hallucinations. The Committee on Drug Abuse of the Council on Psychiatric Services (1987) also noted that, because cocaine stimulates the sympathetic nervous system, premature ventricular heartbeats and death may occur.

Crack is one of the most talked-about drugs. It is a purified and potent form of cocaine produced by heating cocaine with ether ("freebasing"). Crack is sold as small, solid pieces or "rocks." When smoked, crack produces swift and marked euphoria, followed by depression. Johnston and colleagues (1991) found that 1.6 percent of young adults reported having used crack during a twelve-month period.

Crack is a major concern to society for four reasons. First, it is inexpensive and readily obtainable, so large segments of the population can have easy access to the substance. Second, the euphoria of the high from crack is quite intense and immediate, compared

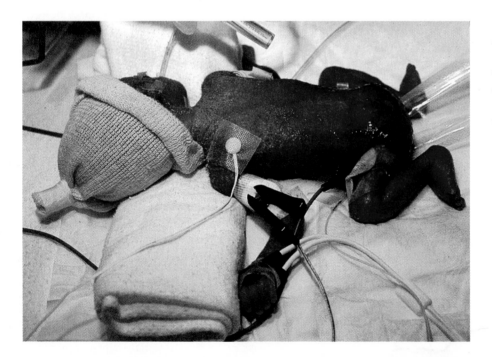

Cocaine has become a "fashionable" drug. It can be eaten, injected intravenously, snorted (inhaled), or smoked. Crack is a potent and highly addictive form of cocaine that is processed and distributed as "rocks" or solid pieces and, as shown here, it is smoked.

with sniffing cocaine. Thus many people prefer crack. Third, users appear to develop a relatively rapid addiction to crack, and they continually seek the substance. Fourth, because of the increasing popularity of the drug and the crimes associated with crack, law enforcement resources have been expanded in the attempt to control its sale, distribution, and use.

Hallucinogens

Hallucinogens are substances that produce hallucinations, vivid sensory awareness, heightened alertness, or perceptions of increased insight. Their use does not typically lead to physical dependence (that is, to increased tolerance or withdrawal reaction), although psychological dependency may occur. Common hallucinogens are marijuana, LSD, and PCP.

Marijuana   The mildest and most commonly used hallucinogen is **marijuana,** also known as "pot" or "grass." Although DSM-IV does not technically consider marijuana a hallucinogen, it does have many of the same effects as hallucinogens. This substance is generally smoked in a cigarette, or "joint." More than 33 percent of the U.S. population (including youngsters) have used marijuana, although it is an illegal substance (National Institute of Drug Abuse, 1991). Marijuana use is most common in the age range of 18 to 30 years and in the male population. As in the case of cigarettes, chronic smoking of marijuana can lead to lung cancer.

The subjective effects of marijuana include feelings of euphoria, tranquility, and passivity. Once the drug has taken effect, subjective time passes slowly, and

Pregnant women who use drugs during pregnancy are likely to have drug-addicted, underweight babies with serious development problems. Pictured here is a "crack baby" going through withdrawal symptoms.

Although marijuana can be abused as a recreational drug, it has been of value in treating patients with certain forms of glaucoma and in reducing the nausea and weight loss often occurring in cancer patients being treated with chemotherapy. Shown here is a medical researcher involved in a glaucoma study.

some users report increased sensory experiences as well as mild perceptual distortions. Prior experience with the drug, expectancy of its effects, and the setting in which marijuana is used influence the precise reactions.

In one experiment, marijuana smokers were given either a marijuana or a placebo cigarette to smoke. Some subjects were told to overcome the drug's effects in performing tasks; others were not told to do so. The researchers wanted to find out whether subjects could control their performance even after marijuana intoxication—that is, whether they could "come down" from a "high" at will. Their results indicated that marijuana intoxication influences the person's ability to estimate time and to remember lists of words. Moreover, motivating subjects to overcome the effects of marijuana improved the subjects' performance at estimating time but not their ability to remember lists of words (Cappell & Pliner, 1973).

Although much controversy has raged over the effects of marijuana, many states have now decriminalized the possession of small quantities of this substance. Marijuana has been helpful in treating some physical ailments, such as certain forms of glaucoma (an eye disorder), and in reducing the nausea of patients being treated with chemotherapy for cancer.

Lysergic Acid Diethylamide (LSD)   LSD or "acid" gained notoriety as a hallucinogen in the mid-1960s. Praised by users as a potent psychedelic, consciousness-expanding drug, LSD produces distortions of reality and hallucinations. "Good trips" are experiences of sharpened visual and auditory perception, height-

ened sensation, convictions that one has achieved profound philosophical insights, and feelings of ecstasy. "Bad trips" include fear and panic from distortions of sensory experiences, severe depression, marked confusion and disorientation, and delusions. Some users report "flashbacks," the recurrence of hallucinations or other sensations days or weeks after taking LSD. Fatigue, stress, or the use of another drug may trigger a "flashback."

LSD is considered a *psychotomimetic* drug because, in some cases, it produces reactions that mimic those seen in acute psychotic reactions. It does not produce physical dependence, even in users who have taken the drug hundreds of times. Aside from its psychological effects, no substantial evidence supports the belief that LSD is dangerous in and of itself. Large doses do not cause death, although there are reports of people who have unwittingly committed suicide while under the influence of LSD. Initially researchers believed that LSD caused chromosomal damage and spontaneous abortions, but such events are probably attributable to impurities in the drug, the use of other drugs, or the unhealthy lifestyles of many users.

Phencyclidine (PCP)   Phencyclidine, also known as PCP, "angel dust," "crystal," "superweed," and "rocket fuel," has emerged as one of the most dangerous of the so-called street drugs. Originally developed for its pain-killing properties, PCP is a hallucinatory drug that causes perceptual distortions, euphoria, nausea, confusion, delusions, and violent psychotic behavior. Reactions to the drug are influenced by dosage, the individual user, and the circumstances in which it is taken. One thing is clear: PCP has in many cases caused aggressive behavior, violence, or death from the taker's recklessness or delusions of invincibility. The drug is illegal, but it is still widely used, often sprinkled on marijuana and smoked.

Spitzer and coworkers (1981, pp. 229–230) described the effects of PCP on a chronic user. As you will see, one long-term effect may have been a personality change.

> The patient is a 20-year-old male who was brought to the hospital, trussed in ropes, by his four brothers. This is his seventh hospitalization in the last two years, each for similar behavior. One of his brothers reports that he "came home crazy" late one night, threw a chair through a window, tore a gas heater off the wall, and ran into the street. The family called the police, who apprehended him shortly thereafter as he stood, naked, directing traffic at a busy intersection. He assaulted the arresting officers, escaped them, and ran home screaming threats at his family. There his brothers were able to subdue him.
>
> On admission the patient was observed to be agitated, his mood fluctuating between anger and fear. He had slurred speech and staggered when he walked. He remained extremely violent and disorganized for the first several days of his hospitalization, then began having longer and longer lucid intervals, still interspersed with sudden, unpredictable periods in which he displayed great suspiciousness, a fierce expression, slurred speech, and clenched fists.
>
> After calming down, the patient denied ever having been violent or acting in an unusual way ("I'm a peaceable man") and said he could not remember how he got to the hospital. He admitted to using alcohol and marijuana socially, but denied phencyclidine (PCP) use except for once, experimentally, three years previously. Nevertheless, blood and urine tests were positive for phencyclidine, and his brother believes "he gets dusted every day."

DSM-IV includes a category for other substance-related disorders. Maladaptive use of substances such as anabolic steroids and nitrous oxide ("laughing gas") are included in this category.

ETIOLOGY OF SUBSTANCE-USE DISORDERS

Why do people abuse substances, despite the knowledge that alcohol and drugs can have devastating consequences in their lives? The answer to this question is complicated by the number of different kinds of substances that are used and the number of factors that interact to account for the use of any one substance.

Many theories have been proposed in the attempt to answer the question. Of these, the major types have been either biogenic in perspective (involving genetic, physiological, and biological factors) or psychological and cultural (involving psychodynamic, personality, sociocultural, or behavioral and cognitive factors). Both perspectives offer valid insights into addiction. The biogenic theories focus on dependence, or the bodily need for alcohol or drugs. The psychological-cultural theories attempt to explain how abuse patterns develop before actual dependence and why addicts who try to stop their habit may relapse and return to substance use. In the case of alcohol, for example, drinking behavior was traditionally believed to be the result of psychological factors, whereas the maintenance of heavy drinking resulted from physical dependence on alcohol. According to this viewpoint, one first drinks because of curiosity; because of exposure to drinking models such as parents, peers, or television characters; and because of the tension-reducing properties of alcohol. After prolonged consumption, however, the person becomes physically dependent and drinks heavily to satisfy bodily needs.

As these statements indicate, traditional theories often assumed that the acquisition and maintenance of substances were largely distinct processes in which psychological factors influenced acquisition and biogenic factors were responsible for maintenance. This assumption is overly simplistic. As you will see shortly, both the acquisition and maintenance of drinking behavior are influenced by a complex interaction of psychological and physical factors. Recent theories have attempted to integrate the psychological and biogenic approaches.

Because of its widespread use, availability, and consequences to society, more research has been conducted on alcohol than on other substances. Most of our discussion therefore centers on alcohol, although we will comment on how different theories may be relevant to the use of substances other than alcohol.

Biogenic Explanations

Because alcohol affects metabolic processes and the central nervous system, investigators have explored the possibility that heredity or congenital factors increase susceptibility to addiction. Alcoholism "runs in families" (Azar, 1995), and 20 to 30 percent of the children of alcoholics eventually develop alcoholism (Research Task Force of the National Institute of Mental Health, 1975). Since children share both genetic and environmental influences with their parents, researchers face the challenge of somehow separating the contributions of these two sets of factors. The role of in utero and neonatal influences must also be determined. Many investigators have attempted to isolate genetic and environmental factors through the use of adoption studies and twin studies.

Several studies have indicated that children whose biological parents were alcoholics but who were adopted and raised by nonrelatives are more likely to develop drinking problems than are adopted children whose biological parents were not alcoholics (Goodwin, 1979; Kanas, 1988). In one study of alcohol abuse among adopted individuals, Cadoret and Wesner (1990) found clear-cut evidence of a genetic factor operating from biological parent to adopted child. However, they also found evidence of environmental influences: Having an alcoholic in the adoptive home also increases the risk of alcohol problems in the adopted person.

Investigators studying the concordance rates for alcoholism among identical and fraternal twins reported similar findings. Although identical twins have higher concordance rates, fraternal twins also have high rates (Rosenthal, 1971). Concordance rates indicate the likelihood that *both* twins have a disorder.

Collectively, these two sets of findings suggest that both heredity and environmental factors are important. Goodwin (1985) speculated that two types of alcoholism may exist: familial and nonfamilial. *Familial alcoholism* shows a family history of alcoholism, suggesting genetic predisposition. This type of alcoholism develops at an early age (usually by the late twenties), is severe, and is associated with an increased risk of alcoholism (but not other mental disorders) among blood relatives. *Nonfamilial alcoholism* does not show these characteristics and is presumably influenced more by environment.

The Search for Specific Genes

The consensus among experts studying alcoholism is that this disorder has a genetic component. Sophisticated new techniques and strategies are being used to localize the responsible genes and to understand how those genes operate (Wijsman, 1990). Recently, a great deal of interest has focused on quantitative trait loci (QTL) analysis (Azar, 1995). QTL analysis attempts to identify the genes that contribute to complex traits such as alcoholism. It involves the selective breeding of animals for certain traits. For example, if the trait being studied were aggression, aggressive rats would be inbred over many generations to produce an extremely aggressive rat. The same sort of inbreeding would take place for passive rats. Investigators would then try to find markers and sites on the rats' DNA that distinguish the aggressive and passive rats. The genes within the sites would be tested and analyzed to determine whether they are responsible for the traits. If similar human genes exist, researchers then could check to see if the genes differ in aggressive and passive human beings. Using this technique, researchers have identified genes that may be responsible for certain traits in alcoholism, such as a preference for alcohol (Azar, 1995).

The Search for Risk Factors

Other researchers have attempted to find risk factors or markers for alcoholism. Risk factors are variables related to, or etiologically significant in, alcoholism. Biological markers involving neurotransmitters in the brain have been found to be related to alcoholism (Kranzler & Anton, 1994; Tabakoff, Whelan & Hoffman, 1990). Another risk factor appears to be sensitivity or responsiveness to alcohol (Schuckit, 1990). Individuals who are not sensitive to alcohol may be able to consume large amounts of it before feeling its effects, and they may therefore be more susceptible to alcoholism.

Being a child of an alcoholic and coming from a family with a history of alcoholism also seem to be risk factors. Noble (1990) compared two groups: high-risk sons of alcoholic fathers and low-risk sons of social drinking fathers. The boys in the two groups were matched for demographic background, and at the start of the study none had ever consumed alcohol or used drugs. The researchers compared central nervous system functioning, using behavioral, neuropsychological, and electrophysiological measures. The central nervous system functioning of both the high-risk boys and their alcoholic fathers differed from that of the low-risk boys and their fathers. Furthermore, the high-risk boys were more likely than low-risk boys to begin drinking. Noble also studied family environments to see if high-risk boys had disturbed family backgrounds. No differences in family background and environment were found. Noble concluded that hereditary factors may be important in alcoholism.

A final area of investigation of the cause of alcoholism has attempted to implicate nutritional or vitamin deficiencies, hormonal imbalances, or abnormal bodily processes. No clear-cut evidence has been found to indicate that these congenital factors are important in human alcoholism.

With respect to other substances such as opiates, tobacco, and LSD, research on the hereditary basis for dependence has not been as extensive as it is for alcohol. Nevertheless, it is conceivable that genetic differences may be a factor in addiction. Some researchers have found racial (and presumably genetic) differences in responses to certain drugs (Rosenblat & Tang, 1987). Asian American, compared to white, clients appear to require smaller dosages of psychotropic medication to achieve the same clinical effects for mental disorders.

Psychodynamic Explanations

A number of psychoanalytic explanations have been proposed for alcoholism. Most hold that childhood traumas (such as an overprotecting mother, maternal neglect, or frustration of dependency needs), especially during the oral stage of development, result in the repression of painful conflicts involving dependency needs (Kanas, 1988). During stress or encounters with situations reminiscent of the original conflicts, symptoms such as anxiety, depression, and hostility begin to occur. Alcohol is seen as (1) releasing inhibitions and allowing the repressed conflicts to be expressed or (2) enabling people to obtain oral gratification and to satisfy dependency needs. Most of the psychoanalytic formulations are based on retrospective clinical case studies rather than empirical data, so their validity is open to question.

Explanations Based on Personality Characteristics

Some researchers believe that certain personality characteristics function as a predisposition, making people vulnerable to alcoholism. Alcoholism has been found to be associated with high activity level, emotionality, goal impersistence, and sociability. Although causality cannot be determined from correlational data, Tarter and Vanyukow (1994) suggest that these characteristics may interact with one's social environment to increase the risk of alcoholism.

Findings regarding a predisposition to drinking are mixed. In one long-term study, researchers found that adolescents reported increased drunkenness when they had (1) lower personal regard for academic achievement, (2) higher tolerance for deviance, (3) more positive reasons in relation to perceived drawbacks for drinking, and (4) more positive reasons for drug use (Jessor & Jessor, 1977). Although these four personality characteristics were significantly correlated with being drunk, the correlations were not strong. Another long-term study (of male drinkers only) found evidence that an unhappy childhood does not cause alcohol abuse, as is popularly believed. Rather, the abuser is unhappy because of heavy drinking (Vaillant & Milofsky, 1982).

In reviews of research on personality and alcoholism, Nathan (1988) and Sher and Trull (1994) have concluded that there is no single alcoholic personality. Nathan has found that only two personality characteristics—antisocial behavior and depression—have been associated with drinking problems. Particularly consistent is the relationship between a childhood or adolescent history of antisocial behavior (such as rejection of societal rules) and alcoholism.

Nathan warned, however, that the role of personality characteristics, including antisocial tendencies and depression, as causal factors in alcoholism cannot be uncritically accepted. Many alcohol abusers do not show antisocial histories, and many antisocial people do not drink excessively. Furthermore, depression may well be a consequence rather than an antecedent of alcohol abuse (that is, problem drinking may cause people to feel depressed). Tarter and Vanyukov (1994) and other researchers who have found personality characteristics (such as emotionality and sociability) associated with alcoholism believe that the effects, if any, of such characteristics are complex and indirect.

Nathan's warning is also pertinent to research that has attempted to find a relationship between personality characteristics and the use of drugs other than alcohol. In the 1960s and 1970s, some researchers hoped to identify a cluster of personality traits that would account for addiction to substances. No such clusters were found, and attempts to find a common pattern of personality traits underlying addiction have failed (Platt, 1986). It is highly unlikely that addiction is caused by a single personality type. (See Critical Thinking for a further discussion of this topic.)

Sociocultural Explanations

Drinking varies according to sociocultural factors such as gender, age, socioeconomic status, ethnicity, religion, and country (American Psychiatric Association, 1994). As mentioned previously, males and young adults consume more alcohol than females and older adults, respectively. Interestingly, consumption tends to increase with socioeconomic status, although alcoholism is more frequent in the middle socioeconomic classes (Kanas, 1988). In terms of religious affiliation, heavier drinking is found among Catholics than among Protestants or Jews. Finally, drinking behavior varies from country to country. In wine-producing countries such as France and Italy, alcohol consumption is high (Goodwin, 1985). Relative to France and Italy, consumption is low in Israel and mainland China, with the United States being moderate in consumption.

Rates of alcoholism may not correspond to per capita consumption of alcohol. For example, in Portugal and Italy where per capita consumption is high, the incidence of alcoholism is relatively low (Kanas, 1988). In the United States and the Soviet Union, alcoholism is high relative to overall consumption levels. Among ethnic groups within the United States, American Indians and Irish Americans are far more likely to become alcoholics than are Americans of Italian, Hispanic, and Asian backgrounds (Sue &

CRITICAL THINKING

Is Drug Use an Indicator of Disturbance?

Many individuals believe that drug users are maladapted and have higher rates of emotional disturbance than nondrug users. Indeed, antisocial personality characteristics are associated with drug use. Does this mean that drug use causes one to become antisocial or maladjusted? Or, is one maladjusted and therefore prone to drug use? When two characteristics—such as drug use and antisocial personality patterns—are related, what kinds of causal inferences can be made?

One way of examining these issues is to conduct a longitudinal study. As mentioned in Chapter 4, longitudinal research evaluates the behaviors of individuals over a period of time. If longitudinal research shows that antisocial behavior occurs *before* drug use, we can be certain that drug use did not cause the antisocial behaviors. Let us imagine that individuals with antisocial tendencies tend to associate with other antisocial peers who may use and encourage drug use. In this case, can we say that drug use is caused by antisocial tendencies?

In a longitudinal study, psychological evaluations (including personality, adjustment, and parent-child assessments) were made of boys and girls at different ages, beginning at age three and continuing to age eighteen. At age eighteen, they were interviewed about the frequency of drug use. The investigators, Shedler and Block (1990), wanted to see if certain psychological characteristics were associated with drug use—characteristics that were present before drug use and therefore could not be caused by drug use. The results were quite striking: Those who frequently used marijuana and had tried at least one other drug were maladjusted, demonstrating alienation, poor control over impulses, and emotional distress. These psychological characteristics were present before and during drug use. Do the results also imply that adolescents who do not use drugs are better adjusted than those who do?

In addition to studying frequent users, the investigators also examined abstainers—adolescents who had never tried marijuana or other drugs—and they studied experimenters, those who had used drugs only a few times. Interestingly, the abstainers were relatively anxious, emotionally constricted, and lacking in social skills. Those who had experimented with drugs occasionally were better adjusted than either the adolescents who used drugs frequently or those who had never used drugs! Parents of abstainers and frequent users also exhibited greater personality problems.

Given the results that those who experiment with drugs are the best adjusted, should we advocate that adolescents occasionally try drugs? Such a position would be inconsistent with the results. Recall from the data that adjustment patterns preceded drug use, so experimenting with drugs will not necessarily cause one to be better adjusted. The point is that we often make mistakes in drawing inferences about cause and effect, and we must be careful not to base practices or policies on these erroneous inferences.

Nakamura, 1984). France has high rates of both consumption and alcoholism. Drinking patterns in France are characterized by moderate alcoholic intake throughout the day, and drunkenness is more permissible there than in Italy. In Italy, drinking wine at meals is common but drinking to become intoxicated is discouraged.

These findings suggest that cultural values play an important role in drinking patterns. The values affect not only the amount consumed and the occasions on which drinking takes place but also the given culture's tolerance of alcohol abuse.

Cultural values and behaviors are usually learned within the family and community. A review of the literature on adolescent drinking led researchers to conclude that teenage problem drinkers are exposed first to parents who are themselves heavy drinkers and then to peers who act as models for heavy consumption (Braucht, 1982). The parents not only consumed a great deal of alcohol but also showed inappropriate

Not surprisingly, drinking is common when it is promoted by cultural practices and values. In Germany, where famous beers are produced and are sources of pride, special occasions such as Oktoberfest encourage celebrating and beer drinking.

behaviors such as antisocial tendencies and rejection of their children. When such children loosened their parental ties, they tended to be strongly influenced by peers who were also heavy drinkers. In addition to acting as role models, parents who consume a great deal of alcohol have been shown to exhibit reduced parental monitoring of the activities of adolescent children and to produce stress and negative affect. These, in turn, make the adolescent more likely to associate with alcohol and drug-using peers and to increase substance usage (Chassin et al., 1993).

As in the case of alcohol, use of other substances shows great variation, and these variations are likely to reflect sociocultural influences. For example, in the United States, lifetime prevalence of drug abuse and dependence is higher among White Americans than among African and Hispanic Americans, although White Americans have lower rates of alcoholism than do the other two groups (Robins & Regier, 1991). Similarly, although Whites are less likely than African or Hispanic Americans to have used heroin during their lifetime, they are more likely to have used hallucinogens and PCP (National Institute of Drug Abuse, 1991).

Individuals are influenced by the group with which they identify and associate. Sussman and his colleagues (1994) found that a good predictor of subsequent smoking in adolescents was their identification with groups in which members smoked. However, smoking did not predict subsequent group identification. This means that if there is a causal relationship between group identification and smoking, group identification and membership lead to smoking.

Behavioral Explanations

Early behavioral explanations for alcohol abuse and dependence were based on two assumptions: (1) alcohol temporarily serves to reduce anxiety and tension, and (2) drinking behavior is learned.

Anxiety Reduction In a classic experiment, researchers induced an "experimental neurosis" in cats (Masserman et al., 1944). After the cats were trained to approach and eat food at a food box, they were given an aversive stimulus (an air blast to the face or an electric shock) whenever they approached the food. The cats stopped eating and exhibited "neurotic" symptoms—anxiety, psychophysiological disturbances, and peculiar behaviors. When the cats were given alcohol, however, their symptoms disappeared and they started to eat. As the effects of the alcohol wore off, the symptoms began to reappear.

The experimenters also found that these cats now preferred "spiked" milk (milk mixed with alcohol) to milk alone. Once the stressful shocks were terminated and the fear responses extinguished, however, the cats no longer preferred spiked milk. Alcohol apparently reduced the cats' anxieties and was used as long as the anxieties were present. (Note that the cats were placed in an *approach-avoidance conflict*. That is, their desire to approach the food box and eat was in conflict with their desire to avoid the air blast or shock.)

An experimenter wanted to test the hypothesis that alcohol reduces the anxiety of conflict—that it resolves conflicts by increasing approach behaviors or

Alcoholism can cause family conflicts and emotional difficulties. The film "When a Man Loves a Woman," starring Meg Ryan and Andy Garcia, illustrates what can happen in a family when alcohol takes over and the healing that can occur when alcoholism is confronted and dealt with.

by decreasing avoidance behaviors. He placed rats in a conflict situation and measured the strengths of approach behaviors and avoidance behaviors before and after the use of alcohol (Conger, 1951). He found that the main effect of alcohol was to reduce avoidance behaviors, and he concluded that alcohol helps resolve conflicts by reducing fear of unpleasant or aversive elements. Many theorists believe that the anxiety-reducing properties of alcohol are reinforcing and therefore largely responsible for maintaining the drinking behavior of the alcoholic.

Learned Expectations A group of researchers (Marlatt, Deming & Reid, 1973) provided evidence that learned expectations also affect consumption. In the process, they challenged the notion that alcoholism is a disease in which drinking small amounts of alcohol leads, in an alcoholic, to involuntary consumption to the point of intoxication. In their study, alcoholics and social drinkers were recruited to participate in what was described as a "tasting experiment." Both the alcoholics and the social drinkers were divided into four groups:

1. Members of the "told alcohol, given alcohol" group were told that they would be given a drink of alcohol and tonic, and they were actually given such a drink.

2. Members of the "told alcohol, given tonic" group were told that they would receive a drink of alcohol and tonic, but they were actually given only tonic.

3. Members of the "told tonic, given alcohol" group were told that they would receive a drink of tonic, but they were actually given an alcohol-and-tonic drink.

4. Members of the "told tonic, given tonic" group were told that they would be given tonic, and they were actually given tonic.

The experimenters used a mixture of five parts tonic and one part vodka for their alcohol-and-tonic drink; these proportions made it difficult to tell whether the drink contained alcohol. At the beginning of the experiment, the participants were "primed" with an initial drink—either alcohol and tonic or tonic only, depending on which group they were in. (That is, the "given alcohol" groups were primed with alcohol, and the "given tonic" groups were primed with tonic.) After the primer drink, participants were told what kind of drink they would next receive. They were free to sample as much of the drink as they wished, alone and uninterrupted.

If alcoholism is a condition in which alcoholics lose control of drinking (a disease model), then those given an alcohol primer should drink more alcohol. Alternatively, if alcoholics learn or expect that alcohol reduces anxiety or enhances feelings of well-being, then those told that they would receive alcohol (whether or not alcohol was actually given) would drink more because they expected alcohol. Participants who were told that they would receive alcohol drank more than those who were told they would receive tonic; and those who actually consumed alcohol did not drink more than those who consumed tonic (Marlatt, Deming & Reid, 1973).

These results suggested that alcoholism is not simply a disease in which a person loses control over drinking. The participants' expectancy had a stronger effect than the actual content of their drinks on how much they consumed. In fact, several people who were given tonic when they believed they were imbibing alcohol acted as though they were "tipsy" from the drinks! The importance of expectancy was also demonstrated in a study of adolescents over a two-year period (Smith et al., 1995). Their drinking pattern was best characterized by a positive feedback model: Those who expected social benefits (such as feelings of confidence and comfort) from drinking drank more. They then endorsed even more positive social benefits, which made even greater consumption more likely. This and other experiments on drinking

Beer manufacturers often use advertisements that associate consumption with partying and having a good time. Some college students, in reaction to this practice, have parties that are alcohol free in an attempt to change this association and to discourage drinking.

behavior imply that psychological factors, such as tension reduction and expectancy, are important in maintaining drinking behavior.

Cognitive Influences   The *tension-reducing model*, which assumes that alcohol reduces tension and anxiety and that the relief of tension reinforces the drinking response, is difficult to test, and research with alcoholics has produced conflicting findings. In fact, prolonged drinking is often associated with increased anxiety and depression (McNamee, Mello & Mendelson, 1968). Although alcoholics who have high blood alcohol levels after drinking may show low muscular tension, they tend to report a high degree of distress (Steffen, Nathan & Taylor, 1974). Alcohol is a sedative that can reduce anxiety, and, ironically, it is possible that the knowledge that one is drinking alcohol can increase one's level of anxiety (Polivy, Schueneman & Carlson, 1976).

Other evidence supports the idea that the tension-reducing model is too simplistic. Steele and Josephs (1988, 1990) found that alcohol can either increase or decrease anxiety, depending on the way alcohol affects perception and thought. When confronted with a stressful situation, people who drank alcohol in the experiment experienced anxiety reduction if they were allowed to engage in a distracting activity. When faced with a stressor, however, those who drank and did not have a distracting activity experienced an increase in anxiety. The investigators argued that the distracting activity allowed drinkers to divert attention from the stressor. Without the distraction, drinkers' attention may have focused on the stressor, which served to magnify their anxiety.

Another study found that different types of tension (electric shock versus social evaluation) produced different results (Marlatt, 1978). When a group of people expected to receive a painful shock, their consumption of alcohol was no greater than that of a control group who expected to receive a nonpainful shock. When a social, rather than a physical, source of tension or anxiety was anticipated (for example, when men were told that they would be rated on their personal attractiveness by a group of women), however, the men tended to consume more alcohol than did a control group who did not expect to be evaluated by others.

Coping responses and expectancy may exert a combined effect. Cooper, Russell, and George (1988) found that stress is related to drinking when individuals expect positive effects from drinking and have coping styles that avoid dealing with anger. In contrast, stress and drinking were negatively correlated among those with little positive expectancy for alcohol and a tendency to actively deal with their anger.

Other investigators (Stacy, Newcomb & Bentler, 1991) found that expectancy is also predictive of drug use.

Relapse: A Source of Evidence

Marlatt (1978) suggested that the type of stressor, the loss of a sense of personal control over situations, and the lack of alternative coping responses influence drinking. As evidence, he indicated his analysis of relapse.

Relapse is the resumption of drinking after a period of voluntary abstinence. A fairly consistent relationship has been found between relapse and time elapsed since last use of a substance, for alcohol, heroin, tobacco, and others (Woody & Cacciola, 1994). Risk of relapse is greatest during the first three months following treatment, becoming less and less likely over time. By the end of three years, relapse is unlikely. One study found that negative emotional states (such as depression, interpersonal conflict, and anxiety) are highly associated with relapse, accounting for 53 percent of relapses among alcoholics trying to quit drinking (Hodgins, El-Guebaly & Armstrong, 1995). Negative emotional states tended to play a role in major relapse (substantial use of the substance), whereas social pressure led to minor relapse (taking just a beer). Negative physical states, urges and temptations, and positive emotional states did not strongly predict relapse. Interestingly, there was a gender difference in the states reported. Women were more likely than men to cite interpersonal conflict and less likely to report emotional states such as depression. This suggests that women may be more vulnerable to social influences than men are in the context of alcohol use and relapse.

Marlatt and Gordon (1985) developed a comprehensive relapse and relapse prevention model. In their view, negative emotional feelings (for example, frustration or anger), social pressure to drink, or temptations (such as walking by a bar) are important preconditions for the resumption of drinking. Such "high-risk" situations make the person vulnerable. If the person has a coping response (a means of resisting social pressure—for instance, by insisting on a soft drink), that response provides an alternative to drinking. Coping responses include assertion (such as saying no when pressured by others to drink), avoidance (such as not walking near a favorite bar), and more satisfactory means of dealing with anger or anxiety. This, in turn, enables the person to feel control over drinking and to continue abstinence. If a person does not have a coping response to the high-risk situation, however, he or she takes that first drink.

A person can obviously stop drinking after one drink. To explain the full-blown resumption of drinking that so often follows an alcoholic's first drink, Marlatt (1978) proposed the notion of an *abstinence violation effect*. That is, once drinking begins, the person senses a loss of personal control. He or she feels weak-willed and guilty and gives up trying to abstain. The abstinence violation effect may also apply to other relapse behaviors, such as overeating, masturbating, and smoking. Treatment to overcome the abstinence violation effect focuses on giving people coping responses for situations in which there is also a high risk of relapse. See Figure 9.4.

In terms of other substances, many researchers and clinicians believed that addiction to certain drugs, such as heroin, could be best explained by biogenic factors such as physical dependence and the attempt to avoid withdrawal symptoms. However, we now know that biogenic explanations alone are not sufficient; the role of learning, expectancy, and situational factors must also be considered.

Withdrawal reactions have been characterized as being no more agonizing than a bad case of the flu (Ausubel, 1961). We also know that heroin addicts who enter a hospital and receive no heroin while hospitalized will stop having withdrawal symptoms in a week or two. Nevertheless, the vast majority who have lost their bodily need for the drug resume heroin use after hospitalization.

These observations emphasize the importance of learning, expectancy, and other situational factors. Further evidence comes from the behavior of Vietnam servicemen who were addicted to heroin. When they returned to the United States, many discontinued its use because they had easier access to alcohol and great difficulty in procuring heroin (Pilisuk, 1975). Schafer and Brown (1991) also found that expectancies were related to marijuana and cocaine use among college students. In a survey of their positive and negative expectancies (for example, relaxation, social facilitation, and cognitive impairment) for the use of marijuana and cocaine, the student users indicated strong positive expectancies.

Thus, as in the case of alcoholism, drug use is a complex phenomenon. Explanatory models must incorporate cognitive and behavioral as well as biogenic approaches.

Overall Theories of the Addiction Process

So far in our discussion, we have cited biogenic, psychodynamic, personality trait, sociocultural, and behavioral approaches to explain alcohol consumption. In the process, we have briefly mentioned how these approaches also explain the development of drug dependence. Recently, some investigators have proposed broad theories that focus on the addiction process

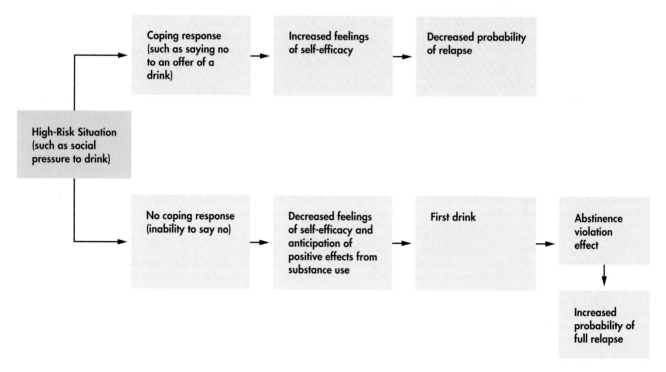

FIGURE 9.4   The Relapse Process   Shown here is Marlatt's model illustrating why some recovering alcoholics or drug abusers either remain abstinent or relapse. Those who encounter high-risk situations (ones that encourage consumption) and have good coping skills develop feelings of self-efficacy and confidence in their ability to avoid consumption and, therefore, have a decreased probability of relapse. On the other hand, those without good coping responses lose confidence and feelings of self-efficacy, which could lead to a relapse. Once this occurs, Marlatt suggests, they feel weak, powerless, or guilty and give up trying to abstain.

Source: Based on Marlatt & Gordon, 1985; Marlatt, 1978.

rather than on a particular substance. In this section, we examine three of these theories.

Solomon's Opponent Process Theory   Solomon (1977) argued that the conditions that cause a person to try a drug have not been identified. The best predictor of drug sampling is drug availability, but drug use is too widespread and drug addiction too rare for the mere sampling of a drug to be a major cause of subsequent addiction. Solomon suggested that the initial reasons for using drugs are complex, varied, and obscure. Most drug use is probably reinforcing at the outset—an attempt to solve some social problem, to respond to peer group influences, to relieve unpleasant emotional states, or to become "high." Then, after continued use, the motivation for drug use changes. The user now must cope with drug craving, a fear of withdrawal, and other acquired motivations. The addict's desire to maintain social relationships and a certain lifestyle may also be a motivating factor.

In other words, Solomon believes that addiction is an acquired motivation, much like other acquired motivations such as love or attachment. To explain the

process, Solomon (1980) proposed the *opponent process theory of acquired motivation.* Consider first the person who has used a drug only a few times: Before taking the drug again, that person, who is not yet addicted, is in a *resting* state. Then, while ingesting the drug, the person experiences a *peak* state (the rush) and euphoria; in other words, the psychopharmacological properties of the drug make the user feel "high." After the effects subside, there may be mild discomfort ("coming down" from the drug). The person may start to crave the drug to combat the discomfort, but the discomfort soon subsides and the person returns to a resting state. For this occasional user, the motivation for use is to achieve the high and to avoid the aversiveness of the craving.

Now consider the chronic user, for whom the process is somewhat different. During the period before the drug is consumed, this person experiences a *craving* for the drug. Then, during ingestion of the drug, the experienced user feels only *contentment* rather than a rush and intense euphoria. And, once the effects of the drug wear off, he or she experiences *withdrawal* reactions and intense physiological or psychological craving (or both), which do not subside until he or she again uses the drug. In essence, the motivation for drug use has changed with experience, from positive to aversive control. A new motivation for drug use has been acquired.

Wise's Two-Factor Model   Wise (1988) also agreed that a single-factor explanation is insufficient. He believes that a two-factor model, involving positive and negative reinforcement, may explain addiction. He theorized that drugs have *positive* reinforcing effects (pleasure or euphoria) through a common biological mechanism. In addition, drugs can independently act as a *negative* reinforcer in that taking the drug can terminate distress or feelings of dysphoria. This theory suggests that either reinforcer results in cravings for the drug. Simply treating the withdrawal symptoms of a drug addict—the negative reinforcement component—is therefore inadequate because the positive reinforcing properties of drug use are not addressed. Wise's theory combines both a behavioral perspective involving learning and reinforcement and a biogenic approach in that the learning is rooted in neural mechanisms.

The theories posited by Solomon and Wise are considerably different. For Solomon, motivation for drugs changes with repeated consumption. In Wise's model, two separate processes help maintain addiction. Nevertheless, each theory points to the problems in conceptualizing addiction as simply one process with one main cause. Another common assumption is that addiction involves both psychological and biogenic components. Future research will probably shed more light on the adequacy of each.

Tiffany's Theory of Automatic Processes   Although Solomon and Wise agreed that the motivation and urge to use drugs are complex, Tiffany (1990) took issue with the role of urges and cravings in drug use. Most theories argued that urges, based on the positive aspects of drug use or on the avoidance of withdrawal, are important in drug-use behavior and in relapse. Research has, however, found only a modest relationship between self-reported urges to use drugs and actual drug use. This led Tiffany to reconceptualize the role of urges. In Tiffany's view, drug-use behaviors are largely controlled by "automatic" processes. Over the course of drug use, addicts develop skills involving drug acquisition and use. The skills are invoked rather automatically so that drug-use behaviors tend to be relatively fast and efficient, repeated without much cognitive attention or effort, and initiated by the presence of certain stimuli. For example, a smoker can quickly and without thought or clumsiness pull out a cigarette, light it, and start smoking. These automatic processes are likely to

occur in certain situations or in the presence of certain stimuli that have in the past been the occasions for smoking (for example, at a party with friends).

Although drug-use behavior is an automatic cognitive process, urges are a nonautomatic process and may not be necessary to explain drug use. They may occur when drug-use plans are hindered (for example, when an alcoholic finds the supply of alcohol has been depleted). To overcome this hindrance, the person must engage in nonautomatic processes that require attention, time, and effort (the alcoholic who no longer has any drinks must find ways of obtaining alcohol). The implications of Tiffany's theory are that urges are not necessary to explain consumption and that once drug-use behaviors become automated, they are highly resistant to change. Thus the theory emphasized the maintenance of behavior rather than the acquisition of drug use, before the development of automatic processes.

These three theories have general relevance for treatment. Clinicians should attend to the course of addiction to understand the motives for addicts, according to Solomon's theory. From the perspective of Wise, clinicians should address the positive *and* negative reinforcement that addicts receive. And according to Tiffany's theory, automatic processes involving abstinence should be inculcated in addicts. Let us now turn to more specific treatment approaches to substance-use disorders.

INTERVENTION AND TREATMENT OF SUBSTANCE-USE DISORDERS

Treatment of substance abusers and addicts depends on both the individual user and the type of drug being used. Most alcohol and drug treatment programs involve two phases: (1) removal of the abusive substance and (2) long-term maintenance without it. In the first phase, which is also referred to as **detoxification,** the user is immediately or eventually prevented from consuming the substance. The removal of the substance may trigger withdrawal symptoms that are opposite in effect to the reactions produced by the drug. For instance, a person who is physically addicted to a central nervous system depressant such as a barbiturate will experience drowsiness, decreased respiration, and reduced anxiety when taking the drug. When the depressant is withdrawn, the user experiences symptoms that resemble the effects of a stimulant—agitation, restlessness, increased respiration, and insomnia. Helping someone successfully cope during withdrawal has been a concern of many treatment strategies dealing with various drugs, particularly in treating heroin addicts. Sometimes, addicts are given medication to alleviate some of the withdrawal symptoms. For example, tranquilizers may be helpful to alcoholics experiencing withdrawal.

In the second phase, intervention programs attempt to prevent the person from returning to the substance (in some rare cases, controlling or limiting the use of the substance). These programs may be community programs, which include sending alcoholics or addicts to a hospital, residential treatment facility, or "halfway house," where support and guidance are available in a community setting. Whatever the setting, the treatment approach may be chemical, cognitive or behavioral, or multimodal. In this section, we discuss these approaches to the treatment of various substance-use disorders and review their effectiveness. We also take a quick look at prevention programs.

Self-Help Groups

Alcoholics Anonymous (AA) is a self-help organization composed of alcoholics who want to stop drinking. Perhaps a million or more alcoholics worldwide participate in the AA program, which is completely voluntary. There are no fees, and the only member-ship requirement is the desire to stop drinking. AA assumes that once a person is an alcoholic, he or she is always an alcoholic—an assumption based on the disease model of alcoholism. Members must recognize that they can never drink again and must concentrate on abstinence, one day at a time. As a means of helping members abstain, each may be assigned a sponsor who provides individual support, attention, and help. Fellowship, spiritual awareness, and public self-revelations about past wrongdoings because of alcohol are encouraged during group meetings.

Some people believe that membership in AA is one of the most effective treatments for alcoholism. A few studies with methodological limitations have found an association between AA attendance and positive treatment outcome (McCrady, 1994). Rigorous outcome studies, however, are difficult to find. Furthermore, it appears that the success rate of AA is not as high as AA members claim it is (Brandsma, 1979). Approximately one-half of the alcoholics who stay in the organization are still abstinent after two years (Alford, 1980), but many drop out of the program and are not counted as failures. Thus, although many people are helped by AA, its success rate has not been firmly established. Spinoffs of AA such as Al-Anon and AlaTeen have been helpful in providing support for adults and teenagers living with alcoholics (Kanas, 1988). There are similar self-help groups for drug abuse (Narcotics Anonymous), although they have not gained the widespread attention and participation seen in AA.

Pharmacological Approach

To keep addicts from using certain substances, some treatment programs dispense other chemical substances. For example, alcohol treatment programs may include the chemical *Antabuse* (disulfiram) to produce an aversion to alcohol. A person who consumes alcohol one to two days after taking Antabuse suffers a severe reaction, including nausea, vomiting, and discomfort. Antabuse has the effect of blocking the progressive breakdown of alcohol so that excessive acetaldehyde accumulates in the body; acetaldehyde causes dysphoria (depression or distress). Most alcoholics will not consume alcohol after ingesting Antabuse. Those who do risk not only discomfort but in some cases death.

While clients are taking Antabuse and are abstinent, psychotherapy and other forms of treatment may be used to help them develop coping skills or alternative life patterns. The families of patients may also be encouraged to work at solving the problems created by the drinking. Knowing that alcohol consumption is unlikely during Antabuse treatment, families do not have to rely solely on the alcoholic's

Alcoholics Anonymous (AA) is a self-help group intended to promote abstinence among alcoholics. Each member has a sponsor who provides support and guidance. During group meetings, such as the one shown here, public self-revelations about past wrong doings, spiritual awareness, and fellowship are encouraged. It has been difficult to evaluate the effectiveness of Alcoholics Anonymous, although informal evaluations have been positive.

promise to stop drinking—a promise that alcoholics often make but are rarely able to keep.

The problem with Antabuse treatment is that alcoholic patients may stop taking the drug once they leave the hospital or are no longer being monitored. And some may drink anyway because they believe the effects of Antabuse have dissipated, because they have forgotten when they last took it, or because they are tempted to drink in spite of the Antabuse.

Chemical treatment may also be used to reduce the intensity of withdrawal symptoms in heroin addicts who are trying to break the drug habit. The drug methadone is prescribed to decrease the intensity of withdrawal symptoms. *Methadone* is a synthetic narcotic chemical that reduces the craving for heroin without producing euphoria (the "high"). It was originally believed that reformed heroin addicts could then quite easily discontinue the methadone at a later date. Although methadone initially seemed to be a simple solution to a major problem, it has an important drawback: It can itself become addicting. The following case illustrates this problem, as well as other facets of the typical two-phase treatment program for heroin addiction.

> After several months of denying the seriousness of his heroin habit, Gary B. finally enrolled in a residential treatment program that featured methadone maintenance, peer support, confrontational therapy, and job retraining. Although at first Gary responded well to the residential program, he soon began to feel depressed. He was reassured by the staff that recovering heroin addicts frequently experience depression and that several treatment options existed. A fairly low dose of tricyclic antidepressant medication was prescribed, and Gary also began supportive-expressive (psychodynamic) therapy.
>
> Psychotherapy helped Gary identify the difficult relationships in his life. His dependence on these relationships and his dependence on drugs were examined for parallels. His tendency to deny problems and to turn to drugs as an escape was pointed out. The therapy then focused on the generation of suitable alternatives to drugs. He worked hard during his therapy sessions and made commendable progress.
>
> For the next three months Gary enjoyed his life in a way that previously had been foreign to him. He was hired by a small restaurant to train as a cook. He was entirely satisfied with the direction in which his life was going until the day he realized that he was eagerly looking forward to his daily methadone dose. Gary knew of people who had become addicted to methadone, but it was still a shock when it happened to him. He decided almost immediately to terminate his methadone maintenance program. The withdrawal process was physically and mentally painful, and Gary often doubted his ability to function without methadone. But by joining a support group composed of others who were trying to discontinue methadone, he was eventually able to complete methadone withdrawal. Gary had never imagined that

the most difficult part of his heroin treatment would be giving up methadone.

It is clear that the use of chemical substances, such as Antabuse or methadone, has not had a dramatic impact in the treatment of addiction. Side effects and potential addiction to chemical treatments are major problems that have to be considered.

In smoking cessation programs, however, one very promising tactic has been the use of nicotine replacement strategy, especially in the application of transdermal nicotine patches, as discussed in the Focus On feature. A patch is applied to the arm, and the nicotine in the patch is absorbed through the skin. Researchers are also experimenting with the effectiveness of directly inhaling nicotine.

Cognitive and Behavioral Approaches

Cognitive and behavioral therapists have devised several strategies for treating alcoholism and other substance-use disorders. Aversion therapy, which is based on classical conditioning principles, has been used for many years. **Aversion therapy** is a conditioning procedure in which the response to a stimulus is decreased by pairing the stimulus with an aversive stimulus. For example, alcoholics may be given painful electric shocks while drinking alcohol, or they may be given *emetics* (agents that induce vomiting) after smelling or tasting alcohol or when they get the urge to drink. After several sessions in which the emetic is used, alcoholics may vomit or feel nauseated when they smell, taste, or think about alcohol.

Imagery has been used as part of **covert sensitization,** an aversive conditioning technique in which the individual imagines a noxious stimulus in the presence of a behavior. Alcoholic patients, for example, are trained to imagine nausea and vomiting in the presence of alcoholic beverages (Cautela, 1966). Covert sensitization has also been used for drug addicts. One difficulty with this technique is the inability of some patients to generalize the treatment—that is, to pair the learned aversive reaction (nausea and vomiting) with the stimulus (taking a particular drug) outside the clinic or hospital setting.

Behavioral Treatment for Cigarette Smoking People who wish to end their addiction to cigarette smoking have used behavioral techniques almost exclusively. Most aversive procedures (such as covert sensitization and shock) have yielded rather disappointing results, but "rapid smoking" appears promising. This technique requires the client to puff a cigarette once every six seconds, until he or she absolutely cannot continue any longer. Its purpose is to pair a highly aversive situation (the feeling of illness that results from

Smoking: Can the Body "Kick the Habit"?

Many people assume that sufficient will power and motivation on the part of smokers, or legal and social sanctions from nonsmokers (such as prohibiting smoking in public facilities), can reduce or eliminate the smoking habit. Judging from current statistics, however, efforts to motivate smokers to quit, to prohibit smoking in certain areas, and to regulate advertising by the tobacco industry have not been successful in achieving that goal. Why do smokers continue to smoke? The answer may lie in the physiological effects of smoking. Even though smokers report feeling more relaxed during smoking, cigarettes act as a stimulant. Heart rate, for instance, increases during smoking. These effects point to the fact that nicotine is a drug. It has been proposed that nicotine is (1) an addictive agent or (2) a pleasure enhancer.

Stanley Schachter, a noted psychologist, argued that people smoke because they are physically addicted to nicotine. In a series of experiments, Schachter (1977) drew two conclusions: First, chronic smokers need their "normal" constant intake of nicotine. When heavy smokers are given low-nicotine cigarettes, they smoke more cigarettes and puff more frequently. Withdrawal symptoms, such as irritability and increased eating, appear when smokers do not receive

their "dose" of nicotine. Second, smoking does not reduce anxiety or calm the nerves. But not smoking increases anxiety and produces withdrawal reactions. Smokers can tolerate less stress when they are deprived of cigarettes than when they are able to smoke. Even with cigarettes, however, smokers do not perform better under stress than nonsmokers. Stress seems to deplete body nicotine, so that smoking is necessary to maintain the nicotine level.

If nicotine addiction maintains cigarette smoking, then supplying smokers with nicotine in a nontobacco product may reduce the need to smoke. Some researchers (Hall et al., 1987) found that giving smokers a nicotine gum was more effective than giving a placebo gum in a stop-smoking program, even if the smokers were not told what substance was in the gum. Fortmann & Killen (1995) also found that smokers who used nicotine gum were more likely to be abstinent and to have lower relapse rates after a one-year follow-up period than were those treated without the gum. Gottlieb and colleagues (1987), however, found that when smokers were led to believe that they had received nicotine gum (whether or not they actually had received it) in a treatment program, they reported fewer withdrawal symptoms and cigarette consumption in a two-

week period than did those who were told they had received no nicotine. Smokers' *belief* about the presence of nicotine was more important in treatment than their actual *ingestion* of nicotine. This study seemed to negate the role of nicotine in treatment and, perhaps, in smoking. The study followed the smokers for only two weeks, however, so the long-term effects of nicotine versus expectancy are unclear.

In a review of the research on nicotine replacement therapy, Lichtenstein and Glasgow (1992) concluded that nicotine gum helps alleviate withdrawal and prevent short-term relapse. Behavioral treatment is most useful in warding off longer-term relapse. However, nicotine gum is not the most effective method of delivering nicotine. The levels of nicotine in the blood can vary considerably, depending on the way the gum is chewed, the number of pieces of gum used, and the ingestion of drinks such as coffee, which may alter the effects of nicotine.

If the treatments involving nicotine gum are limited, are there more effective ways of delivering the nicotine? There has recently been a great deal of interest in nicotine transdermal patches. In this treatment, an adhesive patch, which delivers a standard dose of nicotine during the day, is placed on the upper arm. This method

extremely rapid smoking) with the act of smoking. This is expected to eliminate or reduce the person's desire to smoke. Although rapid smoking has been reasonably effective over both the short and the long term, it is somewhat controversial. Early studies suggested the technique may increase heart rate and blood pressure (Lichtenstein & Glasgow, 1977; Lich-

tenstein & Rodrigues, 1977). A more recent study of smokers with cardiopulmonary disease who engaged in rapid smoking, however, showed that the treatment was effective and did not produce any cardiac complications (Hall et al., 1984).

Another treatment for cigarette smoking is *nicotine fading* (Foxx & Brown, 1979). In this method, the

minimizes problems in delivering a consistent dosage level. Studies comparing the nicotine patch with a placebo patch, in which neither the smokers nor the experimenters knew who had nicotine or placebo patches during treatment (a double-blind study), showed that the nicotine patch is more effective than the placebo patch in smoking cessation (Lichtenstein & Glasgow, 1992).

Without denying the role of nicotine in physical dependence, Lichtenstein (1982) sees the development and maintenance of smoking as a complex process involving a variety of factors. For example, factors such as the availability of cigarettes, curiosity, and smoking models influence the initial use of cigarettes. Then physiological and psychosocial factors such as nicotine addiction and positive consequences maintain smoking. For psychosocial reasons, including health and the expense of smoking materials, the person may try to stop smoking. Withdrawal symptoms and alcohol consumption (former smokers who drink are often tempted to smoke while consuming alcohol), however, are powerful factors motivating the resumption of smoking. Lichtenstein's analysis emphasized the value of multicomponent programs for the treatment and prevention of smoking. His factors are listed in the accompanying table.

A recent view is that the nicotine from smoking may bind to the transmitting end of brain cells (neurons) and release glutamate, one of the key neurotransmitters involved in the pleasure response in the brain ("Nicotine: Powerful Grip on the Brain," 1995). By binding at the transmitter, nicotine's effects may be multiplied in the limbic system of the brain, thereby enhancing the pleasure associated with reproduction, eating, and satisfying the basic drives. Whether smoking is maintained because of addiction or because of pleasure enhancement, quitting smoking through the exercise of will power is no simple matter.

Factors Involved in Smoking Behaviors

Starting (Psychosocial Factors)	Continuing (Psychological and Psychosocial Factors)	Stopping (Psychosocial Factors)	Resuming (Psychosocial and Physiological Factors)
Availability	Nicotine	Health	Withdrawal symptoms
Curiosity	Immediate positive	Expense	Stress and frustration
Rebelliousness	consequences	Social support	Social pressure
Anticipation of	Signals (cues) in	Self-mastery	Alcohol consumption
adulthood	environs	Aesthetics	Abstinence violation
Social confidence	Avoiding negative	Example to others	effect
Social pressure/	effects (withdrawal)		
modeling: peers,			
siblings, parents,			
media			

Source: Lichtenstein, 1982.

client attempts to withdraw gradually from nicotine by progressively smoking cigarette brands that contain less and less nicotine. When clients reach the stage where they are smoking cigarettes that contain only 0.1 milligrams of nicotine, their reduced dependence should enable them to stop altogether (Lichtenstein & Danaher, 1976). A more familiar method is simply to smoke less and less—increasing the interval between cigarettes. Cinciripini and his colleagues (1995) found that systematically increasing the amount of time between using cigarettes was a more effective way of achieving abstinence one year later than were other methods such as going "cold turkey" (abruptly ceasing smoking) or gradually reducing

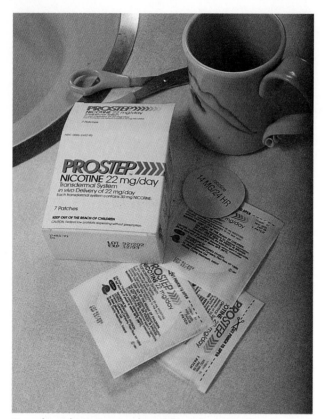

Transdermal nicotine patches such as the ones shown are usually applied to the arm. They deliver nicotine, which is absorbed through the skin. The patches are intended to help smokers quit smoking, by fulfilling the need for nicotine without the use of tobacco.

smoking without any fixed and systematic plan. The scheduled interval method also appeared to be superior in decreasing tension and withdrawal symptoms. The investigators suggest that individuals using this method could plan and bring to bear coping mechanisms to deal with urges to smoke.

Other Cognitive-Behavioral Treatments   Relaxation and systematic desensitization may be useful in reducing anxiety. Almost any aversive conditioning procedure may be effective in treating alcoholism if there is also a focus on enhanced social functioning, resistance to stress, and reduction of anxiety (Nathan, 1976). Some programs incorporate social learning techniques. Cox and Klinger (1988) developed a motivational approach in which alcoholics set important and realistic goals they would like to accomplish. The therapist helps alcoholics achieve these goals and develop a satisfying life without alcohol. Cooper, Russell, and George (1988) found that drinking to cope with emotional problems was a strong factor in

alcohol abuse. They suggested that alcoholics should find more adaptive ways of coping with negative emotions and stress through techniques such as stress management and cognitive restructuring.

Cognitive-behavioral treatments, based on analyses of why addicts experience relapse, have also been tried. Niaura and colleagues (1988) believe that certain cues are strongly associated with substance use (smoking while having coffee, drinking alcohol at a party, and so forth). They suggested that addicts be placed in these situations or in the presence of the cues and prevented from using the substance. In this way, the consumption response to these cues is extinguished. To prevent relapse, some treatment programs help addicts restructure their thoughts about the pleasant effects of drug use (Cooper, Russell & George, 1988). Addicts are taught to substitute negative thoughts for positive ones when tempted to drink. For example, instead of focusing on the euphoria felt from taking cocaine, a person might be taught to say, "I feel an urge to take the substance, but I know that I will feel depressed later on, that many of my friends want me to stop taking it, and that I may get arrested."

The Controlled-Drinking Controversy   A great deal of debate has been generated by the suggestion that it is possible for alcoholics to control their intake and learn to become social drinkers. Proponents of controlled drinking assume that, under the right conditions, alcoholics can learn to limit their drinking to appropriate levels. The finding that alcoholics tend to gulp drinks rather than sip them (as social or moderate drinkers do), to consume straight rather than mixed drinks, and to drink many rather than a few drinks gave investigators clues to behaviors that require modification. Alcoholics were then trained to drink appropriately. In a setting resembling a bar, they were permitted to order and drink alcohol, but they were administered an aversive stimulus for each inappropriate behavior. For example, if the alcoholics gulped drinks or ordered too many, they were given painful electric shocks.

One problem with this technique is that patients need to receive periodic retraining or to learn alternative responses to drinking. Otherwise, they tend to revert to their old patterns of consumption on leaving the treatment program (Marlatt, 1983).

Opponents of controlled drinking generally believe that total abstinence should be the goal of treatment, that controlled drinking cannot be maintained over a period of time, and that alcoholism is a genetic-physiological problem. Furthermore, by trying to teach alcoholics that they can resume and control drinking, proponents are unwittingly contributing to the alcoholics' problems. There have even been questions about the validity of the findings in controlled drinking programs (see Pendery, Maltzman & West, 1982).

Multimodal Treatment

In view of the many factors that maintain drug-use disorders, some treatment programs make systematic use of combinations of approaches. For example, alcoholics may be detoxified through Antabuse treatment and simultaneously receive behavioral training (via aversion therapy, biofeedback, or stress management) as well as other forms of therapy.

Other therapies may include combinations of Alcoholics Anonymous, educational training, family therapy, group therapy, and individual psychotherapy. Proponents of multimodal approaches recognize that no single kind of treatment is likely to be totally effective and that successful outcomes often require major changes in the lives of alcoholics. The combination of therapies that works best for a particular person in his or her particular circumstances is obviously the most effective treatment.

In the case of an amphetamine abuser, the individual may initially be admitted to an inpatient facility for approximately thirty days. There he or she receives individual and group therapy, takes part in occupational and recreational therapy, stress management counseling, and perhaps is introduced to a support group modeled after Alcoholics Anonymous. The patient's spouse may also be asked to participate in the group sessions.

Once the patient has successfully completed this inpatient phase, he or she is scheduled for outpatient treatment. As part of this treatment, the patient is asked to agree to unannounced urine screenings to test for the presence of drugs. The patient is encouraged to continue attending the support group, along with his or her spouse, and to become involved in individual outpatient therapy. Family therapy is the treatment of choice for adolescent substance users (Haley, 1980; Reilly, 1984; Rueger & Liberman, 1984), and it is highly recommended for adults as well. The outpatient program typically continues for about two years.

Prevention Programs

Prevention programs have been initiated to discourage drug and alcohol use before it begins. Campaigns to educate the public about the detrimental consequences of substance use, to reestablish norms against drug use, and to give coping skills to others who are tempted by drug use ("Just say 'no' to drugs") are waged in the media. Other prevention programs take

place in schools, places of worship, youth groups, and families.

Such programs are having some effect. For example, Dent and his colleagues (1995) evaluated the outcome of a junior high school smoking prevention program. One group of students received training focused on (1) resistance to social influence (for example, resisting peer pressure to smoke), (2) information (such as correcting misperceptions of the social image of smokers), (3) information on the physical consequences of smoking, or (4) a combination of the three other approaches. A control group of students was not involved in the training program.

The participants received three initial training sessions and a booster training session given a year later. Two years after the initial three sessions, the students exposed to the training were generally less likely to show increases in smoking and in trying smoking than were students not exposed to the training. The investigators warn that longer-term success may depend on additional training in high school or some other future time. Prevention programs do, however, seem to be an important strategy in reducing substance use.

Effectiveness of Treatment

Research evidence indicates that treatment programs are effective in reducing substance abuse and dependence (McLellan et al., 1994), although outcomes have been quite modest (Woody & Cacciola, 1994) and estimates vary from study to study. About one-third of alcoholic clients remain abstinent one year after treatment. Most opiate-dependent clients and heroin addicts are readdicted within the first year following treatment. The majority of treated smokers return to smoking within one year. Again, relapse occurred most frequently during the first several months of abstinence, and the type of substance is important to consider. Part of the problem in delivering effective treatment is that many individuals with substance-use disorders do not continue treatment (Stark, 1992). However, some individuals recover on their own, without treatment. Other individuals who relapse after treatment subsequently undergo treatment again and become abstinent or develop an ability to control their intake.

Interestingly, McLellan and his colleagues (1994) believe that treatment of substance abuse is effective and find that the same factors predict outcome regardless of the substance used. They examined the outcome of male and female clients in 22 inpatient and outpatient treatment programs for opiate, alcohol, and cocaine dependency. Outcome was assessed six months after treatment, and demographic background, severity of problems, and type of treatment were examined as predictors of outcome. Although a no-treatment control group was not available for comparison purposes, significant and pervasive improvements in reduced substance use, family relations, and adjustment were shown by all groups six months after treatment, and the same factors predicted outcomes regardless of the type of drug problem. The findings suggest that treatment can be helpful and that outcomes are governed by the same client and treatment factors.

SUMMARY

1. Substance abuse and dependence are widespread problems. Substance abuse is a maladaptive pattern of recurrent use over a twelve-month period, during which the person is unable to reduce or cease intake of a harmful substance, despite knowledge that its use causes social, occupational, psychological, medical, or safety problems. Substance dependence is a more serious disorder, involving not only excessive use but also tolerance and withdrawal in many cases.

2. Substance-related disorders vary according to age, gender, and ethnic group. Major categories are depressants, stimulants, and hallucinogens. A large proportion of the U.S. population consumes alcohol, one of the depressants. Alcohol is associated with traffic accidents, absenteeism from work, accidents, violence, and family problems. The consumption of alcohol results in both long-term and short-term psychological and physiological effects. Other depressants such as narcotics, barbiturates, and benzodiazepines can also cause psychological, physiological, or legal problems.

3. In addition to depressants, other categories of psychoactive substances include stimulants and hallucinogens. Stimulants energize the central nervous system, often inducing elation, grandiosity, hyperactivity, agitation, and appetite suppression. Amphetamines and cocaine/crack cocaine, as well as widely used substances such as caffeine and nicotine, are considered stimulants. Abuse and dependency often occur after regular use of stimulants. Hallucinogens, another category of psychoactive substances, often produce hallucinations, altered states of consciousness, and perceptual distortions. Included in this category are marijuana, LSD, and PCP. Drug dependency is relatively rare although abuse may occur. PCP in many cases causes delusions, perceptual distortions, and violent behaviors.

4. There appears to be no single factor that can account for drug abuse or dependence for other substances such as depressants, stimulants, and hallucinogens. In all likelihood, heredity and environmental factors are important. With respect to alcoholism, some research has indicated that heredity, along with environmental factors, plays an important role. Recent experiments have demonstrated the importance of cognitive factors in drinking behavior. The tension-reducing hypothesis alone is inadequate to account for alcoholism because alcohol consumption sometimes results in increased feelings of depression or anxiety. Rather, drinking and alcoholism may be closely related to the type of stress anticipated, the perceived benefits of alcohol, the availability of alternative coping responses in a particular situation, and the drinker's genetic or physiological makeup. For narcotic addiction, both physical and psychological factors are important. Interesting overall theories of addiction have been proposed that emphasize changes in motivation for drug use with chronic consumption, the positive and negative reinforcing effects of drugs, and cognitive factors in maintaining drug use.

5. A variety of treatment approaches have been used, including detoxification, drug therapies, psychotherapy, and behavior modification. Multimodal approaches (the use of several treatment techniques) are probably the most effective. Many alcoholics are helped by treatment, and some achieve abstinence by themselves. The treatment prescribed for other drug users depends on the type of drug and on the user. Heroin addicts usually undergo detoxification fol-

lowed by methadone maintenance and forms of treatment such as residential treatment programs, psychotherapy, cognitive or behavior therapy, and group therapy. Detoxification and occupational, recreational, and family therapies may be suggested for users of other drugs. For addiction to cigarette smoking, aversive procedures including "rapid smoking," nicotine fading (the use of brands containing less and less nicotine), and transdermal nicotine patches have had some success. Prevention programs have also been extensively used in an attempt to discourage substance use. Overall, treatment for substance-use disorders has not been successful. Evidence indicates that relapse is particularly likely during the first three months after treatment, and the risk of relapse decreases as a function of time.

KEY TERMS

alcoholic Person who abuses alcohol and is dependent on it

alcoholism Substance-related disorder characterized by abuse of, or dependency on, alcohol, which is a depressant

amphetamines Drugs that speed up central nervous system activity and produce increased alertness, energy, and, sometimes, feelings of euphoria and confidence; also called "uppers"

aversion therapy Conditioning procedure in which the response to a stimulus is decreased by pairing the stimulus with an aversive stimulus

barbiturate Substance that is a powerful depressant of the central nervous system; commonly used to induce relaxation and sleep; and capable of inducing psychological and physical dependency

cocaine Substance extracted from coca plant; induces feelings of euphoria and self-confidence in users

covert sensitization Aversive conditioning technique in which the individual imagines a noxious stimulus in the presence of a behavior

depressant Substance that causes generalized depression of the central nervous system and a slowing down of responses; a sedative

detoxification Alcohol or drug treatment phase characterized by removal of the abusive substance; after that removal, the user is immediately or eventually prevented from consuming the substance

hallucinogen Substance that produces hallucinations, vivid sensory awareness, heightened alertness, or increased insight

intoxication Condition in which a substance affecting the central nervous system has been ingested and certain maladaptive behaviors or psychological changes, such as belligerence and impaired judgment and functioning, are evident

marijuana The mildest and most commonly used hallucinogen; also known as "pot" or "grass"

narcotics Drugs such as opium and its derivatives—morphine, heroin, and codeine—which depress the central nervous system; act as sedatives to provide relief from pain, anxiety, and tension; and are addictive

polysubstance dependence Substance dependence in which dependency is not based on the use of any single substance but on the repeated use of at least three groups of substances (not including caffeine and nicotine) for a period of twelve months

stimulant Substance that is a central nervous system energizer, inducing elation, grandiosity, hyperactivity, agitation, and appetite suppression

substance abuse Maladaptive pattern of recurrent use that extends over a period of twelve months; leads to notable impairment or distress; and continues despite social, occupational, psychological, physical, or safety problems

substance dependence Maladaptive pattern of use extending over a twelve-month period and characterized by unsuccessful efforts to control use despite knowledge of harmful effects; taking more of substance than intended; tolerance; or withdrawal

substance-related disorders Disorders resulting from the use of psychoactive substances that affect the central nervous system, causing significant social, occupational, psychological, or physical problems, and that sometimes result in abuse or dependence

tolerance Condition in which increasing doses of a substance are necessary to achieve the desired effect

withdrawal Condition characterized by distress or impairment in social, occupational, or other areas of functioning, or physical or emotional symptoms such as shaking, irritability, and inability to concentrate after reducing or ceasing intake of a substance

CHAPTER 10

SEXUAL AND GENDER IDENTITY DISORDERS

S exual and gender-identity disorders encompass a wide range of behaviors. Consider the following cases:

Mary K., a 38-year-old married woman, came for marital therapy at the urging of her husband. Apparently, Mr. K. had become increasingly frustrated at the quality and quantity of their sexual relations which he described as infrequent and "unexciting." He described Mary as "frigid" and as never becoming aroused. Mary stated that, although she would love to please her husband, she never felt "turned on" and had never had an orgasm. She had tried masturbation when young but said the activity "did nothing for me."

Roger recalls that as a young child, he always seemed more interested in "girly things" and activities. He often believed he was a girl, played like a girl, and had no interest in boys' games. Roger often got in trouble for using the women's restroom (because he needed to urinate while sitting), dressing in his sister's clothes, and wearing his mother's make-up. As he became older, Roger could not help believing that nature had played a cruel hoax on him, that he was a woman trapped in a man's body. After much counseling and exploration, Roger became "Rosie" via sex-reassignment surgery. While Rosie eventually married, she regrets not being able to conceive a child.

J.G., a 47-year-old-man, had great difficulty achieving an orgasm unless he was able to hurt his sexual partners. He was obsessed with sadistic sexual acts, which made it difficult for him to concentrate on other matters. He had been married and divorced three times because of his proclivity for hurting his past wives. He could not ejaculate unless he was sticking them with pins, burning them, tying them spreadeagled on the bed, slapping them during intercourse, or biting them so hard that he would draw blood.

These cases illustrate some of the disorders we present in this chapter. We discuss the following DSM-IV categories:

■ *Sexual dysfunctions*, which involve problems of inhibited sexual desire, arousal, and response; Mary K.'s problems fall into this category.

■ *Gender-identity disorders*, which involve an incongruity or conflict between one's anatomical sex and one's psychological feeling of being male or female. Roger/Rosie had such a conflict.

■ *Paraphilias*, which involve sexual urges and fantasies about situations, objects, or people that are not part of the usual arousal pattern that leads to reciprocal and affectionate sexual activity. Mr. J.G.'s activities place him in this category.

In addition to these three DSM categories, we also discuss sexual coercion. We believe the magnitude and seriousness of problems related to sexual coercion in our society warrant such discussion. Public awareness of these problems has heightened in the wake of highly publicized allegations of sexual harassment or assault made against such public figures as William Kennedy Smith, Mike Tyson, Supreme Court Justice Clarence Thomas, and former U.S. Senator Robert Packwood, as well as the infamous "Tailhook" incident involving U.S. Navy aviators.

Before we begin these discussions, however, let's consider another question: How do we decide what "normal" sexual functioning is?

WHAT IS "NORMAL" SEXUAL BEHAVIOR?

Of all the psychological or psychiatric disorders discussed in this text, sexual and gender-identity disorders present the greatest difficulty for those attempting to distinguish between "abnormal" (maladaptive) behavior and nonharmful variances that reflect personal values and tastes markedly different from social norms. What constitutes normal sexual behavior varies widely and is influenced by both moral and legal judgments. For example, the laws of some states define oral-genital sex as a "crime against nature." This view is reflected in a California statute that was repealed as late as 1976:

Oral Sex Perversion—Any person participating in an act of copulating the mouth of one person with the sexual organ of another is punishable by incarceration in the state prison for a period not exceeding 15 years, or by imprisonment in the county jail not to exceed one year.

Another interesting legal definition of normal behavior was implied by a 1943 ruling of the Minnesota

Sexuality is influenced by how different cultures view it. Some societies have very rigid social, cultural, and religious taboos associated with exposure of the human body, while other societies are more open. Pictured here are women from Saudi Arabia, a restricted society, and the United States, an open one.

Supreme Court in the case of *Dittrick* v. *Brown County.* The court upheld the conviction of a father of six as a sexual psychopath because he had an "uncontrollable craving for sexual intercourse with his wife." This "craving" amounted to three or four times a week (Kinsey et al., 1953). It would be difficult today to justify the classification of oral sex as a "perversion." The pioneering work of Kinsey and colleagues revealed that oral sex is widespread, especially among the more highly educated part of the population (Kinsey et al., 1953). Surveys (McBride & Ender, 1977; Young, 1980) have found that most college men and women have engaged in this behavior. And Mr. Dittrick could today base his defense on the views of some current researchers who believe that not having sex often enough indicates a sexual desire disorder. As you can see, legal decisions on sexuality sometimes reflect past moods and morals or questionable and idiosyncratic views.

Classification becomes especially difficult when one compares Western and non-Western cultures, or different time periods within a particular culture. For example, in ancient Greece, homosexuality was not only accepted but encouraged (Arndt, 1991). Among the New Guinea Sambia, a bachelor who does not offer his penis to be sucked by young boys is considered aberrant (Stoller, 1991). In many countries, sex with animals is fairly common among rural youths but is rare among urban boys. And in many parts of Southeast Asia, individuals are afflicted by a disorder called "Koro," characterized by a sudden and intense anxiety that the penis will recede into the body. Thus, it is clear that definitions of sexual disorders are also strongly influenced by cultural norms and values.

If legal, moral, and statistical models fall short of the need for a viable definition of normal sexual behavior, can we resolve the controversy by simply stating that sexual behavior is deviant if it is a threat to society, causes distress to participants, or impairs social or occupational functioning? Using this definition, there would be no objection to our considering rape as deviant behavior; it includes the elements of nonconsent, force, and victimization. But what about sexual arousal to an inanimate object (fetishism), or low sexual drive, or gender identity conflict? These conditions are not threats to society; they may not cause distress to people who experience them; and they may not result in impaired social or occupational functioning. They are deviant simply because they do not fall within "normal arousal and activity patterns." And they are considered deviant even though what constitutes a normal sexual pattern is the subject of controversy (Nevid, Fichner-Rathus & Rathus, 1995).

In short, ambiguities surround all the classification systems, and the controversies will become more obvious as we discuss the three groups of sexual disorders in the remainder of this chapter. Our journey begins with a brief look at the study of human sexuality and the human sexual response cycle.

The Study of Human Sexuality

Because sexual behavior is such an important part of our lives and because so many taboos and myths surround it, people have great difficulty dealing with the topic in an open and direct manner. To some extent, Freud made the discussion of sexual topics more acceptable when he made sex (libido) an important part of psychoanalytic theory. Knowledge of sexual practices and behavior was largely confined to his clinical cases and his speculations from the understanding of social mores, however.

It was not until the contributions of Alfred Kinsey, and colleagues (1948, 1953) that the scientific community and U.S. public were given reliable information on sexual practices and customs. At the time they were published, Kinsey's findings were considered shocking, exciting, provocative, and at times controversial. Later "sex researchers" criticized Kinsey's self-report or questionnaire-interview approaches as being potentially biased. (They dealt with intimate behavior, which might affect the respondent's answers.) Nevertheless, the original Kinsey findings provided valuable baseline data concerning the incidence and prevalence of certain sexual practices.

The field of sex research took another major turn in the late 1960s, when William Masters and Virginia Johnson published their seminal works *Human Sexual Response* (1966) and *Human Sexual Inadequacy* (1970). Instead of relying on interviews or self-report questionnaires, these researchers actually observed sexual behavior of volunteer subjects in the labora-

tory while their physiological responses were carefully monitored. Although some in the U.S. public objected to these studies on moral grounds (observing couples in intercourse, oral sex, and masturbation), Masters and Johnson did much to legitimize the scientific study of sexual behavior. They also dispelled many myths, such as the belief that women were less sexual than men, that simultaneous orgasm between a man and a woman was the ultimate in sex satisfaction, and the myth of vaginal versus clitoral orgasms. But perhaps Masters and Johnson's most important contribution was to give us an understanding of what is now called the "normal" human sexual response cycle, the topic we cover in the next section of this chapter.

Almost three decades after Masters and Johnson's initial work, the *Janus Report* (Janus & Janus, 1993) further increased our knowledge of human sexual practices in the United States. The report, which was greeted enthusiastically by both sex researchers as well as other mental health professionals, summarized

Three major teams of sex researchers have contributed to our understanding of sexual behavior and practices: Dr. Alfred Kinsey and his associates, Masters and Johnson, and the Januses (pictured here).

Sexual Behavior and the Era of AIDS

First identified between 1983 and 1984 in France and the United States, the human immunodeficiency virus (HIV) has been found to cause a chronic and progressive immune deficiency disease called AIDS (acquired immune deficiency syndrome). As of 1992, the Centers for Disease Control (1992) reported that more than 230,000 cases of AIDS had been diagnosed in the United States and estimated that one million persons are currently infected. Because of the long latency between infection and the onset of opportunistic infections, many people who are symptom-free unknowingly pass the HIV virus on through unsafe sex, unsafe needles, birth, and, until recently, blood transfusions (Douce, 1993).

How It Kills The AIDS virus kills white blood cells called T-helper lymphocytes, which are found in the immune system. These lymph-

ocytes are involved in identifying pathogens and instructing other white blood cells (B-lymphocytes) to make antibodies. As the AIDS virus progressively destroys the T-helpers, the body has a weakened ability to fight off "opportunistic diseases" like various kinds of cancer (Kaposi's sarcoma) and pneumonia. These diseases have very little chance of developing in persons with healthy and intact immune systems.

Public Concerns HIV infection has affected far fewer people than have gonorrhea, syphilis, genital herpes, and other sexually transmitted diseases (STDs). For several reasons, however, it has become more of a public concern and obsession. First, there is no known cure for full-blown AIDS. Approximately 92 to 96 percent of those diagnosed between 1978 and 1983 have died, suggesting that AIDS is inevitably fatal (Keeling, 1993).

Equally disturbing is our lack of knowledge concerning what percentage of HIV-infected people will develop AIDS. A consensus is lacking, but many medical researchers believe that the progression is inevitable and will occur within a few short years.

Second, public perceptions of those who are infected with HIV are often negative, condemning, blaming, and stigmatizing (Dworkin & Pincu, 1993). Misguided and phobic reactions include assumptions that someone with an HIV infection is gay, uses drugs, is a prostitute, or engages in immoral sexual acts. Such assumptions blame the victims and force them to hide their condition in shame and despair at a time when they sorely need both medical and psychological help. These assumptions have also proved to be a major barrier in educating the public about HIV and AIDS and in instituting prevention practices.

the findings of a large-scale cross-sectional survey conducted over a nine-year period, between 1983 and 1992. In that survey, the Januses had gathered data concerning the sexual beliefs, thoughts, and behaviors of 1,347 women and 1,418 men. Some of the findings destined to affect our thoughts and behavior include the following:

1. Despite concerns of contracting sexually transmitted diseases (STDs), especially AIDS (see the Focus On feature), frequency of sexual activity has not declined and may have increased.

2. There is no basis for the belief that sexual activity and satisfaction decline among the postmature population (those in their fifties, sixties, and seventies). People sixty-five and older report rates of sexual activity and satisfaction only slightly lower than those of people in their thirties and forties.

3. Education, regional differences, political beliefs, and economic level affect sexual attitudes and practices among both men and women.

The contributions of Freud, Kinsey, Masters and Johnson, and the Januses have given us useful information and perspectives in viewing human sexuality. The works of Masters and Johnson are especially important because treating human sexual dysfunctions requires an understanding of the normal sexual response cycle.

The Sexual Response Cycle

The human sexual response cycle consists of four stages, as illustrated in Figures 10.1 and 10.2: appetitive (desire), excitement, orgasm, and resolution. For accuracy, it is important to note that Masters and Johnson did not posit a separate appetitive stage; they

Although it is true that certain high-risk groups have been identified (gays, intravenous drug abusers, prostitutes, and people receiving contaminated blood, for example), HIV infection is not a function of any group, but the practices that lead to the infection. For example, the belief that HIV is limited only to homosexual contact is a myth—one-third of the women who have AIDS were infected via heterosexual contact (Douce, 1993). AIDS is found in every region of the United States, all over the world, at all economic levels, across all races, and in men, women, and children.

What We Know About HIV Transmission The HIV virus is transmitted in body fluids: blood and blood derivatives, semen, vaginal and cervical secretions, and breast milk. Thus HIV spreads through acts or practices that expose the person to fluids and secretions.

Blood HIV can be transmitted through needle-sharing, accidental injuries resulting in direct exposure to contaminated blood, and transfusion or transplantation of blood, blood derivatives, tissues, or organs in the infected donor. Precautions concerning the use of clean needles, adequate screening and testing of blood and patients, and stringent safeguards in medical care to avoid accidents can do much to prevent contamination.

Mother to fetus or infant An infected mother can transmit HIV to her infant during pregnancy and during breast feeding. It is estimated that 10 to 40 percent of all infants born to HIV-positive mothers will be infected (Keeling, 1993).

Sexual practices HIV can be transmitted during insertive and receptive vaginal and anal intercourse. Among men who have unprotected anal intercourse with one another, the probability of transmission is higher for the receptive partner than for the insertive partner (Darrow, Echenberg & Jaffee, 1987; Detels, English & Vischer, 1989). The risk of transmitting HIV from a man to a woman is greater during anal than during vaginal intercourse (European Study Group, 1992). The risk of transmission from male to female is higher than the risk from female to male during vaginal intercourse. Although

the risk of transmission during fellatio is much lower than during intercourse, some infections have occurred as a result of exposure to semen or pre-ejaculatory fluid. Risk factors are uncertain regarding cunnilingus. No current evidence exists that HIV transmission occurs during kissing of any type, depth, or duration (U.S. Public Health Service, 1986); during oral-anal contact (rimming); during manual-anal contact (fisting); or by touching, massage, and other erotic behavior that does not involve contact with semen, pre-ejaculatory fluid, blood, or vaginal or cervical secretions.

It is clear that AIDS has affected our sexual behavior more than any other sexually transmitted disease. Abstinence is the only guaranteed way to avoid becoming infected when engaging in sex with others. Taking precautions by using condoms, carefully selecting a partner, and engaging in low-risk sexual practices may make sex safer but certainly not safe. As one sex educator put it, "There is no such thing as safe sex, only safer sex."

FIGURE 10.1 **Human Sexual Response Cycle** The studies of Masters and Johnson reveal similar normal sexual response cycles for men and women. Note that women may experience more than one orgasm. Sexual disorders may occur at any of the phases, but seldom at the resolution phase.

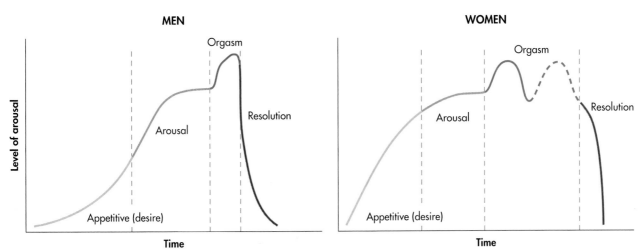

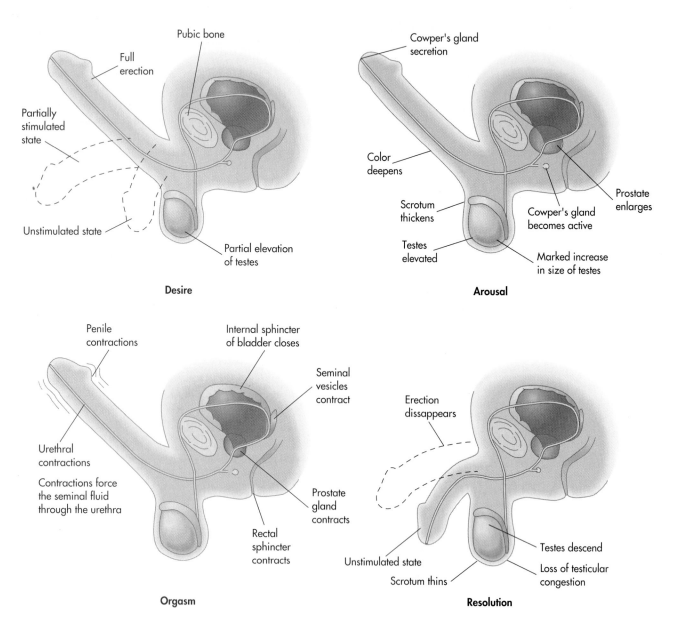

FIGURE 10.2 Genital Changes Associated with Stages of the Human Sexual Response Cycle While we often focus on the differences between men and women, Masters and Johnson found that the physiological responses of both to sexual stimulation are quite similar.

included it with the excitement phase. The work of sex therapist Helen Kaplan (1974) gave us an understanding of how important it is for a person to desire and be sexually ready, thus legitimizing a conceptually distinct state of sexual response.

1. The *appetitive phase* is characterized by the person's desire for sexual activity. The person begins to have thoughts or fantasies surrounding sex. He or she may begin to feel attracted to another person and to daydream increasingly about sex.

2. The *excitement phase* moves out of the appetitive phase when specific and direct sexual stimulation occurs (not necessarily physical). Heart rate, blood pressure, and respiration rate increase. In the male, blood flow increases in the penis, resulting in an erection (see Figure 10.2). The ridge around the head of the penis turns deep purple and the testes enlarge and elevate in preparation for ejaculation. In the female, the breasts swell, nipples become erect, blood engorges the genital region, and the clitoris expands (see Figure 10.2). Vaginal lubrica-

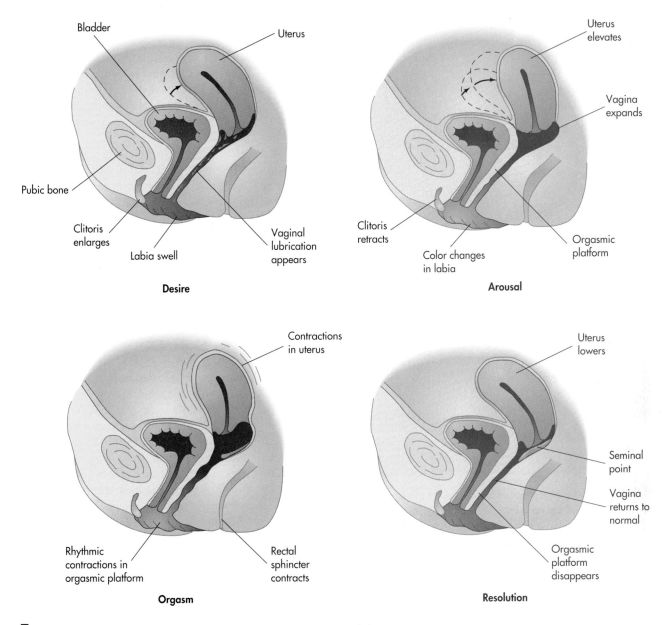

FIGURE 10.2 Genital Changes Associated with Stages of the Human Sexual Response Cycle *(continued)*

tion reflexively occurs, and a sex flush may appear on the skin (usually later in this phase).

3. The *orgasm phase* is characterized by involuntary muscular contractions throughout the body and the eventual release of sexual tension. In the man, muscles at the base of the penis contract, propelling semen through the penis. In the woman, the outer third of the vagina contracts rhythmically. Following orgasm, men enter a refractory period during which they are unresponsive to sexual stimulation for a period of time. However,

women are capable of multiple orgasms with continued stimulation.

4. The *resolution phase* is characterized by relaxation of the body after orgasm. Heart rate, blood pressure, and respiration return to normal.

Problems may occur in any of the four phases of the sexual response cycle, although they are rare in the resolution phase. If problems related to arousal, desire, or orgasm are recurrent and persistent, they may be diagnosed as dysfunctions. We cover this topic in

Debate about whether homosexuality is a life choice or a biologically determined orientation has often been intense and emotional. Recent research, however, seems to support biological determination. Pictured here are Drs. Dean Hammer and Victoria Magnunson as they examine DNA markers trying to locate a possible "gay" gene.

detail later in this chapter, in the section on sexual dysfunctions.

Homosexuality

Just two weeks into his term as president of the United States, Bill Clinton was met by a ferocious backlash from members of Congress, the armed forces and the American public over his stated intention to remove a ban on allowing homosexuals in the military. The controversy and public debate were unprecedented as the White House, Congress, and elected officials were flooded with letters and calls objecting to this action. The objections were not ameliorated when on January 28, 1993, a federal district judge ruled in the highly publicized case of Navy

Petty Officer Keith Meinhold (discharged because of declaring himself gay) that the ban against homosexuals serving in the military was unconstitutional and violated the Constitution's guarantee of equal protection under the law. It was clear from the tone of many statements made at that time that homophobia—the irrational fear of homosexuality—continues to be a major part of these objections.

We debated at length whether to include the topic of homosexuality in the fifth edition of this textbook. Given the level of public misunderstanding and misinformation, however, we believe that it is important to discuss briefly what homosexuality is not. Is homosexuality a mental disorder? The answer is no. The American Psychiatric Association did not include homosexuality in either DSM-III-R or DSM-IV.

DSM-I and DSM-II classified homosexuality as sexual deviance because sexual behavior was considered normal only if it occurred between two consenting adults of the opposite sex. The changing view of homosexuality has been influenced by two main objections. First, many clinicians felt that heterosexual sexuality should not be the standard by which other sexual behaviors are judged. Second, many homosexual people argued that they are mentally healthy and that their sexual preference reflects a normal variant of sexual expression. Research supports these views. In one major study of homosexuality, for example, researchers analyzed data obtained from four-hour interviews with 979 male and female homosexuals and 477 matched controls (Bell & Weinberg, 1978; Bell, Weinberg & Hammersmith, 1981). Most homosexuals accepted their sexual orientation and indicated no regrets at being homosexual.

It is also important to note that while the human sexual response cycle appears equally applicable to a homosexual population, the sexual issues may differ quite dramatically (Strong & DeVault, 1994). For example, problems among heterosexuals most often focus on sexual intercourse, while gay and lesbian sexual concerns focus on other behaviors (aversion toward anal eroticism and cunnilingus). Lesbians and gay men must also deal with societal or internalized homophobia, which often inhibits open expression of their affection toward one another. Finally, gay men are forced to deal with the association between sexual activity and HIV infection. These broader contextual issues may create diminished sexual desire, sexual aversion, and negative feelings toward sexual activity (Strong & DeVault, 1994).

In summary, these conclusions can be reached from the available studies (Bell & Weinberg, 1978; Green et al., 1986; Masters & Johnson, 1979; Strong & DeVault, 1994; Wilson, 1984) on homosexuals and heterosexuals:

- There are no physiological differences in sexual arousal and response between these two groups.

- On measures of psychological disturbance, homosexuals and heterosexuals do not differ significantly from each other.

- Homosexuals do not suffer from gender identity confusions; rather, any gender conflicts they experience are due to societal intolerance to their lifestyles.

- Because of the societal context in which they live (homophobia, health concerns, and other such issues), homosexual sexual concerns may differ significantly from those of heterosexuals.

Nothing more need be said. Homosexuality is not a psychological disorder.

Aging and Sexual Activity

Sexuality during old age is another area of intolerance in our youth-oriented society, where sexual activity is simply not associated with aging. Nevertheless, as we indicated earlier in this chapter, a large percentage of older Americans clearly have active sex lives.

In a study of sexual functioning in 60- to 79-year-old married men, a clear relationship was found between the reported frequency of intercourse at younger ages and at present. The most active respondents reported a present frequency that was 61 percent of their frequency between ages 40 and 59, whereas the least active reported a present frequency of only 6 percent of that between ages 40 and 59. The most active also indicated that they became aroused on seeing women in public situations and in response to visual stimuli. The vast majority (69 percent) felt that sex was important for good health, and most (63 percent) looked on masturbation as an acceptable outlet. Sexual dysfunctions were also more prevalent in the older groups than in younger ones, and the prevalence was affected by the individuals' prior and present sexual activity levels. Of the least active, 21 percent suffered from premature ejaculation, and 75 percent were either impotent or had erectile difficulties. For the most active group, the corresponding percentages were 8 and 19 percent (Martin, 1981). (The results of this study are summarized in Figures 10.3 and 10.4.)

The most recent survey (Janus & Janus, 1993), however, suggested that sexual activity and enjoyment among the older population remains surprisingly high. The Januses survey found that (1) sexual activity of people age 65 and older declined little from their 30- to 40-year-old counterparts, (2) their ability

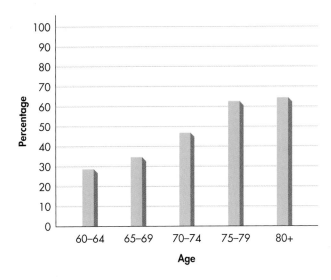

FIGURE 10.3 **Percentage of Men with Erectile Problems, Ages 60 and Older** It is clear that erectile problems increase with age. This increase is most likely attributed to biological rather than psychological reasons.

Source: Data from Diokno, Brown & Herzog, 1990, pp. 197–200.

Contrary to the belief that the elderly lose their sexual desire, studies reveal that sexual desire, love, affection, and mutual regard remain high in the older population.

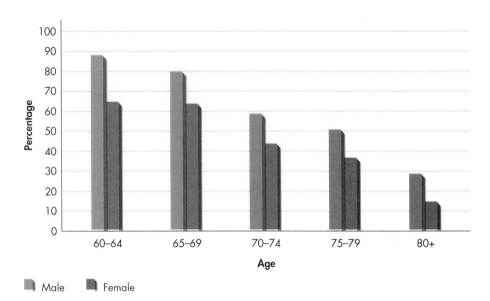

FIGURE 10.4 **Percentages of Men and Women Remaining Sexually Active, Ages 60 and Older** Contrary to many myths about aging and reduced sexual activity, studies reveal that the elderly are surprisingly active. At all age levels, however, men continue to be more sexually active than women. What explanations might account for this difference?

Source: Data from Diokno, Brown & Herzog, 1990, pp. 197–200.

to reach orgasm and have sex diminished very little from their early years, and (3) their desire to continue a relatively active sex life was unchanged.

Physiologically based changes in patterns of sexual arousal and orgasm have been found in people over age 65 (Masters & Johnson, 1966). For both men and women, sexual arousal takes longer. Erection and vaginal lubrication are slower to occur, and the urgency for orgasm is reduced. Both men and women are fully capable of sexual satisfaction if no organic conditions interfere. Many elderly individuals felt that such changes allowed them to experience sex more fully. They reported that they had more time to spend on a seductive buildup, felt positively about their ability to experience unhurried sex-for-joy, and experienced more warmth and intimacy after the sex act (Janus & Janus, 1993).

SEXUAL DYSFUNCTIONS

A **sexual dysfunction** is a disruption of any part of the normal sexual response cycle. Problems in sexual functioning, such as premature ejaculation, low sexual desire, and difficulties in achieving orgasm are

quite common in our society (Strong & DeVault, 1994). To be diagnosed as a dysfunction, the disruption must be recurrent and persistent. DSM-IV also requires that such factors as frequency, chronicity, subjective distress, and effect on other areas of functioning be considered in the diagnosis. As indicated in the disorders chart on page 295, DSM categories for sexual dysfunctions are sexual desire disorders, sexual arousal disorders, orgasmic disorders, and sexual pain disorders. Prevalence of some sexual dysfunctions is summarized in Table 10.1.

Sexual Desire Disorders

Sexual desire disorders are disorders that are related to the appetitive phase and are characterized by a lack of sexual desire. There are two types: *hypoactive sexual desire disorder,* characterized by little or no interest in sexual activities either actual or fantasized, and *sexual aversion disorder,* characterized by an avoidance and aversion to sexual intercourse. Both of these disorders can be lifelong or acquired and may be due to psychogenic or a combination of psychogenic and biogenic factors. Some people may report low sexual desire because of inexperience. Many of these people may not have learned to label or identify their own

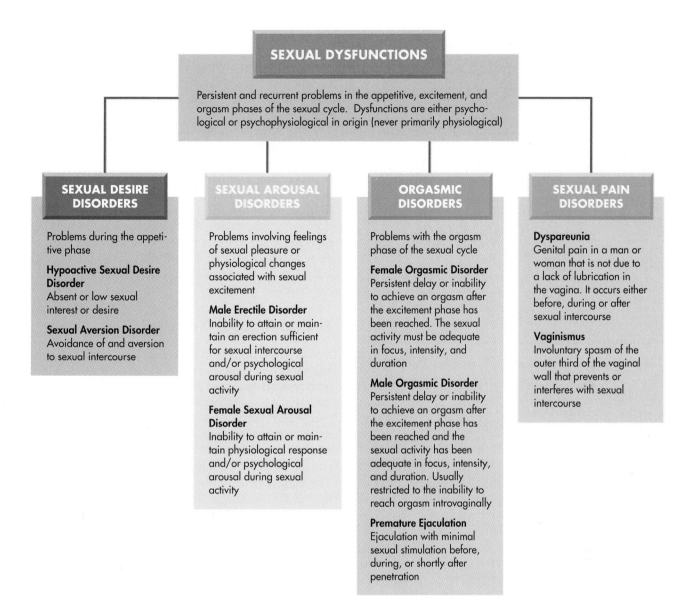

SEXUAL DYSFUNCTIONS

Persistent and recurrent problems in the appetitive, excitement, and orgasm phases of the sexual cycle. Dysfunctions are either psychological or psychophysiological in origin (never primarily physiological)

SEXUAL DESIRE DISORDERS

Problems during the appetitive phase

Hypoactive Sexual Desire Disorder
Absent or low sexual interest or desire

Sexual Aversion Disorder
Avoidance of and aversion to sexual intercourse

SEXUAL AROUSAL DISORDERS

Problems involving feelings of sexual pleasure or physiological changes associated with sexual excitement

Male Erectile Disorder
Inability to attain or maintain an erection sufficient for sexual intercourse and/or psychological arousal during sexual activity

Female Sexual Arousal Disorder
Inability to attain or maintain physiological response and/or psychological arousal during sexual activity

ORGASMIC DISORDERS

Problems with the orgasm phase of the sexual cycle

Female Orgasmic Disorder
Persistent delay or inability to achieve an orgasm after the excitement phase has been reached. The sexual activity must be adequate in focus, intensity, and duration

Male Orgasmic Disorder
Persistent delay or inability to achieve an orgasm after the excitement phase has been reached and the sexual activity has been adequate in focus, intensity, and duration. Usually restricted to the inability to reach orgasm introvaginally

Premature Ejaculation
Ejaculation with minimal sexual stimulation before, during, or shortly after penetration

SEXUAL PAIN DISORDERS

Dyspareunia
Genital pain in a man or woman that is not due to a lack of lubrication in the vagina. It occurs either before, during or after sexual intercourse

Vaginismus
Involuntary spasm of the outer third of the vaginal wall that prevents or interferes with sexual intercourse

arousal levels, may not know how to increase their arousal, and may have a limited expectation for their ability to be aroused (LoPiccolo, 1980).

About 20 percent of the adult population are believed to be suffering from hypoactive sexual desire disorder (DSM-IV). Reports of diminished sexual desire or a lack of sexual desire are more common from women than from men. Some clinicians estimate that 40 to 50 percent of all sexual dysfunctions involve deficits in desire (Southern & Gayle, 1982; Stuart, Hammond & Pett, 1987), and it is now the most common complaint of couples seeking sex therapy (Spector & Carey, 1990). Although people with sexual desire disorders are often capable of experiencing orgasm, they claim to have little interest in, or to derive no pleasure from, sexual activity. In the following

case, relationship problems contributed to the sexual dysfunction:

A 36-year-old woman and her 38-year-old husband were referred by her psychotherapist for sex therapy. The couple had little or no sexual contact over the preceding three years, and the sexual relationship had been troubled and unsatisfactory since the day they met.... Kissing and gentle fondling were enjoyable to both of them, but as their relationship progressed to genital caressing, she became more anxious, despite her being easily orgasmic.... She explained the difficulty as being due to conflict in the relationship. She saw him as angry, controlling and demanding, and very critical of her. Naturally, she did not feel loving or sexually receptive. Correspondingly, he felt angry, resentful, and cheated of a "normal sex life." (Golden, 1988, p. 304)

TABLE 10.1 Prevalence of Selected Sexual Dysfunctions

Disorder	Percentage
Sexual desire disorders	20
Hypoactive (men)	15
Aversion (men)	Rare
Hypoactive (women)	20–35
Erectile dysfunctions	5–10
Inhibited female orgasm	5–10
Inhibited male orgasm	5–10
Premature ejaculation	10–25 (although 1 in every 3 men admit to experiencing it occasionally)

The percentage of sexual disorders in the adult population varies considerably. For example, men rarely suffer from a sexual aversion disorder but are more likely to suffer from premature ejaculation. Women, in contrast to men, suffer more from a hypoactive desire disorder.

In this case, the woman was diagnosed as having inhibited sexual desire. According to DSM-IV, a sexual dysfunction should be diagnosed in such cases because the interpersonal problem is the primary cause of the disturbed functioning. Many people question the legitimacy of these criteria and the categories themselves, however. They challenge the idea that sexual problems stemming from a troubled relationship or from job or academic stress are sufficient to indicate a disorder.

There is an even larger problem in diagnosing these problems. As noted earlier in this chapter, we do not really know what constitutes "normal" sexual desire, and we know little about what frequency of sexual fantasies or activities is "normal." Kinsey, Pomeroy, and Martin (1948) found tremendous variation in reported total sexual outlet, or release. One man reported that he had ejaculated only once in thirty years; another claimed to have averaged thirty orgasms per week for thirty years. After analyzing mean frequencies of orgasm from sex surveys, a group of researchers noted that "a total orgasmic outlet of less than once every two weeks is considered one marker of low desire... unless extenuating circumstances such as a lack of privacy occur" (Schover et al., 1982, p. 616). However, using some average frequency of sexual activity does not seem appropriate for catego-

rizing people as having inhibited sexual desire. One person may have a high sex drive but not engage in sexual activities; another may not have sexual interest or fantasies but may engage in frequent sexual behaviors for the sake of his or her partner (Rosen & Leiblum, 1987).

Furthermore, using number of orgasms (intercourse or masturbation) or desire for orgasms may introduce gender bias into the definition of "normal" sexual desire. The Janus Report indicated that, for all age groups, men masturbate and experience orgasms more than women do (Janus & Janus, 1993). Does this mean that women's sexual desire is less than that of men? Until we can decide on a normal range of sexual desire, we can hardly discover the causes of sexual desire disorders or develop treatment programs for them.

Sexual Arousal Disorders

Sexual arousal disorders are problems occurring during the excitement phase and relating to difficulties with feelings of sexual pleasure or with the physiological changes associated with sexual excitement. In men, inhibited sexual excitement takes the form of **male erectile disorder,** an inability to attain or maintain an erection sufficient for sexual intercourse and/or psychological arousal during sexual activity. The man may feel fully aroused, but he cannot finish the sex act. Although Masters and Johnson (1970) estimated that only about 5 percent of erectile dysfunctions were due to physical conditions, recent studies have found that in more than 30 percent of men, biogenic factors may be involved (Segraves, Schoenberg & Ivanoff, 1983). A primary reason DSM-IV includes general medical conditions as a factor in sexual dysfunctions is that a man may have a minor organic impairment that "makes his erection more vulnerable to being disrupted by psychological, biological, and sexual technique factors" (LoPiccolo & Stock, 1986). The technology does not yet exist, however, to accurately assess a "minor" organic impairment.

Distinguishing between erectile dysfunctions that are primarily biogenic and those that are psychogenic has been difficult. For example, one procedure involves recording nocturnal penile tumescence (NPT). Men who do not display adequate spontaneous erections during sleep suffer from an organic impairment, and psychological causes are thought to predominate in men who have such erections. Unfortunately, considerable overlap in NPT scores has been found between samples of diabetic men with erectile difficulties and normally functioning men in control groups (LoPiccolo & Stock, 1986). Therefore some people diagnosed with organic impotence may actually have a psychologically based impotence. The reverse could also be true.

Primary erectile dysfunction is the diagnosis for a man who has never been able to engage successfully in sexual intercourse. This difficulty often clearly has a psychological origin because many men with this dysfunction can get an erection and reach orgasm during masturbation and can show erection during the REM (rapid eye movement) phase of sleep. In *secondary erectile dysfunction,* the man has had at least one successful instance of sexual intercourse but currently has been unable to achieve an erection and penetration in 25 percent of his sexual attempts (Masters & Johnson, 1970).

> A twenty-year-old college student was suffering from secondary erectile dysfunction. His first episode of erectile difficulty occurred when he attempted sexual intercourse after drinking heavily. Although to a certain extent he attributed the failure to alcohol, he also began to have doubts about his sexual ability. During a subsequent sexual encounter, his anxiety and worry increased. When he failed in this next coital encounter, even though he had not been drinking, his anxiety level rose even more. The client sought therapy after the discovery that he was unable to have an erection even during petting.

The prevalence rate of erectile dysfunction is difficult to determine because it often goes unreported. Clinicians estimate that approximately 50 percent of men have experienced transient impotence (Kaplan, 1974). Of 448 men with sexual dysfunctions treated at the Masters and Johnson sex clinic, 32 were suffering from primary erectile dysfunction and 213 from secondary erectile dysfunction. Our best estimate is that between 10 million and 15 million U.S. men suffer from erectile dysfunction (Leary, 1992). The number of reported cases may be increasing as people feel freer to talk about this problem and as it becomes more acceptable for women to expect greater satisfaction in sexual relationships.

Female sexual arousal disorder is an inability to attain or maintain physiological response and/or psychological arousal during sexual activity. It is characterized by a lack of physical signs of excitement, such as vaginal lubrication or erection of the nipples, or complaints of a lack of pleasure during sexual interactions. As with other sexual dysfunctions, this disorder may be lifelong or acquired and is often the result of negative attitudes about sex or early sexual experiences. Receiving negative information about sex, having been sexually assaulted or molested, and having conflicts with her sexual partner can contribute to the disorder.

> A 38-year-old woman had a satisfying sexual relationship with her husband for many years. Then her husband developed a drinking problem, which created conflict between them. Sexual intercourse started to become aversive to her, and she eventually lost all interest in sex. After her divorce, the woman was disturbed to discover that she was unable to become sexually aroused with other men. A desensitization procedure was used to eliminate her conditioned anxiety toward sexual intercourse. (Wolpe, 1982)

Orgasmic Disorders

An *orgasmic disorder* is an inability to achieve an orgasm after entering the excitement phase and receiving adequate sexual stimulation.

Female Orgasmic Disorder (Inhibited Female Orgasm)

A woman with **female orgasmic disorder,** or *inhibited female orgasm,* experiences persistent delay or inability to achieve an orgasm with stimulation that is "adequate in focus, intensity, and duration" after entering the excitement phase. DSM-III-R included an exception, however: "Some females are able to experience orgasm during noncoital clitoral stimulation, but are unable to experience it during coitus in the absence of manual clitoral stimulation. In most of these females, this represents a normal variation of the female sexual response" (DSM-III-R, p. 294). Whether the lack of orgasm is categorized as a dysfunction or as a "normal variant" is left to the judgment of the clinician. Again, the criteria that define adequate functioning during sexual intercourse are quite controversial.

Inhibited female orgasm may be termed *primary,* to indicate that orgasm has never been experienced, or *secondary,* to show that orgasm has been experienced. Primary orgasmic dysfunction is considered relatively common in women: Perhaps 8 to 10 percent of all women have never achieved an orgasm by any means (Hite, 1976; Kaplan, 1974; Kinsey et al., 1953). This disorder is not equivalent to primary orgasmic dysfunction in males, who often can achieve orgasm through masturbation or by some other means.

Wakefield (1988) argued that inhibited female orgasm actually is rare and exists in less than 1 percent of women. He pointed out that many women do not reach orgasm during initial sexual encounters. In addition, they may not have engaged in masturbation. Wakefield believes that the diagnosis of inhibited orgasm should be made only if the woman has had experiences conducive to eliciting orgasmic responses but still has not had an orgasm.

Male Orgasmic Disorder (Inhibited Male Orgasm)

Male orgasmic disorder, or *inhibited male orgasm,* is the persistent delay or inability to achieve an orgasm after the excitement phase has been reached and sexual activity has been adequate in focus, intensity, and duration. The term is usually restricted to the inability to ejaculate within the vagina, even with full arousal and penile erection. As noted, men who have this dysfunction can usually ejaculate when masturbating. Inhibited orgasm in males is relatively rare, and little is known about it (Dekker, 1993). Treatment is often urged by the wife, who may want to conceive or who may feel (because of the husband's lack of orgasm) that she is not an exciting sexual partner (McCary, 1973).

An examination of the backgrounds of men with this disorder may reveal either the occurrence of some traumatic event or a severely restrictive religious background in which sex is considered evil. Masters and Johnson (1970) gave an example of a man who discovered his wife engaged in sexual intercourse with another man. Although they remained married, he could no longer ejaculate during intercourse.

Premature Ejaculation **Premature ejaculation** is ejaculation with minimal sexual stimulation before, during, or shortly after penetration. It is a relatively common problem, but sex researchers and therapists differ in their criteria for prematurity. Kaplan (1974) defined *prematurity* as the inability of a man to tolerate high (plateau) levels of sexual excitement without ejaculating reflexively. Kilmann and Auerbach (1979) suggested that ejaculation less than five minutes after coital entry is a suitable criterion of prematurity. Masters and Johnson (1970) contended that a man who is unable to delay ejaculation long enough during sexual intercourse to produce an orgasm in the woman 50 percent of the time is a premature ejaculator. The difficulty with the last definition is the possibility that a man may be "premature" with one partner but entirely adequate for another. From the perspective of males, however, surveys suggest that slightly more than one in three men admit to occasional premature ejaculation problems (Spector & Carey, 1990).

Some support has been found for Kaplan's definition. The sexual responsiveness of ten premature ejaculators was compared with that of fourteen normally functioning men, and no differences were found in rate, degree, or amount of arousal, either subjectively or physiologically. The premature ejaculators, however, did ejaculate at lower levels of arousal (Spiess, Geer & O'Donohue, 1984).

The inability to satisfy a sexual partner is a source of anguish for many men. In a campus newspaper column at a midwestern college, premature ejaculation was reported as the largest single source of concern in the realm of male sexual dysfunctions (Werner, 1975). In one sample of married men, 38 percent reported problems of too rapid ejaculation (Nettlebladt & Uddenberg, 1979). Additionally, of the sexually dysfunctional men seeking treatment at a clinic, 29 percent were diagnosed as having premature ejaculation (Hoch et al., 1981).

Sexual Pain Disorders

Sexual pain disorders can be manifested in both males and females in a condition termed **dyspareunia,** which is a recurrent or persistent pain in the genitals before, during, or after sexual intercourse. Dyspareunia is not caused by lack of lubrication or by **vaginismus,** which is an involuntary spasm of the outer third of the vaginal wall, preventing or interfering with sexual intercourse. The incidence of vaginismus is not known, but it is considered very rare.

Several causal factors have been identified in vaginismus. Masters and Johnson (1970) found one or more of the following conditions among many women with this dysfunction: (1) a husband or partner who was impotent; (2) rigid religious beliefs about sex; (3) prior sexual trauma, such as rape; (4) prior homosexual identification; and (5) dyspareunia, or painful intercourse. A history of incestuous molestation is often found in women with this disorder (LoPiccolo & Stock, 1986).

DSM-IV also recognizes the diagnoses of sexual dysfunction due to a general medical condition and substance-induced sexual dysfunction. For example, a man may suffer from an erectile disorder caused by diabetes (a general medical condition) or alcohol abuse (a substance-induced condition).

Etiology and Treatment of Sexual Dysfunctions

Sexual dysfunctions may be due to psychogenic factors alone or a combination of psychological and biogenic factors. They may be mild and transient, or lifelong and chronic. Masters and Johnson (1970) identified some psychological elements in sexual dysfunctions, however, they deemphasized physical factors. Later studies indicate that neurological, vascular, and hormonal factors are important in many cases of sexual dysfunctions (Blakeslee, 1993; Sakheim et al., 1987). In some sexual disorders, organic factors may play a major role in the majority of cases (LoPiccolo, 1985, 1991). Although some of these physical problems may be relatively minor (such as vaginal infections, which cause itching and burning), they may render sexual functioning more susceptible to psychological or social stresses.

Biological Factors and Medical Treatment

Lower levels of testosterone or higher levels of estrogens such as prolactin (or both) have been associated with lower sexual interest in both men and women and with erectile difficulties in men (Bancroft, 1984; Segraves, 1988). Drugs that suppress testosterone levels appear to decrease sexual desire in men (Wincze, Bansal & Malamud, 1986). Conversely, the administration of androgens is associated with reports of increased sexual desire in both men and women (Kaplan, 1974). However, the relationship between hormones and sexual behavior is complex and difficult to understand. People with sexual dysfunctions often have normal testosterone levels.

Medications given to treat ulcers, glaucoma, allergies, and convulsions have also been found to affect the sex drive. Drugs such as hypertensive medication (Rosen, Kostis & Jekelis, 1988) and alcohol (Malatesta et al., 1979) are also associated with sexual dysfunctions, as are illnesses and other physical conditions (Malatesta & Adams, 1984).

Not everyone who takes hypertensive drugs, consumes alcohol, or is ill has a sexual dysfunction. In some people, however, these factors may combine with a predisposing personal history or current stress to produce problems in sexual function. A complete physical work-up—including a medical history, physical exam, and a laboratory evaluation—is a necessary first step in assessment before treatment decisions are made.

For some, a lack of sexual desire may be physiological. One group of women reported no feelings of anxiety about, or aversion to, sexual intercourse. However, they showed significantly lower sexual arousal than did sexually active women during exposure to erotic stimuli. Moreover, participation in therapy did not increase their responsiveness (Wincze, Hoon & Hoon, 1978). The researchers concluded that the absence of sexual arousal in these women is biological, and the appropriate treatment for this condition is unknown. Another physiological factor that may affect sexual functioning is hypersensitivity to physical stimulation (Assalian, 1988). Men who ejaculate prematurely may have difficulty differentiating between ejaculation and its inevitability once the sympathetic nervous system is triggered.

The amount of blood flowing into the genital area is also associated with orgasmic potential in women and erectile functioning in men. In women, masturbation training and Kegel exercises (tightening muscles in the vagina) may increase vascularization of labia, clitoris, and vagina. Vascular problems can hinder blood flow to the penis, producing erectile difficulties. Vascular surgery to increase blood flow has met with limited success because in most cases the problem is due to arteriosclerosis, which affects a number of the small blood vessels (LoPiccolo & Stock, 1986).

If hormone replacement and sex therapy do not appear beneficial, men with organic erectile dysfunction may be given penile implants (Blakeslee, 1993). The penile prosthesis is an inflatable or semirigid device that, once inflated, produces an erection sufficient for intercourse and ejaculation (see Figure 10.5). One study of men with penile implants found that 90 percent would choose it again (Steege, Stout & Carson, 1986). As indicated in the following case, however, a significant number of men report dissatisfaction with the procedure and minimal improvement in their desire for sex.

> Mr. F. was a 54-year-old recovered alcoholic who had received a surgical implant (Scott prosthesis) following a diagnosis of organic impotence. Despite the patient's new-found ability to perform intercourse at will, in the two years following surgery he made infrequent use of the prosthesis. His wife became increasingly distressed by his disinclination to either initiate or respond with any enthusiasm to her overtures for sexual contact. In reviewing the history, it became apparent that his loss of sexual desire had preceded the erectile failure and that the absence of desire appeared to be the primary problem for treatment. Unfortunately, both the urologist and the patient's wife had assumed that once the capacity for intercourse was restored, sexual interest would reemerge unassisted. (Rosen & Leiblum, 1987, p. 153)

Another form of medical treatment for erectile problems is the injection of substances (papaverine and phentolamine) into the penis (Mohr & Beutler, 1990). Within a very short time the man will obtain a very stiff erection, which may last from one to four hours. Although men and their mates have reported general satisfaction with the method (Althof et al., 1987), there are some side effects. There is often bruising of the penis and the development of nodules. Some men find the prolonged erection disturbing in the absence of sexual stimulation.

Psychological Factors and Behavioral Therapy

Psychological causes for sexual dysfunctions may include predisposing or historical factors as well as more current problems and concerns.

Predisposing or Historical Factors

Early experiences can interact with current problems to produce sexual dysfunctions. Traditional psychoanalysts have stressed the role of unconscious conflicts. For exam-

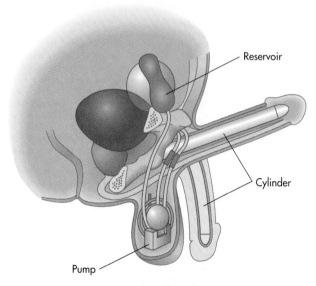

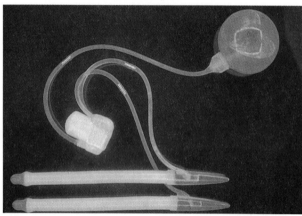

FIGURE 10.5 **Penile Implants** Men who have had penile implants have expressed great satisfaction with their use. The implants are composed of two cylinders placed in the penis with an additional tiny pump inserted near the bladder. By squeezing the pump, fluid is released into the cylinders, thereby inflating the penis. By opening a release valve, the fluid returns to the pump and the penis is deflated.

ple, erectile difficulties and premature ejaculation represent male hostility to women due to unresolved early developmental conflicts involving the parents. Psychodynamic treatment is directed toward uncovering and resolving the unconscious hostility. The results of this approach have been disappointing (Kaplan, 1974; Kilmann & Auerbach, 1979). It seems plausible, however, that the attitudes parents display toward sex and affection and to each other can influence their children's attitudes. For example, women with sexual desire disorders rated their parents' attitude toward sex more negatively than did women

without sexual desire disorders (Stuart, Hammond & Pett, 1987). Being raised in a strict religious environment is also associated with sexual dysfunctions in both men and women (Masters & Johnson, 1970). Traumatic sexual experiences involving incestuous molestations during childhood or adolescence or rape are also factors to consider (Burgess & Holmstrom, 1979; LoPiccolo & Stock, 1986).

Current Factors As we saw in the case featured in the section on sexual desire disorders, current problems may interfere with sexual function. A relationship problem is often a contributing factor, even in the apparent absence of predisposing factors. In a study of fifty-nine women with sexual desire disorders, only eleven had the problem before marriage; the other forty-eight developed it gradually after being married. The women voiced dissatisfaction about their relationship with their husbands, complaining that their spouses did not listen to them. Marital dissatisfaction may have caused them to lose their attraction toward their husbands (Leiblum & Rosen, 1991).

Situational or coital anxiety can interrupt sexual functioning in both men and women. Anxieties over sexual overtures were reported by a group of men with psychogenic erectile dysfunction and included a fear of failing sexually, a fear of being seen as sexually inferior, and anxiety over the size of their genitals. These patients also reported marked increases in subjective anxiety and displayed somatic symptoms such as sweating, trembling, muscle tension, and heart palpitations when asked to imagine engaging in sexual intercourse (Cooper, 1969). In a sample of 275 college men, sexual pressure from a partner was associated with sexual dysfunction. The men most affected were those who identified most heavily with the traditional masculine role (Spencer & Zeiss, 1987).

Factors associated with orgasmic dysfunction in women include having a sexually inexperienced or dysfunctional partner; the crippling fear of performance failure, of never being able to attain orgasm, of pregnancy, or of venereal disease; an inability to accept the partner, either emotionally or physically; and misinformation or ignorance about sexuality or sexual techniques.

Therapy Many approaches have been used to treat sexual dysfunctions, including desensitization (Wolpe, 1973), graded exercises (Stravynski, 1986), masturbation (Kohlenberg, 1974; LoPiccolo & Stock, 1986; Sue, 1978), sex education training (Kilmann et al., 1986), and the modification of sexual expectations (Rosen & Leiblum, 1987). Most general treatment approaches include the following components:

■ *Education* The therapist replaces sexual myths and misconceptions with accurate information about sexual anatomy and function.

■ *Anxiety reduction* The therapist uses procedures such as desensitization or graded approaches to keep anxiety at a minimum. The therapist explains that constantly "observing and evaluating" one's performance can interfere with sexual functioning.

■ *Structured behavioral exercises* The therapist gives a series of graded tasks that gradually increase the amount of sexual interaction between the partners. Each partner takes turns touching and being touched over different parts of the body except for the genital regions. Later the partners fondle the body and genital regions, without making demands for sexual arousal or orgasm. Successful sexual intercourse and orgasm is the final stage of the structured exercises.

■ *Communication training* The therapist teaches the partners appropriate ways of communicating their sexual wishes to each other and also teaches them conflict resolution skills.

Some specific treatments for other dysfunctions are as follows:

1. *Female orgasmic dysfunction* The general approach just described has been successful in treating sexual arousal disorders in women and erectile disorders in men. Masturbation appears to be the most effective way for orgasmically dysfunctional women to have an orgasm. The procedure involves education about sexual anatomy, visual and tactile self-exploration, using sexual fantasies and images, and masturbation, both individually and with a partner. Success rates of 95 percent have been reported with this procedure for women with primary orgasmic dysfunction (LoPiccolo & Stock, 1986). This approach does not necessarily lead to the woman's ability to achieve orgasm during sexual intercourse.

2. *Premature ejaculation* In one technique, the partner stimulates the penis while it is outside the vagina until the man feels the sensation of impending ejaculation. At this point, the partner stops the stimulation for a short period of time and then continues it again. This pattern is repeated until the man can tolerate increasingly greater periods of stimulation before ejaculation (Semans, 1956). Masters and Johnson (1970) and Kaplan (1974) used a similar procedure, called "the squeeze technique." They reported a success rate of nearly 100 percent. The treatment is easily learned.

Although the short-term success rate for treating premature ejaculation is very high, a follow-up study of men after six years of treatment found that relapses were very common (Hawton et al., 1986). More long-term follow-ups of all treatments for the sexual dysfunctions are necessary to judge treatment effectiveness.

3. *Vaginismus* The results of treatment for vaginismus have been uniformly positive (Kaplan, 1974; LoPiccolo & Stock, 1986). The involuntary spasms or closure of the vaginal muscle can be deconditioned by first training the woman to relax, and by then inserting successively larger dilators while she is relaxed, until insertion of the penis can occur.

Evaluation of Behavior Therapy Although early reports on behavioral treatment for sexual dysfunctions were highly positive, later studies have questioned the reports' high success rates (LoPiccolo & Stock, 1986; Malatesta & Adams, 1983). Other researchers have found lower reversal (success) rates than those reported by Masters and Johnson (LoPiccolo et al., 1985).

One long-term outcome study of the results of sexual therapy for 140 couples with a variety of sexual disorders assessed long-term outcome as follows: vaginismus, very good; erectile dysfunction, good; premature ejaculation, surprisingly poor; and sexual desire disorders among women, very poor. Recurrence of the problem during the follow-up period was common; 75 percent of the sample had relapses. Some couples were able to eliminate the problem themselves. Discussing the problem with one's partner, practicing exercises learned during therapy, and reading books on human sexuality were reported to be effective strategies. Ignoring the problem or not having sex were ineffective (Hawton et al., 1986). The results of this study indicated that relapse-prevention procedures (strategies to be employed when problems recur) should be incorporated in sex therapy programs and that new treatment strategies, especially for the sexual desire disorders, should be developed.

GENDER IDENTITY DISORDERS

In contrast to the sexual dysfunctions, which involve any disruption of the normal sexual response cycle, the **gender identity disorders** are characterized by conflict between a person's anatomical sex and his or her gender identity, or self-identification as male or female. These disorders, which are shown in the disor-

GENDER IDENTITY DISORDERS

Disorders involving conflicts between a person's anatomical sex and gender identity, or self identification as male or female

GENDER IDENTITY DISORDER

Strong and persistent cross-gender identification (e.g., desire to be the other gender) and persistent discomfort with one's anatomical sex, which cause significant distress or impairment in social, occupational, or other important areas of functioning (also known as *transsexualism*)

GENDER IDENTITY DISORDER NOT OTHERWISE SPECIFIED

Disorders in gender identity not classifiable as gender identity disorder, such as adults with transient stress-related cross-dressing behavior or individuals who have a persistent preoccupation with castration without a desire to acquire the sex characteristics of the other sex

ders chart above, are relatively rare, and they may appear in adults as well as in children.

DSM-IV groups these disorders into two categories: specified gender identity disorder, and gender identity disorder not otherwise specified. In the speci-

fied category of gender identity disorder—often called **transsexualism**—the person experiences strong and persistent cross-gender identification and persistent discomfort with his or her anatomical sex, creating significant impairment in social, occupational, or

The etiology of gender identity disorder is complex. Although "feminine" behavior in boys and "masculine" behavior in girls can be symptomatic of gender confusion, it does not necessarily lead to gender identity disorder. It is the strength, pervasiveness, and persistence of the identification more than specific behaviors that are the strongest indicators of disorder.

TABLE 10.2 Frequency of Symptoms in 55 Boys with Cross-Gender Preferences (Elicited as Part of a Structured Interview)

Symptom	Number of Boys			
	Present	*Absent*	*Uncertain*	*No Data*
Feminine dressing	50	2	2	1
Aversion to boys' games	50	1	3	1
Desire to be female	43	6	2	4
Girl playmate preference	42	5	3	5
Doll playing	41	5	4	5
Feminine gestures	40	5	5	5
Wearing lipstick	34	12	3	6

Source: Zuger, 1984.

other important areas of functioning. People with this disorder hold a lifelong conviction that nature has played a cruel hoax by placing them in a body of the wrong gender. This feeling produces a preoccupation with eliminating the "natural" physical and behavioral sexual characteristics and acquiring those of the opposite sex.

People with gender identity disorders tend to exhibit gender-role conflicts at an early age and to report transsexual feelings in childhood (Tsoi, 1993). A boy may claim that he will grow up to be a woman, may demonstrate disgust with his penis, and may be exclusively preoccupied with interests and activities considered "feminine." Table 10.2 lists some typical behaviors. Boys with this disorder are frequently labeled "sissies" by their male peers. They prefer playing with girls and generally avoid the rough-and-tumble activities in which boys are traditionally encouraged to participate (Sabilis et al., 1974). They are more likely than normal boys to play with "feminine" toys. They do not differ from girls in this respect (Bates et al., 1979; Rekers & Yates, 1976). Boys with gender disorder show general personality problems in addition to their adoption of opposite gender attitudes and behaviors (Bates, Bentler & Thompson, 1979).

Girls with a gender identity disorder may insist they have a penis and may exhibit an avid interest in rough-and-tumble play. Female transsexuals report being labeled "tomboys" during their childhood. Although it is not uncommon for girls to be considered tomboys, the strength, pervasiveness, and persis-

tence of the cross-gender identification among those with a gender identity disorder are the distinguishing features.

Transsexuals may report little interest in homosexual, heterosexual, or bisexual activities before the diagnosis of transsexualism (Blanchard, 1988). Those who are attracted to members of the same sex do not consider themselves to be homosexuals because they believe they actually are members of the opposite sex. Gender identity disorders are in no way related to homosexuality (Selvin, 1993).

Transsexualism is more common in males than in females. According to various estimates, the prevalence rate of the disorder ranges from one in 100,000 to one in 37,000 among males and from one in 400,000 to one in 100,000 among females (Arndt, 1991).

The not-otherwise-specified gender identity category includes disorders that are not classifiable as a specific gender identity disorder. Examples include children with persistent cross-dressing behavior without the other criteria for gender identity disorder; adults with transient, stress-related cross-dressing behavior; and individuals who have a persistent preoccupation with castration without a desire to acquire the sex characteristics of the other sex.

Etiology of Gender Identity Disorders

The etiology of gender identity disorders is unclear. Because the disorder is quite rare (Zucker, 1990), investigators have focused more attention on other sex-

"Sure I'll play house... Put your apron on"

ual disorders. In all likelihood, a number of variables interact to produce gender identity disorders.

Biogenic Perspective   Are sexual orientation and sex-typed behaviors substantially determined by neurohormonal factors? Reviewing the research in this area, Ellis and Ames (1987) found some support for this view. In our study, male rats were castrated perinatally. This procedure reduces the production of testosterone, which appears to influence the organization of brain centers that govern sexual orientation. The male rats displayed femalelike gender behaviors subsequently. In human females, early exposure to male hormones has resulted in a more masculine behavior pattern. Thus it does appear that gender orientation can be influenced by a lack or excess of sex hormones. In a review of the research, Bancroft (1989) also noted other biologic differences in persons with gender identity disorder: Female transsexuals have been found in some studies to show raised testosterone levels or menstrual irregularities.

Not all research supports the biogenic perspective. Arndt's (1991) review of the biological basis of transsexualism did not yield clear support for the role of neuroendocrine or chromosomal involvement. Children in one study adopted the gender identity of their upbringing, even though it was opposite to their genetic and constitutional makeup (Money, Hampson & Hampson, 1957). The researchers concluded that gender identity is malleable. Because these children had normal hormone levels, their ability to adopt an opposite sex orientation raised doubt that biology alone determines male-female behaviors. Neurohormonal factors are important, but their degree of influence on sexual orientation in human beings may be minor (Hurtig & Rosenthal, 1987).

Psychoanalytic Perspective   Psychoanalysts have written more about other sexual disorders than about transsexualism. In psychoanalytic theory, all sexual deviations symbolically represent unconscious conflicts that began in early childhood (Meyers, 1991). They occur, say psychoanalysts, because the oedipal complex is not fully resolved. The male or female child has a basic conflict between the wish for and the dread of maternal reengulfment (Meyer & Keith, 1991). The conflict results from a failure to deal successfully with separation-individuation phases of life, which creates a gender identity problem. Inability to resolve the oedipal complex is important in gender identity disorder, according to this view.

Behavioral Perspective   Some researchers have hypothesized that childhood experiences influence the development of gender identity disorders (Bernstein et al., 1981). Factors thought to contribute to these disorders in boys include parental encouragement of feminine behavior, discouragement of the development of autonomy, excessive attention and overprotection by the mother, the absence of an older male as a model, a relatively powerless or absent father figure, a lack of exposure to male playmates, and encouragement to cross-dress (Marantz & Coates, 1991; Rekers & Varni, 1977a; Stoller, 1969). A childhood background that results in cross-gender behavior often leads to ostracism and rejection by one's peers; in that case, the only course available to the boy is complete adoption of the already familiar feminine role. Not all males with gender identity disorders describe their fathers as weak or passive, however, nor do they all have excessively attentive mothers (Sabalis et al., 1977).

Treatment of Gender Identity Disorders

Most treatment programs for children identified as having a gender identity disorder include separate components for the child and for his or her parents. The child's treatment begins with sex education. The therapist highlights favorable aspects of the child's physical gender and discusses the child's reasons for avidly pursuing cross-gender activities. The therapist attempts to correct stereotypes regarding certain roles that are "accepted" for one gender and not for the other. Young boys are always assigned to male therapists, which facilitates positive male identification.

Meanwhile, the child's parents receive instruction in the behavior modification practice of reinforcing appropriate gender behavior and extinguishing "inappropriate" behavior (Roberto, 1983). Some therapists help children deal with peer-group ostracism that frequently occurs with those who exhibit strong cross-gender identities and behaviors (Zucker, 1990).

Some success has been reported for behavioral programs that incorporate strategies for modifying sex-typed behavior through modeling and rehearsal. The therapist demonstrates appropriate masculine behavior and mannerisms (modeling) in a number of different situations, and then patients practice (rehearse) their own versions of these behaviors. This is followed by a behavioral procedure that reinforces heterosexual fantasies: Electric shock is applied whenever the person reports transsexual fantasies (Barlow et al., 1979; Khanna, Desai & Channabasavanna, 1987).

In spite of such gains with psychotherapy and behavioral procedures, sex-change operations are indicated for some transsexuals. Prior to surgery, patients may be required to pass the "real-life" test, in which they try to live as completely as possible as members of the opposite gender (Clemmensen, 1990). This requires changing names, clothing, roles, and so on. Almost all patients must deal with reactions from employers, coworkers, friends, and relatives. Successfully "passing" the test paves the way for actual surgical change.

For men, the sex conversion operation begins with removal of the penis and testes. Then plastic surgery constructs female genitalia, including a vagina, cervix, and clitoris. The skin of the penis is used in this construction because the sensory nerve endings that are preserved enable some transsexuals to experience orgasm. The male-to-female operation is nearly perfected and, sometimes, it even fools gynecologists (Stripling, 1986).

Before sex-reassignment surgery, Renee Richards (right), a top-ranked tennis player and coach, was Dr. Richard Raskin (left), a successful ophthalmologist.

Women who want to become men generally request operations to remove their breasts, uterus, and ovaries; some ask for an artificial penis to be constructed. This procedure is much more complicated and expensive than the male-to-female conversion (Fleming et al., 1982). Hormonal treatments to accentuate desired physical and psychological effects can be used instead of, or in conjunction with, surgery (Dickey & Steiner, 1990).

Society often has difficulty in accepting and understanding people who undergo such extreme operations. One 21-year-old male transsexual who was charged with carrying a concealed weapon was placed in a maximum security prison with several thousand men. This person had already had breast implants and was taking hormones (Blank, 1981). The partners of transsexuals also go through self-doubt. One woman, married to a female transsexual scheduled to undergo the woman-to-man operation, wondered if she might be a lesbian and if her three-year-old son (through artificial insemination) would have gender confusion. Because others react negatively, few transsexuals make their condition public (Stripling, 1986).

Some studies of transsexuals indicate positive outcomes for sex-conversion surgery (Fleming et al., 1982; Pauly, 1968). Most females who "changed" to males express satisfaction over the outcome of surgery, although males who "changed" to females are less likely to feel satisfied (Arndt, 1991). Perhaps adjusting to life as a man is easier than adjusting to life as a woman, or reactions of others may be less negative in the case of woman-to-man, rather than man-to-woman, changes. Nevertheless, many transsexuals remain depressed and suicidal after surgery (Hershkowitz & Dickes, 1978; Meyer & Peter, 1979). More than one-half of transsexuals in one study who were offered surgery later changed their minds or became ambivalent about having the operations (Kockott & Fahrner, 1987). Psychotherapy is typically recommended for patients who discover that their problems have not disappeared as a result of the operation (McCauly & Ehrhardt, 1984). Doubts about the benefits of sex-conversion surgery have resulted in a decrease in these procedures.

PARAPHILIAS

Paraphilias are sexual disorders of at least six months' duration, in which the person has either acted on or is severely distressed by recurrent urges or fantasies involving any of the following three categories (see the disorders chart on page 307): (1) nonhuman objects, as in fetishism and transvestic fetishism; (2) nonconsenting others, as in exhibitionism, voyeurism, frotteurism, and pedophilia; and (3) real or simulated suffering or humiliation, as in sadism and masochism. A person who is highly distressed by paraphiliac urges or fantasies but has not acted on them would be diagnosed as having a mild case of the paraphilia.

People in this category often have more than one paraphilia. In one study of sex offenders, researchers found that nearly 50 percent had engaged in a variety of sexually deviant behaviors, averaging between three and four paraphilias, and had committed more than five hundred deviant acts. For example, a substantial number of men who had committed incest had also molested nonrelatives, exposed themselves, raped adult women, and engaged in voyeurism and frotteurism (rubbing against others for sexual arousal; Rosenfield, 1985). Paraphilias are much more prevalent in males than females.

Paraphilias Involving Nonhuman Objects

Fetishism Fetishism comprises an extremely strong sexual attraction and fantasies involving inanimate objects such as female undergarments. The fetish is often employed as a sexual stimulus during masturbation or sexual intercourse. The disorder is rare among women, although milder forms, such as attraction to uniforms, beards, or tall men, are common.

> Mr. M. met his wife at a local church. Some kissing and petting took place but never any other sexual contact. He had not masturbated before marriage. Although he and his wife loved each other very much, he was unable to have sexual intercourse with her since he could not obtain an erection. However, he had fantasies involving an apron and was able to get an erection while wearing an apron. His wife was described as upset over this discovery but was convinced to accept it. The apron was kept hanging somewhere in the bedroom and it allowed him to consummate the marriage. He remembers being forced to wear an apron by his mother during his childhood years. (Kohon, 1987)

Most males find the sight of female undergarments sexually arousing and stimulating; this does not constitute a fetish. An interest in such inanimate objects as panties, stockings, bras, and shoes becomes a sexual disorder when the person is often sexually aroused to the point of erection in the presence of the fetish item, needs this item for sexual arousal during intercourse, chooses sexual partners on the basis of their having the item, or collects these items (Jones, Shainberg & Byer, 1977). In many cases, the fetish item is enough by itself for complete sexual satisfaction through masturbation, and the person does not seek contact with a partner. As a group, people diag-

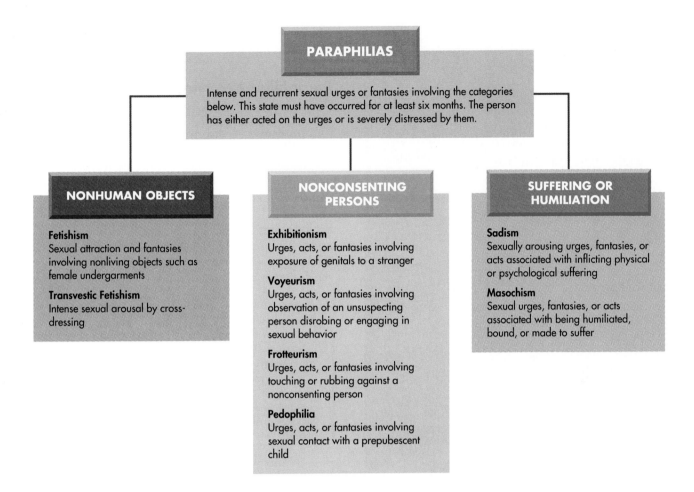

PARAPHILIAS

Intense and recurrent sexual urges or fantasies involving the categories below. This state must have occurred for at least six months. The person has either acted on the urges or is severely distressed by them.

NONHUMAN OBJECTS

Fetishism
Sexual attraction and fantasies involving nonliving objects such as female undergarments

Transvestic Fetishism
Intense sexual arousal by cross-dressing

NONCONSENTING PERSONS

Exhibitionism
Urges, acts, or fantasies involving exposure of genitals to a stranger

Voyeurism
Urges, acts, or fantasies involving observation of an unsuspecting person disrobing or engaging in sexual behavior

Frotteurism
Urges, acts, or fantasies involving touching or rubbing against a nonconsenting person

Pedophilia
Urges, acts, or fantasies involving sexual contact with a prepubescent child

SUFFERING OR HUMILIATION

Sadism
Sexually arousing urges, fantasies, or acts associated with inflicting physical or psychological suffering

Masochism
Sexual urges, fantasies, or acts associated with being humiliated, bound, or made to suffer

nosed with fetishism are not dangerous, nor do they tend to commit serious crimes.

Transvestic Fetishism   A diagnosis of fetishism is not made if the inanimate object is an article of clothing used only in cross-dressing. In such cases, the appropriate diagnosis would be **transvestic fetishism**—intense sexual arousal obtained through cross-dressing (wearing clothes appropriate to the opposite gender). This disorder should not be confused with transsexualism, which is a gender identity disorder in which one *identifies* with the opposite gender. Although some transsexuals and homosexuals also cross-dress, the majority of transvestites are exclusively heterosexual, are married, and have fathered or borne children (Benjamin, 1967). Several aspects of transvestism are illustrated in the following case study:

A 26-year-old graduate student referred himself for treatment following an examination failure. He had been cross-dressing since the age of 10 and attributed his exam failure to the excessive amount of time that he spent doing so (four times a week). When he was younger, his cross-dressing had taken the form of mas-

turbating while wearing his mother's high-heeled shoes, but it had gradually expanded to the present stage in which he dressed completely as a woman, masturbating in front of a mirror. At no time had he experienced a desire to obtain a sex-change operation. He had neither homosexual experiences nor homosexual fantasies. Heterosexual contact had been restricted to heavy petting with occasional girlfriends. (Lambley, 1974, p. 101)

Sexual arousal while cross-dressing is an important criterion in the diagnosis of transvestic fetishism. If arousal is not present or has disappeared over time, a more appropriate diagnosis may be gender identity disorder. This distinction, however, may be difficult to make. Some transsexuals show penile erections to descriptions of cross-dressing (Blanchard, Racansky & Steiner, 1986). Whether sexual arousal occurs in cross-dressing therefore may not serve as a valid distinction between transsexualism and transvestic fetishism. If the cross-dressing occurs only during the course of a gender identity disorder, the person is not considered in the category of transvestic fetishism.

Male transvestites often wear feminine garments or undergarments during sexual intercourse with their

Sexual arousal from such inanimate objects as female undergarments or shoes has become increasingly open and acceptable in our society. Many adult-oriented stores cater to this fetish either by selling these objects directly or by selling magazines, videos, or pictures that display them.

wives, as described by Newman and Stoller (1974, p. 438):

> He continued to have sexual intercourse (while clad in a woman's nightgown) with his wife, while imagining that they were no longer man and wife, but rather two women engaged in a lesbian relationship. He especially enjoyed it when she cooperated with his idea and referred to him by his chosen feminine name.

Many transvestites believe that they have alternating masculine and feminine personalities. In a feminine role, they can play out such behavior patterns as buying nightgowns and trying on fashionable clothes. They may introduce their wives to their female personalities and urge them to go on shopping trips together as women (Buckner, 1970). Other transvestites cross-dress only for the purposes of sexual arousal

and masturbation and do not fantasize themselves as members of the opposite sex.

Paraphilias Involving Nonconsenting Persons

This category of disorders involves persistent and powerful sexual fantasies about unsuspecting strangers or acquaintances. The victims are nonconsenting in that they do not choose to be the objects of the attention or sexual behavior.

Exhibitionism   **Exhibitionism** is characterized by urges, acts, or fantasies about the exposure of one's genitals to a stranger. Often the person wants to shock the unsuspecting victim, as this case shows:

> A nineteen-year-old single white college man reported that he had daily fantasies of exposing and had exposed himself on three occasions. The first occurred when he masturbated in front of the window of his dormitory room, when women would be passing by. The other two acts occurred in his car; in each case he asked young women for directions, and then exposed his penis and masturbated when they approached. He felt a great deal of anxiety in the presence of women and dated infrequently. (Hayes, Brownell & Barlow, 1983)

Exhibitionism is relatively common. The exhibitionist is most often male and the victim female. Surveys of selected groups of young women in the United States have indicated that between one-third and one-half have been victims of exhibitionists (Cox & McMahon, 1978). Although most women did not report any psychological traumas associated with the episodes, about 40 percent indicated being moderately to severely distressed, and 11 percent believed the incident had negatively affected their attitude toward men (Cox, 1988).

Unlike normal (control) subjects, exhibitionists are sexually aroused by sexually neutral scenes such as women knitting, ironing, or sweeping (Kolarsky & Madlatfousek, 1983). Similar findings were obtained by Fedora, Reddon, and Yeudall (1986), who monitored sexual arousal in exhibitionists, normal controls, and nonexhibitionist sex offenders. Only the exhibitionists responded sexually to scenes of fully clothed erotically neutral women. Fedora hypothesized that exhibitionists may be aroused by female uncooperativeness or neutrality.

The main goal of the exhibitionist seems to be the sexual arousal he gets by exposing himself; most exhibitionists want no further contact. However, there may be two types of exhibitionists—those who engage in criminal behavior and those who do not. The former tend to be sociopathic and impulsive, and they may be more likely to show aggression (Forgac & Michaels, 1982; Forgac, Cassel & Michaels, 1984).

Exhibitionists may expect to produce surprise, sexual arousal, or disgust in the victim. The act may involve exposing a limp penis or masturbating an erect penis. In a study of ninety-six exhibitionists, only 50 percent reported that they "almost always" or "always" had erections when exposing, although a large percentage of the men wanted the women to be impressed with the size of their penis. Fantasies about being watched and admired by female observers were common among exhibitionists. More than two-thirds reported that they would not have sex with the victim even if she were receptive (Langevin et al., 1979).

Most exhibitionists are in their twenties—far from being the "dirty old men" of popular myth. Most are married. Their exhibiting has a compulsive quality to it, and they report that they feel a great deal of anxiety about the act. A typical exposure sequence involves the person first entertaining sexually arousing memories of previous exposures and then returning to the area where previous exposures took place. Next, the person locates a suitable victim, rehearses the exposure mentally, and finally exposes himself. As the person moves through his sequence, his self-control weakens and disappears (Abel, Levis & Clancy, 1970). Alcohol use before the act of exhibiting occurs in many cases, perhaps to reduce inhibitions (Arndt, 1991).

Voyeurism Voyeurism comprises urges, acts, or fantasies involving observation of an unsuspecting person disrobing or engaging in sexual activity. "Peeping," as voyeurism is sometimes termed, is considered deviant when it includes serious risk, is done in socially unacceptable circumstances, or is preferred to coitus. The typical voyeur is not interested in looking at his wife or girlfriend; about 95 percent of the cases of voyeurism involve strangers. Observation alone produces sexual arousal and excitement, and the voyeur often masturbates during this surreptitious activity (Katchadourian & Lunde, 1975).

The voyeur is like the exhibitionist in that sexual contact is not the goal; viewing an undressed body is the primary motive. However, a voyeur may also exhibit or use other indirect forms of sexual expression (Abel, Levis & Clancy, 1970). Because the act is repetitive, arrest is predictable. Usually an accidental witness or the victim notifies the police. Potential rapists or burglars who behave suspiciously are often arrested as voyeurs.

The proliferation of sexually oriented television programs, "romance" paperbacks, explicit sexual magazines, and X-rated movies all point to the voyeuristic nature of our society. The growing number of "night clubs" featuring male exotic dancers and attended by women may indicate women's increasing interest in men's bodies and their acknowledgment that it is all right to be sexual.

Frotteurism Whereas physical contact is not the goal of voyeurism, contact is the primary motive in frotteurism. *Frotteurism* involves recurrent and intense sexual urges, acts, or fantasies of touching or rubbing against a nonconsenting person. The touching, not the coercive nature of the act, is the sexually exciting feature. As in the case of the other paraphilias, the person has acted on the urges or is markedly distressed by them.

Pedophilia Pedophilia is a disorder in which an adult obtains erotic gratification through urges, acts, or fantasies involving sexual contact with a prepubescent child. According to DSM-IV, to be diagnosed with this disorder, the person must be at least sixteen

When 1950s' rock star Jerry Lee Lewis married a thirteen-year-old girl, it created a furor in Great Britain, where many considered him a pedophiliac. The public's outrage resulted in the cancellation of many of his concerts, forcing him to return to New York. Lewis was twenty-two at the time of this marriage and not yet divorced from his second wife.

years of age and at least five years older than the victim. Pedophiles may victimize their own children (incest), stepchildren, or those outside the family. Most pedophiles prefer girls, although a few choose prepubertal boys.

Sexual abuse of children is common. Between 20 and 30 percent of women reported having had a childhood sexual encounter with an adult man. And, contrary to the popular view of the child molester as a stranger, most pedophiles are relatives, friends, or casual acquaintances of their victims (Herman & Hirschman, 1981; Zverina et al., 1987).

In most cases of abuse, only one adult and one child are involved, but cases involving several adults or groups of children have been reported. For example, a 54-year-old man, a person who had won a community award for his work with youths, was arrested for child molestation involving boys as young as ten years old. The man encouraged and photographed sexual acts between the boys, including mutual masturbation and oral and anal sex. He then would have sex with one of them (Burgess et al., 1984).

A study of 229 convicted child molesters revealed the following information. Nearly one-fourth of their victims were younger than six years of age. Another 25 percent were ages six to ten, and about 50 percent were ages eleven to thirteen. Fondling the child was the most common sexual behavior, followed by vaginal and oral-genital contact. Bribery was often used to gain the cooperation of the victims (Erickson, Walbek & Seely, 1988). Pedophiles have a relapse rate of approximately 35 percent, the highest among sex offenders (Erickson et al., 1987).

Child victims of sexual abuse show a variety of physical symptoms such as urinary tract infections, poor appetite, and headaches. Reported psychological symptoms include nightmares, difficulty in sleeping, a decline in school performance, acting-out behaviors, and sexually focused behavior. One boy was overheard asking another to take down his pants, which was the request made by the person who had molested him (Burgess, Groth & McCausland, 1981). Some child victims show the symptoms of posttraumatic stress disorder. In a sample of sixty-six victims, forty-five reported experiencing flashbacks of the molestation. They also demonstrated diminished responsiveness to their environment, hyperalertness, and jumpiness (Burgess et al., 1984). The First Person narrative in this chapter discusses child sexual abuse from a prosecutor's point of view.

On psychological tests such as the Minnesota Multiphasic Personality Inventory (MMPI), child molesters tend to have profiles indicating passive-dependent personality, discomfort in social situations, impulsiveness, and alcoholism (Erickson et al., 1987).

Compared with control group members, child molesters are deficient in social skills. They also display a significantly higher fear of negative evaluation (Overholser & Beck, 1986). Some studies found that pedophiles tend to score on the low end of normal on intelligence tests, and some show left hemispheric problems in brain functioning (Langevin, 1990), although brain dysfunction as a cause of the disorder is still speculative. Pedophiles display sexual arousal to slides of young children and report having fantasies involving children during masturbation (Alford et al., 1987). More than 50 percent of one sample of child molesters reported using "hard core" pornography to excite themselves in preparing to commit an offense (Marshall, 1988).

Some cases of child abuse are also incest. We cover that topic in more detail at the end of this chapter.

Paraphilias Involving Pain or Humiliation

Pain and humiliation do not appear to be related to normal sexual arousal. In sadism and masochism, however, they play a prominent role. **Sadism** is a form of paraphilia in which sexually arousing urges, fantasies, or acts are associated with inflicting physical or psychological suffering on others. The word *sadism* was coined from the name of the Marquis de Sade (1740–1814), a French nobleman who wrote extensively about the sexual pleasure he received by inflicting pain on women. The marquis himself was so cruel to his sexual victims that he was declared insane and jailed for twenty-seven years.

Masochism is a paraphilia in which sexual urges, fantasies, or acts are associated with being humiliated, bound, or made to suffer. The word *masochism* is derived from the name of a nineteenth-century Austrian novelist Leopold von Sacher-Masoch, whose fictional characters obtained sexual satisfaction only when pain was inflicted on them.

Sadistic behavior may range from the pretended or fantasized infliction of pain, through mild to severe cruelty toward partners, to an extremely dangerous pathological form of sadism that may involve mutilation or murder. Because of their passive roles, masochists are not considered dangerous. For some sadists and masochists, coitus becomes unnecessary; pain or humiliation alone is sufficient to produce sexual pleasure. As with other paraphilias, DSM-IV specifies that to receive the diagnosis the person must have acted on the urges or be markedly distressed by them.

In a study of 178 sadomasochists (47 women and 131 men), most reported engaging in and enjoying both submissive and dominant roles. Only 16 percent

FIRST PERSON

Mary Kay Barbieri

When I first graduated from law school in 1975, I went to work for King County prosecutor's office in Seattle, Washington. Before that time, cases of child abuse—especially in-family child sexual abuse—were not handled in the criminal justice system. They were treated as "social problems" and handled by Child Protective Services. But around 1975 a movement was afoot to start treating these abuses of children as crimes. Most prosecutors didn't want to handle the cases—they didn't know how to talk to children, they didn't think children could testify in court, and they often didn't believe the children because they didn't understand why they would let the abuse go on for such a long time without telling someone.

I volunteered for all the child sexual abuse cases I could get. I stocked my office with blocks and crayons and big floor cushions and spent hours sitting on the floor with children winning their trust and getting them to tell me about the terrible things that adults had done to them. I was appalled at what I heard from these children. People who were supposed to love or care for them—their parent or stepparent, grandpa or uncle, their teacher or Cub Scout leader or babysitter—these adults were performing every imaginable kind of sexual act with children. They usually started out by bribing the children and then invariably ended up threatening them to keep them from telling. The most common threats were "If you tell they'll think you're bad and they won't love you," or "If you tell I'll kill your mom." Kids always believed these threats, so usually they only disclosed the sexual abuse inadvertently. Fortunately, the school programs that now educate children will disclose abuse sooner.

I learned a lot about bravery from those children. Many of the offenders plead guilty before trial, but many don't, and then the children have to go to court and testify. Courtrooms just aren't made for children: They're big and austere and intimidating even for adults. So, a few days before the trial, I'd take the child to visit the courtroom when it was not in use. I'd have the child sit in the witness chair and swivel around and try out the microphone. I'd tell the child where the judge sat and what the court reporter did, and I'd prepare the child for the fact that the offender would be in court, too. That was always the hardest part, but by this time the child and I had spent a lot of time together and were friends. I'd say, "Don't worry, you don't have to look at him; just look at me instead." I put children as young as three years old on the witness stand. Yes, those children were brave.

I eventually set up a special unit in the prosecutor's office just to handle cases of child sexual abuse. The prosecutors were all trained to work with children and to understand the dynamics of child sexual abuse. As often happens when a program is set up to meet a perceived need, the caseload kept increasing and increasing. The unit became a national model, and my career benefited. Eventually I became the chief prosecutor in charge of the whole sixty-attorney prosecutor's office.

But I missed the kids. I'd always been a little envious of the therapists who worked with children. As a prosecutor my work ended with the trial, while the therapists got to go on helping the children. A lot of the process of preparing children for trial is "doing therapy," but I wished that I could be the one to go on working with the child, helping the child realize that it wasn't his or her fault, and doing the work that needed to be done to keep this experience from haunting the child on into adulthood. Finally I decided that if I wanted to be a therapist, I should become one. I left the practice of law and went to graduate school in clinical and counseling psychology. Now I still get to sit on the floor with blocks and crayons and pillows, and I don't have to stop doing it when the trial is over.

Mary Kay Barbieri was the former chief prosecutor for the King County prosecutor's office in Seattle, Washington. She is now a practicing therapist, specializing in cases involving child sexual abuse.

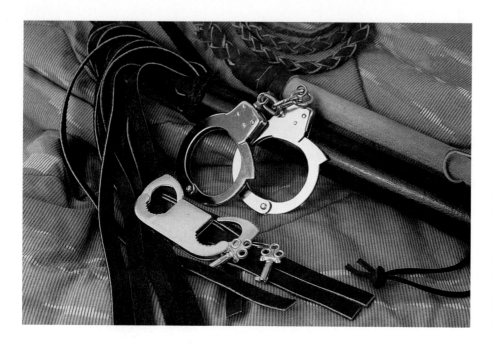

Pain and humiliation are associated with sexual satisfaction in sadism and masochism. Sadism involves inflicting pain on others; masochism involves receiving pain. Instruments used in sadomasochistic activities include handcuffs, whips, chains, and sharp objects.

were exclusively dominant or submissive. Many engaged in spanking, whipping, and bondage (see Table 10.3). Approximately 40 percent engaged in behaviors that caused minor pain using ice, hot wax, biting, or face slapping. Fewer than 18 percent engaged in more harmful procedures, such as burning or piercing. Nearly all respondents reported sadomasochistic (S&M) activities to be more satisfying than "straight" sex (Moser & Levitt, 1987). Most sadomasochists who have been studied report that they do not seek harm or injury but that they find the sensation of utter helplessness appealing (Baumeister, 1988). S&M activities are often carefully scripted and involve role playing and mutual consent by the participants (Weinberg, 1987). In addition, fantasies involving sexual abuse, rejection, and forced sex are not uncommon among both male and female college students (Sue, 1979). Most sadomasochistic behavior among college students involves very mild forms of pain (such as in biting or pinching) that are accepted in our society.

Sadomasochistic behavior is considered deviant when pain, either inflicted or received, is necessary for sexual arousal and orgasm. According to Kinsey and his associates (1953), 22 percent of men and 12 percent of women reported at least some sexual response to sadomasochistic stories. Janus and Janus (1993) reported that 14 percent of men and 11 percent of women have had at least some sadomasochism experiences.

Some cases of sadomasochism appear to be the result of an early experience associating sexual arousal with pain. One masochistic man reported that as a

child he was often "caned" on the buttocks by a school headmaster as his "attractive" wife looked on (Money, 1987). He reported, "I got sexual feelings from around the age of twelve, especially if she was watching" (p. 273). He and some of his schoolmates later hired prostitutes to spank them. Later yet, he engaged in self-whipping.

Although the association of pain and sexual arousal can account for some cases of sadomasochistic behaviors, 80 percent of a sample of sadomasochists did not remember a link between physical punishment during childhood and erotic sensations (Weinberg, 1987). Langevin (1990) and Langevin and associates (1988) found that sadists were more likely than nonsadistic but sexually aggressive men and nonsexual offenders (controls) to have anomalies in the right temporal portions of the brain—brain areas that play a role in sexual behavior. They speculate that brain pathology and life experiences may underlie sadism.

In addition to the paraphilias covered here, DSM-IV lists many others under the category of "not otherwise specified" paraphilias. They include *telephone scatalogia* (making obscene telephone calls) and sexual urges involving corpses *(necrophilia)*, animals *(zoophilia)*, or feces *(coprophilia)*.

Etiology and Treatment of Paraphilias

All etiological theories for the paraphilias must answer three questions (Finkelhor & Araji, 1986). (1) What produced the deviant arousal pattern? (2) Why doesn't the person develop a more appropriate outlet for his or her sexual drive? (3) Why is the behavior not deterred by normative and legal prohibitions? So far, biogenic, psychoanalytic, and behavioral perspectives have provided only partial answers, and a number of behavioral strategies have emerged for treating the paraphilias.

Biogenic Perspective Earlier, we noted that investigators have attempted to find genetic, neurohormonal, and brain anomalies that might be associated with sexual disorders. Some of the research findings conflict; others need replication and confirmation (Nevid et al., 1995). In any event, researchers need to continue applying advanced technological techniques in the study of the biogenic influences on sexual disorders. Even if biogenic factors are found to be important in the cause of these disorders, psychological contributions are also likely to play an important role.

Psychoanalytic Perspective In psychoanalytic theory, all sexual deviations symbolically represent unconscious conflicts that began in early childhood. Castration anxiety is hypothesized to be an important etiological factor underlying transvestic fetishism and exhibitionism, sadism, and masochism. It occurs, say psychoanalysts, when the oedipal complex is not fully resolved. Because the boy's incestuous desires are only partially repressed, he fears retribution from his father in the form of castration. If this is the case, many sexual deviations can be seen as attempts to protect the person from castration anxiety. For example, in transvestic fetishism, acknowledging that women lack a penis raises the fear of castration. To refute this possibility, the male transvestite "restores" the penis to women through cross-dressing. In this manner, he unconsciously represents a "woman who has a penis" and therefore reduces the fear of castration (Shave, 1976). An item of clothing or a particular fetish is selected because it represents a phallic symbol (Arndt, 1991).

Similarly, an exhibitionist exposes to reassure himself that castration has not occurred. The shock that registers on the faces of others assures him that he still has a penis. A sadist may protect himself from castration anxiety by inflicting pain (power equals penis). A masochist may engage in self-castration through the acceptance of pain, thereby limiting the power of others to castrate him. Because castration anxiety stems from an unconscious source, the fear is never completely allayed, however, and so the person feels compelled to repeat deviant sexual acts.

The psychoanalytic treatment of sexual deviations involves helping the patient understand the relation-

Activity	Male	Female
Spanking	79	80
Master-slave relationships	79	76
Oral sex	77	90
Bondage	67	88
Humiliation	65	61
Restraint	60	83
Anal sex	58	51
Pain	51	34
Whipping	47	39
Use of rubber or leather	42	42
Enemas	33	22
Torture	32	32
Golden showers (urination)	30	37

TABLE 10.3 Sadomasochistic Activities, Ranked by Selected Samples of Male and Female Participants

Source: Data from Brewslow, Evans & Langley, 1986.

These sadomasochistic sexual preferences were reported by both male and female respondents. Many more men express a preference for S&M activities, but women who do so are likely to engage in this form of sexual behavior more frequently and with many more partners.

ship between the deviation and the unconscious conflict that produced it. To treat the man whose fetish was wearing an apron before he could engage in sexual intercourse, the therapist used dream analysis and free association. These techniques helped him and the patient understand the "roots" of his behavior, which they interpreted as follows: The apron was made by his mother from a boiler suit that belonged to his father's mother. Because the patient's relationship with his mother produced castration anxiety, the fetish accomplished two purposes. First, it allowed him to reduce castration anxiety by denying that women do not have penises (the apron symbolized a "penis" that was cut out of the body of another woman). Second, a "penis" (the apron) was returned to him (Kohon, 1987). The psychoanalyst helped the patient bring the conflicts into conscious awareness through interpretation. After this, the patient gained insight into his behavior and was able to work through his problem.

Behavioral Perspective Learning theorists stress the importance of early conditioning experiences in the etiology of sexually deviant behaviors. One such conditioning experience is masturbating while engaged in sexually deviant fantasies, combined with lack of social skills that hamper the development of normal sexual patterns. For example, one boy developed a fetish for women's panties at age twelve after he became sexually excited watching girls come down a slide with their underpants exposed. He began to masturbate to fantasies of girls with their panties showing and had this fetish for twenty-one years before seeking treatment (Kushner, 1965). In another example, two young men became sexually aroused while urinating in a semiprivate area after they were surprised by women passing by. The accidental association between sexual arousal and exposure resulted in exhibitionism (McGuire, Carlisle & Young, 1965). These reports must be interpreted carefully because they are extracted from case studies and do not originate from controlled research.

Experimental support for the possible role of conditioning in the development of a fetish was demonstrated by Rachman (1966). Three men were shown a picture of a pair of women's black boots and then were shown slides of nude women, which produced sexual arousal (as measured by penile volume). Initially, the picture of boots did not elicit any increases in penile volume. But after slides of boots and nude women were paired several times (classical conditioning), all three subjects developed conditioned sexual arousal at the sight of the boots alone. Although the conditioned responses were weak, they could have been strengthened by masturbating while the boots were shown.

Laws and Marshall (1990) believe that the conditioning process may involve the concept of "preparedness." Unconditioned and conditioned stimuli, as well as responses and reinforcers, are not associated with equal ease. Organisms appear to be prepared to learn to associate some stimuli with some reinforcers rather than with others. For example, rats can learn to avoid the *taste* of a certain food if they experienced nausea after eating the food. However, they could not learn to associate the *sight* of food (in the absence of tasting it) with nausea, when the sight of food was paired with nausea (Garcia, McGowan & Green, 1972). Thus stimuli may vary in the extent to which they can be conditioned (that is, preparedness). Preparedness may depend on the survival value of the elements to be learned. Under this theory, human beings are less prepared to condition to, or find as sexually attrac-

tive, neutral objects (such as women's boots) than an opposite-sex person. Nevertheless, such conditioning may occur in some people.

Learning approaches to treating sexual deviations have generally involved one or more of the following elements: (1) weakening or eliminating the sexually inappropriate behaviors through processes such as extinction or aversive conditioning; (2) acquiring or strengthening sexually appropriate behaviors; and (3) developing appropriate social skills. The following case illustrates this multiple approach:

> A 27-year-old man with a three-year history of pedophilic activities (fondling and cunnilingus) with four- to seven-year-old girls was treated through the following procedure. The man first masturbated to orgasm while exposed to stimuli involving adult females. He then masturbated to orgasm while listening to a relaxation tape, and then masturbated (but not to orgasm) to deviant stimuli. The procedure allowed the strengthening of normal arousal patterns and lessened the ability to achieve an orgasm while exposed to deviant stimuli (extinction). Measurement of penile tumescence when exposed to the stimuli indicated a sharp decrease to pedophilic stimuli and high arousal to heterosexual stimuli. These changes were maintained over a twelve-month follow-up period. (Alford et al., 1987)

One of the more unique treatments for exhibitionism is the *aversive behavior rehearsal (ABR)* program developed by Wickramasekera (1976). This "shame aversion" technique uses shame or humiliation as the aversive stimulus. The technique requires that the patient exhibit himself in his usual manner to a preselected audience of women. During the exhibiting act, the patient must verbalize a conversation between himself and his penis. He must talk about what he is feeling emotionally and physically and must explain his fantasies regarding what he supposes the female observers are thinking about him.

The developer of ABR believes that exhibitionism often occurs when the person is in a hypnoticlike state. At that time, the exhibitionist's fantasies are extremely active and his judgment is impaired. The ABR method forces him to experience and examine his act while being fully aware of what he is doing (Kilmann et al., 1982).

The results of behavioral treatment have been generally positive, but the majority of the studies involved single subjects. Few control groups were included. Another problem in interpreting the results of these studies becomes apparent when we examine the approaches that were employed. For the most part, several different behavioral techniques were used within each study, so evaluation of a particular technique is impossible.

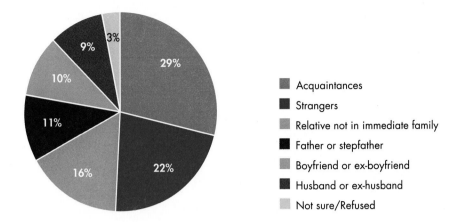

FIGURE 10.6 Who Perpetrates Rape? As these figures suggest, the person who rapes is likely to be known to the victim. Only 22 percent of rapists are strangers and unknown to the victim.

Source: Data from National Victim Center, 1992.

SEXUAL AGGRESSION

Sexual coercion is a broad term used to encompass any or all forms of *sexual pressure* (pleading, arguing, cajoling, or force or threat of force). *Sexual aggression* refers to a narrower class of actions, such as rape, incest, and any type of *sexual activity* (petting, oral-genital sex, anal intercourse, and sexual intercourse) performed against a person's will through the use of force, argument, pressure, alcohol or drugs, or authority (Strong & DeVault, 1994). In this section, we discuss two forms of sexual aggression: rape and incest.

Rape

Considerable controversy exists on whether rape is primarily a crime of violence or sex (Marsh, 1988). Feminists have challenged the belief that rape is an act of sexual deviance; they make a good case that it is truly an act of violence and aggression against women. The principal motive, they believe, is that of power, not sex (Strong & DeVault, 1994). **Rape** is an act of intercourse accomplished through force or threat of force. The Federal Bureau of Investigation (FBI) uses a more limited definition: "Carnal knowledge of a female forcibly and against her consent." This definition fails to include behavior between individuals of the same sex and with males as victim, which certainly does occur. Most states extend their definition of rape to include *statutory rape*—sexual intercourse with a girl younger than a certain age.

FBI statistics reveal that the number of rapes in the United States has risen dramatically—more than 102,000 cases were reported in 1990; that is an average of one rape every five minutes (FBI, 1991; U.S. Senate Committee on the Judiciary, 1991). However, only about 16 percent of reported cases have resulted in a conviction for this crime in past decades. Another 4 percent of those charged with rape were convicted of lesser offenses (Rabkin, 1979). The low conviction rate and the humiliation and shame involved in a rape trial keep many women from reporting rapes, so the actual incidence of the crime is probably much higher than reported. Some experts believe that approximately 90 percent of rapes go unreported (Gibbs, 1991) and that this number is rising faster than reported rapes (U.S. Senate Committee on the Judiciary, 1991).

Some police officers still believe that rape victims are partly to blame because of their manner of dress or behavior, and these officers endorse such statements as "Most charges of rape are unfounded" and "Nice women do not get raped" (LeDoux & Hazelwood, 1985). Estimates based on surveys indicate that as many as one of every five women will be a rape victim at some time during her life (Sorenson & Siegel, 1992). Most rape victims are young women in their teens or twenties, although victims as young as several years old and as old as seventy-three have been reported (Burgess & Holmstrom, 1979). In approximately one-half of all rape cases, the victim is at least acquainted with the rapist and is attacked in the home or in an automobile (Kilpatrick, Veronen & Resick, 1979). Figure 10.6 illustrates the relationships

Rape is an act of violence and aggression. Rape crisis centers and counselors like the women pictured here provide moral, emotional, and often legal support to victims.

between victim and rapist, drawing on data from the National Victim Center. As that figure shows, the form of rape reported most frequently is "acquaintance" or "date" rape, as in the following case:

> Colleen, twenty-seven, a San Francisco office manager, had been involved with her boyfriend for about a year when it happened. After a cozy dinner at her apartment, he suggested that she go to bed while he did the dishes. But a few moments later he stalked into Colleen's bedroom with a peculiar look on his face, brandishing a butcher knife and strips of cloth. After tying her, spread-eagled, to the bed, the formerly tender lover raped her brutally for three hours. When it was all over, he fell soundly asleep. (Seligman et al., 1984, p. 91)

Date rape may account for the majority of all rapes. Many victims may be reluctant to report such an attack; they feel responsible—at least in part—because they made a date with their attacker. Statistics vary as to the incidence of date rapes. Between 8 and 25 percent of female college students have reported that they had "unwanted sexual intercourse," and studies have generally found that most college women had experienced some unwanted sexual activity (Craig, 1990). Estimates vary from study to study because of different definitions of rape and intercourse as presented by the researchers, as well as the willingness or unwillingness of women to participate in surveys or to accurately report their experiences.

Craig (1990) argued that men who try to coerce women into intercourse have certain characteristics. They tend to (1) actively create the situation in which sexual encounters may occur; (2) interpret women's friendliness as provocation or their protests as insincerity; (3) try to manipulate women into sexual favors by using drugs or alcohol; and (4) attribute failures to succeed to perceived negative features of the woman, thereby protecting their egos. Many men who do not rape may also have these characteristics. Indeed, when asked to indicate the likelihood that they would rape if assured that they would not be caught and punished, about 35 percent of college males reported some likelihood and 20 percent indicated fairly high likelihood (Malamuth, 1981).

Should intercourse between a couple be considered rape if the woman did not want to engage in that activity? One police official, in reacting to the high number of rapes reported in his community, noted, "We definitely do not have a serious rape problem in this city. The problem is in the classification. If you took all our rapes one by one, you'd see that nine of ten are a girlfriend-boyfriend thing. These people are known to each other" (Girard, 1984, p. 12). The erroneous assumption made by that police official is that forced intercourse between acquaintances should not be considered rape. Unfortunately, sexual aggression by men is quite common. Fifteen percent of a sample of college men reported that they did force intercourse at least once or twice. Only 39 percent of the men did not admit to any coerced sex (Rapaport & Burkhart, 1984). Of 6,159 male and female students enrolled in thirty-two universities in the United States, more than 50 percent of the women reported being the victims of sexual aggression, and 8 percent of men admitted to committing sexual acts that met the legal definition of rape. Women seldom reported episodes of date rape (Koss, Gidycz & Wisniewski, 1987). Many universities are conducting workshops for students to help them understand that intercourse without consent during a date or other social activity is rape.

Effects of Rape   More than two-thirds of rape victims were not physically injured, 20 percent incurred minor physical injuries, and 4 percent suffered serious injuries (National Victim Center, 1992). However, the psychological scars from rape are often more devastating than the physical damage. Needless to say, rape is highly traumatic. Victims may experience a cluster of emotional reactions that are known as the *rape trauma syndrome;* they include psychological distress, phobic reactions, and sexual dysfunction (Burgess & Holstrom, 1974). These reactions are consistent with *post-traumatic stress disorder (PTSD)* (Bownes, O'Gorman & Sayers, 1991). Two phases have been identified in rape trauma syndrome:

Acute Phase: Disorganization   During this period of several or more weeks, the rape victim may have feelings of self-blame, fear, and depression. It may be characterized by a belief that the victim was responsible for the rape (for example, by not locking the door, wearing provocative clothing, or being overly friendly toward the attacker). The victim may have a strange fear that the attacker will return and anxiety that she may again be raped or even killed. These emotional reactions and beliefs may be directly expressed as anger, fear, rage, anxiety and/or depression or may be hidden. If the latter response occurs, the victim may appear amazingly calm. Beneath this exterior, however, are signs of tension, including headaches, irritability, restlessness, sleeplessness, and jumpiness (Nevid et al., 1995).

Long-Term Phase: Reorganization   This phase may last for several years. The victim begins to deal directly with her feelings and attempts to reorganize her life. Lingering fears and phobic reactions continue, especially to situations or events that remind the victim of the traumatic incident. A host of reactions may be present. In one sample of victims, more than 50 percent reported one or more sexual dysfunctions as the result of the rape; fear of sex and lack of desire or arousal were the most common. Some women recovered quickly, but others reported problems years after the episodes (Gilbert & Cunningham, 1986). A one-year follow-up of rape victims found that they were significantly more fearful than control groups. The fears were selective and involved

things such as darkness and enclosed places—conditions likely to be associated with rape (Calhoun, Atkeson & Resick, 1982). Duration and intensity of fear were also found to be related to perceptions of danger. Attacks in circumstances that the woman had defined as "safe" had a greater emotional impact than attacks in places the women felt were dangerous. Many women drastically changed their perception of how safe the environment really was (Scheppele & Bart, 1983).

In one survey, approximately two-thirds of rape victims reported that they could not resume sexual activity for at least six months (Burgess & Holstrom, 1979b). Their sexual enjoyment was strongly affected. One victim described it this way:

> It depends how I relate to the man. If I'm in a position to enjoy it—a 50-50 thing—then I'm OK. But if I'm feeling that I'm only doing this for him and not for my own enjoyment, then I feel like the incident again. . . . Then sex is bad.

Flashbacks were reported by 50 percent of the sexually active victims. These included fleeting memories that could not be repressed, reliving the experience, and associating the present sex partner with the rapist. Sympathetic understanding, nondemanding affection, and a positive attitude from the partner have been found beneficial. Hugging and gentle caressing are generally satisfying to the victim even if sexual approaches are aversive (Feldman-Summers, Gordon & Meagher, 1979).

In light of the severe sexual and psychological problems that a rape victim can experience, the availability of multiple support systems and counseling becomes very important. Most large cities now have rape crisis centers that provide counseling, as well as medical and legal information, to victims. Trained volunteers often accompany the victim to the hospital and to the police station. Women's organizations have made many hospital personnel and police officers more aware of the trauma of rape and have taught them to behave more sensitively when dealing with victims.

Etiology of Rape   Rape is not specifically listed in DSM-IV as a mental disorder because the act can have a variety of motivations. In an analysis of 133 rapists, Groth, Burgess, and Holstrom (1977) distinguished the three motivational types portrayed in Figure 10.7:

■ The *power rapist,* comprising 55 percent of those studied, is primarily attempting to compensate for feelings of personal or sexual inadequacy by trying to intimidate his victims.

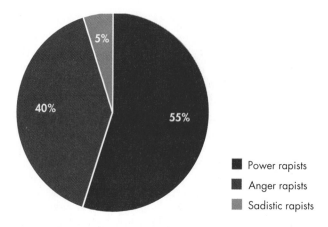

FIGURE 10.7 Three Types of Rapists Rape has less to do with sex than with aggression. These three types of rapists share many characteristics including the need for power, aggressiveness, and a propensity for violence.

Source: Data from Groth, Burgess & Holstrom, 1977.

■ The *anger rapist*, comprising 40 percent of those studied, is angry at women in general; the victim is merely a convenient target.

■ The *sadistic rapist*, comprising only 5 percent of those studied, derives satisfaction from inflicting pain on the victim and may torture or mutilate her.

These findings tend to support the contention that rape has more to do with power, aggression, and violence than with sex. In fact, a study of more than one hundred rapists indicated that 58 percent showed some sexual dysfunction, such as erectile difficulties, during the attack (Groth, Burgess & Holstrom, 1977).

Although these distinctions are of interest, little empirical research was done on the importance of aggressive cues in the sexual arousal of rapists until a study performed by Abel and colleagues (1977). These investigators recorded the degree of penile erection of rapists and nonrapists in response to two-minute audiotapes describing violent and nonviolent sexual scenes. The nonviolent tape described an incident of mutually enjoyable sexual intercourse. The violent tape described a rape in which the man forced himself on an unwilling woman. The rapists were aroused by both tape descriptions, whereas the nonrapists displayed a significantly lesser degree of erection in response to the portrayal of violent sex, preferring the scene involving mutually enjoyable sex. Some rapists in the study also showed strong sexual arousal in response to another tape that was entirely aggressive in content.

Researchers initially thought that only sadists or rapists would show a sexual arousal pattern to audiotapes or slides of aggressive sex. Later studies showed that certain groups of men who are not rapists also respond sexually to aggressive cues. In addition, a portrayal of the woman as taking physical pleasure in the attack also increases sexual response in some men. Here are the results of some of these studies:

1. College men with sadistic tendencies rated slides of women displaying emotional distress (fear, anger, disgust, sadness) as more sexually arousing than did nonsadistic men (Heilbrum & Loftus, 1986).

2. Men who admitted to being more likely to commit rape showed more erections when listening to audiotapes of dramatized sex between nonconsenting participants than when listening to scenes between consenting participants. Men who reported that they were not very likely to rape anyone showed the opposite pattern (Malamuth & Check, 1983).

3. When male students were exposed to a situation in which a woman is portrayed as being initially repelled but later responds sexually to rape, male students (but not females) became less sensitive to rape victims. They viewed the rapist as being less responsible for the act and deserving less punishment. They also showed desensitization to violent sex and were more likely to accept rape myths (Donnerstein & Linz, 1986).

Because of these findings, researchers are raising questions about the effect that media portrayals of violent sex, especially in pornography, have on rape rates. Exposure to such materials may affect attitudes and thoughts and influence patterns of sexual arousal (Malamuth & Briere, 1986). These media portrayals may reflect and affect societal values concerning violence and women.

Baron, Straus, and Jaffee (1988) proposed a "cultural spillover" theory—namely, that rape tends to be high in cultures or environments that encourage violence. The investigators studied the relationship between cultural support for violence, as well as demographic characteristics and rates of rapes in all fifty states. Rates of rape and cultural support for violence were measured in each state. The support for violence was determined by (1) the proportion of individuals who chose magazines and television programs involving violence; (2) the amount of legislation permitting corporal punishment in schools, the number of prisoners sentenced to death, and the number of executions for crimes; (3) National Guard enrollments; and (4) public opinion on such issues as favoring the

The incidence of date rape may be much higher than official figures indicate. The problem has become so serious on college campuses that workshops, such as the one shown here, aimed at education and prevention are often conducted for students. Such programs are also becoming common in high schools.

death penalty, opposing the requirement that gun owners obtain mandatory gun permits, and approving the punching of a stranger in a variety of situations. The researchers also examined demographic variables that could be related to rates of rape in each state, such as percentage of divorced or single males, percentage of women, age of individuals, social class, and race. Results indicated that cultural support for violence was significantly related to the rate of rape, independent of the effects of demographic variables. Having a high proportion of divorced and single men was also related to increased rates of rape. The percentage of African Americans residing in the state was unrelated to rape. The results suggested that when violence is generally encouraged or condoned, there is a "spillover" effect on rape.

As illustrated in the study by Baron, Straus, and Jaffee (1988), researchers are turning their attention to variables other than personality characteristics of rapists. The role of sociocultural variables is gaining increasing attention, particularly by feminists who see rape as a manifestation of male dominance and control of women (Sorenson & White, 1992). Other researchers have proposed integrative models that incorporate many different factors (Barabee & Marshall, 1991; Hall & Hirschman, 1991; Malamuth et al., 1991). See Critical Thinking for a discussion of controversial explanations for rape.

Incest

Incest may be defined as sexual relations between people too closely related to marry legally (Strong & DeVault, 1994); it is nearly universally taboo in human society. Estimates of the incidence of incest range from 48,000 to 250,000 cases per year (Stark, 1984). The incidents of incest most frequently reported to law enforcement agencies involve those between a father and his daughter or stepdaughter. However, the most common incestuous relationship involves brother-sister incest, not parent-child incest (Waterman & Lusk, 1986). Less than 0.5 percent of the women in this study reported sexual contact with their fathers. Mother-son incest seems to be rare. In another study, sexual activities between siblings were again found to be relatively frequent: 15 percent of the women and 10 percent of the men reported that they had had sexual involvement with their siblings. In 75 percent of these cases, mutual consent was involved. About half considered the experience positive; the other half, negative (Finkelhor, 1980).

Most research has focused on father-daughter incest. This type of incestuous relationship generally begins when the daughter is between six and eleven years old, and it continues for at least two years (Stark, 1984). Unlike sex between siblings, father-daughter incest is always exploitative. The girl is espe-

WHY DO MEN RAPE WOMEN?

In 1995, former world heavyweight boxing champ Mike Tyson was released from prison after serving a sentence for raping a beauty contestant in his hotel room. Here was a man who made his living via physical dominance and force. During his trial, "talk radio" and the print media were filled with speculations about his motives and responsibility for the event. Some claimed that Tyson was only minimally responsible because the woman had willingly gone to his hotel room. Others placed the blame on boxing itself, saying the activity condones aggression, even sexual aggression. Still others speculated that Tyson was oversexed, that his testosterone levels were high, or that he acted out because of steroid use.

In science as in the media, many explanations and theories attempt to explain why men rape women. As a useful and interesting class exercise, we invite you to engage in a mock trial based on the Tyson case. There are two major perspectives on rape. After reading about them, divide yourselves into two camps to argue the two viewpoints.

Sociocultural Perspective A variety of views of the causes of rape have been proposed, as noted by Sorenson and White (1992). Some researchers theorized that rape was committed by mentally disturbed men, and studies were initiated to find personality characteristics that might be associated with rape. When Malamuth (1981) published survey results indicating that a significant proportion of men would consider rape if they could get away with it, the view that rapists were simply mentally disturbed individuals began to change.

Sociocultural views then gained favor. Brownmiller (1975) argued that rape was a means of control and dominance, whereby men keep women in a perpetual state of intimidation. This view emphasized a "culture" of male dominance rather than a sexual motive as a primary reason for sexual assault. For example, a permissive attitude toward violence (Baron, Straus & Jaffee, 1988) or rigid gender roles and societal dependency on men (Lisak, 1991) may be factors in rape.

Other theorists believe that social myths embedded in our culture reinforce themes that underlie rape: (a) that women have an unconcious desire to be overpowered and raped; (b) that women "ask for it" by dressing in provocative clothing, visiting a man's room, or going where they should not go; (c) that women could avoid rape if they wanted to; (d) that only "bad girls" get raped; and (d) that women only "cry rape" for revenge (Byers & Enos, 1991; Stock, 1991; Lisak, 1991).

cially vulnerable because she depends on her father for emotional support. As a result, the victims often feel guilty and powerless. Their problems continue into adulthood and are reflected in their high rates of drug abuse, sexual dysfunction, and psychiatric problems (Emslie & Rosenfeld, 1983; Gartner & Gartner, 1988). Incest victims often have difficulty establishing trusting relationships with men. Incestuous relationships that were forceful, intrusive, or of a long duration are more likely to result in long-lasting negative effects (Herman, Russell & Trocki, 1986).

Three types of incestuous fathers have been described (Rist, 1979). The first is a socially isolated man who is highly dependent on his family for interpersonal relationships. His emotional dependency gradually evolves (and expands) into a sexual relationship with his daughter. The second type of incestuous father has a psychopathic personality and is completely indiscriminate in choosing sexual partners. The third type has pedophilic tendencies and is sexually involved with several children, including his daughter. In addition, incest victims have reported family patterns in which the father is violent and the mother is unusually powerless (Herman & Hirschman, 1981). Williams and Finkelhor (1990) noted that some studies have shown that incestuous fathers were more likely than nonincestuous fathers to have experienced childhood sexual abuse themselves, al-

Can you give examples that support or disprove the sociocultural perspective? Does the sociocultural perspective seem accurate to you?

Sociobiological Perspective There are different sociobiological models for sexual aggression and rape. One is that sexual aggression has an evolutionary basis, although biochemical differences between sex offenders and non–sex offenders have not been unequivocally proven (Hall & Hirschman, 1991). Ellis (1991) believes that sex differences have evolved as a means of maximizing the reproduction of the human species. According to this view, men have much more to gain in reproductive terms by being able to pass on their genes rapidly to a large number of women, which increases their chances of having offspring. Men's advantage is women's disadvantage, however. Because women must bear much more of the investment in each offspring before and after birth, natural selection would favor women whose mates are likely to supply a greater share of the investment in offspring. Therefore, it would be advantageous for women to avoid multiple partners and to seek male commitment. Ellis also argued that men's sex drive is stronger than women's, and cited as evidence these three points:

- Men in all societies have higher self-reported desires for copulation and other forms of sexual experiences.

- Males (including males in other species of primates) masturbate more, especially in the absence of sex partners.

- Women are more likely than men to report having sexual intercourse for reasons other than sexual gratification.

Ellis took issue with the view that rape is not a sexual crime. He agreed that rapists often try to obtain sex by actions such as getting women drunk and falsely pledging love; that they use physical force only after these other tactics fail; and that fewer men than women believe rape is motivated by power and anger. Nevertheless, sociobiological theories have difficulty explaining differences in rates of rape in different societies or changes in rates of rape over time, without references to cultural conditions or experiential factors. Ellis believes that the *motivation* for sexual assault is unlearned but that the *behavior* surrounding sexual assault is learned. Thus, sexual motivation (including the drive to rape) is innate. If sexual aggression is reinforced (or not punished), forced copulatory attempts will persist.

Do you think punishment is an effective deterrent to rape? Does the sociobiological perspective seem accurate to you?

Isolating and testing different propositions concerning sexual assault have been difficult. Even so, no one—not even those who believe that men have a stronger biological sexual drive—can excuse or condone such behavior. Research findings suggest that changes in the way men and women relate to one another, attitudes toward violence, and cultural practices can reduce the incidence of rape.

though the phenomenon has not been found in many cases. They also found that incestuous fathers tend to have difficulties in empathy, nurturance, caretaking, social skills, and masculine identification.

Treatment for Incest Offenders and Rapists

Conventional Treatment Imprisonment has been the main form of treatment for incest offenders and for rapists. However, it is more accurate to describe it as punishment since the majority of convicts receive little or no treatment in prison (Goleman, 1992). In some cases of incest, an effort is usually made to keep the family intact for the benefit of the child. Behavioral treatment for sexual aggressors (rapists and pedophiles) generally involves the following steps:

1. Assessing sexual preferences through self-report and measuring erectile responses to different sexual stimuli

2. Reducing deviant interests through aversion therapy (the man receives electric shock when deviant stimuli are presented)

3. Orgasmic reconditioning or masturbating training to increase sexual arousal to appropriate stimuli

4. Social skills training to increase interpersonal competence

5. Assessment after treatment (Marshall et al., 1983)

Although treatment is becoming more sophisticated, questions remain about the effectiveness of these programs. In general, some treatment programs have been effective with child molesters and exhibitionists, although with rapists, treatment outcomes have often been poor (Marshall et al., 1991).

Public revulsion and outrage against incest offenders, pedophiles, and rapists have resulted in a call for severe punishment. A man who had an incestuous relationship with his stepdaughter for seven years was ordered by the judge to receive injections of the hormone progesterone to control his sex drive. This judicial ruling caused an uproar. Some groups believed the punishment was inadequate, some believed it would not work, and others indicated it was "cruel and unusual."

Controversial Treatments Surgical castration has been used to treat sexual offenders in many European countries, and results indicate that rates of relapse have been low (Marshall et al., 1991). An investigation of sex offenders (rapists, heterosexual pedophiles, homosexual pedophiles, bisexual pedophiles, and a sexual murderer) who were surgically castrated reported a decrease in sexual intercourse, masturbation, and frequency of sexual fantasies. However, twelve of the thirty-nine were still able to engage in sexual intercourse several years after being castrated. The rapists constituted the group whose members were most likely to remain sexually active (Heim, 1981).

Chemical therapy, usually involving the hormone Depo-Provera, reduces self-reports of sexual urges in pedophiles but not the ability to show genital arousal. Drugs appear to reduce psychological desire more than actual erection capabilities (Wincze, Bansal & Malamud, 1986). The effectiveness of biological treatment such as surgery and chemotherapy is not known, and controversy obviously continues over the appropriate treatment for incest offenders, pedophiles, and rapists.

SUMMARY

1. One of the difficulties in diagnosing abnormal sexual behavior is measuring it against a standard of normal sexual behavior. No attempt to establish such criteria has been completely successful, but these attempts have produced a better understanding of the normal human sexual response cycle. That cycle has four stages, the appetitive, excitement, orgasm, and resolution phases. Each may be characterized by problems, which may be diagnosed as disorders if they are recurrent and persistent.

2. Many myths and misunderstandings continue to surround homosexuality. The belief that homosexuality is deviant seems to relate more to homophobia than to scientific findings. DSM-IV no longer considers homosexuality to be a psychological disorder.

3. Despite myths to the contrary, sexuality extends into old age. However, sexual dysfunction becomes increasingly prevalent with aging, and the frequency of sexual activity typically declines.

4. Sexual dysfunctions are disruptions of the normal sexual response cycle. They are fairly common in the general population and may affect a person's ability to become sexually aroused or to engage in intercourse. Many result from fear or anxiety regarding sexual activities; the various treatment programs are generally successful.

5. Gender identity disorder involves a strong and persistent cross-gender identification. Transsexuals feel a severe psychological conflict between their sexual self-concept and their gender. Some transsexuals seek sex-conversion surgery, although behavioral therapies are increasingly being used. Gender identity disorder can also occur in childhood. Children with this problem identify with members of the opposite gender, deny their own physical attributes, and often cross-dress. Treatment generally includes the parents and is behavioral in nature.

6. The paraphilias are of three types, characterized by (a) a preference for nonhuman objects for sexual arousal, (b) repetitive sexual activity with nonconsenting partners, or (c) the association of real or simulated suffering with sexual activity. Suggested causes of the paraphilias are unconscious conflicts (the psychodynamic perspective) and conditioning, generally during childhood. Biological factors such as hormonal or brain processes have also been studied, but the results have not been consistent enough to permit strong conclusions about the role of biogenic factors in the paraphilias. Treatments are usually behavioral and are aimed at eliminating the deviant behavior while teaching more appropriate behaviors.

7. Sexual aggression such as rape and incest are not listed in DSM-IV but are serious problems. There appears to be no single cause for these deviations, and rapists seem to have different motivations and personalities. Some researchers feel that sociocultural factors can encourage rape and violence against women; others believe that biogenic factors coupled with sociocultural factors are important in explaining rape. In the case of incest, which involves sexual relations between close relatives, most research has examined father-daughter incest. Several types of incestuous fathers have been identified, which points again to the likelihood that incest is caused by different factors.

KEY TERMS

dyspareunia Recurrent or persistent pain in the genitals before, during, or after sexual intercourse

exhibitionism Disorder characterized by urges, acts, or fantasies about the exposure of one's genitals to a stranger

female orgasmic disorder A sexual dysfunction in which the woman experiences persistent delay or inability to achieve an orgasm with stimulation that is adequate in focus, intensity, and duration after entering the excitement phase; also known as *inhibited orgasm*

fetishism Sexual attraction and fantasies involving inanimate objects, such as female undergarments

frotteurism Disorder characterized by recurrent and intense sexual urges, acts, or fantasies of touching or rubbing against a nonconsenting person.

gender identity disorder Disorder characterized by conflict between a person's anatomical sex and his or her gender identity, or self-identification as male or female

incest Sexual relations between people too closely related to marry legally

male erectile disorder An inability to attain or maintain an erection sufficient for sexual intercourse

male orgasmic disorder The persistent delay or inability to achieve an orgasm after the excitement phase has been reached and sexual activity has been adequate in focus, intensity, and duration; usually restricted to the inability to ejaculate within the vagina (also known as *inhibited male orgasm*)

masochism A paraphilia in which sexual urges, fantasies, or acts are associated with being humiliated, bound, or made to suffer

paraphilias Sexual disorders of at least six months' duration, in which the person has either acted on or is severely distressed by recurrent urges or fantasies involving nonhuman objects, nonconsenting persons, or suffering or humiliation

pedophilia A disorder in which an adult obtains erotic gratification through urges, acts, or fantasies involving sexual contact with a prepubescent child

premature ejaculation Ejaculation with minimal sexual stimulation before, during, or shortly after penetration

rape An act of intercourse accomplished through force or threat of force

sadism Form of paraphilia in which sexually arousing urges, fantasies, or acts are associated with inflicting physical or psychological suffering on others

sexual arousal disorders Problems occurring during the excitement phase and relating to difficulties with feelings of sexual pleasure or with the physiological changes associated with sexual excitement

sexual desire disorders Sexual dysfunctions that are related to the appetitive phase and are characterized by a lack of sexual desire

sexual dysfunction A disruption of any part of the normal sexual response cycle

transsexualism A strong and persistent cross-gender identification and persistent discomfort with one's anatomical sex, which cause significant impairment in social, occupational, or other areas of functioning

transvestic fetishism Intense sexual arousal obtained through cross-dressing (wearing clothes appropriate to the opposite gender); not to be confused with transsexualism

vaginismus Involuntary spasm of the outer third of the vagina wall, preventing or interfering with sexual intercourse

voyeurism Urges, acts, or fantasies involving observation of an unsuspecting person disrobing or engaging in sexual activity

CHAPTER 11

MOOD DISORDERS

All of us have experienced moods involving depression or elation at some time during our lives. The loss of a job or the death of a loved one may result in depression; good news may make us manic (for example, ecstatic, hyperactive, and brazen). How do we know if these reactions are normal or manifestations of a serious mental disorder? In general, we should be concerned if the reaction pervades every aspect of a person's life, persists over a long period of time, or occurs for no apparent reason, for these are signs of a mood disorder.

Mood disorders are disturbances in emotions that cause subjective discomfort, hinder a person's ability to function, or both. Depression and mania are central to these disorders. **Depression** is characterized by intense sadness, feelings of futility and worthlessness, and withdrawal from others. **Mania** is characterized by elevated mood, expansiveness, or irritability, often resulting in hyperactivity.

Depression is quite prevalent in the general population, and it is the most common complaint of individuals seeking mental health care (Gotlib, 1992; Strickland, 1992). Some 10 million Americans, and more than 100 million people worldwide, will experience clinical depression this year. In the large-scale Epidemiologic Catchment Area (ECA) survey, Weissman and her colleagues (1991) found that 2.3 percent of the adult male population and 5 percent of the adult female population in the United States had experienced a mood disorder over a one-year period. Slight ethnic differences were found, but regardless of ethnicity, women were far more likely than men to experience a mood disorder (see Figure 11.1). Lifetime prevalence (the proportion of people who develop severe depression at some point in their lives) ranges from 10 to 25 percent for women and from 5 to 12 percent for men (American Psychiatric Association, 1994). A recent large-scale study has found even higher overall lifetime prevalence rates—reaching almost 20 percent—for all mood disorders among adult Americans (Kessler et al., 1994). Prevalence rates can be expected to differ from study to study because of methodological and conceptual variations; the important point is that depression is relatively common. Moreover, it may be a continuous phenomenon, waxing and waning. After one episode of depression, the likelihood of another is 50 percent; after two episodes, 70 percent; and after three episodes, 90 percent (Munoz et al., 1995). The prevalence of depression has been found to be over ten times higher than that of mania (Robins, Locke & Regier, 1991).

Severe depression does not respect socioeconomic status, educational attainments, or personal qualities; it may afflict rich or poor, successful or unsuccessful, highly educated or uneducated. The following case illustrates one woman's experience:

Amanda is a 39-year-old homemaker with three children, ages 9, 11, and 14. Her husband is the sales manager for an auto agency and the family does well financially and lives comfortably. For years, family life was stable and no serious problems existed between family members. The family could be described as cohesive and loving. However, Jim began to notice that his wife was becoming more and more unhappy and depressed. She constantly said that her life lacked purpose. Jim would try to reassure her, pointing out that they had a nice home and that she had no reason to be unhappy. He suggested that she find some hobbies or socialize more with their neighbors and friends. But Amanda became progressively more absorbed in her belief that her life was meaningless.

After a while, Amanda no longer bothered to keep the house clean, to cook, or to take care of the children. At first Jim thought she was merely in a "bad mood" and that it would pass, but as her lethargy deepened, he became increasingly worried. He thought his wife was either sick or no longer loved him and the children. Amanda told him that she was tired, and that simple household chores took too much energy. She still loved Jim and the children, but said that she no longer had strong feelings for anything. Amanda did show some guilt about her inability to take care of the children and be a wife, but everything was simply too depressing. Life was no longer important, and she just wanted to be left alone. At that point she began to cry uncontrollably. Nothing Jim said could bring her out of the depression or stop her from crying. He decided that she had to see a physician, and he made an appointment for her. Amanda is currently receiving medication and psychotherapy to treat her depression.

In this chapter, we first describe the clinical symptoms of depression and mania, and the two major types of mental disorders—depressive disorders and

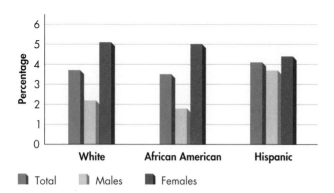

FIGURE 11.1 **One-Year Prevalence of Mood Disorders in the United States** The one-year prevalence rates of major depression and bipolar disorders (not including dysthymia) according to ethnicity and gender are shown. The prevalence is higher among women than men and among ethnic minority groups than Whites.

Source: Data from Weissman et al., 1991.

bipolar disorders. Then we discuss their causes and treatment. In Chapter 12, we examine the very serious problem of suicide—a phenomenon that has been strongly linked to depression.

THE SYMPTOMS OF DEPRESSION AND MANIA

Depression and mania, the two extremes of mood or affect, can be considered the opposite ends of a continuum that extends from deep sadness to wild elation. Of the two, depression is much more prevalent. It appears in 90 percent of all diagnosed cases of mood disorders, and it would be expected to show up in the other 10 percent if they remained untreated.

Clinical Symptoms of Depression

Certain core characteristics are often seen among people with depression. These characteristics may be organized within the four psychological domains used to describe anxiety: the affective domain, the cognitive domain, the behavioral domain, and the physiological domain. Table 11.1 shows this organization and compares the core group symptoms for depression and mania.

Affective Symptoms Depressed mood is the most striking symptom of depression. Depressives experience feelings of sadness, dejection, and an excessive and prolonged mourning. Feelings of worthlessness

and of having lost the joy of living are common. Wild weeping may occur as a general reaction to frustration or anger. Such crying spells do not seem to be directly correlated with a specific situation. Finally, anxiety has been found to frequently accompany depression; the correlation of anxiety and depression is typically in the range of .45 to .75 (Watson et al., 1995).

To illustrate these affective characteristics, the following statements were made by a severely depressed patient who had markedly improved after treatment:

> It's hard to describe the state I was in several months ago. The depression was total—it was as if everything that happened to me passed through this filter which colored all experiences. Nothing was exciting to me. I felt I was no good, completely worthless and deserving of nothing. The people who tried to cheer me up were just living in a different world.

We should note that severe depressive symptoms often occur as a normal reaction to the death of a loved one. This intensive mourning is thought to have a positive psychological function in helping one to adjust. An excessively long period of bereavement accompanied by a preoccupation with feelings of worthlessness, marked functional impairment, and serious psychomotor retardation, however, can indicate a major mood disorder. Cultures vary in the normal duration of bereavement but severe, incapacitating depression rarely continues after the first three months.

Cognitive Symptoms Besides general feelings of futility, emptiness, and hopelessness, certain thoughts and ideas are clearly related to depressive reactions. For example, the person feels a profound pessimism about the future. Disinterest, decreased energy, and loss of motivation make it difficult for the depressed person to cope with everyday situations. Work responsibilities become monumental tasks, and the person avoids them. Self-accusation of incompetence and general self-denigration are common, as are thoughts of suicide. Other symptoms include difficulty in concentrating and in making decisions.

Depression may be considered to be reflected in a cognitive triad, which consists of negative views of the self, of the outside world, and of the future (Beck, 1974). The person has pessimistic beliefs about what he or she can do, about what others can do to help, and about his or her prospects for the future. Some of this triad can be seen in the following self-description of the thoughts and feelings of someone with severe depression:

> The gradual progression to this state of semicognizance and quiescence was steady; it is hard to trace. People and things counted less. I ceased to wonder. I asked a

TABLE 11.1   Symptoms of Depression and Mania

Domain	Depression	Mania
Affective	Sadness, unhappiness, apathy, anxiety, brooding	Elation, grandiosity, irritability
Cognitive	Pessimism, guilt, inability to concentrate, negative thinking, loss of interest and motivation, suicidal thoughts	Flighty and pressured thoughts, lack of focus and attention, poor judgment
Behavioral	Low energy, neglect of personal appearance, crying, psychomotor retardation, agitation	Overactive, speech difficult to understand, talkative
Physiological	Poor or increased appetite, constipation, sleep disturbance, disruption of the menstrual cycle in women, loss of sex drive	High levels of arousal, decreased need for sleep

member of my family where I was and, having received an answer, accepted it. And usually I remembered it, when I was in a state to remember anything objective. The days dragged; there was no "motive," no drive of any kind. A dull acceptance settled upon me. Nothing interested me. I was very tired and heavy. I refused to do most of the things that were asked of me, and to avoid further disturbance I was put to bed again. (Hillyer, 1964, pp. 158–159)

Ezra Pound, one of the most brilliant poets of the twentieth century, suffered a severe depression when he was in his seventies. He told an interviewer bitterly, "I have lived all my life believing that I knew something. And then a strange day came and I realized that I knew nothing, nothing at all. And so words have become empty of meaning. Everything that I touch, I spoil. I have blundered always" (Darrach, 1976, p. 81). Pound stopped writing for years; for days on end, he ceased to speak. For both Hillyer and Pound, motivation, activity, vitality, and optimism had declined drastically.

Behavioral Symptoms   The appearance and outward demeanor of a person is often a telltale sign of depression. The person's clothing may be sloppy or dirty; hair may be unkempt and personal cleanliness neglected. A dull, masklike facial expression may become characteristic. The depressed person moves his or her body slowly and does not initiate new activities. Speech is reduced and slow, and the person may respond with short phrases. This slowing down of all bodily movements, expressive gestures, and spontaneous responses is called *psychomotor retardation.*

Ezra Pound (1885–1972), American poet and expatriate, developed severe depression later in life, and at one point was institutionalized. During his depression, he became extremely pessimistic and derogated much of his work. For a time, he even stopped speaking and writing.

This painting by Vincent Van Gogh, *Portrait of Dr. Gachet*, suggests the extreme melancholy that can characterize the depressive side of manic-depressive disorders.

The person often shows social withdrawal and lowered work productivity. In fact, one of the dominant behavioral symptoms of depression is a low energy level, which has been found to distinguish depressed individuals from nondepressed individuals (Christensen & Duncan, 1995).

Although psychomotor retardation is typical, some people suffering from depression manifest an agitated state and symptoms of restlessness.

Physiological Symptoms The following somatic and related symptoms are frequently found in persons with depression:

1. *Loss of appetite and weight* Some people, however, have increased appetite and gain weight. The loss of appetite often stems from the person's disinterest in eating; food seems tasteless. In severe depression, weight loss can become life threatening.

2. *Constipation* The person may not have bowel movements for days at a time.

3. *Sleep disturbance* Difficulty in falling asleep, waking up early, waking up erratically during the night, insomnia, and nightmares leave the person exhausted and tired during the day. Many dread the arrival of night because it represents a major fatigue-producing battle to fall asleep. Some depressed people show hypersomnia or excessive sleep, however.

4. *Disruption of the normal menstrual cycle in women* Usually, the cycle is prolonged, with possible skipping of one or several periods. The volume of menstrual flow may decrease.

5. *Aversion to sexual activity* Many people report that their sexual arousal dramatically declines.

Clinical Symptoms of Mania

Affective Symptoms In mania, the person's mood is elevated, expansive, or irritable (see Table 1.1). Social and occupational functioning are impaired, as shown in the following case:

Alan was a 43-year-old unmarried computer programmer who had led a relatively quiet life until two weeks before, when he returned to work after a short absence for illness. Alan seemed to be in a particularly good mood. Others in the office noticed that he was unusually happy and energetic, greeting everyone at work. A few days later, during the lunch hour, Alan bought a huge cake and insisted that his fellow workers eat some of it. At first everyone was surprised and amused by his antics. But two colleagues working with him on a special project became increasingly irritated because Alan didn't put any time into their project. He just insisted that he would finish his part in a few days.

On the day that the manager had decided to tell Alan of his colleagues' concern, Alan behaved in a delirious, manic way. When he came to work, he immediately jumped on top of a desk and yelled, "Listen, listen! We aren't working on the most important aspects of our data! I know, since I've debugged my mind. Erase, reprogram, you know what I mean. We've got to examine the total picture based on the input!" Alan then spouted profanities and made obscene remarks to several of the secretaries. Onlookers thought that he must have taken drugs. Attempts to calm him down brought angry and vicious denunciations. The manager, who had been summoned, also couldn't calm him. Finally the manager threatened to fire Alan. At this point, Alan called the manager an incompetent fool and stated that he could not be fired. His speech was so rapid and disjointed that it was difficult to understand him. Alan then picked up a chair and said he was going to smash the computers. Several coworkers grabbed him and held him on the floor. Alan was yelling so loud that his voice was quite hoarse, but he continued to shout and struggle. Two police officers were called, and they had to handcuff him to restrain his movements. Within hours, he was taken to a psychiatric hospital for observation.

Manic people like Alan show boundless energy, enthusiasm, and self-assertion. If frustrated, they may become profane and quite belligerent, as he did.

Cognitive Symptoms   Some of the cognitive symptoms of mania inlcude flightiness, pressured thoughts, lack of focus and attention, and poor judgment. The verbal processes of manic patients reflect their cognitive state. For example, their speech is usually quite accelerated and pressured. They may change topics in mid-sentence or utter irrelevant and idiosyncratic phrases. Although much of what they say is understandable to others, the accelerated and disjointed nature of their speech makes it difficult to follow their train of thought. They seem incapable of controlling their attention, as though they are constantly distracted by new and more exciting thoughts and ideas.

Behavioral Symptoms   Manic patients are often uninhibited, engaging impulsively in sexual activity or abusive discourse. DSM-IV recognizes two levels of manic intensity—hypomania and mania (American Psychiatric Association, 1994). In the milder form, *hypomania,* affected people seem to be "high" in mood and overactive in behavior. Their judgment is usually poor, although delusions are rare. They start many projects, but few if any are completed. When they interact with others, hypomanics dominate the conversation and are often grandiose.

Behaviors are more disruptive in people who suffer from *mania*. Overactivity, grandiosity, and irritability are pronounced; speech may be incoherent; and criticisms or restraints imposed by others are not tolerated. In the more severe form, the person is wildly excited, rants, raves (the stereotype of a wild "maniac"), and is constantly agitated and on the move. Hallucinations and delusions may appear, and the person may be uncontrollable and frequently dangerous to himself or herself or to others. Physical restraint and medication are frequently necessary.

Physiological Symptoms   The most prominent physiological or somatic characteristic is a decreased need for sleep accompanied by high levels of arousal. The energy and excitement these patients show may cause them to lose weight or go without sleep for long periods. Whereas hypomania is not severe enough to cause marked impairment or hospitalization, the mood disturbance in mania is sufficiently severe to cause marked impairment in social or occupational functioning.

CLASSIFICATION OF MOOD DISORDERS

Mood disorders are largely divided into two major categories in DSM-IV: depressive disorders (often referred to as *unipolar disorder*) and bipolar disorder (see the disorders chart on page 330). Once a depressive or manic episode occurs, the disorder is classified into both a category and a subcategory. Let us examine the major categories and subcategories as well as other aspects of the classification scheme.

Depressive Disorders

Depressive disorders in DSM-IV include major depressive disorders, dysthymic disorder, and depressive disorders not otherwise specified. In all of these disorders, there is no history of a manic episode. People who experience a major depressive episode are given the diagnosis of **major depression.** Symptoms should be present for at least two weeks and represent a change from the individual's previous functioning. The symptoms of major depression include a depressed mood or a loss of interest or pleasure, including weight loss or gain, sleep difficulties, fatigue, feelings of worthlessness, inability to concentrate, and recurrent thoughts of death. If the episode is the first one, it is classified as a single episode. For people who have had previous episodes, the disorder is considered a recurrent one. About one-half of those who experience a depressive episode eventually have another episode. In general, the earlier the age of onset, the more likely is a recurrence (Reus, 1988).

If a disorder is characterized by depressed mood but does not meet the criteria for major depression, dysthymic disorder may be diagnosed. In **dysthymic disorder,** the depressed mood is chronic and relatively continual. Typical symptoms include pessimism or guilt, loss of interest, poor appetite or overeating, low self-esteem, chronic fatigue, social withdrawal, or concentration difficulties. Unlike major depression, dysthymia may last for years. Each year, about 10 percent of individuals with dysthymia go on to have a first major depressive episode. In dysthymia, the depressive symptoms are present most of the day and for more days than not during a two-year period (or, for children and adolescents, a one-year period). One study (Myers et al., 1984) found the prevalence of dysthymia to be higher among women than men. Overall, the lifetime prevalence is about 6 percent (American Psychiatric Association, 1994).

Bipolar Disorders

The essential feature of **bipolar disorders** is the occurrence of one or more manic or hypomanic episodes; the term *bipolar* is used because the disorders are usually accompanied by one or more depressive episodes. Symptoms for manic episodes include abnormally and persistently elevated, expansive, or irritable moods lasting at least one week in the case of mania and four

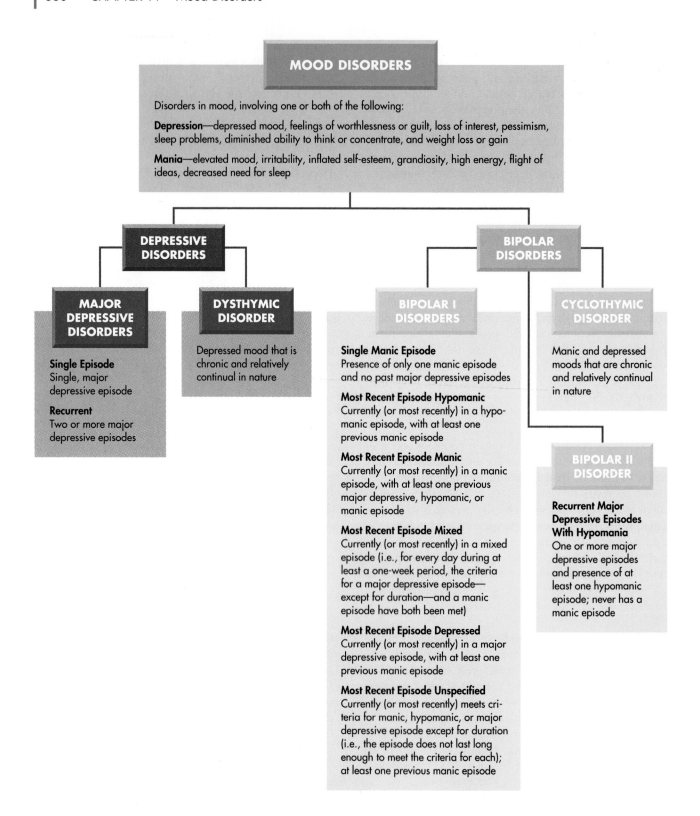

MOOD DISORDERS

Disorders in mood, involving one or both of the following:

Depression—depressed mood, feelings of worthlessness or guilt, loss of interest, pessimism, sleep problems, diminished ability to think or concentrate, and weight loss or gain

Mania—elevated mood, irritability, inflated self-esteem, grandiosity, high energy, flight of ideas, decreased need for sleep

DEPRESSIVE DISORDERS

MAJOR DEPRESSIVE DISORDERS

Single Episode
Single, major depressive episode

Recurrent
Two or more major depressive episodes

DYSTHYMIC DISORDER

Depressed mood that is chronic and relatively continual in nature

BIPOLAR DISORDERS

BIPOLAR I DISORDERS

Single Manic Episode
Presence of only one manic episode and no past major depressive episodes

Most Recent Episode Hypomanic
Currently (or most recently) in a hypomanic episode, with at least one previous manic episode

Most Recent Episode Manic
Currently (or most recently) in a manic episode, with at least one previous major depressive, hypomanic, or manic episode

Most Recent Episode Mixed
Currently (or most recently) in a mixed episode (i.e., for every day during at least a one-week period, the criteria for a major depressive episode—except for duration—and a manic episode have both been met)

Most Recent Episode Depressed
Currently (or most recently) in a major depressive episode, with at least one previous manic episode

Most Recent Episode Unspecified
Currently (or most recently) meets criteria for manic, hypomanic, or major depressive episode except for duration (i.e., the episode does not last long enough to meet the criteria for each); at least one previous manic episode

CYCLOTHYMIC DISORDER

Manic and depressed moods that are chronic and relatively continual in nature

BIPOLAR II DISORDER

Recurrent Major Depressive Episodes With Hypomania
One or more major depressive episodes and presence of at least one hypomanic episode; never has a manic episode

days in the case of hypomania. Grandiosity, decreased need for sleep, flight of ideas, distractibility, and impairment in occupational or social functioning are often observed in persons with the disorder.

As indicated in the disorders chart, bipolar disorders include subcategories that describe the nature of

the disorder. Bipolar I disorders include *single manic episode, most recent episode hypomanic, most recent episode manic, most recent episode mixed, most recent episode depressed,* and *most recent episode unspecified.* Bipolar II disorder includes *recurrent major depressive episodes with hypomania.* Persons in whom manic but not depressive episodes have occurred are extremely rare; in such cases, a depressive episode will presumably appear at some time.

Earlier, we mentioned that the lifetime prevalence of depressive disorders hovers around 15 percent. In comparison, Weissman and colleagues (1991) found the lifetime prevalence rates for bipolar I and II to be 0.8 and 0.5 percent, respectively.

Some people have hypomanic episodes and depressed moods that do not meet the criteria for major depressive episode. If the symptoms are present for at least two years, the individuals are diagnosed with cyclothymic disorder. (For children and adolescents, one year rather than two years is the criterion.) As in the case of dysthymia, **cyclothymic disorder** is a chronic and relatively continual mood disorder, in which the person is never symptom free for more than two months. With a lifetime prevalence between 0.4 and 1 percent, cyclothymia is less common than dysthymia and more common than bipolar disorder. The risk that a person with cyclothymia will subsequently develop a bipolar disorder is 15 to 50 percent (American Psychiatric Association, 1994).

Other Mood Disorders

Mood disorder due to a general medical condition is a disturbance characterized by either (or both) depressed mood or elevated or irritable mood as a direct result of a general medical condition. For example, seriously medically ill patients may exhibit insomnia, weight loss, and depression. This disorder is diagnosed when the symptoms are serious enough to cause significant impairment in social or occupational functioning or marked distress. *Substance-induced mood disorder* is a prominent and persistent disturbance of mood (depression, mania, or both) attributable to the use of a substance or to the cessation of the substance use. Again, it is diagnosed when notable distress and impairment occur.

Symptom Features and Specifiers

To be more precise about the nature of the mood disorders, DSM-IV has listed certain characteristics that may be associated with these disorders. They are important symptom features that may accompany the disorders but are not criteria used to determine diagnosis. *Specifiers* may be used to more precisely describe the major depressive episode. Severity, presence or absence of psychotic features, and remission status may be specified. For example, psychotic features include delusions, hallucinations, and gross impairment in reality testing (an inability to accurately perceive and deal with reality). Their presence tends to predict

Depression is sometimes associated with certain life events or changes. Specifiers are used to more precisely describe the mood disorder. One course specifier indicates whether the depression or mania in women occurs within four weeks of childbirth. If it does, the mood disorder has the specifier "postpartum onset."

a relatively poor diagnosis, more chronicity, and impairment. If a person who is diagnosed with a major depressive episode has psychotic symptoms, the person would receive the diagnosis of major depressive episode with psychotic features. Similarly, major depressive episodes for some of the mood disorders may include (1) *melancholia* (loss of pleasure, lack of reactivity to pleasurable stimuli, depression that is worse in the morning, early morning awakening, excessive guilt, weight loss) and (2) *catatonia,* which is motoric immobility (taking a posture and not moving), extreme agitation (excessive motor activity), negativism (resistance to changing positions), or mutism.

Course Specifiers Course specifiers indicate the cyclic, seasonal, postpartum, or longitudinal pattern of mood disorders. In *rapid cycling* type, which is applicable to bipolar disorders, the manic or depressive episodes have occurred four or more times during the previous twelve months. The episodes may also appear with periods of relative normality in between. In some cases, there may be only partial remission in between the episodes. One patient was reported to demonstrate manic behaviors for almost exactly

In seasonal affective disorder (SAD), depressive symptoms vary with the seasons. One theory for this is that during winter, reduced daylight affects hormone levels, which in turn may induce depression. The woman in this photo is receiving light therapy, which involves exposure to bright light. The treatment appears to be helpful in some cases of SAD.

twenty-four hours, immediately followed by depressive behaviors for twenty-four hours. At the manic extreme, the patient was agitated, demanding, and constantly shouting; the next day, he was almost mute and inactive. The alternating nature of the disorder lasted eleven years (Jenner et al., 1967). Typical manic episodes appear suddenly and last from a few days to months. Depressive episodes tend to last longer.

One of the more interesting course specifiers involves a *seasonal pattern*. For some people, moods are accentuated during certain times. Lehmann (1985) noted that many depressed people find the morning more depressing than the evening. Many individuals also find winter, when days are shorter and darker, more depressing than summer. In seasonal affective

disorder (SAD), serious cases of depression fluctuate according to the season. Although the precise causes for SAD are unclear, it may be that the longer, dark days of winter affect hormonal changes in the body that may somehow affect depression levels. Interestingly, "light therapy" (exposure to bright light) for several hours a day during winter may be helpful for some individuals with SAD (Rosenthal et al., 1985), as may vacations to sunny parts of the country. In some cases of recurrent major depression and bipolar disorder, the onset, end, or change of an episode coincides with a particular time of the year. For example, one man regularly became depressed after Christmas.

Other course specifiers include *postpartum onset* (if depression or mania in women occurs within four weeks of childbirth) and longitudinal course specifiers that indicate the nature of the recurrence and interepisode status of individuals.

Comparison Between Depressive and Bipolar Disorders

Several types of evidence seem to support the distinction between depressive (unipolar) and bipolar disorders (Goodwin & Guze, 1984; Research Task Force of the National Institute of Mental Health, 1975). First, genetic studies have revealed that blood relatives of patients with bipolar disorders have a higher incidence of manic disturbances than do relatives of patients with unipolar disorders. In addition, stronger evidence of genetic or psychophysiological influences exists for bipolar disorders than for unipolar disorders. Second, the age of onset is typically earlier for bipolar disorders (the late twenties) than for unipolar disorders (the mid-thirties). Third, bipolars display psychomotor retardation (a slowing down of movements and speech) and a greater tendency to attempt suicide than do unipolars, whose depressive symptoms often include anxiety. And fourth, bipolars respond to lithium, whereas the drug has little effect on unipolars. However, there is some evidence that the two are not entirely distinct. Relatives of those with unipolar disorders have an increased probability of having unipolar disorders. On the other hand, relatives of those with bipolar disorders have an increased chance of having not only bipolar disorders but unipolar disorders as well (Faraone, Kremen & Tsuang, 1990).

As mentioned earlier, only about 1 percent of the adult population have experienced bipolar disorder, whereas about 8 to 17 percent have at some time experienced a major depressive episode. Unlike major depression, which seems to be more common in females than in males, no apparent gender difference

Mourning over the death of a loved one occurs in all cultures and societies, as illustrated by this group of women gathered in a Zambian cemetery. However, in most cultures, severe and incapacitating depression rarely continues after the first three months. If it does continue longer, then a depressive disorder may have developed.

exists in the frequency of bipolar disorders (Weissman & Klerman, 1977).

THE ETIOLOGY OF MOOD DISORDERS

Despite increasing evidence for a unipolar-bipolar distinction, little is known about what causes the extreme mood changes in the bipolar disorders. Perhaps the regulatory mechanism for maintaining *homeostasis*, or stability of mood, no longer works. Maybe mania is a way of trying to deal with underlying depression. Maybe the apparent euphoria, irritability, and overactivity seen in mania are attempts to deny or ward off depression. In any event, much more is known about what causes depression than about what causes the bipolar disorders, and psychological-sociocultural perspectives focus primarily on depression rather than mania. As indicated earlier, it may be that biological factors play a more prominent role in the etiology of bipolar disorders than in unipolar disorders. Another possibility is that unipolar disorders include more heterogeneous disorders, such that some are more endogenous (internally caused within the organism) rather than exogenous (caused by external precipitating events) in nature. In any event, we focus our discussion of psychological or sociocultural explanations primarily on depression. The section on biogenic explanations covers both unipolar and bipolar disorders, leading into treatment approaches based on those explanations.

Psychological or Sociocultural Approaches to Depression

Over the years, a number of different explanations have been proposed to account for depression. Some of the major theories discussed in this section are psychoanalytic, behavioral, cognitive, cognitive-learning, and sociocultural.

Psychoanalytic Explanations   The psychoanalytic explanation of depression focuses mainly on two concepts: separation and anger. Separation may occur when a spouse, lover, child, parent, or significant other person dies or leaves for one reason or another. But, because depression cannot always be correlated with the immediate loss of a loved one, Freud used the construct of "symbolic loss" to account for depression that did not result directly from a loss. That is to say, the depressed person may perceive any form of rejection or reproach as symbolic of an earlier loss. For example, the withdrawal of affection or support or a rejection can induce depression.

Freud ([1917] 1924) believed that depressed people are excessively dependent because they are fixated in the oral stage. As we discussed in Chapter 2, he viewed the mouth as the primary mechanism by which infants relate to the world, so being fixated at this stage fosters dependency. Being passive and having others fill one's needs (being fed, bathed, clothed, cuddled, and so forth) results in emotional dependency that continues into adult life. Thus, for people fixated in the oral stage, self-esteem depends on other important people in the environment. When a significant loss occurs, the mourner's self-esteem plummets.

Freud also believed that a person in depression fails to follow through the normal process of mourning, which he called "grief or mourning work." In the normal course of mourning, the mourner consciously recalls and expresses memories about the lost person in an attempt to undo the loss. In addition, the mourner is flooded with two strong sets of feelings: anger and guilt. The anger, which arises from the sense of being deserted, can be very strong. The mourner may also be flooded with guilt feelings about real or imagined sins committed against the lost person.

Psychoanalysis has strongly emphasized the dynamics of anger in explaining depression. Many depressed patients have strong hostile or angry feelings, and some clinicians believe that getting clients to express their anger reduces their depression. Such a belief has led some to speculate that depression is really anger turned against the self (Freud, [1917] 1924). Freud suggested that, when a person experiences a loss (symbolic or otherwise), he or she may harbor feelings of resentment and hostility toward the lost person in addition to feelings of love and affection.

There have been relatively few empirical tests of psychoanalytic ideas. One study longitudinally examined whether persons whose spouses had died were less depressed if they directly confronted (that is, performed grief work) rather than avoided dealing with their loss (Stroebe & Stroebe, 1991). Results were equivocal in that performing grief work was inversely related to adjustment for widowers but not for widows. Other studies have shown that loss (death or separation) of significant others in one's life can precipitate depression (Paykel, 1982). However, stressors other than the loss of a significant other may bring about depression, just as the loss of a significant other can lead to disorders other than depression. Anxiety and substance abuse, for example, may follow such losses.

Harlow found that infant monkeys reacted with fear and despair when separated from their mothers. Even monkeys raised with surrogate mothers (in this case, a wire frame covered with terry cloth) exhibited anxiety and despair when separated from them. Psychoanalysts believe that separation can be a cause of depression.

Behavioral Explanations Behaviorists also see the separation or loss of a significant other as important in depression. However, behaviorists tend to see reduced reinforcement as the cause, rather than fixation or symbolic grief, which they view as untestable concepts. When a loved one is lost, an accustomed level of reinforcement (whether affection, companionship, pleasure, material goods, or services) is immediately withdrawn. No longer can one obtain the support or encouragement of the lost person. When this happens, one's level of activity (talking, expressing ideas, working, joking, engaging in sports, going out on the town) is markedly diminished because an important source of reinforcement has disappeared. Thus many behaviorists view depression as a product of inadequate or insufficient reinforcers in a person's life, leading to a reduced frequency of behavior that previously was positively reinforced (Ferster, 1965; Lazarus, 1968; Lewinsohn, 1974a).

As the period of reduced activity (resulting from reduced reinforcement) continues, the person labels himself or herself "depressed." If the new lower level of activity causes others to show sympathy, the depressed person may remain inactive and become chronically "depressed." By being sympathetic about the incident (loss), friends, relatives, and even strangers may be reinforcing the person's current state of inactivity. (This reinforcement for a lower activity level is known as *secondary gain*.) The depression tends to deepen, and the person disengages still further from the environment and further reduces the

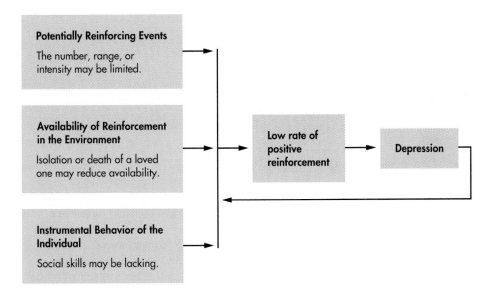

FIGURE 11.2 **Lewinsohn's Behavioral Theory of Depression** If reinforcing events, availability of reinforcement, and instrumental behaviors are limited, the person experiences a low rate of positive reinforcement and may become depressed. In turn, depression leads to a low rate of positive reinforcement by reducing reinforcing events, availability, and so on.

Source: Based on Lewinsohn, 1974a.

chance of obtaining positive reinforcement from normal activity. The result may be continually deepening depression.

Depression has been associated both with low levels of self-reinforcement and with reductions in environmental reinforcements (Heiby, 1983). In other words, when people get less reinforcement from the environment (such as after the death of a loved one) and do not give themselves reinforcement, they are prone to become depressed. Depressed people may lack the skills required to replace lost environmental reinforcements.

This behavioral concept of depression can be elaborated to cover many situations that may elicit depression (such as failure, loss, change in job status, rejection, and desertion). Lewinsohn's model of depression, illustrated in Figure 11.2, is perhaps the most comprehensive behavioral explanation of depression (Lewinsohn, 1974a, 1974b; Lewinsohn & Graf, 1973; Lewinsohn & Libet, 1972; Lewinsohn, Weinstein & Alper, 1970). Along with the reinforcement view of depression, Lewinsohn suggested three sets of variables that may enhance or hinder a person's access to positive reinforcement.

1. *The number of events and activities that are potentially reinforcing to the person.* This number depends very much on individual differences and varies with the biological traits and experiential history of the person. For example, age, gender, or physical attributes may determine the availability of reinforcers. Handsome people are more likely to receive positive attention than those people who look nondescript. Young people are likely to have more social interaction than retirees. A task-oriented person who values intellectual pursuits may not be so responsive as other people to interpersonal or affiliative forms of reinforcement. To such a person, a compliment such as "I like you" may be less effective than "I see you as an extremely competent person."

2. *The availability of reinforcements in the environment.* Harsh environments, such as regimented institutions or remote isolated places, reduce reinforcements.

3. *The instrumental behavior of the individual.* The number of social skills a person can exercise to bring about reinforcement is important. Depressed people lack social behaviors that can elicit positive reinforcements (Lewinsohn, Weinstein & Alper, 1970). They interact with fewer people, respond less, have very few positive reactions, and initiate less conversation. They also feel more uncomfortable in social situations (Youngren & Lewinsohn, 1980), and they elicit depression in others (Hammen & Peters, 1978). Further, depressed people seem to be preoccupied with themselves; they tend to talk about themselves (more so than nondepressed people) without being asked to do

Learning theory suggests that depression may be a product of reduced reinforcement in a person's life. The reduced reinforcement leads to reduced activity levels. Unfortunately, consolation and sympathy from others may sometimes serve to reinforce and maintain depressive behaviors.

so (Jacobson & Anderson, 1982). For this reason or others, nondepressed people may not enjoy talking to those who are depressed and may provide little positive reinforcement to them during social interactions. Depressed individuals may even create conditions that further their depression or drive others away, thereby losing any social reinforcement that others could provide (Coyne, 1976).

A low rate of positive reinforcement in any of these three situations can lead to depression, as Figure 11.2 illustrates. A beautiful person who begins to age may notice declining interest from possible lovers. A person who has recently lost a loved one through divorce or death and has no other friends or family may receive little or no support. And a young student who lacks social skills in heterosexual relationships may be denied the pleasures of such interactions. Behavioral approaches to treating depression might attempt to intervene in any of these conditions.

Lewinsohn also recognized the important role of other factors in depression. For example, Lewinsohn, Hoberman, and Rosenbaum (1988) found that having a prior depressed mood, encountering stress, and being female (as mentioned previously, women are more likely than men to suffer depression) are associated with the occurrence of depressive episodes. Although a low rate of positive reinforcement is a critical feature of his theory, Lewinsohn and colleagues (1985) adopted a more comprehensive view of depression. They believe that an antecedent event such as stress disrupts the predictable and well-established behavior patterns of people's lives. Such disrup-

tions then reduce the rate of positive reinforcements or increase aversive experiences. If individuals are unable to reverse the impact of the stress, they begin to have a heightened state of self-awareness (for example, self-critical, negative expectancies and loss of self-confidence) and to experience depressed affect. With depressed moods, persons then have a more difficult time functioning appropriately, which makes them further vulnerable to depression. Thus Lewinsohn's model attempts to cover not only behavioral elements but also cognitive and emotional consequences.

Behaviorists have made major contributions to the understanding of depression, but, as noted earlier, they and many other theorists have not really given much attention to mania. Acknowledging that biogenic factors may be important in bipolar disorders, Staats and Heiby (1985) believe that learning principles are also involved in mania. They believe that individuals may, because of some behavior (such as performing well using social or interpersonal skills), receive praise and admiration. The euphoria from receiving the praise may elicit further use of the skills, resulting in even more positive consequences. The behaviors then become accelerated and euphoria increases even more—as in a manic state. At some point, however, the behaviors may elicit negative reactions, which sets up conditions for depression.

Cognitive Explanations Some psychologists believe that low self-esteem is the key to depressive reactions. All of us have both negative and positive feelings about what we see as our "self." We like or value certain things about ourselves, and we dislike other things. Some people, especially those who are depressed, have a generally negative self-concept. Such people perceive themselves as inept, unworthy, and incompetent, regardless of reality. If they do succeed at anything, they are likely to dismiss it as pure luck or to forecast eventual failure. Hence a cognitive interpretation of oneself as unworthy may lead to thinking patterns that reflect self-blame, self-criticism, and exaggerated ideas of duty and responsibility.

One major cognitive theory has been advanced by Beck (1976). According to this theory, depression is a primary disturbance in *thinking* rather than a basic disturbance in *mood*. How persons structure and interpret their experiences determines their affective states. If individuals see a situation as unpleasant, they will feel an unpleasant mood. Depressed patients are said to have schemas that set them up for depression. A **schema** is a pattern of thinking or a cognitive set that determines (or colors) a person's reactions and responses. In other words, schemas tend to modify, or color, interpretation of incoming information. In one study, for example, Crowson and Cromwell (1995) gave depressed and nondepressed individuals the choice of listening to positive or negative tape-recorded messages. The researchers found that the nondepressed group was more likely to choose positive messages, whereas the depressed group showed little preference in the messages. Perhaps depression involves schemas that perpetuate negative outlooks and attention to negative messages.

According to this theory, depressives operate from a "primary triad" of negative self-views, present experiences, and the future. Four errors in logic typify this negative schema, which leads to depression and is characteristic of depressives:

1. *Arbitrary inference* The depressed person tends to draw conclusions that are not supported by evidence. For example, a woman may conclude that "people dislike me" just because no one speaks to her on the bus or in the elevator. A man who invites a woman out to dinner and finds the restaurant closed that evening may see this as evidence of his own unworthiness. In both cases, these people draw erroneous conclusions from the available evidence. Depressed people are apparently unwilling or unable to see other, more probable, explanations.

2. *Selected abstraction* The depressed person takes a minor incident or detail out of context and focuses on it, and these incidents tend to be trivial. A person corrected for a minor aspect of his or her work may take the correction as a sign of incompetence or inadequacy—even when the supervisor's overall feedback is highly positive.

3. *Overgeneralization* A depressed person tends to draw a sweeping conclusion about his or her ability, performance, or worth from one single experience or incident. A woman laid off from a job because of budgetary cuts may conclude that he or she is worthless. The comments of a student seen by one of the authors at a university psychology clinic provide another illustration of overgeneralization: When he missed breakfast at the dormitory because his alarm clock didn't ring, the student concluded, "I don't deserve my own body because I don't take care of it." Later, when he showed up late for class through no fault of his own, he thought, "What a miserable excuse for a student I am." When a former classmate passed by and smiled, he thought, "I must look awful today or she wouldn't be laughing at me."

4. *Magnification and minimization* A depressed person tends to exaggerate (magnify) limitations and difficulties and play down (minimize) accomplishments, achievements, and capabilities. Asked to evaluate personal strengths and weaknesses, the person lists many shortcomings or unsuccessful efforts but finds it almost impossible to name any achievements.

All four of these cognitive processes can be seen as results or causes of low self-esteem, which makes the person expect failure and engage in self-criticism that is unrelated to reality. People with low self-esteem may have experienced much disapproval in the past from significant others, such as parents. Their parents or significant others may have responded to them by punishing failures and not rewarding successes or by holding unrealistically high expectations or standards. The following case is an example:

Paul was a twenty-year-old college senior majoring in chemistry. He first came to the student psychiatric clinic complaining of headaches and a vague assortment of somatic problems. Throughout the interview, Paul seemed severely depressed and unable to work up enough energy to talk with the therapist. Even though he had maintained a B+ average, he felt like a failure and was uncertain about his future. His parents had always had high expectations for Paul, their eldest son, and had transmitted these feelings to him from his earliest childhood. His father, a successful thoracic surgeon, had his heart set on Paul's becoming a doctor. The parents saw academic success as very important, and Paul did exceptionally well in school. Although his teachers praised him for being an outstanding student, his parents seemed to take his successes for granted. In fact, they often made statements such as "You can do better."

When he failed at something, his parents would make it obvious to him that they not only were disappointed but felt disgraced as well. This pattern of punishment for failures without recognition of successes, combined with his parents' high expectations, led to the development of Paul's extremely negative self-concept.

Some studies have demonstrated a relationship between cognition and depression. Dent and Teasdale (1988) studied the depression levels and self-schemas (self-descriptions) of the same women at two different periods of time. Women who had negative self-descriptions tended subsequently to have higher levels of depression and to recover more slowly than did women who had less negative self-descriptions. The investigator concluded that although two individuals

According to Seligman, feelings of helplessness can lead to depression. However, if people can learn to control their environment and believe in their ability to succeed, despite difficulties, they can overcome their feelings of helplessness and despair, and begin to lead productive lives again. California Angels' pitcher Jim Abbott won his battle with depression.

may have equal levels of depression, the one who has negative self-schemas may turn out to have a more serious and longer lasting depressive episode.

Further evidence of a link between cognition and depression comes from studies of memory bias. When depressed individuals are given lists of words that vary in emotional content, they tend to recall more negative words than do their nondepressed counterparts. This may indicate a tendency to attend to, and remember, negative and depressing events (Mineka & Sutton, 1992). Even formerly depressed individuals (who have recovered) have a greater tendency to have negative cognitive styles than found among individuals who have never been depressed (Hedlund & Rude, 1995). They presumably have developed negative schemas.

Although the cognitive explanation of depression has merit, it seems too simple. At times, negative cognitions may be the result of, rather than the cause of, depressed moods, as noted by Hammen (1985). That is, one may first feel depressed and then, as a result, have negative or pessimistic thoughts about the world. Hammen also found that a person's schema tends to mediate the relationship between stress and depression. Stress can lead to depression if a person has developed a predisposing schema. Another criticism of cognitive explanations is that many people get depressed, but they do not feel depressed all the time. Yet negative cognitive styles are often hypothesized to be stable or enduring.

Cognitive-Learning Approaches: Learned Helplessness and Attributional Style   Seligman (1975) proposed a unique and interesting view of depression based on cognitive-learning theory. The basic assumption of this approach is that both cognitions and feelings of helplessness are learned, and that depression is **learned helplessness**—an acquired belief that one is helpless and unable to affect the outcomes in one's life. A person who sees that his or her actions continually have very little effect on the environment develops an expectation of being helpless. When this expectation is borne out in settings that may not be controllable, passivity and depression may result.

A person's susceptibility to depression, then, depends on his or her experience with controlling the environment. In his study of helplessness, Seligman discovered strong parallels between the symptoms and causes of helplessness and those for depression (see Table 11.2). He also noticed similarities in cure; one could say that depression is cured when the person no longer believes he or she is helpless.

Seligman described depression as a *belief in one's own helplessness.* Many other investigators have described depression in terms of hopelessness, power-

TABLE 11.2 Similarities Between Learned Helplessness and Depression

	Learned Helplessness	Depression
Symptoms	Passivity	Passivity
	Difficulty learning that response produces relief	Negative cognitive set
	Dissipates in time	Time course
	Lack of aggression	Introjected hostility
	Weight loss, appetite loss	Weight loss, appetite loss
	Social and sexual deficits	Social and sexual deficits
Cause	Learning that responding and reinforcement are independent	Feelings of helplessness
		Belief that responding is useless

Source: Adapted from Seligman, 1975.

lessness, and helplessness. For example, "The severely depressed patient believes that his skills and plans of action are no longer effective for reaching the goals he has set" (Melges & Bowlby, 1969, p. 693). And, according to Seligman (1975, pp. 55–56), "The expectation that an outcome is independent of responding (1) reduces the motivation to control the outcome; (2) interferes with learning that responding controls the outcome; (3) produces fear for as long as the subject is uncertain of the uncontrollability of the outcome, and then produces depression." In general, research has shown that depression is associated with an external locus of control—depressed persons tend to perceive events as being uncontrollable (Benassi, Sweeney & Dufour, 1988).

Attributional Style Seligman's theory of learned helplessness was first published in 1975. Three years later, he and his coworkers revised the model to include more cognitive elements (Abramson, Seligman & Teasdale, 1978). Essentially, they believe that people who feel helpless make *causal attributions* (speculations about why they are helpless). These attributions can be internal or external, stable or unstable, and global or specific. For instance, suppose that a student in a math course receives the same low grades regardless of how much he has studied. The student may attribute the low grades to internal or personal factors ("I don't do well in math because *I'm* scared of math") or to external factors ("The *teacher* doesn't like me, so I can't get a good grade"). The attribution can also be stable ("I'm the type of person who can never do well in math") or unstable ("My poor performance is due to my heavy work load"). Addition-

ally, the attribution can be global or specific. A global attribution ("I'm a poor student") has broader implications for performance than a specific one ("I'm poor at math but good in other subjects"). Abramson and coworkers believe that a person whose attributions for helplessness are internal, stable, and global is likely to have more pervasive feelings of depression than someone whose attributions are external, unstable, and specific (see Figure 11.3). Attributions have been found to be associated with many aspects of life.

Some people tend to have a pessimistic attributional style, explaining bad events (such as failure to pass an examination) in global, stable, and internal terms (such as believing that "I fail in many courses, it always happens to me, and I am stupid"). Attributional style is related to a number of characteristics. People who have pessimistic attributional styles receive lower grades in universities, perform worse as sales agents, and have poorer health (Seligman, 1987).

Seligman and his colleagues developed the Attributional Style Questionnaire to assess attributional style. People are asked to indicate the cause of a number of hypothetical situations. Attributional style can also be reliably determined from a content analysis of verbatim explanations (CAVE), in which the content of an explanation is rated on attributional style. For example, a baseball player who says, "Once in a while I play poorly because of bad breaks, but I always know I'll get my good share of hits," is far more optimistic than one who says, "I'm getting old—my reactions to a pitch have slowed." In an analysis of newspaper quotes from Baseball Hall of Fame players who played between 1900

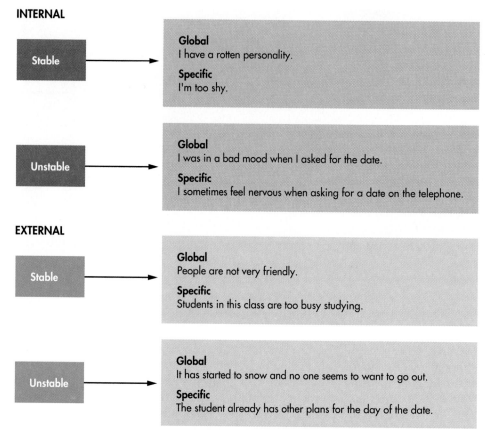

INTERNAL

| Stable | **Global**
I have a rotten personality.
Specific
I'm too shy. |

| Unstable | **Global**
I was in a bad mood when I asked for the date.
Specific
I sometimes feel nervous when asking for a date on the telephone. |

EXTERNAL

| Stable | **Global**
People are not very friendly.
Specific
Students in this class are too busy studying. |

| Unstable | **Global**
It has started to snow and no one seems to want to go out.
Specific
The student already has other plans for the day of the date. |

FIGURE 11.3 Attributional Styles As this figure indicates, attributional styles vary according to whether they are internal or external, stable or unstable, and global or specific. Depressed persons tend to explain failures in terms of internal, global, and stable factors. In the example illustrated here, a depressed student attributes a failure to get a date as the direct result of such factors: "I have a rotten personality."

and 1950, Seligman found that players who had an optimistic attributional style outlived those who were more pessimistic. Zullow and his colleagues (1988) also noted that when President Lyndon Johnson's press conferences contained optimistic phrases, bold presidential actions were taken in the Vietnam War; when he used more pessimistic phrases, the actions were passive.

The implications are that (1) people vary in their attributional styles, (2) attributional style can be assessed, and (3) attributional style may be related to achievements, health, and other behaviors. Obviously, a causal relationship between attributional style and behavior has not been clearly established. But the research suggests that how we explain things may be quite important in our lives.

The learned helplessness model, as well as the attributional style idea, has generated a great deal of research. There is evidence that depressed people make "depressive" attributions and feel that their lives are less controllable than do nondepressives (Raps et al., 1982). As with cognitive theory, however, researchers question whether this model, even with its attributional components, can adequately explain depression, and they also question whether attributions result from or are caused by depression. Cognitions and attributions may be important factors in depression, but the disorder is complex; current models tend to include or explain only particular facets of depression (Hammen, 1985). Helplessness theory (which some investigators have reformulated as the "hopelessness" theory) may explain only a certain type of depression (Abramson, Metalsky & Alloy, 1989; DeVellis & Blalock, 1992). As we mentioned earlier, many researchers believe that an external locus of control is associated with depression, yet Seligman believes that internal attributions are important in depression. Benassi, Sweeny, and Dufour (1988) raise the possibility that internality and externality may be related

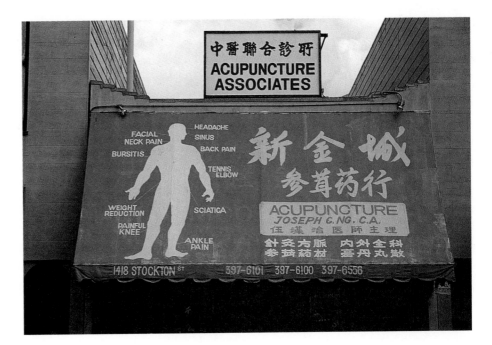

People from different cultures differ in the extent to which the symptoms listed in DSM-IV for disorders are displayed. Chinese with depression often exhibit somatic or bodily complaints instead of depressive symptoms, such as sadness and depression. Chinese medicine and acupuncture are often the preferred forms of treatment for this disorder rather than psychotherapy.

to different types of depression. Depression may be a heterogeneous disorder that can be caused by genetic, biochemical, or social factors.

Sociocultural Explanations Cross-cultural studies of mood disorders have found that prevalence rates and manifestation of symptoms vary considerably among different cultural groups and societies (Goodwin & Guze, 1984). For example, American Indians and Southeast Asians living in the United States appear to have higher rates of depression than other Americans (Chung & Okazaki, 1991; Vega & Rumbaut, 1991). In China, Chinese patients with depression commonly present somatic (bodily) complaints rather than dysphoria (depression, anxiety, or restlessness), which indicates that the expression of symptoms for a particular disorder may differ from culture to culture (Kleinman, 1991). These findings suggest that factors such as culture, social experiences, and psychosocial stressors play an important role in mood disorders. We focus on the role of stressors and resources in mood disorders and then address the issue of the apparent higher rates of depression among women than men.

Stress and Depression Conceptualizations of the role of stress in psychopathology in general and in depression in particular have typically proposed that stress is one of three broad factors that are important to consider: diathesis, stress, and resources or social supports. (See the discussion of stress in Chapter 7.) *Diathesis* refers to the fact that because of genetic or

constitutional or social conditions, certain individuals may have a predisposition or vulnerability to developing depression (Monroe & Simons, 1991). Stress may act as a trigger to activate this predisposition, especially when individuals lack resources to adjust to the stress. Presumably, individuals with low predisposition compared to those with high predisposition require greater levels of stress to become depressed.

The importance of stress in depression has been demonstrated. Multiple studies have shown that severe psychosocial stress, such as the death of a loved one, life-threatening medical condition, and frustration of major life goals, often precedes the onset of major depression (Brown & Harris, 1989; Lewinsohn, Hoberman & Rosenbaum, 1988; Paykel, 1982). This finding has led investigators to ask what kinds of stress lead to depression. Brown and Harris (1989) concluded that one severe stressor is more likely to cause depression than several minor stressors. In other words, several minor stressors do not seem to have the same effect as one very serious stressor. Moreover, in a survey of respondents in a study of stress and depressive symptoms, McGonagle and Kessler (1990) classified stress according to chronicity. Stress that was identified as beginning more than twelve months before the study was considered *chronic*. *Acute* stress was defined as stress beginning within twelve months of the study. The investigators found that chronic stress was more highly related to depression than was acute stress, even though respondents rated both types of stress as being equivalent in terms of severity. Perhaps stress that persists for a

Threatening medical conditions can serve as stressors that may elicit depression in some individuals. Here, a physician is discussing the operation of a portable heart monitor with a woman and her husband, a patient suffering from serious cardiac problems.

long time is viewed as being uncontrollable and stable. Finally, stress also appears to be important in *relapse*—the recurrence of depression after treatment (Krantz & Moos, 1988; Lewinsohn, Zeiss & Duncan, 1989).

Why do some people who encounter stress develop depression while others do not? People may differ in the degree of vulnerability to depression. The vulnerability may be caused by biogenic factors (discussed later), psychosocial factors, or both. Hammen and colleagues (1992) argued that the relationship between stress and depression is complex and interactive. In a longitudinal study of unipolar depressed patients, the investigators found supporting evidence that vulnerability to stress may be influenced by having parents who are dysfunctional and who create stress conditions in the family. In turn, the individuals may fail to acquire adaptive skills and positive self-images, which brings on more stress and, in the face of stress, leads to depression. Therefore, vulnerability may arise from early experiences in the family. (See the Focus On feature for a further discussion of Hammen's ideas.) In addition, the relationship between stress and depression appears to be bidirectional—stress can cause depression, and depression can cause stress (Pianta & Egeland, 1994).

Other investigators have examined social supports or resources as buffers against depression. The assumption is that persons who are exposed to stress may or may not develop depression, depending on whether they have adequate social supports. Holahan and Moos (1991) studied the role of social resources on stress and depression. They collected data on individuals at the beginning and end of a four-year period. Information included personality characteristics, family support (such as helpfulness of family members), stress, and depression. Persons with positive personality traits and family support, compared to those without these characteristics, had less depression four years later, even when initial level of depression (during year one) was controlled. The researchers speculated that personal or family resources help individuals cope and adjust to stress. The effects of social supports were also studied on gay men at risk for AIDS (Hays, Turner & Coates, 1992). The men were assessed as to their level of depression, social supports, and HIV-related symptoms over a one-year period. Results indicated that men who were more satisfied with their social supports were subsequently less likely to suffer from depression.

The research on stress and depression has been impressive. Longitudinal research designs and prospective studies (studies of individuals before their depressive episodes occur) have helped decipher cause-and-effect relationships between stress and depression. The work has also moved from the study of broad variables (for example, stress) to more specific ones (for example, types of stress).

Gender and Depression Depression is far more common among women than among men regardless of region of the world, race and ethnicity, or social class (Strickland, 1992). Although women are more likely than men to be seen in treatment and to be di-

Depression as a Cause of Depression?

Research has shown that stress can trigger a depressive episode. There is increasing evidence that depressed persons may seek or bring about conditions that tend to maintain their depression. Depressed college students were found to choose interaction partners who perceived them unfavorably over those who perceived them favorably. Compared with nondepressed students, they also preferred friends and dating partners who had negative appraisals of them, and they were inclined to seek negative feedback from their roommates (Swann et al., 1992). Depressed people have also been found to be consistently rejected by others (Segrin & Abramson, 1994). Investigators raised the possibility that depressed individuals view themselves negatively. By choosing others who give negative feedback, they verify, stabilize, and make predictable their unfavorable self-images.

In addition to seeking negative feedback, depressed persons may also create stress for themselves. Hammen (1991) conducted a one-year, longitudinal study of women with unipolar depression, bipolar disorder, chronic medical illness, and no illness or disorder. The purpose was to ascertain the relationship between stress and depression. Unipolar, bipolar, and medically ill women had similar levels of stress, which were greater than those encountered by their healthy counterparts. An evaluation of the stressors determined the degree to which their occurrence was certainly or almost certainly independent of the women's behaviors or characteristics, or was likely to be caused by them. For example, some stressors (like being robbed) were considered independent of the women's behaviors, whereas others (such as initiating an argument with another person) were judged to be depen-

dent on the women's behaviors. Women with unipolar depression were more likely than other women to have experienced stressors in which they were contributors and also to have stressors involving interpersonal interactions. Hammen speculated that depressed individuals may help contribute to the stress they encounter, which, in turn, provokes further depression!

This research should not be interpreted as demonstrating that depressed individuals purposely want to further their depressive states. Rather, depressive episodes and the associated negative self-images and cognitions may reduce coping skills, which then lead to situations (such as seeking negative feedback or creating stress for themselves) that in turn lead to further depression.

---

agnosed as depressed, this may not mean that women are more depressed, for several reasons, as noted in Table 11.3. First, women may simply be more likely than men to seek treatment when depressed; this tendency would make the reported depression rate for women higher, even if the actual male and female rates were equal. Second, women may be more willing to report their depression to other people. That is, the gender differences may occur in self-report behaviors rather than in actual depression rates. Third, diagnosticians or the diagnostic system may be biased toward finding depression among women (Caplan, 1995). And fourth, depression in men may take other forms and thus be given other diagnoses, such as substance dependency.

Some clinicians believe that these four possibilities account for only part of the gender difference in depression, and that women really do have higher rates

of depression (Radloff & Rae, 1981). The reasons for these differences are unclear, however. Speculation has involved physiological or social psychological factors.

Genetic or hormonal differences between the sexes were once thought to influence depression. Although biogenic factors may account for the sex differences, relatively little research has been conducted on these factors, and available findings are inconsistent with respect to hormonal changes and depression. This has led researchers to propose social or psychological factors, one of which is the woman's traditional gender role. Women have been encouraged to present themselves as attractive, sensitive to other persons, and passive in relationships (Strickland, 1992). These roles, as well as subservience to men and a lack of occupational opportunities, may produce more depression in women (Bernard, 1976). For the same reason, women may be more likely than men to experience

TABLE 11.3 Explaining the Findings That Rates of Depression Are Higher Among Women Than Among Men

The Gender Differences Only Appear to Be Real Because	The Gender Differences Are Real Because
■ Women may be more likely to seek treatment. ■ Women may be more willing to report their depression to other people. ■ Diagnosticians or the diagnostic system may be gender biased. ■ Men may exhibit depression in different ways and may be given other diagnoses.	■ Genetic or hormonal differences between genders may account for higher depression levels among women. ■ Women are subjected to gender roles that may be unfulfilling and that limit occupational opportunities. ■ Gender roles may lead to feelings of helplessness. ■ Traditional feminine roles may be less successful at eliciting positive reinforcement from others, compared with traditional male roles, which foster assertive and forceful behavior.

Actress Patty Duke suffered for years with bipolar disorder. After appropriate treatment, she now leads a very productive life. Indeed, her insights into her mental disorder have resulted in a revealing book about her own battle with depression and numerous public service messages on the topic.

lack of control in life situations. They may then attribute their "helplessness" to an imagined lack of personal worth. Interestingly, women who are not employed outside the home and who are raising children are particularly vulnerable to depression (Gotlib, 1992). Finally, the traditional feminine gender role behaviors (gentleness, emotionality, and self-subordination) may not be so successful in eliciting reinforcement from others as the assertive and more forceful responses typically associated with males.

In a review of different explanations for the gender differences in depression, Nolen-Hoeksema (1987) concluded that none truly accounts for the observed sex differences in the rates of depression. She hypothesized that the way a person responds to depressed moods contributes to the severity, chronicity, and recurrence of depressive episodes. In her view, women tend to ruminate and amplify their depressive moods, and men dampen or find means to minimize dysphoria. Nolen-Hoeksema (1991) found that when individuals tracked their depressed moods and responses to these moods for one month, women were more likely than men to ruminate in response to depressed moods. Those who tended to ruminate had longer periods of depressed moods, and when tendency to ruminate was statistically controlled, gender differences in duration of depressed moods disappeared.

Egeland and Hostetter (1983) also speculated that responses to depressive moods may affect observed rates of depression. In their study of an Amish religious community in Pennsylvania, they found that

Among the Amish, men and women appear to have similar rates of depression. Egeland and Hostetter (1983) believe that gender roles may affect depression rates. Gender roles, such as working together in the fields, are similar for Amish men and women and may account for the lack of gender differences in rates of depression.

males and females have the same rates for depression. The researchers noted that because Amish men do not show alcoholism or antisocial behaviors, their depression cannot be masked. Additionally, Amish women, like the men, must work outside the home, so engaging in a sick (depressed) role is discouraged. Although role behavior may help explain some of the differences in rates of depression between women and men, it is not clear whether the explanation is enough to account for the vast differences that have been recorded.

The work on sociocultural or psychosocial influences provides a perspective of how cultural, institutional, and environmental conditions affect depression. Now let us turn to theories that are primarily biogenic in nature.

Biological Perspectives on Mood Disorders

Biological approaches to the cause of mood or affective disorders generally focus on genetic predisposition, physiological dysfunction, or combinations of the two.

The Role of Heredity Mood disorders tend to run in families, and the same type of disorder is generally found among members of the same family (American Psychiatric Association, 1994; Perris, 1966; Winokur, Clayton & Reich, 1969). As we have noted in earlier chapters, one way to assess the role of heredity is to compare the incidence of disorders among the biological and adoptive families of people who were adopted early in life and who had the disorders. If heredity is more important, then biological families (which contributed the genetic makeup) should show a high incidence of the disorders. If environment is more important, then adoptive families (which provided the early environment) should show a high incidence. The results of such a comparison indicated that the incidence of mood disorders was higher among the biological families than among the adoptive families; the latter showed an incidence similar to that of the general population (Kety, 1979).

Another way to study the possible genetic transmission of mood disorders is to compare identical and fraternal twins. Nine such studies of twins have been reported. The concordance rate (the probability of one twin having the same disorder as the cotwin) for bipolar disorders was 72 percent for identical twins and 14 percent for fraternal twins. The rate suggests that the genetic component is extremely important, although nongenetic factors also appear important (Baron, 1991). By contrast, the concordance rate for unipolar mood disorders was only 40 percent for identical twins and 11 percent for fraternal twins (Goodwin & Guze, 1984).

Both of these research approaches (and others) consistently turn up evidence of genetic influence on mood disorders. Moreover, the bulk of the research suggests that heredity is a stronger factor in bipolar mood disorders than in unipolar disorders (Reus, 1988).

Egeland and colleagues (1987) have also provided some evidence of genetic involvement in bipolar disorders. Again studying the Amish religious community in Pennsylvania, these investigators found a number of people with bipolar disorders, many of whom had the same ancestors. Using sophisticated techniques, they found that a gene located on a specific region of a chromosome was associated with mood disorders among the Amish. Gershon and colleagues (1989) could not replicate the findings in other populations, although the discrepancy in findings could be a result of the different populations studied. They noted that technological advancements in instrumentation, statistical genetic techniques, and molecular biology have allowed researchers to become increasingly sophisticated in the study of biological aspects of mood disorders.

Although heredity appears to be important, especially in bipolar disorders, researchers show little consensus over the appropriate model for the transmission of affective disorders. Some researchers have proposed that depression is caused by one primary gene rather than many genes; most favor a polygenetic theory over a monogenetic theory (Gershon et al., 1989).

Neurotransmitters and Mood Disorders But how is heredity involved in the major mood disorders? A growing number of researchers believe that genetic factors influence the amounts of *catecholamines*—a group of substances, including norepinephrine, dopamine, and serotonin—which are found at specific sites in the brain. These substances, called **neurotransmitters,** help transmit nerve impulses from one neuron to another. They may mediate between active motor behavior and emotions (Becker, 1974; Weiss, Glazer & Pohorecky, 1975).

Nerve impulses are transmitted from neuron to neuron across *synapses,* which are small gaps between the axon (or transmitting end) of one neuron and the dendrites (or receiving end) of a receptor neuron. In Figure 11.4, Neuron A is the transmitting neuron and Neuron B is the receptor neuron. For a nerve impulse to travel from A to B, the axon at A must release a neurotransmitter into the synaptic gap, thereby stimulating B to fire, or transmit the impulse. According to the *catecholamine hypothesis,* depression is caused by a deficit of specific neurotransmitters at brain synapses; similarly, mania is presumed to be caused by an oversupply of these substances (Bunney et al., 1979; Schildkraut, 1965).

As in other areas, most research has focused on the study of depression. Figure 11.4 illustrates two mechanisms, either of which could cause the amount of neurotransmitters in the synapses to be insufficient: (1) Neurotransmitters are broken down or chemically depleted by the enzyme monoamine oxidase (MAO), which is normally found in the body. (2) Neurotransmitters are reabsorbed by the releasing neuron in the process of *re-uptake.*

Support for the catecholamine hypothesis comes from two lines of research. In the first, researchers have established a connection between levels of neurotransmitters and motor activity. In one study, researchers put rats in stressful situations—for example, a series of inescapable shocks—and found that the level of norepinephrine in the rats' brains was reduced. The animals with these low levels showed "depressive" behaviors, such as motor passivity and an inability to learn avoidance-escape responses. Giving rats a drug that depletes brain norepinephrine also results in motor passivity and an inability to learn (Weiss, Glazer & Pohorecky, 1975).

The second line of support for the catecholamine hypothesis comes from studies of the effects of antidepressant medication on neurotransmitters and on mood changes. Antidepressant medications appear to increase the level of neurotransmitters. One group, the MAO inhibitors, block the effects of MAO in breaking down the neurotransmitters. Another group, the tricyclic drugs, blocks the re-uptake of certain transmitter substances. Fluoxetine (Prozac) seems to block the re-uptake of serotonin in particular.

Further support comes from the study in which rats were subjected to inescapable shocks. If the rats are given a drug that protects against the depletion of norepinephrine, and if this drug is administered before an experience with inescapable shock, the rats become immunized against passivity and poor learning (Weiss, Glazer & Pohorecky, 1975). Clearly, these findings suggest the importance of norepinephrine in depressive behaviors. In addition, they also show that environmental stressors produce biochemical and behavioral changes and, conversely, that biochemical changes can produce behavioral effects similar to those of environmental stressors. Even so, no matter how similar laboratory animals and people may be in various respects, the behavior of animals is not the same as the behavior of human beings. Investigators therefore need more evidence of a direct link between the role of neurotransmitters and depressive behaviors in human beings.

Some evidence implicating neurotransmitters in human depression and mania has been obtained accidentally (Goodwin, 1974). For example, it was dis-

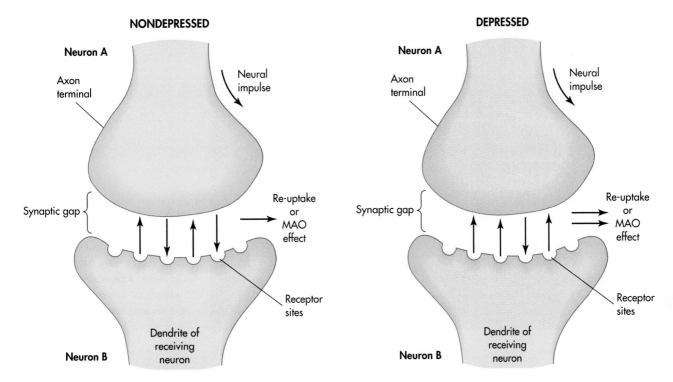

NONDEPRESSED

Neuron A

Axon terminal

Neural impulse

Synaptic gap

Re-uptake or MAO effect

Receptor sites

Dendrite of receiving neuron

Neuron B

DEPRESSED

Neuron A

Axon terminal

Neural impulse

Synaptic gap

Re-uptake or MAO effect

Receptor sites

Dendrite of receiving neuron

Neuron B

FIGURE 11.4   The Catecholamine Hypothesis: A Proposed Connection Between Neurotransmitters and Depression   On the left is a representation of the production of neurotransmitter substances at a synapse between two neurons in the brain of a nondepressed person. Some of the neurotransmitter is reabsorbed by the transmitting neuron in a process known as *re-uptake.* Neurotransmitters are also broken down or chemically depleted by the enzyme monoamine oxidase (MAO), which is normally found in the body (shown on the right). In depressed people, either or both of these two processes may reduce neurotransmitters to a level that is insufficient for normal functioning.

covered that when the drug reserpine was used in treating hypertension, many patients became depressed. (*Reserpine* depletes the level of neurotransmitters in the brain.) Similarly, the drug iproniazid, given to tubercular patients, elevated the mood of those who were depressed. (*Iproniazid* inhibits the destruction of neurotransmitters.) Thus mood levels in human beings were found to vary with the level of neurotransmitters or of neurotransmitter activity in the brain. These variations are consistent with the catecholamine hypothesis.

Some researchers have suggested that the level, or amount, of neurotransmitters present is not the primary factor. They noted that, to travel from one neuron to another, an electrical impulse must release neurotransmitters that stimulate the receiving neuron. The problem may not be the amount of neurotransmitter made available by the sending neuron, but

rather a dysfunction in the reception of the neurotransmitter by the receiving neuron (Sulser, 1979).

Whether mood disorders are caused by a deficiency in the production of neurotransmitter substances, a blunted receptor response, or a more general dysregulation in neurotransmission cannot be resolved at this time. It is also possible that no one cause will be isolated because depression is a heterogeneous collection of subtypes of disorders with differing biological and environmental precursors (Mann, 1989).

Abnormal Cortisol Levels   Considerable interest has also focused on possible abnormalities in neuroendocrine regulation in depressed people. Depressives tend to have high levels of *cortisol,* a hormone secreted by the adrenal cortex. Cortisol levels are measured by the *dexamethasone suppression test (DST).* In

Sleep patterns have been linked to depression. For example, rapid eye movement during sleep occurs more often among depressed than nondepressed individuals. The reasons for this are unclear. Here, a researcher is monitoring a woman's sleep.

this test, patients are given dexamethasone, which normally suppresses the cortisol secretion. Studies in different countries have shown that higher blood levels of cortisol are found in depressives than in normal people (World Health Organization, 1987) and that not suppressing these levels is linked to poorer prognosis for recovery (Reus, 1988). Whether cortisol helps cause depression or is produced by depression, however, is still unclear. Furthermore, measuring cortisol levels accurately has been difficult, and patients with other disorders often exhibit responses similar to those of depressed individuals (Free & Oei, 1989), so questions remain over the value of using the DST as a tool for assessing depression and prognosis.

REM Sleep Disturbances   Findings of a different sort have also aroused interest in the biological or physiological processes of depression. For example, depressed adults differ from nondepressed persons in sleep patterns, particularly in rapid eye movement (REM) sleep. (There are several stages of sleep, and during REM sleep the eyes move rapidly and dreaming occurs.) Depression is linked with a relatively rapid onset of, and an increase in, REM sleep (Goodwin & Guze, 1984). Moreover, reducing the REM sleep of persons with depression seems to help (Vogel et al., 1980). Why sleep patterns are linked to depression is unclear. Monroe, Thase, and Simons (1992) found that some depressed patients experienced severe, acute life stress whereas others did not. REM latency (that is, the time before REM occurs

during sleep) was short among those depressives who did not experience severe life stress. It may be that those with reduced REM latency have a lower threshold for the development of depression, in that less stress is needed to affect depression.

Evaluating the Causation Theories

Three developments have added to our understanding of mood disorders. First, longitudinal or prospective studies have allowed greater insights into the possible causal links between life experiences and depression. Second, technological advancements in psychophysiological tools have enabled researchers to more clearly identify biological markers and processes in mood disorders. Third, researchers are increasingly attentive to the possibility of viewing depression as a heterogeneous collection of disorders. In view of the fact that depression is so common and seemingly influenced by so many factors, the heterogeneous view of the disorder is not surprising. The three developments have, in turn, affected our theories of mood disorders.

The theories of depression presented in this chapter explain certain aspects of the disturbance, but all have weaknesses. According to the psychoanalytic perspective, loss and separation provoke a depressive reaction. But what determines the extent and severity of depression? Fixation at the oral stage, dependency, and symbolic loss are psychoanalytic concepts that are difficult to test. The psychoanalytic assumption that depression may simply be hostility turned inward on the self also seems open to question. When some depressed patients experienced success on experimental tasks, their self-esteem and optimism increased (Beck, 1974). If depression is hostility turned inward, why would success alleviate some of its symptoms?

As we have noted, Beck's idea is that the tendency to think in negative terms helps produce depression. His theory has, over time, become increasingly complex. To what extent is depression caused by depressive thoughts or is the effect of them? Aren't cognitive aspects of depression overemphasized relative to environmental stressors that evoke depression? Lewinsohn's behavioral theory and Seligman's learned helplessness theory are well grounded in research findings. Lewinsohn's work has mainly shown a relationship between depression and inadequate positive reinforcement. But do these low rates of reinforcement actually cause depression? Seligman has shown that learned helplessness and certain attributions can lead to depressive behaviors. However, this model explains only certain kinds of depression—mainly reactions to stress. How can behavioral as well as cognitive theorists present a more convincing account of the development of manic behaviors?

Endogenous (congenital) factors seem to play a crucial role in mood disorders. Although genetic studies have not been extensive, evidence has shown that heredity is involved. The precise genetic mechanisms are not known, but research into biochemical factors or neurotransmitters seems quite promising.

One good way to think about mood disorders is to see them as a range of mood states resulting from an interaction between environmental and biological factors (Kraemer & McKinney, 1979). On one end of the range is mild sadness, then normal grief and the specific affective disorders, and, at the other end of the range are the major mood disorders. Milder instances of depression (or, for that matter, mania) may be more externally caused. In mood disorders in the middle of the spectrum, both external and internal factors may be important. In severe disorders, including psychotic forms of the major mood disorders, endogenous factors may become more prominent (Goodwin, 1977).

THE TREATMENT OF MOOD DISORDERS

Biological approaches to the treatment of mood disorders are generally based on the catecholamine hypothesis. That is, treatment consists primarily of controlling the level of neurotransmitters at brain synapses. Psychological treatment also seems to offer promise for persons with depression.

Biomedical Treatments for Depressive Disorders

Biomedical treatments are interventions that alter the physical or biochemical state of the patient. They include the use of medication and electroconvulsive therapy.

Medication   The drugs that are primarily used to treat unipolar depression are of two general types; both were introduced in the mid-1950s. The *tricyclic antidepressants* (the first group) are still considered the more effective (Klein, Gittelman & Quitkin, 1980), and they seem to be especially effective in endogenous forms of depression (Georgotas, 1985). These drugs seem to block the re-uptake of norepinephrine. When re-uptake is blocked, more norepinephrine is left at the synapses. These higher levels of residual norepinephrine seem to be linked with reduced depressive symptoms. The tricyclics, however, may cause side effects. Reactions include drowsiness, insomnia, agitation, fine tremors, blurred vision, dry mouth, and reduced sexual ability.

The *monoamine oxidase (MAO) inhibitors* (the second group of antidepressants) also work by increasing the level of norepinephrine at the brain synapses. Rather than blocking re-uptake as the tricyclics do, the MAO inhibitors prevent the MAO enzyme (which is normally found in the body) from breaking down norepinephrine that is already available at the synapse.

Although MAO inhibitors, as well as tricyclic antidepressants, affect levels of neurotransmitters, there is growing suspicion that the process is more complicated than previously believed. The drugs may also affect the sensitivity of receptors on the receiving (postsynaptic) neurons.

MAO inhibitors are currently prescribed for depressed patients who have not responded well to treatment with tricyclics. But MAO inhibitors also have many side effects including insomnia, irritability, dizziness, constipation, and impotence. The most serious side effect, however, is tyramine-cheese incompatibility. One normal function of the MAO enzyme is to break down tyramine, a substance found in many cheeses as well as in some beers, wines, pickled products, and chocolate. The MAO inhibitors interfere with this function, so someone who is using one of these drugs must severely restrict his or her intake of tyramine. Failure to do so triggers the tyramine-cheese reaction, which begins with increased blood pressure, vomiting, and muscle twitching and can, if untreated, result in intracranial bleeding followed by death.

Such side effects are a major drawback of the antidepressant drugs, and careful monitoring of the patient's reactions is thus absolutely necessary. Another drawback is that the antidepressant drugs are essentially ineffective during the first two weeks of use, which is a serious concern, particularly where suicide is a danger. As mentioned earlier, the effectiveness of antidepressant drugs may be caused by changes in the sensitivity of postsynaptic receptors. These changes in sensitivity, however, seem to require a couple of weeks to develop.

Klein, Gittelman, and Quitkin (1980) noted that about 65 percent of moderately to severely depressed people improve while taking tricyclics. A review of the effects of selected antidepressant medication from rigorously designed studies, however, suggested that treatment outcomes have probably been overestimated (Greenberg et al., 1992). Although clinicians' ratings of outcome have been high, patients' ratings have been very similar to those patients who were given a placebo. Thus if researchers ask clinicians about the effects of antidepressant medication, they tend to give more favorable ratings than do patients. Another factor to consider is that drug effectiveness may be related to the "type" of depression. Peselow and colleagues (1992) found that depressed patients who were considered high autonomous–low sociotropy personalities (concerned with possible personal failure) had a more favorable response to antidepressant medication than did patients considered high sociotropic–low autonomy personalities (concerned with rejection from others).

More recently, fluoxetine (Prozac) has been widely used for depression because its effects are comparable to those of the tricyclic antidepressants but with fewer unpleasant side effects (Strickland, 1992). Prozac, like the tricyclics, appears to block the re-uptake of serotonin. As noted in Chapter 17, soon after its widespread use, Prozac was accused by some clients and client advocacy groups of precipitating suicides and violent behaviors. Research findings have not supported the accusations (U.S. Department of Health and Human Services, 1991).

Electroconvulsive Therapy   Electroconvulsive therapy (ECT) is generally reserved for patients with severe unipolar depression who have not responded to tricyclics or MAO inhibitors. The procedure is described in Chapter 17; in essence, it consists of applying a moderate electrical voltage to the person's brain for up to half a second. The patient's response to the voltage is a convulsion (seizure) lasting thirty to forty seconds, followed by a five- to thirty-minute coma.

Most seriously depressed patients show at least a temporary improvement after about four ECT treatments (Campbell, 1981). The ECT mechanism is not fully understood; it may operate on neurotransmitters at the synapses, as do antidepressants. Some of the decrease in symptoms may also be due to the amnesia that develops for a short time after the treatment. One major advantage of ECT is that the response to treatment is relatively fast (Gangadhar, Kapur & Kalyanasundaram, 1982). However, common side effects include headaches, confusion, and memory loss. And many patients are terrified of ECT. In about one of every one thousand cases, serious medical complications occur (Goldman, 1988). ECT is controversial, and critics have urged that it be banned as a form of treatment (see Critical Thinking). The Focus On feature (page 352) describes a case in which medication was used in combination with ECT to treat a bipolar affective disorder.

Psychotherapy and Behavioral Treatments for Depressive Disorders

Because the use of antidepressant medication or ECT involves a number of disadvantages, clinicians have sought other approaches to either supplement or replace medical treatment of depression. A variety of psychological forms of treatment have been used, such as psychoanalysis, behavior therapy, and family therapies—all with some success (Hirschfeld & Shea, 1985).

Treatment strategies reflect the theoretical orientation of the therapists. For example, psychoanalysts attempt to have their clients gain insight into unconscious and unresolved feelings of separation or anger. This is accomplished through the therapists' interpretations of the clients' free associations, reports of dreams, resistances, and transferences (see Chapter 17). In contrast, behavioral therapists may believe that reduced reinforcement is responsible for depression. They would attempt to teach clients to increase their exposure to pleasurable events and activities and to improve social skills and interactions.

Two types of treatment—interpersonal psychotherapy and cognitive-behavioral therapy—have been intensively examined for their effectiveness in depressive disorders.

Interpersonal Psychotherapy   Interpersonal psychotherapy is a short-term, psychodynamic-eclectic type of treatment for depression that targets the client's interpersonal relationships and that uses strategies found in psychodynamic, cognitive-behavioral, and

CRITICAL THINKING

Should Electroconvulsive Shock Treatment for Depression Be Banned?

On the editorial page of *USA Today,* two views of electroconvulsive therapy (ECT) were presented:

Shock therapy is gaining new respectibility these days.... But... this drastic, potentially deadly treatment is still far too poorly understood.... Even proponents disagree on how the jolts work, and the cheery benefits are short-lived.... Meanwhile, the long-term effects can be devastating. They include confusion, memory loss, heart failure, and in some patients, death. (Patients, public need full story on shock therapy, *USA Today,* December 8, 1995, p. 12A)

I am astounded at USA TODAY's use of inaccuracies and half-truths this week to malign elec-

troconvulsive therapy, an often lifesaving medical treatment. Thousands of psychiatrists and neuroscientists agree: ECT is a safe and effective treatment for certain serious illnesses. Thousands of patients are living proof. (William Reid, Don't malign treatment, *USA Today,* December 8, 1995, p. 12A)

These opposing viewpoints are not unusual. Testimonies can be obtained from patients and therapists wholeheartedly supporting either the use or the abolition of ECT. Proponents argue that convulsive spasms of the body from ECT have been controlled by muscle relaxants and, although the reasons are unclear, ECT seems to work. Critics are concerned with

confusion, memory loss, and other side effects that may occur, as well as the troublesome inability to explain why ECT works. It is interesting to note that individuals who review the literature on the effectiveness of ECT may come to very different conclusions. Why is this the case? And how do we decide when to ban a certain form of treatment? Clearly, effectiveness is only one factor to consider in evaluations of treatment. What other kinds of information do we need to make a decision? After reading about ECT in this chapter, do you feel it should be banned? (Before answering, you might want to take a quick look at Chapter 17, which also discusses ECT, as well as the Focus On feature.

---

other forms of therapy (Klerman et al., 1984). The assumptions underlying interpersonal psychotherapy are that depression occurs within an interpersonal context and, accordingly, that interpersonal relationship issues must be addressed. The focus is on conflicts and problems that occur in these relationships. Clients gain insight into conflicts in social relationships and strive to change these relationships. For example, by improving communications with others, by identifying role conflicts, and by increasing social skills, clients are able to find relationships more satisfying and pleasant. Although interpersonal psychotherapy resembles psychoanalysis and psychodynamic approaches in acknowledging the role of early life experiences and traumas, it is oriented primarily toward present, not past, relationships. As discussed later, interpersonal psychotherapy has been found to be effective in the treatment of depression.

Cognitive-Behavioral Therapy As its name implies, cognitive-behavioral therapy combines cognitive and behavioral strategies. The cognitive component involves teaching the patient the following (Beck et al., 1979):

■ to identify negative, self-critical thoughts (cognitions) that occur automatically.

■ to note the connection between negative thoughts and the resulting depression.

■ to carefully examine each negative thought and decide whether it can be supported.

■ to try to replace distorted negative thoughts with realistic interpretations of each situation.

Cognitive therapists believe that distorted thoughts cause psychological problems such as depression and

I Am Suffering from Depression

Dr. Norman Endler, a prominent psychologist, stable family man, and chairman of the psychology department at York University, wrote,

> I honestly felt subhuman, lower than the lowest vermin. Furthermore, I was self-deprecatory and could not understand why anyone would want to associate with me, let alone love me....
>
> I was also positive that I was going to be fired from the university because of incompetence and that we could become destitute—that we would go broke.
>
> ... I was positive that I was a fraud and phony and that I didn't deserve my Ph.D. I didn't deserve to have tenure; I didn't deserve to be a full professor; I didn't deserve to be chairman of the psychology department.
>
> ... I couldn't understand how I had written the books and journal articles that I had and how they had been accepted for publication. (Endler, 1982, pp. 45–48)

These comments are from a poignant and very explicit book in which Endler described his experiences with a bipolar disorder and his reactions to treatment. Until the spring of 1977, Endler felt fine. He was at the height of his successful career. He was active in sports and was constantly on the move. In retrospect, Endler had realized that he was hypomanic in the fall of 1976, but not until the following April did he became aware that something was wrong. He had difficulty sleeping and had lost his sex drive. "I had gone from being a winner to feeling like a loser. Depression had turned it around for me. From being on top

of the world in the fall, I suddenly felt useless, inept, sad, and anxious in the spring" (p. 11).

Endler sought treatment and was administered several drugs that did not prove effective. He was then given electroconvulsive therapy (ECT). Endler described his reaction to ECT as well as the way the treatment was administered.

> I was asked to lie down on a cot and was wheeled into the ECT room proper. It was about eight o'clock. A needle was injected into my arm and I was told to count back from 100. I got about as far as 91. The next thing I knew I was in the recovery room and it was about eight-fifteen. I was slightly groggy and tired but not confused. (Endler, 1982, p. 81)

After about seven ECT sessions, his depression lifted dramatically: "My holiday of darkness was over and fall arrived with a bang!" (p. 83).

The next few months were free of depression, and Endler enjoyed everything he did. Later, he realized that he was actually hypomanic during this period also. He was a bit euphoric, energetic, and active; he talked incessantly. Then depression struck again. He recognized that he was experiencing the initial signs of depression and again underwent drug treatment and ECT. This time, however, the treatments were ineffective. Slowly, over the course of about two years, his depression dissipated with the aid of medication.

Endler concludes by offering some advice. First, when people think they are depressed, they should seek treatment immedi-

ately. Second, some combinations of treatments such as psychotherapy, antidepressant drugs, and ECT may be effective. Third, the depressive's family can have an important effect on recovery: When a family member becomes severely depressed, existing family conflicts may become exacerbated. A supportive and understanding family can help a depressed person survive.

> Depression is a common pervasive illness affecting all social classes, but it is eminently treatable. A great deal of heartbreak can be avoided by early detection and treatment. There is nothing to be ashamed of. There is no stigma attached to having an affective disorder. It is unwise to try to hide it and not seek help. I lived to tell and to write about it...
>
> As of this writing ... I have been symptom-free for almost three years.... I am not experiencing an emotional crisis and I hope I never do again.... I am reminded of a telephone conversation I had with my wife.... I mentioned that I had to do a lot of work to finish the first draft of Chapter 11, the last chapter in this book, before I left Stanford at the end of the month. Beatty said to me, "What's so terrible if you don't finish?" That put it all in perspective for me. I intend to live life to the fullest, but carefully. The sun will rise and shine whether or not I finish things today. But it's nice knowing that I did finish the first draft of this book before I left Stanford! (Endler, 1982, pp. 167–169)

Source: Endler, 1982.

Date	Situation	Automatic Thoughts	Emotions	Rational Alternative	Emotion
2/9	I sat home all alone on a Fri. night.	Nobody likes me or I would have been asked out.	Depressed	Most people know that I usually work Fri. nights. Maybe nobody knew I had the night off.	Relief, contentment
2/10	I had trouble understanding my reading assignment.	I must be an idiot. This should be an easy subject.	Depressed, anxious	If I don't understand the material, I bet a number of others don't either.	Calm, determined

FIGURE 11.5　Daily Cognition Chart for a Typical Client with Depression

that changing the distorted thoughts can eliminate the depression.

At the outset of the cognitive therapy, the client is usually asked to begin monitoring his or her negative thoughts and to list them on a chart. It is important for the client to include all the thoughts and emotions associated with each distressing event that takes place each day (see Figure 11.5).

The client brings the chart to the session each week, and the therapist uses it to demonstrate that the client's distress is being caused by his or her own unnecessarily negative thoughts. The client's own rational alternatives to these thoughts are discussed, and the client makes a conscious effort to adopt those alternatives that seem plausible. The goal of the cognitive part of the therapy is to train the client to automatically substitute logical interpretations for self-denigrating thoughts. Cognitive therapists maintain that when a patient's thoughts about himself or herself become more consistently positive, the emotions follow suit.

The second part of the cognitive-behavioral approach is behavior therapy, which is usually indicated in cases of severe depression in which the patient is virtually inactive. One primary assumption underlying this approach is that a depressed person is not doing enough pleasant, rewarding activities. Depressed people tend to withdraw from others when

they belittle themselves; they then interpret their self-imposed social isolation as a sign of being unpopular and inadequate (Lewinsohn, 1977).

To address this problem, depressed patients are asked to keep a daily activity schedule on which they list life events hour by hour and rate the "pleasantness" of each event. When a person is asked to monitor and rate events or activities, activities generally increase in frequency. This in itself is a worthwhile strategy for severely depressed patients; simply getting depressed people to engage in more activities increases the chance that they will become involved in some pleasant, reinforcing events. The patient's chart of this information also helps the therapist spot specific patterns of activity. For instance, a client who insists that he or she does not enjoy anything may rate as "slightly pleasant" time spent outdoors. The therapist would point out this pattern to the client and encourage that person to spend more time outdoors (Beck et al., 1979).

Once the severely depressed client becomes more active, he or she may be asked to attend a social skills training program. Improvements in social skills generally help clients become more socially involved and can make that involvement rewarding (Hersen, Bellack & Himmelhoch, 1980). (See the First Person narrative for one therapist's experience with a client in cognitive-behavioral therapy.)

FIRST
PERSON

Christopher Martell

As a cognitive-behavioral therapist, I look at how people's thought processes and behaviors contribute to mood disorders and help them to change these patterns of thinking and behaving to better cope with life. And, as a psychologist who works with persons who are homosexual, I must always take into account external stressors that affect my clients with mood disorders.

Because gay and lesbian people who "come out" or openly acknowledge their orientation often face homophobia (the irrational fear of homosexuality) and heterosexism (the belief that heterosexuality is the only legitimate sexual orientation) throughout their lives, the social stigma associated with membership in a sexual minority complicates many life situations and psychological conditions that would be difficult to deal with even without such stigmatization. For those who are already predisposed to a mood disorder (major depression, generalized anxiety disorder, and so forth), these societal pressures or traumas make it harder to treat the basic psychological problem.

Joshua,* age 37, presented with complaints of depression and anxiety. He demonstrated all the symptoms of a major depressive episode—loss of pleasure in most activities, a decrease in sexual desire, difficulty sleeping, loss of appetite, fatigue, and blue mood. Because Joshua had also been di-

_____
*Joshua is a fictional character drawn from a composite of a number of clients I've seen.

agnosed with AIDS, though, it was difficult at first to identify the depression as a separate condition. His fatigue and other depressive symptoms are also symptomatic of complications due to AIDS.

Joshua's recent history gave some insight into his depressed state, however. He had decided that he needed to cut back his work hours because of his illness, yet because his illness implied that he was gay he had waited longer than he may have otherwise to inform his employer of the situation. His hesitance was not unusual, given the frequent intolerance and prejudice that exists in the workplace. Joshua wanted to protect his dignity and his job. When he finally decided to approach his supervisor about his illness, he was met with a shocked reaction. Although his supervisor told him that the firm would support him in any way it could, Joshua soon began to notice that important assignments and accounts were being taken away from him. His request for a decrease in hours was becoming a loss of his job altogether. He had taken great pride in his work, had been a stellar em-

---

Both interpersonal psychotherapy and cognitive-behavioral therapy have been found to be effective treatments for depression. In an intensive study, depressed clients were randomly assigned to one of four treatment conditions for four months: interpersonal psychotherapy, cognitive-behavioral therapy, imipramine plus clinical management, and pill-placebo plus clinical management (Elkin, 1994; Elkin et al., 1995). Imipramine, a tricyclic drug, was included in the design because its effectiveness has been studied and the other treatments could be compared with it. The imipramine and pill-placebo conditions were paired with clinical management (in which minimal supportive therapy was provided) because of the ethical need to provide some therapy for clients in the pill-placebo and imipramine conditions. Results indicated that in general the interpersonal psychotherapy, cognitive-

behavioral, and imipramine treatments were equally effective in reducing depression. All were significantly more effective than the pill-placebo condition. However, specific effects were influenced by initial severity of disturbance. In addition, many of the clients showing major improvement at the end of treatment (regardless of treatment condition) had relapsed and were suffering from depression again eighteen months following treatment. Thus interpersonal psychotherapy, cognitive-behavioral therapy, and imipramine appear to be effective, although some of the effects diminish over time.

Hollon, DeRubeis, and Seligman (1992) found that cognitive therapy may reduce the risk of depression episodes that occur after treatment. Depressed clients treated by cognitive therapy were less likely to develop subsequent symptoms of depression than were

ployee, and was commended frequently by his superiors. Although it is hard to say that the response from his boss would have been different if Joshua had been heterosexual and suffering from leukemia, his belief that he was facing discrimination due to his sexual orientation and health status contributed to his depression.

Our therapy focused on his perception of being helpless, his need to confront his employer, and his very real concerns about his illness. As a cognitive therapist, I helped him see where he was distorting reality in a way that made his dysphoria greater. This was no easy task, as he was facing life situations that were truly frightening and traumatic. Joshua felt hopeless—a common aspect of depression. In encouraging him to take control by confronting his employer, reading about treatments for his illness, and developing a plan for daily activities that would keep him from slumping into lethargy, I began the behavioral task of breaking patterns of learned helplessness. We also discussed his beliefs that he was responsible for being sick and that life could have

no meaning or joy because of his illness, and I helped him to disprove these notions.

Although it was very difficult for him to overcome his depression completely, he was better able to cope and we both felt therapy was successful. Nevertheless, we needed to be aware of our parameters. Joshua was dealing not only with depression and fears about his illness, but also with other peoples' fears and prejudice, his internalized homophobia, and multiple losses of friends and loved ones to AIDS.

All therapists need to be sensitive to cultural differences, and the gay and lesbian community is distinct from the heterosexual community socioculturally as well as according to choice of sexual partners. It is as diverse as the heterosexual community. My clients' sexual orientations, for example, feel very normal to them. In terms of stress, however, they may be plagued by learned belief systems that challenge their comfort with their orientation or decision to live according to that orientation.

Those of us who are gay or lesbian professionals and who work

with this population of individuals can only do our small part to change society. We do, however, have an obligation to make sure that the issue of sexual orientation does not obscure the other issues that gay, lesbian, and bisexual persons face. All therapists are responsible for seeing that social and environmental pressures are accounted for in treatment strategies for mood disorders and other psychological problems.

Christopher Martell is a clinical and school psychologist in private practice in Seattle, Washington. His clinical practice focuses primarily on psychotherapeutic interventions with individuals coping with disabilities or chronic illness, depression, and anxiety disorders. He has worked extensively with the gay and lesbian community and is co-chair of the Committee on Lesbian and Gay Concerns for the Washington State Psychological Association.

clients treated pharmacologically. The researchers believe that cognitive changes in explanatory styles and attributions among the clients in cognitive therapy may help prevent depressive symptoms. In fact, cognitive-behavioral techniques have been used in prevention programs. Munoz and his colleagues (1995) found that teaching cognitive-behavioral skills can be helpful in preventing depression.

Treatment for Bipolar Disorders

Although the forms of psychotherapy and behavior therapy used for depressive disorders are also used for bipolar disorders, drugs (especially lithium) are typically given to bipolar clients. Since it was introduced to the United States in 1969, lithium (in the form of lithium carbonate) has been the treatment of choice

for bipolar and manic disorders (Fieve et al., 1976). It is also used as a maintenance drug to prevent or reduce future episodes of bipolar disorder (National Institute of Mental Health, 1985). As noted, the manic phase of bipolar disorder may be caused by too much neurotransmitter (primarily norepinephrine) at brain synapses or by neurotransmitter dysfunction. Lithium decreases the total level of neurotransmitters in the synaptic areas by increasing the re-uptake of norepinephrine into the nerve cells (Barchas et al., 1977).

The generally positive results achieved with lithium have been overshadowed somewhat by reports of distressing side effects (Dubovsky et al., 1982). The earliest danger signals are gastrointestinal complications (such as vomiting and diarrhea), fine tremors, muscular weakness, and frequent urination. The more serious side effects, associated with excessive lithium in the blood, are loss of bladder control, slurred speech, blurred vision, seizures, and abnormal heart rate. Fortunately, accurate measurements of lithium blood levels are easily obtained, and dosages can be adjusted accordingly.

Another problem associated with lithium is lack of patient compliance with the treatment program. For some reason, this problem is consistently worse with bipolar patients taking lithium than with any other group of patients taking any other drug. Bipolar patients often report that they have tried to adjust their lithium dosage by themselves so that they will experience the mania but not the depression of bipolar disorder. Unfortunately, lithium levels cannot be manipulated in this manner. When the dosage is decreased, the initial slightly manic state quickly develops into either a severe manic state or depression.

SUMMARY

1. Severe depression is a major component of the mood disorders; it involves affective, cognitive, behavioral, and physiological symptoms, such as sadness, pessimism, low energy, and sleep disturbances. Mania, which may accompany depression, is characterized by elation, lack of focus, impulsive actions, and almost boundless energy. DSM-IV recognizes hypomania and mania.

2. In bipolar mood disorders, manic episodes occur or alternate with depressive episodes. Depressive disorders (formerly known as unipolar disorders, and including major depression and dysthymic disorder) involve only depression. Psychotic and other features may also appear in persons with severe mood disorders. The depressive disorders are the most common mood disorders; some evidence suggests that they are fairly distinct from the bipolar disorders.

3. Psychological theories of depression have been proposed by adherents of the psychoanalytic, behavioral, cognitive, cognitive-learning, and sociocultural viewpoints, but each has certain weaknesses. Psychoanalytic explanations focus on separation and anger. Behavioral explanations focus on reduced reinforcement following losses. Cognitive explanations see low self-esteem as an important factor. According to the learned helplessness theory of depression, susceptibility to depression depends on the person's experience with controlling the environment. The person's attributional style—speculations about why he or she is helpless—is also important.

4. Sociocultural explanations have focused on cultural factors that influence the rates and symptoms of mood disorders and the role of stress and of social supports. Even though stress often precipitates the occurrence of depression, some people may be more vulnerable to depression, perhaps because of biogenic or psychosocial factors. Furthermore, social supports may provide a buffer against depression. Sociocultural factors have also been used to explain the higher observed rates of depression among women. They include gender role differences that make women more likely than men to amplify depressive symptoms.

5. Genetic and biochemical research has demonstrated that heredity plays a role in depression and mania, probably by affecting neurotransmitter activity or levels in the brain. For example, according to the catecholamine hypothesis, decreases in the amount of norepinephrine causes depression. Sensitivity of neurotransmitter receptors may also be a factor.

6. Biomedical approaches to treating depression focus on increasing the amounts of neurotransmitters available at brain synapses or by affecting the sensitivity of postsynaptic receptors through either medication or electroconvulsive therapy. Different forms of psychological and behavioral treatments have been found to be effective with mood disorders such as cognitive-behavioral treatment, which seeks to replace negative thoughts with more realistic (or positive) cognitions, and interpersonal therapy, which is a short-term treatment focused on interpersonal issues. The most effective treatment for bipolar and manic disorders is lithium, a drug that lowers the level of neurotransmitters at synapses by increasing the reuptake of norepinephrine.

KEY TERMS

bipolar disorder A category of mood disorders characterized by one or more manic or hypomanic episodes and, usually, by one or more depressive episodes

cyclothymic disorder A chronic and relatively continual mood disorder characterized by hypomanic episodes and depressed moods that do not meet the criteria for major depressive episode

depression An emotional state characterized by intense sadness, feelings of futility and worthlessness, and withdrawal from others

depressive disorders DSM-IV category including major depressive disorders, dysthymic disorder, and depressive disorders not otherwise specified; also known as *unipolar disorders* because no mania is exhibited

dysthymic disorder A disorder characterized by chronic and relatively continual depressed mood that does not meet the criteria for major depression

learned helplessness Acquiring the belief that one is helpless and unable to affect the outcomes in one's life

major depression A disorder in which a group of symptoms, such as depressed mood, loss of interest, sleep disturbances, feelings of worthlessness, and an inability to concentrate, are present for at least two weeks

mania An emotional state characterized by elevated mood, expansiveness, or irritability, often resulting in hyperactivity

mood disorders Disturbances in emotions that cause subjective discomfort, hinder a person's ability to function, or both; depression and mania are critical to these disorders

neurotransmitters Substances that help transmit nerve impulses from one neuron to another

schema A pattern of thinking or a cognitive set that determines (or colors) a person's reactions and responses

CHAPTER

12

SUICIDE

Cleopatra, Nirvana's Curt Cobain, Bruno Bettleheim (psychiatrist), Ernest Hemingway, Adolf Hitler, Jim Jones (People's Temple leader), David Koresh (Davidian sect leader), Jack London, Amedeo Modigliani (painter), Marilyn Monroe, Freddie Prinze (comedian), King Saul, Samson, and Virginia Woolf.

What do these individuals have in common? As you may have guessed, they all committed **suicide**—the taking of one's own life. As the following cases reveal, people commit suicide for any number of reasons.

Late one evening Carl Johnson, M.D., left his downtown office, got into his Mercedes 500 SL, and drove toward his expensive suburban home. He was in no particular hurry because the house would be empty anyway; the year before, his wife had divorced him and with their two children had moved back East to her parents' home. Carl was deeply affected. Although he had been drinking heavily for two years before the divorce, he had always been able to function vocationally. For the past several months, however, his private practice had declined dramatically. He used to find his work rewarding, but now he found people boring and irritating. The future looked bleak and hopeless. Carl knew he had all the classic symptoms of depression—he was, after all, a psychiatrist. The garage door opened automatically as he rolled up the driveway. Carl parked carelessly, not even bothering to press the switch that closed the door. Once in the house, he headed directly for the bar in his den; there he got out a bottle of bourbon and three glasses, filled the glasses, and lined them up along the bar. He drank them down, one after the other, in rapid succession. For a good half hour, he stood at the window staring out into the night. Then Carl sat down at his mahogany desk and unlocked one of the drawers. Taking a loaded .38 caliber revolver from the desk drawer, Dr. Carl Johnson held it to his temple and fired.

Possible reasons for suicide: Recent divorce; loss of family life; subsequent depression.

Fifteen-year-old Eric Fadeley was an outstanding athlete in many sports, a top baseball player on both his Little League and high school teams, and a 3.8 grade-point-average student. In September 1992, he killed himself, in his bedroom, with a family handgun. At the funeral his father stated, "Through this whole thing, the main question to ask is 'Why?' Nobody will ever know for sure."

The suicide was even more baffling because Eric had just pitched his team to victory at the Little League Senior Division U.S. championship, was honored the night before by the California Angels at an event called "Night of Champions," had expressed interest in playing for Michigan State and eventually turning pro, and was seen by classmates as tender, kind, and caring. This youngster, who appeared to have everything, revealed in a suicide note that he felt ugly and bad, and felt the intense burden of "making the grade." His mother said that Eric was a perfectionist in everything he did. His sister stated that Eric perhaps could not live up to his own standards.

Possible reasons for suicide: Could not live up to own high standards; felt pressured to excel; felt a failure.

For several months in 1993, the U.S. public became fixated with events that unfolded in Waco, Texas. Followers of a religious sect headed by David Koresh barricaded themselves within a fortresslike building after law enforcement officials attempted to storm the compound. Koresh, a charismatic leader, had predicted a holocaust would strike the world and had warned that mass suicides would occur if law enforcement officers attempted another seige. The outcome is now history; the compound eventually burned to the ground, killing many adults and children. A reconstruction of the events strongly suggests that Koresh and followers set multiple fires throughout the building and chose to die rather than surrender.

Possible reasons for suicide: Collective religious belief in the "rightness" of their cause and actions; belief that death was better than capture and possible mistreatment.

In December 1993, Jenny Williams, a 62-year-old housewife, suffered a severe stroke that resulted in crippling paralysis, loss of speech, and an inability to control her basic eliminative functions. Although she had the full support of her husband, two sons, and a daughter, Mrs. Williams was distressed at having to rely on basic life-support machinery. Although she could not speak, it was clear to her family that she did not want to live this way and that she did not want to be a burden to others. Over several weeks Mrs. Williams's condition improved moderately, until she could move about, with great effort. But she still could not speak or attend to her own needs. She was discharged from the hospital and cared for at home by a part-time nurse and her devoted husband. Two weeks after her discharge, Mrs. Williams took her own life by swallowing a bottle of sleeping pills. Mr. Williams knew of his wife's intention, but he did nothing

While some suicidologists believe that there are commonalities among those who choose to die, it is also true that people take their lives for many different reasons. Ernest Hemingway (left) and Curt Cobain (right) are two such people.

to prevent her suicide. He did not have the heart to go against her wishes.

Possible reasons for suicide: Perception that quality of life was poor; desire to avoid being a burden on her family.

Ten-year-old Tammy Jimenez was the youngest of three children—a loner who had attempted suicide at least twice in the past two years. Tammy's parents always seemed to be bickering about one thing or another and threatening divorce. She and her sisters were constantly abused by their alcoholic father. Finally, in February 1986, Tammy was struck and killed by a truck when she darted out into the highway that passed by her home. The incident was listed as an accident, but her older sister said Tammy had deliberately killed herself. On the morning of her death, an argument with her father had upset and angered her. Her sister said that, seconds before Tammy ran out onto the highway, she had said that she was unwanted and would end her own life.

Possible reasons for suicide: Unhappy family life; child abuse; feelings of being unwanted and unloved.

On October 23, 1983, a lone man in a truck containing six tons of explosives drove up to the U.S. Marine barracks in Beirut, Lebanon. The man, believed to be a Shi'ite Muslim terrorist, did not pause when Marine guards signaled him to stop. Instead, he drove through the entrance barricades and set off a blast that killed himself and 240 American soldiers.

Possible reason for suicide: Belief in killing oneself for a greater good or cause.

Suicide is not only a tragic act, it is a baffling and confusing one as well. Although we have provided possible reasons for the deaths of these individuals, we can never be entirely certain why people knowingly and deliberately end their own lives. The easy and most frequent explanation is that people who kill themselves are suffering from a mental disorder. For example, suicide is usually discussed in conjunction with mood disorders in most abnormal psychology texts. Yet our increasing understanding of suicide suggests that a single unitary explanation is simplistic. Suicide has many causes, and people kill themselves for many different reasons. Our discussion of suicide follows the course charted in Figure 12.1.

We have chosen to provide a separate chapter on suicide for several reasons. First, although suicide is not classified as a mental disorder in DSM-IV, the suicidal person usually has clear psychiatric symptoms. Many persons who suffer from depression, alcohol dependence, and schizophrenia exhibit suicidal thoughts or behavior. Yet suicide does not fall neatly into one of the recognized psychiatric disorders. There is evidence that suicide and **suicidal ideation**—thoughts about suicide—may represent a separate clinical entity. Few, for example, would argue that the topic is not an important domain of the study of abnormal psychology.

The second reason for treating suicide as a separate topic is that increasing interest in suicide appears to warrant study of this phenomenon in its own right. Throughout history, suicide has remained a hidden and mysterious act. People have traditionally avoided discussing it and have participated in a "conspiracy of silence" because of the shame and stigma involved in taking one's life. Mental health professionals as well often find the topic uncomfortable and personally disturbing. Abnormal psychology texts often handle the topic of suicide in a small section along with mood disorders. Over the past several decades, we have learned much about suicide.

Third, we are witnessing increased openness in discussing issues of death and dying, the meaning of suicide, and the right to take one's own life. Some prominent individuals have even gone so far as to advocate "the right to suicide."

And, finally, we need to recognize that suicide is an irreversible act. Once the action has been taken, there is no going back, no reconsideration, and no reprieve. Regardless of the moral stand one takes on this position, the decision to commit suicide is often an ambivalent one, clouded by many personal and social stressors. Many mental health professionals believe that the suicidal person, if taught how to deal with personal and social crisis, would not consciously take his or her own life. As a result, understanding the causes of suicide and what can be done to prevent such an act becomes extremely important to psychologists.

CORRELATES OF SUICIDE

People who commit suicide—who complete their suicide attempts—can no longer inform us about their motives, frame of mind, and emotional state. We have only indirect information, such as case records and reports by others, to help us understand what led them to their tragic act. The systematic examination of existing information for the purpose of understanding and explaining a person's behavior before his or her death is called a **psychological autopsy** (Robins & Kulbok, 1988; Jacobs & Klein, 1993). It is patterned on the *medical autopsy*, which is an examination of a dead body to determine the cause or nature of the biological death. The psychological autopsy attempts to make psychological sense of a suicide or homicide by compiling and analyzing case histories of victims, recollections of therapists, interviews with relatives and friends, information obtained from crisis phone calls, and messages left in suicide notes. Unfortunately,

these sources are not always available or reliable. Only 12 to 34 percent of victims leave suicide notes (Black, 1993; Leenaars, 1992), and many people who commit suicide have never undergone psychotherapy (Fleer & Pasewark, 1982). Explanations from relatives or friends are often distorted because of the emotional impact of the loved one's death.

Despite such weaknesses, the psychological autopsy continues to be used not only because it represents one of the few avenues open to us but because it has broader purposes as well. If psychologists can isolate the events and circumstances that lead to suicide and can identify the characteristics of potential suicide victims, they may be able to prevent other people from performing this irreversible act.

Facts About Suicide

No single explanation is sufficient to account for all types of suicide. Considering the examples at the beginning of this chapter, common sense alone should lead you to the conclusion that Jenny Williams's reasons for taking her own life differ from those of Tammy Jimenez or of the terrorist, Eric Fadeley. In seeking to understand suicide, researchers have focused on events, characteristics, and demographic variables that recur in psychological autopsies and are highly correlated with the act. Our first example, Carl Johnson, fits a particular profile. Higher suicide rates are associated with divorce (National Center for Health Statistics, 1988) and with certain professions (psychiatry in particular). Alcohol is frequently implicated (Rogers, 1992), and men are more likely to kill themselves using firearms than by other means (Kranczer, 1986; NCHS, 1988).

Profiles such as these, as well as those described below, emerge from our increasing knowledge of facts that are correlated with suicide (Berman & Jobes, 1991; Bongar, 1991; Diekstra, 1990; McIntosh, 1991; National Center for Health Statistics, 1988; Rogers, 1990; Shneidman, 1993; U.S. Bureau of the Census, 1988). Let's examine some of them in greater detail. But first, look at Table 12.1, which examines some of the characteristics suicidal individuals share.

Frequency Every 20 to 30 minutes, someone in the United States takes his or her own life. More than 30,000 persons kill themselves each year. Suicide is among the top ten causes of death in the industrialized parts of the world; it is the second or third leading cause of death among young people. Some evidence shows that the number of actual suicides is probably 25 to 30 percent higher than that recorded. Many deaths that are officially recorded as accidental,

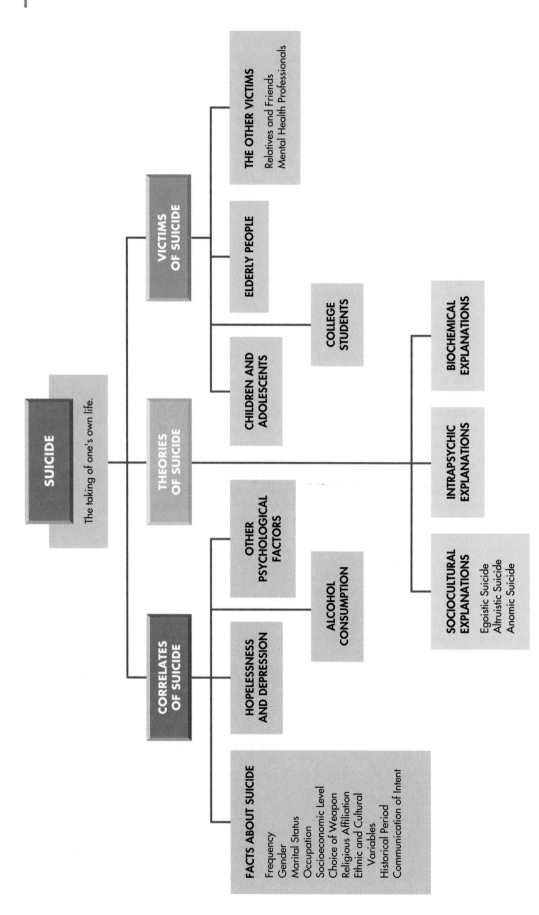

FIGURE 12.1   Suicide

TABLE 12.1 Ten Common Characteristics of Suicide

1. *The common purpose is to seek a solution.* People may believe that suicide represents a solution to an insoluble problem. To the suicidal person, taking one's life is not a pointless or accidental occurrence.

2. *The cessation of consciousness is a common goal.* Consciousness represents constant psychological pain, but suicide represents a termination of distressing thoughts and feelings.

3. *The stimulus for suicide is generally intolerable psychological pain.* Depression, hopelessness, guilt, shame, and other negative emotions are frequently at the basis of a suicide.

4. *The common stressor in suicide is frustrated psychological need.* The inability to attain high standards or expectations may lead to feelings of frustration, failure, and worthlessness. When progress toward goals is blocked, some individuals become vulnerable to suicide.

5. *A common emotion in suicide is hopelessness-helplessness.* Pessimism about the future and a conviction that nothing can be done to improve one's life situation may predispose a person to suicide.

6. *The cognitive state is one of ambivalence.* Although the suicidal person may be strongly motivated to end his or her life, there is usually a desire (in varying degrees) to live as well.

7. *The cognitive state is also characterized by "tunnel vision."* Vision is constricted: The person has great difficulty seeing "the larger picture" and can be characterized as suffering from tunnel vision. People intent on suicide seem unable to consider other options or alternatives. Death is the only way out.

8. *The common action in suicide is escape.* The goal is eggression—escape from an intolerable situation.

9. *The common interpersonal act in suicide is communication of intention.* At least 80 percent of suicides are preceded by either verbal or nonverbal behavioral cues indicating their intentions.

10. *The common consistency is in the area of lifelong coping patterns.* Patterns or habits developed in coping with crisis generally are the same response patterns that are used throughout life. Some patterns may predispose one to suicide.

Source: Shneidman, 1992.

such as single-auto crashes, drownings, or falls from great heights, are actually suicides. According to some estimates, for every person who completes a suicide, eight to ten persons make the attempt.

Children as Victims Recent reports suggest that about 12,000 children between the ages of five and fourteen are admitted to psychiatric hospitals for suicidal behavior every year, and it is believed that twenty times that number actually attempt suicide. Suicides among young people aged fifteen to twenty-four have increased by more than 40 percent in the past decade (50 percent for males and 12 percent for females); suicide is now the second leading cause of death for this group.

College Students as Victims Suicide is the second or third leading cause of death among college students. (More than 10,000 attempt it each year, and more than 1,000 succeed.) The suicide rate for college students is twice as high as that for people not in college. One in five students possesses suicidal thoughts sometime during his or her college career.

Gender The completed suicide rate for men is about three times that for women, although recent findings suggest that many more women are now incurring a higher risk. Among people older than 65, the rate for men is ten times that for women. However, women attempt suicide three times as often as men. The age group beginning at age 65 has the highest suicide rate of all, but men continue to lead in deaths.

Marital Status As Figure 12.2 indicates, the lowest incidence of suicide is found among people who are married, and the highest among those who are divorced. The suicide rates for single and widowed or divorced men are about twice those for women of similar marital status.

Occupation Physicians, lawyers, law enforcement personnel, and dentists have higher-than-average rates of suicide. Among medical professionals, psychiatrists have the highest rate and pediatricians the lowest. Such marked differences raise the question of whether the specialty influences susceptibility or whether a suicide-prone person is attracted to certain specialties.

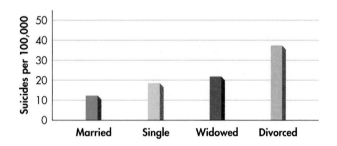

FIGURE 12.2 Marital Status and Suicide per 100,000 Divorced persons are nearly three times more likely to commit suicide. Does a stable marriage somehow tend to immunize people against killing themselves? What other reasons might explain these differences?

Source: Data from McIntosh, 1991.

Socioeconomic Level Suicide is represented proportionately among all socioeconomic levels. Level of wealth does not seem to affect the suicide rate as much as do changes in that level. In the Great Depression of the 1930s, suicide was higher among the suddenly impoverished than among those who had always been poor.

Choice of Weapon Men most frequently choose firearms as the means of suicide; poisoning and asphyxiation via barbiturates are the preferred means

for women. The violent means (which men are more likely to choose) are more certain to complete the act; this partially explains the disproportionately greater number of incomplete attempts by women. Recent studies indicate, however, that women are increasingly choosing firearms and explosives as methods (55.9 percent increase). Some have speculated that this change may be related to a change in role definitions of women in society. Among children younger than fifteen years, the most common suicide method tends to be jumping from buildings and running into traffic. Older children try hanging or drug overdoses. Younger children attempt suicide impulsively and thus use more readily available means.

Religious Affiliation Religious affiliation is correlated with suicide rates. Although the U.S. rate is 12.2 per 100,000, in countries where Catholic Church influences are strong—Latin America, Ireland, Spain, Italy—the suicide rate is relatively low (less than 10 per 100,000). Islam, too, condemns suicide, and the suicide rates in Arab countries are correspondingly low. Where such religious sanctions are absent—for example, where church authority is weaker, as it is in Scandinavian countries, in former Czechoslovakia, and in Hungary—higher rates are observed. Indeed, Hungary has the highest recorded rate of suicide, at 40.7 per 100,000, and Czechoslovakia has a rate of 22.4 per 100,000.

Most religions have strong taboos and sanctions against suicide. In countries where Catholicism and Islam are strong, for example, the rates of suicide tend to be lower than in countries where religious beliefs are not as deeply held.

Ethnic and Cultural Variables   Suicide rates vary among ethnic minority groups in the United States. American Indian groups have the highest rate, followed by White Americans, Mexican Americans, African Americans, Japanese Americans, and Chinese Americans. American Indian youngsters have frighteningly high rates (26 per 100,000) as compared with White youths (14 per 100,000). High rates of alcoholism, a low standard of living, and an invalidation of their cultural lifestyles may all contribute to this tragedy.

Historical Period   Suicide rates tend to decline during times of war and natural disasters, but they increase during periods of shifting norms and values or social unrest, when traditional expectations no longer apply. Sociologists speculate that during wars, people "pull together" and are less concerned with their own difficulties and conflicts.

Communication of Intent   More than two-thirds of the people who commit suicide communicate their intent to do so within three months of the fatal act. (The belief that people who threaten suicide are not serious about it, or will not actually make such an attempt, is ill-founded.) Most people who attempt suicide appear to have been ambivalent about death until the suicide. It has been estimated that fewer than 5 percent unequivocally wish to end their lives.

Hopelessness and Depression

A survey of facts correlated with suicide allows us to learn much about it, but the factors that are probably most closely linked with suicide are hopelessness and depression.

Although it is dangerous to assume that depression causes suicide, a number of studies indicate that the two are very highly correlated (McGuire, 1982; Shneidman, 1992). For example, interest in suicide usually develops gradually, as a result of pleasure loss and fatigue accompanying a serious depressed mood (Hamilton, 1982). Shneidman (1993) has described it as a "psychache," an intolerable pain created from an absence of joy. Studies indicate that 50 to 67 percent of all suicides are related to a primary mood disorder (Whybrow, Akiskal & McKinney, 1984) and that 15 percent of patients suffering mood disorders will eventually kill themselves (Sainsbury, 1982). More recent findings continue to support these statistics (Hawton, 1987). Among both children and adolescents, depression seems to be highly correlated with suicidal behavior (Garland & Zigler, 1993; Kosky, 1983; Rosenthal & Rosenthal, 1984).

While depression is often seen as a leading cause of suicide, recent research suggests that hopelessness is a more powerful factor. When the future looks bleak and dark and pessimism dominates a person's mood, suicide is more likely to be attempted. Here, Boston police officers and EMTs grapple with a man who threatened to jump from a bridge. Fortunately, he was saved.

Such data can lead to the conclusion that depression plays an important role in suicide. Yet other studies indicate that the way this role is manifested is far from simple. For example, patients *seldom* commit suicide while severely depressed (Mendels, 1970). Such patients generally show motor retardation and low energy, which keep them from reaching the level of activity required for suicide. The danger period often comes after some treatment, when the depression begins to lift. Energy and motivation increase, and patients are more likely to carry out the act. Most suicide attempts occur during weekend furloughs from hospitals or soon after discharge, a fact that supports this contention. The risk of suicide seems to be only about 1 percent during the year in which a depressive episode occurs, but it is about 15 percent in subsequent years (Klerman, 1982).

Although depression is undeniably correlated with suicidal thoughts and behavior, the relationship seems very complex. For example, why do some depressed people commit suicide while others do not? The answer may be found in the characteristics of depression and in the factors that contribute to it.

Some believe that hopelessness, or negative expectations about the future, may be the major catalyst in suicide and, possibly, an even more important factor than depression (Weishaar & Beck, 1992). Beck, Emery, and Greenberg (1985) conducted a ten-year study of 207 psychiatric patients who had suicidal thoughts but no recent history of suicidal attempts. Within seventy-two hours after hospital admission, each patient was measured on three variables: hopelessness, depression, and suicidal ideation (thoughts about suicide). During the ten-year period, fourteen patients committed suicide, and the test scores of these people were compared with the others. The investigators found that the two groups did not differ in terms of depression and suicidal ideation, but they did differ in terms of hopelessness. Those who died were more pessimistic about the future than were those who survived. Although the overall results obtained by the scale did not predict suicidal risk, the hopelessness item within the measure did. These findings suggest that therapists should assess all depressed patients' attitudes toward their future to determine how hopeless they feel about it.

Alcohol Consumption

One of the most consistently reported correlates of suicidal behavior is alcohol consumption (Glavin, Franklin & Francis, 1990; Hirschfield & Davidson, 1989; Schuckit, 1994). Indeed, some have even stated that a successful suicide unconnected to alcohol abuse is a rare event (Hatton & Valente, 1984). Alcohol-implicated suicide rates may be as high as 270 per 100,000, which is an astounding 27 times higher than the rate found in the general population (Stillion, McDowell & May, 1989). Many theorists have traditionally argued that alcohol may lower inhibitions related to the fear of death and make it easier to carry out the fatal act. Recent formulations, however, suggest a cognitive link between alcohol use and suicide.

Rogers (1992) argued that the strength of the relationship between alcohol and suicide is the result of *alcohol-induced myopia* (a constriction of cognitive and perceptual processes). This line of reasoning relies heavily on the cognitive characteristics of people who attempt suicide: They are more rigid in their line of

thinking, less flexible in problem solving, and more prone to dichotomous thinking (Shneidman, 1987; 1993). They generally perceive solutions as all or none (life or death) and are myopically incapable of coming up with alternative solutions. Alcohol use by an individual in psychological conflict may increase rather than decrease personal distress. Steele and Josephs (1990) found that alcohol constricts cognitive and perceptual processes. Although alcohol-induced myopia may relieve depression and anxiety by distracting the person from the problem, it is equally likely to intensify the conflict and distress by narrowing the person's focus on the problem. Thus the link between alcohol and suicide may be the result of the myopic qualities of alcohol exaggerating a previously existing constrictive state. If this is true, alcohol is most likely to increase the probability of a suicide in an already suicidal person. Rogers (1992) stated, "The most efficacious and ethically sound intervention in this area would be to promote abstinence by providing information to clients regarding the potential dangers involved in alcohol consumption" (p. 542).

Other Psychological Factors

Although the correlations are not as strong as those of hopelessness and depression, many other psychological factors have been found to be associated with suicide. Findings have consistently revealed that many individuals who commit suicide suffer from a DSM-IV disorder (Litman, 1987; Roy, 1985). Conversely, approximately 15 percent of individuals diagnosed with mood disorders, schizophrenia, and substance abuse attempt to kill themselves (Brent, Perper & Allman, 1987). A review of the literature on suicide also reveals that separation and divorce (Garfinkel & Golumbek, 1983), academic pressures (Priester & Clum, 1992), shame (Shreve & Kunkel, 1991), serious illness (Mackenzie & Popkin, 1987), loss of a job, and other life stresses may be contributing factors.

THEORIES OF SUICIDE

Some clinicians believe that everyone, at one time or another, has wished to end his or her life. Fortunately, most of us do not act on such wishes, even during extreme distress. But why do some people do so? Even though suicide is closely linked to hopelessness and depression, and even though many theories of depression apply to suicide as well, the question cannot be answered easily. We have already discussed how difficult it is to know what causes a person to take his or her life. Generally, such people seem to share a common motive: to gain relief from a life situation that is unbearable. In the search for a more detailed answer, leading explanations have taken sociocultural, intrapsychic, or biochemical perspectives.

Sociocultural Explanations

Early explanations of suicide emphasized its relationship to various social factors. As we saw earlier, rates of suicide vary with age, gender, marital status, occupation, socioeconomic level, religion, and ethnic group. Higher rates are associated with high- and low-status (as opposed to middle-status) occupations, urban living, middle-aged men, single or divorced status, and upper and lower socioeconomic classes (Fremouw, Perczel & Ellis, 1990; National Center for Health Statistics, 1988). In a pioneering work, the French sociologist Emile Durkheim related differences in suicide rates to the impact of social forces on the person (Durkheim, [1897] 1951). He proposed three categories of suicide: egoistic, altruistic, and anomic.

Egoistic Suicide
In Durkheim's view, **egoistic suicide** results from an inability to integrate oneself with society. Failing to maintain close ties with the community deprives the person of the support systems that are necessary for adaptive functioning. Without such support, and unable to function adaptively, the person becomes isolated and alienated from other people.

Altruistic Suicide
Altruistic suicide is motivated by the person's desire to further group goals or to achieve some greater good. Someone may give up his or her life for a higher cause (in a religious sacrifice or the ultimate political protest, for example). Group pressures may make such an act highly acceptable and honored. During World War II, Japanese kamikaze pilots voluntarily dove their airplanes into enemy warships "for the Emperor and the glory of Japan." The self-immolation of Buddhist monks during the Vietnam War and the terrorist truck bombing of the Marine barracks in Lebanon (described at the beginning of this chapter) are likewise in this category.

Anomic Suicide
Durkheim's third category, **anomic suicide**, results when a person's relationship to society is unbalanced in some dramatic fashion. When a person's horizons are suddenly broadened or constricted by unstable conditions, he or she may not be able to handle the change or cope with the new status and may choose suicide as a way out. The suicides of people who lost their personal wealth during the Great Depression or who killed themselves after being freed

from concentration camps at the end of World War II are of this type. Similarly, a person who suddenly and unexpectedly acquires great wealth may be prone to suicide.

Psychosocial explanations may be valid to an extent, but attributing suicide to a single sociological factor (economic depression, residence, or occupation) is too simplistic and mechanistic. As we have noted, correlations do not imply cause-and-effect relationships. Thus Durkheim's three categories are more descriptive than explanatory. Moreover, purely sociological explanations that take into account only one psychosocial factor—group cohesion, for example—omit the intrapsychic dimension of the person's struggles. They fail to explain why only certain members of a group commit suicide and others do not.

During the Vietnam war, people were horrified by scenes of self-immolation by Buddhist monks as a form of protest against the government. This altruistic suicide in 1963 was witnessed by passers-by in the central market of Saigon.

Suicide Notes

Suicide notes represent one source of data used in a psychological autopsy. Research indicates that women are more likely than men to leave notes; that separated or divorced females are more likely than single women to leave notes; that whites are three times more likely to leave notes than are non-whites; and that many suicide notes express intense feelings of self-blame, hatred, and vengeance (Cohen & Fiedler, 1974; Farberow & Simon, 1975; Shneidman & Farberow, 1957). One may conclude from these findings that note-writing behavior in suicides

is correlated with certain demographic variables and that the act of writing is apparently an attempt to influence or manipulate the responses of survivors.

One classification scheme for suicides is based in part on information gleaned from these notes (Shneidman, 1976, 1981). Here are some of the categories, along with illustrative suicide notes.

The *egoistic* suicide is the result of an intrapsychic debate, a struggle within the victim's mind. The victim's inner torment may be philosophical or religious in nature. An example:

Mr. Brown:

. . . It seems unnecessary to present a lengthy defense for my suicide, for if I have to be judged, it will not be on this earth. However, in brief, I find myself a misfit. To me, life is too painful for the meager occasional pleasure to compensate. It all seems so pointless, the daily struggle leading where? Several times I have done what, in retrospect, is seen to amount to running away from circumstances. I could do so now—travel, find a new job, even change vocation, but why? It is Myself that I have been trying to

Intrapsychic Explanations

Early psychological explanations of suicide tended to ignore social factors in favor of intrapsychic ones. In the classical Freudian approach, for example, self-destruction was seen as the result of hostility that is directed inward against the *introjected love object* (the loved one with whom the person has identified). That is, people who kill themselves are really directing anger and the suicidal act against others whom they have incorporated within themselves. If the angry feelings (death instinct) reach murderous proportions, a suicide attempt is the result.

Unfortunately, these ideas are not supported by evidence. Carefully analyzed psychological autopsies indicate that people kill themselves not only for hate and revenge but for a number of other psychological reasons, such as shame, guilt, hopelessness, and pain (Pine, 1981; Shneidman, 1992). An analysis of 165 suicide notes conducted over a 25-year period showed that only 24 percent of the suicides expressed hostile or negative feelings toward themselves, whereas 51 percent expressed positive attitudes and another 25 percent were neutral. The investigators concluded that there is not enough support for believing that hostility is the only cause of suicide (Tuckman,

Kleiner & Lavall, 1959). The Focus On feature contains several suicide notes, as well as an alternative classification scheme.

Biochemical Explanations

Neither a purely sociological nor a purely psychological perspective seems to adequately explain the causes of suicide. Both sociological and psychological factors are probably involved, but other factors seem to be operating as well. For example, you may recall that there is strong evidence that chemical neurotransmitters are associated with depression and mania. Similar evidence shows that suicide is influenced by biochemistry.

Evidence of this link began to accumulate in the mid-1970s, when researchers identified a chemical called *5-hydroxyindoleacetic acid (5HIAA)* (Asberg, Traskman & Thoren, 1976; Stanley & Mann, 1983; Van Praag, 1983). This chemical is produced when serotonin, a neurotransmitter that affects mood and emotions, is broken down in the body. Moreover, some evidence indicates that the serotonin receptors in the brainstem and frontal cortex may be impaired. The spinal fluid of some depressed patients has been found to contain abnormally low amounts of 5HIAA.

escape, and this I can do only as I am about to do! Goodbye!
Bill Smith

The *dyadic* suicide is interpersonal in nature and is influenced primarily by unfulfilled wishes or needs involving a significant other. Frustration, rage, manipulation, and attempts to elicit guilt are common. For example:

Bill,
You have killed me. I hope you are happy in your heart, if you have one which I doubt. Please leave Rover with Mike. Also leave my baby alone. If you don't, I'll haunt you the rest of your life and I mean it and I'll do it.

You have been mean and also cruel. God doesn't forget those things and don't forget that. And

please no flowers; it won't mean anything. Also keep your money.

I want to be buried in Potter's Field in the same casket with Betty. You can do that for me. That's the way we want it. . . .

The *ageneratic* suicide is characteristic of the person who has lost the sense of participating in the transgenerational flow of human life—of belonging to "the scheme of things." Alienation, disengagement, and isolation are involved; the feeling and sense are existential.

To the authorities:
Excuse my inability to express myself in English and the trouble caused. I beg you not to lose time in an inquest upon my body. Just simply record and file it because

the name and address given on the register are fictitious and I wanted to disappear anonymously. No one expects me here nor will be looking for me. I have informed my relatives in America. Please do not bury me! I wish to be cremated and the ashes tossed to the winds. In that way I shall return to the nothingness from which I have come into this sad world. This is all I ask of the Americans for all that I have intended to give them with my coming into this country.
Many thanks,
José Marcia

Source: Shneidman, 1968, pp. 5–8.

Preliminary statistics on patients with low levels of 5HIAA indicated that they are more likely than others to commit suicide, more likely to select violent methods of killing themselves, and more likely to have a history of violence, aggression, and impulsiveness (Edman et al., 1986). Researchers believe that the tendency toward suicide is not a simple link to depression. We already know that depressed patients also exhibit low levels of 5HIAA. What is startling is that low levels of 5HIAA have been discovered in suicidal people without a history of depression, and in suicidal individuals suffering from other mental disorders (Brown et al., 1982; Ninan et al., 1984).

This discovery may lead to a chemical means of detecting people who are at high risk for attempting suicide. However, researchers in this area caution that social and psychological factors also play a role. If, in the future, cerebral serotonin can be detected easily in blood tests, it can be used as a biological marker (a warning sign) of suicide risk (Hawton, 1987). Researchers believe that low 5HIAA content does not cause suicide, but it may make people more vulnerable to environmental stressors (Pines, 1983). And still another caution is in order: This evidence is correlational in nature; it does not indicate whether low levels of 5HIAA are a cause or a result of particular

moods and emotions—or even whether the two are directly related.

VICTIMS OF SUICIDE

In this section we briefly discuss four groups of people who are especially victimized by suicide: the very young, college students, the elderly, and those who are left behind by suicides.

Children and Adolescents

Suicide among the young is an unmentioned tragedy in our society. We have traditionally avoided the idea that some of our young people find life so painful that they consciously and deliberately take their own lives. As in the case of Tammy Jimenez, it may feel easier to call a suicide "an accident." Yet, as many as 250,000 children between the ages of five and fourteen may attempt suicide each year (NCHS, 1993) and approximately 3,000 teenagers successfully end their lives every year (Shaffer & Fisher, 1981). The suicide rate for children younger than fourteen is increasing at an alarming rate, and the rate for adolescents is rising even faster. Indeed, recent figures suggest that adolescent suicides rose by more than 200 percent between 1960 and 1988, compared with a general population increase of 17 percent (Garland & Zigler, 1993; National Center for Health Statistics, 1991). Suicide is now second only to automobile accidents as the leading cause of death among teenagers, and some automobile "accidents" may also really be suicides.

A recent Gallup poll of teenage respondents found that 6 percent admit to a suicide attempt and another 15 percent say they have come close to trying (Freiberg, 1991). Experts on adolescent suicide, however, believe these to be gross underestimates (Berman & Jobes, 1991). The Gallup Organization polled middle-class families (median family income of $41,500) and thus missed certain high-risk groups such as school dropouts. The Gallup study suggested that between 8 and 9 percent of teenagers have engaged in self-harm behavior. The latest available figures revealed that there were 4,924 officially recorded suicides for young people between the ages of fifteen and twenty-four, more than triple the rate in 1957 (Freiberg, 1991).

Characteristics of Childhood Suicides A lack of research on childhood suicides has generally hindered our understanding of why such acts occur. Two studies, however, have helped identify characteristics of suicidal children.

In a retrospective study of admissions to a pediatric hospital emergency room over a seven-year period, researchers identified 505 children and adolescents who had attempted suicide (Garfinkel, Froese & Hood, 1982). This group was compared with a control group of children who were similar in age, gender, and date of admission. The researchers did not, however, compare these children to those who had successfully completed the suicidal act. Some would suggest that unsuccessful attempters differ from successful ones. Nevertheless, children in the group that attempted suicide had the following characteristics:

1. There were three times as many girls as boys, and the boys who attempted suicide were significantly younger than the girls. The gender rates are consistent with adult rates, but the younger age of the boys is not.

2. The clinical symptoms most often shown by both the children and the adolescents were changes in mood and aggressiveness, hostility, or both.

3. Most of the suicide attempts (73 percent) occurred at home, 12 percent in public areas, 7 percent at school, and 5 percent at a friend's house. In 87 percent of the suicide attempts, someone else was nearby—generally parents. The fact that most suicide attempts occur at home implies that parents are in the best position to recognize and prevent suicidal behavior.

4. Most of the attempts were made during the winter months, in the evening or afternoon.

5. Drug overdose was the primary means of attempted suicide, accounting for 88 percent of the attempts. Next, in order, were wrist laceration, hanging, and jumping from heights or in front of moving vehicles.

6. More than 77 percent of the attempts were judged to be of low probability of completion; 21 percent were moderately probable; and slightly more than 1 percent were highly probable. Most attempts were judged to have been made in a way that ensured a high likelihood of rescue. These figures lend credence to the belief that most children who attempt suicide do not really want to end their lives.

The researchers found that the families of the suicidal children were under greater economic stress than the families of the control group. The former had twice the rate of paternal unemployment. Maybe parents who are preoccupied with economic concerns are less readily available to support their children in time of need. Furthermore, fewer than half the families of those who attempted suicide were two-parent families. The families of suicide attempters also had higher rates of medical problems, psychiatric illness, and suicide than control group families. The dominant psychiatric problem was alcohol or drug abuse.

The second study that sheds light on the characteristics of suicidal children also found that family instability and stress and a chaotic family atmosphere were correlated with suicide attempts (Cosand, Borque & Kraus, 1982). Suicidal children seemed to have experienced unpredictable traumatic events and to have suffered the loss of a significant parenting figure before age twelve. Their parents tended to be alcohol or drug abusers who provided poor role models for coping with stress. As in the first study, the child's self-destructive behavior seemed to be a last-ditch attempt to influence or coerce those who threatened his or her psychological well-being. The suicidal children showed considerable anger.

Because such children are at great risk of committing suicide when their problems remain unrecognized and untreated, early detection of their distress signals is vital. Intensive family therapy, including the education of parents with regard to parenting roles, can help. Parents can be taught to recognize the signs of depression, to become aware of their children's after-school activities, and to be cognizant of the role and

Suicide among high-school students is reaching epidemic proportions. One of the dangers parents and teachers need to guard against is copy-cat suicide, a phenomenon in which other students take their lives. To prevent more suicides, schools sometimes initiate programs that help students and faculty cope with their feelings of loss and anger.

accessibility of drugs. In some cases the child may need to be removed from the family.

Mental health professionals and the public need to be aware that the complexion of adolescent suicides is changing at a rapid pace. For example, since the publication of these two studies, two trends are notable. First, the ratio of male to female suicides in 1987 was about 5 to 1, a change from the previous decade's 3-to-1 ratio. Second, youngsters are now selecting more lethal methods of killing themselves (Berman & Jobes, 1991).

Copycat Suicides Considerable attention has recently been directed at multiple or so-called copycat suicides, in which youngsters in a particular school or community seem to mimic a previous suicide (Phillips et al., 1992). For example, within a three-month period in 1985, nine youths ages fourteen to twenty-five killed themselves, all by hanging. All were members of the Shoshone tribe, and all lived in Wind River, Wyoming. In another incident in Omaha, Nebraska, seven high school students attempted suicide within a very short span of time; three were successful ("Suicide Belt," 1986). Likewise, the Bergenfield suicides grabbed headlines in 1987, when two male and two female students killed themselves by inhaling fumes from their car. Their deaths followed that of a friend, who had also committed suicide. This event was unusual because the four signed a suicide pact on a brown paper bag. Tragically, their deaths were in

turn followed by those of two other young women, who used the same method of death (*Newsweek*, 1987).

Although many events, beliefs, and feelings may have contributed to these tragic deaths, suggestion and imitation seem to have played an especially powerful role. Young people may be especially vulnerable, but studies indicate that highly publicized suicides such as those of a celebrity, close friend, relative, coworker, or other well-known person can increase the number of subsequent suicide attempts (Bandura, 1985; Stack, 1987). In the months following Marilyn Monroe's death, for example, suicides increased by some 12 percent. When Nirvana's Curt Cobain committed suicide in 1994, many youth counselors warned about potential imitations from fans. Interestingly, media reports of natural deaths of celebrities are not followed by increases in suicide. Thus it appears that grief, depression, and mourning are not the culprits inducing copycat behaviors.

Although imitative suicides may not be as common as the media suggest, research has indicated that publicizing the event may have the effect of glorifying and drawing attention to it. Thus depressed people may identify with a colorful portrayal, increasing the risk of even more suicides (Phillips & Carstensen, 1986). This pattern appears to be especially true for youngsters who may already be thinking about killing themselves. The stable, well-adjusted teenager does not seem to be at risk in these situations.

Adolescence is often a period of confusing emotions, identity formation, and questioning. It is a difficult and turbulent time for most teenagers, and suicide may seem to be a logical response to the pain and stress of growing up. A suicide occurring in school brings increased risk of other suicides because of its proximity to students' daily life. In such instances, a suicide prevention program should be implemented to let students vent their feelings in an environment equipped to respond appropriately and perhaps even save their lives. Encouragingly, the Gallup survey (1991) reported that 41 percent of schools had programs aimed at suicide prevention (professional counseling services, peer counseling, and special seminars). It is no longer unusual to hear about school programs that are immediately implemented when a tragedy strikes (student suicide, violent death of a student or teacher, natural disaster, for example). One such program is discussed later in this chapter.

College Students

As many as 20 percent of college students have entertained suicidal thoughts during their college careers, and college students represent a high-risk group for young people of this age (Carson & Johnson, 1985). When you consider how well-endowed college students as a group are—with youth, intelligence, and boundless opportunity—you might wonder whether suicide is such a high risk for them because something about the college situation fosters self-destructive acts. Most studies that seek to answer this question have described the characteristics of suicidal students without controlling for the possibility that nonsuicidal students may share the same traits. What is needed is a clear understanding of the characteristics that differentiate suicidal from nonsuicidal students. These characteristics seem to have been pinpointed in several studies where comparison groups were included for controls (Klagsbrun, 1976; Seiden, 1966, 1984a, 1984b).

Characteristics of Student Suicides

At the University of California at Berkeley, a ten-year study found that suicide ranked second only to accidents as the major cause of student deaths (Seiden, 1966, 1984a). Several characteristics of student suicides were distilled from this study. Compared with nonsuicidal students, students who committed suicide

- Tended to be older than the average student by almost four years.

- Were significantly overrepresented among postgraduate students.

- Were more likely to be men, although the proportion of women suicides was higher than among the general population.

- Were more likely to be foreign students and language or literature majors.

- Tended to have better than average academic records as undergraduates, but as postgraduates, were below the graduate grade point average.

In addition, more suicides occurred in February and October (near the beginning of a semester) than in the other months of the year. Thus the notion that suicides occur in response to anxiety over final examinations was not supported by the results. In fact, the danger period appeared to be the start, not the finish, of the school semester. Most of the students committed suicide at their campus residence. Suicides seemed more frequent at larger universities than at smaller ones such as community colleges and small liberal arts colleges. Firearms were the most common means of committing suicide; ingestion of drugs was next. In later studies on other campuses, however, drug overdose was found to be more frequently used than firearms (Klagsbrun, 1976).

Reasons for Student Suicides

These findings (Seiden, 1966; 1984; Klagsbrun, 1976) suggest explanations for student suicides. First, whereas the ratio of male suicides to female suicides is 3 to 1 in the general population, it is 1.5 to 1 for college students. In the past, the comparatively higher rate of suicide among college women may have resulted from conflicting social pressures that accompanied the rapid shift of gender roles among women entering college. Whether this still holds true is certainly debatable. It may be that as women's roles and lifestyles become more similar to men's, so do their suicide rates.

Second, the fact that undergraduates who commit suicide have better scholastic records than the general college population reveals a painful paradox. By objective standards, suicidal students had done well. Friends and relatives report, however, that almost all these students were dissatisfied with their academic performance. They were filled with doubts about their own ability to succeed. One explanation for these feelings is that these students were highly motivated to achieve and had unrealistically high expectations for themselves. One such case occurred at a large Eastern university several years ago. An outstanding young woman, who had consistently made the dean's list and had obtained nearly straight-A grades, leaped to her death from her dormitory room late one winter night. That a student with so much intellectual

Many find it difficult to understand why members of such a privileged group as college students would commit suicide. Unrealistically high internal expectations, excessive pressure from family and friends to excel, and preexisting emotional problems may be some of the causes.

promise could commit such an act seemed inconceivable. Interviews with her friends, family, and fiancé indicated that she had been despondent over receiving a B in one of her courses, which spoiled her unbroken string of A's.

The third explanation of student suicides, which is also related to the previous explanation, is that many suicidal students feel overwhelming shame and disgrace because of their sense of failing others. International students, in particular, are under considerable pressure from families and friends to excel and achieve in this country. Their greatest fear is that they may not fulfill the expectations of their families, who may have sacrificed much to finance their educations. The pressures are even stronger for students from cultures in which it is important to bring honor to the family name (D. W. Sue & D. Sue, 1990). Academic achievement or occupational success reflects creditably on the whole family, not just on the individual. Conversely, unsatisfactory behaviors such as juvenile delinquency, mental illness, and failure in school shame the family. Faced with such pressures, some international students may report only successes to their families and cover up their failures. Needing to constantly reinforce the precariously fabricated image of continuous achievement, and knowing, too, that a day of reckoning will eventually arrive, some students choose suicide.

Finally, it is quite possible that the common denominator among suicidal students may simply be emotional disturbance. The other factors may all play a part, but psychopathology may predispose students to

overreact to them. In fact, according to some theories—mainly products of Western culture—suicide, any suicide, is simply not the act of a rational person. That is, some deviation within the person's personality causes or predisposes him or her to break with reality. Even the Japanese kamikaze pilots and the Shi'ite Muslim terrorists, who sacrificed their lives for a cause, are perceived as mentally disturbed. Not all psychologists agree. Some hold firmly to the belief that a suicide may be culturally sanctioned or may represent a rational response to an intolerable situation.

Elderly People

Aging inevitably results in generally unwelcome physical changes, such as wrinkling and thickening skin, graying hair, and diminishing physical strength. In addition, we all encounter a succession of stressful life changes as we grow older. Friends and relatives die, social isolation may increase, and the prospect of death becomes more real (Kirsling, 1986; Osgood, 1985). Mandatory retirement rules may lead to the need for financial assistance and the difficulties of living on a fixed and inadequate income. Such conditions make depression one of the most common psychiatric complaints of elderly people. And their depression seems to be involved more with "feeling old" than with their actual age or poor physical health.

Suicide seems to accompany depression for older people. Their suicide rates (especially rates for elderly White American men) are higher than those for the

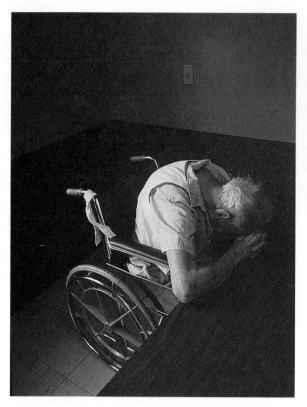

Suicide is less likely to occur among the elderly in cultures that revere, respect, and esteem those of increasing age. For example, Asian countries equate increasing age with greater privilege and status. In the United States, however, growing old is too often associated with declining worth and social isolation. On the left, an elderly man in a nursing home sits alone and isolated. Above, an elderly Ghanan chief is treated with great affection.

general population (McIntosh, 1992); indeed, suicide rates for elderly white men are the highest for any age group (National Center for Health Statistics, 1989). In one study comparing rates of suicide among different ethnic groups, it was found that elderly White Americans committed almost 18 percent of all suicides but comprised only about 11 percent of the population. However, the suicide rate for elderly White Americans has been declining over the past twenty years (McIntosh, 1992). Suicide rates for Chinese Americans, Japanese Americans, and Filipino Americans are even higher than the rate for elderly White Americans. American Indians and African Americans show the lowest rates of suicide among older adults (although both groups are at high risk for suicide during young adulthood).

Of the Asian-American groups, first-generation immigrants were at greatest risk of suicide. One possible explanation for this finding is that the newly arrived Asian Americans had intended to earn money and then return to their native countries. When they found they were unable to earn enough either to return home or to bring their families here, they developed feelings of isolation that increased their risk of suicide. This risk has decreased among subsequent generations of Asian Americans (and, probably, other immigrant groups as well) because of acculturation and the creation of strong family ties.

The Other Victims

Relatives and Friends   When a suicide occurs, our thoughts immediately turn to the person who has taken his or her own life. What unbearable pain was he or she suffering to justify such an end? Yet the true victims of this tragedy are often the relatives and friends who are left behind to face the meaning of this act.

The emotional processes that occur in suicide survivorship are complex. Lukas and Seiden (1990) made the point that the death of a loved one is always painful and traumatic. However, family and friends must cope not only with the suicide but also with a host of unanswered questions about its cause. This stress is compounded by a society that does not sanction an open discussion of suicide; in many cases there is no funeral and a "conspiracy of silence" seems to prevail. Family and friends of the person who committed suicide may become "stuck"—unable to move on with their own lives. In part, this is due to dysfunctional coping mechanisms that individuals may use to protect themselves from devastating feelings and that may abort the normal grieving process (Lukas & Seiden, 1990).

Elisabeth Kübler-Ross (1983), a psychiatrist who has researched and written extensively about death and dying, has outlined a three-stage series of reactions people experience when a family member commits suicide.

Stage 1 The first stage is characterized by shock, denial, and numbness. The act is often incomprehensible to loved ones, who find it difficult to talk about. They tend to avoid using the word *suicide*, and they go through the motions of arranging the funeral as though it had no personal meaning. The depths of pain are too great to be confronted, and family members close themselves off from their feelings. In this stage the bereaved person seems detached from others. Kübler-Ross suggested that friends can help most during this stage by making themselves available both day and night.

Stage 2 In the second stage, family members begin to experience grief. For the spouse especially, anguish is mixed with feelings of anger. He or she now tries to blame someone for something—himself or herself, for example: "Why didn't I see what was happening?" Although expressed as self-blame for the death of one's spouse or child, the true source of this anger is the person who committed suicide. And eventually that anger and rage toward the deceased is expressed: "How could you desert me and our children? How could you do this to us? Why didn't you have the courage to face life? Damn you, why didn't you tell me you were hurting?"

Kübler-Ross believes this second stage is difficult for family and friends to handle. Most people stay away from the suicide victim's parents or spouse, whose rage can often make them quite abusive to everyone. It is important, however, that someone listen, act as a sounding board, and bear the brunt of such anger, because it needs to be expressed and is preferable to denial. The family must be helped to experience the pain, rather than postpone or deny it. They need empathic and understanding people, not sedation. Kübler-Ross says that, in suicide, extreme and prolonged grief can be avoided by not fostering denial. The words *suicide, death,* and *dead* should be used directly, without attempts to soften or disguise them (as in "passed away"). Moreover, it is important for other members of the family to see the corpse, to identify it, and to touch it, so that they face the reality of death.

Stage 3 The last stage is letting go, or completing "unfinished business." In cases of suicide, there is usually much unfinished business to take care of. A husband may think, "I never told her I loved her" or "There's so much we haven't talked about or shared." It is often helpful for the family to say these things to the suicide victim, either at the funeral or in a role-playing situation. Letting go, saying goodbye, and accepting the feelings are important therapy for survivors. (The First Person narrative is a sensitive account of one survivor's experience.)

Mental Health Professionals We have discussed the tragic consequences of suicide from the perspective of suicide victims and their family and friends. Few of us would think that a mental health professional working with a client might also suffer intensely if that person took his or her own life. After all, aren't psychologists supposed to be able to handle such matters without becoming emotionally involved? Furthermore, aren't suicides rare and unlikely to happen to clients undergoing therapy? Not as rare and unlikely as we might hope, according to a nationwide study of 365 psychologists listed in the *National Register of Health Service Providers*. That study was conducted to ascertain the prevalence of client suicides and to determine the impact of such suicides on psychologists (Chemtob et al., 1988).

The study's findings revealed that 22 percent of psychologists had worked with a client who committed suicide. Those psychologists who experienced a client's suicide were asked a number of questions about how it affected their professional practice and personal lives. Many responded that they had become

Elizabeth Kübler-Ross is a world-renowned psychiatrist, author, and lecturer, who has researched and written extensively about death and dying. Among her books are *Living with Death and Dying, On Children and Death,* and *AIDS: The Ultimate Challenge.*

FIRST PERSON

Merryl Maleska Wilbur

When I think about it now, from the context of my normal life, what I did that day seems very odd. Wasn't I aware of the passing cars, the curious onlookers who surely must have stared? And what about my father, parked and waiting just up the road—didn't I worry about what he must be feeling and thinking?

But none of this troubled me at the time. All I knew was that my husband had been buried two days earlier and that this day, this Saturday in June, would have been our sixth wedding anniversary. I needed to be near him. If there was any place in the world that I belonged, it was with him. And so I had thrown myself on the up-turned dirt that marked his grave and for one sweet, calming hour I had lain there, with my face in the ground, talking to him.

"Why did you do it, Carl? Why did it have to get that bad?" Over and over I asked him that question. "There would have been a way, if you could have only waited. You had no right to just get up and do this."

When my father came for me and I had to sit upright and face the blinding light of day, I felt a sudden paralyzing fear. It was as if I had unpeeled layers of my brain and was looking deep inside my own head: I am not going to make it through this. I will go crazy.

I could not know then that exactly one year hence, on the first anniversary of Carl's death, I would drive myself to that same cemetery, stand quietly in front of a newly placed gravestone, and read its inscription aloud to myself; that the tears would come but not in huge engulfing waves; and that when I now asked myself the question why, acknowledgement of a universe and a mystery larger than Carl or me would cause me a long moment of philosophical reflection.

Between those points would lie a year counted by its minutes. I got from one point to the other by

---

more sensitive to suicide-related cues, that they consulted more with their colleagues, and that they were more aware of forensic-legal issues. On a more personal level, the suicides seemed to have a major emotional impact on the therapists; they reported increased concerns with death and dying, intrusive thoughts of suicide, and feelings of anger and guilt toward the clients who had killed themselves.

The investigators found that one in five psychologists can expect to have a patient kill himself or herself and that 39 percent of those who lost one patient can expect to lose another. They contended that client suicides should be acknowledged as an occupational hazard because of their impact on the therapist's professional and personal life. A large proportion of therapists reported symptoms typical of posttraumatic stress disorder lasting longer than six months.

These findings should not be surprising. After all, therapists are just as vulnerable as anyone else. What seems to be needed are resources for psychologists to work through their own experiences of suicide. In addition, training programs in mental health should be initiated to teach trainees and their supervisors how to cope with a client's suicide. The investigators hope that this study will motivate psychology training programs to deal with this issue directly, forcefully, and constructively.

PREVENTING SUICIDE

In almost every case of suicide, there are hints that the act is about to occur. Suicide is irreversible, of course, so preventing it depends very much on early detection and successful intervention (Bongar, 1992; Cantor, 1991; Maltsberger, 1991). Mental health professionals involved in suicide prevention efforts operate under the assumption that potential victims are ambivalent about the act. That is, the wish to die is strong, but there is also a wish to live. Potential rescuers are trained to exert their efforts to preserve life. Part of their success in the prevention process is the ability to assess a client's suicide **lethality**—the probability that a person will choose to end his or her life. Focus On discusses suicidal intervention from the point of view of one of the authors.

something that did not feel at all like courage, although people often called me courageous. Instead, it was a simple but pitiless formula that kept me going. I discovered soon enough that, despite that early panic, I really wasn't going to go crazy. Even after an hour of screaming aloud, I would always be there in my alertness and consciousness. Nor could I seem to do what Carl had done. Ending my life by any one of several specific plans was an idea I carried with me at all moments but could never act through. The formula had its own inexorable logic: If I wasn't going to fall apart and if I couldn't kill myself, then what I was left was having to live.

The choice I made and the things I did that year also seemed to unfold naturally. Like other suicide survivors I met, I found that my guilt was unrelenting. Day after day I put myself on trial, re-viewing the minutiae of my life with Carl, searching for ways in which I had hurt him. The feelings of loss, exaggerated not only by what he had meant to me but because of the suddenness with which he had disappeared, came in great swells. In public, I kept my head down, acted by my own laws and instincts, greeting and smiling at no one; in private I screamed and cried aloud for hours at a time. The way Carl had died, the suicide itself, was so inconceivable that I had a great need to tell the story, to examine it and make it real. With my parents, a new friend who took me into her home, members of a self-help group for suicide survivors, a therapist, colleagues at work, Carl's family—over and over the story I went.

After many months of this, the grief began to change. Although there was no pivotal moment, a breakthrough occurred as I began to recognize that Carl had done something I could not control. He had acted out of who he was; neither my bad moods or nagging—nor my love—could make him be otherwise. Ironically, the fact that his death was a suicide gave me an unusual opportunity, for it helped me accept an essential human separateness. In giving up responsibility for his life, I also found it less and less astonishing that I had my own life and that I could go on without him.

Merryl Maleska Wilbur is a writer and editor. Her husband, Carl, committed suicide in 1982, after working eight years toward a doctoral degree. He was thirty-three.

Working with a potentially suicidal individual is a three-step process that involves (1) knowing what factors are highly correlated with suicide; (2) determining whether there is high, moderate, or low probability that the person will act on the suicide wish; and (3) implementing appropriate actions. People trained in working with suicidal clients often attempt to quantify the "seriousness" of each factor. For example, a person with a *clear suicidal plan* who has *the means (a gun)* to carry out a suicide threat is considered to be in a more lethal state than a recently *divorced* and *depressed* person.

Clues to Suicidal Intent

The prevention of suicide depends very much on the therapist's ability to recognize its signs. Clues to suicidal intent may be demographic or specific. We have already discussed a number of demographic factors, such as the fact that men are three times more likely to kill themselves than are women and that increased age is associated with an increased probability of suicide. And, although the popular notion is that frequent suicidal gestures are associated with less serious intent, most suicides do have a history of making suicide threats; to ignore them is extremely dangerous.

General characteristics often help detect potential suicides, but individual cases vary from statistical norms. What does one look for in specific instances? The amount of detail involved in a suicide threat can indicate its seriousness. A person who provides specific details, such as method, time, and place, is more at risk than one who describes these factors vaguely. Suicidal potential increases if the person has direct access to the means of suicide, such as a loaded pistol. Also, sometimes a suicide may be preceded by a precipitating event. The loss of a loved one, family discord, or chronic or terminal illness may contribute to a person's decision to end his or her life.

A person contemplating suicide may verbally communicate the intent. Some people make very direct statements: "I'm going to kill myself," "I want to die," or "If such and such happens, I'll kill myself." Others make indirect threats: "Goodbye," "I've had it," "You'd be better off without me," and "It's too

A Clinical Approach to Suicide Intervention

As a practicing clinician, I have had the stressful experience of working with suicidal clients; indeed, one of my patients on a psychiatric ward committed suicide when I was serving my internship in 1968. Since that time, I have had to deal with many feelings related to this tragic act, and I have conscientiously kept up with both the literature and clinical work on suicide intervention. Notice that I prefer the word *intervention* rather than *prevention*. I believe that, under certain conditions, individuals have a right to take their own lives. I may intervene in helping them understand their decision, but I do not necessarily view my role as one of prevention.

Despite this philosophical stand, my clinical experience has led me to conclude that, overwhelmingly, the majority of suicidal people do not truly wish to end their lives. When helped to understand the sources of their distress and the resources and options available to them, they inevitably choose life over death. My purpose in discussing this topic is not to debate the ethical merits of suicide or to discuss how one arrives at such a conclusion, but to explain how I, as a mental health professional, approach working with a potentially suicidal client. The setting I am most familiar with is our public schools, where I train and supervise school counselors. Increasingly, many of my trainees are encountering students who express suicidal ideation and threats. Following are some of the clinical thoughts and suggestions that I attempt to impart to them. Interestingly, many of these suggestions are equally valid when applied to friends or relatives who may be contemplating suicide.

1. *Be comfortable discussing suicide.* Many beginning counselors are not comfortable openly and directly discussing suicide with their clients or students. They are afraid that if they open the door to this topic they will inadvertently encourage a suicidal gesture, or that their actions will result in a suicide. Nothing could be further from the truth. My experience has taught me that those who are serious about suicide have entertained those thoughts for some time. Indeed, reluctance to discuss or indirectly allude to possible suicide can have a most devastating effect: It prevents the student from examining himself or herself objectively and reinforces the belief that "only crazy people" entertain these thoughts. Thus the psychological distress for the student may become even more heightened. Furthermore, it also prevents the mental health professional from quickly and accurately ascertaining suicidal risk. Asking direct questions like the following progression is a necessity:

"Are you feeling unhappy and down most of the time?" *(If yes . . .)*

"Do you feel so unhappy that you sometimes wish you were dead?" *(If yes . . .)*

"Have you ever thought about taking your own life?" *(If yes . . .)*

"What methods have you thought about using to kill yourself?" *(If the client specifies a method . . .*

"When do you plan to do this?"

---

much to put up with." On the other hand, cues are frequently very subtle:

> A patient says to Nurse Jones, who is leaving on vacation, "Goodbye, Miss Jones, I won't be here when you come back." If some time afterward Nurse Jones, knowing that the patient is not scheduled to be transferred or discharged prior to her return, thinks about that conversation, she may do well to telephone her hospital. (Danto, 1971, p. 20)

As this example illustrates, verbal expressions must be judged within the larger context of recent events and behavioral cues. We have all, at one time or another, made or heard such statements.

Behavioral clues can be communicated directly or indirectly. The most direct clue is a "practice run," an actual suicide attempt. Even if the act is not completed, *it should be taken seriously;* it often communicates deep suicidal intent that may be carried out in the future. Indirect behavioral clues can include actions such as putting one's affairs in order, taking a lengthy trip, giving away prized possessions, buying a casket, or making out a will, depending on the circumstances. In other words, the more unusual or pe-

Contrary to fears that such an approach will adversely affect the student, I have found that directness diminishes students' distress. Many students are relieved to be able to discuss a taboo topic openly and honestly.

2. *Use the natural barrier against suicide.* Studies reveal that almost all people who commit suicide have made attempts in the past. Most of us have a trained-in barrier against hurting ourselves or taking our own lives. Once a person crosses that barrier, it becomes easier to act against one's moral, ethical, and religious upbringing. Even in students who have made a suicidal gesture, the barrier is never completely gone. When students have never attempted to kill themselves but have thought about ending their lives, the counselor should immediately and forcefully reinforce the barrier to prevent it from being crossed. This can be done in a number of different ways, but generally it involves concrete actions on the part of the counselor.

3. *Take action to affect the client's immediate environment.* If your assessment leads you to believe that you are dealing with a high-risk student, no amount of talk or philosophical debate will help. Although acting in an autocratic manner may be unappealing, a counselor is often required to make decisions and take actions against the wishes of the student. High-risk students should not be allowed to leave the school office without a clear-cut treatment plan and the involvement of responsible parties. Parents may need to be notified immediately, and if they are not cooperative, the school should have specific procedures for involving civil authorities. I tell my students that it is always better to err on the conservative side than to gamble with a person's life.

If, however, your assessment leads you to conclude you are dealing with a low-risk client, other more democratic and less severe actions are possible. For example, two options are involving the student in counseling (within the school) or referring the student to a private practitioner in the community. If you decide to continue a counseling relationship with the student, you may use yourself to reinforce the barrier. I have found, for example, that obtaining an agreement with the student can be a powerful means of blocking suicidal attempts. It may be as simple as extracting a verbal promise that the student will not make any attempt at suicide that week, or as formal as actually signing a behavioral contract, such as this one:

1. I agree not to attempt to kill myself or harm myself from

_____ to

_____ .

2. I agree to get rid of any or all things that may be used to kill myself such as knives, guns, or pills.

3. I agree to immediately call my counselor at

_____ or the Suicide Prevention Center should I feel like hurting myself.

4. I agree to these conditions as a part of my counseling with _____ .

Signed _____

Witnessed _____

Dated _____

Suicide intervention, in some respects, goes against the traditional therapeutic training of most mental health professionals. A potential suicide crisis does not allow the mental health professional either the luxury of time to explore the client's problems or the ease of simply sitting back and behaving in a passive, democratic manner. The actions we choose to take or not take can have major effects on the final outcome of our suicidal clients.

---

culiar the situation, the more likely it is that the action is a cue to suicide.

Crisis Intervention

Suicide prevention can occur at several levels, and the mental health profession has now begun to move in several coordinated directions to establish prevention efforts. At the clinical level, attempts are being made to educate staff at mental health institutions and even at schools to recognize conditions and symptoms that indicate potential suicides (Kneisel & Richards, 1988). For example, a single man older than fifty years of age, suffering from a sudden acute onset of depression and expressing hopelessness, should be recognized by mental health professionals as being at high risk.

When a psychiatric facility encounters someone who fits a particular risk profile for suicide, crisis intervention strategies will most likely be used to abort or ameliorate the processes that could lead to a suicide attempt. Crisis intervention is aimed at providing intensive short-term help to a patient in resolving an immediate life crisis. Unlike traditional psychother-

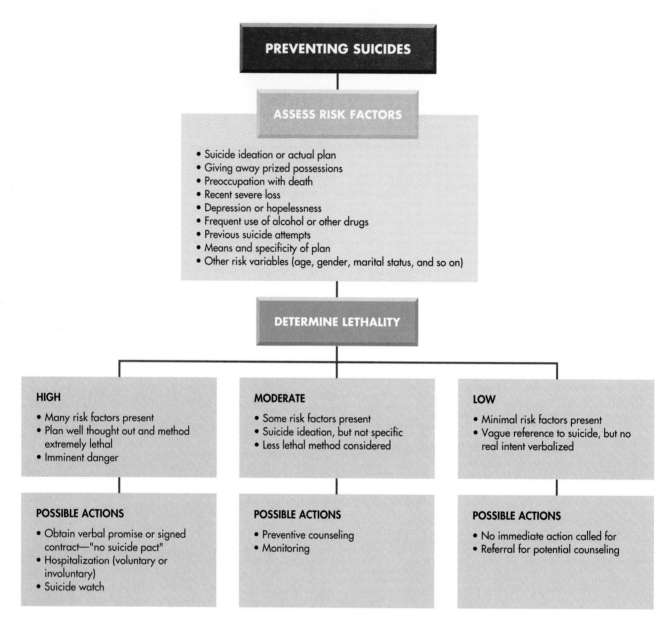

FIGURE 12.3   The Process of Preventing Suicide Suicide prevention involves the careful assessment of risk factors to determine lethality—the probability that a person will choose to end his or her life. Working with a potentially suicidal individual is a three-step process that involves (a) knowing what factors are highly correlated with suicide; (b) determining whether there is high, moderate, or low probability that the person will act on the wish; and (c) implementing appropriate actions.

apy, in which sessions are spaced out and treatment is provided on a more leisurely long-term basis, crisis intervention recognizes the immediacy of the patient's state of mind. The patient may be immediately hospitalized, given medical treatment, and seen by a psychiatric team for two to four hours every day until the person is stabilized and the immediate crisis has passed. In these sessions, the team is very active not only in working with the patient but in taking charge of the person's personal, social, and professional life outside of the psychiatric facility. Much of suicide intervention strategies have been developed through clinical work rather than research because the nature of suicide demands immediate action, as our earlier case study amply demonstrates. Waiting for empirical studies is not a luxury the clinician can afford. Figure 12.3 summarizes the process of assertive risk and determining lethality.

After patients return to a more stable emotional state and the immediate risk of suicide has passed, they are then given more traditional forms of treatment, either on an inpatient or outpatient basis. In addition to the intense therapy they receive from the psychiatric team, relatives and friends may be enlisted to help monitor patients when they leave the hospital. In these cases, the responsible relatives or friends are provided with specific guidelines about how to deal with the patient between treatment team contacts, who to notify should problems arise outside of the hospital, and so forth.

Suicide Prevention Centers

Crisis intervention can be highly successful if a potentially suicidal patient is either already being treated by a therapist or has come to the attention of one through the efforts of concerned family or friends. Many people in acute distress, however, are not formally being treated. Although contact with a mental health agency may be highly desirable, many are unaware of the services available to them. Recognizing that suicidal crises may occur at any time and that preventive assistance on a much larger scale may be needed, a number of communities have established suicide prevention centers.

The first suicide prevention center was established in Los Angeles in 1958 by psychologists Norman L. Farberow and Edwin S. Shneidman. The center first sought patients from the wards of hospitals. Soon, however, its reputation grew, and in little more than a decade, 99 percent of its contacts were by phone (Farberow, 1970). In the last forty years, hundreds of suicide prevention centers patterned after the first one have sprung up throughout the United States. These centers are generally adapted to the particular needs of the communities they serve, but they all share certain operational procedures and goals.

Telephone Crisis Intervention   Suicide prevention centers typically operate twenty-four hours a day, seven days a week. Because most suicide contacts are by phone, a well-publicized telephone number is made available throughout the community for calls at any time of the day or night. Furthermore, many centers provide inpatient or outpatient crisis treatment. If they lack such resources, the centers develop cooperative programs with other community mental health facilities. Most telephone hotlines are staffed by paraprofessionals. All workers are trained in crisis intervention techniques and have been exposed to crisis situations under supervision. Among these techniques are the following:

Suicide prevention centers (SPCs) operate twenty-four hours a day, seven days a week and have well-publicized telephone numbers because most contacts are made by phone. Even though there is controversy about SPC effectiveness, the mental health profession continues to support these centers.

1. *Maintain contact and establish a relationship.*   The skilled worker who establishes a good relationship with the suicidal caller not only increases the caller's chances of working out an alternative solution but also can exert more influence. Thus it is important for the worker to show interest, concern, and self-assuredness.

2. *Obtain necessary information.*   The worker elicits demographic data and the caller's name and address. This information is very valuable in case an urgent need arises to locate the caller.

3. *Evaluate suicidal potential.*   The staff person taking the call must quickly determine the seriousness of the caller's self-destructive intent. Most centers use lethality rating scales to help the worker determine suicide potential. These usually contain questions on age, gender, onset of symptoms, situa-

tional plight, prior suicidal behavior, and the communication qualities of the caller. Staffers also elicit other demographic and specific information that might provide clues to lethality, such as the information discussed in the section on clues to suicidal intent.

4. *Clarify the nature of the stress and focal problem.* The worker must help the caller to clarify the exact nature of the stress, to recognize that he or she may be under so much duress that his or her thinking may be confused and impaired, and to realize that there are other solutions besides suicide. The caller is often disoriented, so the worker *must* be specific to help bring the caller back to reality.

5. *Assess strengths and resources.* In working out a therapeutic plan, the worker can often mobilize the caller's strengths or available resources. In their agitation, suicidal people tend to forget their own strengths. Their feelings of helplessness are so overwhelming that helping them recognize what they can do about a situation is important. The worker explores the caller's personal resources (family, friends, coworkers), professional resources (doctors, clergy, therapists, lawyers), and community resources (clinics, hospitals, social agencies).

6. *Recommend and initiate an action plan.* Besides being supportive, the worker is highly directive in recommending a course of action. Whether the recommendation entails immediately seeing the person, calling the person's family, or referring the person to a social agency the next day, the worker presents a plan of action and outlines it step by step.

This list implies a rigid sequence, but in fact the approach (as well as the order of the steps) is adjusted to fit the needs of the individual caller.

The Effectiveness of Suicide Prevention Centers Today approximately two hundred suicide prevention centers function in the United States, as well as numerous "suicide hotlines" in mental health clinics. Little research has been done on their effectiveness, however, and many of their clients want to remain anonymous.

Nevertheless, some data are available. For example, we know that 95 percent of callers to suicide prevention centers never use the service again (Speer, 1971). This finding may indicate that the service was so helpful that no further treatment was needed or, just as possibly, that callers do not find the centers helpful and feel it is useless to call again. Worse yet, they may have killed themselves after the contact. Another study has shown that potential suicides do

not perceive contact with a prevention center as more helpful than discussion with friends (Speer, 1972). And, if the justification for such centers is based on their ability to offer services to a large number of clients, then the fact that only 2 percent of the people who kill themselves ever contact such a service is disturbing (Weiner, 1969). Furthermore, studies on cities with hotline services provide mixed findings (Lester, 1989; 1991). Some studies found that suicides decreased in a community with hotline services (Miller, Coombs & Leeper, 1984), some found no change (Barraclough, Jennings & Moss, 1977), and others found an increase (Weiner, 1969). However, in cities without prevention centers, the rates increased even more (Lester, 1991).

Before you jump to the conclusion that suicide prevention centers are ineffective, however, note that the studies cited could have been influenced by several factors. For example, cities with and cities without such centers may differ so much that they are not comparable. Additionally, clients may contact these centers only when they are in such great distress that they despair of asking friends for help. They may later perceive their contacts with friends as being more beneficial relative to the distress they feel. Finally, despite the lack of convincing evidence, there is always the possibility that suicide prevention centers do help. Because life is precious, the mental health profession continues to support them.

Community Prevention Programs

Suicide prevention programs also are found at work sites and schools. Increasingly, community leaders have recognized that the suicide of a worker or student has dramatic and stressful emotional effects on fellow workers and students who may have known the victim (Calhoun, Atkeson & Resick, 1982). When a school experiences a suicide, the staff and students quickly learn of the event. This is often followed by emotional upheaval, anxiety, guilt, and severe grieving (Davis, 1985; Praeger & Bernhardt, 1985). Educational institutions now routinely consult mental health professionals after a suicide to help facilitate the natural grieving process; reduce the secrecy, confusion, and rumors surrounding a suicide; and prevent possible copycat suicides.

One interesting and effective form of intervention was developed in response to a particularly violent suicide (Kneisel & Richard, 1988). A fifth- and sixth-grade teacher took her own life by dousing herself with gasoline and igniting herself. Local media coverage was quite intense, and little else was discussed. In responding to this terrible event and the emotional needs of the students, the school assembled a mental health consulting team, comprising two child psychologists trained in crisis intervention and one representative each of the fire department and mayoral task force. The fire department representative was included because of concern about possible increased risk of fire setting among students. The team worked directly with the school psychologist, who already knew the students and staff. The primary goal of the program was to mitigate the effects of the tragedy by providing survivors with an opportunity to express and understand their reactions to the event. To accomplish this goal, the following activities were undertaken:

1. A faculty meeting was called to give teachers a forum in which they could share feelings and information with one another. This session was only partially successful. It gave the team insight into student concerns, but it failed to meet the needs of the faculty.

2. In a classroom discussion, children were given an opportunity to express their feelings and concerns, especially those dealing with fears of death, suicide, and fire. They were reassured that the teacher's decision to kill herself was not based on their behavior and that her death was not their fault. All questions were answered truthfully and in a straightforward manner.

3. Throughout this period of intervention, the school psychologist was available for individual sessions with teachers, staff, and students. Some sought individual sessions because they had an especially close relationship to the victim; others sought help because they were already dealing with personal issues of loss, separation, and abandonment. Some students were referred because they were excessively tearful, withdrawn, or distraught; others were seen because they denied the suicide. Many of these individuals were referred for ongoing follow-up treatment.

After all these meetings, the team met with the principal to plan follow-up actions. A memorial service was held. Parents were sent letters telling them about the suicide and informing them about mental health resources in the community. Written guidelines for suicide prevention were developed and distributed in the school.

Kneisel and Richards concluded that such an institutional response to a suicide minimizes mental health problems among the survivors, restores equilibrium in the school and community, and represents an effective suicide prevention program.

THE RIGHT TO SUICIDE: MORAL, ETHICAL, AND LEGAL IMPLICATIONS

The act of suicide seems to violate much of what we have been taught regarding the sanctity of life. Many segments of the population consider it immoral and provide strong religious sanctions against it. Suicide is both a sin in the canonical law of the Catholic Church and an illegal act according to the secular laws of most countries. Within the United States, many states have laws against suicide and some consider it illegal. Of course, such laws are difficult to enforce because the victims are not around to prosecute. Many are beginning to question the legitimacy of such sanctions, however, and are openly advocating one's right to suicide.

One of the most outspoken critics of suicide prevention programs is Thomas Szasz (1986). He argued that suicide is an act of a moral agent who is ultimately responsible. Szasz opposed coercive methods used by mental health professionals (such as depriving clients of access to the means of suicide, and involuntary hospitalization) to prevent suicide. The taking of one's own life is ultimately the responsibility of the person, not of the mental health professional. By taking actions against a client's wishes, practitioners have allied themselves with the police power of the state and have identified themselves as foes of individual liberty and responsibility. It should be noted that Szasz does not claim that suicide is always good or morally legitimate. Rather, he maintains that we must abstain from empowering agents of the state to use coercion to prevent suicide.

Using another line of reasoning, Doris Portwood believes that elderly people have the right to end their own lives if their continued existence would result in psychological and physical deterioration:

> The choice of suicide is ours to make. It is our life we are giving up, and our death we are arranging. The choice does not infringe on the rights of others. We do not need to explain and excuse. (Portwood, 1978, p. 68)

Portwood contended that these people should be allowed the choice of dying in a dignified manner, particularly if they suffer from a terminal or severely incapacitating illness that would cause misery for their families and friends. Such was the case with Jenny Williams (described at the beginning of this chapter), who chose death over life.

The debate over whether people have the right to end their own lives has become more volatile and controversial recently, focusing on whether others have a right to aid a suicidal person in carrying out a suicide. Is it morally, ethically, and legally permissible

Do People Have a Right to Die?

In 1990 the psychological community was shocked by the suicide of one of their very own, Bruno Bettelheim. During an earlier interview (Fremon, 1991), Bettelheim had revealed some of his own thoughts regarding death and suicide. He stated that he did not fear death but was frightened at the prospect of suffering. At eighty-six years, he had lived a productive and enjoyable life and was fearful he would be kept alive without a purpose. Bettelheim had recently suffered a stroke, was fearful that he would suffer another, and could no longer take part in many of the activities that had brought joy and meaning to his life. He believed that he was living on borrowed time and contemplated meeting with a doctor in The Netherlands who was willing to give him a lethal injection.

From 1989 to 1996, Dr. Jack Kevorkian, a physician, helped nearly twenty people (nearly all women) with chronic debilitating diseases commit suicide. He had invented a "suicide machine" composed of bottles containing chemicals that could be fed intravenously into the arm of the person. The solution could bring instantaneous unconsciousness and quick painless death. His first client, Mrs. J. Adkins, suffered from Alzheimer's disease. She did not want to put her family through the agony of the disease, believed that she had a right to choose death, stated that her act was that of a rational mind, and had the consent of her husband. Two other women who committed suicide did not have diseases that threatened to kill them in the immediate future. One suffered from multiple sclerosis and the other from a pelvic condition that caused severe and constant pain. Several times, charges of homicide were brought against Kevorkian, and in each case they were ultimately dropped. In one ruling, a Michigan judge dismissed the charges on grounds that suicide was not a crime in that state, and therefore assisting suicide cannot be a crime. The legal troubles for Kevorkian are not over, however. A new law in Michigan recently went into effect outlawing "physician-assisted suicides." In his latest trial, a jury found Kevorkian innocent of all charges of assisted suicide.

In November 1992, California citizens had the opportunity of voting on Proposition 161, the Death with Dignity Act. The statewide ballot initiative that would have made it legal for doctors to help their terminally ill patients die was narrowly defeated. However, the State of Oregon recently approved an initiative allowing physician-assisted suicides. The constitutionality of the bill is currently being challenged by opponents. It is obvious that the right to suicide continues to be very controversial and divisive.

What reactions do you have to these three events? Did Bruno Bettelheim have a right to end his own life? What reasons led you to your answer? Does a doctor—or, for that matter, anyone—have a right to help others terminate their lives? What might motivate someone like Dr. Kevorkian to risk censure and imprisonment in helping others to die? If you were a voting-age Californian, would you have voted for or against Proposition 161? Why or why not?

These questions do not have easy answers. Although we may pride ourselves on being social scientists concerned with objective facts in helping provide answers, the topic of suicide raises unavoidable moral, legal, and ethical issues. It is certainly possible for us to study suicide in an academic fashion, but what of the mental health professional who encounters clients who threaten to kill themselves? What if we encounter a friend, classmate, neighbor, or relative who is contemplating suicide? In these situations we cannot be mere observers, for our actions or decisions not to act will reflect our beliefs and values about suicide. Even more close to us is this question: "Might there ever come a time in your life when you would contemplate suicide?" Imagine yourself, like Bettelheim, faced with losing control of your bodily functions, your ability to move about or to read or to feed yourself, and anticipating the onset of multiple strokes. Would you want to be kept alive?

We would like to have you, perhaps with other classmates, consider the three examples above. Can you build a case against suicide prevention? Can you build a case against the right to take one's own life? We hope that you and your classmates will be able to clarify your thoughts and values about suicide. Remember, allowing, respecting, and understanding the diversity of views on this controversial topic is important.

to allow relatives, friends, or physicians to provide support, means, and actions to carry out a suicide (see Critical Thinking)? Two high-profile individuals have fueled the debate by virtue of their actions. Derek Humphrey, former director of the Hemlock Society (an organization that advocates people's right to end their lives), published a best-selling book, *Final Exit* (1991). It is a manual that provides practical information such as drug dosages needed to end one's life; when published it created a national stir. Another individual who has become a household name is Dr. Jack Kevorkian, a physician who has helped nearly twenty people to end their own lives using an invention of his called a "suicide machine."

Ironically, it is the success of medical science that has added fuel to the right-to-die movement. As a part of our remarkable successful efforts to prolong life, this society has also begun to prolong the process of dying. And this prolongation has caused many elderly or terminally ill people to fear the medical decision maker who is intent only on keeping them alive, giving no thought to their desires or dignity. They and many others find it abhorrent to impose on a dying patient a horrifying array of respirators, breathing tubes, feeding tubes, and repeated violent cardiopulmonary resuscitations—procedures that are often futile and against the wishes of the patient and his or her family. Humane and sensitive physicians, who believe that the resulting quality of life will not merit such heroic measures but whose training impels them to sustain life, are caught in the middle of this conflict. A civil or criminal lawsuit may be brought against the physician who agrees to allow a patient to die.

More and more people now believe that individuals ought to have the right to end their own lives, at least in certain circumstances. In cases of obvious terminal illness, when the patient has a short time to live and is suffering unbearable pain, the right-to-die argument seems sensible. In 1976 the California State Assembly became one of the first state legislatures to provide that right to people in such situations. Since then, many other states have passed "living will" laws that offer protection against dehumanized dying and confer immunity on physicians and hospital personnel who comply with a patient's wishes. And, in November 1992, California voters narrowly defeated Proposition 161, the Death with Dignity Act, which would have granted physicians the legal right to help end the lives of terminally ill patients. However, a similar bill was recently passed in Oregon, although its constitutionality is currently being challenged.

Advocates of such laws frequently use the terms *quality of life* and *quality of humanness* as the criteria for deciding between life and death. The meanings of these phrases are, however, somewhat indistinct and subjective. At what point do we consider the quality of life sufficiently poor to justify terminating it? Should people who have been severely injured or scarred (through loss of limbs, paralysis, blindness, or brain injury) be allowed to end their own lives? What about mentally retarded or emotionally disturbed people? Could it be argued that their quality of life is equally poor? Moreover, who will decide whether a

Dr. Jack Kevorkian, a Michigan physician, has assisted in more than twenty suicides. Here, he poses with Marcella Lawrence and Marguerit Tate, two women he helped to die hours before Michigan's governor signed a law banning assisted suicides.

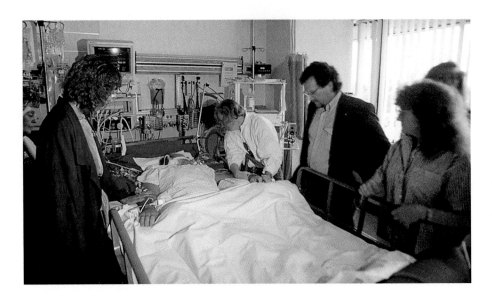

While modern medicine has made incredible advances in prolonging life, many of the procedures simply sustain life without regard to quality. Many terminally ill or elderly patients, wishing to die with dignity, feel they have a basic right to refuse treatment and end their own lives. The ethical and legal considerations are complex.

person is or is not terminally ill? There are many recorded cases of "incurable" patients who recovered when new medical techniques or treatments arrested, remitted, or cured their illnesses. Such questions cannot be answered easily because they deal with ethics and human values.

Yet the mental health practitioner cannot avoid these questions. Like their medical counterparts, clinicians are trained to save people's lives. They have accepted the philosophical assumption that life is better than death, and that no one has a right to take his or her own life. Strong social, religious, and legal sanctions support this belief. Therapists work not only with terminally ill clients who wish to take their own lives but also with disturbed clients who may have suicidal tendencies. These latter clients are not terminally ill but may be suffering severe emotional or physical pain; their deaths would bring immense pain and suffering to their loved ones. Moreover, most people who attempt suicide do not want to die, are ambivalent about the act, or find that their suicidal urge passes when their life situation improves (Bongar, 1991, 1992).

In working with clients who express suicidal wishes, the practicing therapist must confront the following questions (Corey, 1996):

1. Do therapists have a right and responsibility to forcefully protect people from the potential harm that their own decisions may cause?

2. Do therapists have an ethical right to prevent clients from committing suicide when they have clearly chosen death over life?

3. What ethical and legal considerations are involved in right-to-die decisions?

4. Once a therapist determines that a significant risk exists, must some course of action be taken? What are the consequences when a therapist fails to take steps to prevent a suicide?

Of course, these questions are answered differently by different people. We can, however, directly address one of the issues they raise—the legal implications. According to one observer, no clear constitutional or legal statement gives a person the right to choose death. But the Constitution does seem to provide a basis for the right to refuse treatment, even life-saving treatment (Powell, 1982). Despite this apparent contradiction, therapists have a responsibility to prevent suicide if they can reasonably anticipate the possibility of self-destruction. Failure to do so can result in legal liability.

Clearly, suicide and suicide prevention involve a number of important social and legal issues, as well as the personal value systems of clients and their families, mental health professionals, and those who devise and enforce our laws. And just as clearly, we need to know much more about the causes of suicide and the detection of people who are at high risk for suicide, as well as the most effective means of intervention. Life is precious, and we need to do everything possible, within reason, to protect it.

SUMMARY

1. Suicide is both a tragic and puzzling act. In the past, it has often been kept hidden, and relatives and friends of the victim did not speak of it. Mental health professionals now realize that understanding the causes of suicide is extremely important. Much is known about the *facts* of suicide but little about the *why* is understood. Although studies indicate that depression, hopelessness, and excessive alcohol consumption are highly correlated with suicide, the complex relationship between these variables and suicide is not simply one of cause and effect.

2. Early explanations of suicide were based on either a sociocultural or an intrapsychic view. Durkheim identified three categories of suicide on the basis of the nature of the person's relationship to a group. Egoistic suicide results from an inability to integrate oneself with society. Altruistic suicide is motivated by the need to further the goals of the group or to achieve a "higher good." Anomic suicide results when a person's relationship to the group becomes unbalanced in some dramatic fashion. In the intrapsychic view, self-destruction results when hostility toward another person turns inward. More recent evidence has indicated that biochemical factors may be important, but no single explanation seems sufficient to clarify the many facets of suicide.

3. In recent years, childhood and adolescent suicides have increased at an alarming rate. A lack of research has limited our understanding of why children take their own lives. However, the available studies have indicated that those who attempt suicide come from families characterized by psychiatric illness (primarily drug and alcohol abuse), medical problems, suicide, paternal unemployment, and the absence of one parent. Most childhood suicide attempts occur in the home, and drug overdose is the primary means.

4. Suicide among college students is particularly perplexing. Studies have indicated that students who commit suicide can be distinguished from their non-suicidal classmates: they are older and more likely to be postgraduate students, male, language or literature majors, and foreign students. As undergraduates, they have better academic records than their peers. Most college-student suicides occur at the beginning of a semester. They may be related to unrealistically high internal expectations, excessive pressures to excel from family and friends, or simply emotional disturbance.

5. Many people tend to become depressed about "feeling old" as they age, and depressed elderly people often think about suicide.

6. Suicide affects not only the person who commits the act but also the people left behind. Loved ones of the victim frequently respond with denial and shock, followed by grief and anger. The anger may be directed toward the self, but it is usually intended for the person who commits the act. The grief is resolved if and when he or she is able to "let go" of the deceased. Mental health professionals who treat a client who commits suicide also experience psychological distress.

7. Perhaps the best way to prevent suicide is to recognize its signs and intervene before it occurs. People are more likely to commit suicide if they are older, male, have a history of attempts, describe in detail how the act will be accomplished, and give verbal hints that they are planning self-destruction. Crisis intervention concepts and techniques have been used successfully to treat clients who contemplate suicide. Intensive short-term therapy is used to stabilize the immediate crisis. Suicide prevention centers operate twenty-four hours a day to provide intervention services to all potential suicides, especially those not undergoing treatment. Telephone hotlines are staffed by well-trained paraprofessionals who will work with anyone who is contemplating suicide. In addition, these centers provide preventive education to the public. More and more community intervention programs are directed at organizations that may have experienced a suicide. The focus is not only on preventing future suicides but also on helping friends, family, workers, and others affected by the tragedy.

8. The act of suicide raises moral, ethical, and legal concerns. Do people have a right to take their own lives? This question is difficult to answer, particularly when the person is terminally ill and wishes to end his or her suffering. Nevertheless, therapists, like physicians, have been trained to preserve life, and they have a legal obligation to do so.

KEY TERMS

altruistic suicide Suicide that is motivated by a desire to further group goals or to achieve some greater good

anomic suicide Suicide that results when a person's relationship to society is unbalanced in some dramatic fashion

egoistic suicide Suicide that results from an inability to integrate oneself with society

lethality The probability that a person will end his or her life

psychological autopsy The systematic examination of existing information for the purpose of understanding and explaining a person's behavior before his or her death

suicidal ideation Thoughts about suicide

suicide The taking of one's own life

CHAPTER 13

SCHIZOPHRENIA: DIAGNOSIS AND SYMPTOMS

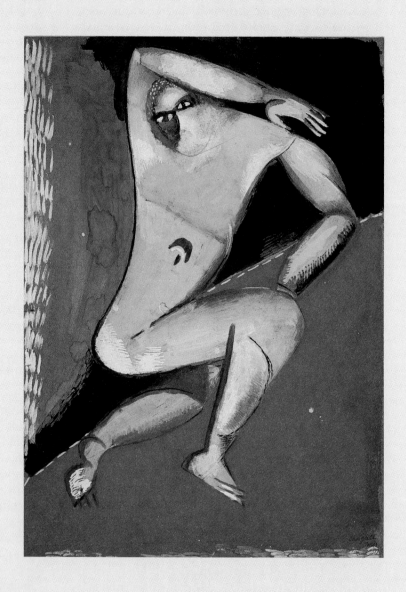

Schizophrenia is a severely disabling disorder. At times, reality becomes so distorted that affected people cannot trust their perceptions and thoughts. Zan Bockes, a woman who completed her undergraduate work between hospitalizations and who eventually entered graduate school, gives a personal account of her struggles with schizophrenia.

> I'd always been very quiet, somewhat of a "loner," usually energetic, and a good student with a particular interest in literature and creative writing, but the illness began disrupting my school work and job performance when I was 19 years old. . . . I increasingly heard voices (which I'd always called "loud thoughts" or "impulses with words") commanding me to take destructive action. I concluded that other people were putting these "loud thoughts" in my head and controlling my behavior in an effort to ruin my life. I smelled blood and decaying matter where no blood or decaying matter could be found (for example, in the classrooms at school). I had difficulty concentrating, I fantasized excessively, and I had trouble sleeping and eating. When I began responding to the voices' commands by breaking windows in my apartment and starting fires, I was committed with a diagnosis of "chronic hebephrenic schizophrenia." . . .
>
> Over those 5 months, I had to deal with occasional hallucinations, recurrent illusions, increased energy. . . and periods during which I found myself indulging in various paranoid and grandiose thought patterns. Since I had learned to recognize these for what they were and had been able to appreciate the ultimate consequences of reacting to them, I was capable of preventing them from drastically affecting my behavior. . . . I recall one recent example of how I prevented further escalation of some irrational suspicions. In March, I became increasingly uneasy about something which I could not pinpoint, until I was quite fearful that some personal disaster was rapidly approaching. On my way to school one day, three large birds passed over me, stalling briefly in the air above my head. In my class, I noticed that a woman in front of me had a large black bag marked with white letters which read, among other things, "URGENT" and "CONFIDENTIAL." I heard a woman in the hallway say, "You won't go to jail." And my professor said during his lecture, "The choices you make are not inevitable," which angered and frightened me because I misunderstood him to mean, "The choices you make are inevitable." These events loomed in my head, and I interpreted them as warnings of impending disaster. With great difficulty, I suppressed my impulses to cry out and strike the nearby professor, and I tried to concentrate on the lecture. I managed to get through class and then hurried to my favorite isolated place on campus to get better control of myself. . . .
>
> I acknowledge that although I have much control over my behavior, and some control over my thinking, and some control over my feelings, there remain a few things over which I have little or no control—for example, hallucinations. The trick is to realize when or if the hallucinations are truly disrupting my thoughts, feelings, and behaviors, and to take appropriate action before things get out of hand. Gradually I am learning where to draw the line—when medication is helpful and necessary and when I can manage safely without it. . . .
>
> As of yet, I still have a long road ahead of me. There is much that I don't understand about schizophrenia, but I realize I am not alone in my lack of knowledge about the illness. . . . Life puts various limitations on each person, but within those limitations, there is always the freedom to make certain choices—an insight that I find relieving as well as revealing. (Bockes, 1987, pp. 40–42)

These few excerpts from Bockes's account illustrate many features of the schizophrenic disorders, which involve disorders of thought or cognition. More specifically, **cognition** consists of the processes of thinking, perceiving, judging, and recognizing. In this chapter we discuss the diagnosis and symptoms of schizophrenia, the different types of schizophrenic disorders, and the course of this disorder. Then, in Chapter 14, we examine the etiology and treatment of schizophrenia.

SCHIZOPHRENIA

Schizophrenia is a group of disorders characterized by severely impaired cognitive processes, personality disintegration, affective disturbances, and social withdrawal. People thus affected may lose contact with reality, may see or hear things that are not actually occurring, or may develop false beliefs about themselves or others.

Schizophrenia receives a great deal of attention for several reasons. First, the disorders are severely disabling and frequently require hospitalization. The financial costs of hospitalization and the psychological

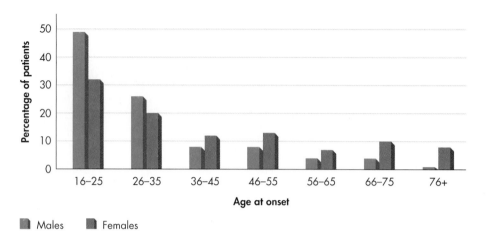

FIGURE 13.1   **Male and Female Schizophrenic Patients—Age of Diagnosis**
Although schizophrenia is characterized by an early age of onset for both males and females, females account for the highest percentage of those receiving the diagnosis after the age of forty.

Source: Castle & Murray, 1993, p. 696.

German psychiatrist Emil Kraepelin (1856–1926) called schizophrenia *dementia praecox* (insanity at an early age). He described many of the disease's features and recognized them as a type of mental disorder.

costs to patients, families, and friends can be enormous. Second, the lifetime prevalence rate of schizophrenia in the United States is about 1 percent, so it affects millions of people directly and males and females equally (Bourdon et al., 1992; Gorwood et al., 1995). And third, the causes of these disorders are not well known, and it has been difficult to find effective treatments. Although DSM-IV tries to present schizophrenia as a distinct disorder, evidence suggests that it is a heterogeneous clinical syndrome with different etiologies and outcomes (Andreasen et al., 1995; Heinrichs, 1993).

The age of onset for schizophrenia occurs earlier in males than in females. As Figure 13.1 indicates, the gender ratio shifts by the mid forties, when the percentage of women receiving this diagnosis is greater than that for men. This trend is especially pronounced in the mid sixties and later (Castle & Murray, 1993). The reason for the gender differences in age of onset is not known (Gorwood et al., 1995). The lifetime prevalence rate for schizophrenia is higher among African Americans (2.1 percent) and lower among Hispanic Americans (0.8 percent). The higher rate among African Americans can be accounted for by their lower socioeconomic status and higher divorce rates, which are independently related with higher rates of schizophrenia (Keith, Regier & Rae, 1991). The lower rate among Hispanic Americans may be due both to the underreporting of symptomatology and to a lower level of help seeking (Dassori, Miller & Saldana, 1995).

History of the Diagnostic Category

What is schizophrenia? Most clinicians agree that the symptoms shown by Zan Bockes (hearing disembodied voices, smelling nonexistent blood and decaying matter, and disturbed thought processes) are consistent with a diagnosis of schizophrenia. The criteria that define this disorder, however, have changed over time. Some who were diagnosed as schizophrenic under criteria used in the past might not receive that diagnosis today.

In 1896 Emil Kraepelin recognized that symptoms such as hallucinations, delusions, and intellectual deterioration were characteristic of a particular disorder whose onset began at an early age. He called this disorder *dementia praecox* (insanity at an early age). Because he believed that the disorder involved some form of organic deterioration, its outcome was considered to be poor. People who recovered from dementia praecox were thought to have been misdiagnosed.

A Swiss psychiatrist, Eugen Bleuler (1911/1950), disagreed with Kraepelin's theory for several reasons. He did not believe that all or even most cases of schizophrenia developed at an early age. The symptoms of schizophrenia were believed to be the result of disordered thought processes affecting the four As: autism (complete self-focus), associations (unconnected ideas), affect (inappropriate emotions), and ambivalence (uncertainty over actions). He argued that the outcome of schizophrenia did not always involve progressive deterioration, and he believed that dementia praecox represented a group of disorders that have different causes. Bleuler also theorized that environmental factors interacting with a genetic predisposition produced the disorder.

Bleuler's definition of schizophrenia was broader than Kraepelin's in that age of onset and the course of the disorder were more variable. DSM-I and DSM-II incorporated the broader definition of schizophrenia and focused on Bleuler's four A's as the criteria. Several international studies (World Health Organization, 1973b; Cooper et al., 1972) revealed that other countries used a stricter definition for schizophrenia. When schizophrenic patients in the United States were rediagnosed according to the international standards, approximately 50 percent were placed into other categories, such as mood, personality disorders, or other psychotic disorders.

This discrepancy with other diagnostic systems forced researchers to reexamine the criteria used to define schizophrenia, and this reexamination resulted in changes in DSM-III and DSM-III-R. "The DSM-III concept is more restrictive in order to identify a group

Eugen Bleuler (1857–1939) was a Swiss psychiatrist who believed that the age of onset and outcomes for schizophrenia were variable. He was the first to use the term "schizophrenia."

that is more homogeneous in regard to differential response to somatic therapy, presence of a familial pattern, a tendency toward onset in early adult life, recurrence, and severe functional impairment" (American Psychiatric Association, 1980, p. 373). But it appears that the pendulum swung too far in narrowing the definition of schizophrenia. The criteria in DSM-III-R (continued in DSM-IV) were considered to be some of the most restrictive among classification systems in the world (Andreasen & Flaum, 1991; Carson, 1991). For example, the symptoms have to be present for at least six months for the diagnosis, compared with only one month according to the tenth revision of the International Classification of Disease (ICD-10) developed by the World Health Organization. Individuals who would be classified as schizophrenic in other countries might not receive that diagnosis with DSM-IV. Although these changes are thought to increase

TABLE 13.1   DSM-IV Criteria for Schizophrenia

A. At least two of the following symptoms lasting for at least one month in the active phase (exception: only one symptom if it involves bizarre delusions or if hallucinations involve a running commentary on the person or two or more voices talking with each other).

1. Delusions

2. Hallucinations

3. Disorganized speech (incoherence or frequent derailment)

4. Grossly disorganized or catatonic behavior

5. Negative symptoms (flat affect, avolition, alogia, or anhedonia)

B. During the course of the disturbance, functioning in one or more areas such as work, social relations, and self-care has deteriorated markedly from premorbid levels (in the case of a child or adolescent, failure to reach expected level of social or academic development).

C. Signs of the disorder must be present for at least six months.

D. Schizoaffective and mood disorders with psychotic features must be ruled out.

E. The disturbance is not substance-induced or caused by organic factors.

diagnostic reliability and validity of research on schizophrenia, they also create difficulties in comparing studies done in the United States under different diagnostic criteria. Problems also occur in cross-cultural comparisons because different countries use ICD-10 instead of DSM-IV. How can you interpret studies on cause and treatment of schizophrenia using different diagnostic criteria?

DSM-IV and the Diagnosis of Schizophrenia

According to the DSM-IV criteria, a diagnosis of schizophrenic disorder should be given only if delusions, auditory hallucinations, or marked disturbances in thinking, affect, or speech are shown. The patient must also have deteriorated from a previous level of functioning concerning work, interpersonal relationships, self-care, or the like. Evidence should show that the disorder has lasted at least six months at some point in the patient's history and has cur-

rently been present for at least one month. Organic mental disorders and affective disorders must be ruled out as causes of the patient's symptoms. (See Table 13.1 for DSM-IV criteria for schizophrenia.)

THE SYMPTOMS OF SCHIZOPHRENIA

Symptoms of schizophrenia include delusions, hallucinations, thought disorder (shifting and unrelated ideas producing incoherent communication), and bizarre behavior. There appears to be three uncorrelated dimensions in schizophrenia (Andreasen et al., 1995; Arndt et al., 1995). The first two, psychoticism (hallucinations and delusions) and disorganization (disorganized speech and behavior, inappropriate affect, motoric disturbances and disorganization, and formal thought disorder), are often described as **positive symptoms.** These symptoms are present during the active phase of the disorder and tend to disappear with treatment. **Negative symptoms,** the third dimension, are associated with inferior premorbid (before the onset of illness) social functioning and carry a poorer prognosis. One such symptom is **flat affect**—little or no emotion in situations where strong reactions are expected. Others include *alogia* (a lack of meaningful speech), *anhedonia* (an inability to feel pleasure), apathy, and *avolition* (an inability to take action or to become goal oriented).

Positive Symptoms

Positive symptoms represent distortions or excesses of normal functioning and include delusions, hallucinations, disorganized communication and thought disturbances, and motor disturbances. With treatment, symptoms diminish in intensity.

Some believe that the positive symptoms indicate a reversible condition and negative symptoms represent irreversible neuronal loss in a structurally abnormal brain (McGlashan & Fenton, 1991). We will discuss in more detail some symptoms associated with schizophrenia.

Delusions   The disordered thinking of schizophrenics may be exhibited in **delusions,** which are false personal beliefs that are firmly and consistently held despite disconfirming evidence or logic (Garety, 1991). Studies have suggested that delusions may differ in their strength and their effect on the person's life. An example of a delusion follows:

> Ms. A., an 83-year-old widow who lived alone for fifteen years, complained that the occupant of an upstairs flat was excessively noisy and that he moved furniture around late at night to disturb her. Over a period of six

months, she developed delusional persecutory ideas about this man. He wanted to frighten her from her home and had started to transmit "violet rays" through the ceiling to harm her and her ten-year-old female mongrel dog. . . . For protection, she placed her mattress under the kitchen table and slept there at night. She constructed what she called an "air raid shelter" for her dog from a small table and a pile of suitcases and insisted that the dog sleep in it. When I visited Ms. A. at her home, it was apparent that the dog's behavior had become so conditioned by that of its owner that upon hearing any sound from the flat upstairs, such as a door closing, it would immediately go to the kitchen and enter the shelter. (Howard, 1992, p. 414)

Ms. A. absolutely believed in her delusion and had little insight into her behavior. Hers was a delusion of persecution, which is one of several types, as listed here.

- *Delusions of grandeur* A belief that one is a famous or powerful person (from the present or the past). Schizophrenic individuals may assume the identities of these other people.

- *Delusions of control* A belief that other people, animals, or objects are trying to influence or take control of one.

- *Delusions of thought broadcasting* A belief that others can hear the thoughts of the individual.

- *Delusions of persecution* A belief that others are plotting against, mistreating, or even trying to kill one.

- *Delusions of reference* A belief that one is always the center of attention, or that all happenings revolve about oneself. Others are always whispering behind one's back, for example.

- *Thought withdrawal* A belief that one's thoughts are being removed from one's mind.

A rare delusion is *Capgras's syndrome* (named after the person who first reported it). It is the belief in the existence of identical "doubles," who may coexist with or replace significant others or the patient. One fourteen-year-old girl, for example, believed that her mother was replaced by an imposter. She also questioned the identities of her brothers and sisters (Kourany & Williams, 1984).

Although it is believed that delusions are firmly held, the strength actually varies from person to person and even within one individual from time to time. For example, one 28-year-old woman was convinced

An individual's exaggerated and firmly held belief about his own importance can be a sign of a delusion of grandeur.

that she was the Virgin Mary. Asked how often she thought of herself in that way, she replied, "Oh, it comes to me now and then." At the other extreme, a 56-year-old man, convinced that he was a government double agent, spent all his waking hours trying to recall how and when he first became involved (Kendler, Glaser & Morgenstern, 1983).

This individual variability suggests the need to reconceptualize delusions. Delusions may not always be held firmly or be disruptive. In a study of nine schizophrenic patients, Brett-Jones, Garety, and Hemsley (1987) found that most were not preoccupied with their delusions. They thought about them "only some of the time." In addition, most indicated that their delusions interfered very little with their daily activities. They responded to contradictory information by ignoring or denying it, and they did not actively test their beliefs. The researchers warned, however, that we should not automatically view the lack of reality testing as pathological. They pointed out that the responses shown by the schizophrenics are "little different from the way that most people deal with evidence concerning beliefs or theories that are important to them" (p. 265). Schizophrenic individuals do appear to manifest deficits in judgment and reasoning in dealing with their delusions. But normal persons have also been found to ignore alternative explanations of their strongly held beliefs (Butler & Braff, 1991).

Schizophenic persons may reach a conclusion on little information, which may be related to the development of unusual beliefs (Maher, 1988). One schizophrenic who was hospitalized developed the delusion that another patient was her grandmother, based on this short conversation:

> "Where do I know you from?" I asked a hefty woman with a tiny face. The woman's short curly hair circled her pudgy face in ringlets. I thought I knew her.
>
> "In the cottage by the sea," said the woman squinting austerely at me, "I was you and you were me."
>
> This enigmatic message must be a piece to the puzzle. I pondered it. Grandma, before she died, had lived by the sea. Suddenly I knew the woman was my grandma. (Anonymous, 1990, p. 356)

In this example, the woman reached the conclusion that the older patient was her grandmother based on the word *sea*. Schizophrenic persons may be attempting to search for a reason for their unusual experiences but are limited in considering different possibilities for their behavior.

People with schizophrenia may be trained to challenge their delusions. One 51-year-old patient believed—with almost 100 percent certainty—that she was younger than twenty and that she was the daughter of Princess Anne. Her therapist asked her to view her delusion as only one possible interpretation of the event. Then they discussed evidence for her belief, and the therapist presented the inconsistencies and irrationality of the belief as well as alternative explanations. After this procedure, the patient reported a large drop in the conviction of her beliefs, stating "I look 50 and I tire more quickly than I use to; I must be 50" (Lowe & Chadwick, 1990, p. 471). She agreed that she was probably older than Princess Anne and therefore could not be her daughter. The patient also learned to react to a voice telling her that she was the mother of another member of the royal family. She disputed the voice and said that it could not possibly be true. Belief modification appears to be a helpful procedure for some schizophrenics, though there is some controversy surrounding this approach, as Focus On illustrates.

Perceptual Distortion Schizophrenics often report **hallucinations,** which are sensory perceptions that are not directly attributable to environmental stimuli. They may claim to see people or objects, to hear voices, or to smell peculiar odors that are not really present. (Note the distinction between hallucinations and delusions: hallucinations are false sensory experiences, whereas delusions are false intellectual experiences.) Hallucinations are not **pathognomonic**—that is, they are not specifically distinctive to this disorder. Persons with certain mood disorders, brief reactive psychoses, and schizophreniform disorders also report hallucinations. But it does appear that individuals with schizophrenia are more likely to report bizarre hallucinations than are persons with other disorders (Goldman et al., 1992).

Hallucinations may involve a single sensory modality or combination of modalities: hearing (*auditory* hallucinations), seeing (*visual* hallucinations), smelling (*olfactory* hallucinations), feeling (*tactile* hallucinations), and tasting (*gustatory* hallucinations). Auditory hallucinations are the most common (Payne, 1992). Hallucinations sometimes accompany and are related to delusional beliefs. For example, a patient who believed that she had committed an unforgivable sin heard imaginary voices saying that she was evil and worthless. This woman became extremely guilt-ridden, distraught, and eventually suicidal in an attempt to atone for the imagined sin.

Auditory hallucinations are one of the symptoms of schizophrenia. The voices are unwanted and often critical and threatening. This nineteenth-century painting by Sir John Millais illustrates that experience.

Should We Challenge Delusions and Hallucinations?

The doctor asked of a patient who insisted that he was dead: "Look. Dead men don't bleed, right?" When the man agreed, the doctor pricked the man's finger, and showed him the blood. The patient said, "What do you know, dead men do bleed after all." (Walkup, 1995, p. 323)

Clinicians have often been unsure about whether to challenge psychotic symptoms. Some believe that the delusions and hallucinations serve an adaptive function and that any attempt to change them would be useless or even dangerous. The example above is supposed to illustrate the futility of using logic in treating people with schizophrenia. However, Walkup and other clinicians (Bentall, Haddock & Slade, 1994; Chadwick et al., 1994; Chadwick & Birchwood, 1994) have found that some clients respond well to challenges to their hallucinations and delusions.

The approach has two phases. In the first, hypothetical contradictions are used to assess how open the patients are to conflicting information. During this phase, pa-tients are introduced to information that might contradict their beliefs, and it is here that their delusions are often weakened.

- A woman, H.J., with auditory hallucinations was asked if her belief in the "voices" would change if it could be determined that they were coming from her. She agreed. She was given a set of industrial earmuffs, which she wore. She still reported hearing voices.

- A woman believed that God was commanding her to kill. She was asked if her belief would be lessened if a priest informed her that God would not ask anyone to kill another person.

In the second phase the therapist issues a verbal challenge, asking clients to give evidence for their beliefs and to develop alternative interpretations. For example, one client claimed that voices were accurate in telling her when her spouse would return. The therapist asked how she might determine her husband's return if the voices were unable to foretell the future. Another patient who claimed he would be killed if he did not comply with auditory commands was told that he has resisted the voices and has not died.

Alternative explanations have been proposed for the hallucinations, such as the possibility that the voices are "self-talk" or thoughts. After cognitive behavioral treatment, most patients report a decrease in the strength of their beliefs in their psychotic symptoms. In H.J.'s case (presented earlier), her degree of certainty about her auditory hallucinations dropped from 100 percent to 20 percent. Although she still heard voices telling her she would die, she learned to disregard them and attributed them as "coming from her head."

Should we challenge psychotic symptoms? We certainly need more research, but for many patients, the answer would seem to be a qualified yes.

Individuals who do not have psychotic symptoms label a stimulus as "real" if it occurs externally and identify stimuli such as thoughts and feelings as internal. In contrast, schizophrenic individuals attribute private events (such as thoughts or self-vocalizations) to sources outside of the individual (Bentall, Haddock & Slade, 1994). These represent hallucinations and delusions. There is some support for the view that auditory hallucinations such as hearing voices are due to subvocalizations by the patient (Bick & Kinsbourne, 1987; Green & Kinsborne, 1990).

Delusions and hallucinations can be extremely distressing to people with schizophrenia as they respond to their internal realities. One college student who suffered auditory hallucinations involving messages from radio and television programs asked, "How can I tell when the radio is really on and when it is my imagination?" This question obviously reflects an attempt to discriminate between reality and hallucinations. Some people have developed ways of coping with their hallucinations. Romme and colleagues (1992) studied 186 schizophrenic individuals who characterized their auditory hallucinations as being primarily negative (although approximately 15 percent were positive), involving voices commenting on their action, and taking over their thinking processes. The investigators found that approximately one-third of these people had developed coping strategies to reduce or even prevent psychotic symptoms. These strategies included

1. *Distraction* Taking a shower, jogging, watching a video, meditating, and so on.

2. *Ignoring* One woman had auditory hallucinations telling her to injure herself. Her husband asked if she would harm herself if their neighbor told her to. She said no and has learned to ignore the voices.

3. *Selective listening* A woman was able to select positive aspects from the voices.

4. *Setting limits* One patient indicated that she had made a deal with the voices: They are allowed expression after 8 P.M., but not during the day. This was successful in removing the impact of the voices.

During acute stages (when the symptoms are most prominent), the person may be so involved in hallucinations that he or she cannot do anything but respond as though they were real. This may be true concerning delusions as well.

Disorganized Communication and Thought Disturbances According to the World Health Organization study (WHO, 1973b; 1981) involving patients from the United States, England, China, India, Denmark, Colombia, Nigeria, and the former Soviet Union and Czechoslovakia, the most common symptom of schiz-

ophrenia is lack of insight. In one study (Amador et al., 1994), more than 57 percent of the participants were either "unaware" or "moderately unaware" of their symptoms (see Figure 13.2). During the active phase of their disorder, people with schizophrenia often cannot recognize that their thinking is disturbed. For example, David Zelt, a psychology graduate student who went through a schizophrenic episode, believed that the CIA was listening to his thoughts and would broadcast them. The student did not question these beliefs. One of his therapists noted, "It was impressive to me to find someone with an exhaustive intellectual knowledge about psychosis and still unable to bring his critical faculties to bear upon the onslaught of ideation" (Zelt, 1981, p. 531). Another individual who had obtained a Ph.D. could not understand the bizarre nature of her hallucinations and delusions, such as being controlled by the television station, having the power to make dogs bark by using mind rays, and receiving brain waves from alien creatures (Payne, 1992). Lack of insight is not by itself enough to justify a diagnosis of schizophrenia, for it is also displayed in other disorders. Investigators are attempting to identify those symptoms that are pathognomonic—specific only to schizophrenia.

Schizophrenic individuals find it difficult to concentrate and to organize incoming information (Penn et al., 1993): "Schizophrenia is frustrating when I can't hold onto my thoughts; when conversation is projected on my mind but won't come out of my

Individuals with schizophrenia may attempt to control their symptoms by engaging in relaxing activities such as jogging meditating, or listening to soothing music, as this man is doing.

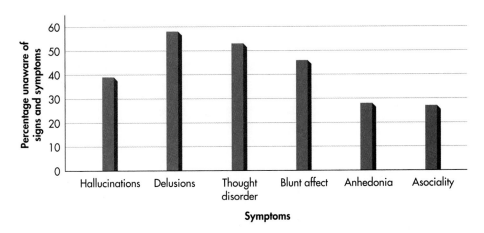

FIGURE 13.2 Schizophrenic Patients' Lack of Awareness of Psychotic Symptoms Most patients with schizophrenia are unaware or only moderately aware that they have symptoms of the disorder. The symptoms they were most unaware of having were delusions, thought disorder, and blunt or flat affect.

Source: Amador et al., 1994, p. 830.

mouth; . . . when my eyes and ears drown in a flood of sights and sounds (McGrath, 1987, p. 38). Although some schizophrenic people appear to realize that they have problems with communication, others are unaware of their disturbance. Chaika (1985) videotaped one man during the active phase of his illness. Later, when the man viewed the tape of himself, he said he never realized he spoke that way.

One investigator wanted to determine if communication deviations could also be found in deaf individuals with schizophrenia. During an interview using sign language, disturbances in thought and communication appeared, as indicated by the following excerpts (Thacker, 1994, p. 821).

Interviewer: ALL POLICE WORLD DISAPPEAR . . . WHAT HAPPENS?

Subject: WHEN WORLD c.e.l.l. c.e.l.l. GROW SPREAD SPREAD LATER YOU KNOW d.o.n.o.s.a.u.r. WALK SIDEWAYS MONKEY RISE UP SLOW.

Like the verbal communication of schizophrenic people who are not deaf, the sign language constructions demonstrated this patient's inability to stay on the topic and to respond to the interviewer's question.

Loosening of Associations   The **loosening of associations**, or *cognitive slippage*, is the continual shifting from topic to topic without any apparent logical or meaningful connection between thoughts. It may be shown by incoherent speech and bizarre and idiosyncratic responses, as indicated in the following example (Thomas, 1995).

Interviewer: "You just must be an emotional person, that's all."

Patient (1): "Well, not very much I mean, what if I were dead. It's a funeral age. Well I um. Now I had my toenails operated on. They got infected and I wasn't able to do it. But they wouldn't let me at my tools." (p. 289)

The beginning phrase in the first sentence appears appropriate to the interviewer's comment. However, the reference to death is not. Slippage appears in the comments referring to a funeral age, having toenails operated on, and getting tools. None of these thoughts are related to the interviewer's observation, and they have no hierarchical structure or organization.

Another person with schizophrenia described the conflict in her thought processes:

I am often caught in guttural struggles with my own voice as I try to get the words out. These aborted thoughts, not lost, but taken over by a more powerful chaos, are among the things that cannot be said. . . . I battle to gain control over the unwieldy words that pour from my mouth, confusing me, frustrating me, and literally tying me down and making me prey once again to the whims of what my brain chooses to allow my lips to utter. (Ruocchio, 1991, pp. 367–368)

In addition, communication may be vague or overly concrete (as opposed to abstract). Some of these characteristics are illustrated in the following patient response to a question:

Q: [What is meant by] "One swallow doesn't make a summer"?

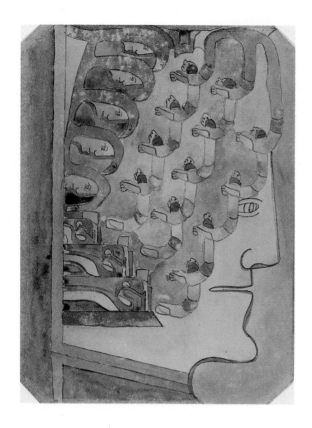

The inner turmoil and private fantasies of schizophrenics are often revealed in their art work. The paintings you see here were created in the 1930s and 1940s by psychiatric patients in European hospitals. They are part of the Prinzhorn collection.

A: That's Oriental. When the first bird in the summer swallows the first worm, then she can start to produce eggs. Which do you think comes first, the chicken or the egg? I think the egg, definitely. And it was fertilized with the sperm, so the sperm came first, too. Which came first, though, the egg or the sperm? (Harrow et al., 1982, p. 666)

Neologisms The speech of some schizophrenic people contains **neologisms,** which are new words formed by combining words in common usage. Their appearance in the speech of a patient almost guarantees a diagnosis of schizophrenia in any country of the world (Kaplan & Sadock, 1981). However, they are a fairly rare symptom. One psychologist asked a patient, "How do you feel today?" The patient responded,

Yes, sir, it's a good day. Full of rainbows you know. They go along on their merry way without concern for asphyxiation or impurities. Yes sir, like unconcerned flappers of the cosmoblue.

The patient's "cosmoblue" is a neologism, a combination of "cosmos" and "blue," the color of the sky. The response is also tangential; instead of answering the question directly, it seems to ramble though a series of asides.

Disorganized Motoric Disturbances The symptoms of schizophrenia that involve motor functions can be quite bizarre. The person may show extreme activity levels (either unusually high or unusually low), peculiar body movements or postures, strange gestures and grimaces, or a combination of these. Like hallucinations, a patient's motoric behaviors may be related to his or her delusions. For example, during a clinical interview one schizophrenic patient kept lowering his chin to his chest and then raising his head again. Asked why he lowered his head in that way, the patient replied that the atmospheric pressure often became too great to bear, and it forced his head down.

Some individuals with this disorder may display extremely high levels of motor activity, moving about quickly, swinging their arms wildly, talking rapidly and unendingly, or pacing constantly. At the other extreme, others hardly move at all, staring out into space (or perhaps into themselves) for long periods of time. The inactive patients also tend to show little interest in others, to respond only minimally, and to have few friends. During periods of withdrawal, they are frequently preoccupied with personal fantasies and daydreams.

The assumption and maintenance of an unusual (and often awkward) body position is characteristic of the *catatonic* type of schizophrenia (to be discussed shortly). A catatonic patient may stand for hours at a time, perhaps with one arm stretched out to the side, or may lie on the floor or sit awkwardly on a chair, staring, aware of what is going on around, but not responding or moving. If a hospital attendant tries to change the patient's position, the patient may either resist stubbornly or may simply assume and maintain the new position.

Negative Symptoms

Negative symptoms have been associated with a poor prognosis and may be the result of structural abnormalities in the brain. Clinicians must be careful to distinguish between *primary symptoms* (symptoms that arise from the disease itself) and *secondary symptoms* (symptoms that may develop as a response to medication and institutionalization). It is the former that researchers are primarily interested in. You may recall

from our earlier discussion that the negative symptoms include *anhedonia* (an inability to feel pleasure), *avolition* (an inability to take action or become goal-oriented), *alogia* (a lack of meaningful speech), and *flat affect* (little or no emotion in situations where strong reactions are expected. A delusional patient, for instance, might explain in detail how parts of his or her body are rotting away but show absolutely no concern or worry through voice tone or facial expression). Beiser and colleagues (1988) reported that more than one-half the schizophrenic patients they studied showed restricted affect ("expressionless face and voice") whatever the topic of discussion. However, flat affect may not be a symptom of the disorder but the result of institutionalization or antipsychotic medications (Lieberman, 1995).

People with schizophrenia often show disturbances in their sense of self and are perplexed about their identity, as the following quotation shows:

> The reflection in the store window—it's me, isn't it? I know it is, but it's hard to tell. Glassy shadows, polished pastels, a jigsaw puzzle of my body, face, and clothes, with pieces disappearing whenever I move. And, if I want to reach out to touch me, I feel nothing but a slippery coldness. Yet I sense that it's me. I just know. (McGrath, 1987, p. 37)

TYPES OF SCHIZOPHRENIA

Five types of schizophrenic disorders are generally recognized: paranoid, disorganized, catatonic, undifferentiated, and residual. (See the disorders chart on page 401.) Although these subtypes have been used traditionally, some clinicians question their value and validity because differences have not been found among them in treatment response, genetics, or long-term outcome (Lieberman, 1995).

Paranoid Schizophrenia

The most common form of schizophrenia is the paranoid type. **Paranoid schizophrenia** is characterized by one or more systematized delusions or auditory hallucinations and the absence of such symptoms as disorganized speech and behavior or flat affect. Delusions of persecution are the most common symptom. The deluded individuals believe that others are plotting against them, are talking about them, or are out to harm them in some way. They are constantly suspicious, and their interpretations of the behavior and motives of others are distorted. A friendly, smiling bus driver is seen as someone who is laughing at them derisively. A busy clerk who fails to offer help is part of a plot to mistreat them. A telephone call that was a

Grossly disorganized behavior in which an individual dresses or behaves in an unusual manner is displayed in some people with schizophrenia. Here, a hospitalized patient showers in her clothes.

wrong number is an act of harassment or an attempt to monitor their comings and goings.

> Mr. A., a 37-year-old Mexican-American Vietnam veteran previously treated at several Veterans Administration hospitals with the diagnosis of paranoid schizophrenia, came to the emergency room stating, "My life is in danger.". . . Mr. A. told a semicoherent story of international spy intrigue that was built around the release of soldiers still missing in action or held as prisoners of war in Vietnam. He believed he was hunted by Vietnamese agents. . . . Mr. A. reported hearing the voices of the men from his company who died. . . . These voices tended to severely criticize and chastise him. He had become so disturbed by these beliefs and auditory hallucinations that he made suicidal efforts to escape the torment. (Glassman, Magulac & Darko, 1987, pp. 658–659)

Individuals with paranoid schizophrenia may be prone to anger since many feel persecuted. A similar disorder, **delusional disorder,** is characterized by persistent, nonbizarre delusions that are not accompanied by other unusual or odd behaviors. It is not a form of schizophrenia, although it is often confused with paranoid schizophrenia. It is described in Focus On.

Disorganized Schizophrenia

Disorganized schizophrenia (formerly called *hebephrenic schizophrenia*) is characterized by grossly disorganized behaviors manifested by disorganized speech and behavior and flat or grossly inappropriate affect (DSM-IV). Behaviors may begin at an early age. People with this disorder act in an absurd, incoherent, or very odd manner that conforms to the stereotype of "crazy" behavior. Their emotional responses to real-life situations are typically flat, but a silly smile and childish giggle may appear at inappropriate times. The hallucinations and delusions of disorganized schizophrenia patients tend to shift from theme to theme rather than remain centered on a single idea, such as persecution or sin. Because of the severity of the disorder, many people affected with disorganized schizophrenia are unable to care for themselves and are institutionalized.

People with this disorder usually exhibit extremely bizarre and seemingly childish behaviors, such as masturbating in public or fantasizing aloud. An example appears in the following excerpt from a clinical interview with a young woman:

> *Therapist:* Do you know why your mother brought you to this clinic?
>
> *Client:* Well, Mom started yelling at me. She gets too excited about things. People are so excited nowadays. You know what I mean?
>
> *Therapist:* What did she yell at you about?
>
> *Client:* Just because I smeared some shit on a painting I was doing for school [silly giggle]. See, the teacher in art class wanted us to do some finger painting at home. She said that we should be creative. I ran out of paint so I thought I would use some shit. After all, it is natural [giggle] and it feels like paint.

Catatonic Schizophrenia

Marked disturbance in motor activity—either extreme excitement or motoric immobility—is the prime characteristic of **catatonic schizophrenia.** Diagnostic criteria include two or more of the following symptoms: motoric immobility or stupor; excessive, purposeless motor activity; extreme negativism (resisting direction)

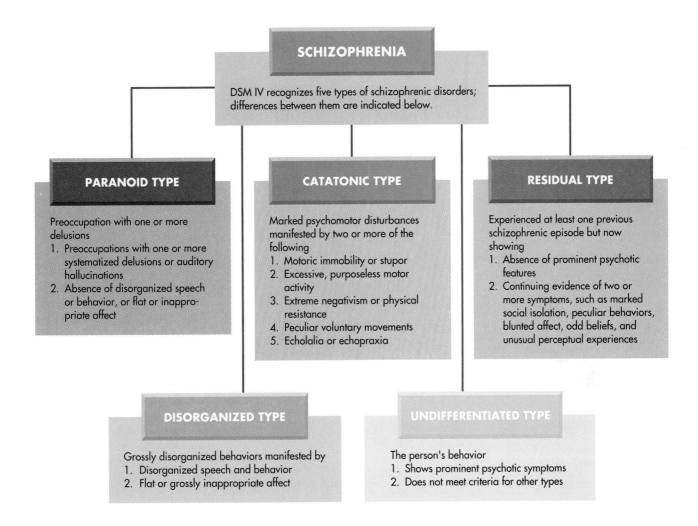

SCHIZOPHRENIA

DSM IV recognizes five types of schizophrenic disorders; differences between them are indicated below.

PARANOID TYPE

Preoccupation with one or more delusions
1. Preoccupations with one or more systematized delusions or auditory hallucinations
2. Absence of disorganized speech or behavior, or flat or inappropriate affect

CATATONIC TYPE

Marked psychomotor disturbances manifested by two or more of the following
1. Motoric immobility or stupor
2. Excessive, purposeless motor activity
3. Extreme negativism or physical resistance
4. Peculiar voluntary movements
5. Echolalia or echopraxia

RESIDUAL TYPE

Experienced at least one previous schizophrenic episode but now showing
1. Absence of prominent psychotic features
2. Continuing evidence of two or more symptoms, such as marked social isolation, peculiar behaviors, blunted affect, odd beliefs, and unusual perceptual experiences

DISORGANIZED TYPE

Grossly disorganized behaviors manifested by
1. Disorganized speech and behavior
2. Flat or grossly inappropriate affect

UNDIFFERENTIATED TYPE

The person's behavior
1. Shows prominent psychotic symptoms
2. Does not meet criteria for other types

or physical resistance; peculiar voluntary posturing or movements; or echolalia (repetition of other people's speech) or echopraxia (repetition of other people's movements). This disorder is quite rare.

People with *excited catatonia* are agitated and hyperactive. They may talk and shout constantly, while moving or running until they drop from exhaustion. They sleep little and are continually "on the go." Their behavior can become dangerous, however, and violent acts are not uncommon. People in *withdrawn catatonia* are extremely unresponsive with respect to motor activity. They show prolonged periods of stupor and mutism, despite their awareness of all that is going on around them. Some may adopt and maintain strange postures and refuse to move or change position. Others exhibit a *waxy flexibility,* allowing themselves to be "arranged" in almost any position and then remaining in that position for long periods of time. During periods of extreme withdrawal, people with catatonic schizophrenia may not eat or control their bladder or bowel functions. Alternating periods

of excited motor activity and withdrawal may occur in this disorder.

Undifferentiated and Residual Schizophrenia

Undifferentiated schizophrenia is diagnosed when the person's behavior shows prominent psychotic symptoms that do not meet the criteria for the paranoid, disorganized, or catatonic categories. These symptoms may include thought disturbances, delusions, hallucinations, incoherence, and severely impaired behavior. Sometimes undifferentiated schizophrenia turns out to be an early stage of another subtype.

The diagnosis of **residual schizophrenia** is reserved for people who have had at least one previous schizophrenic episode but are now showing an absence of prominent psychotic features and continuing evidence of two or more symptoms, such as marked social isolation, peculiar behaviors, blunted affect, odd beliefs, or unusual perceptual experiences. The disorder may

Delusional Disorder

Delusional disorder is often confused with schizophrenia. In both, thought processes are disturbed. Nevertheless, some differences do exist. Delusional disorder involves "nonbizarre" beliefs (situations that could actually occur) that have lasted for at least one month. Also, except for the delusion, the person's behavior is not odd (Yassa & Suranyi-Cadotte, 1993). In schizophrenia, other disturbances in thoughts and perceptions are involved. People with delusional disorder behave normally when their delusional ideas are not being discussed. Common themes in delusional disorders involve

- *Erotomania*—the belief that someone is in love with you; usually the love is romanticized rather than sexual.

- *Grandiosity*—the conviction that you have great, unrecognized talent or have some special ability or relationship with an important individual.

- *Jealousy*—the conviction that

your spouse or partner is being unfaithful.

- *Persecution*—the belief in being conspired or plotted against.

- *Somatic complaints*—convictions of having body odor, being malformed, or being infested by insects or parasites.

The following case illustrates some features of delusional disorders:

Mr. A, a 55-year-old single man was remanded to the Regional Psychiatric Centre. . . . For over 21 years he had pursued a famous female entertainer. . . . He met the entertainer for the first time 21 years ago when she invited him to join her fan club. Since then he has bombarded her with thousands of phone calls, many letters and gifts. . . . Notwithstanding her public denials, he has maintained the belief that she loves him, approves and encourages their relationship. . . . Several things were responsible for 'reinforcing' his behaviour. In particular, she had never returned any of his letters

or gifts. He implied that she communicated with him through her songs but would not elaborate. . . . His identical twin brother still lived at home and also had problems of an emotional nature with a woman. She had to resort to calling the police, but according to Mr. A's mother, "at least he knew when to quit." (Menzies et al., 1995, p. 530)

Erotomania occurs more commonly in females, but most who come to the attention of the law are males. Lack of feedback may play a role in the development of delusional disorder. In a study of people with this disorder, most were characterized as socially isolated, and nearly half had a physical impairment such as deafness or visual problems (Holden, 1987). A decreased ability to obtain corrective feedback, combined with a preexisting personality type that tends toward suspiciousness, may increase the susceptibility of developing delusional beliefs.

be in remission. In any case, the person's symptoms are neither strong enough nor prominent enough to warrant classification as one of the other types of schizophrenia.

Psychotic Disorders Once Considered Schizophrenia

Brief psychotic episodes were considered to represent acute forms of schizophrenia in DSM-II. With DSM-III-R and DSM-IV, people who have "schizophrenic" episodes that last fewer than six months are now diagnosed as having either **brief psychotic disorder** (du-

ration up to one month) or **schizophreniform disorder** (duration more than one month but less than six months). This distinction was made because "there is consistent evidence that people with symptoms similar to those of schizophrenia of less than six months' duration have a better outcome than those with a more prolonged disturbance" (American Psychiatric Association, 1987, p. 207). As we mentioned earlier, the tenth revision of the World Health Organization's International Classification of Disease has a broader definition of schizophrenia, in that it requires that psychotic symptoms be present for only one month.

Differences between these disorders and schizophrenia are shown in Table 13.2. Although there ap-

TABLE 13.2 Comparison of Brief Psychotic Disorder, Schizophreniform Disorders, and Schizophrenia

	Brief Psychotic Disorder	Schizophreniform Disorders	Schizophrenia
Duration	Less than one month	Less than six months	Six months or more
Psychosocial stressor	Always present	Usually present	May or may not be present
Symptoms	Emotional turmoil, psychotic symptoms	Emotional turmoil, vivid hallucinations	Emotional reactions variable; psychotic symptoms
Outcome	Return to premorbid level of functioning	Possible return to earlier, higher level of functioning	Return to earlier, higher level of functioning is uncommon
Familial pattern	No information	Possible increased risk of schizophrenia among family members	Higher prevalence of schizophrenia among family members

pear to be distinct differences, the disorders are often highly similar in characteristics. DSM-IV recommends that the diagnosis of brief psychotic disorder and schizophreniform disorder be "provisional." For example, an initial diagnosis of brief psychotic disorder should change to schizophreniform disorder if it lasts longer than one month and to schizophrenia if it lasts longer than six months. (Approximately two-thirds of those with schizophreniform disorder will later receive a diagnosis of schizophrenia or schizoaffective disorder.) Because duration is the only accurate means of distinguishing among the disorders, questions about the validity of categories have been raised.

Other Psychotic Disorders

Other psychotic disorders include delusional disorder, shared psychotic disorder, and schizoaffective disorder (DSM-IV). Delusional disorder was discussed more fully in the Focus On feature earlier in this chapter. In *shared psychotic disorder,* a person with a close relationship with a delusional (psychotic) individual comes to accept the delusional beliefs. The nonpsychotic individual's delusion tends to weaken if the two are separated. The disorder is relatively rare and is more prevalent among those who are socially isolated. *Schizoaffective disorder* includes both a mood disorder (major depression or bipolar disorder) and the presence of psychotic symptoms "for at least 2 weeks in the absence of prominent mood symptoms" (DSM-IV, p. 295). The prognosis appears to be more positive for this disorder than for schizophrenia.

Catatonic schizophrenia is a rare disorder characterized by disturbances in motor activity. Excited catatonics exhibit great agitation and hyperactivity; withdrawn catatonics (like the woman shown in this picture) may exhibit extreme unresponsiveness or adopt strange postures.

Overwhelming stress such as that existing in a combat situation can produce a brief psychotic disorder. In these cases, the psychotic symptoms disappear in a short time.

THE COURSE OF SCHIZOPHRENIA

It is popularly believed that overwhelming stress can cause a well-adjusted and relatively normal person to experience a schizophrenic breakdown. There are, in fact, recorded instances of the sudden onset of psychotic behaviors in previously well-functioning people. Soldiers have been reported to develop auditory, visual, and tactile hallucinations under combat conditions (Spivak et al., 1992). In most cases, however, the person's *premorbid personality* (personality before the onset of major symptoms) shows some impairment. Similarly, most people with schizophrenia recover gradually rather than suddenly. The typical course of schizophrenia consists of three phases: prodromal, active, and residual.

The *prodromal phase* includes the onset and build-up of schizophrenic symptoms. Social withdrawal and isolation, peculiar behaviors, inappropriate affect, poor communication patterns, and neglect of personal grooming may become evident during this phase. Friends and relatives often consider the person's behavior as odd or peculiar.

Often, psychosocial stressors or excessive demands on a schizophrenic in the prodromal phase result in the onset of prominent psychotic symptoms, or the *active phase* of schizophrenia. In this phase, the person shows the full-blown symptoms of schizophrenia, including severe disturbances in thinking, deterioration in social relationships, and flat or markedly inappropriate affect.

At some later time, the person may enter the *residual phase,* in which the symptoms are no longer prominent. The severity of the symptoms declines, and the individual may show the milder impairment found in the prodromal phase. (At this point, the diagnosis would be residual schizophrenia.) Complete recovery is rare, although long-term studies have shown that many people with schizophrenia can lead productive lives (see Figure 13.3 for different courses of the disease). For whatever reason, recovery rates appear higher in developing countries. See Critical Thinking for a discussion of this phenomenon.

Long-Term Outcome Studies

What are the chances for recovery or improvement from schizophrenia? Kraepelin believed that the disorder follows a deteriorating course. He would have agreed with the following statement concerning the prognosis for schizophrenia: "A complete return to premorbid functioning is unusual—so rare, in fact, that some clinicians would question the diagnosis" (American Psychiatric Association, 1980, p. 185). The chances for improvement or recovery are difficult to evaluate because of the changing definitions for schizophrenia. Before DSM-III, the United States had a very broad definition of schizophrenia. DSM-III and DSM-IV provided a narrower definition. Symptoms of the disorder have to be present for six months for its diagnosis. It makes sense that an individual who does not recover within six months has a more severe condition than one who recovers sooner. We have, therefore, now defined schizophrenia as a chronic condition.

Even with the more restrictive definition for schizophrenia, differences remain in the interpretation of outcome data. Breier and colleagues (1991) pointed to a negative outcome, with 78 percent of schizophrenic patients suffering a relapse and only 20 percent showing good improvement. Carone, Harrow, and Westermeyer (1991) also reported that more than

50 percent of people with schizophrenica had a poor outcome five years after hospitalization. But others believed that the conclusions of these studies "propagate an unduly pessimistic picture of schizophrenia" (Puryear et al., 1992, p. 74). Puryear and colleagues analyzed the data from the Carone study and reinterpreted the findings and offered an alternative conclusion. Instead of stating that more than 50 percent had a poor outcome, they proposed, one could argue that nearly 50 percent had a good or moderately good outcome and that 17 percent of the patients had a complete remission of symptoms within five years. They also pointed out that of the fifty-one patients in the Breier study, thirty-eight were fully employed and sixteen were also working; 20 percent were described as having "good social functioning." Viewed this way, the outcome appears more positive.

Some very long-term studies have also been performed. Ciompi (1980) conducted a 37-year follow-up of 289 schizophrenic patients and found that the long-term prognosis was favorable in 50 percent of patients. With advanced age, there was a "pronounced general tendency toward improvement and recovery." More than one-half the patients were in good physical condition and were employed either full- or part-time. Although the majority still showed evidence of problems with social relationships or independence, most indicated that they felt peaceful and free of conflicts. The findings prompted Ciompi to conclude that "quite contrary to the original—and today still popular—concepts of the nature of schizophrenias, a good majority of definitely 'genuine' schizophrenias (from initial diagnoses) may develop favorably in the long run" (p. 611).

Similar results were obtained in a 22-year follow-up of 502 schizophrenic patients (Huber et al., 1980). Of this group, 22 percent were in complete remission, 43 percent showed only residual symptoms, and 35 percent remained unimproved; 87 percent lived in their homes. Two interesting findings were that the long-term prognosis is unrelated to the original duration of the disorder and that prognosis is more favorable for women than for men.

A criticism that can be leveled against these long-term outcome studies is that they involved patients who were diagnosed according to criteria that preceded DSM-III-R and probably included nonschizophrenic patients who might have a better prognosis. This issue was addressed in a study by Harding and associates (1987). These researchers retrospectively applied DSM-III criteria to schizophrenic patients who were involved in a 32-year, long-term follow-up. These patients from the "back wards" had been ill for an average of sixteen years and had been hospitalized continuously for about six years. Amazingly, the re-

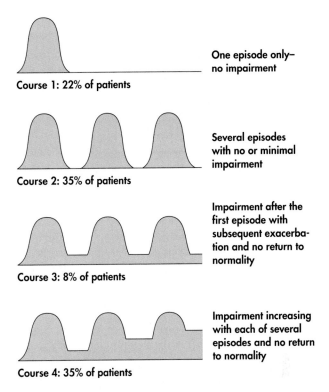

Course 1: 22% of patients — One episode only– no impairment

Course 2: 35% of patients — Several episodes with no or minimal impairment

Course 3: 8% of patients — Impairment after the first episode with subsequent exacerbation and no return to normality

Course 4: 35% of patients — Impairment increasing with each of several episodes and no return to normality

FIGURE 13.3 Some Different Courses Found in Schizophrenia This figure shows four of the many courses that schizophrenia may take. These courses were observed in individuals during a five-year follow-up study (Shepherd, Watt & Falloon, 1989). Some believe that long-term outcomes are even more positive.

searchers found that "for one-half to two-thirds of these subjects who retrospectively met the DSM-III criteria for schizophrenia, long-term outcome was neither marginal but an evolution into various degrees of productivity, social involvement, wellness, and competent functioning" (p. 730).

The results of these studies indicate that the long-term outcome for people with schizophrenia may be more positive than that portrayed by Kraepelin, DSM-III, or DSM-IV. One researcher who reviewed the prognosis of schizophrenia believes there is a "wide spectrum of possible courses that patients follow," many of them being quite positive (Harding, Zubin & Strauss, 1992). The cognitive decline in schizophrenia appears to occur within the first five years of the illness, after which stability and even improvement can occur (Goldberg et al., 1993). Bleuler might have been more correct in indicating a variable and even positive outcome for the disorder. Unfortunately, this optimism has yet to spread to the general public.

CRITICAL THINKING

Schizophrenia in Developing Countries: Recovery or Misdiagnosis?

The following observation appears in DSM-IV: "Individuals with schizophrenia in developing nations tend to have a more acute course and a better outcome than do individuals in industrialized nations" (p. 281). Do people in developing countries who have schizophrenia recover more quickly and fully than individuals in developed countries? If so, why? The World Health Organization examined these questions in a cross-cultural study (Sartorius et al., 1986). The study applied standardized and reliable sets of criteria and found similar prevalence rates for schizophrenia in ten different countries. However, a follow-up of 1,379 persons diagnosed as schizophrenic and described as "remarkably similar in their symptom profiles" in the nine countries revealed that patients in India, Colombia, and Nigeria showed more rapid and more complete recovery than those in London, Moscow, or Washington. Fifty-six percent of schizophrenic people in developing countries had only one episode of the disorder, compared with 39 percent in developed countries.

Severe chronic course was found in 40 percent of those from developed countries, compared with 24 percent in developing countries. Sartorius and colleagues hypothesized that some cultural factor might be responsible for the observed difference in outcome.

Why should patients from developing countries who have less access to modern treatment recover so quickly?

At the present time, the answer to that question is unknown. Some have speculated that in developing countries recovered patients are quickly absorbed into the work force and perform whatever tasks are available (Warner, 1986). Researchers in a follow-up study reported difficulty in interviewing recovered patients because they were often in the fields working. Returning to work may have helped prevent relapses.

Stevens (1987) believes that the higher recovery rate for schizophrenia found in developing countries is due to misdiagnosis. To support her view, she pointed out that in the WHO study, 36 percent of patients in Nigeria and 27 per-

cent in India recovered in less than one month. She conjectured that the illnesses were in actuality either brief psychotic disorders or schizophreniform disorders and not schizophrenia. Although this explanation is certainly plausible, the WHO investigation had found an approximately equal frequency of schizophrenia among the different countries. If misdiagnosis did occur, it must mean that brief psychotic disorders and schizophreniform disorders are more prevalent in developing countries and that schizophrenia occurs less frequently in these countries. This possibility must be examined.

If we define schizophrenia as a "chronic" condition, how could we account for the fact that more than 50 percent of people diagnosed with schizophrenia in developing countries recover after one episode? If schizophrenia is a brain disorder, why is the outcome so different between developing and developed countries? If "culture" is responsible for the more positive outcome in developing countries, how does it influence the course of this disorder?

SUMMARY

1. Schizophrenia is a group of psychotic disorders characterized by severely impaired thinking, personality disintegration, affective disturbances, and social withdrawal. The criteria that differentiate schizophrenia, its subtypes, and other psychotic disorders are specified more precisely in DSM-IV than they have been in the past. However, the criteria must be applied consistently if they are to be effective.

2. The disorders are manifested in positive symptoms such as delusions; perceptual distortion as in hallucinations; disorganized communications and thought disturbances, including loosening of associations, neologisms, attention problems, and disorganized motoric disturbances. Negative symptoms in schizophrenia include anhedonia, avolition, alogia, and flat affect.

3. DSM-IV distinguishes five types of schizophrenia. Paranoid schizophrenia is characterized by persecutory delusions or frequent auditory hallucinations. Disorganized schizophrenia is characterized by disorganized speech and behavior and inappropriate affect. Extreme social impairment and severe regressive behaviors are often seen. The major feature of catatonic schizophrenia is disturbance of motor activity. Patients show excessive excitement, agitation and hyperactivity, or withdrawn behavior patterns. The undifferentiated type includes schizophrenic behavior that cannot be classified as one of the other types, and residual schizophrenia is a category for people who have had at least one episode of schizophrenia but are not now showing prominent symptoms. In addition, other severe disorders may include schizophrenia-like symptoms.

4. The typical course of schizophrenia consists of three phases. In the prodromal phase, the symptoms first begin and build. In the active phase, they become quite prominent. And in the residual phase, they decline in severity. The degree of recovery from schizophrenia is difficult to evaluate, in part because of the changing definitions of the duration of symptoms as a diagnostic criterion. Most schizophrenics recover enough to lead relatively productive lives.

KEY TERMS

brief psychotic disorder Psychotic disorder that lasts no longer than one month

catatonic schizophrenia A schizophrenic disorder characterized by marked disturbance in motor activity—either extreme excitement or motoric immobility; symptoms include motoric immobility or stupor; excessive, purposeless motor activity; extreme negativism or physical resistance; peculiar voluntary movements; or echolalia or echopraxia

cognition The processes of thinking, perceiving, judging, and recognizing

delusion A false belief that is firmly and consistently held despite disconfirming evidence or logic

delusional disorder A disorder characterized by persistent, nonbizarre delusions that are not accompanied by other unusual or odd behaviors

disorganized schizophrenia A schizophrenic disorder characterized by grossly disorganized behaviors manifested by disorganized speech and behavior and flat or grossly inappropriate affect

flat affect Little or no emotion in situations where strong reactions are expected

hallucinations Sensory perceptions that are not directly attributable to environmental stimuli

loosening of associations Continual shifting from topic to topic without any apparent logical or meaningful connection between thoughts

negative symptoms In schizophrenia, symptoms that are associated with inferior premorbid functioning and carry a poorer prognosis than positive symptoms; they include flat affect, poverty of speech, anhedonia, apathy, and avolition

neologisms New words formed by combining words in common usage

paranoid schizophrenia A schizophrenic disorder characterized by one or more systematized delusions or auditory hallucinations and the absence of such symptoms as disorganized speech and behavior or flat affect

pathognomonic Symptoms specific to a disorder

positive symptoms Symptoms that are present during the active phase of schizophrenia and that tend to disappear with treatment; they may include hallucinations and delusions, as well as disorganized speech and behavior, inappropriate affect, and formal thought disorder

residual schizophrenia A category of schizophrenic disorder reserved for people who have had at least one previous schizophrenic episode but are now showing an absence of prominent psychotic features and continuing evidence of two or more symptoms, such as marked social isolation, peculiar behaviors, blunted affect, odd beliefs, or unusual perceptual experiences

schizophrenia A group of disorders characterized by severely impaired cognitive processes, personality disintegration, affective disturbances, and social withdrawal

schizophreniform disorder Psychotic disorder that lasts more than one month but less than six months

undifferentiated schizophrenia A schizophrenic disorder in which the person's behavior shows prominent psychotic symptoms that do not meet the criteria for paranoid, disorganized, or catatonic schizophrenia

CHAPTER 14

SCHIZOPHRENIA: ETIOLOGY AND TREATMENT

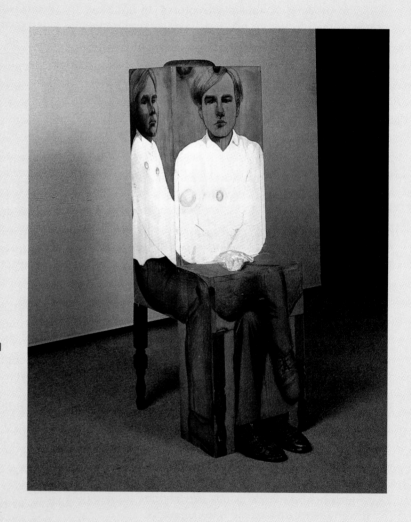

N ew theories of schizophrenia are constantly being advocated. Some are more promising than others. But how do we know which theory, if any, is actually correct? In the following case, Mary McGrath, a person with schizophrenia, expresses her frustration in trying to discover the cause of her disorder.

I know I'm a 37-year-old woman, a sculptor, a writer, a worker. I live alone. I know all of this, but, like the reflection in the glass my existence seems undefined—more a mirage that I keep reaching for, but never can touch.

I've been feeling this way for almost a year now, ever since I was diagnosed a paranoid schizophrenic. Sometimes, though, I wonder if I ever knew myself, or merely played the parts that were acceptable, just so that I could fit in somewhere. . . . There are still occasional episodes of hallucinations, delusions, and terrible fears, and I have medication for these times. It relieves my mental stress, but I hate my bodily responses to it and the dulling of my healthy emotions. Therefore, I stop using the drug as soon as the storms in my mind subside. . . .

I've searched, in library books and in articles about schizophrenia, hoping to find other solutions and answers to my whys, how longs, what's the cure. Some of the information is frightening. . . . Some of it is confusing. . . .Schizophrenia is genetic—no, no, it's surely biochemical—definitely nutritional—sorry, but it's caused by family interactions, maybe stress, etc. Now, with the worship of technological gods, the explanation is that schizophrenia is a brain disease colorfully mapped out by the PET scanner. I suddenly feel that my humanity has been sacrificed to a computer printout, that the researchers have dissected me without realizing that I'm still alive. I'm not comfortable or safe in all their certain uncertainties—I feel they're losing me, the person, more and more.

In the most recently published book I've read, a doctor writes that psychotherapy is useless with schizophrenia. How could he even suggest that, without knowing me, the one over here in this corner, who finds a lot of support, understanding, and acceptance by my therapist? Marianne is not afraid to travel with me in my fearful times. She listens when I need to release some of the "poisons" in my mind. She offers advice when I'm having difficulty with just daily living. She sees me as a human being and not only a body to shovel pills into or a cerebral mass in some laboratory. Psychotherapy is important to me, and it does help. . . .

I'm hopeful about the ongoing research to find an answer to schizophrenia. . . . But I know that I'm the schizophrenic living the experience, and I must look inside myself also for some ways to handle it. I have to be able to see me again as a real person and not a fading reflection. (McGrath, 1987, pp. 37–38)

In this chapter, we consider the different causal theories of schizophrenia, examining genetic, physiological, psychological, and environmental explanations for the disorder. Researchers share Mary McGrath's frustration. Unfortunately, although a great amount of work has been done, no one theory is universally accepted, and each fails to answer all the questions schizophrenia poses. As you will see, methodological flaws and research design limitations restrict the kinds of conclusions that can be drawn about schizophrenia.

We also explore different forms of therapy for schizophrenia. One form of therapy we discuss is **neuroleptics,** antipsychotic drugs that can help treat symptoms of schizophrenia but can produce undesirable side effects, such as symptoms that mimic neurological disorders. Relapse rates remain unacceptably high. As McGrath remarked, her medication kept her "functional," but she also felt "drugged and unreal." Interest in psychotherapy for schizophrenia has revived because most people with this disorder now are hospitalized only temporarily and are then returned to their families. Later in this chapter we discuss some promising new approaches.

ETIOLOGY OF SCHIZOPHRENIA

A thirteen-year-old boy who was having behavioral and academic problems in school was taking part in a series of family therapy sessions. Family communication was negative in tone, with a great deal of blaming. Near the end of one session, the boy suddenly broke down and cried out, "I don't want to be like her." He was referring to his mother, who had been receiving treatment for schizophrenia and was taking antipsychotic medication. He had often been frightened by her bizarre behavior, and he was concerned that his friends would "find out" about her condition. But his greatest fear was that he would inherit the disorder. Sobbing, he turned to the therapist and asked, "Am I going to be crazy, too?"

If you were the therapist, how would you respond? We are constantly exposed to news articles indicating that schizophrenia is produced by an "unfortunate" combination of genes or is due to physical problems in the brain. Does this mean that schizophrenia is only a biological disorder? Some evidence also exists that family communication patterns can influence relapse in schizophrenic individuals. Can the way we interact in a family also precipitate a schizophrenic episode? If so, how? Researchers generally agree that this boy's chances of developing schizophrenia are greater than those of the average person. Why this is so is a subject of controversy. Researchers who favor a biological paradigm tend to favor genetic, brain structure, and biochemical explanations. Other researchers focus primarily on the impact of psychological and social factors in the development of the disorder. We will consider the strengths and weaknesses of the different approaches. At the end of the section on genetics, you should reach your own conclusion about what to tell the thirteen-year-old boy.

HEREDITY AND SCHIZOPHRENIA

Herbert Pardes, president of the American Psychiatric Association, stated, "We have been learning that the genetic factor plays a far greater role in some cases of schizophrenia than we'd ever thought before. . . .There is also evidence of physical or chemical disturbances in the brain" (Ubell, 1989). The importance of genetic influences in the etiology of schizophrenia is no longer a subject of serious debate. Many researchers have suspected this connection for some time. More than thirty years ago, one researcher posed the following challenge to his colleagues:

> You [are] required to write down a procedure for selecting an individual from the population who would be diagnosed as schizophrenic by a psychiatric staff; you have to wager $1,000 on being right. You may not include in your selection procedure any behavioral fact, such as a symptom or trait, manifested by the individual. (Meehl, 1962, p. 827)

According to Meehl, your best chance of winning this wager is to look for someone whose identical twin has already been diagnosed as schizophrenic. This solution reflects the belief that heredity is an important cause in the development of schizophrenia—a belief supported by research (Gottesman, 1991; Heinrichs, 1993; Roberts, 1991).

Problems in Interpreting Genetic Studies

Obtaining a clear picture of the genetic contribution in schizophrenia is not an easy task. To demonstrate a clear link between heredity and schizophrenia, research studies must overcome several major complications, some of which inflate the degree of genetic influence.

1. *Several types of schizophrenia may exist, with different sets of causes and varying degrees of genetic influence.* For example, the risk of developing schizophrenia and related disorders is higher for the child of a schizophrenic parent who does not respond to antipsychotic medication than for the child of a schizophrenic parent who does respond to such medication.

The Genain quadruplets, shown here at age 63, all developed schizophrenia, which is unusual since the concordance rate for the disorder in identical twins is only 50 percent. However, the sisters differed in terms of symptoms, level of recovery, and age of onset. Pictured from left to right are Edna, Wilma, Sarah, and Helen.

Genetic patterns, like those shown in these radiographs, are studied to determine the gene or group of genes responsible for different forms of schizophrenia.

2. *The psychological condition of the nonschizophrenic parent must be considered.* If the other parent had a similar or related disorder, this could increase the genetic risk. One study (Parnas, 1987) found that the mates of schizophrenic people were more likely to have functional psychoses and schizoid, paranoid, or borderline personality disorders before marriage than were mates of nonschizophrenic individuals. If spousal contributions are not considered, genetic influences based only on the mother's diagnosis may be overestimated.

3. *Studies based on severely and chronically ill schizophrenic patients may inflate estimates of genetic influence.* The **concordance rate**—the likelihood that both members of a twin pair will show the same characteristic—for schizophrenia was nearly three times higher among identical twins hospitalized for more than two years than for those hospitalized less than two years (Gottesman, 1991).

4. *Researchers may use differing definitions of concordance.* Some investigators define schizophrenia very narrowly and use the same definition to determine concordance, which would result in lower estimates of genetic influence. Other investigators believe that a number of disorders (such as schizoid and borderline personality disorders and schizophreniform disorders) are genetically related to schizophrenia. Considering concordance to include a diagnosis of schizophrenia or of these other disorders would produce higher estimates of genetic influence.

5. *An interviewer who knows that he or she is interviewing relatives of a schizophrenic might be more likely to find pathology.* Raters involved in genetic studies are often aware of the diagnosis and status (nonblind) of the patients, controls, and the relatives. Studies that do not use blind ratings report higher rates of psychopathology among relatives with disorders than studies that do (Gottesman & Shields, 1982).

In this section, we discuss several kinds of research that link heredity to the schizophrenic disorders. Many of them have one or more of the methodological problems we just discussed.

Studies Involving Blood Relatives

Close blood relatives are genetically more similar than distant blood relatives. For example, first-degree relatives (parents, siblings, child) of the schizophrenic individual share 50 percent of their genes. Second-degree relatives (grandparents, uncles, aunts, nephews) share only 25 percent of their genes. If schizophrenia has a genetic basis, researchers should find more schizophrenia among close relatives of people diagnosed with schizophrenia than among more distant relatives.

Figure 14.1 suggests that this situation is indeed the case. The data are summarized from several major studies on the prevalence of schizophrenia (Gottesman, 1978, 1991). They show that closer blood relatives of people diagnosed with schizophrenia run a

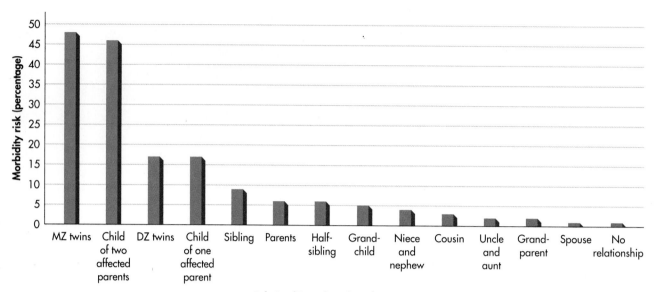

FIGURE 14.1 **Risk of Schizophrenia Among Blood Relatives of Schizophrenics**
This figure reflects the estimate of the lifetime risk of developing schizophrenia—a risk
that is strongly correlated with the degree of genetic influence.
Source: Data from Gottesman, 1978, 1991.

greater risk of developing the disorder. Thus the boy
described earlier has a 12 to 13 percent chance of
being diagnosed with schizophrenia, but his mother's
nieces or nephews have only a 2 to 3 percent chance.
(It should be noted that the risk for the general population is 1 percent.)

Even if well-designed studies pointed to a relationship between degree of genetic relatedness and schizophrenia, however, they still do not clearly demonstrate the role of heredity. Why? Simply because
closer blood relatives are more likely to share the
same environmental factors or stressors as well as the
same genes. To confirm a genetic basis for schizophrenia, research must separate genetic influences from
environmental influences.

Twin Studies

Throughout this text we have described the use of
twin studies by researchers seeking to differentiate between the effects of heredity and those of environment. You may recall that identical, or monozygotic
(MZ), twins are genetically identical, so differences
between two MZ twins are presumably caused by differences in their environments. If reared together, MZ
twins share the same general environment as well as
the same hereditary makeup. But fraternal, or dizygotic (DZ) twins, though born at about the same

time, are not more genetically similar than any other
two siblings, and they may be of different sexes. If
DZ twins are reared together, they share the same
general environment, but their genetic makeup is, on
the average, only 50 percent identical.

In a twin study, concordance rates for a particular
disorder are measured among groups of MZ and DZ
twins. (Recall that a concordance rate is the likelihood both members of a twin pair will show the same
characteristic—in this case, the disorder being studied.) If environmental factors are of major importance, the concordance rates for MZ twins and for
DZ twins should not differ much. If genetic factors
are of prime importance, however, MZ twins should
show a higher concordance rate than DZ twins.

In general, concordance rates for schizophrenia
among MZ twins are two to four times higher than
among DZ twins. This seems to point to a strong genetic basis for the disorder. One study of sixteen pairs
of MZ twins found a concordance rate of zero, however; not one MZ twin of an individual with schizophrenia had the disorder (Tienari, 1963). In fact, concordance rates among MZ twins vary from 0 to 86
percent (Weiner, 1975). How can some twin studies
show little or no genetic influence while other studies
indicate a strong genetic component in schizophrenia?

Again, methodological differences seem to be involved. Consider Table 14.1, which lists the results of

TABLE 14.1   Concordance Rates Found in Twin Studies in the Scandinavian Countries

Study	Country	MZ Pairs		DZ Pairs	
		Number of Pairs	Concordance Rate (percentage)*	Number of Pairs	Concordance Rate (percentage)*
Tienari (1963)	Finland	16	0 (19)	21	5 (14)
Kringlen (1967)	Norway	55	25 (38)	90	10 (19)
Essen-Moller (1970)	Sweden	7	29 (75)	—	— —
Fischer (1973)	Denmark	21	24 (56)	41	10 (19)
Tienari (1975)	Finland	20	15 —	42	7.5 —
Onstad (1991)	Norway	31	48.4 —	28	3.6 —

*The percentages not in parentheses are measured according to a narrow definition of schizophrenia. The percentages in parentheses are concordance rates for a broad definition of schizophrenia. For example, if one twin has schizophrenia and the other twin has a borderline diagnosis, the pair is considered concordant according to the broad definition.

Source: Kringlen, 1980, and Onstad et al., 1991.

several twin studies performed in Scandinavia. Two percentages are given for most entries in the concordance rate columns. The first percentage (not in parentheses) is the rate according to a narrow definition of schizophrenia. The second percentage (in parentheses) is the rate according to a broad defini-

tion that considers disorders such as "latent or borderline" schizophrenia, acute schizophrenic reactions, and schizoid and inadequate personality as concordant. These disorders are part of the schizophrenia spectrum—that is, they are considered to be genetically related to schizophrenia. Note that the Tienari

Identical and fraternal twins are studied to determine the relative importance of genetic factors in schizophrenia and other disorders. Identical twins share the same genes. Thus differences between identical twins can be attributed to differences in their environment rather than in their genetic makeup. Fraternal twins (shown in this photo) share some of the same genes, but no more so than any other pair of siblings.

One of the problems with studying twins is the difficulty of separating heredity factors from environmental influences. Adoption studies are useful because heredity and environmental factors can be clearly differentiated.

(1963) MZ concordance rate of zero would rise to 19 percent if three twins who showed "borderline" psychotic features were counted. In varying degrees, similar changes would take place in the other studies as well.

The broader definition of schizophrenia was used in most studies that reported high concordance rates. Unfortunately, this breadth decreases the diagnostic reliability and validity of twin studies as a whole. The latest twin study by Onstad (1991) used a narrow definition of schizophrenia and reported a concordance rate of 48 percent among MZ twins. A weakness of this study was that ratings were nonblind.

Even though the high concordance rates reported in many earlier studies have been inflated by using the broad definition of schizophrenia, we can conclude that there is clearly some genetic influence in the disorders. This is so whether a strict definition is employed or the schizophrenia spectrum is included. Moreover, it appears that the spectrum disorders are more likely to be found in families with diagnosed schizophrenic members.

Adoption Studies

Even with twin studies, it is difficult to separate the effects of heredity from the effects of environment because twins are usually raised together. Thus when the child of a schizophrenic parent develops schizophrenia, three explanations are possible:

1. The schizophrenic mother or father may have genetically transmitted schizophrenia to the child.

2. The parent, being disturbed, may have provided a stressful environment for the child.

3. The child's schizophrenia may have resulted from a combination of genetic factors and a stressful environment.

In an attempt to sort out the effects of heredity and environment, researchers determined the incidence of schizophrenia and other disorders in a group of people who were born to schizophrenic mothers but who had had no contact with their mothers and had left the maternity hospital within three days of birth (Heston, 1966; Heston & Denny, 1968). This condition eliminated the possibility that contact with the mother increased the chance of developing the disorder. The lives of these people were traced through the records of child-care institutions; all had been adopted by two-parent families. A control group, consisting of people born to nonschizophrenic mothers and adopted through the same child-care institutions, was selected and matched. Information regarding both the at-risk and control groups was collected from many sources (including school records, court

TABLE 14.2 Comparison of Disorders in People Separated from Schizophrenic and Nonschizophrenic Mothers Early in Life

Characteristic	At-Risk Children	Control
Number of individuals	47	50
Males	30	33
Mean age	35.8	36.3
Ratings of mental health/sickness*	65.2	80.1
Number diagnosed as schizophrenic	5	0
Number with mental deficiency (IQ less than 70)	4	0
Number with sociopathic personality	9	2
Number with neurotic personality	13	7
Number spending more than one year in a penal or psychiatric institution	11	2

*A lower score indicates greater severity.
Source: Heston, 1966.

Only children in the high-risk group developed schizophrenia. They were also more likely to receive a diagnosis of mental deficiency, sociopathic personality, and spend more time in an institution than individuals in the control group.

records, and interviews). The people themselves were interviewed and given psychological tests. The results are shown in Table 14.2. Note that five children in the at-risk group were later diagnosed as schizophrenic, compared with none in the control group. These results are highly significant and support a genetic explanation for schizophrenia. The greater incidence of the other disorders such as sociopathic personality among the at-risk group is hard to explain because those disorders are not part of the schizophrenia spectrum.

The study seems to have been well designed. Its only weaknesses involve the diagnostic criteria, which were described as being based on "generally accepted standards" for schizophrenia, and the fact that the schizophrenic mothers "as a group were biased in the direction of severe, chronic disease." (As discussed earlier, genetic factors seem to play a greater role in the more severe cases of schizophrenia.)

Two additional criticisms have been raised, however. First, the schizophrenic mothers received antipsychotic medication during pregnancy, and such drugs present a potential risk to the fetus (*Physician's Desk Reference*, 1994). Second, most families who adopted the child of a schizophrenic mother knew about the mother's disorder. This knowledge could have influenced the adoptive parents' attitude toward the child (Shean, 1987).

Of special interest is the finding that nearly one-half of the at-risk group were "notably successful adults."

The twenty-one experimental subjects who exhibited no significant psychosocial impairment were not only successful adults but in comparison to the control group were more spontaneous when interviewed and had more colorful life histories. They held the more creative jobs: musician, teacher, home-designer; and followed the more imaginative hobbies: oil painting, music, antique aircraft. Within the experimental group there was much more variability of personality and behavior in all social dimensions. (Heston, 1966, p. 825)

Sohlberg (1985) reported similar findings. Approximately 50 percent of "high-risk" children have "healthy personalities" and are "remarkably invulnerable" to schizophrenia. Being "at risk" does not necessarily (or even usually) lead to a negative outcome. Why do some children who have poor familial or environmental backgrounds develop so successfully? Perhaps studies of "stress resistant" children will one day answer this question (Luthar & Zigler, 1991).

TABLE 14.3 Schizophrenia and Spectrum Disorders Among Relatives of Adopted Persons

Group	Schizophrenia (percentage)	Spectrum Disorders (percentage)
Biological relatives of individuals diagnosed with schizophrenia	4.7%	8.2%
Biological relatives of individuals in control group	0	2.5
Adoptive relatives of individuals diagnosed with schizophrenia	0	0
Adoptive relatives of individuals in control group	0	0

Source: Kety et al., 1994.

A diagnosis of schizophrenia is found exclusively in the biological relatives of adoptees who were later diagnosed as schizophrenic. Such a finding indicates that genetic factors are more important than environmental factors in the onset of schizophrenia.

In another study designed to separate hereditary and environmental influences, investigators identified adults who were diagnosed with schizophrenia and who had been adopted in infancy. Then they located both the adoptive parents (the families who had raised the children who became schizophrenic) and the biological parents, who had minimal contact with their children. If environmental factors play the major role in schizophrenia, the adoptive families should be more disturbed than the biological parents. Conversely, if heredity is more important, biological families should show more disturbance than adoptive families. As Table 14.3 indicates, interviews with both sets of families showed a greater prevalence of schizophrenia and spectrum disorders among the biological families (Kety et al., 1994). Similar results were reported in another adoption study by Tienari and others (1994).

Another line of evidence comes from a study of children who had normal biological parents but who were adopted and raised by a parent later diagnosed with schizophrenia (Wender et al., 1977). If environmental factors are of primary importance, these children should be more likely than others to develop schizophrenia. The researchers found no such difference. Thus various adoption studies do indicate that heredity plays a major role in the transmission of schizophrenia.

Studies of High-Risk Populations

Perhaps the most comprehensive way to study the etiology of schizophrenia is to monitor a large group of children over a long time to watch the differences between those who eventually develop schizophrenia and those who do not. This sort of developmental study allows the investigator to see how the disorders develop. But because the prevalence of schizophrenia in the general population is only 1 percent, a prohibitively large group would have to be monitored if a random sample of children were chosen. Instead, investigators have chosen subjects from "high-risk" populations; this increases the probability that a smaller group of subjects will include some who develop schizophrenia.

Mednick's Study The best-known developmental studies are those conducted by Mednick (1970) and Mednick and colleagues (1989), who are still studying about two hundred persons with schizophrenic mothers (the high-risk group) and about one hundred persons with nonschizophrenic mothers (the low-risk control group). The researchers have followed these people for more than twenty-seven years. On the basis of existing data, they have predicted the eventual outcome for both high-risk and low-risk persons. Their prediction, shown in Figure 14.2, is that approximately one-half of the high-risk group may eventually display some form of psychopathology, including but not limited to schizophrenia.

At this time, fifteen of the high-risk individuals have developed schizophrenia; the researchers estimate that another fifteen will later receive this diagnosis. Comparisons of the characteristics of the high-risk individuals who became schizophrenic with those of high-risk individuals who did not develop the disorder revealed that the schizophrenic individuals were more likely to:

■ Have mothers who displayed more severe symptoms of schizophrenia.

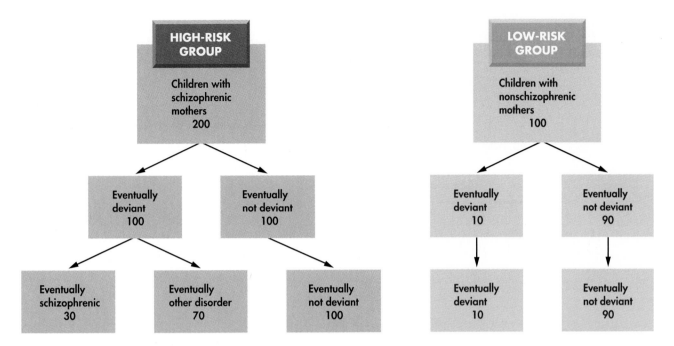

FIGURE 14.2   Predictions About the Development of Deviance and Schizophrenia in High-Risk and Control Children   For more than thirty years, Mednick and Schulsinger have studied about two hundred individuals at high risk for schizophrenia and one hundred individuals at low risk in an attempt to predict the eventual outcome for both groups. As of 1989, fifteen members of the high-risk group had developed schizophrenia.

Source: Mednick & Schulsinger, 1968.

■ Have been separated from their parents and placed in children's homes early in their lives.

■ Have had mothers who had more serious pregnancy or birth complications.

■ Have been characterized by their teachers as extremely aggressive and disruptive.

■ Have a slower autonomic recovery rate (habituate more slowly when exposed to certain stimuli).

It appears that both environmental and biological factors may influence the development of schizophrenia in the high-risk group.

The Israeli Study   Are high-risk children more likely to develop schizophrenia or related disorders if they live with their schizophrenic parent or might they do better when raised in a "healthier" environment? In an attempt to answer this question, an Israeli research team (Ayalon & Mercom, 1985; Marcus et al., 1987; Nagler et al., 1985; Shotten, 1985; Sohlberg, 1985) conducted a **prospective study,** a long-term study of a group of people, beginning before the onset of a disorder, to allow investigators to see how the disorder

develops. The study followed fifty high-risk children (children who had schizophrenic parents). Twenty-five of the children were born and raised in a kibbutz (a collective farm), and the other twenty-five were living in a suburban area with their mentally ill parents. In the kibbutz, all the children lived together. They had regular contact with their parents, but they were raised by child-care workers.

The researchers also included a control group, comprising fifty low-risk children of mentally healthy parents—twenty-five living in the kibbutz and the other twenty-five living in town. Neurophysiological, observational, perceptual-motor, psychophysiological, and behavioral measures were taken at regular intervals.

By the time the high-risk groups reached their thirties, five had received a diagnosis of schizophrenia—two each in the kibbutz and town groups (Ingraham et al., 1995). Kibbutz high-risk individuals were more likely than any other participants to have a major affective disorder, and personality disorders were more frequent in the high-risk groups. No one in the control group was diagnosed as schizophrenic, which again would indicate the importance of a genetic pre-

TABLE 14.4   Lifetime Diagnoses for High-Risk and Control Children in a Kibbutz Environment or at Home

| Group | Number in Group | Schizophrenia | Diagnostic Category | | | |
			Major Affective Disorders	Minor Affective Disorders	Personality Disorders	No Diagnosis
Kibbutz (High Risk)	25	2 (1)	6 (0)	2	3	8 (14)
Town (High Risk)	25	2	1 (0)	5 (1)	5	10 (14)
Kibbutz (Control)	25	0	2 (0)	4 (0)	1	17 (18)
Town (Control)	25	0	1 (0)	4 (0)	1	17 (20)

Note 1: The lifetime prevalence diagnoses indicate whether an individual received a specific diagnosis at any time during the study. The number within the parentheses indicates current diagnostic status.

Note 2: One of the subjects in the kibbutz group with a diagnosis of schizophrenia was free of symptoms at the latest interview and given the status of "no mental illness."

Source: Ingraham et al., 1995.

disposition. Table 14.4 offers a more detailed comparison of the different groups and disorders.

During the 25-year follow-up assessment, most participants who were diagnosed with affective disorder and one who was diagnosed with schizophrenia no longer showed symptoms of these disorders. As Ingraham observed, however, "The most striking finding is the relative absence of severe psychopathology evident at present in most of the subjects" (p. 186). Most of the participants currently do not meet the criteria for affective disorders and most show good adjustment. Living in town or in the kibbutz did not seem to be related to risk factors in developing schizophrenia but may have influenced the expression of major affective disorder.

A number of differences were found in the development of high-risk and control children. High-risk children were more likely to be described as withdrawn, poorer in social relationships, behaving in antisocial ways, uncooperative and incapable of relating to the interviewers, poor at school work, having problems with mood, accident prone, and functioning at lower perceptual-motor levels. Social withdrawal seemed to be the characteristic most related to the risk of developing schizophrenia in the high-risk children (Hans et al., 1992; Mirsky et al., 1995). Nev-

ertheless, the two groups of children overlapped considerably. Deficiencies were shown by only about one-half of the high-risk children. The other half appeared to show "healthy" development.

Environmental factors also appear to be important in schizophrenia. None of the high-risk children who had received "adequate" parenting developed schizophrenia. Approximately 60 percent of the schizophrenic parents provided adequate care for their children.

Conclusions and Methodological Problems   What can we conclude from the high-risk studies? First, there is reasonably strong support for the involvement of heredity in schizophrenia and its associated spectrum disorders. Second, childhood and adolescence may be especially vulnerable periods. Third, schizophrenia seems to result from interaction between the predisposition and environmental factors. Fourth, most high-risk children do not develop the disorder, and most show good adjustment. With this information in mind, what would you tell a thirteen-year-old boy about his chances of developing schizophrenia?

Studies of high-risk subjects are a promising line of research. However, some methodological problems have already been pointed out. First, it may not be possible to generalize results of a study that takes as subjects the offspring of schizophrenic parents. The majority of diagnosed schizophrenics do not have a schizophrenic parent (Gottesman, 1991; Lewine, 1986). Additionally, differences have been found between patients with familial schizophrenia (those with a schizophrenic first-degree relative) and patients with no schizophrenia in the family (Kendler & Hays, 1982). Second, the studies do not include control groups with other psychopathologies; it therefore is hard to decide whether the characteristics found are specific to schizophrenia. For example, some characteristics listed by Mednick and colleagues (1989)—such as pregnancy and birth complications, separation from parents, and problems in school—are also reported for other disorders. Third, there is uncertainty about whether the most relevant variables are being measured. For example, because Mednick and colleagues believe that autonomic reactivity (measured by galvanic skin response) is an important factor in schizophrenia, they have assessed this variable carefully. But they did not assess parent-child interaction, which they considered less important. Fourth, the schizophrenic parents in both high-risk studies were diagnosed according to the criteria used at that time; they might not meet the DSM-IV criteria.

PHYSIOLOGICAL FACTORS IN SCHIZOPHRENIA

Two important areas of research into the causes of schizophrenia focus on brain chemistry and brain pathology. Logically, either could serve as a vehicle for the genetic transmission of schizophrenia, but no substantive evidence to that effect has yet been found. Currently, researchers have found no physiological sign or symptom that leads solely to an invariant diagnosis of schizophrenia. Nonetheless, research in these areas has implications for treatment as well as etiology.

Biochemistry: The Dopamine Hypothesis

Biochemical explanations of schizophrenia have a long history. A century ago, for example, Emil Kraepelin suggested that these disorders result from a chemical imbalance caused by abnormal sex gland secretion. Since then, a number of researchers have tried to show that body chemistry is involved in schizophrenia. Most have failed to do so.

What generally happens is that a researcher finds a particular chemical substance in schizophrenic subjects and does not find it in "normal" controls, but other researchers cannot replicate those findings. In addition, schizophrenic patients differ from normal persons in lifestyle and in food and medication intake, all of which affect body chemistry and tend to confound research results. Table 14.5 summarizes some of the problems associated with current biological research findings.

One promising line of biochemical research has focused on the neurotransmitter dopamine and its involvement in schizophrenia (Davis et al., 1991). According to the **dopamine hypothesis** (discussed briefly in Chapter 2), schizophrenia may result from excess dopamine activity at certain synaptic sites. Support for the dopamine hypothesis has come from research with three types of drugs: phenothiazines, L-dopa, and the amphetamines.

- *Phenothiazines* are antipsychotic drugs that decrease the severity of thought disorders, alleviate withdrawal and hallucinations, and improve the mood of schizophrenic patients. Evidence shows that the phenothiazines reduce dopamine activity in the brain by blocking dopamine receptor sites in postsynaptic neurons.

- *L-dopa* is generally used to treat symptoms of Parkinson's disease, such as muscle and limb rigidity and tremors. The body converts L-dopa to dopamine, and the drug sometimes produces schizophreniclike symptoms. By contrast, the phenothiazines, which reduce dopamine activity, can *produce* side effects that resemble Parkinson's disease.

- *Amphetamines* are stimulants that increase the availability of dopamine and norepinephrine (another neurotransmitter) in the brain. When nonschizophrenic individuals are given continual doses of amphetamines, they show symptoms very much like those of acute paranoid schizophrenia. And very small doses may increase the severity of symptoms in diagnosed schizophrenic patients. Other stimulants, such as caffeine, do not produce these effects.

Thus a drug that is believed to block dopamine reception has the effect of reducing the severity of schizophrenic symptoms, whereas two drugs that increase dopamine availability either produce or worsen these symptoms. Such evidence obviously supports the idea that excess dopamine may cause schizophrenic symptoms.

The evidence is not all positive, however. For example, the dopamine hypothesis might lead us to expect that treating schizophrenia with phenothiazines would be effective in almost all cases. Yet about one-fourth of schizophrenic patients responded very little or not at all to antipsychotic medication (Kane & Freeman, 1994). In a review of studies on dopamine and schizophrenia, Davis and colleagues (1991) argued that the dopamine hypothesis has to be modified

TABLE 14.5   Biological Findings in Schizophrenia and Some Problems Associated with Them

Biological Finding	Problem
Disturbed functioning in dopamine systems	A large minority of people with schizophrenia are not responsive to antipsychotic medications affecting dopamine.
	Other effective medications (Clozapine) work primarily on serotonin, rather than dopamine, system.
	Neuroleptics block dopamine receptors quickly, but relief from symptoms is not seen for weeks.
Ventricular enlargement	Differences are relatively small compared with control groups.
	Reported in only 6 to 40 percent of schizophrenic patients in a variety of studies.
	Also reported in some patients with mood disorders.
Diminished volume of frontal or temporal lobes	Differences are relatively small, compared with control groups.
	About 50 percent of schizophrenic patients fall within range of control groups on this measure.
Low relative glucose metabolism in frontal areas	Participants are generally chronic patients on heavy neuroleptic medications.
	Some evidence indicates that neuroleptics influence cerebral blood flow even in patients who are currently medication free.
Cognitive dysfunctions (visual processing, attention problems, recall memory problems)	Some members of control groups also have such dysfunctions.
	May be a result of medication, hospitalization, or other such variables.
	Validity of measures is questionable.

Source: Compiled from Chua & McKenna, 1995; Faraone et al., 1995; Kane & Freeman, 1994; Vita et al., 1995; Wiesel, 1994.

Although differences have been found in the functioning and structure of the brain in many schizophrenics, the findings are subject to different interpretations.

to explain the discrepant findings. They believe that specific brain areas have to be identified that may be sensitive to either an excess or a deficiency of dopamine. The effectiveness of Clozapine, which acts more on the serotonin than on the dopamine system, indicates that other neurotransmitters may be important in schizophrenia (Syvalahti, 1994).

As noted earlier, schizophrenia may very well be a group of disorders with different causes; this explanation could account for the variable course of the disorders and the uneven responses to phenothiazines. Moreover, researchers may be looking for an oversimplified explanation by focusing on dopamine alone, without considering the interactive functioning of the brain and the biochemical system as a whole. Or perhaps dopamine blockers can influence the symptoms of schizophrenia but not the course of the illness. Obviously, much more remains to be discovered.

Neurological Findings

Abnormal Neurological Findings   Do the symptoms of schizophrenia indicate neurological impairment? This is certainly a possibility. Anywhere from 20 to 65 percent of schizophrenic patients show some signs of neurological abnormalities (Buchsbaum, 1990; Cannon & Marco, 1994; Vita et al., 1991). Again, the wide differences in estimates may indicate problems in the reliability of assessment techniques or may reflect the possibility that different subgroups of people with schizophrenia were assessed.

Some researchers (McGlashan & Fenton, 1991) believe that a group of schizophrenic individuals with predominantly negative symptoms such as flat affect, poverty of speech, and loss of drive display characteristics associated with neuronal loss or deterioration in a structurally abnormal brain. These patients would

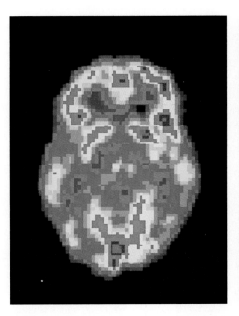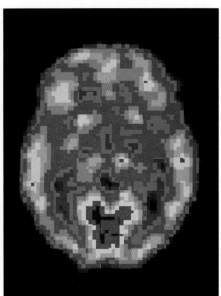

PET scans reveal the amount of neurological activity in specific areas of the brain. Individuals with schizophrenia often display hyperfrontality—that is, less activity is found in the frontal lobes (areas associated with higher thought processes) when compared to individuals without schizophrenia. Note the higher levels of activity (orange and red colors) of the frontal lobes in the normal brain (photo on the left).

be expected to show less responsiveness to antipsychotic medication and have a poorer prognosis. In contrast, schizophrenic individuals with positive symptoms such as hallucinations and delusions do not show brain deterioration but have reversible biochemical abnormalities.

The search for abnormal neurological factors in schizophrenia has intensified as increasingly sophisticated brain-imaging techniques for studying the living brain have been developed. Using these procedures, researchers have found that, compared with members of control groups, people with schizophrenia are more likely to show ventricular enlargement (enlarged spaces in areas of the brain), cerebral atrophy, and a decrease in the size of the thalamus (Andreasen et al., 1994; Chua & McKenna, 1994; Roberts, 1991; Vita et al., 1991; Zipursky, Lim & Pfefferbaum, 1991). Decreased functioning in the frontal lobes and other cerebral areas has also been observed using brain scans (Andreasen et al., 1992; Buchsbaum, 1990). Cerebral glucose metabolism is significantly lower in schizophrenic patients than in their control group counterparts, especially during cognitive tasks (Andreasen et al., 1992; Buchsbaum et al., 1992; Wolkin et al., 1992). Thus, in schizophrenics, areas of the brain involved in attention, planning, and volition seem to be impaired. Interestingly, studies comparing identical twins not concordant for schizophrenia have found that the affected twins had larger ventricles than their co-twins (Suddath et al., 1990). One study comparing cerebral blood flow in identical twins (disconcordant and concordant for schizophrenia) found decreased blood flow only in those with schizophrenia (Berman et al.,

1992). These studies illustrate some of the subtle differences in brain structure and cerebral functioning that have been found in some schizophrenics. The finding that unaffected twins may not show these anatomical or metabolic differences may indicate the impact of environmental factors.

Cognitive Markers People with schizophrenia appear to have information-processing deficits and problems in sustaining attention, recall memory, and visual processing. These characteristics are present during remission as well as during symptomatic periods (Brenner et al., 1992; Liberman & Green, 1992). Researchers have hoped that these characteristics would function as "cognitive markers," indicators of a vulnerability for psychotic episodes. If these "markers" indicate genetic influence, they should also be present in a greater percentage of first-degree relatives than in comparison groups (Green, 1993).

To identify "markers" from transient symptoms, Nuechterlein and colleagues (1992) recommended that we distinguish three sets of characteristics:

1. *Stable vulnerability indicators* These characteristics would be "enduring" or consistently different from those of nonschizophrenic individuals and would be evident before, during, and after schizophrenic episodes. They would not "worsen" during psychotic episodes, they would be genetically determined, and they would occur in much higher frequency in individuals with or at risk for schizophrenia.

2. *Mediating vulnerability factors* These characteristics would be present during both psychotic

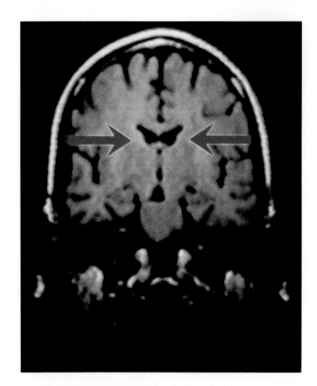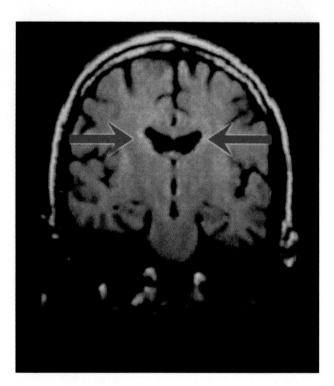

These MRIs are brain images of identical twins, one without schizophrenia and one with schizophrenia. Note that the brain on the right (schizophrenic) has larger ventricles (the butterfly-shaped cavities)—a condition common among schizophrenics.

episodes and remission, but they would become severe during the psychotic episodes. These characteristics are also hypothesized to be genetically determined and to occur at a higher frequency in schizophrenic populations.

3. *Episode indicators* These characteristics would be abnormal during psychotic episodes but would return to normal levels during remission. These characteristics are short-term and a result of the disorder.

This strategy will allow us to separate characteristics that are causal or may function as cognitive markers rather than short-term symptoms due to the disorder. Several tests have been developed to measure some of these deficits. The *Visual Continuous Performance Test,* for example, measures sustained attention to tasks. In one version, subjects monitor a series of letters or numbers and signal when a predetermined stimulus appears. Another test, *Eye Movement Dysfunction Measure,* analyzes how well one's eye follows a target. On both tests, people with schizophrenia show greater impairment than that demonstrated by control samples (Szymansk, Kane & Lieberman, 1991). These information-processing differences have been found consistently in schizo-

phrenic samples. Researchers are not clear, however, on what the findings mean. Perhaps they are cognitive markers.

We cannot answer that question with certainty because there are problems with these identified "markers" for schizophrenia. Impairment on the tests has been associated with certain medications, fatigue, fluctuations in attention, and other physical and psychological disorders (Clementz & Sweeney, 1990). In addition, other psychiatric patients also exhibit stable information-processing differences (Penn et al., 1993). Another difficulty is that the course of schizophrenia is variable, with peaks and valleys, so that it is difficult to identify the particular phase of the disorder for any individual. Because of this, it is difficult to know if we are looking at episode indicators, mediating factors, or stable indicators. Neuropsychological tests may also be unreliable for this population (Heinrichs, 1993).

Although the research strategy Nuechterlein and colleagues suggested seems sound, "enduring" characteristics peculiar to schizophrenia have been difficult to identify. As yet, none of the cognitive markers is specific enough to be included as a criterion in the diagnosis of schizophrenia (Szymanski, Kane & Lieberman, 1991).

Conclusions What can we conclude from studies of brain structure and functioning in schizophrenia? It appears that neurological abnormalities are reported more often in schizophrenic people than in nonschizophrenic individuals and more often in schizophrenic people having negative symptoms. At best, however, these differences are subtle. The observations are intriguing because they highlight the possibility that some subtypes of schizophrenia may be caused by structural brain pathology. Findings that abnormalities in the prefrontal cortex may be a factor are especially interesting because this area is involved with some of the intellectual symptoms associated with schizophrenia.

Interpreting the findings is problematic, however. These neurological abnormalities do not seem to be specific to schizophrenia. They are also found in persons with mood disorders, alcohol and substance abuse, and organic impairment (Shelton et al., 1988; Syvalahti, 1994). After reviewing thirty-nine studies on ventricular size, Van Horn and McManus (1992) concluded, "It [the size difference] is probably too small to be of practical significance in diagnosis" (p. 6). Other problems in interpreting the results of neurophysiological studies include small sample sizes, outdated diagnostic criteria, unreliable assessment techniques, and the potential effects of medication (Bogerts, 1993; Heinrichs, 1993). The search for neurological abnormalities in people with schizophrenia nevertheless is promising.

The research evidence has clearly indicated that schizophrenia is a brain disorder. However, the underlying structure(s) or neuropathological processes have not been identified. Heinrichs (1993) pointed out the many contradictions in the disorder:

1. The presentation of the disorder and its course is varied. Some patients have hallucinations; some have only delusions.

2. Some patients show poor premorbid adjustment in their history, and others seem fine until the disorder strikes.

3. Some patients respond positively to antipsychotic medications, whereas others do not.

4. Neuroanatomical abnormalities are found in some patients but not in others.

5. Genetic factors are important, but they do not seem sufficient for the expression of the disorder.

6. Information-processing deficits are found in most schizophrenic patients, but they are also found in other psychiatric patients.

7. Individuals with brain lesions in the areas of the brain associated with schizophrenia show performance patterns different from those found in people with schizophrenia.

What does this conflicting information mean? Heinrichs believes that "schizophrenia is a heterogeneous illness that, paradoxically, resists subdivision." We need to identify and subdivide the disorder so that we can study the different etiological types. So far, attempts to do so have been largely unsuccessful.

This subject is connected to a device that records the activation of specific areas of the brain during a card sorting task—a measure of abstract thinking. Researchers believe that schizophrenic people do poorly on this task because they may be deficient in the ability to activate the prefrontal cortex (Berman et al., 1992).

ENVIRONMENTAL FACTORS IN SCHIZOPHRENIA

Obviously, genetic and biological research has not yet clarified the cause of the various schizophrenic disorders. Because the concordance rate is less than 50 percent when one identical twin has the disorder, non-shared environmental influences must also play a role (Dilalla & Gottesman, 1995). These influences probably occur early in life (Kendler & Diehl, 1993; Kringlen, 1994). One researcher (Brown, 1994) noted that the states with the highest rates of schizophrenia (see Figure 14.3) are also those with the largest number of cases of Lyme disease or tic-borne encephalitis. Although this correlation may be a coincidence, it illustrates the attempt to identify early environmental factors, such as infections during fetal or perinatal development, which could be related to schizophrenia.

Psychological stressors that may trigger this disorder have also been considered. There are reports of stress-induced hallucinations among individuals facing highly anxiety-arousing circumstances (Spivak et al., 1992), but these episodes were temporary and did not result in diagnoses of schizophrenia. Stressors do appear to be related to probability of relapse (Zubin, Steinhauer & Condray, 1992). As with the biological theories, environmental explanations are not sufficient to explain the etiology of schizophrenia. In this section we consider some of the more developed of these theories—those concerning the role of family dynamics, social class, and cultural differences.

Family Influences

In 1978, a researcher in the field of schizophrenia concluded that "No environmental causes have been found that will invariably or even with moderate probability produce genuine schizophrenia in persons who are unrelated to a schizophrenic individual" (Gottesman, 1978, p. 67). Another researcher echoed this view: "There are no [schizophrenia-producing] environments.... Environmental contributions have little or no specificity" (Fowles, 1984, p. 82). Both researchers believe that unless a person has a genetic predisposition toward schizophrenia, environmental factors have little impact on the development of the disorder. Others strongly disagree. In this section, we consider theories that support psychological factors as either the cause or a contributor to schizophrenia.

Theoretical Constructs Studies of high-risk children have found that those who develop schizophrenia had a negative family environment (Marcus et al., 1987; Tienari et al., 1994). Several theories have attempted to pinpoint patterns of family interaction that could

produce such a disorder. The first was proposed by psychodynamic theorists, who believed that certain behavioral patterns of parents could inhibit appropriate ego development in the child (Alanen, 1994). This, in turn, would make the child vulnerable to the severe regression characteristic of schizophrenia. Attention was focused mainly on the mother, who usually has a great deal of contact with the child. These theorists characterized the **schizophrenogenic** (or schizophrenia-producing) mother as being simultaneously or alternately cold and overprotecting, rejecting and dominating. This behavior pattern led to the development of schizophrenia in the child.

The second theory involving family interaction asked another question: Can some kind of communication pattern produce schizophrenia? This is the **double-bind theory** mentioned in Chapter 2 (Bateson et al., 1956). Proponents suggested that the preschizophrenic child has repeated experiences with one or more family members (usually the mother and father) in which the child receives two contradictory messages. The child cannot discern the parent's meaning and cannot escape the situation. This conflict eventually leads the person to develop difficulty in interpreting other people's communications and in accurately and appropriately conveying his or her own thoughts and feelings.

Assume, for example, that a mother harbors hostile feelings toward her daughter and yet wishes to be a good and loving mother. She might send her child to bed, saying, "You're tired and sleep will do you good." The overt message conveys the mother's concern for her child's health. Her tone of voice, however, is such that the child senses the mother's anger and her desire to be alone. The child then can interpret the contradictory messages in one of two ways (Bateson, 1978): She may correctly interpret her mother's hostility, in which case she is faced with the awful fact that she is not loved or wanted by her mother. Or she may accept the overt message—that she is tired and that her mother cares for her—and then be forced to deny her real understanding of the message. The double bind is that the child is punished whether she discriminates the message correctly or incorrectly.

To survive, the child may resort to self-deception, falsely interpreting her own thoughts as well as those communicated by others. She may develop a false concept of reality, an inability to communicate effectively, withdrawal, and other symptoms of schizophrenia.

Problems with Earlier Research Most studies conducted before the mid-1970s supported the view that communications were less clear and accurate in families with a schizophrenic member than in other fami-

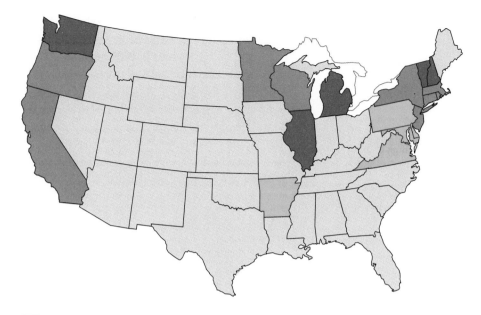

■ States with highest rates of schizophrenia

■ States with highest rates of Lyme disease

■ States with highest rates of schizophrenia and Lyme disease

FIGURE 14.3 **Relationship Between States with Highest Rates of Schizophrenia and Highest Rates of Lyme Disease** This figure shows a strong correspondence between states with the highest rates of schizophrenia and the highest rates of Lyme disease. Some researchers hypothesize that certain viruses in tics can increase susceptibility to schizophrenia.

Source: Adapted from Brown, 1994.

lies. Methodological shortcomings, however, kept researchers from generalizing these results to a relationship between schizophrenia and family dynamics. Two flaws were most common: A family's interactions were studied only after one of its members had been diagnosed as schizophrenic, and studies generally lacked control groups. Thus even if difficult family interaction was correlated with schizophrenia, researchers could not tell which was the cause and which the effect, or whether the correlation was unique to schizophrenia.

Some researchers continue to believe that the family environment may be involved in the onset and course of the disorder. Several prospective studies have found that high-risk children who develop schizophrenia are more likely to have negative family relationships than are high-risk children who do not develop the disorder (Burman et al., 1987; Marcus et al., 1987; Tienari et al., 1994). The importance of parenting was indicated in the Israeli high-risk study discussed earlier in this chapter. Among the high-risk group, none who had received "good parenting" from a schizophrenic parent developed schizophrenia or a spectrum disorder. However, parenting style may also

be a result of how "sick" the child is, a possibility we consider later in the chapter.

Expressed Emotion Current research is directed toward a specific behavior pattern called *expressed emotion (EE)* that is found among some relatives of schizophrenic individuals with schizophrenia. The expressed emotion index is determined by the number of critical comments made by a relative (criticism); the number of statements of dislike or resentment directed toward the patient by family members (hostility); and the number of statements reflecting emotional overinvolvement, overconcern, or overprotectiveness made about the patient (Jenkins & Karno, 1992). For example, high-EE relatives are likely to make a greater number of statements such as "You are a lazy person" or "You've caused our family a lot of trouble" (Rosenfarb et al., 1995). The EE construct strongly predicts the course of the disorder (Karno et al., 1987; Miklowitz, 1994; Mintz, Mintz & Goldstein, 1987). A review of twenty-six studies (Kavanagh, 1992), indicated that the median relapse rate for patients living with high-EE relatives was 48 percent, compared with 21 percent for those living

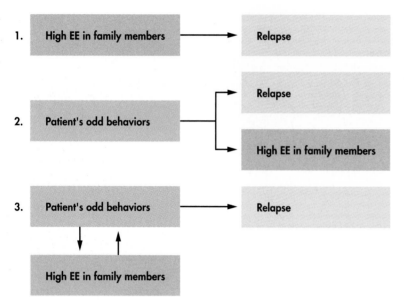

FIGURE 14.4 Possible Relationships Between High Rates of Expressed Emotion and Relapse Rates in Patients with Schizophrenia Although some researchers believe that high expressed emotions among family members are related to relapse rates in schizophrenic patients, the precise relationship has not been determined. This figure shows several ways in which expressed emotions and relapse rates can be related.

with low-EE relatives. That over twice as many people suffer relapses in a high-EE environment than in a low-EE environment indicates the strength of this variable. The importance of expressed emotions was also found among low-income, unacculturated Mexican Americans. High-EE levels in key relatives increased the risk of relapse among remitted schizophrenic patients who returned home after being discharged (Karno et al., 1987).

Although these studies are better designed than those discussed earlier, they are still correlational in nature and are therefore subject to different interpretations. Figure 14.4 indicates three possible interpretations.

1. An environment with high expressed emotions may lead directly to relapse in the schizophrenic family member. Most of the family communication theories of schizophrenia are based on this pattern.

2. A more severely ill individual may produce high-EE communication patterns in relatives. The severity of the illness means that the chances of relapse are high. Schreiber, Breier, and Pickar (1995) found some support for this pattern. They examined the parental emotional response in families who had both schizophrenic and nonschizophrenic children. The parents reacted differently, with more EE communication to the sick child. The researchers hypothesize that expressed emotions may be a response of parents to the "chronic disabling aspect of this illness, and a belief by the parent that increased involvement would facilitate increased functioning of the child" (p. 649).

3. In the bidirectional model, the patient's odd behaviors or symptoms may cause family members to attempt to exert control and to react with frus-

tration, which in turn produce more psychotic symptoms in the patient. An examination of communication patterns in families with schizophrenic patients also shows some support for this view (Rosenfarb et al., 1995).

High-EE communication does not appear to be peculiar to schizophrenia. These patterns have also been found in the families of patients with depression, bipolar disorder, and eating disorders (Kavanagh, 1992). The findings support the view that expressed emotions may, in part, be a reaction of family members to severe illnesses. High-EE communication appears to be more evident in Western families. Studies of the families of patients living in India show much lower levels of expressed emotion than is found in American families (Leff et al., 1990). Not all studies have supported the EE hypothesis and some researchers are voicing concern that the EE hypothesis may be used to blame families for the disorder. Miklowitz (1994) points out that terms such as "high expressed emotions" seem to imply that the relatives are excessively emotional or disturbed in some way. He recommends substituting a term such as "negative affective relationships" to indicate the bidirectional nature of interactions.

Effect of Social Class

Schizophrenia is most common at the lower socioeconomic levels, regardless of whether prevalence is measured relative to patient populations or to general populations. One of the most consistent findings in schizophrenia research is that the disorder is disproportionately concentrated among people in the poorest areas of large cities and in the occupations with the lowest status (Gottesman, 1991). It is five times

Schizophrenia is much more prevalent at lower socioeconomic levels. This may be due to the increased stress of living in poverty, or it could be that individuals with schizophrenia are downwardly mobile due to their inability to function fully. Insufficient social support may also be a contributing factor.

more common in the bottom of the socioeconomic level than in the highest (Keith, Regier & Rae, 1991).

This correlation between social class and schizophrenia has two possible explanations. First, low socioeconomic status is itself stressful. Physical and psychological stressors associated with poverty, a lack of education, menial employment, and the like increase the chance that schizophrenia will develop *(breeder hypothesis)*. Second, schizophrenic and preschizophrenic people tend to drift to the poorest urban areas and the lowest socioeconomic levels because they cannot function effectively elsewhere in society *(downward drift theory)*.

Although one way to test downward drift theory is to determine whether schizophrenic individuals do actually move downward in occupational status, the results of such studies have been inconclusive. Some researchers have found evidence of downward mobility, but others have found none. An alternative research strategy is to compare the occupations of schizophrenic individuals and their fathers. If schizophrenic people generally hold jobs with a lower status than those held by their fathers, a downward drift interpretation would be supported. In several studies, the schizophrenic patients were found to have such lower-status occupations (Gottesman, 1991).

Overall, the evidence seems to support both the breeder hypothesis and downward drift theory. For some people, the stressors and limitations associated with membership in the lowest socioeconomic class facilitate the development of schizophrenia. But for others, low socioeconomic status is a result of the disorder.

Cross-Cultural Comparisons

Schizophrenia appears to be present in all the countries studied by the World Health Organization. The lowest prevalence of the disorder was found in Denmark (1.5 per 10,000) and the highest in India (4.2 per 10,000; Jablensky, 1988). A number of studies found various differences in symptomology, however, and these may result from environmental influences.

Less-developed countries seem to have a greater percentage of "hysterical psychoses," "possession syndromes," and other brief psychotic disorders. These psychoses tend to be rapid in onset and short in duration; they have a good prognosis. The following case from Zimbabwe illustrates some of the characteristics:

> A young teacher was brought to the psychiatric hospital by the police after smashing several plate-glass windows in local shops and breaking the windows of cars parked on the street.... When captured, he was intensely aggressive, spoke incoherently, and claimed voices were talking to him and directing his actions. Following recovery, which required several weeks of treatment with high-dose, high-potency neuroleptics, he told the following story.
>
> Approximately one month prior to onset of his running amok, he consulted a local n'anga [healer] to determine whether the future of his job was secure. The n'anga told him his workmates were jealous of him and might try to harm him. A few weeks later he found a "flash card" in his office. It read, "To die." He knew at once that his colleagues planned to murder him, probably by bewitchment. This episode would not leave his

mind. Hallucinated voices began to echo his thoughts, and his state of wild excitement ensued. (Stevens, 1987, p. 394)

Cases of psychotic reactions after hearing a negative prediction from a healer have been reported in some less-developed countries.

A comparison of the symptoms of hospitalized schizophrenic Americans of Irish and Italian descent found that Irish Americans tended to show less hostility and acting out but more fixed delusions than did Italian Americans. These differences have been attributed to cultural-familial backgrounds: In Irish families, mothers played a very dominant role, were quite strict, and prohibited strong emotional displays; in Italian families, mothers showed the opposite pattern (Opler, 1967). Similarly, Japanese patients hospitalized for schizophrenia are often described as rigid, compulsive, withdrawn, and passive—symptoms that reflect the Japanese cultural values of conformity within the community and reserve within the family (S. Sue & Morishima, 1982).

The content of delusions also seems to be influenced by culture and society. Since the social and political upheavals of the period known as the Cultural Revolution (during the 1960s), a number of new delusions have appeared among Chinese schizophrenic patients (Yu-Fen & Neng, 1981). These include the delusion of leadership lineage, in which patients insist that their parents are people in authority; the delusion of being tested, in which patients believe that their superiors are assessing them to determine whether they are suitable for promotion; the delusion of impending arrest, in which patients assume that they are about to be arrested by authorities; and the delusion of being married, in which a female patient insists that she has a husband even though she is unmarried. Each of these is associated with some facet of the new Chinese society.

Racial differences have also been observed. In a study of 273 schizophrenic patients admitted to hospitals and mental health centers in Missouri over a three-and-a-half-year period, researchers found that African-American patients exhibited more severe symptoms than white patients: angry outbursts, impulsiveness, and strongly antisocial behavior. They also showed greater disorientation and confusion and more severe hallucinatory behaviors, compared with white patients (Abebimpe et al., 1982). These research findings may be interpreted as real differences in symptomology that may have environmental explanations. However, they could also be produced by diagnostic errors. As DSM-IV notes, "There is some evidence that clinicians may have a tendency to overdiagnose Schizophrenia (instead of Bipolar Disorder) in some ethnic groups" (p. 281). Cultural differences between patient and clinician may also produce diagnostic errors—the greater the difference, the greater the likelihood of error. Finally, misdiagnosis can result from racial stereotyping or bias, or from applying diagnostic systems based on white middle-class norms to other racial groups.

THE DIATHESIS-STRESS MODEL OF SCHIZOPHRENIA

As Dilalla & Gottesman (1995) observed after considering identical and fraternal twin studies, "The difference between concordance rates implicates the etiological influence of genetic factors on schizophrenia; the much-less-than-perfect concordance for identical twins also highlights the etiological importance of nonshared environmental factors" (p. 491). Although genetic factors clearly play a major role in this disorder, its appearance may depend on environmental factors.

Researchers have thus developed a general model emphasizing the interaction between genetics and environmental stressors in schizophrenia. This **diathesis-stress model** postulates that a vulnerability to a disorder, either inherited or acquired, combines with the impact of stressors to produce the disorder. Schizophrenia, therefore, develops when a vulnerable person encounters stress and lacks access to the resources or social support systems that he or she needs to cope with it.

A particularly elaborate version of the diathesis-stress model has been developed by Nuechterlein and Dawson (1984) and Nuechterlein (1987). As Figure 14.5 shows, these researchers believe that people with schizophrenia suffer from several "enduring vulnerability characteristics": (1) a predisposition toward poor processing of information and difficulty in sustaining attention, brought on by various thought impairments; (2) overreaction to even mildly aversive stimuli; and (3) lack of adequate social competence and coping skills. These may be the result of dysfunctions in neurotransmitters or brain structure abnormalities.

The vulnerable person may not experience psychotic episodes if he or she has good coping skills, takes antipsychotic medications, or is being raised in a supportive family and has good social support. What might increase the chances of a schizophrenia episode are (1) a family environment in which high EE is present, (2) an environment that is too stimulating, and (3) stressful life events. When the negative factors outweigh positive personal and protective environmental variables, the individual's cognitive functioning becomes overloaded and a feedback loop is created that continually compounds the stress. Eventually schizophrenic symptoms develop.

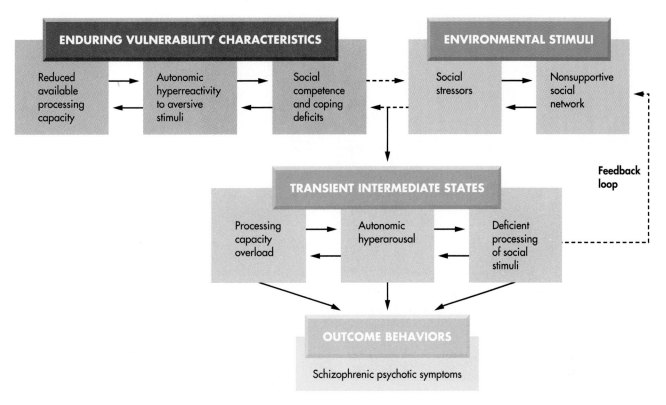

FIGURE 14.5 **The Diathesis-Stress Model** In Nuechterlein and Dawson's model, the vulnerable individual overreacts to environmental stressors that are not buffered by his or her social support system. The feedback loop has the effect of "transforming" such overreactions into added stressors that eventually build up sufficiently to precipitate a schizophrenic episode.

Source: Nuechterlein & Dawson, 1984.

The diathesis-stress model is useful because it calls attention to the role both biological and psychological factors play in schizophrenia. The model also implies that intervention can take many forms. Therapy could involve increasing the "personal protectors" by teaching the individual coping skills and using antipsychotic medication. Family and social interventions can be used to provide a more supportive social environment. In the next section, we discuss the variety of therapeutic approaches based on this model.

THE TREATMENT OF SCHIZOPHRENIA

Through the years, schizophrenia has been "treated" by a variety of means including "warehousing" severely disturbed patients in overcrowded asylums and prefrontal lobotomy, a surgical procedure in which the frontal lobes are disconnected from the remainder of the patient's brain. Such radical procedures were generally abandoned in the 1950s, when the beneficial effects of antipsychotic drugs were discovered. Today

schizophrenia is typically treated with antipsychotic medication along with some type of psychosocial therapy. More severely disordered patients are still hospitalized until they are able to function adequately in society. Many do recover and can function well in society, but are often responded to negatively (see Focus On).

Antipsychotic Medication

Peter was a 29-year-old man with chronic paranoid schizophrenia. . . . When on medication, he heard voices talking about him and felt that his phone was bugged. When off medication, he had constant hallucinations and his behavior became unpredictable. . . . He was on 10 milligrams of haloperidol (Haldol) three times a day. . . . Peter complained that he had been quite restless, and did not want to take the medication. Over the next six months, Peter's psychiatrist gradually reduced Peter's medication to 4 milligrams per day. . . . At this dose, Peter continued to have bothersome symptoms, but they remained moderate. . . . He was no longer restless. (Lieberman, Kopelowicz & Young, 1994, p. 94)

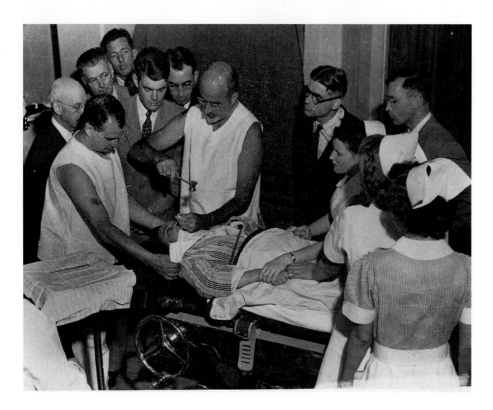

Prefrontal lobotomies, like this one performed by Walter Freedman in 1949, involve the insertion of an instrument resembling an ice pick through the eye socket to sever connections in the frontal lobes of the brain. Because of their poor results, lobotomies have been abandoned as a treatment for schizophrenia.

The use of medication in Peter's case illustrates several points. First, antipsychotic drugs can reduce symptoms. Second, dosage levels should be carefully monitored, and third, side effects can occur as a result of medication.

Most mental health professionals consider the introduction of *Thorazine*, the first antipsychotic drug, the beginning of a new era in treating schizophrenia. For the first time, a medication was available that sufficiently relaxed even violent schizophrenic patients and helped organize their thoughts to the point where straitjackets were no longer needed to contain the individuals. Three decades later, the phenothiazines, which are variations of Thorazine, are still viewed as the most effective drug treatment for schizophrenia. They are not, however, a "cure" for the condition.

The antipsychotic medications (also called *neuroleptics*) are, however, far from perfect and can produce a number of extremely unwelcome side effects that resemble neurological conditions. They quite effectively reduce the severity of the positive symptoms of schizophrenia, such as hallucinations, delusions, bizarre speech, and thought disorders. Most, however, offer little relief from the negative symptoms of social withdrawal, apathy, and impaired personal hygiene (Carpenter et al., 1995; Christison, 1991). Moreover, a "relatively large group" of schizophrenics do not benefit at all from antipsychotic medication (Wiesel, 1994; Silverman et al., 1987). The First Person narra-

tive discusses negative symptoms from an occupational therapist's viewpoint.

A new drug, *Clozapine*, was released for use in the United States in 1990. It has several properties that have generated a great deal of interest. It seems to be effective with individuals who have not responded to other antipsychotic medications and seems to have fewer side effects (Carpenter et al., 1995; Kane, 1991; Meltzer, 1995). There is also some indication that Clozapine may be effective in treating negative symptoms in schizophrenia (Safferman et al., 1991). Its use is carefully monitored because one of its side effects is potentially fatal lesions of the mucous membranes or gastrointestinal system. There is also concern that abrupt discontinuation of the drug will cause more symptom rebound than occurs with other antipsychotic medications (Shore et al., 1995).

Regulation and monitoring of antipsychotic drugs is especially important. Zito and colleagues (1987) found that many of 136 newly admitted schizophrenic patients were given doses in "excess of current guidelines." Women received higher doses of antipsychotic medications than those given to men. In addition, medication was seldom reduced to a maintenance level once the acute stage passed. Segal and colleagues (1992) similarly found that psychiatrists tended to administer higher and higher doses of antipsychotic medications to patients living in halfway houses and other sheltered-care facilities. Nearly one-

Discrimination Against the Mentally Ill

Mental illnesses, especially psychoses such as schizophrenia, are still feared and misunderstood by the public. The resulting discrimination is illustrated by the experiences of a former schizophrenic patient. After he was released from a hospital psychiatric ward, he told his employer about his illness. This marked the beginning of a series of encounters with the general prejudice against former mental patients.

> I was at work only a few days when I was fired but "assured" that I would receive good references. The fact that I had been there for nearly 4 years and [was] a good worker did not matter. (Anonymous, 1981, p. 736)

In applying for a new job, he faced additional problems:

> I also noticed that many job applications would inquire about medical and psychological stability. . . . I learned that honesty is not always the best policy. . . . I am considering graduate school, and there too, questions about past and present psychiatric treatment confront me. . . . The admission forms often request a biographical sketch describing how the student became interested in the field and any personal experiences with psychiatry. This, too, obviously is a Catch-22 position. To admit my personal experiences is to court possible and realistic rejection. I have spoken off the record with an instructor in a well-known school of social work about the situation, and his advice was: "I do not think discussing your hospital experiences would be a plus." [But if] I do not discuss it, I would in a way be compromising my principles. (pp. 736–737)

The former patient partly blames the media for this situation:

> Hardly a month goes by that we do not read a lurid news story of "man goes berserk and kills neighbor" or "former mental patient kills wife." . . . The evidence is overwhelming that the majority of mental patients are, as a class, less dangerous than the "average citizen." . . . Psychotherapy and psychotropic drugs have helped thousands of people to continue to go about their daily lives . . . but at times, I am sure they painfully wonder, for what? (p. 737)

What messages from the mass media have you received about the mentally ill? What do you believe are reasonable restrictions, if any, in hiring or working with persons with schizophrenia?

half received increases in medication during a twelve-year period, and 10 percent received "extreme doses."

Equally disturbing, clinicians are often unaware of possible reactions to the drugs, which include tremors, motor restlessness, anxiety, agitation, extreme terror, and even impulsive suicide attempts (Drake & Ehrlich, 1985). In one study (Weiden et al., 1987) clinicians did not identify motor symptoms such as restlessness, rigidity, and tremors produced by medications. Clinicians identified only one of ten patients showing tardive dyskinesia (involuntary movement disorder). The inability to recognize these symptoms in patients who are medicated is disturbing. Critical Thinking discusses the issue of patients' rights in taking medication.

Because of the severity of some side effects, researchers are trying to identify the groups of schizophrenic patients who do not need maintenance medication. For example, twenty-three chronic schizophrenics who retrospectively met the DSM-III criteria were able to sustain good outcome for an average of fifteen years without maintenance doses of antipsychotic medication. This group had good premorbid and occupational adjustment as well as good social skills. Clearly, then, not all schizophrenic patients require continuous medication. Nevertheless, researchers still need to address the inability to identify the particular groups who do not require maintenance medication (Fenton & McGlashan, 1987).

One approach is to reduce medication and watch for a relapse. Those who function well on a lower dosage might later undergo a trial period in which medication is totally eliminated. In one study conducted over a twelve-month period, reducing dosage levels by 50 percent tripled the relapse rate (32 percent, as opposed to 10 percent on maintenance medication). A tradeoff, however, is that reduced-dose patients showed decreased risk of tardive dyskinesia

FIRST PERSON

Mary Ann Mayer

Schizophrenia—less a diagnosis than a human condition. More than a decade ago I began practicing psychiatric occupational therapy because of my interest in the disease. I remain in practice today because of my respect for the people affiliated with it.

A few days after admission to the psychiatric unit, the psychotic storm that engulfs a schizophrenic patient quiets down and the person emerges, as if from a cocoon. The positive symptoms recede— the command hallucinations, the fear of being stalked or poisoned, hearing one's thoughts whispered by every passerby. But the negative symptoms linger—disturbances in attention, perception, psychomotor behavior, affect, and drive. These are the symptoms that most subtract from the quality of life.

People with schizophrenia are not "crazy"; they have a cognitive disability that robs them of choice and access to the everyday activities you and I take for granted, such as running a household, earning and spending money, and planning for the future. This is why meaningful activity is the treatment method used by occupational therapists; it uses people's assets while helping them cope with their limitations. For some, guided in-

volvement in the activities of daily life can restore meaning, purpose, and identity.

I'm expected to help the schizophrenic person and his or her family understand and manage this disability, reduce environmental barriers to performance, and restore purpose and place in life. I act as an advocate for the patient, explaining to others why that person has difficulty doing certain things. I also assess the schizophrenic individual's environment and try to modify it in ways that optimize that person's performance. Not everything I do works, but anything can work—skills training, simplifying a work site, finding a compatible social group, instilling hope, and showing others alternatives to blaming the schizophrenic person for his or her disability.

The following statements are common misperceptions. One of my responsibilities as an occupational therapist is to interpret a

---

(Johnson et al., 1987). Although a higher relapse rate was associated with a lower level of medication (10 percent of the standard dose), the families of these patients expressed more satisfaction with their adjustment than did the families of patients taking a standard dose. On the lower dose, patients showed greater social competence and adjustment. More than 50 percent remained stable. Researchers also found that negative family attitudes toward the patient were associated with relapse. So dosage reduction, together with careful monitoring, may be useful with some people, but standard dosage levels may be needed in nonsupportive families.

Psychosocial Therapy

Most clinicians today agree that the most beneficial treatment for schizophrenia is some combination of antipsychotic medication and therapy (Hogarty et al., 1991; Leff, 1994; McNally, 1994). This attitude is fairly new, and strict advocates of a medical approach resisted this combination for many years. But even as scientists continued to introduce drugs that effectively

reduced or eliminated many symptoms of schizophrenia, one vital fact became clear: Medicated and adequately functioning schizophrenic people discharged from protective hospital environments were returning to stressful home or work situations. The typical result was repeated rehospitalizations; medication alone was not enough to help these individuals function in their natural environment. Clinicians soon realized that antipsychotic medication had to be supplemented with outpatient therapy.

How do patients with severe mental disorders feel about their experiences with psychotherapy? A random sample of 212 patients from different clinics in Maryland responded to a questionnaire. According to patients with schizophrenia, nearly three-quarters find that individual psychotherapy brings about positive changes in their lives. Although the remaining 28 percent report that it produced no change or had a negative effect, most patients felt that the best treatment was a combination of talking therapy with medication. The study (Coursey, Keller & Farrell, 1995) found that the following aspects of individual therapy were considered most useful. (The numbers in paren-

schizophrenic person's behavior in a way that can be understood by others, thereby encouraging their understanding and support.

Comment: "He just doesn't apply himself. He's always been lazy."

Response: Daily activities can represent an unachievable challenge. Perhaps he's had more experiences of failure than success. Maybe it's not that he won't perform the task, but that he can't manage it alone, yet. He might be too afraid to try.

Comment: "She seems easily distracted and her work is very disorganized."

Response: Is there a quieter place to work? Is supervision available? Let's analyze the job and work with her to find the easiest methods to perform the assigned tasks.

Comment: "When any medication is prescribed, she takes too much. She can be very uncooperative, you know."

Response: Consistent, familiar routines are important. She may not fully understand the cause and effect of certain actions, such as taking too many pills. A medication daily organizer might help.

Comment: "He has a hard time expressing himself and gets very frustrated when people don't understand. Then he withdraws from everyone, including me. That hurts."

Response: Perhaps he's scared of being rejected, which increases his anxiety, making it more difficult for him to express himself. Encouraging him to take his time when he speaks might help him relax and feel less self-conscious.

In addition to positive and negative symptoms, social stigma and exclusion have to be grappled with. All these factors contribute to the need for hospitalization, support, and stabilization. Symptoms can be reduced or compensated for. But social barriers are far more difficult to overcome. Fear and misunderstanding need to be replaced with compassion and acceptance. Schizophrenia is not just an illness, it's also a disability, and schizophrenic people deserve the same respect and support we accord other people with disabilities.

Mary Ann Mayer is a registered occupational therapist at Butler Hospital in Providence, Rhode Island. She evaluates the functional performance of patients, provides rehabilitative activities, and consults with families and caregivers in the community.

theses represent the percentage of patients who agreed with the statement.)

- Therapist gave me practical advice (52 percent)

- Getting in touch with my feelings (45 percent)

- Understanding how I affect other people and how they affect me (25 percent)

- Looking at the ways I usually act and feel and why (24 percent)

- Understanding the impact of my past on what I do now (24 percent)

Most patients felt that the most important quality of a therapist was friendship. It appears that patients with schizophrenia do value psychotherapy.

Institutional Approaches Traditional institutional treatments providing custodial care and medication for schizophrenic patients have yielded poor results, although milieu therapy and behavioral therapy have been found to be more effective. In **milieu therapy,** the hospital environment operates as a community, and patients exercise a wide range of responsibilities, helping to make decisions and to manage the wards. This is in sharp contrast to the passive role schizophrenic patients have had in traditional settings. Social learning programs focus on increasing appropriate self-care behaviors, conversational skills, and role skills, such as job training and ward activities. Undesirable behaviors such as "crazy talk" or social isolation are decreased through reinforcement and modeling techniques. Both approaches have been shown to be effective in helping many schizophrenic people achieve independent living (Falloon, Boyd & McGill, 1984). Living in community homes also has produced positive results. In a study of nearly 100 chronic schizophrenic patients placed in community facilities, almost all improved. They reported more friendships and were less symptomatic than those who remained institutionalized (Leff et al., 1994).

Cognitive-Behavioral Therapy Because schizophrenic people typically lack social skills, training in these skills is almost always part—sometimes the major part—of behavioral therapy. The training emphasizes

Should Patients Have the Right to Refuse Medication?

Should schizophrenics have the right to refuse antipsychotic medications that produce potentially hazardous side effects? Patients in many state hospitals do not have this right. Before you respond to this question, consider this warning, contained in the *Physician's Desk Reference* (1994): "There is no known effective treatment for tardive dyskinesia." That warning represents a major source of concern for patients receiving antipsychotic medications.

Tardive dyskinesia is characterized by involuntary and rhythmic movements of the protruding tongue; chewing, lip smacking, and other facial movements; and jerking movements of the limbs. At risk for this disorder are women, elderly patients, and people who have been treated with antipsychotic medications—also known as neuroleptics—over a long period of time. Women tend to have more severe tardive dyskinesia and a higher prevalence than men do

(Yassa & Jeste, 1992). However, this syndrome is appearing increasingly more often in younger patients and nonpsychotic patients because neuroleptics are now being prescribed to treat anxiety, hyperactivity in children, aggression, and mood disorders.

In one large prospective study, nearly 20 percent of the sample developed tardive dyskinesia after being on the medication for four years. After eight years, 40 percent had tardive dyskinesia (Kane et al.,

---

communication skills and assertiveness. The patient is repeatedly placed in social situations that he or she tends to avoid. Experience with such situations eventually decreases the patient's anxiety concerning them to the point where he or she will seek out, rather than avoid, these situations. This is a crucially important contribution of social skills training because social withdrawal is a major schizophrenic symptom that is untouched by antipsychotic medication. Social skills training has been found to be helpful for chronic schizophrenic patients (Liberman & Green, 1992).

Cognitive approaches have also been used to reduce the impact of delusions, hallucinations, and other thought disorders on the behavior of schizophrenic individuals. Kingdon and Turkington (1991) found that targeting the reduction of psychotic symptoms through the use of a destigmatizing explanation and providing patients with analytic skills were effective. The investigatiors explained that stress often produces such reactions as ideas of reference, paranoid ideas, and misinterpretation of events, and they taught the patients how to analyze their symptoms. For example, patients who heard voices were asked to determine if they were really coming from within their head, and if stress was related to the appearance of the voices. One thirty-year-old man believed that his mind was more full of thoughts than others and that thoughts were transmitted like sound waves.

After going through cognitive therapy, he admitted that his beliefs were theoretically interesting but not realistic. The sixty-four schizophrenic patients treated with this procedure required minimal hospitalization and low levels of medication or no medication. Helping delusional patients to develop the means of critically evaluating their beliefs has also been successful in reducing the impact of their symptoms (Alford & Correia, 1994).

One recent cognitive-behavioral program that has shown promise is *Integrated Psychological Therapy (IPT)*, which identifies the specific cognitive deficits shown by schizophrenic individuals and attempts to remedy them. Several subprograms are involved:

1. *Cognitive differentiation* During this phase, patients learn to discriminate stimulus categories by participating in perceptual tasks. They also learn to form concepts and to retrieve appropriate information.

2. *Social perception* Patients learn to recognize and respond to social cues accurately. They are asked to describe individuals displayed on slides.

3. *Verbal communication* This phase focuses on helping patients learn to understand and evaluate verbal statements. They learn how to have conversations with others.

1986). As Kane and Freeman (1994) have observed, "In patients who are already socially disabled by negative and deficit symptoms, bizarre behavior, and impaired social skills, the addition of embarrassing and stigmatizing involuntary movements of [tardive dyskinesia] is certainly an added obstacle to optimal adjustment in the community" (p. 28). In most cases, the symptoms persist and cannot be eliminated (Glazer, Morgenstern & Douchette, 1991).

The antipsychotic medications may also have some side effects that are reversible. For example, neuroleptics can produce Parkinsonlike symptoms, such as loss of facial expression, immobility, shuffling gait, tremors of the hand, rigidity of the body, and poor postural stability; these symptoms are usually reversible. *Akathisia* (motor restlessness) and *dystonia* (slow and continued contrasting movements of the limbs and tongue), which are also controllable, may appear as well. Patients have described a variety of reactions to the medication: "I feel restless; I cannot keep still; my nerves are jumpy; I feel like jumping out of my skin; my legs just want to keep moving; it's like having ants in my pants" (Sachdev & Loneragan, 1991, p. 383). Other side effects include drowsiness, skin rashes, blurred vision, dry mouth, nausea, and rapid heart beat.

Groups that support the concept of patients' rights argue that forced administration of drugs violates a person's basic freedoms. Yet hospital staff members fear that violent patients may be dangerous to themselves, other patients, and staff if they are not medicated. As the funding of state mental institutions has decreased, the use of medication has increased.

Should patients who admit themselves voluntarily for treatment be able to refuse antipsychotic medications? What about those who are involuntarily committed? Should the state, institution, or psychiatrist be liable for the development of permanent side effects among patients? Can an individual who is currently undergoing a psychotic episode give "consent" to being treated with antipsychotic medications? States and the mental health profession are wrestling with these issues.

4. *Social skills and interpersonal interventions* Patients develop skills for self-care and for coping with community living.

During these last two phases, intensive practice and role-playing are used to develop social skills. IPT has been shown to be more effective than placebo attention activities or routine care. Patients show improvement on tests measuring attention, have decreased scores on psychopathology, and lower hospitalization rates, as compared with control groups at eighteen-month follow-up periods (Brenner et al., 1992).

Interventions Focusing on Expressed Emotions

More than 50 percent of recovering patients now return to live with their families, and new psychological interventions address this fact. Rather than attempting to cure the disorder, most of these approaches try

Supportive counseling or other forms of psychotherapy can supplement drug therapy for schizophrenic patients. Once the patient's psychotic symptoms are under control, a therapist can try to help the patient improve his or her social and coping skills.

The Fountain House in New York provides a sheltered workshop experience for individuals with schizophrenia. Here, they can learn job and interpersonal skills that will allow them greater independence.

to reduce the likelihood of relapse and improve interaction between the patient and family members. These attempts take the form of a two-pronged strategy: (1) disseminating information about the disorder to families of schizophrenic patients and (2) teaching families and the schizophrenic member how to alter their communication patterns, which often includes expressed emotion (EE). In one program, high-EE and low-EE family members meet in a group to talk about specific themes, such as problems faced by families of recovering schizophrenic patients, methods of reducing guilt and responsibility for these patients, and healthy ways of dealing with the stress and frustrations of living with the patients. Vaughn and Leff (1981) and Kavanagh (1992) found that this format successfully reduced EE levels and reduced patients' relapse rates. Falloon (1992) found these procedures to be even more useful when individuals first begin to show symptoms suggestive of a schizophrenic episode. Family intervention approaches based on this model also successfully reduced the rehospitalization rate of male schizophrenic patients in China (Zhang et al., 1994).

It is important that the patient also develop social skills to recognize the emotional responses from family members and learn to respond appropriately (Liberman, Kopelowicz & Young, 1994). Training in family communication patterns should be combined with skills development for individual patients. The positive gains reported from treatment packages that include educating family members, altering communication patterns, and developing social skills and competencies in the patient give an impetus to psychosocial treatments. Family approaches and social skills training have been shown to be much more effective in preventing relapse than is drug treatment alone. Combining family and social skills approaches seems to produce the most positive result (Hogarty et al., 1991).

The combination of medication and the new psychological interventions has provided hope for many schizophrenic patients; continuing research points to an even more promising future. This optimism is reflected in the words of a young pharmacy student who has schizophrenia:

> It would probably shock many people to know that a schizophrenic was in their class, was going to be a pharmacist, and could do a good job. And knowledge of it could cause the loss of many friends and acquaintances. So even now I must write this article anonymously. But I want people to know that I have schizophrenia, that I need medicine and psychotherapy, and at times I have required hospitalization. . . . When you think about schizophrenia next time, try to remember me; there are more people like me out there trying to overcome a poorly understood disease. . . . And some of them are making it. (Anonymous, 1983)

SUMMARY

1. Much research and theorizing has focused on the etiology of schizophrenia, but methodological flaws and research design limitations restrict the kinds of conclusions that can be drawn. Using research strategies such as twin studies and adoption studies, investigators have shown that heredity does influence this group of disorders. The degree of influence is open to question, however; when methodological problems are taken into account, it appears lower than reported. Heredity alone is obviously not sufficient to cause schizophrenia; environmental factors are also involved.

2. The process by which genetic influences are transmitted has not been explained. Attempts to find specific biochemical or neurological differences between schizophrenic and nonschizophrenic people have not yielded many positive findings. The most promising area of research involves the relationship between dopamine (a neurotransmitter) and schizophrenia.

3. The search for an environmental basis for schizophrenia has met with no more success than has the search for genetic influences. Certain negative family patterns, involving parental characteristics or intrafamilial communication processes, seem correlated with schizophrenia. Recent studies have found that high expressed emotions (negative comments), or high EE, from family members are related to relapse in schizophrenic patients.

4. These disorders are most prevalent among people in low-status occupations who live in the poorest areas of large cities, and differences in symptomology seem to be loosely related to cultural variables. The effects of such sociocultural variables, however, are still open to speculation.

5. The research on the etiology of schizophrenia has thus suggested an interaction between genetic and environmental factors. The theoretical diathesis-stress model of schizophrenia considers personal vulnerability, which may be caused by hereditary, biological, or psychological factors. When the vulnerable person is exposed to strong environmental stressors but does not have the resources to cope with them, a schizophrenic episode may result.

6. Schizophrenia seems to involve both biological and physiological factors, and treatment programs that combine drugs with psychotherapy appear to hold the most promise. Drug therapy usually involves the phenothiazines, or antipsychotics. The accompanying psychosocial therapy consists of either supportive counseling or behavior therapy, with an emphasis on social skills training and changing communication patterns among patients and family members.

KEY TERMS

concordance rate The likelihood that both members of a twin pair will show the same disorder

diathesis-stress model A theoretical model postulating that a vulnerability to a disorder, either inherited or acquired, combines with the impact of stressors to produce the disorder

dopamine hypothesis The suggestion that schizophrenia may result from excess dopamine activity at certain synaptic sites

double-bind theory The suggestion that schizophrenia develops as a result of repeated experiences that the preschizophrenic child has with one or more family members (usually the mother and father) in which the child receives contradictory messages

expressed emotion A type of negative communication pattern found in some families with schizophrenic members that is associated with higher relapse rates

milieu therapy A therapy program in which the hospital environment operates as a community and patients exercise a wide range of responsibility, helping to make decisions and to manage wards

neuroleptics Antipsychotic drugs that can help treat symptoms of schizophrenia but can produce undesirable side effects, such as symptoms that mimic neurological disorders

prospective study A long-term study of a group of people, beginning before the onset of a disorder, to allow investigators to see how a disorder develops

schizophrenogenic Causing or producing schizophrenia; a term generally used to describe a parent who is simultaneously or alternately cold and overprotecting, rejecting and dominating

CHAPTER 15

COGNITIVE DISORDERS

n the ring, Muhammad Ali was able to "float like a butterfly, sting like a bee" as he won, lost, and twice regained the world heavyweight boxing championship. Outside the ring he was known for his ego, his wit and rapid-fire speech, and his never-ending rhyming. But it was a different Muhammad Ali who, at age fifty-four and retired from boxing, visited Cuba to donate medicine and supplies on behalf of two American relief organizations. His hands trembled and he could barely speak. He tended to shuffle when he walked; he often seemed remote and expressionless, constantly felt tired, and suffered occasional lapses of memory. Ali often spoke through hand signals that were translated by his wife.

Ali's symptoms resemble those of Parkinson's disease, a brain disorder, but his doctors ruled out that possibility. His disorder was diagnosed as Parkinson's syndrome, meaning that he has many symptoms of Parkinson's disease although he does not have the disorder. Ali's symptoms are probably due to some sort of brain trauma. Anti-Parkinson's medication has reduced the severity of some of the symptoms, but the prognosis is vague.

> As his health has declined, Ali, 54, has been described as a sad figure, a man swallowed up by the body that once challenged the world like a piece of beautiful, controversial art. In fact, he has never been more heroic. All that is left is his humanity as he travels 250 days a year to promote good causes, Islam and peace. (Fainaru, 1996, p. 2)

Like many other individuals, Ali suffers from a **cognitive disorder**—behavioral disturbances that result from transient or permanent damage to the brain. DSM-IV (American Psychiatric Association, 1994) characterizes them as disorders that affect thinking processes, memory, consciousness, perception, and so on and that are caused by brain dysfunction. Psychiatric conditions with associated cognitive symptoms (such as schizophrenia) are not considered in this category or in this chapter.

DSM-IV classifies cognitive disorders (formerly called organic mental syndromes and organic disorders) into four major categories: (1) delirium, (2) dementia, (3) amnestic disorders, and (4) other cognitive disorders (see the disorders chart on p. 440). It also attempts to specify the etiological agent for each disorder.

To some extent, the diagnosis of a cognitive disorder is a process of elimination. For example, delirium is a syndrome in which someone shows a disturbance of consciousness, an inability to maintain attention, memory problems, disorientation, and so on. When the delirium cannot be attributed to another mental disorder (such as a mood disorder) and there is evidence that a general medical condition such as disease or brain trauma is related to the disturbance, it is considered a cognitive disorder. The category of cognitive disorders is somewhat arbitrary because other mental disorders may be associated with cognitive dysfunctions and organic involvement. As you will see, it is often difficult to measure and assess, as well as to discern, the exact causes of the cognitive disorders.

Possible causes of cognitive disorders include aging, trauma, infection, loss of blood supply, substance abuse, and various biochemical imbalances. These may result in cognitive, emotional, and behavioral symptoms that can resemble the symptoms of the mental disorders discussed in preceding chapters.

The overall prevalence of cognitive disorders as found by the ECA study (the largest epidemiological study conducted in the United States) is about 1 percent for severe disorders and 6 percent for mild disorders (George et al., 1991). The study also indicated that prevalence increases with age—for example, the severe cognitive impairment rate for persons aged 75 and older is about 22 times higher than that for persons between the ages of 18 and 34. Gender differences were not meaningful, but one ethnic difference was—African Americans have a higher rate of severe cognitive disorders than is found among either Whites or Hispanic Americans (see Figure 15.1).

Although behavioral disturbance stems from brain pathology, it is influenced by social and psychological factors as well as by the specific pathology. People with similar types of brain damage may behave quite differently, depending on their premorbid personalities, their coping skills, and the availability of such resources as family support systems. Furthermore, people with cognitive impairments often are treated insensitively by other people, so they experience a lot of stress. This stress may add to or modify the symptoms that stem from the disorder.

Physical, social, and psychological factors, therefore, interact in complicated ways to produce the behaviors

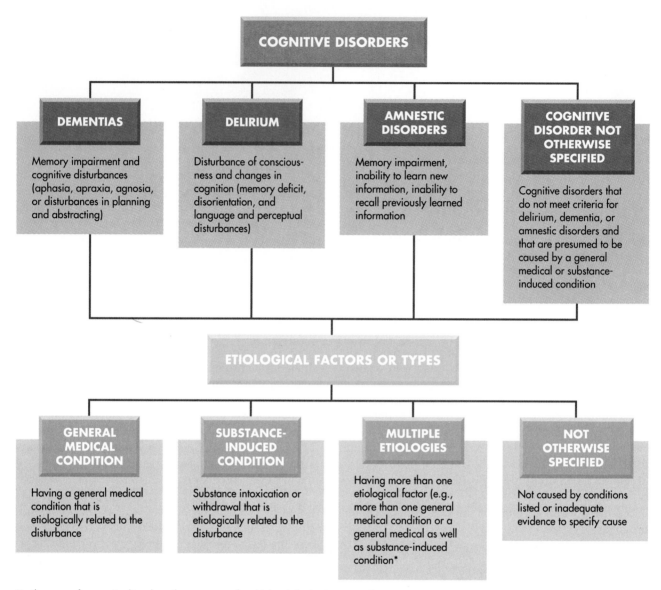

*In the case of amnestic disorders, the category of multiple etiologies is not used.

of people who have cognitive disorders (Binder, 1988). Treatment, too, often requires some combination of physical, medicinal, and psychological therapy; it may include behavior modification and skills training. For some patients who have severe and irreversible brain damage, the only available options may be rehabilitation, modified skills training, and the creation of a supportive environment.

Because the structure of the human brain was discussed in Chapter 2, this chapter focuses primarily on the major causes of cognitive disorders. Before presenting types of cognitive disorders, etiology, and treatment considerations, we will examine some ways to assess brain damage.

THE ASSESSMENT OF BRAIN DAMAGE

Two types of techniques are used to assess brain damage, and both were discussed in Chapter 3. The first consists of psychological tests and inventories that require behavioral responses from the patient and that assess functions such as memory and manual dexterity. These tests are becoming quite sophisticated, in that theories from neuropsychological science and quantitative methods are being applied to find a means to assess brain pathology (Meier, 1992).

The second type of assessment tool is that of neurological tests, which permit more direct monitoring of brain functioning and structure. Using these tools,

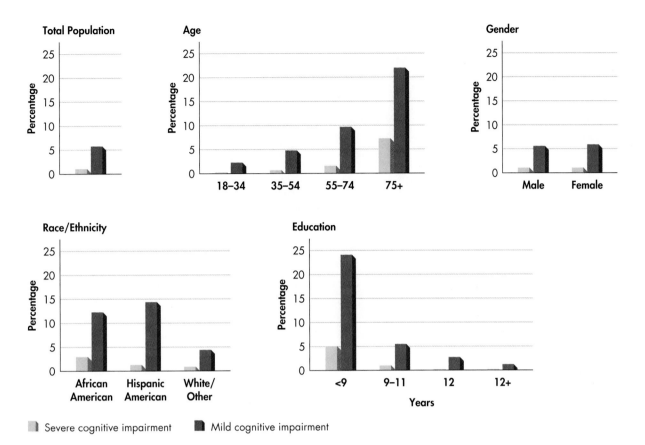

Severe cognitive impairment   Mild cognitive impairment

FIGURE 15.1 **Prevalence of Cognitive Impairment by Demographic Characteristics** Results indicate the prevalence of mild or severe cognitive impairment according to age, gender, race/ethnicity, and educational level. As can be seen, older, as compared to younger, individuals are far more likely to suffer from severe as well as mild cognitive impairment. Whites have lower rates of impairment than do other ethnic groups, and more highly educated persons have lower rates than do less educated persons. Gender appears to be largely unrelated to the prevalence of cognitive impairment. Respondents were administered a cognitive examination as part of the ECA study of adult Americans. Impairment was calculated on the basis of errors occurring during the examination or refusal to answer items on the examination.

Source: Data from George et al., 1991.

researchers and diagnosticians can "look into" the living brain and see evidence of its functions. For example, the **electroencephalograph (EEG)** measures electrical activity of brain cells. **Computerized axial tomography (CAT)** scanning assesses brain damage by means of X-rays and computer technology. Two additional techniques monitor a radioactive substance as it moves through the brain (Boller, Kim & Detre, 1984). In **cerebral blood flow measurement,** the patient inhales a radioactive gas, and a gamma ray camera tracks the gas—and thus the flow of blood—as it moves throughout the brain. In **positron emission tomography (PET),** the patient is injected with radioac-

tive glucose, and the metabolism of glucose in the patient's brain is monitored. This method provides a very accurate means of assessing brain function. A fifth technique produces snapshots of brain anatomy that have striking resolution, almost like a photograph with the skull removed—except that it is accomplished without surgery, exposure to X-rays (as in CAT scans), or ingesting radioactive materials (as in PET scans). In **magnetic resonance imaging (MRI),** the patient is placed in a magnetic field and radio waves are used to produce pictures of the brain. Anatomical areas of the brain are not obscured by bone because bone does not show in the MRI

Muhammad Ali, one of the greatest heavyweight champion boxers, suffers Parkinson-like symptoms, such as slurred speech, shuffling when walking, expressionless facial appearance, and occasional memory lapses. He is seen here in 1994 talking with some Vietnamese boxers at a sports center in Hanoi.

(Frumkin, Palumbo & Naeser, 1994). Each technique has strengths and weaknesses in terms of costs, benefits, and possible side effects (Margolin, 1991). Collectively, these techniques increase diagnostic accuracy in cases of brain damage.

In initial screening for cognitive disorders, clinicians may evaluate cognitive functioning by using the mental status examination (see Chapter 3) or simply asking a patient to give name and place of birth and to repeat phrases or write sentences that the clinician says aloud (Othmer & Othmer, 1994). At that time, and equally important, the clinician assesses the patient's general functioning, personality characteristics, and coping skills, as well as his or her behaviors and emotional reactions, particularly those that differ from reported premorbid functioning. Such an assessment can provide crucial information about brain dysfunction, and it is of utmost importance in planning treatment and rehabilitation.

Localization of Brain Damage

Neurological techniques such as CAT and PET scans and MRI help determine the location and extent of brain damage. But can the location of a damaged or disrupted area of the brain be determined from the type of function loss the patient shows? Neuropsychologists have debated this question for a number of years and have made many attempts to relate functions to specific areas of the brain.

In one study, researchers used CAT scans to examine eighty-seven patients, each of whom had a brain lesion (brain damage) that was localized within one of eight areas of the brain (Golden et al., 1981). Each area was then matched with the particular affected functions. The brain lobes (four in the cerebral cortex) are shown in Figure 15.2; the functions that they seemed to control are listed in Table 15.1. It should be noted that Table 15.1 is not intended to imply a simple one-to-one correspondence between a particular brain area and function.

Note the extensive overlapping of functions, which complicates the assessment of brain damage by determining functional losses. Moreover, as the researchers noted, "no two human brains are identical in appearance or in distribution of the functional organization of psychological skills. Although there are close approximations in most cases, it is not possible to find one-to-one correspondences for specific physical areas related to specific psychological functions from brain to brain" (Golden et al., 1981).

Two processes that may occur within the brain can further complicate the matching of function (or loss of function) with specific brain areas. The first, documented by many experimental and clinical studies, is **diaschisis,** in which a lesion in a specific area of the brain disrupts other intact areas, sometimes even in the other hemisphere.

A possible mechanism for diaschisis is the vast network of neurological pathways connecting the different areas and systems within the brain. These pathways, by which a "message" may be rerouted if it is blocked at a damaged area, may also explain the second process—the recovery of function after an area of

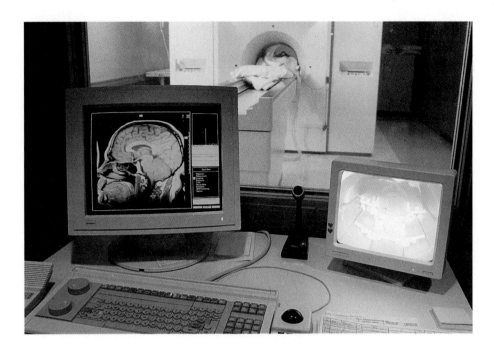

Magnetic resonance imaging can reveal an amazingly detailed image of a person's brain. MRI uses a magnetic field and radiowaves to make pictures of the brain. The pictures are not obscured by the skull because bone does not show through in MRI imaging.

the brain has been damaged. Other explanations for this recovery stress *redundancy,* in which an "unused" portion of the brain takes up the function of the damaged area, or *plasticity,* in which an undeveloped portion of the brain substitutes for the damaged portion. This plasticity would account for the development of language in young children who have left-hemisphere damage. For example, a five-year-old boy whose left hemisphere was removed (to stop his seizures) later developed superior language and intellectual abilities. Because the right hemisphere had not yet become fully specialized, it could develop the structure necessary to support language and intellectual ability (Smith & Sugar, 1975).

Nevertheless, some evidence shows that such a shift of function from one hemisphere to the other may decrease the functional space available for the development of other skills. One person who had left-hemisphere damage at birth did develop normal language ability; his visual-spatial memory, however, was impaired. The development of language may have required functional space normally devoted to visual-spatial ability (Bullard-Bates & Satz, 1983).

The Dimensions of Brain Damage

Brain damage can be evaluated along a continuum of degree, from mild to moderate to severe. In addition, clinicians often use three sets of distinctions in their evaluations: endogenous versus exogenous causes, diffuse versus specific damage, and acute versus chronic conditions.

Endogenous brain damage is caused by something within the person; for example, by loss of blood flow to the brain, which deprives neural tissue of vital oxygen. *Exogenous* brain damage is caused by an external factor, such as a severe blow to the head or poisoning.

FIGURE 15.2 **The Major Areas of the Brain** Four major lobes of the brain are shown. The frontal lobe is located in the front part of the brain. The parietal lobe is found behind the frontal lobe, with the temporal lobe located below the parietal lobe. The occipital lobe lies in the back of the brain. In general, different functions are localized in different areas of the brain (see Table 15.1).

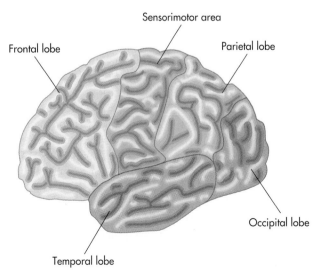

TABLE 15.1 Brain Areas and the Functions They Control

Left Frontal Area	Right Frontal Area
Expression via speech	Motor
Mathematics	Rhythm
Reception of speech	Mathematics

Left Sensorimotor Area	Right Sensorimotor Area
Expression via speech	Motor
Mathematics	Tactile

Left Parietal, Occipital Area	Right Parietal, Occipital Area
Mathematics	Tactile
Expression via speech	Motor
Writing	
Reading	

Left Temporal Lobe	Right Temporal Lobe
Reception of speech	Rhythm
Expression via speech	Motor
Memory	Tactile
Intelligence	

Source: Golden et al., 1981.

The diffuse-specific distinction helps indicate the extent of the brain damage. *Diffuse* damage is rather generalized; it typically involves widespread impairment of functioning, including disorientation, poor memory and judgment, and emotional instability. *Specific* brain damage is fairly localized, usually causing impairment or behavioral consequences that correspond only to the psychological or physiological function of the injured area.

An *acute* brain disorder is not accompanied by significant and permanent brain damage. A high fever or a severe bout of alcoholic intoxication can result in acute brain changes that are reversible and thus temporary. (Note, however, that the ability of the central nervous system to repair itself when damaged is extremely limited.) A *chronic* disorder involves permanent and irreversible brain damage—for example, as a result of the severe lead poisoning caused by a child's eating paint that contains lead.

People with chronic brain disorders may display similar symptoms, but impaired memory is usually the first noticeable sign of a chronic condition. Over time, the person may learn to compensate for many of the other symptoms.

Diagnostic Problems

As noted earlier, diagnosing cognitive disorders is problematic. People who have not suffered brain damage may be diagnosed as having a cognitive disorder. Deeply depressed people often show characteristics similar to those of individuals with cognitive disorders; in particular, the neuropsychological tests used to assess a wide range of functions (including language, cognition, motor functions, and visual-motor functions) were found to be subject to the effects of depression (Sweet, 1983). It is also difficult to distinguish brain-damaged patients from schizophrenic patients by using neuropsychological tests (Portnoff et al., 1983). If a client has symptoms of a mental disorder such as marked depression and if a general medical condition is related to the mood disturbance, the client may be classified as having a mood disorder due to a general medical condition.

Older people are particularly vulnerable to being inaccurately diagnosed as brain-damaged. An aged adult is more likely to perform poorly during assessment testing because of reduced sensory acuity, performance anxiety, fatigue, or failure to understand test instructions. For this reason, tests that differentiate between normal and brain-damaged young adults cannot be assumed to apply to older people. In a study of fifty retired teachers, many scored in the brain-damaged range on the Halstead-Reitan Neuropsychological Test Battery (discussed in Chapter 3), even though they scored in the superior range on the Wechsler Adult Intelligence Scale (WAIS) and functioned very well in their daily lives (Price, Fein & Feinberg, 1980).

To make sure that a particular set of symptoms is indicative of a cognitive disorder, clinicians usually try to determine whether the central nervous system has been damaged or whether a causal agent (such as a poison) is responsible for the symptoms. In some cases, support for a diagnosis of cognitive disorder can come from a patient's positive response to a treatment known to be effective against a particular disorder. For example, a diagnosis of Parkinson's disease is supported by the patient's response to treatment with L-dopa.

Another diagnostic problem is opposite in effect: People who have suffered brain damage may be diagnosed as having a psychological disorder. The following case is an example:

Larry D., age thirty-eight, was an energetic community college teacher and athletic coach and the happily married father of four children. During a particularly busy period, he suffered an apparent seizure while attending a professional conference. Just prior to the seizure, he reported smelling an unusual odor; he then temporarily lost consciousness. Medical evaluations following the episode revealed no obvious cause for Larry's loss of consciousness, and it was assumed to be due to a lack of sleep and general fatigue.

Although he did not pass out again, Larry began to show such symptoms as loss of appetite, difficulty in sleeping, fatigue, and some mental confusion. He became increasingly withdrawn, both from his family and from his professional activities, and he mentioned suicide several times. His family and colleagues became extremely concerned about his behavior. A mental health professional was consulted, and psychiatric hospitalization was recommended. But Larry's condition continued to deteriorate.

At this point, Larry's wife sought a second opinion from the neuropsychology clinic at a local university. The results of neuropsychological testing suggested brain dysfunction originating in the right temporal lobe of the brain. A CAT scan was performed, and a brain tumor was located.

In Larry's case, joint neuropsychological and medical assessment were able to pinpoint the cause of the disorder. Naturally, the course of treatment changed markedly once the brain tumor was discovered. In many cases, as here, an initial neuropsychological assessment or even the initial use of techniques such as CAT scanning may not yield information that clearly points to a brain impairment. For this reason, follow-up testing at regular intervals is often recommended. Such tests also allow the clinician to measure the patient's performance against a base rate to detect significant patterns of deterioration.

TYPES OF COGNITIVE DISORDERS

Four major cognitive disorder categories are listed in DSM-IV: dementia, delirium, amnestic disorders, and cognitive disorders not otherwise specified. In each, clinicians categorize the disorder according to its cause. In general, the causes are classified as due to a general medical condition, a substance-induced condition, multiple etiologies, or conditions not otherwise specified. For example, a client may be given the diagnosis of delirium. If the delirium is caused by the use of psychoactive substances, it is considered to be a case of substance-induced delirium. If the type of substance is identified, it is also specified.

In some cases, individuals also have symptoms of other mental disorders (such as a mood, psychotic, or anxiety disorder) in which there is evidence that the disorder is due to a general medical condition. In this case, DSM-IV lists the disorder within a category appropriate for the symptom pattern. For example, a mood disorder due to a general medical condition is classified under mood disorders, and an anxiety disorder due to a general medical condition is found under the category of anxiety disorders. Neither would be diagnosed as a cognitive disorder.

Dementia

Dementia is characterized by memory impairment and cognitive disturbances, such as *aphasia* (language

Jack Guren, an Alzheimer's patient living in a nursing home, is being visited by his son Peter. Alzheimer's disease is responsible for most cases of dementia among the elderly. Dementia is characterized by multiple and severe cognitive deficits, especially impairment of memory.

disturbance), *apraxia* (inability to carry out motor activities despite intact comprehension and motor function), *agnosia* (failure to recognize or identify objects despite intact sensory function), or disturbances in planning and abstracting in thought processes. The multiple cognitive deficits are severe enough to hinder social and occupational activities and represent a significant decline from a previous level of functioning. People with dementia may forget to finish tasks, the names of significant others, and past events. (The Focus On feature presents the case of an individual with aphasia.) Some people who exhibit dementia also display impulse control problems. They may, for example, disrobe in public or make sexual advances to strangers. Dementia is characterized by gradual onset and continuing cognitive decline.

Dementia can occur for numerous reasons. DSM-IV lists the major etiological categories for dementia as (1) general medical conditions (such as Alzheimer's disease, cerebrovascular disease, Parkinson's disease, brain trauma); (2) substance-induced persisting dementia, in which the symptoms are associated with substance use; (3) multiple etiologies, where more than one factor has caused the disorder (such as a general medical condition and substance use); and (4) dementia not otherwise specified, in which there is insufficient evidence to establish a specific etiology.

About 1.5 million Americans suffer from severe dementia and an additional 1 million to 5 million have mild to moderate forms of the disorder (Read, 1991). Although dementia is most often encountered in older people, only a small proportion of them actually develop this syndrome. Among people over age sixty-five, only 2 to 4 percent have dementia of the Alzheimer's type. (Alzheimer's disease is discussed in detail later in this chapter.) Other types of dementia are even less common. The prevalence of dementia increases with age, with a prevalence of over 20 percent or more in people over the age of eighty-five (American Psychiatric Association, 1994).

Dementia can also occur with delusions, hallucinations, disturbances in perception and communication, and delirium. If these features are predominant, they are noted in the DSM-IV classification.

Dementia is, in fact, associated with a range of disorders. Wells (1978) analyzed the records of 222 patients who displayed dementia as the primary sign, rather than a secondary sign, of a diagnosed disorder. The disorders associated with dementia included Alzheimer's disease, vascular disease, normal pressure hydrocephalus (the accumulation of an abnormal amount of cerebrospinal fluid in the cranium, which can damage brain tissues), dementia in alcoholics, intracranial masses, and Huntington's chorea. These findings have important implications for diagnosis be-

cause such problems as depression, drug toxicity, normal pressure hydrocephalus, and benign intracranial masses can be corrected. Identifying noncorrectable causes of dementia is also important because specific therapeutic intervention may reduce or limit symptoms in some cases.

Delirium

Delirium is characterized by disturbance of consciousness and changes in cognition (memory deficit, disorientation, and language and perceptual disturbances). These impairments and changes are not attributable to dementia. The disorder develops rather rapidly over a course of hours or days. The patient often shows a reduced ability to focus, sustain, or shift attention, and exhibits disorganized patterns of thinking, as manifested by rambling, irrelevant, or incoherent speech. At times there is a reduced level of consciousness and disturbances in the cycle of sleep and waking. The following describes a case of a student who was treated for amphetamine-induced delirium:

> An 18-year-old high-school senior was brought to the emergency room by police after being picked up wandering in traffic on the Triborough Bridge [in New York City]. He was angry, agitated, and aggressive and talked of various people who were deliberately trying to "confuse" him by giving him misleading directions. His story was rambling and disjointed, but he admitted to the police officer that he had been using "speed." In the emergency room he had difficulty focusing his attention and had to ask that questions be repeated. He was disoriented as to time and place and was unable to repeat the names of three objects after five minutes. The family gave a history of the patient's regular use of "pep pills" over the past two years, during which time he was frequently "high" and did very poorly in school. (Spitzer et al., 1981a, p. 36)

Among individuals over age sixty-five who are hospitalized for a general medical condition, about 10 percent exhibit delirium on admission (American Psychiatric Association, 1994). As in the case of dementia, delirium is classified according to its cause: general medical condition, substance-induced condition, multiple etiologies, and not otherwise specified.

Amnestic Disorders

Amnestic disorders are characterized by memory impairment as manifested by an inability to learn new information and an inability to recall previously learned knowledge or past events. As a result, confusion and disorientation occur. The memory disturbance causes major problems in social or occupa-

Aphasia: At a Loss for Words

The loss of motor or sensory functions that are associated with language is known as *aphasia*. Aphasic persons with motor disturbances may have trouble expressing themselves via verbal language (speech aphasia), may be unable to recall the names of familiar objects (nominal aphasia), or may have problems in writing words (manual aphasia). Sensory aphasias include the inability to understand spoken words (auditory aphasia) and the inability to understand written words (visual aphasia or alexia). Aphasic problems may be extremely specific. For example, persons with visual aphasia lose the ability to understand written words, although they have no difficulty in reading the words aloud or in understanding spoken words. Thus, impairment is manifested in listening, speaking, reading, and writing— although not necessarily to the same extent in each area (Chapey, 1994).

Two primary problems in aphasia are the loss of access to words and their meanings, and the inability to retain words and their meanings (Schuell, 1974). Persons with aphasia may become quite emotional and frustrated over their deficits, and this, in turn, can impede efforts at rehabilitation.

The following dialogue illustrates some of the problems involved in aphasia. Albert Harris is a 67-year-old man who suffered a stroke. In addition to physical therapy for his partially paralyzed right side, an effort was made to rehabilitate his speech. Mr. Harris was unable to communicate fully and expressed himself almost exclusively with the words "Mrs. Harris," his wife's name.

Psychologist: Hello, Mr. Harris.

Mr. Harris (responding to psychologist): Hello, Mrs. Harris. Hello, Mrs. Harris.

Psychologist: You look pretty cheerful today.

Mr. Harris: Yes, Mrs. Harris. Ah . . . Ah . . . Ah (apparently trying to elaborate on his response) . . . Yes, Mrs. Harris. Ah . . . Ah (looking disappointed and frustrated).

Psychologist: I know it's hard to say what you want to say.

Mr. Harris: Yes, Mrs. Harris, yes. Things will get better, Mrs. Harris.

Psychologist: You've already shown improvement, don't you think?

Mr. Harris: Mrs. Harris a little bit better, yes. Slow but sure, Mrs. Harris.

Speech therapy and skills training are frequently used to treat aphasia. Although many patients recover from the problem, the reasons for recovery are not well understood. It is possible that other areas of the brain can be trained to compensate for the damaged areas.

---

tional functioning and does not occur exclusively during the course of dementia or delirium. As in the case of dementia and delirium, the etiology is specified. The most common cause of amnestic disorders is Wernicke's encephalopathy, which is probably caused by thiamine deficiency (Conn, 1991).

All three conditions—dementia, delirium, and amnestic disorders—have overlapping symptoms, especially those involving memory deficits. Some important differences distinguish the three, however. In dementia, there is not only memory impairment but also conditions such as aphasia, apraxia, or agnosia. In contrast, the memory dysfunctions that occur in delirium happen relatively quickly, unlike those of dementia, in which functioning gradually declines. In delirium, there is also an impairment of consciousness. In amnestic disorders, the primary symptom involves memory. Figure 15.3 shows the unique characteristics as well as the overlap in cognitive symptoms for the three conditions.

Cognitive disorders that do not meet the criteria for dementia, delirium, or amnestic disorders would be classified as cognitive disorders, not otherwise specified.

ETIOLOGY OF COGNITIVE DISORDERS

Cognitive disorders can be caused by many different factors, and the same factor can result in dementia, delirium, or amnestic disorder. The sources of cognitive disorders discussed here are brain trauma; processes associated with aging, disease, and infection; tumors; epilepsy; and psychoactive substance-induced disorders. Toxic substances, malnutrition, and even brain surgery may also produce cognitive disorders.

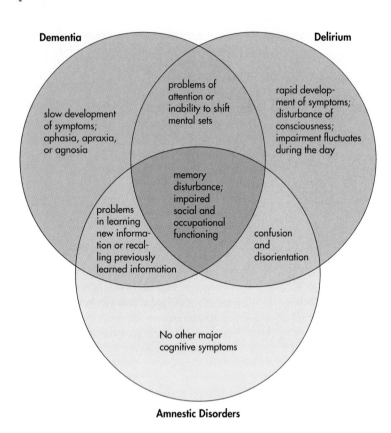

FIGURE 15.3 **Unique and Overlapping Symptoms in Dementia, Delirium, and Amnestic Disorders** Dementia, delirium, and amnestic disorders share some symptoms. The three overlapping circles show the unique and overlapping areas. The symptoms that occur in all three include memory disturbance and impaired functioning. Where the circles do not overlap, symptoms are largely unique. For example, aphasia and apraxia are exhibited in dementia but not in delirium or amnestic disorders. Confusion and disorientation are more likely to occur in delirium and amnestic disorders than in dementia.

Brain Trauma

On September 13, 1848, at Cavendish, Vermont, Phineas Gage was working as foreman of a railroad excavation crew. A premature explosion of a blast sent a tamping iron—a $3\frac{1}{2}$-foot rod about an inch in diameter—through the lower side of Gage's face and out of the top of his head. Exhibiting some convulsions and bleeding profusely, Gage soon regained speech. He was taken to his hotel, where he walked up a flight of stairs to get to his room. Remarkably, Gage survived the trauma, even though there must have been extensive damage to his brain tissue. Later, he appeared to have completely recovered from the accident with no physical aftereffects. However, Gage began to complain that he had a strange feeling, which he could not describe. Soon, his employers and others noticed a marked personality change in him. Although he had been a very capable employee prior to the accident and was known for his affable disposition, Gage now became moody, irritable, profane, impatient, and obstinate. So radically changed was Gage that his friends said that he was "no longer Gage." (Adapted from Harlow, 1868)

A **brain trauma** is a physical wound or injury to the brain, as in the case of Phineas Gage. The severity, duration, and symptoms may differ widely, depending on the person's premorbid personality and on the extent and location of the neural damage. Generally, the greater the tissue damage, the more impaired the functioning. In some cases, however, interactions among various parts of the brain, coupled with brain redundancy, in which different parts of the brain can control a specific function, may compensate for some loss of tissue.

Head injuries are usually classified as concussions, contusions, or lacerations. A *concussion* is a mild brain injury, typically caused by a blow to the head. Blood vessels in the brain are often ruptured, and circulatory and other brain functions may be disrupted temporarily. The person may become dazed or even lose consciousness and, on regaining consciousness, may experience postconcussion headaches, disorientation, confusion, and memory loss. The symptoms are usually temporary, lasting no longer than a few weeks. In some cases, symptoms may persist for months or years, for unknown reasons, without neurological signs of impairment (Binder, 1986).

In a *contusion,* the brain is forced to shift slightly and press against the side of the skull. The cortex of the brain may be bruised (that is, blood vessels may rupture) on impact with the skull. As in concussion, the person may lose consciousness for a few hours or even for days. Postcontusion symptoms often include headaches, nausea, an inability to concentrate, and irritability. Although the symptoms are similar to those of concussion, they are generally more severe and last longer.

More than 8 million Americans suffer head injuries each year, such as concussions, contusions, and lacerations. In order to reduce the risk of head injuries, individuals are advised to wear helmets while riding a bicycle.

Thirteen-year-old Ron G. was catcher for his school baseball team. During a game, one of the players from the other school's team accidentally lost his grip on the bat as he swung at a pitch. The bat hit Ron on the forehead. Although his catcher's mask absorbed some of the blow, the blow knocked Ron out. An hour elapsed before he regained consciousness at a nearby hospital, where he was diagnosed as having a cerebral contusion. Headaches, muscle weakness, and nausea continued for two weeks.

Lacerations are brain traumas in which brain tissue is torn, pierced, or ruptured, usually by an object that has penetrated the skull. When an object also penetrates the brain, death may result. If the person survives and regains consciousness, a variety of temporary or permanent effects may be observed. Symptoms may be quite serious, depending on the extent of damage to the brain tissue and on the amount of hemorrhaging. Cognitive processes are frequently impaired, and the personality may change.

More than eight million Americans suffer head injuries each year, and about 20 percent of these result in serious brain trauma. The majority show deficits in attention and poor concentration, are easily fatigued, and tend to be irritable (Webster & Scott, 1983). Personality characteristics may undergo change in the areas of motivation, subjective emotional experiences, or emotional expressions (Stuss, Gow & Hetherington, 1992). One study examined twenty-three patients with severe traumatic brain injuries (seventeen closed-head injuries, three penetrating missile wounds, two cerebral contusions, and one brainstem contusion)

who had spent an average of twenty days in a coma. Every one displayed a distress syndrome characterized by depression, anxiety, tension, and nervousness—yet they all denied having these feelings (Sbordone & Jennison, 1983). It is, in fact, common for patients with severe traumatic injuries to deny emotional reactions and physical dysfunctions until they begin to recover from their injuries.

Closed-head injuries are the most common form of brain trauma and the most common reason why physicians refer patients younger than age forty to neurologists (Golden et al., 1983). They usually result from a blow that causes damage at the site of the impact and at the opposite side of the head. If the victim's head was in motion before the impact (as is generally the case in automobile accidents), the blow produces a forward-and-back movement of the brain, accompanied by tearing and hemorrhaging of brain tissue. Epilepsy develops in about 5 percent of closed-head injuries and in more than 30 percent of open-head injuries in which the brain tissue is penetrated. Damage to brain tissues in the left hemisphere often results in intellectual disorders, and affective problems more frequently result from damage to brain tissues in the right hemisphere.

Severe brain trauma has long-term negative consequences. Many young adults who are comatose for at least twenty-four hours later experience residual cognitive deficits that interfere with employment and psychosocial adjustment. Recovery from the trauma often does not ensure a return to the victim's premorbid level of functioning. Along with any physical or

The proportion of elderly individuals in the U.S. population is growing rapidly. Increasingly, older Americans are staying healthy and active longer than previous generations. These women are receiving awards for their performances at the U.S. Senior Olympics in Baton Rouge, Louisiana.

mental disabilities produced by the brain damage, motivational and emotional disturbances result from the frustration of coping with these physical or mental deficits. As a consequence, only one-third of patients with severe closed-head injuries can return to gainful employment after traditional rehabilitative therapy (Prigatano et al., 1984).

In one treatment approach, intensive cognitive retraining is combined with psychotherapeutic intervention. This program provides patients with increased awareness and acceptance of their injuries and residual deficits, cognitive retraining to counter selected residual deficits, a repertoire of compensatory skills, and understanding of their emotional and motivational disturbance. When patients in this program were compared with patients in a traditional rehabilitation program, the former showed better neuropsychological functioning, greater improvement in per-

sonality traits, and greater success at work (Prigatano et al., 1984).

Aging and Disorders Associated with Aging

Before discussing the cognitive disorders often associated with aging, it seems appropriate to describe the nature of the older population. A growing proportion of the U.S. population, as well as the world's population, is sixty-five years of age or older (Powell & Whitla, 1994). This group numbered over 31 million of the U.S. population in 1990 (U.S. Department of Commerce, 1991), and by 2010 nearly 15 percent of Americans will be sixty-five years or older and 25 percent will be fifty-five years or older (Warheit, Longino & Bradsher, 1991). The increase is attributable both to longer life expectancy and to the relatively large numbers of people from the "baby boom" generation who were born in the 1940s and who will be elderly by 2010.

Some other characteristics of the population are also noteworthy (American Association of Retired Persons, 1985). First, women outlive men. In 1990, there were 149 women for every 100 men in the older population, as revealed in a 1991 report by the U.S. Department of Commerce. However, men were twice as likely to be married as were the women. Second, about one-fifth of the older population were poor or near-poor. Fully 89 percent were not working or seeking work. Third, statistics indicated that most older people have at least one chronic health condition and many have multiple conditions. The most frequent were arthritis (50 percent), hypertension (39 percent), hearing impairments (30 percent), heart conditions (26 percent), orthopedic impairments (17 percent), and cataracts and sinusitis (15 percent each).

The cognitive disorders most common among the elderly include stroke, Alzheimer's disease, and memory loss. These conditions are correlated with aging, but they also occur among younger people.

Cerebrovascular Accidents or Strokes Although the brain represents only 2 percent of the body's weight, it requires 15 percent of the blood flow and 20 percent of the oxygen (Oliver et al., 1982). A *stroke* or **cerebrovascular accident** is a sudden stoppage of blood flow to a portion of the brain, which leads to a loss of brain function.

Strokes are the third major cause of death in the United States, afflicting more than 400,000 persons annually. Only about 50 to 60 percent of stroke victims survive, and they generally require long-term care while suffering from a variety of mental and sensory-motor disabilities (Oliver et al., 1982). Stroke victims are often frustrated and depressed by their handicaps, and they show greater depression and interpersonal sensitivity than other groups of patients. At least one-fourth of stroke victims appear to develop major depression (Conn, 1991). Moreover, in many cases their depression seems to deepen with time (Magni & Schifano, 1984). Their anxiety about their disabilities occasionally leads to further disability.

The bursting of blood vessels (and the attendant intercranial hemorrhaging) causes 25 percent of all strokes and often occurs during exertion. Victims report feeling that something is wrong within the head, along with headaches and nausea. Confusion, paralysis, and loss of consciousness follow rapidly. Mortality rates for this type of stroke are extremely high.

Strokes may also be caused by the narrowing of blood vessels owing to a buildup of fatty material on interior walls *(atherosclerosis)* or by the blockage of blood vessels. In either case, the result is **infarction,** the death of brain tissue from a decrease in the supply of blood. These strokes often occur during sleep, and the person is paralyzed when he or she awakens. Approximately 20 percent die, 20 percent exhibit full to nearly full recovery, and 60 percent suffer residual disabilities (Lishman, 1978).

The residual loss of function after a stroke usually involves only one side of the body, most often the left. Interestingly, one residual symptom of stroke is a "lack of acknowledgment" of various stimuli to one side. For example, a patient who is asked to copy a pattern may draw half the pattern and may ignore the left side of his or her body (Golden et al., 1983).

Some functional reorganization of the brain may occur after a stroke to compensate for the loss of function. Three months after suffering a stroke owing to cerebral infarction, one patient showed significantly reduced cerebral blood flow in one area. An examination performed one year later showed no abnormalities. The pattern of blood flow, however, suggested increased activation in brain areas surrounding the affected area. It is possible that the patient's clinical improvement was due to brain reorganization in which the function of the destroyed area was taken over by other areas.

A series of infarctions may lead to a syndrome known as **multi-infarct dementia,** which is characterized by the uneven deterioration of intellectual abilities (although some mental functions may remain intact). The specific symptoms of this disruption depend on the area and extent of the brain damage. Both physical and intellectual functioning are usually impaired. The patient may show gradual improvement in intellectual functioning, but repeated episodes of infarction can occur, producing additional disability.

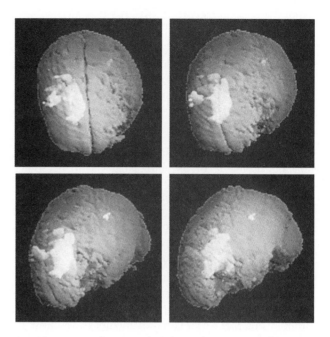

A stroke is a condition in which brain functioning is lost because blood flow to an area of the brain slows or stops. This stoppage is caused by burst or obstructed blood vessels. Shown are three-dimensional images of a brain stroke from four different angles.

Memory Loss in Older People   Memory loss is one of the most obvious symptoms of Alzheimer's disease, which we discuss in depth in the next section. A severe loss of intellectual functioning produced by brain cell deterioration can occur as a result of aging—usually after age seventy-five—although research indicates that age-related decreases in certain cognitive functions can be mitigated in cognitively active persons, such as professors who maintain intellectual activities (Shimamura et al., 1995). Loss of memory may also be shown by elderly people suffering multi-infarct dementia. And finally, occasional loss of memory is part of the normal aging process.

Because memory loss is associated with many disorders as well as normal aging, it is of concern to older adults and yet difficult for clinicians to assess. Consider, for example, the following letter:

Dear Dr. Smyer:

I have toyed with the idea of writing you ever since I heard you speak at the Presbyterian Church a couple of years go. The occasion was one of the series of brown-bag lunches sponsored, I think, by the Area Agency on Aging. You may remember me, since I'm sure you were embarrassed when I substituted one word for another in trying to ask a question about the part inheritance plays in senility. My question made no sense, and you tactfully said, "I don't believe I understand your question," and I repeated it, correctly, saying, "You can see I'm senile already." (I was trying to be funny, but I was not amused.)...

My question, Dr. Smyer, is this: Since I'm sure there must be ongoing research into the problem of senility, would it be of any value to such research if I volunteered as a test subject? At this point, my memory is failing so rapidly, and I suffer such frequent agonies of confusion, that I am at the point of calling on [my physician] for the [drug treatment] he has promised. But I don't want to do so yet if my experience can be of value to someone else, and particularly to the nine daughters of my sisters, ranging in age from 58 to 70, and to my own daughter, 42, who must be wondering if they too are doomed.

Is there any merit to this proposal? I will be most grateful for any advice you can give me. (Smyer, 1984, p. 20)

From her clear, lucid writing (as illustrated in excerpts from her letter) it is obvious that the writer is not suffering from senility. Yet her occasional lapses of memory are causing her to become worried. Smyer pointed out that complaints of memory loss must be examined in light of the person's perception of the event, concurrent factors such as depression or anxiety that might contribute to memory problems, and actual memory behavior. Gallagher and Frankel (1980) have stated their belief that if the Halstead-Reitan Neuropsychological Battery were employed, most normal elderly subjects would be incorrectly identified as brain damaged because no normative standards are established for their age group.

One of the most common reasons for memory loss and confusion in older patients is therapeutic drug in-toxication. People may take several medications that can interact with one another to produce negative side effects (Butler, 1984). Medication often has a stronger effect on older people and takes longer to be cleared from their bodies, yet dosages are often determined by testing on young adults only. In addition, cardiac, metabolic, and endocrine disorders and nutritional deficiencies can produce symptoms resembling dementias.

Losing cognitive and mental capabilities is the symptom of aging most feared by elderly people. One 82-year-old man commented, "It's not the physical decline I fear so much. It's becoming a mental vegetable inside of a healthy body. It is a shame that we can rehabilitate or treat so much of the physical ills, but when your mind goes, there's nothing you can do" (Gatz, Smyer & Lawton, 1980, p. 12). It should be noted that, in general, reports of intellectual decline in aging have been exaggerated. Although tests of intellectual functioning indicate that performance abilities generally start to decline with advancing age, verbal fluency and cognitive skills are relatively stable over time (Gallagher et al., 1980). Intellectual performance on knowledge acquired over the course of the socialization process is fairly stable, whereas fluid abilities (those abilities involving solutions to novel problems or requiring creativity) tend to decline with age (Poon & Siegler, 1991). Ivnik and colleagues (1995) have also found that stability depends on the particular cognitive ability being examined. About 75 percent of older people retain sharp mental function-

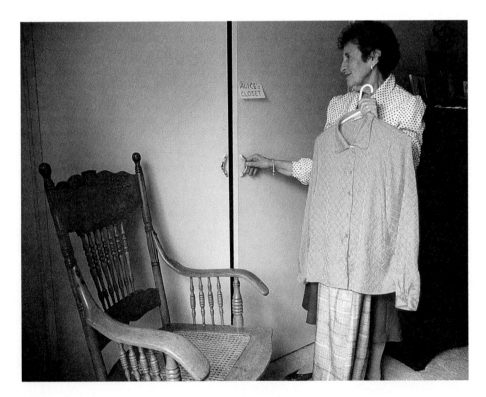

Memory is severely impaired in Alzheimer's disease. A person with the disease may need "reminders" in order to carry out simple chores, such as putting away clothes in a closet. Eventually, a person with Alzheimer's may not recognize loved ones.

CRITICAL THINKING

"Am I Losing It as I Get Older?"

Do you worry about memory loss in elderly individuals that you know or about your own possible memory loss as you become older? Concerns over memory loss as one becomes older are not simply negative stereotypes that younger people have about older people (Craik, 1994). Although age-related declines have often been exaggerated, cognitive performance does diminish with age, and many older individuals are afraid of memory loss. We know some things with certainty. Some cognitive and memory tasks are more likely to decline than others. Some individuals are more affected than others. Engaging in intellectual activities reduces the risk of cognitive decline. And the observed memory loss is a matter of degree—individuals can be placed on a continuum ranging from excellent memory to extremely poor memory as in the advanced stages of Alzheimer's disease.

An important task is to determine if memory loss is a "normal" part of aging or is caused by Alzheimer's disease. In other words, how can we measure and interpret memory loss that is associated with aging? Powell and Whitla (1994) have discussed assessment issues, citing the case of a 69-year-old professor who was concerned that her memory had deteriorated and that she was "losing it." She had difficulty recalling the names of new faculty, could not remember the room number of her classroom, and could not think of the name for the "thing you turn over eggs with." Has her memory deteriorated? How do we know? Some of the strategies to assess cognitive aging include:

1. *Population normative*—comparing a person's cognitive performance with that of the general population. In the case above, we would compare the 69-year-old professor's performance with that of the general population, young and old.
2. *Age-group normative*—comparing a person's cognitive performance with that of others of the same age. Using this approach, we would compare the professor's performance with that of other 69-year-olds.
3. *Reference-group normative*—comparing a person's cognitive performance with others of the same group. Using this tactic, we would compare the professor's performance to that of other faculty members.
4. *Previous functioning*—comparing a person's current cognitive performance with that in the past to see if changes have occurred. In this case, we would measure her present performance with her past performance.

What advantages and disadvantages do you see in each strategy? Is one particular method preferable to the others in trying to determine whether memory changes have taken place? If you were being tested for a cognitive or memory deficit, which would you prefer, and why would you prefer it?

ing, and an additional 10 to 15 percent experience only mild to moderate memory loss (Butler, 1984). Although the structures and biochemistry of the brain are affected in that brain cells and cerebral blood flow are reduced, many researchers nevertheless now believe that the extent of brain atrophy has been overestimated (Duckett, 1991). See Critical Thinking for a further discussion of memory loss.

Alzheimer's Disease

The disorder perhaps most often associated with aging is **Alzheimer's disease,** in which brain tissue atrophies, leading to marked deterioration of intellec-

tual and emotional functioning. It is one of the most prevalent forms of dementia, accounting for almost 80 percent of dementia in older persons (Teri & Wagner, 1992). We have become increasingly aware of the disease because public figures such as former President Ronald Reagan have candidly discussed their condition.

Characteristics of Alzheimer's Disease As noted, there is marked deterioration of intellectual and emotional functioning in Alzheimer's disease. Irritability, cognitive impairment, and memory loss are early symptoms that gradually become worse. Social withdrawal, depression, apathy, delusions, impulsive be-

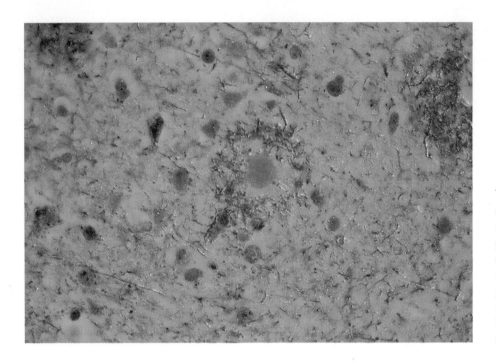

The diseased brain tissue from an Alzheimer's patient shows senile plaques (patches of degenerated nerve endings) located in the gray matter. Some researchers believe that the plaques may interfere with transmission of nerve impulses in the brain, thereby causing the disease's symptoms.

haviors, neglect of personal hygiene, and other symptoms may eventually appear as well. Death usually occurs within five years of the onset of the disorder, which is the fourth leading cause of death in the United States (Francis & Bowen, 1994).

> Elizabeth R., a forty-six-year-old woman diagnosed as suffering from Alzheimer's disease, is trying to cope with her increasing problems with memory. She writes notes to herself and tries to compensate for her difficulties by rehearsing conversations with herself, anticipating what might be said. However, she is gradually losing the battle and has had to retire from her job. She quickly forgets what she has just read, and she loses the meaning of an article after reading only a few sentences. She sometimes has to ask where the bathroom is in her own house and is depressed by the realization that she is a burden to her family. (Clark et al., 1984, p. 60)

The deterioration of memory seems to be the most poignant and disturbing symptom of Alzheimer's disease. The person may at first forget appointments, phone numbers, and addresses. As the disorder progresses, he or she may lose track of the time of day, have trouble remembering recent and past events, and forget who he or she is (Reisberg, Ferris & Crook, 1982). But even when memory is almost gone, contact with loved ones is still important.

> I believe the emotional memory of relationships is the last to go. You can see daughters or sons come to visit, for example, and the mother will respond. She doesn't know who they are, but you can tell by her expression that she knows they're persons to whom she is devoted. (Materka, 1984, p. 13)

Dorothy Coons, whom Materka quoted in the preceding lines, works at the University of Michigan Institute of Gerontology. She predicted that by the year 2000 as many as 4 million persons may be suffering from this disorder (Materka, 1984). The disease affects about 5 to 10 percent of those older than the age of sixty-five and about 20 percent of those older than the age of eighty (Fisher & Carstensen, 1990; Teri & Wagner, 1992).

Alzheimer's Disease and the Brain   Persons with this disease have an atrophy of cortical tissue within the brain, and there is currently no known cure. Autopsies performed on the brains of Alzheimer's victims reveal *neurofibrillary tangles* (abnormal fibers that appear to be tangles of brain tissue filaments) and *senile plaques* (patches of degenerated nerve endings). Both conditions are believed to disrupt the transmission of impulses among brain cells, thereby producing the symptoms of the disorder. Alzheimer's disease is generally considered a disease of the elderly, and its incidence does increase with increasing age. However, it also can attack people in their forties or fifties. It occurs more frequently in women.

Etiology of Alzheimer's Disease   The etiology of Alzheimer's disease is unknown. Many different explanations have been proposed. They include reduced levels of the neurotransmitter acetylcholine in the brain; repeated head injuries; infections and viruses; decreased blood flow in the brain; and other neural and physiological abnormalities (Read, 1991). Some researchers believe that aluminum is the primary cause because high concentrations of the substance have been found in the brains of Alzheimer's patients, increased concentration of aluminum in drinking water is associated with higher incidence of the disease, and aluminum has been experimentally found to pass through the blood-brain barrier, resulting in severe impairment of nerve cells (Yumoto et al., 1995). For a subgroup, heredity may be important. For example, the gene that appears to be responsible for senile plaques and neurofibrillary tangles found in Alzheimer's disease is located on chromosome 21 (Clarke & Clarke, 1987). Furthermore, early onset cases of Alzheimer's disease—those that occur before age sixty-five—may be caused by genetic anomalies (Mullan & Brown, 1994). Although abnormalities are found in the brains of affected individuals, it is not clear if the abnormalities are the cause, effect, or an accompanying condition of Alzheimer's disease. Of course, many different factors may interact to produce the disorder.

Other Diseases and Infections of the Brain

A variety of diseases and infections result in brain damage. As a consequence, behavioral, cognitive, and emotional changes occur (including the development of cognitive disorders).

Parkinson's Disease   **Parkinson's disease** is a progressively worsening disorder characterized by muscle tremors; a stiff, shuffling gait; a lack of facial expression; and social withdrawal. Dementia and depression may develop. It affects about one person out of a thousand, and slightly more men than women have the disease (Rao, Huber & Bornstein, 1992). Parkinson's disease is usually first diagnosed in people between the ages of fifty and sixty. Among persons over age 65, about 1 to 2 percent of individuals are afflicted with the disorder (Pfeiffer & Ebadi, 1994). In some persons, the disorder stems from causes such as infections of the brain, cerebrovascular disorders, brain trauma, and poisoning with carbon monoxide; in other persons, no specific origin can be determined. Some researchers (Kurth & Kurth, 1994) have proposed that genetic predisposition plays a role in the disease, although the evidence is not strong. Death generally follows within ten years of the onset of Parkinson's disease, although some patients have survived for twenty years or longer.

Parkinson's disease seems to be associated with lesions in the motor area of the brainstem and with a diminished level of dopamine in the brain. Some researchers have also found degeneration in the dopaminergic neurons (Tassin et al., 1994). Treatment with L-dopa, which increases dopamine levels, relieves most of its symptoms (Lishman, 1978). Muhammad Ali's Parkinsonlike condition has been treated with Sinemet and Symmetrel, which have the same effect.

AIDS (Acquired Immunodeficiency Syndrome)   The general public knows about the disastrous consequences of AIDS, or acquired immunodeficiency syndrome—the susceptibility to diseases, the physical deterioration, and death, often within several years of infection. Relatively few people, however, know that dementia may be the first sign of AIDS, as one person described in the following:

> It was frightening. It was terrifying. It was terrible headaches, months when I could only stand or lie down. I lost control of one side of my body. I couldn't write. I had lost fine motor control. I also had memory lapses. One time I was in a supermarket and suddenly I couldn't remember how I got there. (Joyce, 1988, p. 38)

Joyce (1988) noted that the vast majority of AIDS patients suffer from some form of dementia. The symptoms involve an inability to concentrate and to perform complex sequential mental tasks. The person may be unable to follow television or movie plots, may miss appointments, and may have hand tremors. Other symptoms include forgetfulness, impaired judgment, and personality disturbances such as anxiety and depression. After initial cognitive symptoms, progression to global cognitive impairment is rather rapid, usually within two months (Tross & Hirsch, 1988).

The dementia can be attributed to three factors. First, the AIDS virus itself reaches the brain at some phase of the infection and may lie dormant for a period of time (Baum & Nesselhof, 1988). When it becomes active, the virus can affect mental as well as physical processes. Second, because AIDS affects the immune system, AIDS-related infections may cause neuropsychological problems. A variety of chemical factors secreted during the course of an immune response may also cause changes in brain-controlled physiological processes (Hall, 1988). Third, depression, anxiety, and confusion can arise from simply knowing that one has AIDS, and experiencing negative reactions from others increases stress for AIDS victims (Kelly & Murphy, 1992). Medication to combat AIDS and its effects may also bring about side effects that influence cognitive functioning. Thus people with AIDS are at high risk for cognitive disorders.

Neurosyphilis (General Paresis)   Syphilis is caused by the spirochete *Treponema pallidum*, which enters

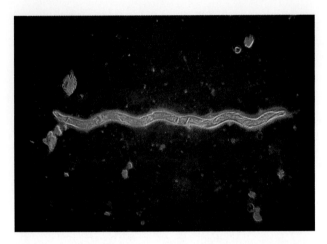

Individuals infected with the syphilis spirochete *Treponema pallidum* (shown here) who go untreated may eventually develop general paresis in which the brain or nervous system is damaged. Dementia and death are likely to occur.

the body through contact with an infected person. This microorganism is most commonly transmitted from infected to uninfected people through intercourse or oral-genital contact. A pregnant woman can also transmit the disease to her fetus, and the spirochete can enter the body through direct contact with mucous membranes or breaks in the skin. Within a few weeks, the exposed person develops a chancre, a small sore at the point of infection, as well as a copper-colored rash. If it is undetected or untreated, the infection spreads throughout the body. There may be no noticeable symptoms for ten to fifteen years after the initial infection, but eventually the body's organs are permanently damaged. In about 10 percent of persons with syphilis who are untreated, the spirochete directly damages the brain or nervous system, causing general paresis.

The most commonly described form of paresis, which includes approximately 18 percent of all cases, has grandiose characteristics: people display expansive and euphoric symptoms along with delusions of power or wealth. A depressive form has also been described, in which the affected person displays all the classic symptoms of depression.

The most frequent course for the illness begins with simple dementia, including memory impairment and early loss of insight. If the disorder remains untreated, the dementia increases, the occasional delusions fade, and the patient becomes quiet, apathetic, and incoherent. Paralysis, epileptic seizures, and death usually occur within five years of the onset of the disease's symptoms.

If syphilis is treated early, however, clinical remission occurs and the patient often can return to work. After five years of treatment, more than one-half of the patients with disorientation, convulsions, tremors,

and euphoria generally lose their symptoms (Golden et al., 1983).

Encephalitis Encephalitis, or sleeping sickness, is a brain inflammation that is caused by a viral infection and that produces symptoms of lethargy, fever, delirium, and long periods of stupor and sleep. Numerous different viruses can lead to encephalitis (Stacy & Roeltgen, 1991). It is not known whether the virus enters the central nervous system directly or whether the brain is hypersensitive to a viral infection at some other site in the body. One form, *epidemic encephalitis,* was widespread during World War I, but the disease is now very rare in the United States. It is still a problem, however, in certain areas of Africa and Asia.

Most cases follow a rapidly developing course that begins with headache, prostration (having to lie down), and diminished consciousness. Epileptic seizures are common in children with encephalitis, and they may be the most obvious symptom. Acute symptoms, as noted earlier, include lethargy, fever, delirium, and long periods of sleep and stupor. When wakeful, the victim may show markedly different symptoms: hyperactivity, irritability, agitation, and seizures. In contrast to past behaviors, a child may become restless, irritable, cruel, and antisocial. A coma, if there is one, may end abruptly. Usually a long period of physical and mental recuperation is necessary, and the prognosis can vary from no residual effects to profound brain damage (Golden et al., 1983).

Meningitis Meningitis is an inflammation of the *meninges,* the membrane that surrounds the brain and spinal cord, and it can result in the localized destruction of brain tissue and seizures. Research on meningitis is complicated because the disorder has three major forms: bacterial, viral, and fungal. In the United States, approximately 400,000 persons develop *bacterial meningitis* annually (Wasserman & Gromisch, 1981). This form generally begins with a localized infection that spreads, via the bloodstream, first to the meninges and then into the cerebrospinal fluid. *Viral meningitis,* which involves symptoms much less serious than those of the bacterial type, is associated with a variety of diseases including mumps, herpes simplex, toxoplasmosis, syphilis, and rubella. *Fungal meningitis* usually occurs in children with such immunological deficiencies as leukemia.

The symptoms of meningitis vary with the age of the patient. In neonates and young infants, the symptoms are nonspecific (fever, lethargy, poor eating, and irritability), which makes diagnosis difficult. In patients older than one year, symptoms may include stiffness of the neck, headache, and cognitive and sensory impairment. All three forms can result in the localized destruction of brain tissue and in seizures, but their incidence is much greater in the bacterial form than in the others (Edwards & Baker, 1981). The outcome is most serious when meningitis is contracted during the neonatal period.

Residual effects of the disorder may include partial or complete hearing loss as a result of tissue destruction (Berlow et al., 1981), mental retardation, and seizures (Snyder et al., 1981). Meningitis also seems to attack the abstract thinking ability of some of its victims.

Huntington's Chorea **Huntington's chorea** is a rare, genetically transmitted disorder characterized by involuntary twitching movements and eventual dementia. Because it is transmitted from parent to child through an abnormal gene, approximately 50 percent of the offspring of an affected person develop this disorder. Recently, scientists have identified the gene that causes the disease, so they are now able to better detect whether a person has inherited the disorder (Saltus, 1993). At this time, Huntington's chorea cannot be treated, so genetic counseling is extremely important in preventing transmission of the disease. However, with technological and scientific advances, researchers hope that the precise nature of the genetic defect can be discovered, leading to prevention and treatment of the disorder (Craufurd, 1994).

The first symptoms usually occur as behavioral disturbances when the person is between the ages of twenty-five and fifty, although some are afflicted before age twenty (Brooks et al., 1987). The first physical symptoms are generally twitches in the fingers or facial grimaces. As the disorder progresses, these symptoms become more widespread and abrupt, involving jerky, rapid, and repetitive movements. Changes in personality and emotional stability also occur. For example, the person may become moody and quarrelsome.

Woody Guthrie, a well-known folk singer and the father of Arlo Guthrie, also a well-known singer, was a victim of Huntington's chorea. His first symptoms were increased moodiness and depression. Later he developed a peculiar manner of walking, and he found it difficult to speak normally. His inability to control his movements was often blamed on alcoholism. On one occasion, his apparent disorientation, walking problems, and disheveled appearance prompted police to arrest him. When his wife sought his release, she was met by a staff psychiatrist who said, "Your husband is a very disturbed man. . . with many hallucinations. He says that he has written a thousand songs." His wife responded by saying, "It is true." The psychiatrist went on: "He also says he has written a book." Guthrie's wife responded, "That is also true." Then the psychiatrist delivered the coup de grace: "He says that a record company has put out

The gene for Huntington's disease was discovered by a team of researchers headed by Nancy Wexler. This discovery increases the likelihood that the disease can, sometime in the future, be prevented or treated. Wexler (on the left) is shown here with Mary Lasker in 1993 after receiving the Albert Lasker Medical Research Award for outstanding public service and achievement in research.

nine records of his songs!" The doctor's voice dripped disbelief. "That is also the truth," she replied (Yurchenco, 1970, pp. 147–148).

Huntington's chorea always ends in death, on the average from thirteen to sixteen years after the onset of symptoms. Early misdiagnoses are given in one-third to two-thirds of persons; schizophrenia is the most common misdiagnosis (Lishman, 1978).

Cerebral Tumors

A **cerebral tumor** is a mass of abnormal tissue growing within the brain. The symptoms depend on which particular area is affected and on the degree to which the tumor increases intracranial pressure. Fast-growing tumors generally produce severe mental symptoms, whereas slow growth may result in few symptoms. Unfortunately, in the latter case, the tumor is often not discovered until death has occurred in a psychiatric hospital. Tumors that affect the temporal area produce the highest frequency of psychological symptoms (Golden et al., 1983).

The most common symptoms of cerebral tumors are disturbances of consciousness, which can range from diminished attention and drowsiness to coma. People with tumors may also show mild dementia and other problems of thinking. Mood changes may also occur from either the direct physical impact of the tumor or the patient's reaction to the problem. Removing a cerebral tumor can produce dramatic results.

> The woman was admitted to a mental hospital, exhibiting dementia and confusion. She responded little to questioning by staff, or to attempts at therapy, even after twelve years of hospitalization. She would simply sit blindly, with her tongue protruding to the right, making repetitive movements of her right arm and leg. She also showed partial paralysis of the left side of her face.
>
> This "left-side, right-side" pattern of symptoms suggested that her condition might be due to a physical problem. Surgery was performed, and a massive brain tumor was discovered and removed. After the operation, the patient improved remarkably. She regained her speech and sight and was able to recognize and converse with her relatives for the first time in twelve years. (Hunter, Blackwood & Bull, 1968)

Epilepsy

Epilepsy is a general term that refers to a set of symptoms rather than to a specific etiology. In particular, **epilepsy** includes any disorder characterized by inter-mittent and brief periods of altered consciousness, often accompanied by seizures, and excessive electrical discharge from brain cells. It is the most common of the neurological disorders; 1 to 2 percent of the population has epileptic seizures at some time during their lives. About 2.5 million children and adults in the United States live with epilepsy or other seizure disorders (McLin, 1992). It also seems to be one of the earliest recognized cognitive disorders: Julius Caesar, Napoleon, Dostoevsky, and Van Gogh are among those who presumably were epileptic.

Epilepsy is most frequently diagnosed during childhood. It can be symptomatic of some primary disorder of the brain without apparent etiology, or it can arise from such causes as hereditary factors, brain tumors, injury, degenerative diseases, and drugs (Lishman, 1978). Epileptic seizures and unconsciousness may last anywhere from a few seconds to several hours; they may occur only a few times during the patient's entire life or many times in one day. And they may involve only a momentary disturbance of consciousness or a complete loss of consciousness—in which case they can be accompanied by violent convulsions and a coma lasting for hours. Alcohol, lack of sleep, fever, a low blood sugar level, hyperventilation, a brain lesion or injury, or general fatigue can all induce an epileptic seizure. Particular musical notes, flickering lights, and emotionally charged situations have also been known to provoke epileptic attacks. Even everyday stress can bring on a seizure (Devinsky, 1994).

Epilepsy can often be controlled, but it cannot be cured. Although people with epilepsy usually behave

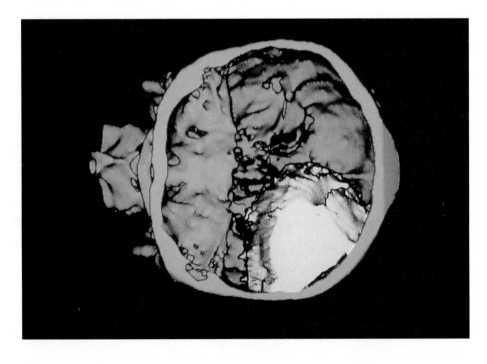

A cerebral tumor is an abnormal tissue growing within the brain. Symptoms depend on the size and location of the tumor. Some are fairly large, such as the one shown in this CAT scan. The most common effects of tumors involve disturbances in consciousness.

and function quite normally between attacks, their chronic, long-term illness is still regarded with suspicion and repugnance by much of society. An attack can be frightening to the afflicted person and observers alike. People with epilepsy face fear and anxiety resulting from the unpredictable nature of their seizures. They are embarrassed by their seeming lack of control over their illness and must deal with society's negative stereotypes concerning epilepsy. Perhaps as a result of these stereotypes concerning epilepsy, approximately 30 to 50 percent of people with epilepsy have accompanying psychological problems (Golden et al., 1983). We shall discuss four types of epilepsy. Each type is associated with a different type of seizure—petit mal, Jacksonian, psychomotor, and grand mal. Although terms such as *tonic-clonic seizures* and *primary generalized-partial seizures* are increasingly used (Devinsky, 1994), the four types give the range of different behaviors that are exhibited during seizures.

Petit Mal Seizures   *Petit mal* ("little illness") *seizures* involve a momentary dimming or loss of consciousness, sometimes with convulsive movements. During an attack, which usually lasts a few seconds, the individual stares blankly. Eyelids flutter, or slight jerking movements may be present, but in general there is little overall movement. After an attack, the person may continue whatever he or she was doing, unaware that a seizure has occurred and that there was a momentary loss of consciousness.

Petit mal seizures are usually seen in children and adolescents; they rarely persist into adulthood. The following description highlights a common problem among petit mal epileptics.

Jack D. is a sixteen-year-old student who was admitted to the outpatient psychiatric service of a large hospital to receive treatment for petit mal epilepsy. Jack and his parents explained that the seizures lasted only a few seconds each but occurred twenty to thirty times a day. His parents were especially concerned because Jack was very eager to get a driver's license; driving a car would be quite dangerous if he were subject to momentary losses of consciousness. Jack was interviewed at a case conference where a group of mental health professionals, medical students, and paraprofessionals discussed his symptoms, the etiology of the disorder, the prognosis, and treatment. During the fifteen-minute interview, Jack experienced two petit mal seizures. The first occurred while he was answering a question. A psychiatrist had asked Jack whether his seizures significantly handicapped him in school. Jack replied, "It really hasn't been that bad. Sometimes I lose track of what the teacher is . . . " At that point, Jack paused. He had a blank stare on his face, and his mouth was slightly opened. After about four seconds, he resumed speaking and said, "Uh,

Epilepsy refers to any disorder that is characterized by intermittent and brief periods of altered consciousness, often accompanied by seizures. It also seems to be one of the earliest recognized organic brain syndromes. Among those who suffered from the disease was Vincent van Gogh, shown here in a self-portrait painted sometime after he had cut off his ear.

writing on the blackboard." A psychologist then asked Jack if he had noticed that he had paused in midsentence. Jack answered that he was not aware of the pause or the brief seizure. Interestingly, several of those present at the case conference later admitted that they too were unaware that a seizure had occurred at that time. They thought Jack's pause was due to an attempt to find the right words.

Later Jack had another seizure that went unnoticed by most of the interviewers. While the resident psychiatrist was elaborating on a question, Jack appeared to be listening. But when the psychiatrist finished, Jack had a puzzled look on his face. He said, "It [a seizure] happened again. I was listening to what you were saying and suddenly you were all finished. I must have blanked out. Could you repeat the question?"

As you can see, such brief interruptions of consciousness may go unnoticed by people interacting with individuals undergoing a petit mal seizure—and sometimes by the individual also. Fortunately the prognosis for Jack was good. Petit mal seizures usually disappear with age and can be controlled with proper medication and treatment.

Jacksonian Seizures

Jacksonian seizures typically begin in one part of the body and then spread to other parts. For example, the hands or feet may first begin to twitch, then the whole arm or leg, and then other parts of the body. Usually the person does not completely lose consciousness unless the seizure spreads to the entire body. At this point, the convulsions resemble those of grand mal epilepsy. Jacksonian seizures are frequently due to a localized and specific brain lesion; surgical removal of the affected area can bring about recovery.

Psychomotor Seizures

About 25 percent of epileptic seizures are psychomotor (Horowitz, 1970). *Psychomotor seizures* are characterized by a loss of consciousness, during which the person engages in well-organized and normal-appearing behavioral sequences. For example, one person undergoing a psychomotor attack lost consciousness while he was mowing his lawn. During the next hour, he went into his house, changed into swim trunks, and proceeded to take a swim in his pool. An hour later, when he came out of the "trance," he did not recall how he had gotten into the pool. His last memory was of mowing the lawn. The behaviors can be a source of great embarrassment, such as disrobing at work (Devinsky, 1994).

The disturbance in consciousness typically lasts for a brief period of time, usually just a few minutes; occasionally, however, it may affect someone for days. Although it was originally believed that many people were prone to violence during such seizures, violence is actually quite rare. It has been exaggerated because of some reports in which violence was emphasized.

Some investigators have suggested that there is a relationship between psychomotor epilepsy and psychotic or schizophrenic behaviors (Glaser, Newman & Schafer, 1963; Stevens et al., 1969). The artist Van Gogh is supposed to have cut off his ear during a psychomotor attack. And the defense attorneys for Jack Ruby, who killed Lee Harvey Oswald (the alleged assassin of President John F. Kennedy), argued that Ruby had epileptic seizures and consequently was not responsible for his actions. But such accounts provide a misleading view of epilepsy. In only a very few cases have acts of violence been related to epileptic seizures.

Grand Mal Seizures

The most common and dramatic type of epileptic seizure is the *grand mal* ("great illness") *seizure.* Although this type usually lasts no longer than a few minutes, it typically consists of four distinct phases. A majority of people experiencing grand mal seizures report that they experience an *aura* (an unusual sensory experience that provides a warning of an impending convulsion) before the loss of consciousness. The aura lasts only a few seconds and signals the onset of a seizure. During this first phase, the person feels physical or sensory sensations such as headaches, hallucinations, mood changes, dizziness, or feelings of unreality. During the *tonic* phase, the individual becomes unconscious and falls to the ground. The muscles become rigid and the eyes remain open. During the third or *clonic* phase, jerking movements result from the rapid contraction and relaxation of body muscles. These movements may be so violent that the persons bruise their heads on the ground, bite their tongues, or vomit. Fourth and finally, the muscles relax and a *coma* ensues, lasting from a few minutes to several hours. When the individual awakens, he or she may feel exhausted, confused, and sore. Some people report that they awaken relieved and refreshed.

Grand mal attacks may occur daily or be limited to only once or twice during an entire lifetime. In rare cases, grand mal attacks may occur in rapid succession (a condition known as *status epilepticus*) and result in death if untreated.

Etiological Factors

As we have noted, the epilepsies have been attributed to a wide range of factors, including brain tumors, head injuries, biochemical imbalances, physical illness, and stress. Somehow these result in excessive neuronal discharge within the brain. Sometimes the discharge appears to be quite localized and results in focal seizures or twitching in isolated parts of the body. Generalized seizures are presumably caused by general cortical discharge, and the effects involve the whole body.

Some researchers have investigated the hypothesis that genetic or personality factors predispose people to epilepsy. Evidence has shown that the concordance rate for epilepsy is greater among identical than among fraternal twins, and that seizures are much more frequent among family members of a person with epilepsy than among unrelated people (Devinsky, 1994). However, heredity may not be a necessary or sufficient condition for the onset of epilepsy. With respect to personality factors, no single type of personality has been associated with epilepsy. Although personality disturbances are correlated with some cases of epilepsy, it is unclear whether personality factors predispose people to epilepsy or whether epilepsy influences personality development. Another possibility is that the person is under great stress because of the condition and because of the stigma attached to the disorder. This stress, rather than either the disorder or its causes, may affect the personalities of those who have epilepsy.

Use of Psychoactive Substances

Using psychoactive substances (see Chapter 9) can result in cognitive disorders (dementia, delirium, or amnestic disorder). The substances have effects on the nervous system. Most people diagnosed as having a cognitive disorder involving psychoactive substances also have problems concerning substance use. The most common psychoactive substances that can lead to cognitive disorders are alcohol, amphetamines, caffeine, marijuana, cocaine, hallucinogens, inhalants, nicotine, opioids, PCP, and sedatives.

TREATMENT CONSIDERATIONS

Because cognitive disorders can be caused by many different factors and are associated with different symptoms and dysfunctions, treatment approaches have varied widely. The major interventions have been surgical, medical, psychological, and environmental. Most treatment programs are comprehensive in nature, providing patients with medication, rehabilitation, therapy, and environmental modifications (see Cohen & Weiner, 1994). Surgical procedures may be used to remove cerebral tumors, relieve the pressure caused by tumors, or restore ruptured blood vessels. Psychotherapy may help patients deal with the emotional aspects of these disorders. And some patients who have lost motor skills can be retrained to compensate for their deficiencies or can be retaught these skills. Sometimes, patients with cognitive disorders need complete hospital care. We'll examine the use of medication and cognitive and behavioral approaches in more detail.

Medication

Drugs can prevent, control, or reduce the symptoms of brain disorders, as in the use of L-dopa in Parkinson's disease. Medication is of the most benefit in controlling some symptoms of cognitive disorders. For example, more than 50 percent of the people with epilepsy can control their seizures with medication such as Dilantin; another 30 percent can reduce the frequency of seizures. However, side effects can occur, such as a decrease in the speed of motor responding, tremors, weight gain, and swollen gums (Dodrill &

Matthews, 1992; Hauser, 1994). Only 20 percent of epileptics are not helped by the medications (Epilepsy Foundation of America, 1983). Sometimes medication is used to control emotional problems that may accompany cognitive impairment. Teri and Wagner (1992) have shown that antidepressant drugs can alleviate the depression found in many patients with Alzheimer's disease.

Cognitive and Behavioral Approaches

The cognitive therapeutic approaches appear to be particularly promising. As an example, researchers have hypothesized that the impaired attention and concentration shown by head-injured people result from the disruption of private speech, which regulates behavior and thought processes (Luria, 1982). One therapeutic program uses self-instructional training to enhance the self-regulation of speech and behavior (Webster & Scott, 1983). The program was used to treat a 24-year-old construction worker who had been in a coma for four days as a result of a car accident. Tests showed him to have poor recall, poor concentration, and attentional difficulties; he couldn't concentrate on any task for a long period of time. He also complained that intrusive nonsexual thoughts kept him from maintaining an erection during intercourse.

The patient was told to repeat the following self-instructions aloud before doing anything:

1. "To really concentrate, I must look at the person speaking to me."

2. "I also must focus on what is being said, not on other thoughts which want to intrude."

3. "I must concentrate on what I am hearing at any moment by repeating each word in my head as the person speaks."

4. "Although it is not horrible if I lose track of conversation, I must tell the person to repeat the information if I have not attended to it." (Webster & Scott, 1983, p. 71)

After he had learned to use these vocalized instructions (actually, he rephrased them in his own words), he was taught to repeat them subvocally before each task. His concentration and attention soon improved greatly, and he returned to his former job. He also successfully blocked intrusive thoughts during sexual intercourse by focusing on his partner. Such self-vocalizations often increase a person's effectiveness at the task at hand (Kohlenberg & Tsai, 1991).

A similar program was developed to eliminate the anger response brain-injured people sometimes display, either as a result of the brain damage or in reaction to their deficits. One 22-year-old patient had suffered a severe head trauma in a motorcycle accident at age sixteen. After two months of intensive medical treatment, he had returned home to live with his parents. There he showed outbursts of anger toward people and objects, a low frustration level, and impulsiveness. These behaviors led to many failures in a vocational rehabilitation program. Medication did not help control his outbursts.

A stress inoculation program was developed for this patient. Twelve 30-minute sessions, spread over three weeks, focused on the following areas:

1. *Cognitive preparation* The function and appropriateness of anger were explained, as were alternatives to being destructive. The situations that produced anger were identified, and appropriate responses were demonstrated.

2. *Skills acquisition* The patient was taught to stop himself from becoming angry, to reevaluate anger-evoking situations, and to use self-verbalizations that were incompatible with the expression of anger.

3. *Application training* A hierarchy of situations evoking anger was developed. The patient role-played and practiced the use of cognitive and behavioral skills to cope with progressively greater anger-evoking stimuli. He also used these techniques in the hospital setting and received feedback about his performance.

Before treatment, the patient had averaged about three outbursts each week. No outbursts at all were recorded immediately after treatment, and a follow-up five months later indicated that the gain had been maintained. He found a part-time job as a clerk and was living independently.

An interesting seizure prevention program using classical conditioning was reported by Efron (1956, 1957). For example, one woman, suffering from grand mal seizures, learned to prevent the occurrence of the tonic (body extended and stiff) and clonic (rapid alternation of muscle contraction and relaxation) phases by sniffing an unpleasant odor during the initial stage of an attack. The odor was first presented to the woman while she stared at a bracelet. After the smell was paired with the bracelet over a period of several days, the bracelet alone was enough to elicit thoughts of the unpleasant odor. At that point the patient could stop a seizure by staring at her bracelet when she felt the attack starting. Eventually she could cut an attack short by just thinking about the bracelet. Other behavior modification and biofeedback techniques have also been helpful in reducing seizure activity (Devinsky, 1994).

Environmental Interventions and Caregiver Support

The effects of many cognitive disorders are largely irreversible. This raises the issue of how family and friends can assist those with cognitive disorders. There are a variety of means by which people with these disorders may be helped to live comfortably and with dignity while making use of those abilities that remain. The following interventions have been proposed by Butler (1984):

1. To preserve the patient's sense of independence and control over his or her life, the environment must be modified to make it safer. Rails can be installed to allow the patient to move freely in the house. A chair that is easy to get into and out of, a remote-control device for the television set, and guard rails for the bathtub will help the patient do things for himself or herself. The patient should be encouraged to make as many personal decisions as possible—to choose which clothing to wear and which activities to take part in—even if the choices are not always perfect.

2. Continued social contacts are important, but visits by friends and relatives should be kept short so that the patient does not feel pressured to continue the social interaction. Visits should not involve large groups of individuals, which could tend to overwhelm the patient.

3. Diversions, such as going out for a walk, are important. It is better to stroll through a calm and peaceful area than to visit a crowded shopping mall, where the environment tends to be unpredictable.

4. Tasks should be assigned to the patient to increase his or her sense of self-worth. These tasks may not be completed to perfection, but they will provide a very important sense of having contributed. In addition, older people can be taught the use of memory aids and other strategies to facilitate remembering.

The family and friends who provide care may, themselves, need support (see the First Person narrative). They often feel overwhelmed, helpless, frustrated, anxious, or even angry at having to take care of someone with a cognitive impairment. They may

FIRST PERSON

Marie Smart

I have been a social service professional for more than two decades and have specialized in the care of the elderly and their families for almost half that time. For the past several years I have worked almost exclusively with families afflicted with Alzheimer's disease or a related disorder. I am a family counselor with the Sanders-Brown Center on Aging at the University of Kentucky and a member of the clinical care team of the Alzheimer's Disease Research Center there. We see patients and their families in the neurology clinic for the initial evaluation of a memory problem and then every six months for follow-up purposes. I am available on an as-needed basis to these families by telephone or in person in my office or their homes. My work with them involves helping accurately assess and evaluate the nature and extent of the dementia, educating the caregivers about their loved one's illness, and then providing ongoing counseling and support to these families as they live with Alzheimer's disease.

My role in counseling with these families is varied. For some of them, I am a "safe listener," the person to whom they can express their strongest feelings about the stresses of caregiving and know that it won't go beyond me. For these folks, often a good listener is the most they need. I have sessions with other family caregivers educating them about the disease itself and helping them identify different and hopefully more effective approaches to caring. With still other families, I am the mediator who helps them consider and appreciate the caregiving strengths of each member of the family and then works with them to develop an acceptable care plan that can include all of them. My counseling frequently involves helping families make difficult decisions—whether to move their loved one out of a lifelong home, how to get them to stop driving, when and how to take over money management tasks, whether to place them in a nursing home and if so, which one to choose. My goal is not to make decisions for these families but to help them feel secure about their ability to make their own decisions.

I am involved with an elderly couple who have been married for over fifty years. She has Alzheimer's disease and frequently now doesn't recognize "that man" who spends so much time with her. She calls their daughter at bedtime each evening to ask her about the appropriateness of going to bed with "that man." The daughter has learned to offer reassurance in words and concepts that work for her mother. She tells her mother that she thinks it's okay for the man to be there: He's very nice and polite, "He's cute and he has money." With that reassurance, this wife of fifty-plus years is able to relax and let her husband help her prepare for bed.

Then there is the son and his wife and their three teenagers who are caring for his mother. She lives in the home with them; her granddaughter gave up her room so "Granny" would have a room of her own. Granny has reached the point in her disease where she no longer understands how to use the different eating utensils. She can manage only a spoon. When this family gathers at the table for their meals, there is only a spoon at each person's place. They refuse to do something that might make Granny feel different or inferior.

Another couple with whom I work are much younger and have been devoted square dancers for a number of years. Though he now has Alzheimer's disease and often does not recognize his home or his wife or daughter, the husband can still dance. At those times when he becomes very agitated, his wife has learned to play their favorite square dance music. With that he begins to dance and his agitation is relieved. He doesn't miss a step.

We say at our Center that "when you've worked with one Alzheimer family, you've worked with *one* Alzheimer family." Every family has different strengths and needs. Some of them have developed coping skills that help them meet their caregiving challenges without what they perceive to be any great difficulty. Others of these families quickly learn new and previously unthought of ways to care for a loved one with a cognitive disorder. Other families aren't ever able to make the adjustments in their lives to cope successfully with the trauma of their diseases.

It is my privilege to provide support and education and counseling to each of these families. From them I receive support and education and reinforcement of my valuing of the elderly and their families.

Marie Smart is a family therapist at the Sanders-Brown Center on Aging at the University of Kentucky.

worry about how to take proper care of a loved one who has a cognitive disorder or feel guilty if the loved one gets injured or deteriorates under their care. Role relationships may change. For example, the role of parent and child may be reversed when a parent becomes disabled in that the child may now become the primary caregiver (Feldman et al., 1994). In all of these circumstances, caregivers should learn as much as possible about the disorder and the means of taking care of loved ones, realize that the role of a caregiver is stressful, and receive personal support (such as through self-help groups composed of other caregivers).

SUMMARY

1. Cognitive disorders are behavioral disturbances that result from transient or permanent damage to the brain. The effects of brain damage vary greatly. The most common symptoms include impaired consciousness and memory, impaired judgment, orientation difficulties, and attentional deficits. The effects can be acute (often temporary) or chronic (long term); the causes can be endogenous (internal) or exogenous (external); and the tissue damage can be diffuse or specific (localized). Assessing brain damage is complicated because its symptoms are often similar to those of functional disorders.

2. DSM-IV lists four major types of cognitive disorders: dementia, delirium, amnestic disorders, and other cognitive disorders. In dementia, memory is impaired and cognitive functioning declines as revealed by aphasia (language disturbance), apraxia (inability to carry out motor activities despite intact comprehension and motor function), agnosia (failure to recognize or identify objects despite intact sensory function), or disturbances in planning, organizing, and abstracting in thought processes. Delirium is a condition in which there is an impairment in consciousness with reduced ability to focus, sustain, or shift attention. Changes in cognition (memory deficit, disorientation, and language or perceptual disturbance) are observed, and the disorder develops rather rapidly over a course of hours or days. Amnestic disorders are characterized by memory impairment as manifested by the inability to learn new information and the inability to recall previously learned knowledge or past events. Finally, cognitive impairments that do not meet the criteria for the other three are classified as other cognitive disorders.

3. Many different agents can cause cognitive disorders; among these are physical wounds or injuries to the brain, processes of aging, diseases that destroy brain tissue (such as neurosyphilis and encephalitis), and brain tumors. Epilepsy is characterized by intermittent and brief periods of altered consciousness, frequently accompanied by seizures, and excessive electrical discharge by neurons. Psychoactive substances can also cause cognitive disorders.

4. Treatment strategies include corrective surgery and cognitive and behavioral training. Medication is often used, either alone or with other therapies, to decrease or control the symptoms of the various cognitive disorders. Caregivers can learn to provide assistance to loved ones with cognitive disorders.

KEY TERMS

Alzheimer's disease A dementia in which brain tissue atrophies, leading to marked deterioration of intellectual and emotional functioning

amnestic disorders Disorders characterized by memory impairment as manifested by inability to learn new information and the inability to recall previously learned knowledge or past events

brain trauma A physical wound or injury to the brain

cerebral blood flow measurement A technique for assessing brain damage in which the patient inhales radioactive gas, and a gamma ray camera tracks the gas—and thus the flow of the blood—as it moves throughout the brain

cerebral tumor A mass of abnormal tissue growing within the brain

cerebrovascular accident A sudden stoppage of blood flow to a portion of the brain, leading to a loss of brain function; also called *stroke*

cognitive disorders Behavioral disturbances that result from transient or permanent damage to the brain

computerized axial tomography (CAT) A neurological test that assesses brain damage by means of X-rays and computer technology

delirium A syndrome in which there is a disturbance of consciousness and changes in cognition, such as memory deficit, disorientation, and language and perceptual disturbances

dementia A syndrome characterized by memory impairment and cognitive disturbances, such as aphasia, apraxia, agnosia, or disturbances in planning or abstracting in thought processes

diaschisis A process in which a lesion in a specific area of the brain disrupts other intact areas

electroencephalograph (EEG) A neurological test that assesses brain damage by measuring the electrical activity of brain cells

encephalitis Brain inflammation that is caused by a viral infection and that produces symptoms of lethargy, fever, delirium, and long periods of stupor and sleep; also known as *sleeping sickness*

epilepsy Any disorder characterized by intermittent and brief periods of altered consciousness, often accompanied by seizures, and excessive electrical discharge from brain cells

Huntington's chorea A rare, genetically transmitted degenerative disease characterized by involuntary twitching movements and eventual dementia

infarction The death of tissue resulting from a decrease in the supply of blood serving that tissue

magnetic resonance imaging (MRI) A technique to assess brain functioning, using a magnetic field and radio waves to produce pictures of the brain

meningitis Inflammation of the meninges, the membrane that surrounds the brain and spinal cord; can result in the localized destruction of brain tissue and seizures

multi-infarct dementia Dementia characterized by uneven deterioration of intellectual abilities and resulting from a number of cerebral infarctions

Parkinson's disease A progressively worsening dementia characterized by muscle tremors; a stiff, shuffling gait; a lack of facial expression; and social withdrawal

positron emission tomography (PET) A technique for assessing brain damage in which the patient is injected with radioactive glucose and the metabolism of the glucose is monitored

CHAPTER 16

DISORDERS OF CHILDHOOD AND ADOLESCENCE AND MENTAL RETARDATION

he disorders of childhood and adolescence encompass a wide variety of behavioral problems, ranging from severe disturbances affecting many aspects of behavior to the less-severe developmental disturbances that are typically confined to a given area. Between 11 to 14 percent of the 63 million children and adolescents in the United States have a serious emotional or behavioral problem. The annual cost for treatment is more than $1.5 billion (Kazdin, 1993; Weisz et al., 1992). Fewer than 50 percent receive any form of treatment (Saxe, Cross & Silverman, 1988). Children and adolescents are, in fact, subject to many "adult" disorders discussed in previous chapters.

In this chapter, we discuss some of the problems that arise primarily during the earlier stages of life. We begin with severe disturbances that were formerly known as "childhood psychoses"; then we examine several less-disabling disorders of childhood and adolescence. Eating disorders tend to develop during adolescence and are also discussed in this chapter. We conclude the chapter with a discussion of mental retardation.

PERVASIVE DEVELOPMENTAL DISORDERS

The **pervasive developmental disorders** are severe childhood disorders in which qualitative impairment in verbal and nonverbal communication and social interaction are the primary symptoms. These disorders affect psychological functioning in such areas as language, social relationships, attention, perception, and affect. They include autistic disorder, Rett's disorder, childhood disintegrative disorder, Asperger's disorder, and pervasive developmental disorders not otherwise specified. The pervasive developmental disorders differ distinctly from the psychotic conditions observed in adolescents and adults. For example, the childhood disorders do not include such symptoms as hallucinations, delusions, the loosening of associations, or incoherence. A child showing these symptoms probably would be diagnosed with schizophrenia.

The impairments shown in the pervasive developmental disorders are not simply delays in develop-

ment but are distortions that would not be normal at any developmental stage. We begin our discussion with autistic disorder.

Autistic Disorder

Jim, currently twenty-nine years old, received a diagnosis of autism during his preschool years. His parents reported that Jim was not "cuddly." He would stiffen when touched and preferred being alone. Touching was not tolerated until the age of twenty-three. Jim found touching aversive because it produced soundlike sensations as well as tactile sensations. This was confusing to him. In talking about his reactions, Jim found it difficult to discuss sensations because he believed that his sensory and perceptual sensations were different from others. On responding to external stimuli he replied, "Sometimes the channels get confused, as when sounds come through as color. Sometimes I know that something is coming in somewhere, but I can't tell right away what sense it's coming through..." (Cesaroni & Garber, 1991, p. 305). Jim engaged in stereotyped movements involving rocking and twirling. He can now consciously control these behaviors, but they still occur when he is tired and not consciously aware. Any environmental change was very distressing to him. He strongly responded to the sale of the family car as the "loss of a family member." Jim feels different from others and is unable to understand social signals. He describes himself as "communication impaired." He is most comfortable when communication is concrete but not when different subjects or informal conversation occurs. Relationships are enormously difficult to form because of the communication problems. His inability to establish contact is reflected in his poem:

I built a bridge
out of nowhere, across nothingness
and wondered if there would be something
    on the other side.
I built a bridge
out of fog, across darkness
and hoped that there would be light on the other side.
I built a bridge
out of despair, across oblivion
and knew that there would be hope on the other side.
I built a bridge
out of helplessness, across chaos
and trusted that there would be strength
    on the other side.

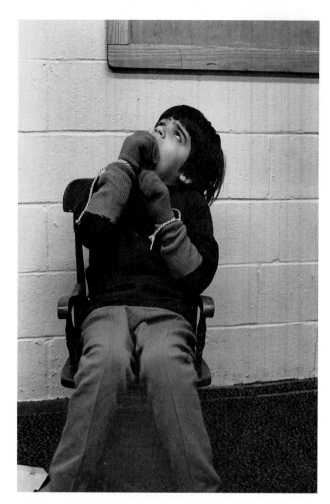

Children with autism have no interest in others and may exhibit self-injurious behaviors. Here a boy's hands are covered to prevent him from hurting himself.

I built a bridge
out of hell, across terror
and it was a good bridge, a strong bridge,
a beautiful bridge.
It was a bridge I built myself
with only my hands for tools, my obstinacy for supports,
   my faith for spans, and my blood for rivets.
I built a bridge, and crossed it,
but there was no one there to meet me on the other side.
(Cesaroni & Garber, 1991, p. 312)

In 1943 Leo Kanner, a child psychiatrist, described a group of children who shared certain symptoms with other psychotic children but who also displayed some unique behaviors. Kanner called the syndrome *infantile autism,* from the Greek *autos* ("self"), to reflect the profound aloneness and detachment of these children. A highly unusual symptom of autistic children is their extreme lack of responsiveness to adults: "The child is aware of people . . . but considers them not dif-ferently from the way he (or she) considers the desk, bookshelf, or filing cabinet" (Kanner & Lesser, 1958, p. 659).

The puzzling symptoms displayed by the children Kanner described fit the diagnostic criteria for **autistic disorder** in DSM-IV—qualitative impairment in social interaction and/or communication; restricted, stereotyped interest and activities; and delays or abnormal functioning in a major area before the age of three. Figure 16.1 illustrates some characteristics of autistic children. Autistic disorder is quite rare—about four to seven cases in every 10,000 children. It occurs three or four times more frequently in boys than in girls (Gillberg, 1992).

Impairments   The impairments found with this disorder occur in three major areas: social interactions, verbal and nonverbal communication, and activities and interests (American Psychiatric Association, 1994; Gillberg, 1992; Klin, Volkmar & Sparrow, 1992).

■ *Social Interactions*   Unusual lack of interest in others is a primary aspect of this disorder. Autistic individuals interact as though other people were unimportant objects, and they show little interest in establishing friendships, imitating behaviors, or playing games (Stone & Lemanek, 1990). As a result, children with autistic disorder fail to develop peer relationships. Disturbances may be displayed in body postures, gestures, facial expressions, and eye contact.

Autistic children appear to be unaware of other people's identity and emotions. Frith (1991) hypothesized that they lack a theory of mind, that they do not or cannot understand that others think and feel. This lack produces an inability to empathize with others. They appear not to need physical contact with or emotional response from their caretakers. For example, although autistic children are as likely as other children to smile when they successfully complete a task, they are much less likely to look at an adult to convey this feeling (Kasari et al., 1993). The social interactive component is missing. In one study (Klin, 1991), autistic, mentally retarded, and normally developing children could choose to listen to their mothers' speech or to the buzz of conversation in a cafeteria. The children in the two comparison groups all showed a strong preference for their mothers' voices. Autistic children were more likely either to prefer the buzzing conversation tape or to show no preference for either selection. Autistic infants are usually content to be left alone and do not show an anticipatory response to being picked up.

■ *Verbal and Nonverbal Communication* About 50 percent of autistic children do not develop speech. Those who do generally show oddities such as *echolalia* (echoing what has previously been said). One child constantly repeated the words "How do you spell relief?" without any apparent reason. In addition, the child may reverse pronouns. For example, "you" might be used for "I," and "I" for "me." Even when they can speak, such children may be unable to, or unwilling to, initiate conversations. Autistic children also use more nonsensical and idiosyncratic language than that of matched controls (Volden & Lord, 1991). Autistic individuals do learn to use a variety of gestures to communicate. However, they seem to lack those that reflect mental states such as consolation or embarrassment (Happe, 1994).

■ *Activities and Interests* Autistic children engage in few activities. They often have unusual repetitive habits such as spinning objects, whirling themselves, or fluttering or flapping their arms. They may show intense interest in self-induced sounds or in staring at their hands and fingers. They may stare into space and be totally self-absorbed. Minor changes in the environment may produce rages and tantrums. Autistic children show a lack of imaginary activities. They rarely engage in behaviors such as caring for a doll, talking on a "telephone," or pretending to drink from an empty cup (Atlas & Lapidus, 1987).

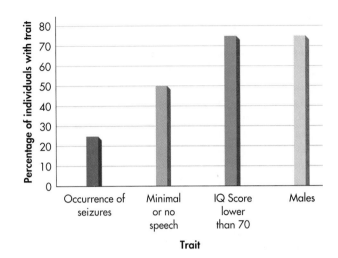

FIGURE 16.1 **Some Characteristics of Autistic Individuals** Biological factors appear to be implicated by the unique characteristics shown in autism.

Source: Data from Dawson & Castelloe, 1992.

As many as three-fourths of autistic children have IQ scores lower than 70. High-functioning autistic people such as Jim or the person played by Dustin Hoffman in the movie *Rain Man* account for only a minority of people with this disorder—about 20 percent—who have average to above-average intelligence (Freeman, 1993; Gillberg, 1988). In the past, some theorists, including Kanner, believed that children

Because autistic children have verbal language difficulties, nonverbal methods such as sign language have been tried as means of communication, with limited success.

with autism are unusually bright. They based their beliefs on two phenomena. First, some of them display *splinter skills*—that is, they often do well with drawings, puzzle construction, and rote memory but perform poorly on verbal tasks and tasks requiring language skills and symbolic thinking. Second, they often display unusual abilities. One Chinese boy with autism could identify the day of the week for different dates and convert the Gregorian calendar to the Chinese calendar. He also knew the lottery numbers and their drawing dates for the last three months; the titles of songs in the popular charts for the last ten years and their dates of release; and the numbers and routes of buses throughout the city (Ho, Tsang & Ho, 1991). Autistic children who score in the mentally retarded range on IQ tests but who have specific and unusual abilities have been described as "autistic savants."

Diagnosis Autism might seem to be easy to diagnose, given its unique characteristics. Yet questions have been raised about whether it is a distinct entity. Gillberg (1992) pointed out three problems in diagnosis: (1) many different medical conditions can produce the behavioral characteristics of autism, (2) the autistic symptom profile has been found in children with and without signs of neurological impairments, and (3) autistic disorder shares several characteristics with other disorders that involve social and communication impairment. In addition, symptoms can vary widely among autistic children, especially with regard to developmental age and level of functioning. Some

researchers (Brook & Bowler, 1992) believe that the degree of social impairment differentiates children with autistic disorder from children with other related disorders.

Because no specific etiological factor has been identified and because symptoms of the disorder overlap with other pervasive developmental disorders, there is confusion over when to use the term *autism*.

Autistic children are often diagnosed as only mentally retarded. Autistic symptoms may not be recognized. The two disorders often coexist. Still, there are ways to distinguish children with both autism and mental retardation from children with mental retardation alone. For example, children with autistic disorder exhibit splinter skills much more often than children with mental retardation. Also, children with mental retardation are more likely to relate to others and to be more socially aware than are autistic children with both autism and mental retardation.

Research on Autism Research on social unresponsiveness and the unusual communication patterns of autistic children tends to confirm clinical observations in some limited areas. For example, even very young infants can distinguish between male and female and between child and adult, an ability that suggests responsiveness and attention to social cues. Autistic children, however, have been described as more interested in inanimate objects than in human beings. Hobson (1987) was interested in this social unresponsiveness and wanted to find out if such children noticed people's age and gender. The researcher matched

Can good parenting prevent the occurrence of autism? Research seems to indicate that parents are not responsible for this disorder.

FIGURE 16.2   Where Will Sally Look? Most autistic children appear to be unable to understand the viewpoint of others and do poorly on experiments that focus on other people's thoughts and beliefs.

Source: Newsweek, Aug. 14, 1995, p. 67.

seventeen autistic and seventeen nonautistic control children, and exposed them to videotapes of nonhuman stimuli (bird, dog, train, and car) and videotapes of people (boy, girl, man, and woman), presented one at a time. Before, during, and after the videotaped presentations, the children were asked to match the object or person with five schematic drawings. Both the autistic and control children correctly matched videotapes of nonhuman stimuli with the schematic drawings at least 75 percent of the time. Yet on the videotapes involving people, autistic children were highly inaccurate in choosing the correct face, whereas control children continued to achieve 75 percent accuracy. Autistic children do appear to be unattentive to human characteristics. Another study found similar results. Autistic children did a better job of discriminating between pictures of buildings than between faces (Boucher & Lewis, 1992). They also had difficulty responding to people according to qualities, such as age or gender. Hobson cited an example of a middle-aged autistic man who talked to babies, children, and elderly people with the same style of speech. This lack of social attentiveness has been shown experimentally but the reason for this has not been found.

As mentioned earlier, some theorists (Baron-Cohen, Leslie & Frith, 1985; Tager-Flusberg & Sullivan, 1994; Frith, 1991) believe that individuals with autism lack a "theory of mind," that they are unable to attribute mental states to others or to understand that others think and have feelings. As Cowley (1995) described it, "Their worlds are peopled not by fellow beings with thoughts, feelings and agendas but by skin-covered bags that approach and withdraw unpredictably" (p. 67). They are unable to apply mental states to others resulting in an inability to lie, to deceive, or to understand jokes. Parents have said their autistic child "[is] embarrassingly honest,"

"wouldn't know what a white lie was," "tells jokes but they don't make any sense," and "knows you laugh at the end of [a joke]" (Leekham & Prior, 1994).

An experiment performed by Baron-Cohen, Leslie, and Frith demonstrated that autistic children were unable to recognize mistaken beliefs in others. The participants in the experiment were autistic children who were matched with a control group of normal four-year-olds and children with Down syndrome. The children were shown a scenario (see Figure 16.2) in which a character, Sally, hides a marble and then leaves the room. While Sally is gone, another child moves the marble to another container. Then Sally returns to get her marble. The children are asked where they think Sally will look for the marble. Approximately 86 percent of the control group children answered correctly. Sally would look at the place where she had hidden the marble. In the autistic group, however, only 20 percent of the children answered correctly. The remaining 80 percent chose the place where they knew the second child had hidden the marble.

Studies such as these are interpreted as indicating that autistic individuals are unable to understand that others think and have beliefs. This inability to appreciate other people's mental states appears to be long-lasting. Autistic children who showed this deficit displayed unchanged performance seven years later, even though their experience had increased (Holroyd & Baron-Cohen, 1993). Even when autistic children "pass" tests in identifying thoughts in others, they do not demonstrate the ability to apply this skill in real-life situations (Leekham & Prior, 1994).

Although we are learning more about the symptoms of autism, many questions remain. What causes the bizarre and puzzling abnormalities that are seen in children with autism? Why do they lack social responsiveness? After a brief discussion of other pervasive developmental disorders, we consider the causes, prognosis, and treatment of autism.

Other Pervasive Developmental Disorders

About 22 in 10,000 children show some but not all of the characteristics of autistic disorder, and they also show severe social impairment (Brook & Bowler, 1992). These children would receive a diagnosis from one of the new categories of the pervasive developmental disorders. The diagnosis may be Rett's disorder, childhood disintegrative disorder, Asperger's disorder, or pervasive developmental disorder not otherwise specified. Characteristics of these disorders often overlap with autistic disorder (see the disorders chart on page 473. Rett's disorder, childhood disintegrated disorder, and Asperger's disorder are new categories which appear in DSM-IV. Some psychologists question whether they should be considered distinctive disorders or merely variants of autistic disorder. Manjiviona and Prior (1995) believe, for example, that people diagnosed with Asperger's disorder are actually high-functioning autistic individuals. Gillberg (1994) argues that Rett's syndrome is a neurological condition, that some cases are characterized by autistic symptoms, and that it therefore should not be listed as a pervasive developmental disorder.

Little research exists on children with these diagnoses. To see the difficult diagnostic issues involved, consider the following case of a girl who was videotaped by her parents several times from birth to two years and seven months (Eriksson & de Chateau, 1992).

> During the first year of her life the girl showed normal development (smiled, laughed, babbled, waved bye-bye to parents, and played peek-a-boo). During the second year she spoke few words. She sat on the floor and played with a book in a stereotyped manner and showed little response to her parents. After two years of age, she was withdrawn, spoke no words except meaningless phrases from songs. She was preoccupied with rocking or spinning her mother's hair. Computerized axial tomography scans, magnetic resonance imaging, and electroencephalogram readings were normal. No physical condition was found to be associated with her condition.

Would you diagnose this child as suffering from autistic disorder or one of the following pervasive developmental disorders?

1. *Rett's disorder* This disorder is characterized by normal development for at least five months and an onset of symptoms between five and forty-eight months, including a marked delay and impairment of language and/or social skills. Stereotyped hand movements, poor coordination, and deceleration of head growth occur. This condition has been diagnosed only in females.

2. *Childhood disintegrative disorder* These disorders are characterized by at least two years of normal development in social relationships, verbal and nonverbal communication, motor skills, play, and bowel or bladder control, followed by severe impairment and deterioration in two or more of these skills. Other symptoms of autistic disorder develop (impairment in social interaction, interest, and communication, and repetitive stereotyped behaviors).

3. *Asperger's disorder* Children with this disorder have severe impairment in social interactions and skills, limited repetitive behaviors, and lack of emotional reciprocity. They show no significant delay in language and cognitive development.

4. *Pervasive developmental disorder not otherwise specified* This category is for cases that are not typical in terms of age of onset or specific behavior pattern. Pervasive and severe impairment in reciprocal social interactions occurs, as do communication abnormalities and limited interests and activities. These children do not, however, meet the full criteria for autistic disorder.

As you can see, diagnosis involving the specific pervasive developmental disorders is difficult, and the appropriate criteria for each is still evolving. Further research will help determine the usefulness of these categories.

Etiology

Little research has been done on Rett's disorder, childhood disintegrative disorder, and Asperger's syndrome since they are new to DSM-IV. Our discussion of etiology will therefore be confined to autistic disorder. There are four major etiological groupings in autism (Gillberg, 1992): (1) familial autism, (2) autism related to a medical condition, (3) autism associated with nonspecific brain dysfunction, and (4) autism without a family history or associated brain dysfunction. One very puzzling aspect of this disorder is that different factors are associated with different cases (Folstein & Rutter, 1988; Gillberg, 1992; Volkmar et al., 1988). How the syndrome of autism can develop from so many different conditions is not known. One important implication of the four sets of conditions is that no single cause for autism is likely to be found.

PERVASIVE DEVELOPMENTAL DISORDERS

Qualitative impairment in verbal and nonverbal communication and social interaction are primary symptoms.

AUTISTIC DISORDER

Qualitative impairment in social interaction (lack of eye contact, failure to develop peer relationships, lack of social empathy or reciprocity)

Qualitative impairment in communication (delay or lack of spoken language, inability to converse, idiosyncratic language, lack of play)

Restricted, stereotyped interest and activities (stereotyped movements, compulsive adherence to rituals, preoccupation with parts of objects)

Delays or abnormal functioning in one of the above major areas before the age of three

RETT'S DISORDER

Normal development for at least five months

Onset between 5 and 48 months
- Deceleration of head growth
- Loss of previously acquired movements and development of stereotyped hand movements
- Loss of social engagement (may regain later)
- Appearance of poorly coordinated movements
- Marked delay and impairment in language
- Diagnosed only in females

CHILDHOOD DISINTEGRATIVE DISORDER

Normal development for at least two years

Loss of previously acquired skills in two or more of
- Language
- Social skills
- Bowel or bladder control
- Play
- Motor skills

Qualitative impairment in social interaction

Qualitative impairment in communication

Restricted, stereotyped interest and activities

ASPERGER'S DISORDER

Qualitative impairment in social interaction

Repetitive, stereotyped interest and activities

No significant delay in language

No delay in cognitive development (appropriate self-help skills, adaptive behaviors, and curiosity)

PERVASIVE DEVELOPMENTAL DISORDER NOT OTHERWISE SPECIFIED

Severe and pervasive impairment in reciprocal social interaction or restricted, stereotyped interests

Does not fully meet onset age, specific behavior pattern, or other criteria for any specific pervasive developmental disorder

Because of the early lack of normal development and distinct social and cognitive deficits, researchers increasingly believe that autism results from organic rather than psychosocial factors. However, the earliest explanations for autism involved parent-child relationships.

Psychoanalytic Theories Psychodynamic theories of autism stress the importance of deviant parent-child interactions in producing this condition. Kanner (1943), who named the syndrome, concluded that cold and unresponsive parenting is responsible for the development of autism. He described the parents as "successfully autistic," "cold, humorless perfectionists who preferred reading, writing, playing music, or thinking" (p. 663). These individuals "happened to defrost long enough to produce a child" (Steffenburg & Gillberg, 1989). Kanner has changed his position and now believes the disorder is "innate."

Psychological factors are implicated in many disorders, but they do not seem to be involved in autism. Unfortunately, many mental health professionals continue to inflict guilt on parents who already bear the burden of raising an autistic child. Parents of autistic children show much stress and are particularly concerned about the well-being of their children after they can no longer take care of them (Koegel et al., 1992). In light of current research, no justification exists for allowing parents to think they caused their child's autism.

Family and Genetic Studies   Few family or genetic studies have been conducted on autism, and the studies that have been done are methodologically flawed. This is not surprising because the disorder is so rare.

About 2 to 9 percent of siblings of autistic children are also autistic, which is one to two hundred times greater than the rate found in the general population (Bolton et al., 1994; Ritvo et al., 1989; Smalley & Asarnow, 1990). These findings are supportive of some genetic influences. A well-controlled twin study was performed by Folstein and Rutter (1977). They recruited fraternal and identical twins, some of whom were discordant and some concordant. (That is, in some pairs both twins were autistic; in others only one twin had the disorder.) Identification as identical or fraternal was determined through blood analysis, and diagnoses were made without knowing who the twins' siblings were or whether the twins were fraternal or identical. The concordance rate for twenty-one pairs of twins was 36 percent for identical twins and 0 percent for fraternal twins. An interesting finding of the Folstein and Rutter study is that seven of the disconcordant identical twins showed some language impairment—one characteristic of autism. Some type of inherited cognitive or semantic impairment may be associated with autism (Brook & Bowler, 1992). Folstein and Rutter also believe that the diathesis-stress model could account for some of their findings. Among the seventeen disconcordant twin pairs, twelve cases involved a birth complication for the autistic twin. So a predisposition interacting with an environmental stressor may result in the disorder.

Central Nervous System Impairment   Autistic disorder appears to be a neurodevelopmental disorder involving some form of inherited brain dysfunction (Rutter, 1994). However, what is confusing is that autistic disorder seems to be associated with many organic conditions (Bolton et al., 1989; Ghaziuddin et al., 1992), none of which are specific only to autism. Conditions such as the fragile X chromosome (malformation of the X chromosome), tuberous sclerosis (a congenital hereditary disease associated with brain tumors), neurofibromatosis (tumors of the peripheral nerves), phenylketonuria (PKU), and intrauterine rubella (measles) have been reported among children with autistic disorder. These diseases affect the central nervous system, but most people undergo them without developing autism.

That so many organic conditions are associated with autism has caused some researchers to search for central nervous system impairment—possibly in the left hemisphere, which is associated with cognition and language. Results have been mixed. Researchers have reported some differences in brain structure between autistic and nonautistic individuals (Courchesne et al., 1988; Courchesne, 1995). For example, Hashimoto and his colleagues (1995) found that certain parts of the brainstem and cerebellum are significantly smaller in autistic patients than in members of control groups. However, other researchers found no difference in similar comparisons (Garber & Ritvo, 1992). An examination of the regional cerebral blood flow in autistic individuals also failed to reveal an abnormal pattern (Ghaziuddin et al., 1992). No consistent pattern of impairment has yet been found, which is perhaps to be expected, given the different subgroups of autism. Rutter and colleagues (1994) believe that some of the confusion is due to including samples of "atypical" autism and other pervasive developmental disorders in studies of autism. Each of these may have etiological components that differ from those of "true" autism. The etiological picture may become clearer once the distinctions among the different pervasive developmental disorders are accepted.

Biochemical Studies   Researchers are also interested in the role that neurotransmitters may play in autistic disorder. But the studies are difficult to interpret because they often use different intellectual and behavioral measures, and they may study different subgroups of autistic people (DuVerglas, Banks & Guyer, 1988). Nevertheless, some autistic children do have elevated serotonin and dopamine levels. Ritvo and colleagues (1984) reported elevated blood serotonin levels in a minority of autistic patients. The significance of this elevation is still not clear, but it suggests a promising line of research.

Prognosis

The prognosis for children with pervasive developmental disorders is mixed. Those with severe mental retardation have a poorer outcome. The prognosis is somewhat better for those who are considered high functioning with good verbal skills. Approximately 25 percent are able to function in a supported environment. Another 25 percent will be able to live independently, although social impairment continues (Freeman, 1993). In a follow-up of twenty-two high-functioning persons aged eighteen or older, six were competitively employed, thirteen were in supervised employment or in special school programs, and three were unemployed and not in school (Venter, Lord & Schopler, 1992). Some cases of highly significant improvement have been reported. Temple Grandin overcame the symptoms of autistic disorder to earn a doctorate in animal science and is now a recognized leader in the field of livestock handling (Ratey, Grandin & Miller, 1992).

Treatment

Because patients with these disorders have communication or social impairments, pervasive developmental disorders are very difficult to treat. Therapy with the parents, family therapy, drug therapy, and behavior modification techniques are all currently being used. Although they may improve social adjustment somewhat, overall success has been limited. Intensive behavior modification programs seem the most promising treatment.

Drug Therapy The antipsychotic medication haloperidol can produce modest reductions in withdrawal, stereotypical movements, and fidgetiness. However, long-term use produces movement problems and other side effects in many children (Gadow, 1991). Recently, fenfluramine has been found to increase attention span and decrease hyperactivity in some autistic children. This medication inhibits the uptake of serotonin by nerve terminals and blocks dopamine receptors (Campbell, 1988). Other studies, however, have found few positive effects of fenfluramine compared with placebos (Campbell et al., 1987). Treatment with medication has produced mixed results.

Behavior Modification Behavior modification procedures have been used effectively to eliminate echolalia, self-mutilation, and self-stimulation. They also have effectively increased attending behaviors, verbalizations, and social play through social interaction training (Oke & Schreibman, 1990; Plienis et al., 1987).

Young children with autism seem to make significant intellectual and language gains in early intervention programs. A follow-up study of autistic children treated by Lovaas (1987) using an intensive behavior modification program indicated that most of the children had improved and that about one-half obtained intellectual test scores in the normal range. Harris and colleagues (1991) also found that a one-year behavioral language intensive educational program for preschool autistic children resulted in average IQ score gains of 19 points.

Nevertheless, certain symptoms of social impairment generally remain. Even high-functioning adults with autistic disorder display problem behaviors involving inappropriate communication and poor interpersonal skills. One group of high-functioning autistic adults had problems obtaining employment because of behaviors such as rudely terminating or interrupting conversations, walking sideways, or waving arms in a robotlike fashion. Through behavioral interventions, these adults were able to become competitively employed, although some oddities of behavior remained (Burt, Fuller & Lewis, 1991).

OTHER DEVELOPMENTAL DISORDERS

How do we know whether a child has a childhood disorder? Such decisions are often based on vague and arbitrary interpretations of the extent to which a given child deviates from some "acceptable" norm. And, as some critics have observed, the decision frequently depends on the tolerance of the referring agent. Kanner (1960) pointed out that many childhood problems are transient and that "a multitude of early breathholders, nose-pickers, and casual masturbators" develop into normal adults. If a child is brought to a mental health clinic, the difficulties will be interpreted as "far out of proportion to their role as everyday problems of the everyday child." Cultural factors also play a role in the types of problems identified. In Thailand, where aggression is discouraged and values such as peacefulness, politeness, and deference are encouraged, clinic referrals are primarily for overcontrolled behaviors (fearfulness, sleep problems, somatization). In the United States, where independence and competitiveness are emphasized, problems generally involve undercontrolled behaviors (disobedience, fighting, arguing) (Tharp, 1991). Table 16.1 compares some problem behaviors reported by teachers in four different countries.

The less-severe childhood and adolescent disturbances cover a wide range of problems. We will now discuss some of the more common disorders, which include disruptive disorders and attention deficit hyperactive disorder, separation-anxiety disorders, tic disorders, eating disorders, and mental retardation.

DSM-IV also recognizes a variety of other childhood disorders, many of which focus on impairments or disturbed patterns in language development. These are summarized in Table 16.2.

Problems with Diagnosis

Has DSM-IV done much to improve the reliability and validity of the diagnosis of childhood disorders? Unfortunately, criticisms similar to those presented by Kanner remain. Guidelines for assessing the type of behavior and the degree of deviation necessary for a given diagnosis remain vague and depend on "clinical judgment." Controversy exists over the number or types of behavior that is needed for a diagnosis. If the diagnosis is too easy to make, false positives will

TABLE 16.1   Behavioral Symptoms Reported by Teachers of Children in Four Countries (in Percent)

Source	Rutter et al. (1974)				Minde (1977)	McGee et al. (1985)		Ekblad (1990)	
Year	1974				1977	1982		1984	
Place	England				Uganda	New Zealand		China	
Informant	Teacher				Teacher	Teacher		Teacher	
Age group (years)	10				7–15	7		11–13	
Population	Nonimmigrant		West Indian		Ugandan	New Zealand		Chinese	
Gender	Boys	Girls	Boys	Girls	Both	Boys	Girls	Boys	Girls
Number	873	816	172	182	577	491	449	139	127
Behavioral disturbances									
Hyperactivity	30.5	17.9	49.5	32.4	15.0	33.0	17.4	13.7	2.4
Tics, twitches	8.3	3.6	7.0	5.5	6.7	5.5	4.9	0.7	0.0
Nailbiting	17.5	14.7	13.9	10.4	7.2	3.9	6.4	7.9	1.6
Thumbsucking	5.1	6.4	2.9	8.2	3.8	4.9	7.4	7.9	0.0
Stuttering	8.2	2.4	10.5	1.1	5.8	5.3	2.7	2.9	2.4
Aggressiveness	24.3	13.9	51.7	34.1	12.8	22.4	14.9	19.4	3.9
Depression	18.5	15.5	26.2	31.8	19.4	11.8	15.6	6.5	2.4
Anxiety	32.5	30.0	32.0	25.3	17.2	36.0	31.6	5.0	0.8
Phobias	28.5	26.1	32.0	35.7	9.9	27.5	28.3	7.2	6.3
Lying	12.5	6.3	30.2	25.3	10.1	11.8	8.7	16.6	2.4
Theft	3.4	1.7	13.4	13.2	4.4	5.3	4.2	1.4	0.8
Truancy	5.6	1.9	5.2	1.6	7.3	1.2	0.4	4.3	0.0

Source: Ekblad, 1990.

Reports of behavioral symptoms vary according to country. Teachers of West Indian children reported the most aggression in their students, while teachers of Chinese students reported students to have few problems with anxiety.

occur, and children will be stigmatized. If the diagnosis is too difficult, individuals who need help will not be identified. The correct balance has been difficult to determine for many childhood disorders. The clinician must decide whether problem behaviors are present and then whether they are "excessive," "maladaptive," or "inappropriate" for the developmental level. Even mental health professionals have difficulty making such judgments. Whether a problem exists is often "in the eye of the beholder."

ATTENTION DEFICIT/HYPERACTIVE DISORDERS AND DISRUPTIVE BEHAVIOR DISORDERS

These disorders involve symptoms that are often socially disruptive and distressing to others (see the disorders chart on page 478). They include attention deficit/hyperactive disorders (ADHD), conduct disorder, and oppositional defiant disorder. These disorders often occur together and have overlapping symptoms. Without intervention, these disorders tend to persist

(Farmer, 1995; Fergusson, Horwood & Lynskey, 1995). In a longitudinal study of "hard to manage" preschoolers followed from age three until school entry and to age nine, 67 percent showed clinically significant problems at age six and met the criteria for one of the disorders in this category (Campbell & Ewing, 1990). The children displayed problem behaviors such as inattention, overactivity, and aggression, and they required supervision. Early identification and intervention are necessary to interrupt the negative course of these disorders.

Raising a child with a disruptive behavior disorder is difficult. Parents report more negative feelings about parenting, higher stress levels, and a more negative impact on their social life than do parents of normally developing children (Donenberg & Baker, 1993).

Attention Deficit/Hyperactive Disorders

Ron, an only child, was always on the go as a toddler and preschooler. He had many accidents because of his continual climbing and risk-taking. Temper outbursts were frequent. In kindergarten Ron had much difficulty

TABLE 16.2   Other Childhood Disorders

Disorder	Prevalence	Course	Etiology
Learning Disorders Achievement in reading, math, or writing below that expected for age, education, and intelligence level.	Approximately 5 percent of public school children. Reading disorders are more common in males.	Impairment is usually apparent by first or second grade. School dropout rate is higher than average. Early intervention is often successful.	Reading and other learning disorders are more common in first-degree biological relatives of individuals with learning disorders.
Expressive Language Disorder Impairment in communication, such as limited speech, poor vocabulary, or unusual word order that is not appropriate for the developmental age. May be developmental (no associated neurological condition) or acquired (result of a medical condition).	About 3 to 5 percent of children. Developmental type is more common in males and is usually identified by age three.	Fifty percent of development type grow out of it. Acquired type can occur at any age, and prognosis depends on severity of neurological problem.	Some evidence of family history of communication or language disorder in developmental type. No such evidence in acquired type.
Phonetic Disorder Failure to use developmentally appropriate sounds in language. May omit certain sounds in words or misarticulate certain letters (*l, r, s, z, th, ch,* and so on).	Approximately 2 to 3 percent of six- and seven-year-olds have this disorder. Milder forms are more prevalent.	Milder forms may recover spontaneously. More severe forms require therapy.	Family history found in some forms of phonetic disorder.
Stuttering Disturbances in the fluency of speech that is inappropriate for the developmental level. Often related to stress.	Approximately 1 percent of children. Males are three times more likely to receive the diagnosis.	Onset is generally between the ages of two and seven and is gradual. Most recover spontaneously before the age of sixteen.	Studies indicate some evidence of genetic factors.
Encopresis Repeated defecation in inappropriate places by child who is at least four years old. Usually involuntary.	Approximately 1 percent of five-year-olds; more common in males.	May recur intermittently; is rarely chronic.	Inadequate toilet training or psychosocial stress.
Enuresis Repeated urination into clothes or bedding. Usually involuntary.	Among five-year-olds, present in 7 percent of males, 3 percent of females	Usually begins by age five. Most remit spontaneously. Only 1 percent continue into adulthood.	About 75 percent have first-degree biological relative with the same disorder.

Source: Based on DSM-IV.

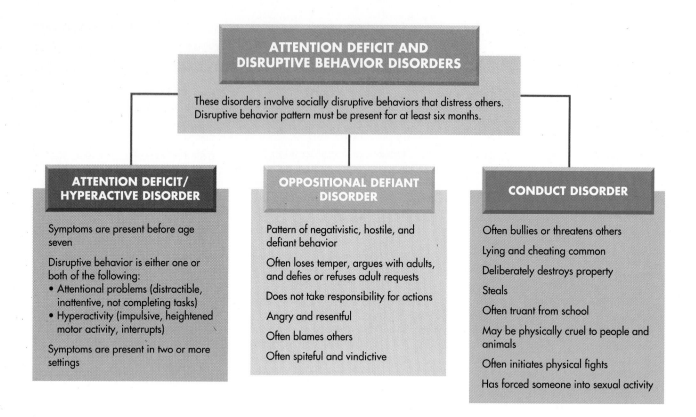

staying seated for group work and in completing projects. The quality of his work was poor. In the first grade, Ron was referred to the school psychologist for evaluation. Although his high activity level and lack of concentration were not so pronounced in this one-on-one situation, his impulsive approach to tasks and short attention span were evident throughout the interview. Ron was referred to a local pediatrician who specializes in attention deficit disorders. The pediatrician prescribed Ritalin, which helped reduce Ron's activity level.

Attention deficit/hyperactive disorders (ADHD) are characterized by socially disruptive behaviors—either attentional problems or hyperactivity—that are present before age seven and persist for at least six months. *Hyperactivity* is a confusing term because it refers to both a diagnostic category and behavioral characteristics. Children who are "overactive" or who have "short attention spans" are often referred to as "hyperactive" even though they may not meet the diagnostic criteria for this disorder. Whether a child is merely overactive or has ADHD is often difficult to determine.

Three types of attention deficit hyperactive disorders are recognized:

■ *ADHD, predominantly hyperactive-impulsive type* is characterized by behaviors such as heightened motoric activity (fidgeting and squirming), short attention span, distractibility, impulsiveness, and lack of self-control.

■ *ADHD, predominantly inattentive type* is characterized by problems such as distractibility, difficulty with sustained attention, inattention to detail, and difficulty completing tasks. Children with attentional deficits tend to have less-severe conduct problems and impulsivity than children with the hyperactive form of ADHD. Instead, they are more likely to be described as sluggish, daydreamers, anxious, and shy; they respond to lower doses of stimulants than do children with hyperactivity (Frick & Lahey, 1991).

■ *ADHD, combined type* is probably the most common form of the disorder. In this case, the criteria for both the hyperactive and inattentive types are met.

A confusing aspect of attention deficit/hyperactive disorders is their inconsistency. Attentional deficit or excessive motor activity are not necessarily always evident, nor are they displayed in all situations. In one study, ADHD boys showed greater motor activity during academic tasks but did not differ from control boys during lunch, recess, and physical education activities (Porrino et al., 1983). Thus a child might be identified as hyperactive in one situation but not in others. To receive a diagnosis of ADHD, the individual must display these characteristics in two or more situations (DSM-IV). Some investigators (Luk, Lueng & Yuen, 1991; Schachar, 1991) believe that "pervasive" hyperactivity (displayed in different situations) may be a different form, a more severe type, or "true" ADHD. Pervasive ADHD appears to be a risk factor in developing a conduct disorder (McArdle, O'Brien & Kolvin, 1995).

ADHD is relatively common. Estimates of its prevalence range from 5 to 20 percent, with boys four times as likely to receive this diagnosis as girls (Lewinsohn et al., 1993; Shaywitz & Shaywitz, 1991). The wide range in its estimated prevalence shows the difficulty encountered in diagnosing the condition. It is a persistent disorder. Children with ADHD continue to show problems with impulsivity, family conflicts, and attention during adolescence. This is especially likely if a disruptive disorder is also present (Barkley et al., 1991). Improvements seem to occur during the ages of sixteen to twenty-one. Those less likely to improve had a concurrent conduct disorder (Klein, 1987).

The prognosis in children with only attentional problems is more promising. Some 40 percent of the children display attentional problems at some point in their lives but in only about 5 percent does it persist (Palfrey et al., 1985).

ADHD is associated with many behavioral and academic problems. Children with this disorder are more likely to need to attend special classes or schools, drop out of school, become delinquent, and have problems with the law (Lambert, 1988; Lambert et al., 1987). Hyperactive boys have fewer problems in structured situations where they are self-directed. They have more difficulty in less-structured situations or in activities demanding sustained attention.

Because they tend to display coercive and critical styles, they are disliked by their peers (Buhrmester et al., 1992).

Several conclusions can be reached concerning the studies just cited. First, in most cases, ADHD does appear to persist until adolescence. Yet improvements do occur; during late adolescence, most no longer meet the criteria for the disorder. Second, the prognosis seems to depend on the presence or absence of other disruptive disorders. If conduct disorder or oppositional disorder occurs concurrently with ADHD, problems in adjustment are more likely to continue into adulthood. Third, the symptoms of ADHD seem to have the greatest impact on academic performance and peer relationships. Fourth, the prognosis for the attentional form of ADHD is relatively positive.

Etiology   Many researchers believe that the symptoms of overactivity, short attention span, and impulsiveness suggest central nervous system involvement. In fact, many conditions thought to cause neurological impairment such as lead poisoning, chromosomal abnormalities, and fetal alcohol syndrome have been associated with ADHD (Hynd et al., 1991). The areas of the brain thought to be involved in ADHD are the reticular activating system (attention), frontal lobes (voluntary control of attention), and the temporal-parietal regions (involuntary attention; Schaughency & Hynd, 1989). Research, however, including attempts to identify brain impairment, has produced equivocal or negative findings. Part of the reason for conflicting findings is that ADHD appears to com-

Many researchers believe that neurotoxins, such as lead, or food additives, such as sugar, are causal factors in ADHD.

prise several different types. Only those with pervasive hyperactivity may show neurological deficits (Luk, Lueng & Yuen, 1991; Schachar, 1991).

Some researchers believe that certain foods or food additives produce physiological changes in the brain or other parts of the body, resulting in hyperactive behaviors. This view was promoted by Feingold (1977), who developed a diet excluding these substances. Sugar is also suspected as a causal factor in ADHD (Chollar, 1988). Approximately 45 percent of physicians have recommended low-sugar diets for ADHD children (Bennett & Sherman, 1983). Many parents have tried the recommended diets on their children, and many claim that their children's behavior improved. But parental expectations or treating the children differently (going shopping with them to buy only certain foods) might result in behavioral changes. In one study (Hoover & Millich, 1994), mothers were told that their "sugar-sensitive" sons had just received a drink that contained sugar or a sugar substitute (placebo). All children received only the sugar substitute. The mothers were asked to rate the behavior of their sons, as viewed during a videotaped play session. The mothers who believed their sons ingested sugar rated the sons as significantly more hyperactive, even though the videotapes recorded no increases in motor activity in the sons. Clearly, expectations can also result in misperceptions.

To determine whether certain chemicals or sugars are implicated in hyperactivity, carefully controlled double-blind studies have also been conducted. Some of these studies involved a "biological challenge test." In this design, the diets of the children were alternated so that some of the time they ate food with the additive and other times without. The parents were not aware of the type of food they were giving their children. Reviews of such studies showed that eliminating food additives or certain chemicals from the diets of hyperactive children had little effect on their behavior (Consensus Development Panel, 1982; Milich & Pelham, 1986; Wolraich, Wilson & White, 1995).

Family variables also seem related to ADHD, although it is not clear whether genetic or environmental factors or a combination are involved. Evidence supporting the hypothesis of genetic transmission includes the higher prevalence rates for the disorder in the first- and second-degree relatives of children with ADHD and higher concordance rates for this disorder among identical twins (Gillis et al., 1992; Knopf, 1984). Rutter and colleagues (1990) believe that a conclusion of genetic influences is premature and that environmental factors could be involved in ADHD.

Treatment Most children with ADHD have been treated with drug therapy. Stimulants in particular in-

crease attention span and improve academic performance (Fischer & Newby, 1991; Gadow, 1991; Tannock, Schachar & Logan, 1995). Approximately 70 percent of children with ADHD respond positively to stimulant medication; 30 percent show no response or become worse when taking medication. The drugs seem to treat the symptoms of ADHD rather than its causes, however, so drug therapy alone does not produce any long-term benefits. Changes tend to be short-lived or to persist only as long as medication continues, and only a subset of major problems is affected (Whalen & Henker, 1991). Medication has also been found to reduce prosocial behaviors in ADHD boys and did not markedly reduce aversive behaviors (Buhrmester et al., 1992).

Satterfield, Hoppe, and Schell (1982) believe that using medication alone may be harmful because drug therapy fails to address such problems as antisocial behavior, poor peer relationships, and learning difficulties. In fact, some studies that compared medication and behavior therapy in treating ADHD report that combining the two treatments produces the most positive results (Carlson et al., 1992; DuPaul & Barkley, 1993). Other clinicians have suggested that both physicians and therapists should pay more attention to family dynamics and child management problems rather than rely solely on pharmacological intervention (Prior, Leonard & Wood, 1983). The Focus On feature elaborates on some issues surrounding drug therapy. Self-instructional procedures, modeling, role playing, classroom contingency management programs, and parent training programs have been useful in dealing with the problems of ADHD and have been found as effective as drug therapy (Abramowitz & O'Leary, 1991; Whalen & Henker, 1991).

Oppositional Defiant Disorder

Oppositional defiant disorder (ODD) is characterized by a negativistic, argumentative, and hostile behavior pattern. The child often loses his or her temper, argues with adults, and defies or refuses adult requests. The child may refuse to do chores and refuse to take responsibility for his or her actions. The defiant behavior is directed primarily toward parents, teachers, and other people in authority. Anger, resentment, blaming others, and spiteful and vindictive behavior are common. Although confrontation often occurs, it does not involve the more serious violations of the rights of others that are involved in conduct disorders (American Psychiatric Association, 1993).

Oppositional defiant disorder is a relatively new category and is certainly one of the more controversial childhood disorders. It is often difficult to separate this disorder from milder forms of conduct disorder and from normal developmental difficulties in

Are We Overmedicating Children?

A large number of medications are being prescribed to treat childhood disorders. They include tranquilizers, stimulants, and antipsychotic medication. Researchers have been especially concerned regarding the use of stimulants for attention deficit hyperactivity disorder, or ADHD. About 90 percent of the estimated 1.5 to 2.5 million children diagnosed with this disorder receive Ritalin or other drugs as treatment (Guttman, 1995). Opponents describe the use of medications as a "Band Aid" approach or a "chemical straitjacket" to ensure ease of management (Hutchens & Hynd, 1987).

In Georgia, a mother with an ADHD child filed suit against the Gwinnett County School District and the American Psychiatric Association. She charged that the school had insisted that her son be given Ritalin and that the medication made him suicidal and violent. The American Psychiatric Association was included in the charge because the diagnosis was based on DSM-III criteria. The mother's attorney claimed that the diagnostic criteria were too general and that they resulted in misidentification. In another case, involving a fifteen-year-old boy convicted of killing a classmate with a baseball bat, the defense attorney claimed that Ritalin contributed to the boy's act. In addition, five other suits involving medical malpractice for prescribing Ritalin were filed in Massachusetts (Cowart, 1988).

Several questions are raised. Are medications such as Ritalin effective in treating the specific disorders? Are medications being prescribed too freely? Ritalin production has increased ninefold from 1985 to 1995 (Guttman, 1995). Is there adequate assessment or evaluation to determine if medication is appropriate? Is there adequate monitoring of the effects of the drug and identification of possible side effects? A number of studies have indicated that stimulant medication such as Ritalin can help reduce some ADHD symptoms. However, nearly one-third of people with ADHD do not show positive results when given stimulant medication (Poling, Gadow & Cleary, 1991). Clinicians recommend that Ritalin be prescribed only after a comprehensive diagnostic and evaluation procedure. The particular symptom or symptoms to be treated should be identified and the dosage modified if necessary. Unfortunately, a large percentage of physicians and psychiatrists do not follow these guidelines (DuPaul & Barkley,

1993). In the case of the fifteen-year-old boy convicted of homicide, the pediatrician who prescribed the Ritalin was reported to have monitored the boy only through yearly physical exams.

Prescribing any medication also necessitates the communication of possible side effects and contraindications to the patient and parent. Stimulants, for example, should not be used for children with tics, glaucoma, or seizure disorders (Hutchens & Hynd, 1987). It is estimated that 15 percent of children with Tourette's syndrome (a severe tic disorder) might not have developed this disorder if stimulant medication had not been prescribed. If tics occur, the medication should be discontinued.

Medication has certainly been helpful in treating a variety of childhood disorders such as ADHD. However, medications should be employed only after carefully evaluating and monitoring their effects. Are we overmedicating our children? Barry Garfinkel, a physician and the director of Child and Adolescent Psychiatry at the University of Minnesota, answers, "We just don't have a good way to judge that" (Cowart, 1988, p. 2521).

children and adolescents (Paternite, Loney & Roberts, 1995). Most children and adolescents go through a period or several periods of defiant behaviors. ODD is not recognized or described as a separate disorder in the mental disorders section of the International Classification of Diseases, Tenth Revision (ICD-10), a classification system used by many other countries.

The symptoms of ODD can be found in several different childhood disorders. One study of preadolescent schoolchildren found that 15.8 percent met the criteria for oppositional defiant disorder (Pfeffer et al., 1987). This percentage in a normal population seems high and may reflect the fact that many children and adolescents show some signs of oppositional defiant disorder. In DSM-IV, a criterion indicating that the problem causes "significant impairment in social or academic functioning" was added to try to discriminate between "normal" and "pathological" defiance. ODD is associated with parent-child conflict, the espousing of unreasonable beliefs, and negative

Many adolescents with conduct disorder deliberately destroy or deface property. They generally have a history of antisocial behavior, beginning when they were children.

family interactions (Barkley et al., 1992). Because DSM-IV has attempted to raise the threshold for the diagnosis of ODD, it is not clear how this will affect conclusions of studies using a lower threshold.

Conduct Disorders

Charles was well known to school officials for his many fights with peers. After a stabbing incident at school, he was put on probation and then transferred to another junior high school. Two months later, at age fourteen, Charles was charged with armed robbery and placed in a juvenile detention facility. He had few positive peer contacts at the juvenile facility and seemed unwilling or unable to form close relationships. Some progress was achieved with a behavioral contract program that involved positive reinforcement from adults and praise for refraining from aggression in handling conflicts. He was transferred to a maximum-security juvenile facility when he seriously injured two of his peers, whose teasing had angered him. Charles completed a vocational training program in this second facility, but he couldn't hold a regular job. He was sent to prison following a conviction for armed robbery.

Conduct disorders are characterized by a persistent pattern of antisocial behaviors that violate the rights of others. Many children and adolescents display isolated instances of antisocial behavior, but this diagnosis is given only when the behavior is repetitive and persistent. Conduct disorders include behaviors such as bullying, lying, cheating, fighting, temper tantrums, destruction of property, stealing, setting fires, cruelty

to people and animals, assaults, rape, and truant behavior. The pattern of misconduct must last for at least six months to warrant this diagnosis (DSM-IV). The prevalence of conduct disorders is estimated to range from 3 to 10 percent of children and adolescents and is four to five times more prevalent in males than in females (Kazdin, 1987; Lewinsohn et al., 1993). Two types of conduct disorder are recognized: (1) childhood onset type (at least one conduct problem occurs before age ten) and (2) adolescent onset type (conduct problem occurs after age ten). Early onset for both boys and girls is related to more serious offending and chronicity. Less serious involvement and being limited to adolescent years is associated with later onset (Tolan & Thomas, 1995).

Conduct disorders in adolescence represent a serious societal problem. In the United States, approximately 83,000 juveniles are housed in correctional institutions for antisocial behaviors, and 1.75 million were arrested in 1990 (Zigler, Taussig & Black, 1992). Parents often report the following pattern in the development of the disorder: early arguments, stubbornness, and tantrums, oppositional behaviors leading to fire setting and stealing and then truancy, vandalism, and substance abuse (Robins, 1991). Oppositional defiant disorder often precedes the development of conduct disorders and often exists concurrently with ADHD. Although many childhood disorders remit over time, children are unlikely to outgrow conduct disorders. Of concern is the increase in violence among young people. Homicide is the second leading cause of death among children and ado-

TABLE 16.3 Effect of Parental Criminal Records on Adopted Sons		
Parents with Criminal Records		**Sons with Criminal Records (Percent)**
Biological Parents	**Adoptive Parents**	
No criminal record	No criminal record	13.5
No criminal record	Criminal record	14.7
Criminal record	No criminal record	20
Criminal record	Criminal record	24.5

Source: Adapted from Mednick, 1985.

The criminal status of the biological parent appears to have greater influence on criminality of sons than the criminal status of adoptive parents.

lescents. African American males between the ages of fourteen and nineteen are especially at risk; they are ten times more likely to die of homicide than are white males of the same age (Hammond & Yung, 1993).

Prognosis for conduct disorders is poor; they often lead to criminal behavior, antisocial personality, and problems in marital and occupational adjustment during adulthood (Kazdin, Siegel & Bass, 1992). Many people with these disorders show early involvement with alcohol and illegal drugs (Lynskey & Fergusson, 1995). A large percentage of offending delinquent adolescents later become adult criminals. Nearly all adult offenders have a history of repeated antisocial behavior as children, and about 25 percent develop an antisocial personality disorder (Robins, 1991). The key factor associated with negative outcome is aggression. Highly aggressive children tend to remain aggressive over time, whereas other childhood adjustment problems show much less stability (Lerner et al., 1988). A particularly negative sign is sexually aggressive behaviors. Individuals who engage in sexual assaults are more likely to show subsequent violence (both sexual and nonsexual) than are individuals who commit nonsexual violence (Rubenstein et al., 1993). Prognosis is better for males who have higher IQ scores and whose parents do not have antisocial personalities (Lahey et al., 1995). Females also have a better prognosis.

Etiology   Psychoanalysts interpret antisocial and delinquent behaviors in children as symptoms of an underlying anxiety conflict in the child. This conflict results from an inadequate relationship with the par-

ents; the problem behaviors can be produced by either emotional deprivation or overindulgence. In the first case, the parents offer the child little affection or concern, so childhood conflicts are not resolved and the superego does not develop adequately. The lack of a strong conscience increases the likelihood of aggressive and antisocial behaviors. The child becomes unable to form close personal relationships with others.

Genetic factors may also be involved. Boys with conduct disorders are more likely to have antisocial parents at a higher than normal rate (Hinshaw, 1987), but the reason for this higher rate could be either genetic or social. Mednick (1985) tried to isolate influences by comparing the adult criminal records of children adopted early in life and the records of their biological and adoptive parents (the sample comprised 14,427 adopted children). If genetic factors are important, the biological parents would have the greatest influence on subsequent criminal behavior on the adoptees. If environmental influences are the most important, the records of adoptive parents should have the greatest impact. As Table 16.3 shows, adopted sons whose biological parents have criminal records are more likely to also have criminal records. These results support the view of a genetic predisposition in criminality. However, social factors were also important. The highest rate occurred when a criminal record existed for both the biological and adoptive parents. In addition, children born to parents of low socioeconomic status had the highest rates of criminality no matter what type of adoptive family they lived with. Convictions among children adopted into lower-class families were more frequent than among those adopted into higher-class families. As Mednick observed, "Regardless of genetic background, improved social conditions seem to reduce criminality" (1985, p. 60). But Rutter and colleagues (1990) cautioned that these studies are based on criminal acts, not on a diagnosis of conduct disorder. Very little is actually known about genetic influences for conduct disorder.

Patterson (1986) believes that antisocial behaviors are the result of the parents' failure to effectively punish misbehavior. In his work with families of conduct-disordered children, he noticed that when a parent requested something from or criticized the child, the child would counterattack. This would result in the parents' withdrawal from the conflict. The child's failure to learn to respect authority generalizes to the school setting, resulting in academic failure and poor peer relations. Patterson concluded that the specific factors that contribute to the development of antisocial behaviors include (1) a lack of parental monitoring (increases in unsupervised street time were associated with increased rates of antisocial behaviors), (2) inconsistent disciplinary practices, (3) failure to use positive management techniques or to teach social process skills, and (4) failure to teach the skills necessary for academic success (listening, compliance, following directions, and so on). Although Patterson focused primarily on the learning aspects in the etiology of conduct disorders, he also supported the view that predisposing factors such as difficult child temperament may increase the need for parents to learn and consistently apply appropriate management skills.

Treatment Although conduct disorders and group delinquency have resisted traditional forms of psychotherapy, training in social and cognitive skills appears promising. One program (Kolko, Loar & Sturnick, 1990), for example, focused on helping aggressive boys develop verbal skills to enter groups, play cooperatively, and provide reinforcement for peers. The cognitive element included using problem-solving skills to identify behavior problems, generate solutions to them, and select alternative behaviors. In addition, the children learned positive social skills through viewing videotapes and role-playing with therapists and peers. Role-playing was continued until mastery was achieved. Each child also practiced the skill in the classroom. Participants reported fewer feelings of loneliness, lower amounts of problem behaviors, and greater social competence. In a one-year follow-up, children involved in the program still engaged in more appropriate social behaviors than they had before treatment.

Even greater success has been found with parent management training (Patterson, 1986; Webster-Stratton, 1991). In these programs, specific skills are taught so that the parents learn how to establish appropriate rules for the child, implement consequences, and reward positive behaviors. The parents first practice their newly learned skills on simple problems and gradually work on the more difficult problems as they become more proficient in management techniques. Patterson's program has evolved over a period of twenty years of work with problem children. Success

Puerto Rican children with behavior problems may respond better to culturally congruent counseling, such as Cuento therapy. Folk tales from their culture are used as examples and models of different adaptive responses to problem situations.

has been reported, and treatment changes have been maintained even for periods as long as four years after treatment (Kazdin, 1987). The combination of both building cognitive and social skills and parent management training appears to produce the most marked and durable changes in conduct disordered children (Kazdin, Siegel & Bass, 1992).

ANXIETY DISORDERS

Children and adolescents suffer from a variety of problems involving chronic anxiety—fears, nightmares, school phobia, shyness, timidity, and lack of self-confidence. Children with these disturbances display exaggerated autonomic responses and are apprehensive in new situations, preferring to stay at home or in other familiar environments. They report more negative thoughts about events and are overly self-critical (Bell-Dolan & Wessler, 1994). In contrast with the disruptive behavior disorders, which are socially disruptive and undercontrolled, the anxiety disorders are considered to be internalizing or overcontrolled. Higher distress scores are obtained from those with internalizing disorders than from those with externalizing disorders (McGee & Stanton, 1992).

The prognosis or course of internalizing disorders, even without treatment, is very promising (Esser, Schmidt & Woerner, 1990). Some researchers believe that specific personality patterns may predispose a child toward developing anxiety and other childhood disorders (see the Focus On feature).

Children who suffer from a **separation anxiety disorder (SAD)** show excessive anxiety when separated from parents or home. They constantly seek their parents' company and may worry too much about losing them. Separation may produce physical symptoms, such as vomiting, diarrhea, and headaches. During separation, the child will often express negative emotions, such as by crying (Shouldice & Stevenson-Hinde, 1992). To receive a diagnosis of separation anxiety disorder, a child must display at least three of the following symptoms:

1. Excessive anxiety about separation from the attachment figure.

2. Unrealistic fear that the attachment figures will be harmed.

3. Reluctance to attend school.

4. Persistent refusal to go to sleep unless the attachment figure is nearby.

5. Persistent avoidance of being alone.

6. Nightmares involving themes of separation.

It is normal for young children to feel distress when separated from their primary caretakers. Only when the distress is severe and prolonged is a diagnosis of separation anxiety disorder made.

7. Repeated physical complaints when separated.

8. Excessive distress when separation is anticipated.

This pattern must last at least four weeks and must occur before the age of eighteen (DSM-IV) to be diagnosed as a disorder. Children with this disorder tend to come from caring and close-knit families. During adolescence, the most frequent symptoms involve physical complaints on school days (Francis, Last & Strauss, 1987). Separation anxiety disorder may be a risk factor in developing a panic disorder (Battaglia et al., 1995).

One type of separation anxiety disorder that has been studied extensively is *school phobia*. The physical symptoms may occur merely at the prospect of having to go to school. In a sample of high school students, about 6 percent of females and 2.5 percent of males indicated having had this disorder sometime in their life (Lewinsohn et al., 1993). School refusal is common among children referred for treatment. It occurs more frequently in European-American children than in African-American children and is more common in children from lower socioeconomic backgrounds (Last & Perrin, 1993).

Personality and Behavior: The Temperament-Environment Fit Model

For many childhood disorders, there is increasing interest in the temperament-environment fit model. Research continues to support the view that temperament is an important factor in adjustment. In a longitudinal study conducted by Chess and Thomas (1984), about 10 percent of the children studied showed a negative reaction to new situations and were emotionally reactive. These "difficult" children showed greater adjustment difficulties later in life. Tendencies toward "shyness" also appear early in development. Kagan (1987) and Kagan & Snidman (1991) found that some children showed behavioral inhibitions, such as being cautious around strangers. In addition, they had high heart rates in response to mild mental stress. These early reactions persisted. Other differences in temperament may include characteristics such as depressive mood and need for stimulation. The child's temperament may predispose that individual to develop a specific disorder. For example, a child with behavioral inhibition may develop an anxiety disorder, or a "difficult" child may develop a disruptive behavior. Three-year-old children identified as "hard to manage" were likely to display problems involving hyperactivity, defiance, or aggression at age nine (Campbell & Ewing, 1990). Whether a child develops a problem, however, also depends on environmental factors and parental skills. If parents are inexperienced, cannot adjust to the child's temperament, have personal difficulties and stresses that influence their parenting skills, or are inconsistent with the child, the chances of problem behaviors occurring greatly increase (Carey, 1986; Chess, 1986).

Temperament and the environment can affect one another. Difficult infants elicit more confrontation and conflict with their mothers (Lee & Bates, 1985). Environmental changes can also affect the child's temperament. Kagan (1987) reported that 40 percent of the "inhibited" children became more outgoing. This change was associated with parental encouragement for the child to approach stressful situations.

What are the implications of the temperament-environment fit model? First, more research would be directed toward (1) individual differences in temperament, (2) the neurobiological bases for these differences, and (3) the interaction between temperament and environment. This would help identify both the children who are at risk for developing a disorder and the type of disorder they are most likely to develop. Psychotherapeutic interventions and parenting style may have to be altered to "fit" the child's temperament. For example, approaches that might be effective with a difficult child (being firm and consistent) may be inappropriate with an "inhibited" child.

Darcy's school phobias were first manifested while riding in the car with her mother on the second day of school. She began to cry and hold on to her mother, scream hysterically, and plead not to be taken to school. Once at school, Darcy screamed and kicked to avoid being taken into the building, and then to her classroom. Darcy's mother sat with the child in class and attempted to reassure her that school was pleasant and enjoyable. When the mother got up to leave the room, Darcy immediately began to cry, scream, and grab her mother's arm to prevent her from returning home. (Kolko, Ayllon & Torrence, 1987, p. 251)

Psychoanalytic explanations of school phobia stress the overdependence of the child on the mother. The reluctance to attend school is not seen as a fear of school but as anxiety over separation from the mother. If separation anxiety is the primary etiological factor in this disorder, however, it should occur in the early school history of the child. But many cases of school phobia do not develop until the third or fourth grade. Also, these children often do not display "separation anxiety" in other situations that require separation from their mothers.

School phobia has also been explained in terms of learning principles. Parents are important sources of reinforcement during a child's preschool period. Going to school requires a child to develop new skills and to encounter uncertain and anxiety-arousing situations. If a parent reinforces the child's fears (for example, by continually warning the child not to get lost), the child may seek refuge away from school, where the kind of reinforcement he or she received earlier in life is available.

For young children treated with most forms of psychotherapy, the prognosis for separation anxiety disorder is very good. But separation anxiety that devel-

The expression shown by the girl in this painting, *The Dead Mother and the Little Girl,* by Edvard Munch, illustrates the overwhelming distress a child feels when a parent dies. Loss of a major attachment figure can result in depression in children

ops during adolescence may be more resistant to change.

CHILDHOOD DEPRESSION

> David had a history of depressive reactions to unpleasant events since infancy, which had become increasingly severe. Two events seemed to have produced affective pain and to have triggered the depressive acting out which led to his referral: One was a cerebral stroke suffered by his maternal grandmother with whom he was very close, and the second was learning of his mother's fourth pregnancy. . . . His parents described him as fearful, socially isolated, and as making self-deprecating statements. His behavior at the time of referral was passive, quiet, and motorically slow, punctuated with occasional hostile outbursts. Suicidal ideation surfaced for several months—twice during the course of therapy. (O'Connor, 1987, p. 106)

The five-year-old boy just described displays many symptoms of depression. Although DSM-IV does not list childhood depression in the childhood disorders (it would be diagnosed as a mood disorder), major depressive episodes can begin very early in life, even in infancy. Estimates of childhood depression range from 27 to 52 percent in clinical populations (Winnett et al., 1987). During a five-year longitudinal study of third-grade children, the percentage of children who scored at a "serious" level of depression ranged from 4.9 percent to 11.3 percent (Nolen-Hoeksema, Girgus & Seligman, 1992). Children who were depressed during the first year of the study tended to also be depressed throughout the five-year period. Correlated with depressive scores were stressful life events, high levels of helplessness in social and academic situations, and a more pessimistic explanatory style. Depression is also reported in adolescents, with girls reporting more depressive symptoms than boys (Weiss et al., 1992).

In a sample of one thousand preschool children who were referred to a child development center, fewer than 1 percent evidenced a major depression. Symptoms of depression expressed by this group involved feelings of sadness, loss of appetite, sleep difficulties, fatigue, and other somatic complaints. Kashani and Carlson (1987) believe that a pattern of frequent somatic complaints may indicate depression in preschoolers. Environmental factors were also important. All children who were depressed had been abused or seriously neglected, as compared with 22 percent of control children. Depressed children were also more likely to live in a broken home (100 percent versus 33 percent).

Depressed mood is more prevalent during adolescence. Moderate to intense depressive symptoms were reported in 10 percent of adolescent boys and 40 percent of adolescent girls. Clinical depression is found in about 42 percent of psychiatric samples of adolescents and about 7 percent of nonclinical samples (Petersen et al., 1993).

Clearly, depression does occur in childhood and adolescence. Children are especially vulnerable to environmental factors because they lack the maturity and skills to deal with various stresses. Conditions such as poor or inconsistent parenting, parental illness, loss of an attachment figure, and neglect or abuse often produce lowered self-esteem and increased vulnerability to depression. Depressed children show many of the same characteristics exhibited by depressed adults. They have more negative self-concepts and are more likely to engage in self-blame and self-criticism (Jaenicke et al., 1987). Programs involving social skills training, cognitive behavioral therapy (Winnett et al., 1987), and supportive therapy (O'Connor, 1987) have been effective in treating childhood depression.

TIC DISORDERS

> Saul Lubaroff, a disc jockey in Iowa City, is able to deliver smooth news reports on the weather, news, and sports. However, whenever he turns off his microphone, an explosive, involuntary stream of obscenities follow. In high school, his classmates would mock and threaten him. Even today, his outbursts are highly embarrassing to him. He has shouted "HEY" and "I MASTURBATE" in a fancy restaurant. However, Saul does have control while he is on the air. He indicates that "I have no problem announcing. I can turn off my 'noises' for 20 to 25 seconds, sometimes up to two minutes." (Dutton, 1986, p. c1)

Saul Lubaroff has a chronic tic disorder. **Tics** are involuntary, repetitive, and nonrhythmic movements or vocalizations. Transient and chronic tic disorders and Tourette's syndrome comprise this group of disorders. Most individuals with tic disorders report bodily sensations or urges that precede the tic (Leckman, Walker & Cohen, 1993).

Chronic Tic Disorder

Most tics in children are *transient* and disappear without treatment. If a tic lasts longer than four weeks but less than one year, it is diagnosed as a **transient tic disorder**. A diagnosis of **chronic tic disorder** is given when the tic or tics last more than a year. Chronic tic disorders may persist into and through adulthood.

The most common tics are eye blinking and jerking movements of the face and head, although sometimes the extremities and larger muscle groups may be involved. In tic disorders, the movements, which are normally under voluntary control, occur automatically and involuntarily. Examples of tics reported in the literature include eye blinking, facial grimacing, throat clearing, head jerking, hiccoughing, foot tapping, flaring of the nostrils, flexing of the elbows and fingers, and contractions of the shoulders or abdominal muscles. Vocal tics can range from coughing, grunting, and sniffing to repeating words.

Approximately 15 to 23 percent of children have single, transient tics; their occurrence usually peaks at age seven. Diagnoses of tic disorders can be made only in retrospect because there is no way of determining whether a tic will disappear or develop into a chronic tic disorder or Tourette's syndrome (Gadow, 1986; Golden, 1987).

Tourette's Syndrome

> P. first exhibited features of GTS [Gilles de la Tourette's syndrome] at the age of six years when she started to twitch her nose. She went on to develop a variety of motor and vocal tics as well as echolalia. Diagnosis of GTS was made when she was twelve, at which time it was noted that the tics could be triggered by coughing and sniffing. When she heard these noises she would experience an irresistible urge to tic. (Commander, Corbett & Ridley, 1991, p. 877)

According to DSM-IV, a diagnosis of **Tourette's syndrome** requires that "both multiple motor and one or more vocal tics have been present at some time during the illness, although not necessarily concurrently" (American Psychiatric Association, 1993, p. 80). Tourette's syndrome usually begins in childhood, between the ages of two and thirteen. This puzzling disorder is characterized by facial and body tics, which increase in frequency and intensity as the person grows older, and by grunting and barking sounds that generally develop into explosive *coprolalia*, the compulsion to shout obscenities. Stress increases the severity of these symptoms (Silva et al., 1995). The disorder is relatively rare, with a prevalence of four to five cases per 10,000 people; it occurs two to three times more frequently in males than in females (DSM-IV).

Researchers have not yet determined whether Tourette's syndrome differs from the tic disorders. However, studies seem to suggest that the two are quite similar. For example, Corbett (1971) studied data on groups of children and adults suffering from single or multiple tics, tics with vocalizations, and tics with coprolalia (Tourette's syndrome). These three groups displayed no significant differences in IQ scores, psychiatric symptoms, or EEG readings. The prognosis was more favorable for those with single or multiple tics (94 percent improved) than for those with Tourette's syndrome. About 30 to 40 percent of those who have Tourette's syndrome recover fully by late adolescence. Another 30 percent show significant improvement; symptoms remain severe for about one-third (Robertson, 1994).

Etiology and Treatment

Anxiety and stress seem to be primary factors in producing, maintaining, and exacerbating tic disorders. In the psychodynamic view, tics represent underlying aggressive or sexual conflicts. For example, eye blinking may represent attempts to block out thoughts of the "primal scene" (intercourse between the child's parents) or other anxiety-evoking stimuli. Although tics do appear early in life, when the fixation of sexual or aggressive impulses is most likely to occur, little support has been found for this explanation.

According to the learning theorists, tics are conditioned avoidance responses initially evoked by stress. These responses become habit through reinforcement when they reduce anxiety. The therapeutic technique of negative practice or massed practice is based on this viewpoint. The technique requires that the person perform the tic intentionally, over and over again. This forced practice of the behavior produces fatigue, which inhibits the response. The tic gradually acquires aversive properties, so not performing the tic becomes reinforcing. In general, behavioral or other psychological therapies are ineffective (Leckman, Walker & Cohen, 1993).

Both multiple tics and Tourette's syndrome appear to be transmitted in families. If a parent has a tic disorder, there is an increased risk that the children will also have the disorder (Rutter et al., 1990). This relationship may be due to either genetic or environmental factors—or perhaps to both. Some also believe that tic disorders are related genetically to obsessive-compulsive disorder (George et al., 1993; Leonard et al., 1992). Other researchers, however, have not found a relationship between these disorders (Black et al., 1992).

Interestingly, as many as 50 percent of children with Tourette's syndrome also meet the criteria for attention deficit hyperactive disorder, which might reflect a genetic link between the two disorders (Golden, 1987). As we noted earlier in the chapter, treating ADHD with stimulants may precipitate Tourette's syndrome: Such treatment should be avoided if a familial history of tic disorder is present and should be discontinued in other cases if tics appear in the patient (Gadow, 1991).

Several investigators believe that Tourette's syndrome may stem from an impairment of the central nervous system involving the dopamine system (Malison et al., 1995). Reported therapeutic success with the drug haloperidol, which acts on the dopamine receptors, supports this view (Gadow, 1991). However, there have also been reports that drug treatment has had unfavorable results (Bauer & Shea, 1984). In addition, haloperidol produces some negative side effects in children and could lead to motor dysfunctions such as tardive dyskinesia.

EATING DISORDERS

Eating problems are becoming more prevalent in the United States, especially among younger people. It is estimated that 35 percent of women engage in binge eating, 8 percent attempt to control their weight through self-induced vomiting, and nearly 6 percent abuse laxatives (Kendler et al., 1991a). Eating problems may be a result of both the availability of many attractive high-calorie foods and the American pursuit of thinness. Preoccupation with weight and body dimensions may become so extreme that it develops into one of the eating disorders—anorexia nervosa or bulimia (see the disorders chart for anorexia nervosa and bulimia nervosa on page 490).

There is often a confusion between eating behaviors and an eating disorder. For example, binge eating occurs in a large number of individuals but is not in itself enough for a diagnosis of bulimia. The diagnosis is given only when it coexists with a severely negative body image, dissatisfaction with body size and appearance, and inappropriate compensatory activities after eating (Rosen, Reiter & Orosan, 1995; Williamson et al., 1995).

Anorexia Nervosa

The patient was a 25-year-old woman who had a diagnosis of anorexia nervosa since she was 12 years old. She came in for therapy because of complaints of "having her whole life revolve around her eating symptoms." Her highest weight has been 110 pounds and her lowest, 56 pounds. To control her weight, she uses laxatives, exercises excessively, and induces vomiting. Her prognosis is "extremely guarded." (Baker & Webb, 1987)

Anorexia nervosa is characterized by a refusal to maintain a body weight above the minimum normal weight for one's age and height; an intense fear of becoming obese, which does not diminish with weight loss; body image distortion; and, in girls, the absence of at least three consecutive menstrual cycles otherwise expected to occur. A person with this bizarre and puzzling disorder literally engages in self-starvation. Even when skeletal in appearance, such patients deny the seriousness of their physical condition. As Bruch (1978, p. 209) noted, people with this disorder "vigorously defend their often gruesome emaciation as not being too thin. . . . They identify with the skeleton-like appearance, actively maintain it, and deny its abnormality." The inability to objectively assess one's physical condition is characteristic of anorexia nervosa. Because they believe they are overweight, anorexic patients deny that their weight loss is a problem. Their concern about weight is reflected in frequent thoughts such as "I'm getting fatter and fatter" (Cooper & Fairburn, 1992). Some controversy exists over whether a disturbance in body image perception is necessary for the diagnosis. Although about 75 percent of anorexic patients did show a distorted body image, the remainder did not (Horne, Van Vactor & Emerson, 1991).

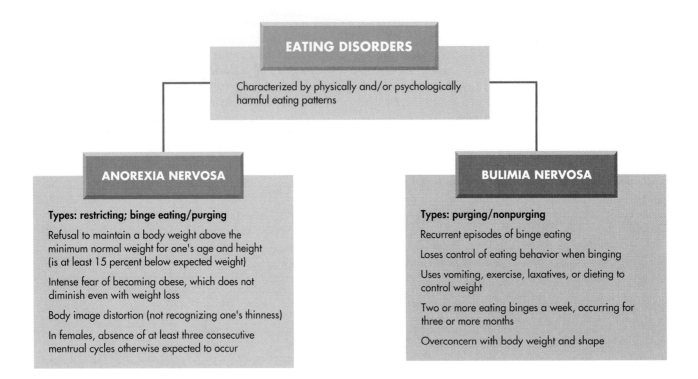

EATING DISORDERS

Characterized by physically and/or psychologically harmful eating patterns

ANOREXIA NERVOSA

Types: restricting; binge eating/purging

Refusal to maintain a body weight above the minimum normal weight for one's age and height (is at least 15 percent below expected weight)

Intense fear of becoming obese, which does not diminish even with weight loss

Body image distortion (not recognizing one's thinness)

In females, absence of at least three consecutive mentrual cycles otherwise expected to occur

BULIMIA NERVOSA

Types: purging/nonpurging

Recurrent episodes of binge eating

Loses control of eating behavior when binging

Uses vomiting, exercise, laxatives, or dieting to control weight

Two or more eating binges a week, occurring for three or more months

Overconcern with body weight and shape

Christy Henrich, a former world-class gymnast died in 1994 from anorexia-related complications at the age of 22. Henrich, seen here a year before her death, shows visible signs of her illness.

Self-starvation produces a variety of physical complications along with weight loss. Anorexic patients often exhibit cardiac arrhythmias because of electrolyte imbalance; about 80 percent display low blood pressure and slow heart rates. Rates as low as 25 beats per minute have been reported (De Zwaan & Mitchell, 1993). In addition, the heart muscle is often damaged and weakened because the body may use it as a source of protein during starvation. One result of such complications is a mortality rate of approximately 10 percent (American Psychiatric Association, 1993).

There are two subgroups of patients with anorexia. Of 105 patients hospitalized with this disorder, 53 percent had lost weight through constant fasting *(restricting type)*; the remainder had periodically resorted to binge eating followed by purging or vomiting *(binge eating/purging type)*. Although both groups displayed a vigorous pursuit of thinness, some differences were found. The restricting anorexics were more introverted and tended to deny that they suffered hunger and psychological distress. The binge/purging type were more extroverted; reported more anxiety, depression, and guilt; admitted more frequently to having a strong appetite; and tended to be older.

Although anorexia has been known for more than one hundred years, it is receiving increased attention, owing to greater public knowledge of the disorder and the apparent increase in its incidence. The disorder occurs primarily in adolescent girls and young women, and only rarely in males. Estimates of its prevalence range from 0.4 to 0.7 percent of the female population (Lewinsohn et al., 1993; Pope, Hudson & Yurgelun-Todd, 1984). The rate peaks among 15- to 19-year-olds (Frombonne, 1995). One disturbing finding is an increase in early-onset anorexia, in girls between the ages of eight and thirteen (Lask & Bryant-Waugh, 1992). The causes for this condition are similar to those in women and include the pursuit of thinness, preoccupation with body weight and shape, disparagement of body shape, low self-esteem, and perfectionism.

Bulimia Nervosa

> The 22-year-old single female had uncontrollable binge eating episodes for 7 years. She made herself vomit after binging. Binge eating episodes were followed by strict dieting during which she would only eat "healthy" foods such as fruits. She showed excessive preoccupation with weight and appearance. Specific foods were chosen for the binge and included ice cream, chocolate candy, cookies, shortbread, licorice, bananas, milk, diet 7-up, and tea. She would dress in comfortable clothing, arrange the food on a tray, and eat while reading. The food was consumed in about fifteen minutes. (Jansen et al., 1989)

Bulimia nervosa is an eating disorder characterized by recurrent episodes of binge eating (the rapid consumption of large quantities of food) at least twice a week for three months, during which the person loses control over eating and uses vomiting, laxatives, and excess exercise to control weight. A persistent overconcern with body image and weight also characterizes this disorder. Eating episodes may be stopped when abdominal pain develops or by self-induced vomiting. Frequent weight fluctuations of more than ten pounds often are caused by alternating binges and fasts.

Bulimic subjects overestimate their body size (Williamson, Cubic & Gleaves, 1993) and are afraid to gain weight. When asked to imagine gaining five pounds, a group of bulimic subjects showed pronounced motoric, heart rate, and muscle tension changes (Cutts & Barrios, 1986). Compared with nonbulimic women at similar weight levels, bulimic women exhibited greater psychopathology, more external locus of control, lower self-esteem, and a lower sense of personal effectiveness on questionnaires (Shisslak, Pazda & Crago, 1990). They also have a negative self-image, feelings of inadequacy, dissatisfaction with their bodies, and a tendency to perceive events as more stressful than most people would (Vanderlinden, Norre & Vandereycken, 1992). We should note that these characteristics of diagnosed bulimics may be a result of their loss of control over eating patterns, however, rather than the causes of the disorder.

Bulimic people realize that their eating patterns are not normal and are frustrated by that fact. They become disgusted and ashamed of their eating and hide it from others. Some do not eat during the day but lose control and binge in late afternoon or evening. The loss of self-control over eating is typical of bulimics (Cooper & Fairburn, 1992). Weight is controlled through vomiting or the use of laxatives. The vomiting, or purging, produces feelings of relief and, often, a commitment to a severely restrictive diet—one that ultimately fails.

Bulimia is much more prevalent than anorexia, although prevalence estimates depend on the sample being described. These estimates range from 2 to 4 percent of the general population (Kendler et al., 1991). An additional 10 percent of women reported some symptoms but did not meet all the criteria for the diagnosis (Drewnowski, Yee & Krahn, 1988). The incidence of bulimia appears to be increasing in women and is especially prevalent in urban areas (Hoek et al., 1995). Few males exhibit the disorder, presumably because there is less cultural pressure for them to remain thin.

A person's weight seems to have little to do with whether the individual develops bulimia. Of a sample of forty women with the disorder, twenty-five were of normal weight, two were overweight, one was obese, and twelve were underweight. These women averaged about twelve binges per week, and the estimated calories consumed in a binge could be as high as 11,500. Typical binge foods were ice cream, candy, bread or toast, and donuts.

People with this disorder use a variety of measures to control the weight gain accompanying binge eating. These include fasting, self-induced vomiting, diet pills, laxatives, and exercise (Kendler et al., 1991). Side effects and complications may result from the self-induced vomiting or the excessive use of laxatives. The effects of vomiting include swollen parotid glands, which produces a puffy facial appearance. Vomited stomach acid can erode tooth enamel. Possible gastrointestinal disturbances include esophagitis and gastric and rectal irritation. Vomiting also lowers potassium, which can weaken the heart and cause arrhythmia and cardiac arrest.

Some evidence has shown that bulimics eat not only out of hunger but also as an emotionally soothing response to distressing thoughts or external stressors. As noted earlier, women with this disorder tend to perceive events as more stressful than most people would. Such difficulties may lead them to consume food for gratification, as Sandy, a bulimic actress-singer, reported: "I would stuff down my feelings with the food. . . . I used the food as a catalyst to flush my feelings down the toilet and watch them go away. It was numbing" (Bartlett, 1984, p. 1).

Is Our Society Creating Eating Disorders?

There appears to be a dramatic increase in eating disorders during the last twenty years, which is correlated with our society's emphasis on thinness and attractiveness. In the 1980s alone, we spent close to $30 billion on diet foods, programs, and books. Liposuction is the leading cosmetic surgical procedure (Brownell, 1991). Equating thinness with success and attractiveness has taken a toll, however, especially among women. As many as 64 percent of college women exhibit symptoms of eating disorders and even more are dissatisfied with their body shape (Mintz & Betz, 1988).

What role has society played in eating disorders and why do they appear primarily in Western societies? Eating disorders are rare in China, Singapore, Malaysia, and Hong Kong (Lee, Hsu & Wing,

1992) and in other non-Western cultures (Bhadrinath, 1990). Root (1990) believes that thinness represents success and control in Western societies. Other societies do not place such emphasis on thinness. Is it possible that eating disorders are culture-bound syndromes and are attempts by women to resolve identity issues?

As psychologists, we are interested in the etiology or causes of problems. What do you think about the position that the "pursuit of thinness" is a culture-bound phenomenon? Do contemporary women gain status or identity through their physical appearance? Why have Western cultures been so susceptible to eating disorders? Do you think eating disorders will increase in the future in other societies? If society continues to equate desirable char-

acteristics with thinness, how can we change its message? How have African Americans been able to insulate themselves from this standard?

The women's movement stressed the importance of ability over appearance. Why, given the greater freedom and power that women have gained, is there an increase in the importance of appearance?

We are also beginning to see more physically attractive men in the mass media. (In one study of 25 college men with an eating disorder, they showed a dissatisfaction with their body image and used vomiting, laxatives and exercise to control their weight, [Olivardia et al., 1995].) Will this cause a dramatic increase in eating disorders in men?

Etiology of Eating Disorders

Both social and psychological factors are probably important in the etiology of eating disorders. Yager, Landsverk, and Edelstein (1987) believe that the eating disorders result from the sociocultural demand for thinness in females, which produces a preoccupation with weight. Society's increasing emphasis on thinness over the last twenty years has been accompanied by an increasing incidence of eating disorders (Ruderman & Besbeas, 1992). This standard of thinness results in the belief that approval and self-worth are dependent upon body size and shape (Mizes & Christiano, 1995).

Some believe that eating disorders are a culture-bound syndrome found only in Western cultures (see Critical Thinking). Some countries or groups that have been exposed to Western values show an increasing concern over eating. Asian female adoles-

cents born in Britain also have concerns over body shape and eating (Hill & Bhatti, 1995). Among Pakistani adolescent girls, those who were the most exposed to Western culture had the highest rates of abnormal eating attitudes (Mumford, Whitehouse & Choudry, 1992). Interestingly, African Americans appear to be somewhat insulated from the thinness standard. Few African American women appear to have an eating disorder (Dolan, 1991). In a survey involving university students, they expressed less concern about weight, felt less social pressure to be thin, and chose a significantly heavier ideal body size than white women. African American men were more willing than white men to date heavier women (Powell & Kahn, 1995). African Americans appear to be able to ignore the white media messages that equate thinness with beauty. Table 16.4 compares some differences in body image and weight concerns among African American and white women.

TABLE 16.4   Differences in Body Image and Weight Concerns Among African American and White Females

Concern	African American Females	White American Females
Satisfied with current weight or body shape	70 percent	11 percent
Body image	Perceive selves to be thinner than they actually are.	Perceive selves to be heavier than they actually are.
Attitude toward dieting	Better to be a little overweight than underweight (65 percent of respondents in a survey).	Need to diet to produce a slender body. Fear of being overweight.
Definition of beauty	Well groomed, "style," and overall attractiveness. Beauty is the right "attitude and personality."	Slim; 5'7"; 100 to 110 pounds. Perfect body can lead to success and the good life.
Being overweight	Of those who were overweight, 40 percent considered their figures attractive or very attractive.	Those who considered selves as not having a weight problem were 6 to 14 pounds under the lower limit of the "ideal" weight range.
Age and beauty	Believed they would get more beautiful with age (65 percent chose this response).	Beauty is fleeting and decreases with age.

Source: From Desmond et al., 1989; Kumanyika, Wilson & Guiford-Davenport, 1993; Parker et al., 1995; Rand & Kuldau, 1990.

One possibility researchers have looked at is whether body dissatisfaction is specific or distinctive to eating disorders. The answer appears to be no. Young women without eating disorders display a high degree of body dissatisfaction that is "striking and disturbing" (Klemchuk, Hutchinson & Frank, 1990). Many women have a distorted image of the size of their waist, thighs, and hips, overestimating to a much greater extent than men do (Thompson, 1986). They see themselves as heavier than they are and have

"Beauty" contests equating physical appearance with attractiveness and success can program a thinness standard. Here preschool girls learn at an early age what society values, especially in females. Some theorists believe that a preoccupation with thinness and appearance leads to eating disorders.

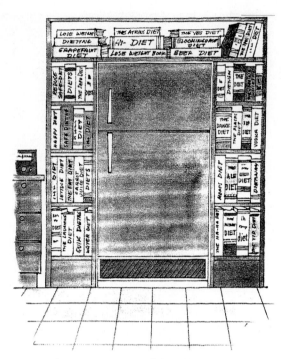

The preoccupation of American society.

as an ideal body image a picture of a much thinner woman. A study of more than two thousand women found that they wanted to weigh about nine pounds less than their current weight (Drewnowski, Yee & Krahn, 1988). Most men seem to equate their current body shape with their ideal shape (Fallon & Rozin, 1985).

A preoccupation with thinness appears to develop by early adolescence. A study of 288 girls between the ages of ten and fifteen found that girls wanted thinner bodies than they thought boys found attractive. They did not consider themselves overweight, however, and displayed less body dissatisfaction than did older women (Cohn et al., 1987).

Women in their twenties have a much higher standard of thinness than girls do. This might indicate that a need to be increasingly thin begins to develop in adolescence and becomes deeply ingrained when the young woman reaches full adulthood. Especially intriguing is the finding by Cohn and colleagues (1987) that adolescent girls were aware that their "ideal" body shape was thinner than the body shape they thought boys preferred.

Variables other than being attractive to men must be involved. An independent standard of thinness might be one factor. Some support for this view was found by Silverstein and Perdue (1988). They found that women equated thinness with attractiveness. In addition, being slim was also associated with professional success and intelligence. Immaturity, passive-aggression, and a self-defeating behavior pattern were

found in patients with anorexia nervosa and bulimia nervosa. They tended to displace their emotional conflicts onto somatic concerns (Scott & Baroffio, 1986). Although it is widely believed that sexual abuse is a causal factor in eating disorders, several studies have failed to find such a connection (Conners & Morse, 1993; Pope & Hudson, 1992; Pope et al., 1994).

Another line of inquiry has interested some researchers. Rates of affective disorders are higher in the relatives of individuals with eating disorders than in control relatives, and some investigators believe that eating disorders represent an expression of an affective disorder (Rutter et al., 1990). Depression often accompanies eating disorders. One interesting finding is that binge eating, purging, and mood varied seasonally among patients with bulimia nervosa (Blouin et al., 1992). The researchers hypothesize that for some bulimics, a relationship with seasonal affective disorder may exist. The cycle of bingeing and purging may be associated with light availability. At this point, we still do not know the precise relationship between affective disorders and eating disorders. Some therapists believe that depression is the result, not the cause, of anorexia or bulimia (Vanderlinden, Norre & Vandereycken, 1992).

Other researchers are searching for genetic influences in eating disorders. Kendler and associates (1991) examined identical and fraternal twins to estimate the role of genetics in bulimia nervosa. They reported concordance rates of 22.9 percent and 8.7 percent respectively, which suggested a modest genetic influence.

Treatment of Eating Disorders

As you have seen, eating disorders, especially anorexia nervosa, can be life threatening. The first goal of therapy is for the anorexic patient to gain weight to ensure that the body is not endangered by electrolyte imbalance and weakened muscles caused by starvation (American Psychiatric Association, 1993). Either a medical or a behavioral inpatient weight-gain program can be implemented. The medical approach generally involves complete bed rest and either intravenous or nasogastric (tube through the nose) feeding. The behavioral approach is designed to encourage weight gain through the use of such positive reinforcers as television or telephone privileges, visits from family and friends, mail, and access to street clothes. The particular reinforcers used to reward weight gain, depend, of course, on the likes and dislikes of the patient. Weight-gain plans are generally aimed at increases of up to one pound per day (see First Person for an account of a treatment program). Once the anorexic patient has gained sufficient weight

FIRST PERSON

Karen J. Shaw

Why in the world would you want to work in that unit? This was the response I received from many of my friends when I informed them that I would be leaving the medical-surgical unit to work on the Eating Disorder Program (EDP) within my hospital. It became apparent to me that many nurses view psychiatric nursing as an uncomplicated job. However, my experience is entirely different. I had never worked as intensely as I do now, and I have never had a more rewarding and enjoyable job.

The EDP is located on the north wing of the medical-surgical floor, giving it a definite hospital atmosphere. Patients have regular beds rather than hospital beds, though, so the room resembles a dormitory. Most of our patients' time is spent in the large group room,

which looks like a combined living room and dining room. We follow a fairly rigid daily structure. Most meals are eaten in the group room and are supervised by a staff person. We ask that patients refrain from using the bathroom for one hour after meals. During the one-hour post-meal supervision, staff people on the unit run various groups. The EDP also provides individual and family therapy.

Sara (not her real name) was admitted to the EDP during her summer break from college. She was anxious and frightened, as evidenced by her words and tears. Sara shared with the staff and other patients that she felt she could no longer deal with her eating disorder, that it was "controlling her." Sara said that she felt overwhelmed with guilt after any meal or snack and would excuse herself to the bathroom to purge. She complained of many physical symptoms: cold hands and feet, heart palpitations, amenorrhea, dental deterioration, fatigue, and extreme labile emotions.

One of the first goals on the EDP is to enable a patient like Sara to complete 100 percent of her meals and snacks. Once a patient's nutrition is improved, he or she is less food-oriented and more able to focus closely on personal behavior. For example, once Sara began to eat all her portioned food, she was able to explore how she had felt growing up in her family as the youngest child. Sara reported that her older sister was very difficult, causing the family

much concern and worry. Consequently, Sara always tried to identify how her parents would like her to behave, and then do so. As a result, Sara had difficulty understanding her own needs and wants.

Therapy enabled Sara to identify her feelings and begin to communicate them in a more appropriate manner. She learned to recognize factors that would trigger a binge/purge cycle and to develop new coping strategies. Sara was very pleased with herself because within the last five years this was the longest period of time she had refrained from purging.

Sara was discharged from the EDP after one month of therapy. She was not totally cured, but she had gained insight and had learned a myriad of coping strategies to confront life's difficulties. One year after Sara's discharge, she sent a letter to the unit expressing that she has had some slips, but she is "getting on with her life" by identifying her feelings and using the various strategies that she had learned on the unit. Enclosed was a photograph of Sara and another former patient. I saw two beautiful women smiling at me, appearing ready to deal with life. I ask you, "Wouldn't you like a job like mine?"

Karen J. Shaw is a psychiatric nurse at Hahnemann Hospital in Brighton, Massachusetts.

to become an outpatient, family therapy sessions may be implemented. Experience has shown that this approach helps maintain the treatment gains achieved in the hospital.

Approximately 50 percent of treated anorexics recover completely (remain within the normal weight range), and another 30 to 40 percent show some weight gain but remain underweight (American

Psychiatric Association, 1993; Anderson, Hedblom & Hubbard, 1983; Lask & Bryant-Waugh, 1992). For the most part, these percentages do not include patients who were treated with the family therapy approach; expectations are that it will improve overall therapeutic results.

Bulimia has been successfully treated through psychotherapy and through antidepressant medication

(American Psychiatric Association, 1993). A somewhat novel treatment is the psychoeducational group approach, which combines behavioral and educational techniques. Clients are told that to eliminate binges they must eat regularly. They are taught how to anticipate the urge to binge and how to either prevent or delay binges. Clients also learn to delay purging for as long as possible after an eating binge (in which case they may not require purging at all) and then to go back to eating regularly. Each binge is considered an isolated incident, rather than part of a pattern.

Cognitive-behavior approaches have also been effective in increasing self-efficacy in bulimics developing a sense of self-control. Bulimics learn to replace urges to binge with exercise, relaxation, or other alternative behaviors (Fairburn et al., 1991; Fairburn et al., 1995; Garner et al., 1993). Common components of cognitive-behavioral treatment plans are encouraging the consumption of three or more balanced meals, reducing rigid food rules and body image concerns, and developing cognitive and behavioral strategies. This approach was as successful as antidepressant medication in treating bulimia nervosa, although combined treatment was the most effective (Agras et al., 1992).

MENTAL RETARDATION

A teenager with mental retardation told his fellow students, during a high school assembly, how he felt about his handicap:

> My name is Tim Frederick. . . . I would like to tell you what it is like to be retarded. . . . I am doing this so that you might be able to understand people like me. I do chores at home. I have to take care of all the animals—twelve chickens, three cats, a dog, three goldfish, and a horse. That's a lot of mouths to feed. . . . After I graduate from school, I hope to live in an apartment. . . . The hardest thing is when people make fun of me. I went to a dance a few weeks ago, and no girl would dance with me. Can you guys imagine how you would feel if that happened to you? Well, I feel the same way. (Smith, 1988, pp. 118–119)

How mental retardation is perceived is undergoing a fundamental change. Until recently, it was considered a hopeless condition that required institutionalization. Tim Frederick's mother was told that her son's development would be delayed and he might never be able to walk or talk. We now know that the effects of mental retardation are variable and that with training, even people who are severely handicapped can make intellectual and social gains.

The Association for Retarded Citizens, an advocacy organization, has estimated that 75 percent of children with mental retardation can become completely self-supporting adults if given appropriate education and training. Another 10 to 15 percent have the potential to be self-supporting. The challenge is to develop appropriate programs to ensure the greatest success. The movement away from institutionalization will continue to create greater contact between people with mental retardation and the general population. In 1967, more than 200,000 people with mental handicaps lived in public institutions. By 1984, this number had decreased to 110,000 (Landesman & Butterfield, 1987). It is now widely accepted that mentally retarded people should have the opportunity to live, work, learn, and develop relationships with nonretarded people in integrated settings. People are beginning to question assumptions about what individuals with mental retardation can do. A dance troupe called "Images in Motion," composed of individuals with IQ scores between 30 and 60, has won rave reviews (Walker, 1991). The next frontier will be fuller integration of people into the social fabric (Wolfensberger, 1988).

Diagnosing Mental Retardation

About 7 million or more persons in the United States are mentally retarded, with IQ scores of about 70 or less (Madle, 1990). The definition of **mental retardation** in DSM-IV includes the following criteria:

1. *Significant subaverage general intellectual functioning* (this ordinarily means an IQ score of 70 or less on an individually administered IQ test).

2. *Concurrent deficiencies in adaptive behavior* (social and daily living skills, degree of independence lower than would be expected by his or her age or cultural group).

3. *Onset before age eighteen* (subaverage intellectual functioning arising after age eighteen is typically categorized as dementia).

Common characteristics that accompany mental retardation are dependency, passivity, low self-esteem, low frustration tolerance, depression, and self-injurious behavior (American Psychiatric Association, 1994). The more severe levels of mental retardation are associated with speech difficulties, neurological disorders, cerebral palsy, and vision and hearing problems (McQueen et al., 1987).

Issues Involved in Diagnosing Mental Retardation Arguments have been raised against the use of IQ scores to determine mental retardation, especially among members of ethnic minority groups. The validity of IQ scores is questionable especially when they are used to test members of minority groups. This controversy has resurfaced with the publication of *The Bell Curve* by Herrnstein and Murray (1994) which attributes the poorer performance of African Americans on IQ tests to genetic factors. Frisby (1995), however, points out that alternative explanations for IQ performance can be made (see Table 16.5). IQ tests also may measure familiarity with mainstream middle-class culture, not intelligence. Jane Mercer (1988) argued that the IQ test has been inappropriately used and that it is unfair to attempt to "measure" intelligence by using items drawn from one culture to test individuals from a different cultural group. In addition, IQ tests do not acknowledge the positive coping characteristics of the disadvantaged.

In 1979, ruling in the *Larry P. v. Riles* case, Judge Peckham held that IQ tests were culturally biased and were not to be used in decisions regarding the placement of African American children in classes for the educable mentally retarded. He broadened his decision in 1986 by saying that IQ tests could not be used to determine the educational needs of African American children as part of a comprehensive educational program—even with parental consent. His decision was challenged by the mother of an African American child who requested IQ testing. She argued that this was a case of reverse discrimination since IQ tests can be administered for special education services to European Americans, Hispanic Americans, Asian Americans, and American Indians. On September 1, 1992, Judge Peckham reversed his 1986 ruling. IQ tests can again be used with African American children as part of a special education assessment. However, the 1979 ruling still holds. They cannot be used to place African American children in classes for the mentally retarded.

Levels of Retardation   DSM-IV specifies four different levels of mental retardation, which are based only on IQ score ranges, as measured on the revised Wechsler scales (WISC-R and WAIS-R): (1) mild (IQ score 50–55 to 70), (2) moderate (IQ score 35–40 to 50–55), (3) severe (IQ score 20–25 to 35–40), and (4) profound (IQ score below 20 or 25). Social and vocational skills and degree of adaptability may vary greatly within each category. Table 16.6 contains estimates of the number of people within each level in the United States.

It should be noted that the American Association on Mental Retardation (AAMR), unlike the American Psychiatric Association and DSM-IV, no longer uses a classification of mental retardation based on levels of

TABLE 16.5   Alternative Explanations for Lower Performance by African Americans on IQ Tests

Disadvantage/Oppression Explanations

Legacy of slavery
Teacher racism/prejudice
Inadequate schools
- Lack of funds, resources
- Lack of parental involvement

Inadequate home environment
- Poverty
- Lack of opportunities to learn
- Deficient mother-child interactions
- Lack of parental support
- Lack of academic role models

Cultural Difference Explanations

Cultural bias in tests
- Lack of African Americans in standardization samples
- Preference for "dynamic" vs. "static" testing
- Item loading on white middle-class culture
- Different race of the examiner from test taker
- Lack of "test-wiseness"

Afrocentric home/Eurocentric school mismatch
- Active opposition to "white" cultural values
- Lack of cultural competence in teachers
- Lack of multicultural curricula
- Preference for cooperative vs. competitive learning
- Preference for African American English vs. standard English
- African American behavioral/learning style

Psychological Maladjustment Explanations

Expectancy of failure due to low teacher expectations
Low self-esteem (negative self-concept)
- Caused by segregation from whites
- Caused by integration with whites

Lack of motivation to achieve
Test/performance anxiety
Learned helplessness
Negative peer pressure (burden of acting white)

Source: Adapted from Frisby, 1995.

intellectual functioning as revealed in IQ scores. Instead, AAMR classifies the intensity of needed support (how much support the person needs to function in the environment) rather than assesses the level of intellectual deficit (Dawson, 1992). However, the

TABLE 16.6 Estimated Number of Mentally Retarded People by Level

Level	Range Wechsler IQ	Percentage of All Mentally Retarded	Number
Mild	50–70	85	6,075,000
Moderate	35–49	10	715,475
Severe	20–34	3–4	250,400
Profound	0–19	1–2	107,300

Note: Estimates based on percentages from the American Psychiatric Association (1993) and applied to the normal probability distribution of intelligence based on a U.S. population of 210 million.

AAMR accepts an IQ cutoff point of 75, which is higher than the 70 in DSM-IV. Unfortunately the higher IQ score used by AAMR may lead a greater number of persons to be labeled mentally retarded because of their different cultural or social backgrounds.

Etiology of Mental Retardation

Mental retardation is thought to be produced by environmental factors (such as poor living conditions), by genetic or biogenic factors, or by a combination of the two. Biogenic factors in mental retardation include genetic variations, genetic abnormalities, metabolic disorders, malnutrition, infection, or prematurity. Environmental conditions such as a blow to the head causing brain trauma can also directly affect the brain. Table 16.7 presents some of the predisposing factors associated with mental retardation.

Environmental Factors   Certain features of the environment may contribute to retardation. Among these are the absence of stimulating factors or situations, a lack of attention and reinforcement from parents or significant others, and chronic stress and frustration. In addition, poverty, lack of adequate health care, poor nutrition, and inadequate education place children at a disadvantage. A lower socioeconomic status generally implies a lower mean group IQ score (Ardizzone & Scholl, 1985).

Genetic Factors   Genetic factors in mental retardation include genetic variations and genetic abnormalities (Thapar et al., 1994). As noted earlier, mental retardation may be caused by normal genetic variation. In a normal distribution of traits, some individuals will have significantly lower intelligence scores than others. No organic or physiological anomaly associated with mental retardation is found in this type of retardation. Researchers have suggested that the normal range of intelligence lies between the IQ scores of 50 and 150, and that some individuals simply lie on the lower end of this normal range (Zigler, 1967). In any case, the majority of people classified as mildly retarded have normal health, appearance, and physical abilities.

Mental retardation that is caused by genetic anomalies is rare and generally is more severe. Those who are profoundly retarded (about 1 to 2 percent of those who are retarded) may be so intellectually deficient that constant and total care and supervision are necessary. Many also have significant sensorimotor impairment (Irwin & Gross, 1990) and are confined to a bed or wheelchair by the congenital defects that produced the retardation. Even with teaching, there is minimal, if any, acquisition of self-help skills among these individuals. Their mortality rate during childhood is extremely high, with more than one-half dying before age twenty (Ramer & Miller, 1992). Associated physical problems such as neuromuscular disorders, impairment of vision or hearing, and seizures may coexist (Irwin & Gross, 1990).

Down syndrome is a condition produced by the presence of an extra chromosome (trisomy 21, an autosomal, or nonsex, chromosome) and resulting in mental retardation and distinctive physical characteristics. It may occur as often as once in every thousand live births (Thapar et al., 1994). About 10 percent of children with severe or moderate retardation show this genetic anomaly. As Figure 16.3 illustrates, the prevalence rate increases dramatically with the age at

TABLE 16.7   Predisposing Factors Associated with Mental Retardation

Factor	Percentage of Cases	Examples
Heredity	5	Errors of metabolism (Tay-Sachs), single gene abnormalities (tuberous sclerosis), chromosome aberrations (translocation Down syndrome, fragile X syndrome)
Alteration of embryonic development	30	Chromosomal changes (Down syndrome, trisomy 21), prenatal damage due to toxins (FAS), infections
Pregnancy and perinatal complications	10	Malnutrition, prematurity, hypoxia, traumas, infections
Infancy or childhood medical conditions	5	Traumas, infections, lead ingestion
Environmental influences and other mental conditions	15–20	Social, linguistic, and nurturance deprivation. Severe mental disorders (autistic disorder)
Etiology unknown	30–40	Etiological factors cannot be identified

Source: Based on DSM-IV.

which the mother gives birth (U.S. Department of Health and Human Services, 1995).

The well-known physical characteristics of Down syndrome are short in-curving fingers, short broad hands, slanted eyes, furrowed protruding tongue, flat and broad face, harsh voice, and incomplete or delayed sexual development. Cosmetic surgery (consisting mostly of modifying tongue size) is being used

FIGURE 16.3   Rate of Down Syndrome Births   This figure shows the rate of live Down syndrome births by mothers' ethnicity and age. For all groups, the rate of Down syndrome births increases after the maternal age of 30.

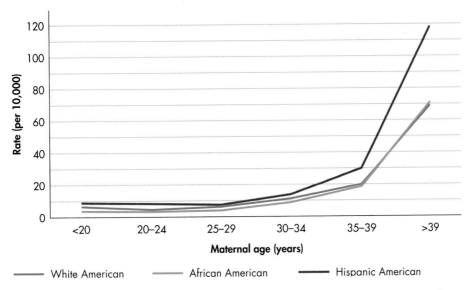

Source: Data from U.S. Department of Health and Human Services, Center for Disease Control, 1995.

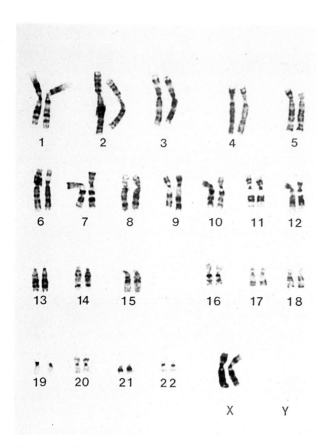

Three sets of chromosomes in the number 21 chromosome set (trisomy 21) can be seen in this photograph. The extra chromosome is responsible for Down syndrome.

with some Down syndrome children in an effort to make their physical appearance more nearly normal and to allow them to speak more clearly and to eat more normally. The procedure is intended to allow Down syndrome people to fit in as much as possible with their peers to enhance their social interactions and communication abilities (May & Turnbull, 1992). People with Down syndrome who live past age forty are at high risk for developing Alzheimer's disease. The gene responsible for the conditions of *amyloid plaques* (patches of degenerated nerve endings) and neurofibrillary tangles (fibers that appear to be tangles of brain tissue filaments) found in Alzheimer's disease, is located on chromosome 21, indicating a possible relationship between Down syndrome and Alzheimer's disease (Clarke & Clarke, 1987). People who have Down syndrome show a greater intellectual decline after the age of 35 than do other individuals with mental retardation (Young & Kramer, 1991). Congenital heart abnormalities are also common in people with Down syndrome, causing a high mortality rate. Recent surgical procedures have improved

the probability of surviving these heart defects and have resulted in both a longer life expectancy and a healthier life (Carr, 1994).

Prenatal detection of Down syndrome is possible through **amniocentesis,** a screening procedure in which a hollow needle is inserted through the pregnant woman's abdominal wall and the amniotic fluid is withdrawn from the fetal sac. This procedure is performed during the fourteenth or fifteenth week of pregnancy. The fetal cells from the fluid are cultivated, and within three weeks, these cells can be tested to determine whether Down syndrome is present. This procedure involves some risk for both mother and fetus, so it is employed only when the chance of finding Down syndrome is high—as, for example, with women older than age thirty-five. Remember, however, that the greater percentage of babies with Down syndrome are born to younger mothers, and yet testing for Down syndrome through amniocentesis occurs primarily among older women.

A procedure that allows earlier detection of Down syndrome is *chorionic villus sampling.* Tests are made of cells on the hairlike projections (villi) on the sac that surrounds the fetus and can be performed after the ninth week of pregnancy (Pueschel, 1991).

Other, less-common genetic anomalies include Turner's syndrome, Klinefelter's syndrome, phenylketonuria (PKU), Tay-Sachs disease, and cretinism.

Nongenetic Biogenic Factors Mental retardation may be caused by a variety of environmental mishaps that can occur during the prenatal period (from conception to birth), the perinatal period (during the birth process), and the postnatal period (after birth). During the prenatal period, the developing organism is susceptible to viruses and infections (such as German measles), drugs, radiation, poor nutrition, and other nongenetic influences.

Increasing attention is being focused on the problem of mental deficits related to alcohol consumption during pregnancy. Some children born to alcoholic mothers have **fetal alcohol syndrome (FAS),** a group of congenital physical and mental defects including small body size and *microcephaly,* an anomaly whose most distinguishing feature is an unusually small brain. Such children are generally mildly retarded, but many are moderately retarded or of average intelligence. Those with normal intelligence seem to have significant academic and attentional difficulties, however, as well as a history of hyperactivity and behavioral deficits (Streissguth, 1993). Smoking and poor nutrition may increase the likelihood that an alcoholic mother will have FAS offspring. Available information suggests that one case of FAS occurs in each 750

Alcohol consumption by women during pregnancy is one of the most common causes of mental retardation and can result in fetal alcohol syndrome.

live births, which places alcohol among the most common causes of retardation for which an etiology can be determined (Streissguth et al., 1980). Among the different ethnic groups in the United States, the rate of FAS is especially high among American Indians (U.S. Department of Health and Human Services, 1995).

During the perinatal period, mental retardation can result from birth trauma, prematurity, or asphyxiation. After birth or during the postnatal period, head injuries, infections, tumors, malnutrition, and ingesting toxic substances such as lead can cause brain damage and consequent mental retardation. Compared with prenatal factors, however, these hazards account for only a small proportion of organically caused mental retardation. The most common birth condition associated with mental retardation is prematurity and low birth weight. Although most premature infants develop normally, approximately 20 percent show signs of neurological problems reflected in learning disabilities and mental retardation (Pound, 1987). In a study of more than 53,000 U.S. women and their children, researchers found that low birth weight was generally associated with low IQ scores. The average IQ score of children who had birth weights between 26 ounces and 52.5 ounces was 86, whereas those with birth weights between 122 ounces and 140 ounces had an average IQ score of 105 (Broman, Nichols & Kennedy, 1975).

Although most types of mental retardation now have decreasing incidence rates, mental retardation owing to postnatal causes is on the increase. For example, direct trauma to the head produces hemorrhaging and tearing of the brain tissue, often as the result of an injury sustained in an automobile accident or from child abuse. Depending on the definition of child abuse, estimates of the number of cases of child abuse per year range from 35,000 to 1.9 million. Of this group, a large percentage are subjected to violent abuse that could cause serious injury (Gelard & Sanford, 1987). The authors of a British study of child abuse go so far as to argue that violence-induced handicaps should be recognized as a major cause of retardation: "Children rendered mentally handicapped as a result of abuse may account for more cases than PKU. The consequences are frequently more severe than those of Down syndrome" (Buchanan & Oliver, 1977, p. 465).

Programs for People with Mental Retardation

Early Intervention Programs such as Head Start have not produced dramatic increases in intellectual ability among at-risk children (those from low-income families). But long-term follow-up studies have found that they do produce positive results (Royce, Lazar & Darlington, 1983; Zigler & Bergman, 1983). Children who participated in early intervention programs were found to perform better in school than nonparticipants, and the difference between the two groups continued to widen until the twelfth grade. In addi-

Here, a woman with Down syndrome is working successfully at McDonald's. Many mentally retarded individuals can lead productive and satisfying lives.

tion, a greater proportion of the participants in early intervention finished high school, which no doubt helped them obtain and hold better jobs.

The families of participants were also positively influenced by the programs. They rated the programs as personally helpful, spent more time working with their children on school tasks, and perceived their children as becoming happier and healthier. There is continuing optimism about the efficacy of such programs, even though two well-known studies that re-

ported large increases in IQ scores (the studies of Heber & Garber, 1975, and Skeels, 1966) were found to have serious methodological flaws (Longstreth, 1981; Page, 1972).

Employment Programs People with mental handicaps can achieve more than was previously thought. The parents of a teenage boy, for example, were told that he would always be childlike and that the only job he would ever be fit for was stringing beads.

Individuals with mental retardation living in group homes learn many social and practical skills that enable them to lead semi-independent lives.

Another person with moderate retardation, who spent most of his time staring at his hands and rubbing his face, also appeared to have a dismal future. Both of these men now have paying jobs, one as a janitor and the other as a dishwasher. Programs designed to help people with mental handicaps learn occupational skills are largely responsible for the improved outcome of these men and others like them (McLeod, 1985). Gains made in social and vocational skills appear to be maintained or increased in follow-up studies (Foxx & Faw, 1992).

Living Arrangements There has been an increase in the deinstitutionalization of people with mental retardation. More of them are being placed in group homes or in situations where they can live independently or semi-independently within the community. The idea is to provide the "least restrictive environment" that is consistent with their condition and that will give them the opportunity to develop more fully. Although the implication seems to be that institutions are bad places, they do not have uniformly negative effects. Nor do group homes always provide positive experiences. What seems to be most important are program goals; programs that promote social interaction and the development of competence have positive effects on the residents of either institutions or group homes (Tjosvold & Tjosvold, 1983).

Nontraditional group arrangements, in which a small number of people live together in a home, sharing meals and chores, provide increased opportunity for social interactions. These "normalized" living arrangements were found to produce benefits such as increased adaptive functioning, improved language development, and socialization (Kleinberg & Galligan, 1983; MacEachron, 1983). Many of these positive behaviors, however, were already part of the residents' repertoires; what they need are systematic programs that will teach them additional living skills (Kleinberg & Galligan, 1983). Merely moving retarded people from one environment to another does not alone guarantee that they will be taught the skills that they need. Nonetheless, properly planned and supported deinstitutionalization does provide persons with mental retardation the opportunity to experience a more "normal" life.

SUMMARY

1. Pervasive developmental disorders include autistic disorder, Rett's disorder, childhood disintegrative disorder, Asperger's disorder, and pervasive developmental disorder not otherwise specified.

2. Autistic disorder is characterized by an extreme lack of responsiveness and by language and speech deficits. It appears early in life and seems to have genetic, not psychological, causes.

3. Parents' behaviors do not cause autism. The prognosis for the pervasive development disorders is poor. Behavior modification procedures have yielded promising results, but evidence has suggested that long-term (if not lifelong) treatment is needed.

4. Developmental problems are reported in both "normal" children and children who are clinic patients. Attention deficit hyperactivity disorder, or ADHD (characterized by overactivity, restlessness, distractibility, short attention span, and impulsiveness) is a somewhat common problem. Three types of ADHD are recognized: predominantly hyperactive-impulsive; predominantly inattentive, and combined. Although ADHD may be produced by organic problems, many children diagnosed as "hyperactive" do not show pathological neurological signs. Drugs have been used extensively to treat this disorder, but the use of behavior modification and self-control methods is increasing.

5. Oppositional defiant disorder (ODD) is characterized by a pattern of hostile, defiant behavior toward authority figures. Children with ODD do not display the more serious violations of others' rights that are symptomatic of conduct disorders. The latter constitute one of the few childhood conditions that show a clear continuity with adult problems. Unfortunately, the prognosis is poor. Possible causes of the antisocial behaviors include emotional deprivation or overindulgence; genetic factors; the learning, reinforcement, and modeling of aggression; and the influence of the family.

6. Children may also suffer from a variety of problems related to anxiety and depression. Children with separation-anxiety disorder show excessive anxiety, including physical symptoms, when they are separated from parents and home. Children's anxiety reactions are usually transitory and disappear with age. Depression also occurs in childhood and becomes more prevalent during adolescence.

7. Tics and other stereotyped movements often occur in children and adolescents. In most cases, tics are transient and disappear with or without treatment. Tics that last longer than a year are diagnosed as chronic tic disorders. A more severe problem is Tourette's syndrome, which may involve organic problems and last into adulthood. Drugs and behavior therapy have been only partially successful in treating tic disorders.

8. The eating disorders, anorexia nervosa and bulimia, are becoming more prevalent in the United States. Anorexia involves a loss of body weight through self-starvation, body image distortion, and an intense fear of becoming obese that does not diminish with weight loss. Anorexics have poor self-esteem and may use their bizarre behavior as a way to control others. Bulimia is characterized by episodes of binge eating followed by self-induced vomiting or purging. The excessive weight consciousness of anorexic and bulimic patients may be a result of societal emphasis on thinness, especially for women. The disorders are treated primarily by reinforcing desirable behaviors.

9. DSM-IV identifies four different levels of mental retardation, which are based only on IQ scores: mild (IQ score 50 to 70), moderate (IQ score 35 to 49), severe (IQ score 20 to 34), and profound (IQ score below 20). Causes of retardation include environmental factors, normal genetic processes, genetic anomalies, and other biogenic abnormalities such as physiological or anatomical defects. Most mental retardation does not have an identifiable organic cause and is associated with only mild intellectual impairment.

10. The vast majority of those with mental retardation can become completely self-supporting with appropriate education and training. Public schools provide special programs for children and adolescents; even people who are severely retarded are given instruction and training in practical self-help skills. Various approaches—behavioral therapy in particular—are being used successfully to help retarded people acquire needed "living" skills.

KEY TERMS

amniocentesis A screening procedure in which a hollow needle is inserted through the pregnant woman's abdominal wall and amniotic fluid is withdrawn from the fetal sac; used during the fourteenth or fifteenth week of pregnancy to determine the presence of Down syndrome

anorexia nervosa An eating disorder characterized by a refusal to maintain a body weight above the minimum normal weight for the person's age and height; an intense fear of becoming obese, which does not diminish with weight loss; body image distortion; and in girls, the absence of at least three consecutive menstrual cycles otherwise expected to occur

attention deficit/hyperactivity disorders (ADHD) Disorders of childhood and adolescence characterized by socially disruptive behaviors—either attentional problems or hyperactivity—that are present before age seven and persist for at least six months

autistic disorder A severe childhood disorder characterized by qualitative impairment in social interaction and/or communication; restricted stereotyped interest and activities; and delays or abnormal functioning in a major area before the age of three

bulimia nervosa An eating disorder characterized by recurrent episodes of binge eating (the rapid consumption of large quantities of food) at least twice a week for three months, during which the person loses control over eating and uses vomiting, laxatives, and excess exercise to control weight

chronic tic disorder Childhood-onset disorder characterized by involuntary, repetitive, and nonrhythmic movements or vocalizations that last longer than one year

conduct disorders Disorders of childhood and adolescence characterized by a persistent pattern of antisocial behaviors that violate the rights of others; repetitive and persistent behaviors include bullying, lying, cheating, fighting, temper tantrums, destruction of property, stealing, setting fires, cruelty to people and animals, assaults, rape, and truant behavior

Down syndrome A condition produced by the presence of an extra chromosome (trisomy 21) and resulting in mental retardation and distinctive physical characteristics

fetal alcohol syndrome (FAS) A group of congenital physical and mental defects found in some children born to alcoholic mothers; symptoms include small body size and microcephaly, in which the brain is unusually small and mild retardation may occur

mental retardation Significant subaverage general intellectual functioning accompanied by concurrent deficiencies in adaptive behavior, with onset before age eighteen

oppositional defiant disorder (ODD) A childhood disorder characterized by a pattern of negativistic, argumentative, and hostile behavior in which the child often loses his or her temper, argues with adults, and refuses adult requests; refusal to take responsibility for action, anger, resentment, blaming others, and spiteful and vindictive behavior are common, but serious violations of others' rights are not

pervasive developmental disorders Severe childhood disorders in which qualitative impairment in verbal and nonverbal communication and social interaction are the primary symptoms; include autistic disorder, Rett's disorder, childhood disintegrative disorder, Asperger's disorder, and pervasive developmental disorder not otherwise specified

separation anxiety disorder A childhood disorder characterized by excessive anxiety concerning separation from parents and home

tics Involuntary, repetitive, and nonrhythmic movements or vocalizations

Tourette's syndrome A childhood disorder characterized by multiple motor and one or more verbal tics that may develop into coprolalia (compulsion to shout obscenities)

Transient tic disorder Childhood-onset disorder characterized by involuntary, repetitive, and nonrhythmic movements or vocalizations that last longer than four weeks but less than one year

CHAPTER 17

INDIVIDUAL AND GROUP THERAPY

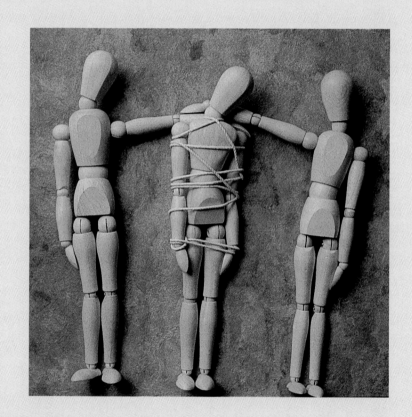

A t some time in our lives, all of us have experienced personal, social, and emotionally distressing problems. Although many of us have been fortunate enough to handle such difficulties on our own, others have been greatly helped by discussing them with someone who could reassure and advise. People have always relied on friends, relatives, members of the clergy, teachers, and even strangers for advice, emotional and social support, approval, and validation. However, this function has been taken over by psychotherapists (Zilbergeld, 1983). In fact, psychotherapists have even been called the "secular priests" of our society (London, 1964a, 1986).

In preceding chapters, we have examined a wide variety of disorders, ranging from personality disturbances to schizophrenia. We have also examined the treatment approaches that seem to help people suffering from these disorders. In this chapter, we provide a more rounded view of the various techniques used to treat psychopathology: biology-based approaches, individual psychotherapy (both insight and action approaches), and group and family therapies. We end the chapter with a brief examination of community psychology.

BIOLOGY-BASED TREATMENT TECHNIQUES

Biological or somatic treatment techniques use physical means to alter the patient's physiological state and hence the person's psychological state (Lickey & Gordon, 1991). The basic philosophy underlying this approach can be traced to ancient times, beginning with the practices of trephining (see Chapter 1) and bleeding and purging (laxatives and emetics) unwanted substances from the body. These primitive and barbaric methods of treatment have given way to more enlightened and benign forms. As our understanding of human physiology and brain functioning has increased, so has our ability to provide more effective biologically based therapies for the mentally ill. Three such techniques are examined here: electroconvulsive therapy, psychosurgery, and psychopharmacology (medication or drug therapy).

Electroconvulsive Therapy

Many people consider physically shocking the patient's body an abhorrent form of treatment. But such treatment can be used successfully to treat certain mental disorders. This is especially true for severe depressive reactions, where it can effect quite dramatic improvements (National Institute of Mental Health, 1985; Scovern & Kilmann, 1980).

The first therapeutic use of shock was *insulin shock treatment,* introduced in the 1930s by psychiatrist Manfred Sakel. Insulin was injected into the patient's body, drastically reducing the blood sugar level. The patient then went into convulsions and coma. The behavior of some schizophrenic patients improved after awakening from this shock treatment.

Also in the 1930s, another psychiatrist, Lazlo von Meduna, hypothesized that schizophrenia and epileptic seizures are antagonistic (seizures seem to prevent schizophrenic symptoms) and that by inducing convulsions in schizophrenics he could eliminate their bizarre behaviors. Meduna injected patients with the drug *metrazol* to induce the seizures. Neither insulin nor metrazol shock treatment was very effective, however, and their use declined with the advent of electroconvulsive therapy.

In 1938, two Italian psychiatrists, Ugo Cerletti and Lucio Bini, introduced **electroconvulsive therapy (ECT)**, or electroshock treatment. ECT is the application of electric voltage to the brain to induce convulsions. The patient lies on a padded bed or couch and is first injected with a muscle relaxant to minimize the chance of self-injury during the later convulsions. Then 65 to 140 volts of electricity are applied to the temporal region of the patient's skull, through electrodes, for 0.1 to 0.5 seconds. Convulsions occur, followed by coma. On regaining consciousness, the patient is often confused and suffers a memory loss for events immediately before and after the ECT. Research indicates that unilateral shock (applying shock to only one hemisphere) causes less confusion and memory loss and is just as effective as bilateral shock (Abrams & Essman, 1982; Horne et al., 1985).

ECT is much more useful in treating depression than in treating schizophrenia, against which it provides at best only temporary relief (Berkowitz, 1974).

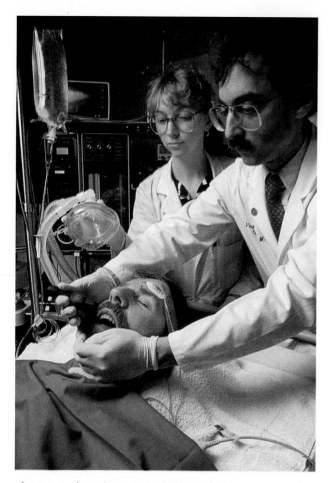

Electroconvulsive therapy involves the administration of electric shock to the brain. The treatment appears to be effective especially with severe depression, although the precise reasons for its effectiveness are unclear.

But how ECT acts to improve depression is still unclear. Some researchers believe ECT alters brain chemistry through suppressing the hormone cortisol (Fink, 1982; Grunhaus et al., 1987). You may recall from Chapter 11 that high levels of cortisol have been found in the blood of patients with some forms of depression, and that some researchers believe these people may be unable to suppress the production of cortisol. Other investigators have suggested that ECT is so aversive that some patients get better simply to avoid treatment. Or perhaps shocks stimulate certain neurotransmitters in the brain, leading to increased activity and improved mood. Another possibility is that depressed patients feel better after experiencing ECT because they see the shocks as punishment for perceived sins. Whatever the mechanism, ECT seems to be effective against severe depression (Abrams, 1988). Indeed, psychologist Norman Endler (1990) wrote a

biography about his own struggle with depression and how ECT greatly helped his recovery. Evidence suggests that the treatment is particularly useful for endogenous cases of depression—those in which some internal cause can be determined (Klerman et al., 1994; see also Chapter 11).

For several reasons, the use of ECT declined in the 1960s and 1970s, despite its success. First, there is concern that ECT might cause permanent damage to important parts of the brain. Indeed, animals who have undergone ECT treatment show brain damage. Would it be unreasonable to expect similar damage in human beings? Second, a small percentage of patients fracture or dislocate bones during treatment. Although modern techniques have reduced pain and side effects (the convulsions are now almost unnoticeable), many patients anticipate a very unpleasant experience. Third, clinicians often argue that the "beneficial changes" initially observed in patients after ECT do not persist over the long term. Fourth, the abuses and side effects of ECT have been dramatized—often sensationally—in the mass media. In the movie *One Flew Over the Cuckoo's Nest,* for instance, ECT was administered repeatedly to the hero because he would not conform to regulations while in a mental hospital (such use of ECT is now illegal and probably nonexistent). Fifth, and most important, recent advances in medication have diminished the need for ECT, except in the treatment of profoundly depressed patients for whom medications act too slowly. Objections to ECT were so strong that in 1982, citizens in Berkeley, California, voted to ban its use in the city. This ban was, however, subsequently overturned by the courts. Because the procedure is so controversial and so little is known about how and why it works, ECT should be used only as a last resort.

The 1980s saw a slight increase in the use of ECT for carefully selected patients. About 33,000 psychiatric patients undergo ECT each year (National Institute of Mental Health, 1985). Severe depression in old age and the depressed stages of bipolar disorders are most responsive to shock therapy.

Psychosurgery

As noted in Chapter 15, damage to brain tissue can dramatically alter a person's emotional characteristics and intellectual functioning. In the 1930s, the Portuguese neurologist Egas Moniz theorized that destroying certain connections in the brain, particularly in the frontal lobes, could disrupt psychotic thought patterns and behaviors. During the 1940s and 1950s, **psychosurgery**—brain surgery performed for the purpose of correcting a severe mental disorder—became increasingly popular. The treatment was used most often with schizophrenic and severely depressed patients, although many patients with personality and anxiety disorders also underwent psychosurgery.

Psychosurgery is a term applied to several procedures or techniques. *Prefrontal lobotomy* involves drilling holes in the skull. A leukotome (a hollow tube that extrudes a cutting wire) is inserted through the holes to cut nerve fibers between the frontal lobes and the thalamus or hypothalamus. In *transorbital lobotomy,* the instrument is inserted through the eye socket, eliminating the need to drill holes in the skull. In a *lobectomy,* some or all of the frontal lobe is removed (to treat such disorders as brain tumors). Parts of the brain may also be subjected to electrical *cauterization* (searing or burning), which destroys selected brain tissue. Psychosurgical techniques have been refined to the point where it is possible to operate on extremely small and contained areas of the brain. For example, videolaserscopy allows the surgeon to use a video camera in making extremely small incisions with a laser (Cowley, 1990).

Critics of psychosurgical procedures have raised both scientific and ethical objections. In the case of lobotomies, for example, initial reports of results were enthusiastic, but later evaluations indicated that the patient's improvement or lack of improvement was independent of the psychosurgical treatment. In addition, serious negative and irreversible side effects were frequently observed (Valenstein, 1986). Although postlobotomy patients often became quite manageable, calm, and less anxious, many emerged from surgery with impaired cognitive and intellectual functioning, were listless (even vegetative), or showed uninhibited impulsive behavior. Some such patients were described as "robots" or "zombies." A small number suffered from continuing seizures and, in rare cases, some died from the surgery. Finally, because psychosurgery always produces permanent brain damage, some critics called for a halt to this form of treatment on humanitarian grounds.

Although surgery is a widely accepted form of treatment for some organic brain disorders such as tumors, its use to treat functional mental disorders has declined drastically since the late 1960s. Both the scientific and ethical objections cited earlier and an increased reliance on medication contributed to its demise. Nowadays, psychosurgery is considered only as a last resort, in the most intractable cases of dangerous pathological behavior. On the whole, this severe restriction and regulation of its use seems wise. The First Person narrative in this chapter discusses some experiences one therapist had with other treatment methods that are no longer used to combat the effects of mental illness.

Psychopharmacology

Psychopharmacology is the study of the effects of drugs on the mind and on behavior; it is also known as *medication* or *drug therapy.* The use of medications has generally replaced shock treatment and psychosurgery for treating serious behavior disorders. Since the 1950s medication has been a major factor in allowing the early discharge of hospitalized mental patients and permitting them to function in the community. Medication is now widely used throughout the United States: More mental patients receive drug therapy than receive all other forms of therapy combined, and it is estimated that we spend more than $500 million annually on antianxiety drugs alone (Baldessarini & Cole, 1988).

Table 17.1 lists the generic and brand names of the drugs most frequently prescribed to treat psychological disorders. The alarming rise in the use of minor tranquilizers has become a major concern to society because of possible abuses and their addictive quali-

TABLE 17.1 Drugs Most Commonly Used in Drug Therapy

Category	Generic Name	Brand Name
Antianxiety drugs	Meprobamate	Miltown, Equanil
	Chlordiazepoxide	Librium
	Diazepam	Valium
Antipsychotic drugs	Alprozolam	Xanac
	Chlorpromazine	Thorazine
	Trifluoperazine	Stelazine
	Thioxanthene	Haldol, Prolixin
	Clozapine	Clozaril
Antidepressants	Phenelzine	Nardil
	Isocarboxazid	Marplan
	Tranylcypromine	Parnate
	Imipramine	Tofranil
	Doxepin	Sinequan
	Amitriptyline	Elavil
	Fluoxetine	Prozac
Antimanic drugs	Lithium	Eskalith

FIRST PERSON

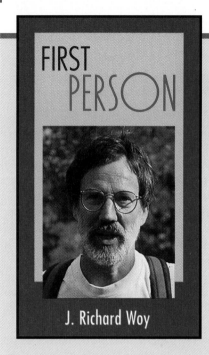

J. Richard Woy

I will never forget my first exposure to people suffering from severe mental disorders, nor will I forget my first involvement in the care and treatment of mental illness. Those first experiences had a strong effect on me, and I was both horrified and fascinated by what I saw.

These experiences occurred just after my graduation from college in 1964. In order to get some first-hand experience in the field before starting a doctoral program in clinical psychology, I worked for several months as a "psychiatric attendant" at a private mental hospital.

The mental health field in 1964 was in the middle of a major transition. Some mental hospitals were already relying heavily on the recently introduced and powerful new psychotropic medications. Others were more cautious and continued a primary reliance on traditional treatment methods—some of which have disappeared entirely since then.

The mental hospital where I worked was old and very conservative in its practices, and I realized later that I had witnessed a kind of living museum, the last vestiges of an earlier era in the treatment of mental illness. Wearing a starched white jacket and carrying an impressive set of very large keys, I escorted patients from one locked portion of the hospital to another, supervised patients on the ward, and assisted doctors and nurses in their various treatments.

Three treatment practices made particular impressions on me. The first was the practice of doing "cold wet packs" in conjunction with electroconvulsive shock therapy. "Shock therapy" was done early every Tuesday and Thursday morning. Each patient first was asked to take off all of his or her clothes and to lie down on a padded rolling cart. We then tightly wrapped each patient from head to foot in wet sheets that had been soaked in cold water. Each patient then lay in the "cold wet pack" for a period of fifteen minutes to a half hour. During this time the room looked like it was filled with mummies. Then I and three other attendants rolled each patient individually into the treatment room where we removed the sheets that were wrapped around the patient's arms and legs. While each of the four of us held one of the patient's limbs, the doctor placed an electrode on each side of the patient's head and then administered the electrical charge, producing an immediate and violent seizure and physical convulsions. We held onto the patient's arms and legs so that the powerful muscular spasms would not cause injury. After the treatment, we rolled patients back to the recovery room, where they

---

ties. Some researchers have also noted that gender bias may operate in the extent to which they are prescribed for women. Studies indicate that women receive twice as many antianxiety medication prescriptions than are given to men; that although women comprise only slightly more than one-half of the patients seen by psychiatrists, they receive 73 percent of all prescriptions; and that male psychiatrists prescribe medication twice as often as their female counterparts (Cypress, 1980; Hohmann et al., 1988; Rossiter, 1983).

We discuss four major categories of medication in this section. These are the antianxiety drugs (or minor tranquilizers), the antipsychotic drugs (or major tranquilizers), the antidepressant drugs (which relieve depression by elevating one's mood), and antimanic drugs such as lithium. Many of these will be familiar to you from our earlier discussions in the context of a specific disorder.

Antianxiety Drugs (Minor Tranquilizers) Before the 1950s, barbiturates were often prescribed to relieve anxiety. *Barbiturates* are sedatives that have a calming effect but that are also highly addictive. Many people who take barbiturates develop a physical tolerance to these medications and require increasing doses to obtain the same effects. An overdose can result in death, and discontinuing the medication can produce agonizing withdrawal symptoms. Moreover, physical and mental disturbances such as muscular incoordination and mental confusion can result even from normal dosages. For these reasons, the barbiturates were replaced with antianxiety drugs almost as soon as the latter became available.

During the 1940s and 1950s, the propanediols (meprobamate compounds) and benzodiazepines took over as the preferred medications. Researchers first developed *meprobamate* (the generic name of Mil-

gradually returned to a waking condition. The electroconvulsive shock therapy was intended to reduce both manic and depressive symptoms, and the cold wet packs were believed to enhance the effectiveness of the shock treatments.

The second treatment method was called "hydrotherapy." This treatment was administered in a specially constructed room that was tiled from floor to ceiling and looked much like a shower room. However, the only fixtures in the room were sets of metal and leather fasteners on one wall and a powerful adjustable nozzle like those on a fire engine on the opposite wall. Treatment consisted of shackling one or more nude patients spread-eagled on one wall and pummeling them with powerful jets of water from the large nozzle. The physical assault of the water jets was intended to shock depressed patients out of their depression.

I don't recall what the third treatment was called. It also occurred in a specially constructed room that was tiled from floor to ceiling. The only thing in the room was a very large bathtub that was

constructed so that warm water would continually circulate through it, much like a jacuzzi. However, the tub had a heavy canvas cover on top of it with a single hole at one end, and the cover could be securely fastened down with straps and buckles. An agitated patient was confined in the tub for several hours at a time with only his or her head sticking out through the hole in the top. The purpose of the treatment was to reduce the patient's agitation through the soothing effects of immersion in the warm water. I or another attendant remained with the patient to be sure he or she was safe and was instructed to record everything the patient said and to say nothing.

This hospital was not a backwater or a snake pit. Located in a suburb of a major city, it had an excellent facility on an attractive and spacious campus, had competent and caring staff, was affiliated with a major university medical school, and drew its patients primarily from the wealthy and well to do. Furthermore, in retrospect it is clear to me that the patients I met suffered from the most serious

and profound of the mental disorders, including schizophrenia, major depression, manic-depressive disorders, and the like.

Nevertheless, I was disturbed by the methods just described even at the time. The emphasis on physically controlling and constraining patients against their will, even to the extent of tying them up, seemed excessive to me and made me very uncomfortable. These methods seemed to me to be demeaning and to involve a loss of personal dignity that left me feeling guilty and embarrassed. I'm glad that I have never seen those three treatment methods used again in all the years since 1964.

J. Richard Woy spent ten years as a researcher and administrator at the National Institute of Mental Health. He is currently head of JRW Associates, a management consulting firm in Boston that serves health and human service organizations. In addition, Dr. Woy publishes, teaches, and maintains a clinical practice.

town and Equanil) for use as a muscle relaxant and anxiety reducer. Within a few years, it was being prescribed for patients who complained of anxiety and nervousness or had psychosomatic problems. Soon other antianxiety drugs, the benzodiazepines (Librium and Valium) also entered the market. Studies suggest that the benzodiazepines work by binding to specific receptor sites at the synapses and blocking transmission, which is another piece of evidence that supports the hypothesis that anxiety, like many other mental conditions, is linked to brain structure and physiology (Hayward, Wardle & Higgitt, 1989).

The antianxiety medications can be addictive and can impair psychomotor skills; discontinuing them after prolonged usage at high doses can result in withdrawal symptoms (Bassuk, Schoonover & Gelenberg, 1983; Levenson, 1981). But they are considered safer than barbiturates, and there is little doubt that they

effectively reduce anxiety and the behavioral symptoms of anxiety disorder.

The major problem of the minor tranquilizers is the great potential for overuse and overreliance. Because of its selective ability to diminish anxiety and leave adaptive behavior intact, Valium has become the drug most often prescribed in all medicine. In addition, about one in ten adults uses antianxiety drugs at least once a year (Uhlenhuth et al., 1983), and people have become more receptive to their use in relieving psychological problems (Clinthorne et al., 1986). Almost everyone feels anxious at one time or another, and the antianxiety drugs are effective, readily available, low in cost, and easy to administer. They are a quick, easy alternative to developing personal coping skills. As a result, people tend to choose the short-term relief offered by these medications, over the long-term but more gradual gains of developing the ability to manage stress and to learn to solve one's own problems.

Antipsychotic Drugs (Major Tranquilizers) Although the antianxiety medications seem to relax and reduce anxiety in patients, they have minimal impact on the hallucinations and distorted thinking of schizophrenic and highly agitated patients. In 1950 a synthetic sedative was developed in France. This medication, *chlorpromazine* (the generic name of Thorazine), had an unexpected tranquilizing effect, which decreased patients' interest in the events taking place around them. Some two million patients used Thorazine in less than a year after its introduction. Chlorpromazine also seemed to reduce psychotic symptoms (believed to be a biochemical effect of blocking dopamine receptors). Thereafter, a number of other major tranquilizers were developed, mainly for administration to patients with schizophrenia. (Chapter 14 discusses medication as a treatment for schizophrenia.)

Those who conduct research on medication treatment (and, for that matter, on psychotherapy) must control for **placebo effects.** These are positive responses to a drug or other experimental condition that result from the patient's understanding of the drug's action, from faith in the doctor, or from other psychological factors unrelated to the medication's specific physiological action. Similarly, those who evaluate any form of treatment or psychotherapy must be aware that patients' expectancy of improvement and the attention received from a doctor could influence improvement rates if controls are not part of the research design. A particular treatment is usually considered effective if it results in greater improvement than would result from giving a patient a *placebo*—a chemically inert or inactive substance.

Several experimental studies have demonstrated the efficacy of antipsychotic drugs in treating schizophrenia (Klerman et al., 1994). A review of many large-scale controlled studies indicates that the beneficial effects of Thorazine, Stelazine, Prolixin, and other antipsychotic drugs have allowed institutions to release thousands of chronic "incurable" mental patients throughout the country (Lickey & Gordon, 1991; Wender & Klein, 1981). When hospitalized schizophrenic patients were given *phenothiazines* (a class of major tranquilizers), they showed more social interaction with others, better self-management, and less agitation and excitement than when they were given placebos.

Despite their recognized effectiveness, antipsychotic drugs do not always reduce anxiety, and they can produce side effects. Patients may develop psychomotor symptoms resembling those of Parkinson's disease, sensitivity to light, dryness of the mouth, drowsiness, or liver disease. After at least six months of continuous treatment with antipsychotic drugs, some patients (usually patients older than forty years of age) develop tardive dyskinesia—a disorder characterized by involuntary movement of the head, tongue, and extremities (Kane & Smith, 1982).

Patients discharged from hospitals typically show only marginal adjustments to community life, and psychotic symptoms usually return when the medication is discontinued. As a result, the rehospitalization rate is high. Nevertheless, medication or drug therapy is very important in treating schizophrenia, and nearly all psychiatric institutions use it. Antipsychotic drugs have dramatically increased the proportion of schizophrenic patients who can return and function in the community, even though such patients may show residual symptoms.

Antidepressant Drugs As in the case of antipsychotic drugs, the development of antidepressants was aided by a fortunate coincidence. During the 1950s, clinicians noticed that patients treated with the antituberculosis medication *iproniazid* became happier and more optimistic. When tested on depressed patients, the medication was found to be effective as an antidepressant. Unfortunately, liver damage and fatalities caused by the medication were relatively high. Continued interest in antidepressants has led to the identification of two large classes of the compounds: monoamine oxidase (MAO) inhibitors and tricyclics.

Monoamine oxidase inhibitors are antidepressant compounds believed to correct the balance of neurotransmitters in the brain. A number of the MAO inhibitors such as *phenelzine* were found to be less dangerous but similar in effect to iproniazid. It is hypothesized that the MAO inhibitors work primarily to correct a deficiency in concentrations of neurotransmitters in the brain. They block the action of monoamine oxidase, thereby preventing the breakdown of norepinephrine and serotonin. As you may recall from Chapters 1 and 11, the lack of these neurotransmitters at pertinent synaptic sites has been implicated in depression. Although the MAO inhibitors relieve depression, they produce certain toxic effects and require careful dietary monitoring. (Certain foods and other drugs when taken with an MAO inhibitor could cause severe illness.)

More frequently used in cases of depression are the **tricyclics,** antidepressant compounds that relieve symptoms of depression and seem to work like the MAO inhibitors but produce fewer of the side effects associated with prolonged drug use. The medication *imipramine,* a tricyclic, has been at least as effective as psychotherapy in relieving the symptoms of depression (Elkin et al., 1995).

Prozac is a controversial drug used to treat depression. Some observers claim that it can induce suicide or violent behavior. In fact, the "Prozac defense" has been used in criminal trials involving murder. The accusations, however, have not been supported by research findings, and Prozac is still widely used.

Until recently, the tricyclics were the most widely used medication in treating depression. The medication that may replace tricyclics as the preferred medication for treating depression is fluoxetine hydrochloride, better known as Prozac. It works by inhibiting the central nervous system's neuronal uptake of serotonin. When originally introduced, Prozac was thought to be a relatively safe medication with minimal addictive characteristics and few dangers associated with high overdoses. Its side effects were reported to be relatively mild and included nervousness, insomnia, and nausea (Cole & Bodkin, 1990). However, Prozac became the center of a controversy because of its association with suicide and violent behavior (Cole & Bodkin, 1990; Food and Drug Administration, 1991; Papp & Gorman, 1990; Teicher, Glad & Cole, 1990). Claims that it increased suicidal and violent acting-out behavior quickly brought Prozac to the attention of the public ("20/20" [television program], 1992); that a patient took Prozac has even been used as a defense in homicide trials.

The bad press received by Prozac and concerns for the safety of individuals prompted a special FDA Psychopharmacological Drug Advisor Committee meeting in 1991 (U.S. Department of Health & Human Services, 1991). The committee heard testimony from patients, advocacy groups, and other interested parties, and it reanalyzed selected studies. It concluded that there was no credible link showing an increase in suicidal tendencies or violent behavior in patients who use Prozac. They noted that suicidal tendencies are often a manifestation of depression and that reports of increased violent behaviors after taking

Prozac were the result of a difference in reporting practices. Despite these conclusions, it is safe to say that controversy surrounding the effects of Prozac will continue. The positive outcome from this may be a closer monitoring of medication usage by researchers and mental health practitioners.

Antimanic Drugs *Lithium* is another mood-controlling (antimanic) medication that has been very effective in treating bipolar disorders, especially mania (Bassuk, Schoonover & Gelenberg, 1983; Klerman et al., 1994). About 70 to 80 percent of manic states can be controlled by lithium. It also controls depressive episodes. How lithium works remains highly speculative. One hypothesis is that it somehow limits the availability of serotonin and norepinephrine at the synapses and produces an effect opposite from that of the antidepressants. Yet lithium's ability to relieve depression appears to contradict this explanation. Other speculations involve electrolyte changes in the body, which alters neurotransmission in some manner.

Strangely enough, lithium, which is administered as a salt, has no known physiological function. Yet with proper administration of lithium—a single tablet in the morning and another in the evening—patients' manic and depressive cycles can be modulated or prevented. However, cautions limit its use in treating bipolar disorders. First, it is largely preventive and must be taken before symptoms appear. Once a manic or depressive state occurs, lithium's effect is minimal. Second, it is often extremely difficult to determine a patient's appropriate dosage. The effective dosage level often borders on toxicity, which can cause convulsions, delirium, and other bad effects. So careful and constant monitoring of the lithium level in a patient's blood is very important.

Psychopharmacological Considerations   A major issue in psychopharmacology is deciding which medication to use with which kind of patient under what circumstances. For example, although imipramine is more effective with long-standing and severe depressions without specific situational causes, antidepressants often do not begin to help patients until two to three weeks after treatment begins. If rapid improvement is necessary, ECT may be used to treat a severely depressed or suicidal patient as a last resort.

The use of antidepressants, antianxiety drugs, and antipsychotics has greatly changed therapy. Patients who take them report that they feel better, that symptoms decline, and that overall functioning improves. Long periods of hospitalization are no longer needed in most cases, and patients are more amenable to other forms of treatment, such as psychotherapy. Remember, however, that medications do not cure mental disorders. Some would characterize their use as "control measures," somewhat better than traditional hospitalization, "straightjackets," or "padded cells." Furthermore, medications seem to be most effective in treating "active" symptoms such as delusions, hallucinations, and aggression and much less effective with "passive" symptoms like withdrawal, poor interpersonal relationships, and feelings of alienation. And, finally, medication does not help patients improve their living skills. A large number of patients discharged from mental hospitals require continuing medication to function even minimally in the community. Unfortunately, many of them do not continue to take their medication after leaving the hospital. Some do not realize the importance of continued and timely medication. Others are unable to pay for medication, either individually or through an insurance plan. Others' lifestyles are not conducive to taking the medications. Once they discontinue their medications, patients may again experience the same disorder that led to their hospitalization.

PSYCHOTHERAPY

In most cases, biological treatments such as medication are used as an adjunct to psychotherapy. But beyond general agreement that psychotherapy is an internal approach to treating psychopathology, involving interaction between one or more clients and a therapist, there is little consensus on exactly what else it is. Psychotherapy has been called "a conversation with a therapeutic purpose" (Korchin, 1976); it has also been called "the talking cure" or the "purchase of friendship" (Schofield, 1964). One observer has suggested that psychotherapy can be variously defined by goals, procedures, and methods; by those who practice it; or by the relationship formed in therapy (Reisman, 1971).

For our purposes, **psychotherapy** may be defined as the systematic application, by a trained and experienced professional therapist, of techniques derived from psychological principles, for the purpose of helping psychologically troubled people. We cannot be more succinct or precise without getting involved in specific types of therapy. Depending on their perspective and theoretical orientation, therapists may seek to modify attitudes, thoughts, feelings, or behaviors; to facilitate the patient's self-insight and rational control of his or her own life; to cure mental illness; to enhance mental health and self-actualization; to make clients "feel better"; to remove a cause; to change a self-concept; or to encourage adaptation. Psychotherapy is practiced by many different kinds of people in many different ways—a fact that seems to preclude establishing a single set of standard therapeutic procedures. And—despite our emphasis on the scientific basis of therapy—in practice it is often more art than science.

Diverse psychotherapies do seem to share some common therapeutic factors. In one study the investigators examined fifty publications on psychotherapy and found that the characteristics common to most of them were (1) development of a therapeutic alliance, (2) opportunity for catharsis, (3) acquisition and practice of new behaviors, and (4) the clients' positive expectancies (Grencavage & Norcross, 1990). These characteristics are very consistent with those proposed by Korchin (1976):

■ *Psychotherapy is a chance for the client to relearn.* Many people say to their psychotherapists, "I know I shouldn't feel or act this way, but I just can't help it." Psychotherapy provides a chance to unlearn, relearn, develop, or change certain behaviors or levels of functioning.

■ *Psychotherapy helps generate the development of new, emotionally important experiences.* A person questioning the value of psychotherapy may ask, "If I talk about my problems, how will that cause me to change, even though I may understand myself better? I talk things over now, with friends." But psychotherapy is not merely a "talking cure." It involves the reexperiencing of emotions that clients may have avoided, along with the painful and helpless feelings fostered by these emotions. This *experiencing* allows relearning as well as emotional and intellectual insight into problems and conflicts.

Culturally Appropriate Mental Health Services

The United States is one of the most ethnically diverse societies in the world (Aponte & Crouch, 1995; Comas-Diaz & Griffith, 1988). Although this diversity is enriching, it also challenges our mental health system. Many ethnic minorities find mainstream mental health services alien to their cultural values and traditions. Consequently, they avoid using services, prematurely terminate their connections, or find treatment unhelpful. To decrease the disparity between the cultural backgrounds of clients and treatment practices, some therapists provide orientation sessions to explain to clients what they can expect from therapy (Acosta, 1984). Another strategy is to tailor treatment to the cultural background of clients, so that the services are less strange or alien to clients.

In San Francisco, which has a large Asian American population, one hospital made an effort to develop services that would be ap-

propriate to this population. San Francisco General Hospital created a special psychiatric ward for severely disturbed Asian clients (Lee, 1985). Mental health staff who were knowledgeable about Asian cultures and who spoke Asian languages were hired. The ward's decor reflected an Asian influence, and patients received Asian diets (such as rice and tea). Information was provided in English and Asian languages. The treatment programs were modified so that they would be more consistent with the cultural backgrounds of clients. For example, because Asian cultural values emphasize the role of family, members of clients' families were encouraged to visit the clients and to participate in treatment. These strategies seem to be successful, at least in terms of service utilization. Whereas Asians represented only 10 percent of the client population in 1981, this figure had increased to 34 percent by 1984.

Another mental health program in an inner-city area of Miami also provided culturally consistent forms of treatment, in this case designed to serve a multiethnic population, primarily African Americans, African Caribbeans, Cubans, and Puerto Ricans (Bestman, 1986). Clients were treated by a team of mental health workers that included staff knowledgeable and familiar with the clients' culture. For those clients who believed in folk or indigenous healers, the mental health team asked such folk healers to collaborate in the treatment process.

In addition to these programs, a variety of other innovative treatment programs have been created in other cities to offer more adequate mental health services to a diverse ethnic population. There is evidence that culturally responsive programs have an effect in lowering treatment dropout rates and in facilitating positive treatment outcomes (Sue et al., 1991).

■ *A therapeutic relationship exists.* Therapists have been trained to listen, show empathic concern, be objective, value the client's integrity, communicate understanding, and use their professional knowledge and skills. Therapists may provide reassurance, interpretations, self-disclosures, reflections of the client's feelings, or information, each at appropriate times. As a team, therapist and client are better prepared to venture into frightening areas that the client would not have faced alone.

■ *Clients in psychotherapy have certain motivations and expectations.* Most people enter therapy with both anxiety and hope. They are frightened by their emotional difficulties and by the prospect of treatment, but they expect or hope that therapy will be helpful.

The goals and general characteristics of psychotherapy as described seem admirable, and most people consider them so. Nevertheless, psychotherapy itself has been criticized as being biased and inappropriate to the lifestyles of many clients, including members of minority groups. Indeed, as the Focus On feature points out, mental health programs have been exploring ways to be more culturally appropriate to members of ethnic groups.

First we will discuss individual psychotherapy, in which one therapist treats one client at any one time, and then group and family therapy. We will also distinguish between insight- and action-oriented approaches to individual therapy. This distinction separates approaches that stress awareness, understanding, and consciousness of one's own motivations (that is, insight) from those approaches that stress actions, such as changing one's behavior or thoughts (London, 1964a). The first set includes the psychoanalytic and humanistic-existential therapies, whereas the second set involves mainly behavioral therapies. Despite this variety of approaches, many therapists use similar treatment strategies. And, as noted in Chapter 1, many therapists choose relevant techniques from all the various "pure" approaches to develop the most effective integrative approach for each particular client.

INSIGHT-ORIENTED APPROACHES TO INDIVIDUAL PSYCHOTHERAPY

The theoretical bases of the major insight-oriented psychotherapies were discussed in Chapter 2. Here we briefly review these theoretical bases and then discuss the most common treatment techniques.

Psychoanalysis

According to Freud's theory of personality, people are born with certain instinctual drives, urges that constantly seek to discharge or express themselves. As the personality structure develops, conflicts occur among the id, ego, and superego. If conflicts remain unresolved, they will resurface during adulthood. The relative importance of such an unresolved conflict depends on the psychosexual stage (oral, anal, phallic, or genital) in which it occurs. The earlier the stage in which an unresolved conflict arises, the greater the conflict's effect on subsequent behaviors. Repressing unacceptable thoughts and impulses (within the unconscious) is the primary way that people defend themselves against such thoughts.

Psychoanalytic therapy, or psychoanalysis, seeks to overcome defenses so that (1) repressed material can be uncovered, (2) the client can achieve insight into his or her inner motivations and desires, and (3) unresolved childhood conflicts can be controlled. Psychoanalysis requires many sessions of therapy over a long period of time. It may not be appropriate for certain types of people, such as nonverbal adults, young children who cannot be verbally articulate or reasonable, schizoid people, those with urgent problems requiring immediate reduction of symptoms, and the mentally retarded (Fenichel, 1945).

Psychoanalysts traditionally use four methods to achieve their therapeutic goals: free association and dream analysis, analysis of resistance, transference, and interpretation.

Free Association and Dream Analysis   In **free association** the patient says whatever comes to mind, regardless of how illogical or embarrassing it may seem, for the purpose of revealing the contents of the patient's unconscious. Psychoanalysts believe the material that surfaces in this process is determined by the patient's psychic makeup and that it can provide some understanding of the patient's conflicts, unconscious processes, and personality dynamics. Simply asking patients to talk about their conflicts is fruitless because they have repressed the really important material from their consciousness. Instead, reports of dreams, feelings, thoughts, and fantasies reflect a patient's psychodynamics; the therapist's tasks are to encourage continuous free association of thoughts and to interpret the results.

Similarly, dream analysis is a very important therapeutic tool that depends on psychoanalytic interpretation of hidden meanings in dreams. Freud is often credited with referring to dreams as "the royal road to the unconscious." According to psychoanalytic theory, when people sleep, defenses and inhibitions of the ego weaken, allowing unacceptable motives and feelings to surface. This material comes out in the disguised and symbolic form of a dream. The portion we remember is called the *manifest content,* and the deeper, unacceptable impulse is the *latent content.* The therapist's job is to uncover the disguised symbolic meanings and let the patient achieve insight into the anxiety-provoking implications.

Analysis of Resistance   Throughout the course of psychoanalytic therapy, the patient's unconscious may try to impede the analysis in a process known as **resistance,** by preventing the exposure of repressed material. In free association, for example, the patient may suddenly change the subject, lose the train of thought, go blank, or become silent. Such resistance may also show up in a patient's late arrival or failure to keep an appointment. A trained analyst is alert to telltale signs of resistance because they indicate that a sensitive area is being approached. The therapist can make therapeutic use of properly interpreted instances of resistance to show the patient that repressed material is coming close to the surface and to suggest means of uncovering it.

Transference   When a patient begins to perceive, or behave toward, the therapist as though the therapist were an important person in the patient's past, the process of transference is occurring. In **transference** the patient reenacts early conflicts by carrying over and applying to the therapist feelings and attitudes that the patient had toward significant others—primarily parents—in the past. These feelings and attitudes then become accessible to understanding. They may be positive, involving feelings of love for the analyst, or negative, involving feelings of anger and hostility.

Part of the psychoanalyst's strategy is to remain "unknown" or ambiguous, so that the client can freely develop whatever kind of transference is required. The patient is allowed, even encouraged, to develop unrealistic expectations and attitudes regarding the therapist. These expectations and attitudes are used as a basis for helping the patient deal realistically with painful early experiences. In essence, a miniature neurosis is re-created; its resolution is crucial to the therapy.

At the same time, the therapist must be careful to recognize and control any instances of *countertransference*. In this process, the therapist—who is also a human being with feelings and fears—transfers those feelings to the patient. This is one reason why Freud believed so strongly that all psychoanalysts need to undergo psychoanalysis themselves.

Interpretation Through interpretation—the explanation of a patient's free associations, reports of dreams, and the like—a sensitive analyst can help the patient gain insight (both intellectual and emotional) into his or her repressed conflicts. By pointing out the symbolic attributes of a transference relationship or by noting the peculiar timing of symptoms, the therapist can direct the patient toward conscious control of unconscious conflicts.

The following example shows the timely interpretation of an important instance of transference:

Sandy (the patient): John [her ex-husband] was just like my father. Always condemning me, always making me feel like an idiot! Strange, the two of them—the most important men in my life—they did the most to screw me up. When I would have fun with my friends and come home at night, he would be sitting there—waiting—to disapprove.

Therapist (male): Who would be waiting for you?

Sandy: Huh?

Therapist: Who's the "he" who'd be waiting?

Sandy: John—I mean, my father—you're confusing me now. . . . My father would sit there—smoking his pipe. I knew what he was thinking, though—he didn't have to say it—he was thinking I was a slut! Someone—who, who was a slut! So what if I stayed up late and had some fun? What business was it of his? He never took any interest in any of us. (Begins to weep.) It was my mother—rest her soul—who loved us, not our father. He worked her to death. Lord, I miss her. (Weeps uncontrollably.)—I must sound angry at my father. Don't you think I have a right to be angry?

Therapist: Do you think you have a right to be angry?

Sandy: Of course, I do! Why are you questioning me? You don't believe me, do you?

Therapist: You want me to believe you.

Sandy: I don't care whether you believe me or not. As far as I'm concerned, you're just a wall that I'm talking to—I don't know why I pay for this rotten therapy.—Don't you have any thoughts or feelings at all? I know what you're thinking—you think I'm crazy—you must be laughing at me—I'll probably be a case in your next book! You're just sitting there—smirking—making me feel like a bad person—thinking I'm wrong for being mad, that I have no right to be mad.

Therapist: Just like your father.

Sandy: Yes, you're just like my father.—Oh my God! Just now—I—I—thought I was talking to him.

Therapist: You mean your father.

Sandy: Yes—I'm really scared now—how could I have—can this really be happening to me?

Therapist: I know it must be awfully scary to realize what just happened—but don't run away now, Sandy. Could it be that your relationship with your father has affected many of the relationships you've had with other men? It seems that your reaction to me just now, and your tendency to sometimes refer to your ex-husband as your father—

Sandy: God!—I don't know—what should I do about it?—Is it real?

Modern Psychoanalysis In Chapter 2, we noted the contemporary changes in theoretical formulations of psychoanalytic theory, especially the increased importance of the ego (ego autonomy theorists) and past interpersonal relationships (object relations theorists). Among the ego autonomy theorists were people such as Anna Freud, Heinz Hartmann, and Erik Erikson, who believed that cognitive processes of the ego were often constructive, creative, and productive (independent from the id). Likewise, object relations theorists such as Melanie Klein, Margaret Mahler, Otto Kernberg, and Heinz Kohut stressed the importance of interpersonal relationships and the child's separation from the mother as important in one's psychological growth. The contributions of these theorists and practitioners expanded and loosened the rigid therapeutic techniques of traditional psychoanalysis. Today, very few psychodynamic therapists practice traditional psychoanalysis. Most are more active in their sessions, restrict the number of sessions they have with clients, place greater emphasis on current rather than past factors, and seem to have adopted a number of client-centered techniques in their practice.

The Effectiveness of Psychoanalysis Psychoanalysis has been criticized for a number of reasons. Psychoanalysts tend to select certain kinds of clients for treatment, usually those who are young, white, and highly educated (Garfield, 1994). This means that psychoanalysis has been limited in addressing the needs of a larger population. Providing operational definitions for such constructs as the unconscious and the libido have been problematic, making it extremely difficult to confirm the various aspects of the theory. For example, psychoanalytic theory suggests that neurotic or anxiety symptoms are caused by underlying emotional conflicts. (DSM in the past had a diagnostic category for "neurotic disorders," which is no longer used. Psychoanalysts often refer to neuroses or neurotic disorders because the disorders have played an important role in conceptualizing psychoanalytic views.) When these symptoms are eliminated without removing the conflict, the person merely expresses the neurosis in other ways and shows other symptoms—a phenomenon known as *symptom substitution*. Many researchers, particularly behavior therapists, assert that it is possible to eliminate neurotic or anxiety symptoms without symptom substitution occurring. Furthermore, they contend that when the symptoms are eliminated, the neurosis or anxiety disorder is cured. Thus, psychoanalysis has encountered many problems despite its vast influence in the field of psychotherapy. While it is still widely practiced, many therapists do not strictly follow all psychoanalytic procedures, preferring psychodynamic or ego psychological modifications. Many psychotherapists predict that psychoanalysis will decline in use in the future (Norcross & Freedheim, 1992).

Humanistic-Existential Therapies

In contrast to the psychic determinism implicit in psychoanalysis, the humanistic-existential therapies stress the importance of self-actualization, self-concept, free will, responsibility, and the understanding of the client's phenomenological world. The focus of therapy is on qualities of "humanness"; human beings cannot be understood without reference to their personal uniqueness and wholeness. Among the several humanistic-existential therapies are person-centered therapy, existential analysis, and gestalt therapy.

Person-Centered Therapy Carl Rogers, the founder of person-centered therapy, believed that people could develop better self-concepts and move toward self-actualization if the therapist provided certain therapeutic conditions. These are the conditions in which clients use their own innate tendencies to grow, to actively negotiate with their environment, and to realize their potential. Therefore, therapists must accept clients as people, show empathy and respect, and provide unconditional positive regard for them. A therapist should not control, inhibit, threaten, or interpret a client's behaviors. These actions are manipulative, and they undermine the client's ability to find his or her own direction.

Person-centered therapy thus emphasizes the kind of person the therapist should be in the therapeutic relationship rather than the precise techniques to use in therapy. Particular details of this therapeutic approach were discussed in Chapter 2.

Existential Analysis **Existential analysis** follows no single theory or group of therapeutic techniques. Instead, it is concerned with the person's experience and involvement in the world as a being with consciousness and self-consciousness. Existential therapists believe that the inability to accept death or nonbeing as a reality restricts self-actualization. In contemporary society, many people feel lonely and alienated; they lose a sense of the meaning of life, of self-responsibility, and of free will. This state of mind is popularly called "existential crisis." The task of the therapist is to engage clients in an encounter in which they can experience their own existence as being real. The encounter should involve genuine sharing between partners, in which the therapist, too, may grow and be influenced. When clients can experience their existence and nonexistence, then feelings of responsibility, choice, and meaning reemerge. (Again, see Chapter 2 for additional details.)

Existential approaches to therapy are strongly philosophical in nature. They have not received any research scrutiny because many existential concepts and methods are difficult to define operationally for research purposes. Furthermore, existential therapists point out that therapist and client are engaged in a complex encounter that cannot be broken down into components for empirical observation, so research studies are incapable of assessing the impact of therapy. Although impressive case histories indicate its effectiveness, little empirical support for existential analysis exists.

Gestalt Therapy The German word *gestalt* means "whole." As conceptualized by Fritz Perls in 1969, **gestalt therapy** emphasizes the importance of a person's total experience, which should not be fragmented or separated. Perls believed that when affective and cognitive experiences are isolated, people lack full awareness of their complete experience.

In gestalt therapy, clients are asked to discuss the totality of the here-and-now. Only experiences, feelings, and behaviors occurring in the present are stressed. Past experiences or anticipated future experiences are brought up only in relation to current feelings. Interestingly, Perls was originally trained as a psychoanalyst, but he later rejected Freudian theory.

He did, however, incorporate dream analysis in his work. Dreams, too, are interpreted in relation to the here-and-now. As a means of opening clients to their experiences, therapists encourage clients to

1. make personalized and unqualified statements that help them "act out" their emotions. For example, instead of hedging by saying, "It is sometimes upsetting when your boss yells at you," a client is encouraged to say "I get scared when my boss yells at me."

2. exaggerate the feelings associated with behaviors to gain greater awareness of their experiences and to eliminate intellectual explanations for them.

3. role-play situations and then focus on what was experienced during the role playing.

Like existential analysis, gestalt therapy has generated little research. Thus it is difficult to evaluate its effectiveness. Proponents of gestalt therapy are convinced that clients are helped, but sufficient empirical support has never emerged. (You might be interested in reading Perls's remarkable book *Gestalt Therapy Verbatim* [1969] for a fuller explanation of this approach.)

ACTION-ORIENTED APPROACHES TO INDIVIDUAL PSYCHOTHERAPY

The principles underlying the action-oriented or behaviorist approaches to abnormal behavior were discussed in depth in Chapter 2. Treatment based on classical conditioning, operant conditioning, observational learning, and cognitive-behavioral processes has gained widespread popularity (Norcross & Freedheim, 1992). Behavior therapists typically use a variety of techniques, many of which were discussed in preceding chapters. This section presents a selection of the most important behavioral techniques.

Classical Conditioning Techniques

Using the classical conditioning principles described in Chapter 2, Joseph Wolpe (1973) used systematic desensitization as treatment for anxiety. This technique attempts to reduce anxiety in response to a stimulus situation by eliciting in the given situation an alternative response that is incompatible with anxiety. For example, if a woman is afraid of flying in a jet plane, her anxiety response could be reduced by training her to relax while in airplanes.

Systematic desensitization typically includes training in relaxation, the construction of a fear hierarchy,

TABLE 17.2 A Systematic Desensitization Fear Hierarchy for a Client with a Fear of Flying

Scene	Fear Rating
1. Encountering turbulence while flying	99
2. Flying at 35,000 feet	95
3. Taking off	90
4. Fastening the seatbelt	85
5. Boarding the plane	80
6. Waiting to board the plane	60
7. Taking a taxi to the airport	40
8. Packing for trip	25
9. Making airline reservations	20
10. Thinking about a trip involving flying	10

and the combination of relaxation and imagined scenes from the fear hierarchy. This process is described in detail in Chapter 5, but we can illustrate the process using the example of the woman who wants to overcome her fear of flying. The therapist would first train her to relax, probably employing a progressive relaxation method in which the muscles are alternately tensed and relaxed (Jacobson, 1964). Working with the therapist, the client would construct a fear hierarchy for flying, rating the level of fear in various scenarios on a scale of 1 to 100, as in Table 17.2. Notice that self-reported anxiety increases as the task approaches, and a high level of fear occurs in response to a scene in which the plane is shaking due to turbulence while flying. If there are large increases in anxiety from one consecutive scene to the next, other scenes may be constructed that occupy an intermediate position. For example, a twenty-point difference occurs in Table 17.2 between scenes 5 and 6 (and between scenes 6 and 7). The client and therapist may find another scene that the client rates as being fifty points on the hierarchy—for example, she might imagine getting a boarding pass and checking in her luggage. The client is then asked to *imagine* herself in each of these situations. Most clients experience anxiety when they imagine such situations, and it is obviously more convenient to imagine them than to actually go through them. If the client is actually present in the fear-provoking situations, the approach

Flooding is a technique used to reduce anxiety by placing the client in the real-life anxiety-provoking situation. For example, a client with a fear of heights may be taken to the top of a tall building. The client experiences intense anxiety but the imagined consequences, such as falling off the building, do not occur. According to classical conditioning principles, the anxiety and fear should then begin to extinguish.

is known as an *in vivo* approach. The development of a fear hierarchy is important in systematic desensitization when an in vivo approach is not used.

Once the person is able to relax, the therapist asks the client first to imagine a low-anxiety scene (such as making flight reservations) and to relax at the same time. The client then proceeds up the fear hierarchy, imagining each situation in order. If a particular situation elicits too much anxiety, the client is told to return to a less anxiety-provoking one. This procedure is repeated until the client can imagine the entire hierarchy without anxiety.

Behavior therapists believe that systematic desensitization is more effective than psychotherapy for cer-

tain kinds of problems such as simple phobias; it certainly requires fewer sessions to achieve desired results (Wolpe, 1973). Systematic desensitization has stimulated a great deal of research, and its efficacy in reducing fears has been well documented. Some researchers question the need for certain procedural aspects of the treatment approach. For example, Wolpe's rather rigid format for desensitization may be unnecessary, and alternatives to relaxation, such as talking about the fear or listening to soothing music, may be used in the process (Nathan & Jackson, 1976; Sue, 1972).

Flooding and Implosion Two other techniques that use the classical conditioning principles of extinction are flooding and implosion (Levis, 1985; Stampfl & Levis, 1967). The two are very similar. **Flooding** attempts to extinguish fear by placing the client in a real-life anxiety-provoking situation at full intensity. **Implosion** attempts to extinguish fear by having the client imagine the anxiety-provoking situation at full intensity. The difference between systematic desensitization and flooding and implosion lies in the speed with which the fearful situation is introduced to the client. Systematic desensitization introduces it more slowly. Flooding and implosion require the client to immediately confront the feared situation in its full intensity. The belief is that the client's fears will be extinguished if he or she is not allowed to avoid or escape the situation. In flooding, for example, a client who is afraid of heights may be taken to the top of a tall building, mountain, or bridge and physically prevented from leaving. Some studies have indicated that flooding effectively eliminates specific fears such as phobias (Foa & Kozak, 1986). In implosion therapy, the client is forced to imagine a feared situation. For example, a therapist might ask a client who is afraid of flying to close her eyes and imagine the following:

> You are flying in an airplane. Suddenly the plane hits an air pocket and begins to shake violently from side to side. Meal trays fly around, and passengers who do not have their seatbelts fastened are thrown from their seats. People start to scream. As you look out the window, the plane's wing is flying by. The pilot's frantic voice over the loudspeaker is shouting: "Prepare to crash, prepare to crash!" Your seatbelt breaks and you must hang on for dear life, while the plane is spinning around and careening. You can tell that the plane is falling rapidly. The ground is coming up toward you. The situation is hopeless—all will die.

Presumably the client feels intense anxiety, after which she is told to "wake up." Repeated exposure to such a high level of anxiety eventually causes the stimulus to lose its power to elicit anxiety and leads to extinction.

These cigarette smokers are taking an aversive conditioning class to quit smoking. They have been asked to puff their cigarettes at a very rapid pace, which usually brings on nausea. Repeated pairings of rapid smoking and feelings of nausea may result in an aversion to smoking.

The developers of implosion and flooding believe that they can be effective, though some clients find the procedures too traumatic and discontinue treatment. In general, these methods have not been scrutinized as carefully as systematic desensitization has been, but they appear to be equally effective with clients with phobias (Emmelkamp, 1994).

Aversive Conditioning   In **aversive conditioning**, a widely used classical conditioning technique, the undesirable behavior is paired with an unpleasant stimulus to suppress the undesirable behavior. For example, it has been used to modify the smoking behaviors of heavy smokers. In the rapid smoking technique, smokers who are trying to quit are asked to puff cigarettes at a fast rate (perhaps a puff every 6 or 7 seconds). Puffing at this rate usually brings on nausea, so the nausea from puffing is associated with smoking behaviors. After repeated pairings, many smokers find cigarette smoke aversive and are more motivated to quit (Glasgow & Lichtenstein, 1987).

Aversive conditioning has also been applied to alcoholics, drug addicts, and people with sexual disorders, again with varying degrees of success. The noxious stimuli have included electric shock, drugs, odors, verbal censure, and reprimands. Some aversive conditioning programs also provide positive reinforcement for alternative behaviors that are deemed appropriate (Emmelkamp, 1994).

Several problems have been encountered in the use of aversive conditioning. First, because noxious stimuli are used, many people in treatment discontinue therapy, as in the smoking-reduction program just described. Second, aversive methods often suppress the undesirable behavior only temporarily, especially when punishment for those behaviors is applied solely in a laboratory situation that bears little resemblance to real life. Third, the client may become anxious and hostile. And some critics argue that punishment is unethical or has the potential for misuse and abuse. Partially as a response to these criticisms, as well as for practical reasons, some therapists advocate the use of *covert sensitization*. Like implosion, it requires imagining the aversive situation along with the behavior one is trying to eliminate (Cautela, 1966, 1967). A person who wants to stop smoking may be asked to imagine a smoke-filled room, becoming nauseated, suffocating, and dying slowly of lung cancer and emphysema.

Operant Conditioning Techniques

Behavior modification using operant methods has flourished, and many ingenious programs have been developed. As in the case of classical conditioning, only a few important examples are presented here.

Token Economies   Treatment programs that reward patients with tokens for appropriate behaviors are known as **token economies** (Kazdin, 1980). The tokens may be exchanged for hospital privileges, food, or weekend passes. The goal is to modify patient behaviors using a secondary reinforcer (the tokens). In much the same way, money operates as a secondary reinforcer for people who work.

Three elements are necessary to a token economy: (1) the designation by hospital staff of certain patient behaviors as desirable and reinforceable; (2) a medium of exchange, such as coinlike tokens or tallies on a piece of paper; and (3) goods, services, or privileges that the tokens can buy. It is up to the hospital staff to dispense the tokens for desirable patient behaviors (Ullman & Krasner, 1975). In one psychiatric hospital ward, tokens could be exchanged for hospital passes, cigarettes, food, television viewing, and the choice of dining room tablemates. Patients were given tokens for good grooming and neat physical appearance, and for washing dishes and performing other chores. Although the program markedly improved the behavior of schizophrenic patients, the previously reinforced activities decreased when tokens were no longer given (Ayllon & Azrin, 1968). This finding supported the conclusion that tokens were responsible for the success. Other studies have also indicated that token economy systems are effective with chronic hospitalized patients who are considered resistant to treatment (Paul, 1982). Token economies also tend to raise staff morale (Ullman & Krasner, 1975).

Token economy programs are used in a variety of settings, with such different types of people as juvenile delinquents, schoolchildren, retarded people, and patients in residential community homes (Kazdin, 1994). Although such programs have been extremely successful in modifying behaviors in institutional settings, problems remain. Some patients do not respond to token economies. Complex behaviors, such as those involving language, are difficult to modify with this technique. A final criticism is that desirable patient behaviors that are exhibited in a hospital may not be continued outside the hospital setting.

Punishment   When less drastic methods are ineffective, punishment is sometimes used in treating autistic and schizophrenic children. In an early study, Lovaas (1977; Lovaas, Schaeffer & Simmons, 1965) attempted to modify the behaviors of five-year-old identical twins, both diagnosed with schizophrenia. The children had shown no response to conventional treatment and were largely unresponsive in everyday interpersonal situations. They showed no reaction to speech and did not themselves speak. They did not recognize adults or each other, and they engaged in temper tantrums, self-destructive behaviors, and inappropriate handling of objects. The experimenters decided to use electric shock as a punishment for the purpose of modifying the children's behaviors. A floor gridded with metal tape was constructed so that a painful but not physically damaging shock could be administered to their bare feet. By turning the shock on and off, the experimenters were able to condition desired behaviors in the children. Affectionate responses such as kissing and hugging were developed, and tantrum behaviors were eliminated—all via the use of shock as an aversive stimulus. Lovaas (1987) has also used a loud "No" as well as a slap to the thigh of a child to reduce undesirable or self-destructive behaviors.

Lovaas's work has shown that operant conditioning is a powerful technique for changing the behavior of autistic children who have failed to respond to other forms of treatment. Because of the ethical issues raised by the use of electric shocks, however, use of this punishment technique has declined in recent years.

Observational Learning Techniques

As discussed in Chapter 2, *observational learning* is the acquisition of new behaviors by watching them. The process of demonstrating these behaviors to a person or audiences is called *modeling*. Modeling has been shown to be effective in helping people acquire more appropriate behaviors. In one experiment, young adults who showed an intense fear of snakes were assigned to four groups:

1. The *live modeling with participation* group watched a live model who initiated progressively more fear-evoking activities with the snake. Subjects were then guided to imitate the model and were encouraged to touch the snake, first with a gloved hand and then with a bare hand.

2. The *symbolic modeling* group underwent relaxation training and then viewed a film in which children and adults were seen handling snakes in progressively more fear-evoking circumstances.

3. The *systematic desensitization* group received systematic desensitization treatment for snake phobias.

4. The *control* group received no treatment.

Before treatment, the approach behaviors of all four groups of participants toward snakes were equally few. After treatment, the ability to approach and touch snakes had increased for members of all treated groups, who performed better than individuals in the control group. Group 1, in which treatment was live modeling with participation, showed the greatest change: Nearly all its members voluntarily touched the snake (Bandura, Blanchard & Ritter, 1969).

Observation of models who verbalize how to perform a task and who make a few mistakes while completing the task has been found to be more effective than viewing models who do not verbalize or who perform with no anxiety or mistakes (Braswell & Kendall, 1988).

The modeling of behaviors shown in films has been successfully used in medical and dental practices to reduce fears of medical procedures (Wilson & O'Leary, 1980), in teaching social and problem-solving skills (Bellack, Hersen & Himmelnoch, 1983; Braswell & Kendall, 1988), and in reducing compulsions and phobias (Rachman & Hodgson, 1980).

Cognitive-Behavioral Therapy

In Chapter 2, we discussed in some detail how cognitive-behavioral approaches believe that psychopathology stems from irrational, faulty, negative, and distorted thinking or self-statements that a person makes to himself or herself. As a result, most cognitive approaches share several elements. First, cognitive restructuring is used to change a client's irrational, self-defeating, and distorted thoughts and attitudes to more rational, positive, and appropriate ones. Second, skills training is used to help clients learn to manage and overcome stress. Third, problem solving provides clients with strategies for dealing with specific problems in living.

Initially, Albert Ellis's rational-emotive therapy, or RET (1962) was not well received by therapists. Attitudes soon changed, however, when the behaviorists became increasingly interested in mediating cognitive processes. In addition, RET and the behavioral strategies are similar in a number of ways. For example, RET incorporates cognitive restructuring, skills training, and problem-solving skills. Cognitive restructuring specifically is used to help clients deal with their irrational thoughts and beliefs. For example, a client's belief that he or she should be loved by everyone is attacked directly by the therapist: "What is so awful about not being loved by everyone? If your father doesn't love you, that's his problem!" Once the client begins to restructure his or her thoughts, the therapist begins the task of helping the client learn new ways to appraise and evaluate situations. Last, homework assignments (behavioral rehearsal) are given to help the client learn new strategies to deal with situations.

Aaron Beck (1976, 1985; Beck & Weishaar, 1989) has also been a major contributor to cognitive behavioral therapy. Originally using this approach to treat depression, he extended his treatment to other disorders such as anxiety and phobias (Beck, 1985; Beck, Emery & Greenberg, 1985). Beck holds that emotional disorders

TABLE 17.3 Beck's Cognitive Triad of Depression

Negative View of Self—"I'm Worthless"

Believing that one is worthless, defective, inadequate, and undesirable. A depressed person may interpret negative events as being caused by personal inadequacies and failures.

Negative View of the World— "Everything Bad Happens to Me"

Perceiving the world and one's environment as being unreceptive, frustrating, and demanding. A depressed person may see the world in the most pessimistic and cynical manner.

Negative View of the Future—"Nothing Is Ever Going to Change"

Perceiving the future as hopeless and believing that negative events will continue to occur. The depressed person believes that one is helpless and powerless to improve the situation in the future.

are primarily caused by negative patterns of thought, which he labels the "cognitive triad"—errors in how we think about ourselves (such as "I'm worthless"), our world ("Everything bad happens to me"), and our future ("Nothing is ever going to change") (see Table 17.3). Whereas RET engages the client in a rational or socratic "debate," Beck's approach emphasizes the client's capacity for self-discovery. Less hurried and confrontive, the therapist and client work as a team to uncover underlying assumptions, to test them in the client's everyday life situations, and to determine by logical means whether they are valid. As in systematic desensitization, smaller challenges are assigned first and more difficult ones are tackled as successes are experienced.

Other variations of cognitive-behavioral methods have been developed, and all are based on similar assumptions. For example, stress inoculation therapy was developed by Meichenbaum (Meichenbaum, 1985; Meichenbaum & Cameron, 1982). The assumption behind stress inoculation training is that people can be taught better ways to handle life stresses. Meichenbaum uses cognitive preparation and skill acquisition, rehearsal, application, and practice.

Cognitive-behavioral therapy shows much promise. Studies have indicated successful use of rational emotive therapy (Lipsky, Kassinove & Miller, 1980),

Beck's approach (Kovacs et al., 1981), and stress inoculation therapy (Denicola & Sandler, 1980; Meichenbaum, 1985). Furthermore, some evidence suggests that the approaches may be at least as effective as medication or drug therapy for certain situational and specific depressions (Hollon & Beck, 1994; Lipman & Kendall, 1992; Simons et al., 1986). In one survey of psychotherapists, cognitive-behavioral approaches were rated as a therapeutic orientation that will continue to grow in popularity (Norcross & Freedheim, 1992).

Behavioral Medicine

Behavioral medicine (or health psychology) integrates behavioral and biomedical science. The two fields merged because people realized that psychological factors were often related to the cause and treatment of physical illnesses (Brownell, 1982). The term *psychobiology* has also been used to address the importance of viewing the totality of the human condition (both biology and experience) in explaining and understanding behavior (Dewsbury, 1991). The goal of behavioral medicine is to help people change their lifestyles to prevent illness or to enhance the quality of their lives. As discussed in Chapter 7, heart disease, strokes, and cancer have been correlated with lack of exercise, diet, smoking, alcohol consumption, and other behaviors of a particular lifestyle. Behavioral medicine makes people aware of the effects of these behaviors and helps them to develop healthier patterns of living.

One way to do this is through **biofeedback therapy,** which combines physiological and behavioral approaches. A patient receives information, or feedback, regarding particular autonomic functions such as heart rate, blood pressure, and brain wave activity and is rewarded for influencing those functions in a desired direction. Monitoring devices supply the information; the rewards vary, depending on the patient and the situation. Studies have found that biofeedback therapy can help reduce high blood pressure (Blanchard, 1994).

In an early study, researchers attempted to help patients with essential hypertension (elevated blood pressure) lower their systolic pressure. They used an operant conditioning feedback system in which patients saw a flash of light and heard a tone whenever their systolic blood pressure decreased. They were told that the light and tone were desirable and were given rewards—slides of pleasant scenes and money—for achieving a certain number of light flashes and tones. The patients gradually reduced their blood pressure at succeeding biofeedback sessions. When they reached the point where they were unable to reduce their pressure further for five consecutive sessions, the experiment was discontinued (Benson et al., 1971).

Meyer Friedman in 1984 reported a study in which coronary patients who changed their lifestyles drastically reduced their recurrence of heart attacks. The investigation discovered that 95 percent of patients who suffer heart attacks exhibit what is called "Type A" behavior (discussed in Chapter 7), which is character-

Biofeedback is a technique in which a client is attached to various monitoring devices and receives information or feedback regarding particular autonomic functions, such as heart rate, blood pressure, and brain wave activity. The client is given a reward (that is, positive feedback) for being able to somehow control the functions. Here, a client with hypertension is learning to reduce his blood pressure.

ized by time urgency (the compulsion to finish tasks early, be early for appointments, and always race against the clock), attempts to perform several tasks at once, a propensity to anger quickly when others do not perform as expected, and rapid speech and body movements. The patients in Friedman's Recurrent Coronary Prevention Project learned, through counseling and practice drills, to control and change their Type A behaviors. Although the Type A hypothesis has proven to have a number of shortcomings (Friedman & Booth-Kewley, 1988), behavioral medicine techniques, which focus on lifestyle changes, have proven very beneficial. Some of these are listed here:

1. *Establish priorities.* It is important for each of us to determine where to put our time and energies. Establishing a daily or weekly priority list, including everything that must be done, is a helpful strategy. If time is limited, learn to postpone the low-priority items without feeling guilty.

2. *Avoid stressful situations.* Do not put yourself in situations that involve unnecessary stress. For example, if you know that a particular traffic route involves constant tie-ups, consider another time for your commuting or take another route. Remember, we can and do have control over much of our lives.

3. *Take time out for yourself.* We all need to engage in activities that bring pleasure and gratification. Whether they involve going fishing, playing cards, talking to friends, or taking a vacation, they are necessary for physical and mental health. And they give the body time to recover from the stresses of everyday life.

4. *Exercise regularly.* Exercise is effective in reducing anxiety and increasing tolerance for stress. Furthermore, a healthy body gives us greater energy to cope with stress and greater ability to recover from a stressful situation.

5. *Eat right.* You have heard this advice before, but it happens to be excellent advice: Eat well-balanced meals that are high in fiber and protein but low in fat and cholesterol. Nutritional deficiencies can lower our resistance to stress.

6. *Make friends.* Good friends share our problems, accept us as we are, and laugh and cry with us. Their very presence enables us to reduce or eliminate much of the stress we may be experiencing.

7. *Learn to relax.* A major finding of stress management research is that tense, "uptight" people are more likely to react negatively to stress than are relaxed people. Relaxation can do much to com-

bat the autonomic effects of anxiety and stress; thus the various relaxation techniques are helpful in eliminating stress.

Behavioral medicine approaches have also been used to address a wide range of problems, including chronic pain, recurring headaches, and insomnia.

EVALUATING INDIVIDUAL PSYCHOTHERAPY

Both insight- and action-oriented approaches have attracted firm followers and loud critics. Behavioral therapists, for example, believe that this approach has solid theoretical support and empirical justification; that it provides a rapid means of changing behaviors; and that (unlike the insight-oriented approaches) it includes specific goals, procedures, and means of assessing its effectiveness. Critics have argued that behavioral therapy is dehumanizing, mechanical, and manipulative; that its relationship to learning theory is more apparent than real; and that it is applicable only to a narrow range of problems.

Whether one argues for either insight- or action-oriented therapies depends largely on whether one believes that human behavior is determined primarily by internal or external factors. Interestingly, Norcross and Freedheim (1992) surveyed a group of prominent psychotherapists and psychotherapy researchers about which therapeutic orientations would grow or decline in use during the next decade. As indicated in Figure 17.1, the respondents predicted that theoretical integration, eclecticism, and cognitive orientations would gain popularity, while psychoanalysis and transactional analysis would decrease in use.

Eysenck's Criticisms of Psychotherapy

More than forty years ago, Hans Eysenck (1952) concluded that there was *no evidence that psychotherapy facilitates recovery* from what were then classified as neurotic disorders. According to the criteria he used, patients receiving no formal psychotherapy recovered at least as well as those who were treated! Since that time, others have also claimed that psychotherapy's success has been oversold and that both its practitioners and its clients are wasting time, money, and effort. Some opponents feel so strongly that they advocate a "truth in packaging" policy: Prospective clients should be warned that "Psychotherapy will probably not help you very much."

Critics of the Eysenck study raise several objections. First, it is not clear that the groups of treated

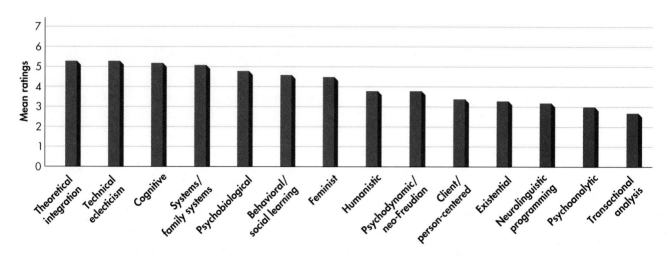

FIGURE 17.1   Predictions of the Theoretical Orientations of the Future
These ratings are averages compiled from the responses of prominent psychotherapists and psychotherapy researchers who were asked to predict the use of various psychotherapeutic orientations in the next decade. The ratings were made on a scale ranging from 1 (representing great decrease) to 7 (representing great increase).
Source: Data from Norcross & Freedheim, 1992.

and untreated patients were comparable in demographic variables, such as age, socioeconomic class, and race—factors associated with prognosis. Second, the improvement criteria applied to the untreated patients (discharge rate, return to work, lack of complaints) are not the same as those used by many psychotherapists, who aim for far more substantial personality changes. Furthermore, the criteria Eysenck used to calculate improvement for patients in psychoanalysis were such that he underestimated the rate of improvement. In fact, one critic showed it was possible to come up with an improvement rate of more than 80 percent for psychoanalysis—using Eysenck's data (Bergin, 1971). Finally, was the "untreated" group really untreated? We know that disturbed people often seek help from relatives, friends, or members of the clergy during times of stress. A form of psychotherapy may have been rendered by these other sources. In addition, later studies revealed that Eysenck's high spontaneous remission rates did not hold up and may be closer to 40 to 45 percent rather than 70 percent (Bergin & Lambert, 1978).

Do Outcome Studies Accurately Reflect Psychotherapy?   In a thought-provoking article, Persons (1991) pointed out that past outcome studies showing no positive effects from psychotherapy or no difference in outcome in the use of different therapies may have suffered from a major methodological flaw. She argued that psychotherapy outcome studies do not ac-

curately represent current models of psychotherapy. Her argument is based on three lines of reasoning.

1. *Outcome studies fail to carry out a theory-driven psychological assessment of clients.*   Instead, in an attempt to meet a single diagnostic category like dysthymia (depression), assessment of disorders is based on narrow criteria, using a particular standard or inventory. Such assessments assume that patients possess the same problem and that their cases differ only in severity. Real psychotherapy, in contrast, is often quite personal and individualized and attempts to understand the comprehensive multitude of problems encountered by patients. For example, depressed patients typically manifest problems associated with aspects of their lives such as family, work, and social isolation. Outcome studies frequently ignore such difficulties when focusing only on a single diagnostic term. In addition, outcome studies ignore theoretical approach and focus on diagnosis. In actual clinical practice, assessment strategies are determined by the theoretical model used and its constructs. The psychodynamic model collects information about the patient's core conflicts; the behavioral model collects information about antecedents and consequences related to the behavioral problem; and the cognitive model collects information concerning dysfunctional cognitive processes. Treatment is based not so much on the diagnostic category as on the underlying mechanisms described in the theory.

2. *Assessment and treatment in outcome studies are separate, whereas in actual therapy they are inseparable.* Persons (1991) argued that clinicians believe that assessment is intimately and inextricably linked to treatment. The process of therapy involves assessing the patient's problems, designing a therapy program, assessing the progress, and using the information to revise the treatment as needed. This interplay is continual and requires ongoing assessment and change in treatment.

3. *In outcome studies, treatment is standardized, whereas actual clinical practice requires treatment to be individualized.* Persons' third criticism is that studies aimed at comparing or determining the effectiveness of therapy make every effort to see that the treatment received by patients in a given treatment condition is the same (standardized). Such manipulations do not reflect clinical reality.

Taken together, these three points lead Persons to conclude that contemporary outcome studies do not accurately represent psychotherapy.

Meta-analysis and Effect Size A form of statistical analysis *(meta-analysis)* has been found to be an extremely useful tool in analyzing therapy outcome studies. Meta-analysis allows us to analyze a large number of different studies by looking at *effect size,* a term that refers to treatment-produced change. To determine effect size, researchers subtract the mean of the control group from the mean of the treatment group. The difference is then divided by the standard deviation of the control group. The larger the numerical figure obtained, the larger is the effect of the treatment. Ideally, this comparison of effect size in many studies allows us to determine the effectiveness of different treatment approaches. It is important to note that meta-analysis is controversial; it has both staunch supporters (Shapiro & Shapiro, 1983; Smith, Glass & Miller, 1980) and detractors (Erwin, 1986; Paul, 1985).

Meta-analytic studies strongly support the conclusion that psychotherapy is effective, and they allow one to estimate how large the effect is. Figure 17.2 graphically displays the effect of treatment, based on two meta-analytic studies (Lambert & Bergin, 1994). As can be seen, individuals who receive psychotherapy are better off than 79 percent of individuals who receive no treatment. Those receiving minimal treatment (for example, a placebo) are better off than 66 percent of the people in no-treatment control groups.

Many reviews of outcome research have indicated that psychotherapy is effective and that people who are treated show more and larger desirable changes

Hans Eysenck started a controversy by asserting in 1952 that there was no evidence that psychotherapy was effective. Research, however, indicates that psychotherapy *is* effective and that the real issues concern types of treatment and their suitability for clients and their particular circumstances.

than those who do not receive formal psychotherapy (Garfield & Bergin, 1994; Sloane et al., 1975; Smith & Glass, 1977; Smith, Glass & Miller, 1980). In addition, the largest gains in treatment tend to occur within the first few months and tend to endure (Lambert, Shapiro & Bergin, 1986; Nicholson & Berman, 1983; Smith, Glass & Miller, 1980). Howard (1994) argues that psychotherapy is one of the best documented and most studied treatment interventions and that research clearly attests to its beneficial impact in people's lives.

We believe that psychotherapy *is* valuable. We also believe its maximal value is attained not unreservedly accepting or rejecting any group of treatments, either behavioral or insight-oriented, but by searching for the best match that can be made among therapist, client, and situational variables. The Critical Thinking

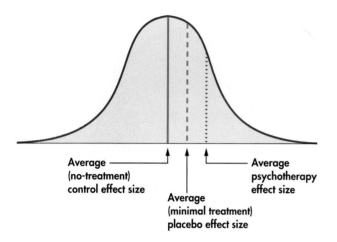

FIGURE 17.2   Effect Sizes for Psychotherapy, Placebo, and No-Treatment Groups *Effect size* is the result of calculations that reflect the changes produced by treatment. The effect size of psychotherapy is much higher than that of the placebo condition, which in turn is higher than the no-treatment condition. In terms of percentage improved, the figure can be interpreted as follows: The average client undergoing a placebo treatment is better off than 66 percent of the no-treatment controls; the average client undergoing psychotherapy appears to be better off than 79 percent of the no-treatment controls.

Source: Based on Lambert & Bergin, 1994.

feature discusses some options that should be considered in choosing a therapist.

GROUP, FAMILY, AND MARITAL THERAPY

The classic form of psychotherapy involves a one-to-one relationship between one therapist and one client. **Group therapy** is a form of therapy that involves the simultaneous treatment of two or more clients and may involve more than one therapist. Its increasing popularity stems from certain economic and therapeutic advantages: Because the therapist sees several clients at each session, he or she can provide much more mental health service to the community. And, because several clients participate in the sessions, the cost to each person is noticeably reduced. Saving time and money is important, but the increasing use of group therapy seems also to be related to the fact that many psychological difficulties are basically interpersonal in nature—they involve relationships with others, and these problems are best treated within a group rather than individually.

Most of the techniques of individual psychotherapy are also used in group therapy. Rather than repeat them here, we will first discuss some general features of group therapy and family and marital therapy.

Group Therapy

Group Member 1: What you just said really makes me angry, Frank. You're blaming me for something you should be responsible for.

Frank [a group member]: I was just pointing out that you never contribute to the decision-making process. I wasn't blaming you! What's your problem anyway?

Group Member 1: There you go again! I don't have a problem with the group exercises. When they go wrong, I try to see what happened and why. If it's my fault, I'll try to correct it—okay?

Frank: If the shoe fits, wear it!

Group Member 1: Damn! It's no use trying to talk to you. Why do you always blame others?

Frank (angrily): Piss on you! It seems like you're the only one who thinks that way. I totally reject your accusations!

Group Member 2 (hesitantly): Frank, you do blame others a lot—

Frank: Shit! Do I have to put up with another conspirator?

Group Member 3: I don't think he's the only one in the group who sees you that way. For the past few times I've been angry at you too. You make me and the others feel incompetent and anxious. Last week you made fun of me when I talked about my problems with Janice.

Frank (somewhat bewildered): I wasn't making fun of you. Why are you so defensive?

Therapist: Frank, we have at least three members in this group who are giving you feedback about your behavior and how it affects them. Maybe you should check out how the others feel and think about your behavior.

Frank: Well—I don't want to waste our time—there are more important things—

Therapist: It's important for us to give and ask for feedback from one another. I know it's hard sometimes, but that's one part of learning about ourselves: If it's OK with you, I'd like to start—

Frank (quietly): It's okay.

There are now a great variety of group therapies, reflecting the many dimensions along which a therapeutic group may be characterized. (The Focus On fea-

CRITICAL THINKING

What Kind of Therapist Do You Want?

In general, people who experience emotional and behavioral problems benefit from psychotherapy. Yet benefits often vary according to client, therapist, and treatment characteristics. Given this fact, it is surprising that many individuals in need of therapy do little prior thinking about the kind of therapist they would like to see or about how and where to find "good" therapists.

If you were depressed or anxious, what kind of therapist would you like to find? What characteristics are important to you? What characteristics do you consider to be relatively unimportant? Why? The answers to these questions are complex and vary from person to person. Let us examine some of the factors that might be important and then provide an example of the kind of issues that can be raised.

■ *Demographic characteristics of the therapist* These include age, gender, educational and experiential background, ethnicity,

and other similar characteristics. For example, would you mind seeing a therapist who had just recently completed training in psychotherapy?

■ *Overall reputation and professional standing* How can you determine how effective or successful a therapist is?

■ *Experience with clients having problems similar to yours* Does it matter whether the therapist specializes in your problem or is a general practitioner?

■ *Therapeutic orientation* (such as psychoanalytic, behavioral, spiritual, and so on) Would you want to work with a therapist who believes that meditation is the primary tool to use against mental disorders?

■ *Interpersonal style* (such as humorous, serious, formal, informal, dominant, and submissive) Would you like a therapist who provides only minimal verbal responses in order to allow you all the time to talk?

■ *Values and beliefs* If you were a Christian fundamentalist, how comfortable would you feel working with an agnostic therapist?

Undoubtedly, many other important factors and issues can be listed. Your preferences will reflect your culture, feelings, beliefs, and your needs.

In "A Buyer's Guide to Psychotherapy," psychotherapist Frank Pittman (1994) considers the client as a consumer who should not be afraid to ask questions of therapists in order to ascertain if they seem suitable. He recommends that the consumer should hire a therapist who has worked effectively with people the consumer knows, who leads a life that seems desirable to the consumer, and who treats a consumer with respect. In other words, Pittman argues that clients should become informed and selective in choosing a therapist.

---

ture presents several types of groups.) One obvious dimension is the type of people who comprise the group. In marital and family therapy, they are related; in most other groups, they are initially strangers. Group members may share various characteristics. Groups may be formed to treat older clients, unemployed workers, or pregnant women; to treat clients with similar psychological disturbances; or to treat people with similar therapeutic goals.

Therapeutic groups also differ with regard to psychological orientation and treatment techniques,

number of members, frequency and duration of meetings, and the role of the therapist or group leader. Some groups work without a leader. Others have leaders who play active or passive roles within the group. Moreover, the group may focus either on interrelationships and the dynamics of interaction or on the individual members. And groups may be organized to *prevent* problems as well as to solve them; for example, group therapy has been suggested for divorced people who are likely to encounter stress (Bloom, Asher & White, 1978).

Some Types of Therapy Groups

Human Relations Training Groups Some groups focus on helping people increase their sensitivity to others and improve their human relations skills so that they can be more efficient and responsive in their relationships with others—particularly in schools or business organizations. The group leader focuses on group processes (such as how members are relating to one another and what is happening in the group) and encourages members to be open, honest, and flexible. Rather than dominating the sessions, the leader helps members develop their own ideas (Korchin, 1976).

Encounter Groups Drawing on certain principles of sensitivity training, Carl Rogers conceived of encounter groups as vehicles to facilitate human growth and development (greater ef-fectiveness, openness, spontaneity, and flexibility) through encounter experiences. Encounter groups encourage freedom of expression and the reduction of defensiveness. The group leader acts as a facilitator, refusing to direct the group authoritatively or to manipulate group activities. Merely by providing a climate of respect and freedom, the group helps members develop trust and become less defensive and allows greater freedom to grow and use positive experiences. Although Rogers observed that group members are initially frustrated and anxious over the lack of group structure and direction, they later begin to feel freedom and trust.

Self-Help Groups Self-help groups bring people together so that they can help one another cope more effectively with some personal or life-disrupting problems by exchanging psychological support, information, and resources. In this sense, group members are "prosumers"—that is, both providers and consumers of services (Borkman, 1990). Informal self-help groups have always existed. Alcoholics Anonymous is one self-help group with which most people are familiar. Indeed, as former U.S. Surgeon General C. Everett Koop and others recognized, such groups are a community resource that can provide immense social supports. The rapid growth of self-help groups reflects the growing belief that people can help themselves and others (Levine & Perkins, 1987).

Transactional Analysis Transactional analysis (TA) is a group therapy technique based on the assumption that people play certain "games" that hinder development of genuine and deep interpersonal

---

Commonalities of Group Therapy Despite their wide diversity, successful groups and group approaches share several features that promote beneficial change in clients (Kottler & Brown, 1992; Yalom, 1970).

First, the group experience allows each client to become involved in a social situation and to see how his or her behavior affects others. In the group dialogue that begins this section, Frank is slowly and painfully being asked to examine the impact of his behavior on others. He may easily dismiss unpleasant feedback about his behavior from one member as inaccurate, but it is much more difficult to do so when others reinforce the feedback (agreeing that Frank externalizes his problems and avoids responsibility for his own behavior). Once the group member can view his or her interactions realistically, problems can be identified and then resolved.

Second, in group therapy the therapist can see how clients respond in a real-life social and interpersonal context. In individual therapy, the therapist either must rely on what clients say about their social relationships or must assess those relationships on the basis of client-therapist interactions. But data gathered thus are often unrepresentative or inaccurate. In the group context, response patterns are observed rather than communicated or inferred. For example, Frank's therapist could see and hear him try to blame his fellow group members with such statements as "What's your problem anyway?" "I totally reject your accusations!" "Why are you so defensive?"

Third, group members can develop new communication skills, social skills, and insights. (This is one of the most powerful mechanisms of group therapy.) The group provides an environment for imitative learning and practice. Frank's group members can show him that his statements and behaviors indicate defensiveness and that they affect others negatively. He may then be able to change his interpersonal behavior by imitating other group members and practicing better social and communication skills with them.

relationships. These games have disguised goals, which are usually related to the need for recognition. The game of "one-up-man-ship" is an example: Person A may approach person B to get help with a problem. B sincerely attempts to help A by offering advice and sympathy, taking on the role of therapist. A rejects the advice and points out its flaws. B offers alternative advice, only to have it rejected again. B then feels helpless and perhaps guilty for letting A down. A is "one up" over B, who has been "put down" and has become apologetic. Thus Person A has accomplished a transactional role reversal.

Underlying TA is the idea that people adopt certain roles (child, adult, and parent) that reflect their ego states (Berne, 1972). "Spoiled brat" behavior or excessive dependency indicates the child role; the adult role is characterized by mature and rational behavior; and the parent role is a controlling one, in which the person treats others like children. In many marriages, one spouse often acts as parent (domi-nating, commanding), while the other adopts the role of child (incapable, immature). Berne felt that such interpersonal transactions hinder the development of authentic relationships. The purpose of TA therapy is first to make the client aware of the games he or she is playing and then to eliminate them and allow more authentic means of expression, more meaningful relationships with others, and better life adjustment. Transactional analysis may be used for families or for unrelated people in group therapy.

Assertiveness Training Groups

Assertiveness training groups use behavioral therapy techniques to help people who want to assert or express themselves better. Many people feel unable to express hostility, criticism, or warmth. In assertiveness training, people are constantly reminded of the negative consequences of nonassertive behaviors and are encouraged to act out and practice assertive skills (both in the group sessions and outside of the sessions).

Assertiveness training has been unfairly characterized as a breeding ground for the development of overly critical and hostile people. The actual intent is to train people to express themselves appropriately.

Psychodrama Jacob Moreno (1946) was among the first to use the term *group therapy* in his writings. He developed psychodrama, a form of group therapy in which patients and other people role-play situations. When clients act out current or anticipated situations, they become aware of their feelings, and they can rehearse techniques for working out their problems. Others may play supporting roles, so that the client can fully act out the situation and interact with them. At times the client and another person may exchange roles, so that the client can understand the motives and behaviors of other people with whom he or she interacts.

Self-help groups allow individuals with common goals or problems to come together for mutual assistance, support, and communication. This self-help group was organized to support efforts for persons with disabilities to achieve independent living.

Fourth, groups often help their members feel less isolated and fearful about their problems. Many clients enter therapy because they believe that their problems are unique: no one else could possibly be burdened with such awful impulses, evil or frightening thoughts, and unacceptable ways. The fear of having others find out how "sick" they are may be as problematic to clients as their actual disorders. But when they suddenly realize that their problems are common, that others also experience them, and that others have similar fears, their sense of isolation is eased. This realization allows group members to be more open about their thoughts and feelings.

Finally, groups can provide their members with strong social and emotional support. The feelings of intimacy, belonging, protection, and trust (which members may not be able to experience outside the group) can be a powerful motivation to confront one's problems and actively seek to overcome them. The group can be a safe environment in which to share one's innermost thoughts and to try new adaptive behaviors without fear of ridicule or rejection.

Evaluating Group Therapy   Clients are sometimes treated in group and individual psychotherapy simultaneously. There are no simple rules for determining when one or the other, or both, should be employed. The decision is usually based on the therapist's judgment, the client's wishes, and the availability (or unavailability) of one treatment or the other. Of course, people who are likely to be disruptive are generally excluded from group therapy.

As desirable as it would be to base decisions regarding treatment techniques on the observed effectiveness of group therapy, little substantial research has been done on that topic. Reviews of studies have suggested that group therapy results in improvement, compared to no treatment or placebo treatment (Bednar & Kaul, 1978; 1994; Kaul & Bednar, 1986). The problems encountered in evaluating the success of group therapy include all those problems involved in assessing individual therapy, compounded by group variables and the behaviors of group members. Indeed, some have even questioned whether group therapy is really any different from individual therapy because the same therapeutic variables are involved (Hill, 1990).

Group therapy also has some disadvantages. For example, groups cannot give intensive and sustained attention to the problems of individual clients (Korchin, 1976). Moreover, clients may not want to share some of their problems with a large group, and the sense of intimacy with one's therapist is often lost in a group. Group pressures may prove too strong for some members, or the group may adopt values or behaviors that are themselves deviant. And, in leaderless groups, the group members may not recognize or be able to treat psychotic or potentially suicidal people.

Family Therapy

Johnny is a seven-year-old boy, attractive and energetic, who came to the attention of the school psychologist midway through his third year in grade school. He had been a good student in the first and second grades, but his schoolwork and attention span deteriorated dramatically at the beginning of the third year. Among the symptoms noticed by his teacher were multiple fears, tardiness, and failure to complete school assignments.

Johnny's mother, Mrs. B., was contacted by his teacher several times in the three months before Johnny was referred to the psychologist. Mrs. B. reported that her son had become school-phobic only this year, and that she had tried unsuccessfully to reassure Johnny that there was nothing to fear. Nevertheless, getting Johnny to school was a daily struggle; he overslept, ate breakfast at a snail's pace, and took what seemed like hours to wash and get dressed. When she dropped him off at school, he would cry and beg to be taken back home. Mr. B. noted that Johnny was younger than his classmates and wondered whether his son was simply finding the work too demanding.

Both parents were obviously concerned about their son. They were subsequently referred to a reputable child psychologist, who saw the family together several times. After their third session, both parents reported a marked improvement in Johnny's behavior. The therapist suggested that Johnny be seen individually for a period of time but also recommended marital counseling for the parents. Mr. B. vigorously objected to that suggestion and stated that there was nothing wrong with their marriage; the problem was helping Johnny overcome his school phobia and helping him cope with the pressures of school. At the urging of the wife, however, they did seek marital counseling, attending four sessions before Mr. B. abruptly terminated treatment. His reason was that the counseling was not helping with the family relationships and that, in fact, he and his wife had begun to argue and express anger at one another. In addition, shortly after Mr. and Mrs. B. had sought counseling, Johnny had reverted to his earlier fears and behaviors. The husband felt that the marital therapy had diverted their attention from the real problem—Johnny.

Family therapy may be broadly defined as group therapy that seeks to modify relationships within a family to achieve harmony (Foley, 1989). We use this definition to include all forms of therapy that involve more than one family member in joint sessions, including marital therapy and parent-child therapy. The important point is that the focus is not on an individual but on the family as a whole. Family therapy is based on three assumptions: (1) it is logical and economical to treat together all those who exist and

Family therapy is a group therapy approach whose goal is to modify relationships within a family unit to achieve harmony. The family, rather than an individual member of the family, is the focus of treatment.

operate within a system of relationships (here, the primary nuclear family); (2) the problems of the "identified patient" are only symptoms, and the family itself is the client; and (3) the task of the therapist is to modify relationships within the family system.

These basic tenets have arisen from the repeated observations of therapists who have worked with individuals and families. Johnny's case illustrates them nicely. Both parents saw their son as the "identified patient" and the problem. Even the teacher and school psychologist saw the problem as one of adjustment for Johnny. Attempts to treat Johnny individually had to fail because the problem lay in the family system. For example, marital therapy revealed basic antagonisms and conflicts between Mr. and Mrs. B., but as long as Johnny was the identified patient, the parental problems could be covered up. When Johnny improved with therapy and the focus shifted to the marital relationship, many of the husband-wife problems were uncovered. To maintain the family's stability, Johnny, who sensed that the relationship was getting worse, became phobic again.

Johnny's return to phobic behavior is typical of family dynamics, and it actually serves several functions for the entire family. First, Johnny again becomes the center of attention and helps ward off a possible divorce. Second, the husband and wife can avoid examining their own relationship and its problems. Third, the status quo of the system is maintained.

Obviously, as long as the family members are treated as individuals, little progress will be made.

The family is a social system that needs to be treated as a whole. Mr. and Mrs. B. would probably benefit not only from therapy involving the entire family but from marital therapy as well.

Two general classes of family therapy have been identified: the *communications approach* and the *systems approach* (Foley, 1989). Let us look briefly at each of them.

The Communications Approach   The communications approach to family therapy is based on the assumption that family problems are communication difficulties. Many family communication problems are both subtle and complex. Family therapists may have to concentrate on improving not only faulty communications but also interactions and relationships among family members (Satir, 1967). The way in which rules, agreements, and perceptions are communicated among members may also be important (Haley, 1963).

The therapist's role in repairing faulty family communications is active but not dominating. He or she must seek to show family members how they are now communicating with one another; prod them into revealing what they feel and think about themselves and other family members and what they want from the family relationship; and convince them to practice new ways of responding.

The Systems Approach   People who favor the systems approach to family therapy also consider communication important, but they especially emphasize the interlocking roles of family members (Minuchin, 1974). Their basic assumption is that the family system itself contributes to pathological behavior in the family. As in Johnny's case, a family member becomes "sick" because the family system requires a sick member. Treating that person outside the system may result in transitory improvement, but once the client returns to the family system, he or she will be forced into the "sick role" again. Thus family systems therapy is directed at the organization of the family. It stresses accurate assessment of family roles and dynamics and intervention strategies to create more flexible or changed roles that foster positive interrelationships.

Marital Therapy

Marital therapy is a treatment aimed at helping couples understand and clarify their communications, role relationships, unfulfilled needs, and unrealistic or unmet expectations. Marital therapy has become an increasingly popular treatment for couples who find that the quality of their relationship needs improvement. Indeed, seeing only one partner has proven less effective in resolving interpersonal problems than seeing both together (Gurman & Kniskern, 1978). Marital therapists work on the assumption that it is normal for any couple in an intense long-term relationship to experience conflicts. For example, the husband may find it difficult to express affectionate feelings toward his wife, who may have a strong need to be nurtured and loved. Or the couple may be locked in a power struggle involving financial decisions. Or the wife may resent a husband who shows any sign of weakness because the man she married was supposed to be "strong and invulnerable." In all these cases, marital therapy attempts to clarify and improve the communications, interactions, and role relationships between the couple. Note that it is not the purpose of marital therapy to "save a marriage," as many couples believe when they first enter treatment. The decision to remain together, separate, or divorce is a decision that must be made by the couple. The role of the therapist is to help the couple understand the nature of their relationship, how it may be contributing to conflicts and unhappiness, their available options, and, if they want, how to work toward a healthier and happier marriage.

Here is an example of how a marital therapy session might run:

Therapist: Betty [the wife], I wonder if the last two sessions have been helpful to you in saying more openly what you think and feel.

Husband: Well, I think she's feeling better about the sessions, but there's been no big change in how she relates to the kids.

Therapist: Is that right, Betty?

Husband: Of course it is. She's always been afraid of—

Therapist (interrupting): I'd like to hear from Betty.

Wife: Well—Leonard [the husband]—he's not exactly right—I have—.

Husband: She tried, but nothing's happened.

Therapist (to Leonard): Do you realize that several times now you've spoken for your wife and cut her off when I've directed questions to her? I wonder if this is something that frequently happens with you and your wife?

Husband: I wasn't doing that. I was just trying to help my wife clarify her thoughts and feelings.

Wife: But—you don't—you only make me feel worse.

Husband: Betty does need a lot of—.

Therapist: What did your wife just say to you?

Husband: Huh! Uh—she said something about—about not feeling well—I think—Isn't that right?

Wife: I said you make me feel like a child who can't think or feel for myself.

Therapist (after a long silence): What do you think your wife is saying to you? Can you paraphrase it?

Husband: She's saying that I make her feel incompetent—or dumb.

Therapist: I wonder, Betty, if you could turn to Leonard now, and tell him exactly how you feel. Did he hear what you said?

Wife: You do make me feel stupid and incompetent, when—when you always speak for me. Don't you realize that I'm my own person with my own feelings and thoughts!

Husband (to therapist): I didn't realize—that my wife or that—I was doing that—I'm sorry if—if—.

Therapist: Don't tell me, tell your wife.

Husband (to wife): I'm sorry—for—for—I didn't know that's what I was doing.

Research on the effects of family and marital therapy has been consistent in pointing to the value of therapy compared with no-treatment and alternative-treatment control groups. However, as Alexander, Holtzworth-Munroe, and Jameson (1994) have noted, research studies have generally not been rigorous in design; they often lacked appropriate control groups, follow-up periods of outcome, or good measures of outcome. As a result, no strong conclusions are warranted at this time.

SYSTEMATIC INTEGRATION AND ECLECTICISM

The therapies discussed in this chapter share the common goal of relieving human suffering. Yet as we have seen, they differ considerably in their basic conception of psychopathology and in the methods they use to treat mental disorders. Many theories and techniques seem almost diametrically opposed to one another. For example, early criticisms of psychoanalysis concentrated on the mystical and unscientific nature of its explanation and treatment of behavioral pathology. Most of these criticisms came from behaviorists, who were likewise attacked by psychoanalysts as being superficial and concerned with "symptom removal" rather than with the cure of "deeper conflicts in the psyche." There have been attempts at rapprochement between psychoanalysis and behavior therapy (Davis, 1983; Goldfried, Greenberg & Marmar, 1990; Marmor & Woods, 1980; Murray, 1983; Wachtel, 1982). But even these sophisticated attempts have come under fire as being empirically and theoretically inconsistent (Yates, 1983).

As we stated in Chapter 1, most practicing clinicians consider themselves eclectics (Garfield & Bergin, 1994). It appears that relying on a single theory and a few techniques is correlated with inexperience; the more experienced the clinician, the greater the diversity and resourcefulness used in a session (Norcross & Prochaska, 1988). *Therapeutic eclecticism* has been defined as the "process of selecting concepts, methods, and strategies from a variety of current theories which work" (Brammer & Shostrom, 1982, p. 35). An example is the early "technical eclecticism" of Lazarus (1967). This approach has now been refined into a theoretical model called *multimodal behavior therapy* (Lazarus 1967, 1984). Although behavioral in basis, it embraces many cognitive and affective concepts as well.

The eclectic model calls for openness and flexibility, but it can also encourage the indiscriminate, haphazard, and inconsistent use of therapeutic techniques and concepts. As a result, therapists who call themselves eclectic have been severely criticized as confused, inconsistent, contradictory, lazy, and unsystematic (Goldfried & Safran, 1986; Patterson, 1980). The resulting negative reception of the term *eclecticism* has led to other terms (including *creative synthesis*, *masterful integration*, and *systematic eclecticism*) that are more positively associated with attempts to integrate, to be consistent, to validate, and to create a unique and personalized theoretical position. Indeed, evidence indicates that practitioners prefer the term *integrative* to *eclectic* (Norcross & Prochaska, 1988).

There is, of course, no single integrative theory or position. Rather, an integrative approach recognizes that no one theory or approach is sufficient to explain and treat the complex human organism. All the therapies that we have discussed have both strengths and weaknesses; no one of them can claim to tell "the whole truth." The goal of the eclectic approach is to integrate those therapies that work best with specific clients who show specific problems under specific conditions. Thus in one sense, all therapists are eclectics—that is, each has his or her own personal and unique approach to therapy.

COMMUNITY PSYCHOLOGY

It is difficult to discuss psychotherapy and intervention without reference to the context in which services are provided. The context involves people living in families and communities and functioning within social, economic, educational, political, religious, and health institutions. **Community psychology** is an approach to mental health that takes into account the influence of environmental factors and that encourages the use of community resources and agencies to eliminate conditions that produce psychological problems. It is concerned with the promotion of well-being and the prevention of mental disturbance. Pertinent issues include managed health care and the prevention of psychopathology.

Managed Health Care

The delivery of mental health services is headed for major changes. Concerns have been expressed over the rising costs of medical and mental health care, the uncertainty of treatment outcome, and the inadequacies in the delivery of treatment to certain segments of the population, such as older individuals and members of ethnic minority groups (see the Focus On feature on page 515). As Figure 17.3 indicates, only a small proportion of individuals with mental disorders seek care from the mental health system, and changes are needed to make services accessible, available, and affordable.

Reform is occurring in several ways. The following are among the most important. First, mental health care will be shifted to health maintenance organizations (HMOs), which operate to reduce as much cost as possible. At the same time, traditional fee-for-service financing of services will diminish. Many HMOs are turning to managed-care companies to administer their mental health benefit plans. Second, care providers will emphasize short-term treatment, intended to

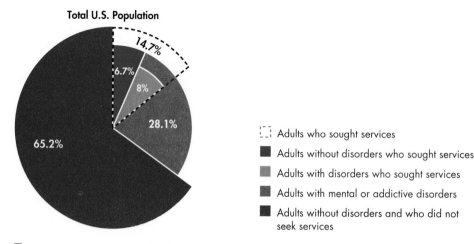

Total U.S. Population

14.7%

6.7%

8%

28.1%

65.2%

⸢⸣ Adults who sought services

■ Adults without disorders who sought services

■ Adults with disorders who sought services

■ Adults with mental or addictive disorders

■ Adults without disorders and who did not seek services

FIGURE 17.3   Use of Mental Health Services Among Individuals with Mental or Addictive Disorders   In the ECA survey of adult Americans, 28.1 percent of the sample said they were experiencing or had experienced a mental or addictive disorder during the previous year. During that year, 14.7 percent of Americans sought mental health services. Because many of those who sought services did not meet the criteria for a mental disorder, only 8 percent of the population had both a mental or addictive disorder and sought services. Thus only 28.5 percent of those with mental or addictive disorders used services (8 percent divided by 28.1 percent).

Source: Data from Regier et al., 1993.

enable the client to function, rather than long-term treatment that attempts to "cure" the client. Third, individuals with master's degrees and others who do not have doctorates will increasingly provide services formerly provided by therapists with M.D.'s or Ph.D.'s. Because doctoral providers' services cost more, they will be less in demand. Fourth, the effectiveness and cost-efficiency of treatments and of clini-

cians must be continually assessed to reduce cost and inefficiency. Accountability and quality assurance will be emphasized to an even greater degree than in the past.

While there is general consensus that problems have existed in the mental health system, managed care has not been enthusiastically embraced by many mental health professionals. For example, there are

Community psychologists are concerned about community institutions and the effectiveness of services provided. In the past, patients were often confined in mental hospitals under substandard living conditions, like those shown here. Community psychology is concerned not only with improving mental health services but also with the strengthening of other community resources such as churches, schools, and law enforcement agencies.

concerns that health maintenance organizations may attempt to reduce costs simply by reducing the quality or extent of services, expending little effort on preventing problems, hiring providers to give cheap services, and gaining a much stronger voice than providers of services in determining treatment for clients (Karon, 1995). Clients may have a difficult time obtaining more long-term care. In adapting to the reforms in mental health care, some have pointed out the need for focused training of mental health care providers. These reforms could ensure that clinical health psychologists' educational background includes behavioral medicine and health psychology, as well as clinical psychology. Other skills in health assessment and intervention and outcome assessment are also needed (Belar, 1995).

Reform is also taking place in other ways. For example, the American Psychological Association has endorsed the principle that clinical psychologists with proper training should be able to prescribe medication for patients with mental disorders (Martin, 1995), although some psychologists oppose such a move (Hayes, 1995). Another facet of the reform movement is a systematic attempt that is being made to identify those treatments that have been empirically validated as being effective (Task Force on Promotion and Dissemination of Psychological Procedures, 1995). It is hoped that the effort will make it possible to establish standards for client and therapist treatment decisions based on scientific research.

"Manualized" treatment programs are also gaining popularity. These programs have manuals that instruct therapists (particularly those using cognitive and cognitive-behavioral approaches) to conduct treatment in a planned, systematic, and guided fashion. The assumption is that following treatment manuals will reduce possible ineffective discretionary practices that therapists use when they base procedures largely on therapist judgment. Thus the field of clinical psychology, as well as the other fields involved in mental health, is changing, and with this change come opportunities as well as conflicts.

Prevention of Psychopathology

Preventing psychopathology is one of the most innovative functions of community psychology. Prevention programs are attempts to maintain health rather than to treat sickness. The main emphasis is on reducing the number of new cases of mental disorders, the duration of disorders among afflicted people, and the disabling effects of disorders. These three areas of prevention have been called *primary, secondary,* and *tertiary* prevention (Cowen, 1983).

Primary Prevention **Primary prevention** is an effort to lower the incidence of new cases of behavioral disorders by strengthening or adding to resources that promote mental health and by eliminating community characteristics that threaten mental health. As an example of the former, Project Head Start was initiated in 1964 with the goal of setting up a new and massive preschool program to help neglected or deprived children develop social, emotional, and intellectual skills. Examples of the latter are efforts to eliminate discrimination against members of minority groups to help them fulfill their potential. Both techniques—introducing new resources and eliminating causal factors—can be directed toward specific groups of people or toward the community as a whole.

Munoz and colleagues (1982, 1995) have been systematically attempting to prevent depression in a communitywide project and in primary care patients. The communitywide project was particularly interesting. During a two-week period, nine televised programs intended to prevent depression were broadcast in San Francisco. Each program lasted for four minutes and showed viewers some coping skills, such as how to think positively, engage in rewarding activities, and deal with depression. Telephone interviews were conducted with 294 San Francisco residents. Some respondents were interviewed one week before the television segments were shown; others were interviewed one week after; and still others were interviewed both before and after the segments. Information about respondents' depression levels was collected during the interviews. (For those who were interviewed before and after the segments, the depression measure was administered twice.) Respondents who were interviewed after the televised segments were also asked to indicate whether they had watched any of the segments. Results indicated that those who saw the segments exhibited a significantly lower level of depression than that found among the nonviewers. The results, however, held only for respondents who had some symptoms of depression to begin with. Watching the television programs did not change the depression levels of those who initially (before the segments) reported little depression.

The results indicated that a communitywide prevention program can be beneficial. A large proportion (approximately one-third) of the viewers had some symptoms of depression, and this group showed fewer symptoms after viewing the programs. The long-term effects of the programs were not assessed. Another problem in the study was that those who benefited from the programs exhibited some initial symptoms. If they were clinically diagnosable as being depressed, the intervention might be considered

Groups and organizations often use the media to reach out to people with emotional problems. These communications reinforce the idea that problems can be prevented and offer help in how to go about it. A suicide-awareness group is using this billboard to get its message across to people in trouble.

secondary rather than primary prevention. (Secondary prevention is discussed in the next section.) Nevertheless, the San Francisco study demonstrated the effects of large-scale interventions that may help disorders.

Evidence also exists that early, primary prevention efforts can be successful in reducing the incidence of juvenile delinquency. Zigler, Taussig, and Black (1992) noted that few treatment and rehabilitation programs for juvenile delinquents have had much effect. In their review of early intervention programs aimed at children, they found evidence that these programs, intended to promote social and intellectual competence, have had an expected positive effect on preventing delinquency. The investigators speculated that gaining competence may snowball to generate further success in other aspects of life and prevent delinquency.

Although interest in primary prevention continues to grow, resistance to prevention is also strong. First, only through prospective and longitudinal research can developmental processes in primary prevention be uncovered (Lorion, 1990). Primary prevention is future-oriented, in that the benefits of the effort are not immediately apparent. Second, primary prevention competes with traditional programs aimed at treating people who already show emotional disturbances. Third, prevention may require social and environmental changes so that stressors can be reduced or resources can be enhanced. Most mental health workers are either unable or unwilling to initiate such changes; many others doubt that people have the abil-

ity to modify social structures. Fourth, funding for mental health programs has traditionally been earmarked for treatment. Prevention efforts constitute a new demand on the funding system. And fifth, primary prevention requires a great deal of planning, work, and long-term evaluation. This effort alone discourages many from becoming involved.

Secondary Prevention **Secondary prevention** is an attempt to shorten the duration of mental disorders and to reduce their impact. If the presence of a disorder can be detected early and an effective treatment can be found, it is possible to minimize the impact of the disorder or to prevent its developing into a more serious and debilitating form. For example, classroom teachers can play an important role in secondary prevention by identifying children who are not adjusting to the school environment. Once identified, such children can be helped by teachers, parents, or school counselors.

In practice, there are a number of problems with secondary prevention. First, traditional diagnostic methods are often unreliable and provide little insight into which treatment procedures to use. It has been suggested that more specialized diagnostic techniques be used, perhaps focusing on certain behaviors or on demographic characteristics that may be related to psychopathology (Zax & Spector, 1974). Second, once a disorder is detected, it is often difficult to decide what form of treatment will be most effective with a particular patient. Third, prompt treatment is frequently unavailable because of the shortage of

Because of client demand, some mental health clinics have waiting lists. Clients, therefore, may not receive immediate treatment unless it is an emergency. Drop-in centers and walk-in clinics like this one allow individuals easy and quick access to services.

mental health personnel and the inaccessibility of services. Indeed, many mental health facilities have long lists of would-be patients who must wait months before receiving treatment. "Walk-in" clinics, crisis intervention facilities, and emergency telephone lines have been established in an attempt to provide immediate treatment.

Tertiary Prevention   The goal of **tertiary prevention** is to facilitate the readjustment of the person to community life after hospital treatment for a mental disorder (Felner et al., 1983). Tertiary prevention focuses on reversing the effects of institutionalization and on providing a smooth transition to a productive life in the community. Several programs have been developed to accomplish this goal. One involves the use of "passes," whereby hospitalized patients are encouraged to leave the hospital for short periods of time. By spending gradually increasing periods of time in the community (and then returning each time to the hospital), the patient can slowly readjust to life away from the hospital while still benefiting from therapy.

Psychologists can also ease readjustment to the community by educating the public about mental disorders. Public attitudes toward mental patients are often based on fears and stereotypes. Factual information can help modify these attitudes so that patients will be more graciously accepted. This help is especially important for the family, friends, and business associates of patients, who must interact frequently with them. A more difficult problem to deal with is the growing backlash against the discharge of former

mental patients into nursing homes or rooming houses in the community. Many community members feel threatened when such patients live in their neighborhoods. Again, education programs may help dispel community members' fears and stereotypes.

SUMMARY

1. A variety of psychotherapeutic or treatment procedures are used to change behaviors, modify attitudes, and facilitate self-insight. Biological (or somatic) treatments use physical means to alter the bodily and psychological states of patients. The use of electroconvulsive therapy (ECT), or electroshock, has diminished but is still used for some severely depressed patients. Because psychosurgery permanently destroys brain tissue, it too is now rarely used and strictly regulated. One reason for the declining use of ECT and psychosurgery is a correspondingly greater reliance on medication or drug therapy. Antianxiety drugs reduce anxiety, antipsychotic drugs help control or eliminate psychotic symptoms, antimanic drugs reduce mania, and antidepressants effectively reduce depression. Medication has enabled many patients to function in the community and to be more amenable to other forms of treatment, particularly insight-oriented and behavioral therapy.

2. The insight-oriented therapeutic approaches include psychoanalytic therapy, person-centered therapy, existential analysis, and gestalt therapy. These approaches provide the patient with an opportunity to develop better levels of functioning, to undergo new and emotionally important experiences, to develop a therapeutic relationship with a professional, and to relate personal thoughts and feelings.

3. Action-oriented or behavior therapies (based on classical conditioning, operant conditioning, modeling, and cognitive restructuring) have been applied to a variety of disorders. Behavioral assessment, procedures, goals, and outcome measures are more clearly defined and more easily subjected to empirical investigation than are insight-oriented approaches. Two promising approaches are behavioral medicine and stress resistance training, which combine behavioral, cognitive, medical, and social knowledge.

4. Some critics claim that the effectiveness of psychotherapy—of whatever orientation—has not been demonstrated. Results from numerous studies and meta-analyses of these studies have pointed to the beneficial impact of treatment. The real issue, however, may be one of finding the best combination of therapies and situational variables for each client.

5. Although critics argue that behavior therapy is dehumanizing, limited to a narrow range of human problems, and mechanical, proponents consider behavior modification both effective and efficient.

6. Group therapy involves the simultaneous treatment of more than one person. Many psychological difficulties are interpersonal in nature, and the group format allows the therapist and clients to work in an interpersonal context. Family and marital therapies consider psychological problems as residing within the family rather than in one individual. The communications approach to family therapy concentrates on improving family communications, whereas the systems approach stresses the understanding and restructuring of family roles and dynamics.

7. Most practicing therapists are eclectic or integrative in perspective. They try to select therapeutic methods, concepts, and strategies from a variety of current theories that work. Being eclectic is sometimes criticized as being haphazard and inconsistent, but every therapist who fits the therapy to the client is, in fact, eclectic.

8. In discussing therapeutic intervention, it is also important to be aware of broader mental health efforts involving community psychology or community mental health. Several developments are necessary to consider. First, a growing trend in the delivery of mental health services is managed health care. Under managed health care, consideration will be given to cost-effectiveness of services and short-term care. While many mental health providers are critical of managed care, others have called for changes in the role and services given by providers. Second, the mental health field is also grappling with issues involving prescription privileges for psychologists, using empirical validation of treatments as a guideline for delivery services, and employing treatment manuals in the practice of psychotherapy and behavioral modification. Third, in addition to treatment, primary, secondary, and tertiary forms of prevention are important in our efforts to enhance mental health and well-being.

KEY TERMS

aversive conditioning A classical conditioning technique in which an undesirable behavior is paired with an unpleasant stimulus to suppress the undesirable behavior

biofeedback therapy A therapeutic approach combining physiological and behavioral approaches, in which a patient receives information regarding particular autonomic functions and is rewarded for influencing those functions in a desired direction

community psychology An approach to mental health that takes into account the influence of environmental factors and that encourages the use of community resources and agencies to eliminate conditions that produce psychological problems

electroconvulsive therapy (ECT) The application of electric voltage to the brain to induce convulsions; used to reduce depression; also called *electroshock therapy*

existential analysis A therapeutic approach that is concerned with the person's experience and involvement in the world as a being with consciousness and self-consciousness

family therapy Group therapy that seeks to modify relationships within a family to achieve harmony

flooding A behavioral treatment that attempts to extinguish fear by placing the client in a real-life anxiety-provoking situation at full intensity

free association A psychoanalytic method during which the patient says whatever comes to mind, regardless of how illogical or embarrassing it may seem, for the purpose of revealing the contents of the patient's unconscious

gestalt therapy A humanistic-existential approach to therapy that emphasizes the importance of a person's total experience, which should not be fragmented or separated

group therapy A form of therapy that involves the simultaneous treatment of two or more clients and may involve more than one therapist

implosion A behavioral treatment that attempts to extinguish a fear by having the client imagine the anxiety-provoking situation at full intensity

marital therapy A treatment aimed at helping couples understand and clarify their communications, role relationships, unfulfilled needs, and unrealistic expectations

monoamine oxidase (MAO) inhibitor An antidepressant compound believed to correct the balance of neurotransmitters in the brain

person-centered therapy A humanistic therapy that emphasizes the kind of person the therapist should be in the therapeutic relationship, rather than the precise techniques to use in therapy

placebo effects Positive responses to a drug or other experimental condition that result from the patient's understanding of the drug's effect, faith in the doctor, or other psychological factors unrelated to the medication's specific physiological action

primary prevention An effort to lower the incidence of new cases of behavioral disorders by strengthening or adding to resources that promote mental health and by eliminating community characteristics that threaten mental health

psychopharmacology The study of the effects of drugs on the mind and on behavior; also known as *medication* and *drug therapy*

psychosurgery Brain surgery performed for the purpose of correcting a severe mental disorder

psychotherapy The systematic application, by a trained and experienced professional therapist, of techniques derived from psychological principles, for the purpose of helping psychologically troubled people; includes both insight-oriented and action-oriented therapies

resistance During psychoanalysis, the process in which the patient unconsciously attempts to impede the analysis by preventing the exposure of repressed material; tactics include silence, late arrival, failure to keep an appointment, and others

secondary prevention An attempt to shorten the duration of mental disorders and to reduce their impact

tertiary prevention Efforts to facilitate the readjustment of the person to community life after hospital treatment for a mental disorder

token economy A treatment program, based on principles of operant conditioning, that rewards patients for appropriate behaviors with tokens, which can then be exchanged for hospital passes, special privileges, food, or weekend passes

tricyclics Antidepressant compounds that relieve symptoms of depression and that seem to work like the MAO inhibitors but produce fewer side effects

transference During psychotherapy, a process in which the patient reenacts early conflicts by carrying over and applying to the therapist feelings and attitudes that the patient had toward significant others (primarily parents) in the past

LEGAL AND ETHICAL ISSUES IN ABNORMAL PSYCHOLOGY

Public interest in the workings of the legal system has never been more pronounced than it has been since the O. J. Simpson trial, with its controversial outcome. Millions of Americans have been introduced to such legal terminology as *inadmissible evidence, sidebar conferences, presumption of innocence, Fifth-Amendment rights, due process,* and *beyond a reasonable doubt.* Likewise, this high-profile case led to speculation not only about Simpson's guilt or innocence but about his state of mind. If he did kill his ex-wife, Nicole Brown Simpson, and her friend, Ronald Goldman, what could have motivated him to do so? Jealousy? Need for control? An ultimate extension of his wife-battering behaviors? And were these acts premeditated or impulsive, born of extreme and uncontrollable rage?

In the end, the jury found O. J. Simpson not guilty, ending some of the public speculation about these particular crimes. But trials like the Simpson trial take place daily, in courtrooms around the country. And in those trials, forensic psychologists play an important role in determining the state of mind of defendants and/or participating in decisions and actions of the legal system (Stromberg, Lindberg & Schneider, 1995). Dr. Lenore Walker, for example, was originally scheduled to be called by the Simpson defense (see the First Person narrative on page 546). In the past, psychologists dealt primarily with evaluation of competency and issues related to criminal cases. Now, however, their expanded roles include giving expert opinions on child custody, organic brain functioning, traumatic injury, suicide, and even deprogramming activities. And just as psychologists have influenced decisions in the legal system, they have also been influenced by mental health laws passed at local, state, and federal levels. The following case examples illustrate the complex relationship between mental health issues and the law.

For five months between 1977 and 1978, Los Angeles was terrorized by a series of murders of young women whose bodies were left on hillsides. All the women had been raped and strangled; some had been brutally tortured. The public and press dubbed the culprit the Hillside Strangler, and a massive hunt for the killer ensued. A major break occurred one year after the Los Angeles murders, when 27-year-old Kenneth Bianchi was arrested for two unrelated murders of college students in Bellingham, Washington. His fingerprints matched those found at the scene of the Hillside murders.

Bianchi was an unlikely murder suspect because many who knew him described him as dependable and conscientious—"the boy next door." Furthermore, despite the strong evidence against Bianchi, he insisted that he was innocent. Police noticed that he was unable to remember much of his past life. During interviews in which hypnosis was used, a startling development occurred: Bianchi exhibited another personality (Steve). Steve freely admitted to killing the women, calling Ken a "turkey," and laughing at Ken's ignorance of his existence.

On August 20, 1989, two brothers, Erik and Lyle Menendez, killed their parents, entertainment executive José Menendez, and Mary Louise (Kitty) Menendez. The brothers, then eighteen and twenty-one, admitted emptying their two pump-action Mossbert shotguns into their parents. Prosecutors claimed that the brothers killed their millionaire parents to inherit the family's fortune; indeed, just days after the slayings, the brothers went on a shopping spree charging purchases onto their credit cards. As support for their case, the prosecution played tapes of the Menendez brothers' therapy sessions in which they confessed to the killings.

The defense, however, argued that the killings were due to (a) an irrational fear that their lives were in danger, (b) years of sexual molestation by the father, (c) constant physical abuse and intimidation, and (d) threats that they would be killed if the "family secret" was ever exposed. The defense portrayed the brothers as "the victims" who endured years of sexual, psychological, and physical abuse and who, as a result, killed out of "mind-numbing, adrenalin-pumping fear." The prosecution argued for a first-degree murder conviction and sought the death penalty. The brothers were tried separately, and in each case the jury was deadlocked, unable to reach a verdict. The brothers were retried and a second jury convicted them of first-degree murder in March 1996. They were sentenced to life in prison without possibility of parole.

She was a well-known "bag lady" in the downtown Oakland area who by night slept on any number of park benches and in store fronts. By day she could be seen pushing her Safeway shopping cart full of boxes, extra clothing, and garbage, which she collected from numerous trash containers. According to her only surviving sister, the woman had lived this way for nearly ten years and had been tolerated by local merchants. Over the past six months, however, the woman's behavior had become progressively intolerable. She had always talked to

Confessed Hillside Strangler Kenneth Bianchi is shown giving testimony against his cousin Angelo Buono. From 1977 to 1978, both men raped, tortured, and murdered a number of young Los Angeles women. Wanting to use the insanity plea, in order to get a reduced sentence, Bianchi tried to convince psychiatrists that he was a multiple personality. His scheme failed, he was found guilty of murder and sentenced to life in prison without parole.

herself, but recently she had begun shouting and screaming at anyone who approached her. Her use of profanity was graphic, and she often urinated and defecated in front of local stores. She was occasionally arrested and detained for a short period of time by local law-enforcement officials, but she always returned to her familiar haunts. Finally, her sister and several merchants requested that the city take action to commit her to a mental institution.

In 1968, Prosenjit Poddar, a graduate student from India studying at the University of California at Berkeley, sought therapy from the student health services for depression. Poddar was apparently upset over what he perceived to be a rebuff from a female student, Tatiana Tarasoff, whom he claimed to love. During the course of treatment, Poddar informed his therapist that he intended to purchase a gun and kill the woman. Judging Poddar to be dangerous, the psychologist breached the confidentiality of the professional relationship by informing the campus police. The police detained Poddar briefly, but freed him because he agreed to stay away from Tarasoff. On October 27, Poddar went to Tarasoff's home and killed her, first wounding her with a gun and then stabbed her repeatedly with a knife.

A male therapist said, "I remember the incident quite clearly. I was seeing a female student for a therapy session at the university counseling center. Jennifer, a 22-year-old senior, was in extreme distress as she mourned

the loss of her younger sister. She was not only grieving about her sister's death, but she was also attempting to cope with her own feelings of guilt. Jennifer had been the driver when she was broadsided by another car on the passenger side. Both her sister and the driver of the other car were killed instantaneously.

"I had been working with Jennifer for nearly 3 months and had found her bright, vivacious, and extremely attractive. I had entertained sexual fantasies about her, and I felt conflicted about my feelings. During one particular session, Jennifer's pain seemed especially intense. I could feel the depths of her grief and sorrow. Without thinking, I pulled my chair next to her, placed my arms around her, and pulled her to my chest, where she wept uncontrollably. I could feel myself becoming sexually aroused as I struggled to maintain my professional composure."

In Chapter 1, we defined *abnormal psychology* as the scientific and objective approach to describing, explaining, predicting, and treating behaviors that are considered strange and unusual. All five of the preceding examples of behavior fit this definition well, and we can clearly see their clinical implications. What is less clear to many is that clinical or mental health issues can often become legal and ethical ones as well. This is most evident in the Kenneth Bianchi (Hillside Strangler) case. If his attorneys could prove that he was insane, Bianchi could be judged "not guilty by reason of insanity." Yet how do we determine whether a person is insane or sane? What criteria do we use? If we call on experts as in the Bianchi case, we find that professionals often disagree with one another. Might defendants in criminal trials attempt to fake mental disturbances to escape guilty verdicts?

Related to this question is the case of the Menendez brothers. If their claim is true that they suffered from years of excessive abuse, do such reasons excuse them from the moral or legal obligations of a wrongful act? Increasingly, lawyers are using clients' claims of child abuse, domestic violence, and other psychological traumas to explain the criminal actions of their clients. In 1994, a jury found Lorena Bobbitt not guilty of charges related to cutting off her husband's penis because she had suffered physical and sexual abuse throughout her married life. Should people like the Menendez brothers and Lorena Bobbitt be held responsible for their actions? And what about defendants who are mentally ill and found to be insane? What should the state do with them? Such questions lead us into the area of criminal commitment and legal rulings that force mental health practitioners to go beyond clinical concepts defined in DSM-IV.

The example of the homeless woman raises issues of civil commitment. When should a person who has committed no crime but who appears severely disturbed be institutionalized? Certainly, defecating and urinating in public are disgusting to most people and are truly unusual behaviors, but are they enough to deprive someone of her civil liberties? What are the procedures for civil commitment? What happens to people once they are committed?

In the first three examples, the focus of legal and ethical issues tends to be on the individual or defendant. Mental health issues become legal ones (1) when decisions must be made about involuntary commitment to mental hospitals, (2) when competence to stand trial is in doubt, (3) when an accused person bases his or her criminal defense on insanity or diminished mental capacity, and (4) when the rights of mental patients are legally tested.

In the *Tarasoff* case, the focus of legal and ethical concern shifts to the therapist. When is a therapist legally and ethically obligated to breach patient-therapist confidentiality? In this case, had the therapist done enough to prevent a potentially dangerous situation from occurring? According to all previous codes of conduct issued by professional organizations such as the American Psychological Association, and according to accepted practice in the field, many would answer yes. Yet in 1976 the California Supreme Court ruled that the therapist should have warned not only the police but also the likely victim.

The ruling has major implications for therapists in the conduct of therapy. One implication is also related to the earlier cases. How does a therapist predict that another person is dangerous (to self, to others, or to society)? To protect himself or herself from being sued, does the therapist report all threats of homicide or suicide? Should a psychologist warn clients that not everything they say is privileged or confidential? How will this affect the clinical relationship?

Erik (right) and Lyle Menendez killed their parents in August 1989. The defense argued that the brothers killed out of fear of their father and trauma suffered from years of sexual and physical abuse from him. The brothers were tried separately, and both cases resulted in hung juries. After a second trial, the brothers were found guilty.

FIRST PERSON

Lenore E. A. Walker

When I was a graduate student in psychology, I never dreamed that I would be practicing psychology in the courtrooms of our nation. Trained as a scientist-practitioner, I learned how to take complex psychological questions, provide scientific psychological analysis to them, and then apply the answers to people's lives. Yet, that is exactly what I do as a forensic psychologist: I use the study of human behavior to help judges, juries, and attorneys answer legal questions. I try to educate them in the area of my expertise, which is how interpersonal violence affects a person's state of mind and what it would take to remediate their psychological injuries.

My first chance to give expert witness testimony as a psychologist came in 1977. I had given a speech at a large conference in Seattle, Washington, about the psychology of domestic violence and had stressed the need for social change to stop men's violence against women and children. Someone in the audience then asked me a question about how to protect all those women and children who were being killed by men whose violence was escalating right now. These women did not have the time to wait until social change occurred. I responded quickly by stating, "Any woman who thought she was about to die should have the right to kill the man to protect herself and her children!" And, I promised I would help provide a defense for her. Little did I know that the next day the reporters in the audience would headline my comments. "Noted Psychologist Will Defend Battered Women Who Kill in Self-Defense!" the wire services screamed out. By the time I returned home I had my first case. When that jury found Miriam Griegg "not guilty" because it was a *justifiable homicide,* I knew I was hooked on teaching and applying psychology in the legal system. Since that time I have explained the cycle of violence hundreds of times.

Each couple's pattern of violence can be measured on a graph and then used to explain why the woman had a *reasonable perception* of *imminent danger.* It is important that in most states self-defense is measured by this standard: Killing someone may be justified (not excused as it would be if an insanity defense was used) if it can be proven that the defendant acted in a reasonable way. Interestingly, the definition of *imminent* also had to be clarified in order for women's defensive violence to be better understood. Imminent means "about to happen," "on the brink of occurring" rather than "immediate" or "right now." Case

---

Last, but not least, we come to ethical issues related to therapist conduct. The male therapist who experienced a strong sexual attraction to his client, Jennifer, may have been tempted to act on his feelings. Yet, it was obvious that such behavior would be considered unethical and might compromise his role as a therapist. Worst yet, what possible psychological harm might the therapist inflict upon his client by acting on his fantasies? Is sexual intimacy with clients a major problem in the profession?

We address some of these questions and issues in greater depth in this chapter. We begin by examining some of the issues of criminal and civil commitment. Then we look at patient rights and deinstitutionalization. We end by exploring the legal and ethical parameters of the therapist-client relationship, taking a final look at ethical issues related to cultural pluralism and the mental health profession.

CRIMINAL COMMITMENT

A basic premise of criminal law is that all of us are responsible beings who exercise free will and are capable of choices. If we do something wrong, we are responsible for our actions and should suffer the consequences. **Criminal commitment** is the incarceration of an individual for having committed a crime. Abnormal psychology accepts different perspectives on free will; criminal law does not. Yet criminal law does recognize that some people lack the ability to discern the ramifications of their actions because they are mentally disturbed. Although they may be technically guilty of a crime, their mental state at the time of the offense exempts them from legal responsibility. Let us explore the landmark cases that have influenced this concept's evolution and application. These cases are summarized in Figure 18.1.

law created by state supreme court justices helped redefine these terms so that they are better applied to the typical behavior of women's self-defense.

My research on factors that were likely to predict the development of *learned helplessness* in battered women and children are also used in court to demonstrate to the jury which factors the particular defendant showed during a clinical evaluation.

Today we also use the concept of battered woman syndrome, which includes both the psychological impact of the trauma on a particular battered woman (most commonly labeled as a posttraumatic stress disorder) as well as the dynamics of domestic violence, which include the discussions of the cycle of violence and the woman's perception of danger. This testimony helps judges and juries understand behavior of battered women and children that might otherwise seem incomprehensible.

In my most famous case, I was asked to help O. J. Simpson's defense attorneys understand the psychological dynamics of domestic violence to help prepare his defense. I was also asked to perform a clinical evaluation of O. J. Simpson to better understand the pattern of the client's cognitive, emotional, and behavioral functioning. The psychological tests and interviews did not reveal any information that would be persuasive of whether O. J. Simpson killed his former wife, Nicole Brown, and her friend, Ron Goldman. There are no statistical data to predict that one particular batterer would actually kill his abused partner, even though we do know that if the man does kill the woman, it is most likely at the point of separation when other high-risk factors are also present. However, there are cases where the woman either is killed or kills in self-defense, even though there has never been a physically violent incident. We also know that if a woman is killed by her current or former partner, she is most likely to have been battered by him before the murder. However, we cannot tell which battered woman would be killed before it occurs. So, if one hundred battered women were placed in one room and their batterers were placed in another room and we knew that one woman would be killed by her batterer, we could not pick out either the woman who would die or the man who would kill her. We could place about 25 of the batterers and battered women in rooms labeled "high-risk," but we could not say with certainty that the woman who ends up dead would come from that room or from another. Psychology has not yet reached the point where we can make any better predictions. Although I was never called to testify in the Simpson case, I was prepared to talk about what the scientific and clinical research could tell the jury to assist them in making their decision.

Lenore E. A. Walker, Ed.D., is a licensed psychologist in independent practice with Walker & Associates, in Denver, Colorado, and is executive director of the Domestic Violence Institute. Her psychology interests have concentrated on women's mental health issues and on stopping all forms of violence against women and children.

The Insanity Defense

The concept of "innocent by reason of insanity" has provoked much controversy among legal scholars, mental health practitioners, and the general public (Shapiro, 1984). The insanity defense is a legal argument used by defendants who admit they committed a crime but plead not guilty because they were mentally disturbed at the time the crime was committed. The insanity plea recognizes that under specific circumstances people may not be held accountable for their behavior. One of the public's greatest fears is that such a plea might be used by a guilty individual to escape criminal responsibility. This fear is further reinforced by findings that people acquitted of crimes because of insanity spend less time in psychiatric hospitals than convicted people spend in prison (Kahn & Raufman, 1981; Pasework, Pantel & Steadman, 1982). Some point to the Kenneth Bianchi case as a prime example of the danger of the misuse of this insanity plea.

The question confronting the state prosecutors, defense attorney, and mental health experts in the Bianchi case was whether the defendant was a shrewd, calculating, cold-blooded murderer or a true multiple personality. It is important to note, however, that any number of psychiatric conditions may be used in an insanity plea.

Psychologist Martin Orne, an internationally recognized expert on hypnosis, was asked by the prosecution to examine Bianchi. Orne knew that Bianchi was either a multiple personality or a clever liar. He reasoned that if Bianchi was pretending, he would be highly motivated to convince others that he was a multiple personality. Orne thought that if he told Bianchi that multiple personalities rarely show just

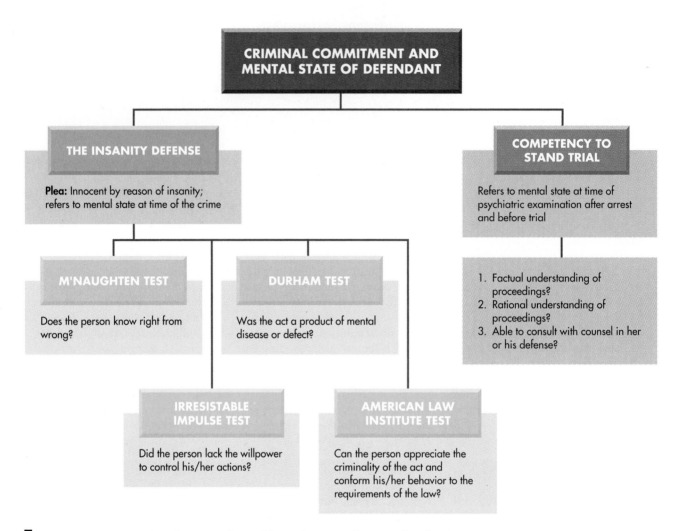

FIGURE 18.1 Landmark Cases That Address the Mental State of Defendants

two distinct personalities, Bianchi might show still an-other personality to convince Orne that his was a true case. After hinting to Bianchi in the waking state that two personalities are rare, Orne placed Bianchi under hypnosis. Bianchi took the bait. Another personality—Billy—emerged. (Other experts were unable to draw out more than two personalities.)

Orne also noticed that Bianchi's behaviors were unusual for someone under hypnosis. For example, during one session Orne wanted Bianchi to halluci-nate the presence of his attorney, so he suggested to Bianchi that his attorney was sitting in the room. Bianchi immediately got up and shook hands with his (hallucinated) attorney. Orne then asked whether his attorney was shaven. Bianchi responded, "Oh, no. Beard. God, you can see him. You must be able to see him" (*Frontline*, "The Mind of a Murderer," Part 2, 1984, p. 11). These behaviors are unusual for the fol-lowing reasons. First, multiple personalities almost never shake hands spontaneously because that re-

quires a tactile hallucination. Bianchi would have to imagine not only seeing his attorney but also feeling the touch of his hand. Second, the statement, "You can see him. You must be able to see him," seemed to be excessive and to be aimed at convincing Orne that Bianchi really saw his attorney. Orne believed that Bianchi was faking. His work, coupled with other ev-idence, forced a change in Bianchi's plea from "not guilty by reason of insanity" to "guilty." Unfortu-nately, the rare but highly publicized cases—such as those of the Hillside Strangler, John Hinckley (the person who attempted to assassinate Ronald Reagan), and the Menendez brothers—seem to have the great-est impact and to provoke public outrage and suspi-cion (Rogers, 1987).

Legal Precedents   In this country, a number of differ-ent standards are used as legal tests of insanity. One of the earliest is the ***M'Naghten Rule.*** In 1843, Daniel M'Naghten, a grossly disturbed woodcutter from

Glasgow, Scotland, claimed that he was commanded by God to kill the English prime minister, Sir Robert Peel. He killed a lesser minister by mistake and was placed on trial, where it became obvious that M'Naghten was quite delusional. Out of this incident emerged the M'Naghten Rule, which has popularly been referred to as the "right-wrong" test. The ruling held that people could be acquitted of a crime if it could be shown that, at the time of the act, they (1) had such defective reasoning that they did not know what they were doing or (2) were unable to comprehend that the act was wrong. The first part of the standard refers to a person being unaware of the *nature* of an act (for example, strangling a person but believing that he or she was squeezing a lemon) or the *quality* of an act (a disturbed person's belief that it would be amusing to cut off someone's head to watch him or her search for it in the morning) due to mental impairment (Shapiro, 1984). The M'Naghten Rule has come under tremendous criticism from some who regard it as being exclusively a cognitive test (knowledge of right or wrong), which does not consider volition, emotion, and other mental activity (Rogers, 1987; Shapiro, 1984). Further, it is not often easy to evaluate a defendant's awareness or comprehension.

The second major precedent that strengthened the insanity defense was the **irresistible impulse test.** In essence, the doctrine says that a defendant is not criminally responsible if he or she lacked the will power to control his or her behavior. Combined with the M'Naghten Rule, this rule broadened the criteria for using the insanity defense. In other words, a verdict of not guilty by reason of insanity could be obtained if it was shown that the defendant was unaware of or did not comprehend the act (M'Naghten Rule) or was irresistibly impelled to commit the act. Criticisms of the irresistible impulse defense revolve around what constitutes an irresistible impulse. Shapiro (1984) asked the question, "What is the difference between an *irresistible* impulse (*unable* to exert control) and an *unresisted* impulse (*choosing* not to exert control)?" For example, is a person with a history of antisocial behavior unable to resist his or her impulses, or is he or she choosing not to exert control? Neither the mental health profession nor the legal profession has answered this question satisfactorily.

In the case of *Durham v. United States* (1954), the U.S. Court of Appeals broadened the M'Naghten Rule with the so-called products test. An accused person was not considered criminally responsible if his or her unlawful act was the *product* of mental disease or defect. It was Judge David Bazelon's intent to (1) give the greatest possible weight to expert evaluation and testimony and (2) allow mental health professionals to define mental illness. The ***Durham* standard,** also

Psychologist Martin Orne (right) is shown here in 1976 with attorney F. Lee Bailey. Orne, an international expert on hypnosis, was the psychologist who exposed Kenneth Bianchi's fraudulent claim of multiple personality disorder. Increasingly, psychologists are being called upon to tesitfy in court cases.

has its drawbacks. The term "product" is vague and difficult to define because almost anything can cause anything (as you have learned by studying the many theoretical viewpoints in this text). Leaving the task of defining mental illness to mental health professionals often results in having to define mental illness in every case. In many situations, relying on psychiatric testimony only serves to confuse the issues because both the prosecution and defense present psychiatric experts, who often present conflicting testimony (Otto, 1989). Interestingly, Judge Bazelon eventually recognized these problems and withdrew support for it.

In 1962, the **American Law Institute (ALI)**, in its Model Penal Code, produced guidelines to help jurors determine the validity of the insanity defense on a case-by-case basis. The guidelines combined features from the previous standards.

1. A person is not responsible for criminal conduct if at the time of such conduct as a result of mental disease or defect he lacks substantial capacity either to appreciate the criminality of his conduct or to conform his conduct to the requirements of the law.

2. As used in the Article, the terms "mental disease or defect" do not include an abnormality manifested by repeated criminal or otherwise antisocial conduct. (Sec. 401, p. 66)

It is interesting to note that the second part of this guideline was intended to eliminate the insanity defense for people diagnosed as antisocial personalities.

With the attempt to be more specific and precise, the ALI guidelines moved the burden of determining criminal responsibility back to the jurors. As we have seen, previous standards, particularly the *Durham* standard, gave great weight to expert testimony, and many feared that it would usurp the jury's responsibilities. By using phrases such as "substantial capacity," "appreciate the criminality of his conduct," and "conform his conduct to the requirements of the law," the ALI standard was intended to allow the jurors the greatest possible flexibility in ascribing criminal responsibility.

In some jurisdictions, the concept of *diminished capacity* has also been incorporated into the ALI standard. As a result of a mental disease or defect, a person may lack the *specific intent* to commit the offense. For example, a person under the influence of drugs or alcohol may commit a crime without premeditation or intent; a person who is grief-stricken over the death of a loved one may harm the one responsible for the death. Although diminished capacity has been used primarily to guide the sentencing and disposition

of the defendant, it is now introduced in the trial phase as well.

Such was the trial of Dan White, a San Francisco supervisor who killed Mayor George Moscone and Supervisor Harvey Milk on November 27, 1978. White blamed both individuals for his political demise. During the trial, his attorney used the now famous "Twinkies defense" (White gorged himself on junk food such as Twinkies, chips, and soda) as partial explanation for his client's actions. White's attorney attempted to convince the jury that the high sugar content of the junk food affected his cognitive and emotional state and was partially to blame for his actions. Because of the unusual defense (the junk food diminished his judgment), White was convicted only of voluntary manslaughter and sentenced to less than eight years in jail. Of course, the citizens of San Francisco were outraged by the verdict and never forgave Dan White. Facing constant public condemnation, he eventually committed suicide after his release.

Guilty, but Mentally Ill Perhaps no other trial has more greatly challenged the use of the insanity plea than the case of the *United States v. Hinckley* (1982). John W. Hinckley, Jr.'s attempt to assassinate President Ronald Reagan, and Hinckley's subsequent acquittal by reason of insanity, outraged the public as well as legal and mental health professionals. Even before the shooting, the increasingly successful use of the insanity defense had been a growing concern in both legal circles and the public arena. Many had begun to believe that the criteria for the defense were too broadly interpreted. These concerns were strong, even though findings indicate that the insanity defense is used in less than 1 percent of cases; that its use is rarely successful; and that few fake or exaggerate their psychological disorders (Steadman et al., 1993; Callahan et al., 1991).

For quite some time, the Hinckley case aroused such strong emotional reactions that calls for reform were rampant. The American Psychiatric Association (1983), the American Medical Association (Kerlitz & Fulton, 1984), and the American Bar Association (1984) all advocated a more stringent interpretation of insanity. As a result, Congress passed the Insanity Reform Act of 1984, which based the definition of insanity totally on the individual's ability to understand what he or she did. The American Psychological Association's position on the insanity defense ran counter to these changes (Rogers, 1987). Its position is that even though a given verdict might be wrong, the standard is not necessarily wrong.

Nevertheless, in the wake of the *Hinckley* verdict, some states have adopted alternative pleas, such as "culpable and mentally disabled," "mentally disabled,

John Hinckley, Jr., was charged with the attempted murder of President Ronald Reagan. His acquittal by reason of insanity created a furor among the American public over use of the insanity defense. The outrage forced Congress to pass the Insanity Reform Act.

but neither culpable nor innocent," and "guilty, but mentally ill." These pleas are attempts to separate mental illness from insanity and to hold people responsible for their acts. Despite attempts at reform, however, states and municipalities continue to use different tests of insanity with varying outcomes, and the use of the insanity plea remains controversial. (See the Focus On feature.)

One noted psychiatrist, Thomas S. Szasz, argued not only against the insanity defense but against involuntary commitment as well (Szasz, 1963, 1986). Szasz made the case that mental illness is a myth, that the label has been used throughout history to deprive people of their civil liberties, and that the behaviors of people are ultimately their own responsibility. To label a criminal act as "mental illness" is to take responsibility away from them (a violation of their civil liberties) and to act on behalf of the state. Such actions are a threat to individual liberty and responsibility. Szasz also argued that labeling a person insane potentially masks the social ills of a society that may have led to the so-called insane act. Very concerned with the use of psychiatry in political oppression, Szasz believes that psychiatric labels allow "the state" to discredit dissenting opinions or behaviors.

Competency to Stand Trial

The term **competency to stand trial** refers to a defendant's mental state at the time of psychiatric examination after arrest and before trial. It has nothing to do with the issue of criminal responsibility, which refers to an individual's mental state or behavior at the time

of the offense. Three criteria are usually used to judge whether a person is competent to stand trial (Shapiro, 1984):

1. Does the defendant have a factual understanding of the proceedings?

2. Does the defendant have a rational understanding of the proceedings?

3. Can the defendant rationally consult with counsel in presenting his or her own defense?

Given this third criterion, a defendant who is suffering from a paranoid delusion and believes that his attorney is conspiring with the prosecution could not stand trial because a serious impairment exists.

It is clear that many more people are committed to prison hospitals because of incompetency determinations than are acquitted on insanity pleas (Steadman, 1979; Rogers, 1987; Steadman, et. al., 1993). Competency to stand trial is important to ensure that a person understands the nature of the proceedings and is able to help in his or her own defense. After all, it would be unfair to try a person incapable of self-defense. Although determination of competency is meant to protect mentally disturbed people and to guarantee preservation of criminal and civil rights, being judged incompetent to stand trial may have unfair negative consequences as well. A person may be committed for a long period of time, denied the chance to post bail, and isolated from friends and family, all without having been found guilty of a crime.

Was Ellie Nesler Insane When She Shot Daniel Driver to Death?

The Presenting Facts Forty-one-year-old Ellie Nesler shot to death 35-year-old Daniel Driver on April 2, 1993, in a Jamestown, California, courtroom. She fired her weapon into the victim five times. The weapon had been smuggled into the courtroom. Driver was on trial for molesting Nesler's six-year-old son. The defense claimed that Nesler was insane at the time of the act.

Nesler's trial was separated into two phases: (a) nature and type of crime and (b) her state of mind at the time of the crime. In August, the jury acquitted her of murder (both first- and second-degree) but convicted her of voluntary manslaughter (she killed in the heat of passion). In the second part of the trial the jury found Nesler legally sane when she committed the act. Despite the jury's determination that Nesler was sane, they did concede that some mental disorders existed and expressed hope that she would receive psychological therapy.

Defense Arguments In Favor of an Insanity Finding The defense presented evidence and an overall theory that Nesler experienced such mounting pressures and conflicts that her ability to distinguish between right and wrong was impaired. The defense argued that she "snapped" and said her act was that of "an insane mind." To explain Nesler's state of mind, they presented the following points:

Nesler had lived with a history of fear, trauma, and violence. They recounted her witnessing countless occasions on which her drunken father thrashed her mother; her attempts to shield and protect her mother and two younger sisters from her father; her own molestation at the age of three and the sexual abuse that occurred later at the hands of at least three other men; and her childhood thoughts of suicide.

The most important piece of the puzzle presented by the defense was Nesler's discovery that her own son had also been molested and her

guilt that she shared the blame— Nesler had unwittingly entrusted the six-year-old child to Driver (a convicted child molester).

The defense argued that during Driver's three-year flight from the law, Nesler's son Danny had lived in constant fear that he would be harmed by the accused assailant. Indeed, on the morning when he was scheduled to testify, Danny was so distraught and fearful that he vomited.

The defense contended that Nesler saw "secret signs" from routine comments of her friends and relatives that ordered her to kill Driver. As a result, she took the pistol (smuggled in) from her sister's purse and killed Driver.

The defense had a number of mental health professionals present their views of Nesler's mental health. The diagnoses varied, but among them were posttraumatic stress disorder and brief reactive psychosis.

Such a miscarriage of justice was the focus of a U.S. Supreme Court ruling in 1972 in the case of *Jackson v. Indiana*. In that case, a severely retarded, brain-damaged person who could neither hear nor speak was charged with robbery but was determined incompetent to stand trial. He was committed indefinitely, which in his case probably meant for life, because it was apparent by the severity of his disorders that he would never be competent. His lawyers filed a petition to have him released on the basis of deprivation of **due process**—the legal checks and balances that are guaranteed to everyone, such as the right to a fair trial, the right to face accusers, the right to present evidence, the right to counsel, and so on. The U.S. Supreme Court ruled that a defendant cannot be

confined indefinitely solely on the grounds of incompetency. After a reasonable time, a determination must be made as to whether the person is likely or unlikely to regain competency in the foreseeable future. If, in the hospital's opinion, the person is unlikely to do so, the hospital must either release the individual or initiate civil commitment procedures.

CIVIL COMMITMENT

Sometimes action seems necessary when people are severely disturbed and exhibit bizarre behaviors that can pose a threat to themselves or others. **Civil commitment** is the involuntary confinement of a person

Prosecution Arguments in Favor of Sanity The prosecution pointed out that Nesler did not act like an insane person. Her behavior leading up to her actions appeared planned and deliberate. She had the ability to distinguish right from wrong and chose the latter course. One juror, for example, stated, "We couldn't understand how she could be insane before and sane after. We felt if she was insane she would have run in there and started shooting, not walked the whole length of the hall." The prosecution presented some powerful evidence indicating that Nesler knew precisely what she was doing.

Nesler admitted that she waited to see if Driver would "cop a plea" and that she had searched his eyes for remorse before firing. She had checked, in a cryptic manner, to see if a deputy she had befriended would get in trouble if Driver was killed, and she had made sure no children would witness the shooting. Were these the actions of an insane person? The prosecution produced equally impressive mental health professionals who argued that Nesler was sane.

Discussion Questions and Group Exercise With other students from your class, form small groups and address this question: Was Nesler sane or insane? Present arguments in favor and against your verdict.

Can your group come to a consensus? An extremely enlight-ening exercise is to use a chart (similar to the one below) and to apply the four legal tests of insanity to this case. Would your verdict (guilty or not guilty by reason of insanity) on Ellie Nesler differ or remain the same in the four situations? Why?

	M'Naghten Rule	Irresistible Impulse	Durham Rule	ALI Guidelines
Verdict				
Guilty	___	___	___	___
Not Guilty	___	___	___	___

For each test, indicate your response by checking the guilty or not guilty verdict.

judged to be a danger to himself or herself, even though the person has not committed a crime. Factors relevant to civil commitment are displayed in Figure 18.2. The commitment of a person in acute distress may be viewed as a form of protective confinement (Bednar et al., 1991; Ponterotto, 1987) and a concern for the psychological and physical well-being of that person or others (Everstine & Everstine, 1983). Hospitalization is considered in the case of potential suicide or assault, bizarre behavior, destruction of property, and severe anxiety leading to loss of impulse control (Hipple & Hipple, 1983).

Involuntary hospitalization should, however, be avoided if at all possible because it has many potentially negative consequences. Ponterotto (1987) sum-marized these consequences as the lifelong social stigma associated with psychiatric hospitalization, major interruption in the person's life, losing control of his or her life and being dependent on others, and loss of self-esteem and self-concept. To this we would add a possible loss or restriction of civil liberties—a point that becomes even more glaring when we consider that the person has actually committed no crime at all.

Criteria for Commitment

States vary in the criteria used to commit a person, but there do appear to be certain general standards. It is not enough that a person be mentally ill: Additional

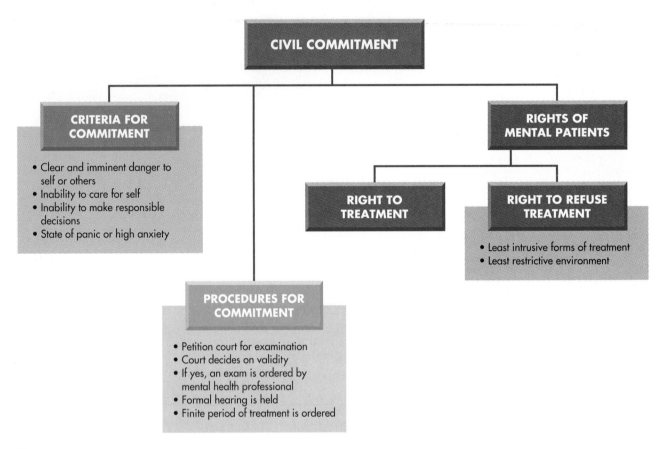

FIGURE 18.2 Factors in the Civil Commitment of a Nonconsenting Person

conditions need to exist before hospitalization is considered (Turkheimer & Parry, 1992).

1. *The person presents a clear and imminent danger to self or others.* An example is someone who is displaying suicidal or bizarre behavior that places him or her in immediate danger (walking out on a busy freeway). Threats to harm someone or behavior viewed to be assaultive or destructive are also grounds for commitment.

2. *The person is unable to care for himself or herself or does not have the social network to provide for such care.* The details vary, but states generally specify an inability to provide sufficient

   ■ Food (Person is malnourished, food is unavailable, and person has no feasible plan to obtain it.)

   ■ Clothing (Attire is not appropriate for climate or is dirty or torn, and person has no plans for obtaining others.)

   ■ Shelter (Person has no permanent residence, insufficient protection from climatic conditions,

and no logical plans for obtaining adequate housing.)

Most civil commitments are based primarily on this criterion.

3. *The person is unable to make responsible decisions about appropriate treatment and hospitalization.* As a result, there is a strong chance of deterioration.

4. *The person is in an unmanageable state of fright or panic.* Such people may believe and feel that they are on the brink of losing control.

Certainly the example of the homeless lady in the beginning of the chapter would seem to fulfill the second and possibly third criteria. In the past, commitments could be obtained solely on the basis of mental illness and a person's need for treatment, which was often determined arbitrarily. Increasingly, the courts have tightened up civil commitment procedures and have begun to rely more on a determination of whether the person presents a danger to self or others. How do we determine this possibility? Many people would not consider the homeless woman a danger to herself or others. Some, however, might believe that she could be assaultive to others and injurious to herself. Disagreements among the public may be understandable, but are trained mental health professionals more accurate in their predictions? Let's turn to that question.

Assessing Dangerousness   Most studies have indicated that mental health professionals have difficulty predicting whether their clients will commit dangerous acts and that they often overpredict violence (Monahan, 1981; McNiel & Binder, 1991; Monahan & Walker, 1990). The fact that civil commitments are often based on a determination of **dangerousness**—the person's potential for doing harm to himself or herself or to others—makes this conclusion even more disturbing. The difficulty in predicting this potential seems linked to four factors.

1. It is quite apparent that the rarer something is, the more difficult it is to predict. As a group, psychiatric patients are not dangerous! While there is some evidence that individuals suffering from severe psychotic disorders may have slightly higher rates of violent behavior (Monahan, 1993) than those found in the general population, it should not be a major concern. A frequent misconception shared not only by the public but by the courts is that mental illnesses are in and of themselves dangerous. Studies have indicated that few psychotic patients are assaultive: estimates range from 10 percent of hospitalized patients to about 3 percent in outpatient clinics (Tardiff, 1984; Tardiff & Koenigsburg, 1985; Tardiff & Sweillam, 1982). Homicide is even rarer, and a psychiatric patient is no more likely to commit a homicide than is someone in the population at large (Monahan, 1981).

2. It appears that violence is as much a function of the context in which it occurs as it is of the person's characteristics. Although it is theoretically possible for a psychologist to accurately assess an individual's personality, one has little idea about the situations in which people will find themselves. Shapiro (1984) advocated that the mental health professional needs to help the court define the term *dangerous* so that testimony can be restricted to a description of the patient's personality and kinds of situations in which personality may deteriorate, lead to assaultive behavior, or both (see the Focus On feature).

3. Probably the best predictor of dangerousness is past criminal conduct or a history of violence or aggression. Such a record, however, is frequently

The Constitution guarantees legal representation and due process to everyone, including mental patients who have often been deprived of their rights. In recent years, court decisions have more clearly defined the criteria under which individuals can be committed and how they must be treated once confined to a mental facility.

ruled irrelevant or inadmissible by mental health commissions and the courts.

4. The definition of dangerousness is itself unclear. Most of us would agree that murder, rape, torture, and physical assaults are dangerous. But are we confining our definition to physical harm only? What about psychological abuse or even destruction of property?

Procedures in Civil Commitment

Despite the difficulties in defining dangerousness, once someone believes that a person is a threat to himself or herself or to others, civil commitment procedures may be instituted. The rationale for this action is that it (1) prevents harm to the person or to others, (2) provides appropriate treatment and care, and (3) ensures due process of law (that is, legal hearing). In most cases, people deemed in need of protective confinement can be convinced to *voluntarily* commit themselves to a period of hospitalization. This process is fairly straightforward, and many believe that it is the preferred one (Ponterotto, 1987). *Involuntary* commitment occurs when the client does not consent to hospitalization.

Predicting Dangerousness: The Case of Serial Killers and Mass Murderers

Jeffrey L. Dahmer admits to killing his first victim in 1978 near his boyhood home. After killing his second victim, Dahmer states that he began to lose control of his necrophilia, a desire to have sex with the dead. Over a period of years until 1991 when he was arrested, he killed fifteen other men or young boys. Not only did he murder them, but he often killed them in hideous and torturous fashion. Once they were dead he would have sex with them, dismember their bodies, and feed upon them in cannibalistic fashion. Dahmer pleaded "not guilty by reason of mental disease or defect," but he was subsequently found guilty and was killed by another inmate in prison.

In the worst mass shooting in the United States, 35-year-old George Hennard smashed his pickup truck through a restaurant window, leaped out of the truck, and fired a high-powered automatic weapon into a lunch-time crowd. On that sunny afternoon in October 1991, Hennard killed twenty-two innocent patrons and workers in Killeen, Texas. Shortly after the slaughter, he put a bullet through his head and killed himself.

These examples of serial killers and mass murderers often make us wonder why such people were never identified as being potentially dangerous. Jeffrey Dahmer, for example, tortured animals as a small boy and was arrested in 1988 for molesting a child. Even though his father suspected his son was dangerous, Jeffrey Dahmer was released. And there appears to be sufficient evidence to suggest that mass murderer Hennard was a feared man who often acted in a paranoid way. In both situations, aberrant thoughts and behaviors appeared to go unrecognized or ignored.

Lest we be too harsh on psychologists and law-enforcement officials, it is important to realize that few serial killers or mass murderers willingly share their deviant sexual or asocial fantasies. Furthermore, many of the problems in predicting whether a person will commit dangerous acts lie in (1) limited knowledge concerning the characteristics associated with violence, (2) lack of a one-to-one correspondence between danger signs and possible violence, (3) increasing knowledge that violent behavior is most often the result of many variables, and (4) recogni-

---

Involuntary commitment can be a temporary emergency action or a longer period of detention that is determined at a formal hearing. All states recognize that cases arise in which a person is so grossly disturbed that immediate detention is required. Because formal hearings may take a long time, delaying commitment might prove adverse to the person or to other individuals.

Formal civil commitment usually follows a similar process, regardless of the state in which it occurs. First, a concerned person such as a family member, therapist, or family physician petitions the court for an examination of the person. If the judge believes there is responsible cause for this action, he or she will order an examination. Second, the judge appoints two professionals with no connection to each other to examine the person. In most cases, the examiners are physicians or mental health professionals. Third, a formal hearing is held in which the examiners testify to the person's mental state and potential danger. Others, such as family members, friends, or therapists, may also testify. The person is also allowed to speak on his or her behalf and is represented by counsel. Last, if it is determined that the person must enter treatment, a finite period may be specified; periods of six months to one year are common. Some states, however, have indefinite periods subject to periodic review and assessment.

Protection Against Involuntary Commitment We have said that involuntary commitment can lead to a violation of civil rights. Some have even argued that criminals have more rights than the mentally ill. For example, a person accused of a crime is considered innocent until proven guilty in a court of law. Usually, he or she is incarcerated only after a jury trial, and only if a crime is committed (not if there is only the possibility or even high probability of crime). Yet, a mentally ill person may be confined without a jury trial and without having committed a crime if it is thought possible that he or she might do harm to self or others. In other words, the criminal justice system will not incarcerate a person because he or she *might* harm someone (they must already have done it), but

tion that incarceration—both criminal and civil—cannot occur on the basis of "potential danger" alone. Nevertheless, our limited experiences with mass murderers and serial killers have produced patterns and profiles of interest to mental health practitioners and law-enforcement officials. It is important to note, however, that the profiles of mass murderers and serial killers contain some major differences and similarities. Some of these are discussed as follows:

Profile of Serial Killers   Serial killers are usually white males, and they often suffer from some recognized psychiatric disorder, such as sexual sadism, antisocial personality, extreme narcissism, and borderline personality disorder. Few are psychotic, and psychoses do not appear to be the cause of their compulsion to kill. Almost all, however, entertain violent sexual fantasies and have experienced traumatic sex at a young age. Their earlier years are troubled with family histories of abuse, alcoholism, and criminal activity. Dahmer, for example, was sexually molested as a youngster. Most serial killers seem to exhibit little remorse for their victims, have little incentive to change, and seem to lack a value system. The compulsion to kill is often associated with what has been described as "morbid prognostic signs" (Schlesinger, 1989): breaking and entering for nonmonetary purposes; unprovoked assaults and mistreatment of women; a fetish for female undergarments and destruction of them; showing hatred, contempt, or fear of women; violence against animals, especially cats; sexual identity confusion, including underlying homosexual feelings; a "violent and primitive fantasy life"; and sexual inhibitions and preoccupation with rigid standards of morality (Youngstrom, 1991, p. 32).

Profile of Mass Murderers   Mass murderers are usually men who are social isolates and seem to exhibit inadequate social and interpersonal skills. They have been found to be quite angry and to be filled with rage. The anger appears to be cumulative and is triggered by some type of event, usually a loss. For example, it may be the loss of a job or a relationship that is seen as being catastrophic to the person. Most have strong mistrust of people and entertain paranoid fantasies such as a wide-ranging conspiracy against them. They tend to be rootless and have few support systems such as family, friends, or religious or fraternal groups. Many researchers believe that the number of mass murders will increase as firearms proliferate in our society. Other social correlates affecting mass murders are an increasing sense of rootlessness in the country, general disenchantment, and loneliness. The more random the killings, the more disturbed, delusional, and paranoid the person is likely to be.

---

civil commitment *is* based on possible future harm. It can be argued that in the former case, confinement is punishment, while in the latter case it is treatment (for the individual's benefit). For example, it is often argued that mentally ill people may be incapable of determining their own treatment, and that once treated, will be grateful for the treatment they received. If people resist hospitalization, they are thus being irrational, which is a symptom of their mental disorder.

Critics do not accept this reasoning. They point out that civil commitment is for the benefit of those initiating commitment procedures (society), and not for the individual. Even after treatment, people rarely appreciate it. These concerns have raised and heightened sensitivity toward patient welfare and rights, resulting in a trend toward restricting the powers of the state over the individual.

Rights of Mental Patients   Many people in the United States are concerned about the balance of power among the state, our mental institutions, and our citizens. The U.S. Constitution guarantees certain "inalienable rights" such as trial by jury, legal representation, and protection against self-incrimination. As indicated in Chapter 1, the mental health profession has great power, which may be used wittingly or unwittingly to abridge individual freedom. In recent decades, some courts have ruled that commitment for any purpose constitutes a major deprivation of liberty that requires due process protection.

Until 1979, the level of proof required for civil commitments varied from state to state. In a case that set legal precedent, a Texas man claimed that he was denied due process because the jury that committed him was instructed to use a lower standard than "beyond a reasonable doubt" (more than 90 percent sure). The appellate court agreed with the man, but when the case finally reached the Supreme Court in April 1979 *(Addington v. Texas)*, the court ruled that the state must only provide "clear and convincing evidence" (approximately 75 percent sure) that a person is mentally ill and potentially dangerous before that person can be committed. Although it is important to

Convicted serial killer Jeffrey Dahmer killed at least seventeen men and young boys over a period of many years. Besides torturing many of his victims, Dahmer admitted to dismembering them and devouring their bodies in a celebration of cannibalism. Although Dahmer had been imprisoned in 1988 for sexual molestation, it would have been difficult to predict his degree of dangerousness. Despite an attempt to use the insanity plea, Dahmer was found guilty in 1994, imprisoned, and subsequently killed by another inmate.

note that confinement requires a higher standard than advocated by most mental health organizations, this ruling represented the first time that the Supreme Court considered any aspect of the civil commitment process (Shapiro, 1984). Under the advocacy of President Jimmy Carter, the U.S. Congress in 1980 passed the Mental Health Systems Act, protecting mental patients' rights and liberties (see Table 18.1).

Due to decisions in several other cases (*Lessard v. Schmidt*, 1972, Wisconsin Federal Court; and *Dixon v. Weinberger*, 1975), states must provide the **least restrictive environment** for people. This means that people have a right to the least restrictive alternative to freedom that is appropriate to their condition. Only patients who cannot adequately care for themselves are confined to hospitals. Those who can function acceptably should be given alternative choices, such as boarding homes and other shelter.

Right to Treatment   One of the primary justifications for commitment is that treatment will improve a person's mental condition and increase the likelihood that he or she will be able to return to the community. If we confine a person involuntarily and do not provide the means for release (therapy), isn't this deprivation of due process? Several cases have raised this problem as a constitutional issue. Together, they have determined that mental patients who have been involuntarily committed have a **right to treatment**—a right to receive therapy that would improve their emotional state.

In 1966, in a lawsuit brought against St. Elizabeth's Hospital in Washington, D.C. *(Rouse v. Cameron)*, the court held that (1) right to treatment is a constitutional right and (2) failure to provide treatment cannot be justified by lack of resources. In other words, a mental institution or the state could not use lack of funding facilities or labor power as reasons for not providing treatment. Although this decision represented a major advance in patient rights, the ruling provided no guidelines for what constitutes treatment.

This issue was finally addressed in 1972 by U.S. District Court Judge Frank Johnson in the Alabama Federal Court. The case *(Wyatt v. Stickney)* involved a mentally retarded boy who not only failed to receive treatment but had to live in an institution that was unable to meet even minimum standards of care. Indeed, the living conditions in two of the hospital buildings resembled those found in early asylums of the eighteenth century. Less than 50 cents a day was spent on food for each patient; the toilet facilities were totally inadequate and filthy; patients were crowded in group rooms with minimal or no privacy; and personnel (one physician per two thousand patients) and patient care were practically nonexistent.

Judge Johnson not only ruled in favor of the right to treatment, but also specified standards of adequate treatment, such as staff-patient ratios, therapeutic environment conditions, and professional consensus about appropriate treatment. The court also made it clear that mental patients could not be forced to work (scrub floors, cook, serve food, wash laundry, and so on) or to engage in work-related activities aimed at maintaining the institution in which they lived. This practice, widely used in institutions, was declared unconstitutional. Moreover, patients who volunteered to perform tasks had to be paid at least the minimum wage to do them instead of merely being given token

TABLE 18.1 The Patient Bill of Rights

1. Right to appropriate treatment in a supportive environment which minimizes restriction of a person's liberty.
2. Right for reasonable explanation of the care and treatment process.
3. Right to refuse treatment if informed, voluntary, and written consent has not been obtained (unless in emergencies).
4. Right to be free from restraint or seclusion unless an emergency situation exists and written orders from a responsible mental health professional have been obtained.
5. Right to have access to one's own mental health records.
6. Right to have access to telephone, mail, visitation, and private conversations.
7. Right to exercise these rights and others without fear of reprisal.
8. Right to confidentiality of personal records.

Under the advocacy of President Jimmy Carter, Congress passed the Mental Health Systems Act in 1980, which outlined the rights of mental patients. This bill was intended to protect patients from being deprived of their individual rights and liberties. Some of these rights are listed here.

allowances or special privileges. This landmark decision ensures treatment beyond custodial care and protection against neglect and abuse.

Another important case (tried in the U.S. District Court in Florida), *O'Connor v. Donaldson* (1975), has also had a major impact on the right-to-treatment issue. It involved Kenneth Donaldson, who at age forty-nine was committed for twenty years to the Chattahoochee State Hospital on petition by his father. He was found to be mentally ill and dangerous. Throughout his confinement, Donaldson petitioned for release, but Dr. O'Connor, the hospital superintendent, determined that the patient was too dangerous. Finally, Donaldson threatened a lawsuit and was reluctantly discharged by the hospital after fourteen years of confinement. He then sued both O'Connor and the hospital, winning an award of $20,000. The monetary award is insignificant compared with the significance of the ruling. Again, the court reaffirmed the client's right to treatment. It ruled that Donaldson did not receive appropriate treatment and said that the state cannot constitutionally confine a nondangerous person who is capable of caring for himself or herself outside of an institution or who has willing friends or family to help. Further, it said that physicians as well as institutions are liable for improper confinements.

One major dilemma facing the courts in all cases of court-ordered treatment is what constitutes treatment. As discussed in earlier chapters, treatment can range from rest and relaxation to psychosurgery, medication, and aversion therapy. Mental health professionals believe that they are in the best position to evalu-

In 1972 Judge Frank M. Johnson issued a landmark decision dealing with patient rights in the case of *Wyatt v. Stickney.* The ruling provided guidelines to mental hospitals about what constituted appropriate treatment. Prior to the ruling, patients were often hospitalized without adequate therapeutic treatment. Johnson later served as FBI director.

ate the type and efficacy of treatment, a position supported by the case of *Youngberg v. Romeo* (1982). The court ruled that a mentally retarded boy, Nicholas Romeo, had a constitutional right to "reasonable care and safety," and it deferred judgment to the mental health professional as to what constitutes therapy.

Right to Refuse Treatment Patients frequently refuse medical treatment on religious grounds or because the treatment would only prolong a terminal illness. In many cases, physicians are inclined to honor such refusals, especially if they seem based on reasonable grounds. But should mental patients have a right to refuse treatment? At first glance, it may appear that this question does not make sense. After all, why commit patients for treatment and then allow them to refuse it? Furthermore, isn't it possible that mental patients may be incapable of deciding what is best for themselves? For example, a man with a paranoid delusion may refuse treatment because he believes the hospital staff is plotting against him. If he is allowed to refuse medication or other forms of therapy, his condition may deteriorate more. The result is that the client becomes even more dangerous or incapable of caring for himself outside of hospital confinement (Stone, 1975).

Proponents of the right to refuse treatment argue, however, that many forms of treatment, such as medication or electroconvulsive therapy (ECT), may have long-term side effects, as discussed in earlier chapters. They also point out that involuntary treatment is generally much less effective than treatment accepted voluntarily (Shapiro, 1984). People forced into treatment seem to resist it, thereby nullifying the potentially beneficial effects.

The case of *Rennie v. Klein* (1978) involved several state hospitals in New Jersey that were forcibly medicating patients in nonemergency situations. The court ruled that people had a constitutional right to refuse treatment (psychotropic medication) and to be given due process. In another related case, *Rogers v. Okin* (1979), a Massachusetts court supported these guidelines. Both cases made the point that psychotropic medication was often used only to control behavior or as a substitute for treatment. Further, the decisions noted that drugs might actually inhibit recovery.

In these cases, the courts supported the right to refuse treatment under certain conditions and have extended the least restrictive alternative principle to include *least intrusive forms of treatment*. Generally, psychotherapy is considered less intrusive than somatic or physical therapies (ECT and medication). Although this compromise may appear reasonable, other problems present themselves. First, how do we define an intrusive treatment? Are insight therapies as intrusive as behavioral techniques (punishment and aversion procedures)? Second, if patients are allowed to refuse certain forms of treatment and if the hospital does not have alternatives for them, can clients sue the institution? These questions are still unanswered.

DEINSTITUTIONALIZATION

Deinstitutionalization is the shifting of responsibility for the care of mental patients from large central institutions to agencies within local communities. When originally formulated in the 1960s and 1970s, the concept excited many mental health professionals. Since its inception, many state-run hospitals have experienced a greater than 50 percent reduction in the hospital population and a 75 percent decrease in the average daily number of committed patients (Mechanic, 1987; Turkheimer & Parry, 1992). The impetus behind deinstitutionalization came from several quarters.

First, there has been (and still is) a feeling that large hospitals provide mainly custodial care, that they produce little benefit for the patient, and that they may even impede improvement. Court cases discussed earlier (*Wyatt v. Stickney* and *O'Connor v. Donaldson*) exposed the fact that many mental hospitals are no better than "warehouses for the insane." Institutionalization was accused of fostering dependency, promoting helplessness, and lowering self-sufficiency in patients. The longer patients were hospitalized, the more likely they were to remain hospitalized, even if they had improved (Wing, 1980). Further, symptoms such as flat affect and nonresponsiveness, which were thought to be clinical signs of schizophrenia, may actually result from hospitalization.

Second, the issue of patient rights has received increasing attention. As already discussed, recent legal decisions have mandated that patients live in the least restrictive environments. Mental health professionals became very concerned about keeping patients confined against their will and began to discharge patients whenever they approached minimal competencies. It was believed that **mainstreaming**—integrating mental patients as soon as possible back into the community—could be accomplished by providing local outpatient or transitory services (such as board-and-care facilities, halfway houses, churches). In addition, advances in tranquilizers and other drug treatment techniques made it possible to medicate patients, which made them manageable once discharged.

Third, insufficient funds for state hospitals have almost forced these institutions to release patients back

Should this homeless man be considered mentally disturbed and committed to an institution? Is he a danger to himself or to others? Residents in the neighborhood where Larry Hogue lives claim that he has been frightening people for years. He has been arrested numerous times for threatening people and damaging property but he has never been permanently confined.

into communities. Overcrowded conditions made mental health administrators view the movement favorably; state legislative branches encouraged the trend, especially because it reduced state costs and funding.

What has been the impact of deinstitutionalization on patients? Its critics believe that deinstitutionalization is a policy that allows states to relinquish their responsibility to care for patients unable to care for themselves. There are alarming indications that deinstitutionalization has been responsible for placing or "dumping" on the streets up to one million former patients who should have remained institutionalized (Toro & Wall, 1991). The majority appear severely disabled, have difficulty coping with daily living, suffer from schizophrenia, and are alcoholic (Lamb, 1984; Toro & Wall, 1991; Fischer & Breakey, 1991). Recently, two federal reports *(Outcasts on Mainstreet* and *Caring for People: Conclusions for Research)* have examined the issue of the homeless mentally ill (Observer, 1992). They paint a distressing picture of the fragmented nature of existing programs to assist millions of mentally ill citizens.

Thus it is becoming apparent that many mentally ill people are not receiving treatment. Approximately 750,000 mentally ill now live in nursing homes, board-and-care homes, or group residences (Applebaum, 1987). The quality of care in many of these places is marginal, forcing continuing and periodic rehospitalization of the mentally ill (Turkheimer & Parry, 1992). The mentally ill constitute a substantial portion of the homeless population (Fischer & Breakey, 1991; Levine & Rog, 1990).

Much of the problem with deinstitutionalization appears to be the community's lack of preparation and resources to care for the chronically mentally ill. Many patients lack family or friends who can help them make the transition back into the community; many state hospitals do not provide patients with adequate skills training; many discharged patients have difficulty finding jobs; many find substandard housing worse than the institutions from which they came; many are not adequately monitored and receive no psychiatric treatment; and many become homeless (Westermeyer, 1987). It is difficult to estimate how many discharged mental patients comprise the burgeoning ranks of the homeless. We do know that homelessness in the United States, especially in large, urban areas, is increasing at an alarming pace (Kondratas, 1991; Toro et al., 1991). Certainly, it is not difficult to see the number of people who live in transport terminals, parks, flophouses, homeless shelters, cars, and storefronts. It is hard to determine how many of the homeless, like the woman discussed at the beginning of this chapter, have been deinstitutionalized before adequate support services were present

Homelessness has become one of the great social problems of urban communities. Many believe that deinstitutionalization has contributed to the problem although it is not clear what proportion of homeless people are mentally ill. Scenes like this one, however, are becoming all too common.

in a community. We do know, however, that the homeless have significantly poorer psychological adjustment and higher arrests and conviction records (Lamb, 1984). The solution, although complex, probably does not call for the return to the old institutions of the 1950s but rather for the provision of more and better community-based treatment facilities and alternatives (Kiesler, 1991).

For patients involved in alternative community programs, the picture appears somewhat more positive. After reviewing reports of experimental studies on alternative treatment, a group of researchers concluded that such patients fared at least as well as those in institutions. Where differences were found, they favored the alternative programs (Braun et al., 1981). Such studies are few, however, and much remains to be done if deinstitutionalized patients are to be provided with the best supportive treatment.

THE THERAPIST-CLIENT RELATIONSHIP

The therapist-client relationship involves a number of legal, moral, and ethical issues. In our examination of confidentiality and privileged communication, we will explore many of these areas.

Confidentiality and Privileged Communication

Basic to the therapist-patient relationship is the premise that therapy involves a deeply personal association in which clients have a right to expect that

whatever they say will be kept private. Therapists believe that genuine therapy cannot occur unless clients trust their therapists and believe they will not divulge confidential communications. Without this guarantee, clients may not be completely open with their thoughts and may thereby lose the benefits of therapy. This raises several questions. First, what professional ethics and legal statutes govern the therapist-client relationship? Under what conditions can a therapist breach the confidentiality of the relationship? Second, what if, in a conflict between clinical issues (need for trust) and legal ones (need to disclose), the therapist chooses trust? What are the consequences? Third, if a therapist decides to disclose information to a third party, what effects can the disclosure have on the therapist-client relationship? Last, how can a therapist discuss the limits of confidentiality in a way that would be least likely to disrupt the therapeutic relationship?

Confidentiality is an ethical standard that protects clients from disclosure of information without their consent. Generally, mental health organizations publish codes of ethics endorsing confidentiality in the therapist-client relationship. The American Psychological Association (1991) ethics code specifies:

Psychologists disclose confidential information only as required by law, or where permitted by law, for a valid purpose such as: (1) to provide needed professional services to the patient or client, (2) to obtain appropriate professional consultations, (3) to protect the patient or client or others from harm, or (4) to obtain payment for services, in which instance, disclosure is limited to the minimum necessary to achieve the purpose (1991).

Furthermore, the public also seems to believe in the importance of confidentiality in the therapeutic relationship. In one study, it was found that 74 percent of respondents thought everything told to a therapist should be confidential; indeed, 69 percent believed that whatever they discussed was never disclosed (Miller & Thelen, 1986).

Confidentiality is an ethical, not a legal, obligation. **Privileged communication,** a narrower legal concept, protects privacy and prevents the disclosure of confidential communications without a client's permission (Corey, Corey & Callanan, 1993; Herlicky & Sheeley, 1988). It must be kept in mind that the "holder of the privilege" is the client, not the therapist. In other words, if a client waives this privilege, the therapist has no grounds for withholding information. Shapiro (1984) pointed out that our society recognizes how important certain confidential relationships are and protects them by law. These relationships are the husband-wife, attorney-client, pastor-congregant, and therapist-client relationships. Psychiatric practices are regulated in all fifty states, including the District of Columbia, and forty-two states have privileged communication statutes (Herlicky & Sheeley, 1988).

Exemptions from Privileged Communication Although states vary considerably, all states recognize certain situations in which communications can be divulged. Corey and associates (1984, 1993) summarized these conditions:

1. In situations that deal with civil or criminal commitment or competency to stand trial, the client's right to privilege can be waived. For example, a court-appointed therapist who determines that the client needs hospitalization for a psychological disorder may disclose the results of the examination to an appropriate third party.

2. Disclosure can also be made when a client sees a therapist and introduces mental condition as a claim or defense in a civil action. For example, a woman who sues an employer for harassment and uses "mental distress" to justify her claim may force the therapist to disclose information relevant to her claim.

3. When the client is younger than sixteen years of age and information leads the therapist to believe that the child has been a victim of crime (incest, rape, or child abuse), the therapist must provide that information to the appropriate child protective services agency.

4. When criminal action is involved, the therapist is again obligated to disclose information related to that action.

5. When the therapist has reason to believe that a client presents a danger to himself or herself (possible injury or suicide) or may potentially harm someone else, the therapist must act to ward off the danger.

Clearly privilege in communication is not absolute. It involves the delicate balance between the individual's right to privacy and the public's need to know certain information (Leslie, 1991). Problems arise when we try to determine what the balance should be and how important various events and facts are. Originally, Max Siegel (a former president of the American Psychological Association) argued that under no circumstances should the confidential nature of the therapeutic relationship ever be breached. Clinical concerns are paramount and should be given greatest weight (Siegel, 1979). Others have challenged the position that confidentiality is necessary for effective treatment (Denkowski & Denkowski, 1982). Clearly, the issues are complex. The rights of both clients and the general public must be protected, and the courts must decide when the rights of one group conflict with those of the other.

The Duty-to-Warn Principle

At the beginning of the chapter, we briefly described the case of Prosenjit Poddar (*Tarasoff v. Board of Regents of the University of California*, 1976), a graduate student who killed Tatiana Tarasoff after notifying his therapist that he intended to take her life. Before the homicide, the therapist had decided that Poddar was dangerous and likely to carry out his threat, and had notified the director of the Cowell Psychiatric Clinic that the client was dangerous. He also informed the campus police, hoping that they would detain the student. Surely the therapist had done all that could be reasonably expected. Not so, ruled the California Supreme Court. In the *Tarasoff ruling,* the court stated that when a therapist determines, according to the standards of the mental health profession, that a patient presents a serious danger to another, the therapist is obligated to warn the intended victim. The court went on to say that the protective privilege ends where public peril begins.

Criticism of the Duty-to-Warn Principle This ruling seems to place the therapist in the unenviable role of being a double agent (Bednar et al., 1991). Therapists have an ethical and legal obligation to their clients, but they also have legal obligations to society. Not only can these dual obligations conflict with one another, but they can be quite ambiguous. Many situations exist in which state courts must rule to clarify

CRITICAL THINKING

Does the Duty-to-Warn Principle Apply to AIDS?

George, a 24-year-old graduate student, had known for some time that he was HIV-infected. He entered counseling at the university psychiatric services center because of extreme feelings of guilt associated with his dishonesty in not disclosing his infection to a woman-student with whom he had recently become intimate. He had hidden his medical condition from family, friends, and past lovers because of the social stigma involved and the fear that others would find out that he had often engaged in bisexual relationships. On numerous occasions, George had unprotected sex with his partners, but he had started to use condoms with his current woman-friend. However, she did not like condoms and

had encouraged George to avoid their use in love-making. Several times, George had complied with her request.

If you were George's therapist, what would you do? What ethical or legal obligations do you have toward George and toward the larger society? Should you maintain the confidentiality of the therapeutic relationship or inform others about George's HIV condition? If you choose to disclose this information, whom would you notify? From your reading in the section on the *Tarasoff* decision, are there any guidelines that could help you decide? Before reading further, take a few minutes to contemplate your answers to these questions.

Under the Family Education Rights and Privacy Act (McGowan,

1991), student records are confidential and strong prohibitions worn against releasing information. HIV- and AIDS-positive students are guaranteed confidentiality because of their rights to privacy. In addition, a public diagnosis of HIV or AIDS may stigmatize the student and subject him or her to social ostracism and discrimination. Proponents of maintaining confidentiality believe that any violation of the therapeutic trust would decrease the likelihood that students will discuss their health status with a counselor. They believe it would be more beneficial in the long run if the counselor explored with students their motives for concealing their condition and encouraged them to discuss it with their sexual partners.

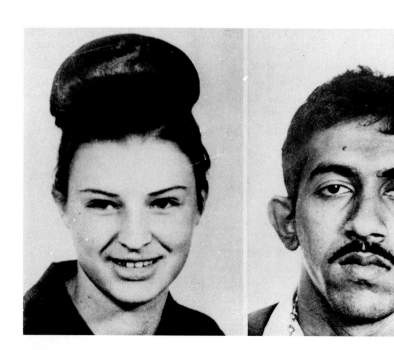

Tatiana Tarasoff, a college student, was stabbed to death in 1969 by Prosenjit Poddar, a graduate student at the University of California at Berkeley. Although Poddar's therapist notified the university that he thought Poddar was dangerous, the California Supreme Court ruled that the therapist should have warned the victim as well.

Others, however, have less faith in the counselor's ability to convince infected students to be honest with their partners (Hoffman, 1991). Studies indicate that dishonesty about one's sexual history and infectious state is quite common (Kegeles, Catania & Coates, 1988): Among gay or bisexual men who were diagnosed as HIV positive, 12 percent said they did not plan to tell their primary sexual partners; 27 percent said they would not tell their nonprimary partners. In another study of heterosexual men, 20 percent said they would lie about being seropositive, and 35 percent said they had lied to female partners about their past sexual behavior (Elias, 1988). Some counselors would argue that breaking confidentiality is a small price to pay when an unknowing partner may be receiving the equivalent of a death sentence.

So far there have been no legal tests of the *Tarasoff* decision and its relationship to HIV infection (Cohen, 1990; Knapp & Vande-Creek, 1990). The decision, however, does have important ramifications for a therapist's decision to breach confidentiality. Hoffman (1991) outlined three criteria important in that decision:

1. A (fiduciary) special relationship of trust must exist between the counselor and client. A therapeutic relationship fulfills this criteria.

2. There must be an identifiable potential victim. Remember, the duty to warn extends only to identifiable victims rather than to all persons whom the client could conceivably infect. Anonymous partners or casual partners who are unknown to the counselor would not fall within the duty to protect principle. Partners who live with the person under a monogamous or exclusive relationship would most likely meet this criterion.

3. The assessment of dangerousness must be made. Three factors need to be clarified under this criteria: (a) the certainty of an HIV infection in the client, (b) the extent to which the client engages in behaviors that carry a high risk of HIV transmission, and (c) the use or nonuse of safer sex techniques.

In light of the above criteria, how would you apply these to the case of George? Perhaps it would be helpful to divide yourselves into smaller groups to discuss these issues and come to a decision. Remember, even with these criteria, many gray areas exist. For example, not all sexual practices are high risk with regard to transmission. Thus not all sexual practice necessitates a legal obligation to report. As mentioned, there have been no legal tests of the *Tarasoff* criteria in HIV-infected persons, and the APA Ethical Guidelines make no mention of confidentiality and HIV (Melton, 1988).

the implications and uncertainties of the "duty-to-warn" rule (Fulero, 1988; see Critical Thinking).

Siegel (1979) loudly criticized the Tarasoff ruling, stating that it was a "day in court for the law and not for the mental health professions." He reasoned that if confidentiality had been an absolute policy, Poddar might have been kept in treatment, thus ultimately saving Tarasoff's life. Other mental health professionals have echoed this theme in one form or another. Hostile clients with pent-up feelings and emotions may be less likely to act out or become violent when allowed to ventilate their thoughts. The irony, according to critics, is that the duty-to-warn principle may actually be counterproductive to its intent to protect the potential victim.

Another controversial issue surrounding the duty-to-warn principle relates not just to determining danger but to when that determination should be made. Stimulated mainly by the *Tarasoff* ruling, mental health professionals and government and private in-

stitutions have begun to develop guidelines for dealing with dangerous clients. These guidelines have several common elements. One is the recognition that the therapist's principal duty is to the client and that confidentiality is a crucial aspect of the therapeutic relationship. Another is that therapy necessarily encourages people to engage in open dialogue with the therapist and to share their innermost thoughts and feelings. It is not unusual for clients to voice thoughts about ending their own lives or harming others. Relatively few of these threats are actually carried out, and therapists are not expected to routinely report all of them.

A third common element in the guidelines for dealing with dangerous clients is that the duty-to-warn principle can be invoked only in the most extraordinary circumstances. During the therapy session, however, the therapist should continue to treat the client and, if therapeutically appropriate, should attempt to dissuade the client from the threatened violence. A final point is that somewhere in the therapy process, the therapist must discuss the limits of confidentiality and inform the client about the possible actions he or she must take to protect a third party. In other words, professionals are obligated to inform their clients that they have a duty to warn others about the threatened actions of their clients. Although some therapists fear that such actions might prevent the client from being open and honest, one study seemed to suggest that informing clients about the limits of confidentiality had little impact in inhibiting clients' disclosures (Muehleman, Pickens & Robinson, 1985).

Sexual Relationships with Clients

Traditionally, mental health practitioners have emphasized the importance of separating their personal and professional lives. They reasoned that therapists need to be objective and removed from their clients because becoming emotionally involved with them was nontherapeutic. Having a personal relationship with a client may make the therapist less confrontive, allow the therapist to fulfill his or her own needs at the expense of the client, and unintentionally allow the therapist to exploit the client because of his or her position (Corey et al., 1984, 1993). Some people question the belief that a social or personal relationship is necessarily antitherapeutic (Burton, 1972). Although it is not within the scope of this section for us to debate the issue, matters of personal relations with clients are being increasingly raised, especially when they deal with erotic and sexual intimacies with clients.

Sexual misconduct of therapists is considered to be one of the most serious of all ethical violations. Indeed, virtually all professional organizations condemn sexual intimacies in the therapist-client relationship (see Table 18.2).

But what are the practitioners' thoughts about sexual intimacies with clients? How often does it really occur? Who does what to whom? Some studies indicate that being sexually attracted to a client or engaging in sexual fantasy about one is not uncommon among therapists (Pope, Tabachnick & Keith-Spiegel, 1987; Pope & Tabachnick, 1993). Furthermore, complaints to state licensing boards about sexual misconduct by therapists have increased significantly (Zamichow, 1993). While these are indisputable facts, the vast majority of psychologists are able to control their sexual feelings and to behave in a professional manner.

In an early nationwide study of 500 male and 500 female psychologists, Holroyd and Brodsky (1977) reported that 5.5 percent of male therapists and 0.6 percent of female therapists have had sexual intercourse with clients. Sexual intimacy is almost always

between male therapists and female clients. Of those who had sexual intercourse with clients, 80 percent were likely to repeat the practice. Of those responding, 88 percent of female and 70 percent of male therapists believed that erotic contact is never beneficial to clients. However, 4 percent of the respondents thought that erotic contact with clients was beneficial. Although in the minority, these therapists took the position that sexual intimacy may be beneficial to clients because it validates the clients as sexual beings, frees them from inhibitions and guilt, and allows them to enjoy their sexuality.

Critics of these arguments find them weak and self-serving. First, sexual intimacy represents an abuse of the therapist's power. Clients who discuss the most intimate aspects of their lives (sexual desires and struggles) are very vulnerable, and it is extremely easy for therapists to take advantage of their clients' trust and to exploit it. Second, sexual intimacy fosters dependency in clients, who look toward the therapist as an "ideal" and as someone who has "the answers." An individual's personal therapeutic goals become subordinate to a desire to please the therapist or to live up to his or her standards. Third, objectivity may also be lost. When therapists become sex partners, they cease to be therapists. Fourth, clients often feel exploited, used, embittered, and angry. Their self-esteem is also harmed.

Statistics on the harmful effects of sexual intimacy on clients have supported these conclusions. In a survey of 559 clients who became sexually involved with their therapists, 90 percent were deemed adversely affected (Bouhoutsos et al., 1983). The harm included mistrust of opposite-gender relationships, hospitalizations, deterioration of their relationships with primary partners, and suicide. Many victims of therapist-client sexual contact had responses that seemed similar to the rape syndrome, the battered-spouse syndrome, and symptoms displayed by victims of child abuse (Pope, 1988; Pope & Vetter, 1991; Sherman, 1993). The Committee on Women in Psychology of the American Psychological Association (1989) took the position that sexual relationships between therapists and clients are never the fault of the client and that the therapist can never be excused for sexual misconduct.

Most professional organizations and states have procedures for filing and processing ethical complaints related to sexual intimacies between therapist and client. In the state of California, the Board of Medical Quality Assurance—the parent organization of the Psychology Examining Committee—has power to suspend or revoke the licenses of therapists who engage in sexual misconduct with their clients. Furthermore, clients always have legal recourse to sue their therapists for malpractice. Therapists who en-

TABLE 18.2   Policy Statements on Sexual Intimacy Between Therapists and Clients

American Psychological Association (1992)

Psychologists do not engage in sexual intimacies with current patients or clients.

Psychologists do not accept as patients or clients persons with whom they have previously engaged in sexual intimacies.

Psychologists do not engage in sexual intimacies with a former therapy patient or client for at least two years after cessation or termination of professional services.

The American Psychiatric Association (1989)

The necessary intensity of the therapeutic relationship may tend to activate sexual and other needs and fantasies on the part of both patient and therapist, while weakening the objectivity necessary for control. Sexual activity with a patient is unethical. Sexual involvement with one's former patients generally exploits emotions deriving from treatment and therefore almost always is unethical.

The American Association for Counseling And Development (1988)

The member will avoid any type of sexual intimacies with clients. Sexual intimacies with clients are unethical.

The National Association of Social Workers (1990)

The social worker should under no circumstances engage in sexual activities with clients.

The American Association for Marriage and Family Therapy (1991)

Sexual intimacy with clients is prohibited. Sexual intimacy with former clients for two years following the termination of therapy is prohibited.

The American Psychoanalytic Association (1983)

Sexual relationships between analyst and patient are antithetical to treatment and unacceptable under any circumstances. Any sexual activity with a patient constitutes a violation of this principle of ethics.

All mental health organizations have developed ethical principles and codes of conduct for their members. Sexual intimacies with clients have become a focus of serious debate. Concerns about dual role conflicts, abuse of power, potential psychological harm to clients, and the image of the therapeutic professions have resulted in strong statements by professional organizations.

gage in sex with clients have few arguments they can use in court because the courts have generally rejected claims of consent (Austin, Moline & Williams, 1990). Many cases of misconduct, however, probably go unreported because of the client's shame and guilt over their "complicity." In any case, the consensus is that sexual intimacy with clients is unethical, antitherapeutic, and detrimental.

CULTURAL PLURALISM AND THE MENTAL HEALTH PROFESSION

Increasingly, mental health providers are coming into contact with clients who differ from them in terms of race, culture, and ethnicity (Sue, Arredondo & McDavis, 1992). The 1990 U.S. Census reveals that the United States is fast undergoing some very radical demographic changes. It is estimated that by the year

2000, over one-third of the population will be composed of racial/ethnic minorities, with an even higher proportion (45 percent) in our public schools; within several decades, today's racial minorities will become the majority (Sue, 1991; Johnston & Packer, 1987). These estimates are based upon two observed trends. The first is differing birth rates between European Americans and American minority groups. For example, European Americans average 1.7 children per mother. African Americans average 2.4 children per mother; Mexican Americans, 2.9; Vietnamese Americans, 3.4; Hmong Americans, 11.9. The second trend is that of immigration patterns, with increases in immigrants from Asian and Latin American countries.

Many mental health professionals assert that the prevailing concepts of mental health and mental disorders are culture bound, and that the prevailing theories of therapy are based on values specific to a middle-class, white, highly individualistic, and ethno-

The demographic landscape of the United States is changing at a very rapid pace. Within several short decades, racial and ethnic minorities will become a numerical majority. The implications are that therapists will come into increasing contact with clients who differ from them in terms of race, ethnicity, and culture. Multicultural psychology has become an important field for the mental health profession.

centric population (D. W. Sue & D. Sue, 1990; Special Populations Task Force of the President's Commission on Mental Health, 1978; D. W. Sue & D. Sue, 1990). As a result, misdiagnosis and inappropriate treatments often victimize ethnic minority clients. Underutilization of traditional mental health facilities and premature termination by culturally different clients have been well documented in the past (Sue, Allen & Conaway, 1975; Sue et al., 1974). As we have stated elsewhere (Sue & Sue, 1990), "The services offered are frequently antagonistic or inappropriate to the life experiences of the culturally different client; they lack sensitivity and understanding, and they are oppressive and discriminating toward minority clients." (p. 7).

These ethical and professional concerns are reflected in the most recent *Ethical Principles of Psychologists and Code of Conduct of the American Psychological Association* (APA, 1992). Below are some of the more pertinent principles:

Psychologists are aware of cultural, individual, and role differences, including those due to age, gender, race, ethnicity, national origin, religion, sexual orientation, disability, language, and socioeconomic status. Psychologists try to eliminate the effect on their work of biases based on those factors, and they do not knowingly participate in or condone unfair discriminatory practices (*Principle D: Respect for People's Rights and Dignity*, pp. 1599–1600).

Where differences of age, gender, race, ethnicity, national origin, religion, sexual orientation, disability, language, or socioeconomic status significantly affect psycholo-

gists' work concerning particular individuals or groups, psychologists obtain the training, experience, consultation or supervision necessary to ensure the competence of their services, or they make appropriate referrals (*General Standards: Human Differences*, p. 1601).

Psychologists attempt to identify situations in which particular interventions or assessment techniques or norms may not be applicable or may require adjustment in administration or interpretation because of factors such as individuals' gender, age, race, ethnicity, national origin, religion, sexual orientation, disability, language, or socioeconomic status (*Evaluation, Assessment, or Intervention: Use of Assessment in General and with Special Populations*, p. 1603).

These ethical principles make it clear that working with culturally different clients is unethical unless the mental health professional has adequate training and expertise in multicultural psychology. From an ethical perspective, mental health professionals have a moral and professional responsibility as follows (Sue & Sue, 1990): (a) to become aware of and deal with the biases, stereotypes, and assumptions that support their practice; (b) to become aware of the culturally different client's values and world view; and (c) to develop appropriate intervention strategies that take into account the social, cultural, historical, and environmental influences of culturally different clients.

The increased awareness of multicultural influences in our understanding of abnormal psychology is reflected in the most recent version of the *Diagnostic and Statistical Manual of the American Psychiatric Association* (DSM-IV). For the first time since its publication in 1952, DSM is acknowledging the importance of culture in the diagnosis and treatment of mental disorders. A new section on culturally related features describes culture-specific symptom patterns, preferred idioms for describing distress, and prevalence information. The clinician is given specific guidance on how clinical presentation of disorders among various ethnic and cultural groups may vary. DSM-IV also contains a section dealing with culture-bound syndromes unique to particular groups, cultures, or societies. Appendix I in DSM-IV presents many of these culture-bound syndromes, the cultures in which they were first described, and, possibly, related DSM-IV categories. The inclusion of cultural issues is intended to enhance the cross-cultural applicability of DSM-IV and to reduce clinicians' possible bias stemming from their own cultural backgrounds.

In further recognition of the importance of cultural differences in psychotherapy, the Office of Minority Affairs of the American Psychological Association (APA, 1991) has published *Guidelines for Providers of Psychological Services to Ethnic, Linguistic, and Culturally Diverse Populations*. This document makes it clear that service providers need to become aware of how their own culture, life experiences, attitudes, values, and biases have influenced them. It also emphasizes the importance of culture and environmental factors in diagnosis and treatment, and it insists that therapists respect and consider using traditional healing approaches intrinsic to a client's culture. Finally, it suggests that therapists learn more about cultural issues and seek consultation when confronted with cultural-specific problems.

SUMMARY

1. Legal interpretations of insanity are always changing. Historically, several interpretations have been applied. The M'Naghten Rule holds that people can be acquitted of a crime if it can be shown that their reasoning was so defective that they were unaware of their actions, or if aware of their actions, were unable to comprehend the wrongness of them. The irresistible impulse test holds that people are innocent if they are unable to control their behavior. The *Durham* decision acquits people if their criminal actions were products of mental disease or defects. The American Law Institute guidelines state that people are not responsible for a crime if they lack substantial capacity to appreciate the criminality of their conduct or to conform their conduct to the requirements of the law. Weaknesses in the standards and public outrage with the acquittal of some highly publicized people (such as John Hinckley, Jr.) have re-

sulted in movements to restrict use of the insanity defense. The "guilty, but mentally ill" plea is an attempt to separate mental illness from insanity and to hold people responsible for their actions.

2. The phrase "competency to stand trial" refers to defendants' mental state at the time they are being examined. It is a separate issue from criminal responsibility, which refers to past behavior at the time of the offense. Accused people are considered incompetent if they have difficulty understanding the trial proceedings or cannot rationally consult with attorneys in their defense. Although competency to stand trial is important in ensuring fair trials, being judged incompetent can have negative consequences, such as unfair and prolonged denial of civil liberties.

3. Concern with denial of civil liberties is also present in civil commitment cases. People who have committed no crime can be confined against their will if it can be shown that (a) they present a clear and imminent danger to themselves or others, (b) they are unable to care for themselves, (c) they are unable to make responsible decisions about appropriate treatment and hospitalization, and (d) they are in an unmanageable state of fright or panic. Courts have tightened criteria and rely more than ever on the concept of dangerousness. Mental health professionals have great difficulty in predicting dangerousness because dangerous acts depend as much on social situations as on personal attributes, and because the definition is unclear.

4. Concern with patients' rights has become an issue because many practices and procedures seem to violate constitutional guarantees. As a result, court rulings have established several important precedents. First, the standard of proof for commitment is "clear and convicing evidence." Second, commitment laws are now designed to provide patients with the "least restrictive environment," which does not necessarily involve hospitalization. Third, patients have a right to treatment (as opposed to custodial care) and a right to a humane environment (this latter ruling was a reaction to inhumane and abhorrent conditions that existed in some hospitals). Last, patients also have a right to refuse treatment in certain situations. The courts have used the "less intrusive forms of treatment" concept in applying their rulings.

5. During the 1960s and 1970s, the policy of deinstitutionalization became popular: the shifting of responsibility for the care of mental patients from large central institutions to agencies within the local community. Deinstitutionalization was considered a promising answer to the "least restrictive environment" ruling and to monetary problems experienced

by state governments. Critics, however, have accused the states of "dumping" former patients and avoiding their responsibilities under the guise of mental health innovations.

6. Most mental health professionals believe that confidentiality is crucial to the therapist-client relationship. Exceptions to this privilege include situations that involve (a) civil or criminal commitment and competency to stand trial, (b) a client's initiation of a lawsuit for malpractice or a civil action where the client's mental condition is introduced, (c) the belief that child abuse has occurred to a client younger than sixteen, (d) a criminal action, or (e) the danger of a client to himself or herself or to others. Although psychologists have always known that privileged communication is not an absolute right, the *Tarasoff* decision makes therapists responsible for warning a potential victim to avoid liability.

7. Mental health professionals are beginning to recognize that ethical and moral values permeate the therapeutic process. The most controversial issues involve erotic and sexual intimacy. Sexual intimacy with clients is almost universally condemned by therapists as immoral, unethical, and antitherapeutic. Patients who are sexually victimized by their therapists suffer emotionally. Patients who are sexually victimized by their therapists suffer emotionally. While it is not unusual for therapists to harbor sexual fantasies about their clients, few act out their feelings or compromise their therapeutic roles.

8. Major demographic changes are forcing mental health professionals to consider culture, ethnicity, gender, and socioeconomic status as powerful variables in (a) the manifestation of mental disorders and (b) the need to provide culturally appropriate intervention strategies for minority groups. Increasingly, mental health organizations are taking the position that it is unethical to treat members of minority groups without adequate training and expertise in cross-cultural psychology.

KEY TERMS

American Law Institute (ALI) code A test of legal insanity that combines both cognitive and motivational criteria. Its purpose is to give jurors increased latitude in determining the sanity of the accused

civil commitment The involuntary confinement of a person judged to be a danger to himself or herself or to others, even though the person has not committed a crime

competency to stand trial A judgment that a defendant has a factual and rational understanding of the proceedings and can rationally consult with counsel in presenting his or her own defense; refers to the defendant's mental state at the time of psychiatric examination

confidentiality An ethical standard that protects clients from disclosure of information without their consent; an ethical obligation of the therapist

criminal commitment Incarceration of an individual for having committed a crime

dangerousness A person's potential for doing harm to himself or herself or to others

deinstitutionalization The shifting of responsibility for the care of mental patients from large central institutions to agencies within local communities

due process Legal checks and balances that are guaranteed to everyone (the right to a fair trial, the right to face accusers, the right to present own evidence, the right to counsel, and so on)

Durham **standard** A test of legal insanity which asks whether the person was overcome by an irresistible impulse

insanity defense The legal argument used by defendants who admit they have committed a crime but plead not guilty because they were mentally disturbed at the time the crime was committed

irresistible impulse test One of the tests of insanity, which states that a defendant is not criminally responsible if he or she lacked the will power to control his or her behavior

least restrictive environment A person's right to the least restrictive alternative to freedom that is appropriate to his or her condition

mainstreaming Integrating mental patients as soon as possible back into the community

M'Naghten Rule A cognitive test of legal insanity that inquires whether the accused knew right from wrong when he committed the crime

privileged communication In therapy, protects privacy and prevents the disclosure of confidential communications without a client's permission; a legal obligation of the therapist

right to treatment Mental patients who have been involuntarily committed have a right to receive therapy that would improve their emotional state

Tarasoff **ruling** Commonly referred to as the "duty-to-warn" principle, it obligates mental health professionals to break confidentiality when their clients pose clear and imminent danger to another person

GLOSSARY

abnormal behavior Behavior that departs from some norm and that harms the affected individual or others

abnormal psychology The scientific study whose objectives are to describe, explain, predict, and control behaviors that are considered strange or unusual

acute stress disorder Exposure to a traumatic stressor that results in dissociation, reliving the experience, and attempts to avoid reminders of the events and that lasts for more than two and less than thirty days

agoraphobia An intense fear of being in public places where escape or help may not be readily available; in extreme cases, a fear of leaving one's home

alcoholic Person who abuses alcohol and is dependent on it

alcoholism Substance-related disorder characterized by abuse of, or dependency on, alcohol, which is a depressant

altruistic suicide Suicide that is motivated by a desire to further group goals or to achieve some greater good

Alzheimer's disease A dementia in which brain tissue atrophies, leading to marked deterioration of intellectual and emotional functioning

American Law Institute (ALI) code A test of legal insanity that combines both cognitive and motivational criteria. Its purpose is to give jurors increased latitude in determining the sanity of the accused.

amnestic disorders Disorders characterized by memory impairment as manifested by inability to learn new information and inability to recall previously learned knowledge or past events

amniocentesis A screening procedure in which a hollow needle is inserted through the pregnant woman's abdominal wall and amniotic fluid is withdrawn from the fetal sac; used during the fourteenth or fifteenth week of pregnancy to determine the presence of Down syndrome

amphetamines Drugs that speed up central nervous system activity and produce increased alertness, energy, and, sometimes, feelings of euphoria and confidence; also called "uppers"

analogue study An investigation that attempts to replicate or simulate, under controlled conditions, a situation that occurs in real life

anomic suicide Suicide that results when a person's relationship to society is unbalanced in some dramatic fashion

anorexia nervosa An eating disorder characterized by a refusal to maintain a body weight above the minimum normal weight for the person's age and height; an intense fear of becoming obese, which does not diminish with weight loss; body image distortion; and, in females, the absence of at least three consecutive menstrual cycles otherwise expected to occur

antisocial personality disorder A personality disorder characterized by a failure to conform to social and legal codes, by a lack of anxiety and guilt, and by irresponsible behaviors

anxiety Feelings of fear and apprehension

anxiety disorder A disorder that meets one of three criteria: the anxiety itself is the major disturbance; the anxiety is manifested only in particular situations; or the anxiety results from an attempt to master other symptoms

assessment With regard to psychopathology, the process of gathering information and drawing conclusions about the traits, skills, abilities, emotional functioning, and psychological problems of an individual

asthma A respiratory disorder that results from constriction of the airways in the lungs owing to muscle tone changes in the airways, excessive mucous secretion, edema, or inflammation

attention deficit hyperactivity disorders (ADHD) Disorders of childhood and adolescence characterized by socially disruptive behaviors—either attentional problems or hyperactivity—that are present before age seven and persist for at least six months

autistic disorder A severe childhood disorder characterized by qualitative impairment in social interaction and/or communication; restricted stereotyped interest and activities; and delays or abnormal functioning in a major area before the age of three

aversion therapy Conditioning procedure in which the response to a stimulus is decreased by pairing the stimulus with an aversive stimulus

aversive conditioning A classical conditioning technique in which an undesirable behavior is paired with an unpleasant stimulus to suppress the undesirable behavior

avoidant personality disorder A personality disorder characterized by a fear of rejection and humiliation and a reluctance to enter into social relationships

axon At the end of a neuron, a long, thin extension that sends signals to other neurons

barbiturate Substance that is a powerful depressant of the central nervous system; commonly used to induce relaxation and sleep; and capable of inducing psychological and physical dependency

base rate A phenomenon's natural occurrence in the population studied

behavioral medicine A number of disciplines that study social, psychological, and lifestyle influences on health

behavioral models Theories of psychopathology that are concerned with the role of learning in abnormal behavior

biofeedback therapy A therapeutic approach, combining physiological and behavioral approaches, in which a patient receives information regarding particular autonomic functions and is rewarded for influencing those functions in a desired direction

biofeedback training   A therapeutic technique in which the person is taught to voluntarily control a particular physiological function, such as heart rate or blood pressure

biogenic view   The belief that mental disorders have a physical or physiological basis

biological markers   Biological indicators of a disorder that may or may not be causal

biopsychosocial approach   The belief that biological, psychological, and social factors must all be considered in explaining and treating mental disorders

bipolar disorder   A category of mood disorders characterized by one or more manic or hypomanic episodes and, usually, by one or more depressive episodes

body dysmorphic disorder   A somatoform disorder that involves preoccupation with an imagined physical defect in a normal-appearing person, or an excessive concern with a slight physical defect

borderline personality disorder   A personality disorder characterized by intense fluctuations in mood, self-image, and interpersonal relationships

brain pathology   Dysfunction or disease of the brain

brain trauma   A physical wound or injury to the brain

brief psychotic disorder   Psychotic disorder that lasts no longer than one month

bulimia nervosa   An eating disorder characterized by recurrent episodes of binge eating (the rapid consumption of large quantities of food) at least twice a week for three months, during which the person loses control over eating and uses vomiting, laxatives, and excess exercise to control weight

case study   Intensive study of one individual that relies on observation, psychological tests, and historical and biographical data

catatonic schizophrenia   A schizophrenic disorder characterized by marked disturbance in motor activity—either extreme excitement or motoric immobility; symptoms include motoric immobility or negativism or physical resistance; peculiar voluntary movements; or echolalia or echopraxia

cathartic method   The therapeutic use of verbal expression to release pent-up unconscious conflicts

cerebral blood flow measurement   A technique for assessing brain damage, in which the patient inhales radioactive gas, and a gamma ray camera tracks the gas—and thus the flow of the blood—as it moves throughout the brain

cerebral tumor   A mass of abnormal tissue growing within the brain

cerebrovascular accident   A sudden stoppage of blood flow to a portion of the brain, leading to a loss of brain function; also called *stroke*

chronic tic disorders   Childhood-onset disorders that last longer than one year and are characterized by involuntary, repetitive, and nonrhythmic movements or vocalizations

civil commitment   The involuntary confinement of a person judged to be a danger to himself or herself or to others, even though the person has not committed a crime

classical conditioning   A principle of learning, in which involuntary responses to stimuli are learned through association

classification system   With regard to psychopathology, a system of distinct categories, indicators, and nomenclature for different patterns of behavior, thought processes, and emotional disturbances

cluster headache   Excruciating headache that tends to occur on one side of the head near the eye, producing tears and a blocked nose

cocaine   Substance extracted from the coca plant; induces feelings of euphoria and self-confidence in users

cognition   The processes of thinking, perceiving, judging, and recognizing

cognitive disorders   Behavioral disturbances that result from transient or permanent damage to the brain

cognitive model   A principle of learning holding that conscious thought mediates, or modifies, an individual's emotional state and/or behavior in response to a stimulus

community psychology   An approach to mental health that takes into account the influence of environmental factors and that encourages the use of community resources and agencies to eliminate conditions that produce psychological problems

competency to stand trial   A judgment that a defendant has a factual and rational understanding of the proceedings and can rationally consult with counsel in presenting his or her own defense; refers to the defendant's mental state at the time of psychiatric examination

compulsion   The need to perform acts or to dwell on thoughts to reduce anxiety

computerized axial tomography (CAT)   Neurological test that assesses brain damage by means of x-rays and computer technology

concordance rate   The likelihood that both members of a twin pair will show the same disorder

conditioned response (CR)   In classical conditioning, the learned response made to a previously neutral stimulus that has acquired some of the properties of another stimulus with which it has been paired

conditioned stimulus (CS)   In classical conditioning, a previously neutral stimulus that has acquired some of the properties of another stimulus with which it has been paired

conduct disorders   Disorders of childhood and adolescence characterized by a persistent pattern of antisocial behaviors that violate the rights of others; repetitive and persistent behaviors include bullying, lying, cheating, fighting, temper tantrums, destruction of property, stealing, setting fires, cruelty to people and animals, assaults, rape, and truant behavior

confidentiality   An ethical standard that protects clients from disclosure of information without their consent; an ethical obligation of the therapist

continuous amnesia   An inability to recall any events that have occurred between a specific time in the past and the present time; the least common form of psychogenic amnesia

conversion disorder   A somatoform disorder in which there are complaints of physical problems or impairments of sensory or motor functions controlled by the voluntary nervous system, all suggesting a neurological disorder but with no underlying cause

coronary heart disease (CHD) A narrowing of the arteries in or near the heart, resulting in the restriction or partial blockage of the flow of blood and oxygen to the heart

correlation The extent to which variations in one variable are accompanied by increases or decreases in a second variable

covert sensitization Aversive conditioning technique in which the individual imagines a noxious stimulus occurring in the presence of a behavior

criminal commitment Incarceration of an individual for having committed a crime

cultural relativism The belief that what is judged to be normal or abnormal may vary from one cultural context to another

cultural universality The belief that the origin, process, and manifestation of disorders are equally applicable across cultures

cyclothymic disorder A chronic and relatively continual mood disorder characterized by hypomanic episodes and depressed moods that do not meet the criteria for major depressive episode

dangerousness A person's potential for doing harm to himself or herself or to others

decompensation Loss of the ability to deal successfully with stress, resulting in more primitive means of coping

defense mechanisms In psychoanalytic theory, ego-protection strategies that shelter the individual from anxiety, operate unconsciously, and distort reality

deinstitutionalization The shifting of responsibility for the care of mental patients from large central institutions to agencies within local communities

delirium A syndrome in which there is disturbance of consciousness and changes in cognition, seen as memory deficit, disorientation, and language and perceptual disturbances

delusion A false belief that is firmly and consistently held despite disconfirming evidence or logic

delusional disorder A disorder characterized by persistent, nonbizarre delusions that are not accompanied by other unusual or odd behavior

dementia A syndrome characterized by memory impairment and cognitive disturbances, such as aphasia, apraxia, agnosia, or disturbances in planning or abstraction in thought processes

dendrites Rootlike structures that are attached to the body of the neuron and that receive signals from other neurons

dependent personality disorder A personality disorder characterized by reliance on others and unwillingness to assume responsibility

dependent variable A variable that is expected to change when an independent variable is manipulated in a psychological experiment

depersonalization disorder A dissociative disorder in which feelings of unreality concerning the self or the environment cause major impairment in social or occupational functioning

depressant Substance that causes generalized depression of the central nervous system and a slowing down of responses; a sedative

depression An emotional state characterized by intense sadness, feelings of futility and worthlessness, and withdrawal from others

depressive disorders DSM-IV category including major depressive disorders, dysthymic disorder, and depressive disorders not otherwise specified; also known as *unipolar disorders* because no mania is exhibited

detoxification Alcohol or drug treatment phase characterized by removal of the abusive substance; after that removal, the user is immediately or eventually prevented from consuming the substance

diaschisis A process in which a lesion in a specific area of the brain disrupts other intact areas

diathesis-stress model A theoretical model postulating that vulnerability to a disorder, either inherited or acquired, combines with the impact of stressors to produce the disorder

diathesis-stress theory The theory that a *predisposition to develop mental illness*—not mental illness itself—is inherited and that this predisposition may or may not be activated by environmental forces

disorganized schizophrenia A schizophrenic disorder characterized by grossly disorganized behaviors manifested by disorganized speech and behavior and flat or grossly inappropriate affect

dissociative amnesia A dissociative disorder characterized by the partial or total loss of important personal information, sometimes occurring suddenly after a stressful or traumatic event

dissociative disorders Mental disorders in which a person's identity, memory, or consciousness is altered or disrupted; include dissociative amnesia, dissociative fugue, dissociative identity disorder (multiple personality disorder), and depersonalization disorder

dissociative fugue Confusion over personal identity accompanied by unexpected travel away from home; also called *fugue state*

dissociative identity disorder A dissociative disorder in which two or more relatively independent personalities appear to exist in one person; formerly known as *multiple-personality disorder*

dopamine hypothesis The suggestion that schizophrenia may result from excess dopamine activity at certain synaptic sites

double-bind theory The suggestion that schizophrenia develops as a result of repeated experiences that the preschizophrenic child has with one or more family members (usually the mother and father) in which the child receives two contradictory messages

Down syndrome A condition produced by the presence of an extra chromosome (trisomy 21) and resulting in mental retardation and distinctive physical characteristics

drug therapy See *psychopharmacology* The treatment of mental disorders with drugs

DSM I, II, III, III-R, IV The diagnostic and statistical manuals of mental disorders published by the American

Psychiatric Association; they contain the diagnostic categories and criteria for differential diagnosis of abnormal behavior

due process Legal checks and balances that are guaranteed to everyone (the right to a fair trial, the right to face accusers, the right to present own evidence, the right to counsel, and so)

Durham standard A test of legal insanity which asks whether the person was overcome by an irresistible impulse

dyspareunia Recurrent or persistent pain in the genitals before, during, or after sexual intercourse

dysthymic disorder A disorder characterized by chronic and relatively continual depressed mood that does not meet the criteria for major depression

egoistic suicide Suicide that results from an inability to integrate oneself with society

electroconvulsive therapy (ECT) The application of electric voltage to the brain to induce convulsions; used to reduce depression; also called *electroshock therapy*

electroencephalograph (EEG) A neurological test that assesses brain damage by measuring the electrical activity of brain cells

encephalitis Brain inflammation that is caused by a viral infection and that produces symptoms of lethargy, fever, delirium, and long periods of stupor and sleep, also known as *sleeping sickness*

epidemiological research The study of the rate and distribution of mental disorders in a population

epilepsy Any disorder characterized by intermittent and brief periods of altered consciousness, often accompanied by seizures, and excessive electrical discharge from brain cells

essential hypertension Chronic high blood pressure, usually with no known organic cause; the most common disease in the United States

etiology The causes or origins of a disorder

exhibitionism Disorder characterized by urges, acts, or fantasies about the exposure of one's genitals to strangers

existential analysis A therapeutic approach that is concerned with the person's experience and involvement in the world as a being with consciousness and self-consciousness

existential approach A set of attitudes that has many commonalities with humanism but is less optimistic, focusing (1) on human alienation in an increasingly technological and impersonal world, (2) on the individual in the context of the human condition, and (3) on responsibility to others as well as to oneself

exorcism Ritual in which prayer, noise, emetics, and extreme measures such as flogging and starvation were used to cast evil spirits out of an afflicted person's body

experiment A technique of scientific inquiry in which a prediction—an experimental hypothesis—is made about two variables; the independent variable is then manipulated in a controlled situation, and changes in the dependent variable are measured

experimental hypothesis A prediction concerning how an independent variable affects a dependent variable in an experiment

exposure therapy A therapy technique in which the patient is introduced to encounters (can be gradual or rapid) with the feared situation

expressed emotion A type of negative communication pattern that is found in some families with schizophrenic members and that is associated with higher relapse rates

factitious disorders Disorders in which symptoms of physical or mental illnesses are deliberately induced or simulated with no apparent incentive

family dynamics The day-to-day "operation" of the family system, including communication among its members

family systems model A model of psychopathology that emphasizes the family's influence on individual behavior

family therapy Group therapy that seeks to modify relationships within a family to achieve harmony

female orgasmic disorder A sexual dysfunction in which the woman experiences persistent delay or inability to achieve an orgasm with stimulation that is adequate in focus, intensity, and duration, after entering the excitement phase; also known as *inhibited orgasm*

fetal alcohol syndrome (FAS) A group of congenital physical and mental defects found in some children born to alcoholic mothers; symptoms include small body size and microcephaly, in which the brain is unusually small and mild retardation may occur

fetishism Sexual attraction and fantasies involving inanimate objects, such as female undergarments

field study An investigative technique in which behaviors and events are observed and recorded in the natural environment

flat affect Little or no emotion in situations where strong reactions are expected

flooding A therapeutic technique that involves continued *in vivo* (actual) or imagined exposure to a highly fear-arousing situation; a form of exposure therapy

free association A psychoanalytic method during which the patient says whatever comes to mind, regardless of how illogical or embarrassing it may seem for the purpose of revealing the contents of the patient's unconscious

frotteurism Disorder characterized by recurrent and intense sexual urges, acts, or fantasies of touching or rubbing against a nonconsenting person

fugue state See *dissociative fugue*

gender identity disorder Disorder characterized by conflict between a person's anatomical sex and his or her gender identity, or self-identification as male or female

general adaptation syndrome (GAS) A three-stage model for understanding the body's physical and psychological reactions to biological stressors

generalized amnesia An inability to remember anything about one's past life

generalized anxiety disorder (GAD) Disorder characterized by persistent high levels of anxiety and excessive worry over many life circumstances

genetic linkage studies Studies that attempt to determine whether a disorder follows a genetic pattern

genotype A person's genetic makeup

gestalt therapy A humanistic-existential approach to therapy that emphasizes the importance of a person's total experience, which should not be fragmented or separated

group therapy A form of therapy that involves the simultaneous treatment of two or more clients and may involve more than one therapist

H pylori *Helicobacter pylori*; the form of bacteria believed to be the cause of peptic ulcers

hallucinations Sensory perceptions that are not directly attributable to environmental stimuli

hallucinogen Substance that produces hallucinations, vivid sensory awareness, heightened alertness, or increased insight

hardiness A concept developed by Kobasa and Maddi that refers to a person's ability to deal well with stress

histrionic personality disorder A personality disorder characterized by self-dramatization, the exaggerated expression of emotions, and attention-seeking behaviors

humanism Philosophical movement that emphasizes human welfare and the worth and uniqueness of the individual

humanistic perspective The optimistic viewpoint that people are born with the ability to fulfill their potential and that abnormal behavior results from disharmony between the person's potential and his or her self-concept

Huntington's chorea A rare, genetically transmitted degenerative disease characterized by involuntary twitching movements and eventual dementia

hypochondriasis A somatoform disorder characterized by persistent preoccupation with one's health and physical condition, even in the face of physical evaluations that reveal no organic problems

hypothesis A conjectural statement, usually describing a relationship between two variables

iatrogenic Unintended effects of therapy; a change in behavior resulting from a medication prescribed or a psychological technique employed by the therapist

implosion A behavioral treatment that attempts to extinguish a fear by having the client imagine the anxiety-provoking situation at full intensity

impulse control disorder A disorder in which the person fails to resist an impulse or temptation to perform some act that is harmful to the person or to others; the person feels tension before the act and released after it

incest Sexual relations between people too closely related to marry legally

independent variable A variable or condition that an experimenter manipulates to determine its effect on a dependent variable

infarction The death of tissue resulting from a decrease in the supply of blood serving that tissue

inhibited male orgasm See *male orgasmic disorder*

inhibited female orgasm See *female orgasmic disorder*

insanity defense The legal argument used by defendants who admit they have committed a crime but plead not guilty because they were mentally disturbed at the time the crime was committed

intermittent explosive disorder Impulse control disorder characterized by separate and discrete episodes of loss of control over aggressive impulses, resulting in serious assaults on others or destruction of property

intoxication Condition in which a substance affecting the central nervous system has been ingested and certain maladaptive behaviors or psychological changes, such as belligerence and impaired functioning, are evident

irresistible impulse test One test of insanity, which states that a defendant is not criminally responsible if he or she lacked the will power to control his or her behavior

kleptomania An impulse control disorder characterized by a recurrent failure to resist impulses to steal objects

law of effect The principle that behaviors associated with positive consequences will be repeated and behaviors associated with unpleasant consequences will be reduced

learned helplessness Acquiring the belief that one is unable to affect the outcomes in one's life

least restrictive environment A person's right to the least restrictive alternative to freedom that is appropriate to his or her condition

lethality The probability that a person will end his or her life

life-change model An explanation of stress that assumes that all changes in a person's life—large or small, desirable or undesirable—can act as stressors and that the accumulation of small changes can be as powerful as one major stressor

localized amnesia The most common type of amnesia; an inability to recall all the events that happened during a specific period, often centered on some highly painful or disturbing event

loosening of associations Continual shifting from topic to topic without any apparent logical or meaningful connection between thoughts

magnetic resonance imaging (MRI) A technique to assess brain functioning, using a magnetic field and radio waves to produce pictures of the brain

mainstreaming Integrating mental patients as soon as possible back into the community

major depression A disorder in which a group of symptoms, such as depressed mood, loss of interest, sleep disturbances, feelings of worthlessness, and an inability to concentrate, are present for at least two months

male erectile disorder An inability to attain or maintain an erection sufficient for sexual intercourse

male orgasmic disorder Persistent delay or inability to achieve an orgasm after the excitement phase has been reached and sexual activity has been adequate in focus, intensity, and duration; usually restricted to an inability to ejaculate within the vagina (also known as *inhibited male orgasm*)

malingering Faking a disorder to achieve some goal, such as an insurance settlement

managed health care A term that refers to the industrialization of health care, whereby large organizations in the private sector control the delivery of services

mania   An emotional state characterized by elevated mood, expansiveness, irritability, often resulting in hyperactivity

marijuana   The mildest and most commonly used hallucinogen; also known as "pot" or "grass"

marital therapy   A treatment aimed at helping couples understand and clarify their communications, role relationships, unfulfilled needs, and unrealistic expectations

masochism   A paraphilia in which sexual urges, fantasies, or acts are associated with being humiliated, bound, or made to suffer

mass madness   Group hysteria, in which large numbers of people exhibit similar symptoms that have no apparent cause

medication   See *psychopharmacology*

meningitis   Inflammation of the meninges, the membrane that surrounds the brain and spinal cord; can result in the localized destruction of brain tissue and seizures

mental retardation   Significant subaverage general intellectual functioning accompanied by concurrent deficiencies in adaptive behavior, with onset before age eighteen

migraine headache   Severe headache characterized by constriction of cranial arteries, followed by dilation of the cerebral blood vessels, resulting in moderate to severe pain

milieu therapy   A therapy program in which the hospital environment operates as a community and patients exercise a wide range of responsibility, helping to make decisions and to manage wards

M'Naughten rule   A cognitive test of legal insanity that inquires whether the accused knew right from wrong when he or she committed the crime

model   An analogy used by scientists, usually to describe or explain a phenomenon or process that they cannot directly observe

modeling   The process of learning by observing models and later imitating them; also known as *vicarious conditioning*

modeling therapy   A therapeutic approach to phobias in which the person with the phobia observes a model in the act of coping with, or responding appropriately in, the fear-producing situation

monoamine oxidase (MAO) inhibitor   An antidepressant compound believed to correct the balance of neurotransmitters in the brain

mood disorders   Disturbances in emotions that cause subjective discomfort, hinder a person's ability to function, or both; depression and mania are central to these disorders

moral treatment movement   A shift to more humane treatment of the mentally disturbed; its initiation is generally attributed to Philippe Pinel

multicultural psychology   A field of psychology that stresses the importance of culture, race, ethnicity, gender, age, socioeconomic class, and other similar factors in its efforts to understand and treat abnormal behavior

multi-infarct dementia   Dementia characterized by uneven deterioration of intellectual abilities and resulting from a number of cerebral infarctions

multiple personality disorder   See *dissociative identity disorder*

narcissistic personality disorder   A personality disorder characterized by an exaggerated sense of self-importance, an exploitative attitude, and a lack of empathy

narcotic   Drugs such as opium and and its derivatives—morphine, heroin, and codeine—which depress the central nervous system; act as sedatives to provide relief from pain, anxiety, and tension; and are addictive

negative symptoms   In schizophrenia, symptoms that are associated with premorbid social functioning and carry a poorer prognosis than positive symptoms; they include flat affect, poverty of speech, anhedonia, apathy and avolution

neo-Freudians   Therapists who broke away from Freud and formulated psychological models of their own but whose ideas were strongly influenced by Freud's psychoanalytic model; also called *post-Freudians*

neologisms   New words formed by combining words in common usage; often invented by schizophrenics

neuroleptics   Antipsychotic drugs that can help treat symptoms of schizophrenia but can produce undesirable side effects, such as symptoms that mimic neurological disorders

neurons   Nerve cells that transmit messages throughout the body

neurotransmitters   Chemical substances released by axons of sending neurons and involved in the transmission of neural impulses to the dendrites of receiving neurons

object relations   Past interpersonal relations that shape and affect the individual's current interactions with people

observational learning theory   A theory of learning that holds that an individual can acquire behaviors simply by watching other people perform them

obsession   An intrusive and repetitive thought or image that produces anxiety

obsessive-compulsive disorder   Disorder characterized by intrusive and repetitive thoughts or images, or by the need to perform acts or dwell on thoughts to reduce anxiety

obsessive-compulsive personality disorder   A personality disorder characterized by perfectionism, a tendency to be interpersonally controlling, devotion to details, and rigidity

operant behavior   A voluntary and controllable behavior that "operates" on an individual's environment

operant conditioning   A theory of learning, applying primarily to voluntary behaviors, that holds that these behaviors are controlled by the consequences that follow them

operational definitions   Definitions of the variables under study

oppositional defiant disorder (ODD)   A childhood disorder characterized by a pattern of negativistic, argumentative, and hostile behavior in which the child often loses his or her temper, argues with adults, and refuses adult requests; refusal to take responsibility for actions, anger, resentment, blaming others, and spiteful and vindictive behavior are common, but serious violations of other's rights are not

organicity   Damage or deterioration in the central nervous system

pain disorder A somatoform disorder characterized by reports of severe pain that has no physiological or neurological basis, is greatly in excess of that expected with an existing condition, or lingers long after a physical injury has healed

panic disorder Anxiety disorder characterized by severe and frightening episodes of apprehension and feelings of impending doom

paranoid personality disorder A personality disorder characterized by unwarranted suspiciousness, hypersensitivity, and a reluctance to confide in others

paranoid schizophrenia A schizophrenic disorder characterized by one or more systematized delusions or auditory hallucinations and the absence of such symptoms as disorganized speech and behavior or flat affect

paraphilias Sexual disorders of at least six months' duration, in which the person has either acted on, or is severely distressed by, recurrent urges or fantasies involving nonhuman objects, nonconsenting persons, or suffering or humiliation

Parkinson's disease A progressively worsening dementia characterized by muscle tremors; a stiff, shuffling gait; lack of facial expression; and social withdrawal

pathognomonic Symptoms specific to a disorder

pathological gambling An impulse control disorder in which the essential feature is a chronic and progressive failure to resist impulses to gamble

pedophilia A disorder in which an adult obtains erotic gratification through urges, acts, or fantasies involving a prepubescent child

peptic ulcer An open sore within the digestive system

personality disorder A disorder characterized by inflexible and maladaptive personality traits that cause significant functional impairment or subjective distress for the individual

person-centered therapy A humanistic therapy that emphasizes the kind of person the therapist should be in the therapeutic relationship rather than the precise techniques to use in therapy

pervasive developmental disorders Severe childhood disorders in which qualitative impairment in verbal and nonverbal communication and social interaction are the primary symptoms; include autistic disorder, Rett's disorder, childhood disintegrative disorder, Asperger's disorder, and pervasive developmental disorder not otherwise specified

phenotype The observable results of the interaction of a person's genotype and the environment

phobia A strong, persistent, and unwarranted fear of some specific object or situation

placebo effects Positive responses to a drug or other experimental condition that result from the patient's understanding of the drug's effect, faith in the doctor, or other psychological factors unrelated to the medication's specific physiological action

pleasure principle Usually associated with the id in Freudian theory; the impulsive, pleasure-seeking aspect of our being that seeks immediate gratification of instinctual needs regardless of moral or realistic concerns

polysubstance dependence Substance dependence in which dependency is not based on the use of any single substance but on the repeated use of at least three groups of substances (not including caffeine and nicotine) for a period of twelve months

positive symptoms Symptoms that are present during the active phase of schizophrenia and that tend to disappear with treatment; they may include hallucinations and delusional, as well as disorganized speech and behavior, inappropriate affect, and formal thought disorders

positron emission tomography (PET) A technique for assessing brain damage, in which the patient is injected with radioactive glucose and the metabolism of the glucose is monitored

post-Freudians See *neo-Freudians*

posthypnotic amnesia An inability to recall events that occurred during hypnosis

posttraumatic stress disorder (PTSD) An anxiety disorder that lasts for more than thirty days; develops in response to a specific extreme stressor; characterized by intrusive memories of the traumatic event, emotional withdrawal, and heightened autonomic arousal

premature ejaculation Ejaculation with minimal sexual stimulation before, during, or shortly after penetration

primary prevention An effort to lower the incidence of new cases of behavioral disorders by strengthening or adding to resources that promote mental health and by eliminating community characteristics that threaten mental health

privileged communication In therapy, protects privacy and prevents the disclosure of confidential communications without a client's permission; a legal obligation of the therapist

prognosis A prediction of the future course of a particular disorder

projective personality test A personality assessment technique in which the test taker is presented with ambiguous stimuli and is asked to respond to them in some way

prospective study A long-term study of a group of people, beginning before the onset of a disorder, to allow investigators to see how the disorder develops

psychoanalysis Therapy based on the Freudian view that unconscious conflicts must be aired and understood by the patient if abnormal behavior is to be eliminated

psychoanalytic model The view that adult disorders arise from traumas or anxieties originally experienced in childhood but later repressed because they are too threatening for the adult to face

psychodiagnosis An attempt to describe, assess, and systematically draw inferences about an individual's psychological disorder

psychogenic view The belief or theory that mental disorders are caused by psychological and emotional factors, rather than organic factors

psychological autopsy The systematic examination of existing information for the purpose of understanding and explaining a person's behavior before his or her death

psychological tests and inventories A variety of standardized test instruments used to assess personality, maladaptive behavior, development of social skills, intellectual abilities, vocational interest, and cognitive impairment

psychometrics Mental measurement, including its study and techniques

psychopathology Clinical term meaning abnormal behavior

psychopharmacology The study of the effects of drugs on the mind and on behavior; also known as *medication* and *drug therapy*

psychophysiological disorder Any physical disorder that has a strong psychological basis or component

psychosexual stages In psychoanalytic theory, the sequence of stages—oral, anal, phallic, latency, and genital—through which human personality develops

psychosurgery Brain surgery performed for the purpose of correcting a severe mental disorder

psychotherapy The systematic application, by a trained and experienced professional therapist, of techniques derived from psychological principles, for the purpose of helping psychologically troubled people; includes both insight-oriented and action-oriented therapies

pyromania An impulse control disorder having as its main feature deliberate and purposeful fire setting on more than one occasion

rape An act of intercourse accomplished through force or threat of force

reactivity A change in the way a person usually responds, triggered by the person's knowledge that he or she is being observed or assessed

reality principle Usually associated with the ego in Freudian theory; an awareness of the demands of the environment and of the need to adjust behavior to meet these demands

relaxation training A therapeutic technique in which the person acquires the ability to relax the muscles of the body in almost any circumstances

reliability The degree to which a procedure or test will yield the same result repeatedly, under the same circumstances

residual schizophrenia A category of schizophrenic disorder reserved for people who have had at least one previous schizophrenic episode but are now showing an absence of prominent psychotic features and continuing evidence of two or more symptoms, such as marked isolation, peculiar behaviors, blunted affect, odd beliefs, or unusual perceptual experiences

resistance During psychoanalysis, the process in which the patient unconsciously attempts to impede the analysis by preventing the exposure of repressed material; tactics include silence, late arrival, or failure to keep an appointment, and others

right to treatment The concept that mental patients who have been involuntarily committed have a right to receive therapy that would improve their emotional state

sadism Form of paraphilia in which sexually arousing urges, fantasies, or acts are associated with inflicting physical or psychological suffering

schema The set of underlying assumptions that is heavily influenced by a person's experiences, values, and perceived capabilities and that influences how he or she interprets events

schizoid personality disorder A personality disorder characterized by social isolation, emotional coldness, and indifference to others

schizophrenia A group of disorders characterized by severely impaired cognitive processes, personality disintegration, affective disturbances, and social withdrawal

schizophreniform disorder Psychotic disorder that lasts more than one month but less than six months

schizophrenogenic Causing or producing schizophrenia; a term generally used to describe a parent who is simultaneously or alternately cold and overprotecting, rejecting and dominating

schizotypal personality disorder A personality disorder characterized by peculiar thoughts and behaviors and by poor interpersonal relationships

scientific method A method of inquiry that provides for the systematic collection of data through controlled observation and for the testing of hypotheses

secondary prevention An attempt to shorten the duration of mental disorders and to reduce their impact

selective amnesia An inability to remember certain details of an incident

self-actualization An inherent tendency to strive toward the realization of one's full potential

self-concept An individual's assessment of his or her own value and worth

self-report inventories An assessment tool that requires test takers to answer specific written questions or to select specific responses from a list of alternatives

separation anxiety disorder (SAD) A childhood disorder characterized by excessive anxiety over separating from parents and home

sexual arousal disorders Problems occurring during the excitement phase and relating to difficulties with feelings of sexual pleasure or with the physiological changes associated with sexual excitement

sexual desire disorders Sexual dysfunctions that are related to the appetitive phase and are characterized by a lack of sexual desire

sexual dysfunction A disruption of any part of the normal sexual response cycle

single-subject experiment An experiment performed on a single individual in which some aspect of the person's own behavior is used as a control or baseline for companies with future behaviors

sleeping sickness See *encephalitis*

social phobia An intense, excessive fear of being scrutinized in one or more social situations

somatization disorder A somatoform disorder in which the person chronically complains of a number of bodily symptoms that have no physiological basis; complaints include at least four symptoms in different sites, two gastrointestinal symptoms, one sexual symptom, and one pseudoneurologic symptom

somatoform disorders Mental disorders that involve physical symptoms or complaints that have no physiological basis; include somatization disorder, conversion disorder, pain disorder, hypochondriasis, and body dysmorphic disorder

specific phobia An extreme fear of a specific object or situation; a phobia that is not classified as either agoraphobia or a social phobia

stimulant Substance that is a central nervous system energizer, inducing elation, grandiosity, hyperactivity, agitation, and appetite suppression

stress An internal response to a stressor

stressor An external event or situation that places a physical or psychological demand on a person

stroke See *cerebrovascular accident*

substance abuse Maladaptive pattern of recurrent use that extends over a period of twelve months; leads to notable impairment or distress; and continues despite social, occupational, psychological, physical, or safety problems

substance dependence Maladaptive pattern of use extending over a twelve-month period and characterized by unsuccessful efforts to control use, despite knowledge of harmful effects; taking more of substance than intended; tolerance; or withdrawal

substance-related disorders Disorders resulting from the use of psychoactive substances that affect the central nervous system, causing significant social, occupational, psychological, or physical problems, and that sometimes result in abuse or dependence

sudden death syndrome Unexpected abrupt death that seems to have no specific physical basis

suicidal ideation Thoughts about suicide

suicide The taking of one's own life

synapse A minute gap between the axon of the sending neuron and the dendrites of the receiving neuron

syndrome A cluster of symptoms that tend to occur together and that are believed to represent a particular disorder with its own unique cause, course, and outcome

systematic desensitization A behavioral therapy technique in which relaxation is used to eliminate the anxiety associated with phobias and other fear-evoking situations

Tarasoff ruling Commonly referred to as the "duty-to-warn" principle; obligates mental health professionals to break confidentiality when their clients pose clear and imminent danger to another person

tension headache A headache thought to be produced by prolonged contraction of the scalp and neck muscles, resulting in vascular constriction

tertiary prevention Efforts to facilitate the readjustment of the person to community life after hospital treatment for a mental disorder

theory A group of principles and hypotheses that together explain some aspect of a particular area of inquiry

therapy A program of systematic intervention whose purpose is to modify a client's behavioral, affective (emotional), or cognitive state

tics Involuntary, repetitive, and nonrhythmic movements or vocalizations

token economy A treatment program, based on principles of operant conditioning, that rewards patients for appropriate behaviors with tokens, which can then be exchanged for hospital passes, special privileges, food, or weekend passes

tolerance Condition in which increasing doses of a substance are necessary to achieve the desired effect

Tourette's syndrome A childhood disorder characterized by multiple motor and one or more verbal tics that may develop into coprolalia (compulsion to shout obscenities)

transaction model of stress Explanation of stress that states that stress resides neither in the person alone nor in the situation alone, but rather in a transaction between the two

transference During psychotherapy, a process in which the patient reenacts early conflicts by carrying over and applying to the therapist feelings and attitudes that the patient had toward significant others (primarily parents) in the past

transient tic disorder Childhood onset disorder characterized by involuntary, repetitive, and nonrhythmic movements or vocalizations that last longer than four weeks but less than one year

transsexualism Strong and persistent cross-gender identification and persistent discomfort with one's anatomical sex, which cause significant impairment in social, occupational, or other areas of functioning

transvestic fetishism Intense sexual arousal obtained through cross-dressing (wearing clothes appropriate to the opposite gender); not to be confused with transsexualism

trephining An ancient surgical technique in which part of the skull was chipped away to provide an opening through which evil spirits could escape

trichotillomania An impulse control disorder characterized by an inability to resist impulses to pull out one's own hair

tricyclics Antidepressant compounds that relieve symptoms of depression and that seem to work like MAO inhibitors but produce fewer side effects

unconditional positive regard A humanistic concept referring to love and acceptance of an individual, regardless of his or her behavior

unconditioned response (UCR) In classical conditioning, the unlearned response made to an unconditioned stimulus

unconditioned stimulus (UCS) In classical conditioning, the stimulus that elicits an unconditioned response

undifferentiated schizophrenia A schizophrenic disorder in which the person's behavior shows prominent psychotic symptoms that do not meet the criteria for paranoid, disorganized, or catatonic schizophrenia

unipolar disorder See *depressive disorders*

vaginismus Involuntary spasm of the outer part of the vaginal wall, preventing or interfering with sexual intercourse

validity The extent to which a test or procedure actually performs the function it was designed to perform

vicarious conditioning See *modeling*

voyeurism Urges, acts, or fantasies involving observation of an unsuspecting person disrobing or engaging in sexual activity

withdrawal Condition characterized by distress or impairment in social, occupational, or other areas of functioning, or physical or emotional symptoms such as shaking, irritability, and inability to concentrate after reducing or ceasing intake of a substance

REFERENCES

Abebimpe, V. R., Chu, C. C., Klein, H. E., & Lange, M. H. (1982). Racial and geographic differences in the psychopathology of schizophrenia. *American Journal of Psychiatry, 139,* 888–891.

Abel, G. G., Barlow, D. H., Blanchard, E. B., & Guild, D. (1977). The components of rapists' sexual arousal. *Archives of General Psychiatry, 34,* 895–903.

Abel, G. G., Levis, D. J., & Clancy, J. (1970). Aversion therapy applied to taped sequences of deviant behavior in exhibitionism and other sexual deviations: A preliminary report. *Journal of Behavior Therapy and Experimental Psychiatry, 1,* 59–66.

Abels, G. (1975). *The double bind: Paradox in relationships.* Unpublished doctoral dissertation, Boston University.

Abels, G. (1976). Researching the unresearchable: Experimentation on the double bind. In C. E. Sluzki & D. C. Ransom (Eds.), *Double bind: The foundation of the communication approach to the family.* New York: Grune & Stratton.

Abels, N. (1986). Proceedings of the American Psychological Association, Incorporated, for the year 1985: Minutes of the Annual Meeting of the Council of Representatives. *American Psychologist, 41,* 631–663.

Abramowitz, A. J., & O'Leary, S. G. (1991). Behavioral interventions for the classroom: Implications for students with ADHD. *School Psychology Review, 20,* 220–234.

Abrams, R. (1988). *Electroconvulsive treatment: It apparently works, but how and at what risks are not yet clear.* New York: Oxford University Press.

Abrams, R., & Essman, W. B. (1982). *Electroconvulsive therapy.* Jamaica, NY: Medical & Scientific Books.

Abramson, L. Y., Metalsky, G. I., & Alloy, L. B. (1989). Hopelessness in depression: A theory-based subtype of depression. *Psychological Review, 96*(2), 358–372.

Abramson, L. Y., Seligman, M. E. P., & Teasdale, J. D. (1978). Learned helplessness in humans: Critique and reformulation. *Journal of Abnormal Psychology, 87,* 49–74.

Acierno, R., Hersen, M., Van-Hasselt, V. B. & Ammerman, R. T. (1991). Remedying the Achilles heel of behavior research and therapy: Prescriptive matching of intervention and psychopathology. *Journal of Behavior Therapy and Experimental Psychiatry, 25,* 179–188.

Acosta, F. X. (1984). Psychotherapy with Mexican Americans: Clinical and empirical gains. In J. L. Martinez & R. H. Mendoza (Eds.), *Chicano psychology* (pp. 163–189). New York: Academic Press.

Adler, J., & Gosnell, M. (1979, December 31). A question of fraudulent fever. *Newsweek,* p. 65.

Adler, J., Hager, M., Zabarsky, M., Jackson, T., Friendly, D. T., & Abramson, P. (1984, April 23). The fight to conquer fear. *Newsweek,* pp. 66–72.

Agras, W. S., Rossiter, E. M., Arnow, B., Schneider, J. A., Telch, C. F., Raeburn, S. D., Bruce, B., Perl, M. & Koran, L. M. (1992). Pharmacologic and cognitive-behavioral treatment for bulimia nervosa: A controlled comparison. *American Journal of Psychiatry, 149,* 82–87.

Ahles, T. A., Cassens, H. L., & Stalling, R. B. (1987). Private body consciousness, anxiety and the perception of pain. *Journal of Behavior Therapy and Experimental Psychiatry, 18,* 215–222.

Alanen, Y. O. (1994). An attempt to integrate the individual-psychological and interactional concepts of the origins of schizophrenia. *British Journal of Psychiatry, 164,* 56–61.

Aldridge-Morris, R. (1989). *Multiple personality. An exercise in deception.* Hove, United Kingdom: Erlbaum.

Alexander, F. (1950). *Psychosomatic medicine.* New York: Norton.

Alexander, F. G., & Selesnick, S. T. (1966). *The history of psychiatry.* New York: Harper & Row.

Alexander, J. F., Holtzworth-Munroe, A., & Jameson, P. (1994). The process and outcome of marital and family therapy: Research review and evaluation. In A. E. Bergin & S. L. Garfield (Eds.), *Handbook of psychotherapy and behavior change* (pp. 595–630). New York: Wiley.

Alexander, J. R., Lerer, B., & Baron, M. (1992). Ethical issues in genetic linkage studies of psychiatric disorders. *British Journal of Psychiatry, 160,* 98–102.

Alford, B. A., & Correia, C. J. (1994). Cognitive therapy for schizophrenia: Theory and empirical status. *Behavior therapy, 25,* 17–33.

Alford, G. S., Morin, C., Atkins M., & Schuen, L. (1987). Masturbatory extinction of deviant sexual arousal: A case study. *Behavior Therapy, 18,* 265–271.

Allison, R. B., & Schwartz, T. (1980). *Minds in many pieces: The making of a very special doctor.* New York: Rawson, Wade.

Alter-Reid, K., Gibbs, M. S., Lachenmeyer, J. R., Sigal, J., & Massoth, N. A. (1986). Sexual abuse of children: A review of the empirical findings. *Clinical Psychology Review, 6,* 249–266.

Althof, S. E., Turner, L. A., Levine, S. B., Risen, C., Kursch, E. D., Bodner, D., & Resnick, M. (1987). Intracavernosal injection in the treatment of impotence: A prospective study of sexual, psychological, and marital functioning. *Journal of Sex and Marital Therapy, 13,* 155–167.

Amador, X. F., Falum, M., Andreasen, N. C., Strauss, D. H., Yale, S. A., Clark, S. C., & Gorman, J. M. (1994). Awareness of illness in schizophrenia and schizoaffective and mood disorders. *Archives of General Psychiatry, 51,* 826–836.

American Association for Counseling and Development. (1988). *Ethical Standards* (rev. ed.). Alexandria, VA: American Association for Counseling and Development.

American Association for Marriage and Family Therapy. (1991). *AAMFT code of ethics.* Washington, DC: American Association for Marriage and Family Therapy.

American Association of Retired Persons. (1985). *A profile of older Americans: 1985.* Washington, DC: American Association of Retired Persons.

American Bar Association. Standing Committee on Association Standards for Criminal Justice. (1984). *Criminal justice and mental health standards.* Chicago: American Bar Association.

American Cancer Society (1993). *Cancer facts and figures–1993.* Atlanta: American Cancer Society.

American Heart Association (1993). *Heart facts.* Dallas: American Heart Association.

American Psychiatric Association. (1952). *Diagnostic and statistical manual of mental disorders* (1st ed.). [DSM-I]. Washington, DC: American Psychiatric Association.

American Psychiatric Association. (1968). *Diagnostic and statistical manual of mental disorders* (2nd ed.). [DSM-II]. Washington, DC: American Psychiatric Association.

American Psychiatric Association (1980). *Diagnostic and statistical manual of mental disorders* (3rd ed.). [DSM-III]. Washington, DC: American Psychiatric Association.

American Psychiatric Association. (1983). American Psychiatric

Association statement on the insanity defense. *American Journal of Psychiatry, 140,* 681–688.

American Psychiatric Association. (1987). *Diagnostic and statistical manual of mental disorders* (3rd ed.). [DSM-III-R]. Washington, DC: American Psychiatric Association.

American Psychiatric Association. (1989). *The principles of medical ethics, with annotations especially applicable to psychiatry.* Washington, DC: American Psychiatric Association.

American Psychiatric Association. (1993). *DSM-IV Draft Criteria.* Washington, DC: American Psychiatric Association.

American Psychiatric Association. (1993). Practice guideline for eating disorders. *American Journal of Psychiatry, 150,* 212–228.

American Psychiatric Association (1994). *Diagnostic and statistical manual of mental disorders* (4th ed.). [DSM-IV]. Washington, DC: American Psychiatric Association.

American Psychiatric Association (1994). *Diagnostic and statistical manual of mental disorders* (4th ed.). Washington, DC: American Psychiatric Association.

American Psychoanalytic Association. (1983). *Principles of ethics for psychoanalysts and provisions for implementation of the principles of ethics for psychoanalysts.* New York: American Psychoanalytic Association.

American Psychological Association. (1989). *Ethical principles of psychologists.* Washington DC: American Psychological Association.

American Psychological Association. (1991). Draft of APA ethics code. *APA Monitor, 22,* 30–35.

American Psychological Association. (1992). Ethical principles of psychologists and code of conduct. *American Psychologist, 47,* 1597–1611.

American Psychological Association. (1993). Guidelines for providers of psychological services to ethnic, linguistic, and culturally diverse populations. *American Psychologist, 48,* 45–48.

Anastasi, A. (1982). *Psychological testing.* New York: Macmillan.

Anderson, A., Hedblom, J., & Hubbard, F. (1983). A multidisciplinary team treatment for patients with anorexia nervosa and their families. *International Journal of Eating Disorders, 2,* 181–192.

Andreasen, N. C. (1984). *The broken brain.* New York: Harper & Row.

Andreasen, N. C. (1989). Nuclear magnetic resonance imaging. In N. C. Andreasen (Ed.), *Brain imaging: Applications in psychiatry* (pp. 67–121). Washington, DC: American Psychiatric Press.

Andreasen, N. C., Arndt, S., Alliger, R., Miller, D., & Flaum, M. (1995). Symptoms of schizophrenia: Methods, meanings, and mechanisms. *Archives of General Psychiatry, 52,* 341–351.

Andreasen, N. C., Arndt, S., Swayze, V. W., II., Cizadlo, T., Flaum, M., O'Leary, D., Ehrhardt, J. C., & Yuh, W. T. C. (1994). Thalamic abnormalities in schizophrenia visualized through magnetic resonance image averaging. *Science, 266,* 294–298.

Andreasen, N. C., & Flaum, M. (1991). Schizophrenia: The characteristic symptoms. *Schizophrenia Bulletin, 17,* 27–48.

Andreasen, N. C., Rezai, K., Alliger, R., Swayze, V. W., II., Flaum, M., Kirchner, P., Cohen, G., & O'Leary, D. S. (1992). Hypofrontality in neuroleptic-naive patients and in patients with chronic schizophrenia. *Archives of General Psychiatry, 49,* 943–958.

Angell, M. (1985). Disease as a reflection of the psyche. *New England Journal of Medicine, 312,* 1570–1572.

Angrist, B., Rotrosen, J., & Gershon, S. (1980). Responses to apomorphine and amphetamine, and neuroleptics in schizophrenia subjects. *Psychopharmacology, 67,* 31–38.

Anonymous. (1981). First person account: The quiet discrimination. *Schizophrenia Bulletin, 7,* 739.

Anonymous. (1983). First person account: Schizophrenia—A pharmacy student's view. *Schizophrenia Bulletin, 9,* 152–155.

Anonymous. (1990). First person account: A pit of confusion. *Schizophrenia Bulletin, 16,* 355–359.

Anthony, J. C., & Helzer, J. E. (1991). Syndromes of drug abuse and dependence. In L. N. Robins & D. A. Regier (Eds.), *Psychiatric disorders in America: The Epidemiologic Catchment Area study* (pp. 116–154). New York: Free Press.

Antoni, M. H., Baggett, L., Ironson, G. I., La Perriere, A., August, S., Klimas, N., Schneiderman, N., & Fletcher, M. A. (1991). Cognitive-behavioral stress management intervention buffers distress responses and immunologic changes following notification of HIV-I seroposity. *Journal of Consulting and Clinical Psychology, 59,* 906–915.

Antony, M., Brown, T. A., & Barlow, D. H. (1992). Current perspectives on panic and panic disorder. *Current Directions, 1,* 79–82.

Aplin, D. Y., & Kane, J. M. (1985). Variables affecting pure tone and speech audiometry in experimentally simulated hearing loss. *British Journal of Audiology, 19,* 219–228.

Aponte, J. F., & Crouch, R. T. (1995). The changing ethnic profile of the United States. In J. F. Aponte, R. Y. Rivers, & J. Wohl (Eds.), *Psychological interventions and cultural diversity* (pp. 1–18). Needham, MA: Allyn & Bacon.

Applebaum, P. S. (1987). The right to refuse treatment with antipsychotic medications: Retrospect and prospect. *American Journal of Psychiatry, 145,* 413–419.

Ardizzone, J., & Scholl, G. T. (1985). Mental retardation. In G. T. Scholl (Ed.), *The school psychologist and the exceptional child.* Reston, VA: Council for Exceptional Children.

Arkonac, O., & Guze, S. (1963). A family study of hysteria. *New England Journal of Medicine, 268,* 239–242.

Arlow, J. A. (1991). Derivative manifestations of perversions. In G. I. Fogel & W. A. Myers (Eds.), *Perversions and near-perversions in clinical practice* (pp. 59–74). New Haven, CT: Yale University Press.

Arndt, S., Andreasen, N. C., Flaum, M., Miller, D., & Nopoulous, P. (1995). A longitudinal study of symptom dimensions in schizophrenia. *Archives of General Psychiatry, 52,* 352–360.

Arndt, W. B., Jr. (1991). *Gender disorders and the paraphilias.* Madison, CT: International Universities Press.

Aronson, T. A. (1987). A naturalistic study of imipramine in panic disorder and agoraphobia. *American Journal of Psychiatry, 144,* 1014–1019.

Ash, P. (1949). The reliability of psychiatric diagnosis. *Journal of Abnormal and Social Psychology, 44,* 272–276.

Asmundson, G. J. G., & Norton, G. R. (1993). Anxiety sensitivity and its relationship to spontaneous and cued panic attacks in college students. *Behaviour Research and Therapy, 31,* 199–201.

Assalian, P. (1988). Clomipramine in the treatment of premature ejaculation. *Journal of Sex Research, 24,* 213–215.

Associated Press. (1994, January 30). Long-term HIV survivors intrigue scientists. *Bellingham Herald,* p. A10.

Astin, M. C., Ogland-Hand, S. M., Foy, D. W., & Coleman, E. M. (1995). Posttraumatic stress disorder and childhood abuse in battered women: Comparisons with maritally distressed women. *Journal of Consulting and Clinical Psychology, 63,* 308–312.

Atkinson, D. R., Morten, G., & Sue, D. W. (1993). *Counseling American minorities.* Dubuque, IA: Brown & Benchmark.

Atlas, J. A., & Lapidus, L. B. (1987). Patterns of symbolic expression in subgroups of the childhood psychoses. *Journal of Clinical Psychology, 43,* 177–188.

Austin, K. M., Moline, M. M., & Williams, G. T. (1990). *Confronting malpractice: Legal and ethical dilemmas in psychotherapy.* Newbury Park, CA: Sage.

Ausubel, D. P. (1961). Causes and types of narcotic addiction: A psychosocial view. *Psychiatric Quarterly, 35,* 523–531.

Ayalon, M., & Mercom, H. (1985). The teacher interview. *Schizophrenia Bulletin, 11,* 117–120.

Ayllon, T., & Azrin, N. H. (1968). *The token economy: A motivational system for therapy and rehabilitation.* New York: Appleton-Century-Crofts.

Azar, B. (1995). Several genetic traits linked to alcoholism. *APA Monitor, 26,* 21–22.

Bacon, N. M. K., Bacon, S. F., Atkinson, J. H., Slater, M. A. (1994). Somatization symptoms in chronic low back pain patients. *Psychosomatic Medicine, 56*, 118–127.

Bahnson, C. B. (1981). Stress and cancer: The state of the art. *Psychosomatics, 22*, 207–209.

Baker, L. A., & Clark, R. (1990). Introduction to special feature on genetic origins of behavior: Implications for counselors. *Journal of Counseling and Development, 68*, 597–605.

Baldessarini, R. J., & Cole, J. O. (1988). Chemotherapy. In A. M. Nicholi, Jr. (Ed.), *The new Harvard guide to psychiatry*. Cambridge, MA: Harvard University Press.

Ball, J. D., Archer, R. P., Gordon, R. A., & French, J. (1991). Rorschach depression indices with children and adolescents: Concurrent validity findings. *Journal of Personality Assessment, 57*, 465–476.

Balon, R., Pohl, R., Yeragani, V. K., Rainey, J. M., & Berchou, R. (1988). Follow-up study of control subjects with lactate- and isoproterenol-induced panic attacks. *American Journal of Psychiatry, 145*, 238–241.

Bancroft, J. (1984). Testosterone therapy for low sexual interest and erectile dysfunctions in men: A controlled study. *British Journal of Psychiatry, 14*, 146–151.

Bancroft, J. (1989). *Human sexuality and its problems*. New York: Churchill-Livingstone.

Bandler, R., & Grinder, J. (1979). *The structure of magic*. Palo Alto, CA: Science and Behavior Books.

Bandura, A. (1969). *Principles of behavior modification*. New York: Holt, Rinehart & Winston.

Bandura, A. (1985). *Social foundations of thought and action*. Englewood Cliffs, NJ: Prentice-Hall.

Bandura, A., Blanchard, E., & Ritter, B. (1969). Relative efficacy of desensitization and modeling approaches for inducing behavioral, affective, and attitudinal changes. *Journal of Personality and Social Psychology, 13*, 173–199.

Bandura, A., & Rosenthal, T. L. (1966). Vicarious classical conditioning as a function of arousal level. *Journal of Personality and Social Psychology, 3*, 54–62.

Bandura, A., & Walters, R. H. (1963). *Social learning and personality development*. New York: Holt, Rinehart & Winston.

Baratz, S., & Baratz, J. (1970). Early childhood intervention: The social sciences base of institutional racism. *Harvard Educational Review, 40*, 29–50.

Barbaree, H. E., & Marshall, W. L. (1991). The role of male sexual arousal in rape: Six models. *Journal of Consulting and Clinical Psychology, 59*, 621–630.

Barber, J. P., & Luborsky, L. (1991). A psychodynamic view of simple phobias and prescriptive matching: A commentary. *Psychotherapy, 28*, 469–472.

Barchas, J., Berger, P., Ciaranello, R., & Elliott, G. (1977). *Psychopharmacology: From theory to practice*. New York: Oxford University Press.

Barkley, R. A., Anastopoulous, A. D., Guevremont, D. C., & Fletcher, K. E. (1992). Adolescents with attention deficit hyperactivity disorder: Mother-child-adolescent interactions, family beliefs and conflicts, and psychopathology. *Journal of Abnormal Child Psychology, 20*, 263–288.

Barkley, R. A., Fischer, M., Edelbrock, C., & Smallish, L. (1991). The adolescent outcome of hyperactive children diagnosed by research criteria–III. Mother-child interactions, family conflicts and maternal psychopathology. *Journal of Child Psychology and Psychiatry, 32*, 233–255.

Barlow, D. H. (1991). Introduction to the special issue on diagnoses, dimensions, and DSM-IV: The science of classification. *Journal of Abnormal Psychology, 100*, 243–244.

Barlow, D. H., Abel, G., & Blanchard, E. (1979). Gender identity change in transsexuals. *Archives of General Psychiatry, 36*, 1001–1007.

Baron, L., Straus, M. A., & Jaffee, D. (1988). Legitimate violence, violent attitudes, and rape: A test of the cultural spillover theory. In R. A. Prentky and V. L. Quisey (Eds.), *Human sexual aggression: Current perspectives. Annals of the New York Academy of Sciences, 528* (pp. 79–110). Salem, MA: New York Academy of Sciences.

Baron, M. (1991). Genetics of manic depressive illness: Current status and evolving concepts. In P. R. McHugh & V. A. McKusick (Eds.), *Genes, brain, and behavior* (pp. 153–164). New York: Raven Press.

Baron-Cohen, L., Leslie, A. M., & Frith, U. (1985). Does the autistic child have a "theory of mind"? *Cognition, 21*, 37–46.

Barraclough, B. M., Jennings, C., & Moss, J. R. (1977). Suicide prevention by the Samaritans: A controlled study of effectiveness. *Lancet, 2*, 237–238.

Barrett, G. V., & Depinet, R. L. (1991). A reconsideration of testing for competence rather than for intelligence. *American Psychologist, 46*, 1012–1024.

Barsky, A. J., Cleary, P. D., Sarnie, M. K., & Klerman, G. L. (1993). The course of transient hypochondriasis. *American Journal of Psychiatry, 150*, 484–488.

Barsky, A. J., Wool, C., Barnett, M. C., & Cleary, P. D. (1995). Histories of childhood trauma in adult hypochondriacal patients. *American Journal of Psychiatry, 151*, 397–401.

Barsky, A. J., & Wyshak, G. (1990). Hypochondriasis and somatosensory amplification. *British Journal of Psychiatry, 157*, 404–409.

Barsky, A. J., Wyshak, G., & Klerman, G. L. (1991). In reply. *Archives of General Psychiatry, 48*, 955–956.

Barsky, A. J., Wyshak, G., & Klerman, G. L. (1992). Psychiatric comorbidity in DSM-III-R hypochondriasis. *Archives of General Psychiatry, 49*, 101–108.

Bartlett, K. (1984, August 26). Bulimia: The secret that becomes a compulsion. *Ann Arbor News*, p. F1.

Bass, E., & Davis, L. (1988). *The courage to heal*. New York: Harper & Row.

Bassuk, E. L., Schoonover, S. C., & Gelenberg, A. J. (1983). *The practitioner's guide to psychiatric drugs* (2nd ed.). New York: Plenum.

Bates, J. E., Bentler, P. N., & Thompson, S. K. (1979). Gender-deviant boys compared with normal and clinical control boys. *Journal of Abnormal Child Psychology, 7*, 243–259.

Bateson, G. (1978). The birth of a matrix or double-bind and epistemology. In M. M. Berger (Ed.), *Beyond the double bind*. New York: Brunner/Mazel.

Bateson, G., Jackson, D., Haley, J., & Weakland, J. (1956). Toward a theory of schizophrenia. *Behavioral Science, 1*, 251–264.

Battaglia, M., Bertella, S., Politi, E., Bernardeschi, L., Perna, G., Gabriele, A., & Bellodi, L. (1995). Age at onset of panic disorder: Influence of familial liability to the disease and of childhood separation anxiety. *American Journal of Psychiatry, 152*, 1362–1364.

Bauer, A. M., & Shea, T. M. (1984). Tourette's syndrome: A review and educational implications. *Journal of Autism and Developmental Disorders, 14*, 69–80.

Baum, A., & Nesselhof, S. E. A. (1988). Psychological research and the prevention, etiology, and treatment of AIDS. *American Psychologist, 43*(11), 900–906.

Bauman, W. & Melnyk, W. T. (1994). A controlled comparison of eye movements and finger tapping in the treatment of test anxiety. *Journal of Behavior Therapy and Experimental Psychiatry, 25*, 29–33.

Baumeister, A. A. (1987). Mental retardation. *American Psychologist, 42*, 796–800.

Baumeister, R. F. (1988). Masochism as escape from self. *Journal of Sex Research, 25*, 28–59.

Beal, E. (1978). Use of the extended family in the treatment of multiple personality. *American Journal of Psychiatry, 135*, 539–543.

Beam, E., III (1995). Helicobacter pylori and peptic ulcer disease. *Clinician Reviews, 5*, 51–70.

Beck, A. T. (1962). Reliability of psychiatric diagnosis: A critique of systematic studies. *American Journal of Psychiatry, 119,* 210–216.

Beck, A. T. (1970). Cognitive therapy: Nature and relationship to behavior therapy. *Behavior Therapy, 1,* 184–200.

Beck, A. T. (1974). The development of depression: A cognitive model. In R. J. Friedman & M. M. Katz (Eds.), *The psychology of depression: Contemporary theory and research.* New York: Wiley.

Beck, A. T. (1976). *Cognitive therapy and emotional disorders.* New York: International Universities Press.

Beck, A. T. (1985). Cognitive therapy, behavior therapy, psychoanalysis, and pharmacotherapy: A cognitive continuum. In M. Mahoney & A. Freeman (Eds.), *Cognition and psychotherapy.* New York: Plenum Press.

Beck, A. T. (1991). Cognitive therapy. *American Psychologist, 46,* 368–375.

Beck, A. T., Emery, G., & Greenberg, R. L. (1985). *Anxiety disorders and phobias: A cognitive perspective.* New York: Basic Books.

Beck, A. T., Freeman, A., & Associates. (1990). *Cognitive therapy of personality disorders.* New York: Guilford Press.

Beck, A. T., Kovacs, M., & Weissman, A. (1979). Assessment of suicidal ideation: The Scale for Suicide Ideation. *Journal of Consulting and Clinical Psychology, 47,* 343–352.

Beck, A. T., Rush, A., Shaw, B., & Emery, G. (1979). *Cognitive therapy of depression.* New York: Guilford Press.

Beck, A. T., Ward, C. H., Mendelson, M., Mock, J. E., & Erbaugh, J. (1961). An inventory for measuring depression. *Archives of General Psychiatry, 4,* 561–571.

Beck, A. T., & Weishaar, M. E. (1989). Cognitive therapy. In R. J. Corsini & D. Wedding (Eds.), *Current psychotherapies* (pp. 285–320). Itasca, IL: Peacock.

Becker, J. (1974). *Depression: Theory and research.* Washington, DC: Winston-Wiley.

Bednar, R. L., Bednar, S. C., Lambert, M. J., & Waite, D. R. (1991). *Psychotherapy with high-risk clients: Legal and professional standards.* Pacific Grove, CA: Brooks/Cole.

Bednar, R. L., & Kaul, T. J. (1978). Experiential group research: Current perspectives. In S. L. Garfield & A. E. Bergin (Eds.), *Handbook of psychotherapy and behavior change: An empirical analysis* (2nd ed.). New York: Wiley.

Bednar, R. L., & Kaul, T. J. (1994). Experiential group research: Can the canon fire? In A. E. Bergin & S. L. Garfield (Eds.), *Handbook of psychotherapy and behavior change* (pp. 631–663). New York: Wiley.

Beiser, M., Fleming, J. A. E., Iacono, W. G., & Lin, T.-Y. (1988). Redefining the diagnosis of schizophreniform disorder. *American Journal of Psychiatry, 145,* 695–700.

Belar, C. (1995). What distinguishes clinical health psychology, rehabilitation psychology, and neuropsychology? *Professional Psychology: Research and Practice, 26,* 349–351.

Belfer, P. L., & Glass, C. R. (1992). Agoraphobic anxiety and fear of fear: Test of a cognitive-attentional model. *Journal of Anxiety Disorder, 6,* 133–146.

Bell, A. P., & Weinberg, M. S. (1978). *Homosexualities: A study of diversity among men and women.* New York: Simon & Schuster.

Bell, A. P., Weinberg, M. S., & Hammersmith, S. K. (1981). *Sexual preference: Its development in men and women.* Bloomington: Indiana University Press.

Bell-Dolan, D., & Wessler, A. E. (1994). Attribution style of anxious children: Extensions from cognitive theory and research on adult anxiety. *Journal of Anxiety Disorders, 8,* 79–94.

Bellack, A. S., & Hersen, M. (1980). *Introduction to clinical psychology.* New York: Oxford University Press.

Bellack, A. S., Hersen, M., & Himmelhoch, J. M. (1983). A comparison of social skills training. *Behavior Research & Therapy, 21,* 101–108.

Benassi, V. A., Sweeney, P. D., & Dufour, C. L. (1988). Is there a

relation between locus of control orientation and depression? *Journal of Abnormal Psychology, 97*(3), 357–367.

Bender, L. (1938). A visual-motor Gestalt test and its clinical use. *American Orthopsychiatric Association Research Monographs,* No. 3.

Benjamin, H. (1967). Transvestism and transsexualism in the male and female. *Journal of Sex Research, 3,* 107–127.

Benjamin, L. S., & Wonderlich, S. A. (1994). Social perceptions and borderline personality disorder: The relation to mood disorders. *Journal of Abnormal Psychology, 103,* 610–624.

Bennett, L. F. C., & Sherman, R. (1983). Management of childhood "hyperactivity" by primary care physicians. *Journal of Developmental and Behavioral Pediatrics, 4,* 88–93.

Bennett, P., & Carroll, D. (1990). Stress management approaches to the prevention of coronary heart disease. *British Journal of Clinical Psychology, 29,* 1–12.

Bennett, P., Wallace, L., Carroll, D., & Smith, N. (1991). Treating type A behaviours and mild hypertension in middle-aged men. *Journal of Psychosomatic Research, 35,* 209–223.

Bennun, I., & Schindler, L. (1988). Therapist and patient factors in the behavioural treatment of phobic patients. *British Journal of Clinical Psychology, 27,* 145–150.

Benson, H., Shapiro, D., Tursky, B., & Schwartz, G. (1971). Decreased systolic blood pressure through operant conditioning techniques in patients with essential hypertension. *Science, 173,* 740–742.

Bentall, R. P., Haddock, G., & Slade, P. D. (1994). Cognitive behavioral therapy for persistent auditory hallucinations: From theory to therapy. *Behavior Therapy, 25,* 51–66.

Bergin, A. E. (1971). The evaluation of therapeutic outcomes. In A. E. Bergin & S. L. Garfield (Eds.), *Handbook of psychotherapy and behavior change: An empirical analysis.* New York: Wiley.

Bergin, A. E., & Lambert, M. J. (1978). The evaluation of therapeutic outcomes. In S. L. Garfield & A. E. Bergin (Eds.), *Handbook of psychotherapy and behavior change: An empirical analysis* (2nd ed.). New York: Wiley.

Berkowitz, A., & Perkins, H. W. (1988). Personality characteristics of children of alcoholics. *Journal of Consulting and Clinical Psychology, 56,* 206–209.

Berkowitz, N. J. (1974). Up-to-date review of theories of shock therapies. *Diseases of the Nervous System, 35,* 523–527.

Berlow, S. J., Caldarelli, D. D., Matz, G. J., Meyer, D. H., & Harsch, G. G. (1981). Bacterial meningitis and SHL. *Laryngoscope, 4,* 1445–1452.

Berman, A. L., & Jobes, D. A. (1991). *Adolescent suicide: Assessment and intervention.* Washington, DC: American Psychological Association.

Berman, K. F., Torrey, E. F., Daniel, D. G., & Weinberger, D. R. (1992). Regional cerebral blood flow in monozygotic twins disconcordant and concordant for schizophrenia. *Archives of General Psychiatry, 49,* 927–934.

Bernard, J. (1976). Homosociality and female depression. *Journal of Social Issues, 32,* 213–238.

Berne, E. (1972). *What do you say after you say hello?* New York: Grove Press.

Bernstein, S. M., Steiner, B. W., Glaisler, J. T. D., & Muir, C. F. (1981). Changes in patients with gender identity problems after parental death. *American Journal of Psychiatry, 138,* 41–45.

Bersoff, D. N. (1981). Testing and the law. *American Psychologist, 36,* 1047–1057.

Bestman, E. W. (1986). Cross-cultural approaches to service delivery to ethnic minorities: The Miami model. In M. R. Miranda & H. H. Kitano (Eds.), *Mental health research and practice in minority communities: Development of culturally sensitive training programs* (pp. 199–226). Washington, DC: U.S. Government Printing Office.

Bhadrinath, B. R. (1990). Anorexia nervosa in adolescents of Asian extraction. *British Journal of Psychiatry, 156,* 565–568.

Bick, P. A., & Kinsbourne, M. (1987). Auditory hallucinations and subvocal speech in schizophrenic patients. *American Journal of Psychiatry, 144,* 222–225.

Bilken, D. (1990). Communication unbound: Autism and praxis. *Harvard Educational Review, 60,* 219–314.

Binder, L. M. (1986). Persisting symptoms after mild head injury: A review of the postconcussive syndrome. *Journal of Clinical and Experimental Neuropsychology, 8,* 323–346.

Binder, R. L. (1988). Organic mental disorders. In H. H. Goldman (Ed.), *Review of general psychiatry* (pp. 252–265). Norwalk, CT: Appleton & Lange.

Black, D. W., Noyes, R., Goldstein, R. B., & Blum, N. (1992). A family study of obsessive-compulsive disorder. *Archives of General Psychiatry, 49,* 362–368.

Black, S. T. (1993). Comparing genuine and simulated suicide notes: A new perspective. *Journal of Consulting and Clinical Psychology, 67*(4), 699–702.

Blakeslee, S. (1993, June 2). New therapies are helping men to overcome impotence. *New York Times,* p. C12.

Blanchard, E. B. (1992). Psychological treatment of benign headache disorders. *Journal of Consulting and Clinical Psychology, 60,* 537–551.

Blanchard, E. B., & Andrasik, F. (1982). Psychological assessment and treatment of headache: Recent developments and emerging issues. *Journal of Consulting and Clinical Psychology, 50,* 859–879.

Blanchard, E. B., Hickling, E. J., Taylor, A. E., Forneris, C. A., Loos, W., & Jaccard, J. (1995). Effects of varying scoring rules of the clinician-administered PTSD Scale (CAPS) for the diagnosis of post-traumatic stress disorder in motor accident victims. *Behaviour Research and Therapy, 33,* 471–475.

Blanchard, E. B., Hickling, E. J., Vollmer, A. J., Loos, W. R., Buckley, T. C., & Jaccard, J. (1995). Short-term follow-up of post-traumatic stress symptoms in motor accident victims. *Behaviour Research and Therapy, 33,* 369–377.

Blanchard, R. (1988). Nonhomosexual gender dysphoria. *Journal of Sex Research, 24,* 188–193.

Blanchard, R., Racansky, I. G., & Steiner, B. W. (1986). Phallometric detection of fetishistic arousal. *Journal of Sex Research, 22,* 452–462.

Blank, R. J. (1981). The partial transsexual. *American Journal of Psychiatry, 35,* 107–112.

Bligh, S., & Kupperman, P. (1993). Brief report: Facilitated communication evaluation procedure accepted in a court case. *Journal of Autism and Developmental Disorders, 23,* 553–551.

Bliss, E. L. (1980). Multiple personalities: A report of 14 cases with implications for schizophrenia and hysteria. *Archives of General Psychiatry, 39,* 823–825.

Bliss, E. L. (1984). Hysteria and hypnosis. *Journal of Nervous and Mental Disease, 172,* 203–208.

Bliss, E. L., Larson, E. M., & Nakashima, S. R. (1983). Auditory hallucinations and schizophrenia. *Journal of Nervous and Mental Disease, 171,* 30–33.

Bloom, B. L., Asher, S. J., & White, S. W. (1978). Marital disruption as a stressor: A review and analysis. *Psychological Bulletin, 85,* 867–894.

Blouin, A., Blouin, J., Aubin, P., Carter, J., Goldstein, C., Boyer, H., & Perez, E. (1992). Seasonal patterns of bulimia nervosa. *American Journal of Psychiatry, 149,* 73–81.

Blum, K., Noble, E. P., Sheridan, P. J., Montgomery, A., Ritchie, T., Jagadeeswaran, P., Nogami, H., Briggs, A. H., & Cohn, J. B. (1990). Allelic association of human dopamine D2 receptor gene in alcoholism. *Journal of the American Medical Association, 263,* 2055–2060.

Bockes, Z. (1987). "Freedom" means knowing you have a choice. In *Schizophrenia: The experiences of patients and families* (pp. 40–42). Rockville, MD: National Institute of Mental Health.

Boersma, K., Den Hengst, S., Dekker, J., & Emmelkamp, P. M. G. (1976). Exposure and response prevention in the natural environment: A comparison with obsessive-compulsive patients. *Behaviour Research and Therapy, 14,* 12–24.

Bogerts, B. (1993). Recent advances in the neuropathology of schizophrenia. *Schizophrenia Bulletin, 19,* 431–440.

Bohman, M., Cloninger, R., von Knorring, A., & Sigvardsson, S. (1984). An adoption study of somatoform disorders. *Archives of General Psychiatry, 41,* 872–878.

Bolger, N., & Schilling, E. A. (1991). Personality and the problems of everyday life: The role of neuroticism in exposure and reactivity to daily stress. *Journal of Personality, 59,* 355–386.

Bolgrad, M. (1984). Family systems approaches to wife battering: A feminist critique. *American Journal of Orthopsychiatry, 54,* 558–568.

Bolgrad, M. (1986). A feminist examination of family systems models of violence against women in the family. In J. C. Hansen & M. Ault-Riche (Eds.), *Women and family therapy* (pp. 34–50). Rockville, MD: Aspen Systems.

Boll, T. J. (1983). Neuropsychological assessment. In I. B. Weiner (Ed.), *Clinical methods in psychology.* New York: Wiley.

Boller, F., Kim, Y., & Detre, T. (1984). Assessment of temporal lobe disorder. In P. E. Logue & J. M. Schear (Eds.), *Clinical neuropsychology.* Springfield, IL: Thomas.

Bolton, P., Macdonald, H., Pickles, A., Rios, P., Goode, S., Crowson, M., Bailey, A., & Rutter, M. (1994). A case-control family history of autism. *Journal of Child Psychology and Psychiatry, 35,* 877–900.

Bolton, P., Rutter, M., Butler, L., & Summers, D. (1989). Females with autism and the fragile x. *Journal of Autism and Developmental Disorders, 19,* 473–476.

Bongar, B. (1991). *The suicidal patient: Clinical and legal standards of care.* Washington, DC: American Psychological Association.

Bongar, B. (1992). Effective risk management and the suicidal patient. *Register Report, 18,* 1–3, 21–27.

Boon, S., & Draijer, N. (1993). Multiple personality disorder in the Netherlands: A clinical investigation of 71 patients. *American Journal of Psychiatry, 150,* 489–494.

Booth, G. K. (1988). Disorders of impulse control. In H. H. Goldman (Ed.), *Review of general psychiatry* (pp. 381–390). Norwalk, CT: Appleton & Lange.

Booth, R., & Rachman, S. (1992). The reduction of claustrophobia I. *Behaviour Research and Therapy, 30,* 207–221.

Borkman, T. (1990). Self-help groups at the turning point: Emerging egalitarian alliances with the formal health care system? *American Journal of Community Psychology, 18*(2), 321–332.

Boucher, J., & Lewis, Y. (1992). Unfamiliar face recognition in relatively able autistic children. *Journal of Child Psychology and Psychiatry, 33,* 843–859.

Bouhoutsos, J., Holroyd, J., Lerman, H., Forer, B. R., & Greenberg, M. (1983). Sexual intimacy between psychotherapists and patients. *Professional Psychology: Research and Practice, 14,* 185–196.

Bourdon, K. H. (1992). Estimating the prevalence of mental disorders in U.S. adults from the Epidemiologic Catchment Area survey. *Public Health Reports,* pp. 663–667.

Bourdon, K. H., Rae, D. S., Locke, B. Z., Narrow, W. E. & Regier, D. A. (1992). Estimating the prevalence of mental disorders in U.S. adults from the Epidemiologic Catchment Area Survey. *Public Health Reports, 107,* 663–668.

Bourne, E. J. (1990). *The anxiety and phobia workbook.* Oakland, CA: New Harbinger.

Bownes, I. T., O'Gorman, E. C., & Sayers, A. (1991). Assault characteristics and post-traumatic stress disorder in rape victims. *Acta Psychiatrica Scandinavica, 83,* 27–30.

Bozzuto, J. C. (1975). Cinematic neurosis following *The Exorcist. Journal of Nervous and Mental Disease, 161,* 43–48.

Bradford, J. W., & Smith, S. M. (1979). Amnesia and homicide: The Padula case and a study of thirty cases. *Bulletin of the American Academy of Psychiatry and Law, 7,* 219–231.

Brady, K. T., Austin, L., & Lydiard, R. B. (1991). Body dysmorphic disorder: The relationship to obsessive-compulsive disorder. *Journal of Nervous and Mental Disease, 178,* 538–539.

Brammer, L. M., & Shostrom, E. (1982). *Therapeutic psychology.* Englewood Cliffs, NJ: Prentice-Hall.

Brandsma, J. (1979). *Outpatient treatment of alcoholism.* Baltimore: University Park Press.

Braswell, L., & Kendall, P. C. (1988). Cognitive-behavioral methods with children. In K. S. Dobson (Ed.), *Handbook of cognitive-behavioral therapies* (pp. 167–213). New York: Guilford Press.

Braucht, G. (1982). Problem drinking among adolescents: A review and analysis of psychosocial research. In National Institute on Alcohol Abuse and Alcoholism, *Alcohol Monograph 4: Special Population Issues.* Washington, DC: U.S. Government Printing Office.

Braun, P., Kochonsky, G., Shapiro, R., Greenberg, S., Gudeman, J. E., Johnson, S., & Shore, M. F. (1981). Overview: Deinstitutionalization of psychiatric patients: A critical review of outcome studies. *American Journal of Psychiatry, 138,* 736–749.

Breier, A., Albus, M., Pickar, D., Zahn, T. P., Wolkowitz, O. M., & Paul, S. M. (1987). Controllable and uncontrollable stress in humans: Alterations in mood and neuroendocrine and psychophysiological function. *American Journal of Psychiatry, 144,* 1419–1425.

Breier, A., Schreiber, J. L., Dyer, J., & Pickard, D. (1991). National Institute longitudinal study of chronic schizophrenia. *Archives of General Psychiatry, 48,* 239–246.

Bremner, J. D., Southwick, S. M., Johnson, D. R., Yehuda, R., & Charney, D. S. (1993). Childhood physical abuse and combat-related posttraumatic stress disorder in Vietnam veterans. *American Journal of Psychiatry, 150,* 235–239.

Brenner, H. D., Hodel, B., Roder, V., & Corrigan, P. (1992). Treatment of cognitive dysfunctions and behavioral deficits in schizophrenia. *Schizophrenia Bulletin, 18,* 21–26.

Brent, D. A., Perper, J. A., & Allman, C. J. (1987). Alcohol, firearms, and suicide among youth. *JAMA: The Journal of the American Medical Association, 257,* 3369–3372.

Breslau, N., Davis, G. C., & Andreski, P. (1995). Risk factors for PTSD-related traumatic events: A prospective analysis. *American Journal of Psychiatry, 152,* 529–535.

Breslau, N., Davis, G. C., Andreski, P., & Peterson, E. (1991). Traumatic events and posttraumatic stress disorder in an urban population of young adults. *Archives of General Psychiatry, 48,* 216–222.

Brett-Jones, J., Garety, P., & Hemsley, D. (1987). Measuring delusional experiences: A method and its application. *British Journal of Clinical Psychology, 26,* 257–265.

Breuer, J., & Freud, S. (1957). *Studies in hysteria.* New York: Basic Books. (Originally published 1895.)

Brewslow, N., Evans, L., & Langley, J. (1986). Comparisons among heterosexual, bisexual, and homosexual male sadomasochists. *Journal of Homosexuality, 13,* 83–107.

Briere, J. (1992). Methodological issues in the study of sexual abuse effects. *Journal of Consulting and Clinical Psychology, 60,* 196–203.

Brislin, R. (1993). *Understanding culture's influence on behavior.* New York: Harcourt Brace Jovanovich.

Broman, S. H., Nichols, P. L., & Kennedy, W. A. (1975). *Preschool IQ: Prenatal and early developmental correlates.* Hillsdale, NJ: Erlbaum.

Bromet, E. J. (1984). Epidemiology. In A. S. Bellack & M. Hersen (Eds.), *Research methods in clinical psychology* (pp. 266–282). New York: Pergamon Press.

Brook, S. L., & Bowler, D. M. (1992). Autism by another name? Semantic and pragmatic impairments in children. *Journal of Autism and Developmental Disorders, 22,* 61–81.

Brooks, D. S., Murphy, D., Janota, I., & Lishman, W. A. (1987). Early-onset Huntington's chorea. *British Journal of Psychiatry, 151,* 850–852.

Brown, G. L., Ebert, M., Goyer, P., Jimerson, D. C., Klein, W. J., Bunney, W. E., & Goodwin, F. K. (1982). Aggression, suicide, and serotonin: Relationships to CSF amine metabolites. *American Journal of Psychiatry, 139,* 741–746.

Brown, G. R., & Anderson, B. (1991). Psychiatric morbidity in adult inpatients with childhood histories of sexual and physical abuse. *American Journal of Psychiatry, 148,* 55–61.

Brown, G. W., & Harris, T. O. (1989). Depression. In G. W. Brown & T. O. Harris (Eds.), *Life events and illness* (pp. 49–93). New York: Guilford Press.

Brown, J. S., Jr. (1994). Geographic correlation of schizophrenia to ticks and tick-borne encephalitis. *Schizophrenia Bulletin, 20,* 755–775.

Brown, T. A., & Cash, T. F. (1990). The phenomenon of nonclinical panic: Parameters of panic fear, and avoidance. *Journal of Anxiety Disorders, 4,* 15–29.

Brownell, K. D. (1982). Behavioral medicine. In C. M. Franks, G. T. Wilson, P. C. Kendall, & K. D. Brownell (Eds.), *Annual Review of Behavior Therapy: Theory and Practice* (Vol. 8). New York: Guilford Press.

Brownell, K. D. (1991). Dieting and the search for the perfect body: Where physiology and culture collide. *Behavior Therapy, 22,* 1–12.

Brownmiller, S. (1975). *Against our will: Men, women, and rape.* New York: Simon & Schuster.

Bruch, H. (1978). Obesity and anorexia nervosa. *Psychosomatics, 19,* 208–221.

Bruch, M. A., & Heimberg, R. G. (1994). Differences in perceptions of parental and personal characteristics between generalized and nongeneralized social phobics. *Journal of Anxiety Disorders, 8,* 155–168.

Bryant, R. A., & McConkey, K. M. (1989). Visual conversion disorder: A case analysis of the influence of visual information. *Journal of Abnormal Psychology, 98,* 326–329.

Buchanan, A., & Oliver, J. E. (1977). Abuse and neglect as a cause of mental retardation. *British Journal of Psychiatry, 131,* 458–467.

Buchsbaum, M. S. (1990). The frontal lobes, basal ganglia, and the temporal lobes as sites for schizophrenia. *Schizophrenia Bulletin, 16,* 379–389.

Buchsbaum, M. S., Haier, R. J., Potkin, S. G., Nuechterlein, K., Bracha, H. S., Katz, M., Lohr, J., Wu, J., Lottenberg, S., Jerabeck, P. A., Trenary, M., Tafalla, R., Reynolds, C., & Bunney, W. E., Jr. (1992). Frontostriatal disorder of cerebral metabolism in never-medicated schizophrenics. *Archives of General Psychiatry, 49,* 935–942.

Buchsbaum, M. S., Potkin, S. G., Siegel, B. V., Lohr, J., Katz, M., Gottschalk, L. A., Gulasekaram, B., Marshall, J. F., Lottenberg, S., Teng, C. Y., Abel, L., Plon, L., & Bunney, W. E., Jr. (1992). Striatal metabolic rate and clinical response to neuroleptics in schizophrenia. *Archives of General Psychiatry, 49,* 966–974.

Buckner, H. T. (1970). The transvestic career path. *Psychiatry, 33,* 381–389.

Buhrmester, D., Whalen, C. K., Henker, B., McDonald, V., & Hinshaw, S. P. (1992). Prosocial behavior in hyperactive boys: Effects of stimulant medication and comparison with normal boys. *Journal of Abnormal Child Psychology, 20,* 103–121.

Bullard-Bates, P. C., & Satz, P. (1983). A case of pathological left-handedness. *Clinical Neuropsychology, 5,* 128–135.

Bunney, W. E., Pert, A., Rosenblatt, J., Pert, C. B., & Gallaper, D. (1979). Mode of action of lithium: Some biological considerations. *Archives of General Psychiatry, 36,* 898–901.

Burgess, A. W., Groth, A. N., & McCausland, M. P. (1981). *American Journal of Orthopsychiatry, 51,* 110–119.

Burgess, A. W., Hartman, C. R., McCausland, M. P., Powers, P. (1984). Response pattern in children and adolescents exploited through sex rings and pornography. *American Journal of Psychiatry, 141,* 656–662.

Burgess, A. W., & Holmstrom, L. L. (1979). Rape: Sex disruption and recovery. *American Journal of Orthopsychiatry, 49,* 648–657.

Burman, B., Mednick, S. A., Machon, R. A., Parnas, J., & Schulsinger, F. (1987). Children at high risk for schizophrenia: Parents and offspring perceptions of family relationships. *Journal of Abnormal Psychology, 96,* 364–366.

Burt, D. B., Fuller, S. P., & Lewis, K. R. (1991). Brief report: Competitive employment of adults with autism. *Journal of Autism and Developmental Disorders, 21,* 237–242.

Burt, V. L., Whelton, P., Roccella, E. J., Higgins, M., Horan, M. J., & Labarthe, D. (1995). Prevalence of hypertension in the U.S. adult population: Results from the Third National Health and Nutrition Examination Survey, 1988–1991. *Hypertension, 25,* 305–313.

Burton, A. (1972). *Interpersonal psychotherapy.* Englewood Cliffs, NJ: Prentice-Hall.

Buss, A. H. (1966). *Psychopathology.* New York: Wiley.

Butcher, J. N. (1990). *The MMPI-2 in psychological treatment.* New York: Oxford University Press.

Butcher, J. N. (1995). Item content in the interpretation of the MMPI-2. In J. N. Butcher (Ed.), *Clinical personality assessment: Practical approaches* (pp. 302–316). New York: Oxford University Press.

Butler, G., Cullington, A., Munby, M., Amies, P., & Gelder, M. (1984). Exposure and anxiety management in the treatment of social phobia. *Journal of Consulting and Clinical Psychology, 52,* 642–650.

Butler, G., Fennell, M., Robson, P., & Gelder, M. (1991). Comparison of behavior therapy and cognitive behavior therapy in the treatment of generalized anxiety disorder. *Journal of Consulting and Clinical Psychology, 59,* 167–175.

Butler, G., Gelder, M., Hibbert, G., Cullington, A., & Klimes, I. (1987). Anxiety management: Developing effective strategies. *Behaviour Research and Therapy, 25,* 517–522.

Butler, R. N. (1984). Senile dementia: Reversible and irreversible. *Counseling Psychologist, 12,* 75–79.

Butler, R. W., & Braff, D. L. (1991). Delusions: A review and integration. *Schizophrenia Bulletin, 17,* 633–645.

Byers, E. S., & Eno, R. J. (1991). Predicting men's sexual coercion and aggression from attitudes, dating history, and sexual response. *Journal of Psychology and Human Sexuality, 4*(3), 55–70.

Cadoret, R. J., & Cain, C. (1981). Environmental and genetic factors in predicting adolescent antisocial behavior in adoptees. *Psychiatric Journal of the University of Ottawa, 6,* 220–225.

Cadoret, R. J., & Wesner, R. B. (1990). Use of the adoption paradigm to elucidate the role of genes and environment and their interaction in the genesis of alcoholism. In C. R. Cloninger & H. Begleiter (Eds.), *Genetics and biology of alcoholism* (pp. 31–42). Cold Spring Harbor, NY: Cold Spring Harbor Laboratory Press.

Calamari, J. E., Faber, S. D., Hitsman, B. L., & Poppe, C. J. (1994). Treatment of obsessive compulsive disorder in the elderly. *Journal of Behavior Therapy and Experimental Psychiatry, 25,* 95–104.

Calhoun, K. S., Atkeson, B. M., & Resick, P. A. (1982). A longitudinal examination of fear reactions in victims of rape. *Journal of Counseling Psychology, 29,* 655–661.

Callahan, L. A., Steadman, H. J., McGreevy, M. A., & Robbins, P. C. (1991). The volume and characteristics of insanity defense pleas: An eight-state study. *Bulletin of the American Academy of Psychiatry and the Law, 19*(4), 331–338.

Campbell, M. K. (1988). Fenfluramine treatment of autism. *Journal of Child Psychology and Psychiatry, 29,* 1–10.

Campbell, M. K., Small, A. M., Palij, M., Perry, R., Polonsky, B. B., Lukashok, D., & Anderson, L. T. (1987). The efficacy and safety of fenfluramine in autistic children: Preliminary analysis of a double-blind study. *Psychopharmacology Bulletin, 23,* 123–127.

Campbell, R. J. (1981). *Psychiatric dictionary* (5th ed.). New York: Oxford University Press.

Campbell, S. B., & Ewing, L. J. (1990). Follow-up of hard-to-manage preschoolers: Adjustment at age 9 and predictors of continuing symptoms. *Journal of Child Psychology and Psychiatry, 31,* 871–889.

Cannon, T. D., & Marco, E. (1994). Structural brain abnormalities as indicators of vulnerability to schizophrenia. *Schizophrenia Bulletin, 20,* 89–100.

Cantor, P. (1991). Developmental perspective on prevention and treatment of suicidal youth. In A. A. Leenaars (Ed.), *Life span perspectives of suicide: Time-lines in the suicide process.* New York: Plenum.

Caplan, P. J. (1995). *They say you're crazy.* Reading, MA: Addison-Wesley.

Cappell, H., & Pliner, P. (1973). Volitional control of marijuana intoxication: A study of the ability to "come down" on command. *Journal of Abnormal Psychology, 82,* 428–434.

Cardena, E., & Spiegel, D. (1993). Dissociative reactions to the San Francisco Bay Area earthquake of 1989. *American Journal of Psychiatry, 150,* 474–478.

Carey, G. (1992). Twin imitation for antisocial behavior: Implications for genetic and family environment research. *Journal of Abnormal Psychology, 101,* 18–25.

Carey, W. B. (1986). Interactions of temperament and clinical conditions. In M. Wolraich & D. Routh (Eds.), *Advances in developmental and behavioral pediatrics.* Greenwich, CT: JAI Press.

Carlson, C. L., Pelham, W. E. Jr., Milich, R., & Dixon, J. (1992). Single and combined effects of methylphenidate and behavior therapy on the classroom performance of children with attention-deficit hyperactivity disorder. *Journal of Abnormal Child Psychology, 20,* 213–232.

Carlson, E. B., & Rosser-Hogan, R. (1991). Trauma experiences, posttraumatic stress, dissociation, and depression in Cambodian refugees. *American Journal of Psychiatry, 148,* 1548–1551.

Carone, B. J., Harrow, M., & Westermeyer, J. F. (1991). Post-hospital course and outcome in schizophrenia. *Archives of General Psychiatry, 48,* 247–253.

Carpenter, W. T., Conley, R. R., Buchanan, R. W., Breier, A., & Tamminga, C. A. (1995). Patient response and resource management: Another view of clozapine treatment of schizophrenia. *American Journal of Psychiatry, 152,* 827–832.

Carr, A. T. (1974). Compulsive neurosis: A review of the literature. *Psychological Bulletin, 81,* 311–318.

Carr, E. G. (1977). The motivation of self-injurious behavior: A review of some hypotheses. *Psychological Bulletin, 84,* 800–816.

Carr, J. (1994). Annotation: Long-term outcome for people with Down syndrome. *Journal of Child Psychology and Psychiatry, 35,* 425–439.

Carson, N. D., & Johnson, R. E. (1985). Suicidal thoughts and problem-solving preparation among college students. *Journal of College Student Personnel, 26,* 484–487.

Carson, R. C. (1991). Dilemmas in the pathway of the DSM-IV. *Journal of Abnormal Psychology, 100,* 302–307.

Carter, M. M., Hollon, S. D., Carson, R., & Shelton, R. C. (1995). Effects of a safe person on induced distress following a biological challenge in panic disorder with agoraphobia. *Journal of Abnormal Psychology, 104,* 156–163.

Cassileth, B. R., Lusk, E. J., Miller, D. S., Brown, L. L., & Miller, C. (1985). Psychosocial correlates of survival in advanced malignant disease? *New England Journal of Medicine, 312,* 1551–1555.

Castle, D. J., & Murray, R. M. (1993). The epidemiology of late-onset schizophrenia. *Schizophrenia Bulletin, 22,* 691–699.

Cautela, J. R. (1966). Treatment of compulsive behavior by covert sensitization. *Psychological Record, 16,* 33–41.

Cautela, J. R. (1967). Covert sensitization. *Psychological Reports, 20,* 459–468.

Centers for Disease Control (1981). *Morbidity and Mortality Weekly Report, 30,* 582.

Centers for Disease Control (1992, June 30). *HIV AIDS survey report.* Atlanta, GA: Author.

Cesaroni, L., & Garber, M. (1991). Exploring the experience of autism through firsthand accounts. *Journal of Autism and Developmental Disorders, 21,* 303–313.

Chadwick, P., & Birchwood, M. (1994). The omnipotence of voices: A cognitive approach to auditory hallucinations. *British Journal of Psychiatry, 164,* 190–201.

Chadwick, P. D. J., Lowe, C. F., Horne, P. J., & Higson, P. J. (1994). Modifying delusions: The role of empirical testing. *Behavior Therapy, 25,* 35–49.

Chaika, E. (1985). Crazy talk. *Psychology Today, 19,* 30–35.

Chambless, D. M. (1993). Division of Clinical Psychology. *Task force on promotion and dissemination of psychological procedures.* A report adopted by the Division 12 Board—October 1993. Unpublished document.

Chapey, R. (1994). Assessment of language disorders in adults. In R. Chapey (Ed.), *Language intervention strategies in adult aphasia* (pp. 80–120). Baltimore: Williams & Wilkins.

Chapman, L. J., & Chapman, J. P. (1967). Genesis of popular but erroneous psychodiagnostic observations. *Journal of Abnormal Psychology, 72,* 193–204.

Chassin, L. C., Pillow, D. R., Curran, P. J., Molina, B. S., & Berrera, M. (1993). Relation of parental alcoholism to early adolescent substance use: A test of three mediating mechanisms. *Journal of Abnormal Psychology, 102,* 3–19.

Chemtob, C. M., Hamada, R. S., Bauer, G., Torrigue, R. Y., & Kinney, B. (1988). Patient suicide: Frequency and impact on psychologists. *Professional Psychology: Research and Practice, 19*(4), 416–420.

Chesney, M. A. (1993). Health psychology in the twenty-first century: Acquired immunodeficiency syndrome as a harbinger of things to come. *Health Psychology, 12,* 259–268.

Chess, S. (1986). Commentary on the difficult child. *Pediatrics in Review, 8,* 35–37.

Chess, S., & Thomas, A. (1984). *Origins and evolution of behavior disorders.* New York: Brunner/Mazel.

Chodoff, P. (1987). Letters to the editor. *American Journal of Psychiatry, 144,* 124.

Chollar, S. (1988). Food for thought. *Psychology Today, 22,* 30–34.

Christensen, L., & Duncan, K. (1995). Distinguishing depressed from nondepressed individuals using energy and psychosocial variables. *Journal of Consulting and Clinical Psychology, 63,* 495–498.

Christison, G. W., Kirch, D. G. & Wyatt, R. J. (1991). When symptoms persist: Choosing among alternative somatic treatments for schizophrenia. *Schizophrenic Bulletin, 17,* 217–245.

Chua, S. E., & McKenna, P. J. (1995). Schizophrenia: A brain disease? A critical review of structural and functional cerebral abnormality in the disorder. *British Journal of Psychiatry, 166,* 563–582.

Chung, R., & Okazaki, S. (1991). Counseling Americans of Southeast Asian descent: The impact of the refugee experience. In C. C. Lee & B. L. Richardson (Eds.), *Multicultural issues in counseling: New approaches to diversity* (pp. 107–126). Alexandria, VA: American Association for Counseling and Development.

Cinciripini, P. M., Lapitsky, L., Seay, S., Wallfisch, A., Kitchens, K., & Van Vunakis, H. (1995). The effects of smoking schedules on cessation outcome: Can we improve on common methods of gradual and abrupt nicotine withdrawal? *Journal of Consulting and Clinical Psychology, 63,* 388–400.

Ciompi, L. (1980). Long-term study on the course of life and aging of schizophrenics. *Schizophrenia Bulletin, 6,* 606–618.

Clark, D. M. (1986). A cognitive approach to panic. *Behaviour Research and Therapy, 24,* 461–476.

Clark, M., Gosnell, M., Hager, M., Shapiro, D., Norris, E., & Gordon, J. (1988, Spring). Headaches: How to ease the pain. *Newsweek on Health,* pp. 12–21.

Clark, M., Gosnell, M., Witherspoon, J., Huck, J., Hager, M., Junkin, D., King, P., Wallace, A., & Robinson, T. (1984, December 3). A slow death of the mind. *Newsweek,* pp. 56–62.

Clarke, A. D. B., & Clarke, A. M. (1987). Research on mental handicap, 1957–1958: A selective review. *Journal of Mental Deficiency Research, 31,* 317–328.

Clarkin, J. F., Marziali, E., & Munroe-Blum, H. (1991). Group and family treatments for borderline personality disorder. *Hospital and Community Psychiatry, 42,* 1038–1043.

Cleckley, J. (1976). *The mask of sanity* (5th ed.). St. Louis, MO: Mosby.

Clementz, B. A., & Sweeney, J. A. (1990). Is eye movement dysfunction a biological marker for schizophrenia? A methodological review. *Psychological Bulletin, 108,* 77–92.

Clemmensen, L. H. (1990). The "real-life test" for surgical candidates. In R. Blanchard & B. W. Steiner (Eds.), *Clinical management of gender identity disorders in children and adults* (pp. 119–136). Washington, DC: American Psychiatric Press.

Clinthorne, J. K., Cisin, I. H., Balter, M. B., Mellinger, G. D., Uhlenhuth, E. H. (1986). Changes in popular attitudes and beliefs about tranquilizers: 1970–1979. *Archives of General Psychiatry, 43,* 527–532.

Cloitre, M., Shear, M. K., Cancienne, J., & Zeitlin, S. B. (1994). Implicit and explicit memory for catastrophic associations to bodily sensation words in panic disorder. *Cognitive Therapy and Research, 18,* 225–240.

Clomipramine Collaborative Study Group (1991). Clomipramine in the treatment of patients with obsessive-compulsive disorder. *Archives of General Psychiatry, 48,* 730–738.

Cloninger, C. R. (1991). D2 dopamine receptor gene is associated but not linked with alcoholism. *Journal of the American Medical Association, 266,* 1833–1834.

Cloninger, C. R., Reich, T., Sigvardsson, S., Von Knorring, A. L., & Bohman, M. (1986). The effects of changes in alcohol use between generations or the inheritance of alcohol abuse. In American Psychological Association (Ed.), *Alcoholism: A medical disorder: Proceedings of the 76th Annual Meeting of the American Psychological Association.*

Coffman, J. A. (1989). Computed tomography in psychiatry. In N. C. Andreasen (Ed.), *Brain imaging: Applications in psychiatry* (pp. 1–65). Washington, DC: American Psychiatric Press.

Cohen, A. M., & Weiner, W. J. (Eds.) (1994). *The comprehensive management of Parkinson's disease.* New York: Demos Publications.

Cohen, E. D. (1990). Confidentiality, counseling, and clients who have AIDS: Ethical foundations of a model rule. *Journal of counseling and development, 68,* 282–286.

Cohen, M. J., Rickles, W. H., & McArthur, D. L. (1978). Evidence for physiological response stereotypy in migraine headaches. *Psychosomatic Medicine, 40,* 344–354.

Cohen, S., & Williamson, G. M. (1991). Stress and infectious disease in humans. *Psychological Bulletin, 109,* 5–24.

Cohen, S. L., & Fiedler, J. E. (1974). Content analyses of multiple messages in suicide notes. *Life-Threatening Behavior, 4,* 75–95.

Cohn, L. D., Adler, N. E., Irwin, C. E., Jr., Millstein, S. G., Kegeles, S. M., & Stone, G. (1987). Body-figure preferences in male and female adolescents. *Journal of Abnormal Psychology, 96,* 276–279.

Cole, J. O., & Bodkin, J. A. (1990). Antidepressant drug side effects. *Journal of Clinical Psychiatry, 51,* 21–26.

Comas-Diaz, L., & Griffith, E. E. (Eds.). (1988). *Clinical guidelines in cross-cultural mental health.* New York: Wiley.

Comings, D. E., & Comings, B. G. (1987). Hereditary agoraphobia and obsessive-compulsive behaviour in relatives of patients with Gilles de la Tourette's syndrome. *British Journal of Psychiatry, 151,* 195–199.

Comings, D. E., Comings, B. G., Muhleman, G., Dietz, B., Shahbahrami, D., Task, D., Knell, E., Kocsis, P., Baumgarten, R., Kovacs, B. W., Levy, D. L., Smith, M., Borison, R. L., Evans, D. D., Klein, D. N., MacMurray, J., Toak, J., Sverd, J., Glysin, R., & Flanagan, S. D. (1991). The dopamine D2 receptor locus as a modifying gene in neuropsychiatric disorders. *Journal of the American Medical Association, 266,* 1793–1800.

Commander, M., Corbett, J., & Ridley, C. (1991). Reflect tics in two patients with Gilles de la Tourette syndrome. *British Journal of Psychiatry, 159,* 877–879.

Conger, J. J. (1951). The effects of alcohol on conflict behavior in the albino rat. *Quarterly Journal of Studies on Alcohol, 12,* 1–30.

Conn, D. K. (1991). Delirium and other organic mental disorders. In J. Sadavoy, L. W. Lazarus, & L. F. Jarvik (Eds.), *Comprehensive review of geriatric psychiatry* (pp. 11–336). Washington, DC: American Psychiatric Press.

Conners, M. E., & Morse, W. (1993). Sexual abuse and eating disorders: A review. *International Journal of Eating Disorders, 13,* 1–11.

Consensus Development Panel. (1982). Defined diets and childhood hyperactivity. *Clinical Pediatrics, 21,* 627–630.

Cook, E. W., III, Hodes, R. L., & Lang, P. J. (1986). Preparedness and phobia: Effects of stimulus content on human visceral conditioning. *Journal of Abnormal Psychology, 95,* 195–207.

Coons, P. M. (1986). Treatment progress in twenty patients with multiple personality disorder. *Journal of Nervous and Mental Disease, 174,* 715–721.

Coons, P. M. (1988). Misuse of forensic hypnosis: A hypnotically elicited false confession with the apparent creation of a multiple personality. *International Journal of Clinical and Experimental Hypnosis, 36,* 1–11.

Coons, P. M. (1994). Confirmation of childhood abuse in child and adolescent cases of multiple personality disorder and dissociative disorder not otherwise specified. *Journal of Nervous and Mental Disease, 182,* 461–464.

Coons, P. M., & Bowman, E. S. (1993). Dissociation and eating. *American Journal of Psychiatry, 150,* 171–172.

Coons, P. M., & Bradley, K. (1985). Group psychotherapy with multiple personality patients. *Journal of Nervous and Mental Diseases, 173,* 515–521.

Coons, P. M., Milstein, V., & Marley, C. (1982). EEG studies of two multiple personalities and a control. *Archives of General Psychiatry, 39,* 823–825.

Cooper, A., & McCormack, W. A. (1992). Short-term group treatment for adult children of alcoholics. *Journal of Counseling Psychology, 39,* 350–355.

Cooper, A. J. (1969). A clinical study of coital anxiety in male potency disorders. *Journal of Psychosomatic Research, 13,* 143–147.

Cooper, J. E., Kendell, R. E., Gurland, B. J., Sharp, L., Copeland, J. R. M., & Simon, R. (1972). *Psychiatric diagnosis in New York and London.* Maudsley Monograph Series No. 20. London: Oxford University Press.

Cooper, J. R., Bloom, F. E., & Roth, R. H. (1986). *The biochemical basis of neuropharmacology* (5th ed.). New York: Oxford University Press.

Cooper, M. J., & Fairburn, C. G. (1992). Thoughts about eating, weight and shape in anorexia nervosa and bulimia nervosa. *Behaviour Research and Therapy, 30,* 501–511.

Cooper, M. L., Russell, M., & George, W. H. (1988). Coping, expectancies, and alcohol abuse: A test of social learning formulations. *Journal of Abnormal Psychology, 97,* 218–230.

Corbett, J. A. (1971). The nature of tics and Gilles de la Tourette's syndrome. *Journal of Psychosomatic Research, 15,* 32.

Corey, G. (1991). *Theory and practice of counseling and psychotherapy.* Pacific Grove, CA: Brooks/Cole.

Corey, G. (1995). *Theory and practice of counseling and psychotherapy* (5th ed.). Pacific Grove, CA: Brooks/Cole.

Corey, G. (1996). *Theory and practice of counseling and psychotherapy.* Pacific Grove, CA: Brooks/Cole.

Corey, G., Corey, M. S., & Callanan, P. (1993). *Issues and ethics in the helping professions* (3rd ed.). Pacific Grove, CA: Brooks/Cole.

Corlis, R., & Rabe, P. (1969). *Psychotherapy from the center: A humanistic view of change and of growth.* Scranton, PA: International Textbook.

Cosand, B. J., Bourque, L. B., & Kraus, J. F. (1982). Suicide among adolescents in Sacramento County, California 1950–1979. *Adolescence, 17,* 917–930.

Cottone, R. R. (1992). *Theories and paradigms of counseling and psychotherapy.* Boston: Allyn & Bacon.

Council on Scientific Affairs (1985). Scientific status of refreshing recollection by the use of hypnosis. *Journal of the American Medical Association, 253,* 1918–1923.

Courchesne, E. (1995). New evidence of cerebellar and brainstem hypoplasia in autistic infants, children, and adolescents: The MR imaging study by Hashimoto and colleagues. *Journal of Autism and Developmental Disorders, 25,* 19–22.

Courchesne, I., Yeung-Courchesne, R., Press, G. A., Hesselink, J. R., & Jernigan, T. L. (1988). Hypoplasia of cerebellar vermal lobules VI and VII in autism. *New England Journal of Medicine, 318,* 1349–1354.

Coursey, R. D., Keller, A. B., & Farrell, E. W. (1995). Individual psychotherapy and persons with serious mental illness: The clients' perspective. *Schizophrenia Bulletin, 21,* 283–299.

Cowart, V. S. (1988). The ritalin controversy: What made this drug's opponents hyperactive. *Journal of the American Medical Association, 259,* 2521–2523.

Cowen, E. L. (1983). Primary prevention in mental health: Past, present, and future. In R. D. Felner, L. A. Jason, J. N. Moritsugu, & S. S. Farber (Eds.), *Preventive psychology: Theory, research and practice.* New York: Pergamon Press.

Cowley, G. (1990, February 12). Hanging up the knife. *Newsweek,* pp. 58–59.

Cowley, G. (1995). Blind to other minds. *Newsweek,* August 14, p. 67

Cox, B. J., Fergus, K. D., & Swinson, R. P. (1994). Patient satisfaction with behavioral treatments for panic disorder with agoraphobia. *Journal of Anxiety Disorders, 8,* 193–206.

Cox, D. J., & McMahon, B. (1978). Incidence of male exhibitionism in the United States as reported by victimized college students. *International Journal of Law and Psychiatry, 1,* 453–457.

Cox, W. J., & Kenardy, J. (1993). Performance anxiety, social phobia, and setting effects in instrumental music students. *Journal of Anxiety Disorders, 7,* 49–60.

Cox, W. M., & Klinger, E. (1988). A motivational model of alcohol use. *Journal of Abnormal Psychology, 97,* 168–180.

Coyne, J. C. (1976). Depression and the response of others. *Journal of Abnormal Psychology, 85,* 186–193.

Craig, M. E. (1990). Coercive sexuality in dating relationships: A situational model. *Clinical Psychology Review, 10,* 395–424.

Craig, T. K. J., Boardman, A. P., Mills, K., Daly-Jones, O., & Drake, H. (1993). The South London Somatizing Study I: Longitudinal course and the influence of early life experiences. *British Journal of Psychiatry, 163,* 579–588.

Craig, T. K. J., Drake, H., Mills, K., & Boardman, A. P. (1994). The South London Somatizing Study II: Influence of stressful life events and secondary gain. *British Journal of Psychiatry, 165,* 248–258.

Craik, F. I. (1994). Memory changes in normal aging. *Current Directions in Psychological Science, 3,* 155–158.

Crandall, C. S., Preisler, J. J., & Aussprung, J. (1992). Measuring life event stress in the lives of college students: The Undergraduate Stress Questionnaire (USQ). *Journal of Behavioral Medicine, 15,* 627–662.

Craske, M. G. (1991). Phobic fear and panic attacks: The same emotional states triggered by different cues? *Clinical Psychology Review, 11,* 599–620.

Craske, M. G., Glover, D., & DeCola, J. (1995). Predicted versus unpredicted panic attacks: Acute versus general distress. *Journal of Abnormal Psychology, 104,* 214–223.

Craufurd, D. (1994). Molecular biology of Huntington's Disease. In F. Owen & R. Itzhaki (Eds.), *Molecular and cell biology of neuropsychiatric diseases* (pp. 1–24). New York: Chapman and Hall.

Crowe, R. R., Noyes, R., Jr., Pauls, D. L., & Slymen, D. (1983). A family study of panic disorder. *Archives of General Psychiatry, 40,* 1065–1069.

Crowson, J. J., & Cromwell, R. L. (1995). Depressed and normal individuals differ both in selection and in perceived tonal quality of positive-negative messages. *Journal of Abnormal Psychology, 104,* 305–311.

Cummings, N. A. (1995). Behavioral health after managed care: The next golden opportunity for professional psychology. *Register Report, 20,* 1, 30–33.

Curnan, J. W., Jaffe, H. W., Hardy, A. M., Morgan, W. M., Selik, R. M., & Dondero, J. (1990). Epidemiology of HIV infection and AIDS in the United States. In M. C. McClellan (Ed.), *AIDS education* (pp. 23–29). New York: Center on Evaluation, Development and Research, Phi Delta Kappa.

Curtis, G. C. (1981). Sensory experiences during treatment of phobias by in vivo exposure. *American Journal of Psychiatry, 138,* 1095–1097.

Cutts, T. F., & Barrios, B. A. (1986). Fear of weight gain among bulimic and nondisturbed females. *Behavior Therapy, 17,* 626–636.

Cypress, B. K. (1980). *Characteristics of visits to female and male physicians: The national ambulatory medical care survey, 1977.* Hyattsville, MD: National Center for Health Statistics.

Dahlstrom, W. G., & Welsh, G. S. (1965). *An MMPI handbook.* Minneapolis: University of Minnesota Press.

Danto, B. L. (1971, Fall). Assessment of the suicidal person in the telephone interview. *Bulletin of Suicidology,* 48–56.

Darrach, D. (1976, March 8). Poetry and poison. *Time.*

Darrow, W. W., Echenberg, D. F., Jaffe, H. W. (1987). Risk factors for human immunodeficiency virus infections in homosexual men. *American Journal of Public Health, 77,* 479–483.

Darwin, C. (1859). *On the origin of species by means of natural selection.* London: Murray.

Dassori, A. M., Miller, A. L., & Saldana, D. (1995). Schizophrenia among Hispanics: Epidemiology, phenomenology, course, and outcome. *Schizophrenia Bulletin, 21,* 303–310.

Davey, G. C. L., Forster, L., & Mayhew, G. (1993). Familial resemblances in disgust sensitivity and animal phobias. *Behaviour Research and Therapy, 31,* 41–50.

Davidson, J., Allen, J. G., & Smith W. H. (1987). Complexities in the hospital treatment of a patient with multiple personality disorder. *Bulletin of the Menninger Clinic, 51,* 561–568.

Davidson, J. R. T., & Foa, E. B. (1991). Diagnostic issues in the posttraumatic stress disorder: Considerations for DSM-IV. *Journal of Abnormal Psychology, 100,* 346–355.

Davis, J. D. (1983). Slaying the psychoanalytic dragon: An integrationist's commentary on Yates. *British Journal of Clinical Psychology, 22,* 133–134.

Davis, J. M. (1985). Suicidal crisis in schools. *School Psychology Review, 14,* 313–324.

Davis, K. L., Kahn, R. S., & Ko, G. (1991). Dopamine in schizophrenia: A review and reconceptualization, *American Journal of Psychiatry, 148,* 1474–1486.

Davis, M. C., Mathews, K. A., Meilahn, E. N., & Kiss, J. E. (1995). Are job characteristics related to fibrinogen levels in middle-aged women? *Health Psychology, 14,* 310–318.

Davison, G. C., Williams, M. E., Nezami, E., Bice, T. L., & DeQuattro, V. (1991). Relaxation, reduction in angry articulated thoughts, and improvements in borderline essential hypertension and heart rate. *Journal of Behavioral Medicine, 14,* 453–468.

de Gobineau, A. (1915). *The inequality of human races.* New York: Putnam.

De La Fuente, R. (1990). The mental health consequences of the 1985 earthquakes in Mexico. *International Journal of Mental Health, 19,* 21–29.

De Zwaan, M., & Mitchell, J. E. (1992). Medical complications of anorexia nervosa and bulimia nervosa. In A. S. Kaplan & P. E. Garfinkel (Eds.), *Medical issues and the eating disorders* (pp. 60–100). New York: Brunner/Mazel.

Dekker, J. (1993). Inhibited male orgasm. In W. O'Donohue & J. H. Geer (Eds.), *Handbook of sexual dysfunctions: Assessment and treatment* (pp. 279–301). Boston: Allyn & Bacon.

Denicola, J., & Sandler, J. (1980). Training abusive parents in child management and self-control skills. *Behavior Therapy, 11,* 263–270.

Denkowski, K. M., & Denkowski, G. C. (1982). Client-counselor confidentiality: An update of rationale, legal status, and implications. *Personnel and Guidance Journal, 60,* 371–375.

Dent, C. W., Sussman, S., Stacy, A. W., Craig, S., Burton, D., & Flay, B. R. (1995). Two-year behavior outcomes of Project Towards No Tobacco Use. *Journal of Consulting and Clinical Psychology, 63,* 676–677.

Dent, J., & Teasdale, J. D. (1988). Negative cognition and the persistence of depression. *Journal of Abnormal Psychology, 97(1),* 29–34.

DeSilva, P. (1988). Phobias and preparedness: Replication and extension. *Behaviour Research and Therapy, 26,* 97–98.

Desmond, S., Price, J., Hallinan, C., & Smith, D. (1989). Black and White adolescents' perceptions of their weight. *Journal of School Health, 59,* 353–358.

Detels, R., English, P., Visscher, B. R., (1989). Seroconversion, sexual activity, and condom use among 2915 sero-negative men followed for up to 2 years. *Journal of AIDS, 2,* 77–83.

Deutsch, A. (1949). *The mentally ill in America* (2nd ed.). New York: Columbia University Press.

DeVellis, B. M., & Blalock, S. J. (1992). Illness attributions and hopelessness depression: The role of hopelessness expectancy. *Journal of Abnormal Psychology, 101(2),* 257–264.

Devinsky, O. (1994). *A guide to understanding and living with epilepsy.* Philadelphia: F. A. Davis.

Dewsbury, D. A. (1991). Psychobiology. *American Psychologist, 46,* 198–205.

Dick-Barnes, M., Nelson, R. O., & Aine, C. J. (1987). Behavioral measure of multiple personality: The case of Margaret. *Journal of Behavior Therapy and Experimental Psychiatry, 18,* 229–239.

Dickey, R., & Steiner, B. (1990). Hormone treatment and surgery. In R. Blanchard & B. W. Steiner (Eds.), *Clinical management of gender identity disorders in children and adults* (pp. 137–158). Washington, DC: American Psychiatric Press.

Diekstra, R. F. (1990). Suicidal behavior in adolescents and young adults: The international picture. *Crisis, 10,* 16–35.

DiLalla, D. L., & Gottesman, I. I. (1995). Normal personality characteristics of identical twins discordant for schizophrenia. *Journal of Abnormal Psychology, 104,* 490–499.

Diokno, A. C., Brown, M. B., & Herzog, A. R. (1990). Sexual function in the elderly. *Archives of Internal Medicine, 150,* 197–200.

Dodrill, C. B., & Matthews, C. G. (1992). The role of neuropsychology in the assessment and treatment of persons with epilepsy. *American Psychologist, 47,* 1139–1142.

Dohrenwend, B. P., & Dohrenwend, B. S. (1982). Perspectives on the past and future of psychiatric epidemiology: The 1981 Rema Lapouse Lecture. *American Journal of Public Health, 72,* 1271–1279.

Dohrenwend, B. P., Dohrenwend, B. S., Gould, M. S., Link, B., Neugebauer, R., & Wunsch-Hitzig, R. (1980). *Mental illness in the United States: Epidemiological estimates.* New York: Praeger.

Dolan, B. (1991). Cross-cultural aspects of anorexia nervosa and bulimia: A review. *International Journal of Eating Disorders, 10,* 67–69.

Dollinger, S. J. (1983). A case of dissociative neurosis (depersonalization disorder) in an adolescent treated with family therapy and behavior modification. *Journal of Consulting and Clinical Psychology, 15,* 479–484.

Domb, Y., & Beaman, K. (1991). Mr. X—A case of amnesia. *British Journal of Psychiatry, 158,* 423–425.

Donenberg, G., & Baker, B. L. (1993). The impact of young children with externalizing behaviors on their families. *Journal of Abnormal Child Psychology, 21,* 179–198.

Dong, Q., Yang, B., & Ollendick, T. H. (1994). Fears in Chinese children and adolescents and their relations to anxiety and depression. *Journal of Child Psychology and Psychiatry, 35,* 351–363.

Donnerstein, E., & Linz, D. (1986). Mass media sexual violence and male viewers. *American Behavioral Scientist, 29,* 601–618.

Dorfman, D. D. (1978). The Cyril Burt question: New findings. *Science, 201,* 1177–1186.

Dorken, H., Stapp, J., & VandenBos, G. (1986). Licensed psychologists: A decade of major growth. In H. Dorken & Associates (Eds.), *Professional psychology in transition: Meeting today's challenge* (pp. 3–19). San Francisco: Jossey-Bass.

Douce, L. A. (1993). AIDS and HIV: Hopes and challenges for the 1990s. *Journal for Counseling and Development, 71,* 259–260.

Draguns, J. G. (1985). Psychological disorders across cultures. In P. Pedersen (Ed.), *Handbook of cross-cultural counseling and therapy.* Westport, CT: Greenwood Press.

Drake, R. E., & Ehrlich, J. (1985). Suicide attempts associated with akathisia. *American Journal of Psychiatry, 142,* 499–501.

Dressler, W. W., Dos Santos, J. E., & Viteri, F. E. (1986). Blood pressure, ethnicity, and psychosocial resources. *Psychosomatic Medicine, 48,* 509–519.

Drewnowski, A., Yee, D. K., & Krahn, D. D. (1988). Bulimia in college women: Incidence and recovery rates. *American Journal of Psychiatry, 145,* 753–755.

Drummond, L. M., & Matthews, H. P. (1988). Obsessive-compulsive disorder occurring as a complication in benzodiazepine withdrawal. *Journal of Nervous and Mental Disease, 176,* 688–691.

Dryden, W. (1989). Albert Ellis: An efficient and passionate life (an interview with Albert Ellis). *Journal of Counseling and Development, 67,* 539–546.

Du Verglas, G., Banks, S. R., & Guyer, K. E. (1988). Clinical effects of fenfluramine on children with autism: A review of the research. *Journal of Autism and Developmental Disorders, 18,* 297–308.

Dubovsky, S., Franks, R., Lifschitz, M., & Coen, R. (1982). Effectiveness of verapamil in the treatment of a manic patient. *American Journal of Psychiatry, 139,* 502–504.

Duckett, S. (1991). The normal aging human brain. In S. Duckett (Ed.), *The pathology of the aging human nervous system* (pp. 1–19). Philadelphia: Lea & Febiger.

DuPaul, G. J., & Barkely, R. A. (1993). Behavioral contributions to psychopharmacology: The utility of behavioral methodology in medication treatment of children with attention deficit hyperactivity disorder. *Behavior Therapy, 24,* 47–65.

Durkheim, E. (1951). *Suicide.* New York: Free Press. (Originally published 1897.)

Dutton, J. (1986, September 30). Doctors seek reason for bizarre syndrome. *Bellingham Herald,* p. C1.

Dworkin, S. H., & Pincu, L. (1993). Counseling in the era of AIDS. *Journal of Counseling and Development, 71,* 275–281.

Eaton, W. W., Dryman, A., & Weissman, M. M. (1991). Panic and phobia. In L. N. Robins & D. A. Regier (Eds.), *Psychiatric disorders in America: The Epidemiologic Catchment Area study* (pp. 155–179). New York: Free Press.

Eaton, W. W., Holzer, C. E., III, Von Korff, M., Anthony, J. C., Helzer, J. E., George, L., Brunam, A., Boyd, J. H., Kessler, L. G., & Locker, B. Z. (1984). The design of the Epidemiologic Catchment Area surveys. *Archives of General Psychiatry, 41,* 942–948.

Eberlin, M., McConnachie, G., Ibel, S., & Volpe, L. (1993). Facilitated communication: A failure to replicate the phenomenon. *Journal of Autism and Developmental Disorders, 23,* 507–530.

Edelson, J. L., Miller, D. M., Stone, G. W., & Chapman, D. G. (1985). Group treatment for men who batter. *Social Work Research and Abstracts, 21,* 18–21.

Edman, G., Asberg, M., Levander, S., & Schalling, D. (1986). Skin conductance habituation and cerebrospinal fluid 5-hydroxyindoleactic acid in suicidal patients. *Archives of General Psychiatry, 43,* 586–592.

Edwards, M. S., & Baker, C. J. (1981). Meningitis infections in children. *Journal of Pediatrics, 99,* 540–545.

Edwards, S., & Dickerson, M. (1987). On the similarity of positive and negative intrusions. *Behaviour Research and Therapy, 25,* 207–211.

Efron, R. (1956). The effect of olfactory stimuli in arresting uncinate fits. *Brain, 79,* 267–281.

Efron, R. (1957). The conditioned inhibitions of uncinate fits. *Brain, 80,* 251–262.

Egeland, J. A., Berhard, D. S., Pauls, D. L., Sussex, J. N., Kidd, K. K., Allen, C. R., Hostetter, A. M., & Housman, D. E. (1987). Bipolar affective disorders linked to DNA markers on chromosome 11. *Nature, 325,* 783–787.

Egeland, J. A., & Hostetter, A. M. (1983). Amish study, I: Affective disorders among the Amish. *American Journal of Psychiatry, 140,* 56–61.

Ehlers, A., Margraf, J., Roth, W. T., Taylor, C. G., & Birbaumer, N. (1988). Anxiety induced by false heart rate feedback in patients with panic disorder. *Behaviour Research and Therapy, 26,* 1–11.

Eisenberg, M. M. (1978). *Ulcers.* New York: Random House.

Eisenberg, M. M. (1989). *Ulcers.* New York: Random House.

Ekblad, S. (1990). The children's behaviour questionnaire for completion by parents and teachers in a Chinese sample. *Journal of Child Psychology and Psychiatry, 31,* 775–791.

Elias, M. (1988, August 15). Many lie about AIDS risk. *USA Today,* p. D–1.

Elkin, I. (1994). The NIMH Treatment of Depression Collaborative Research Program: Where we began and where we are. In A. E. Bergin & S. L. Garfield (Eds.), *Handbook of psychotherapy and behavior change* (4th ed., pp. 114–142). New York: Wiley.

Elkin, I., Gibbons, R. D., Shea, M. T., Sotsky, S. M., Watkins, J. T., Pilkonis, P. A., & Hedeker, D. (1995). Initial severity and differential treatment outcome in the National Institute of Mental Health Treatment of Depression Collaborative Research Program. *Journal of Consulting and Clinical Psychology, 63,* 841–847.

Ellason, J. W., & Ross, C. A. (1995). Positive and negative symptoms in dissociative identity disorder and schizophrenia: A comparative analysis. *Journal of Nervous and Mental Disease, 183,* 236–241.

Ellenberger, H. F. (1972). The story of "Anna O.": A critical review with new data. *Journal of the History of the Behavior Sciences, 8,* 267–279.

Ellickson, P. L., Hays, R. D., & Bell, R. M. (1992). Stepping through the drug use sequence: Longitudinal scalogram analysis of initiation and regular use. *Journal of Abnormal Psychology, 101,* 441–451.

Ellingson, R. (1954). Incidence of EEG abnormality among patients with mental disorders of apparently nonorganic origin: A critical review. *American Journal of Psychiatry, 111,* 363–375.

Elliott, C. H., & Jay, S. M. (1987). Chronic pain in children. *Behaviour Research and Therapy, 25,* 263–271.

Ellis, A. (1962). *Reason and emotion in psychotherapy.* New York: Stuart.

Ellis, A. (1971). *Growth through reason.* Palo Alto, CA: Science and Behavior Books.

Ellis, A. (1973). Are cognitive behavior therapy and rational therapy synonymous? *Rational Living, 8,* 8–11.

Ellis, A. (1979). Rational-emotive therapy: Research data that support the clinical and personality hypotheses of RET and other modes of cognitive-behavior therapy. In A. Ellis & J. M. Whiteley (Eds.), *Theoretical and empirical foundations of rational emotive therapy* (pp. 101–173). Monterey, CA: Brooks/Cole.

Ellis, A. (1984). Rational-emotive therapy. In R. J. Corsini (Ed.), *Current psychotherapies*. Itasca, IL: Peacock.

Ellis, A. (1987). A sadly neglected cognitive element in depression. *Cognitive Therapy and Research, 11,* 121–146.

Ellis, A. (1989). Rational-emotive therapy. In R. J. Corsini & D. Wedding (Eds.), *Current psychotherapies* (pp. 197–238). Itasca, IL: Peacock.

Ellis, A. (1991). Rational-emotive treatment of simple phobias. *Psychotherapy, 28,* 452–456.

Ellis, L., & Ames, M. A. (1987). Neurohormonal functioning and sexual orientation: A theory of homosexuality-heterosexuality. *Psychological Bulletin, 101,* 233–258.

Ely, D. L., & Mostardi, R. A. (1986). The effects of recent life events stress, life assets, and temperament pattern on cardiovascular risk factors for Akron city police officers. *Journal of Human Stress, 12,* 77–91.

Embry, C. (1990). Psychotherapeutic interventions in chronic posttraumatic stress disorder. In M. E. Wolf & A. D. Mosmain (Eds.), *Posttraumatic stress disorder: Etiology, phenomenology and treatment.* Washington, DC: American Psychiatric Press.

Emmelkamp, P. M. (1994). Behavior therapy with adults. In A. E. Bergin & S. L. Garfield (Eds.), *Handbook of psychotherapy and behavior change* (pp. 379–427). New York: Wiley.

Emmelkamp, P. M. G., and Beens, H. (1991). Cognitive therapy with obsessive-compulsive disorder: A comparative evaluation. *Behaviour Research and Therapy, 29,* 293–300.

Emslie, G. J., & Rosenfeld, A. (1983). Incest reported by children and adolescents hospitalized for severe psychiatric problems. *American Journal of Psychiatry, 140,* 108–111.

Endler, N. (1982). *Holiday of darkness.* New York: Wiley.

Endler, N. (1990). *Holiday of darkness: A psychologist's journey out of his depression* (rev. ed.). Toronto: Wall & Thompson.

Enright, M. F., Welch, B. L., Newman, R., & Perry, B. M. (1990). The hospital: Psychology's challenge in the 1990s. *American Psychologist, 45,* 1057–1058.

Epilepsy Foundation of America (1983). *Questions and answers about epilepsy.* Landover, MD: Epilepsy Foundation of America.

Erickson, W. D., Luxenberg, M. G., Walbek, N. H., & Seely, R. K. (1987). Frequency of MMPI two-point code types among sex offenders. *Journal of Consulting and Clinical Psychology, 55,* 566–570.

Erickson, W. D., Walbek, N. H., & Seely, R. K. (1988). Behavior patterns of child molesters. *Archives of Sexual Behavior, 17,* 77–86.

Ericksson, A. S., & Chateau, P. (1992). Brief report: A girl aged two years and seven months with autistic disorder videotaped from birth. *Journal of Autism and Developmental Disorders, 22,* 127–129.

Erikson, E. H. (1968). *Identity: Youth and crisis.* New York: Norton.

Erwin, E. (1986). Establishing causal connections: Meta-analysis and psychotherapy. *Midwest Studies in Philosophy, 9,* 421–436.

Esman, A. H. (1994). Child abuse and multiple personality disorder. *American Journal of Psychiatry, 151,* 948.

Essen-Möller, E. (1970). Twenty-one psychiatric cases and their MZ co-twins: A thirty years' follow-up. *Acta Geneticae Medicae et Gemellologiae, 19,* 315–317.

Esser, G., Schmidt, M. H., & Woerner, W. (1990). Epidemiology and course of psychiatric disorders in school-age children: Results of a longitudinal study. *Journal of Child Psychology and Psychiatry, 31,* 243–263.

Eth, S., & Pynoos, R. S. (1985). Developmental perspective on psychic trauma in childhood. In C. R. Figley (Ed.), *Trauma and its wake* (pp. 36–52). New York: Brunner/Mazel.

European Study Group on Heterosexual Transmission of HIV. (1992). Comparison of female to male and male to female transmission of HIV in 563 stable couples. *British Medical Journal, 304,* 809–813.

Everstine, D. S., & Everstine, L. (1983). *People in crisis: Strategic therapeutic interventions.* New York: Brunner/Mazel.

Exner, J. E. (1983). Rorschach assessment. In I. B. Weiner (Ed.), *Clinical methods in psychology.* New York: Wiley.

Exner, J. E. (1990). *A Rorschach workbook for the Comprehensive System* (2nd ed.). Asheville, NC: Rorschach Workshops.

Eysenck, H. J. (1952). The effects of psychotherapy: An evaluation. *Journal of Consulting Psychology, 16,* 319–324.

Eysenck, H. J. (1957). *Dynamics of anxiety and hysteria.* London: Routledge & Kegan Paul.

Eysenck, H. J., & Rachman, S. (1965). *The causes and cures of neurosis.* San Diego: Knapp.

Fagan, J., & McMahon, P. P. (1984). Incipient multiple personality in children: Four cases. *Journal of Nervous and Mental Disease, 172,* 26–36.

Fainaru, S. (1996, January 29). Ali shares his greatness with Cubans. *Boston Globe,* p. 2.

Fairburn, C. G., Jones, R., Peveler, R. C., Carr, S. J., Solomon, R. A., O'Connor, M. E., Burton, J., & Hope, R. A. (1991). Three psychological treatments for bulimia nervosa: A comparative trial. *Archives of General Psychiatry, 48,* 463–469.

Fairburn, C. G., Norman, P. A., Welch, S. L., O'Connor, M. E., Doll, H. A., & Peveler, R. C. (1995). A prospective study of bulimia nervosa and the long-term effects of three psychological treatments. *Archives of General Psychiatry, 52,* 304–312.

Fallon, A. E., & Rozin, P. (1985). Sex differences in perceptions of desirable body shape. *Journal of Abnormal Psychology, 94,* 102–105.

Falloon, I. R. H. (1992). Early intervention for first episodes of schizophrenia: A preliminary exploration. *Psychiatry, 55,* 4–15.

Falloon, I. R. J., Boyd, J. L., & McGill, C. W. (1984). *Family care of schizophrenia.* New York: Guilford Press.

Faraone, S. V., Kremen, W. S., Lyons, M. J., Pepple, J. R., Seidman, L. J., & Tsuang, M. T. (1995). Diagnostic accuracy and linkage analysis: How useful are schizophrenia spectrum phenotypes? *American Journal of Psychiatry, 152,* 1286–1290.

Faraone, S. V., Kremen, W. S., & Tsuang, M. T. (1990). Genetic transmission of affective disorders: Quantitative models and linkage analysis. *Psychological Bulletin, 108,* 109–127.

Farberow, N. L. (1970). Ten years of suicide prevention—Past and future. *Bulletin of Suicidology, 6,* 5–11.

Farberow, N. L., & Simon, M. D. (1975). Suicide in Los Angeles and Vienna. In N. L. Farberow (Ed.), *Suicide in different cultures* (pp. 185–204). Baltimore: University Park Press.

Farley, F. (1986). World of the type T personality. *Psychology Today, 20,* 45–52.

Farmer, E. M. Z. (1995). Extremity of externalizing behavior and young adult outcomes. *Journal of Child Psychology and Psychiatry, 36,* 617–632.

Farrell, A. D., Stiles-Camplair, P., & McCullough, L. (1987). Identification of target complaints by computer interview: Evaluation of the computerized assessment system for psychotherapy evaluation research. *Journal of Consulting and Clinical Psychology, 55,* 691–700.

Fauman, M. A. (1994). *Study guide to DSM-IV.* Washington, DC: American Psychiatric Press.

Fava, G. A., Zielezny, M., Savron, G., Grandi, S. (1995). The long-term behavioral treatment for panic disorder with agoraphobia. *British Journal of Psychiatry, 166,* 87–92.

Federal Bureau of Investigation (1991). *Uniform crime reports.* Washington, DC: U.S. Department of Justice.

Fedora, O., Reddon, J. R., & Yeudall, L. T. (1986). Stimuli eliciting sexual arousal in genital exhibitionists as possible clinical application. *Archives of Sexual Behavior, 15,* 417–427.

Feingold, B. F. (1977). Behavioral disturbances linked to the ingestion of food additives. *Delaware Medical Journal, 49,* 89–94.

Feldman, R. G., Mosbach, P., Thomas, C., & Perry, L. M. (1994). Psychosocial factors in the treatment of Parkinson's disease: A contextual approach. In A. M. Cohen & W. J. Weiner (Eds.), *The comprehensive management of Parkinson's disease* (pp. 193–208). New York: Demos Publications.

Feldman-Summers, S., Gordon, P. E., & Meagher, J. R. (1979). The impact of rape on sexual satisfaction. *Journal of Abnormal Psychology, 88,* 101–105.

Feldman-Summers, S., & Pope, K. S. (1994). The experience of "forgetting" childhood abuse: A national survey of psychologists. *Journal of Consulting and Clinical Psychology, 62,* 636–639.

Felner, R. D., Jason, L. A., Moritsugu, J., & Farber, S. S. (1983). Preventive psychology: Evolution and current status. In R. D. Felner & L. A. Jason (Eds.), *Preventive psychology: Theory, research and practice.* New York: Pergamon Press.

Fenichel, O. (1945). *The psychoanalytic theory of neuroses.* New York: Norton.

Fenton, W. S., & McGlashan, T. H. (1987). Sustained remission in drug-free schizophrenic patients. *American Journal of Psychiatry, 144,* 1306–1309.

Fergusson, D. M., Horwood, L. J., & Lynskey, M. T. (1995). The stability of disruptive childhood behaviors. *Journal of Abnormal Child Psychology, 23,* 379–396.

Ferster, C. B. (1965). Classification of behavior pathology. In L. Krasner & L. P. Ullman (Eds.), *Research in behavior modification.* New York: Holt, Rinehart & Winston.

Fieve, R., Dunner, D., Kumbaraci, et al. (1976). Lithium carbonate prophylaxis in three subtypes of primary affective disorder. *Pharmakopsychiatri Neuropsychopharmakol, 9,* 100–107.

Figley, C. R. (Ed.). (1985). *Trauma and its wake* (pp. 53–69). New York: Brunner/Mazel.

Fink, M. (1982). ECT in anxiety: An appraisal. *American Journal of Psychotherapy, 36,* 371–378.

Finkelhor, D. (1980). Sex among siblings: A survey on prevalence, variety, and effects. *Archives of Sexual Behavior, 9,* 171–194.

Finkelhor, D., & Araji, S. (1986). Explanations of pedophilia: A four-factor model. *Journal of Sex Research, 22,* 145–161.

Fischer, D. G., & Elnitsky, S. (1990). A factor analytic study of two scales measuring dissociation. *American Journal of Clinical Hypnosis, 32,* 201–207.

Fischer, M. (1973). Genetic and environmental factors in schizophrenia: A study of schizophrenic twins and their families. *Acta Psychiatrica Scandinavica,* Supplement 238.

Fischer, M., & Newby, R. F. (1991). Assessment of stimulant response in ADHD children using a refined multimethod clinical protocol. *Journal of Clinical Child Psychology, 20,* 232–244.

Fischer, P. J., & Breakey, W. R. (1991). The epidemiology of alcohol, drug, and mental disorders among homeless persons. *American Psychologist, 46,* 1115–1128.

Fisher, J. E., & Carstensen, L. L. (1990). Behavior management of the dementias. *Clinical Psychology Review, 10,* 611–629.

Fishman, S. M., & Sheehan, D. V. (1985). Anxiety and panic: Their cause and treatment. *Psychology Today, 19,* 26–32.

Fitts, S. N., Gibson, P., Redding, C. A., & Deiter, P. J. (1989). Body dysmorphic disorder: Implications for its validity as a DSM-III-R clinical syndrome. *Psychological Reports, 64,* 655–658.

Fleer, J., & Pasewark, R. A. (1982). Prior public health agency contacts of individuals committing suicide. *Psychological Reports, 50,* 1319–1324.

Fleming, I., Baum, A., Davidson, L. M., Rectanus, E., & McArdle, S. (1987). Chronic stress as a factor in physiologic reactivity to challenge. *Health Psychology, 6,* 221–237.

Fleming, M. Z., MacGowan, B. R., Robinson, L., Spitz, J., & Salt, P. (1982). The body image of the post-operative female-to-male transsexual. *Journal of Consulting and Clinical Psychology, 50,* 461–462.

Foa, E. B., & Kozak, M. J. (1986). Emotional processing of fear: Exposure to corrective information. *Psychological Bulletin, 99,* 20–35.

Foa, E. B., & Kozak, M. J. (1995). DSM-IV field trial: Obsessive-compulsive disorder. *American Journal of Psychiatry, 152,* 90–96.

Foa, E. B., Rothbaum, B. O., Riggs, D. S., & Murdock, T. B. (1991). Treatment of posttraumatic stress disorder in rape victims: A comparison between cognitive-behavioral procedures and counseling. *Journal of Consulting and Clinical Psychology, 59,* 715–723.

Foley, V. (1989). Family therapy. In R. J. Corsini & D. Wedding (Eds.), *Current psychotherapies* (pp. 455–500). Itasca, IL: Peacock.

Folstein, S., & Rutter, M. (1977). Infantile autism: A genetic study of 21 twin pairs. *Journal of Child Psychology, 18,* 297–321.

Folstein, S., & Rutter, M. (1988). Autism: Familial aggregation and genetic implications. *Journal of Autism and Developmental Disorders, 18,* 3–30.

Food and Drug Administration. (1991, October 18). *Talk Paper: Antidepressants Update.* Rockville, MD: United States Department of Health and Human Services.

Forbes, D., Creamer, M., & Rycroft, P. (1994). Eye movement desensitization and reprocessing in posttraumatic stress disorder: A pilot study using assessment measures. *Journal of Behavior Therapy and Experimental Psychiatry, 25,* 113–120.

Fordyce, W. E. (1982). A behavioral perspective on chronic pain. *British Journal of Clinical Psychiatry, 21,* 313–320.

Fordyce, W. E. (1988). Pain and suffering: A reappraisal. *American Psychologist, 43,* 276–283.

Foreyt, J. P. (1987). Behavioral medicine. In G. T. Wilson, C. M. Franks, P. C. Kendall, & J. P. Foreyt (Eds.), *Review of behavior therapy: Theory and practice* (Vol. 2, pp. 154–176). New York: Guilford Press.

Forgac, G. E., Cassel, C. A., & Michaels, E. J. (1984). Chronicity of criminal behavior and psychopathology in male exhibitionists. *Journal of Clinical Psychology, 40,* 827–832.

Forgac, G. E., & Michaels, E. J. (1982). Personality characteristics of two types of male exhibitionism. *Journal of Abnormal Psychology, 91,* 287–293.

Fortmann, S. P., & Killen, J. D. (1995). Nicotine gum and self-help behavioral treatment for smoking relapse prevention: Results from a trial using population-based recruitment. *Journal of Consulting and Clinical Psychology, 63,* 460–468.

Foxx, R., & Brown, R. (1979). Nicotine fading and self-monitoring for cigarette abstinence or controlled smoking. *Journal of Applied Behavior Analysis, 12,* 111–125.

Foxx, R. M., & Faw, G. D. (1992). An eight-year follow-up of three social skills training studies. *Mental Retardation, 30,* 63–66.

Frances, A. J., First, M. B., Widiger, T. A., Miele, G. M., Tilly, S. M., Davis, W. W., & Pincus, H. A. (1991). An A to Z guide to DSM-IV conundrums. *Journal of Abnormal Psychology, 100,* 407–412.

Francis, G., Last, C. G., & Strauss, C. C. (1987). Expression of separation anxiety disorder: The roles of age and gender. *Child Psychiatry and Human Development, 18,* 82–89.

Francis, P. T., & Bowen, D. M. (1994). Neuronal pathology in relation to molecular biology and treatment of Alzheimer's disease. In F. Owen & R. Itzhaki (Eds.), *Molecular and cell biology of neuropsychiatric diseases* (pp. 24–54). New York: Chapman and Hall.

Franklin, D. (1987). The politics of masochism. *Psychology Today, 21,* 51–57.

Franklin, J. A. (1987). The changing nature of agoraphobic fears. *British Journal of Clinical Psychology, 26,* 127–133.

Franks, C. M. (1990). Behavior therapy: An overview. In C. M. Franks, G. T. Wilson, P. C. Kendall, & J. P. Forest (Eds.), *Review of behavior therapy: Theory and practice* (Vol. 12). New York: Guilford.

Free, M. L., & Oei, T. P. S. (1989). Biological and psychological processes in the treatment and maintenance of depression. *Clinical Psychology Review, 9*, 653–688.

Freedman, D. X. (1984). Psychiatric epidemiology counts. *Archives of General Psychiatry, 41*, 931–933.

Freeman, B. J. (1993). The syndrome of autism: Update and guidelines for diagnosis. *Infants and Young Children, 6*, 1–11.

Freeston, M. H., & Ladouceur, R. (1993). Appraisal of cognitive intrusions and response style: Replication and extension. *Behaviour Research and Therapy, 31*, 185–191.

Freiberg, P. (1991). Suicide in family, friends is familiar to too many teens. *APA Monitor, 22*, 36–37.

Freinkel, A., Koopman, C., & Spiegel, D. (1994). Dissociative symptoms in media eyewitnesses of an execution. *American Journal of Psychiatry, 151*, 1335–1339.

Fremon, C. (1991, January 27). Love and death. *Los Angeles Times Magazine*, pp. 17–35.

Fremouw, W. J., Perczel, W. J., & Ellis, T. E. (1990). *Suicide risk: Assessment and response guidelines*. Elmsford, New York: Pergamon.

Freud, S. (1905). Psychical (or mental) treatment. In J. Strachey (Ed.), *The complete psychological works* (Vol. 7). New York: Norton.

Freud, S. (1909/1959). *Beyond the pleasure principle*. New York: Bantam.

Freud, S. (1924). Mourning and melancholia. In J. Riviere (Trans.), *Collected papers* (Vol. 4). London: Hogarth Press. (Original work published 1917.)

Freud, S. (1938). The psychopathology of everyday life. In A. B. Brill (Ed.), *The basic writings of Sigmund Freud*. New York: Modern Library.

Freud, S. (1949). *An outline of psychoanalysis*. New York: Norton.

Freud, S., & Breuer, J. (1895). Studies on hysteria. In J. Strachey (Ed.), *The standard edition of the complete psychological works of Sigmund Freud* (Vol. 2). London: Hogarth Press, 1962.

Frick, P. J., & Lahey, B. B. (1991). Nature and characteristics of attention-deficit hyperactivity disorder. *School Psychology Review, 20*, 163–173.

Friedman, A. P. (1979). Characteristics of tension headache: Profile of 1,420 cases. *Psychosomatics, 20*, 451–461.

Friedman, H. S., & Booth-Kewley, S. (1988). The "disease prone" personality: A meta-analytic view of the construct. *American Psychologist, 42*, 539–555.

Friedman, M. (1984). *Treating Type A behavior and your heart*. New York: Knopf.

Friedman, M., & Rosenman, R. H. (1974). *Type A behavior*. New York: Knopf.

Friedrich, J. (1985, January 7). Seven who have succeeded. *Time*, pp. 41–45.

Frisby, C. L. (1995). When facts and orthodoxy collide: The bell curve and the robustness criterion. *School Psychology Review, 24*, 12–19.

Frischholz, E. J., Braun, B. G., Lipman, L. S., & Sachs, R. (1992). Suggested posthypnotic amnesia in psychiatric patients and normals. *American Journal of Clinical Hypnosis, 35*, 29–39.

Frith, U. (1991). *Autism and Asperger syndrome*. Cambridge: Cambridge University Press.

Fritz, G. K., Rubenstein, S., & Lewiston, N. J. (1987). Psychological factors in fatal childhood asthma. *American Journal of Orthopsychiatry, 57*, 253–257.

Frombonne, E. (1995). Anorexia nervosa: No evidence of an increase. *British Journal of Psychiatry, 166*, 462–471.

Frumkin, N. L., Palumbo, C. L., & Naeser, M. A. (1994). Brain imaging and its application to aphasia rehabilitation: CT and MRI. In R. Chapey (Ed.), *Language intervention strategies in adult aphasia* (47–79). Baltimore: Williams & Wilkins.

Fulero, S. M. (1988). Tarasoff: 10 years later. *Professional Psychology: Research and Practice, 19*, 184–190.

Funk, S. C. (1992). Hardiness: A review of theory and research. *Health Psychology, 11*, 335–345.

Furlong, F. W. (1991). Credibility of patients in psychiatric research. *American Journal of Psychiatry, 148*, 1423.

Fyer, A. J., Liebowitz, M. R., Gorman, J. M., Campeas, R., Levin, A., Davies, S. O., Goetz, D., & Klein, D. (1987). Discontinuation of Alprazolam treatment in panic patients. *American Journal of Psychiatry, 144*, 303–308.

Gadow, K. D. (1986). *Children on medication* (Vol. 1). San Diego: College-Hill Press.

Gadow, K. D. (1991). Clinical issues in child and adolescent psychopharmacology. *Journal of Consulting and Clinical Psychology, 59*, 842–852.

Gallagher, D., & Frankel, A. S. (1980). Depression in (an) older adult(s): A moderate structuralist viewpoint. *Psychotherapy: Theory, Research, and Practice, 17*, 101–104.

Gallahorn, G. E. (1981). Borderline personality disorders. In J. R. Lion (Ed.), *Personality disorders: Diagnosis and management*. Baltimore: Williams & Wilkins.

Galton, F. (1869). *Hereditary genius: An inquiry into its laws and consequences*. London: Macmillan.

Gamble, E., & Elder, S. (1983). Multimodal biofeedback in the treatment of migraine. *Biofeedback and Self-Regulation, 8*, 383–392.

Ganellen, R. J. (1988). Specificity of attributions and overgeneralization in depression and anxiety. *Journal of Abnormal Psychology, 97*, 83–86.

Gangadhar, B., Kapur, R., & Kalyanasundaram, S. (1982). Comparison of electroconvulsive therapy with imipramine in endogenous depression: A double blind study. *British Journal of Psychiatry, 141*, 367–371.

Garber, H. J., & Ritvo, E. R. (1992). Magnetic resonance imaging of the posterior fossa in autistic adults. *American Journal of Psychiatry, 149*, 245–247.

Garcia, J. (1981). The logic and limits of mental aptitude testing. *American Psychologist, 36*, 1172–1180.

Garcia, J., McGowan, B. K., & Green, K. F. (1972) Biological constraints on conditioning. In A. H. Black & W. F. Prokasy (Eds.), *Classical conditioning II: Current research and theory*. New York: Appleton-Century-Crofts.

Garety, P. (1991). Reasoning and delusions. *British Journal of Psychiatry, 159*, 14–18.

Garfield, S. L. (1994). Research on client variables in psychotherapy. In A. E. Bergin & S. L. Garfield (Eds.), *Handbook of psychotherapy and behavior change* (pp. 190–228). New York: Wiley.

Garfield, S. L., & Bergin, A. E. (1994). Introduction and historical overview. In A. E. Bergin & S. L. Garfield (Eds.), *Handbook of psychotherapy and behavior change* (pp. 3–18). New York: Wiley.

Garfinkel, B. D., Froese, A., & Hood, J. (1982). Suicide attempts in children and adolescents. *American Journal of Psychiatry, 139(10)*, 1257–1261.

Garfinkel, B. D., & Golumbek, H. (1983). Suicidal behavior in adolescence. In H. Golumbek & B. D. Garfinkel (Eds.), *The adolescent and mood disturbance*. New York: International Universities Press.

Garland, A. F., & Zigler, E. (1993). Adolescent suicide prevention: Current research and social policy implications. *American Psychologist, 48*, 169–182.

Garner, D. M., Rockert, W., Davis, R., Garner, M. V., Olmsted, M. P., & Eagle, M. (1993). Comparison of cognitive-behavioral and supportive-expressive therapy for bulimia nervosa. *American Journal of Psychiatry, 150*, 37–46.

Garretson, D. J. (1993). Psychological misdiagnosis of African Americans. *Journal of Multicultural Counseling and Development, 21*, 119–126.

Gartner, A. F., & Gartner, J. (1988). Borderline pathology in post-incest female adolescents. *Bulletin of the Meninger Clinic, 52*, 101–113.

Gatz, M. (1990). Interpreting behavioral genetic results: Suggestions for counselors and clients. *Journal of Counseling and Development, 68*, 601–605.

Gatz, M., Smyer, M. A., & Lawton, M. P. (1980). The mental health system and the older adult. In L. W. Poon (Ed.), *Aging in the 1980s*. Washington, DC: American Psychological Association.

Gawin, F. H. (1991). Cocaine addiction: Psychology and neurophysiology. *Science, 251*, 1580–1586.

Gaynor, J., & Hatcher, C. (1987). *The psychology of child firesetting*. New York: Brunner/Mazel.

Gelard, M. S., & Sanford, E. E. (1987). Child abuse and neglect: A review of the literature. *School Psychology Review, 16*, 137–155.

Gelernter, C. S., Uhde, T. W., Cimbolic, P., Arnkoff, D. B., Vittone, B. J., Tancer, M. E., & Bartko, J. J. (1991). Cognitive-behavioral and pharmacological treatments of social phobia. *Archives of General Psychiatry, 48*, 938–945.

Gelertner, J., O'Malley, S., Risch, N., Kranzler, H. R., Krystal, J., Merikangas, K., Kennedy, J., & Kidd, K. K. (1991). No association between an allele at the D2 dopamine receptor gene (DRD2) and alcoholism. *Journal of the American Medical Association, 266*, 1801–1807.

Genest, M., Bowen, R. C., Dudley, J., & Keegan, D. (1990). Assessment of strategies for coping with anxiety: Preliminary investigations. *Journal of Anxiety Disorders, 4*, 1–14.

George, D. T., Ladenheim, J. A., & Nutt, D. J. (1987). Effect of pregnancy on panic attacks. *American Journal of Psychiatry, 144*, 1078–1079.

George, L. K., Landerman, R., Blazer, D. G., Anthony, J. C. (1991). Cognitive impairment. In L. N. Robins & D. A. Regier (Eds.), *Psychiatric disorders in America: The Epidemiologic Catchment Area study* (pp. 291–327). New York: Free Press.

George, M. S., & Ballenger, J. C. (1992). The neuroanatomy of panic disorder: The emerging role of the right parahippocampal region. *Journal of Anxiety Disorder, 6*, 181–188.

George, M. S., Trimble, M. R., Ring, H. A., Sallee, F. R., & Robertson, M. M. (1993). Obsessions in obsessive-compulsive disorder with and without Gilles de la Tourette's syndrome. *American Journal of Psychiatry, 150*, 93–97.

Georgotas, A. (1985). Affective disorders: Pharmacotherapy. In H. I. Kaplan & B. J. Sadock (Eds.), *Comprehensive textbook of psychiatry* (4th ed., pp. 821–833). Baltimore: Williams & Wilkins.

Gerin, W., Milner, D., Chawla, S., & Pickering, T. G. (1995). Social support as a moderator of cardiovascular reactivity in women: A test of the direct effects and buffering hypotheses. *Psychosomatic Medicine, 57*, 16–22.

Gerin, W., Pieper, C., Levy, R., & Pickering, T. G. (1992). Social support in social interaction: A moderator of cardiovascular reactivity. *Psychosomatic Medicine, 54*, 324–336.

Gershon, E. S., Berrettini, W. H., Nurnberger, J. I., Jr., & Goldin, L. R. (1989). Genetic studies of affective illness. In J. J. Mann (Ed.), *Models of depressive disorders: Psychological, biological, and genetic perspectives* (pp. 109–142). New York: Plenum.

Ghaziuddin, M., Tsai, L., Eilers, L., & Ghaziuddin, N. (1992). Brief report: Autism and herpes simplex encephalitis. *Journal of Autism and Developmental Disorders, 22*, 107–113.

Ghosh, A., & Marks, I. M. (1987). Self-treatment of agoraphobia by exposure. *Behavior Therapy, 18*, 3–16.

Gibbs, N. (1991, June 3). When is it rape? *Time*, pp. 48–54.

Gilbert, B., & Cunningham, J. (1986). Women's post-rape sexual functioning: Review and implications for counseling. *Journal of Counseling and Development, 65*, 71–73.

Gillberg, C. (1988). The neurobiology of infantile autism. *Journal of Child Psychology and Psychiatry, 29*, 257–266.

Gillberg, C. (1992). Autism and autistic-like conditions: Subclasses among disorders of empathy. *Journal of Child Psychology and Psychiatry, 33*, 813–842.

Gillberg, C. (1994). Debate and argument: Having Rett syndrome in ICD-10 PDD category does not make sense. *Journal of Child Psychology and Psychiatry, 35*, 377–378.

Gillie, D. (1977). The IQ issue. *Phi Delta Kappan, 58*, 469.

Gillis, J. J., Gilger, J. W., Pennington, B. F., & DeFries, J. C. (1992). Attention deficit in reading-disabled twins: Evidence for a genetic etiology. *Journal of Abnormal Child Psychology, 20*, 303–315.

Girard, F. (1984, August 5). State crime data called flawed, late. *Detroit News*, pp. 1, 12.

Glaser, G. H., Newman, R. J., & Schafer, R. (1963). Interictal psychosis in psychomotor-temporal lobe epilepsy: An EEG psychological study. In G. H. Glaser (Ed.), *EEG and behavior*. New York: Basic Books.

Glasgow, R. E., & Lichtenstein, E. (1987). Long-term effects of behavioral smoking cessation intervention. *Behavior Therapy, 18*, 297–324.

Glassman, J. N. S., Magulac, M., & Darko, D. F. (1987). Folie a famille: Shared paranoid disorder in a Vietnam veteran and his family. *American Journal of Psychiatry, 144*, 658–660.

Glavin, D. K., Franklin, J., & Francis, R. J. (1990). Substance abuse and suicidal behavior. In S. Blumenthal & D. Kupfer (Eds.), *Suicide over the life cycle: Risk factors, assessment, and treatment of suicidal patients* (pp. 177–204). Washington, DC: American Psychiatric Press.

Glazer, W. M., Morgenstern, H., & Doucette, J. T. (1991). The prediction of chronic persistent versus intermittent tardive dyskinesia. *British Journal of Psychiatry, 158*, 822–828.

Gloger, S., Grunhaus, L., Gladic, D., O'Ryan, F., Cohen, L. & Codner, S. (1989). Panic attacks and agoraphobia: Low dose clomipramine treatment. *Journal of Clinical Pharmacology, 9*, 28–32.

Goff, D. C. (1993). Reply to Dr. Armstrong. *Journal of Nervous and Mental Disease, 181*, 604–605.

Goff, D. C., & Simms, C. A. (1993). Has multiple personality disorder remained consistent over time? *Journal of Nervous and Mental Disease, 181*, 595–600.

Goldberg, T. E., Hyde, T. M., Kleinman, J. E., & Weinberger, D. R. (1993). Course of schizophrenia: Neuropsychological evidence for a static encephalopathy. *Schizophrenia Bulletin, 19*, 797–802.

Golden, C. J. (1989). The Nebraska Neuropsychological Children's Battery. In C. R. Reynolds & E. Fletcher-Janzen (Eds.), *Handbook of clinical child neuropsychology* (pp. 193–204). New York: Plenum Press.

Golden, C. J., Graber, B., Blose, I., Berg, R., Coffman, J., & Bloch, S. (1981). Differences in brain densities between chronic alcoholic and normal control patients. *Science, 211*, 508–510.

Golden, C. J., Moses, J. A., Coffman, J. A., Miller, W. R., & Strider, F. D. (1983). *Clinical neuropsychology*. New York: Grune & Stratton.

Golden, C. J., Moses, J. A., Fishburne, F. J., Engum, E., Lewis, G. P., Wisniewski, A. M., Conley, F. K., Berg, R. A., & Graber, B. (1981). Cross-validation of the Luria-Nebraska Neuropsychological Battery for the presence, lateralization, and location of brain damage. *Journal of Consulting and Clinical Psychology, 49*, 491–507.

Golden, C. J., & Vincente, P. J. (Eds.). (1983). *Foundation of clinical neuropsychology*. New York: Plenum Press.

Golden, G. S. (1987). Tic disorders in childhood. *Pediatrics in Review, 8*, 229–234.

Golden, J. (1988). A second look at a case of inhibited sexual desire. *Journal of Sex Research, 25,* 304–306.

Goldenberg, H., & Goldenberg, I. (1995). Family therapy. In R. J. Corsini & D. Wedding (Eds.), *Current psychotherapies* (5th ed.). Itasca, IL: Peacock.

Goldfried, M. R., & Davison, G. C. (1976). *Clinical behavior therapy.* San Francisco: Holt, Rinehart & Winston.

Goldfried, M. R., Greenberg, L. S., & Marmar, C. (1990). Individual psychotherapy: Process and outcome. *Annual Review of Psychology* (Vol. 41, pp. 659–688). Palo Alto, CA: Annual Reviews.

Goldfried, M. R., & Safran, J. D. (1986). Future directions in psychotherapy integration. In J. C. Norcross (Ed.), *Handbook of eclectic psychotherapy* (pp. 463–483). New York: Brunner/Mazel.

Golding, J. M., Smith, G. R., & Kashner, T. M. (1991). Does somatization disorder occur in men? *Archives of General Psychiatry, 48,* 231–235.

Goldman, D., Hien, D. A., Haas, G. L, Sweeney, J. A., & Frances, A. J. (1992). Bizarre delusions and DSM-III-R schizophrenia. *American Journal of Psychiatry, 149,* 494–499.

Goldman, H. H. (1988). Psychiatric epidemiology and mental health services research. In H. H. Goldman (Ed.), *Review of general psychiatry* (pp. 143–156). Norwalk, CT: Appleton & Lange.

Goldman, H. H., & Foreman, S. A. (1988). Psychiatric diagnosis and psychosocial formulation. In H. H. Goldman (Ed.), *Review of general psychiatry* (pp. 136–142). Norwalk, CT: Appleton & Lange.

Goldman, M. J., & Gutheil, T. G. (1991). Bruxism and sexual abuse. *American Journal of Psychiatry, 148,* 1089.

Goleman, D. (1976). Why your temples pound. *Psychology Today, 10,* 41–47.

Goleman, D. (1992). Therapies offer hope for sex offenders. *New York Times,* pp. C1, C11.

Goma, M., Perez, J., & Torrubia, R. (1988). Personality variables in antisocial and prosocial disinhibitory behavior. In T. E. Moffitt & S. A. Mednick (Eds.), *Biological contributions to crime causation* (pp. 211–222). Boston: Martinus Nijhoff Publishers.

Goodwin, D. W. (1979). Alcoholism and heredity. *Archives of General Psychiatry, 36,* 57–61.

Goodwin, D. W. (1985). Alcoholism and alcoholic psychoses. In H. I. Kaplan & B. J. Sadock (Eds.), *Comprehensive textbook of psychiatry/IV* (pp. 1016–1025). Baltimore: Williams & Wilkins.

Goodwin, D. W., & Guze, S. B. (1984). *Psychiatric diagnosis* (3rd ed.). New York: Oxford University Press.

Goodwin, F. (1974). On the biology of depression. In R. J. Friedman & M. M. Katz (Eds.), *The psychology of depression: Contemporary theory and research.* Washington, DC: V. H. Winston & Sons.

Goodwin, F. K. (1977). Diagnosis of affective disorders. In M. Jarvik (Ed.), *Psychopharmacology in the practice of medicine.* New York: Appleton-Century-Crofts.

Gorwood, P., Leboyer, M., Jay, M., Payan, C., & Feingold, J. (1995). Gender and age of onset in schizophrenia: Impact of family history. *American Journal of Psychiatry, 152,* 208–212.

Gossett, T. F. (1963). *The history of an idea in America.* Dallas: Southern Methodist University Press.

Gotlib, I. H. (1992). Interpersonal and cognitive aspects of depression. *Current Directions in Psychological Science, 1*(5), 149–154.

Gottesman, I. I. (1978). Schizophrenia and genetics: Where are we? Are you sure? In L. C. Wynne, R. L. Cromwell, & S. Matthysse (Eds.), *The nature of schizophrenia: New approaches to research and treatment* (pp. 59–69). New York: Wiley.

Gottesman, I. I. (1991). *Schizophrenia genesis.* New York: W. H. Freeman & Co.

Gottesman, I. I., & Shields, J. (1982). *Schizophrenia: The epigenetic puzzle.* New York: Cambridge University Press.

Gottlieb, A. M., Killen, J. D., Marlatt, G. A., & Taylor, C. B. (1987). Psychological and pharmacological influences in cigarette smoking withdrawal: Effects of nicotine gum and expectancy on smoking withdrawal symptoms and relapse. *Journal of Consulting and Clinical Psychology, 55,* 606–608.

Gould, S. J. (1994, November 28). Curveball. *New Yorker,* 139–149.

Graham, J. R. (1990). *MMPI-2: Assessing personality and psychopathology.* New York: Oxford University Press.

Green, B. L., Wilson, J. P., & Lindy, J. D. (1985). Conceptualizing PTSD: A psychosocial framework. In C. R. Figley (Ed.), *Trauma and its wake* (pp. 53–69). New York: Brunner/Mazel.

Green, M. F. (1993). Cognitive remediation in schizophrenia: Is it time yet? *American Journal of Psychiatry, 150,* 178–187.

Green, M. F., & Kinsbourne, M. (1990). Subvocal activity and auditory hallucinations: Clues for behavioral treatments? *Schizophrenia Bulletin, 16,* 617–625.

Green, R., Mandel, J. B., Hotvedt, M. E., Gray, J., & Smith, L. (1986). Lesbian mothers and their children: A comparison with solo parent heterosexual mothers and their children. *Archives of Sexual Behavior, 15,* 167–184.

Greenberg, R. P., Bornstein, R. F., Greenberg, M. D., & Fisher, S. (1992). A meta-analysis of antidepressant outcome under "blinder" conditions. *Journal of Consulting and Clinical Psychology, 60*(5), 664–669.

Greene, R. L. (1991). *The MMPI-2/MMPI: An interpretive manual.* Boston: Allyn & Bacon.

Greer, S., & Morris, T. (1975). Psychological attributes of women who develop breast cancer: A controlled study. *Journal of Psychosomatic Research, 19,* 147–153.

Grencavage, L. M., & Norcross, J. C. (1990). Where are the commonalities among the therapeutic common factors? *Professional Psychology: Research and Practice, 21,* 372–378.

Grier, W., & Cobbs, P. (1968). *Black rage.* New York: Basic Books.

Grinker, R. R., & Robbins, F. P. (1954). *Psychosomatic case book.* New York: Blakiston.

Gross, P. R., & Eifert, G. H. (1990). Components of generalized anxiety: The role of intrusive thoughts vs worry. *Behaviour Research and Therapy, 28,* 421–428.

Groth, A. N., Burgess, A. W., & Holstrom, L. (1977). Rape: Power, anger, and sexuality. *American Journal of Psychiatry, 134,* 1239–1243.

Grove, M. W., Lebow, B. S., Clementz, B. A., Cerri, A., Medus, C., & Iacono, W. G. (1991). Familial prevalence and coaggregation of schizotypy indicators: A multitrait family study. *Journal of Abnormal Psychology, 100,* 115–121.

Grunhaus, L., Zelnick, T., Albala, A., Rabin, D., Haskett, R. F., Zis, A. P., & Greden, F., Jr. (1987). Serial dexamethasone suppression tests in depressed patients treated only with electroconvulsive therapy. *Journal of Affective Disorders, 13,* 233–240.

Guerin, P. J., Jr., & Chabot, D. R. (1992). Development of family systems theory. In D. K. Freedheim (Ed.), *History of psychotherapy* (pp. 225–260). Washington, DC: American Psychological Association.

Gurman, A. S., & Kniskern, D. P. (1978). Research on marital and family therapy: Progress, perspective, and prospect. In S. L. Carfield & A. E. Bergin (Eds.), *Handbook of psychotherapy and behavior change: An empirical analysis* (2nd ed.). New York: Wiley.

Guttmacher, L. B., & Nelles, C. (1984). In vivo desensitization alteration of lactate-induced panic: A case study. *Behavior Therapy, 15,* 369–372.

Guttman, M. (1995, October 27–29). The Ritalin generation. *USA Weekend,* pp. 4–6.

Haley, J. (1963). *Strategies of psychotherapy.* New York: Grune & Stratton.

Haley, J. (1977). *Problem-solving therapy.* San Francisco: Jossey-Bass.

Haley, J. (1980). *Leaving home*. New York: McGraw-Hill.

Haley, J. (1987). *Problem-solving therapy* (2nd ed.). New York: Jossey-Bass.

Hall, C. S., & Lindzey, G. (1970). *Theories of personality*. New York: Wiley.

Hall, G. C. N., & Hirschman, R. (1991). Toward a theory of sexual aggression: A quadripartite model. *Journal of Consulting and Clinical Psychology, 59*, 662–669.

Hall, J. E. (1995). A perspective on the evolving health care environment: Quality, integrity, reliability and value. *Register Report, 20*, 2–3.

Hall, N. R. S. (1988). The virology of AIDS. *American Psychologist, 43*(11), 907–913.

Hall, R. G., Sachs, D. P. L., Hall, S. M., & Benowitz, N. L. (1984). Two-year efficacy and safety of rapid smoking therapy in patients with cardiac and pulmonary disease. *Journal of Consulting and Clinical Psychology, 52*, 574–581.

Hall, S. M., Havassy, B. E., & Wasserman, D. A. (1990). Commitment to abstinence and acute stress in relapse to alcohol, opiates, and nicotine. *Journal of Consulting and Clinical Psychology, 58*, 175–181.

Hall, S. M., Havassy, B. E., & Wasserman, D. A. (1991). Effects of commitment to abstinence, positive moods, stress, and coping on relapse to cocaine use. *Journal of Consulting and Clinical Psychology, 59*, 526–532.

Hall, S. M., Tunstall, C. D., Ginsberg, D., Benowitz, N. L., & Jones, R. T. (1987). Nicotine gum and behavioral treatment: A placebo controlled trial. *Journal of Consulting and Clinical Psychology, 55*, 603–605.

Hamilton, M. (1982). Symptoms and assessment of depression. In E. S. Paykel (Ed.), *Handbook of affective disorders* (pp. 3–11). New York: Guilford.

Hammen, C. (1991). Generation of stress in the course of unipolar depression. *Journal of Abnormal Psychology, 100*(4), 555–561.

Hammen, C., Davilla, J., Brown, G., Ellicott, A., & Gitlin, M. (1992). Psychiatric history and stress: Predictors of severity of unipolar depression. *Journal of Abnormal Psychology, 101*(1), 45–52.

Hammen, C., & Peters, S. (1978). Interpersonal consequences of depression: Responses to men and women enacting a depressed role. *Journal of Abnormal Psychology, 87*, 322–332.

Hammen, C. L. (1985). Predicting depression: A cognitive-behavioral perspective. In P. Kendall (Ed.), *Advances in cognitive-behavioral research and therapy* (Vol. 4). New York: Academic Press.

Hammond, W. R., & Yung, B. (1993). Psychology's role in the public health–response to assaultive violence among young African-American men. *American Psychologist, 48*, 142–154.

Hanback, J. W., & Revelle, W. (1978). Arousal and perceptual sensitivity in hypochondriacs. *Journal of Abnormal Psychology, 87*, 523–530.

Hans, S. L., Marcus, J., Henson, L., Auerbach, J. G., & Mirsky, A. F. (1992). Interpersonal behavior of children at risk for schizophrenia. *Psychiatry, 55*, 314–335.

Happe, F. G. E. (1994). Annotation: Current psychological theories of autism: The "theory of mind" account and rival theories. *Journal of Child Psychology and Psychiatry, 35*, 215–229.

Harding, C. M., Brooks, G. W., Ashikaga, T., Strauss, J. S., & Breier, A. The Vermont Longitudinal Study of Persons with Severe Mental Illness, II: Long-term outcome of subjects who retrospectively met DSM-III criteria for schizophrenia. *American Journal of Psychiatry, 144*, 727–735.

Harding, C. M., Zubin, J., & Strauss, J. S. (1992). Chronicity in schizophrenia: Revisited. *British Journal of Psychiatry, 161*, 27–37.

Hare, R. D. (1968). Psychopathy, autonomic functioning and the orienting responses. *Journal of Abnormal Psychology, 73*, 1–24.

Hare, R. D. (1970). *Psychopathy: Theory and research*. New York: Wiley.

Hare, R. D. (1975). Anxiety, stress, and psychopathy. In I. Sarason & C. Spielberger (Eds.), *Stress and anxiety* (Vol. 2). Washington, DC: Hemisphere Publishing.

Hare, R. D., Hart, S. D., & Harpur, T. J. (1991). Psychopathology and the DSM-IV criteria for antisocial personality disorder. *Journal of Abnormal Psychology, 100*, 391–398.

Harlow, J. M. (1868). Recovery from the passage of an iron bar through the head. *Publication of the Massachusetts Medical Society, 2*, 327.

Harpur, T. J., & Hare, R. D. (1994). Assessment of psychopathy as a function of age. *Journal of Abnormal Psychology, 103*, 604–609.

Harpur, T. J., Hare, R. D., and Hakstian, A. R. (1989). Two-factor conceptualization of psychopathology: Construct validity and assessment implications. *Psychological Assessment: A Journal of Consulting and Clinical Psychology, 1*, 6–17.

Harris, E. L., Noyes, R., Crowe, R. R., & Chaudhry, D. R. (1983). Family study of agoraphobia. *Archives of General Psychiatry, 40*, 1061–1064.

Harris, P. R. (1980). *Promoting health–preventing disease: Objectives for the nation*. Washington, DC: U.S. Government Printing Office.

Harris, S. L., Handleman, J. S., Gordon, R., Kristoff, B., & Fuentes, F. (1991). Changes in cognitive and language functioning of preschool children with autism. *Journal of Autism and Developmental Disorders, 21*, 281–290.

Harrow, M., Grossman, L. S., Silverstein, M. L., & Meltzer, H. Y. (1982). Thought pathology in manic and schizophrenic patients. *Archives of General Psychiatry, 39*, 665–671.

Hart, S. D., & Hare, R. D. (1989). Discriminant validity of the psychopathology checklist in a forensic psychiatric population. *Psychological Assessment: A Journal of Consulting and Clinical Psychology, 1*, 211–218.

Hashimoto, T., Tayama, M., Murakawa, K., Yoshimoto, T., Miyazaki, M., Harada, M., & Kuroda, Y. (1995). Development of brainstem and cerebellum in autistic patients. *Journal of Autism and Developmental Disorders, 25*, 1–18.

Hatcher, S. (1989). A case of doll phobia. *British Journal of Psychiatry, 155*, 255–257.

Hathaway, S. R., & McKinley, J. C. (1943). *Manual for the Minnesota Multiphasic Personality Inventory*. New York: Psychological Corporation.

Hatton, C. L., & Valente, S. M. (1984). *Suicide assessment and intervention* (2nd ed.). Norwalk, CT: Appleton-Century-Crofts.

Hauff, E., & Vaglum, P. (1994). Chronic posttraumatic stress disorder in Vietnamese refugees. *Journal of Nervous and Mental Disease, 182*, 85–90.

Hauser, W. A. (1994). The distribution of mild and severe forms of epilepsy. In M. R. Trimble & W. E. Dodson (Eds.), *Epilepsy and quality of life* (pp. 249–257). New York: Raven Press.

Hawton, K. (1987). Assessment of suicide risk. *British Journal of Psychiatry, 150*, 145–153.

Hawton, K., Catalan, J., Martin, P., & Fagg, J. (1986). Long-term outcome of sex therapy. *Behaviour Research and Therapy, 24*, 665–675.

Hayes, S. (1995). *Now the battles are substantive*. Reno: Content Press.

Hayes, S. C., Brownell, K. D., & Barlow, D. H. (1983). Heterosexual skills training and covert sensitization: Effects on social skills and sexual arousal in sexual deviants. *Behaviour Research and Therapy, 21*, 383–392.

Hayes, S. C., & Zettle, R. D. (1979). The mythology of behavioral training. *Behavior Therapist, 2*, 5–6.

Hays, R. B., Turner, H., & Coates, T. J. (1992). Social support, AIDS-related symptoms, and depression among gay men. *Journal of Consulting and Clinical Psychology, 60*(3), 463–469.

Hayward, P., Wardie, J., & Higgitt, A. (1989). Benzodiazepine research: Current findings and practical consequences. *British Journal of Psychiatry, 28*, 307–327.

Heath, R. G., Guschwan, A. F., & Coffey, J. W. (1970). Relation of taraxein to schizophrenia. *Diseases of the Nervous System, 31,* 391–395.

Heber, R., & Garber, H. (1975). The Milwaukee project: A study of the use of familial retardation to prevent cultural-familial retardation. In B. Z. Friedlander, G. M. Sterrit, & G. E. Kirk (Eds.), *Exceptional infant, Vol. 3: Assessment and intervention.* New York: Brunner/Mazel.

Hedlund, S., & Rude, S. S. (1995). Evidence of latent depressive schemas in formerly depressed individuals. *Journal of Abnormal Psychology, 104,* 517–525.

Heiby, E. M. (1983). Depression as a function of the interaction of self- and environmentally controlled reinforcement. *Behavior Therapy, 14,* 430–433.

Heilbrun, A. B., Jr., & Loftus, M. P. (1986). The role of sadism and peer pressure in the sexual aggression of male college students. *Journal of Sex Research, 22,* 320–332.

Heim, N. (1981). Sexual behavior of castrated sex offenders. *Archives of Sexual Behavior, 10,* 11–19.

Heinrichs, R. W. (1993). Schizophrenia and the brain. *American Psychologist, 48,* 221–233.

Hekmat, H., Lubitz, R., & Deal, R. (1984). Semantic desensitization: A paradigmatic intervention approach to anxiety disorders. *Journal of Clinical Psychology, 40,* 463–466.

Helms, J. E. (1992). Why is there no study of cultural equivalence in standardized cognitive ability testing? *American Psychologist, 47,* 1083–1101.

Helzer, J. E., Burnam, A., & McEvoy, L. T. (1991). Alcohol abuse and dependence. In L. N. Robins & D. A. Regier (Eds.), *Psychiatric disorders in America: The Epidemiologic Catchment Area study* (pp. 81–115). New York: Free Press.

Hendin, H., Pollenger, A., Singer, P., & Ulman, R. (1981). Meanings of combat and the development of posttraumatic stress disorder. *American Journal of Psychiatry, 131,* 1490–1493.

Herbert, J. D., Hope, D. A., & Bellack, A. S. (1992). Validity of the distinction between generalized social phobia and avoidant personality disorder. *Journal of Abnormal Psychology, 101,* 332–339.

Herlicky, B., & Sheeley, V. L. (1988). Privileged communication in selected helping professions: A comparison among statutes. *Journal of Counseling & Development, 65,* 479–483.

Herman, J., & Hirschman, L. (1981). Families at risk for father-daughter incest. *American Journal of Psychiatry, 38,* 967–970.

Herman, S., Russell, D., & Trocki, K. (1986). Long-term effects of incestuous abuse in childhood. *American Journal of Psychiatry, 154,* 1293–1296.

Herrnstein, R. (1971, September). IQ. *Atlantic Monthly,* pp. 43–64.

Herrnstein, R. (1982). IQ. *Atlantic Monthly,* pp. 43–64.

Herrnstein, R. J., & Murray, C. (1994). *The bell curve: Intelligence and class structure in American life.* New York: Free Press.

Herschkowitz, S., & Dickes, R. (1978). Suicide attempts in a female-to-male transsexual. *American Journal of Psychiatry, 135,* 368–369.

Hersen, M., Bellack, A., & Himmelhoch, J. (1980). Treatment for unipolar depression with social skills training. *Behavior Modification, 4,* 547–556.

Heston, L. L. (1966). Psychiatric disorders in foster-home-reared children of schizophrenic mothers. *British Journal of Psychiatry, 122,* 819–825.

Heston, L. L., & Denny, D. (1968). Interactions between early life experience and biological factors in schizophrenia. In D. Rosenthal & S. Kety (Eds.), *The transmission of schizophrenia.* New York: Pergamon Press.

Heston, L. L., & White, J. A. (1991). *The vanishing mind.* New York: W. H. Freeman.

Hibbert, G. (1984). Ideational components of anxiety: Their origin and content. *British Journal of Psychiatry, 144,* 618–624.

Hill, A. J., & Bhatti, R. (1995). Body shape perception and dieting in preadolescent British Asian girls: Links with eating disorders. *International Journal of Eating Disorders, 17,* 175–183.

Hill, D., & Watterson, D. (1942). Electroencephalographic studies of the psychopathic personality. *Journal of Neurology and Psychiatry, 5,* 47–64.

Hills, C. E. (1990). Is individual therapy process really different from group therapy process: The jury is still out. *Counseling Psychologist, 18,* 126–130.

Hillyer, J. (1964). Reluctantly told. In B. Kaplan (Ed.), *The inner world of mental illness.* New York: Harper & Row.

Hinshaw, S. (1987). On the distinction between attentional deficits/hyperactivity and conduct problems/aggression in child psychopathology. *Psychological Bulletin, 101,* 443–463.

Hipple, J. L., & Hipple, L. B. (1983). *Diagnosis and management of psychological emergencies.* Springfield, IL: Thomas.

Hirschfeld, R. M., & Davidson, L. (1989). Clinical risk factors for suicide. *Psychiatric Annals, 18,* 628–635.

Hirschfeld, R. M., & Shea, T. (1985). Affective disorders: Psychosocial treatment. In H. I. Kaplan & B. J. Sadock (Eds.), *Comprehensive textbook of psychiatry* (4th ed., pp. 786–810). Baltimore: Williams & Wilkins.

Hite, S. (1976). *The Hite report.* Chicago: Dell.

Ho, D. D., Neumann, A. U., Perelson, A. S., Chen, W., Leonard, J. M., & Markowitz, M. (1995). Rapid turnover of plasma virions and CD4 lymphocytes in HIV-1 infection. *Nature, 373,* 123–126.

Ho, E. D. F., Tsang, A. K. T., & Ho, D. Y. F. (1991). An investigation of the calendar calculation ability of a Chinese calendar savant. *Journal of Autism and Developmental Disorders, 21,* 315–327.

Ho, M. K. (1987). *Family therapy with ethnic minorities.* Newbury Park, CA: Sage Publications.

Hobson, R. P. (1987). The autistic child's recognition of age- and sex-related characteristics of people. *Journal of Autism and Developmental Disorders, 17,* 63–79.

Hoch, Z., Safir, M. P., Peres, Y., & Stepler, J. (1981). An evaluation of sexual performance—Comparison between sexually dysfunctional and functional couples. *Journal of Sex and Marital Therapy, 7,* 195–206.

Hodgins, D. C., El-Guebaly, N., & Armstrong, S. (1995). Prospective and retrospective reports of mood states before relapse to substance use. *Journal of Consulting and Clinical Psychology, 63,* 400–407.

Hodgson, R. J., & Rachman, S. (1972). The effects of contamination and washing in obsessional patients. *Behavior Research and Therapy, 10,* 111–117.

Hoehn-Saric, R., Pearlson, G. D., Harris, G. J., Machlin, S. R., & Camargo, E. E. (1991). Effects of fluoxetine on regional cerebral blood flow in obsessive-compulsive patients. *American Journal of Psychiatry, 148,* 1243–1245.

Hoek, H. W., Bartelds, A. I. M., Bosveld, J. J. F., Van der Graaff, Y., Limpens, V. E. L., Maiwald, M., & Spaaij, C. J. K. (1995). Impact of urbanization on detection rates of eating disorders. *American Journal of Psychiatry, 152,* 1272–1278.

Hoffman, M. A. (1991). Counseling the HIV-infected client: A psychosocial model for assessment and intervention. *The Counseling Psychologist, 19,* 467–542.

Hofmann, S. G., Ehlers, A., & Roth, W. T. (1995). Conditioning theory: A model for the etiology of public speaking anxiety? *Behaviour Research and Therapy, 33,* 567–571.

Hogarty, G. E., Anderson, C. M., Reiss, D. J., Kornblith, S. J., Greenwald, D. P., Ulrich, R. F., & Carter, M. (1991). Family psychoeducation, social skills training, and maintenance chemotherapy in the aftercare treatment of schizophrenia. *Archives of General Psychiatry, 48,* 340–347.

Hohmann, A. A., Larson, D. B., Thompson, J. W., & Beardsley, R. S. (1988, November). *Psychotropic medication prescription in U.S. ambulatory medical care.* Paper presented at the American Public Health Association Annual Meeting, Boston, Massachusetts.

Holahan, C. J., & Moos, R. H. (1991). Life stressors, personal and social resources, and depression: A 4-year structure model. *Journal of Abnormal Psychology, 100*(1), 31–38.

Holcomb, H. H., Links, J., Smith, C., & Wong, D. (1989). Positron emission tomography: Measuring the metabolic and neurochemical characteristics of the living human nervous system. In N. C. Andreasen (Ed.), *Brain imaging: Applications in psychiatry* (pp. 235–370). Washington, DC: American Psychiatric Press.

Holden, C. (1986). Proposed new psychiatric diagnoses raise charges of gender bias. *Science, 231,* 327–328.

Holden, N. L. (1987). Late paraphrenia or the paraphrenias? A descriptive study with a 10-year follow-up. *British Journal of Psychiatry, 150,* 635–639.

Hollender, M. H. (1980). The case of Anna O.: A reformulation. *American Journal of Psychiatry, 137,* 797–800.

Hollon, S. D., & Beck, A. T. (1994). Cognitive and cognitive-behavioral therapies. In A. E. Bergin & S. L. Garfield (Eds.), *Handbook of psychotherapy and behavior change* (pp. 428–466). New York: Wiley.

Hollon, S. D., DeRubeis, R. J., & Seligman, M. E. P. (1992). Cognitive therapy and the prevention of depression. *Applied and Preventive Psychology, 1,* 89–95.

Hollon, S. D., Shelton, R. C, & Loosen, P. T. (1991). Cognitive therapy and pharmacotherapy for depression. *Journal of Consulting and Clinical Psychology, 59*(1), 88–99.

Holmes, T. H., & Rahe, R. H. (1967). The social readjustment rating scale. *Journal of Psychosomatic Research, 11,* 213–218.

Holmes, T. S., & Holmes, T. H. (1970). Short-term intrusion into the life style routine. *Journal of Psychosomatic Research, 14,* 121–132.

Holroyd, J., & Brodsky, A. (1977). Psychologists' attitudes and practices regarding erotic and nonerotic physical contact with patients. *American Psychologist, 32,* 839–843.

Holroyd, S., & Baron-Cohen, S. (1993). Brief report: How far can people with autism go in developing a theory of mind? *Journal of Autism and Developmental Disorders, 23,* 379–385.

Holt, R. R. (1962). The logic of the romantic point of view in personology. *Journal of Psychoanalysis, 38,* 377–402.

Hoover, D. W., & Milich, R. (1994). Effects of sugar ingestion expectancies on mother-child interactions. *Journal of Abnormal Child Psychology, 22,* 501–515.

Horne, R. L., Pettinati, H. M., Sugerman, A. A., & Varga, E. (1985). Comparing bilateral to unilateral electroconvulsive therapy in randomized study with EEG monitoring. *Archives of General Psychiatry, 42,* 1087–1092.

Horne, R. L., Van Vactor, C., & Emerson, S. (1991). Disturbed body image in patients with eating disorders. *American Journal of Psychiatry, 148,* 211–215.

Horowitz, M. J. (1970). *Psychosocial function in epilepsy.* Springfield, IL: Thomas.

Horwath, E., Johnson, J., & Horning, C. D. (1993). Epidemiology of panic disorder in African-Americans. *American Journal of Psychiatry, 150,* 465–469.

Horwitz, A. V., & White, H. R. (1987). Gender role orientations and styles of pathology among adolescents. *Journal of Health and Human Behavior, 28,* 158–170.

Hovanitz, C. A., & Wander, M. R. (1990). Tension headache: Disregulation at some levels of stress. *Journal of Behavioral Medicine, 13,* 539–560.

Howard, K. (1994). Quality assurance in psychotherapy: An application of research to clinical cases. In Scientific Program Committee (Ed.), *Proceedings of the 16th International Congress of Psychotherapy,* Seoul: Korean Academy of Psychotherapists.

Howard, R. (1992). Folie a deux involving a dog. *American Journal of Psychiatry, 149,* 414.

Huber, G., Gross, G., Schuttler, R., & Linz, M. (1980). Longitudinal studies of schizophrenic patients. *Schizophrenia Bulletin, 6,* 592–605.

Hudgens, A. (1979). Family-oriented treatment of chronic pain. *Journal of Marital and Family Therapy, 5,* 67–78.

Hudson, J. I., Manoach, D. S., Sabo, A. N., & Sternbach, S. E. (1991). Recurrent nightmares in posttraumatic stress disorder: Association with sleep paralysis, hypnopompic hallucinations, and REM sleep. *Journal of Nervous and Mental Disease, 179,* 572–573.

Hugdahl, K., Frederickson, M., & Ohman, A. (1977). Preparedness and arousability determinants of electrodermal conditioning. *Behaviour Research and Therapy, 15,* 345–353.

Hull, J. C., & Bond, C. F. (1986). Social and behavioral consequences of alcohol consumption and expectancy: A meta-analysis. *Psychological Bulletin, 99,* 347–360.

Hunter, R., Blackwood, W., & Bull, J. (1968). Three cases of frontal meningiomas presenting psychiatrically. *British Medical Journal, 3,* 9–16.

Hunter, R., & Macalpine, I. (1963). *Three hundred years of psychiatry, 1535–1860.* London: Oxford University Press.

Hurtig, A. L., & Rosenthal, I. M. (1987). Psychological findings in early treated cases of female pseudohermaphroditism caused by virilizing congenital adrenal hyperplasia. *Archives of Sexual Behavior, 16,* 209–223.

Hutchens, T. A., & Hynd, G. W. (1987). Medications and the school-age child and adolescent: A review. *School Psychology Bulletin, 16,* 527–542.

Hutchings, B., & Mednick, S. A. (1977). Criminality in adoptees and their adoptive and biological parents: A pilot study. In S. A. Mednick & K. L. Christianson (Eds.), *Biosocial bases of criminal behavior.* New York: Garden Press.

Hynd, G. W., Hern, K. L., Voeller, K. K., & Marshall, R. M. (1991). Neurobiological basis of attention-deficit hyperactivity disorder. *School Psychology Review, 20,* 174–186.

Ingraham, L. J., Kugelmass, S., Frenkel, E., Nathan, M., & Mirsky, A. F. (1995). Twenty-five–year follow-up of the Israeli high-risk study: Current and lifetime psychopathology. *Schizophrenia Bulletin, 21,* 183–192.

Irwin, A., & Gross, A. M. (1990). Mental retardation in childhood. In M. Hersen & C. G. Last (Eds.), *Handbook of child and adult psychopathology* (pp. 325–336). New York: Pergamon Press.

Irwin, M., Daniels, M., Smith, T. L., Bloom, E., & Weiner, H. (1987). Impaired natural killer cell activity during bereavement. *Brain, Behavior, and Immunity, 1,* 98–104.

Isenberg, S. A., Lehrer, P. M., & Hochron, S. (1992). The effects of suggestion and emotional arousal on pulmonary function in asthma: A review and a hypothesis regarding vagal medication. *Psychosomatic Medicine, 54,* 192–216.

Ivnik, R. J., Smith, G. E., Malec, J. F., Petersen, R. C., & Tangalos, E. G. (1995). Long-term stability and intercorrelations of cognitive abilities in older persons. *Psychological Assessment, 7,* 155–161.

Jablenski, A. (1988). Epidemiology of schizophrenia. In P. Bebbington and P. McGuffin (Eds.), *Schizophrenia: The major issues* (pp. 19–35). London: Heinemann Medical Books.

Jackson, M., & Claridge, G. (1991). Reliability and validity of a psychotic traits questionnaire (STQ). *British Journal of Psychiatry, 30,* 311–323.

Jacobs, D., & Klein, M. E. (1993). The expanding role of psychological autopsies. In A. A. Leenaars (Ed.), *Suicidology.* Northvale: Jason Aronson Inc.

Jacobsen, P. B., Bovbjerg, D. H., Schwartz, M. D., Hudis, C. A., Gilewski, T. A., & Norton, L. (1995). Conditioned emotional distress in women receiving chemotherapy for breast cancer. *Journal of Consulting and Clinical Psychology, 63,* 108–114.

Jacobson, E. (1938). *Progressive relaxation*. Chicago: University of Chicago Press.

Jacobson, E. (1964). *Self-operations control*. New York: Lippincott.

Jacobson, E. (1967). *Tension in medicine*. Springfield, IL: Thomas.

Jacobson, N. S., & Anderson, E. A. (1982). Interpersonal skill and depression in college students: An analysis of the timing of self-disclosures. *Behavior Therapy, 13*, 271–282.

Jaenicke, C., Hammen, C., Zupan, B., Hiroto, D., Gordon, D., Adrian, C., & Burge, D. (1987). Cognitive vulnerability in children at risk for depression. *Journal of Abnormal Child Psychology, 15*, 559–572.

James, G. D., Yee, L. S., Harshfield, G. A., Blank, S. G., & Pickering, T. G. (1986). The influence of happiness, anger, and anxiety on the blood pressure of borderline hypertensives. *Psychosomatic Medicine, 48*, 502–508.

Janoff-Bulman, R. (1985). Aftermath of victimization: Rebuilding shattered assumptions. In C. R. Figley (Ed.), *Trauma and its wake* (pp. 15–31). New York: Brunner/Mazel.

Jansen, A., Van Den Hout, M. A., De Loof, C., Zandbergen, J., & Griez, E. (1989). A case of bulimia successfully treated by cue exposure. *Journal of Behavior Therapy and Experimental Psychiatry, 20*, 327–332.

Janssen, K. (1983). Treatment of sinus tachycardia with heart-rate feedback. *Psychiatry and Human Development, 17*, 166–176.

Janus, S. S., & Janus, C. L. (1993). *The Janus report on sexual behavior*. New York: Wiley.

Jawed, S. Y. (1991). A survey of psychiatrically ill Asian children. *British Journal of Psychiatry, 158*, 268–270.

Jellinek, E. M. (1971). Phases of alcohol addiction. In G. Shean (Ed.), *Studies in abnormal behavior*. Chicago: Rand McNally.

Jenike, M. A., Baer, L., Summergrad, P., Weilburg, J. B., Holland, A., & Seymour, R. (1989). Obsessive-compulsive disorder: A double-blind, placebo controlled trial of clomipramine in 27 patients. *American Journal of Psychiatry, 146*, 1328–1330.

Jenkins, J. H, & Karno, M. (1992). The meaning of expressed emotion: Theoretical issues raised by cross-cultural research. *American Journal of Psychiatry, 149*, 9–21.

Jenner, F. A., Gjessing, L. R., Cox, J. R., Davies-Jones, A., Hullin, R. R., & Hanna, S. M. (1967). A manic-depressive psychotic with a persistent forty-eight-hour cycle. *British Journal of Psychiatry, 113*, 895–910.

Jensen, A. (1969). How much can we boost IQ and school achievements? *Harvard Educational Review, 39*, 1–123.

Jessor, R., & Jessor, S. L. (1977). *Problem behavior and psychosocial development: A longitudinal study of youth*. New York: Academic Press.

Johnson, D. A. W., Ludlow, J. M., Street, K., & Taylor, R. D. W. (1987). Double-blind comparison of half-dose and standard-dose flupenthixol decanoate in the maintenance treatment of stabilized out-patients with schizophrenia. *British Journal of Psychiatry, 151*, 634–638.

Johnson, W. G. (1990). Multifactorial diseases and other disorders with non-Mendelian inheritance. In H. E. Hendrie, L. G. Mendelsohn, & C. Readhead (Eds.), *Brain aging: Molecular biology, the aging process and neurodegenerative disease* (pp. 5–19). Bern, Germany: Hans Huber Publishers.

Johnson, L. D., O'Malley, P. M., & Bachman, J. G. (1991). *Drug use among American high school seniors, college students and young adults, 1975–1990* (Vols. 1 & 2). Rockville, MD: National Institute on Drug Abuse.

Johnston, W. B., & Packer, A. H. (1987). *Workforce 2000: Work and workers for the twenty-first century*. Indianapolis, IN: Hudson Institute.

Jones, J. M. (1995). Headache: Benign or catastrophic? *Physician Assistant, 19*, 25–44.

Jones, K. L., Shainberg, L. W., & Byer, C. O. (1977). *Sex and people*. New York: Harper & Row.

Joseph, E. (1991). Psychodynamic personality theory. In K. Davis, H. Klar, & J. J. Coyle (Eds.), *Foundations of psychiatry*. Philadelphia: Saunders.

Joseph, S. A., Brewin, C. R., Yule, W., & Williams, R. (1993). Causal attributions in posttraumatic stress in adolescents. *Journal of Child Psychology and Psychiatry, 34*, 247–253.

Joyce, C. (1988). Assault on the brain. *Psychology Today, 22*, 38–44.

Julkunen, J., Idanpaan-Heikkila, U., & Saarinen, T. (1993). Components of type A behavior and the first-year prognosis of a myocardial infarction. *Journal of Psychosomatic Research, 37*, 11–18.

Kagan, D. M., & Squires, R. L. (1984). Eating disorders among adolescents: Patterns and prevalence. *Adolescence, 19*, 15–29.

Kagan, J., Reznick, J. S., & Snidman, N. (1987). The physiology and psychology of behavioral inhibition in children. *Child Development, 58*, 1459–1473.

Kagan, J., & Snidman, N. (1991). Temperamental factors in human development. *American Psychologist, 46*, 856–862.

Kahn, A. U., Staerk, M., & Bonk, C. (1974). Role of counterconditioning in the treatment of asthma. *Journal of Psychosomatic Research, 18*, 88–92.

Kahn, M. W., & Raufman, L. (1981). Hospitalization versus imprisonment and the insanity plea. *Criminal Justice and Behavior, 8*(4), 483–490.

Kallman, W. M., Hersen, M., & O'Toole, D. H. (1975). The use of social reinforcement in a case of conversion reaction. *Behavior Therapy, 6*, 411–413.

Kamarck, T., & Jennings, J. R. (1991). Biobehavioral factors in sudden cardiac death. *Psychological Bulletin, 109*, 42–75.

Kanas, N. (1988). Psychoactive substance use disorders: Alcohol. In H. H. Goldman (Ed.), *Review of general psychiatry* (pp. 286–298). Norwalk, CT: Appleton & Lange.

Kane, J. M. (1991). New developments in the pharmacologic treatment of schizophrenia: Editor's introduction. *Schizophrenia Bulletin, 17*, 193–195.

Kane, J. M., & Freeman, H. L. (1994). Towards more effective antipsychotic treatment. *British Journal of Psychiatry, 165*, 22–31.

Kane, J. M., & Smith, J. M. (1982). Tardive dyskinesia: prevalence and risk factors, 1959–1979. *Archives of General Psychiatry, 39*, 473–481.

Kane, J. M., Woerner, M., Borenstein, M., Wegner, J., & Lieberman, J. (1986). Investigating the incidence and prevalence of tardive dyskinesia. *Psychopharmacology Bulletin, 22*, 254–258.

Kanfer, F. H., & Phillips, J. S. (1969). A survey of current behavior therapies and a proposal for classification. In C. M. Franks (Ed.), *Behavior therapy: Appraisal and status*. New York: Wiley.

Kanner, L. (1943). Autistic disturbances of affective content. *Nervous Child, 2*, 217–240.

Kanner, L. (1960). Do behavior symptoms always indicate psychopathology? *Journal of Child Psychological Psychiatry, 1*, 17–25.

Kanner, L., & Lesser, L. I. (1958). Early infantile autism. *Pediatrics Clinic of North America, 5*, 711–730.

Kaplan, H. I., & Sadock, B. J. (1981). *Modern synopsis of comprehensive textbook of psychiatry* (3rd ed.). Baltimore: Williams & Wilkins.

Kaplan, H. S. (1974). No nonsense therapy for six sexual malfunctions. *Psychology Today, 8*, 76–80, 83, 86.

Kaplan, M. (1983). A woman's view of DSM-III. *American Psychologist, 38*, 786–792.

Karno, M., & Golding, J. M. (1991). Obsessive-compulsive disorder. In L. N. Robins & D. A. Regier (Eds.), *Psychiatric disorders in America: The Epidemiologic Catchment Area study* (pp. 204–219). New York: Free Press.

Karno, M., Hough, R. L., Burnam, A., Escobar, J. I., Timbers, D. M., Santana, F., & Boyd, J. H. (1987). Lifetime prevalence of specific psychiatric disorders among Mexican Americans and non-Hispanic whites in Los Angeles. *Archives of General Psychiatry, 44,* 695–701.

Karno, M., Jenkins, J. H., De la Selva, A., Santana, F., Telles, C., Lopez, S., & Mintz, J. (1987). Expressed emotion and schizophrenic outcome among Mexican-American families. *Journal of Nervous and Mental Disease, 175,* 143–151.

Karon, B. P. (1995). Provision of psychotherapy under managed health care: A growing crisis and national nightmare. *Professional Psychology: Research and Practice, 26,* 5–9.

Kasari, C., Sigman, M. D., Baumgartner, P., & Stipek, D. J. (1993). Pride and mastery in children with autism. *Journal of Child Psychology and Psychiatry, 34,* 353–362.

Kashani, J. H., & Carlson, G. A. (1987). Seriously depressed preschoolers. *American Journal of Psychiatry, 144,* 348–350.

Kaszniak, A. W., Nussbaum, P. D., Berren, M. R., & Santiago, J. (1988). Amnesia as a consequence of male rape: A case report. *Journal of Abnormal Psychology, 97,* 100–104.

Katchadourian, H. A., & Lunde, D. T. (1975). *Fundamentals of human sexuality* (2nd ed.). New York: Holt, Rinehart & Winston.

Katerndahl, D. A., & Realini, J. P. (1993). Lifetime prevalence of panic states. *American Journal of Psychiatry, 150,* 246–249.

Katschnig, H. & Amering, M. Long-term treatment risk/benefit ratio and therapeutic outcome. *Clinical Neuropharmacology, 15,* 178–179.

Katz, J. (1985). The sociopolitical nature of counseling. *Counseling Psychologist, 13,* 615–624.

Kaufman, A. S., Kamphaus, R. W., & Kaufman, N. L. (1985). The Kaufman Assessment Battery for Children (K-ABC). In C. S. Newmark (Ed.), *Major psychological assessment instruments* (pp. 249–276). Boston: Allyn & Bacon.

Kaufman, A. S., & Kaufman, N. L. (1983). *Kaufman Assessment Battery for Children.* Circle Pines, MN: American Guidance Services.

Kaul, T. J., & Bednar, R. L. (1986). Experiential group research: Results, questions, and suggestions. In S. L. Garfield and A. E. Bergin (Eds.), *Handbook of psychotherapy and behavior change: An evaluative analysis.* New York: Wiley.

Kavanagh, D. J. (1992). Recent developments in expressed emotions and schizophrenia. *British Journal of Psychiatry, 160,* 601–620.

Kawachi, I., Sparrow, D., Vonkonas, P. S., & Weiss, S. T. (1994). Symptoms of anxiety and risk of coronary heart disease: The Normative Aging Study. *Circulation, 90,* 2225–2229.

Kazdin, A. E. (1980). *Behavior modification in applied settings* (2nd ed.). Homewood, IL: Dorsey.

Kazdin, A. E. (1987). Treatment of antisocial behavior in children: Current status and future directions. *Psychological Bulletin, 102,* 187–203.

Kazdin, A. E. (1993). Adolescent mental health: Prevention and treatment programs. *American Psychologist, 48,* 127–141.

Kazdin, A. E. (1994). Psychotherapy for children and adolescents. In A. E. Bergin & S. L. Garfield (Eds.), *Handbook of psychotherapy and behavior change* (pp. 543–594). New York: Wiley.

Kazdin, A. E., Siegel, T. C., & Bass, D. (1992). Cognitive problem-solving skills training and parent management training in the treatment of antisocial behavior in children. *Journal of Consulting and Clinical Psychology, 60,* 733–747.

Keane, T. M., Fairbank, J. A., Caddell, J. M., Zimering, R. T., & Bender, M. E. (1985). A behavioral approach to assessing and treatment of posttraumatic stress disorder in Vietnam veterans (pp. 257–294). In C. R. Figley (Ed.), *Trauma and its wake.* New York: Brunner/Mazel.

Keeling, R. P. (1993). HIV disease: Current concepts. *Journal of Counseling and Development, 71,* 261–274.

Kegeles, T., Catania, J., & Coates, T. (1988). Intentions to communicate positive HIV status to sex partners (letters to the editor). *Journal of the American Medical Association, 259,* 216–217.

Keith, S. J., Regier, D. A., & Rae, D. S. (1991). Schizophrenic disorders. In L. N. Robins & D. A. Regier (Eds.), *Psychiatric Disorders in America* (pp. 33–52). New York: Free Press.

Kellner, R. (1982). Psychotherapeutic strategies in hypochondriasis: A clinical study. *American Journal of Psychotherapy, 36,* 146–157.

Kellner, R. (1985). Functional somatic symptoms and hypochondriasis. *Archives of General Psychiatry, 42,* 821–833.

Kellner, R., Hernandez, J., & Pathak, D. (1992). Hypochondriacal fears and beliefs, anxiety, and somatization. *British Journal of Psychiatry, 160,* 525–532.

Kelly, J. A., & Murphy, D. A. (1992). Psychological interventions with AIDS and HIV: Prevention and treatment. *Journal of Consulting and Clinical Psychology, 60*(4), 576–585.

Kendler, K. S. (1988). Familial aggregation of schizophrenia and schizophrenic spectrum disorders. *Archives of General Psychiatry, 45,* 377–383.

Kendler, K. S., & Diehl, S. R. (1993). The genetics of schizophrenia: A current, genetic-epidemiologic perspective. *Schizophrenia Bulletin, 19,* 261–284.

Kendler, K. S., Glaser, W. M., & Morgenstern, H. (1983). Dimensions of delusional experience. *American Journal of Psychiatry, 140,* 466–469.

Kendler, K. S., & Hays, P. (1982). Familial and sporadic schizophrenia: A symptomatic, prognostic, and EEG comparison. *American Journal of Psychiatry, 139,* 1557–1562.

Kendler, K. S., MacLean, C., Neale, M., Kessler, R., Heath, A., & Eaves, L. (1991). The genetic epidemiology of bulimia nervosa. *American Journal of Psychiatry, 148,* 1627–1637.

Kendler, K. S., Neale, M. C., Kessler, R. C., Heath, A. C., & Eaves, L. J. (1992a). Generalized anxiety disorder in women. *Archives of General Psychiatry, 49,* 267–271.

Kendler, K. S., Neale, M. C., Kessler, R. C., Heath, A. C., & Eaves, L. J. (1992b). The genetic epidemiology of phobias in women. *Archives of General Psychiatry, 49,* 273–281.

Kendler, K. S., Silberg, J. L., Neale, M. C., Kessler, R. C., Heath, A. C., & Eaves, L. J. (1991). The family history method: Whose psychiatric history is being measured? *American Journal of Psychiatry, 148,* 1501–1504.

Kerlitz, I., & Fulton, J. P. (1984). *The insanity defense and its alternatives: A guide to policy makers.* Williamsburg, VA: National Center for State Courts.

Kernberg, O. (1976). Technical considerations in the treatment of borderline personality organization. *Journal of the American Psychoanalytic Association, 24,* 795–829.

Kernberg, O. F. (1975). *Borderline conditions and pathological narcissism.* New York: Jason Aronson.

Kessler, R. C., McGonagle, K. A., Zhao, S., Nelson, C. B., Hughes, M., Eshleman, S., Wittchen, H.-U., & Kendler, K. S. (1994). Lifetime and twelve-month prevalence of DSM-III-R psychiatric disorders in the United States. *Archives of General Psychiatry, 51,* 8–19.

Kety, S. S. (1979). Disorders of the human brain. *Scientific American, 241,* 202–214.

Kety, S. S., Wender, P. H., Jacobsen, B., Ingraham, L. J., Jansson, L., Faber, B., & Kinney, D. K. (1994). Mental illness in the biological and adoptive relatives of schizophrenic adoptees. *Archives of General Psychiatry, 51,* 442–455.

Keyes, D. (1981). *The minds of Billy Milligan.* New York: Bantam.

Khanna, S., Desai, N. G., & Channabasavanna, S. M. (1987). A treatment package for transsexualism. *Behavior Therapy, 2,* 193–199.

Kiecolt-Glaser, J. K., Dura, J. R., Speicher, C. E., Trask, O. J., & Glaser, R. (1991). Spousal caregivers of dementia victims: Longitudinal changes in immunity and health. *Psychosomatic Medicine, 53,* 345–362.

Kiecolt-Glaser, J. K., & Glaser, R. (1988). Psychological influences on immunity: Implications for AIDS. *American Psychologist, 43,* 892–898.

Kiecolt-Glaser, J. K., & Glaser, R. (1992). Psychoneuroimmunology: Can psychological interventions modulate immunity? *Journal of Consulting and Clinical Psychology, 60,* 569–575.

Kiecolt-Glaser, J. K., & Glaser, R. (1993). Mind and immunity. In D. Goleman & J. Gurin (Eds.), *Mind/body medicine* (pp. 39–64). New York: Consumer Reports Books.

Kiecolt-Glaser, J. K., & Glaser, R. (1995). Psychoneuroimmunology and health consequences: Data and shared mechanisms. *Psychosomatic Medicine, 57,* 269–274.

Kiecolt-Glaser, J. K., Glaser, R., Dyer, C., Shuttleworth, E. C., Ogrocki, P., & Speicher, C. E. (1987). Chronic stress and immune function in family care-givers of Alzheimer's disease victims. *Psychosomatic Medicine, 49,* 523–535.

Kiesler, C. A. (1991). Homelessness and public policy priorities. *American Psychologist, 46,* 1245–1252.

Kilmann, P., Sabalis, R., Gearing, M., Bukstel, L., & Scovern, A. (1982). The treatment of sexual paraphilias: A review of the outcome research. *Journal of Sex Research, 18,* 193–252.

Kilmann, P. R., & Auerbach, R. (1979). Treatments of premature ejaculation and psychogenic impotence: A critical review of the literature. *Archives of Sexual Behavior, 8,* 81–100.

Kilmann, P. R., Mills, K. H., Caid, C., Davidson, E., Bella, B., Milan, R., Drose, G., Boland, J., Follingstad, D., Montgomery, B., & Wanlass, R. (1986). Treatment of secondary orgasmic dysfunction: An outcome study. *Archives of Sexual Behavior, 15,* 211–229.

Kilpatrick, D. G., Veronen, L. J., & Best, C. L. (1985). Factors predicting psychological distress among rape victims (pp. 113–141). In C. R. Figley (Ed.), *Trauma and its wake.* New York: Brunner/Mazel.

Kilpatrick, D. G., Veronen, L. J., & Resick, P. A. (1979). The aftermath of rape: Recent empirical findings. *American Journal of Orthopsychiatry, 49,* 658–669.

King, A. C., Taylor, C. B., Albright, C. A., & Haskells, W. L. (1990). The relationship between repressive and defensive coping styles and blood pressure responses in healthy, middle-aged men and women. *Journal of Psychosomatic Research, 34,* 461–471.

King, D. W., King, L. A., Gudanowski, D. M., & Vreven, D. L. (1995). Alternative representations of war zone stressors: Relationships to posttraumatic stress disorder in male and female Vietnam veterans. *Journal of Abnormal Psychology, 104,* 184–196.

King, N. J., Gullione, E., Tonge, B. J., & Ollendick, T. H. (1993). Self-reports of panic attacks and manifest anxiety in adolescents. *Behaviour Research and Therapy, 31,* 11–116.

King, R. M., & Wilson, G. V. (1991). Use of a diary technique to investigate psychosomatic relations in atopic dermatitis. *Journal of Psychosomatic Research, 35,* 697–706.

Kingdon, D. G., & Turkington, D. (1991). The use of cognitive behavior therapy with a normalizing rationale in schizophrenia. *Journal of Nervous and Mental Disease, 179,* 207–211.

Kinsey, A. C., Pomeroy, W. B., & Martin, C. E. (1948). *Sexual behavior in the human male.* Philadelphia: W. B. Saunders.

Kinsey, A. C., Pomeroy, W. B., Martin, C. E., & Gebhard, P. H. (1953). *Sexual behavior in the human female.* Philadelphia: Saunders.

Kinzie, J. D., Frederickson, R. H., Ben, R., Fleck, J., & Karls, W. (1984). Posttraumatic stress disorder. *American Journal of Psychiatry, 141,* 645–650.

Kirkpatrick, D. R. (1984). Age, gender and patterns of common intense fears among adults. *Behavior Research and Therapy, 22,* 141–150.

Kirsling, R. A. (1986). Review of suicide among elderly persons. *Psychological Reports, 59,* 359–366.

Klagsbrun, F. (1976). *Too young to die: Youth and suicide.* Boston: Houghton Mifflin.

Klein, D., Gittelman, R., & Quitkin, F., et al. (1980). *Diagnosis and drug treatment of psychiatric disorders: Adults and children* (pp. 268–404). Baltimore: Williams & Wilkins.

Klein, E., & Uhde, T. W. (1988). Controlled study of Verapamil for treatment of panic disorder. *American Journal of Psychiatry, 145,* 431–434.

Klein, R. G. (1987). Prognosis of attention deficit disorder and its management in adolescence. *Pediatrics in Review, 8,* 216–222.

Kleinberg, J., & Galligan, B. (1983). Effects of deinstitutionalization on adaptive behavior of mentally retarded adults. *American Journal of Mental Deficiency, 88,* 21–27.

Kleinman, A. (1991, April). *Culture and DSM-IV: Recommendations for the introduction and for the overall structure.* Paper presented at the Conference on Culture and DSM-IV, Pittsburgh.

Kleinmutz, B. (1967). *Personality measurement: An introduction.* Homewood, IL: Dorsey.

Klemchuk, H. P., Hutchins, C. B., & Frank, R. I. (1990). Body dissatisfaction and eating-related problems on the college campus. *Journal of Counseling Psychology, 37,* 297–305.

Klerman, G. L. (1982). Practical issues in the treatment of depression and mania. In E. S. Paykel (Ed.), *Handbook of affective disorders.* New York: Guilford Press.

Klerman, G. L., Weissman, M. M., Markowitz, J., Glick, I., Wilner, P. J., Mason, B., & Shear, M. K. (1994). Medication and psychotherapy. In A. E. Bergin & S. L. Garfield (Eds.), *Handbook of psychotherapy and behavior change* (pp. 734–782). New York: Wiley.

Klerman, G. L., Weissman, M. M., Rounsavelle, B. J., & Chevron, E. S. (1984). *Interpersonal psychotherapy of depression.* New York: Basic Books.

Klin, A. (1991). Young autistic children's listening preferences in regard to speech: A possible characterization of the symptom of social withdrawal. *Journal of Autism and Developmental Disorders, 21,* 29–42.

Klin, A., Volkmar, F. R., & Sparrow, S. S. (1992). Autistic social dysfunction: Some limitations of the theory of mind hypothesis. *Journal of Child Psychology and Psychiatry, 33,* 861–876.

Kline, M., Frances, A., Davis, W. W., Pincus, H. A., & Comer, R. J. (1993). *DSM-IV: 1993 update.* New York: W. H. Freeman and Company.

Klopfer, B., & Davidson, H. (1962). *The Rorschach technique.* New York: Harcourt, Brace & World.

Klosko, J. S., Barlow, D. H., Tassinari, R., & Cerny, J. A. (1990). A comparison of Alprazolam and behavior therapy in the treatment of panic disorder. *Journal of Consulting and Clinical Psychology, 58,* 77–84.

Kluft, R. P. (1982). Varieties of hypnotic interventions in the treatment of multiple personality. *American Journal of Clinical Hypnosis, 24,* 230–240.

Kluft, R. P. (1987a). Dr. Kluft replies. *American Journal of Psychiatry, 144,* 125.

Kluft, R. P. (1987b). First-rank symptoms as a diagnostic clue to multiple personality disorder. *American Journal of Psychiatry, 144,* 293–298.

Knapp, S., & VandeCreek, L. (1990). Application of the duty to protect to HIV-positive patients. *Professional Psychology: Research and Practice, 21,* 161–166.

Kneisel, P. J., & Richards, G. P. (1988). Crisis intervention after the suicide of a teacher. *Professional Psychology: Research and Practice, 19,* 165–169.

Knopf, I. J. (1984). *Childhood psychopathology* (2nd ed.). Englewood Cliffs, NJ: Prentice-Hall.

Knott, J., Platt, E., Ashley, M., & Gottlieb, J. (1953). A familial evaluation of the electroencephalogram of patients with primary behavior disorder and psychopathic personality. *EEG and Clinical Neurophysiology, 5,* 363–370.

Kobasa, S. C., Hilker, R. J., & Maddi, S. R. (1979). Psychological hardiness. *Journal of Occupational Medicine, 21,* 595–598.

Kockott, G., & Fahrner, E.-M. (1987). Transsexuals who have not undergone surgery: A follow-up study. *Archives of Sexual Behavior, 16,* 511–522.

Koegel, R. L., Screibman, L., Loos, L. M., Dirlich-Wilheim, H., Dunlap, G., Robbins, F. R., & Plienis, A. J. (1992). Consistent stress profiles in mothers of children with autism. *Journal of Autism and Developmental Disorders, 22,* 205–216.

Kohlenberg, R. J. (1973). Behavioristic approach to multiple personality: A case study. *Behavior Therapy, 4,* 137–140.

Kohlenberg, R. J. (1974). Directed masturbation and the treatment of primary orgasmic dysfunction. *Archives of Sexual Behavior, 3,* 349–356.

Kohlenberg, R. J., & Tsai, M. (1991). *Functional analytic psychotherapy.* New York: Plenum.

Kohler, F. W., Strain, P. S., Hoyson, M., Davis, L., Donina, W. M., & Rapp, N. (1995). Using a group-oriented contingency to increase social interactions between children with autism and their peers. *Behavior Modification, 19,* 10–32.

Kohon, G. (1987). Fetishism revisited. *International Journal of Psycho-Analysis, 68,* 213–228.

Kolarsky, A., & Madlatfousek, J. (1983). The inverse rule of preparatory erotic stimulation in exhibitionists: Phallometric studies. *Archives of Sexual Behavior, 12,* 123–148.

Kolb, L. C. (1987). A neuropsychological hypothesis explaining posttraumatic stress disorder. *American Journal of Psychiatry, 144,* 989–995.

Kolko, D. J., Ayllon, T., & Torrance, C. (1987). Positive practice routines in overcoming resistance to the treatment of school phobia: A case study with follow-up. *Journal of Behavior Therapy and Experimental Psychiatry, 18,* 249–257.

Kolko, D. J., & Kazdin, A. E. (1991). Children who set fires. *Journal of Clinical Child Psychology, 20,* 191–201.

Kolko, D. J., Loar, L. L., & Sturnick, D. (1990). Inpatient social-cognitive skills training groups with conduct disordered and attention deficit disordered children. *Journal of Child Psychology and Psychiatry, 31,* 734–748.

Kondratas, A. (1991). Ending homelessness. *American Psychologist, 46,* 1226–1231.

Kopelman, M. D. (1987). Amnesia: Organic and psychogenic. *British Journal of Psychiatry, 144,* 293–298.

Korchin, S. J. (1976). *Modern clinical psychology.* New York: Basic Books.

Kosky, R. (1983). Childhood suicidal behavior. *Journal of Child Psychology and Psychiatry, 24,* 457–468.

Koss, M. P., Gidycz, C. A., & Wisniewski, N. (1987). The scope of rape: Incidence and prevalence of sexual aggression and victimization in a national sample of higher education students. *Journal of Consulting and Clinical Psychology, 55,* 162–170.

Kottler, J. A., & Brown, R. W. (1992). *Introduction to therapeutic counseling.* Belmont, CA: Brooks/Cole.

Kourany, R. F. C., & Williams, B. V. (1984). Capgras' syndrome with dysmorphic delusion in an adolescent. *Psychosomatics, 25,* 715–717.

Kovacs, M., Rush, A., Beck, A., & Hollon, S. (1981). Depressed outpatients treated with cognitive therapy or pharmacotherapy. *Archives of General Psychiatry, 38,* 33–39.

Kraemer, G. W., & McKinney, W. T. (1979). Interactions of pharmacological agents which alter biogenic amine metabolism and depression: An analysis of contributing factors within a primate model of depression. *Journal of Affective Disorders, 1,* 33–54.

Kraepelin, E. (1923). *Textbook of psychiatry* (8th ed.). New York: Macmillan. (Originally published 1883.)

Kramer, B. (1973, November 16). Mass hysteria: An age-old illness still crops up in modern times. *Wall Street Journal,* p. 36b.

Krantz, S. E., & Moos, R. H. (1988). Risk factors at intake predict nonremission among depressed patients. *Journal of Consulting and Clinical Psychology, 56(6),* 863–869.

Kranzler, H. R., & Anton, R. F. (1994). Implications of recent neuropsychopharmacologic research for understanding the etiology and development of alcoholism. *Journal of Consulting and Clinical Psychology, 62,* 1116–1126.

Kringlen, E. (1980). Schizophrenia: Research in Nordic countries. *Schizophrenia Bulletin, 6,* 566–578.

Kringlen, E. (1994). Theory of schizophrenia: Comments. *British Journal of Psychiatry, 164,* 62–64.

Kübler-Ross, E. (1983). *On death and dying.* New York: MacMillan.

Kuch, K., Cox, B. J., Evans, R., & Shulman, I. (1994). Phobias, panic, and pain in fifty-five survivors of road vehicle accidents. *Journal of Anxiety Disorders, 8,* 181–187.

Kumanyika, S., Wilson, J., & Guilford-Davenport, M. (1993). Weight-related attitudes and behaviors of Black women. *Journal of the American Dietetic Association, 93,* 416–422.

Kurth, J. H., & Kurth, M. C. (1994). Role of monoamine oxidase genetics in the etiology of Parkinson's disease. In A. Lieberman, C. W. Olanow, M. B. Youdin, & K. Tipton (Eds.), *Monoamine oxidase inhibitors in neurological diseases* (pp. 113–126). New York: Marcel Dekker.

Kushner, M. (1965). The reduction of a long-standing fetish by means of aversive conditioning. In L. P. Ullmann & L. Krasner (Eds.), *Case studies in behavior modification.* New York: Holt, Rhinehart & Winston.

Kushner, M. G., Riggs, D. S., Foa, E. B., & Miller, S. M. (1992). Perceived controllability and the development of posttraumatic stress disorder (PTSD) in crime victims. *Behaviour Research and Therapy, 31,* 105–110.

Lacey, J. I., Bateman, D. E., & Van Lehn, R. (1953). Autonomic response specificity. *Psychosomatic Medicine, 15,* 8–21.

LaGreca, A. M., & Stringer, S. A. (1985). The Wechsler Intelligence Scale for Children–Revised. In C. S. Newmark (Ed.), *Major psychological assessment instruments* (pp. 277–322). Boston: Allyn & Bacon.

Lahey, B., Hartdagen S. E., Frick, P. J., McBurnett, K., Connor, R., & Hynd, G. W. (1988). Conduct disorder: Parsing the confounded relation to parental divorce and antisocial personality. *Journal of Abnormal Psychology, 97,* 334–337.

Lahey, B. B., Loeber, R., Hart, E. L., Frick, P. J., Applegate, B., Zhang, Q., Green, S. M., & Russo, M. R. (1995). Four-year longitudinal study of conduct disorders in boys: Patterns and predictors of persistence. *Journal of Abnormal Psychology, 104,* 89–93.

Lai, J. Y., & Linden, W. (1992). Gender anger expression style, and opportunity for anger release determine cardiovascular reaction to and recovery from anger provocation. *Psychosomatic Medicine, 54,* 297–310.

Laker, B. (1992, April 14). A nightmare of memories. *Seattle Post-Intelligencer,* pp. C1–C2.

Lamb, H. R. (1984). Deinstitutionalization and the homeless mentally ill. *Hospital Community Psychiatry, 35,* 899–907.

Lambert, M. J., & Bergin, A. E. (1994). The effectiveness of psychotherapy. In A. E. Bergin & S. L. Garfield (Eds.), *Handbook of psychotherapy and behavior change* (pp. 143–189). New York: Wiley.

Lambert, M. J., Shapiro, D. A., & Bergin, A. E. (1986). The effectiveness of psychotherapy. In S. L. Garfield & A. E. Bergin (Eds.), *Handbook of psychotherapy and behavior change* (3rd ed., pp. 157–212). New York: Wiley.

Lambert, N. M. (1988). Adolescent outcomes for hyperactive children. *American Psychologist, 43,* 786–799.

Lambert, N. M., Hartsough, C. S., Sassone, D., & Sandoval, J. (1987). Persistence of hyperactivity symptoms from childhood to adolescence and associated outcomes. *American Journal of Orthopsychiatry, 57,* 22–23.

Lambley, P. (1974). Treatment of transvestism and subsequent coital problems. *Journal of Behavior Therapy and Experimental Psychiatry, 5,* 101–102.

Landesman S., & Butterfield, E. C. (1987). Normalization and de-institutionalization of mentally retarded individuals. *American Psychologist, 42,* 809–816.

Lane, W. D., & Kern, R. M. (1987). Multidimensional treatment of a 14-year-old anorexia nervosa patient. *Journal of Child and Adolescent Psychotherapy, 4,* 211–215.

Langer, E. J., & Rodin, J. (1976). The effects of choice and enhanced personal responsibility for the aged: A field experiment in an institutional setting. *Journal of Personality and Social Psychology, 34,* 191–198.

Langevin, R. (1990). Sexual anomalies and the brain. In W. L. Marshall, D. R. Laws, & H. E. Barbaree (Eds.), *Handbook of sexual assault: Issues, theories, and treatment of the offender* (pp. 103–114). New York: Plenum Press.

Langevin, R., Bain, J., Wortzman, G., Hucker, S., Dickey, R., & Wright, P. (1988). Sexual sadism: Brain, blood, and behavior. In R. A. Prentky and V. L. Quisey (Eds.), *Human sexual aggression: Current perspectives. Annals of the New York Academy of Sciences, 528* (pp. 79–110). Salem, MA: New York Academy of Sciences.

Langevin, R., Paitich, D., Ramsay, G., Anderson, C., Kamrad, J., Pope, S., Geller, G., Pearl, L., & Newman, S. (1979). Experimental studies of exhibitionism. *Archives of Sexual Behavior, 8,* 307–331.

Laraia, M. T., Stuart, G. W., Frye, L. H., Lydiard, R. B., & Ballenger, J. C. (1994). Childhood environment of women having panic disorder with agoraphobia. *Journal of Anxiety Disorders, 8,* 1–17.

Lask, B., & Bryant-Waugh, R. (1992). Early-onset anorexia nervosa and related eating disorders. *Journal of Child Psychology and Psychiatry, 33,* 281–300.

Last, C. G., Hersen, M., Kazdin, A., Orvaschel, H., & Perrin, S. (1991). Anxiety disorders in children and their families. *Archives of General Psychiatry, 48,* 928–934.

Last, C. G., & Perrin, S. (1993). Anxiety disorders in African-American and white children. *Journal of Abnormal Child Psychology, 21,* 153–162.

Laudenslager, M. L., Ryan, S. M., Drugan, R. C., Hyson, R. L., & Maier, S. F. (1983). Coping and immunosuppression: Inescapable but not escapable shock suppresses lymphocyte proliferation. *Science, 220,* 568–570.

Laughlin, H. P. (1967). *The neuroses.* Washington, DC: Butterworth.

Laws, D. R., & Marshall, W. L. (1990). A conditioning theory of the etiology and maintenance of deviant sexual preference and behavior. In W. L. Marshall, D. R. Laws, & H. E. Barbaree (Eds.), *Handbook of sexual assault: Issues, theories, and treatment of the offender* (pp. 209–230). New York: Plenum Press.

Lazarus, A. A. (1967). In support of technical eclecticism. *Psychological Reports, 21,* 415–416.

Lazarus, A. A. (1968). Learning theory and the treatment of depression. *Behavior Research and Therapy, 6,* 83–90.

Lazarus, A. A. (1977). Has behavior therapy outlived its usefulness? *American Psychologist, 32,* 550–554.

Lazarus, A. A. (1983). *Psychological stress.* New York: McGraw-Hill.

Lazarus, A. A. (1984). Multimodel therapy. In R. J. Corsini (Ed.), *Current psychotherapies.* Itasca, IL: Peacock.

Lazarus, R. S. (1983). *Psychological stress.* New York: McGraw-Hill.

Leary, W. E. (1992, December 10). Medical panel says most sexual impotence in men can be treated without surgery. *New York Times,* p. D20.

Leckman, J. F., Walker, D. E., & Cohen, D. J. (1993). Premonitory urges in Tourette's syndrome. *American Journal of Psychiatry, 150,* 98–102.

LeDoux, J. C., & Hazelwood, R. R. (1985). Police attitude and beliefs toward rape. *Journal of Police Science Administration, 13,* 211–220.

Lee, C. L., & Bates, J. E. (1985). Mother-child interaction at age two years and perceived difficult temperament. *Child Development, 56,* 1314–1325.

Lee, E. (1985). Inpatient psychiatric services for Southeast Asian refugees. In T. C. Owan (Ed.), *Southeast Asian mental health: Treatment, prevention, services, training, and research* (pp. 307–328). Washington, DC: U.S. Government Printing Office.

Lee, S., Hsu, L. K., & Wing, Y. K. (1992). Bulimia nervosa in Hong Kong Chinese patients. *British Journal of Psychiatry, 161,* 545–551.

Leekam, S. R., & Prior, M. (1994). Can autistic children distinguish lies from jokes? A second look at second-order belief attribution. *Journal of Child Psychology and Psychiatry, 35,* 901–915.

Leenaars, A. A. (1992). Suicide notes, communication, and ideation. In R. W. Maris, A. L. Berman, J. T. Maltsberger, & R. I. Yufit (Eds.), *Assessment and prediction of suicide.* New York: Guilford.

Leff, J. (1994). Working with the families of schizophrenic patients. *British Journal of Psychiatry, 164,* 71–76.

Leff, J., Thornicroft, G., Coxhead, N., & Crawford, C. (1994). The TAPS project. 22: A five-year follow-up of long-stay psychiatric patients discharged to the community. *British Journal of Psychiatry, 165,* 13–17.

Leff, J., Wig, N. N., Bedi, H., Menon, D. K., Kuipers, L., Korten, A., Ernberg, G., Day, R., Sartorius, N., & Jablenski, A. (1990). Relatives' expressed emotion and the course of schizophrenia in Chandigarh. *British Journal of Psychiatry, 156,* 351–356.

Lehmann, H. E. (1985). Affective disorders: Clinical features. In H. I. Kaplan & B. J. Sadock (Eds.), *Comprehensive textbook of psychiatry/IV* (pp. 786–810). Baltimore: Williams & Wilkins.

Lehrer, P. M., Sargunaraj, D., & Hochron, S. (1992). Psychological approaches to the treatment of asthma. *Journal of Consulting and Clinical Psychology, 60,* 639–643.

Leiblum, S. R., & Rosen, R. C. (1991). Couples therapy for erectile disorders: Conceptual and clinical considerations. Special issue: The treatment of male erectile disorders. *Journal of Sex and Marital Therapy, 17,* 147–159.

Leichtman, M. (1995). Behavioral observations. In J. N. Butcher (Ed.), *Clinical personality assessment: Practical approaches* (pp. 251–266). New York: Oxford University Press.

Lelliott, P. T., Marks, I. M., Monteiro, W. O., Tsakiris, L. F., & Noshirvani, H. (1987). Agoraphobics 5 years after imipramine and exposure. *Journal of Nervous and Mental Disease, 175,* 599–605.

Lenzenweger, M. F., Cornblatt, B. A., and Putnick, M. (1991). Schizotypy and sustained attention. *Journal of Abnormal Psychology, 100,* 84–89.

Leonard, H. L., Lenane, M. C., Swedo, S. E., Rettew, D. C., Gershon, E. S., & Rapoport, J. L. (1992). Tics and Tourette's disorder: A 2- to 7-year follow-up of 54 obsessive-compulsive children. *American Journal of Psychiatry, 149,* 1244–1251.

Leong, F. (1986). Counseling and psychotherapy with Asian-Americans: Review of the literature. *Journal of Counseling Psychology, 33,* 196–206.

Lerner, J. V., Hertzog, C., Hooker, K. A., Hassibi, M., & Thomas, A. (1988). A longitudinal study of negative emotional states.

Lerner, P. M. (1995). Assessing adaptive capacities by means of the Rorschach. In J. N. Butcher (Ed.), *Clinical personality assessment: Practical approaches* (pp. 317–328). New York: Oxford University Press.

Lesieur, H. R. (1989). Current research into pathological gambling and gaps in the literature. In H. J. Shaffer, S. A. Stein, B. Gambino, & T. N. Cummings (Eds.), *Compulsive gambling: Theory, research, and practice* (pp. 223–248). Lexington, MA: Lexington Books.

Leslie, R. (1991, July/August). Psychotherapist-patient privilege clarified. *The California Therapist,* 11–19.

Lester, D. (1989). *Can we prevent suicide?* New York: AMS Press.

Lester, D. (1991a). Do suicide prevention centers prevent suicide? *Homeostasis in Health and Disease, 33(4),* 190–194.

Lester, D. (1991b). The etiology of suicide and homicide in urban and rural America. *Journal of Rural Community Psychology, 2(1),* 15–17.

Levenkron, J. C., Cohen, J. D., Mueller, H. S., & Fisher, E. B. (1983). Modifying the type A coronary-prone behavior pattern. *Journal of Consulting and Clinical Psychology, 51,* 192–204.

Levenson, A. J. (1981). Basic psychopharmacology. New York: Springer.

Levenstein, C., Prantera, C., Varvo, V., Scribano, M. L., Berto, E., Luzi, C., & Andreoli, A. (1993). Development of the Perceived Stress Questionnaire: A new tool for psychosomatic research. *Journal of Psychosomatic Research, 37,* 19–32.

Levine, D. S., & Willner, S. G. (1976, February). The cost of mental illness, 1974. *Mental Health Statistical Note No. 125* (pp. 1–7). Washington, DC: National Institute of Mental Health.

Levine, I. S., & Rog, D. J. (1990). Mental health services for homeless mentally ill persons: Federal initiatives and current service trends. *American Psychologist, 45,* 963–968.

Levine, M., & Perkins, D. V. (1987). *Principles of community psychology: Perspectives and applications.* New York: Oxford University Press.

Levis, D. J. (1985). Implosive therapy: A comprehensive extension of conditioning theory of fear/anxiety to psychology. In S. Reiss & R. R. Bootzin (Eds.), *Theoretical issues in behavior therapy.* New York: Academic Press.

Lewine, R. (1986). Familial and nonfamilial schizophrenia? *American Journal of Psychiatry, 143,* 1064–1065.

Lewinsohn, P. M. (1974). A behavioral approach to depression. In R. J. Friedman & M. M. Katz (Eds.), *The psychology of depression: Contemporary theory and research.* New York: Wiley.

Lewinsohn, P. M. (1977). The behavioral study and treatment of depression. In M. Hersen, R. M. Eisler, & P. M. Miller (Eds.), *Progress in behavior modification.* New York: Academic Press.

Lewinsohn, P. M., & Graf, M. (1973). Pleasant activities and depression. *Journal of Consulting and Clinical Psychology, 41,* 261–268.

Lewinsohn, P. M., Hoberman, H. M., & Rosenbaum, M. (1988). A prospective study of risk factors for unipolar depression. *Journal of Abnormal Psychology, 97(3),* 251–264.

Lewinsohn, P. M., Hoberman, H. M., Teri, L., & Hautzinger, M. (1985). An integrative theory of depression. In S. Reiss & R. R. Bootzin (Eds.), *Theoretical issues in behavioral therapy* (pp. 331–359). Orlando, FL: Academic Press.

Lewinsohn, P. M., Hopps, H., Roberts, R. E., Seeley, J. R., & Andrews, J. A. (1993). Adolescent psychopathology: I. Prevalence and incidence of depression and other DSM-III-R disorders in high school students. *Journal of Abnormal Psychology, 102,* 133–144.

Lewinsohn, P. M., & Libet, J. (1972). Pleasant events, activity schedules, and depression. *Journal of Abnormal Psychology, 79,* 291–295.

Lewinsohn, P. M., Weinstein, M. S., & Alper, T. (1970). A behavioral approach to the group treatment of depressed persons: A methodological contribution. *Journal of Chemical Psychology, 26,* 525–532.

Lewinsohn, P. M., Zeiss, A. M., & Duncan, E. M. (1989). Probability of relapse after recovery from an episode of depression. *Journal of Abnormal Psychology, 97,* 387–398.

Ley, R. (1992). The many faces of Pan: Psychological and physiological differences among three types of panic attacks. *Behaviour Research and Therapy, 30,* 347–357.

Li-Repac, D. (1980). Cultural influences on clinical perceptions: A comparison between Caucasian and Chinese-American therapists. *Journal of Cross-Cultural Psychology, 11(3),* 327–342.

Liberini, P., Faglia, L., Salvi, F., & Grant, R. P. J. (1993). Cognitive impairment related to conversion disorder: A two-year follow-up study. *Journal of Nervous and Mental Disease, 181,* 325–327.

Liberman, R. P., & Green, M. F. (1992). Whither cognitive-behavioral therapy for schizophrenia. *Schizophrenia Bulletin, 18,* 27–35.

Liberman, R. P., Kopelowicz, A., & Young, A. S. (1994). Biobehavioral treatment and rehabilitation of schizophrenia. *Behavior Therapy, 25,* 89–107.

Liberman, R. P., Mueser, K. T., & DeRisi, W. J. (1989). *Social skills training for psychiatric patients.* Elmsford, NY: Pergamon Press.

Lichtenstein, E. (1982). The smoking problem: A behavioral perspective. *Journal of Consulting and Clinical Psychology, 50,* 804–819.

Lichtenstein, E., & Danaher, B. (1976). Modification of smoking behavior: A critical analysis of theory, research, and practice. In M. Hersen, R. Eisler, & P. Miller (Eds.), *Progress in behavior modification: 3.* New York: Academic Press.

Lichtenstein, E., & Glasgow, R. E. (1977). Rapid smoking: Side effects and safeguards. *Journal of Consulting and Clinical Psychology, 45,* 815–821.

Lichtenstein, E. & Glasgow, R. E. (1992). Smoking cessation: What we have learned over the past decade? *Journal of Consulting and Clinical Psychology, 60,* 518–527.

Lichtenstein, E., & Rodrigues, M. (1977). Long-term effects of rapid smoking treatment for dependent cigarette smokers. *Addictive Behaviors, 2,* 109–112.

Licky, M. E., & Gordon, B. (1991). *Medicine and mental illness.* New York: W. H. Freeman.

Lieberman, J. A. (1995). Signs and symptoms. *Archives of General Psychiatry, 52,* 361–363.

Light, K. C., Brownley, K. A., Turner, J. R., Hinderliter, A. L., Girdler, S. S., Sherwood, A., & Anderson, N. B. (1995). Job status and high-effort coping influence work blood pressure in women and Blacks. *Hypertension, 25,* 554–559.

Lindsay, W. R., Gamisu, C. V., McLaughlin, E., Hood, E. M., & Espie, C. A. (1987). A controlled trial of treatments for generalized anxiety. *British Journal of Clinical Psychology, 26,* 3–15.

Linehan, M. M. (1987). Dialectical behavior therapy for borderline personality disorder. Theory and method. *Bulletin of the Menninger Clinic, 51,* 261–276.

Lipman, A. J., & Kendall, P. C. (1992). Drugs and psychotherapy: Comparison, contrasts, and conclusions. *Applied and Preventive Psychology, 1,* 141–148.

Lipsitt, D. R. (1983). The Munchausen mystery. *Psychology Today, 17,* 78–79.

Lipsky, M. J., Kassinove, H., & Miller, N. J. (1980). Effects of rational-emotive therapy, rational role reversal and rational-emotive imagery on the emotional adjustment of community mental health center patients. *Journal of Consulting & Clinical Psychology, 48,* 366–374.

Lisak, D. (1991). Sexual aggression, masculinity, and fathers. *Signs, 16,* 238–262.

Lishman, W. A. (1978). *The psychological consequences of cerebral disorder.* Oxford, England: Blackwell.

Litman, R. E. (1987). Hospital suicides: Lawsuits and standards. *Suicide and Life-Threatening Behavior, 12,* 212–220.

Livesley, W. J., Schroeder, M. L., Jackson, D. N., & Jang, K. L. (1994). Categorical distinctions in the study of personality disorder: Implications for classification. *Journal of Abnormal Psychology, 103,* 6–17.

Livnat, S., & Felton, D. L. (1985). To the editor. *New England Journal of Medicine, 313,* 1357.

Loeber, R. (1990). Development and risk factors of juvenile antisocial behavior and delinquency. *Clinical Psychology Review, 10,* 1–42.

Loftus, E. F. (1993). The reality of repressed memories. *American Psychologist, 48,* 518–537.

Loftus, E. F., Garry, M., Brown, S. W., & Rader, M. (1994). Near-natal memories, past-life memories, and other memory myths. *American Journal of Clinical Hypnosis, 37*, 176–182.

Loftus, E. F., Garry, M., & Feldman, J. (1994). Forgetting sexual trauma: What does it mean when 38 percent forget? *Journal of Consulting and Clinical Psychology, 62*, 1177–1181.

London, P. (1964). *Modes and morals of psychotherapy.* New York: Holt, Rinehart & Winston.

Longstreth, L. E. (1981). Revisiting Skeels's final study: A critique. *Developmental Psychology, 17*, 620–625.

Lopez, S. R. (1989). Patient variable biases in clinical judgment: Conceptual overview and methodological considerations. *Psychological Bulletin, 106*, 1–20.

Lopez, S. R., & Hernandez, P. (1987). When culture is considered in the evaluation and treatment of Hispanic patients. *Psychotherapy, 24*, 120–126.

LoPiccolo, J. (1985). Advances in diagnosis and treatment of male sexual dysfunction. *Journal of Sex and Marital Therapy, 11*, 215–232.

LoPiccolo, J. (1991). Post-modern sex therapy for erectile failure. In R. C. Rosen & S. R. Leiblum (Eds.), *Erectile failure: diagnosis and treatment.* New York: Guilford.

LoPiccolo, J., & Stock, W. E. (1986). Treatment of sexual dysfunction. *Journal of Consulting and Clinical Psychology, 54*, 158–167.

LoPiccolo, L. (1980). Low sexual desire. In S. R. Leiblum & L. A. Pervin (Eds.), *Principles and practice of sex therapy.* New York: Guilford Press.

Lorion, R. P. (1990). Developmental analyses of community phenomena. In P. Tolan, C. Keys, F. Chertok, & L. Jason (Eds.), *Researching community psychology* (pp. 32–41). Washington, DC: American Psychological Association.

Lovaas, O. I. (1977). *The autistic child: Language development through behavior modification.* New York: Halsted Press.

Lovaas, O. I. (1987). Behavioral treatment and normal educational and intellectual functioning in young autistic children. *Journal of Consulting and Clinical Psychology, 55*, 3–9.

Lovaas, O. I., Schaeffer, B., & Simmons, J. Q. (1965). Building social behavior in autistic children by use of electric shock. *Journal of Experimental Research in Personality, 1*, 99–109.

Lowe, C. F., & Chadwick, P. D. J. (1990). Verbal control of delusions. *Behavior Therapy, 21*, 461–479.

Luk, S. L., Leung, P. W. L., & Yuen, J. (1991). Clinical observations in the assessment of pervasiveness of childhood hyperactivity. *Journal of Child Psychology and Psychiatry, 32*, 833–850.

Lukas, C., & Seiden, H. M. (1990). *Silent grief: Living in the wake of suicide.* New York: Bantam Books.

Luparello, T., Lyons, H. A., Bleecker, E. R., & McFadden, E. R. (1968). Influences of suggestion on airway reactivity in asthmatic subjects. *Psychosomatic Medicine, 30*, 819–825.

Luria, A. R. (1982). *Language and cognition.* New York: Oxford University Press.

Lydiard, R. B., Brady, K. T., & Austin, L. S. (1994). To the editor. *American Journal of Psychiatry, 151*, 462.

Lykken, D. F. (1957). A study of anxiety in the sociopathic personality. *Journal of Abnormal and Social Psychology, 55*, 6–10.

Lykken, D. T. (1982). Fearlessness: Its carefree charm and deadly risks. *Psychology Today, 16*, 20–28.

Lynn, S. J., & Nash, M. R. (1994). Truth in memory: Ramifications for psychotherapy and hypnotherapy. *American Journal of Clinical Hypnosis, 36*, 194–206.

Lynskey, M. T., & Fergusson, D. M. (1995). Childhood conduct problems, and adolescent alcohol, tobacco, and illicit drug use. *Journal of Abnormal Child Psychology, 23*, 281–302.

MacEachron, A. E. (1983). Institutional reform and adaptive functioning of mentally retarded persons: A field experiment. *American Journal of Mental Deficiency, 88*, 2–12.

Machover, K. (1949). *Personality projection in the drawing of the human figure: A method of personality investigation.* Springfield, IL: Thomas.

MacKenzie, K. R. (1994). Using personality measurements in clinical practice. In P. T. Costa & T. A. Widiger (Eds.), *Personality disorders and the five-factor model of personality* (pp. 237–250). Washington, DC: American Psychological Association.

Mackenzie, T. B., & Popkin, M. K. (1987). Suicide in the medical patient. *International Journal of Psychiatry in Medicine, 17*, 3–22.

Maddi, S. R. (1972). *Personality theories.* Homewood, IL: Dorsey.

Madle, R. A. (1990). Mental retardation in adulthood. In M. Hersen & C. G. Last (Eds.), *Handbook of child and adult psychopathology* (pp. 337–352). New York: Pergamon Press.

Magni, G., & Schifano, F. (1984). Psychological distress after stroke. *Journal of Neurology, Neurosurgery and Psychiatry, 47*, 567–568.

Maher, B. A. (1966). *Principles of psychopathology.* New York: McGraw-Hill.

Maher, B. A. (1988). Anomalous experiences and delusional thinking: The logic of explanations. In T. F. Oltmanns & B. A. Maher (Eds.), *Delusional beliefs.* New York: Wiley.

Maher, W. B., & Maher, B. A. (1985). Psychopathology: I. From ancient times to the eighteenth century. In G. A. Kimble & K. Schlesinger (Eds.), *Topics in the history of psychology* (Vol. 2). Hillsdale, NJ: Erlbaum.

Mahler, M. S. (1979). *The selected papers of Margaret S. Mahler* (Vol. 2). New York: Aronson.

Mahoney, M. J. (1977). Reflections on the cognitive-learning trend in psychotherapy. *American Psychologist, 32*, 5–13.

Malamuth, N. M. (1981). Rape proclivity among males. *Journal of Social Issues, 37*, 138–157.

Malamuth, N. M., & Briere, J. (1986). Sexual violence in the media: Indirect effects on aggression against women. *Journal of Social Issues, 42*, 75–92.

Malamuth, N. M., & Check, J. V. P. (1983). Sexual arousal to rape depictions: Individual differences. *Journal of Abnormal Psychology, 92*, 55–67.

Malamuth, N. M., Sockloskie, R. J., Koss, M. P., & Tanaka, J. S. (1991). Characteristics of aggressors against women: Testing a model using a national sample of college students. *Journal of Consulting and Clinical Psychology, 59*, 670–681.

Malatesta, V. J., & Adams, H. E. (1984). The sexual dysfunctions. In H. E. Adams & P. B. Sutker (Eds.), *Comprehensive handbook of psychopathology* (pp. 725–776). New York: Plenum Press.

Malatesta, V. J., Pollack, R. H., Wilbanks, W. A., & Adams, H. E. (1979). Alcohol effects on the orgasmic-ejaculatory response in human males. *Journal of Sex Research, 15*, 101–107.

Malison, R. T., McDougle, C. J., Van Dyck, C. H., Scahill, L., Baldwin, R. M., Seibyl, J. P., Price, L. H., Leckman, J. F., & Innis, R. B. (1995). ^{123}IB-CIT SPECT imaging of striatal dopamine transporter binding in Tourette's disorder. *American Journal of Psychiatry, 152*, 1359–1361.

Mallick, M. J., Whipple, T. W., & Huerta, E. (1987). Behavioral and psychological traits of weight conscious teenagers: A comparison of eating disordered patients and high- and low-risk groups. *Adolescence, 22*, 157–168.

Mallinckrodt, B., McCreary, B. A., & Robertson, A. K. (1995). Co-occurrence of eating disorders and incest: The role of attachment, family environment, and social competencies. *Journal of Counseling Psychology, 42*, 178–186.

Maltsberger, J. T. (1991). The prevention of suicide in adults. In A. A. Leenaars (Ed.), *Life span perspectives of suicide: Time-lines in the suicide process.* New York: Plenum.

Manderscheid, R. W., & Sonnenschein, M. A. (1992). *Mental health, United States, 1992.* Rockville, MD: U.S. Department of Health and Human Services.

Manjiviona, J., & Prior, M. (1995). Comparison of Asperger syndrome and high-functioning autistic children on a test of motor impairment. *Journal of Autism and Developmental Disorders, 25*, 23–39.

Mann, J. J. (1989). Neurobiological models. In J. J. Mann (Ed.), *Models of depressive disorders: Psychological, biological, and genetic perspectives* (pp. 143–177). New York: Plenum Press.

Mannuzza, S., Klein, R. G., Bonagura, N., Malloy, P., Giampino, T. L., & Addalli, K. A. (1991). Hyperactive boys almost grown up. *Archives of General Psychiatry, 48,* 77–83.

Marantz, S. (1985, May 12). In the eyes of his public Ali is still the greatest. *Boston Globe,* p. 63.

Marantz, S., & Coates, S. (1991). Mothers of boys with gender identity disorder: A comparison of matched controls. *Journal of the American Academy of Child and Adolescent Psychiatry, 30,* 310–315.

Marchione, K., Michelson, L., Greenwald, M., & Dancu, C. (1987). Cognitive behavioral treatment of agoraphobia. *Behaviour Research and Therapy, 25,* 319–328.

Marcus, J., Hans, S. L., Nagler, S., Auerbach, J. G., Mirsky, A. F., & Aubrey, A. (1987). Review of the NIMH Israeli kibbutz-city study and the Jerusalem Infant Developmental study. *Schizophrenia Bulletin, 13,* 425–437.

Margolin, R. (1991). Neuroimaging. In J. Sadavoy, L. W. Lazarus, & L. F. Jarvik (Eds.), *Comprehensive review of geriatric psychiatry* (pp. 245–271). Washington, DC: American Psychiatric Press.

Margraf, J., Barlow, D. H., Clark, D. M., & Telch, M. J. (1993). Psychological treatment of panic: Work in progress on outcome, active ingredients, and follow-up. *Behaviour Research and Therapy, 31,* 1–8.

Margraf, J., Ehlers, A., & Roth, W. T. (1987). Panic attacks associated with perceived heart rate acceleration: A case report. *Behavior Therapy, 18,* 84–89.

Margraf, J., Ehlers, A., Roth, W. T., Clark, D. B., Sheikh, J., Agras, W. S., & Taylor, C. B. (1991). How "blind" are double-blind studies? *Journal of Consulting and Clinical Psychology, 59,* 184–187.

Marks, I. M. (1983). Are there anticompulsive or antiphobic drugs? Review of the evidence. *British Journal of Psychiatry, 143,* 338–347.

Marks, I. M. (1987). *Fears, phobias, and rituals.* New York: Oxford University Press.

Marks, I. M., Gray, S., Cohen, D., Hill, R., Mawson, D., Rammn, E. & Stern, R. S. (1983). Imipramine and brief therapist-aided exposure in agoraphobics having self-improvement homework. *Archives of General Psychiatry, 40,* 153–162.

Marlatt, G. A. (1978). Craving for alcohol, loss of control and relapse: A cognitive-behavioral analysis. In P. E. Nathan & G. A. Marlatt (Eds.), *Experimental and behavioral approaches to alcoholism.* New York: Plenum.

Marlatt, G. A. (1983). The controlled-drinking controversy: A commentary. *American Psychologist, 38,* 1097–1110.

Marlatt, G. A., Demming, B., & Reid, J. (1973). Loss-of-control drinking in alcoholics: An experimental analogue. *Journal of Abnormal Psychology, 81,* 233–241.

Marlatt, G. A., & Gordon, J. R. (1985). *Relapse prevention: Maintenance strategies in the treatment of addictive behaviors.* New York: Guilford Press.

Marlowe, N. I. (1992). Pain sensitivity and headache: An examination of the central theory. *Journal of Psychosomatic Research, 36,* 17–24.

Marmar, C. R. (1988). Personality disorders. In H. H. Goldman (Ed.), *Review of general psychiatry* (pp. 401–424). Norwalk, CT: Appleton & Lange.

Marmor, J., & Woods, S. M. (1980). *The interface between the psychodynamic and behavioral therapies.* New York: Plenum Medical.

Marmot, M. G., & Syme, S. L. (1976). Acculturation and coronary heart disease in Japanese-Americans. *American Journal of Epidemiology, 104,* 225–247.

Marquis, J. N. (1991). A report on seventy-eight cases treated by eye movement desensitization. *Journal of Behavior Therapy and Experimental Psychiatry, 22,* 187–192.

Marsh, J. C. (1988). What have we learned about legislative remedies for rape? In R. A. Prentky and V. L. Quisey (Eds.), *Human sexual aggression: Current perspectives. Annals of the New York Academy of Sciences, 528* (pp. 79–110). Salem, MA: New York Academy of Sciences.

Marshall, W. L. (1988). Behavioral indices of habituation and sensitization during exposure to phobic stimuli. *Behaviour Research and Therapy, 26,* 67–77.

Marshall, W. L., Earls, C. M., Segal, Z., & Durke, J. (1983). A behavioral program for the assessment and treatment of sexual aggressors. In K. D. Craig & R. J. McMahon (Eds.), *Advances in clinical behavior therapy* (pp. 148–174). New York: Brunner/Mazel.

Marshall, W. L., Jones, R., Ward, T., Johnston, P., & Barbaree, H. E. (1991). Treatment outcome with sex offenders. *Clinical Psychology Review, 11,* 465–486.

Martin, C. E. (1981). Factors affecting sexual functioning in 60–79-year-old married males. *Archives of Sexual Behavior, 10,* 399–420

Martin, S. (1995). APA to pursue prescription privileges. *APA Monitor, 26,* 6.

Maser, J. D., Kaelber, C., & Weise, R. E. (1991). International use and attitudes toward DSM-III and DSM-III-R: Growing consensus in psychiatric classification. *Journal of Abnormal Psychology, 100,* 271–279.

Maslow, A. H. (1954). *Motivation and personality.* New York: Harper & Row.

Masserman, J., Yum, K., Nicholson, J., & Lee, S. (1944). Neurosis and alcohol: An experimental study. *American Journal of Psychiatry, 101,* 389–395.

Masters, W. H., & Johnson, V. E. (1966). *Human sexual response.* Boston: Little, Brown.

Masters, W. H., & Johnson, V. E. (1970). *Human sexual inadequacy.* London: Churchill.

Masters, W. H., & Johnson, V. E. (1979). *Homosexuality in perspective.* Boston: Little, Brown.

Masterson, J. F. (1981). *The narcissistic and borderline disorders: An integrated developmental approach.* New York: Brunner/Mazel.

Matarazzo, J. D. (1986). Computerized clinical psychological test interpretations. Unvalidated plus all mean and no sigma. *American Psychologist, 41,* 14–41.

Matarazzo, J. D. (1992). Psychological testing and assessment in the 21st century. *American Psychologist, 47,* 1007–1018.

Matchett, G., & Davey, G. C. L. (1991). A test of a disease-avoidance model of animal phobias. *Behaviour Research and Therapy, 29,* 91–94.

Materka, P. R. (1984). Families caring, coping with Alzheimer's disease. *Michigan Today, 16,* 13–14.

Mattick, R. P., & Peters, L. (1988). Treatment of severe social phobia: Effects of guided exposure with and without cognitive restructuring. *Journal of Consulting and Clinical Psychology, 56,* 251–260.

Mavissakalian, M. (1987). The placebo effect in agoraphobia. *Journal of Nervous and Mental Disease, 175,* 95–99.

Mavissakalian, M., Michelson, L., & Dealy, R. S. (1983). Pharmacological treatment of agoraphobia: Imipramine with programmed practice. *British Journal of Psychiatry, 143,* 348–355.

May, D. C., & Turnbull, N. (1992). Plastic surgeons' opinions of facial surgery for individuals with Down syndrome. *Mental Retardation, 30,* 29–33.

May, R. (1967). *Psychology and the human dilemma.* New York: Van Nostrand.

McArdle, P., O'Brien, G. O., & Kolvin, I. (1995). Hyperactivity: Prevalence and relationship with conduct disorder. *Journal of Child Psychology and Psychiatry, 36,* 297–303.

McBride, M. C. (1990). Autonomy and the struggle for female identity: Implications for counseling women. *Journal of Counseling and Development, 69,* 22–26.

McBride, M. C., & Ender, K. L. (1977). Sexual attitudes and behavior among college students. *Journal of College Student Personnel, 18,* 183–187.

McCann, B. S., Woofolk, R. L., & Lehrer, P. M. (1987). Specificity in response to treatment: A study of interpersonal anxiety. *Behaviour Research and Therapy, 25,* 129–136.

McCary, J. L. (1973). *Human sexuality.* New York: Van Nostrand.

McCauley, E., & Ehrhardt, A. A. (1984). Follow-up of females with gender identity disorders. *Journal of Nervous and Mental Disease, 172,* 353–358.

McConaghy, N. (1983). Agoraphobia, compulsive behaviours, and behaviour completion mechanisms. *Australian and New England Journal of Psychiatry, 17,* 170–179.

McCord, W., & McCord, J. (1964). *The psychopath: An essay on the criminal mind.* Princeton, NJ: Van Nostrand.

McCormick, R. A., and Taber, J. I. (1988). Attributional style in pathological gamblers in treatment. *Journal of Abnormal Psychology, 97,* 368–370.

McCracken, L. M., & Larkin, K. T. (1991). Treatment of paruresis with in vivo desensitization: A case report. *Journal of Behavior Therapy and Experimental Psychiatry, 22,* 57–62.

McCrady, B. S. (1994). Alcoholics Anonymous and behavior therapy: Can habits be treated as diseases? Can diseases be treated as habits? *Journal of Consulting and Clinical Psychology, 62,* 1159–1166.

McCrae, R. R. (1994). A reformulation of Axis II: Personality and personality-related problems. In P. T. Costa & T. A. Widiger (Eds.), *Personality disorders and the five-factor model of personality* (pp. 303–310). Washington, DC: American Psychological Association.

McGee, R., & Stanton, W. R. (1992). Sources of distress among New England adolescents. *Journal of Child Psychology and Psychiatry, 33,* 999–1010.

McGeer, P. L., & McGeer, E. G. (1980). Chemistry of mood and emotions. *Annual Review of Psychology, 31,* 273–307.

McGlashan, T. H., & Fenton, W. S. (1991). Classical subtypes for schizophrenia: Literature review for DSM III. *Schizophrenia Bulletin, 17,* 609–622.

McGoldrick, M., Pearce, J., & Giordano, J. (Eds.). (1982). *Ethnicity and family therapy.* New York: Guilford Press.

McGonagle, K. A., & Kessler, R. C. (1990). Chronic stress, acute stress, and depressive symptoms. *American Journal of Community Psychology, 18*(5), 681–706.

McGowan, S. (1991, November). Confidentiality and the ethical dilemma. *Guidepost, 34,* 1, 6, 10.

McGrath, M. E. (1987). *Where did I go? Schizophrenia: The experiences of patients and families.* Rockville, MD: National Institutes of Health.

McGuire, D. (1982). The problem of children's suicide: Ages 5–14. *International Journal of Offender Therapy and Comparative Criminology, 26,* 10–17.

McGuire, R. J., Carlisle, J. M., & Young, B. G. (1965). Sexual deviations as conditioned behavior: A hypothesis. *Behavior Research and Therapy, 2,* 185–190.

McIntosh, J. L. (1991). Epidemiology of suicide in the U.S. In A. A. Leenaars (Ed.), *Lifespan perspectives of suicide.* New York: Plenum.

McIntosh, J. L. (1992). Epidemiology of suicide in the elderly. *Suicidal and Life-Threatening Behavior, 22*(1), 15–35.

McKeon, P., & Murray, R. (1987). Familial aspects of obsessive-compulsive neurosis. *British Journal of Psychiatry, 151,* 528–534.

McLarnon, L. D., & Kaloupek, D. G. (1988). Psychological investigation of genital herpes recurrence: Prospective assessment and cognitive-behavioral intervention for a chronic physical disorder. *Health Psychology, 1,* 231–249.

McLellan, A. T., Alterman, A. I., Metzger, D. S., Grissom, G. R., Woody, G. E., Luborsky, L., & O'Brien, C. P. (1994). Similarity of outcome predictors across opiate, cocaine, and alcohol treatments: Role of treatment services. *Journal of Consulting and Clinical Psychology, 62,* 1141–1158.

McLeod, B. (1985). Real work for real pay. *Psychology Today, 19,* 42–50.

McLin, W. M. (1992). Introduction to issues in psychology and epilepsy. *American Psychologist, 47*(9), 1124–1125.

McNally, R. J. (1994). Introduction to the special series: Innovations in cognitive-behavioral approaches to schizophrenia. *Behavior Therapy, 25,* 1–4.

McNamee, H. B., Mello, N. K., & Mendelson, J. H. (1968). Experimental analysis of drinking patterns of alcoholics: Concurrent psychiatric observations. *American Journal of Psychiatry, 124,* 1063–1069.

McQueen, P. C., Spence, M. W., Garner, J. B., Pereira, L. H., & Winson, E. J. T. (1987). Prevalence of major mental retardation and associated disabilities in the Canadian Maritime Provinces. *American Journal of Mental Deficiency, 91,* 460–466.

Mead, M. (1949). *Male and female.* New York: Morrow.

Meares, A. (1979). Mind and cancer. *Lancet, 22,* 978.

Mechanic, D. (Coordinator). (1978). Report of the task panel on the nature and scope of the problems. In *President's Commission on Mental Health* (Vol. 2, pp. 1–138). Washington, DC: U.S. Government Printing Office.

Mednick, S. A. (1970). Breakdown in individuals at high risk for schizophrenia: Possible predispositional perinatal factors. *Mental Hygiene, 54,* 50–63.

Mednick, S. A. (1985). Crime in the family tree. *Psychology Today, 19,* 58–61.

Mednick, S. A., Cannon, T., Parnas, J., & Schulsinger, F. (1989). 27 year follow-up of the Copenhagen high-risk for schizophrenia project: Why did some of the high-risk offspring become schizophrenic? *Schizophrenia Research, 2,* 14.

Mednick, S. A., & Christiansen, K. O. (Eds.). (1977). *Biosocial bases of criminal behavior.* New York: Gardner Press.

Mednick, S. A., & Kandel, E. (1988). Genetic and perinatal factors in violence. In T. E. Moffitt & S. A. Mednick (Eds.), *Biological contributions to crime causation* (pp. 40–54). Boston: Martinus Nijhoff.

Mednick, S. A., & Schulsinger, F. (1968). Some premorbid characteristics related to breakdown in children with schizophrenic mothers. In D. Rosenthal & S. Kety (Eds.), *The transmission of schizophrenia.* New York: Pergamon Press.

Meehl, P. E. (1962). Schizotaxia, schizotypia, schizophrenia. *American Psychologist, 17,* 827–838.

Meichenbaum, D. H. (1977). *Cognitive-behavior modification: An integrative approach.* New York: Plenum.

Meichenbaum, D. H. (1985). *Stress-inoculation training.* New York: Pergamon Press.

Meichenbaum, D. H., & Cameron, R. (1982). Cognitive behavior therapy. In G. T. Wilson & C. M. Franks (Eds.), *Contemporary behavior therapy: Conceptual and empirical foundations.* New York: Guilford Press.

Meier, M. J. (1992). Modern clinical neuropsychology in historical perspective. *American Psychologist, 47*(4), 550–558.

Melges, F., & Bowlby, J. (1969). Types of hopelessness in psychopathological process. *Archives of General Psychiatry, 20,* 690–699.

Melton, G. B. (1988). Ethical and legal issues in AIDS-related practice. *American Psychologist, 43,* 941–947.

Meltzer, H. Y. (1995). Clozapine: Is another view valid? *American Journal of Psychiatry, 152,* 821–825.

Mendels, J. (1970). *Concepts of depression.* New York: Wiley.

Menzies, R. G., & Clarke, J. C. (1995). Danger expectancies and insight in acrophobia. *Behaviour Research and Therapy, 33,* 215–221.

Menzies, R. P. D., Fedoroff, J. P., Green, C. M., & Isaacson, K. (1995). Prediction of dangerous behavior in male erotomania. *British Journal of Psychiatry, 166,* 529–536.

Mercer, J. R. (1979). *System of Multicultural Pluralistic Assessment (SOMPA): Technical manual*. New York: Psychological Corporation.

Mercer, J. R. (1988). Death of the IQ paradigm: Where do we go from here? In W. J. Lonner & V. O. Tyler (Eds.), *Cultural and ethnic factors in learning and motivation: Implications for education*. Bellingham, WA: Western Washington University.

Merskey, H. (1992). The manufacture of personalities: The production of multiple personality disorder. *British Journal of Psychiatry, 160,* 327–340.

Merskey, H. (1995). Multiple personality disorder and false memory syndrome. *British Journal of Psychiatry, 166,* 281–283.

Messinger, H. B., Sperlings, E. L. H., Vincent, A. J. P., & Libbink, J. (1991). Headache and family history, *Cephalalgia, 11,* 13–18.

Meyer, J., & Peter, D. (1979). Sex reassignment: Follow-up. *Archives of General Psychiatry, 36,* 1010–1015.

Meyer, R. G. (1989). *The clinician's handbook*. Needham Heights, MA: Allyn & Bacon.

Meyer, R. G., & Osborne, Y. V. H. (1982). *Case studies in abnormal behavior*. Boston: Allyn & Bacon.

Meyer, T. J., & Mark, M. M. (1995). Effects of psychosocial interventions with adult cancer patients: A meta-analysis of randomized experiments. *Health Psychology, 14,* 101–108.

Meyer, W. S., & Keith, C. R. (1991). Homosexual and preoedipal issues in the psychoanalytic psychotherapy of a female-to-male transsexual. In C. W. Socarides & V. D. Volkan (Eds.), *The homosexualities and the therapeutic process* (pp. 75–96). Adison, CT: International Universities Press.

Meyers, W. A. (1991). A case history of a man who made obscene telephone calls and practiced frotteurism. In G. I. Fogel & W. A. Myers (Eds.), *Perversions and near-perversions in clinical practice* (pp. 109–126). New Haven, CT: Yale University Press.

Mezzich, J. E., & Good, B. (1991, April 11). *Cultural proposals for the DSM-IV multiaxial formulation*. Paper presented at the Conference on Culture and DSM-IV, Pittsburgh.

Michelson, L., Mavissakalian, M., & Marchione, K. (1988). Cognitive, behavioral, and psychophysiological treatment of agoraphobia: A comparative outcome investigation. *Behavior Therapy, 19,* 97–120.

Michelson, L. K., & Marchione, K. (1991). Behavioral, cognitive, and pharmacological treatments of panic disorder with agoraphobia: Critique and synthesis. *Journal of Consulting and Clinical Psychology, 59,* 100–114.

Michenbaum, D. H. (1986). Metacognitive methods of instruction: Current status and future prospects. *Special Services in the Schools, 3*(1–2), 23–32.

Miklowitz, D. J. (1994). Family risk indicators in schizophrenia. *Schizophrenia Bulletin, 20,* 137–148.

Milich, R., & Pelham, W. E. (1986). Effects of sugar ingestion on the classroom and playground behavior of attention deficit disordered boys. *Journal of Consulting and Clinical Psychology, 54,* 714–718.

Miller, D. J., & Thelen, M. H. (1986). Knowledge and beliefs about confidentiality in psychotherapy. *Professional Psychology, 17,* 15–19.

Miller, H. L., Coombs, D. W., & Leeper, J. D. (1984). An analysis of the effects of suicide prevention facilities on suicide rates in the United States. *American Journal of Public Health, 74,* 340–343.

Miller, J. B. (1976). *Toward a new psychology of women*. Boston: Beacon Press.

Miller, N. E. (1974). Applications of learning and biofeedback to psychiatry and medicine. In A. M. Freedman, H. I. Kaplan, & B. J. Sadock (Eds.), *Comprehensive textbook of psychiatry* (2nd ed.). Baltimore: Williams & Wilkins.

Miller, S. D., & Triggiano, P. J. (1992). The psychophysiological investigation of multiple personality disorder: Review and update. *American Journal of Clinical Hypnosis, 35,* 47–61.

Miller, T. Q., Turner, C. W., Tinsdale, R. S., Posavac, E. J., &

Dugoni, B. L. (1991). Reasons for the trend toward null findings in research on Type A behavior. *Psychological Bulletin, 110,* 469–485.

Millon, T. (1973). *Theories of psychopathology and personality*. Philadelphia: Saunders.

Millon, T. (1975). Reflections on Rosenhan's "On being sane in insane places." *Journal of Abnormal Psychology, 84,* 456–461.

Millon, T. (1981). *Disorders of personality: DSM-III-R, Axis II*. New York: Wiley-Interscience.

Millon, T. (1983). The DSM-III: An insider's perspective. *American Psychologist, 38,* 804–814.

Millon, T. (1994). Personality disorders: Conceptual distinctions and classification issues. In P. T. Costa & T. A. Widiger (Eds.), *Personality disorders and the five-factor model of personality* (pp. 279–301). Washington, DC: American Psychological Association.

Millon, T., & Everly, G. S. (1985). *Personality and its disorders*. New York: Wiley.

Milstein, V. (1988). EEG topography in patients with aggressive violent behavior. In T. E. Moffitt & S. A. Mednick (Eds.), *Biological contributions to crime causation* (pp. 121–134). Boston: Martinus Nijhoff.

Mineka, S., & Sutton, S. K. (1992). Cognitive biases and the emotional disorders. *Psychological Science, 3*(1), 65–69.

Mintz, J., Mintz, L., & Goldstein, M. (1987). Expressed emotion and relapse in first episodes of schizophrenia. *British Journal of Psychiatry, 151,* 314–320.

Mintz, L. B., & Betz, N. E. (1988). Prevalence and correlates of eating disordered behaviors among undergraduate women. *Journal of Counseling Psychology, 35,* 463–471.

Minuchin, S. (1974). *Families and family therapy*. Cambridge, MA: Harvard University Press.

Mirsky, A. F., Kugelmass, S., Ingraham, L. J., Frenkel, E., & Nathan, M. (1995). Overview and summary: Twenty-five–year follow-up of high-risk children. *Schizophrenia Bulletin, 21,* 227–237.

Mischel, W. (1968). *Personality and assessment*. New York: Wiley.

Mizes, J. S., & Christiano, B. A. (1995). Assessment of cognitive variables relevant to cognitive behavioral perspectives on anorexia nervosa and bulimia nervosa. *Behaviour Research and Therapy, 33,* 95–105.

Modestin, J. (1992). Multiple personality disorder in Switzerland. *American Journal of Psychiatry, 149,* 88–92.

Mohr, D. C., & Beutler, L. E. (1990). Erectile dysfunction: A review of diagnostic and treatment procedures. *Clinical Psychology Review, 10,* 123–150.

Monahan, J. (1981). *The clinical prediction of violent behavior*. Rockville, MD: National Institute of Mental Health.

Monahan, J. (1993). Limiting therapist exposure to Tarasoff liability: Guidelines for risk containment. *American Psychologist, 48*(3), 242–250.

Monday, J., Montplaisir, J., & Malo, J.-L. (1987). Dream process in asthmatic subjects with nocturnal attacks. *American Journal of Psychiatry, 144,* 638–640.

Money, J. (1987). Masochism: On the childhood origin of paraphilia, opponent-process theory, and antiandrogen therapy. *Journal of Sex Research, 23,* 273–275.

Money, J., Hampson, J. G., & Hampson, J. L. (1957). Imprinting and establishing gender role. *Archives of Neurological Psychiatry, 77,* 333–336.

Monroe, M., & Simons, A. D. (1991). Diathesis-stress theories in the context of life stress research: Implications for the depressive disorders. *Psychological Bulletin, 110*(3), 406–425.

Monroe, S. M., Thase, M. E., & Simons, A. D. (1992). Social factors and the psychobiology of depression: Relations between life stress and rapid eye movement sleep latency. *Journal of Abnormal Psychology, 101*(3), 528–537.

Montgomery, R. W., & Ayllon, T. (1994). Eye movement desensitization across subjects: Subjective and physiologic measures of treatment efficacy. *Journal of Behavior Therapy and Experimental Psychiatry, 25,* 217–230.

Mooney, J. (1988, November 18). A flight from pain for Vietnam veterans. *Seattle Post-Intelligencer,* p. B2.

Moore, S., Donovan, B., & Hudson, A. (1993). Brief report: Facilitator-suggested conversational evaluation of facilitated communication. *Journal of Autism and Developmental Disorders, 23,* 541–551.

Moore, S., Donovan, B., Hudson, A., Dykstra, J., & Lawrence, J. (1993). Brief report: Evaluation of eight case studies of facilitated communication. *Journal of Autism and Developmental Disorders, 23,* 531–540.

Moreno, J. L. (1946). *Psychodrama.* New York: Beacon.

Morey, L. C. (1988). Personality disorders in DSM-III and DSM-III-R: Convergence, coverage, and internal consistency. *American Journal of Psychiatry, 145,* 573–577.

Morey, L. C., & Ochoa, E. S. (1989). An investigation of adherence to diagnostic criteria: Clinical diagnosis of the DSM-III personality disorders. *Journal of Personality Disorders, 3,* 180–192.

Morgan, S. B., & Brown, T. L. (1988). Luria-Nebraska Neuropsychological Battery–Children's Revision: Concurrent validity with three learning disability subtypes. *Journal of Consulting and Clinical Psychology, 56,* 463–466.

Moser, C., & Levitt, E. E. (1987). An exploratory-descriptive study of a sadomasochistically oriented sample. *Journal of Sex Research, 23,* 322–337.

Moss, R. A. (1986). The role of learning history in current sick-role behavior and assertion. *Behaviour Research and Therapy, 24,* 681–683.

Mrazek, D. A. (1993). Asthma: Stress, allergies, and the genes. In D. Goleman & J. Gurin (Eds.), *Mind/body medicine* (pp. 193–205). New York: Consumer Reports Books.

Muehleman, T., Pickens, B. K., & Robinson, F. (1985). Informing clients about the limits to confidentiality, risks, and their rights: Is self-disclosure inhibited? *Professional Psychology: Research and Practice, 16,* 385–397.

Mukherjee, S., Shukla, S., Woodle, J., Rosen, A. M., & Olarte, S. (1983). Misdiagnosis of schizophrenia in bipolar patients: A multiethnic comparison. *American Journal of Psychiatry, 140,* 1571–1574.

Mullan, M., & Brown, F. (1994). The clinical features of Alzheimer's disease and the search for clinico-aetiologic correlates. In D. Nicholson (Ed.), *Anti-dementia agents: Research and prospects for therapy* (pp. 1–12). San Diego: Academic Press.

Mumford, D. B., Whitehouse, A. M., & Choudry, I. Y. (1992). Survey of eating disorders in English-medium schools in Lehore, Pakistan. *International Journal of Eating Disorders, 11,* 173–184.

Munoz, R. F., Glish, M., Soo-Hoo, T., & Robertson, J. (1982). The San Francisco mood survey project: Preliminary work toward the prevention of depression. *American Journal of Community Psychology, 10,* 317–330.

Munoz, R. F., Ying, Y. W., Bernal, G., Perez-Stable, E. J., Sorenson, J. L., Hargreaves, W. A., Miranda, J., & Miller, L. S. (1995). Prevention of depression with primary care patients: A randomized controlled trial. *American Journal of Community Psychology, 23,* 199–222.

Muris, P., Merckelbach, H., & de Jong, P. J. (1995). Exposure therapy outcome in spider phobics: Effects of monitoring and blunting coping styles. *Behaviour Research and Therapy, 33,* 461–464.

Murphree, O. D., & Dykman, R. A. (1965). Litter patterns in the offspring of nervous and stable dogs: I. Behavioral tests. *Journal of Nervous and Mental Disorders, 141,* 321–332.

Murray, E. J. (1983). Beyond behavioral and dynamic therapy. *British Journal of Clinical Psychology, 22,* 127–128.

Murray, H. A., & Morgan, H. (1938). *Explorations in personality.* New York: Oxford University Press.

Myers, J. K., Weissman, M. M., Tischler, G. L., Holzer, C. E., Leaf, P. J., Orvaschel, H., Anthony, J. C., Boyd, J. H., Burke, J. D., Kramer, M., & Stoltzman, R. (1984). Six-month prevalence of psychiatric disorders in three communities. *Archives of General Psychiatry, 41,* 959–967.

Myers, W. A. (1992). Body dysmorphic disorder. *American Journal of Psychiatry, 149,* 718.

Nagler, S., Marcus, J., Sohlberg, S. C., Lifshitz, M., & Silberman, E. K. (1985). Clinical observation of high-risk children. *Schizophrenia Bulletin, 11,* 107–111.

Nash, M. R., Drake, S. D., Wiley, S., & Khalsa, S. (1986). Accuracy of recall by hypnotically age-regressed subjects. *Journal of Abnormal Psychology, 95,* 298–300.

Nathan, P., & Jackson, A. (1976). Behavior modification. In I. Weiner (Ed.), *Clinical methods in psychology.* New York: Wiley.

Nathan, P. E. (1976). Alcoholism. In H. Leitenberg (Ed.), *Handbook of behavior modification and behavior therapy.* Englewood Cliffs, NJ: Prentice-Hall.

Nathan, P. E. (1988). The addictive personality is the behavior of the addict. *Journal of Consulting and Clinical Psychology, 56,* 183–188.

Nathan, P. E. (1991). Substance use disorders in the DSM-IV. *Journal of Abnormal Psychology, 100,* 356–361.

National Association of Social Workers. (1990). *Code of ethics* (rev. ed.). Silver Springs, MD: Author.

National Center for Health Statistics (1988). Advance report of final mortality statistics, 1986. *NCHS Monthly Vital Statistics Report, 37*(6). Hyattsville, MD: U.S. Public Health Service.

National Center for Health Statistics (1989). *Vital statistics of the United States, 1987 (Vol. 2): Mortality.* Washington, DC: U.S. Government Printing Office.

National Center for Health Statistics (1991). *Vital statistics of the United States (Vol. 2): Mortality–Part A [for the years 1966–1988].* Washington, DC: U.S. Government Printing Office.

National Center for Health Statistics (1993). Advance report of final mortality statistics, 1991. *Monthly Vital Statistics Report, 42*(2). Hyattsville, MD: U.S. Public Health Service.

National Institute of Mental Health. (1985). *Mental Health: United States, 1985.* Washington, DC: U.S. Government Printing Office.

National Institute of Mental Health. (1991). *Panic disorder.* Washington, DC: U.S. Government Printing Office.

National Institute on Drug Abuse. (1991). *National household survey on drug abuse: Main findings 1990.* Washington, DC: U.S. Government Printing Office.

National Victim Center (1992). *Rape in America: A Report to the Nation.* Charleston, SC: Crime Victims Research and Treatment Center.

Neale, J. M., & Oltmanns, T. F. (1980). *Schizophrenia.* New York: Wiley.

Nelson-Gray, R. O. (1991). DSM-IV: Empirical guidelines from psychometrics. *Journal of Abnormal Psychology, 100,* 308–315.

Nettlebladt, P., & Uddenberg, N. (1979). Sexual dysfunction and sexual satisfaction in 58 married Swedish men. *Journal of Psychosomatic Research, 23,* 141–148.

Neugebauer, R. (1979). Medieval and early modern theories of mental illness. *Archives of General Psychiatry, 36,* 477–483.

Nevid, J. S., Fichner-Rathus, L., & Rathus, S. A. (1995). *Human sexuality.* Boston: Allyn & Bacon.

Newman, L. E., & Stoller, R. J. (1974). Nontranssexual men who seek sex reassignment. *American Journal of Psychiatry, 131,* 437–441.

Newmark, C. S. (1985). The MMPI. In C. S. Newmark (Ed.), *Major psychological assessment instruments* (pp.11–64). Boston: Allyn & Bacon.

Niaura, R. S., Rohsenow, D. J., Binkoff, J. A., Monti, P. M., Pedraza, M., & Abrams, D. B. (1988). Relevance of cue reactivity to understanding alcohol and smoking relapse. *Journal of Abnormal Psychology, 97,* 133–152.

Nichols, M. (1984). *Family therapy.* New York: Gardner Press.

Nicholson, R. A., & Berman, J. S. (1983). Is follow-up necessary in evaluating psychotherapy? *Psychological Bulletin, 93,* 261–278.

Nicotine: Powerful grip on the brain. (1995, September 22). *Los Angeles Times,* pp. A1, A37.

Nigg, J. T., Lohr, N. E., Westen, D., Gold, L. J., & Silk, K. R. (1992). Malevolent object representations in borderline personality disorder and major depression. *Journal of Abnormal Psychology, 101,* 61–67.

Noble, E. P. (1990). Alcoholic fathers and their sons: Neuropsychological, electrophysiological, personality, and family correlates. In C. R. Cloninger & H. Begleiter (Eds.), *Genetics and biology of alcoholism* (pp. 159–170). Cold Spring Harbor, NY: Cold Spring Harbor Laboratory Press.

Noble, J., & McConkey, K. M. (1995). Hypnotic sex change: Creating and challenging a delusion in the laboratory. *Journal of Abnormal Psychology, 104,* 69–74.

Nolen-Hoeksema, S. (1987). Sex differences in unipolar depression: Evidence and theory. *Psychological Bulletin, 101,* 259–282.

Nolen-Hoeksema, S. (1991). Responses to depression and their effects on the duration of depressive episodes. *Journal of Abnormal Psychology, 100*(4), 569–582.

Nolen-Hoeksema, S., Girgus, J. S., & Seligman, M. E. (1992). Predictors and consequences of childhood depressive symptoms: A 5-year longitudinal study. *Journal of Abnormal Psychology, 101,* 405–422.

Norcross, J. C., & Freedheim, D. K. (1992). Into the future: Retrospect and prospect in psychotherapy. In D. K. Freedheim (Ed.), *History of psychotherapy: A century of change* (pp. 881–900). Washington, DC: American Psychological Association.

Norcross, J. C., & Prochaska, J. O. (1988). A study of eclectic (and integrative) views revisited. *Professional Psychology: Research and Practice, 19,* 170–174.

Norton, G. R., Cox, B. J., Asmundson, G. J. G., & Maser, J. D. (1995). The growth of research on anxiety disorders during the 1980s. *Journal of Anxiety Disorders, 9,* 75–85.

Nuechterlein, K. H. (1987). Vulnerability models for schizophrenia: State of the art. In H. Hafner, W. F. Gattaz, & W. Janzarik (Eds.) *Search for the causes of schizophrenia.* Heidelberg: Springer-Verlag, 1987.

Nuechterlein, K. H., & Dawson, M. E. (1984). A heuristic vulnerability/stress model of schizophrenic episodes. *Schizophrenic Bulletin, 10,* 300–311.

Nuechterlein, K. H., Dawson, M. E., Gitlin, M., Ventura, J., Goldstein, M. J., Snyder, K. S., Yee, C. M., & Mintz, J. (1992). Developmental processes in schizophrenic disorders: Longitudinal studies of vulnerability and stress. *Schizophrenia Bulletin, 18,* 387–425.

Nussbaum, N. L., & Bigler, E. D. (1989). Halstead-Reitan neuropsychological test batteries for children. In C. R. Reynolds & E. Fletcher-Janzen (Eds.), *Handbook of clinical child neuropsychology* (pp. 181–191). New York: Plenum Press.

O'Connor, K. (1987). The interaction of hostile and depressive behaviors: A case study of a depressed boy. *Journal of Child and Adolescent Psychotherapy, 3,* 105–108.

O'Kearney, R. O. (1993). Additional considerations in the cognitive-behavioral treatment of obsessional ruminations—A case study. *Journal of Behavior Therapy and Experimental Psychiatry, 24,* 357–365.

Observer. (1992, July). *The severely mentally ill and the homeless mentally ill.* Washington, DC: American Psychological Society, 14–15.

Office of Technical Assessment. (1983). *The effectiveness of costs of alcoholism treatment.* Washington, DC: U.S. Congress.

Ofshe, R. J. (1992). Inadvertent hypnosis during interrogation: False confession due to dissociative state; mis-identified multiple personality and the satanic cult hypothesis. *International Journal of Clinical and Experimental Hypnosis, XL,* 125–156.

Ohaeri, J. U., & Odejide, O. A. (1994). Somatization symptoms among patients using primary health care facilities in a rural community in Nigeria. *American Journal of Psychiatry, 151,* 728–731.

Ohman, A., & Soares, J. J. F. (1993). On the autonomic nature of phobic fear: Conditioned electrodermal responses to masked fear-relevant stimuli. *Journal of Abnormal Psychology, 102,* 121–132.

Okazaki, S., & Sue, S. (1995). Cultural considerations in psychological assessment of Asian Americans. In J. N. Butcher (Ed.), *Clinical personality assessment: Practical approaches* (pp. 107–119). New York: Oxford University Press.

Oke, N. J., & Schreibman, L. (1990). Training social imitations to a high-functioning autistic child: Assessment of collateral behavior change and generalization in a case study. *Journal of Autism and Developmental Disorders, 20,* 479–497.

Olivardia, R., Pope, H. G., Mangweth, B., & Hudson, J. I. (1995). Eating disorders in college men. *American Journal of Psychiatry, 152,* 1279–1285.

Oliver, J., Shaller, C. A., Majovski, L. V., & Jacques, S. (1982). Stroke mechanisms: Neuropsychological implications. *Clinical Neuropsychology, 4,* 81–84.

Ollendick, T. H., & King, N. J. (1991). Origins of childhood fears: An evaluation of Rachman's theory of fear acquisition. *Behaviour Research and Therapy, 29,* 117–123.

Onstad, S., Skre, I., Edvardsen, J., Torgersen, S., & Kringlen, E. (1991). Twin concordance for DSM-III-R schizophrenia. *Acta Psychiatrica Scandinavica, 83,* 395–401.

Opler, M. K. (1967). *Culture and social psychiatry.* New York: Atherton Press.

Orr, S. P., Lasko, N. B., Shalev, A. Y., & Pitman, R. K. (1995). Physiologic responses to loud tones in Vietnam veterans with posttraumatic stress disorder. *Journal of Abnormal Psychology, 104,* 75–82.

Osgood, M. J. (1985). *Suicide in the elderly: A practitioner's guide to diagnosis and mental health intervention.* Rockville, MD: Aspen.

Öst, L.-G. (1987). Age of onset in different phobias. *Journal of Abnormal Psychology, 96,* 223–229.

Öst, L.-G. (1992). Blood and injection phobia: Background and cognitive, physiological, and behavioral variables. *Journal of Abnormal Psychology, 101,* 68–74.

Öst, L.-G., & Hugdahl, K. (1981). Acquisition of phobias and anxiety response patterns in clinical patients. *Behaviour Research and Therapy, 19,* 439–447.

Öst, L.-G., & Westling, B. E. (1995). Applied relaxation vs. cognitive behavior therapy in the treatment of panic disorder. *Behaviour Research and Therapy, 33,* 145–158.

Othmer, E., & Othmer, S. C. (1994). *The clinical interview using DSM-IV. Volume 1: Fundamentals.* Washington, DC: American Psychiatric Press.

Otto, R. K. (1989). Bias and expert testimony of mental health professionals in adversarial proceedings: A preliminary investigation. *Behavioral Science and Law, 7,* 267–273.

Overholser, J. C., & Beck, S. (1986). Multimethod assessment of rapists, child molesters, and three control groups in behavioral and psychological measures. *Journal of Consulting and Clinical Psychology, 54,* 682–687.

Page, E. B. (1972). Miracle in Milwaukee: Raising the IQ. *Educational Researcher, 1,* 3–16.

Paley, A.-M. (1988). Growing up in chaos: The dissociative response. *American Journal of Psychoanalysis, 48,* 72–83.

Palfrey, J. S., Levine, M. D., Walker, D. K., & Sullivan, M. (1985). The emergence of attention deficits in early childhood: A prospective study. *Developmental and Behavioral Pediatrics, 6,* 339–348.

Pallack, M. (1995). Managed care's evolution during the health care revolution. *National Psychologist, 4,* 12.

Papp, L., & Gorman, J. M. (1990). Suicidal preoccupation during fluoxetine treatment. *American Journal of Psychiatry, 147,* 1380.

Papp, L. A., Klein, D. F., Martinez, J., Schneier, F., Cole, R., Liebowitz, M. R., Hollander, E., Fyer, A. J., Jordan, F., & Gorman, J. M. (1993). Diagnostic and substance specificity of carbon-dioxide-induced panic. *American Journal of Psychiatry, 150,* 250–257.

Parker, S., Nichter, M., Vuckovic, N., Sims, C., & Ritenbaugh, C. (1995). Body image and weight concerns among African-American and White adolescent females: Differences that make a difference. *Human Organization, 54,* 103–114.

Parnas, J. (1987). Assortative mating in schizophrenia: Results from the Copenhagen high-risk study. *Psychiatry, 50,* 58–64.

Pasework, R. A., Pantel, M. L., & Steadman, H. J. (1982). Detention and rearrest rates of persons found not guilty by reason of insanity and convicted felons. *American Journal of Psychiatry, 139*(7), 892–897.

Pasnau, R. O. (1984). Clinical presentations of panic and anxiety. *Psychosomatics, 25,* 4–9.

Paternite, C. E., Loney, J., & Roberts, M. A. (1995). External validation of oppositional disorder and attention deficit disorder with hyperactivity. *Journal of Abnormal Child Psychology, 23,* 453–469.

Patrick, C. J., Cuthbert, B. N., & Lang, P. J. (1994). Emotion in the criminal psychopath: Fear image processing. *Journal of Abnormal Psychology, 103,* 523–534.

Patterson, C. H. (1980). *Theories of counseling and psychotherapy.* New York: Harper & Row.

Patterson, G. R. (1986). Performance models for antisocial boys. *American Psychologist, 41,* 432–444.

Patterson, S. M., Matthews, K. A., Allen, M. T., & Owens, J. F. (1995). Stress-induced hemoconcentration of blood cells and lipids in healthy women during acute psychological stress. *Health Psychology, 14,* 319–324.

Paul, G. L. (1985). Can pregnancy be a placebo effect: Terminology, designs, and conclusions in the study of psychosocial and pharmacological treatments of behavioral disorders. In L. White, B. Tursky, & G. Schwartz (Eds.), *Placebo: Clinical phenomenon and new insights.* New York: Guilford Press.

Pauli, P., Marquardt, C., Hartl, L., Nutzinger, D. O., Holzl, R., & Strian, F. (1991). Anxiety induced by cardiac perceptions in patients with panic attacks: A field study. *Behaviour Research and Therapy, 29,* 137–145.

Pauly, I. B. (1968). The current status of the change of sex operation. *Journal of Nervous and Mental Diseases, 147,* 460–471.

Paykel, E. S. (Ed.). (1982). *Handbook of affective disorders.* New York: Guilford Press.

Payne, R. L. (1992). First person account: My schizophrenia. *Schizophrenia Bulletin, 18,* 725–728.

Pedersen, P. B. (1987). Ten frequent assumptions of cultural bias in counseling. *Journal of Multicultural Counseling and Development, 15,* 16–24.

Pendery, M. L., Maltzman, I. M., & West, L. J. (1982). Controlled drinking by alcoholics? New findings and a reevaluation of a major affirmative study. *Science, 217,* 169–175.

Penn, D. L., Van Der Does, W., Spaulding, W. D., Garbin, C. P., Linszen, D., & Dingemans, P. (1993). Information processing and social cognitive problem solving in schizophrenia. *Journal of Nervous and Mental Disease, 181,* 13–20.

Perls, F. (1969). *Gestalt therapy verbatim.* Moab, UT: Real People Press.

Perodeau, G. M. (1984). Married alcoholic women: A review. *Journal of Drug Issues, 14,* 703–720.

Perris, C. (1966). A study of bipolar (manic-depressive) and unipolar recurrent depressive psychosis. *Acta Psychiatrica Scandinavica* (Suppl. 194).

Perse, T. L., Greist, J. H., Jefferson, J. W., Rosenfeld, R., & Dar, R. (1987). Fluovoxamine treatment of obsessive-compulsive disorder. *American Journal of Psychiatry, 144,* 1543–1548.

Persky, V. W., Kempthorne-Rawson, J., & Shekelle, R. B. (1987). Personality and the risk of cancer: 20 years follow-up of the Western Electric Company. *Psychosomatic Medicine, 49,* 435–449.

Persons, J. B. (1986). The advantages of studying psychological phenomena rather than psychiatric diagnosis. *American Psychologist, 41,* 1252–1260.

Persons, J. B. (1991). Psychotherapy outcome studies do not accurately represent current models of psychotherapy: A proposed remedy. *American Psychologist, 46,* 99–106.

Peselow, E. D., Robins, C. J., Sanfilipo, M. P., Block, P., & Fieve, R. R. (1992). Sociotropy and autonomy: Relationship to antidepressant drug treatment response and endogenous-nonendogenous dichotomy. *Journal of Abnormal Psychology, 101*(3), 479–486.

Petersen, A. C., Compas, B. E., Brooks-Gunn, J., Stemmler, M., Ey, S., & Grant, K. E. (1993). Depression in adolescence. *American Psychologist, 48,* 155–168.

Pfeffer, C. R., Zuckerman, S., Plutchik, R., & Mizruchi, M. S. (1987). Assaultive behavior in normal school children. *Child Psychiatry and Human Development, 17,* 166–176.

Pfeiffer, R. F., & Ebadi, M. (1994). Pharmacologic management. In A. M. Cohen & W. J. Weiner (Eds.), *The comprehensive management of Parkinson's disease* (pp. 9–38). New York: Demos Publications.

Phares, E. J. (1984). *Clinical psychology: Concepts, methods, and professions.* Homewood, IL: Dorsey.

Philips, H. C. (1983). Assessment of chronic tension headache behavior. In R. Melzack (Ed.), *Pain measurement and assessment* (pp. 155–165). New York: Raven Press.

Philips, H. C. (1987). Avoidance behavior and its role in sustaining chronic pain. *Behaviour Research and Therapy, 25,* 273–279.

Phillips, D. P., & Carstensen, L. L. (1986). Clustering of teenage suicides after television news stories about suicide. *New England Journal of Medicine, 315,* 685–689.

Phillips, D. P., Van Voorhees, C. A., & Ruth, T. E. (1992). The birthday: Lifeline or deadline? *Psychosomatic Medicine, 54,* 532–542.

Phillips, K. A. (1991). Body dysmorphic disorder: The distress of imagined ugliness. *American Journal of Psychiatry, 148,* 1138–1149.

Phillips, K. A., McElroy, S. L., Keck, P. E., Pope, H. G., Jr., & Hudson, J. I. (1993). Body dysmorphic disorder: 30 cases of imagined ugliness. *American Journal of Psychiatry, 150,* 302–308.

Phillips, K. A., Pope, H. G., Jr., McElroy, S. L., Hudson, J. I., & Keck, P. E., Jr. (1994). Dr. Phillips and colleagues reply. *American Journal of Psychiatry, 151,* 461–462.

Physicians' Desk Reference (1994). *Physicians' Desk Reference* (48th ed.). Oradell, NJ: Medical Economics Company.

Piacentini, J., Gitow, A., Jaffer, M., Graael, F., & Whitaker, A. (1994). Outpatient behavioral treatment of child and adolescent obsessive-compulsive disorder. *Journal of Anxiety Disorders, 8,* 277–289.

Pianta, R. C., & Egeland, B. (1994). Relation between depressive symptoms and stressful life events in a sample of disadvantaged mothers. *Journal of Consulting and Clinical Psychology, 62,* 1229–1234.

Pierce, K. A., & Kirkpatrick, D. R. (1992). Do men lie on fear surveys? *Behaviour Research and Therapy, 30,* 415–418.

Pigott, T. A., & Murphy, D. L. (1991). In reply. *Archives of General Psychiatry, 48,* 858–859.

Pilisuk, M. (1975). The legacy of the Vietnam veteran. *Journal of Social Issues, 31*(4), 3–12.

Pine, C. J. (1981). Suicide in American Indian and Alaskan native tradition. *White Cloud Journal, 2,* 3–8.

Pines, M. (1983, October). *Science,* pp. 55–58.

Pittman, F. (1994, January/February). A buyer's guide to psychotherapy. *Psychology Today*, pp. 50–53, 74, 76–78, 80–81.

Platt, J. J. (1986). *Heroin addiction: Theory, research, and treatment*. New York: Wiley.

Plienis, A. J., Hansen, D. J., Ford, F., Smith, S., Jr., Stark, L. J., & Kelly, J. A. (1987). Behavioral small group training to improve the social skills of emotionally-disordered adolescents. *Behavior Therapy, 18*, 17–32.

Plonin, R. (1989). Environment and genes: Determinant of behavior. *American Psychologist, 44*, 105–111.

Poling, A., Gadow, K. D., & Cleary, J. (1991). *Drug therapy for behavior disorders*. New York: Pergamon Press.

Polivy, J., Schueneman, A. L., & Carlson, K. (1976). Alcohol and tension reduction: Cognitive and physiological effects. *Journal of Abnormal Psychology, 85*, 595–600.

Pollard, C. A., Pollard, H. J., & Corn, K. J. (1989). Panic onset and major events in the lives of agoraphobics: A test of continuity. *Journal of Abnormal Psychology, 98*, 318–321.

Ponterotto, J. G. (1987). Client hospitalization: Issues and considerations for the counselor. *Journal of Counseling and Development, 65*, 542–546.

Ponterotto, J. G., & Casas, J. M. (1991). *Handbook of racial/ethnic minority counseling research*. Springfield, IL: Thomas.

Poon, L. W., & Siegler, I. C. (1991). Psychological aspects of normal aging. In J. Sadovoy, L. W. Lazarus, & L. F. Jarvik (Eds.), *Comprehensive review of geriatric psychiatry* (pp. 117–145). Washington, DC: American Psychiatric Press.

Pope, H. G., Jr., & Hudson, J. I. (1992). Is childhood sexual abuse a risk factor for bulimia nervosa? *American Journal of Psychiatry, 149*, 455–463.

Pope, H. G., Jr., Hudson, J. I., & Yurgelun-Todd, D. (1984). Anorexia nervosa and bulimia among 300 suburban women shoppers. *American Journal of Psychiatry, 141*, 292–294.

Pope, H. G., Jr., Mangweth, B., Negrao, A. B., Hudson, J. I., & Cordas, T. A. (1994). Childhood sexual abuse and bulimia nervosa: A comparison of American, Austrian, and Brazilian women. *American Journal of Psychiatry, 151*, 732–737.

Pope, K. S. (1988). How clients are harmed by sexual contact with mental health professionals: The syndrome and its prevalence. *Journal of Counseling and Development, 67*, 222–226.

Pope, K. S., & Tabachnick, B. G. (1993). Therapists' anger, hate, fear, and sexual feelings: National survey of therapist responses, client characteristics, critical events, formal complaints, and training. *Professional Psychology: Research and Practice, 24*(2), 142–152.

Pope, K. S. Tabachnick, B. G., & Keith-Spiegel, P. (1987). Ethics of practice: The beliefs and behaviors of psychologists as therapists. *American Psychologist, 42*(11), 993–1166.

Pope, K. S., & Vetter, V. A. (1991). Prior therapist-patient sexual involvement among patients seen by psychologists. *Psychotherapy, 28*(3), 429–438.

Porrino, L. J., Rapoport, J. L., Behar, D., Sceery, W., Ismond, D. R., & Bunney, W. E. (1983). A naturalistic assessment of the motor activity of hyperactive boys. *Archives of General Psychiatry, 40*, 681–687.

Portnoff, L. A., Golden, C. J., Wood, R. E., & Gustavson, J. L. (1983). Discrimination between schizophrenic and parietal lesion patients with neurological tests of parietal involvement. *Clinical Neuropsychology, 5*, 175–178.

Portwood, D. (1978, January). A right to suicide. *Psychology Today, 2*, 66–74.

Pound, E. J. (1987). Children and prematurity. In A. Thomas & J. Grimes (Eds.), *Children's needs: Psychological perspectives* (pp. 441–450). Washington, DC: National Association of School Psychologists.

Powell, A. D., & Kahn, A. S. (1995). Racial differences in women's desires to be thin. *International Journal of Eating Disorders, 17*, 191–195.

Powell, C. J. (1982, August). *Adolescence and the right to die:*

Issues of autonomy, competence, and paternalism. Paper presented at the meeting of the American Psychological Association, Washington, DC.

Powell, D. H., & Whitla, D. K. (1994). Normal cognitive aging: Toward empirical perspectives. *Current Directions in Psychological Science, 3*, 27–31.

Praeger, S. G., & Bernhardt, G. R. (1985). Survivors of suicide: A community in need. *Family and Community Health, 3*, 62–72.

President's Commission on Mental Health. (1978). *Report from the President's Commission on Mental Health*. Washington, DC: U.S. Government Printing Office.

Pribor, E. F., & Dinwiddie, S. H. (1992). Psychiatric correlates of incest in childhood. *American Journal of Psychiatry, 149*, 52–56.

Price, L. J., Fein, G., & Feinberg, I. (1980). Neurological assessment of cognitive function in the elderly. In L. W. Poon (Ed.), *Aging in the 1980's*. Washington, DC: American Psychological Association.

Prichard, J. C. (1837). *Treatise on insanity and other disorders affecting the mind*. Philadelphia: Haswell, Barrington & Haswell.

Priester, M. J., & Clum, G. A. (1992). Attributional style as a diathesis in predicting depression, hopelessness, and suicide ideation in college students. *Journal of Psychopathology and Behavioral Assessment, 14*(2), 111–122.

Prigatano, G. P., Fordyce, D. J., Zeiner, H. K., Roueche, J. R., Pepping, M., & Wood, B. C. (1984). Neuropsychological rehabilitation after closed head injury in young adults. *Journal of Neurology and Neuropsychology, 47*, 505–513.

Prior, M., Leonard, A., & Wood, G. (1983). A comparison study of preschool children diagnosed as hyperactive. *Journal of Pediatric Psychology, 8*, 191–207.

Pruzinsky, T., & Borkovec, T. D. (1990). Cognitive and personality characteristic of worriers. *Behaviour Research and Therapy, 28*, 507–512.

Pueschel, S. M. (1991). Ethical considerations relating to prenatal diagnosis of fetuses with Down syndrome. *Mental Retardation, 29*, 185–190.

Puryear, D. A., Carson, C., Fuentes, R., & Valls, T. (1992). Subjective conclusions about schizophrenia. *Archives of General Psychiatry, 49*, 74.

Putnam, F. W., Guroff, J. J., & Silberman, E. K. (1986). The clinical phenomenon of multiple personality: Review of one hundred recent cases. *Journal of Clinical Psychiatry, 47*, 285–293.

Quay, H. C. (1965). Psychopathic personality as pathological stimulation seeking. *American Journal of Psychiatry, 122*, 180–183.

Rabkin, J. G. (1979). The epidemiology of forcible rape. *American Journal of Orthopsychiatry, 49*, 634–647.

Rabkin, J. G., McGrath, P. J., Quitkin, F. M., Tricamo, E., Stewart, J. W., & Klein, D. F. (1990). Effects of pill-giving on maintenance of placebo response in patients with chronic depression. *American Journal of Psychiatry, 147*, 1622–1626.

Rabkin, J. G., Williams, J. B. W., Remien, R. H., Goetz, R., Kertzner, R., & Gorman, J. M. (1991). Depression, distress, lymphocyte subsets, and human immunodeficiency virus symptoms on two occasions in HIV-positive homosexual men. *Archives of General Psychiatry, 48*, 11–119.

Rachman, S. (1966). Sexual fetishism: An experimental analogue. *Psychological Record, 16*, 293–296.

Rachman, S., & DeSilva, P. (1987). Abnormal and normal obsessions. *Behaviour Research and Therapy, 16*, 233–248.

Rachman, S., & Hodgson, R. (1980). *Obsessions and compulsions*. Englewood Cliffs, NJ: Prentice-Hall.

Rachman, S., Lopatka, C., & Levitt, K. (1987). Panic: The link between cognitions and bodily symptoms–I. *Behavior Research and Therapy, 25*, 411–423.

Rachman, S., Lopatka, C., & Levitt, K. (1988). Experimental analysis of panic–II. Panic patients. *Behaviour Research and Therapy, 26,* 33–40.

Rachman, S., Marks, I. M., & Hodgson, R. (1973). The treatment of obsessive-compulsive neurotics by modeling and flooding in vivo. *Behaviour Research and Therapy, 13,* 271–279.

Radloff, L. S., & Rae, D. S. (1981). The components of the sex difference in depression. In R. G. Simmons (Ed.), *Research in community and mental health* (Vol. 2). Greenwood, CT: JAI Press.

Rahe, R. H. (1994). The more things change . . . *Psychosomatic Medicine, 56,* 306–307.

Rahe, R. H., & Arthur, R. J. (1978). Life change and illness studies: Past history and future directions. *Journal of Human Stress, 4,* 3–15.

Ramer, J. C., & Miller, G. (1992). Overview of mental retardation. In G. Miller & J. C. Ramer (Eds.), *Static encephalopathies of infancy and childhood* (pp. 1–10). New York: Raven Press.

Ramirez, A. J., Craig, T. K. J., Watson, J. P., Fentiman, I. S., North, W. R. S., & Rubens, R. D. (1989). Stress and relapse in breast cancer. *British Medical Journal, 298,* 291–293.

Rand, C., & Kuldau, J. (1990). The epidemiology of obesity and self-defined weight problem in the general population: Gender, race, age, and social class. *International Journal of Eating Disorders, 9,* 329–343.

Rao, S. M., Huber, S. J., & Bornstein, R. A. (1992). Emotional changes with multiple sclerosis and Parkinson's disease. *Journal of Consulting and Clinical Psychology, 60(3),* 369–378.

Rapaport, K., & Burkhart, B. R. (1984). Personality attitudinal characteristics of sexually coercive college males. *Journal of Abnormal Psychology, 93,* 216–221.

Rapee, R. M. (1995). Psychological factors influencing the affective response to biological challenge procedures in panic disorder. *Journal of Anxiety Disorders, 9,* 59–74.

Rappaport, J., & Cleary, C. P. (1980). Labeling theory and the social psychology of experts and helpers. In M. S. Gibbs, J. R. Lachenmyer, & J. Sigal (Eds.), *Community psychology: Theoretical and empirical approaches.* New York: Gardner Press.

Raps, C. S., Peterson, C., Reinhard, K. E., Abramson, L. Y., & Seligman, M. E. P. (1982). Attributional styles among depressed patients. *Journal of Abnormal Psychology, 91,* 102–108.

Raskin, M., Pecke, H. V. S., Dickman, W., & Pinsker, H. (1982). Panic and generalized anxiety disorders. *Archives of General Psychiatry, 39,* 687–689.

Ratey, J. J., Grandin, T., & Miller, A. (1992). Defense behavior and coping in an autistic savant: The story of Temple Grandin, PhD. *Psychiatry, 55,* 382–391.

Ratican, K. L. (1992). Sexual abuse survivors: Identifying symptoms and special treatment considerations. *Journal of Counseling and Development, 71,* 33–38.

Rauch, S. L., Jenike, M. A., Alpert, N. M., Baer, L., Breiter, H. C. R., Savage, C. R., & Fischman, A. J. (1994). Regional cerebral blood flow measured during symptom provocation in obsessive-compulsive disorder using oxygen 15-labeled carbon dioxide and positron emission tomography. *Archives of General Psychiatry, 51,* 62–70.

Read, S. (1991). The dementias. In J. Sadavoy, L. W. Lazarus, & L. F. Jarvik (Eds.), *Comprehensive review of geriatric psychiatry* (pp. 287–309). Washington, DC: American Psychiatric Press.

Reading, C., & Mohr, P. (1976). Biofeedback control of migraine: A pilot study. *British Journal of Social and Clinical Psychology, 15,* 429–433.

Red Horse, Y. (1982). A cultural network model: Perspectives for adolescent services and paraprofessional training. In S. M. Manson (Ed.), *New directions in prevention among American Indian and Alaskan Native communities* (pp. 173–184). Portland, OR: Oregon Health Sciences University.

Rees, L. (1964). The importance of psychological, allergic, and infective factors in childhood asthma. *Journal of Psychosomatic Research, 1,* 253–262.

Regan, J., & LaBarbera, J. D. (1984). Lateralization of conversion symptoms. *American Journal of Psychiatry, 141,* 1279–1280.

Regier, D. A., Boyd, J. H., Burke, J. D., Rae, D. S., Myers, J. K., Kramer, M., Robins, L. N., George, L. K., Karno, M., & Locke, B. Z. (1988). One-month prevalence of mental disorders in the U.S.: Based on five Epidemiologic Catchment Area (ECA) sites. *Archives of General Psychiatry, 45,* 977–986.

Regier, D. A., Goldberg, I. O., & Taube, C. A. (1978). The de facto U.S. mental health services systems: A public health perspective. *Archives of General Psychiatry, 35,* 685–693.

Regier, D. A., Narrow, W. E., Rae, D. S., Manderscheid, R. W., Locke, B. Z., & Goodwin, F. K. (1993). The de facto U.S. Mental and Addictive Disorders Service System: Epidemiologic Catchment Area prospective one-year prevalence rates of disorders in services. *Archives of General Psychiatry, 50,* 85–94.

Reich, J. (1987). Sex distribution of DSM-III personality disorders in psychiatric outpatients. *American Journal of Psychiatry, 144,* 485–488.

Reid, W. H. (1981). The antisocial personality and related symptoms. In J. R. Lion (Ed.), *Personality disorders: Diagnosis and management.* Baltimore: Williams & Wilkins.

Reilly, D. (1984). Family therapy with adolescent drug abusers and their families: Defying gravity and achieving escape velocity. *Journal of Drug Issues, 14,* 381–389.

Reisberg, B., Ferris, S. H., Crook, T. (1982). Signs, symptoms, and course of age-associated cognitive decline. In S. Corkin, K. L. Davis, J. H. Growdon, E. Usdin, & R. J. Wurtman (Eds.), *Alzheimer's disease: A report of progress.* New York: Raven Press.

Reiser, D. E. (1988). The psychiatric interview. In H. H. Goldman (Ed.), *Review of general psychiatry* (pp. 184–192). Norwalk, CT: Appleton & Lange.

Reisman, J. (1971). *Toward the integration of psychotherapy.* New York: Wiley.

Reiss, S., Levitan, G. W., & Szyszko, J. (1982). Emotional disturbance and mental retardation: Diagnostic overshadowing. *American Journal of Mental Deficiency, 86,* 567–574.

Reiss, S., Peterson, R. A., Gursky, D. M., & McNally, R. J. (1986). Anxiety sensitivity, anxiety frequency, and the prediction of fearfulness. *Behaviour Research and Therapy, 24,* 1–8.

Reissman, F. (1962). *The culturally deprived child.* New York: Harper & Row.

Rekers, G. A., & Varni, J. W. (1977a). Self-monitoring and self-reinforcement processes in a pre-transsexual boy. *Behaviour Research and Therapy, 15,* 177–180.

Rekers, G. A., & Yates, C. E. (1976). Sex-typed play in feminoid boys versus normal boys and girls. *Journal of Abnormal Child Psychology, 4,* 1–8.

Renfrey, G. & Spates, C. R. (1994). Eye movement desensitization: A partial dismantling study. *Journal of Behavior Therapy and Experimental Psychiatry, 25,* 231–239.

Reschly, D. J. (1992). Mental retardation: Conceptual foundations, definitional criteria, and diagnostic operations. In S. R. Hooper, G. W. Hynd, & R. E. Mattison (Eds.), *Developmental disorders: Diagnostic criteria and clinical assessment* (pp. 23–67). Hillsdale, NJ: Lawrence Erlbaum Associates.

Research Task Force of the National Institute of Mental Health. (1975). *Research in the service of mental health* (DHEW Publication No. ADM 75–236). Washington, DC: U.S. Government Printing Office.

Reus, V. I. (1988). Affective disorders. In H. H. Goldman (Ed.), *Review of general psychiatry* (pp. 332–348). Norwalk, CT: Appleton & Lange.

Reynolds, C. R., Kamphaus, R. W., & Rosenthal, B. L. (1989). Applications of the Kaufman Assessment Battery for Children (K-ABC) in neuropsychological assessment. In C. R. Reynolds & E. Fletcher-Janzen (Eds.), *Handbook of clinical child neuropsychology* (pp. 181–191). New York: Plenum Press.

Rhoades, E. R., Marshal, M., Attneave, D., Echohawk, M., Bjork, J., & Beiser, M. (1980). Mental health problems of American Indians seen in outpatient facilities of the Indian Health Services, 1975. *Public Health Reports, 96*, 329–335.

Ridley, C. R. (1995). *Overcoming unintentional racism in counseling and therapy.* Thousand Oaks, CA: Sage.

Rimm, D. C., Janda, L. H., Lancaster, D. W., Nahl, M., & Dittmar, K. (1977). An exploratory investigation of the origin and maintenance of phobias. *Behaviour Research and Therapy, 15,* 231–238.

Rimm, D. C., & Masters, J. C. (1979). *Behavior therapy: Techniques and empirical findings* (2nd ed.). New York: Academic Press.

Riskind, J. H., Moore, R., & Bowley, L. (1995). The looming of spiders: The fearful perceptual distortion of movement and menace. *Behaviour Research and Therapy, 33,* 171–178.

Rist, K. (1979). Incest: Theoretical and clinical views. *American Journal of Orthopsychiatry, 49,* 680–691.

Ritvo, E. R., Freeman, B. J., Yuwiler, A., Geller, E., Yokota, A., Schroth, P., & Novak, P. (1984). Study of fenfluramine in outpatients with the syndrome of autism. *Journal of Pediatrics, 105,* 823–828.

Ritvo, E. R., Jorde, L. B., Mason-Brothers, A., Freeman, B. J., Pingree, C., Jones, M. B., McMahon, W. M., Petersen, B., Jenson, W. R. & Mo, A. (1989). The UCLA-University of Utah epidemiologic survey of autism: Recurrent risk estimates and genetic counseling. *American Journal of Psychiatry, 146,* 1032–1036.

Roberto, L. (1983). Issues in diagnosis and treatment of transsexualism. *Archives of Sexual Behavior, 12,* 445–473.

Roberts, G. W. (1991). Schizophrenia: A neuropathological perspective. *British Journal of Psychiatry, 158,* 8–17.

Robertson, J., Wendiggensen, P., & Kaplan, I. (1983). Toward a comprehensive treatment for obsessional thoughts. *Behaviour Research and Therapy, 21,* 347–356.

Robertson, M. M. (1994). Annotation: Gilles de la Tourette syndrome–An update. *Journal of Child Psychology and Psychiatry, 35,* 597–611.

Robins, L. N. (1966). *Deviant children growing up: A sociological and psychiatric study of sociopathic personality.* Baltimore: Williams & Wilkins.

Robins, L. N. (1991). Conduct disorder. *Journal of Child Psychology and Psychiatry, 32,* 193–212.

Robins, L. N., Helzer, J. E., Weisinann, M. M., Orvaschel, H., Gruenberg, E., Burke, J. D., & Regier, D. A. (1984). Lifetime prevalence of specific psychiatric disorders in three sites. *Archives of General Psychiatry, 41,* 949–958.

Robins, L. N., & Kulbok, P. (1988). Epidemiological studies in suicide. *Psychiatric Annual, 18,* 619–627.

Robins, L. N., Locke, B. Z., & Regier, D. A. (1991). An overview of psychiatric disorders in America. In L. N. Robins & D. A. Regier (Eds.), *Psychiatric disorders in America: The Epidemiologic Catchment Area study* (pp. 328–366). New York: Free Press.

Robins, L. N., & Regier, D. A. (Eds.) (1991). *Psychiatric disorders in America: The Epidemiologic Catchment Area study.* New York: Free Press.

Robins, L. N., Tipp, J., & Przybeck, T. (1991). Antisocial personality. In L. N. Robins & D. A. Regier (Eds.), *Psychiatric disorders in America: The Epidemiologic Catchment Area study* (pp. 258–290). New York: Free Press.

Robinson, J. P., Shaver, P. R., & Wrightsman, L. S. (Eds.). (1991). *Measures of personality and social psychological attitudes.* San Diego, CA: Academic Press.

Rodin, J., & Langer, E. J. (1977). Long-term effects of a control-relevant intervention with the institutionalized aged. *Journal of Personality and Social Psychology, 35,* 897–902.

Rogers, C. R. (1951). *Client-centered therapy.* Boston: Houghton Mifflin.

Rogers, C. R. (1959). A theory of therapy, personality, and interpersonal relationships, as developed in client-centered framework. In S. Koch (Ed.), *Psychology: A study of science* (Vol. 3). New York: McGraw-Hill.

Rogers, C. R. (1961). *On becoming a person.* Boston: Houghton Mifflin.

Rogers, C. R. (1980). *A way of being.* Boston: Houghton Mifflin.

Rogers, C. R. (1987). The underlying theory: Drawn from experiences with individuals and groups. *Counseling and Values, 32,* 38–45.

Rogers, J. R. (1990). Female suicide: The trend toward increased lethality in method of choice and its implications. *Journal of Counseling and Development, 69,* 37–41.

Rogers, J. R. (1992). Suicide and alcohol: Conceptualizing the relationship from a cognitive-social paradigm. *Journal of Counseling and Development, 70,* 540–543.

Rogers, R. (1987). APA's position on the insanity defense. *American Psychologist, 42,* 840–848.

Roland, C. B. (1993). Exploring childhood memories with adult survivors of sexual abuse: Concrete reconstruction and visualization techniques. *Journal of Mental Health Counseling, 15,* 363–372.

Rollason, D. H., Jr. (1995). Clinical asthma: Fundamental concepts of diagnosis and treatment. *Physician Assistant,* Supplement, 3–15.

Romme, M. A., Honig, A., Noorthoorn, E. O., & Escher, A. D. M. A. C. (1992). Coping with hearing voices: An emancipatory approach. *British Journal of Psychiatry, 161,* 99–103.

Root, M. P. (1990). Disordered eating in women of color. *Sex Roles, 22,* 525–536.

Roper, G., & Rachman, S. (1976). Obsessive-compulsive checking: Experimental replication and development. *Behaviour Research and Therapy, 14,* 25–32.

Roper, G., Rachman, S., & Marks, I. M. (1975). Passive and participant treatment in obsessive-compulsive neurotics. *Behaviour Research and Therapy, 13,* 271–279.

Rosen, J. C., Reiter, J., & Orosan, P. (1995a). Cognitive-behavioral body image therapy for body dysmorphic disorder. *Journal of Consulting and Clinical Psychology, 63,* 263–269.

Rosen, J. C., Reiter, J., & Orosan, P. (1995b). Assessment of body image in eating disorders with the body dysmorphic disorder examination. *Behaviour Research and Therapy, 33,* 77–84.

Rosen, R. C., Kostis, J. B., & Jekelis, A. W. (1988). Beta-blocker effects on sexual function in normal males. *Archives of Sexual Behavior, 17,* 241–255.

Rosen, R. C., & Leiblum, S. R. (1987). Current approaches to the evaluation of sexual desire disorders. *Journal of Sex Research, 23,* 141–162.

Rosenblat, R., & Tang, S. W. (1987). Do Oriental psychiatric patients receive different dosages of psychotropic medication when compared with Occidentals? *Canadian Journal of Psychiatry, 32,* 270–274.

Rosenfarb, I. S., Goldstein, M. J., Mintz, J., & Nuechterlein, K. H. (1995). Expressed emotion and subclinical psychopathology observable within the transactions between schizophrenic patients and their family members. *Journal of Abnormal Psychology, 104,* 259–267.

Rosenfield, A. H. (1985). Discovering and dealing with deviant sex. *Psychology Today, 19,* 8–10.

Rosenhan, D. L. (1973). On being sane in insane places. *Science, 179,* 250–258.

Rosenthal, D. (1970). *Genetic theory and abnormal behavior.* New York: McGraw-Hill.

Rosenthal, D. (1971). *Genetics of psychopathology.* New York: McGraw-Hill.

Rosenthal, J., & Jacobson, L. (1968). *Pygmalion in the classroom.* New York: Holt, Rinehart & Winston.

Rosenthal, N. E., Sack, D. A., Carpenter, C. J., Parry, B. L.,

Mendelson, W. B., & Wehr, T. A. (1985). Antidepressant effects of light in seasonal affective disorder. *American Journal of Psychiatry, 142,* 163–170.

Rosenthal, P., & Rosenthal, S. (1984). Suicidal behavior by preschool children. *American Journal of Psychiatry, 141,* 520–525.

Ross, C. A., Anderson, C., Fleisher, W. P., & Norton, G. R. (1991). The frequency of multiple personality disorder among psychiatric inpatients. *American Journal of Psychiatry, 148,* 1717–1720.

Rossiter, L. F. (1983). Prescribed medicines: Findings from the National Medical Care Expenditure Survey. *American Journal of Public Health, 73,* 1312–1315.

Rothbaum, B. O., Foa, E. B., Murdock, T., Riggs, D., & Walsh, W. (1990). Post-traumatic stress disorders in rape victims. Unpublished manuscript.

Rothenberg, R. B., & Aubert, R. E. (1990). Ischemic heart disease and hypertension: Effects of disease coding on epidemiologic assessment. *Public Health Reports, 105,* 47–52.

Roy, A. (1985). Suicide in doctors. *Psychiatric Clinics of North America, 8,* 377–387.

Roy, A., Adinoff, B., Roehrich, L., Lamparski, D., Custer, R., Lorenz, V., Barbaccia, M., Guidotti, A., Cost, E., & Linnoila, M. (1988). Pathological gambling: A psychobiological study. *Archives of General Psychiatry, 45,* 369–373.

Roy-Byrne, P. P., Geraci, M., & Uhde, T. W. (1986). Life events and course of illness in patients with panic disorder. *American Journal of Psychiatry, 143,* 1033–1035.

Royce, J. M., Lazar, I., & Darlington, R. B. (1983). Minority families, early education, and later life changes. *American Journal of Orthopsychiatry, 53,* 706–720.

Rubinstein, M., Yaeger, C. A., Goodstein, C., & Lewis, D. O. (1993). Sexually assaultive male juveniles: A follow-up. *American Journal of Psychiatry, 150,* 262–265.

Ruderman, A. J., & Besbeas, M. (1992). Psychological characteristics of dieters and bulimics. *Journal of Abnormal Psychology, 101,* 383–390.

Rueger, D., & Liberman, R. (1984). Behavioral family therapy for delinquent and substance-abusing adolescents. *Journal of Drug Issues, 14,* 403–417.

Ruocchio, P. J. (1991). First person account: The schizophrenic inside. *Schizophrenia Bulletin, 17,* 357–360.

Rutter, M. (1994). Debate and argument: There are connections between brain and mind and it is important that Rett syndrome be classified somewhere. *Journal of Child Psychology and Psychiatry, 35,* 379–381.

Rutter, M., MacDonald, H., LeCouteur, A., Harrington, R., Bolton, P., & Bailey, A. (1990). Genetic factors in child psychiatric disorders–II. Empirical findings. *Journal of Child Psychology and Psychiatry, 31,* 39–83.

Sabalis, R. F., Frances, A., Appenzeller, S. N., & Moseley, W. B. (1974). The three sisters: Transsexual male siblings. *American Journal of Psychiatry, 131,* 907–909.

Sabalis, R. F., Staton, M. A., & Appenzeller, S. N. (1977). Transsexualism: Alternative diagnostic etiological considerations. *American Journal of Psychoanalysis, 37,* 223–228.

Sachdev, P., & Loeragan, C. (1991). The present status of akathisia. *Journal of Nervous and Mental Disease, 179,* 381–391.

Sackeim, H. A., & Vingiano, W. (1984). Dissociative disorders. In S. Turner & M. Hersen (Eds.), *Adult psychopathology and diagnosis.* New York: Wiley.

Safferman, A., Lieberman, J. A., Kane, J. M., Szymanski, S., & Kinon, B. (1991). Update on the clinical efficacy and side effects of clozapine. *Schizophrenia Bulletin, 17,* 247–261.

Saigh, P. A. (1987). In vivo flooding of an adolescent's posttraumatic stress disorder. *Journal of Clinical Child Psychology, 16,* 147–150.

Sainsbury, P. (1982). Suicide: Epidemiology and relationship to depression. In J. K. Wing & Y. L. Wing (Eds.), *Cambridge handbook of psychiatry: Psychoses of uncertain aetiology* (pp. 134–140). Cambridge, England: Cambridge University Press.

Sakheim, D. K., Barlow, D. H., Abrahamson, D. J., & Beck, J. G. (1987). Distinguishing between organogenic and psychogenic erectile dysfunction. *Behavior Research and Therapy, 25,* 379–390.

Sakheim, D. K., Hess, E. P., & Chivas, A. (1988). General principles for short-term inpatient work with multiple personality disorder patients. *Psychotherapy, 25,* 117–124.

Salim, A. S. (1987). Stress, the adrenergic hypothalamovagal pathway, and the aetiology of chronic duodenal ulceration. *Journal of Psychosomatic Research, 31,* 231–237.

Salkovskis, P. M., & Harrison, J. (1984). Abnormal and normal obsessions–A replication. *Behaviour Research and Therapy, 22,* 549–552.

Salkovskis, P. M., & Warwick, H. M. C. (1986). Morbid preoccupations, health anxiety and reassurance: A cognitive-behavioral approach to hypochondriasis. *Behavior Research and Therapy, 24,* 597–602.

Salley, R. D. (1988). Subpersonalities with dreaming functions in a patient with multiple personalities. *Journal of Nervous and Mental Disease, 176,* 112–115.

Saltus, R. (1993, March 24). Huntington's disease gene is identified. *Boston Globe,* pp. 1, 20.

SAMHSA. (1995). Survey shows youth drug abuse up. *SAMHSA News, 3,* 11, 20.

Sanavio, E. (1988). Obsessions and compulsions: The Padua Inventory. *Behaviour Research and Therapy, 26,* 169–177.

Sanders, B., & Giolas, M. H. (1991). Dissociation and childhood trauma in psychologically disturbed adolescents. *American Journal of Psychiatry, 148,* 50–54.

Sanderson, C., & Clarkin, J. F. (1994). Use of the NEO-PI personality dimensions in differential treatment planning. In P. T. Costa & T. A. Widiger (Eds.), *Personality disorders and the five-factor model of personality* (pp. 219–236). Washington, DC: American Psychological Association.

Sarason, I. G., Johnson, J. H., & Siegel, J. M. (1978). Assessing the impact of life changes: Development of the Life Experiences Survey. *Journal of Consulting and Clinical Psychology, 46,* 932–946.

Sarbin, P. R., & Cole, W. C. (1979). Hypnosis and psychopathology: Replacing old myths with fresh metaphors. *Journal of Abnormal Psychology, 88,* 506–526.

Sartorius, N., Jablensky, A., Korten, A., Ernberg, G., Anker, M., Cooper, J. E., & Day, R. (1986). Early manifestations and first-contact incidence of schizophrenia in different cultures. *Psychological Medicine, 16,* 909–928.

Satir, V. (1967). A family of angels. In J. Haley & L. Hoffman (Eds.), *Techniques of family therapy.* New York: Basic Books.

Satow, R. (1979). Where has all the hysteria gone? *Psychoanalytic Review, 66,* 463–477.

Satterfield, J. H., Hoppe, C. M., & Schell, A. M. (1982). A prospective study of delinquency in 110 adolescent boys with attention deficit disorder and 88 normal adolescent boys. *American Journal of Psychiatry, 139,* 795–798.

Saxe, L., Cross, T., & Silverman, N. (1988). Children's mental health. *American Psychologist, 43,* 800–807.

Sbordone, R. J., & Jennison, J. H. (1983). A comparison of the OBD-168 and MMPI to assess the emotional adjustment of traumatic brain-injured inpatients to their cognitive deficits. *Clinical Neuropsychology, 5,* 87–88.

Scarr, S., Webber, P. L., Weinberg, R. A., and Wittig, M. A. (1981). Personality resemblance among adolescents and their parents in biologically related and adoptive families. *Journal of Personality and Social Psychology, 40,* 885–898.

Schachar, R. (1991). Childhood hyperactivity. *Journal of Child Psychology and Psychiatry, 32,* 155–191.

Schacht, T. E. (1985). DSM-III and the politics of truth. *American Psychologist, 40,* 513–521.

Schacht, T. E., & Nathan, P. E. (1977). But is it good for the psychologists? Appraisal and status of DSM-III. *American Psychologist, 32,* 1017–1025.

Schachter, S. (1977). Nicotine regulation in heavy and light smokers. *Journal of Experimental Psychology (General), 106,* 5–12.

Schachter, S., & Latane, B. (1964). Crime, cognition, and the autonomic nervous system. *Nebraska Symposium on Motivation, 12,* 221–274.

Schacter, D. L. (1986). Amnesia and crime. *American Psychologist, 41,* 186–295.

Schaef, A. W. (1981). *Women's reality: An emerging female system in the white male society.* Minneapolis: Winton Press.

Schaefer, H. H. (1970). Self-injurious behavior: Shaping "head banging" in monkeys. *Journal of Applied Behavior Analysis, 3,* 111–116.

Schaefer, H. H., & Martin, P. L. (1969). *Behavioral therapy.* New York: McGraw-Hill.

Schafer, J., & Brown, S. A. (1991). Marijuana and cocaine effect expectancies and drug use patterns. *Journal of Consulting and Clinical Psychology, 59,* 558–565.

Schaughency, E. A., & Hynd, G. W. (1989). Attention and impulse control in attention deficit disorders (ADD). *Learning and Individual Differences, 1,* 423–449.

Scheppele, K. L., & Bart, P. B. (1983). Through women's eyes: Defining danger in the wake of sexual assault. *Journal of Social Issues, 39,* 63–80.

Schildkraut, J. J. (1965). The catecholamine hypothesis of affective disorders: A review of supporting evidence. *American Journal of Psychiatry, 122,* 509–522.

Schleifer, S. J., Keller, S. E., Camerino, M., Thornton, J. C., & Stein, M. (1983). Suppression of lymphocyte stimulation following bereavement. *Journal of the American Medical Association, 250,* 374–377.

Schlesinger. L. (1989). *Sex murder and sex aggression.* New York: Wiley.

Schmauk, F. J. (1970). Punishment, arousal, and avoidance learning. *Journal of Abnormal Psychology, 76,* 325–335.

Schmidt, H. O., & Fonda, C. P. (1956). The reliability of psychiatric diagnosis: A new look. *Journal of Abnormal and Social Psychology, 52,* 262–267.

Schnurr, P. P., Friedman, M. J., & Rosenberg, S. D. (1993). Premilitary MMPI scores as predictors of combat-related PTSD symptoms. *American Journal of Psychiatry, 150,* 479–483.

Schoeneman, T. J. (1984). The mentally ill witch in textbooks of abnormal psychology: Current status and implications of a fallacy. *Professional Psychology, 15,* 299–314.

Schofield, W. (1964). *Psychotherapy: The purchase of friendship.* Englewood Cliffs, NJ: Prentice-Hall.

Schover, L. R., Friedman, J. M., Weiler, S. J., Heiman, J. R., & LoPiccolo, J. (1982). Multiaxial problem-oriented system for sexual dysfunctions. *Archives of General Psychiatry, 39,* 614–619.

Schreiber, F. R. (1973). *Sybil.* Chicago: Regnery.

Schreiber, J. L., Breier, A., & Pickar, D. (1995). Expressed emotion: Trait or state? *British Journal of Psychiatry, 166,* 647–649.

Schuckit, M. A. (1990). A prospective study of children of alcoholics. In C. R. Cloninger & H. Begleiter (Eds.), *Genetics and biology of alcoholism* (pp. 183–194). Cold Spring Harbor, NY: Cold Spring Harbor Laboratory Press.

Schuckit, M. A. (1994). A clinical model of genetic influences in alcohol dependence. *Journal of Studies on Alcohol, 55,* 5–17.

Schuell, H. (1974). *Aphasia theory and therapy: Selected lectures and papers of Hildred Schuell.* Baltimore: University Park Press.

Schulsinger, F. (1972). Psychopathy: Heredity and environment. *International Journal of Mental Health, 1,* 190–206.

Schwartz, L., Slater, M. A., & Birchler, G. R. (1994). Interpersonal stress and pain behaviors in patients with chronic pain. *Journal of Consulting and Clinical Psychology, 62,* 861–864.

Schwartz, R., & Geyer, S. (1984). Social and psychological differences between cancer and noncancer patients: Cause or consequence of the disease? *Psychotherapy and Psychomatics, 41,* 195–199.

Scott, M. J., & Stradling, S. G. (1994). Post-traumatic stress disorder without the trauma. *British Journal of Clinical Psychology, 33,* 71–74.

Scott, R. L., & Baroffio, J. R. (1986). An MMPI analysis of similarities and differences in three classifications of eating disorders: Anorexia nervosa, bulimia, and morbid obesity. *Journal of Clinical Psychology, 42,* 708–713.

Scovern, A. W., & Kilmann, P. R. (1980). Status of electroconvulsive therapy: A review of the outcome literature. *Psychological Bulletin, 87,* 260–303.

Segal, S. P., Cohen, D., & Marder, S. R. (1992). Use of antipsychotic medication in sheltered-care facilities. *American Journal of Public Health, 47,* 39–46.

Segraves, R. T. (1988). Hormones and libido. In R. C. Rosen & S. R. Leiblum (Eds.), *Sexual desire disorders.* New York: Guilford.

Segraves, R. T., Schoenberg, H. W., & Ivanoff, J. (1983). Serum testosterone and prolactin levels in erectile dysfunction. *Journal of Sex and Marital Therapy, 9,* 19–26.

Segrin, C., & Abramson, L. Y. (1994). Negative reactions to depressive behaviors: A communication theories analysis. *Journal of Abnormal Psychology, 103,* 655–668.

Seiden, R. H. (1966). Campus tragedy: A study of student suicide. *Journal of Abnormal and Social Psychology, 71,* 389–399.

Seiden, R. H. (1984a). Death in the West—A regional analysis of the youthful suicide rate. *Western Journal of Medicine, 140,* 969–973.

Seiden, R. H. (1984b). The youthful suicide epidemic. *Public Affairs Report, 25,* 1.

Seligman, J., Huck, J., Joseph, N., Namuth, T., Prout, L. R., Robinson, T. L., & McDaniel, A. L. (1984, April 9). The date who rapes. *Newsweek,* pp. 91–92.

Seligman, M. E. P. (1971). Phobias and preparedness. *Behavior Therapy, 2,* 307–320.

Seligman, M. E. P. (1975). *Helplessness.* San Francisco: Freeman.

Seligman, M. E. P. (1987). Stop blaming yourself. *Psychology Today, 21,* 30–32, 34, 36–39.

Selvin, I. P. (1993). The incidence and prevalence of sexual dysfunctions. *Archives of Sexual Behavior, 19*(4), 389–408.

Selye, H. (1956). *The stress of life.* New York: McGraw-Hill.

Selye, H. (1982). Stress: Eustress, distress, and human perspectives. In S. B. Day (Ed.), *Life stress* (pp. 3–13). New York: Van Nostrand Reinhold.

Semans, J. H. (1956). Premature ejaculation: A new approach. *Southern Medical Journal, 49,* 353–357.

Semenchuk, E. M., & Larkin, K. T. (1993). Behavioral and cardiovascular responses to interpersonal challenges among male offspring of essential hypertensives. *Health Psychology, 12,* 416–419.

Shaffer, D., & Fisher, P. (1981). The epidemiology of suicide in children and young adolescents. *Journal of the American Academy of Child Psychiatry, 21,* 545–565.

Shafran, R., Booth, R., & Rachman, S. (1993). The reduction of claustrophobia–II: Cognitive analysis. *Behaviour Research and Therapy, 31,* 75–85.

Shahar, A., & Marks, I. (1980). Habituation during exposure treatment of compulsive rituals. *Behavior Therapy, 11,* 397–401.

Shahidi, S., & Salmon, P. (1992). Contingent and non-contingent biofeedback training for type A and B health adults: Can type As relax by competing? *Journal of Psychosomatic Research, 36,* 477–483.

Shapiro, D. A., & Shapiro, D. (1983). Meta-analysis of comparative therapy outcome studies: A replication and refinement. *Psychological Bulletin, 92,* 581–594.

Shapiro, D. L. (1984). *Psychological evaluation and expert testimony.* New York: Van Nostrand Reinhold.

Shapiro, F. (1989). Eye movement desensitization procedure: A new treatment for post-traumatic stress disorder. *Journal of Behavior Therapy and Experimental Psychiatry, 20,* 211–217.

Shapiro, J. P. (1991). Interviewing children about psychological issues associated with sexual abuse. *Psychotherapy, 28,* 55–65.

Shapiro, L., Rosenberg, D., Lauerman, J. F., & Sparkman, R. (1993, April 19). Rush to judgment. *Newsweek,* pp. 54–60.

Shapiro, M. K. (1991). Bandaging a "broken heart:" Hypnoplay therapy in the treatment of multiple personality disorder. *American Journal of Clinical Hypnosis, 34,* 1–9.

Shave, D. (1976). Transsexualism as a manifestation of orality. *American Journal of Psychoanalysis, 36,* 57–66.

Shaywitz, S. E., & Shaywitz, B. A. (1984). Evaluation and treatment of children with attention deficit disorders. *Pediatrics in Review, 6,* 99–109.

Shaywitz, S. E., & Shaywitz, B. A. (1991). Introduction to the special series on attention deficit disorder. *Journal of Learning Disabilities, 24,* 68–71.

Shean, G. (1987) *Schizophrenia.* Cambridge, MA: Winthrop Publishers.

Shear, M. K., Ball, G., Fitzpatrick, M., Josephson, S., Klosko, J., & Frances, A. (1991). Cognitive-behavioral therapy for panic: An open study. *Journal of Nervous and Mental Disease, 179,* 468–472.

Shedler, J., & Block, J. (1990). Adolescent drug use and psychological health: A longitudinal inquiry. *American Psychologist, 45,* 612–630.

Sheehan, P. W., Grigg, L., & McCann, T. (1984). Memory distortion following exposure to false information in hypnosis. *Journal of Abnormal Psychology, 93,* 259–265.

Shelton, R. C., Karson, C. N., Doran, A. R., Pickar, D., Bigelow, L. B., & Weinberger, D. R. (1988). Cerebral structural pathology in schizophrenia: Evidence for a selective prefrontal cortical defect. *American Journal of Psychiatry, 145,* 154–163.

Shepherd, M., Watt, D., Falloon, I. R. F., & Smeeton, N. (1989). The natural history of schizophrenia: A five-year follow-up study of outcome and prediction in a representative sample of schizophrenics. *Psychological Medicine, 15,* 1–46.

Sher, K. J., & Trull, T. J. (1994). Personality and disinhibitory psychopathology: Alcoholism and antisocial personality disorder. *Journal of Abnormal Psychology, 103,* 92–102.

Sherman, C. (1993). Behind closed doors: Therapist-client sex. *Psychology Today, 26*(3), 64–72.

Shimamura, A. P., Berry, J. M., Mangels, J. A., Rusting, C. L., & Jurica, P. J. (1995). Memory and cognitive abilities in university professors: Evidence for successful aging. *Psychological Science, 6,* 271–277.

Shine, K. I. (1984). Anxiety in patients with heart disease. *Psychosomatics, 25,* 27–31.

Shisslak, C. M., Pazda, S. L., & Crago, M. (1990). Body weight and bulimia as discriminators of psychological characteristics among anoretic, bulimic, and obese women. *Journal of Abnormal Psychology, 99,* 380–384.

Shneidman, E. S. (1968). *Classifications of suicide phenomena: Bulletin of suicidology.* For the National Institute of Mental Health, Alcohol, Drug Abuse, and Mental Retardation, U.S. Department of Health, Education, and Welfare. Washington, DC: U.S. Government Printing Office.

Shneidman, E. S. (1976). A psychological theory of suicide. *Psychiatric Annals, 6,* 51–66.

Shneidman, E. S. (1981). Suicide thoughts and reflections: 1960–1980. *Suicide and Life-Threatening Behavior, 11,* 197–360.

Shneidman, E. S. (1987). A psychological approach to suicide. In G. VandenBos & B. Bryant (Eds.), *Cataclysms, crises, and catastrophes: Psychology in action* (pp. 151–183). Washington, DC: American Psychological Association.

Shneidman, E. S. (1992). What do suicides have in common? Summary of the psychological approach. In B. Bongar (Ed.), *Suicide: Guidelines for assessment, management, and treatment.* New York: Oxford University Press.

Shneidman, E. S. (1993). *Suicide as psychache: A clinical approach to self-destructive behavior.* Northvale, NJ: Jason Aronson.

Shneidman, E. S., & Farberow, N. L. (Eds.). (1957). *Clues to suicide.* New York: McGraw-Hill.

Shockley, W. (1972). Negro IQ deficit. *Journal of Criminal Law and Criminology, 7,* 530–543.

Shore, D., Matthews, S., Cott, J., & Lieberman, J. A. (1995). Clinical implications of clozapine discontinuation: Report of an NIMH workshop. *Schizophrenia Bulletin, 21,* 333–337.

Shore, J. H. (1988). *American Indian and Alaskan Native Mental Health Research, 1,* 3–4.

Shotten, J. H. (1985). The family interview. *Schizophrenia Bulletin, 11,* 112–116.

Shouldice, A., & Stevenson-Hinde, J. (1992). Coping with security distress: The Separation Anxiety Test and attachment classification at 4.5 years. *Journal of Child Psychology and Psychiatry, 33,* 331–348.

Shreve, B. W., & Kunkel, M. A. (1991). Self-psychology, shame, and adolescent suicide: Theoretical and practical considerations. *Journal of Counseling and Development, 69,* 305–311.

Shuey, A. (1966). *The testing of Negro intelligence.* New York: Social Science Press.

Sibler, E., Hamburg, D. A., Coelho, G. V., Murphy, E. B., Rosenberg, M., & Perle, L. I. (1961). Adaptive behavior in competent adolescents. *Archives of General Psychiatry, 5,* 354–365.

Siegel, M. (1979). Privacy, ethics, and confidentiality. *Professional Psychology, 10,* 249–258.

Siegel, R. A. (1978). Probability of punishment and suppression of behavior in psychopathic and nonpsychopathic offenders. *Journal of Abnormal Psychology, 87,* 514–522.

Siegel, S. (1990). Drug anticipation and drug tolerance. In M. Lader (Ed.), *The psychopharmacology of addiction.* New York: Wiley.

Siever, L. J. (1981). Schizoid and schizotypal personality disorders. In J. R. Lion (Ed.), *Personality disorders: Diagnosis and management.* Baltimore: Williams & Wilkins.

Siever, L. J., Davis, K. L., & Gorman, L. K. (1991). Pathogenesis of mood disorders. In K. Davis, H. Klar, & J. T. Coyle, *Foundations of psychiatry.* Philadelphia: Saunders.

Silva, R. R., Munoz, D. M., Barickman, J., & Friedhoff, A. J. (1995). Environmental factors and related fluctuation of symptoms in children and adolescents with Tourette's disorder. *Journal of Child Psychology and Psychiatry, 36,* 305–312.

Silverman, J. M., Mohs, R. C., Davidson, M., Losonczy, M. F., Keefe, R. S. E., Breitner, J. C. S., Sorokin, J. E., & Davis, K. L. (1987). Familial schizophrenia and treatment response. *American Journal of Psychiatry, 144,* 1271–1276.

Silverman, L. H. (1976). Psychoanalytic theory: "The reports of my death are greatly exaggerated." *American Psychologist, 31,* 621–637.

Silverstein, B., & Perdue, L. (1988). The relationship between role concerns, preference of slimness, and symptoms of eating problems among college women. *Sex Roles, 18,* 101–160.

Simon, G. E., & Vonkorff, M. (1991). Somatization and psychiatric disorder in the NIMH Epidemiologic Catchment Area study. *American Journal of Psychiatry, 148,* 1494–1500.

Simons, A. D., Murphy, G. E., Levine, J. L., & Wetzel, R. D. (1986). Cognitive therapy and pharmacotherapy for depression: Sustained improvement over one year. *Archives of General Psychiatry, 43,* 43–48.

Simonton, O. C., Mathews-Simonton, S., & Creighton, J. (1978). *Getting well again: A step-by-step, self-help guide to overcoming cancer for patients and their families.* Los Angeles: Tarcher.

Skeels, H. M. (1966). Adult status of children with contrasting early life experiences. *Monographs of the Society for Research in Child Development, 31.*

Skinner, B. F. (1990). Can psychology be a science of mind? *American Psychologist, 45*, 1206–1210.

Sloane, R. B., Staples, F. R., Cristol, A. H., Yorkston, N. J., & Whipple, K. (1975). *Psychotherapy versus behavior therapy.* Cambridge, MA: Harvard University Press.

Smalley, S. L., & Asarnow, R. F. (1990). Brief report: Cognitive subclinical markers in autism. *Journal of Autism and Developmental Disorders, 20*, 271–278.

Smith, A., & Sugar, O. (1975). Development of above normal language and intelligence 21 years after left hemispherectomy. *Neurology, 25*, 813–818.

Smith, D. (1982). Trends in counseling and psychotherapy. *American Psychologist, 37*, 802–809.

Smith, D., & Kraft, W. A. (1983). DSM-III: Do psychologists really want an alternative? *American Psychologist, 38*, 777–785.

Smith, D. E., & Landry, M. J. (1988). Psychoactive substance use disorders: Drugs and alcohol. In H. H. Goldman (Ed.), *Review of general psychiatry* (pp. 266–285). Norwalk, CT: Appleton & Lange.

Smith, G. T., Goldman, M. S., Greenbaum, P. E., & Christiansen, B. A. (1995). Expectancy for social facilitation from drinking: The divergent paths of high-expectancy and low-expectancy adolescents. *Journal of Abnormal Psychology, 104*, 32–40.

Smith, K. (1988, May). Loving him was easy. *Reader's Digest,* pp. 115–119.

Smith, M. B. (1950). The phenomenological approach in personality theory: Some critical remarks. *Journal of Abnormal and Social Psychology, 45*, 516–522.

Smith, M. L., & Glass, G. V. (1977). Meta-analysis of psychotherapy outcome studies. *American Psychologist, 32*, 752–760.

Smith, M. L., Glass, G. V., & Miller, T. I. (1980). *The benefits of psychotherapy.* Baltimore: The Johns Hopkins University Press.

Smith, T. W., Turner, C. W., Ford, M. H., Hunt, S. C., Barlow, G. K., Stults, B. M., & Williams, R. R. (1987). Blood pressure reactivity in adult male twins. *Health Psychology, 6*, 209–220.

Smyer, M. A. (1984). Life transitions and aging: Implications for counseling older adults. *Counseling Psychologist, 12*, 17–28.

Snyder, R. D., Stovring, J., Cushing, A. H., Davis, L. E., & Hardy, T. L. (1981). Cerebral infarction in childhood bacterial meningitis. *Journal of Neurology, Neurosurgery, and Psychiatry, 44*, 581–585.

Snyder, S. (1986). *Drugs and the brain.* New York: Scientific American Library.

Sohlberg, S. C. (1985). Personality and neuropsychological performance of high-risk children. *Schizophrenia Bulletin, 11*, 48–65.

Solano, L., Costa, M., Salvati, S., Coda, R., Aiuti, F., Mezzaroma, I., & Bertini, M. (1993). Psychosocial factors and clinical evolution in HIV-1 infection: A longitudinal study. *Journal of Psychosomatic Research, 37*, 39–51.

Solkoff, N., Gray, P., & Keill, S. (1986). Which Vietnam veterans develop posttraumatic stress disorders? *Journal of Clinical Psychology, 42*, 687–698.

Solomon, R. L. (1977). An opponent-process theory of motivation: The affective dynamics of drug addiction. In J. D. Maser & M. E. Seligman (Eds.), *Psychopathology: Experimental models.* San Francisco: Freeman.

Solomon, R. L. (1980). The opponent-process theory of acquired motivation: The costs of pleasure and the benefits of pain. *American Psychologist, 35*, 691–712.

Sorenson, S. B., & Siegel, J. M. (1992). Gender, ethnicity, and sexual assault: Findings from a Los Angeles study. *Journal of Social Issues, 48*, 93–104.

Sorenson, S. B., & White, J. W. (1992). Adult sexual assault: Overview of research. *Journal of Social Issues, 48*, 1–8.

Southern, S., & Gayle, R. (1982). A cognitive behavioral model of hypoactive sexual desire. *Behavioral Counselor, 2*, 31–48.

Southworth, S., & Kirsch, I. (1988). The role of expectancy in exposure-generated fear reduction in agoraphobia. *Behaviour Research and Therapy, 26*, 113–120.

Spanos, N. P. (1978). Witchcraft in histories of psychiatry: A critical analysis and an alternative conceptualization. *Psychological Bulletin, 85*, 417–439.

Spanos, N. P., Menary, E., Gabora, N. J., DuBreuil, S. C., & Dewihirst, B. (1991). Secondary identity enactments during hypnotic past-life regression: A sociocognitive perspective. *Journal of Personality and Social Psychology, 61*, 308–320.

Spector, I. P., & Carey, M. P. (1990). Incidence and prevalence of sexual dysfunctions: A critical review of the empirical literature. *Archives of Sexual Behavior, 19*, 389–408.

Speer, D. C. (1971). Rate of caller re-use of a telephone crisis service. *Crisis Intervention, 3*, 83–86.

Speer, D. C. (1972). *An evaluation of a telephone crisis service.* Paper presented at the meeting of the Midwestern Psychological Association, Cleveland, Ohio.

Spence, S. H. (1991). Cognitive-behavioral therapy in the treatment of chronic occupational pain in the upper limbs: A 2 year follow-up. *British Journal of Psychiatry, 29*, 503–509.

Spencer, S. L., & Zeiss, A. M. (1987). Sex roles and sexual dysfunction in college students. *Journal of Sex Research, 23*, 338–347.

Spiegler, M. D. (1983). *Contemporary behavioral therapy.* Palo Alto, CA: Mayfield Publishing.

Spiess, W. F., Geer, J. H., & O'Donohue, W. T. (1984). Premature ejaculation: Investigation of factors in ejaculatory latency. *Journal of Abnormal Psychology, 93*, 242–245.

Spitzer, R. L. (1975). On pseudoscience in science, logic in remission, and psychiatric diagnosis: A critique of Rosenhan's "On being sane in insane places." *Journal of Abnormal Psychology, 84*, 442–452.

Spitzer, R. L. (1981). The diagnostic status of homosexuality in DSM-III: A reformation of the issues. *American Journal of Psychiatry, 138*, 210–215.

Spitzer, R. L., Gibbon, M., Skodol, A. E., Williams, J. B., & First, M. B. (1994). *DSM-IV casebook.* Washington, DC: American Psychiatric Press.

Spitzer, R. L., Skodol, A. E., Gibbon, M., & Williams, J. B. W. (1981). *DSM-III casebook.* Washington, DC: American Psychiatric Association.

Spitzer, R. L., & Williams, J. B. (1987). Introduction. In American Psychiatric Association, *Diagnostic and statistical manual of mental disorders* (3rd ed. [DSM-III]). Washington, DC: American Psychiatric Association.

Spivak, B., Trottern, S. F., Mark, M., Bleich, A., & Weizman, A. (1992). Acute transient stress-induced hallucinations in soldiers. *British Journal of Psychiatry, 160*, 412–414.

Srole, L., & Fischer, A. K. (1980). The midtown Manhattan longitudinal study vs. "the mental paradise lost" doctrine: A controversy joined. *Archives of General Psychiatry 37*(2), 209–221.

Srole, L., Langer, T. S., Michael, S. T., Opler, M. K., & Rennie, T. A. (1962). *Mental health in the metropolis: The midtown Manhattan study.* New York: McGraw-Hill.

Staats, A. W., & Heiby, E. M. (1985). Paradigmatic behaviorism's theory of depression: Unified, explanatory, and heuristic. In S. Reiss & R. R. Bootzin (Eds.), *Theoretical issues in behavioral therapy* (pp. 279–330). Orlando, FL: Academic Press.

Stack, S. (1987). Celebrities and suicide: A taxonomy and analysis, 1948–1983. *American Sociological Review, 52*, 401–412.

Stacy, A. W., Newcomb, M. D., & Bentler, P. M. (1991). Cognitive motivation and drug use: A 9-year longitudinal study. *Journal of Abnormal Psychology, 100*, 502–515.

Stacy, M., & Roeltgen, D. (1991). Infection of the central nervous system in the elderly. In S. Duckett (Ed.), *The pathology of the aging human nervous system* (pp. 374–392). Philadelphia: Lea & Febiger.

Stampfl, T., & Levis, D. (1967). Essentials of implosive therapy: A learning-theory-based psychodynamic behavioral therapy. *Journal of Abnormal Psychology, 72*, 496–503.

Stanley, M., & Mann, J. J. (1983). Increased serotonin-z binding sites in frontal cortex of suicide victims. *Lancet, 2*, 214–216.

Stanley, M. A., & Turner, S. M. (1995). Current status of pharmacological and behavioral treatment of obsessive-compulsive disorder. *Behavior Therapy, 26,* 163–186.

Starcevic, V., Fallon, S., & Uhlenhuth, E. H. (1994). The frequency and severity of generalized anxiety disorder symptoms. *Journal of Nervous and Mental Disease, 182,* 80–84.

Stark, E. (1984). The unspeakable family secret. *Psychology Today, 18,* 38–46.

Stark, M. J. (1992). Dropping out of substance abuse treatment: A clinically oriented review. *Clinical Psychology Review, 12,* 93–116.

Stavig, G. R., Igra, A., & Leonard, A. R. (1988). Hypertension and related health issues among Asian and Pacific Islanders in California. *Public Health Report, 103,* 28–37.

Steadman, H. J. (1979). *Beating a rap: Defendants found incompetent to stand trial.* Chicago: University of Chicago Press.

Steadman, H. J., Monahan, J., Robbins, P. C., Appelbaum, P., Grisso, T., Klassen, D., Mulvey, E. P., & Roth, L. (1993). From dangerousness to risk assessment: Implications for appropriate research strategies. In S. Hodgins (Ed.), *Mental disorder and crime.* New York: Sage Publications.

Steege, J. F., Stout, A. L., & Carson, C. C. (1986). Patient satisfaction in Scott and small-Carrion penile implant recipients: A study of 52 patients. *Archives of Sexual Behavior, 15,* 171–177.

Steele, C. M., & Josephs, R. A. (1988). Drinking your troubles away II: An attention-allocation model of alcohol's effect on psychological stress. *Journal of Abnormal Psychology, 97,* 196–205.

Steele, C. M., & Josephs, R. A. (1990). Alcohol myopia: Its prized and dangerous effects. *American Psychologist, 45,* 921–933.

Steffen, J. J., Nathan, P. E., & Taylor, H. A. (1974). Tension-reducing effects of alcohol: Further evidence and methodological considerations. *Journal of Abnormal Psychology, 83,* 542–547.

Steffenburg, S., & Gillberg, C. (1989). The etiology of autism. In C. Gillberg (Ed.), *Diagnosis and treatment of autism* (pp. 63–82). New York: Plenum Press.

Stein, M., Miller, A. H., & Trestman, R. L. (1991). Depression, the immune system, and health and illness. *Archives of General Psychiatry, 48,* 171–177.

Steketee, G., & White, K. (1990). *When once is not enough.* Oakland, CA.: New Harbinger Publications.

Steptoe, A. (1991). Invited review: The links between stress and illness. *Journal of Psychosomatic Research, 35,* 633–644.

Stern, J., Murphy, M., & Bass, C. (1993). Personality disorders in patients with somatisation disorder: A controlled study. *British Journal of Psychiatry, 163,* 785–789.

Stern, R. S., Lipsedge, M. A., & Marks, I. M. (1973). Thought-stopping of neutral and obsessive thoughts: A controlled trial. *Behavior Research and Therapy, 11,* 659–662.

Stevens, J. (1987). Brief psychoses: Do they contribute to the good prognosis and equal prevalence of schizophrenia in developing countries? *British Journal of Psychiatry, 151,* 393–396.

Stevens, J., Mark, B., Erwin, F., Pacheco, P., & Suematsu, K. (1969). Deep temporal stimulation in man. *Archives of Neurology, 21,* 157–169.

Stevens, J. H., Turner, C. W., Rhodewalt, F., & Talbot, S. (1984). The type A behavior pattern and carotid artery atherosclerosis. *Psychosomatic Medicine, 46,* 105–113.

Stewart, W. F., Lipton, R. B., Celentano, D. D., & Reed, M. L. (1992). Prevalence of migraine headache in the United States. *Journal of the American Medical Association, 267,* 64–69.

Stillion, M. J., McDowell, E. E., & May, J. H. (1989). *Suicide across the life span: Premature exits.* Washington, DC: Hemisphere Publishing.

Stock, W. E. (1991). Feminist explanations: Male power, hostility, and sexual coercion. In E. Grauerholz and M. A. Koralewski (Eds.), *Sexual coercion: A sourcebook on its nature, causes, and prevention* (pp. 61–73). Lexington, MA: Lexington Books.

Stoller, R. J. (1969). Parental influences on male transsexualism. In R. Green & J. Money (Eds.), *Transsexualism and sex reassignment.* Baltimore: Johns Hopkins University Press.

Stoller, R. J. (1991). The term *perversion.* In G. I. Fogel & W. A. Myers (Eds.), *Perversions and near-perversions in clinical practice* (pp. 36–58). New Haven, CT: Yale University Press.

Stone, A. A. (1975). *Mental health and law: A system in transition.* Rockville, MD: National Institute of Mental Health.

Stone, W. L., & Lemanek, K. L. (1990). Parental report of social behaviors in autistic preschoolers. *Journal of Autism and Developmental Disorders, 20,* 513–522.

Stravynski, A. (1986). Indirect behavioral treatment of erectile failure and premature ejaculation in a man without a partner. *Archives of Sexual Behavior, 15,* 355–360.

Streissguth, A. P. (1994). A long-term perspective of FAS. *Alcohol Health and Research World, 18,* 74–81.

Streissguth, A. P., Landesman-Dwyer, S., Martin, J. C., & Smith, D. W. (1980). Teratogenic effects of alcohol in humans and laboratory animals. *Science, 209,* 353–361.

Strickland, B. R. (1992). Women and depression. *Current Directions in Psychological Science, 1*(4), 132–135.

Stripling, S. (1986, August 3). Crossing over. *Seattle Post Intelligencer,* pp. K1–K2.

Stroebe, M., & Stroebe, W. (1991). Does "grief work" work? *Journal of Consulting and Clinical Psychology, 59*(3), 479–482.

Stromberg, C., Lindberg, D., & Schneider, J. (1995, January). A legal update on forensic psychology. *The Psychologists' Legal Update, No. 6.* Washington, DC: National Register of Health Service Providers in Psychology.

Strong, B., & DeVault, C. (1994). *Human sexuality.* Mountain View, CA: Mayfield Publishing.

Strupp, H. H., & Hadley, S. W. (1977). *Psychotherapy for better or worse: An analysis of the problem of negative effects.* New York: Jason Aronson.

Stuart, F. M., Hammond, D. C., & Pett, M. A. (1987). Inhibited sexual desire in women. *Archives of Sexual Behavior, 16,* 91–106.

Stuss, D. T., Gow, C. A., & Hetherington, C. R. (1992). "No longer Gage": Frontal lobe dysfunction and emotional changes. *Journal of Consulting and Clinical Psychology, 60*(3), 349–359.

Suddath, R. L., Christison, G. W., Torrey, E. F., & Weinberger, D. R. (1990). Cerebral anatomical abnormalities in monozygotic twins discordant for schizophrenia. *New England Journal of Medicine, 322,* 789–794.

Sue, D. (1972). The role of relaxation in systematic desensitization. *Behaviour Research and Therapy, 10,* 153–158.

Sue, D. (1978). The use of masturbation in the in vivo treatment of impotence. *Journal of Behavior Therapy and Experimental Psychiatry, 9,* 75–76.

Sue, D. (1979). Erotic fantasies of college students during coitus. *Journal of Sex Research, 15,* 299–305.

Sue, D. W. (1991). A model for cultural diversity training. *Journal for Counseling and Development, 70,* 99–105.

Sue, D. W. (1995). Toward a theory of multicultural counseling and psychotherapy. In J. A. Banks & C. A. Banks, *Handbook of research on multicultural education.* New York: Macmillan.

Sue, D. W., Arredondo, P., & McDavis, R. J. (1992). Multicultural competencies/standards: A pressing need. *Journal of Counseling and Development, 70*(4), 477–486.

Sue, D. W., Ivey, A. E., & Pedersen, P. B. (1996). *A theory of multicultural counseling and psychotherapy.* Pacific Grove, CA: Brooks Cole.

Sue, D. W., & Sue, D. (1990). *Counseling the culturally different* (2nd ed.). New York: Wiley.

Sue, S., & Abe, J. (1988). *Predictors of academic achievement among Asian American and white students.* New York: The College Board.

Sue, S., Allen, D., & Conaway, L. (1975). The responsiveness and quality of mental health care to Chicanos and Native Americans. *American Journal of Community Psychology, 45,* 11–118.

Sue, S., Fujino, D., Hu, L., Takeuchi, D. T., & Zane, N. (1991). Community mental health services for ethnic minority groups: A test of the cultural responsiveness hypothesis. *Journal of Consulting and Clinical Psychology, 59,* 533–540.

Sue, S., & Morishima, J. K. (1982). *The mental health of Asian Americans.* San Francisco: Jossey-Bass.

Sue, S., & Nakamura, C. Y. (1984). An integrative model of physiological and social/psychological factors in alcohol consumption among Chinese and Japanese Americans. *Journal of Drug Issues, 14,* 349–364.

Suicide belt. (1986, February 24). *Time, 116*(9), 56.

Sullivan, H. S. (1953). In H. S. Perry & M. L. Gawel (Eds.), *The interpersonal theory of psychiatry.* New York: Norton.

Sulser, F. (1979). Pharmacology: New cellular mechanisms of antidepressant drugs. In S. Fielding & R. C. Effland (Eds.), *New frontiers in psychotropic drug research.* Mount Kisco, NY: Futura.

Sundberg, N. D., Taplin, J. R., & Tyler, L. E. (1983). *Introduction to clinical psychology.* Englewood Cliffs, NJ: Prentice-Hall.

Sussman, S., Dent, C. W., McAdams, L. A., Stacy, A. W., Burton, D., & Flay, B. R. (1994). Group self-identification and adolescent cigarette smoking: A one-year prospective study. *Journal of Abnormal Psychology, 103,* 576–580.

Swann, W. B., Jr., Wenzlaff, R. M., Krull, D. S., & Pelham, B. W. (1992). Allure of negative feedback: Self-verification strivings among depressed persons. *Journal of Abnormal Psychology, 101*(2), 193–306.

Swartz, M., Landerman, R., George, L. K., Blazer, D. G., & Escobar, J. (1991). Somatization disorder. In L. N. Robins and D. A. Regier (Eds.), *Psychiatric disorders in America.* New York: The Free Press, 220–255.

Swedo, S. E., Rapoport, J. L., Leonard, H., Lenane, M., & Cheslow, D. (1989). Obsessive-compulsive disorder in children and adolescents. *Archives of General Psychiatry, 46,* 335–341.

Sweet, J. J. (1983). Confounding effects of depression on neuropsychological testing: Five illustrative cases. *Clinical Neuropsychology, 5,* 103–108.

Syvalahti, E. K. G. (1994). I. The theory of schizophrenia: Biological factors in schizophrenia. *British Journal of Psychiatry, 164,* 9–14.

Szasz, T. (1986). The case against suicide prevention. *American Psychologist, 41,* 806–812.

Szasz, T. S. (1961). *The myth of mental illness: Foundations of a theory of personal conduct.* New York: Hoeber-Harper.

Szasz, T. S. (1963). *Law, liberty, and psychiatry.* New York: Macmillan.

Szasz, T. S. (1987). Justifying coercion through theology and therapy. In J. K. Zeig (Ed.), *The evolution of psychotherapy.* New York: Brunner/Mazel.

Szymanski, S., Kane, J. M., & Lieberman, J. A. (1991). A selective review of biological markers in schizophrenia. *Schizophrenia Bulletin, 17,* 99–111.

Tabakoff, B., Whelan, J. P., & Hoffman, P. L. (1990). Two biological markers of alcoholism. In C. R. Cloninger & H. Begleiter (Eds.), *Genetics and biology of alcoholism* (pp. 195–204). Cold Spring Harbor, NY: Cold Spring Harbor Laboratory Press.

Tager-Flushberg, H., & Sullivan, K. (1994). Predicting and explaining behavior: A comparison of autistic, mentally retarded, and normal children. *Journal of Child Psychology and Psychiatry, 35,* 1059–1075.

Tannock, R., Schachar, R., & Logan, G. (1995). Methylphenidate and cognitive flexibility: Dissociated dose effects in hyperactive children. *Journal of Abnormal Child Psychology, 23,* 235–257.

Tarasoff vs. The Regents of the University of California, 17 Cal. 3d 435, 551 P.2d, 334, 131 Cal. Rptr. 14, 83 Ad. L. 3d 1166 (1976).

Tardiff, K. (1984). Characteristics of assaultive patients in private psychiatric hospitals. *American Journal of Psychiatry, 141,* 1232–1235.

Tardiff, K., & Koenigsberg, H. W. (1985). Assaultive behavior among psychiatric outpatients. *American Journal of Psychiatry, 142,* 960–963.

Tardiff, K., & Sweillam, A. (1982). Assaultive behavior among chronic inpatients. *American Journal of Psychiatry, 139,* 212–215.

Tarter, R. E., & Vanyukov, M. (1994). Alcoholism: A developmental disorder. *Journal of Consulting and Clinical Psychology, 62,* 1096–1107.

Task Force on Promotion and Dissemination of Psychological Procedures (1995). Training in and dissemination of empirically-validated psychological treatments: Report and recommendations. *Clinical Psychologist, 48,* 3–23.

Tassin, J. P., Trovero, F., Blanc, G., Herve, D., & Glowinski, J. (1994). Interactions between noradrenaline and dopamine neurotransmission in the rat prefrontal cortex and their consequences on dopaminergic subcortical function. In M. Briley & M. Marien (Eds.), *Noradrenergic mechanisms in Parkinson's disease* (pp. 107–125). Ann Arbor, MI: CRC Press.

Tavris, C. (1991). The mismeasure of woman: Paradoxes and perspectives in the study of gender. In J. D. Goodchilds (Ed.), *Psychological perspectives on human diversity in America* (pp. 91–136). Washington, DC: American Psychological Association.

Taylor, E. H. (1990). The assessment of social intelligence. *Psychotherapy, 27,* 445–457.

Taylor, S. E. (1983). Adjustments to threatening events: A theory of cognitive adaptation. *American Psychologist, 38,* 1161–1173.

Teicher, M. H., Glod, C., & Cole, J. O. (1990). Emergence of intense suicidal preoccupation during fluoxetine treatment. *American Journal of Psychiatry, 147,* 207–210.

Telch, M. J., Lucas, J. A., & Nelson, P. (1989). Nonclinical panic in college students: An investigation of prevalence and symptomatology. *Journal of Abnormal Psychology, 98,* 300–306.

Telch, M. J., Tearnan, B. H., & Taylor, C. B. (1983). Antidepressant medication in the treatment of agoraphobia: A critical review. *Behaviour Research and Therapy, 21,* 505–517.

Tellegen, A., Lykken, D. T., Bouchard, T. J., Jr., Wilcox, K. J., Segal, N. L., and Rich, S. (1988). Personality similarity in twins reared apart and together. *Journal of Personality and Social Psychology, 54,* 1031–1039.

Teri, L., & Wagner, A. (1992). Alzheimer's disease and depression. *Journal of Consulting and Clinical Psychology, 60*(3), 379–391.

Terman, L. M. (1916). *The measurement of intelligence.* Boston: Houghton Mifflin.

Terman, L. M., & Merrill, M. A. (1960). *Stanford-Binet intelligence scale.* Boston: Houghton Mifflin.

Terr, L. C. (1991). Childhood traumas: An outline and overview. *American Journal of Psychiatry, 148,* 10–20.

Thacker, A. J. (1994). Formal communication disorder: Sign language in deaf people with schizophrenia. *British Journal of Psychiatry, 165,* 818–823.

Thapar, A., Gottesman, I. I., Owen, M. J., O'Donovan, M. C., & McGuffin, P. (1994). The genetics of mental retardation. *British Journal of Psychiatry, 164,* 747–758.

Tharp, R. G. (1991). Cultural diversity and treatment of children. *Journal of Consulting and Clinical Psychology, 59,* 799–812.

Theorell, T., Blomkvist, V., Jonsson, H., Schulman, S., Berntorp, E., & Stigendal, L. (1995). Social support and the development of immune function in human immunodeficiency virus infection. *Psychosomatic Medicine, 57,* 32–36.

Thiers, N. (1988, August 1). Murder rampant in America: Professionals respond. *Guidepost, 51,* 1, 4, 5.

Thigpen, C. H., & Cleckley, H. M. (1984). On the incidence of multiple personality disorder: A brief communication. *International Journal of Clinical and Experimental Hypnosis, 32,* 63–66.

Thigpen, C. H., & Cleckley, H. (1957). *The three faces of Eve.* Kingsport, TN: Kingsport Press.

Thomas, A., Chess, S., & Birch, H. G. (1968). *Temperament and behavior disorders in children.* New York: New York University Press.

Thomas, A., & Sillen, S. (1972). *Racism and psychiatry.* New York: Brunner/Mazel.

Thomas, P. (1995). Thought disorder or communication disorder: Linguistic science provides a new approach. *British Journal of Psychiatry, 166,* 287–290.

Thompson, J. K. (1986). Larger than life. *Psychology Today, 20,* 39–44.

Thorndike, R. L., Hagen, E. P., & Sattler, J. M. (1986). *The Stanford-Binet intelligence scale: Guide for administration and scoring* (3rd ed.). Chicago: Riverside.

Thorpe, G., & Burns, L. (1983). *The agoraphobic syndrome.* Chichester, England: Wiley.

Tienari, P. (1963). Psychiatric illness in identical twins. *Acta Psychiatrica Scandinavica, 39* (Supplement 171).

Tienari, P., Wynne, L. C., Moring, J., Lahti, I., Naarala, M., Sorri, A., Wahlberg, K.-E., Saarento, O., Seitamaa, M., Kaleva, M., & Laksy, K. (1994). The Finnish adoptive family study of schizophrenia: Implications for family research. *British Journal of Psychiatry, 164,* 20–26.

Tierney, J. (1988, July 3). Research finds lower-level workers bear brunt of workplace stress. *Seattle Post Intelligencer,* pp. K1–K3.

Tiffany, S. T. (1990). A cognitive model of drug urges and drug-use behavior: Role of automatic and nonautomatic processes. *Psychological Review, 97,* 147–168.

Tjosvold, D., & Tjosvold, M. M. (1983). Social psychological analysis of residences for mentally retarded persons. *American Journal of Mental Deficiency, 88,* 28–40.

Tobin, J. J., & Friedman, J. (1983). Spirits, shamans, and nightmare death: Survivor stress in a Hmong refugee. *American Journal of Orthopsychiatry, 53,* 439–448.

Tolan, P. H., & Thomas, P. (1995). The implications of age of onset for delinquency risk II: Longitudinal data. *Journal of Abnormal Child Psychology, 23,* 157–180.

Tollefson, G. D., Rampey, A. H., Potvin, J. H., Jenike, M. A., Rush, A. J., Dominguez, R. A., Koran, L. M., Shear, M. K., Goodman, W., & Genduso, L. A. (1994). A multicenter investigation of fixed-dose fluoxetine in the treatment of obsessive-compulsive disorder. *Archives of General Psychiatry, 51,* 559–567.

Torgersen, S. (1983). Genetic factors in anxiety disorders. *Archives of General Psychiatry, 40,* 1085–1089.

Toro, P. A. & Wall, D. D. (1991). Research on homeless persons: Diagnostic comparisons and practice implications. *Professional psychology: Research and practice, 22,* 479–488.

Treiber, F. A., McCaffrey, F., Musante, L., Rhodes, T., Davis, H., Strong, W. B., & Levy, M. (1993). Ethnicity, family history of hypertension and patterns of hemodynamic reactivity in boys. *Psychosomatic Medicine, 55,* 70–77.

Triandis, H. C. (1983). Essentials of studying cultures. In D. Landis & R. W. Brislin (Eds.), *Handbook of intercultural training.* New York: Pergamon Press.

Tross, S., & Hirsch, D. A. (1988). Psychological distress and neuropsychological complications of HIV infection and AIDS. *American Psychologist, 43*(11), 929–934.

Trull, T. J. (1995). Borderline personality disorder features in nonclinical young adults: 1. Identification and validation. *Psychological Assessment, 7,* 33–41.

Tsoi, W. F. (1993). Male and female transsexuals: A comparison. *Singapore Medical Journal, 33*(2), 182–185.

Tuckman, J., Kleiner, R., & Lavell, M. (1959). Emotional content of suicide notes. *American Journal of Psychiatry, 16,* 59–63.

Turkheimer, E., & Parry, C. D. H. (1992). Why the gap? *American Psychologist, 47,* 646–655.

Turner, J. A., & Clancy, S. (1988). Comparison of operant behavioral and cognitive-behavioral group treatment for chronic low back pain. *Journal of Consulting and Clinical Psychology, 56,* 261–266.

Turner, S. M., Beidel, D. C., & Jacob, R. G. (1994). Social phobia: A comparison of behavior therapy and atenolol. *Journal of Consulting and Clinical Psychology, 62,* 350–358.

Turner, S. M., Beidel, D. C., & Townsley, R. M. (1992). Social phobia: A comparison of specific and generalized subtypes and avoidant personality disorder. *Journal of Abnormal Psychology, 101,* 326–331.

Turner, S. M., Jacob, R. G., & Morrison, R. (1984). Somatoform and factitious disorders. In H. E. Adams and P. B. Sutker (Eds.), *Comprehensive handbook of psychiatry* (pp. 307–348). New York: Plenum Press.

Tyrer, P., Lee, I., & Alexander, J. (1980). Awareness of cardiac function in anxious, phobic, and hypochondriacal patients. *Psychological Medicine, 10,* 171–174.

U.S. Bureau of the Census. (1988). *Statistical abstract of the United States* (108th ed.). Washington, DC: U.S. Government Printing Office.

U.S. Department of Commerce (1991). *1990 Census Profile.* Washington, DC: U.S. Bureau of the Census.

U.S. Department of Health and Human Services. (1991). *Depression: What you need to know.* Rockville, MD: NIMH 60-FL-1485-0.

U.S. Department of Health and Human Services (1995a). Down syndrome prevalence at birth–United States, 1983–1990. *Morbidity and Mortality Weekly Report, 43,* 617–623.

U.S. Department of Health and Human Services (1995b). Update: Trends in fetal alcohol syndrome. *Morbidity and Mortality Weekly Report, 44,* 249–251.

U.S. Department of Health, Education and Welfare. (1971). *The alcoholism report: The authoritative newsletter for professionals.* Washington, DC: U.S. Government Printing Office.

U.S. Senate Committee on the Judiciary (1991). Violence against women: The increase of rape in America 1990. *Response to the Victimization of Women and Children, 14* (79, No. 2), 20–23.

Uba, L. (1994). *Asian Americans: Personality patterns, identity, and mental health.* New York: Guilford.

Ubell, E. (1989, December 3). They're closing in on mental illness. *Parade Magazine,* pp. 6–7.

Uhlenhuth, E. H., Balter, M. B., Mellinger, G. D., Cisin, I. H., & Clinthorne, J. (1983). Symptom checklist syndromes in the general population. *Archives of General Psychiatry, 40,* 1167–1173.

Ullmann, L. P., & Krasner, L. (1965). Introduction. In L. P. Ullmann & L. Krasner (Eds.), *Case studies in behavior modification.* New York: Holt, Rinehart & Winston.

Ullmann, L. P., & Krasner, L. (1975). *A psychological approach to abnormal behavior* (2nd ed.). Englewood Cliffs, NJ: Prentice-Hall.

United States Public Health Service. (1986). *Surgeon general's report on acquired immune deficiency syndrome.* Washington, DC: U.S. Department of Health and Human Services.

Update (1988): Sudden unexplained death syndrome among southeast Asian refugees–United States. *Morbidity and Mortality Weekly Report, 37,* 569–570.

Vaillant, G. E. (1975). Sociopathy as a human process: A viewpoint. *Archives of General Psychiatry, 32,* 178–183.

Vaillant, G. E. (1994). Ego mechanisms of defense and personality psychopathology. *Journal of Abnormal Psychology, 103,* 44–50.

Vaillant, G. E., & Milofsky, E. S. (1982). The etiology of alcoholism. *American Psychologist, 37,* 494–503.

Vaillant, G. E., & Perry, J. C. (1985). Personality disorders. In H. I. Kaplan & B. J. Sadock (Eds.), *Comprehensive textbook of psychiatry* (4th ed., pp. 958–986). Baltimore: Williams & Wilkins.

Valenstein, E. S. (1986). *Great and desperate cures: The rise and decline of psychosurgery and other radical treatments for mental illness.* New York: Basic Books.

Van Der Molen, G. M., Van Den Hout, M. A., Vroemen, J., Lousberg, H., & Griez, E. (1986). Cognitive determinants of lactate-induced anxiety. *Behaviour Research and Therapy, 24,* 677–680.

Van Evra, J. P. (1983). *Psychological disorders of children and adolescents.* Boston: Little, Brown.

Van Horn, J. D., & McManus, I. C. (1992). Ventricular enlargement in schizophrenia. *British Journal of Psychiatry, 160,* 687–697.

Van Oppen, P., De Haan, E., Van Balkom, A. J. L. M., Spinhoven, P., Hoogduin, K., & Van Dyck, R. (1995). Cognitive therapy and exposure in vivo in the treatment of obsessive disorder. *Behaviour Research and Therapy, 33,* 378–390.

Van Pragg, H. M. (1983). CSF 5-H1AA and suicide in non-depressed schizophrenics, *Lancet, 2,* 977–978.

Vanderlinden, J., Norre, J., & Vandereycken, W. (1992). *A practical guide to the treatment of bulimia nervosa.* New York: Brunner/Mazel.

Vaughn, C., & Leff, J. (1981). Patterns of emotional response in relatives of schizophrenic patients. *Schizophrenia Bulletin, 7,* 43–45.

Vazquez, M. I., & Buceta, J. M. (1993). Effectiveness of self-management programmes and relaxation training in the treatment of bronchial asthma: Relationships with trait anxiety and emotional attack triggers. *Journal of Psychosomatic Medicine, 37,* 71–81.

Vega, W., & Rumbaut, R.G. (1991). Ethnic minorities and mental health. *Annual Review of Sociology, 17,* 351–383.

Venter, A., Lord, C., & Schopler, E. (1992). A follow-up study of high-functioning autistic children. *Journal of Child Psychology and Psychiatry, 33,* 489–507.

Visintainer, M. A., Volpicelli, J. R., & Seligman, M. E. P. (1982). Tumor rejection in rats after inescapable or escapable shock. *Science, 216,* 437–439.

Vita, A., Bressi, S., Perani, D., Invernizzi, G., Giobbio, G. M., Dieci, M., Garbarini, M., Del Sole, A., & Fazio, F. (1995). High-resolution SPECT study of regional cerebral blood flow in drug-free and drug-naive schizophrenic patients. *American Journal of Psychiatry, 152,* 876–882.

Vita, A., Dieci, M., Giobbio, G. M., Azzone, P., Garbini, M., Sacchetti, E., Cesana, B. M., & Cazzullo, C. L. (1991). CT scan abnormalities and outcome in chronic schizophrenia. *American Journal of Psychiatry, 148,* 1577–1579.

Vogel, G., Vogel, F., McAbee, R., & Thurmond, A. (1980). Improvement of depression by REM sleep deprivation. *Archives of General Psychiatry, 37,* 247–253.

Vogler, R. E., & Bartz, W. R. (1983). *The better way to drink.* New York: Simon & Schuster.

Volden, J., & Lord, C. (1991). Neologisms and idiosyncratic language in autistic speakers. *Journal of Autism and Developmental Disorders, 21,* 109–130.

Volkmar, F. R., Cicchetti, D. V., Dykens, E., Sparrow, S. S., Leckman, J. F., & Cohen, D. J. (1988). An evaluation of the Autism Behavior checklist. *Journal of Autism and Developmental Disorders, 18,* 81–97.

Wachtel, P. L. (1977). *Psychoanalysis and behavior therapy.* New York: Basic Books.

Wachtel, P. L. (1982). Vicious circles: The self and the rhetoric of emerging and unfolding. *Contemporary Psychoanalysis, 18,* 280–282.

Wakefield, J. (1988). Female primary orgasmic dysfunctions: Masters and Johnson versus DSM-III-R on diagnosis and incidence. *Journal of Sex Research, 24,* 363–377.

Wakefield, J. C. (1992). The concept of mental disorder. *American Psychologist, 47,* 373–388.

Walder, C. P., McCracken, J. S., Herbert, M., James, P. T., & Brewitt, N. (1987). Psychological intervention in civilian flying phobia. *British Journal of Psychiatry, 151,* 494–498.

Waldstein, S. R., Manuk, S. B., Ryan, C. M., & Muldoon, M. F. (1991). Neurophysiological correlates of hypertension: Review and methodological considerations. *Psychological Bulletin, 110,* 451–468.

Walen, S., Hauserman, N. M., & Lavin, P. J. (1977). *Clinical guide to behavior therapy.* Baltimore: Williams & Wilkins.

Walker, L. E. (1991). Post-traumatic stress disorder in women: Diagnosis and treatment of battered woman syndrome. *Psychotherapy, 28,* 21–29.

Walkup, J. (1995). A clinically based rule of thumb for classifying delusions. *Schizophrenia Bulletin, 21,* 323–331.

Ward, C. H., Beck, A. T., Mendelson, M., Mock, J. E., & Erbaught, J. K. (1962). The psychiatric nomenclature: Reasons for diagnostic disagreement. *Archives of General Psychiatry, 7,* 198–205.

Warheit, G. J., Longino, C. F., & Bradsher, J. E. (1991). Sociocultural aspects. In J. Sadavoy, L. W. Lazarus, & L. F. Jarvik (Eds.), *Comprehensive review of geriatric psychiatry* (pp. 99–116). Washington, DC: American Psychiatric Press.

Warner, R. (1986). Hard times and schizophrenia. *Psychology Today, 20,* 50–51.

Warren, C. A. B. (1982). *The court as a last resort: Mental illness and the law.* Chicago: University of Chicago Press.

Wartik, N. (1994, February). Fatal attention. *Redbook,* pp. 62–69.

Warwick, H. M. C., & Marks, I. M. (1988). Behavioural treatment for illness phobia and hypochondriasis. *British Journal of Psychiatry, 152,* 239–241.

Wasserman, E., & Gromisch, D. (1981). *Survey of clinical pediatrics.* New York: McGraw-Hill.

Waterman, J., & Lusk, R. (1986). Scope of the problem. In K. MacFarlane (Ed.), *Sexual abuse of young children: Evaluation and treatment* (pp. 3–14). New York: Guilford Press.

Watkins, B., & Bentovim, A. (1992). The sexual abuse of male children and adolescents: A review of current research. *Journal of Child Psychology and Psychiatry, 33,* 197–248.

Watkins, E. C., & Peterson, P. (1986). Psychiatric epidemiology: Its relevance for counselors. *Journal of Counseling and Development, 65,* 57–59.

Watson, C. G., & Buranen, C. (1979). The frequencies of conversion reaction symptoms. *Journal of Abnormal Psychology, 88,* 209–211.

Watson, D., Weber, K., Assenheimer, J. S., Clark, L. A., Strauss, M. E., & McCormick, R. A. (1995). Testing a tripartite model: I. Evaluating the convergent and discriminant validity of anxiety and depression symptom scales. *Journal of Abnormal Psychology, 104,* 3–14.

Watson, J. B., & Rayner, R. (1920). Conditioned emotional responses. *Journal of Experimental Psychology, 3,* 1–14.

Weakland, J. H. (1960). The "double-bind" hypothesis of schizophrenia and three-party interaction. In D. D. Jackson (Ed.), *The etiology of schizophrenia.* New York: Basic Books.

Webster, J. S., & Scott, R. P. (1983). The effects of self-instruction training in attention deficit following head injury. *Clinical Neuropsychology, 5,* 69–74.

Webster-Stratton, C. (1991). Annotation: Strategies for helping families with conduct disordered children. *Journal of Child Psychology and Psychiatry, 32,* 1047–1062.

Wechsler, D. (1981). *Wechsler Adult Intelligence Scale.* New York: Harcourt, Brace, Jovanovich.

Weddington, W. W. (1979). Single case study: Conversion reaction in an 82-year-old man. *Journal of Nervous and Mental Diseases, 167,* 368–369.

Weiden, P. J., Mann, J. J., Haas, G., Mattson, M., & Frances, A. (1987). Clinical nonrecognition of neuroleptic-induced movement disorders: A cautionary study. *American Journal of Psychiatry, 144,* 1148–1553.

Weinberg, T. S. (1987). Sadomasochism in the United States: A review of recent sociological literature. *Journal of Sex Research, 23,* 50–69.

Weiner, B. (1975). On being sane in insane places: A process (attributional) analysis and critique. *Journal of Abnormal Psychology, 84,* 433–441.

Weiner, H. (1991). From simplicity to complexity (1950–1990): The case of peptic ulceration–II. Animal studies. *Psychosomatic Medicine, 53,* 491–516.

Weiner, I. B. (1995). How to anticipate ethical and legal challenges in personality assessments. In J. N. Butcher (Ed.), *Clinical personality assessment: Practical approaches* (pp. 95–106). New York: Oxford University Press.

Weiner, I. W. (1969). The effectiveness of suicide prevention programs. *Mental Hygiene, 53,* 357–373.

Weintraub, W. (1981). Compulsive and paranoid personalities. In J. R. Lion (Ed.), *Personality disorders: Diagnosis and management.* Baltimore: Williams & Wilkins.

Weishaar, M. E., & Beck, A. T. (1992). Clinical and cognitive predictors of suicide. In R. W. Maris, A. L. Berman, J. T. Maltsberger, & R. I. Yufit (Eds.), *Assessment and prediction of suicide.* New York: Guilford.

Weiss, B., Weisz, J. R., Politano, M., Carey, M., Nelson, W. M., & Finch, A. J. (1992). Relations among self-reported depressive symptoms in clinic referred children versus adolescents. *Journal of Abnormal Psychology, 101,* 391–397.

Weiss, D. S. (1988). Personality assessment. In H. H. Goldman (Ed.), *Review of general psychiatry* (pp. 221–232). Norwalk, CT: Appleton & Lange.

Weiss, J. M., Glazer, H. I., & Pohorecky, L. A. (1975). Coping behavior and neurochemical changes: Alternative explanation for the original "learned helplessness" experiments. In G. Serban & A. Ling (Eds.), *Relevance of the animal model to the human.* New York: Plenum.

Weissberg, M. (1993). Multiple personality disorder and iatrogenesis: The cautionary tale of Anna O. *International Journal of Clinical and Experimental Hypnosis, XLI,* 15–34.

Weissman, M. M. (1993). The epidemiology of personality disorders: A 1990 update. *Journal of Personality Disorders, Supplement 1,* 44–62.

Weissman, M. M., Bruce, M. L., Leaf, P. J., Florio, L. P., & Holzer, C. (1991). Affective disorders. In L. N. Robins & D. A. Regier (Eds.), *Psychiatric disorders in America: The Epidemiologic Catchment Area study* (pp. 53–80). New York: Free Press.

Weissman, M. M., & Klerman, G. L. (1977). Sex differences and the epidemiology of depression. *Archives of General Psychiatry, 34,* 98–111.

Weisz, J. R., Weiss, B., & Donenberg, G. R. (1992). The lab versus the clinic: Effects of child and adolescent psychotherapy. *American Psychologist, 12,* 1578–1585.

Welgan, P. R. (1974). Learned control of gastric acid secretions in ulcer patients. *Psychosomatic Medicine, 36,* 411–419.

Wells, C. E. (1978). Role of stroke in dementia. *Stroke, 9,* 1–3.

Wender, P. H., & Klein, D. F. (1981, February). The promise of biological psychiatry. *Psychology Today, 15,* 25–41.

Wender, P. H., Rosenthal, D., Rainer, J. D., Greenbill, L., & Sarlan, M. B. (1977). Schizophrenics' adopting parents. *Archives of General Psychiatry, 34,* 777–784.

Werner, A. (1975). Sexual dysfunction in college men and women. *American Journal of Psychiatry, 132,* 164–168.

Westen, D. (1991). Cognitive-behavioral interventions in the psychoanalytic psychotherapy of borderline personality disorders. *Clinical Psychology Review, 11,* 211–230.

Westermeyer, J. (1987). Public health and chronic mental illness. *American Journal of Public Health, 77,* 667–66°.

Wetzel, R. D., Guze, S. B., Cloninger, C. R., Martin, R. L., & Clayton, P. J. (1994). Briquet's syndrome (hysteria) is both a somatoform and a "psychoform" illness: A Minnesota Multiphasic Personality Inventory study. *Psychosomatic Medicine, 56,* 564–569.

Whalen, C. K., & Henker, B. (1991). Therapies for hyperactive children: Comparisons, combinations, and compromises. *Journal of Consulting and Clinical Psychology, 59,* 126–137.

White, G. M. (1982). The role of cultural explanations in "somatization" and "psychologization." *Social Science Medicine, 16,* 1519–1530.

White, J. L., & Parham, T. A. (1990). *The psychology of Blacks.* Englewood Cliffs, NJ: Prentice-Hall.

Whitehead, W. E. (1993). Gut feelings: Stress and the GI tract. In D. Goleman and J. Gurin (Eds.), *Mind/body medicine* (pp. 161–175). New York: Consumer Reports Books.

Whitehill, M., DeMeyer-Gapin, S., & Scott, T. J. (1976). Stimulus seeking in antisocial preadolescent children. *Journal of Abnormal Psychology, 85,* 101–104.

Whittal, M. L., Suchday, S., & Goetsch, V. L. (1994). The panic attack questionnaire: Factor analysis of symptom profiles and characteristics of undergraduates who panic. *Journal of Anxiety Disorders, 8,* 237–245.

Whittenmore, H. (1992, September 20). He broke the silence. *Parade Magazine,* pp. 8–9.

Whybrow, P. C., Akiskal, H. S., & McKinney, W. T., Jr. (1984). *Mood disorders: Toward a new psychobiology.* New York: Plenum.

Wickramasekera, I. (1976). Aversive behavior rehearsal for sexual exhibitionism. *Behavioral Therapy, 1,* 167–176.

Widiger, T. A., & Frances, A. J. (1994). Toward a dimensional model for the personality disorders. In P. T. Costa & T. A. Widiger (Eds.), *Personality disorders and the five-factor model of personality* (pp. 19–40). Washington, DC: American Psychological Association.

Widiger, T. A., Frances, A. J., Pincus, H. A., Davis, W. W., & First, M. B. (1991). Toward an empirical classification for the DSM-IV. *Journal of Abnormal Psychology, 100,* 280–288.

Widiger, T. A., & Shea, T. (1991). Differentiation of Axis I and Axis II disorders. *Journal of Abnormal Psychology, 100,* 399–406.

Widiger, T. A., & Spitzer, R. L. (1991). Sex bias in the diagnosis of personality disorders: Conceptual and methodological issues. *Clinical Psychology Review, 11,* 1–22.

Widiger, T. A., Trull, T. J., Clarkin, J. F., Sanderson, C., & Costa, P. T. (1994). A description of the DSM-III-R and DSM-IV personality disorders with the five-factor model of personality. In P. T. Costa & T. A. Widiger (Eds.), *Personality disorders and the five-factor model of personality* (pp. 41–58). Washington, DC: American Psychological Association.

Widom, C. S. (1976). Interpersonal and personal construct systems in psychopaths. *Journal of Consulting and Clinical Psychology, 44,* 614–623.

Widom, C. S. (1977). A methodology for studying noninstitutionalized psychopaths. *Journal of Consulting and Clinical Psychology, 45,* 674–683.

Wiens, A. N. (1983). The assessment interview. In I. B. Weiner (Ed.), *Clinical methods in psychology.* New York: John Wiley.

Wiesel, F.-A. (1994). II. The treatment of schizophrenia. *British Journal of Psychiatry, 164,* 65–70.

Wijsman, M. (1990). Linkage analysis of alcoholism: Problems and solutions. In C. R. Cloninger & H. Begleiter (Eds.), *Genetics and biology of alcoholism* (pp. 317–326). Cold Spring Harbor, NY: Cold Spring Harbor Laboratory Press.

Wilding, T. (1984). Is stress making you sick? *American Health, 6,* 2–5.

Williams, L. M., & Finkelhor, D. (1990). The characteristics of incestuous fathers: A review of recent studies. In W. L. Marshall, D. R. Laws, & H. E. Barbaree (Eds.), *Handbook of sexual assault. Issues, theories, and treatment of the offender* (pp. 231–256). New York: Plenum Press.

Williams, R. (1974). The problem of match and mismatch. In L. Miller (Ed.), *The testing of black children.* Englewood Cliffs, NJ: Prentice-Hall.

Williams, R. B., Benson, H., & Follick, M. J. (1985). To the editor. *New England Journal of Medicine, 312,* 1356–1357.

Williams, R. B., Jr., Barefoot, J. C., Haney, T. L., Harrell, F. E., Jr.,

Blumenthal, J. A., Pryor, D. B., & Peterson, B. (1988). Type A behavior and angiographically documented coronary atherosclerosis in a sample of 2,289 patients. *Psychosomatic Medicine, 50,* 139–152.

Williamson, D. A., Barker, S. E., Bertman, L. J., & Fleaves, D. H. (1995). Body image, body dysmorphia, and dietary restraint: Factor structure in nonclinical subjects. *Behaviour Research and Therapy, 33,* 85–93.

Williamson, D. A., Cubic, B. A., & Gleaves, D. H. (1993). Equivalence of body image disturbances in anorexia and bulimia nervosa. *Journal of Abnormal Psychology, 102,* 177–180.

Wilson, G. T. (1984). Clinical issues and strategies in the clinical practice of behavior therapy. In C. M. Franks, G. T. Wilson, K. D. Brownell, & P. Kendall (Eds.), *Annual review of behavior therapy: Theory and practice* (p. 8). New York: Guilford Press.

Wilson, G. T., & O'Leary, K. D. (1980). *Principles of behavior therapy.* Englewood Cliffs, NJ: Prentice-Hall.

Wilson, M. L., Wilson, D. B., & White, J. W. (1995). The effect of sugar on behavior or cognition in children. *Journal of the American Medical Association, 274,* 1617–1621.

Wilson, M. S., & Meyer, E. (1962). Diagnostic consistency in a psychiatric liaison service. *American Journal of Psychiatry, 19,* 207–209.

Wincze, J. P., Bansal, S., & Malamud, M. (1986). Effects of medrox progesterone acetate on subjective arousal, arousal to erotic stimulation, and nocturnal penile tumescence in male sex offenders. *Archives of Sexual Behavior, 15,* 293–305.

Wincze, J. P., Hoon, E. F., & Hoon, P. W. (1978). Multiple measure analysis of women experiencing low sexual arousal. *Behaviour Research and Therapy, 16,* 43–49.

Wing, J. K. (1980). Social psychiatry in the United Kingdom: The approach to schizophrenia. *Schizophrenia Bulletin, 6,* 557–565.

Winnett, R. L., Bornstein, P. H., Cogsuell, K. A., & Paris, A. E. (1987). Cognitive-behavioral therapy for childhood depression: A levels-of-treatment approach. *Journal of Child and Adolescent Psychotherapy, 4,* 283–286.

Winokur, G., Clayton, P. J., & Reich, T. (1969). *Manic depressive illness.* St. Louis: Mosby.

Winton, E. C., Clark, D. M., & Edelmann, R. J. (1995). Social anxiety, fear of negative evaluation, and the detection of negative emotion in others. *Behaviour Research and Therapy, 33,* 193–196.

Wise, R. A. (1988). The neurobiology of craving: Implications for understanding and treatment of addiction. *Journal of Abnormal Psychology, 97,* 118–132.

Wittchen, H.-U., Zhao, S., Kessler, R. C., & Eaton, W. W. (1994). DSM-III-R generalized anxiety disorder in the National Comorbidity Survey. *Archives of General Psychiatry, 51,* 355–364.

Wittkower, E. C., & Rin, H. (1965). Cultural psychiatric research. In W. Caudell & T. Lin (Eds.), *Mental health research in Asia and the Pacific.* Honolulu: East-West Center Press.

Wolfensberger, W. (1988). Common assets of mentally retarded people that are commonly not acknowledged. *Mental Retardation, 26,* 63–70.

Wolraich, M. L., Wilson, D. B. & White, J. W. (1995). The effect of sugar on behavior or cognition in children. *Journal of the American Medical Association, 274,* 1617–1621.

Wolkin, A., Sanfilipo, M., Wolf, A. P., Angrist, B., Brodie, J. D., & Rotrosen, J. (1992). Negative symptoms and hypofrontality in chronic schizophrenia. *Archives of General Psychiatry, 49,* 959–965.

Wolpe, J. (1958). *Psychotherapy by reciprocal inhibition.* Stanford, CA: Stanford University Press.

Wolpe, J. (1973). *The practice of behavior therapy.* New York: Pergamon.

Wolpe, J. (1982). *The practice of behavior therapy* (3rd ed.). Elmsford, NY: Pergamon Press.

Wolpe, J., & Abrams, J. (1991). Post-traumatic stress disorder overcome by eye-movement desensitization. *Journal of Behaviour Therapy and Experimental Psychiatry, 22,* 39–43.

Wood, C. (1986). The hostile heart. *Psychology Today, 20,* 10–12.

Woody, G. E., & Cacciola, J. (1994). Review of remission criteria. In T. A. Widiger, A. J. Frances, H. A. Pincus, M. B. First, R. Ross, & W. Davis (Eds.), *DSM-IV Sourcebook: Volume 1* (pp. 67–80). Washington, DC: American Psychiatric Association.

World Health Organization. (1973a). *Manual of the international statistical classification of diseases, injuries and causes of death* (Vol. 1). Geneva: World Health Organization.

World Health Organization. (1973b). *Report on the international pilot study of schizophrenia* (Vol. 1). Geneva: World Health Organization.

World Health Organization. (1981). *Current state of diagnosis and classification in the mental health field.* Geneva: World Health Organization. Used by permission of the World Health Organization, Geneva.

World Health Organization. (1987). The Dexamethasone Suppression Test in depression. *British Journal of Psychiatry, 150,* 459–462.

Wyler, A. R., Masuda, M., & Holmes, T. H. (1971). Magnitude of the life events and seriousness of illness. *Journal of Psychosomatic Medicine, 33,* 115–122.

Yager, J., Landsverk, J., & Edelstein, C. K. (1987). A 20-month follow-up of 628 women with eating disorders, I: Course and severity. *American Journal of Psychiatry, 144,* 1172–1177.

Yalom, I. D. (1970). *The theory and practice of group psychotherapy.* New York: Basic Books.

Yapko, M. D. (1994). Suggestibility and repressed memories of abuse: A survey of psychotherapists' beliefs. *American Journal of Clinical Hypnosis, 36,* 163–171.

Yassa, R., & Jeste, D. V. (1992). Gender differences in tardive dyskinesia: A critical review of the literature. *Schizophrenia Bulletin, 18,* 701–715.

Yassa, R., & Suranyi-Cadotte, B. (1993). Clinical characteristics of late-onset schizophrenia and delusional disorder. *Schizophrenia Bulletin, 19,* 701–707.

Yates, A. (1983). Behavior therapy and psychodynamic psychotherapy: Basic conflict or reconciliation and integration? *British Journal of Clinical Psychology, 22,* 107–125.

York, D., Borkovec, T. D., Lasey, M., & Stern, R. (1987). Effects of worry and somatic anxiety induction on thoughts, emotion, and physiological activity. *Behaviour Research and Therapy, 25,* 523–526.

Young, E. C., & Kramer, B. M. (1991). Characteristics of age-related language decline in adults with Down syndrome. *Mental Retardation, 29,* 75–79.

Young, M. (1980). Attitudes and behavior of college students relative to oral-genital sexuality. *Archives of Sexual Behavior, 9,* 61–67.

Youngren, M. A., & Lewinsohn, P. M. (1980). The functional relation between depression and problematic interpersonal behavior. *Journal of Abnormal Psychology, 89,* 333–341.

Youngstrom, N. (1991). Spotting serial killer difficult, experts note. *APA Monitor, 22*(10), 32.

Yu-Fen, H., & Neng, T. (1981). Transcultural investigation of recent symptomatology of schizophrenia in China. *American Journal of Psychiatry, 138,* 1484–1486.

Yumoto, S., Kakimi, S., Ogawa, Y., Nagai, H., Imamura, M., & Kobayashi, K. (1995). Aluminum neurotoxicity and Alzheimer's disease. In I. Hanin, M. Yoshida, & A. Fisher (Eds.), *Alzheimer's and Parkinson's diseases: Recent developments* (pp. 223–229). New York: Plenum Press.

Yurchenco, H. (1970). *A mighty hard road: The Woody Guthrie story.* New York: McGraw-Hill.

Zamichow, N. (1993, February 15). The dark corner of psychology. *Los Angeles Times,* p. A1.

Zax, M., & Spector, G. A. (1974). *An introduction to community psychology.* New York: Wiley.

Zelt, D. (1981). First person account: The messiah quest. *Schizophrenia Bulletin, 7,* 527–531.

Zhang, M., Wang, M., Li, J., & Phillips, M. R. (1994). Randomized-control trial of family intervention for 78 first-episode male schizophrenic patients. An eighteen-month study in Suzhou, Jiangsu. *British Journal of Psychiatry, 165,* 96–102.

Zheng, Y.-P., & Lin, K.-M. (1994). A nationwide study of stressful life events in mainland China. *Psychosomatic Medicine, 56,* 296–305.

Zigler, E. (1967). Familial mental retardation: A continuing dilemma. *Science, 155,* 292–298.

Zigler, E., & Bergman, W. (1983). Discerning the future of early childhood intervention. *American Psychologist, 38,* 893–905.

Zigler, E., Taussig, C., & Black, K. (1992). Early childhood intervention: A promising preventative for juvenile delinquency. *American Psychologist, 47,* 997–1006.

Zilbergeld, B. (1983). *The shrinking of America.* Boston: Little, Brown.

Zilboorg, G., & Henry, G. W. (1941). *A history of medical psychology.* New York: Norton.

Zipursky, R. B., Lim, K. O., & Pfefferbaum, A. (1991). Brain size in schizophrenia. *Archives of General Psychiatry, 48,* 179–180.

Zito, J. M., Craig, T. J., Wanderling, J., & Siegel, C. (1987). Pharmaco-epidemiology in 136 hospitalized schizophrenic patients. *American Journal of Psychiatry, 144,* 778–782.

Zubin, J., Steinhauer, S. R., & Condray, R. (1992). Vulnerability to relapse in schizophrenia. *British Journal of Psychiatry, 161,* 13–18.

Zucker, K. J. (1990). Gender identity disorders in children: Clinical descriptions and natural history. In R. Blanchard & B. W. Steiner (Eds.), *Clinical management of gender identity disorders in children and adults* (pp. 1–24). Washington, DC: American Psychiatric Press.

Zuger, B. (1984). Early effeminate behavior in boys: Outcome and significance for homosexuality. *Journal of Nervous and Mental Disease, 172,* 90–97.

Zullow, H. M., Oettingen, G., Peterson, C., & Seligman, M. E. (1988). Pessimistic explanatory style in the historical record: Caving LBJ, presidential candidates, and East versus West Berlin. *American Psychologist, 43,* 673–682.

Zverina, J., Lachman, M., Pondelickova, J., & Vanek, J. (1987). The occurrence of atypical sexual experience among various female patient groups. *Archives of Sexual Behavior, 16,* 321–326.

CREDITS

Chapter 10: p. 286: *(left)* David Austen/Stock Boston; *(right)* McGlynn/The Image Works. **p. 287:** Yvonne Hemsy/Gamm Liaison. **p. 290:** Dennis Brack/Black Star. **p. 292:** Dennis Brack/Black Star. **p. 293:** Cleo/The Picture Cube, Inc. **p. 300:** *(bottom)* Thomas Bishop/Custom Medical Stock Photo. **p. 302:** *(left)* Martin Rogers/Stock Boston; *(right)* Frank Siteman/Stock Boston. **p. 304:** Cartoonists and Writers Syndicate. **p. 305:** *(both)* AP/Wide World Photos. **p. 308:** Custom Medical Stock Photo. **p. 309:** The Bettmann Archive. **p. 312:** Custom Medical Stock Photo. **p. 316:** B. Mahoney/The Image Works. **p. 319:** Crandall/The Image Works.

Chapter 11: p. 327: The Bettmann Archive. **p. 328:** Giraudon/Art Resource. **p. 331:** Robert Eckert Jr./Stock Boston. **p. 332:** John Griffin/The Stock Shop. **p. 333:** A. Ramey/Stock Boston. **p. 334:** Harlow Primate Lab. **p. 336:** H. Gans/The Image Works. **p. 338:** H. Gans/The Image Works. **p. 338:** M. Grecco/The Stock Shop. **p. 341:** Barbara Alper/Stock Boston. **p. 342:** Robert Rathe/Stock Boston. **p. 344:** AP/Wide World of Photos. **p. 345:** Steve Leonard/Tony Stone World Wide. **p. 348:** Yoav Levy/Tony Stone World Wide. **p. 352:** *Focus On 11.2* From Endler, N.S., Holiday of Darkness. Copyright © 1982. Reprinted by permission of John Wiley & Sons, Inc. **p. 339:** *Table 11.2* From Seligman, Martin E.P., Helplessness: On Depression, Development, and Death. Copyright © 1975. Used by permission of W.H. Freeman.

Chapter 12: p. 360: *(left)* Ken Hayman/Black Star; *(right)* Jay Blakesberg/Sygma. **p. 364:** *(left)* Mangino/The Image Works; *(right)* Shepard Sherbell/SABA. **p. 365:** J. Mahoney/The Image Works. **p. 367:** UPI/Bettmann. **p. 371:** UPI/Bettmann. **p. 373:** Walter Bibikow/The Image Bank. **p. 374:** *(left)* B. Daemmrich/The Image Works; *(right)* Christiana Dittman/Rainbow. **p. 375:** UPI/Bettmann. **p. 381:** M. Antman/The Image Works. **p. 385:** Reuters/Bettmann. **p. 386:** Mark Richards/Photo Edit.

Chapter 13: p. 390: The Bettmann Archive. **p. 391:** The Bettmann Archive. **p. 393:** Cartoonist and Writers Syndicate. **p. 394:** Art Resource. **p. 396:** Bill Gallery/Stock Boston. **p. 397:** *Figure 13.2* From Amador, X.F. et al., "Awareness of illness in schizophrenia and schizoaffective and mood disorders," *Archives of General Psychiatry*, 51, p. 830. Copyright © 1994 American Medical Association. Used by permission. **p. 398:** (Three photos) Prinzhorn Sammlung/Foto Klinger. **p. 400:** Mary Ellen Mark. **p. 403:** Monkmeyer/Grannitus. **p. 404:** M. Edrington/The Image Works.

Chapter 14: p. 410: Edna Murlock. **p. 411:** Julie Houck/Stock Boston JHKO29OC. **p. 413:** Alan Becker/Image Bank. **p. 414:** Bob Daemmrich/Stock Boston. **p. 421:** *(left)* Hank Morgan/Rainbow; *(right)* Hank Morgan/Science Source/Photo Researchers. **p. 422:** National Institute of Mental Health. **p. 423:** Burt Glinn/Magnum Photos, Inc. **p. 427:** John Sohm/The Image Works. **p. 430:** UPI/Bettmann. **p. 435:** James Prince/Photo Researchers. **p. 411:** Christopher Morris/Black Star.

Chapter 15: p. 442: Corbis/Bettmann. **p. 443:** Owen Franken/Stock Boston. **p. 445:** James Schnepf/Gamma Liaison. **p. 449:** Lawrence Migdale/Stock Boston. **p. 450:** Bob Daemmrich/Stock Boston. **p. 451:** Cemax Inc. Phototake. **p. 452:** Rhoda Sidney/Stock Boston. **p. 454:** Science Source/Photo Researchers. **p. 456:** Dr. David Chase/CNRI/Phototake. **p. 457:** Sygma. **p. 458:** CNRI/Phototake. **p. 459:** Bridgeman/Art Resource.

Chapter 16: p. 468: Joel Gordon. **p. 469:** Alan Carey/Phototake. **p. 470:** Lawrence Mogdale/Stock Boston. **p. 476:** *Table 16.1* From "The children's behaviour questionnaire for completion by parents and teachers in a Chinese sample," by S. Ekblad, *Journal of Child Psychology and Psychiatry*, 31, pp. 775–791. Copyright © 1990. Reprinted by permission of *The Journal of Child Psychology and Psychiatry and Allied Disciplines*. **p. 477:** *Table 16.2* From "Crime in the Family Tree" by S.A. Mednick, 1985, *Psychology Today*, 19, 58–61. Reprinted with permission from *Psychology Today Magazine*. Copyright © 1985 (Sussex Publishers, Inc.). **p. 479:** Seth Resnick/Stock Boston. **p. 482:** Phil McCarten. **p. 484:** Migdale/Photo Researchers. **p. 485:** Tom McCarthy/The Picture Cube. **p. 487:** Scala Art Resource. **p. 490:** Reuters. **p. 493:** Tim Barnwell/The Image Works. **p. 494:** Cartoonists and Writers Syndicate. **p. 497:** *Table 16.5* "Alternative Explanations for Black Scholastic Underachievement Relative to Whites" from *School Psychology Review*, 1995, Vol. 24, No. 1. Copyright © 1995 by the National Association of School Psychologists. Reprinted by permission of the publisher. **p. 500:** Custom Medical Stock Photo. **p. 501:** C.S. Gray/The Image Works. **p. 502:** *(top)* James Shaffer/Photo Edit; *(bottom)* M. Greenlar/The Image Works.

Chapter 17: p. 508: W & D McIntyre/Photo Researchers. **p. 520:** Brad Nelson/Phototake Inc. **p. 520:** Jacques Chenet/Woodfin Camp and Associates. **p. 521:** John Chiasson/Gamma Liaison. **p. 524:** David Attie/The Stock Shop. **p. 527:** Topsham/The Image Works. **p. 531:** Bob Daemmrich/The Image Works. **p. 533:** Bob Daemmrich/The Image Works. **p. 536:** Jack Spratt/The Image Works. **p. 538:** M. Siluk/The Image Works. **p. 539:** Bob Daemmrich/Stock Boston.

Chapter 18: p. 544: UPI/Bettmann. **p. 545:** Reuters/Bettmann. **p. 549:** UPI/Bettmann. **p. 551:** UPI/Bettmann Newsphoto. **p. 555:** John Running/Stock Boston. **p. 558:** SABA. **p. 559:** UPI/Bettmann. **p. 561:** AP/Wide World Photos. **p. 562:** P.J. Griffiths/Magnum Photos Inc. **p. 564:** AP/Wide World Photos. **p. 568:** Bob Daemmrich/Stock Boston.

Name Index

SUBJECT INDEX